Hacker's Guide to Visual FoxPro© 6.0

Tamar E. Granor
Ted Roche

Hentzenwerke Publishing

Published by:
Hentzenwerke Publishing
980 East Circle Drive
Whitefish Bay, WI 53217

Hentzenwerke Publishing books are available through booksellers and directly from the publisher.
Contact Hentzenwerke Publishing at:
414.332.9876
414.332.9463 (fax) or
www.hentzenwerke.com

Hacker's Guide™ to Visual FoxPro© 6.0
By Tamar E. Granor & Ted Roche
Technical Editor: Doug Hennig
Contributor: Steven Black
Copy Editor: Jeana Randell
Cover Art: Robert Griffith

ISBN: 0-96550-936-2

Manufactured in the United States of America

Dedicated to the proposition that
all men and women are created equal.

Contents

The body
Of
Benjamin Franklin
Printer
(Like the cover of an old book
Its contents torn out
And stripped of its lettering and gilding)
Lies here, food for worms.
But the work shall not be lost
For it will (as he believed) appear once more
In a new and more elegant edition
Revised and corrected
by
The Author.

Benjamin Franklin, *Epitaph on Himself*, 1728

Foreword to the Second Edition

I was thrilled that Tamar and Ted decided to update their *Hacker's Guide* for Visual FoxPro 6.0. The easily understandable style of the *Guide* will help Fox developers come up to speed quickly on the wonderful new features in VFP 6. I continue to enjoy the way they examine each and every feature, even the potential "gotchas".

An innovation of the 6.0 Guide is the HTML Help version that comes on CD. You'll have all the fabulous content of the *Hacker's Guide* in the easily searchable Table of Contents and Index of HTML Help. I appreciate the fact that I can still sit in my comfortable easy chair and read straight through the book, and yet I have the *Guide's* valuable information at my fingertips when I'm using VFP at my desk.

Tamar and Ted, thanks again for sharing your knowledge with the Fox community.

Susan Graham
Former Visual FoxPro Program Manager
Microsoft Developer Division

Foreword to the First Edition

When I first learned that Tamar and Ted were planning to "take the plunge" and write a Visual FoxPro book, I couldn't have been more pleased. Tamar's ability to explain complex concepts is well known, as is Ted's depth of knowledge about many aspects of the product.

In the *Hacker's Guide to Visual FoxPro for Windows*, Tamar and Ted make the learning curve much flatter for novice users of Visual FoxPro, as well as for those who are already fairly comfortable with the product. They discuss concepts new to the Xbase developer (such as Object Oriented Programming), as well as old concepts with new guise (no more READs!). They also present a great deal of information in their reference component, which is the heart of the book. However, my favorite section is "Franz and Other Lists—a collection of lists containing information one can never seem to find in the Help file (it's usually there, but it can be hard to find). And don't miss the section on Frequently Asked Questions.

As in the articles they've written and in the talks they've given, Tamar and Ted provide technical information, strategies and source code on a Companion Disk. They provide clear and concise explanations of complex subjects such as SQL, the new event model and parameterized views. I especially appreciate the real-life examples of why to use a feature in a particular way. It truly aids in understanding.

Even though the content of this book is basically technical, the style of this *Hacker's Guide* is informal, quite amusing, and is a particularly easy read. How many of you get the reference in the title *Controls and KAOS*?

It has been my pleasure to work with Tamar and Ted on the many FoxPro beta cycles I've managed over the past few years. (Nobody has read our Help File and docs as thoroughly as Tamar has!) Their insights and opinions have helped us improve each of our products, and this perspective is demonstrated to great advantage in the *Hacker's Guide*. This book will be a valuable resource to Visual FoxPro users.

Susan Graham
Visual FoxPro Program Manager
Microsoft Developer Division

Acknowledgments for the Second Edition

As with the original Hacker's Guide, lots of people have made this book better. We'll start right off the bat by thanking all the people we thanked the first time around. (See the acknowledgments for the first edition for their names.) It was a lot easier (though not as much as we'd hoped) to write this book when we started with 800 solid pages.

Our technical editor for this edition, Doug Hennig, improved the book in many ways. He caught us when we were sloppy or lazy, shared his extensive knowledge with us, and even fixed many of our grammatical mistakes (though we're still not sure we agree with him about when you need "that" and when you don't). Jeana Frazier, our copy editor, was all that we could ask and more. She managed to improve our writing without changing the meaning, and was flexible about style issues without letting us run wild.

Steven Black again contributed his expertise, updating his original masterful work on the Builders and Wizards, and letting his zest for the Class Browser and Component Gallery produce an in-depth guide to these complex tools.

A number of people let us know about mistakes and misprints in both the original Hacker's Guide and early versions of this one. Thanks to Steven Black, Chaim Caron, Dan Freeman, Doug Hennig, Paul Maskens, Andrew Ross MacNeill, Tom Piper, Hale Pringle, Hans Remiens, Brad Schulz, Edwin Weston and Gene Wirchenko. If we left your name out of this list, it doesn't mean that your contribution didn't count, only that you've caught us in another mistake.

Similarly, a lot of people pointed out VFP problems with words like "you might want to include this in the Hacker's Guide." We can't possibly list all of those people here, but your contributions are appreciated and they all make this a better book.

A few people offered us so much wisdom that we must include their names (or they'll come after us). Thanks, in no particular order, to Christof Lange, Mac Rubel, Drew Speedie (technical editor for the first edition), Jim Booth, Gary DeWitt, Steve Dingle, Dan Freeman, and everyone else who taught us something, made a point clear, or asked a hard question that made us rethink an issue.

Thanks to the contributors of material for the disk: Sue Cunningham, the Wyoming Silver Fox, Toni Feltman, Jim Hollingsworth, Ryan Katri, Ken Levy, Andrew Ross MacNeill, Guy Pardoe, the late Tom Rettig, and Randy Wallin.

The folks at Microsoft have been remarkably helpful and kind to a couple of people who make a habit of pointing out what's wrong with their product. Special thanks to Susan Graham (now formerly of Microsoft), Calvin Hsia, Robert Green, Randy Brown, John Rivard, Allison Koeneke, and the hard-working beta team: Phil Stitt, Jim Saunders, Hong-Chee Tan, Steve Pepitone, Dave Kappl and Steve Klem for putting up with our incessant questions and the whole VFP team (including some people who don't actually work for Microsoft) for giving us this great toy to pound on. Similarly, the DevCon '98 speakers helped to plug a few holes in our knowledge and give us some ideas about what you could do with this version of VFP.

Thanks, too, to the other teams at Microsoft responsible for the tools we used to build this book. The Word team produced Service Release 2 just in time to fix some of the most horrific bugs with generating HTML from Word. Despite our many grumblings about its shortcomings, Word is one of the world's most powerful word processors, and its capability to do Automation made assembly of the book and the HTML Help file a far easier process. Thanks, too, to Word MVP's and/or CSP's Cindy Meister, Colleen Macri, George Mair and Chris Woodman for their help in figuring out how to get Word to do what we wanted rather than what *it* wanted.

Many people encouraged the creation of some sort of hypertext documentation. HTML Help came along just at just the right time to be used for this version of the book. The HTML Help team has done an incredible job with a product whose specs won't sit still, treating us to versions 1.0, 1.1, 1.1a and 1.1b in less than a year. Thanks to

Dan Freeman and Steven Black for their insistence on its value, Stephen Le Hunte for his incredible HTML Reference Library, and to the wonderful folks on the WINHLP-L mailing list for explaining it all, especially Help MVPs Cheryl Lockett Zubak and Dana Cline, and list contributor Patrick Sheahan for his hack to make the Fonts button appear.

As always, the VFP beta testers taught us a lot, showed us all kinds of strange behaviors, and made the whole process a lot more fun. Thanks, too, to all of the readers of our first version, for the encouraging words and support.

We're not sure what to say to our good friend, Whil Hentzen, who's been crazy enough to take on publishing books as a sideline to his software development business. Guess "thanks for everything, Whil" will have to do. Special thanks, also, to Whil's wife, Linda, who holds it all together and fits right in with the gang, and to Tamar's husband, Marshal, for making a lot of things happen in the background as we were in the last stages of getting this book out the door.

Finally, once again, we have to thank the two people who got us into this in the first place, Woody Leonhard and Arnold Bilansky. Perhaps thanks are also due to an anonymous cab driver in Toronto who let us do all the talking the day we met so we could discover we were friends.

On a personal level, life doesn't stop while you spend nearly a year writing a book and we each owe a lot to the people around us.

Once again, my family has had too little of me for too long. I owe my husband, Marshal, and sons, Solomon and Nathaniel, more than I can possibly explain for their love, patience (especially while I talked about things they knew nothing about), and help. As before, my extended family and good friends have been supportive and helpful throughout, as have the people at Advisor.

Tamar

Through the year of turning this crazy idea into the book before you, life went on. Thanks to Ellen, my dear wife, for putting up with it all. You are my strength and my inspiration. Thanks, Steve, for entertaining yourself for nearly a year. Thanks and farewell to my best beta tester, Chloe. Thanks to my coworkers at Blackstone for their suggestions, support and encouragement.

Ted

Acknowledgments for the First Edition

As with any work of this sort, a lot of people have contributed to this book in many different ways. We'll take the chance of thanking them by name, knowing we're bound to leave someone out. Whoever you are, we really do appreciate whatever you did.

Two people have made this a substantially better book. Drew Speedie, our technical editor, kept us honest, pushed us harder, and offered many gentle suggestions based on his own hard-won expertise. Steve Black may know more about Visual FoxPro's Builders and Wizards than anyone alive except their designers (maybe even more than them, too). Thanks to him, the chapter on that subject is a true hacker's delight.

Many other folks turned the light on for us or made us look harder at something or just plain told us what we needed to know. Thanks to: the Toms - Rombouts and Rettig - for filling the holes in the history of Xbase; Dan Pollak, beta tester extraordinaire and true Hacker, who figured out a bunch of stuff we missed; Mac Rubel off whom many thoughts and ideas were bounced, especially in the area of error handling; Doug Hennig, for helping Ted through the database container; Harve Strouse who helped Tamar finally to understand Present Value and Future Value (at least long enough to write about them); Tom Meeks who made sense of DrawMode and its friends; Nancy Jacobsen, who educated us about colors and made us think hard about what a user interface should be; Ken Levy and Paul Bienick for their help in getting us to understand the Browser and OLE Automation; Andy Neil, the master of multi-user; Brad Schulz, PrintMaster, for his help on printing issues; Tamar's father (the retired Math teacher), who helped her make sense of MOD()'s weird behavior with negative numbers; the Visual FoxPro Beta tester community, who pushed and prodded and poked and showed us all kinds of ways VFP could be used and abused. Thanks to all of the DevCon '95 speakers, each of whom brought their own talents and perspectives to bear on this wonderful product, and produced wonderfully lucid sessions with a product still not done.

We have (at least until this book comes out) many friends at Microsoft. Our respect for the group that built Visual FoxPro is tremendous—this is an awesome product—and we thank them all. Special thanks to a few people who helped us in various ways—Susan Graham, Erik Svenson, Gene Goldhammer, Randy Brown, Calvin Hsia.

A few people kindly helped us to fill the disk. Thanks to: Sue Cunningham, Walt Kennamer, Roy L. Gerber, Andy Griebel, James Hollingsworth, Ken Levy, Andrew Ross MacNeill, Tom Rettig, Randy Wallin and Ryan Katri, Rick Strahl, and our friends at Flash, Micromega and Neon.

Our thanks to all the FoxFolk who allowed us to include their records in our sample data.

Dealing with Addison-Wesley has been nothing like the stories we hear about publishers. Our editor, Kathleen Tibbetts, has been helpful and pleasant throughout. Working with Woody Leonhard was a special bonus. Thanks, too, to Arnold Bilansky, who first suggested we take on this book together.

On to more personal thanks.

Solomon and Nathaniel have had nearly a year of "Mom'll take care of it after the book." Hey, guys, it's after the book - I'll take care of it now. My husband, Marshal, has gone way above and beyond the call of duty in taking on extra responsibilities and letting me work on "the book, the book, the book." He also has an amazing knack to know when I need to hear "of course, you can do that" and when I need the challenge of "gee, I don't know if you can do that." I couldn't have done this without him.

My extended family (Ezekiels, Granors and Fishbeins) have all contributed in tangible and intangible ways. Special thanks to my parents who never once said to me (at least not about work), "Girls can't do that."

So many of my friends have helped out by driving carpool, watching my kids, letting me moan, and more that I can't begin to name names. You know who you are and I really do appreciate it. I owe you all a lot.

Editing a monthly magazine while writing a book while beta-testing a massive product definitely falls into the major league stress category. Everyone at Advisor has been understanding and helpful.

Tamar

This book was only possible through the love and support of my family. My wife Ellen has tolerated more long hours and stress than any spouse should have to put up with. She is the wind beneath my wings. Thanks to son Steve, for letting Dad finish "The Book." Thanks, too, to my extended family for their support, especially my dad, who knew I could write long before I did.

Ted

Who Needs This Book?

We love Visual FoxPro. We'd rather use it to develop applications than any other product we've ever worked with.

But (isn't there always a "but"?) Visual FoxPro's not perfect. Some parts of the language don't work as they should. Others do what they're supposed to, but we can't imagine why anyone thinks you'd want to do that. And some pieces do exactly what they're supposed to and it's a good thing to do, but it's hard as heck to understand. We should add that the Visual FoxPro documentation is good—in fact, it gets better with each new version—but there are still too many places where it's wrong or incomplete.

Enter this book. This is the book for the times when you've done it just as the manual shows, but it still doesn't work and you're running out of hair to pull out. It's for those days when you think you've found a command that does what you need, but you can't make any sense of what Help has to say about it. We'll tell you how it really works or why you shouldn't do it the way the manual shows—or tell you that it doesn't work at all, and show you how to do it another way.

What This Book Is Not

This is an "intermediate-level" book. This book is not a replacement for the online help or the Language Reference manual. It's a supplement. If something works the way it's documented, we won't repeat all the gory details. Instead, we summarize that and tell you anything the manual doesn't tell you.

On the other hand, if a command or function or property or event or method doesn't work as documented or if the documentation doesn't make sense, we dig down and explain it in detail. And, of course, in those cases, we still tell you the stuff the manual doesn't say.

This book is not the way to begin learning Visual FoxPro. Other books out there, including Whil Hentzen's book in this series, are designed to teach you Visual FoxPro. If you're new to Visual FoxPro, get one of those and work your way through it. Then get this book to help you move on.

This book is not an advanced application framework. There are several good commercial frameworks available that will provide you with all the code you need to start plugging your information into their systems and getting working apps out the other end. In fact, VFP 6 even comes with a decent framework you can use right away. We like and work with several of the frameworks, and we do not intend to duplicate their work here. Instead, we try to provide an advanced reference when you need to step outside the framework's box, or need to troubleshoot something the framework isn't doing right. You may also use this book to develop your own framework, but that exercise, as our profs loved to say, is left to the student.

We assume you're already familiar with the basics of Visual FoxPro, that you know how to use the Power Tools, and that you've spent some time with the product. Although we cover some introductory material, it's not at the level you'd want if you're a beginner.

So Who Does Need This Book?

Immodestly, we say anyone who's serious about working in Visual FoxPro needs this book at his or her side. Once you've gotten past the "Help, I don't know where to begin" stage and spent some time working with Visual FoxPro, you're ready. As soon as you've spent a long day and a sleepless night fighting one of the less-than-intuitive behaviors or trying to make something work that just plain doesn't, you're probably well past ready.

In putting together both the first and second editions of this book, we've learned a tremendous amount about what's going on under the hood. Our copies of the original *Hacker's Guide* are well thumbed and starting to look pretty ratty. We're ready to replace them with this version at our respective desks. We hope you find reading it as informative as we have writing it.

Hacking the Hacker's Guide

In any book of this size, there are bound to be mistakes, omissions, or places we just missed the mark. If you think you've caught us on one of these, drop us an email and we'll check it out for the next edition. (Tamar_Granor@compuserve.com or TedRoche@compuserve.com)

While we do love tracking down FoxPro problems, we're both too busy to do it on a one-to-one basis except for our clients and closest friends. So, if you need help with a particularly complex problem or general advice about how to proceed, please take advantage of one or more of the wonderful online resources for VFP. There's a list of them in "Back o' da Book." (Who knows? You may find one of us there anyway.)

> For what appears truth to the one may appear to be error to the other.

Mahatma Gandhi, 1922

Tamar E. Granor

Elkins Park, Pennsylvania

Ted Roche

Contoocook, New Hampshire

How To Use This Book

> Insert flap (A) in slot (B). Turn crank (C) so that teeth (D) engage with flap (A).
>
> Every Instruction Manual You've Ever Used

"So how do you use a book like this? We don't imagine that many of you will sit down and read it cover to cover. Of course, if you're the type who reads language reference manuals sequentially, be our guest."

We wrote those words in the first edition of this book. Since then, we've learned that a lot of you *are* the type who read language manuals in order. A surprising number of people have told us that they read the original *Hacker's Guide* from front to back before turning it into a reference book. We're flattered and astonished.

Nonetheless, we still think that most of you have a few other things to do with your time, so this edition is still organized so that you don't have to read it all before you can put it to work.

The book is divided into five sections. The first, "Wow, What a Concept!" is an overview of Visual FoxPro, organized by the various components of the language: Xbase traditions and assumptions, SQL, OOP, data structures, Web support, and more. We recommend you read it, even if you've been working with FoxPro since FoxBase days. We hope you'll find a few little nuggets tucked away in there.

The second section, "Ship of Tools," looks at Visual FoxPro's Power Tools, including some of our favorite tips and tricks for working with the tools, with more in-depth coverage of debugging and source control.

Section 3, "Franz and other Lists," is a somewhat random assortment of lists—from hardware suggestions, to things that sure feel like bugs when you run into them, to optimization tips. A lot of what was in this section in the first edition has migrated into other parts of the book this time around. In particular, many of the "It's a Feature, Not a Bug" items have been moved into the appropriate entries in the reference section to make them easier to find.

After you finish with all those appetizers, Section 4 is the main course. It's a complete reference to Visual FoxPro's commands, functions, properties, events and methods. We've even thrown in a few operators like "%" and "&".

This is the part of the book we really don't expect you to sit down and read sequentially. It's organized alphabetically so you can find the command that's driving you nuts. However, in the interest of our sanity and yours, not to mention saving a few trees, we've grouped related commands together. So, when you get to a particular command, all you may find is "See SomeOtherCommand." It's in there, but it's where we think it belongs logically.

Finally, Section 5 is for those daring souls who want to take the product a little further. It covers the various Active technologies as they relate to VFP (some are like siblings, while others are more like that annoying second cousin you wish would go away) and two incredibly deep tools, the Class Browser and Component Gallery. On the CD, you'll also find a wealth of information about VFP's Builder and Wizard technologies.

Help! I Need Some CD

After the original *Hacker's Guide* came out, lots of people asked us whether we could make it available in some online format (ranging from Windows Help to PDF to HTML to who knows what). They wanted access to the contents no matter where they were, without having to carry the book along. While we sympathized (especially when we were on the road ourselves), we just didn't have the resources to do the job.

This time around, we've planned a digital version from the beginning. The CD included with the book contains a complete copy of the book in HTML Help format.

HTML Help is Microsoft's latest version of Help and you need it for VFP 6's Help file, so we figured it was a safe bet that all our readers would have it. (If you don't, you can download what you need from the Microsoft Web site. We'd tell you where, but they changed the address three times while we were writing the book, so searching for "HTML Help" will get you there faster.)

For the curious, let us add that we created both the book and the Help file using Automation from VFP (where we track the progress of the book) to Word. In addition, we used VFP to do extensive post-processing on the generated HTML, parsing it and applying textmerge with VFP's lightning-fast string manipulation features.

Feel free to copy the Help file onto your hard drive (even more than one, if you have multiple machines yourself), but please do us the courtesy of not sharing it with everyone you know. (You will find appropriate copyright notices in there.) We've put a tremendous amount of time into this book, and illegal copies deprive us of the income to pay for that time.

I Think Icon

We have pretty mixed emotions about icons—they're great as a supplement to text, but not as a replacement. (After all, humans didn't spend centuries going from written text to pictographs; it was the other way around.) The icons in this book flag those portions of the text you'll want to pay particular attention to if you're having problems, trying to understand why Microsoft makes it work this way, or just skimming for cool features of Visual FoxPro. Here are the icons we use in the book and their meanings. You'll find the icons that appear only in the HTML Help file in "How to Use This Help File."

This ugly creature identifies bugs, both the ones that Microsoft recognizes and the ones we think are bugs, even though Microsoft says they're just fine. We were pleased to find that we were able to remove a lot of these critters that appeared in the first edition. We were less pleased to find plenty of new ones to add.

This doodad is supposed to say "design" to you. We use it whenever something is less than intuitive but not wrong, just hard to understand. We also use it sometimes when we think the design stinks.

This one probably speaks for itself. It's for stuff we think is incredibly cool ("cool", we think, should be the official adjective of Visual FoxPro). These things are jaw-droppers—enjoy them.

Code-dependent

When we started writing the first edition of this book, we noticed that each of us had somewhat different coding conventions. Nothing major, but some real differences, especially in what we like to capitalize. Since our styles were pretty readable and since the skill of being able to read code written by different people is an important one, we chose not to change our varied styles.

After writing together for nearly four years, our styles have converged somewhat, but there are still differences. So you may find what appear to be inconsistencies among the examples. We think each individual example is internally consistent. (We're sure you'll let us know, if not.)

Many of the examples show class definitions in code. Others show code to assign values to various properties in forms. The truth is that we usually don't do it that way—we use the Designers. But code makes better examples. Just about any class you see in code here can be created as a visual class, too.

Who Ever Heard of a Sin Tax?

We're capable of drawing the kind of syntax diagrams contained in the FoxPro manuals. In fact, we learned in school how to draw even more obscure syntax diagrams than that. For this book, though, we wanted to present the syntax of each command in the least threatening way possible. So, we use a simpler notation than the manuals. The flip side is that our notation is a little bit ambiguous.

Here are the rules we're using. FoxPro keywords use either all uppercase or mixed case. For the most part, Xbase-style keywords are in uppercase, while OOP-type keywords are mixed.

Vertical bars ("|") indicate choices—pick one or the other, but not both. Square brackets ("[ ]") indicate options—use it or not, your choice. Those two are the same as in the manuals.

What we didn't do was use angle brackets ("< >") to enclose the things you need to substitute into commands. Most of the time, you can recognize them because they begin with a single lowercase letter to indicate their type ("c" for character, "n" for numeric, and so on). It does get confusing when a command requires something like a filename or table name that isn't any of those types. Names are shown in mixed case (which can be confused with OOP-style keywords).

For the most part, we've tried to use meaningful names in our diagrams so you can see what a command or function is looking for, even without reading further.

A Class Act

In the reference entries on Visual FoxPro's base classes, you'll find charts showing properties, events and methods for that class. Rather than showing you every single PEM for every single base class, we've chosen to include only those that are special for that class. So, none of the classes list Top or Left in their reference entries—those are pretty much the same across the board. On the other hand, Style means something different to just about every class that has it, so you'll find it listed in several of the base class sections.

For a complete list of the PEMs of any base class, check Help.

Version Mania

Writing about software in the '90s is like chasing a moving target. This edition of the book was written about the initial release version of Visual FoxPro 6.0. We won't be surprised if, by the time you're reading it, there's been at least one service release. We fervently hope that, by that point, they'll have fixed lots of the bugs we tell you about. But we don't really think so. The worst of them will be fixed, but lots of these problems have been around for eons.

On your mark! Get set! Go hack!

How to Use the Help File

Help a man against his will and you do the same as murder him.

Horace, *Ars Poetica*

We should probably start by saying that we were as surprised as you when the first version of VFP 6 we saw turned up with a brand new kind of help. We wondered what was wrong with Windows Help. Is HTML Help just more evidence of Microsoft's single-mindedness on the path to the Internet?

As we've worked with HTML Help over the past year, it's grown on us. It still has lots of maturing to do, but the basic structure is sound and the process for producing it is simpler than for the traditional Windows Help. Ted, in particular, has spent many hours digging in and learning to work with this creature.

We believe that HTML Help is Microsoft's help of the future (at least until they invent the next "help of the future"); therefore, we chose it as the medium for the electronic version of the *Hacker's Guide*. However, one of our biggest gripes about HTML Help is that it doesn't come with "Help on Help." Fortunately, we did find a separate help file for HTML Help on Microsoft's Web site and we've included it on this CD. Of course, it's in HTML Help format, too, so if you don't know how to use HTML Help, it may not be much help. All things considered, this section is devoted to teaching you how to use the *Hacker's Guide* help file effectively. It covers both things specific to this help file and a number of the tricks we've learned to make working with HTML Help easier. Do check Microsoft's help file, too, for additional tidbits.

All the things we said in "How to Use this Book" apply to the help file as well, though we suspect that most of you (at least of the ones who bought both the book and the CD) won't choose the help file as the right way to read the front and back of the book. It's the reference section that really is effective this way.

Getting There

The first challenge you may run into with HTML Help is getting it to run. HTML Help depends on many of the same DLLs as Microsoft's Internet Explorer (IE). In fact, IE is really just a simple shell around the DLLs that render HTML, interpret scripts, provide navigation, and the rest of the features we have begun to take for granted on the Web. For this reason, the easiest way to be sure your computer has the correct files to run HTML Help is to install Internet Explorer. Some folks go ballistic upon hearing this, but please understand—IE does not *have* to have an icon on the desktop, it does not *have* to be the default browser, and it does *not* take up significantly more space than is required to install all the gew-gaws needed for HTML Help. Even if you are convinced that IE is just another step in Microsoft's plan for world domination, installing it is the easiest way to read HTML Help files.

You can install IE from the Visual Studio disks, if you got that package, download it from Microsoft's Web site, or install it from countless other CDs available from Microsoft. We encourage you to get the latest version to be sure you have the most recent fixes for bugs and security problems. In addition, you might want to consider installing HTML Help Workshop and HTML Help Runtime Update (Hhupd.EXE) also available on Microsoft's Web site. (We don't give links here, because we're sure they'll change within a month or two. But the main search page at Microsoft should be able to turn them up.) Both of these files install updated OCX and DLL files that may make reading the help file a more positive experience.

What's In There?

A structure becomes architectural, and not sculptural, when its elements no longer have their justification in nature.

Guillaume Apollinaire, *The Cubist Painters*

Like so many applications these days, HTML Help has two panes. The left pane controls what you see in the right pane. The left pane has three pages (tabs): Contents, Index, and Search. The right pane contains one chunk of the book at a time—a chapter from the front or back of the book or a listing from the reference section.

The pages in the left pane have two things in common. First, each provides a way of getting to the entry you want. Second, each includes a way of re-synching the list if you jump around using links.

In the reference section, the items in the See Also listing are links. Just click on them to go to the named item.

If you'd like to make more room for the content, you can adjust the ratio between the two panes by dragging the bar between them left or right. You can also get rid of the left pane by clicking the Hide button. Non-intuitively and inexplicably (and totally the opposite of what Internet Explorer does), clicking Hide shrinks HTML Help to the size of the right pane. You can then stretch it out (or maximize it) to make the right pane (guess it's not really the "right pane" at that moment) bigger. Use the Show button to make the left pane reappear.

As in a browser, the Back and Forward buttons take you back one action. (Interestingly, it appears that scrolling sometimes counts as an action, so you may find yourself at the bottom of the page rather than the top. We kind of think this is a good thing.) Pressing Backspace is the same as clicking the Back button. We haven't been able to find a single keystroke replacement for Forward; however, you can use Alt+O to open the Options menu, and then press F for Forward.

HTML Help demonstrates the confusion at Microsoft these days when it comes to interface design. The top of the HTML Help form contains no true menu (text prompts dropping down lists of options). Neither is what's there truly a toolbar, as it cannot be undocked. Worst of all, just to prove they know how to mangle a metaphor but good, the Options button on the thing-that's-not-a-toolbar does call a drop-down menu.

But wait, you say—I use the MSDN viewer to look at FoxPro's native help file, and it has a menu. It does indeed, and for a simple reason: You are not looking at the native HTML Help interface. The MSDN viewer is a custom application Microsoft developed to present its documentation for Visual Studio. The MSDN viewer has several features (like a true menu) that we would have liked to integrate into the *Hacker's Guide* help, but we haven't been able to find documentation on how Microsoft did that.

I'd Be Content To Do That

> Strong and content I travel the open road.
>
> Walt Whitman, *Song of the Open Road*

The Contents page shows you the table of contents for the book. It looks an awful lot like the one in the printed version. If you want to go through the book sequentially, this is the page for you.

In the listing for the Reference section, every command, function, class, property, event, method, and system variable is included (along with some of the more unusual operators). We didn't write a separate Reference entry for each item, though—they're logically grouped. In the book, looking up some items gets you to a "See something else" and you have to flip pages to find that one. In the help file, that's not necessary. Choosing an item from the Contents list takes you right to the appropriate Reference section.

We've also added to the Contents list some keywords that aren't commands, just to make them easier to find. So you can go to ENDCASE and click, and it'll bring up the entry for DO CASE, for example.

When you click a link in the right pane, the Contents list keeps up with you. It always highlights the item you're now looking at.

Index, Outdex

> And for the citation of so many authors, 'tis the easiest thing in nature. Find out one of these books with an alphabetical index, and without any farther ceremony, remove it verbatim into your own . . .
>
> Miguel de Cervantes, *Prologue to Don Quixote*

The Index page is the same as the Reference portion of the Contents list, except for two things. First, it provides a text box to let you type in what you're looking for. Second, when you click on a link in the right pane, the Index doesn't follow along. So you can come back to where you were in the Index after wandering down a path of links.

The Search text box offers incremental search—that is, you start typing and it jumps to the first item that matches what you've typed so far. Unfortunately, there seem to be some bugs in the search algorithm—it has trouble with similar items in different cases. For example, if you type "alias", the highlight lands on the Alias property, shown in the Index as "Alias". However, if you add a left parenthesis (so your search string is now "alias("), the highlight does *not* move to "ALIAS()", as it should. You can see the same bug in the VFP 6 help file. We hope the HTML Help people fix it soon.

Choosing the Display button on the Index page takes you back (in the right pane) to the currently highlighted item in the Index. Clicking Locate on the toolbar/menu brings up the Contents list with the item that's currently displayed in the right pane highlighted in the Contents list.

The Search is On

> The philosophic spirit of inquiry may be traced to brute curiosity, and that to the habit of examining all things in search of food.
>
> W. Winwood Reade, *The Martyrdom of Man*

The Search page lets you look for things in ways we didn't consider. Type in any string, press Enter (or choose the List Topics button) and a list of items containing your string appears. Then choose the one you want to see.

As with the Index page, the Search page doesn't keep up with you as you follow links. Instead, it patiently sits there displaying the matches from the last search. As on the Index page, choosing the Display button returns you to the highlighted item in the list. The Locate button also behaves as it does on the Index page, taking you to the Contents page with the current item highlighted.

A couple of pointers when using the Search tab. The search engine is not the brightest star in the heavens, and many common VFP phrases stump its somewhat limited intellect. First, it ignores non-alphabetic characters, so searching for #DEFINE finds DEFINE MENU and DEFINE WINDOW, as well as #DEFINE. Second, we suspect the help authors had some special intentions for parentheses, as we have never been able to include them without getting "The syntax of the search query is incorrect." This is maddening when searching for something like USER(), because every use of "user" comes up if you do not include the parentheses.

Enclose phrases in quotation marks to locate topics that contain that exact phrase.

You can use the Boolean operators AND, OR and NOT as well as the NEAR operator to limit your search, but only one operator to an expression, please. Use "ugly" AND "interface" to locate that one section, "ugly" NOT "interface" for the others, "Julian" OR "Gregorian" for calendar discussions.

The Key to the Future

> Woe unto you, lawyers! for ye have taken away the key of knowledge
>
> *The Bible*

We're both touch typists and, as a result, like to keep our hands on the keyboard (not to mention the physical wear and tear of moving the arm back and forth between keyboard and mouse). It turns out you can do pretty much everything in HTML Help with the keyboard, but it ain't easy to figure it out. Some of the keyboard shortcuts are pretty obscure, and, to make matters worse, the relevant topic in the Help for HTML Help is called "Use accessibility shortcut keys." Sounds like something that's only for those with physical disabilities, doesn't it? How about calling it "Keyboard shortcuts"?

The one that took us the longest to find (in fact, we didn't find it until we got the help file) is moving focus from the left to the right pane. We tried everything we could think of (tabs, shift+tabs, arrows, shift+arrows, you name it), even asking other people, and came up empty. It turns out the magic key is F6. Now that's intuitive, isn't it?

Once you get to the right pane, you can use the keyboard to navigate within the entry and to follow a link. Once you follow a link, for some reason, it takes two tabs to land on the first link in the new section. Same thing when you back up. We're not sure where focus is when you get there or after that first tab.

To go back from right to left, you can use F6 again. In addition, all three pages of the left pane have hot keys.

Not only are many of the keystrokes unintuitive, but some of them don't work as documented and others don't seem to be documented at all. For instance, the Help for HTML Help says that Alt+LeftArrow and Alt+RightArrow close and open folders, respectively. What they actually seem to do is navigate back and forth in the history list (far more useful). To open and close folders, use + and – when the appropriate item is highlighted. Totally undocumented is that Shift+LeftArrow and Shift+RightArrow move you up and down a level in the Contents hierarchy. It's worth spending some time trying various keystrokes to see what they do. You can't damage anything by doing so, so why not check it out?

Icon Take Much More

HTML Help offers the capability to set the icon of each topic to have its own individual bitmap. We decided not to go hog-wild, and just kept to a few different ones. The book icon is for the Front of the book. Each major section appears as a folder. The individual sections appear as a text icon. The icon for every language item or chapter that's new in VFP 6 is marked in the Contents listing with a red star. There is one last set of icons that we hope appears nowhere in the final version: During beta testing, missing sections were marked with icons of little pencils writing in the text (to indicate that we were still working on them).

Just the Way You Want It

> Custom, then, is the great guide of human life.
>
> David Hume, *An Enquiry Concerning Human Understanding*

We had many difficult design decisions to make in creating the help file. If for some reason you cannot abide our choices in fonts, font sizes or colors, all is not lost. There is a technique to override what is presented in HTML Help, but it's a little strange. You set your font and color options through the Internet Options dialog of Internet Explorer (also available in Control Panel). You'll find the directions in the Help for HTML Help. That means, of course, that your changes affect every HTML Help file you use and all of your IE work. Not good. Although using the same choices across applications is generally a good thing, so is letting people make specific choices for specific applications.

In addition, the choices in the IE dialog don't include font size. To be specific, you can tell it to ignore the font size specified in the original, but you can't choose your favorite font size there. To make things easier on your eyes, the font button on the toolbar/menu lets you cycle through five different font sizes to find the one that works best for you. The Font button is a hack—obviously, the code is somewhere within the HTML Help engine, but there is no way to add it to your help file using the HTML Help Workshop interface. The good news is that we got it to work; the bad news is that we haven't figured out if it has a keyboard shortcut.

You can also modify what's available on the Contents page. The context menu for that page contains a Customize item. When you choose it, a Customize dialog appears with a wizard that lets you limit the items shown to those introduced in particular versions of FoxPro. So, if you want to know what's new in VFP 6, choose the Custom option button on the first page, and then uncheck everything except Visual FoxPro 6.0 on the second. When you finish the wizard, Contents shows you only the items that were introduced in VFP 6. (We've chosen to leave all of the front and back of the book chapters available, no matter which subset you're in.) To restore the list to include all items, either choose the All option button or check every version.

LoOKs LIke a RaNSom NoTE

At first glance, the alphabetical listings of language elements on the Contents and Index pages look like someone forgot to proofread it. Some items are all caps, some are mixed case, some have parentheses, others don't, and sometimes the same item appears more than once.

Relax—there *is* method to our madness. Due to its long evolution and liberal borrowing from other languages (see "It's Always Been That Way" for details), VFP has not only an assortment of traditions in terms of capitalization, but also quite a few keywords that have multiple meanings. We've done our best to sort things out so you can find what you need.

Here are our rules (which we tried to follow universally). Xbase and SQL commands, functions and keywords are listed in ALL CAPS. Properties, events, methods and other OOP keywords use Mixed Case. Functions are shown with trailing parentheses. Events and methods are not.

So, for example, NewObject is a method, while NewObject() is a function. (They're both new in VFP 6.) Similarly, Alias refers to the property, and ALIAS() is the function. DEBUG is a command and Debug is a property.

For the most part, this system provides us with a unique string for each language item. But once in a while, it breaks down. For example, there's a Run event and a Run method. In those cases, we've included the additional information needed to clarify things.

What all this means, in practice, is that after you've typed enough to get to the right word, sometimes you'll have to press an extra down arrow or two to get to the item you want.

Keep it Handy

> More helpful than all wisdom is one draught of
> simple human pity that will not forsake us.
>
> George Eliot, *The Mill on the Floss*, 1860

We've been working with beta versions of the help file for some time, trying to get it right and make it as useful as possible. It didn't take us long to figure out that keeping a shortcut to HackFox.CHM on the desktop means that it's only a double-click away. We also find that we live on the Index page most of the time, so that we can quickly find the section we want. The combination of the shortcut and the index is even faster than grabbing our well-worn copies of the original *Hacker's Guide*. We hope you find it as useful as we do.

Section 1: Wow, What a Concept!

> Ignorance is preferable to error; and he is less remote from the truth who believes nothing, than he who believes what is wrong.
>
> Thomas Jefferson, *Notes on the State of Virginia*, 1781-1785

Section 1 introduces the major themes of Visual FoxPro, starting with its history and covering the fundamentals of each of its major sub-languages. Think of it as the "If it's Tuesday, this must be Belgium" Tour of Visual FoxPro.

"It's Always Been That Way"

> The past is but the beginning of a beginning, and all that is and has been is but the twilight of the dawn.
>
> H. G. Wells, *The Discovery of the Future*, 1901

"In the beginning"—isn't that how histories normally begin? But what is the beginning of Visual FoxPro? It has bits and pieces from so many different languages and technologies that there's no one beginning. Visual FoxPro is a true hybrid.

One bit of lineage is clearer than the rest, though, and that's FoxPro's Xbase heritage. For that, there's at least a partial beginning. "In the beginning, there was the dot."

In this beginning, it was 1975 and a programmer named Wayne Ratliff was working at the Jet Propulsion Laboratory (JPL) in Pasadena, California. He wanted to participate in the football pool, but felt he needed to really work over the statistics to have a fair shot at winning. Naturally, he wanted to use a computer to help him. Somehow, he got sidetracked into exploring programming languages. Along the way, he was introduced to microcomputers and to an internal language at JPL called JPLDIS.

In 1978, Ratliff started writing his microcomputer version of JPLDIS (developed by Jeb Long and others). Along the way, he omitted some commands, added some and modified others. The language was called Vulcan, as a tribute to Star Trek. Ratliff began licensing Vulcan in 1979.

When marketing Vulcan became too much for Ratliff, he made a deal with George Tate and Hal Lashlee to take over the marketing. They brought in an ad man named Hal Pawluk who gave the product a new name, dBASE II, and named the company Ashton-Tate. dBASE II started shipping in 1981. (By the way, note that there never was a dBASE I nor an Ashton. You can probably win a few bucks on those.)

Eventually, Ratliff and co-worker Jeb Long left JPL to work full-time with a team of programmers on a new version of dBASE (to be called dBASE III). As part of that process, it was ported to the IBM PC. dBASE III was finally released in June 1984.

A Fox in the Hen House

> The fox knows many things, but the hedgehog knows one great thing.
>
> Archilochus, Early seventh century B.C.

In the midst of all this, a computer science professor at Bowling Green University named Dave Fulton got a consulting contract for which dBASE II seemed the appropriate tool. But, when the work was done, the resulting system was too slow. Fulton and his group decided the solution was to write their own, faster version of dBASE II. The product they created was a marketing failure (through no fault of their own), but from the ashes of that product, the runtime libraries were salvaged in hopes that some commercial gain could be made from them.

The result was FoxBase, one of a number of dBASE clones that hit the market. The difference between FoxBase and many of the others was that it survived and found its own niche.

Once dBASE III appeared, Fulton's group geared up to apply the Fox magic to it. FoxBase+ shipped in July 1986. A little more than a year later, FoxBase+ 2 was released, with dBASE III Plus compatibility. FoxBase+ 2 also included a number of tools to aid in application development. One of them, FoxView, let the developer lay out screens visually, then generate code for that layout. The code was generated by running a script written in another tool called FoxCode, which meant the same layout could result in many different programs.

Suited to Everyone

Suspicion all our lives shall be stuck full of eyes;
For treason is but trusted like the fox.

William Shakespeare, *King Henry the Fourth*

Back in Perrysburg, Ohio (home of Fox Software), the development team was hard at work on a Macintosh version of FoxBase+.

In developing the Mac version, many of the programmers found a real liking for the Mac's interface. So, Fulton and the gang decided to bring many of the benefits of the Mac to PC programmers. Work started on FoxPro in the fall of 1988.

Not coincidentally, dBASE IV, the successor to dBASE III Plus, was released in October 1988. The new FoxPro would be dBASE IV-compatible, but for the first time, the decision was made to deviate from total compatibility. Instead, the new FoxPro would be better. Naturally, it would still be faster. It turned out that making FoxPro better than dBASE IV wasn't all that hard—the initial release of dBASE IV was terribly buggy and poorly received. (By this time, Ashton-Tate had a number of problems. George Tate had died in 1984 and the company never really recovered.)

It was also in the fall of 1988 that Ashton-Tate filed a lawsuit against Fox Software for infringing on their copyright of the dBASE language. It took more than two years and the acquisition of Ashton-Tate by Borland before this issue was dropped.

FoxPro 1.0 was released in November 1989, still including the FoxView-FoxCode pair for designing input screens. FoxPro remained true to its Xbase roots, but incorporated lots of new commands for using windows and menus. The Mac influence was definitely felt. FoxPro 1.0 also added the first of many sub-languages: the low-level file functions that let you manipulate files as streams of characters. The term "low-level" is something of a misnomer because these really just provide the same file input/output capabilities most programming languages have, but they are lower-level than FoxPro's other input/output facilities.

A Two-Oh Punch

The delight that consumes the desire,
The desire that outruns the delight.

Algernon Charles Swinburne, *Dolores*, 1866

Naturally, the new capabilities offered in FoxPro 1.0 weren't enough for the FoxPro community. The FoxPro user interface included all kinds of neat widgets like push buttons, radio buttons, scrollable lists, and so forth. It didn't take long for FoxPro developers to start clamoring for access to these goodies.

FoxPro 2.0 was the response to these demands. It appeared in July 1991, and featured a collection of so-called "Power Tools." Developers were told to use the new Project Manager, Screen Builder, Menu Builder, Report Writer and so forth to design and build applications. For the first time, anything you could do with the Power Tools could be done with code, too. Best of all, the Power Tools stored their data in regular FoxPro tables and, in the case of the Screen Builder and Menu Builder, used regular FoxPro code to convert that metadata into programs. Like the earlier FoxView and FoxCode, this open architecture meant you could roll your own, if you chose, without needing to learn the arcane syntax of the template language. This was all made possible with the addition of very few commands, comprising a textmerge sub-language.

Another new language was introduced into FoxPro in this version. FoxPro 2.0 featured four SQL commands (CREATE TABLE, CREATE CURSOR, INSERT INTO and SELECT). Up to this point, all new commands had pretty much followed the Xbase style. But this group came from an entirely different background—not quite the other side of the tracks, but a whole different way of thinking about code, a non-procedural way. With the SQL commands, you indicate what you want, but not how to get there; FoxPro figures that out internally. This "set-oriented" view of data opens FoxPro up to opportunities both in larger-scale Xbase applications and in new client-server venues, which would have been difficult, if not impossible, to reach without the SQL syntax.

FoxPro 2.0 also introduced the infamous "foundation READ," which could be used as part of a structure to provide so-called "event-driven" programs. These applications, which are the norm today, allow a user to begin one task, leave it unfinished while moving on to another, then freely switch between the two, or even three, four or 15 tasks. The foundation READ of FoxPro 2.0, while kludgy in the extreme, was the beginning of the path to the rich event model of Visual FoxPro.

Crossroads

FoxPro 2.0 was very well received and won lots of awards. But was that enough for FoxPro users? Of course not! They kept asking for more. One of the big things they asked for was versions of FoxPro on platforms other than DOS. FoxBase+/Mac users felt left out because DOS users had now had two major upgrades and they hadn't. Plus, Windows was looking more and more important.

So, the next task for the Fox group was to cross the road—that is, to make FoxPro cross-platform. Work proceeded simultaneously on the Windows and DOS versions of FoxPro 2.5 through 1991 and 1992. The 1991 Developer's Conference (DevCon) featured demos of both the Windows and Unix versions of FoxPro then in development. At the 1992 DevCon, almost every presenter used the then-in-beta Windows version.

In March 1992, the Fox world shook when it was announced that Microsoft and Fox were to merge. Given their relative sizes and importance, it was clear that "merger" was a euphemism for "acquisition." However, the story was that the development team including Dave Fulton would make the move to Redmond. The merger became final in June and by fall, nearly all of the former Fox employees had trekked cross-country.

FoxPro 2.5 for Windows and for DOS were released in January 1993. They included a "Transporter" for moving applications between the two platforms. The Mac and Unix versions were promised to follow soon. Some folks complained that the Windows version wasn't a true Windows product, but they were answered by those who pointed out that "true Windows products" don't work cross-platform. Other than those needed for cross-platform operation or for new Windows capabilities, FoxPro 2.5 didn't introduce many new commands and functions.

So What's "Soon" Anyway?

> With foxes we must play the fox.
>
> Thomas Fuller

While DOS and Windows developers learned to write cross-platform applications, Mac and Unix developers waited and waited. It wasn't until the spring of 1994 that FoxPro/Mac made its appearance. FoxPro/Unix never made it in version 2.5. By the time that product was ready in August 1994, the ante had been upped to 2.6 across the board.

Version 2.6 was an interesting project. Its primary reason for existence was to attract dBASE users before dBASE 5 for DOS and dBASE for Windows shipped. A bunch of new commands were added to create 2.6—almost every one of them was labeled "for dBASE compatibility," whether or not it was actually useful. Most didn't even rate their own entry in the Help file. And some, despite their downplaying by Microsoft, were truly useful additions to the language.

In the summer of 1994, the family was finally completed with the release of FoxPro 2.6 for Unix. That was the only FoxPro for Unix that ever was.

Third Time's the Charm ... Or is it?

> High thoughts must have high language.
>
> Aristophanes, *Frogs*, 405 B.C.E.

By 1994, the programming world was changing. On the data side, client-server was the next big thing. Programming-wise, it was object orientation. So, of course, Microsoft decided to include both in the next version of FoxPro. They also updated the name to be in line with their other development tools, and FoxPro 3.0 became Visual FoxPro 3.0.

Visual FoxPro still contains all the Xbase commands it ever had (and more), the "low-level file function" sub-language, the textmerge sub-language, and the SQL sub-language with lots of additions. But wait, there's more.

The major new language in Visual FoxPro is that of OOP, Object-Oriented Programming. There's also a sub-language for client-server operation. Altogether, Visual FoxPro 3.0 contained more than 1,000 commands, functions, system variables, properties, events and methods. It was released in June 1995. The initial version of VFP had some serious problems. Because the product was released before Windows 95 and most of the computing world still worked in 16-bit versions of Windows, this 32-bit application had to cooperate with the Win32S subsystem to run under Windows 3.1 and Windows for Workgroups. A lot of people found that combination less than stable.

In many ways, it makes sense to think of VFP 3.0 as actually being "version 1" of a new product. Major portions of the product were brand-new code, from the object orientation to the new controls like grids. And, as with most version 1's, it didn't take long for updates to come along. The first one, VFP 3.0a, was released only in the Far East as the enhancements it offered were related to dealing with the languages used in that part of the world. However, in December of 1995, Microsoft released version 3.0b, which fixed a number of bugs in 3.0, as well as added support for double-byte character sets (the kind used for Japanese and Chinese and other languages that use pictographs rather than strings of characters to make words).

A Mac version of 3.0 was released in May 1996. Though it was initially popular, its extreme slowness and hardware hunger, together with Microsoft's lukewarm support, made it something of a niche product. Mac enthusiasts kept waiting for an improved version, but it never appeared and we don't think there'll ever be another Mac version of VFP.

Whatever Happened to Version 4?

> Glorious, stirring sight! The poetry of motion! The *real* way to travel! The *only* way to travel! Here today—in next week tomorrow! Villages skipped, towns and cities jumped—always somebody else's horizons! O bliss! O poop-poop! O my! O my!
>
> Kenneth Grahame, *The Wind in the Willows*, 1908

VFP 3.0b was barely out the door before the development team started getting serious about what we figured would be VFP 4.0. Wrong again. To bring FoxPro into synch with Microsoft's other development products, the version after 3.0b was 5.0.

Where the first version of VFP focused on improving the programming language, most of the focus for this version went into the developer tools. VFP 5 featured a new debugger, color-coded syntax, an improved editor, and integration with source control tools (especially Microsoft's Visual SourceSafe). There were language improvements, too, of course, including offline views and a bunch of new properties. In addition, VFP 5 can be an Automation server as well as a client, and you can build custom automation servers with it, too.

VFP 5.0 was released in August 1996. Like so many versions before it, an update wasn't too long in the making.

Version 5.0a was released in December 1996. It was primarily a bug-fix release. The most notable thing about it was its inclusion in the Visual Studio product. Visual Studio combined Microsoft's developer products (including Visual Basic, Visual C++, Visual InterDev, Visual SourceSafe and, of course, Visual FoxPro, and more) into a single package. In this first version, pretty much the only common thing about the products in the box is that they're in the same box and share an installation routine. But the history of the Office product line suggests that the products will grow more together as time passes.

Since 5.0a, there have been two minor revisions to VFP, included in Visual Studio Service Packs. As of this writing, the latest version is build 415, with a release date of October 21, 1997.

Now We Are Six

This book covers Visual FoxPro 6. VFP 6 is part of Visual Studio 6, as well as an independent product.

The big changes in this version are focused in several areas. The first big change primarily affects developers—it's the ability to address projects programmatically. In addition, a lot of work has been done to make VFP a stronger player in the component world. Among other things, VFP 6 is better at hosting ActiveX controls than its predecessors and supports OLE drag and drop. There's lots of other new stuff, too—cool new functions, additional properties, and more.

By now, lots of things work differently in different versions of VFP. Wherever possible, we point that out and let you know where it's working and where it's broken.

So Now What?

> Strengthen me by sympathizing with my strength, not my weakness.
>
> A. Bronson Alcott, *Table Talk*, 1877

The proliferation of sub-languages is a key factor in developing in Visual FoxPro. There are several ways to tackle almost anything you might want to do. We'll point this out over and over again and let you know where we think one approach is better than others.

The remaining chapters in this section introduce each of Visual FoxPro's major sub-languages. Each covers the basic terminology and the fundamental assumptions you need to understand when dealing with that group of commands.

DBF, FPT, CDX, DBC—Hike!

> Let's look at the record.
>
> Alfred E. Smith, 1928

The transition from the FoxPro 2.x model of the universe to the Visual FoxPro mindset was pretty revolutionary on a lot of fronts. While we cringe to use the hackneyed and overused term, the introduction of databases in Visual FoxPro was a major paradigm shift and one that took some getting used to. The introduction of the database container, local and remote views, vast improvements in client-server connectivity, and a slew of new data types, commands, and functions was mind-boggling. We'll try to give you an overview of the data changes here, and refer you to areas where you can get more information throughout the book.

If you're coming from an Xbase background, you might think you're encountering some NewSpeak in Visual FoxPro, but it's all for a good cause. Individual DBF files used to be referred to as "databases" but now, a better term, that used by Visual FoxPro, is to call individual DBF files "tables" and the new DBC a "database container" or just "database" for short. While it's frustrating to try to change terminology you've been using for years, we've found it does lead to greater understanding of the new scheme of Visual FoxPro. Not only that, but the new names bring us in line with the rest of the relational database world.

The Database Container

A database container (DBC file) is a Visual FoxPro table that links together the tables, indexes, views and special code associated with your data. When a table is added to a database, many new features become available. You can define code to validate individual fields or entire records before they are saved, each with its own individual error message. A default value and caption can be specified for each field.

Database containers also allow you to specify *persistent relations*, saving hours of tedium in system development. These relations form the basis for enforcement of relational integrity (RI) at the database level, through the use of stored procedures and record-level triggers. In addition to RI enforcement, our own program code can be triggered on the insertion of a new record, the updating of an existing record, or the deletion of a record. Program code can also run at the field level, specifying default values, validation rules and error messages. Individual fields can have default captions and control classes assigned to them.

All of these features are controlled by the database engine itself, with no need for the developer to write supporting code. Even cooler, all of these features are available when directly editing the table, like in a Browse. This promises far greater reliability and integrity for the data we use.

Better Tables

Cool new features have been added to the DBF table, too. A table can be "free," not associated with a particular database, or it can be "contained" within a DBC. This "containership" is not the same as, say, Access's monolithic MDB files—no data from the tables is actually stored within the DBC, just links to the tables, views and other elements. This structure is like the Project Manager, which holds references to source documents but not the documents themselves.

Whether free or contained, tables have gained new features: several new field types, the capability to store NULL values within fields, and the ability to flag character or binary data in fields not to be translated between different language versions of Visual FoxPro.

The New Database Container

Xbase programmers have gotten into a rut. In every application, in every screen, in every routine, they've had to code the same functionality. "Customer.DBF is related to Orders.DBF by the Cust_ID field." "Customer mailing address state needs to be validated against the States.DBF table." "Every time a record is added to the AR table, run the routine to post an audit trail record." If the developer forgets one of these rules in just one place in an application, the consistency of the data is in jeopardy and a long, arduous troubleshooting session is sure to result. To compound the error, it's possible that these rules are in place in all programs, but a database change made interactively by a programmer or user can still be responsible for bad data. What a headache!

Visual FoxPro's competition, the Relational DataBase Management Systems (RDBMSs) and Client-Server systems, have developed solutions to these problems. RDBMSs have made leaps and bounds in functionality in the past few years, while the basic data model of Xbase hasn't changed since the development of dBASE. With the release of Visual FoxPro, Microsoft determined it was time for an improvement in the basic model. Visual FoxPro introduces some new terminology and some incredible power in the form of the new DBC databases. As we mentioned above, we used to call each individual DBF file a database, but this terminology is not really consistent with most other database management systems. Besides, those folks with their poky-slow RDBMSs would sneer at us: "That's not a real database—where are the persistent relations? Relational Integrity? Security? Triggers? Stored Procedures?"

It's in there.

The new Visual FoxPro databases contain and support:

- Tables—DBF files specially marked for use only within a database.

- Long, long, long table and field names (128 characters!).
- Field-level validation functions, default values, error message text and comments.
- Record-level validation.
- Separate trigger functions for insert, update and delete.
- Primary and candidate keys.
- Persistent relationships—define a relation once and it is preserved.
- Local views—updateable cursors spanning multiple tables.
- Remote views—easy access to data stored within other DBMSs.
- Stored procedures—common method code accessible from all procedures within the DBC.

Tables added to a DBC can have long names associated with the table itself and its constituent fields. These names are stored in the DBC database container.

Triggers and stored procedures are Visual FoxPro code fragments that run automatically when their associated event occurs. Field-level procedures fire when a field is modified. Record-level procedures fire when an attempt is made to commit a new record to a file, update an existing record, or delete a record from a table.

Primary and candidate keys both uniquely distinguish a record from all others. Indexes designated as either of these don't accept duplicate values, but instead generate an error message.

Persistent relationships can be defined once within the DBC, and are then available throughout the system. When tables engaged in a persistent relationship are brought into the data environment of a form or report, the relationship is brought with them. While the relationship can be modified in each place it exists, if the most common relationship is defined within the DBC, far less work is needed in each subsidiary form and report to put a system together.

After creating tables and their relationships within the DBC, run the Relational Integrity Builder by issuing the command Modify Database and then choosing Edit Referential Integrity from the Database menu or the context menu. The Relational Integrity Builder appears. When you are done and choose OK, the builder regenerates the RI stored procedures needed to ensure Relational Integrity in the database.

Views are cursors on warp speed. A view is defined like a SQL SELECT, allowing you to join multiple tables (and use their persistent relations, if set), select the output fields, and order and group records just like a SELECT. But views are really cool because they can be updateable, so changes made to the records in the resulting cursor can be "written through" onto the tables. This has fantastic implications for new methods of manipulating and updating data.

Remote views have all the coolness of the Local views just mentioned, with a simple but profound variation—the data is not Visual FoxPro data. Using ODBC, the Connection Designer, and the View Designer, Visual FoxPro has become, in one swell foop, one of the most powerful clients in a client-server relationship. Even cooler, because both local and remote views can be defined, a Visual FoxPro client-server system can be designed, prototyped and tested on local data stores, and converted to remote data storage when ready to go into production. This is a big attraction to developers who want to work on client-server systems on their client site, but don't want or need to set up servers in their own offices. For more information on using client-server architectures, see "Your Server Will Be With You in a Moment."

Had enough views yet? There's one more variation on the theme: offline views. An offline view is defined as any other, but it allows an operator to actually "check out" a set of records, make changes, and then re-synchronize with the original source. This is a cool feature for "road warriors," anyone who needs to disconnect from the main network, go on the road, do some work, and then reconnect and update the main files.

Finally, stored procedures allow programming code for the triggers and rules, as well as any other associated code, to be stored within the DBC. For example, the Referential Integrity Builder's code for performing cascaded updates or deletes is placed in the stored procedures area. This is also where you can place code that otherwise might be a "calculated field," an item wisely not supported within the data model, or a UDF. For example, the routine to format a postal code based on the country is a routine you might include within your main DBC to produce the effect of a calculated field on your customer table. Rather than requesting Customer.PostalCode, you could specify CustPostCode(Customer.PostalCode) and get the built-in code to do the work. This has advantages over a stand-alone UDF because it's always available when the data is. The downside is that this code is only available for the current SET DATABASE database, so stored procedures are not a replacement for stand-alone or procedure libraries. They are, however, still a great place to store database-specific code.

Compatibility—The Good, the Bad and the Ugly

> Consistency is the last refuge of the unimaginative.
>
> Oscar Wilde

The best—and the worst—feature of Xbase is the cross-compatibility (sometimes) of the basic file structures. It's great news if you're trying to tie together an analysis piece in a spreadsheet with a data-entry product written in a front-end language and output via a third-party reporting tool, but it's hell when you're trying to hide the payroll figures.

Cross-compatibility has allowed the development of "clone" products, which perform many of the functions of the original, but either extend the functionality or improve the performance. (Fox was originally an example of both—see "It's Always Been That Way"). In addition, this compatibility allowed the development of a third-party marketplace where add-on products—database repair tools, viewers, and translators—could flourish.

The flip side of compatibility is that, like the cop when someone else is speeding, it's never there when you need it. DBFs created by one product (such as FoxPro 2.x) might not be readable in another (FoxBASE+) because of enhancements to the language, and backward (but not forward) compatibility.

We will not repeat the file extensions table, found under "File Extensions and File Types" in Help. However, we do recommend you use a good introductory FoxPro book to review the formats of PJX/PJT projects, SCX/SCT screens, FRX/FRT reports, and LBX/LBT labels.

There are a few file extensions and structures you might not see described elsewhere, but you should be aware of them. If you are called upon to examine (or exhume) applications written in another Xbase language, you might see and need to examine these files:

Extension	Purpose
BAK	Backup files—sometimes DBFs, sometimes something else.
DBC/DCT & DCX	VFP database (table, memo and index, respectively).
DBT	dBASE III memo files.
FKY	Perhaps "function key"?—macro files, documented in the Help topic "Macro File Structure." Check out PLAY MACROS in the Reference section for our thoughts on these macros.
FMT	Format files (text/program files of @ ... SAY/GET commands).

NDX, IDX	Clipper or FoxBASE/FoxPro standalone indexes, compact or non-compact.
MEM	Memory variable files: see "SAVE TO" and "RESTORE FROM" commands.
MDX	dBASE IV compound indexes.
NTX, NDX	Clipper and dBASE indexes, respectively.

A Rose By Any Other Name

You might think a DBF is a DBF, but alas, this is not so. Tables created with older products, such as FoxBASE and dBASE III, have the DBF extension, but may not be fully compatible with Visual FoxPro. Visual FoxPro DBFs cannot be read with these products, either. The first clue you may get is an error when attempting to USE a table. FoxPro determines this by reading the first byte in the DBF file (see the SYS(2029) function). If the byte is wrong, the dreaded "Not a table" message appears.

Visual FoxPro continues the tradition of backward-compatibility, since it can read DBF files created with earlier products. However, in order to facilitate linking with DBC database containers, Visual FoxPro introduced changes to the DBF header structure that make Visual FoxPro DBFs unreadable with earlier products. If you need to "regress" a Visual FoxPro table to an earlier format, you can use the TYPE FOX2X keywords with the COPY TO command.

Header Structure, bytes 0 – 31	
Location	**Meaning**
0	DBF Type, reported by SYS(2029).
1, 2, 3	Date last updated as YY, MM, DD. See LUPDATE(). Yes, astute reader, this is a Y2K problem, but resolved in VFP 6.
4, 5, 6, 7	Number of records, returned by RECCOUNT().
8, 9	Location of first data record, also HEADER().
10, 11	Record length, returned by RECSIZE().
12 – 27	Unused.
28	Bit 1: is there a structural CDX? Bit 2: is there an associated memo file? Bit 3: is this file used as a DBC?
29	Code page signature. See CPZero.PRG for translation of these values to code page values.
30, 31	Unused.

Field Records: one for each field in the table, each 32 bytes long	
Offset	**Meaning**

0 – 10	Field name, padded with CHR(0).
11	Field type, same values as TYPE().
12, 13, 14, 15	Starting location of field within record.
16	Length of the field (binary), like FSIZE().
17	Decimal length, if applicable.
18	Field-level flags: Bit 1: is this a "system" (hidden) field? Bit 2: is this field nullable? Bit 3: is this field NOCPTRANS?
19 – 31	Unused.

End of table header	
CHR(13)	Terminating character to indicate end of field information.
263 bytes	"Backlink" containing the path and filename of the database container that owns this table. CHR(0) if a free table.

The tables above show the internal structure of a Visual FoxPro table. Several VFP traits are of key interest. Byte 0, the so-called "signature byte," is always 48 (hexadecimal 0x30) for Visual FoxPro tables. Byte 28 was used in earlier FoxPro versions to designate that a CDX file was used by storing a CHR(01) in that location. This has been expanded in VFP to include whether a memo file is used for memo or general field information and also whether the table is a database container. This is accomplished by adding 2 for memo fields and 4 for DBCs. A similar pattern of "bit flags" occurs for each field record stored in the header. Byte 18 of each field record contains three bit flags: bit 0 indicates whether the field is displayed or is a hidden ("system") field; bit 1 flags whether the field can store null values; and bit 2 determines whether the field is translated to the current code page or treated as binary data.

Nulls

> What is man in nature? Nothing in relation to the infinite, everything in relation to nothing, a mean between nothing and everything.
>
> Blaise Pascal, *Pensées*, 1670

How many answers can there be to a simple question? How about three? "Yes, No, and I Don't Know." For years, Xbase had no good way to store the "I Don't Know" answer for many fields. Logical fields were restricted to .T. and .F. A character field left empty was indistinguishable from one for which the value was unknown. Numeric values were treated as zeroes if they were not filled in.

So what, you ask? Who needs them? Consider this case: you ask 10 septuagenarians their age. Eight answer: 72, 78, 73, 76, 70, 79, 72, 74. Two refuse to answer. You plug your eight answers into a field named AGE and issue the command CALCULATE AVG(AGE) for the 10 people. What's your answer? 59.4. Now, who's going to believe that? If, instead, you REPLACE AGE WITH .NULL. for the two people who refused to answer, your average is a far more believable 74.25. Nulls are very useful in many statistical calculations.

Nulls can be used in any field designated as nullable. Fields can be made nullable by checking the box at the right edge of the field description within the Table Designer, or by using the NULL keyword in CREATE TABLE or ALTER TABLE. Fields in remote views from server systems can be defined as nullable by their DBMS server, and this carries over into the view.

Understanding how nulls work within calculations is important. If any of the fields or memory variables within your system are allowed to take on the null value, you must anticipate how this value can affect calculations, functions and processing within your application. The ISNULL() function can be used to test for the presence of a null value, and the NVL() function can substitute another value (such as zero or a blank) for a value found to be .NULL. Why can't we just test a variable to see if it is equal to .NULL.? This gets back to the concept at the beginning of this section: .NULL. means "I don't know." What's the value of a mathematical expression involving .NULL.? I don't know—.NULL. One half of .NULL.? I don't know—.NULL. Is .NULL. equal to .NULL.? I don't know—.NULL. The first three characters of .NULL.? I don't know—.NULL.

Null values "propagate" through functions—if any value is not known, the result can't be known. We can't test an unknown value against another value (even another unknown) and know if they're equal. Hence the need for an ISNULL() function.

Because null values can propagate through the calculations of a system, we discourage their indiscriminate use. Carefully bracket your use of them to test and properly handle the null values. When a null value is appropriate for the data design, nothing else will do. We applaud the fact that Visual FoxPro has been endowed with this cool feature.

An interesting feature is how nulls are actually stored within a table. Since many of the field types can hold any value from 0x00 to 0xFF in each byte, it is impossible to store null values within the current disk space allocated for each field. Instead, Microsoft created a new field, called _NullFlags. _NullFlags is a "system" field, using the new byte 18, bit 0 flag in the field record portion of the file header, shown above. This field contains a bitmap, one bit for each nullable field in the table, in the physical order of the fields in the table. If a field is to be null, the associated bit is set on (to one). This seems awfully kludgy to us, but it does work, and reliably—physically rearranging the order of fields in the table, or programmatically using only some fields with SET FIELDS TO doesn't seem to trip it up. There doesn't seem to be any way within the language to access _NullFlags directly (our hacker instincts made us try), which is probably all for the best. However, having hidden, system fields in a table, which don't show up in a DISPLAY STRUCTURE, and which can trip up your space calculations (see the reference sections on AFIELDS() and RECSIZE()) is not what we consider a great leap forward. In this era of "what do you know and when did you know it," a little more in the way of full disclosure should be expected.

Take a Memo, Miss Jones

Memo and general fields store their data in a separate file, the FPT. It makes sense, since memo field data can be of varied lengths, from an empty note to a monstrous embedded WinWord dissertation. Storing this data in a separate, non-fixed-length format should minimize the use of disk space. However, poor tuning or cleanup practices can lead to severe memo field bloat. Here are two tips to minimize the "out of disk space" blues.

Each time data is written to a memo field, new blocks are added to the end of the FPT, data is added to them, and then the pointer contained within the memo header is updated to point at the new data. The old data remains within the file, and the space it occupied is not reclaimed. Over a period of time, memo fields can grow beyond control without containing that much information. This is the dreaded "memo field bloat." The relatively new ADDITIVE clause of the REPLACE command does not alleviate this, it just makes it easier to tack one more sentence onto the end of a long memo—internally, the same process occurs.

In development, you can reclaim the space with the command PACK MEMO. This packs the file in place, replacing the memo field with a far more compact one. However, as we discuss in "Commands to Use Only Interactively," the PACK command leaves the developer in the dark if something goes wrong in mid-flight. See that section for suggested work-arounds.

VFP provides the SET BLOCKSIZE command to allow you to tune and optimize your use of memo fields. BLOCKSIZE accepts a numeric argument: passing it 1 through 32 creates blocks of 512 bytes times that number; a number greater than 32 creates blocks of that number of bytes. A new option, SET BLOCKSIZE TO 0, stores the memo blocks as individual bytes, rather than as blocks. It seems to us that this method wastes the least "slack space" at the end of each memo, but might in some circumstances lead to greater overhead in processing and reading millions of teeny little blocks. We're not sure where the breakpoint is between the speed of I/O and the speed of the processor overhead, and like many other benchmark items, we encourage you to try it in your environment with your machines and data, to see what works out best for you.

dBASE III had a somewhat different method of storing the memo fields (general fields did not exist) in the DBT file. FoxPro can read and write DBT files, but should you choose to COPY a table containing a DBT memo, the new file will have an FPT memo field instead.

But We Speak Icelandic Here

Nothing could be worse than porting an application to a new platform, tweaking all the forms and programs to handle the new (or missing) features and then discovering the data is unreadable. But this was exactly what happened to many FoxPro developers as they brought their information from DOS to Windows in the 2.5 release. What happened?

What happened was code pages. A code page is the translation table that the computer uses to translate each of the characters stored on disk—8 little bits, storing one of 256 different patterns—into the single character we're used to seeing on the screen. While some of these codes are pretty standardized, people who speak any one of the thousands of languages other than English use a different code page to represent their characters. Code pages can be loaded and manipulated in DOS using the NLSFUNC, CHCP and MODE commands. A typical U.S. code page is 437 for DOS and 1252 for Windows.

In most database applications, code page translation would be a one-step, pain-in-the-neck translation from the "old" way to the "new" way, but FoxPro, thanks to its cross-platform application, supports access from multiple code pages, perhaps one on a Windows box and one on a Macintosh, simultaneously. Remarkably, it accomplishes this feat, pretty much transparently, through the use of a code page byte, stored within DBF headers and also stored as part of compiled code.

That sounds like the happy end to the story, right? We should all ride off into the sunset now. Well, it's not always that simple, pardner.

What happens if you're storing data in a field in some sort of a packed or encrypted format, where you use all 256 byte combinations, and you need to share that data with someone whose code page differs from yours? Well, without any other actions, the other user will read your data and see different numbers, translated courtesy of the Visual FoxPro engine, automatically and transparently. It's not a bug, it's a feature.

Luckily, there's a solution to this one. As part of the definition of a table at creation (see CREATE TABLE) or while maintaining a table (see ALTER TABLE), a field can be flagged as NOCPTRANS, which tells the FoxPro engine "Hands off! Don't mess with this one."

Note that the NOCPTRANS flag stored within the table itself is automatically set for Double, Integer, Datetime and Currency fields, even though it can't (and shouldn't!) be set ON or OFF programmatically for these field types. That's because the values in these fields are stored in a binary/packed format, and translation would lead to some awfully funny numbers.

Date Math

Date math is really cool. Amaze your friends, astound your competition, baffle the crowd with your ability to glibly say, "Of course, everyone knows there have been over 340,000 days since the signing of the Magna Carta, and in that time, blah blah blah..." while simply calculating:

```
? date() - {^1215-06-15}
```

A note about the curly braces above. One of the more common questions we hear is about these funny looking things, and why expressions such as:

```
{"06/" + ALLTRIM(STR(RAND ()*30)) + "/90"}
```

return empty dates. The key to understanding these braces is to understand that they are delimiters, wrapping around a set of characters and giving FoxPro an idea what's contained inside, but they are not functions with the power to evaluate their contents. Just as double and single quotes delimit a character expression, curly braces designate a date or datetime expression. Use a conversion function, such as CTOD() or DATE(), to evaluate a character function and return a date.

The second strange thing most veteran Xbase developers will notice is the prefixed caret and the strange ordering of YYYY-MM-DD. This is the strict date format, stealthily introduced into the product in Visual FoxPro 5.0. In VFP 6, the SET STRICTDATE command provides us with some ability to audit existing code and detect potential Year 2000 compatibility problcms. See "Strictly Speaking..." below for more details.

There are practical uses for this neat technology, too. Calculating 30-60-90-day aging on an account is a piece of cake. A number of days can be added or subtracted from a date, or one date can be subtracted from another to return the difference in days. The various parts of the date can be returned using the DAY(), MONTH and YEAR() functions for numeric calculation or CMONTH() and CDOW() functions for character display. Dates can be converted to character format (DToC()) or from character to date (DToC()) relatively easily.

In Visual FoxPro, dates are stored within tables as eight characters of the format YYYYMMDD. Obviously, this practically limits dates to the range of Year Zero to 9999, but that should be long enough for most of the business processes we hope to model in VFP.

A few cautions are in order. In the "good old days," we often extracted portions of a date using substring functions, modified it, and plunked it back into the value, as in the following:

```
* BAD CODE *
* Calculate the last day of the month for a supplied date dDate
nMonth=VAL(LEFT(DtoC(dDate),2)) + 1  && increment the month
nYear = VAL(RIGHT(DtoC(dDate),2))    && extract the year
if nMonth = 13
  nMonth = 1
  nYear = nYear + 1
endif
* Now create a new date, the first of next month, and decrement it one day
* to get the last date of the current month
return CtoD(STR(nMonth,2)+"/01/"+STR(nYear,2)) -1
```

Pretty clever, huh? This worked great for many small U.S.-centric companies in the 1980s, but with the coming internationalization of trade, this code is far too bigoted to make it in the '90s. The assumptions (and we all know what an assumption does, right?) that the first two characters of a date are the month, the last are the year and the middle is the day, all separated by slashes, are Stone Age logic. Check out the SET DATE command—you can bet that your branch offices in Toronto and London have. Make no assumptions about the internal position of digits within a date. Let's try this again. Trapped in a dBase III world, we could just rewrite the function, preserving the state of SET DATE, SET MARK and SET CENTURY, changing them as needed, dissecting and reassembling a date, and then resetting the SET variables again, but there's a far more graceful way, using newer FoxPro functions:

```
* Dlast() - Return the last day of the month from supplied dDate
dNewDate = GOMONTH(dDate,1)  && add a month to the date
dNewDate = dNewDate - DAY(dNewDate)  && subtract the number of days in month
return dNewDate
```

On the Other Hand...

You can do some really dumb things with date calculations. The date and datetime field types are really meant for storing contemporary date times, and are inappropriate for storing date/time fields in historical, archeological, astronomical or geological time spans. It's overly precise to try to store the start of the Jurassic era in a date field, and in fact, it's impossible to store dates Before the Common Era (BCE) or BC. Since no one really seems to know what time it is, even dates as recent as four centuries ago make the precision of the date math functions questionable.

For example, GOMONTH() won't go back further than the year 1753, the year after England took on the "Gregorian shift" of the calendar, jumping 11 days overnight and adding the bizarre leap year rules of "every four, except in years ending in 00's, except those divisible by 400." Okay, got it? Sheesh. Star-dates had better be easier than this. So GOMONTH() works for Mozart, but falls apart for Bach.

It's not just GOMONTH(), either. Adding and subtracting enough days yields wild results too. For example: {^1999-7-5} – 730246 yields "03/00/0000". Yes, DAY() verifies this date is Day Zero, and YEAR() says Year Zero. Hmmph.

Stick with the recent past, present and future, and you should be okay.

It's About Time, It's About Dates...

> My object all sublime
> I shall achieve in time—
> To make the punishment fit the crime.
>
> Sir W. S.Gilbert, *The Mikado*, 1885

A new field type, datetime, was introduced in VFP 3. While primarily intended as a compatibility feature for ease of use with similar fields in tables in a client-server environment, datetimes offer the intrepid FoxPro programmer some neat opportunities.

Datetime is stored as an eight-byte field. Supposedly the first four bytes store the date and the last four store the time. We haven't hacked this one apart, but we'd love to hear from the hackers who do.

Like currency fields stored without a unit of measure, we suggest there may be problems of determining just when this time occurred—there is no "time zone" designation. Is this GMT, Eastern Daylight Savings Time, or Bering? If you anticipate dealing with a database with multiple time zones, we suggest you consider a region-to-GMT offset table and store all times as absolute GMT datetimes for ease of calculation.

Datetimes, like dates, can be specified explicitly by using curly braces. As we explain above, delimiters don't work as conversion functions, evaluating the expression given to them, but rather just indicate constants. Nonetheless, Visual FoxPro is pretty clever, accepting any of the standard date delimiters (slash, dot or hyphen) and either 12- or 24-hour formatted time, regardless of the settings of SET MARK TO or SET HOURS. The order of the month, day and year, however, must be the same as that set by SET DATE. The only exception to that is the use of the strict date form described above. In that case, the order of the date or datetime is always in the form:

{^YYYY-MM-DD[,][HH[:MM[:SS]][A|P]]}

That syntax diagram also is a little misleading. It appears that you could supply only an hours component and the datetime would resolve. But, in fact, you get an error message. If you include only the hours component, you must either include the comma separating the date from the time, or follow the hours with a colon to have VFP interpret your datetime constant without error.

Strictly Speaking...

> Mere facts and names and dates communicate more than we suspect.
>
> Henry David Thoreau, *Journals*

Visual FoxPro 5 introduced the idea of "strict" date entry with the cleverly named StrictDateEntry property. The property allows "loose" data entry where we depend upon the machine to interpret the varieties of hyphens, dashes and slashes we throw at it. At the same time, the Fox team added a curveball: a new format for loose StrictDateEntry that allows the data-entry operator to override the preformatted date sequence by preceding the date with a caret. Following the caret, the date is always interpreted in a consistent manner: year, month, day, and, in the case of datetime values, hour, minute and second.

This innovation in VFP 5 laid the groundwork for the introduction in VFP 6 of the SET STRICTDATE command. This command, essential for ensuring Year 2000 compliance in code, generates errors at compile time, and optionally at runtime, reporting that code contains dates that can be ambiguous. Since the ordering of day, month and year is determined by SET DATE, both in the runtime and development environments, "constants" (as well as expressions using the date conversion functions like CTOD()) can be interpreted in more than one way. The SET STRICTDATE command flags these variable constants unless they, too, now use the strict date format of caret, year, month, day. For conversion from string to date or datetime, the DATE() and DATETIME() functions have been beefed up.

Float, Double, Integer, Numeric and Currency—What's in a Number

There are a number (sorry) of different fields in Fox, all of which seem to store the same or similar data. The reason for this is primarily backward and sideways compatibility with previous Fox and Xbase products. There are some differences, however...

Float

Seems to be same as numeric. Float exists to allow compatibility with other database products that treated numeric and float fields differently. Visual FoxPro treats them no differently internally.

Double

Always seems to store as length 8, but allows you to change decimal places from zero to 18. A fixed format used primarily for client-server compatibility, it's manipulated internally the same as any other numeric by FoxPro, but stored differently.

Integer

Integer is probably one of the most useful new data types introduced in Visual FoxPro 3.0. Stored in only four bytes on disk, the field has a range from –2147483647 to plus 2147483647. If you need to track whole numbers only, this can be a compact and efficient way to do it. We find these fields to be ideal as primary keys, since they're small and form smaller indexes, and also are easy to manipulate and increment. They're also the fastest way to join tables in a SQL SELECT.

Numeric

A numeric field allows up to 20 numeric digits to be entered, but one space is occupied by the decimal place, if used. Microsoft describes accuracy as 16 digits, but 14 seems closer to the truth. Check this out:

```
lnNumeric = 98765432109876543210  && Here's 20 digits
* In VFP 3, you'll see these numbers with no
* digits to the left of the decimal point and
* with exponents of 20. In VFP 5 and 6, Microsoft adopted the
* more common syntax of making the mantissa a single digit shown below:
? lnNumeric                      && displays 9.8765432109876E+19
? str(lnNumeric)                 && displays 9.876E+19
? str(lnNumeric,16)              && displays 9.876543210E+19
? str(lnNumeric,20)              && displays 9.8765432109876E+19
? str(lnNumeric,25)              && displays 9.87654321098763900OE+19
```

Numeric fields are stored in character format, as ".98765432109876E+20".

Currency

> Only one fellow in ten thousand understands the currency question, and we meet him every day.
>
> Kin Hubbard

A currency field is a fixed numeric field, always stored as eight bytes, with four decimal places. These fields are marked by default as NOCPTRANS, since the data is packed. Currency is a funny field type. Just as datetime stores a time without a time zone, currency stores a value without a unit. Also like datetime, this field type was introduced primarily for compatibility with client-server databases. But is this currency in dollars, Euros, or yen? An international application needs to know if it's running in Zurich or New Delhi.

Like datetime, currency introduces some new functions and delimiters into the language. NTOM() and MTON() convert numerics to currency and vice versa. The dollar-sign delimiter preceding a numeric literal forces the type to currency.

Math involving currency and other numerics introduces a new kink. What's the result of multiplying two currency values—a numeric or a currency value? What about trigonometry on these values? We could engage in quite a diatribe on the meaning of unitless and "unit-ed" variables being processed together, but it doesn't really matter—Microsoft has a method to its madness, and while it might be different from what we would've come out with, it works under most circumstances: basic four-function math (addition, subtraction, multiplication and division) involving currency gives results in currency. Exponentiation and trigonometry yield numerics.

Logical

> “Contrariwise,” continued Tweedledee, “if it was so, it might be; and if it were so, it would be; but as it isn't, it ain't. That's logic.”
>
> Lewis Carroll, *Through the Looking-Glass*, 1872

Not too much has changed with the logical field type since the FoxPro 2.x days. With the introduction of NULLs, described above, a logical field can contain a third value, .NULL., as well as the standard values of .T. and .F. (Okay, it's true they could contain a fourth state of BLANK, but we strongly argue against it). Logical fields take up one byte in a table, even though they really only need a single bit. With the data compression Microsoft implemented in double, datetime, currency, and integer fields, as well as shrinking the size of the memo and general fields from 10 bytes to four, we're surprised they didn't try to implement some sort of byte-and-offset addressing for storing multiple logical fields in a single byte as well.

Hip Hip Array!

Arrays are not truly a different type of variable, but they are a method of aggregating several values, of the same or different types, into one place. Arrays make it easier to handle things like disk directories (ADIR()), field descriptions (AFIELDS()) and object properties, events and methods (AMEMBERS()). Arrays can be used to hold data on its way to and from tables—SCATTER, GATHER and INSERT all support array clauses. Understanding how to manipulate these arrays, especially how they are referenced by different functions, is an important aspect of Visual FoxPro programming.

Arrays come in two flavors—one-dimensional and two-dimensional—distinguished by the number of subscripts supplied with them. However, internally, both array types are stored the same way, and functions that work with one type work with the other as well. This can lead to some confusion. Suppose you create an array:

```
LOCAL ARRAY aRay[2,5]
```

We would view this array as a table of two rows and five columns, and on the whole, Visual FoxPro would be willing to go along with us on this. But if we try to locate a value that we know is in the third element of the second row by using the ASCAN() function:

```
aRay[2,3] = "My value"
? ASCAN(aRAY,"My value")
```

Visual FoxPro returns 6! Well, what would you expect? 2? 3? Since Visual FoxPro is limited to returning a single value from a function, it returns the ordinal number of the element in the array. We can use the function ASUBSCRIPT() to get the appropriate row and column values:

```
? ASUBSCRIPT(aRay,ASCAN(aRay,"My value"),1)   && returns 2
? ASUBSCRIPT(aRay,ASCAN(aRay,"My value"),2)   && returns 3
```

Even more interesting, we can just use the single digit returned. The fact is that FoxPro is willing to use any combination of rows and columns we supply to reference an element as long as we do not exceed the defined number of rows:

```
? aRay[6]     && displays "My Value"
? aRay[1,6]   && also displays "My value"
? aRay[2,3]   && "My value" again
? aRay[6,1]   && Whoa! Errors with "Subscript is outside defined range"
```

You can determine the number of rows and columns of an array by using the ALEN() function.

You can change the dimensions of an array on the fly by issuing another DIMENSION, LOCAL ARRAY or PUBLIC statement, depending on the scope of your variable. Redimensioning does not erase the values of the array, but it can rearrange them in some pretty funny ways. The values originally assigned to the array in ordinal form are reassigned to the new array in the same order. This can result in some pretty useless looking arrays, with values slipping diagonally across the columns. Instead, try out our aColCopy() function (under ACOPY() in the Reference section) for a better way to do this.

Many functions also redimension arrays automatically to fit the contents of the function. As a general rule, functions redimension arrays to fit only those values the function returns. Typically, the array is created or redimensioned only if the function has something to put in it. We note in the Reference section where functions don't follow these thumbrules.

The array manipulations you'll often want to do are inserting and deleting rows from the array, and you'll probably suspect that AINS() and ADEL() are the functions to do this. Foolish mortal. AINS() does, in fact, create a row of new values (all initialized to .F.), but it does this by pushing the following rows down, until the last falls off the array into the bit bucket. ADEL() reverses the process, causing rows of elements to move up over the deleted one, and leaving an empty row at the bottom. In both cases, a call to DIMENSION or its equivalent before or after the function, respectively, will complete what you need to do. Again, more information on this, and the far less simple column operations, is available in the Reference section, under the associated functions, as well as in the overview "Array Manipulation."

Passing an Array

An array can only be passed to another routine using explicit referencing. That means the array name must be preceded with the symbol "@" when passed as a parameter. Forgetting to append this symbol causes only the first element of the array to be passed; this is one of our favorite programming omissions that drive us mad trying to troubleshoot.

An array passed by reference, as we explain in "It's Always Been That Way" really has only one occurrence in memory, and all changes performed by called routines have their effect on this one array. Caution is called for.

International Settings: Using the Control Panel

> Henry IV's feet and armpits enjoyed an international reputation.
>
> Aldous Huxley

There's a wonderful though little used resource for international settings—dates, times, currency, etc.—available through the Windows Control Panel, in the Regional Settings applet. These dialogs are available to your users, and you don't have to maintain the code! What you do have to do is check to see if your users have modified them. In Windows 3.1 we used the Windows API function GetProfileString() to get values from the [intl] section of Win.INI. In the jet-setting 32-bit world of the late '90s, check out the Registry under HKEY_CURRENT_USER\Control Panel\International and modify the behavior of your application appropriately. See SET SYSFORMATS for more information on using the user's Windows settings.

General Fields: Object Linking and Embedding

> I drink to the general joy of the whole table.
>
> William Shakespeare, *Macbeth*

General fields are Visual FoxPro's implementation of the technology formerly known as "Object Linking and Embedding," then "OLE," and then "Active" something or other. While the marketeers don't seem to be happy with any name they've thought of so far, the idea of this portion of the implementation remains the same: provide a portal between FoxPro and some other application (the "OLE Server") and store the information about that link and the data shared here.

OLE, er, Active, er, this stuff is no cakewalk. For many of the gory details, see the section "Active Something" as well as the individual reference sections for APPEND GENERAL, MODIFY GENERAL, OLEControl and OLEBoundControl.

A couple of cautions here. General fields contain several pieces of information: all contain "display data," and have either a path to data (for linked data) or the embedded data itself. The "display" or "presentation" data is a raw BMP that Visual FoxPro uses to show that the field is occupied. In Word 2.0, this was the big blue W logo. Word 6.0 allows you to store a representation of the first page of a document. MS Graph shows—surprise!—the graph. But some OLE severs can be a problem. Graphics servers, which store pictures, are usually forced to provide Visual FoxPro with a BMP for presentation data, even if their graphic is in another format (like the far more compact JPG format). This BMP can be HUGE—a large image rendered in 24-bitplanes (roughly a bazillion colors) can take megabytes of space. This space is used even if the data is only linked to the field! Anticipate a large amount of storage space if you choose to link very large or very high-resolution documents. Consider other techniques (such as just storing the path and filenames in a character field, and using a cursor to hold one image at a time) if disk space is a concern.

One last note about general fields. A general field is nothing more than a special form of the memo field that contains binary data, including a "wrapper" around the data that tells FoxPro who to call to manipulate this data—the OLE server. When data is called up and changed and saved back to the memo field, new blocks of the memo field are allocated for the new data, and the old blocks are internally marked as not used. These old blocks are never reused. What happens over a period of time is that the memo file will grow and grow and grow. To alleviate this problem, you can consider using the PACK MEMO command to shrink the file (but only after reading the cautions in "Commands Never to Use") or use the equivalent COPY/SELECT, RENAME, DELETE routine to refresh the file.

File storage within Visual FoxPro is similar to earlier versions of FoxPro, but with some powerful enhancements provided by the Database Container. New fields and field capabilities have been added. Some compatibility has been lost, but we feel the benefits of the new features far outweigh the limitations, and that workarounds are available for most of the incompatibilities.

Xbase Xplained

> To him who looks upon the world rationally, the world in its turn presents a rational aspect. The relation is mutual.
>
> Georg Wilhelm Friedrich Hegel, *Philosophy of History*, 1832

FoxPro's oldest heritage is its Xbase heritage. As we said in "It's Always Been That Way," Xbase has a long and varied history. This section explains the basic language concepts that derive from that history.

dBase was originally conceived primarily as an interactive language. Because of this, many of the older commands' default behavior focuses on interactive results, with optional clauses available to use the command programmatically.

Do You Work Here?

The nature of a relational database like FoxPro is that you need to work with many tables at once. You couldn't get much work done if you had access to only one table at a time. Xbase handles this by providing multiple work areas, each capable of handling one table and its related indexes.

The available number of work areas has been one of the carrots manufacturers have used in the Xbase competition. In ancient Xbase history, there were two work areas. By dBase III Plus and FoxBase+, 10 work areas were provided and each table could be opened with up to seven index files. In FoxPro 2.5, the number of available work areas went up to 225. Since you'd run out of file handles long before you could open 225 different tables, you'd think that would be sufficient for anyone's needs, even if some tables are open several times. But Visual FoxPro raised the stakes again, providing 32,767 work areas. Yes, 32K work areas! (In fact, there are 32,767 work areas per data session. More on data sessions later.) While this seems extravagant (in fact, ridiculous) at first glance, it leaves room for a lot of things going on behind the scenes which weren't there before. Visual FoxPro's buffering and multiple data sessions require a lot more work areas than ever before. Remember that each file still needs one or more file handles (See "Hardware and Software Recommendations"), so while you can open the same tables many times, you still can't open 400 tables at once—not that you'd ever want to.

It's also interesting that Visual FoxPro's databases, a much newer concept than tables, don't require work areas. We guess Microsoft found a better way to handle this internally. There's no documented limit on how many databases you can open simultaneously, but databases require file handles (three, actually—one each for DBC, DCT and DCX) so you are typically limited to fewer than 30 on a system with file handles of 100, or around 80 on a system with 255 handles.

Work areas are numbered from 1 to 32767 and can be referenced by number, as in:

```
SELECT 27
```

Doing so is usually a bad idea, except when hacking from the command window. Similarly, it is poor form to refer to the first 10 work areas by the letters A–J, a historical vestige of the days when there were only 10 work areas.

Once a table is open in a work area, you should refer to that work area by the table's alias, like this:

```
SELECT Customer
```

Before that, it doesn't matter which work area you use. You can get to the lowest available work area by issuing:

```
SELECT 0
```

or to the highest available work area (why? we dunno, but you can) with:

```
SELECT SELECT(1)
```

To open a table in the lowest available work area, there are two choices. As above, you can use SELECT 0:

```
SELECT 0
USE MyTable
```

or you can incorporate the 0 in the USE command:

```
USE MyTable IN 0
```

There is one subtle (and undocumented) difference between those two sequences. The first leaves you in the work area containing the newly opened MyTable. The second leaves you in whatever work area you were in before. It opens the table, then returns to the current work area. We can't tell you how many times we've fallen into this trap.

As the previous paragraph implies, you're "in" one work area at a time. That is, one work area is always current.

You can refer to fields of the table open in that work area without aliasing them. Also, many commands are scoped (see below) to the current work area.

To make a different work area current, you SELECT it, preferably by using the alias of the table open in that work area:

```
SELECT MyOtherTable
```

To close the table open in a work area, issue USE with no alias:

```
USE   && closes the table in the current work area
```

Or specify an alias to close that one:

```
USE IN MyTable && closes the table opened with alias "MyTable"
```

So What's Your Point?

Xbase (unlike SQL) is a record-based language. Just as Xbase always believes one work area is the "current" area, one record in each table is also "current." So, in each open table, Xbase maintains a record pointer. The record pointer always points to a single record. Many commands operate on the record pointed to.

Lots of Xbase commands move the record pointer. Some are specifically designed to move the pointer, while others do it more or less as a side effect. The second type is discussed in the next section, "Scope, FOR, WHILE (and Santa) Clauses."

Commands designed to move the record pointer can be further divided into two groups: those that move it based on position and those that move it based on content. GO and SKIP fall into the position category, while LOCATE, CONTINUE and SEEK are in the content category.

Both GO and SKIP are affected by an active index order. If you've SET ORDER TO something other than 0, GO TOP and GO BOTTOM move to the top and bottom of the current order, respectively. (However, they can do so pretty slowly. See "Faster than a Speeding Bullet" for hints on doing this better.)

Only GO <n> is absolute. It moves to the record whose record number is <n>, regardless of any order. This, of course, makes GO <n> nearly useless. Its only real utility is in returning the record pointer to a previous position after a command has moved it. For example:

```
nHoldRec=RECNO()
COUNT FOR category="Oddities"
GO nHoldRec
```

Unfortunately, even that simple piece of code won't always work. If the record pointer is at EOF() before the COUNT, the GO fails. Instead, you have to do it like this:

```
nHoldRec=IIF(EOF(),0,RECNO())
COUNT FOR category="Oddities"
IF nHoldRec=0
   GO BOTTOM
   SKIP
ELSE
   GO nHoldRec
ENDIF
```

Except in the situation above, stay away from referring to records by their record numbers. Record numbers are a volatile thing. If you delete some records and pack the table, the record numbers change. The real point is that you don't need record numbers. FoxPro has plenty of other tools to find a particular record.

Scope, FOR, WHILE (and Santa) Clauses

Xbase commands operate on groups of records—a group may be as small as one record or as large as an entire table. There are three ways to specify which records are affected by an Xbase command. They are Scope, the FOR clause and the WHILE clause. All three reflect the record order-based nature of Xbase processing.

Almost all the record processing commands that originated in Xbase accept all three clauses. The group includes DELETE, RECALL, REPLACE, LIST, DISPLAY, AVERAGE, COUNT, SUM, CALCULATE, LABEL FORM, REPORT FORM, SCAN and LOCATE, as well as some others.

The next few sections describe each of the record-selection mechanisms. Then, "Combining the Clauses" talks about their interactions.

A Grand Scope

The designers of Xbase provided several ways of choosing a group of records based on their position in the table: choosing all the records in a table, choosing a single record, choosing several records in sequence, and choosing all the records from the present location to the end of the table. They grouped these four choices together and called them "scope." You specify them by including the appropriate clause, respectively: ALL, RECORD <n>, NEXT <n>, or REST. Note that <n> means a record number for RECORD, but means "how many" for NEXT. Also, be aware that NEXT and REST are interpreted according to the current index order. Commands that accept a scope clause use a default scope if no scope term is included. Those commands that have the potential to be destructive default to NEXT 1. Commands that can't do any damage to the database's records generally default to ALL. For example, DELETE and REPLACE have a default scope of NEXT 1, while LIST and REPORT default to ALL.

You'll find that you use ALL and NEXT quite a bit, while RECORD and REST seem somewhat antiquated in a set-based world. In fact, there are some good times to use REST, but we haven't used RECORD in years.

FOR Better or FOR Worse

The FOR clause allows a command to process records based on content, regardless of the position of the record in the table.

Prior to FoxPro 2.0, this made a FOR clause something to be avoided at all costs. With Rushmore optimization, FOR clauses can be very fast. (That's "FOR better.") However, if a FOR expression can't be optimized, it can ruin performance. (That's "FOR worse.")

FOR accepts a logical expression and processes all records for which that expression is true. This makes it just the thing for getting a list of all customers in the UK:

```
BROWSE FOR Country = "UK"
```

or for replacing all occurrences of a misspelled string with the correctly spelled version:

```
REPLACE LastName WITH "Quayle" FOR LastName="Quail" AND NOT IsBird
```

Note that giving REPLACE a FOR (or WHILE) clause changes its default scope to ALL.

Any command including a FOR clause may be optimizable. See "Faster Than a Speeding Bullet" for hints on how to optimize these commands.

WHILE Away the Hours

WHILE is used when records are already ordered the way you want. It processes records starting with the current record and continues until it encounters a record that doesn't meet the condition.

WHILE is handy for things like totaling all the detail records of an invoice:

```
SELECT Detail
SET ORDER TO InvId
SEEK Invoice.InvId
SUM DetAmt WHILE InvId=Invoice.InvId TO InvTotal
```

or changing the area code for all the people with a particular phone exchange:

```
SELECT People
* Tag Phone is on the actual phone number field;
```

```
* area code is a separate field.
SET ORDER TO Phone
SEEK "555"
REPLACE AreaCode WITH "610" WHILE Phone="555"
```

Our first version of the SEEK, then REPLACE WHILE example, ran into a nasty, subtle problem in working with ordered data. We planned to show changing the ZIP code field for everyone in a particular zip code (something that actually happened to Tamar a few years ago). The code looks like this:

```
SET ORDER TO zip
SEEK "19117"
REPLACE Zip WITH "19027" WHILE Zip="19117"
```

But, using this approach, you can't do that. With order set to zip code, once you change the zip code field for a record, it moves to its new position. In the example, as soon as one record gets the new zip code, it moves to join the other "19027"s. Unless you're particularly lucky, when the record pointer moves forward, it's no longer on a "19117" record and the REPLACE ends. You can run into the same problem when you SCAN with order set.

To do the zip code replacement, you need to use REPLACE FOR instead:

```
REPLACE Zip WITH "19027" FOR Zip="19117"
```

When you use WHILE, you need to position the record pointer to the beginning of the group of records you want to process. When you finish, the record pointer is on the first record that doesn't match the criteria.

Combining the Clauses

Scope, FOR and WHILE can be combined in a single command. The interactions are logical, but not necessarily intuitive.

First, realize that FOR has an implied (or default) scope of ALL. Any command containing FOR without a scope clause or a WHILE clause checks all records. This means it's not necessary to use the ALL keyword here:

```
REPLACE ALL vegetable WITH "Lettuce" FOR vegetable = "Broccoli"
```

If no other scope is included, and there's no WHILE clause, the record pointer is left at EOF() after a FOR clause.

WHILE has an implied scope of REST, but it may stop short of the end of the file if the WHILE condition is no longer met.

So, what happens when you combine these babies? Adding scope to either FOR or WHILE means that it behaves as it usually does, but only processes records in the specific scope. So:

```
BROWSE NEXT 20 FOR State = "Confusion"
```

displays all of the next 20 records that meet the FOR criteria, but it does *not* display the next 20 records that do.

Combining FOR and WHILE seems contradictory, but actually it's not. The key to understanding such a command is knowing that the WHILE is in charge with the FOR just helping out. In other words, we process records until we find one that fails the WHILE test, but we only process those that pass the FOR test. For example:

```
SELECT Employee
SET ORDER TO GroupId
SEEK "     2"
LIST First_Name, Last_Name WHILE GroupId = SPACE(5)+"2" FOR NOT EMPTY(Photo)
```

lists only those employees in group 2 for whom we have a photo on file.

As we mentioned above, a few commands accept only FOR and not WHILE. LOCATE accepts both a FOR and a WHILE clause, but the FOR clause is required in that case. That is, to find group 2 employees with photos, you can:

```
LOCATE FOR NOT EMPTY(Photo) WHILE GroupId = SPACE(5)+"2"
```

but you can't use WHILE to look for all the group 2 people, like this:

```
LOCATE WHILE GroupId = SPACE(5)+"2"
```

This behavior makes some sense. Using just WHILE with LOCATE isn't very useful. You might as well use SKIP and test the condition. WHILE requires the records to be in order anyway, so LOCATE WHILE is overkill. However, we might want to search only in a specific group of records for the first meeting a condition. LOCATE FOR with a WHILE clause does that for us.

Shall I Compare Thee to a Summer Day?

One of the most confusing aspects of Xbase is the way string comparison works. The Xbase way is to compare strings only to the end of the right-hand string. If they match up to that point, they're considered equal.

Given Xbase's interactive history, it's not really bad behavior. When you're searching for a particular record or want to find all the records that match a given string, it's kind of nice to not have to type out the whole string to match. But in programs, this behavior can be a disaster.

The SET EXACT command controls string comparisons for Xbase commands. For more than you ever wanted to know about this subject, check out SET EXACT in the reference section.

Operator, Operator, Give Me Number Nine

> "Reeling and Writhing, of course, to begin with," the Mock Turtle replied, "and the different branches of Arithmetic—Ambition, Distraction, Uglification, and Derision."
>
> Lewis Carroll, *Alice's Adventures in Wonderland*, 1865

Remember seventh grade (or maybe it was sixth or eighth) when you learned a mnemonic that went something like "Please Excuse My Dear Aunt Sally?" Right about now, you're probably scratching your head and saying, "Oh, sure, those are the Great Lakes, right?," or "Yeah, that sounds familiar, but what's it about?" unless, like us, you remember this kind of stuff forever, and you're sitting there saying "Sure, parentheses, exponents, multiplication, division, addition, subtraction." You got it: the mnemonic provides the order of precedence of numeric operators. That is, when you see:

```
3 + 7 * 4
```

you know that it's 31, not 40, because multiplication comes before addition (except in the dictionary). On the other hand:

```
(3 + 7) * 4
```

is 40 because parentheses come before any other operators. When there are multiple operators at the same level, they're evaluated left to right.

In Xbase, there are a bunch of other operators besides arithmetic operators. Comparison operators (=, <>, <, >, <=, >=, and $) are used to compare values (big surprise). Logical operators (AND, OR, NOT) are used to combine logical expressions (often comparisons).

Some of the operators used for arithmetic can also be applied to other data types (all of them for double, integer and currency, + and - for characters, - for dates and datetimes). There's also one additional arithmetic operator (%, which is the same as MOD()) that applies to numeric, double, integer and currency values.

The arithmetic precedence rules have been extended to cover the full set of operators. Arithmetic operators used on other types have the same precedence as when they're used with numbers. The % has the same precedence as multiplication and division.

The complete precedence rules for FoxPro are somewhat different than those in some other programming languages. In particular, logical operators come below arithmetic and comparison operators:

- Parentheses

- Exponentiation
- Multiplication/Division/Modulo
- Addition/Subtraction
- Comparison
- NOT
- AND
- OR

Maybe the FoxPro version of the old mnemonic should be "Please Excuse Miss Daisy Mae And Sally Combing Nits All October?" Maybe not.

Just Some Routine Inquiries, Ma'am

A subroutine (or sub-program, as some folks call them) is a program that is called from another program, performs a task, and then returns to the calling program, which picks up where it left off. We like to think of the original routine as getting moved to the back burner until the subroutine finishes executing, then it comes back to the front burner again.

Like many programming languages, FoxPro has two kinds of subroutines: procedures and functions. The big difference in using them is that a function returns a value while a procedure doesn't, so a function call can appear as part of an expression while a procedure call cannot.

By the way, many people refer to functions and even procedures as UDFs for "user-defined functions." This is to distinguish them from FoxPro's built-in functions. Historically, there have been some places where a built-in function could be used, but a UDF could not, though we can't think of any in Visual FoxPro.

In many programming languages, there's a distinction drawn between procedures and functions: a subroutine is one or the other. Not so in FoxPro. Here, any subroutine can be either a procedure or a function. In fact, it's not the name you give the subroutine when you define it (either PROCEDURE MyRoutine or FUNCTION MyRoutine) that determines whether it's a procedure or function: it's the way you call it. That is, the same subroutine can be called as a function sometimes and as a procedure at others. Like this:

```
DO MyRoutine with Param1, Param2
```

or

```
? MyRoutine(Param1, Param2)
```

Why does this matter? Two reasons. One we already mentioned: functions return a value. When you call a function as a procedure, the return value is thrown away. (When you call a procedure as a function, and there's no return value, the function returns .T.)

Throughout Xbase history, when you called a routine as a function (with the parentheses at the end), you had to do something with the result. You couldn't write:

```
MyRoutine()
```

Instead, you needed to either assign the result to a variable, use it in an expression, display it, or throw it out. Here are examples of each:

```
MyResult = MyRoutine()   && value assigned to MyResult
IF MyRoutine() > 7 ...   && value tested
? MyRoutine()            && value displayed
= MyRoutine()            && value thrown out
```

The equal notation in the last example says to run the function and throw away the return value. The only reason to do it that way is if you're running the function for what it does and not for what it returns—that is, for its side effects. (More on side effects later.)

Starting in VFP5, you can cut to the chase and just call the function without doing anything with the result.

Pass the Parameters, Please

The other important distinction between procedures and functions has to do with parameter passing. Parameters are the way one routine communicates with another. Think of the name of a subroutine as being an instruction to do something. Then, the parameters are the items the instruction applies to. Let's look at a built-in function as an example:

```
UPPER(LastName)
```

says "Apply the UPPER function to the LastName field and return the result." Since UPPER() converts whatever you give it to uppercase, you get back something like this:

```
"GATES"
```

Sometimes the routine needs several pieces of information to carry out its task. For example, the built-in function SUBSTR() returns part of a character string you pass it (that is, a substring). It accepts two or three parameters: the string to work on, the place the substring starts, and, if you want, the length of the substring. Here's an example:

```
SUBSTR("The quick Visual FoxPro jumped over the slower dogs", ;
       11, 13)
```

returns:

```
Visual FoxPro
```

A subroutine must indicate what parameters it expects to receive. There are three ways to do so: the PARAMETERS statement, the LPARAMETERS statement, and by listing them in parentheses in the routine's header line (PROCEDURE or FUNCTION declaration). The PARAMETERS statement creates the parameters as private variables, while the other two methods create them as local variables. (See "Scope It Out!" below for the distinction between private and local.)

There are two ways of passing parameters: by value and by reference. The passing method indicates whether the subroutine can affect the original item passed to the routine.

If you want to be technical about it, the parameters specified in the subroutine are called "formal parameters," while the items you pass are called "actual parameters." The method of passing parameters determines whether the actual parameters change when the formal parameters are changed.

Got it? Neither did we, nor did our students the first few times. So let's not be technical about it. Think of it this way, instead: When you pass by value, the items you pass are copied to the parameters listed in the subroutine. Any changes to the parameters don't affect the items in the call. When you pass by reference, FoxPro makes an internal connection between the items you pass and the parameters, so changes to the parameters ripple back to the items you passed.

In fact, it turns out that the names of the two methods are pretty informative. When you pass by value, the value of the item is passed, not the item itself. When you pass by reference, FoxPro creates a reference to the original item. Better now?

Now here's the sneaky part. Ordinarily, you don't explicitly specify the parameter passing method—it's implied by the subroutine call. Functions pass parameters by value; procedures pass by reference. Remembering that it's the call that determines whether it's a procedure or a function, that's a major implication. The same routine may behave very differently, depending how you call it.

Here's a very simple example. We usually check parameters at the beginning of a routine to make sure they're the right type and have realistic values. Suppose the beginning of a subroutine looks like this:

```
PROCEDURE ProcessDate
PARAMETER dInput

IF TYPE('dInput')<>"D"
   dInput=DATE()
ENDIF
* now do whatever
```

Now look at these two calls to the routine:

```
MyDate = "Sandy"
? ProcessDate( MyDate )
```

or

```
MyDate="Sandy"
DO ProcessDate WITH MyDate
```

In the first case, the variable MyDate isn't affected by the error checking in the routine. In the second case, MyDate gets changed to today's date (and isn't Sandy's mother surprised?).

Normally, this isn't a problem since most routines are called either as procedures or as functions, not both. So let's move on to another issue.

There's a principle of structured programming that says functions shouldn't have "side effects." This means that functions should accept some parameters, do some processing and return a value—without changing anything in the environment. (It reminds us of the Scouting maxim for visiting the wilderness—"Take only pictures, leave only footprints.")

This is why parameters are passed to functions by value. (There is one case, discussed below, where it's essential to pass by reference.) Anyway, suppose you don't have any principles and you want to pass a parameter to a function by reference. Can you do it?

Of course you can—this is FoxPro, after all. In fact, there are not one, but two ways. One is global while the other is local. The global approach uses a SET command—SET UDFPARMS. You can SET UDFPARMS TO VALUE (the default) or TO REFERENCE. When you do so, all subsequent function calls use the specified method.

The local approach is to prefix the actual parameter (the item you're passing) with the "@" symbol. For example:

```
=MyFunction(@MyVariable)
```

calls MyFunction, passing MyVariable by reference.

On the whole, we prefer local approaches to local problems. Remember that environmental slogan, "Think Globally, Act Locally"? The same thing applies here. Consider the overall effects of your actions, but take the actions over the smallest possible scope. The problem with SET UDFPARMS is that it can have unexpected effects. Suppose you change it to REFERENCE and call a function. Suppose that function in turn calls another function, which expects its parameters to be passed by value. The inner function may change one of its parameters (not expecting that to affect anything outside the function), which in turn changes the results of the function you called. What a mess.

No, we didn't forget the one case where you have to pass by reference. When you specify an array in a function call (with UDFPARMS set to VALUE), only the first element of the array is passed. Makes it a little hard to, say, total the array elements. To pass an entire array to a function, you must pass by reference. So, a call to our fictional array totaling function would look like:

```
nTotal=SumArray(@aMyArray)
```

What about the flip side—suppose you want to pass by value to a procedure. Surprisingly, there's only one, local, way to do it—no equivalent of SET UDFPARMS in sight. All it takes is to turn the actual parameter into an expression. This is best demonstrated by the fact that you can pass constants to a procedure. For example, the following is a valid procedure call:

```
DO MyProcedure WITH 14, 29, 93, "Hike"
```

as long as MyProcedure expects four parameters.

But how do you turn a variable into an expression? Simple: put parentheses around it and it becomes something that FoxPro evaluates before passing. Voila—pass by value. Here's an example:

```
DO MyOtherProcedure WITH (MyVariable), (MyOtherVariable)
```

We've noticed in the last few years that more and more programmers (ourselves included) have a tendency to use only functions and not procedures. This is partly a consequence of object-oriented programming (methods, after all, feel an awful lot like functions). We're not sure yet whether this is a good thing or a bad thing. Since many of the routines we write actually do something other than returning a value, calling them as functions certainly does violate the old rule about side effects. If nothing else, be sure to document the effects your code has on the environment.

Two's Company ... Three's Even Better

FoxPro has allowed you to pass fewer parameters than a routine expects for quite a long time. The actual parameters are matched to the formal parameters (those declared with a PARAMETERS or LPARAMETERS statement) one by one, and the extra formal parameters at the end get initialized to .F. The PARAMETERS() function (and the superior PCOUNT()) tells you how many parameters were actually passed, so you can give the rest useful defaults.

In Visual FoxPro, things are even better, though more confusing, too. You can choose to omit actual parameters even if they're not at the end of the list. Just put in a comma placeholder and the corresponding formal parameter gets initialized to .F.

While we welcome this change because it means parameters can be grouped logically instead of based on the likelihood of needing them, it also introduces new complexity. It used to be simple. Check PARAMETERS() and you knew that everything after that had defaulted to .F. Now that's not enough. You have to check each parameter to make sure it's got a value of the right type. Of course, that's a good idea in any case, since you can also pass the wrong type anyway.

Mom Was Right

The mess you can cause with SET UDFPARMS leads to an observation about subroutines in general. They should make no assumptions about the environment in which they're called and should clean up after themselves. This means a routine shouldn't expect a certain variable to exist or that any SET commands (like SET EXACT or SET DELETED) will have particular values. If it changes any of those, it should set them back to their original values before exiting. Routines following these rules will be welcome in any programming neighborhood.

Can You Offer a Subroutine a Good Home?

There are at least three places you can store subroutines in FoxPro. Each routine can be stored in its own PRG file (for performance implications, see "Faster than a Speeding Bullet"), a routine can be stored with the program that uses it, or you can group a bunch of routines together into a "procedure file" (which can contain functions as well as procedures).

Prior to FoxPro 2.0, separate PRG files were too much trouble to manage. You had to remember where possibly hundreds of little programs could be found. So, most people stored subroutines used by only one program with that program, and more widely used subroutines were stored in a procedure file. But there were problems with that approach, since only one procedure file could be used at a time, and there was no way to save the name of the current procedure file before switching to another.

The Project Manager changed all that. It remembered where you left a function so you didn't have to. Suddenly, keeping every routine in a separate PRG file became feasible. Several well-respected FoxPro developers suggested directory structures to aid in this endeavor. Others offered programs to automate the process of breaking a procedure file into its component parts.

With Visual FoxPro, the waters have been muddied. The SET PROCEDURE command now supports an ADDITIVE clause, so multiple procedure files can be set. On the other hand, the Project Manager is still happy to do the work for you. Finally, object orientation means that code is stored with data for anything defined as an object and the database allows some code to be stored there as well.

Our preference is still for stand-alone PRG files for code that isn't object method code.

Scope it Out!

> Desiring this man's art, and that man's scope,
> With what I most enjoy contented least;
> Yet in these thoughts myself almost despising,
> Haply I think on thee.
>
> William Shakespeare, *Sonnet 29, l. 7*

By now, it should be no surprise that the word "scope" has two distinct meanings in FoxPro. One is discussed above in "Scope, FOR, WHILE (and Santa) Clauses." The other (which has nothing to do with the first) applies to visibility of variables.

Variables in FoxPro have three possible scopes: public, private and local. They vary as to which routines (other than the one in which the variable was created) can see and change the variable.

Doing it in Public

Public variables are exhibitionists. They're visible in every routine in an application except any that have an identically named private or local variable. Anybody can use their value; anybody can change it.

Any variable you create in the Command Window is public. Otherwise, to create public variables, you need to use the PUBLIC keyword. In older versions of FoxPro, PUBLIC was picky—if the variable existed when you tried to make it public, you got an error message. Although VFP no longer complains about this, most FoxPro programmers make it a habit to write it this way:

```
RELEASE PublicVar
PUBLIC PublicVar
```

The RELEASE doesn't do any harm if the variable doesn't exist already, but protects you if it does. Variables created this way start out life as logical with a value of .F.

Public variables stick around until you explicitly release them. It's not good enough to say RELEASE ALL, either. You've got to list them out, one by one, in order to release them (unless you do in the Command Window, where RELEASE ALL does release all public variables—go figure). That's as good a reason as any to stay away from public variables.

Actually, you should keep public variables to a minimum. As with SET commands, they're often a global solution to a local problem. Frequently, creating a private variable at the appropriate level in your program will give you the same results.

There is one "gotcha" involving public variables. If you pass a public variable by reference (see "Pass the Parameters, Please"), that variable is hidden within the called routine. This means a reference to the variable within the called routine gives an error message. This is just another reason to avoid public variables as much as possible.

It's a Private Affair

The term "private variable" is really a misnomer. These variables aren't private. (In fact, local variables behave as the name private implies; see below.) Private variables are visible in the routine that creates them and all routines lower in the calling chain, unless those routines have their own private or local variable of the same name.

Let us run that by you again. When you declare a private variable, it hides any variables of the same name that were created higher in the calling chain, but can be seen by routines lower in the calling chain.

Hmm, how about an example? Suppose you have a routine MyRoutine that creates a variable called MyVar, then calls a subroutine called MySub. MySub can see MyVar and act on it. However, if MySub declares its own private version of MyVar, MyRoutine's MyVar is hidden and MySub acts only on its own version of MyVar. Here's some code to demonstrate the point:

```
* MyRoutine.PRG

MyVar1 = 7
MyVar2 = 10

? "In MyRoutine before calling MySub", MyVar1, MyVar2

* Note that MyVar1 and MyVar2 are NOT passed as parameters
DO MySub

? "In MyRoutine after calling MySub", MyVar1, MyVar2

RETURN

PROCEDURE MySub

PRIVATE MyVar2
MyVar2 = 2

? "In MySub before doubling", MyVar1, MyVar2

MyVar1 = 2 * MyVar1
MyVar2 = 2 * MyVar2

? "In MySub after doubling", MyVar1, MyVar2
RETURN
```

If you run this program, you'll see that MyVar1 ends up with a value of 14, but MyVar2 (in MyRoutine) remains 10. So, using private variables, you can hide information from a higher-level routine, but not from a lower level.

If you don't specify otherwise, variables are created private. Private variables are released when you return from the routine that created them. You can explicitly release them sooner with the RELEASE command.

You can explicitly make a variable private by declaring it with the PRIVATE keyword. You must do this if a variable of the same name exists at a higher level in the calling chain.

Unlike PUBLIC and LOCAL, though, declaring a variable PRIVATE doesn't create the variable—it just means that if you create that variable, it will be private. This makes some sense when you notice that PRIVATE can take a skeleton and make all variables matching that skeleton private—the others take only a specified list of variables. The skeleton allows you to do things like this:

```
PRIVATE ALL LIKE j*
```

which means any variable you create beginning with J is private.

Local Initiative

Prior to Visual FoxPro, public and private were the only choices for variables. Visual FoxPro adds local variables, which makes writing black-box code much easier.

Local variables can be seen only in the routine that creates them. No other routine can access or change them. This makes them perfect for all those bookkeeping tasks you need in a routine, like loop counters, holding part of a string, and so forth.

Here's an example to demonstrate why local variables are much easier to work with than private variables.

Suppose you have a routine that sums a specified subset of an array. That is, you pass the array, a starting element and the number of elements to sum, and the function returns the sum of those elements. Here's the function:

```
* ArraySum.PRG
* Return the sum of a specified group of elements
* of an array.

LPARAMETERS aInput, nStart, nNum
   * aInput = Array to Sum
   * nStart = Element to start
   * nNum = Number of elements to sum

LOCAL nCnt,nSum
   * nCnt = Loop Counter
   * nSum = running total

* Do some error checking
* Complete checking would also make sure each array element
* summed is numeric.

IF TYPE("nStart") <> "N" OR nStart < 1
   nStart = 1
ENDIF

IF TYPE("nNum") <> "N" OR nStart + nNum - 1 > ALEN(aInput)
   nNum = ALEN(aInput) - nStart + 1
ENDIF

nSum = 0

FOR nCnt = nStart TO nStart + nNum - 1
   nSum = nSum + aInput[nCnt]
ENDFOR

RETURN nSum
```

If you have a numeric array called MyArray and want to total the third through eighth elements, you'd issue this call:

```
? ArraySum(@MyArray,3,6)
```

Now suppose you need a function that totals each row of a two-dimensional array. You could write all the summing code again or you could take advantage of the code you've already written. The following function calls on ArraySum to total each row and just stores the result. It takes advantage of the fact that FoxPro represents all arrays internally as one-dimensional. (See "Hip, hip, array" in "DBF, FPT, CDX, DBC—Hike!" for more on that subject.) For good measure, the function returns the number of rows.

```
* SumRows.PRG
* Sum each row of an array, returning the results
* in a one-column array

LPARAMETERS aInput, aOutput
   * aInput = Array with rows to be summed
   * aOutput = One-dimensional array of sums

LOCAL nCnt, nRowCnt, nColCnt
   * nCnt = loop counter
   * nRowCnt = number of rows in input
   * nColCnt = number of columns in input

nRowCnt = ALEN(aInput, 1)
nColCnt = ALEN(aInput, 2)

* dimension aOutput appropriately
DIMENSION aOutput(nRowCnt)

FOR nCnt = 1 TO nRowCnt
```

```
   aOutput[nCnt] = ArraySum(@aInput, nColCnt * (nCnt - 1) + 1, nColCnt)
ENDFOR

RETURN nRowCnt
```

If you have a two-dimensional array called My2DArray, you'd get the row totals like this:

```
DIMENSION MyTotals[1]
= SumRows(@My2DArray, @MyTotals)
```

The key point here is that, in writing SumRows, we didn't have to worry about what variables ArraySum used. Since SumRows made all its variables local, no routine that it calls can damage its environment. Think of local variables as "a piece of the rock" for your routines.

You create local variables with the LOCAL keyword. Local variables are released when you complete the routine in which they were created. You can create local arrays, as well as scalars, using LOCAL. Newly created local variables have logical type and a value of .F.

You may have noticed the LPARAMETERS declaration in those two functions. LPARAMETERS is also an addition in Visual FoxPro. It creates formal parameters as local variables, protecting them in the same way that LOCAL protects variables.

We recommend all procedures and functions use local variables and local parameters for all internal tasks. Use private variables only when you explicitly want lower-level routines to have access to those variables—for example, when SCATTERing fields for a form (something you don't really need to do in VFP).

SQL - The Original

> You taught me language; and my profit on 't
> Is, I know how to curse: the red plague rid you,
> For learning me your language!
>
> William Shakespeare, *The Tempest*, 1611–1612

SQL, which stands for Structured Query Language, is a set-based language. Unlike Xbase, which cares about individual records, SQL is interested mostly in groups of records. (The Xbase concept most similar to SQL's point of view is the FOR clause.) The name "SQL" is read by some folks as a series of letters ("ess queue ell") and by others as "sequel"—we use either one, depending on the phase of the moon, though we lean more toward the latter these days.

The biggest difference between SQL and Xbase is that Xbase is procedural while SQL is not. In Xbase, you have to tell the computer exactly what to do to get from point A to point B—without step-by-step instructions, Xbase has no clue. SQL, on the other hand, lets you tell it what you want and figures out how to give it to you. This is most apparent with SELECT-SQL, which lets you tell what records should be placed in a result set without having to navigate the tables containing them.

In database theory, languages for manipulating databases are divided into two sets: the Data Definition Language (DDL) and the Data Manipulation Language (DML). Despite its name, SQL (like Xbase) incorporates both.

SQL first poked its way into FoxPro 2.0 with two DDL commands (CREATE TABLE and CREATE CURSOR) and two DML commands (SELECT and INSERT). Naturally, this wasn't enough for FoxPro users and they immediately started clamoring for more. Visual FoxPro finally added to the set, with the addition of both DDL and DML commands.

The most recently added data-definition command (new in VFP 3) is ALTER TABLE, an extremely powerful command that lets you add and remove fields and indexes, set various properties of fields, and create persistent relations among tables. All this in one command—no wonder its syntax diagram occupies nearly a full page.

CREATE TABLE has been significantly enhanced in Visual FoxPro, too. Its syntax diagram is also pretty hefty.

VFP 3.0 also introduced two new SQL data manipulation commands: DELETE and UPDATE. DELETE is fairly similar to the Xbase version of DELETE, though it has a few wrinkles of its own. (See its entry in the "Visual FoxPro Reference" for the nasty details.) UPDATE is a lot like Xbase's REPLACE, though again there are some differences, primarily in syntax. What makes these two commands such welcome additions is that you can use exactly the same commands on FoxPro data and on data originating from other sources. Besides, all those folks who've been writing SQL code in other languages really want to do it their way.

VFP 5 didn't add any new SQL commands to the language, but it seriously enhanced our old favorite, SELECT. Queries now offer the chance to lay out joins explicitly and to use the various flavors of outer joins. VFP 5 also gave us the ability to limit SELECT's result set by number or percent of matching records, though this isn't quite as powerful as it sounds.

So Which One Do I Use?

In theory, you could do all your data definition and manipulation using only FoxPro's SQL commands. Or you could ignore the SQL commands and use only the traditional Xbase commands. We know people who prefer either approach, including some who'll zealously campaign for their chosen method.

We don't recommend either, though, for two reasons. Some things are easier to do in Xbase while others are easier in SQL. (And some work best with a marriage of the two.) If you're using one approach and your code starts to seem convoluted, step back and see if you can use the other. For example, if a process takes five successive complex queries, stop and think about whether you can do it by setting relations instead.

The second reason we can't arbitrarily recommend one approach over the other is speed: some things are faster in Xbase; others are faster in SQL. There's really no way to tell which approach is faster without testing. Any time you can think of both procedural and SQL solutions, you should probably test both solutions to see which runs faster. Sometimes, the results will surprise you.

Is a Cursor Someone Who Uses Bad Words?

In addition to tables, SQL works with data in cursors. The term "cursor" is shorthand for "CURrent Set Of Records."

In FoxPro, a cursor is similar to a table, though it has some differences. The most important difference is that cursors are temporary. When you close them, they disappear into thin air, never to be seen again—at least not until you create them again from scratch.

There are three ways to actively create cursors in FoxPro, one of them available only in Visual FoxPro. As you'd expect, the CREATE CURSOR command creates cursors. You list the fields you want and their characteristics and FoxPro does the rest, thoughtfully leaving the new cursor open in the current work area.

SELECT-SQL also can create cursors to hold query results. Cursors created this way are read-only. (You can do a trick to make them read-write, but it's no longer relevant with the advent of views; see "Your Server will be With You in a Moment.")

The VFP-only method for creating cursors is to open a view. By definition, all SQL views use cursors. When you issue USE <viewname>, the underlying query is executed and the results put in a cursor. Views may be updateable, depending on how they're defined.

In addition to these three types of cursors, there's also a tendency in VFP to refer to any open table, cursor or view as a cursor—hence, functions like CursorSetProp().

Work Areas? What Work Areas?

> Oh, why don't you work
> Like other men do?
>
> Anonymous, *Hallelujah, I'm a Bum*, c. 1907

Unlike Xbase, SQL has no concept of a current work area. Each SQL command, instead, indicates what table it's working on. Tables are opened automatically if they're not already open and, when appropriate, they're secretly reopened.

Even though they don't officially recognize work areas, several of the SQL commands do change the current work area. Both CREATE commands (CREATE CURSOR and CREATE TABLE) leave you in the previously empty work area containing the newly created object. If you send query results to a cursor or table, SELECT makes the work area containing the results current.

INSERT INTO, DELETE and UPDATE don't change work areas, but they do open the table if it's not already open.

Who Needs Consistency Anyway?

> Consistency is contrary to nature, contrary to life.
> The only completely consistent people are the dead.
>
> Aldous Huxley

The seven SQL commands available in Visual FoxPro have no fewer than three different ways of referring to the table (or tables) they operate on.

SELECT and DELETE use a FROM clause to list tables. INSERT uses INTO. The others don't have a special keyword—the table name simply follows the command itself (as in CREATE TABLE Inconsistent ...). We can't blame Microsoft (or even Fox) for this one, though, because the commands do conform in this respect to the ANSI standard for SQL. This is a good place to point out that, while FoxPro's SQL commands are ANSI-compliant in some respects, they deviate in others. The bottom line is, if you're familiar with ANSI SQL, you'll want to check the FoxPro manuals or help before you start coding.

WHERE, Oh WHERE, Can My Data Be?

Three of the four DML commands in FoxPro's version of SQL use a WHERE clause to determine which records are affected. WHERE is essentially identical to the Xbase FOR clause, with minor variations in string comparisons (see SET ANSI and SET EXACT) and operator syntax. In DELETE and UPDATE, WHERE filters the table. In SELECT, WHERE both filters the data and can specify join conditions used to combine records from multiple tables (but see "Won't you JOIN me?" below).

The WHERE clause can contain any valid logical condition. To optimize these commands, make sure tags exist for each expression involving a field that appears in the WHERE clause and there's a tag on DELETED() if you use SET DELETED ON.

Won't You JOIN Me?

Unlike VFP's other SQL commands, SELECT can involve multiple tables directly. (Other commands may include multiple tables through sub-queries, but not in the listing of tables.) When there is more than one table, you need to indicate how to match up records from the different tables. In VFP 3 and earlier versions of FoxPro, you did this in the WHERE clause along with your filter conditions. Beginning in VFP 5, you can also use the ANSI JOIN syntax to specify how to combine tables.

The advantage of the new syntax is that it lets you specify outer joins (where unmatched records in one or more tables are included in the result) as well as the inner joins that WHERE lets you include. For the details on the JOIN syntax, see the entry for SELECT-SQL in the "Visual FoxPro Reference."

No Room at the Top

> Set thine house in order.
>
> *The Second Book of Kings*, 20:1

Because SQL is set-based, certain concepts fundamental to Xbase don't have exact analogues in SQL. SQL usually doesn't care where a record is in the table; there's no such thing as a SQL record number. When you manipulate records with SQL commands, you mostly do it based on the records' contents, not their position. SQL has no NEXT or REST clauses.

Similarly, FoxPro's version of SQL doesn't know from first and last (or, as we call them in Xbase, TOP and BOTTOM). Before VFP 5, there was no way to say "the first 10" or "the most recent 25." VFP 5 added TOP n and TOP n PERCENT syntax to SELECT, but its utility is quite limited—the clause applies to the overall query results, not to each group within the result. When you need "the first 10" or whatever in each group of records, you have to use a hybrid approach that combines SQL with Xbase's record number to produce the desired results. It requires a multi-step process and you still need enough space to select all the matching records first. (Tamar published the solution to this one in the March '94 issue of *FoxPro Advisor*.)

OOP is Not an Accident!

> The poetical language of an age should be the current language heightened, to any degree heightened and unlike itself, but not ... an obsolete one.
>
> Gerard Manley Hopkins, 1879

We've been hearing about Object-Oriented Programming (OOP) for more than 20 years. At first, it was just theory. Then, we started hearing about this language called SmallTalk. In the last few years, OOP's been everywhere, and the claims of who has it and how it will revolutionize programming have grown louder and louder.

So what is OOP? Why is it important? And will it really change the way we program?

Object-Oriented Programming is a different way of looking at programming than the procedural approach found in traditional programming languages. (It's different than the "give me what I want—I don't care how" approach of SQL, too.) Conventional programming languages look at the world in terms of actions—first you figure out what to do, then you figure out what to act on. OOP looks at the world in terms of objects—first you figure out what objects you want, then you figure out what actions the objects should take.

OOP is not a replacement for everything you have learned about making a computer work up to this point. We know naysayers who claim you need to throw out everything you've done before and start from scratch. That's just not true. OOP is a better, more realistic way of looking at the processes and entities and their interactions, modeling them, describing them, abstracting them and enhancing them, but it does not change the requirements of our systems to perform the functions they do. It just looks at packaging them differently. Consider the FoxPro 2.x way of maximizing a window: ZOOM WINDOW MyWindow MAX. You start out by indicating the action you want to take (ZOOM WINDOW), then indicate what object to apply the action to (MyWindow).

The OOP equivalent is MyWindow.WindowState = 2. You start out by indicating that you want to deal with MyWindow, then you narrow it down to MyWindow's WindowState. Finally, you indicate what you're doing—setting that state to 2 (which is maximized).

This may seem like only a minor syntactic difference, but in fact, we're really turning the whole process on its head. The hidden difference here is the change from passive elements to active elements. In procedural code, windows, controls, and so on are all passive things that we act on with commands. In OOP, windows, controls and so on are active objects that know how to do things—we simply tell them what we want them to do. (See "The Message is the Medium" below for more on this.)

It's worth noting that this difference is also the major one between the DOS and GUI worlds. In DOS, you use a Command-Object syntax: What shall I do? and, by the way, who should I do it to? In graphical environments like Windows and Mac, you choose a thing and then decide what to do to it. It's not a surprise, then, that the big move to object orientation has come with the move to GUIs—it's much easier to program when your language works like your environment.

The Object of My Affections

> Nothing can have value without being an object of utility.
>
> Karl Marx, *Capital*

Not surprisingly, the basic unit in OOP is an object. An object is an entity that has some characteristics and knows how to do some things. For example, a form is an object. So is a check box or a grid.

The formal name for the object's characteristics is *properties*. The official name for the things it knows how to do is *methods*. (There are some special methods called *events* that react to user and system actions—see "A Gala Event" for more on this subject.)

Object orientation is really packaging. We put the properties together with the methods so the object is self-contained. To use the object, you don't need to depend on anything outside the object itself. This essential feature of object orientation is called *encapsulation*—that's one of several rather intimidating words you'll find floating around the OOP world.

Encapsulation is really pretty simple. Instead of putting data in one place and code that operates on it in another (the traditional procedural division), you package them together, so when you have one, you also have the other. If you've ever worked with abstract data types, you're familiar with this concept. If not, we suspect it'll grow on you pretty quickly.

Don't confuse the data that's encapsulated in objects with your database data. Although there's talk about object-oriented database management systems, we're not dealing with those here. The properties of an object are its data; the methods are the code.

A Class Act

> To be an Englishman is to belong to the most exclusive class there is.
>
> Ogden Nash

Where do objects come from? Well, there's the Mama object and the Papa object and they get together with the birds and the bees and nature takes its course. Oops, wrong kind of object.

So where do objects come from? We don't just pull them out of thin air. Instead, we base each object on a class. The class forms a blueprint or template for the object, and we can create as many objects as we'd like, based on a single class. (More on where these class things come from below.)

The class definition determines what properties and methods an object has. Every object based on a particular class has the same set of properties and methods. What distinguishes one object from another is the values of those properties. (For example, one check box might have its caption to the left while another has the caption to the right. All that's been changed is the value of the Alignment property.)

Visual FoxPro provides two ways of defining classes: in code and through the Visual Class Designer. (Actually, there's a third way—using the Form Designer—but that's really a variation on using the Class Designer.) In either case, though, you do the same kinds of things: Specify the properties and methods of the class, and indicate initial values for the properties.

The act of creating an object based on a class is called *instantiation*; the object created is called an *instance* of the class.

That's Quite an Inheritance

> I would rather make my name than inherit it.
>
> William Makepeace Thackeray

Suppose you have a class that's almost what you want for some purpose, but not quite. The procedural thing to do is to copy the class and make the changes you need.

But then you're stuck with two different classes to maintain. What if you find a bug in the original? You have to remember to change not just the original, but the copy you modified. And what if you then need another class a little different than either the original or the modified version? You copy and change it again. Now you've got three things to maintain. And it keeps getting worse and worse.

One of the most powerful features of object orientation is the ability to create subclasses of existing classes. The subclass inherits the properties and methods of the original, but allows you to make changes. Most important of all, changes to the original class are inherited by the subclass.

Inheritance is the second of the three characteristics a language must have to be considered object-oriented. (It's also the one missing from Visual Basic—VB is considered to be object-based, not object-oriented.)

So where do all these classes come from anyway? No, not Mama and Papa classes—you've been dozing through our explanation. All classes, ultimately, are descendants of one of the base classes built into the language. In the case of Visual FoxPro, we've been supplied with a rich set of base classes from which all of our classes are built. More on these a little later.

Our favorite example of inheritance is pretty simple. Say you work for LargeCo, a large corporation, and there's a corporate standard for input forms. The standard includes the corporate logo as wallpaper. Then, LargeCo is gobbled up by EvenLarger Corporation, which declares that all forms must have its corporate logo as wallpaper.

In FoxPro 2.x, you might have handled the original requirement by saving a screen containing just the logo and copying it as the basis for all your new screens. Works great until EvenLarger comes along—then, you have to go back to every screen you've created and change the wallpaper.

Okay, how does this work in Visual FoxPro? You start off by subclassing VFP's base form class. In your subclass, you set up the wallpaper with LargeCo's corporate logo. Now, whenever you need a new form, you subclass it from your corporate form and start building. Doesn't seem so different from what you did in FoxPro 2.x.

But here's the payoff. Along comes EvenLarger—what do you have to do? You go back to your original subclass (the one based on VFP's form class). You change the wallpaper to the new corporate logo and voila! All your other forms inherit the change. That's right—with inheritance, you make the change once!

So are you sold yet? We are.

Inheritance is actually even more powerful. Not only does a subclass inherit the properties and methods of the class it's based on, it also inherits the code in the methods. You can override that code by specifying different code for the same method of the subclass. If you don't override, it's as if you'd put the inherited code right in the subclass' method. (See "Hierarchies and Lower-archies" below for how to have the best of both worlds.)

Polymorphism is Mighty Morphism

There's one more key feature of object orientation, and its name is even more obscure than encapsulation or inheritance. This one is *polymorphism.*

Actually, though, this one's pretty simple. It means that different objects can have methods with the same name. The methods don't have to behave the same way (though it's a good idea for them to do similar things).

In other words, you no longer have to struggle to come up with unique names for minor variations on a theme. Every object can have a Print method—no more PrintInv, PrintCust, PrintThis, PrintThat. Just issue SomeObject.Print and that object gets printed.

The Message is the Medium

Okay, we've defined all the buzzwords and talked about objects and classes, but how does all this fit together? The key is in *message passing*. No, not the like the kind that got you in trouble with your second-grade teacher. Well, maybe like that, actually.

The basic idea in OOP is that objects know how to take care of themselves. They contain all their data and a set of actions to perform on that data. But sometimes, they need something from another object to get the job done or they have information that another object needs. So they send a message to the other object, asking that object to do something, asking for information from that object, or telling the other object something important. These correspond roughly to invoking a method of another object, checking a property value from another object, and changing a property value in another object.

You can access a property of any object by giving the object's name, then a period ("."), then the property name. For example, the Picture property (which provides the wallpaper) of a form called MyForm is referenced with:

```
MyForm.Picture
```

To change a property, simply assign it a new value. To give MyForm the Fox bitmap for wallpaper, you'd write something like:

```
MyForm.Picture = "F:\VFP\Fox.BMP"
```

To store the current value of MyForm's picture property in a memory variable, perhaps so it could be changed and later restored, you'd write something like:

```
cCurPict = MyForm.Picture
```

You reference methods similarly. Use the object name, a period, and the method name. If the method accepts parameters, enclose them in parentheses. Parentheses are optional if you're not passing parameters, but we recommend always using them when calling methods. To call MyForm's Refresh method, for example, you can write:

```
MyForm.Refresh
```

or

```
MyForm.Refresh()
```

We like the second form better because it makes it clear that Refresh is a method.

The Protection Racket

> Woman must not depend upon the protection of man, but must be taught to protect herself.
>
> Susan B. Anthony

Some objects have properties or methods that can be dangerous in the wrong hands. The way you prevent these dangers is by marking those properties and methods as "protected." Protected properties and methods can be accessed only by methods of the same object.

If other objects need access to the value of a protected property, you can provide a method (not protected) whose sole function is to return that value.

For example, the disk for this book contains a class designed to keep track of connections to remote servers. That class uses an array to contain the connection information and has a property indicating how many connections it's currently tracking. Letting the outside world touch that counter property would be suicidal for this class. Instead, that property is protected and there's a Count method that returns the current connection count.

Some OOP theorists believe that all access to properties should come through methods, that no object should be able to directly read or change the properties of another. Visual FoxPro does not follow that philosophy by default, but you can design your classes to do so, if you wish. (See "Assign of the Times" below for another approach to this problem.)

Hide and No Seek

> Society is a masked ball, where every one hides his real character, and reveals it by hiding.
>
> Ralph Waldo Emerson, *The Conduct of Life*, 1860

In VFP 5 and later, you can go even farther to protect properties and methods from outside abuse by marking them as "hidden." Protected properties and methods can be seen in subclasses of the original class; hidden properties and methods cannot. They can be seen only in objects of the class that creates them.

The hidden characteristic seems particularly useful when you're building classes to be distributed without source. You can keep some properties and methods from even being visible in subclasses and use them for internal bookkeeping. Unfortunately, VFP keeps this approach from being as useful as it should because hidden methods can't even be accessed indirectly through calls up the class hierarchy. (See "Climbing Trees" below for an explanation of such calls.)

Assign of the Times

> Remember that you are an actor in a drama, of such a part as it may please the master to assign you, for a long time or for a little as he may choose.
>
> Epictetus, *Encheiridion, no. 17.*

We said above that some people think one object should never directly change the properties of another. The reason is that the object being changed doesn't know it's being changed. VFP 6 gives your objects the opportunity to know when they're being changed and even when they're being used (a feature we might have found handy at some time in our lives).

Each property can have two events associated with it automatically: an Access method and an Assign method. When a property has an Access method (the method name is propertyname_Access), that method is called whenever someone reads the value of the property. An Assign method (named propertyname_Assign) is called whenever someone changes the value of the property. You can put code in these methods to prevent the access or assign, to log it, or to do anything else you want.

Hierarchies and Lower-archies

> In a hierarchy, every employee tends to rise to his level of incompetence.
>
> Laurence J. Peter, *The Peter Principle*, 1969

One of the most confusing aspects of object-oriented programming is that there are two different hierarchies at work. We mentioned above that you can create subclasses based on existing classes. In fact, you can do this over and over again, building a tree (the computer science kind of tree, not the nature kind of tree) of classes of as many levels as you'd like.

At the top of this tree, known as the class hierarchy, are Visual FoxPro's base classes—more on those a little further along. The next level contains subclasses derived directly from base classes. At the next level are subclasses derived from the subclasses one level up. And so on and so forth.

The reasonably standard OOP term for the class one level up the hierarchy is *superclass*. For reasons we can't comprehend, Visual FoxPro instead calls the class one level up the hierarchy the *parentclass*. Reminds us of the old joke, "How many Microsofties does it take to change a lightbulb?" — "None, they just declare darkness the new standard."

Inheritance applies to the class hierarchy. An object based on a class at the bottom of the tree has properties and methods specified for that class, plus it inherits any properties and methods of its parentclass, and those of the parentclass of its parentclass (you might call it the grandparentclass) and so on, all the way back to the root of the tree.

When a method of an object is called, the class the object is based on is checked. If it has code for that method, the code is executed. If there's no code there, we start climbing the class hierarchy, looking for an ancestor of this class that has code for the specified method. As soon as we find some code for that method, we execute it and stop. But until we find it, we keep climbing the tree until we reach the Visual FoxPro base class the object is ultimately derived from. Even if no code is specified anywhere on the tree, if the base class has some default behavior, like redrawing the object upon invocation of the Refresh method, that behavior occurs. (Actually, that base behavior normally occurs even if there's code somewhere in the hierarchy—see "Ain't Nobody's Default But My Own?" below.)

Contain Yourself

Now what about the other hierarchy we mentioned? This comes from the fact that one object can contain another. For example, a form is an object (based on the Visual FoxPro Form base class). A form usually contains all kinds of other objects like text boxes, check boxes, grids, and so forth. Some of the objects in a form can contain other objects. For example, a grid contains columns, which in turn can contain headers and controls.

So the second hierarchy is the containment hierarchy. This is the map of what's inside of what. The most important point about the containment hierarchy is that inheritance has nothing to do with it at all. Objects do not inherit anything from their containers or from the objects they contain.

The second most important thing about the containment hierarchy is that the term "parent" is used here, too. (This is one reason we're frustrated by Microsoft's choice of parentclass over superclass.) The parent of an object is the object that contains it. For example, the parent of a column is the grid containing that column. The parent of a text box might be a form. Don't confuse "parent" with "parentclass"—they really are two different things.

One other terminology note: The objects inside another object are called *members* of the containing object. The term "members" is also used more broadly to refer to the properties and methods of an object, as well as the objects it contains.

Climbing Trees

At various times, we need to climb each of the hierarchies. Let's start with the class hierarchy. Say you're defining a subclass and, for some method, you want to do everything the parentclass does, but then do a few more things. Your first instinct might be to copy all the code from that method of the parentclass into the corresponding method of the new subclass. Why shouldn't you do this?

What happens if you have to change the parentclass' behavior? If you've done cut-and-paste to the subclass, you're out of luck. The changes aren't inherited.

So what should you do? Call the parentclass' method explicitly from the subclass' method. There are two ways to do this. One way uses a notational trick, since you can normally only call methods of objects, not of classes. A special operator "::" lets you call up the class hierarchy—the notation is:

```
ClassName::Method
```

The second way to call up the class hierarchy is by using the DoDefault() function. This function, which can only be used in method code, calls the same method one level up the hierarchy—it was added in VFP 5.

Both DoDefault() and the "::" operator let you have your cake and eat it, too. A subclass' method can call the same method of its parentclass, then do some more work. Or, if you prefer, do the extra stuff first, then call the parentclass' method. Or both: Do something, call the parentclass' method, then do something else.

Moving around the container hierarchy is actually a lot more common. To send a message from one object to another, you have to be able to find the recipient. You can do that by walking down the container hierarchy until you reach the object you want. For example, to refer to a spinner named spnDays on a page called pagPage1 of a page frame called pgfCalendar of a form called frmWhoKnows, you write:

```
frmWhoKnows.pgfCalendar.pagPage1.spnDays
```

What a mouthful!

You want class definitions to be as reusable as possible. Because you might create many instances of a single class, you don't know when you're writing code what the name of the actual object will be. You also may not know what the parent of an object is. For example, a text box might be contained by a form, a column or a page (of a page frame).

A special operand, This, lets you refer to the current object without knowing its name. The Parent operator lets you move one level up the container hierarchy without knowing what's up there. For example, to find the name of the parent of the current object, you'd write:

```
This.Parent.Name
```

You can use Parent repeatedly to climb multiple levels:

```
This.Parent.Parent.Parent.Left
```

gives you the left edge of the object three levels up in the hierarchy. If This is a check box in a column of a grid on a page of a page frame, that expression would refer to the page's Left property.

Because you don't always know how deep in the hierarchy you'll be, This has two cousins, ThisForm and ThisFormSet, which let you jump quickly to the top of the container hierarchy. Then you can climb back down one level at a time. Say you want to address the button cmdSave that's on the current form. You can reference it with:

```
ThisForm.cmdSave
```

without worrying about where you are now on the form.

Base Clef

> All fantasy should have a solid base in reality.
>
> Sir Max Beerbohm, *Zuleika Dobson*, 1911

Visual FoxPro comes with a set of built-in classes known as the base classes. FoxPro's base classes cannot be changed, but most of them can be subclassed. In fact, we recommend that one of the first things you do is subclass all the input controls and build your own forms and form classes from your subclassed controls, rather than from FoxPro's base class controls. We suggest you do this even if you change not one thing about the control because someday, you're going to want to make changes. (In VFP 6, Microsoft has provided a set of "one-off" classes to start from, so you don't have to do this yourself anymore.) If you've used the base classes in your forms, there'll be a lot of work ahead.

There are several ways to break the Visual FoxPro base classes into groups. The biggest division seems to be between containers and non-containers. Containers can hold other objects while non-containers can't—simple enough. There's also the question of whether a class can be subclassed in the Class Designer. Then, some classes are visible while others aren't. Finally, different classes came into the language at different times. The table below shows all of Visual FoxPro's base classes and classifies them according to all four criteria.

Base Class	Container?	Subclass-able in CD?	Visible?	Version Introduced
ActiveDoc	No	Yes	No	VFP 6
Checkbox	No	Yes	Yes	VFP 3
Column	Yes	No	Yes	VFP 3
CommandButton	No	Yes	Yes	VFP 3
CommandGroup	Yes	Yes	Yes	VFP 3
ComboBox	No	Yes	Yes	VFP 3
Container	Yes	Yes	Yes	VFP 3
Control	Yes	Yes	Yes	VFP 3
Cursor	No	No	No	VFP 3
Custom	Yes	Yes	No	VFP 3
DataEnvironment	Yes	No	No	VFP 3
Editbox	No	Yes	Yes	VFP 3
Form	Yes	Yes	Yes	VFP 3
FormSet	Yes	Yes	Yes	VFP 3
Grid	Yes	Yes	Yes	VFP 3
Header	No	No	Yes	VFP 3
Hyperlink	No	Yes	No	VFP 6
Image	No	Yes	Yes	VFP 3
Label	No	Yes	Yes	VFP 3
Line	No	Yes	Yes	VFP 3
ListBox	No	Yes	Yes	VFP 3
OLEBoundControl	No	Yes	Yes	VFP 3
OLEControl	No	Yes	Yes	VFP 3

OptionButton	No	No in VFP 3 Yes in VFP 5 and VFP 6	Yes	VFP 3
OptionGroup	Yes	Yes	Yes	VFP 3
Page	Yes	No	Yes	VFP 3
Pageframe	Yes	Yes	Yes	VFP 3
ProjectHook	No	Yes	No	VFP 6
Relation	No	No	No	VFP 3
Separator	No	No in VFP 3 Yes in VFP 5 and VFP 6	Yes	VFP 3
Shape	No	Yes	Yes	VFP 3
Spinner	No	Yes	Yes	VFP 3
Textbox	No	Yes	Yes	VFP 3
Timer	No	Yes	No	VFP 3
ToolBar	Yes	Yes	Yes	VFP 3

The table points out some of the terminology problems in Visual FoxPro. We have a base class named Control. We also refer to the various objects that let users enter data as "controls." And, in fact, something derived from the base class Control might just be a control, but so are a lot of other things. Why couldn't they have picked a different name?

Similarly, there's a base class called Container, but a lot of the other base classes are containers, too. Doesn't English have enough words to go around? Do we have to overload a few of them so badly?

To complicate this particular issue even further, Container and Control are very similar classes. They're both designed to let you create complex controls (the input kind) built out of multiple objects. The difference is that objects based on Control don't allow other objects access to the contained items, while objects based on Container do. In other words, using Control as the basis for an object is kind of like protecting all its member objects.

Not Quite All There

Since in true OOP, every class can be subclassed, we like to think of those base classes that can't be subclassed in the Class Designer as being "half-classed." For the most part, each of these classes is a necessary component of some container class. You can subclass these classes in code, but you still can't incorporate your subclasses in the containers (or subclasses of them) that normally contain the base classes. For example, you can subclass Grid, but your subclass will still be made up of Columns, which will still contain Headers. Similarly, Pageframes always contain Pages; you can't base a Pageframe subclass on a subclass of Page.

Even with CommandButtons and OptionButtons (which you can subclass visually), when you make a CommandGroup or an OptionGroup, it's always built of CommandButtons or OptionButtons—you can't build it out of a subclass.

We can see the reason for this limitation, but we keep hoping it will go away.

The details of each of the base classes are discussed in the Reference section, so we won't go into them here.

Ain't Nobody's Default But My Own?

Certain behaviors are built into Visual FoxPro's base classes. For example, when you press a key, that keystroke is placed in the keyboard buffer. When there are tables or views in the DataEnvironment, you don't need to write code to open them and set up the specified relations. Generally, these behaviors are tied to certain events. The keystroke entering the keyboard buffer is part of the KeyPress event. Opening tables and setting relations is part of the OpenTables method (which behaves more like an event in many ways).

Even if you override the method code for these events with your own code, these default behaviors occur anyway. And that's a good thing. You wouldn't want to have to code your own version of putting a keystroke in the keyboard buffer or opening the tables in the DE. Nor would you want to have to call up to the base class every time you override a method.

But, once in a while, you want to override the default behavior as well. Perhaps you want to eat the keystroke because you're doing something special with it. Sure enough, there's a way to handle it. To prevent an event from firing its default base class behavior, put the keyword NoDefault somewhere in the method for that event. Since the base class default behavior always happens last, NoDefault can go anywhere in the method code.

NoDefault and DoDefault() are two more places where the words used for things cause confusion. Given their names, it's not unreasonable to think that they're exact opposites. It's not unreasonable; unfortunately, it's also not true. NoDefault turns off the *built-in* behavior of a method; it has no effect on user code. DoDefault() executes the code for a method one level up the class hierarchy and can cause the built-in behavior to occur. It's not at all uncommon to have both NoDefault and DoDefault() in the same method code. The most common reason to combine them is to make the built-in behavior happen sooner. For example, we sometimes issue NoDefault followed by DoDefault() at the beginning of the OpenTables method. Then, we can add some code to do things like create indexes for views that were opened.

Taking Some Extension Classes

At the same time as VFP has been OOP-ified, so have a lot of other parts of the programming world. In particular, many of the tools for allowing applications to interact now use object-oriented techniques. This includes ActiveX and various data access technologies, like RDO and ADO.

What this means to you is that you'll find yourself writing OOP-y code not just to handle tasks in VFP, but to handle much of the interaction with other applications. For example, Automation with Word or Excel involves creating an automation object and then setting properties and calling methods. So does using ADO to access non-VFP data.

In addition, a number of objects that are accessible directly from VFP (that is, without having to explicitly create them) are really ActiveX objects. For example, the Project and File objects added in VFP 6 use ActiveX technology. You can't subclass them in VFP, but you talk to them through properties and methods.

Give Me the Whole ScOOP

We've just skimmed the surface on object orientation here. After working with it for several years now, the OOP way of looking at things feels pretty natural to us. So many tasks are performed more simply using OOP.

But using OOP effectively is more than just a code thing. Designing applications to take advantage of OOP requires a new way of looking at them. We're still working our way up that learning curve. Check the appendices for some references on object-oriented analysis and design.

Controls and KAOS

> Who controls the past controls the future;
> who controls the present controls the past.
>
> George Orwell, *Nineteen Eighty Four*

Controls in Visual FoxPro are not just a new name for the SAYs and GETs of earlier Xbase languages—they are far more. Controls are full-fledged participants in the interactions with users. Understanding the intricate ways in which the properties, events and methods are evaluated and executed is essential to grasping how Visual FoxPro works. In this section, we'll discuss what controls are and some of the features common to controls. We'll go on to look briefly at each control (you'll find more in the Reference section), and discuss where it's appropriately used. At the end of the section, we'll discuss how the built-in characteristics of controls can be extended to create more complex and customized controls, tailored to meet your clients' needs, capable of interacting with your users in ways beyond those anticipated by Visual FoxPro's designers.

What's a control?

Most controls are objects that are manipulated, like light switches, sliders or radio buttons, and hence can be thought of as computer representations of real-world controls. This metaphor falls a bit short, however, for some controls, such as the timer, which doesn't have a visual representation, is invisible to the end user, and can't be "grasped." For our purposes, we think a sufficient definition is that controls are the objects on forms that perform specific actions when acted upon by an event generated by the user interface, program code or the system.

Controls can be placed on a form in a number of ways. The simplest is to use the Form Controls toolbar. However, some of the other approaches offer more power, including dragging fields from the Data environment or controls from the Component Gallery. Properties, events and methods contain the information that determines what a control looks like, what characteristics it has, and what it should do when acted upon. Hence, the control's appearance and behavior is *encapsulated* within the control—one of the key principles of object-oriented programming. (See "OOP is Not an Accident" for more on the principles of object orientation and how they're implemented in Visual FoxPro.) The properties of forms and controls are changed through the Property Sheet. Their events and methods can be customized using the method code editor.

While there appear to be a dazzling number of properties, events and methods associated with the collection of controls (in fact, there are more than 2,200 combinations of controls with properties, events and methods), many of the properties, events and methods are common to most controls and perform the same function (or a very similar function) for most of them. Hence, they can be understood just as easily with a blanket statement rather than repeating something like "The Top property determines how far from the top of its container the control appears" in each control's reference section. In fact, we don't repeat that information in the Reference section of this book. The tables there list only those PEMs (that's common shorthand for "properties, events and methods") that are of particular interest for that control. The VFP Help does contain complete lists for each control.

Here is a quick synopsis of the most common PEMs.

Common Control Properties

A property is nothing more than a characteristic of an object. Properties describe things like the object's height, width, color, and whether the object should have certain capabilities, such as being enabled or being visible. Properties are manipulated in Visual FoxPro in pretty much the same manner as memory variables, and can be thought of in many respects as private memory variables scoped to a single control.

There are two common ways to manipulate the properties of a control: at runtime using assignment commands and during development using the design mode tools. (In fact, you can manipulate properties programmatically at design time, too. See "Builders and Wizards and Bears, Oh My!" on the CD for more on this.) To refer to properties programmatically, use the "dot notation" explained in "OOP is Not an Accident"—as in:

```
ThisForm.PageFrame1.Page7.Command1.Caption = "OK"
```

Properties are assigned visually using the Property Sheet. Formally, Microsoft calls this the "Properties Window" but we've gotten used to the "Sheet" terminology, especially since this window is often set to be "always on top" (see the right-click menu for that option)—something that seems more intuitive for a sheet than a window. We've heard it variously called the "Properties Form," "Property List," "Properties Sheet," "Property Sheet" and "PropSheet." We think all are fine, as long as folks know what you're talking about. Let's review some of the more common properties and what they are usually used for:

The **Name** property of a control does what it says: tells you the control's Name. You use the name to refer to the control programmatically.

Parent provides an object reference to the object containing the control. For a control sitting right on a form, for example, Parent holds a reference to the form. For a control on a page of a page frame, Parent contains a reference to the page. Parent helps you climb up from the control you're on to the outside world. This is the containership hierarchy, not to be confused with the inheritance hierarchy—see ParentClass, below, for that.

Value holds whatever the control currently contains, generally some variation on the user's input. **ControlSource** lets you bind the control's Value to a field, variable or property—when Value changes, so does the item named in ControlSource.

The control's location and size are specified with the **Top**, **Height**, **Left** and **Width** properties. All of these measurements are expressed in units determined by the object's **ScaleMode**—either pixels or foxels. (Stick with pixels—we haven't come across any good reasons to use foxels.)

Font characteristics are specified with the **FontName**, **FontSize**, **FontBold**, **FontUnderline**, **FontStrikethru** and **FontItalic** properties—almost all controls have these. The **FontCondense**, **FontExtend**, **FontOutline** and **FontShadow** properties are oddballs, included for compatibility with the Macintosh but having no effect on Windows fonts.

The **Comment** and **Tag** properties have no designed use. They're there to provide a place to leave notes or do whatever you want. We haven't seen very many people actually use these properties. On the whole, it seems better to add custom properties as needed. The term Tag, by the way, is a carryover from Visual Basic, and is not at all related to the tags Visual FoxPro uses in its indexes.

The **Enabled** property determines whether an object is capable of reacting to external events like clicking, typing, or tabbing to a control. This is the equivalent under most circumstances of FoxPro 2.x's SHOW GET ... ENABLE | DISABLE.

Color settings for a control can be specified in a number of ways. The most obvious are the properties **BorderColor**, **ForeColor** and **BackColor**, with their equivalents of **DisabledForeColor** and **DisabledBackColor**, which apply when the object's Enabled property is False. However, in most cases you'll want to use the **ColorSource** property instead, so the control's colors are based on system-wide choices. A number of controls also have other color settings that affect particular aspects of their appearance (such as **ItemForeColor** and **FillColor**).

The **BaseClass**, **Class**, **ParentClass** and **ClassLibrary** properties describe the pedigree and history of a control, and are fixed at the time a control is created. These allow you, at runtime or design time, to examine the lineage of a control and act appropriately.

A couple of properties help you hook your controls into your Help system. **HelpContextID** and **WhatsThisHelpID** each contain an identifier for the control that can link to a Help entry.

Every VFP object has the **Application** property. It contains an object reference to the instance of Visual FoxPro in which that object was created. For self-contained applications (the kind that use only VFP), there's not too much for this property. However, when a VFP application is started by another application, this reference gives you a handle to the VFP engine. (See "It was Automation, You Know" for an explanation of why another application might run a VFP application.)

Common Control Events

Events introduce some difficulties in talking about Visual FoxPro. When we speak of "adding code to the MouseDown event," it is easy for our audience to sense that an event is somehow a different kind of thing from a method. This is a linguistic issue, not a complication of Visual FoxPro. An event is an occurrence that is communicated to your application. This event might be the fact that the mouse is passing over a control, or that a timer's Interval has elapsed. When your application, via the underlying FoxPro engine, receives this message, a method with the same name as the event is run automatically. So when we talk about modifying the MouseDown event, we are really speaking of "the method associated with the MouseDown event." Events happen. There is nothing we can do about them and certainly nothing modifiable about them. We're not going to keep trying to say "The method associated with the MouseDown event," but since we do want to distinguish an automatically run event from a method, like most VFP developers, we shorten it to "the MouseDown event."

Init and **Destroy** events occur when an object is created and destroyed. These two events fire only once in the life of a control. This is a good place to establish settings that the control depends on, and to clean up these settings upon the control's release.

The **Error** event is the place to put a local routine designed to handle errors that the control might generate. This is a great place to put specific code in your custom controls when you anticipate that the user might be able to perform some error-causing action. You can handle it internally and gracefully within the control, making the control a more useful black-box object, and, again, encapsulating the object's behavior. For example, a disk drive combo box, where you select the drive to which you save your file, could be a useful custom class. The picker itself should detect the disk not being inserted, and handle the error with a message box rather than passing control on to a default error handler. On the whole, we expect little code to end up in this event. Under no circumstances should you consider cutting and pasting the same complex code to handle every conceivable error into all of your top-level subclasses' Error events. Instead, we expect to use Error as part of a larger error-handling scheme. (See Error in the Reference section.)

The **InteractiveChange** and **ProgrammaticChange** events allow you to include code in the control to react to a user's or program's actions immediately, creating a more responsive system.

Other interactions are handled by events such as **MouseDown**, **MouseUp**, **Click**, **RightClick**, **DblClick**, **Drag**, and **KeyPress**. (Some more esoteric interactions are handled by events such as **MiddleClick** and **MouseWheel**.) Most of these events are pretty self-explanatory, although the sequence in which they occur might not always be apparent. An easy way to trace the firing sequence of events is to use the Event Tracking option in the Debugger, run the form, try some things and then examine the results. For example, clicking a command button in a command group (one which previously did not have the focus) can fire a blizzard of events. In this example, a check box called Check1 had focus before the click—we've also pulled out the whole series of MouseMove firings that occurred en route to the button, and left only the last one.

```
form1.commandgroup1.command2.MouseMove(0, 0, 186, 66)
form1.commandgroup1.MouseMove(0, 0, 186, 66)
form1.commandgroup1.command2.When()
form1.commandgroup1.When()
form1.check1.LostFocus()
form1.commandgroup1.command2.GotFocus()
form1.commandgroup1.Message()
form1.commandgroup1.command2.MouseDown(1, 0, 186, 66)
form1.commandgroup1.MouseDown(1, 0, 186, 66)
form1.Paint()
form1.commandgroup1.command2.MouseUp(1, 0, 186, 66)
form1.commandgroup1.MouseUp(1, 0, 186, 66)
form1.commandgroup1.InteractiveChange()
form1.commandgroup1.command2.Click()
```

```
form1.commandgroup1.command2.Valid()
form1.commandgroup1.Valid()
form1.commandgroup1.command2.When()
form1.commandgroup1.When()
form1.commandgroup1.Message()
form1.commandgroup1.Click()
```

Other common events include **Resize**, which fires when a container's size is changed, and **GotFocus** and **LostFocus**, which fire when a control receives and loses focus.

In VFP 6, controls have a bunch of events whose names begin with OLE. These events handle actions related to OLE drag and drop.

VFP 6 also adds a new wrinkle to events with Access and Assign. These events can be attached to any property and fire when the property is either read or changed. Because the existence of these events is under developer control, they add a new dimension to controls. (See the Reference section for details.)

Common Control Methods

Methods are similar to events, in that they contain a block of code to be executed. The main difference is that events are triggered by something outside the direct control of the developer, but methods are called explicitly. Compared to events and properties, there are not many common methods. That's because methods are really the determining factor in creating a unique control—unique behaviors of an object indicate that it needs to be considered a unique control. This is one of the reasons that Microsoft decided to combine the FoxPro 2.x "Invisible Button" and "Push Button" controls into a single CommandButton in VFP; they are functionally identical, differing only in a few properties. However, ComboBox and ListBox are two separate controls. Although they share a number of methods, there are enough differences between them to justify separate structures.

The **ZOrder** method sends the specified control to the front or back of its group of overlapping controls. ZOrder moves items along the Z-axis, the third dimension we simulate on our monitors. But ZOrder is not just for appearance; it also affects the firing order of some events—see the ZOrder entry in the Reference section for more details on this. Some controls contain their own ordering properties (such as Page frame's PageOrder)—those properties determine the horizontal (X-axis) or vertical (Y-axis) order of the contents. ZOrder determines the depth (Z-axis) order.

Move allows movement of controls on a form under programmatic control. **Drag** and **OLEDrag** initiate native drag and drop and OLE drag and drop, respectively.

The **Refresh** method redisplays a control, also firing the Refresh method of any contained controls.

SetFocus moves the focus programmatically to the control (similar to the function performed by the _CUROBJ memory variable in FoxPro 2.x).

AddObject, **NewObject** and **RemoveObject** allow the addition or subtraction of controls from container objects. **CloneObject** creates a duplicate of the control inside the same container.

The **SaveAsClass** method is pretty cool. It allows us to save the definition of any control to a class library, both at design time and at runtime! This can be really useful in an interactive development session, where you can programmatically alter a live object's properties until you get them just right, and then save your result right from the Command Window, putting the live form into a visual class library.

The **SetAll** method programmatically sets a property of all objects or objects of a particular class within a container. **ResetToDefault**, added in VFP 3.0b, lets you return a property to its default value—very handy, since a control is created faster when properties are set to default than when they're explicitly assigned the default value.

AddProperty, new in VFP 6, lets you add properties to an object at runtime. **ReadExpression**, **ReadMethod**, **WriteExpression**, and **WriteMethod** let you examine and change properties and methods programmatically.

Except for WriteMethod, they're available at runtime, as well as design time.

ShowWhatsThis displays the WhatsThisHelp for the control.

The remainder of methods built into Visual FoxPro are typically contained in only a few objects, and are more appropriately discussed in the reference section for that object.

Visual FoxPro Controls

Controls can be broken down into groups in a number of ways. We have chosen to focus on them from the end user's point of view—what the end user is going to use each control for. This isn't an exhaustive view of them; it would take another book at least as long as this one to explore all the capabilities of each. We're trying to focus more on the use of each control and to provide some pointers. Further information about specific controls can be found in the Reference section.

Text-based controls: TextBox, EditBox and Spinner

These controls allow you to enter one item of text. A text box, a fancy descendent of our plain old GET objects, is typically restricted to a few words or phrases, occupying a single line of form real estate. An edit box, typically bound to a memo field, allows free-form entry of a variable-length block of text from one word to a large narrative, providing scrollbars as necessary. Spinners are used for numeric entries and allow both direct text entry and selection by means of up or down arrows.

Choices: CheckBox, ComboBox, ListBox and OptionGroup

These controls allow the user to select the most appropriate answer or answers from a set of choices. Check boxes are used for on/off, true/false-type answers. Option groups also allow only one answer, though typically from a larger number of choices. Combo boxes and list boxes allow the choice of one or more answers from a list. Normally, check boxes and option groups are defined during the design of a form to have a particular shape and prompts. The two kinds of lists, on the other hand, tend to be more flexible, allowing population at runtime. The nice thing about the Visual FoxPro object model is that the properties of these objects are available at runtime, so the rules above are typical guidelines and not carved in stone.

Check boxes, in the Windows interface, normally are used just as an on/off, true/false switch. Occasionally, though, a check box is used as a button that immediately fires further actions, such as calling up a dialog. (See the Project Class check box on the Projects page of VFP's Options dialog, for example.) Our take is that this use of a check box, even when the prompt ends in an ellipsis, is bad design, since it confuses users. Use buttons when you need them and save check boxes for indicating if something is or it isn't.

Option groups also allow only one choice, and are typically sized and populated with their choices at design time. You can arrange the choices in any visual configuration—you're not limited to rows, columns or even grids of them.

Combo boxes, formerly known as drop-downs or popups, take up little real estate when inactive. List boxes take a larger piece of screen space, but allow the user to see several options at once. Both combo boxes and list boxes can be populated from a number of sources, ranging from a hard-coded list entered at design time to a list programmatically generated at runtime from an array, table or query. Both can handle multi-column lists. List boxes have the added advantage of allowing for multiple selection, and for the addition of mover bars to let the user move things around in the list. Combo boxes, on the other hand, can be configured to allow the user to enter data not on the list. Whichever you use, keep in mind that these controls are meant for choosing from small- to medium-sized lists and not for choosing among thousands or tens of thousands of options. Your users will *not* be amused as they scroll through the choices one at a time (and, despite the incremental search available in both controls, some users will scroll through one at a time). In general, list boxes are suited to somewhat larger sets of choices than combo boxes.

Using combos and lists with a huge number of items has been a perennial source of bugs and performance issues in FoxPro. VFP 3 had problems with multi-selection of more than about 60 items on a list; FoxPro 2.x actually crashes under some conditions with 600 or more items in the list. Not only is this poor interface design for us, but it is also difficult for the Fox team to program in the Windows environment. Avoid very large data sets for these controls if at all possible.

Actions: CommandButton, Timer and Hyperlink

The action controls are used to fire an action immediately upon selection.

Command buttons are variously referred to as "push buttons" or just "buttons." (For whatever reason, option buttons are rarely, if ever, called just "buttons.") Command buttons can show text or a bitmap, or be invisible to create a "hot" region on the form. (Don't confuse the last option with the Visible property—an invisible button is still an active participant in the form, but any control with its Visible property set to False is both invisible and disabled.)

Timer controls might seem like a bit of an odd duck in this category, but timers are unique no matter how you categorize things. They are the only invisible controls that directly cause actions to occur, unlike the more passive Custom class objects. But they do cause actions, which is why we plunked them here. Timers are a welcome addition to our arsenal, allowing us to dynamically take a look at the current state of a form to check status, update displays, and so forth.

Hyperlinks, new in VFP 6, are also unusual. Like timers, they're invisible, but unlike timers, they don't have any special events that fire on their own. What they do have, though, is a couple of methods useful for manipulating a browser. The most important is NavigateTo, which can open a browser looking at a particular Web page or file.

Containers: Grid, Column, PageFrame, Page, CommandGroup, Container, Control and Toolbar

Containers are objects that can contain other controls. A container class is a great place to put a chunk of code that should affect all of the contained objects, like the logic to turn off navigation buttons when at the top or bottom of the data set, or to disable visually contained controls when their container is disabled.

Grids contain columns, which in turn contain other controls. They're normally used to display the contents of a table, like the Browse of old. Unlike Browse, grids are incredibly configurable, with the ability to use different controls for different data, change colors and fonts on the fly, and much more. They're also incredibly difficult to get just right for data entry—many of the developers we know would rather climb Mount Everest than configure a grid for entering data. As a display device, though, or a tool to select a particular record, they're hard to beat. A fellow developer was heard to say, after evaluating a number of other ActiveX data grids, that the only thing worse than the VFP Grid was any other choice.

Page frames allow the creation of tabbed or tabless sets of pages. The hottest thing around when VFP 3 first came on the scene, tabbed dialogs have already fallen out of favor to some extent, but they still have their uses. A page frame contains pages, which contain controls.

Command groups contain sets of command buttons. These seemed terribly important when VFP was new, but much less so now. Using individual buttons provides more control and greater flexibility. Bundling command buttons with other controls like check boxes and combos in a container provides nearly all the benefits of command groups, but with added flexibility.

The other three classes in this category, Container, Control and Toolbar, are not exactly controls in their own right, but they are container objects. Controls (isn't this confusing?) and toolbars cannot be directly created from the Form Controls toolbar, unlike the other controls listed in this section, including Containers.

Yet another mangled piece of overloaded terminology here. The Container class is one of a number of classes, all of which are referred to as "container classes." To confuse matters more, Control is a class, but "controls" refers to a whole set of classes, and "control" is a general-purpose term for any member of that set. We try to distinguish between the individual Container class and the set of container classes, and between the Control class and the controls, with our use of capitalization, but, as in the heading above, we don't always succeed. It looks like we're stuck with these names for the long term, so bear with us.

Containers and Controls seem to be very similar. Each is essentially a box with the standard set of properties and events: border, background and foreground color and style, size and location, mouse events, and so forth. Both can contain other controls. The difference between the two is that a Container object contains other controls whose properties can be manipulated at design time and runtime, while a Control hides the individual controls it contains from manipulation. Control allows you to create true "black box" controls whose innards are hidden from manipulation except through your predefined interface, while Container is more of a grouping mechanism.

A Toolbar is a funny thing. Sometimes it behaves like a form. Sometimes it's more like a control or a container (lowercase) control. Unlike the other visual objects, there is no separate Toolbar Designer power tool. You create a toolbar by defining a class for it, either visually or through code, and then add it to a form set or create it in code. A surprising collection of objects can be added to a toolbar. Most common are command buttons, separators, option buttons, combo boxes and check boxes, with both kinds of buttons and check boxes normally using a graphical style. (Check out Word's Formatting toolbar to see all of those control types.) However, the Class Designer allows the addition of pretty much every VFP control except grids to a toolbar. That can lead to some pretty strange looking toolbars. In some versions of VFP, some pretty strange things start to happen, too, when out-of-the-ordinary controls are thrown on a toolbar. See the Reference section for details.

Graphical Elements: Image, Line, Shape and Separator

These graphical items can be used to segregate related areas, draw on the form, display images, or separate related groups of buttons on a toolbar. Unlike the graphical elements in FoxPro 2.x and the Box and Line methods of forms, these are full participants in the form, and can react to clicks and drag-and-drop events. (We are amused that Separators are on the Form Controls toolbar when you can't put them on a form. But the same toolbar is used in the Class Designer; in addition, a toolbar can be added to a formset in the Form Designer, so it does make sense.)

ActiveX: OLEBoundControl and OLEControl

VFP's ActiveX container controls have some very special functionality: They allow Visual FoxPro to open a window into another application, and to control the display and functionality of that application. OLEControls also are used to add third-party ActiveX controls to forms, giving the form capabilities beyond those (or better designed than those) built into VFP.

It's worth noting that Microsoft created a bit of a mess for itself by including the term "OLE" in the names of these classes. Since they did that, "OLE" has been transformed into "ActiveX"—you'll see a reflection of this in the ToolTip and status bar message if you pass the mouse over these items on the Form Controls toolbar.

User Interface Issues with Controls

Much has been written about the importance of good user interface design, and we don't want to beat the issue to death here. (Well, since we're both pretty passionate on this subject, actually we do want to beat it to death, but we won't.) Check out the appendices for some suggested reading on this topic if you haven't dealt with this before. A clean, easily understood and consistent user interface can enhance users' confidence in their abilities with your system, and improve their opinion that they are dealing with a polished and professional application.

The most important user interface principle to bear in mind with controls is consistency throughout an application. If a command button with a printer icon calls up a print dialog on one form, a check box with the same icon in another form should not toggle an option that determines whether the output of an action should be printed. The user is bound to call you, swearing the application isn't working the way it did yesterday. All forms should share similar prompts—when completing a form, the users should not have to vacillate between selecting "Close," "Cancel," "OK" or "Quit" button prompts, if the resulting action on the different forms is the same.

Think about the way your application is to be used. If the predominant use of a form is for high-volume, heads-down data entry, requiring the user to switch from keyboard to mouse to keyboard is murder on efficiency. On the other hand, a form more likely to be used by someone trolling for new relationships between the pieces of information should be tailored to the more creative "What happens if I click here and select this" operation of a click-happy mouse user.

Another consideration is accessibility. All controls in your systems should be accessible by several means. The minimum is to provide keyboard and mouse access. In many cases, you'll also want a shortcut key and perhaps a menu option. This is a convenience for power users, who will discover these shortcuts and use them to run your application faster. But this is more than an issue of sophistication. Many of your users will have a preference for the keyboard over the mouse, or vice versa, and the application should be accessible to them. In addition, users with limited visual or motor skills should be able to operate your application. As more companies become sensitive to this issue of making provisions for their disabled workforce, this issue will become more prominent. Microsoft itself has jumped onto this bandwagon in the last few years and now offers accessibility guidelines for applications. The bottom line is that you should plan and design your application from the beginning to accommodate as many interface styles as reasonably practical.

Finally, let the user know what is going on. Nothing raises the stress level of a user more quickly than a system that wanders off and appears to hang when they tell it do go do something. If your application will take a while to complete a step, change the mouse pointer to an hourglass, display a progress thermometer or tell the user that the operation will take some time to complete. Give the user a chance to cancel long operations if she doesn't have the time or resources to complete a step. Let the user be in charge.

User interface design is not a subject that comes naturally to many of us. Study some of your favorite applications to see how they handle your actions. Maybe more important, study some applications you hate, to see what makes them so miserable to use—and be sure not to do those things in your applications. Read some references in the field. Above all, make the user feel comfortable, confident and in control.

Extending the Reach of Controls

The most profound aspect of the many facets of Visual FoxPro is that the developer is not limited to the functionality built into the language, but rather that this functionality is the basis from which the developer can extend the capabilities of Visual FoxPro to the needs of the client. This is true in many different ways, including controls.

Custom controls are useful in a number of circumstances. Because controls in an object-oriented hierarchy inherit behavior and characteristics from their parents, a class hierarchy can make it far easier to distribute changes throughout a system. For example, changing all the command buttons in a system to use FixedSys rather than Arial is just a matter of changing the FontName property in the parent class definition upon which all of your buttons are built. In addition, encapsulating small bits of thoroughly tested code at various stages of the class tree ensures a more robust and bug-free final result. Once you have written solid code for a Next button, preserve that button in a class library and use that class wherever the button is needed. If you find a bug in the behavior, you can fix it in one place. If you need additional functionality in some places, you can subclass and refine the class definition.

Creating a custom control is easy. Build the control you want, using a blank form in the Form Designer. Click the control to select it, and then select the "Save As Class" option from the File menu. Select a name and location for the Visual Class Library in which you'd like to store your custom controls and save it. If you prefer, you can just start with the Class Designer—it looks a lot like the Form Designer, except that the Run (!) button on the toolbar is disabled.

There are several ways to use your own controls in the Form and Class Designers. First, the View Classes button (the one that looks like books) on the Form Controls toolbar lets you choose among various sets of classes. You can add your own class libraries using the Add option provided by that button. To make a particular library available all the time, register it using the Controls page of the Tools-Options dialog. These visual class libraries are registered and stored in the Windows Registry, under the entry HKEY_CURRENT_USER\ Software\ Microsoft\ VisualFoxPro\ <version number>\Options\VCXList. (Fill in 3.0, 5.0 or 6.0 for <version number>.)

We strongly recommend that you never use the base classes that come with Visual FoxPro. Create your own set of custom controls, consisting of all controls available in the default Form Control Toolbar but subclassed one level. In VFP 6, such a set of controls is provided for you in the _base library found in the FFC subdirectory of your VFP home directory. We (and all the experts we know) recommend you do this because the base class controls supplied by Microsoft cannot be customized and cannot have custom properties or methods attached to them, whereas the subclassed group you have created (or the ones in _base) have that ability. (In fact, you'll probably want to subclass further to give you the ability to change things on an application level, as well.)

One of the things we find frustrating about VFP is that you can't make changes across all the controls. If you want to use 24-point Haettenschweiler throughout all your development, you have to change it in each of your "base" classes (the ones we just told you to create). Of course, once you do so, you're done, and when you come to your senses, it's not too hard to change back to something reasonable again. However, we'd like it even more if all the VFP base classes derived from a single class, where this kind of change could be made once. We actually suspect that, internally, this may be true in VFP 6, but we have no external evidence to back it up.

Custom controls can be built from more than one component. The Reference section contains an example (under "Container") for Shapes, where two shapes and a Text box are combined to form a thermometer control. These controls can be turned into a custom class as described above—just select all of the controls you want to combine, and select "Save As Class". Visual FoxPro automatically dumps the selected controls into a Container control as part of saving them into a visual class library. As before, if you know what you want, you can just use the Class Designer in the first place, drop a Container on it, and add what you need. Remember to use your subclasses to create these complex objects—any base class object you used as part of a custom control cannot have additional properties or methods attached to it.

Controls are the only means our users have to communicate with our applications. It's important to provide them with a rich, consistent and helpful set of tools with which to do their jobs. Visual FoxPro's powerful built-in controls, combined with the object-oriented structure that allows us to customize and build upon the capabilities of those controls, provides us with the means of delivering the tools our clients need.

A Gala Event

> The great events of life often leave one unmoved...
>
> Oscar Wilde

Death to the Foundation Read! Long live READ EVENTS!

What is an event? What do we need to do about it? The FoxPro family was a leader in the Xbase world in moving from a procedural application to an event-driven interface, even in DOS. With Visual FoxPro, FoxPro became fully attuned to the rich event model of the underlying Windows interface. Visual FoxPro can create far more responsive applications, and applications that are more consistent with the behaviors of other Windows programs. We'll examine the different events that are possible, under what circumstances they occur and what code is appropriate for each of them.

What's an Event?

Simply put, events happen. In OOP terms, an event is an occurrence outside your control about which one of your objects is notified with a message. An event can be system-generated, user-initiated, or caused by another object in the application. When Windows handles the resizing of a form, it sends a message perceived by the form as a Resize event. When the user clicks on a control, the control receives a Click event. When a Timer control in your application counts down its elapsed time, a Timer event fires.

As we discussed in "Controls and KAOS," there is no difference between the code contained in an event and that in a method. When we talk of modifying "the Mouse event," it's shorthand for "the code contained in the method associated with the Mouse event." We won't apologize for using this shorthand, nor do we expect to stop.

The set of events is fixed. Unlike methods, it isn't possible to design your own custom events. Although you can customize the code that occurs (or specify that nothing occurs) when an event happens, you cannot create additional events. (Visual FoxPro lacks the WithEvents options of Visual Basic to add events from ActiveX controls). Luckily, Visual FoxPro has provided us with such a rich event model that few events are missing. (In fact, VFP 6 offers more on this front than previous versions with the addition of Access and Assign methods. See the Reference section.)

How to Handle Events

In days gone by, it was a major undertaking to get FoxPro to just stop and let the user direct what was to happen next. Xbase was originally designed as a procedural language, where the program demanded input and then performed its process. The emphasis has shifted over the years, with improving user interfaces, toward an event-driven system, where the tables are turned in such a way that it is the user who seems to be controlling events and the computer that responds. The shift in FoxPro to this new way of doing business has been a gradual and not altogether smooth transition.

Several alternative event-handling methods have been proposed over the years, and each has its proponents. Until the release of Visual FoxPro, there were good reasons why each method might have been desirable under some circumstances. A simple looping structure, checking for a keystroke, could be used as a basis for the application. Several means of detecting a keystroke, using WAIT, INKEY(), CHRSAW() or READ could respond to the event. In FoxPro 2.0, an alternative, named the Foundation Read (and quickly nicknamed "The Mother Of All Reads," or MOAR, for short) became popular. This READ worked without any corresponding GETs, causing the READ VALID code snippet to fire when an event occurred. Several elegant application frameworks were developed based on this parlor trick. But, like the techniques before them, this method could be tricky to implement under some circumstances, and had kinks and limitations. Visual FoxPro solved the need for these artificial constructs by allowing our applications to become part of the native event loop of the FoxPro engine. In essence, we can now tell FoxPro "Just wait until something happens, or we tell you it's time to quit."

The READ EVENTS command sets the event handler in action after establishing your environment. There was some discussion that a more suitable command would have been "WAIT HERE," but WAIT is already overloaded. Just what should Visual FoxPro do if someone issued WAIT HERE NOWAIT "What now?" TO lcFred AT 10,10? Or perhaps "ENERGIZE!" (but some dumb bunny's already cornered the market on that one) or "MAKE IT SO" (but Paramount might sue)? So, READ EVENTS it is. It doesn't READ anything at all, and EVENTS go right past it without a raised brow, but that's the command to start the ball rolling.

When you're done in Visual FoxPro and ready to close up shop, CLEAR EVENTS is the command to tell READ EVENTS to stop whatever it has been doing. CLEAR is one of the most heavily overloaded commands in the language, releasing everything from class libraries cached in memory to DLL declarations to menu items defined with @ ... PROMPT or even CLEARing the screen. We would have preferred newer, cleaner terminology, like "STOP" or "ALL DONE", but no one asked us.

It's Not My Default!

When an event occurs, you probably want to provide some code for it to run. When the user clicks on a button, or a timer times out, you need to provide code to describe what happens next. That's easy. You can do that. You're a programmer, right? We spend most of the rest of the book telling you how to do that. But what happens when you don't want any code to run, or perhaps want absolutely nothing at all to happen? If the code fragment for the event you're concerned with is left blank, the same event for the control's parent class is searched to find code to run. If there's nothing there, the same event in the parent's parent class is searched, and so on and so forth. Even if there's no code for that event anywhere in the inheritance hierarchy (that's what determines who gets Uncle Scrooge's millions, right?), there's often some default behavior associated with the event. For example, by default, when the user presses a key, the KeyPress event fires—the default behavior is to put the key in the keyboard buffer. To get a control to do nothing, not even the default behavior, you issue the NoDefault command, valid only in methods.

User interface events occur even when NoDefault is issued. For example, when a command button is clicked, the button is visually depressed (guess it needs a good therapist). Check boxes and option buttons display when they have been toggled. If you want no action from one of these controls at all, NoDefault is not for you—use the When event to return .F. for a complete lack of response.

We run into another situation a lot: We need to let the normal action of the class occur, but we just need to do one teensy-weensy thing besides that. Normally, when you put code in an event, the search described above doesn't happen. That is, once you add some code, the parent class isn't checked for code in that event. The parent class' code is said to be *overridden.* (The fortunate exception here is that the built-in behavior of the event always occurs, even if there's code, unless you specifically suppress it with NODEFAULT.) In the bad old days, we'd just cut and paste the code from one class to another, and then modify it, but these are the good new days. The newer (and better) way to do this is to perform what code we need, and then call on the code from the parent class (or its parent or its parent or ...). Or, if it's more appropriate in your situation, call the code from the parent class (or its parent or ... you get the idea) and then perform your custom code.

There are two ways to call the code from the parent class. In VFP 5 and 6, use DoDefault(). Put DoDefault() in any method and it calls the same method in the parent class (and yes, you can pass parameters).

In all versions of VFP (though we'd only use this version in VFP 3), you can use the operator :: to call up one level in the class hierarchy. The simple version is just:

```
NameOfTheParentClass::NameOfTheMethod
```

but if you want code that works anywhere, anytime, use:

```
LOCAL cMethodName
cMethodName = SUBSTR(PROGRAM(),1+RAT(".",PROGRAM()))
= EVALUATE(This.ParentClass+"::" + cMethodName)
```

This calls the method of the parent class from which this class is derived, reinstating the "normal" code hierarchy as if no code were present in the class.

Obviously, either form can be a real time-saving device, since many subclasses differ in just one aspect from the parent, and the parent code can be called before, after, or even in the middle of the custom code written for this subclass. More importantly, though, calling up the hierarchy makes your classes more maintainable. Imagine changing code near the top of the class hierarchy and finding it doesn't affect some of the objects derived from that class! Wouldn't that be frustrating? More importantly, wouldn't that defeat the primary object of object orientation—reduced maintenance? By always calling up the hierarchy, except when you explicitly want to override the normal behavior, you know what to expect when you use a particular subclass.

In some cases, you might want to simply change the time at which the built-in behavior of the VFP base classes (like putting a character in the keyboard buffer or opening tables) occurs. The built-in behaviors normally occur after all the custom code in an event, but there are times when you want VFP to do its thing before your code, or in the middle of your code. For those situations, you can combine DoDefault() and NoDefault. Issue DoDefault() at the point at which you want the built-in behavior. Issue NoDefault at any point in the code (or at least, any point that actually gets executed). We like to put the two together to make it clear what's going on, though.

Finally, we should point out that there's nothing magical about either keyword. Like anything else in FoxPro, they only take effect if they get executed. So, you can write code that figures out what's going on and suppresses base behavior or calls up the class hierarchy only when it's appropriate.

"Ready, Aim, Fire"

In order to have your code perform as you expect it to, it's essential that you understand the order and the circumstances in which a particular event's code will be called. For the purposes of this discussion, we break up the VFP classes into four groups: general non-container controls, containers, forms and form sets, and the rest (which includes some classes that don't have anything to do with forms). Most of the event model discussions can be explained by looking at individual controls, but some events only make sense (or only occur) in terms of higher-level objects.

Non-container Controls

Init fires when the object is first created or "instantiated." This method is similar to the "constructor" methods of other object-oriented languages. (It differs from constructors in that it doesn't actually create the object.) If the object should be populated with data at runtime, or if its properties should be altered based on the present circumstance in the user's environment (say, her selection of currency values calls for a change to InputMask, or his color set calls for a change to the contrasting colors of a control), Init is the place to do it.

Despite the fact that Init code is the first to run after an object has been created, we have been able to change the properties of an object in the Init of another object that fires before the Init of the targeted object. However, trying the same code in the form's Load event generates the expected "Unknown member" error. We suspect that all of the objects are instantiated first, then their Inits are run in the same order. We don't recommend depending on this undocumented behavior, though it has remained the same for three versions.

Destroy fires when the object is released in one of three situations: the container is being released (like a form closing), a release method is fired, or all references to the object go out of scope.

An Error event fires when an error occurs in a method of the control (or in a program or ActiveX control method called from a method of the control) and the Error method contains any code (at any level of its class hierarchy). The method can call a global event handler object, or assume the responsibility for dealing with an anticipated error, handling it locally for greater encapsulation of the control's behavior.

Other events fire when the corresponding user actions occur. For example, a control's MouseMove event fires when the mouse passes over the control. GotFocus fires when the control receives the focus, and so forth.

Containers

A container behaves very much like other controls. It has similar, if not identical, events associated with it. Init occurs when the object is created, Destroy when it is released. Error fires when an error occurs, and the user interface events (MouseOver, Drag, Click) fire as they do for the non-containers. The difference between a container and other controls is the sequence of event firings for the container and its contained controls.

Init events start with the innermost controls. This makes sense once you realize that a container cannot perform its actions until its contents exist. (Yeah, we guess you could argue that you can't put the controls anywhere until the container exists, but that's not how it works.) Therefore, objects are created from the inside out. If a text box is placed in the column of a grid and that grid is on the page of a page frame in a form, the sequence of Init firings is: text box, column, grid, page, page frame, and finally form. This is probably counter-intuitive to our mental models of a form; first you get a box, then you fill it with stuff, right? But there is some logic to the idea that first you create the individual controls and then you can run the routines from the container that affect them all.

Destroy events fire in the opposite order, from the outside in, as if the container is imploding. This, too, makes some sense from a programming point of view, since the destruction of the container forces the things inside to go "ka-blooie," too.

Containers and their contained controls also share some user interface events. The amount of sharing and interaction between the two objects depends on how tightly bound the two objects are to each other. For example, when a text box is placed on a page or in a column of a grid, that text box pretty much has free reign over what occurs on its turf. Once the object gains the focus, events are within the domain of that control. Once focus is lost, the container can then fire related events, such as the AfterRowColChange event in a grid.

On the other hand, "dedicated" container controls that hold only one type of control, such as option groups and command groups, tend to be much more involved in interactions with their contents. When the mouse is moved over a command button in a command group, the MouseMove event of the button fires first, followed by the MouseMove event of the button group. See "Controls and KAOS" for the sequence of events when a button in a button group is clicked—the key point is that some events fire at both the button and the group levels.

Forms, FormSets and Toolbars

Forms, form sets and toolbars are just big containers. Like the other controls before them, they have Init, Destroy and Error, as well as Click, DblClick and the other Mouse events. But they also have some additional events and features.

The data environment's OpenTables and CloseTables methods fire automatically (despite the fact that they're methods) if automatic opening of tables has been selected using the cleverly named AutoOpenTables and (you'll never guess) AutoCloseTables properties. In this case, these two methods behave more like events than methods. If manually initiated opening or closing is selected, explicit calls to the OpenTables and CloseTables methods are required to open and close tables. The BeforeOpenTables and AfterCloseTables events fire immediately before and after (respectively) the tables are opened or closed.

We found BeforeOpenTables a hard event to understand at first. BeforeOpenTables fires immediately before the tables are actually opened, but after the OpenTables method has been called and the custom code in it has run. Placing a DEBUGOUT in each of the methods gives the unintuitive sequence OpenTables, then BeforeOpenTables, but in fact, the BeforeOpenTables event is fired because the OpenTables code is preparing to actually open the tables. (You can't use Event Tracking to test this sequence because OpenTables isn't an event.) The key point is that BeforeOpenTables fires *not* before the OpenTables method, but before that method's default behavior of opening tables occurs.

In any event (pun intended), the data environment events are wrapped around the form, so that the form has data available from the time it starts until it finishes.

The Load event fires before all other form events, including the initial data environment events, offering a handy place to take care of form-wide settings. Unload is the last event on the form to fire, although the data environment's Destroy events occur after the form is long gone. Activate and Deactivate fire when the form or toolbar gets the focus (is "activated") or loses the focus. The Paint event fires in toolbars or forms whenever the object needs to be redrawn because of the removal of an overlying object or a change in the size of the object or its contents. The QueryUnload event, unique to forms, allows the form to sense the reason it's being released and either prevent incorrect actions, or ensure that all processing is complete before the form terminates.

Other Objects

VFP 6 introduces some new objects that don't fit into any of the categories above: ActiveDoc, Hyperlink and ProjectHook. All have Init, Destroy and Error events. Hyperlink has no additional events (and we're sort of inclined to think of it as a non-container control), but the other two classes each have some events that are different from any others in VFP.

Active docs have several events that let them interact with their "host" (that is, the browser in which they're running). The Run event fires when the active doc has been created and is ready to go. It's essentially the "main program" of the active doc. ShowDoc and HideDoc fire when their names say—when the active doc application becomes visible or invisible. CommandTargetQuery and CommandTargetExec fire when the user performs actions in the host, to offer the active doc a chance to respond. Finally, ContainerRelease fires when the host lets go of the active doc.

Project hooks have events that fire when the user (developer, in this case, presumably) acts on the associated project. QueryAddFile, QueryModifyFile, QueryRemoveFile and QueryRunFile fire when the specified action occurs on a file in the project—issuing NoDefault in one of those methods prevents the action from taking place. BeforeBuild and AfterBuild are also well named because they fire when a build is initiated and when it's completed. You shouldn't need to deal with any of these events at runtime, since project hooks are essentially a design-time creation.

The Whole Event

Let's run through the whole event loop now, just to tie it all together. Your user has started your application. You've run the startup routine, perhaps instantiating a number of application-wide objects. These might include an Application object, to contain application-wide preferences, keep track of the current status and get the ball rolling. Other objects your application might use are a Security object, to accept a login and password and to dole out permissions as requested; a Data Manager object, to control the flow of data to and from your various forms; a Form Manager object, to keep track of active forms and handle any interactions among them; and an Error Handler object, to take care of errors not dealt with locally. (In VFP 6, take a look at the classes in the _framewk library found in the Wizards subdirectory to get a sense of how you can distribute responsibilities in an application. Be forewarned: This is complex code, though quite well written. Don't expect to fully understand it on the first pass.)

Once everything is set up the way it should be, your program issues the READ EVENTS command to get the event loop started, and your application sits back and waits for the user to pick something to do. The user chooses a form to work on, and the form begins.

The data environment starts the ball rolling by optionally setting up a private data session for this form, opening the tables, setting up relations, and instantiating cursors. OpenTables (if it has code) and BeforeOpenTables fire first and the tables get opened. The Load event of the form or form set fires next. This is the first form event, and a place to put code that should run before the rest of the form gets to work, such as settings to be used throughout the form. There follows a flurry of Init events—first the data environment and its contents (from the inside out), and then controls from the innermost outward, by ZOrder within a container level, are created. This ends finally with the Init of the form, and is followed by the Activate event of the form. Next, the Refresh methods are called (by whom? Refresh is a method, not an event), one for each control and for the form itself, from the outside in. Finally, the control designated to be the first on the form (by TabIndex) fires its When clause, to make any last-minute changes before it accepts the focus. If the When returns .T. (or nothing at all—.T. is assumed), the GotFocus events fire—first the form's, then any container's, and finally the control's. And there we sit, waiting for the next action.

While a control is sitting on a form, snoozing, waiting for something to happen, no events fire, except perhaps the Timer event of a timer control. When the user tabs to a control, or brings his mouse over a control, that's when the fun begins. If the mouse was used to select a control, the MouseMove event can be the first to sense the approach of the user's pointer. (If both container and contained controls have code in their MouseMove events, the container can even prepare the controls for the arrival of the mouse. But watch out—MouseMove fires a lot. Too much code there could slow things down. On a fairly powerful machine, 50,000 repetitions of a totally empty loop were enough to result in some visual oddities.) The When event determines whether the object is allowed to gain focus; if When returns .F., the events stop here for now. Once it's been confirmed that the new object can have the focus, the last object's LostFocus event runs. Next up are the new object's GotFocus and Message events.

What goes on when the user is within the domain of an individual control depends to some extent on what the control is and what it is capable of doing. A simple command button can sense and react to MouseDown, MouseUp, Click and Valid events, all from a single mouse click, but we find we usually put code only in the Click event. Although it is nice to have the other options there, we suspect that many of the events don't see much use except when designing very specific interfaces per clients' requests. A more complex control, like a combo box or a grid, can have a richer set of interactions with the user. We leave the specifics of each control's behavior to the Reference section, but cover below exactly which controls have which events.

Finally, the user wants to leave our form. We usually provide our users with a Close button for that purpose. But they can also select the Close option from the form's control menu or the close ("X") button on the title bar. In the last two cases, the QueryUnload event occurs, letting us detect the user's desire to quit, so we can ensure the same handling that occurs when he uses the Close button. If QueryUnload lets the form close, the form's Destroy event fires, followed by the Destroy events of the objects on the form. The form's Unload event follows the Destroy events of all contained objects. The data environment then shuts down. If the data environment's AutoCloseTables property is set true, the tables close and the AfterCloseTables event fires. (If, on the other hand, AutoCloseTables is false, the tables close only if the CloseTables method is called programmatically.) The data environment's Destroy events follow. Like its associated form, the data environment implodes, firing first the data environment's Destroy, and then the Destroy events of any contained relations and cursors.

Event, Event—Who's Got the Event?

So, with 35 different base classes and 69 events to choose from, how's a body to know which classes support which events? Well, we suppose you could just open them up in the Form or Class Designer and check it out, but we've saved you the trouble by putting together this table. The events are listed in reverse order based on how many base classes have them.

Event	Object(s)	Meaning
Init	All base classes in VFP 6. In earlier versions, some classes omitted this event.	Fires when the object is created and can accept parameters. If Init returns .F., the object is not created. Contained objects fire before containers, in the order added; see ZOrder in the reference section.
Error	All base classes in VFP 6. In earlier versions, some classes omitted this event.	Fires when an error occurs in the method of an object. Receives the error number, method name and line number. If there's no code here or in its class hierarchy, the error handler established with ON ERROR, or as a last resort, the built-in VFP "Cancel Ignore Suspend" dialog, fires.
Destroy	All base classes in VFP 6. In earlier versions, some classes omitted this event.	Code runs just before an object is released. Containers fire before contents.
DragOver, DragDrop	All base classes except ActiveDoc, Column, Cursor, Custom, DataEnvironment, FormSet, Header, Hyperlink, ProjectHook, Relation, Separator, and Timer	Fire during and on completion, respectively, of a native VFP drag and drop operation. Each receives parameters to accept a reference to the data being dragged and the mouse coordinates.
MouseMove	All base classes except ActiveDoc, Cursor, Custom, DataEnvironment, FormSet, Hyperlink, OLEControl, OLEBoundControl, ProjectHook, Relation, Separator, and Timer	Tracks mouse movement over an object. Receives status of Ctrl, Alt, and Shift keys, as well as left, middle and right mouse button statuses.

Event	Object(s)	Meaning
MouseWheel	All base classes except ActiveDoc, Cursor, Custom, DataEnvironment, FormSet, Hyperlink, OLEControl, OLEBoundControl, ProjectHook, Relation, Separator, and Timer	Fires on use of the rotating wheel available on some pointing devices. Receives parameters indicating direction of movement, current position, and the status of the Ctrl, Alt and Shift keys.
MouseDown, MouseUp, Click	All base classes except ActiveDoc, Column, Cursor, Custom, DataEnvironment, FormSet, Hyperlink, OLEControl, OLEBoundControl, ProjectHook, Relation, Separator, and Timer	Fire when the user uses the left (primary) mouse button. Typically detected in the order shown.
RightClick, MiddleClick	All base classes except ActiveDoc, Column, Cursor, Custom, DataEnvironment, FormSet, Hyperlink, OLEBoundControl, OLEControl, ProjectHook, Relation, Separator, and Timer	Fires when the right or middle mouse button, respectively, is clicked. These are not preceded by MouseDown and MouseUp events.
OLEDragOver, OLEDragDrop	All base classes except ActiveDoc, Column, Cursor, Custom, DataEnvironment, FormSet, Header, Hyperlink, OLEBoundControl, OLEControl, Relation, Separator, and Timer	Fire during and on completion, respectively, of an OLE drag and drop operation. Receive parameters describing the drag action in progress, including a reference to the dragged data object.
OLEGiveFeedback	All base classes except ActiveDoc, Column, Cursor, Custom, DataEnvironment, FormSet, Header, Hyperlink, OLEBoundControl, OLEControl, Relation, Separator, and Timer	Fires for the drag source of an OLE drag and drop each time the OLEDragOver event fires for a drop target. Allows the source to control the potential results of a drop and the icon in use.
OLEStartDrag, OLECompleteDrag	All base classes except ActiveDoc, Column, Cursor, Custom, DataEnvironment, FormSet, Header, Hyperlink, OLEBoundControl, OLEControl, ProjectHook, Relation, Separator, and Timer	Fire for the drag source of an OLE drag and drop when the operation starts and when it ends. OLEStartDrag lets the data source indicate valid actions. OLECompleteDrag lets it respond to whatever occurred.
OLESetData	All base classes except ActiveDoc, Column, Cursor, Custom, DataEnvironment, FormSet, Header, Hyperlink, OLEBoundControl, OLEControl, ProjectHook, Relation, Separator, and Timer	Fires for the drag source of an OLE drag and drop when the drop target requests data. Receives a reference to the data object and the format requested by the drop target.

Event	Object(s)	Meaning
DblClick	All base classes except ActiveDoc, Column, CommandButton, Cursor, Custom, DataEnvironment, FormSet, Hyperlink, OLEControl, OLEBoundControl, ProjectHook, Relation, Separator, and Timer	Fires when the user double-clicks.
UIEnable	CheckBox, ComboBox, CommandButton, CommandGroup, Container, Control, EditBox, Grid, Image, Label, Line, ListBox, OLEBoundControl, OLEControl, OptionButton, OptionGroup, PageFrame, Shape, Spinner, TextBox	Fires when control becomes visible or invisible because of activation or deactivation of the page it sits on in a page frame. Receive a parameter that indicates whether the page is being activated (.T.) or deactivated (.F.). We think that separate UIEnable and UIDisable events would be more consistent with the rest of the event model.
GotFocus, LostFocus	CheckBox, ComboBox, CommandButton, Container, Control, EditBox, Form, ListBox, OLEBoundControl, OLEControl, OptionButton, Spinner, TextBox	GotFocus occurs when the control is tabbed to or clicked on. When fires before, and determines whether, GotFocus fires. LostFocus fires when another control is clicked on or tabbed to, and that control succeeds in gaining the focus using its When event.
When	CheckBox, ComboBox, CommandButton, CommandGroup, EditBox, Grid, ListBox, OptionButton, OptionGroup, Spinner, TextBox	Good old When, a useful carryover from FoxPro 2.x, fires before GotFocus. A control can't have the focus unless When says it's okay. When also fires on each up-arrow and down-arrow keystroke while scrolling through a list box, but does not fire while scrolling in a combo box (use InteractiveChange for that).
Valid	CheckBox, ComboBox, CommandButton, CommandGroup, EditBox, Grid, ListBox, OptionButton, OptionGroup, Spinner, TextBox	Valid usually fires when a change is made. Even if no changes are made, tabbing though a combo box, edit box or text box fires its Valid event. Returning a numeric value from Valid determines the next control to get focus. Zero forces focus to stay on the current control without firing the ErrorMessage event; negative returns move back through the tab order; positive values move forward.

Event	Object(s)	Meaning
ErrorMessage, Message	CheckBox, ComboBox, CommandButton, CommandGroup, EditBox, ListBox, OptionButton, OptionGroup, Spinner, TextBox	When Valid returns .F., ErrorMessage fires to display an error message. We hardly ever use this—we handle the problem in the Valid, prompting the user if necessary, and use the return of zero in Valid to handle this. Message is an old-fashioned way of putting text on the status bar—consider StatusBar and StatusBarText instead.
KeyPress	CheckBox, ComboBox, CommandButton, EditBox, Form, ListBox, OptionButton, Spinner, TextBox	Allows processing of input keystroke-by-keystroke, rather than waiting for input to be completed.
Moved, Resize	Column, Container, Control, Form, Grid, OLEBoundControl, OLEControl, PageFrame, Toolbar	Fire when the object has been moved or resized, respectively.
InteractiveChange, ProgrammaticChange	CheckBox, ComboBox, CommandGroup, EditBox, ListBox, OptionGroup, Spinner, TextBox	What UPDATED() always should have been, but at a finer level. Fires each time a change is made to a control's Value, even before focus has shifted from the control. InteractiveChange detects user changes; ProgrammaticChange fires on changes performed in code.
Activate, Deactivate	Form, FormSet, Page, Toolbar	Occur when container gets the focus or the Show method is called, and when it loses the focus or the Hide method is called, respectively.
RangeHigh, RangeLow	ComboBox, ListBox, Spinner, TextBox	These events have two distinct uses, both of them outdated. For text boxes and spinners, can be used to prevent out-of-range entries. Don't do it this way—use Valid instead. For combo boxes and list boxes, these are used only in forms converted from FoxPro 2.x to indicate the first element and number of elements settings.
DownClick, UpClick	ComboBox, Spinner	Not to be confused with MouseDown, fires when the down or up arrow of a spinner is pressed or, for combos, when the arrows on the scrollbar are used.
Load, Unload	Form, FormSet	Load is the first form event to fire, before Init, Activate and GotFocus. Load fires for the form set before the form. Unload is the last form event to fire, reversing the order: form first and then form set.

Event	Object(s)	Meaning
Paint	Form, Toolbar	Fires when the item is repainted. CAUTION: don't Resize or Refresh an object in its Paint event—a "cascading" series can occur!
Scrolled	Form, Grid	Fires when the user uses the scrollbars. Parameter indicates how the scrollbars were used.
BeforeOpenTables, AfterCloseTables	Data Environment	Wrappers around the automatic behavior of the Data Environment. Occur before and after tables are automatically opened and closed, respectively.
BeforeRowColChange, AfterRowColChange	Grid	Fire before the Valid of the row or column of the cell being left, and after the When of the cell being moved to, respectively.
Deleted	Grid	Fires when the user marks or unmarks a row for deletion.
DropDown	ComboBox	Fires when user opens the list part of the combo box.
Timer	Timer	Fires when a timer is enabled and its Interval has passed.
BeforeDock, AfterDock, Undock	ToolBar	Microsoft missed a great chance here for a property to tell you which toolbars are attached just below the menu—a WhatsUpDock property. These events probably won't shock you: BeforeDock fires before a toolbar is docked, AfterDock after the fact and Undock when the toolbar is moved from a docked position.
QueryUnload	Form	Fires when a form is released other than through a call to its Release method or explicit release of the referencing variable. Allows testing of the ReleaseType property to determine how the form is being released and takes appropriate action.
BeforeBuild, AfterBuild	ProjectHook	Fire before and after a project is built, whether through the interface or the Build method.
QueryAddFile, QueryModifyFile, QueryRemoveFile, QueryRunFile	ProjectHook	Fire when the specified action is taken on a file in the project. NODEFAULT in the method prevents the indicated action.

Event	Object(s)	Meaning
ShowDoc, HideDoc	ActiveDoc	Fire when the user navigates to or from an active document application, respectively.
Run	ActiveDoc	Fires when an active document application is all set up and ready to go. Use it to start the application doing something useful.
CommandTargetQuery, CommandTargetExec	ActiveDoc	Fire when the user of an active document application in a browser begins or completes an action in the browser that might be handled by the application.
ContainerRelease	ActiveDoc	Fires when the browser holding an active document application lets go of the application. Allows the app to figure out what to do next.
ReadActivate, ReadDeactivate, ReadShow, ReadValid, ReadWhen	Form	Based on the FoxPro 2.x READ model, these work only in the "compatibility" modes. Ignore them unless you're converting older apps.

Add Your Own Events

In addition to the events provided by the designers, VFP 6 lets us add our custom events. Sort of. The new Access and Assign methods let us attach code to any property of any object. The Access method for a property fires when the property's value is read; the Assign method fires when a value is stored to the property (whether or not it's actually changed). In addition, the This_Access method fires whenever any property of the object is read or written.

We consider these events even though their names are "Access method" and "Assign method," because they fire on their own under specified circumstances. That makes them events, by us. If we did add these to the table above, they'd have to go at the top, since not only does every object support them, but for the property-specific versions, a given object can have as many Access methods and as many Assign methods as it has properties.

How to Mangle the Event Model

There are a few items, especially those which have been retained in Visual FoxPro "for backward compatibility" that can cause some real difficulties with the new event model. We cover a few of them here for your consideration. We think these are some of the first items you should be looking at revising if you're moving a FoxPro 2.x application to Visual FoxPro.

On Key Label commands

An ON KEY LABEL command defines an action to be performed as soon as the keystroke is received. Unlike keyboard macros and keystrokes processed in input controls, "OKLs," as they are often called, are processed immediately, interrupting the current processing between two lines of code. If these routines do not restore the environment to exactly the condition it was in before the OKL initiated, the results, as Microsoft likes to say, can be unpredictable. Disastrous is more like it. We recommend trying newer alternatives, like the KeyPress event of the affected controls, rather than depending on being able to control all the side effects of this shot-in-the-dark.

ON Commands In General

ON commands are a different kind of event handler. ON KEY reacts to each keystroke, ON ESCAPE to pressing the ESCape key and ON KEY = only to a specific keystroke (with a READ to be in effect). Give up on these. Use the newer Visual FoxPro events. While there are exceptions—Christof Lange's very clever Y2K solution is one of them—generally speaking, anything done with the old ON model can be done in a more extensible, supportable way with the new event model. ON ERROR and ON SHUTDOWN are the necessary exceptions that prove the rule.

BROWSEs

Integrating BROWSE with READ was the sought-after Holy Grail of FoxPro 2.x. BROWSE, arguably one of the most powerful commands in the language, was a bit testy about sharing the stage with READs. Because BROWSEs did not make it easy to detect when they were activated and deactivated, it was difficult to properly manage them within a READ situation. Although several plausible solutions were advanced, most were very sensitive to changes in the environment and difficult to work with. With the advent of grids in Visual FoxPro, these complexities have been eliminated (and totally new ones introduced), as should BROWSEs from your application code. If you haven't heard enough of this topic, tune in to "Commands Never to Use" for more.

"Your Server Will Be With You In A Moment"

> If we do not lay out ourselves in the service of mankind whom should we serve?
>
> Abigail Adams, 1778

Client-Server: definitely one of the buzzwords of the nineties. Or is that two of the buzzwords—we haven't figured out yet whether "client-server" is one word or two. We're not alone in this. A salesman for a major vendor asked to define client-server a few years ago responded, "Client-server? Why, that's whatever it is I'm selling today."

So why all the fuss about client-server? Because most organizations have their data spread out over multiple machines in at least as many formats. Client-server is advertised as the ticket to using all that data without forcing everyone to use the same applications or having to convert everything to a common format.

UDA, ODBC, ADO, OLEDB, DAO, RDO, I Don't Know!

We noticed a trend several years ago, surfing the Microsoft Web site. Where previously there had been little or no talk about database issues, now we were starting to see some action. WebDb, DAO and RDO were the first, then OLE DB, ADO and UDA. Acronymomania! From little attention, Microsoft turned its attention from the Office suite and network wars first to the Internet and then to the enterprise. Like drinking from a firehose, suddenly we were drowning in new terminology, 1.0 products and "preview" betaware. With Visual Studio 6, we are starting to see the first stable products of this craze, and we think you should be watching them, too. But for now, the best course is to consider "classic" client-server development, and wait for the tools to catch up with the marketeers. We'll take a deeper look at the promise of all those acronyms and a few more (like MTS and COM+) a little later, in "n-Tiers of a Clown," below.

Let's race back to the present. In Microsoft's world, client-server and database connectivity is implemented through ODBC, or "Open DataBase Connectivity." ODBC is to databases what Print Manager is to printers. Just as Print Manager and appropriate drivers let you send all sorts of documents to whatever printers you want, ODBC, together with a set of drivers, lets you use data from whatever database management system you want in an assortment of applications. Installing Visual FoxPro or your application installs the ODBC Administrator applet and a bunch of drivers, if you let it. You can get other (and perhaps more up-to-date) drivers from the manufacturers of the DBMS you need to talk to.

Visual FoxPro provides two methods of performing client-server: views and SQL Pass-Through. Views are everyman's entree to the client-server world. You can grab server data, manipulate it in FoxPro, then return it to the server. SQL Pass-Through gives you more control at the cost of more responsibility. You communicate with the server through a special set of functions—you can pass commands directly to the server to be executed. (SQL

Pass-Through is an updated version of what the Connectivity Kit provided in FoxPro 2.x.)

So What's a Server, Anyway?

A client is to me a mere unit, a factor in a problem.

Sir Arthur Conan Doyle, Sherlock Holmes in *The Sign of Four*

Let's get some basic terminology down. Start with "client" and "server." The server's the one who has the data you want. It might be a mainframe on the other side of the world, SQL Server on your network, or Paradox on your machine. The server is also called the "back end." Server data is sometimes referred to as "remote" data.

The client is the one who wants the data—in our case, your Visual FoxPro application. The client is sometimes called the "front end." Data that originates in the client is called "native" or "local" data.

ODBC is the translator here. It sits between the client and the server and converts the client's requests into a form the server understands. Then it converts the server's responses back into the client's format.

A key ODBC concept is a "data source"—an application and a database it owns. When you want to get your hands on server data, you tell ODBC what data source to use. For testing purposes, our favorite is Microsoft Access with the ODBC 2.0 drivers pointing at a doctored-up copy of Access' sample Northwind Traders database. (You might want to use this method, too—it's a simple and cheap way to get some experience with client-server capabilities on a single machine.) We call this data source "Access with ODBC 2.0" (which is a lousy name for it, but we started doing that before we understood). Whenever we want to play with the Northwinds database, we just refer to the "Access with ODBC 2.0" data source. (The doctoring here is to remove embedded spaces in the names of the Northwinds tables and fields. In defiance of pretty much every other DBMS out there, Access lets you use spaces in names of things. Kind of like Visual FoxPro's long names, which also let you embed spaces in table and view names. In both cases, while Visual FoxPro can handle it, it's generally more trouble than it's worth.)

You can define a data source that doesn't point at a particular database, but then you'll get prompted to specify one every time you open that data source.

All of this terminology can be misleading, since for some data sources, such as an Access table on your local machine, the data is neither remote, nor is there truly any process running you can call a server. Using ODBC to connect to this data source is not truly "client-server" in its pure sense, but, thanks to the abstraction of ODBC, it will appear exactly the same to the consumer of the data, the client. This abstraction of interfaces is key to letting us prototype a client-server application using a "one-tier" ODBC data source.

Data From Afar and From Anear

'Tis distance lends enchantment to the view.

Thomas Campbell, Pleasures of Hope

Views are a very cool idea. They let you take data from a variety of sources and handle it all pretty much the same way. Once you get your hands on the data, you don't have to worry about where it came from.

A view is a subset of the data in a database, organized in a way that makes sense for a particular operation. Often, data in a view is denormalized to make it easier to report on or more logical for the user who's working with it.

Views in FoxPro can be based on remote data, native data or a combination of the two. This makes it possible to process data without regard to the original source of the data. From your application's perspective, the data in the view is just data; it doesn't know or care whether it started out in FoxPro, Access, SQL Server or Joe's Original Database.

Data in a view can be updated. It's your choice whether the updated data gets passed back to the original data source and, if so, when that happens. By definition, all the fields in a view are updateable locally (in Visual FoxPro). It's your responsibility not to let users make updates that don't get passed to the server. Having their updates thrown away tends to make most users a little grouchy, so ensure that your interface makes it clear when data is updateable and when it is not.

Views are based on queries. A view is defined by specifying a query that collects the data to populate the view. Like so much else in Visual FoxPro, this can be done either by command or using the visual tools (in this case, the View Designer, known for short as the VD—we can't believe they left this name in, but at least they didn't name their whole product this way).

It's much easier to create views with the VD than in code, but you have to accept the serious limitations of working within the VD. In Visual FoxPro 5, in a move to make VFP more ANSI-SQL compatible by supporting the new JOIN clause, Microsoft broke the View Designer badly. Because of the way join clauses form intermediate results between tables, multiple joins to the same tables (such as a parent with two sibling children) often cannot be expressed properly by the Designer. It complains while saving a view that it will not be editable again, or gripes that columns cannot be found. Fortunately, we have the coded method to fall back on. When you create views in code (using CREATE SQL VIEW), you generally need a long series of calls to DBSETPROP() to establish update criteria. We think the best solution is a hybrid approach. Get as far as you can with the VD, coding your simple views, then use the cool utility GENDBC (which ships with FoxPro) to get the code to create the view. Make further modifications to the code, run it, and you've got your view.

You can also create parameterized views. With these, one or more variables appear in the query's WHERE clause preceded by "?". When you open the view, the value of those variables is substituted into the query. No big deal, right? Except that, if the variable doesn't exist, the user is prompted for a value. Imagine a view that pulls out all customers in a single country. Rather than writing separate versions for each country, or some deviously tricky, macroized routine you'll never figure out how to debug, you use a parameter for the country and the user fills it in at runtime. If the query parameter does exist, the user isn't prompted, so if you prefer to create your own dialog for the user, or can derive the parameterized value from the environment, you can create the parameter and refresh the view yourself. We often find ourselves coding this trick in calls to the Refresh() function.

A Forward Pass

> For I will pass through the land of Egypt this night …
>
> Exodus

SQL Pass-Through (or SPT) is for those who need to be in control. Instead of simply defining a view once and opening it as needed, with SPT you send the necessary commands to the server each time you want to see some data.

SPT works a lot like FoxPro's low-level file functions. You open a connection, which gives you a handle. After that, you refer to the connection by the handle and call on appropriate functions to communicate with the server. When you're done, you close the connection.

By providing more or less direct access to the server, SPT also lets you handle administrative functions on the server end of things. You can even perform tasks like creating tables on the server. Definitely, this mode is for those who know what they're doing.

What you can actually do depends on the server. Different servers have different capabilities. You'll need to learn the capabilities and liabilities of the servers you want to work with.

I've Got Connections

> In historic events, the so-called great men are labels giving names to events, and like labels they have but the smallest connection with the event itself.
>
> Leo Tolstoy, *War and Peace*

To access remote data, you need a data source. You also have various options regarding the way Visual FoxPro interacts with that data source. Since you're likely to want to do it the same way over and over again, FoxPro lets you create what it calls a connection.

A connection is simply the name of a data source, along with various properties, stored and assigned a name. When you create a view or open a communication channel with SPT, one of your options is to use a named connection. Without it, you have to specify the data source and all the appropriate properties. Individual views can have their connection specified in the CREATE VIEW command or within the VD interface (look under Advanced Options on the Query menu pad). Sharing a connection is the preferred option in a production environment, because connections consume valuable resources on the server. In addition, some servers are licensed by connection, rather than by user, and an errant application can consume many more connections than necessary, limiting the number of users.

The Connection Designer lets you specify connections more or less visually. You can create connections in code with (what else?) the CREATE CONNECTION command. Connect and disconnect with (brace yourself) SQLConnect() and SQLDisconnect().

Developers raise a legitimate concern that connection definitions are stored within the DBC and could include user IDs and passwords to access back-end databases. We agree. There are good solutions out there as well. First, don't store the password with the Connection. Either ask the operator for it at runtime, or store it in an encrypted field.

Buzzwords? You Want Buzzwords?

> The chief merit of language is clearness, and we know that nothing detracts so much from this as do unfamiliar terms.
>
> Galen, *On the Natural Faculties*

There are a number of items you can set to control access to remote data. Some of them apply only with SPT, while others affect views as well. Naturally, all of them come with long-winded terminology. Most of these settings apply to a connection, but some are properties of individual views or cursors.

Everything in Synch

The first choice you have (for SPT or named connections only) is whether to use synchronous or asynchronous processing. In English, this means whether you have to wait for the command to finish or you get control back right away.

Synchronous processing is what we're all pretty much used to. You issue a command and when it's done, you go on. With asynchronous processing, you have to keep asking the server if it's done. So why would you want to do this? If the command will take a long time, asynchronous processing lets you update the display (or even do other stuff) while you wait. It's like taking a book along to the doctor's office.

With asynchronous processing, you keep issuing the same command over and over until it returns a non-zero value. The bonus is what else you put in the loop that issues the command.

A Nice Big Batch

The next option is relevant only when you're dealing with a server that lets you send multiple commands at once.

(SQL Server does this; Access doesn't.) When you do that, you have a choice of waiting for the whole group of commands to finish (Batch processing) or starting things off with the first command and then coming back to ask for results of the others (non-Batch). This one also applies only to SPT and named connections.

As with asynchronous processing, non-batch lets you do things in between and keep the user updated on progress. In this case, you start the commands, and then use SQLMoreResults() each time you want results from a command after the first.

Although synchronous/asynchronous and batch/non-batch sound just about the same, they're really not. Synchronous/asynchronous relate to a single command; batch/non-batch control a group of commands.

In fact, you can mix and match the two. Any of the four combinations of these two settings is permitted. Here are the choices and what they do:

Synchronous batch processing means you can start a group of commands and control doesn't return until all the commands have been processed. When control returns, a cursor has been created for each result set generated by the commands.

Asynchronous batch processing means you start a group of commands and keep reissuing the original call (SQLEXEC()) until it returns something other than zero. At this point, there's a cursor for each result set generated.

Synchronous non-batch means you start a group of commands. Control returns when the first command is done and there's a cursor containing that result set. You call SQLMoreResults() for each subsequent result set.

Asynchronous non-batch is the most complicated, but gives you the most control. You start a group of commands. You reissue the original command until you get a non-zero value, at which point you've got the first result set. Then, you issue SQLMoreResults() repeatedly for each additional result set. Each time SQLMoreResults() returns 1, you know you've got another result set. When it returns 2, you know you're done.

But Wait, There's More

Progressive Fetching—sounds like something a '90s kind of dog would do. Actually, it means you get control back while the server keeps on sending the rest of the records. This one's easy to test. Just create a view with a few thousand records in it (say, based on the OrderDetails table in Northwinds). When you USE the view from the Command Window, watch what happens in the status bar. You get control back with only 100 records in the cursor, and you can go right ahead and Browse that cursor right away. But if you keep watching the status bar, you'll see the record count going up and up until it's reached the actual table size.

You can set the number of records that get fetched at a time. You also control whether data in memo and general fields is retrieved up front, or not until you need it. Waiting until you need it speeds up the initial query at the cost of a slight delay when you want to edit a memo or general field.

Another setting lets you control the maximum number of records returned by the server. You get back the first however many records the server finds and the rest are ignored.

The complete list of properties for remote data access is covered under the DBSetProp(), CursorSetProp() and SQLSetProp() functions.

It's Been a Pleasure Transacting Business with You

Visual FoxPro's built-in transactions let you protect your data when storing it. For example, you can wrap storage of an invoice and its detail records in a transaction. If storage of any one record fails, the whole transaction can be rolled back, preventing partial data from being stored.

FoxPro's transactions don't affect storage of remote data. If the server you're dealing with supports transactions natively, use SQLSetProp() to set Transactions to Manual; without that setting, each individual SQL statement is wrapped in an individual transaction. It's far more likely that you'll want to ensure that whole batches of updates happen together. You can control the remote transactions with the SQLCommit() and SQLRollBack() functions. Remember, though, if you've assumed the responsibility of controlling transactions, you'd better remember to finish them! An uncommitted transaction is automatically rolled back if it's not completed before the connection is lost. Also, transactions typically place a heavy burden on servers, forcing them to hold locks on a number of records and slowing processes for other applications accessing the server. Get in there, start your transaction, make your data changes and get out as quickly as possible, in order to get optimum performance from your server.

To Err is Human

SQL Pass-Through functions handle errors somewhat differently than most FoxPro commands. In fact, error handling for SPT functions is similar to that for the low-level file functions they resemble. Unlike the LLFFs, though, the SPT functions don't have their own dedicated error function—instead, they cooperate with the AError() function.

Rather than triggering a FoxPro error (or the specified error handler), the SPT functions return a negative number when they fail. According to Help, they return -1 when there's a "connection-level" error and -2 when there's an "environment-level" error. We haven't been able to generate an environment-level error, but maybe we just haven't tried the right destructive things.

We've also run into a few situations where an SPT function does go to the FoxPro error handler rather than returning a negative result. Passing bogus SQL sometimes generates the #1526 Connectivity error. Check out a few of the errors in the 1520's and 30's for items you'll need to beware of. SQLDisconnect(), in particular, yells for help when you try to shut down a nonexistent connection or a connection that's in use.

It looks like you usually get FoxPro's error hander when FoxPro itself can detect the error, and you get a negative result when ODBC or the server finds the error. We sure wish it were uniform. This hybrid mix makes writing an error handler much harder. Your overall error handler has to be prepared to deal with some client-server errors, but any SPT code has to check each return value and call on an error handler if a negative value pops up.

In spite of this weakness, we're very satisfied with Visual FoxPro's client-server capabilities. We see a lot of client-server work out there and are really glad that Visual FoxPro can now jump right into the fray.

n-Tiers of a Clown

If you talk to a cutting-edge developer about client-server work, you're likely to get the reaction "Bah! Client-server? Way too limited! We're into n-tier applications now." It sounds way cool, but what does this mean?

The tiers in application development refer to the different independent processes performing data manipulations in an application. A one-tier application, like classic FoxPro applications using DBFs, Access applications with MDB files, or even Word or Excel, involves a client application that reads and writes to a file. While there might be a "server" somewhere out on the network providing file services, there is no other intelligent process intervening between the client and the data. Two-tier applications, on the other hand, have a client application, one that typically interacts with the user, talking to the server application that processes the queries and allows (or disallows) updates to the data. Client-server allows centralized processing of data queries and the centralization of all logic that is needed to determine whether an update should be applied to the database.

What more could we possibly ask for? A two-tier application sounds like it has solved all problems. Client applications perform the locally intensive work of presenting the user interface, while a "big-iron" server can do heavy-duty queries with, what is to the server, local data. In addition, the server can provide a "firewall" of protection to make sure that bad data doesn't get into the system, maintaining referential integrity and perhaps security as well.

Well, there are a few chinks in the armor. First, server products typically each have their own proprietary languages, usually extensions to SQL, and well, frankly, they stink. While they're good at protecting their data and performing routine tasks like queries and triggers, they aren't built for processing complex business logic ("if the customer has ordered more than $X from categories A, B and C within the last 90 days, not counting closeouts and specials, their shipping is free, unless..."), nor is there any easy way to transmit complex messages from the back end to the client. No client likes to be told "Update rejected," but that's about what you can get from a lot of client-server systems.

The other problem with client-server is the problem model they were designed to solve—big, hefty servers with dumb little terminals—is outdated. While a large shop can field a symmetric multi-processing, RAID-5 server with a gigabyte of RAM and 100 gig of drive space, it's most likely being hit by Pentium II workstations with 64 MB of RAM themselves, not shabby machines. The idea that one box, even with eight processors on it, can do all of the heavy lifting for hundreds of high-powered users is a very poor use of resources.

Enter n-tier. The idea of an n-tier model is that the database server just serves the data. Its job in life is downsized from a one-stop shop to a big, dumb brute that serves data as rapidly as possible, performs queries, fires triggers and ensures relational integrity. Middle tiers come into play—*tiers* with an 's'—there might be more than one, hence we're not talking about three tiers, but *n*, in the sense of 1, 2, 3, 4, ... *n* objects between you and the data. A middle tier object is where the business rules get placed—an object with clearly defined interfaces and a specific task to which it's been assigned. By creating multiple objects through which the data passes, we can simplify the tasks of each object, and by using an object technology that lets us manage these objects, we can field the individual objects on whichever platform makes the most sense in terms of efficiency and distribution of processing.

So now we need a technology that can create objects with simple interfaces, manage them across an enterprise and allow us to do distributed processing? Is this possible? Ta-da! Microsoft to the rescue with COM and DCOM. Check out "It was Automation, You Know" and "Active Something" for some ideas on where these technologies are and where they are going.

Much ADO About Nothing?

As we mentioned earlier, Microsoft has gone ga-ga over data. We're somewhat glad for the attention, but a little concerned whenever the Microsoft Marketeers get an idea. And this one's a whopper.

Microsoft is pitching Universal Data Access (UDA) as the solution for all things data. Just like Microsoft's claims in years past of the WOSA (Windows Open System Architecture) umbrella for all things Windows, or the Windows At Work solution for everyone's office microwave, we skeptically feel this is a combination of a good idea with a dose of marketing hyperbole. The key technologies behind UDA are (get your acronym seat belt on!) ADO, OLE DB and ODBC. What are these? ADO, Active Data Objects, are high-level COM components that provide basic data services within the familiar COM programming model. OLE DB is the underlying technology that ADO uses to reach data. OLE DB, in turn, uses either native OLE DB providers or ODBC to reach the data sources.

So why would we want to go to all this trouble to get to data when we can already do it quite well natively? Well, there are a number of situations where we can see ADO having a distinct advantage over the built-in FoxPro one-tier and two-tier models. First, ADO presents a very simple model. Second, ADO recordsets are COM objects that can be passed from one object to the next with no dependence on work areas or knowledge of how to manipulate a cursor. Not only can ADO be passed between local objects, but these lightweight objects, through the wonders of DCOM, can be transferred over a variety of network protocols, including the Internet.

In addition, languages that lack a native database engine, like Visual Basic or Visual J++, will flock to this new technology, which effectively gives them a data engine to work with. If we want to play in the exciting new world of components with these tools, we need to learn to speak the lingua franca as well.

The last piece in this puzzle is MTS. Now that we have this gaggle of objects slinging ADO recordsets from place to place and complex transactions being attempted, how do we coordinate all of this? The Microsoft Transaction Server, MTS, is the piece that completes the puzzle. This server, running on a Windows NT Server machine, allows us to parcel out and load-balance resource dispensers of middle-tier objects and back-end connections in a manner somewhat akin to the TP monitors of the mainframe model. MTS is the crown jewel that will link all of the ADO, DCOM, COM, and OLE DB technologies into a grand whole that Microsoft is calling COM+, the star player of their Digital Nervous System (DNS) and Distributed interNet Architecture (DNA). (We're pretty nervous ourselves about the idea of a digital *nervous* system. Wouldn't want trembling fingers on the red button.)

Whew! Had enough acronyms yet? We sure have! What's the bottom line here?

Where Are They Going To Go Today?

> I fear we have awoken the sleeping giant.
>
> Admiral Yamamoto, on hearing of the success of his Pearl Harbor attack

Microsoft has noticed data. Having all but cornered the market on office productivity software, on an uphill climb to take over network operating systems, and skirmishing to make the Internet its own, Microsoft has chosen to open yet another war front by attempting to wrest the enterprise applications from the mainframe and mini-computer crowd. To do that, Microsoft has to get a lot better at working with data, and the efforts in DNA, ADO and you name it are signs that Microsoft is making its move. Considering Microsoft's track record, we have little doubt they'll succeed. So we'll keep an eye on their progress, and think you should, too.

In the meantime, we'll continue using FoxPro to deliver the most powerful desktop applications on the planet.

"It Was Automation, You Know"

> Besides black art, there is only automation and mechanization.
>
> Federico García Lorca, 1936

Have you ever been working in one application and really needed some capability from another? Say, you were creating a report in FoxPro, but really needed Word's formatting prowess? Or maybe you needed to do calculations on a few items of data contained in a set of spreadsheets? We sure have, more times than we can count.

In the real world, many of the things people want to do aren't segregated into discrete kinds of tasks. Sure, sometimes all you want to do is write a letter or total some numbers. But more often, you want to create a complex report with pictures and maybe some spreadsheet data and so forth. (Heck, even our respective kids do this sort of thing for school these days.)

Finding a way to handle interaction among applications has been computing's equivalent of searching for the Rosetta Stone since not too long after the PC was introduced. Various approaches have been tried over the years.

First, we had applications that could read data in other formats or write their own data out in a format another application could understand. That helped, but it didn't solve the problem.

Next up, we got the integrated applications, like Framework, Q&A, ClarisWorks and Microsoft Works. These tried to throw all the apps you might need into a single package. The price was that none of the apps inside was particularly powerful, and they could only talk to each other through common file formats, though they knew something about each other's formats.

Until the Windows world, that was pretty much it. Windows brought us Dynamic Data Exchange (DDE), which let one application order another around. Progress, but it was awfully hard to use. Windows also introduced Object Linking and Embedding (OLE). That gave us a way to combine data from different applications into a single document, but still didn't quite solve the problem.

Then along came Automation (called OLE Automation at the time, until Microsoft decided that the term "OLE" wasn't snazzy enough for them, so they dropped it). Automation lets one application speak directly to another in a simple object-based way, and makes it easy to work with data from multiple applications at the same time.

We love Automation! In fact, this book was assembled using Automation. We wrote it using Word (a word processor did seem like the most appropriate choice). Each chapter, as well as each entry in the reference section, was stored in a separate document. (That's 800-odd documents, if you're counting.) Of course, being FoxPro programmers, we tracked the progress of each document using a set of VFP tables.

Eventually, we finished, though not by the time that we're writing this. (That was a sentence only Raymond Smullyan could love.) But how do you turn over 800 documents into a book? Automation to the rescue. Using our VFP tables to drive the process, we told Word to open each document and put it in the right place. The HTML Help version of the book was similarly assembled with added complications based on the need to convert Word documents to HTML files. We used Automation for the first edition of this book, too, and were amazed how easily, accurately and quickly an error-prone, tedious operation was completed.

As Automation itself has become more common, Microsoft has morphed OLE into ActiveX and, more recently, ActiveX into COM (Component Object Model). COM gives us the ability to talk not just to other applications, but to an assortment of operating system objects as well. Clearly, Automation brings us much closer to the lingua franca. But how do you use it?

Putting Automation to Work

> Far and away the best prize that life offers is the chance to work hard at work worth doing.
>
> Theodore Roosevelt, 1903

The good news is that if you're comfortable with VFP's object-oriented syntax, having one object call another's methods, and manipulating behavior by changing properties, Automation is easy. It's just another set of objects, each with its own properties and methods.

The bad news is that, for each application you want to talk to, you have to learn a new object model. Each one has its own objects in their own hierarchy, and some of it is pretty obscure (not to mention underdocumented).

You may have already won a million dollars. No, wait a minute! That's Ed McMahon's line. Let's try again. You may have already worked with some Automation objects. The Project object introduced in VFP 6 is an Automation object, as are the DataObjects used in OLE drag and drop, and the Objects collection found in many of the VFP container classes.

Most Automation objects, though, don't make themselves available quite so transparently. You have to go out and grab the object you want (using CreateObject() or GetObject()). Once you have a reference to it, though, you can do all kinds of things, from opening documents with the application to saving them to sending data from VFP to the other application to bringing the other application's data into VFP.

But Where Did Automation Come From?

Automation offers the opportunity to start moving our applications away from the one-app-does-it-all method of writing huge applications, toward an application design where more of the components are pulled off the shelf and the job of the application developer becomes one of identifying the correct components and providing the glue to bring them together. Much of the productivity gain of the Industrial Age came from the availability of cheap, interchangeable parts available in large quantities from many vendors. OLE Automation may lead to a similar availability of component parts for our applications.

Automation is similar in many ways to the Dynamic Data Exchange (DDE) protocol it's eclipsing. Both require applications on each end to carry on a conversation. Both require one of the applications to initiate the conversation (the client), and one to respond (the server). (This is an unfortunate choice of terms, as client-server means something completely different in the world of database management systems.) There are also differences—OLE is implemented by a new engine, and in a different way, than DDE is. OLE has the opportunity of being a visible as well as invisible participant in the ongoing events.

Automation is a replacement for DDE, but a far richer and more visual replacement. In exchange, it also tends to be far more resource-intensive. Automation allows direct dialogue between applications, giving the programmer the opportunity to take advantage of the strengths of the different applications making up the total client solution. In this way, Automation can be thought of as an Inter-application or Windows batch language.

Automation was introduced in the OLE 2.0 standard. The Microsoft Office Development Kit for Office 95 states that "Different applications expose different objects in different ways." This is an understatement. Every application we've worked with has its own unique implementation of Automation. We are seeing improvement, however: Microsoft has standardized on VBA for their Office applications, and is trying to bring similar object models to other applications as well. VBA has been licensed by a number of third-party vendors, too. But many tools, both within and outside Microsoft, lag behind, with weird implementations, actions that fire on setting property values, strange callback schemes, and hard-to-decipher error messages. Nonetheless, despite the frustrations of having to learn to speak a new language with each application, the power of Automation promises to bring new levels of functionality and features to our applications.

I'd Rather Fight Than Switch

So is DDE dead? Nope, not by a long shot. While Automation has supplanted DDE in many applications and has become the more stable and reliable of the two, many third-party applications are just now getting on board the Automation bandwagon. Other applications may never need to make the switch, so the older DDE means of communication will still be needed for some time. If you have an application running satisfactorily using DDE, we can't recommend that you switch. On the other hand, if you have a DDE link to an application that keeps failing or crashing or just not working, press the vendor for an Automation solution (or shop for a vendor offering one) and see if that makes for a more solid solution.

Using FoxPro as a Client

Visual FoxPro works quite well as the client in an Automation conversation, directing the work of other Automation servers. It's quite impressive to see the database-processing power of Visual FoxPro augmented by the features of Word, Excel or Visio (or whatever Automation server you need to use). There are three commands to initiate Automation: CreateObject(), NewObject() and GetObject().

CreateObject() is used to create new objects (surprised, huh?) based on either Visual FoxPro class definitions (base classes or class definitions in programs, procedures or VCXs) or from OLE objects defined in the Windows Registry.

```
oObjectHandle = CreateObject(OLEClassName)
```

NewObject() sure sounds similar to CreateObject(), doesn't it? It does essentially the same thing for COM objects. Its main advantage for VFP-coded classes is that the class library can be specified as part of the NewObject() call.

GetObject() is used to access a pre-existing object, and is used only for Automation, unlike the overloaded CreateObject() above.

```
oObjectHandle = GetObject(cFileName, cClassName)
```

In most cases, only the filename must be supplied—COM matches the file up to its appropriate server. In the case where a file might have more than one server that could work with it, or where the file has a non-standard extension that doesn't specify the server, cClassName can be used to indicate which class to use.

Once an object has been instantiated, it can be manipulated using the properties and methods it "exposes" through COM. The next section illustrates the kind of interfaces that may be presented.

One note on the syntax you'll encounter below. Some commands and property references use the Object property. This isn't really a Visual FoxPro property; it's a means of clarifying that you want to speak to the server contained within an OLE control, rather than the OLE control itself. This syntax is required only when an OLE server object and the OLE control have a property or method with the same name—use Object to make it clear that you mean the contained OLE server's property or method, and not that of the container.

Automation with the Office Applications

> When I give a man an office, I watch him carefully to see whether he is swelling or growing.
>
> Woodrow Wilson, 1916

Word 97 changed everything from the challenges we described in our original *Hacker's Guide.* Where Word 6.0 exposed only a single "Word.Basic" object and you had to manipulate all of the Word features through a difficult interface, Word 97 introduced a rich object model that made it easy to work with just the feature set you need.

We've heard many complaints that every example of Automation anyone can find uses the same example: Open Word, load and print a document, and close Word. It's not only boring, it's trivial and useless. So we've got a better solution: We won't show you an example at all. The easy examples are, well, easy, and the tough ones are way too specific. Here's a little bit of advice instead.

First, take advantage of the Help provided with the product. The table of contents of Word's Help includes an item way at the bottom called "Microsoft Word Visual Basic Reference." Other Office products have similar topics. These are your best friends as you stick your toes into the waters of automating the Office applications.

If you're going to get into Office Automation in a big way, get the best references out there. Microsoft publishes a monstrous set of books detailing every nook and cranny of the interface. If you're just starting out, the "Mastering" CD series may also be worth considering. Start slowly, and build your way up. A number of other authors have written killer books on using the Office tools. Our litmus test is pretty easy: Recall a problem you encountered in automating Office that took a while to resolve. Go to your local bookstore and check the indexes and tables of contents of the books to see if you can solve the problem. Read the section involved. If you understand the solution and like the writing style, buy the book. If they can't solve a problem you've already run into, what are the chances they'll solve any others? Take a pass.

Our favorite way to start an Automation programming session is to start in the tool we want to automate and record the sequence of actions. The easiest way to learn to program Word is to record a macro of the steps you need to take, and then translate it into matching VFP code. Unfortunately, there isn't a one-to-one correspondence from the VBA code into the code VFP uses via Automation because VBA allows the use of named arguments.

In languages that support only positional arguments (like FoxPro), parameters are passed to a function in a specific order, and elements not needed for that call are left empty or placeholders are supplied, as in this example:

```
Do MyFunc with "One","Two","Three", , , , "Seven"
```

But in languages that support named arguments, you can pass only those parameters that are needed, by preceding each with the parameter name, like this:

```
MailMerge .CheckErrors = 0, .Destination = 3, .MergeRecords = 0
```

While somewhat more self-documenting, this notation is wordier and is more difficult to work with using Automation, which supports only the positional form. Versions of Word prior to Word 97 didn't always document the correct positional form, and additional documentation needed to be dug out of the Microsoft documentation dungeons. With the latest version, they seem to have done a much better job of covering the language.

Digging Into Other Servers

You will no doubt be called upon to automate other servers. The good news is that, even if the books supplied with a server seem lacking in essential details, most of what you need to know to automate a server is built in to the server and its supporting files. Using the Class Browser or another OLE-snooping tool (see below), you should be able to determine the interface of the server, the constants it uses, and the parameters it requires in its method calls. Type Libraries, typically with extensions of TLB and OLB, are the files an application uses to register itself on your machine. The libraries contain the definitions of method names, parameters and constants added to the Registry and made available to calling programs to validate their method calls. You, too, can access this information, with a variety of tools.

First, the Class Browser can open and examine Type Libraries. Click the Open icon, and drop down the listing of file types—note that both TLB and OLB files are listed.

A second means to view Type Libraries is to use the Visual Basic or VBA Object Browsers. (In Word, Tools/Macro/VB Editor gets you to the Visual Basic editor. Select Tools/References, pick the COM component you want to examine, and then press F2 to bring up the Object Browser.) The VB Object Browser has several features missing from the Class Browser, including the ability to display the values of constants from the Type Library. Knowing the constants is essential, because often the documentation that comes with the product shows code using those constants; often the only place to find those constants is in the type library.

If these tools aren't enough, you can really get down and dirty with the OLE View tool that comes with Visual Studio. It's normally installed as part of the standard Visual Studio install. It lets you examine OLE interfaces in some detail, down to the GUID numbers and the Access and Assign interfaces for each exposed member.

One last tool, and we'll let you on your way. The FoxTLib ActiveX control is installed as part of the FoxPro development system, and we suspect its main purpose in life is to supply typelib information to the Class Browser. If there's information you can't get via the Class Browser, why not give a shot at accessing it yourself using this control? Documentation for the tool is supplied in the main Visual FoxPro help file. Happy hacking!

Turning the Tables

> It is not real work unless you would rather be doing something else.
>
> J. M. Barrie, 1922

Like so much else these days, Automation looks at the world in terms of clients and servers. The application that starts the conversation and says, "Hey, you! I want to talk to you" is the client. The application on the other end of the line, the one saying "Yeah? What's up, man?" is the server. In our various examples above, VFP was always the client, telling Word to assemble our book or telling Excel to hand over some data so it could be stored in a table for further processing. And, in fact, in VFP 3, that was your only choice. FoxPro could be an Automation client only.

In VFP 5, Microsoft added an interesting capability. They allowed VFP to be used as an Automation server. So, other applications can call on VFP to hand over some data or whatever's called for. You can even call on the VFP Automation server from inside VFP, using the built-in Application object (or the system variable that references it, _VFP). The application object's DoCmd, Eval and SetVar methods let you execute a VFP command, evaluate an expression, and assign a value to a variable, creating it if necessary, respectively.

For fun, call on VFP 6 from VFP 3 by issuing:

```
oVFP = CreateObject("VFP.Application")
```

Then, use the oVFP reference and its methods to execute VFP 6 code in VFP 3. Well, it's not really in VFP 3, any more than a command you send to Word through Automation is executing in VFP. But it is fun. However, there's not much practical use for this particular ability, because you have to have VFP 6 to do it. Why would you bother with VFP 3 when VFP 6 is available?

More importantly, because VFP is an Automation server, other applications can call up and say, "Run this query and hand me the results" or "Here's some new data for you. Please store it where it belongs." We're also fairly certain that, without the ability to act as an Automation server, VFP couldn't play with OLE drag and drop, one of the coolest additions in VFP 6.

Would You Care for a Custom Server?

He serves his party best who serves his country best.

Rutherford B. Hayes, *Inaugural Address*, 1877

However, working with VFP through its Application interface can get a little tedious. You can manipulate properties and even objects in an OOP way, but to execute any custom code, you're stuck with the DoCmd, Eval and SetVar methods. While you can do just about anything, it doesn't take too long to get tedious this way.

If the goal is to have access to a fixed set of operations, there's another way to go. Instead of working with the whole VFP Automation object, use VFP to build a custom class with methods for the things you want to do. Have VFP build it into a server for you (by declaring it OLEPublic). Then, you can instantiate your server object from other applications, and call on its methods to do what needs to be done.

An Automation server is a DLL or EXE created in FoxPro. It presents COM interfaces that can be manipulated by other programs. So how do you create those interfaces? How do you create the DLL or EXE? How do you choose between DLL or EXE, for that matter? And finally, once you've solved all that, how do you distribute your Automation server to the world?

All objects you want to make accessible through COM must be created as part of a VFP project. The process of building a project into an EXE or DLL creates the appropriate Registry entries and the additional files needed to turn a VFP program or class into a COM object.

COM interfaces are nothing more than method calls, just like the ones we're used to making. It's the packaging that's different. All classes containing interfaces you want to make public must be declared with the keyword OLEPUBLIC. For classes defined in code, this keyword is used in the DEFINE CLASS statement; for visually designed classes, the OLE Public check box must be checked in the Class Info dialog. Once you've defined a class as OLE Public, you'll probably want to tweak the class definition a bit so only those PEMs you want accessible to the outside world are visible via COM. In the Class Designer, check Protected on the Members tab for all those PEMs you want to keep internal to the object. Public members are exposed as part of the COM interface. If you're defining the class in code, use the Protected keyword for the properties and methods to hide.

In your method, it's pretty much business as usual. You define the parameters for the method to receive, perform the processing code, and return a result. Essentially, there's no difference in the behavior of FoxPro code within a COM server; it's just running in the runtime as far as it is concerned. Since you're running as a COM object, however, there are a few additional considerations you need to keep in mind.

First, make sure that your code doesn't attempt to interact with the user. Since a COM object is instantiated invisibly, there is nowhere to ask the user "Are you sure?" questions. Make sure your code doesn't call any dialogs. You also need to turn off the implicit ones. Remember to SET SAFETY OFF if you're deleting or overwriting files. Scan your code carefully. Some statements will surprise you. SET HELP TO, for example, will probably work fine on your development system but hang on your client's workstation. Why? SET HELP TO tries to set help to the default FoxHelp.CHM—what you probably mean to do is SET HELP OFF. Visual FoxPro 6.0 introduces a new function, SYS(2335), which prevents your server from invisibly hanging when a dialog appears. Instead, it generates an error, which your error handler should be able to record. Then, you can safely and cleanly terminate your server, if appropriate.

EXE or DLL? Only Your Hairdresser Knows for Sure.

I am not an adventurer by choice but by fate.

Vincent Van Gogh, 1886

The Build dialog in the Project Manager includes options for building both EXEs and DLLs. Both of these apply to COM. (Of course, BUILD EXE also applies to other applications.) An EXE, known as an *Out-of-Process* server, runs in its own memory space, while a DLL, or *In-Process* server, shares memory space with the application that instantiates it. You need to create your COM server as an EXE if you're going to make it available remotely. For other machines to invoke the COM server on a server machine, it needs to run on that server machine in its own memory space.

Another reason for choosing an EXE over a DLL is stability. If a COM server runs into problems and errors out, hangs, or just plain dies, an EXE usually crashes its own space, but only causes an error in the client calling it. A crash in a DLL-based server usually brings down the whole process—client, server and all.

There's a down side to using EXEs, of course. Since the client application and the server are in different processes, there is a significant amount of overhead in the interprocess communication that takes place. Also, if the EXE needs to load from disk and start each time it is called, there can be a significant wait (called a "latency period") before the EXE is ready to serve. Under heavy loads, this latency can become a bottleneck.

A DLL has the opposite benefits, with equivalent liabilities. Because a DLL is running in the same memory space, the communication carries far less overhead. But running a FoxPro DLL, especially inside a FoxPro application, does introduce some tricky issues. The Fox DLL shares the same VFP runtime with its hosting client, which means that they share the same DEFAULT, TALK and other global settings. Be very careful to preserve and restore any settings you change when crafting a FoxPro DLL. Like a guest in someone else's house, make sure you put back what you move and disturb as little as possible. (Of course, that's always good advice when programming.) Take advantage of scoping and privatizing your behavior, using private data sessions and minimal variable scope to minimize the effects on the host application.

Distributing Your COM Server

> Our society distributes itself into Barbarians, Philistines and Populace; and America is just ourselves with the Barbarians quite left out, and the Populace nearly.
>
> Matthew Arnold, *Culture and Anarchy*, 1869

A COM server can be bundled up and shipped using the Setup Wizard, just like any other application. In the second step of the wizard, pick "COM Components" and follow the prompts to add your servers to the list displayed. In-Process (DLL) servers have no options, but with Out-of-Process (EXE) servers, you can specify several options as to how the install should proceed. Check the Help file for more details.

How to Troubleshoot

> People struggled on for years with "troubles," but they almost always succumbed to "complications."
>
> Edith Wharton, *Ethan Frome*, 1911

Troubleshooting COM components can be a bear because they don't have a visible interface you can use for direct debugging. A DLL produces a "Feature not available" error if you attempt to suspend or debug in the middle of one of its procedures, even if you've instantiated it in the FoxPro development environment. Our advice: debug in advance as much as possible, and set up a robust error handler to dump all of the environmental information you can find into an error log when an error occurs. That way, even though live debugging is unavailable, you should have sufficient evidence to deduce the source of the problem.

COM & DCOM

DCOM, or Distributed COM, is the latest shipping version of COM. (COM+ is still in the vaporware stages—we'll look at that a little further along). What does DCOM give us?

Distributed COM is built into Windows NT 4.0 and Windows 98 and is available for Windows 95 as a free download from the Microsoft site. DCOM allows you to call for a service, using the same terminology you would for any object invocation, but the service actually runs on another machine! This opens up some great possibilities for distributed computing—where a few fast, powerful machines, or machines with special resources, could provide their services to other clients. DCOM can let you create "farms" of machines to provide computing-intensive services with one centralized computer providing the interface to the calling machines, acting in effect as a pooling manager. In fact, that is one of the major features of Microsoft Transaction Server (MTS), a key component in the COM+ architecture: acting as pool manager for the resources required.

You don't need to do anything special to your application or server to take advantage of DCOM. When you're ready to ship the software, just select the DCOM options from within the Setup Wizard. At installation time, the installer must know the details of where the service is available—network address and network protocol—in order to configure the client machine. Check the VFP Help files for details on installing and configuring DCOM servers.

Using VFP in an n-Tier Architecture

Microsoft's current marketing pitch, COM+, is an application architecture that uses COM components and the COM interface for all layers of an n-tier application model. (See "n-Tiers of a Clown" in "Your Server Will Be With You in a Moment" for more on the n-tier model.) We welcome these developments, and feel that VFP has a place to play, both as a heavy-duty front-end tool and as a middle layer serving business rules between the client and the data services. However, we advise caution before leaping into this new solution.

First, you want to make sure that your application really needs the power of an n-tier solution. While the architecture seems attractive, we've discovered that the complexity of design, management and testing of our applications is proportionate to the number of interfaces we need to support. As more components are introduced into the mix, it becomes more complex to anticipate and properly code the ability to handle failures of single components, error passing between layers, and many other issues.

Second, realize that the architecture is more theory than reality in some places. Microsoft states that the full COM+ architecture will not be in place until Windows NT 5 ships (at this point, sometime in 1999, well after we write this). While versions of most of the components are available now, they have very low version numbers—1.0 and 2.0—that inspire us to caution.

Finally, there are serious questions about how well the architecture will scale. It is easy to do demos of Northwind Traders or the Pubs data sample from SQL Server and post a few records. If you are interested in n-tier architecture, though, you probably are dealing with much larger tables, much higher transaction rates, and some serious performance requirements. We recommend that early in your design of an n-tier system, you set up some bench tests to give you an idea of the hardware and software components that will be needed to meet your requirements.

"Ah, What a Tangled Web We Weave"

The Internet. Unless you've been hiding in a cave for most of the past decade, you know that the Internet, and particularly the World Wide Web, has captured the lion's share of the publicity in the computer world. What is it about the Web that has attracted so much attention? What can we FoxPro developers do to capture some portion of this market? And what *should* we do?

This is not a primer on the technologies of the Internet—there are many fine books on that subject. Nor is it an in-depth examination of the techniques needed to assemble a robust VFP Web-based application—that's well covered in Rick Strahl's awesome *Internet Applications with Visual FoxPro 6.0,* part of the Essentials series that also includes the fine volume you're reading now. Our goal is to give you a brief overview of the stuff that's involved, and then we'll dig into the stuff you can do with Visual FoxPro.

HTML is Just Text!

The idea behind the Web is that specially formatted plain old text can be used as the communication medium between any two computers. With special formatting marks to designate relative font size, italics, font strength, and so forth, each computer application can read the text and render it in a means appropriate for its display device. The basic language involved is Hypertext Markup Language, HTML. It consists of *tags*, usually in begin-end pairs, set off from the main text with greater-than and less-than brackets, which set the format of the text between them. Tags are typically reduced to a few mnemonic characters, so <I> stands for italic and <BR> for line break. When paired, the ending tag begins with a slash. So, text wrapped in the <STRONG> and </STRONG> tags appears as strong text (usually represented by bold).

Right away, you should be realizing that HTML itself is pretty plain vanilla, and that, if text manipulation is all that's involved, well, Visual FoxPro's textmerge capabilities, as well as some new version 6.0 enhancements like StrToFile(), make VFP an ideal language for generating HTML. True enough. But wait, there's more...

HTML serves adequately as a markup language for generating static pages. It isn't a typographer's dream, being limited to a few relative font sizes and a couple of simple enhancements—bold, italic and so forth. In addition, basic HTML supports simple input via text boxes, command buttons, option buttons and combos. But that's about the limit of the language. In order to get much further than that, you need to look into extensions to the basic language and into scripting languages.

We love standards. That's why we have so many. HTML is no exception. Over its short lifetime, it has gone through a number of revisions, with version 3.2 the currently accepted standard and 4.0 coming along close on its heels. It's important that you know what your customers will be using to access your Web pages so you can ensure your pages don't present content they're unable to read. Different browsers and different versions of the same browser support different versions of HTML and the various extensions. HTML 4.0 and Dynamic HTML (DHTML for short) are the latest cool languages—if you're dealing with an in-house application, or can limit your customer base to those with the latest compatible browsers, this is what you'll want to code in.

Script Me a Part

For more sophisticated work than layout, enter scripting languages. Scripts are blocks of code in HTML that run within their interpreter. Java, JavaScript (no relation), VBScript and ECMAScript (the European Community standard of JavaScript) are among the more popular. These scripts perform many of the interesting things that go on within a displayed page, such as highlighting areas as the mouse floats over them. Scripts can be client-side—that is, run in the user's browser—or server-side, running on the Web server to modify the HTML before it's sent to the client browser.

There are a bunch of scripting languages, and they present many of the same compatibility issues as do the varied versions of HTML. Java is considered to be the "universal" language "for" browsers. Developed and licensed by Sun Microsystems, Java took the world by storm a few years ago. We're a little envious of the Java language, because it was built from the ground up as a new language with the latest technological bells and whistles and none of the baggage of supporting legacy applications that many languages suffer from today. At the same time, it's faced great challenges in being developed to run within a "Java Virtual Machine" (JVM) on any number of otherwise incompatible platforms, running on each platform securely and efficiently. Quite a task. With Java, Sun likes to claim you can "Code once, run everywhere." We look forward to a few more revisions of the JVMs until we reach that goal, but now Java is a little closer to "Code once, debug everywhere," as one wag put it. Nonetheless, if you are coding an application for a limited number of platforms, Java may be the leading choice.

Serve It Up!

Okay, so now you've got some idea of what you want to present and what languages you'll use to present it. Now, how do you get that cool Web site up onto that World Wide Web? First, obviously, you need a connection into the Internet. While many larger firms have full-time Internet access in-house, a number of smaller firms depend on an outside vendor, an Internet Service Provider (ISP) to host and maintain their Web sites. Choosing whether to use an ISP or supporting a Web server in-house is primarily an economic decision, but whichever way you go, make sure that the server you are using can support the server-side work you'll want to perform. Many ISPs run their machines on UNIX or other operating systems that won't support FoxPro runtimes or ISAPI interfaces.

In a typical Web site scenario, clients connect to your Web site, requesting a particular Web page via a Uniform Resource Locator (URL). Your server receives this request, finds the specified page, and returns it. The actual mechanism for finding the page depends on the request. If it was just for "somepage.html", the server can just pull a static page off disk. If the request includes specific keywords, it triggers the server to run certain programs and return the HTML those programs generate. Like every other aspect of Web technology we've talked about so far, yes, there are many techniques to choose from, and yes, different solutions have advantages and disadvantages, compatibility issues and limitations.

As we've said before, we can't possibly go into all of the details of all the ways a server can interact with data, but here are some basics to give you an idea of what's out there.

CGI—Common Gateway Interface—really is the common way to interface to Internet servers. You've probably seen "cgi" in URLs while browsing the Internet. CGI is a standardized interface to communicate with servers—you can count on it being available on pretty much any server out there. If your site is hosted on an ISP, there's very little chance this interface is not supported, whether they run IIS on Windows NT or the Apache server on Linux, or JoeBob's WonderServer on some operating system you've never heard of.

ISAPI, the Internet Server Application Programming Interface, is a proposed Microsoft standard; it requires a far more intimate connection between the application and the server. CGI scripts run as individual executables for each request made of the server, potentially bogging down the server under very heavy traffic. ISAPI is a single DLL running in the server's space, and is capable of handling multiple requests and queuing results. While performance may be improved by eliminating inter-application communication and multiple EXE startups, you trade this for a DLL capable of crashing the server if it misbehaves.

What Does the Fox Do?

Okay, by now we expect you're totally dazzled and frazzled on this whole Internet thing. There are clients and servers, scripts and protocols, lots of things to consider. But FoxPro's end of this thing is pretty simple: generate HTML. That's easy. Here's a trivial sample:

```
* MakeHTML

SET TEXTMERGE TO main.html
SET TEXTMERGE ON NOSHOW
\<HTML>
\<HEAD>
\<META NAME="Generator" CONTENT="Microsoft Visual FoxPro">
\<META NAME="Date" CONTENT="<<DATETIME()>>" >
\<TITLE>Demonstration HTML</TITLE>
\</HEAD>
\<BODY>
\<H1> This is a demonstration of HTML </H1>
\</BODY>
\</HTML>

SET TEXTMERGE OFF
SET TEXTMERGE TO
```

This program generates a small file named Main.HTML, which displays "This is a demonstration of HTML" in large letters, when opened in a browser. Ho-hum. It's hard to get clients to pay you for this sort of stuff. But notice the eighth line of the routine, where DATETIME() is automatically evaluated by the textmerge process, as part of generating the text file. No, clients won't pay you for the time of day (though we hope they'll give you time of day), either, but they will pay you for converting their data into HTML, and that's exactly what you can do with Fox and textmerge.

There are two things the client might want to consider, with two different solutions and levels of difficulty and expense. If the client is interested in posting information on their Web site in "real enough time" (last month's sales figures, a list of items in inventory, relatively static information), it probably makes sense to consider generating the static information off-line and transferring it to the Web server as Web pages. If, on the other hand, the client needs information online and up-to-date, FoxPro is up to working as part of an online Web service. We'll look at both of those options in the next few sections.

We'll take on the static items first—the capability of generating HTML for transfer to a Web site. Then, we'll look at the options for generating HTML live and on-demand.

"Save as HTML" Menu Option

You may have noticed that, in VFP 6, the File menu has the welcome addition of a *Save As HTML* option, but it seems to be disabled much of the time. This option is available only while creating or modifying menus, forms or reports, but much of the underlying engine is available to developers at any time. Let's take a look at what it does first, and then look at the how.

When editing a menu, selecting Save As HTML generates a file listing all prompts and messages for the menu. We're really not sure why. We can't see a lot of use for such a thing, unless a developer was then to go in and edit all of the HTML into links to various parts of the application. But it doesn't strike us as a particularly appealing user interface.

With a form, the Save As HTML option generates an HTML file closely matching the layout of the original form. When translating a program from network-based VFP runtimes to an Internet-based Web design, we can see this as an attractive step. However, the Save As option doesn't support a number of VFP controls: Container, Grid, Image, Line, PageFrame, Shape or Spinner. For those, you have to go in and edit the generated HTML manually to get what you want, or consider writing your own modifications to the supplied GenHTML.

The Save As HTML option also works for reports: The option appears to generate an ASCII output file and then converts that by adding the required HTML headings, wrapping <PRE> formatting tags around the displayed text, and converting spaces to their equivalent non-breaking spaces by adding the code . The ugly   codes take up a lot of space and probably aren't necessary if the reports already use a non-proportional font—the default seems to set it to Courier.

How do these functions work? Setting a breakpoint on PROGRAM() = "GENHTML" gives it away. Each of these options calls the program set in _GENHTML; by default, it's GenHTML.PRG in the VFP home directory.

The Magic of GenHTML

With code like this, there's no need for comments—NOT!

```
oSaveEnvironment=NEWOBJECT("_SaveEnvironment")
lcProgramPath=JUSTPATH(LOWER(SYS(16)))+"\"
lcHTMLVCX=IIF(VERSION(2)=0,"",HOME()+"FFC\")+"_HTML.vcx"
lcOutFile=IIF(VARTYPE(tcOutFile)=="C",LOWER(ALLTRIM(tcOutFile)),"")
IF NOT EMPTY(lcOutFile) AND EMPTY(JUSTEXT(lcOutFile))
   lcOutFile=FORCEEXT(lcOutFile,"htm")
ENDIF
lnShow=IIF(VARTYPE(tnShow)=="N" OR ;
       VARTYPE(tnShow)=="I",MIN(MAX(INT(tnShow),0),5),0)
lcSourceVarType=VARTYPE(tvSource)
```

We suspect GenHTML is a slick and elegant program with a whole bunch of real cool features. We say "suspect" instead of "know" because no one but the whiz kids at Microsoft who wrote it have a clue what it does! There's a lovely header at the beginning of the file that describes the various parameters that can be passed to the function, and we suspect that with a few months of testing and tweaking, we will find GENHTML to be a handy tool. But, our past few months have been spent documenting the other 1,615 topics for this book. We hope some other hackers will come along and do the same for this tool.

We can see some real power in this tool and wish it were better documented.

A few hints: the program uses the various _HTM* classes that are part of the FoxPro Foundation Classes found in HOME()+"\FFC". It also depends upon styles and directives stored in GenHTML.DBF in the FoxPro root directory. Good luck, spelunkers! Let us all know what you find!

We anticipate that GenHTML will be one of our main avenues for generating HTML from FoxPro. But FoxPro is going to interact with the Internet in many more ways than just being a passive server of text data! First, we anticipate the need to have our applications call up a browser directly. We also can see situations where our application may be running *within* a browser. The Hyperlink control, covered next, solves the first problem, while Active Documents and the remainder of this section look at various ways we can interact live with the Internet.

HyperLink Control

The HyperLink control can be placed on a FoxPro form or within a FoxPro class in order to access the Web by passing an address to its Navigate method. We can see many good uses for these, such as linking tech support information on Help or About forms directly into your Technical Support Web site. Other uses include providing additional navigation within Active Documents, or starting up a browser to display other information—see "HTML is Not Just for Web Pages Anymore!" below.

Active Documents

Active Documents were all the rage when the Fox team started putting together the list of goodies for Visual FoxPro 6. "Tahoe," as it was known in those days, would have Active Documents as well, catching up with the ActiveDocs of Visual Basic 5.0. Not only that, but ActiveDocs in Visual FoxPro would not just be VFP forms running in a browser, but entire Visual FoxPro *applications,* capable of doing everything their network-bound apps could do.

Well, it sounded good in theory. And in fact, Active Documents have some remarkable features. But don't give up your favorite HTML editor just yet—ActiveDocs are not going to become the Next Big Thing on the Internet. The good news is that a properly constructed VFP application that can run as a standalone network application can also run as an ActiveDoc. With careful negotiation with its hosting browser (currently, you have your choice of any version of Internet Explorer 4.01 you want to work with), the app can share menu items and give the browser clues as to how to handle various requests from the user.

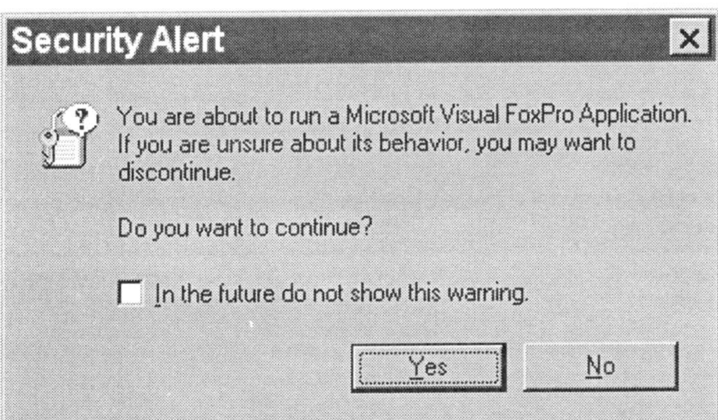

Figure 1-1: Is there an app whose behavior you are sure of?

The bad news? First, Active Documents have no special way to handle data. They require a network connection to the data just like regular applications. Without a special means of transferring data over HTTP, such as ADO, these applications must have some sort of a network attachment to the data source. If your users are willing to set up a bunch of network mappings while they're on the Internet, it is feasible to use ActiveDocs over the Internet, but what's the point? You can do the same thing without the browser container, and with a little less overhead. Finally, and perhaps more importantly, running an ActiveDoc is the same as running a FoxPro executable—the client workstation needs to have the FoxPro runtime files loaded. Very few casual browsers to your site are going to be interested in a multi-megabyte download. On the other hand, customers who could gain significant benefit from this, or "roaming users" who can be configured in the office before going on the road, could find this mechanism to be a useful one.

We can live with the warning the application gives us on startup (shown in figure 1-1), rude as it is. But without a means of transferring data or running on client machines without the VFP runtime, ActiveDocs are likely to end up as curiosities used only in a few very specialized applications. They certainly won't have the general usage we hoped they would.

Web Publishing Wizard

We often think of wizards as simplistic programs with few options that generate basic documents, but usually not tools powerful enough to use for "real" production work. The Web Publishing Wizard may be the exception that proves this rule. This cool tool lets you pull data from the application of your choice and generate HTML to display it as you wish. In addition, the wizard can generate a PRG to re-create the HTML on demand with updated data. Cool!

This wizard is a pretty slick device. It starts out in the usual fashion with the "pick a table, select your fields, select the order" routine that most developers can do in their sleep. But in step 3, the power of this little tool begins to shine. In addition to being able to pick from a set of five data layout templates, there are 26 styles that can be applied to them. Each of the data layouts has an option dialog with a page frame full of settings. Using the "Advanced" dialog, you can go even further, specifying a Cascading Style Sheet, background image, or even additional HTML elements you want added to the page. Finally, step 3 also has a Preview button. Whew! This page is like an applet unto itself, with three levels of modal dialogs sometimes appearing.

If you survive the gauntlet of step 3, you're almost done. Step 4 gives you the usual "finish line" options of running the page, viewing the code, or saving it for later. Choosing the last option saves code that looks something like the following:

```
* -- Generated Web Wizard Script File --
*
* A unique record has been created in GENHTML.DBF with your settings.
* This record can be referenced by the ID specified in the
* DO (GENHTML) command below.

LOCAL lnSaveArea
lnSaveArea=SELECT()
SELECT 0

SELECT Topic,Ngroup,Version FROM "E:\HACKFOX97\STATUS\ALLCANDF.DBF" ;
  ORDER BY Ngroup INTO CURSOR webwizard_query

IF EMPTY(_GENHTML)
   _GENHTML='GenHTML.PRG'
ENDIF
DO (_GENHTML) WITH "E:\HACKFOX97\STATUS\ALLCANDF.HTM",ALIAS(),2,,"_RXL0WSC1J"

IF USED("webwizard_query")
  USE IN webwizard_query
ENDIF
SELECT (lnSaveArea)
```

The Web Publishing Wizard offers us some really powerful capabilities. By saving all of our preferences in the GENHTML table, the wizard is, in effect, a What You See Is What You Get (WYSIWYG) editor for publishing Fox data on the Web. Rather than settling for the feeble Select statement generated by the wizard, we can substitute any generated query, filtered table or parameterized view request to populate the source table, even perhaps receiving our search parameters from another Web page. Then, we can leave it all to GenHTML to format and generate the HTML.

A few cautions are in order. If you're using the Tabular Hierarchical data layout, the Web page is generated with an ActiveX control (the Tabular Data Control, Tdc.OCX) and a comma-separated value (CSV) version of the table. You'll need to install the TDC on those client machines that don't already have it, and make sure that you put the CSV file in a place accessible to the Web site. Finally, for any of the Web pages, the wizard seems to generate the graphics with unique names but leaves them in the Wizards\Graphics\ subdirectory of the FoxPro home directory. Plan on moving them, and updating the HTML, when installing them on your Web server.

Don't confuse FoxPro's Web Publishing Wizard with the same-named Microsoft Web Publishing Wizard. The first is an application that runs within FoxPro and gives us HTML and the PRGs to create them. The latter is a program for uploading Web pages to a remote Web server.

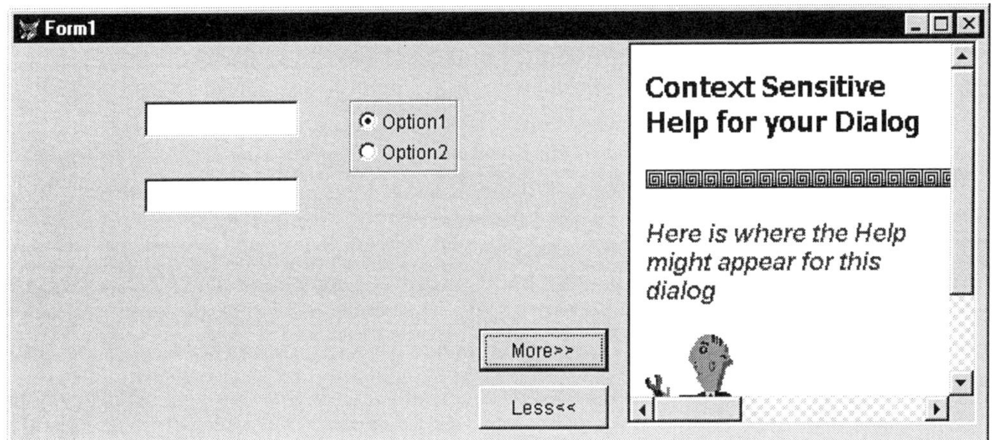

Figure 1-2: A Web Browser control added to your form gives you the ability to display richly formatted materials within your forms.

HTML is Not Just for Web Pages Anymore!

Just because HTML was originally designed for Web pages doesn't mean that its use should be restricted to that purpose. The Web browser technology provides us with widgets that are ideal as viewers, not only as standalone applications, but also as *components* within our applications. Ken Levy's Web site has some excellent demonstrations of what he calls WebExplorerX, a technique that binds a Microsoft Web Browser control onto a FoxPro form. Two tricks are needed to get it to run: Issue SYS(2333) to turn off VTable binding, and add NODEFAULT to the Refresh method of the control. Then, you can call the control's Navigate2() method and pass it the URL you want it to display. The URL does not have to be a Web page—it can be an HTML page on a local disk (called with the FILE:\\ protocol), a GIF or JPG, or any file for which a viewer add-on has been installed—you could let the user preview Word documents, Acrobat files, or any other files with viewers available. Figure 1-2 should give you some ideas.

WWW Search Page Wizard

Microsoft ships two samples with Visual FoxPro, meant to be used as online Web server components. The WWW Search Page Wizard uses Microsoft's elderly "Internet Data Connector" technology to transfer data between the Web server and the database application. This technology is fairly simplistic, swapping information between the server and the data application using files on disk as data-transfer mechanisms and semaphores. While it is a simple and robust model, it cannot support the scalability some sites require. (That's why Microsoft developed the ISAPI technology, which we'll look at in the next section.)

The WWW Search Page Wizard was first available as a free download from the Microsoft Web site several months after Visual FoxPro 3.0 shipped, and hasn't changed much. Nonetheless, the basic functionality it presents may be enough to get your Web application started. Like all of the wizards included with version 6.0, source code is also included so you can see how things are put together.

This wizard presents the typical wizard interface and coaches you through the process of creating a query to be performed against a single table. The query has to be an exact match against an indexed field. The wizard generates the code to return a result set, either in a formatted HTML page or as a downloadable text file for the client. The basic wizard engine allows you to pick your table (or ODBC data source, our preference), post a simple query against the page, specifying the single field to be queried, and allows you to pick from a variety of formats for the resulting page. For many simple operations, like a stock lookup against an inventory table, this is all you might need to do. If this was all it was capable of doing, this would be dead-end technology, great for dog-and-pony-show demos but not suitable for the real world. Let's look at the pieces a little closer and see what we can do for customization.

First, in order to support this technology, a VFP server, Server.App, needs to be running on the Web server. This server is supplied with the Search Page Wizard, in the HOME() + "Tools\InetWiz" directory. This is the tool that gets the requests from the Web server, evaluates what needs to be done, goes and does it, and then returns the record set to the Web server. To get it running on the server, all you need to do is copy it to a directory on the server, start it up, and fill in the directories it needs to work with in the form that appears.

The wizard generates three files, with the extensions HTM, HTX and IDC. The HTM file is the query page presented to the operator. This is standard HTML, editable in any text editor. The HTX file serves as a template for the returned data, specifying the format. It is also in HTML, with some markers to indicate where field values should be placed. The IDC file is the data request actually submitted to the server, with the operator's parameters filled in. The IDC file represents the Internet Data Connector, the message containing information on the data source, the template to use for a return value, and the SQL to execute against the data source. A sample IDC looks like:

```
Datasource:
Template: MVP.HTX
SQLStatement:
+SELECT  Iid, Cfirst, Clast, Cspecialty
+ FROM 'MVP'
+ WHERE cLast = '%SearchParam%'
Maxrecords: 10
```

Note that the wizard allows you to specify not only native FoxPro tables, but also ODBC data sources. The SQL statement passed to the VFP server, as generated by the wizard, tends to be simplistic, but there is no reason a developer cannot use far more advanced logic and the entire array of SQL commands: UPDATE, INSERT and DELETE within the IDC format.

We called Internet Data Connector format "elderly" earlier, and it's true that it's one of the first technologies for Web-based data to come from Microsoft, nearly three years ago. Many of its comrades, like dbWeb, have all but disappeared from the Microsoft arsenal, or have been so mutated and renamed that they are no longer recognizable. But we think IDC still has a little life left in it, and may be just the thing for developing simple, low-maintenance Web sites.

FoxISAPI

Buried deep down in the samples is the FoxISAPI sample—check under HOME(2) + "Servers\Foxisapi." This provides yet another newer, more modern way to access Fox logic from the Web. Unlike many Microsoft technologies, though, this one is available from other Web server vendors as well. The idea behind ISAPI is that a product that runs in the same process space as the Web server itself can eliminate much of the interprocess communication overhead of a Web application.

FoxISAPI.DLL runs within the Web server and it talks to FoxPro Automation Servers. Two server samples are included. There's FoxWeb, a simple demonstration of Automation in code. Then there's FoxIS, a pretty slick sample of how an Automation server can have both a FoxPro front end and generate HTML for a Web-based view. It uses the classic employee table example, but the Web interface is pretty impressive. (See Figure 1-3.) Like the IDC example above, studying the source code can give you lots of ideas about how to implement similar technologies to solve your own problems. You can use the FoxISAPI.DLL as a tool for your own custom FoxPro Web server applications.

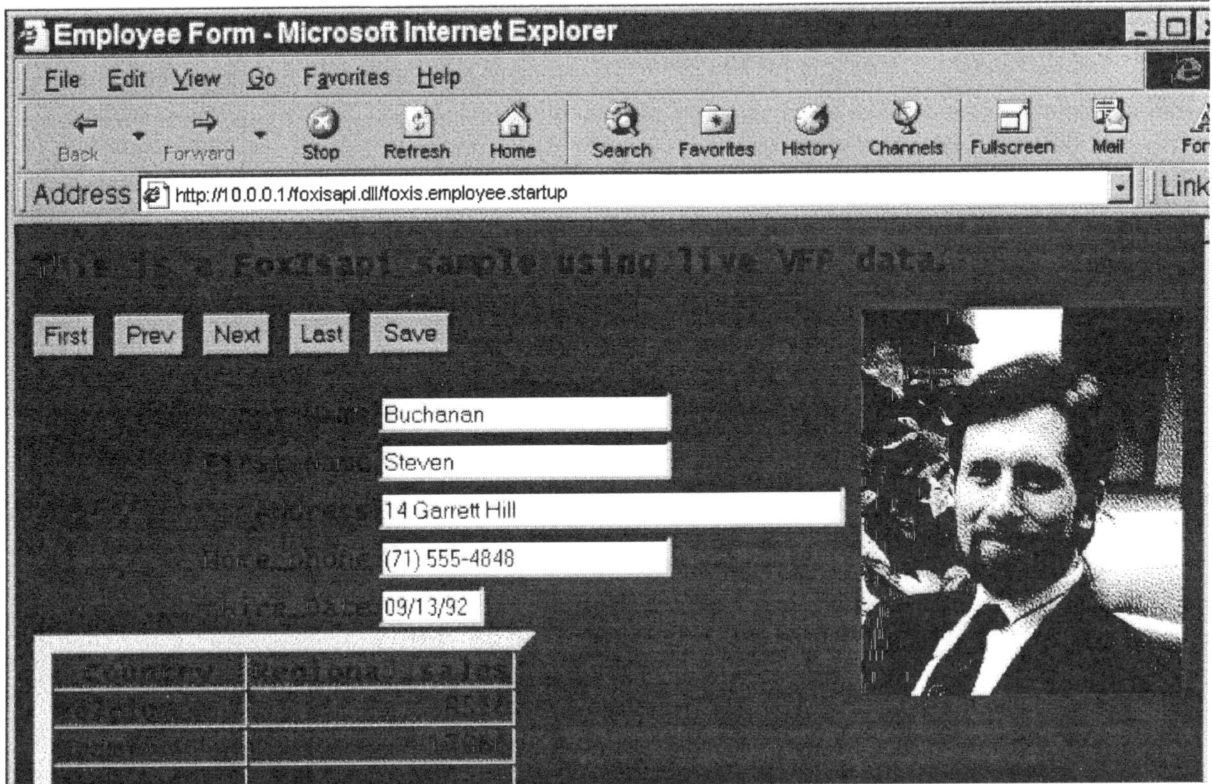

Figure 1-3: The FoxISAPI sample pulls out all the stops to demonstrate VFP as a legitimate Web server database engine.

Make sure to read the section of the Help file titled "FoxISAPI Automation Server Samples" in order to understand all the capabilities of this cool tool.

Tell Me More, Tell Me More

When you're ready to know more about working with VFP and the Web, there are plenty of resources out there. Before you leave the comfort of your office, take a look at all the information that comes with FoxPro. Check out the Solutions sample for good examples of Active Documents, hyperlinks and HTML generation. Read through the documentation on HTML, the wizards and the new HTML capabilities of Visual FoxPro 6. If you're testing out the servers, read through the documentation a few times, and make sure you do your testing on a machine other than your production server. Until you have mastered the intricacies of working with Web servers, it is likely you'll need to start and stop the machine a few times, and you'll also want to make sure you've worked the bugs out of updating data before you go live.

A browse through the Internet can give you more high-quality materials on HTML, Web design and Web applications than we could possibly list here. One source we do recommend is Ken Levy's ClassX.Com. Last time we checked, Ken had just overhauled his site and re-created the entire thing to run off XML, yet another new technology, the eXtensible Markup Language, that's still somewhere in our future. Check out his WebExplorerX and ScreenX technologies as well—only Ken could have found a way to have a live Web page appear as the background in the VFP development environment.

Other Commercial Fox Application Tools

Finally, you need to realize that the tools Microsoft supplies with Visual FoxPro most likely are missing some capabilities you will need. The Web Publishing Wizards and the FoxISAPI samples are not intended as end-alls and be-alls as much as demonstrations of technology—proof that the ability to do the work of Web services is present and feasible in Visual FoxPro. In order to develop Web applications capable of supporting large commercial applications, it's reasonable to look outside the Visual FoxPro box for commercial applications or frameworks capable of providing many of the foundation pieces and the key technical support needed to deliver world-class applications.

Several vendors advertise in the FoxPro magazines and frequent the FoxPro forums, newsgroups and Web sites. A simple search of the Web will get you dozens of hits. Finally, there is life beyond Microsoft. We're really not qualified to talk about a lot of it, but searches of the Web should lead you to many other vendors with many nifty products to sell. Since FoxPro comes with a competent ODBC driver, nearly any Web development environment should be able to access FoxPro tables directly. With Visual FoxPro's capabilities for creating COM components, you should be able to achieve mixed development environments that include the business rules and processing you developed in FoxPro.

> We stand today on the edge of a new frontier—the frontier of the 1960s, a frontier of unknown opportunities and perils, a frontier of unfulfilled hopes and threats. . . . The new frontier of which I speak is not a set of promises—it is a set of challenges.
>
> John F. Kennedy, July 13, 1960

The frontier of the Web may truly turn out to be as earth-shaking a change as the changes of the 1960s. The promise of ubiquitous access and the ability to gather information from widely disparate sources may have a profound effect, not just on us nerds cranking code, but on the entire civilization.

Section 2: Ship of Tools

Man is a tool-using animal…Without tools he is nothing, with tools he is all.

Thomas Carlyle, *Sartor Resartus*, 1833-1834

Section 2 discusses in brief the Power Tools—the key to using Visual FoxPro effectively. You'll find our favorite tips and tricks for using the Power Tools here, too, and an introduction to integrating source control with VFP development.

When Should You Use the Power Tools?

Always.

No Ifs, Ors, Buts or Howevers. Any questions?

Okay, maybe there are some Ifs, Ors, Buts and Howevers. Let's explore the question in a little more depth...

What's a Power Tool?

Long, long ago, in a land far away, Xbase was a command-line language. A not-very-user-friendly dot greeted you on an empty startup screen, and you were left to your own devices to create screens, reports, menus and other interface elements. Programmers spent their hours with graph paper, trying to calculate how many fields could be fit on a page, how many characters in each prompt. Hours were wasted drawing, erasing and redrawing these prototype screens, and more hours consumed trying to transfer them from paper to screen.

Evolution brought primitive tools—first to reports, then to menus and screens. Like many of the innovations introduced into the language, third-party add-on tools were first on the scene, adding features desperately needed into the product. These third-party tools allowed you to develop a sample screen, perhaps in a template language, and offered a method to translate these templates into your Xbase language of choice.

FoxBase was one of the first Xbase languages to add template generation into the product. The first attempt, with the FoxCode product, introduced yet another template language and a generator to write FoxBase code. Although it worked quite well, learning yet another language just to code screens was a burden, and acceptance was not universal. The FoxPro product broke new ground, in bringing everything under the FoxPro language's domain. Design tools built into FoxPro created tables (in the standard DBF format) and then generation programs, also written in FoxPro, read these tables and created executable FoxPro code. Although this may seem like an inefficient and time-consuming process, in fact, the open nature of the generation process allowed FoxPro programmers to intervene in the process, customizing the underlying tables and generation programs to extend the results of the generated objects in ways Fox Software, and later, Microsoft, never anticipated. One of the most famous of these, Ken Levy's GENSCRNX program, allowed additional capabilities within screen programs, such as screen elements becoming visible under only certain conditions, or 3-D effects added without programmer painting.

The overall concept behind the power tools is pretty straightforward. You use a visual design tool to lay out the form, label or report you want. The design tool saves your design into a series of DBF records. These DBF records can then either be generated into code, in the case of 2.x forms or menus, or interpreted at runtime, in the case of labels and reports. The open nature of this design-generate cycle leaves the doors open to innovative developers who can take the core "engines" and drive them in ways not anticipated (or perhaps needed) at the time the tools were designed. This idea of allowing extensibility of the core product in new ways was a key concept behind FoxPro 2.x, and it continues in Visual FoxPro with its accessible design storage, user-extensible data structures, and open Wizard and Builder engines.

With Visual FoxPro, Microsoft has turned the tables a bit, but still leaves us with lots of room to customize the process to our own ends. In the 2.x model, we used built-in objects, placed them on an input or output form, and then added code to get them to behave the way we wanted them to. We needed to intercept the generation process to customize the objects beyond the basic options that were provided for us. In the VFP model, we are not limited to using the objects that Microsoft wants us to use. Rather, we can create our own powerful custom controls, pre-programmed to do what we need them to do, and use them on our forms. We don't need to create our objects by hand-crafting them; they can come from pre-built Visual Class Libraries. We don't even have to set their basic options ourselves—we can build our own Wizards to do that. After creating these objects, we can run our custom Builders on them to tweak them the way we'd like them. (See the CD version of the book for the "Wizards and Builders and Bears, Oh My" section, which details these wonderful tools.)

"I hand-coded it myself before, and I'll hand-code it now," a few diehards out there say. Well, let's see if we can give you a few more reasons to reconsider your stand...

Cross-Platform Transportability

Most VFP developers snicker at the thought of cross-platform transportability, now that it has become clear that Microsoft intends to release and support Visual FoxPro on its Win32 platform only. But cross-platform does not mean both Win95 and WinNT. The tables of the power tools are not just for the use of the power tools, but can be used by developers as a repository of design information. Having forms, menus and reports designed with the power tools gives us access to their designs, in our FoxPro programs, so that we can generate the HTML, SGML, XML, or whatever-ML an application may call for. Power tools store design meta-data, a commodity that promises to become more valuable over time.

Upgradability

There have been numerous versions of Fox to date, and we hope to see a few more. Each upgrade has added capabilities, features, language enhancements, and also occasionally required some changes to the basic structure of some of the power tools' tables. This can be performed automatically as part of the upgrade; but don't expect Microsoft to come out with a code parser to graze through your volumes of code and try to introduce new features into it. Processing tables, on the other hand, is far easier. A power tool user will find it easier to get to the next upgrade.

Enhancements

We are eagerly looking forward to a number of third parties coming out with add-ons for Visual FoxPro. We anticipate that most, if not all, of these add-ons—new custom visual classes, business rules managers, Builders, Wizards, and so forth—will expect and perhaps require your code to be properly encased in the power tool format. Don't miss out on the great work of others. Avoid the 'Not Invented Here' syndrome and leverage the work of others into delivering the best application for your clients.

These Are Not Your Father's Power Tools

> Civilization advances by extending the number of important operations which we can perform without thinking about them.
>
> Alfred North Whitehead, *An Introduction to Mathematics*, 1911

When you walk into a hardware store, there's generally no question about what's a power tool and what's not. If it has a cord, or uses batteries or gas, it's a power tool. If you make it go by the sweat of your brow, it's not.

In Visual FoxPro, the lines aren't quite as simple. There are a number of items that could be called "power tools" or not. We choose to take a fairly broad view and include in our list anything that at least partially automates a task you'd otherwise have to do by hand.

We're not going to give you step-by-step (or even general) instructions on using each of the power tools. We assume you've read the documentation or an introductory book. Instead, we concentrate here on the stuff you might have missed—shortcuts, neat tricks, and new ways of working.

As with everything else in FoxPro, there are various ways the Power Tools can be categorized. It turns out that, for the most part, the design team has done a pretty good job of pigeonholing the tools just by assigning them names, so we'll use that breakdown. (They've definitely done a better job of this than the 2.x team did—remember Screen Builder, Report Writer and Label Designer?)

Designers

Generally, Designers are tools that let you point-and-click to create something for which you'd otherwise have to write code. They let you work visually instead of worrying about syntax. They also let you see results as you go, although you might be seeing intermediate results (as in the Form Designer, where you can tell what the form looks like, but not how it works).

By our count, Visual FoxPro has 11 Designers: Form, Class, Report, Label, Menu, Database, Table, View, Query, Connection and Data environment. The Form and Class Designers are quite similar, as are the Report and Label Designers, and the View and Query Designers.

There's one more tool that's not named "Designer," but we think belongs in this category. That's the Expression

Builder, which lets you design an expression. It's certainly not a builder, and in some ways it's just barely a power tool. (It's kind of like a battery-operated screwdriver. It has power, but not much.) But, if we call it a power tool at all, it's more of a designer than anything else.

Wizards

The magical name given to these tools seems a little strong, but they are useful helpers. They serve the same purpose as the Experts and Assistants that those other big software companies provide.

Wizards walk you through a task, taking care of the details so you don't have to remember all the steps. They're a one-shot deal—once you've run a particular wizard, you can't rerun it on the results.

Different versions of VFP have different numbers of wizards. They cover a wide range of tasks, from laying out a form to documenting your code to preparing an app for distribution to scaling data up to SQL Server or Oracle. Rather than listing them all here, we'll point out that you can find out which ones you've got by examining the table Wizard.DBF in the WIZARDS subdirectory of the main Visual FoxPro directory.

The wizard system in Visual FoxPro is extensible in two ways. You can add your own wizards. You can also add formatting styles to be used in those wizards where it's relevant (the various form and report wizards). Both of these topics are covered in "Wizards and Builders and Bears, Oh My!" —found on the CD.

We think the wizards are an area neglected by too many developers. Those of us who have grown up (and grown old) using the product dismiss them as "training wheels for newbies." But, in fact, the wizards present simple, automated ways to perform some complex tasks. VFP 6 has some improvements in this area, especially the new Application Wizard and Application Builder, as well as with the inclusion of the foundation classes. Project hooks also seem to us to offer new opportunities for wizard and builder creators, since it's now easy to hook right into project management.

One other note about wizards. The Documentation Wizard is the replacement for the old FoxDoc application documenter. (As of VFP 6, the source code for the wizards and builders is provided with the product, so you can make changes if you don't like the way they work. All the code is in two ZIP files in HOME() + "Tools\Xsource\".)

Builders

Builders are like wizards, only much better. We can't figure why wizards got the flashy name while "Builders" is so prosaic.

The simplest definition of a builder is a "re-entrant wizard." They're similar to wizards, in that they guide you through a complex task, letting you focus on the desired result rather than how to get there. Unlike wizards, though, you can go back again. You can apply the same builder to the same object over and over, until you get it just right.

Like wizards, builders are extensible; you can add your own. " Builders and Wizards (and Bears, Oh My!)" explains how.

As with wizards, the exact set of builders supplied varies from one version to the next. However, in all versions, all but one of the supplied builders relate to creating forms and their controls. The exception is the Referential Integrity Builder, which helps you set up appropriate triggers in your databases.

As with wizards, you can find the list of installed builders by examining a table—in this case, Builder.DBF. It's also found in the WIZARDS subdirectory.

On the whole, now that we've been using VFP for several years, we find we're using builders a lot less than we anticipated. We suspect that's generally true, and that most people who use builders regularly are using homegrown builders, not the ones that come with the product.

It's actually quite easy to write simple builders that use SYS(1270) or AMouseObj() to get a reference to an object and then do something to it behind the scenes. The hard part is putting on an attractive interface and making them work in general, rather than specific, cases.

Managers

Actually, that should be "manager"—there's only one of these, the Project Manager. But it's a humdinger. The Project Manager is where you'll live when you're working on an application. It organizes the components of your application and gives you quick access to the other power tools. And, of course, it lets you build an APP or EXE file.

System Dialogs

There are a whole bunch of FoxPro dialogs you can incorporate into your applications. We think of these as power tools because they save you from having to write your own dialogs. We mentioned the Expression Builder above—it's accessible via the oddball GETEXPR command. The rest of these are, more sensibly, function calls. Here's the list. Before you spend too much time trying to write your own dialogs, you might want to look through this list and consider using one of these. See the Reference section for details on using each.

- GetColor() displays a variant of the Windows Color Picker.
- GetCP() displays the Code Page dialog.
- GetDir() displays the Select Directory dialog.
- GetFile() and LocFile() both display the Open File dialog, but LocFile() looks for a specified file first and only displays the dialog if it can't be found.
- GetFont() displays the Font selection dialog.
- GetPict() displays the Open dialog specially configured to choose pictures. This one is significantly improved in VFP 6, where it lets you look at just about any graphic format you can come up with, and where the Preview option has sensibly become a check box again instead of a button.
- GetPrinter() and SYS(1037) both display printer dialogs. SYS(1037) displays the Print Setup dialog that lets you choose a printer and paper type and orientation. In VFP 5 and 6, GetPrinter() displays the printer selection dialog.
- PutFile() displays the Save As dialog.

Doing it the Windows Way

Back in FoxPro 2.x and even in VFP 3, using the system dialogs through the GetWhatever functions listed above seemed incredibly forward-thinking. But the proliferation of ActiveX over the last few years means that, for a lot of those tasks and a whole bunch more that aren't listed above, there are better ways. For example, the Common Dialogs control gives you access to the native Open File, Save File and Printer dialogs, with a lot more control than GetFile(), PutFile() and SYS(1037) offer you.

ActiveX controls are available for all kinds of things. You can replace the status bar, put a calendar onto a form, use treeviews and listviews (the main interface elements of Windows Explorer), or even put a Web browser into your application. A lot of ActiveX controls come with Visual FoxPro, more get installed by other things you might have on your system, and thousands are available for sale, usually in packages of related items.

The fact that ActiveX controls get installed on your development machine by just about every application you install these days does raise one problem. Most controls have pretty strict rules about licensing and redistribution. When you're designing a form, it's hard to know whether you have a particular control because it came with VFP and, therefore, you can distribute it with your apps, or it's there because the last applet you downloaded brought it along, and you only have rights to use it on your machine. Be sure to check this stuff out before you base your whole interface metaphor on some cool control you found lurking. (You can look at the help files that come with the controls by dropping the control on a form and right-clicking, then choosing Help. At least some of them give you a clue about what can be distributed and what can't. Also, check the root Visual Studio directory for a file called Redist.TXT that indicates, in accordance with your license agreement (ours is named Eula.TXT on disk 1) which files can be redistributed.

OOP Tools

One of the most powerful of the power tools is the Class Browser, which lets you explore and manage the contents of class libraries. New in VFP 6 is the Component Gallery, which organizes not just class libraries, but all kinds of files. The big secret is that the Class Browser and the Component Gallery are really the same tool (which is why there's a button in each that switches to the other). Properties control which face it puts on when you call it.

In its Class Browser guise, this tool lets you look at the structure of classes as well as perform maintenance on class libraries. The Component Gallery provides tools for organizing all kinds of files into logical groups. For more on these tools, see "Hacking the Class Browser and Component Gallery" in "But Wait! There's More!"

It's worth noting, by the way, that the Browser/Gallery is written in VFP. (In VFP 6, source code is provided.)

Odds and Ends

The remaining power tools can't be easily categorized. In fact, we're not exactly sure what they are. But they add power to our development efforts, so here they are:

The updated Debugger probably ranks as a power tool, though the old one available in VFP 3 certainly doesn't. For sure, the new-to-VFP 6 Coverage Analyzer is a power tool. Both the Debugger and the Coverage Analyzer are discussed in "Productive Debugging."

The tools we're not sure have power are GENDBC (which generates code to re-create a DBC), the Converter (to bring FoxPro 2.x projects and screens into VFP), and the Data Session window (the window formerly known as "View").

The Tools subdirectory of VFP contains a number of other goodies, including Ted's favorite, Filer, which gives you a cousin of Explorer's Find dialog inside VFP. There's also HexEdit that provides a hex editor (surprise), letting you twiddle bits and bytes by hand. Be careful with that one. The Tools directory also contains the Transformer, which lets you move older applications to VFP.

In addition, definitely not power tools, but more like a filled toolbox, VFP 6 includes a ton of classes for all kinds of tasks and an extensible application framework. Use the Component Gallery to check out the parts that Microsoft has supplied you with.

A Tip O' the Hat

Here are our hints for working more productively. We start out with those that apply pretty generally, then hone in on tool-specific tips.

Right-Click

Just about everywhere in VFP, in just about every mode, right-click brings up a menu of context-specific choices. Beginning in VFP 5, that context menu even lets you do things like highlight a block of code and run it on the fly. Wherever you go, try a right-click and see what happens.

Do be careful—on many of the right-click menus, the first choice is "Cut" and it's pretty easy to choose it by accident. Worse yet, Undo doesn't always undo the cut. If you've created an ON KEY LABEL RightMouse in some of your routines, you'll probably want to ditch it about now, especially if it ends with KEYBOARD "{ENTER}".

If you're having problems with right-click menus always coming up as "Move Here/Copy Here/Cancel," instead of something context-appropriate, the problem is that FoxPro is detecting your click as a MouseDown-Drag-MouseUp. Try rearranging your mouse setup, tweaking on the driver, or being really, really careful not to move the mouse as you press the button. There really are more options than that on the menu!

Drag and Drop

Again, drag and drop is widely supported in VFP and, with VFP 6, even between VFP and other applications. You can drag a class from the Project Manager to the Form Designer to put an instance of that class on the form. You can even drag a table from Explorer into the Command Window and it gets opened and BROWSEd. As with right-clicks, try dragging and dropping all over the place and see what you get.

Layout Toolbar

The Form, Class, Report and Label Designers all work with the Layout toolbar. This handy contraption lets you line things up neatly and match object sizes. It sounds so easy, but was so hard in 2.x.

Always On Top

The Property Sheet, the Class Browser/Component Gallery, and torn-off tabs in the Project Manager all give you a way to make them be "Always on Top." In VFP 3 and with torn-off tabs in all versions, push in the pushpin and you can't put anything on top of that window. In later versions, right-click and select "Always on Top." If you're still working in 640x480 mode and probably even in 800x600, you'll never want to do this. As we mentioned in "Hardware Recommendations," 640x480 is probably an unrealistic video mode for working in Visual FoxPro, and this nice feature illustrates the problem well.

That's One Option

The Tools-Options dialog includes an amazing array of choices for configuring both your working environment and the results. Spend some time experimenting there.

Be aware that the changes you make in this dialog are in effect only for the current session (except for Field Mapping, which is persistent). To make the others stick, click on Set As Default in the dialog. But watch out! Even though you can see only one page at a time, Set As Default stores the current settings for all the pages. (This stuff is stored in the Registry.) We haven't found a way to store just a few settings, short of editing the Registry, not one of our favorite tasks. Also, check out the new-to-VFP 6 SYS(3056) function for rereading those settings.

Query/View Field Lists

You almost never need to visit the Fields page in the Query and View Designers. Instead, use the top pane, which shows the tables in the query or view. You can double-click on fields there to choose them. Beware—the result depends on which page is on top. With the Join, Filter, Update Criteria or Miscellaneous pages on top, fields are added to the Fields list. With Order By topmost, the field is added to both the list of selected fields and the ordering list. When Group By is on top, the field is added only to the grouping criteria. (The set of pages is different in VFP 3, but the results are the same.)

You can also add fields to the various lists by dragging and dropping. You can even add multiple fields by highlighting them, and then dragging them into the destination list.

Double-clicking in the Selected Fields list of the Fields page removes the field from the Selected Fields list.

Class Browser Tricks

The Class Browser isn't just for classes. You can open forms there, too. Just choose Form or All files from the List files of type dropdown in the Open dialog. If you choose Project or Application and then pick one of those, the class libraries and forms for that project are opened. You can also browse objects of other types, such as ActiveX controls.

It might not be obvious that you can use the keyboard to navigate through the Class Browser (and its symbiotic twin, the Component Gallery), but in fact, a combination of tabs and arrow keys does let you get pretty much everywhere.

You can test VFP classes while you're looking at them. Highlight the desired class in the hierarchy, and then drag the icon that appears just above the hierarchy onto the screen. An instance of the class is created as a member of the screen. You can access it as _SCREEN.<classname>1. For example, if you drop the icon for a class called Yowza onto the screen, you can address it as _SCREEN.Yowza1.

The Class Browser gets close to providing Visual FoxPro with "two-way tools." Click the "View Class Code" button and a window opens, showing an equivalent class definition in code. Although the code generated isn't always executable as-is (it takes some shortcuts), it's great for debugging and documentation, not to mention its value as an aid to help you understand how things get put together.

The Browser is itself an object with properties, events and methods. You can change all kinds of things about its behavior by modifying its properties or invoking its methods. Check out the various Class Browser topics in Help to see what properties are available.

Like so much about Visual FoxPro, the Class Browser is extensible. The button that looks like it's got blocks on it gives you access to "add-ins"—programs that you register with the Browser and can then activate from inside it. Use the Browser's AddIn method to register an add-in—check Help for the details.

Take a really good look at the Browser itself. It's a tremendous example of what you can do with Visual FoxPro. (Try resizing it—notice how everything gets neatly rearranged. Also, in VFP 6, note the splitter that lets you size each panel as you like.)

Report/Label Designer changes

The Visual FoxPro Report and Label Designers look an awful lot like their FoxPro 2.x counterparts, but there are some neat new features hidden inside.

First, although the RD and LD haven't been OOP-ified, they do have a Data environment. We're not real clear on how a non-object can contain an object, but we're not complaining because it means we never have to write driver programs for reports again. Instead of using a program to set up the data for a report, do your setup in the Data environment. (We find we often put views in there.) Like forms, reports can operate in a private data session.

Again, although report objects don't have PEMs like their form counterparts, reports and labels themselves have acquired a set of events. Each band of the report now has the ability to execute a function "On Entry" and "On Exit." Think of these as GotFocus and LostFocus for report bands—they'll let you display thermometers (without resorting to tricks like FOR UpdateTherm() in the REPORT FORM command that actually runs the thing) or update data as the report executes. Double-click on the band bar (the gray bar with the name of the band on it) to bring up the dialog that lets you specify these.

Perhaps the most welcome change to the Report Designer in VFP is the ASCII keyword to the TO FILE option of REPORT FORM. Finally, you can send reports to a text file without worrying about printer-driver garbage!

Project Manager Mania

You'll spend a lot of time in the Project Manager. It's incredibly versatile.

You can choose whether double-click on an item opens the item for editing or executes it. The Tools-Options dialog's Projects page has option buttons for the two choices. It also lets you decide whether you want to be prompted to use wizards every time you create something new. That page also lets you configure your interaction with a source code provider. (See "A Source is a Source, Of Course, Of Course" for more on source code control.)

The Project Manager can be collapsed into something resembling a toolbar. In that state, you can open a single tab or tear off the tabs to put them where you want them. In either case, the tab can be resized. The PM remembers each tab's size.

You can provide a description for any item in the project using the Edit Description option on the Project menu (and the PM's context menu). The description you enter appears in the bottom panel of the PM when the item is highlighted. No more frantically trying to remember what "Arpmt02.PRG" does. For classes, the description shown in the Project Manager is the same one you can enter in the Class Designer's Class Info dialog. You can enter it either place and see it in both.

The Version button in the PM's Build dialog gives you access to the same version information used by commercial applications. You can set up your app with version number, copyright, and so forth that'll show up when the user chooses Properties in Explorer. You can also grab this version information to use in your application's About dialog using AGetFileVersion() in VFP 6 or the FoxTools' GetFileVersion() function in VFP 5.

Expression Builder Tricks

The Expression Builder has its own set of preferences, hidden away under the Options button on the misnamed "Builder." These preferences are saved in the current resource file, and allow the Builder's popups to be restricted to just those functions you'd like the user to be able to manipulate. You can also specify whether system memory variables are visible, and how aliases get added to expressions. Because anyone can access these options, it's not exactly foolproof security, but it can be an aid in guiding the user. See the Reference section's entry on GETEXPR for more on this command.

Toolbar Techniques

Right-click in any toolbar and you get a list of system toolbars. Choose one and it appears.

Double-click in a docked toolbar to undock it. Double-click in an undocked toolbar and it re-docks wherever you last had it docked (by default, at the top).

Toolbars sometimes seem to disappear. Usually, the problem is that they are docked somewhere off-screen (or far enough off that you can't find them). We haven't found a command to fix this, but you can do it by brute force. Use the View menu to close the toolbar in question. SET RESOURCE OFF and open the resource file. Find the record for this toolbar (Id="TTOOLBAR" and Name is the toolbar's name). Delete the record and pack the file. Close the resource file and SET RESOURCE ON. When you bring up that toolbar again, it'll be in its initial, default location.

Form Designer Hints

If you're designing forms for users who work at a lower video resolution than you, make sure you don't make things too big. The Forms page of the Tools-Options dialog lets you set a maximum design area to any of the most common Windows video modes. Limiting a form to 640 x 480 doesn't prevent you from creating forms with insufficient room because of all of your added menus, status bars, toolbars and other miscellaneous ornamentation, so you should still test your application in the lower resolution for ease of use. (Try to keep form height to 390 pixels or less to account for all these factors.)

Always test your applications in both large and small fonts so that, no matter which way your users set up their machines, things look right. (We're pretty sure Microsoft doesn't always remember to do this, since Tamar habitually uses large fonts and frequently finds graphic glitches in MS apps.) On this front, don't ever, under any circumstances, use 8-point MS Sans Serif in your forms. It doesn't scale properly between large and small fonts. TrueType fonts are almost always a better choice.

If you're always annoyed by the Prompt to Save Changes dialog when you run a form right from the Designer (well, gee, what else would you want to do?), get rid of it by unchecking that item in the Tools-Options dialog. (Thanks to our good friend Mac Rubel for this one.)

There are two ways to set the tab order for controls. One is by Shift+clicking on each control in the order you want it (as in FoxPro/DOS). The other is by using a list with movers (as in FoxPro 2.x/Windows). You choose which method you want in the Tools-Options dialog—again, the Forms page is used.

Know the grid of lines that appears on the background in the Form Designer (or for form classes in the Class Designer)? You can control that. By default, the grid lines are 12 pixels apart in each direction. You can change that for a particular form by using the Set Grid Scale item on the Format menu, or for all new forms using the Forms page of the Tools-Options dialog. This option is not only used for the Snap to Grid feature, but it is also used when you copy and paste an object with the Ctrl+C, Ctrl+V shortcuts—the copy appears one grid increment to the right and below the original.

When you're writing code in a method window, right-click and choose Object List to avoid having to type long object references. Just choose the object you're interested in and an appropriate reference is added at the cursor position.

You can run a form directly from the Form Designer using the ! button on the Standard toolbar. In VFP 3, that was it for this capability, but it keeps getting better and better. In VFP 5, another button was added that lets you go back to the Designer from the running form. In fact, anytime you run a form from the Form Designer, closing it takes you back to the Designer. But, in VFP 5, you had to make sure that the form window itself was on top in order to click the !. Not anymore. In VFP 6, not only can you click ! no matter which window is on top (the form, the property sheet, or a method code window), but when you return to the Form Designer, the last method code window you were working in is still open and it's on top.

Speaking of methods, the METHOD keyword of MODIFY FORM and MODIFY CLASS is a real time-saver, too! If you're repeatedly in the run-test-crash-code cycle, consider adding the option of MODIFY FORM YourForm METHOD YourMethod if you keep going back to tweak on the same chunk of code.

Draw Me a Map

One of the truly powerful changes in VFP 5 was the addition of field mapping. In VFP 3, when you dragged a field from the DE or the Project Manager onto a form, you got a text box based on the VFP base text box class. When you dragged a table, you got a grid based on the base grid class.

However, using the base classes is a bad idea. It's always better to use a subclass at least one level down the hierarchy in case you need to make some global changes (like getting rid of MS Sans Serif, 8).

Field mapping lets you specify the classes used when you drag a field or table onto a form. It also lets you specify the form class used by default when you issue CREATE FORM. You set up your mappings in, where else, the Tools-Options dialog, save them as defaults, and forget about it. (We tend to forget about it so much that we're occasionally surprised to find ourselves working with a test form that isn't based on VFP's form class.) You can use a project hook to swap the settings you want in and out when a form is opened and closed. However, if you open multiple projects at the same time and they have different settings, there's no way to ensure that the right settings are in place as you move among the forms.

A View To Kill For

The View window has changed since FoxPro 2.x. The biggest change is that it's now called the Data Session window. There are no more work area numbers (guess the design team didn't think anyone wanted to scroll through 32,767 of 'em) and the "Setup" button is now the "Properties" button. (We're not at all happy about the extra steps to get to the Table Designer, but that's another story.) The other options, for SETtings, default file paths, and international settings, have been moved to the Tools-Options dialog. Curiously, issuing the SET command still brings up the View Window, even though all the SETtings have moved on.

With no work area numbers, opening a table through the view window no longer closes a table. Even if an alias is highlighted, when you choose Open, FoxPro automatically puts the table you choose in a new work area.

Open tables are listed in reverse order of being opened—that is, the most recently opened appears at the top and the one you opened first shows up last.

Color Us Happy

Another big change introduced in VFP 5 was syntax coloring. This means that, as you type code, whether in an editing window or the Command Window, it gets colored based on VFP's interpretation of it. You can control the colors used with the Syntax Coloring page of the Tools-Options dialog.

The syntax coloring mechanism appears to be a simple lookup, not a sophisticated parser. So, it can't tell that you're using a keyword as a table name. For that matter, it can't even tell that a comment has been continued to a new line. Nonetheless, we love it, and when on occasion we're forced to use older versions of FoxPro, we find it hard to read the dull black code we see there.

Edit Me This

Aside from syntax coloring, the editor was seriously enhanced in VFP 5. The context menu includes the ability to comment or uncomment a block of code, as well to indent and unindent a block of code. A dialog is available to teleport you instantly to any function or procedure within the code. You can set the character string used to denote a comment, though this is one of the few things *not* available through the Tools-Options dialog. To change the comment character, you have to edit the Registry—the key you're looking for is:

HKEY_CURRENT_USER\Software\Microsoft\VisualFoxPro\6.0\Options\EditorCommentString

Substitute the appropriate version number in there.

If you hate having BAK files all over your disk, right-click in an editing window and choose Properties. The dialog there lets you decide whether backups should be created on every save. (This one is a bit of a toss-of-the-coin. We rarely go back to those files, but when we do, we're really glad they're there. Of course, more often, we don't realize that we've fouled up until we're several saves beyond the critical mistake.)

That dialog also lets you decide what font your editing windows use, so you can blow things up if, like us, you're starting to find 10-point type a little hard to work with. You can also decide whether to show line and column positions while editing. We like them on for PRG files, but off for TXT, where we generally have word-wrap on. You can even set the size of a tab for indentation. (That one's a mixed bag since the Tab key inserts actual tabs, not spaces. You might not want those in your code.)

As with the Tools-Options dialog, it's a good idea to check out Edit Properties every now and then to remind yourself what's there.

Macro and Cheese

Visual FoxPro includes a keyboard macro recorder that lets you record, edit, play back, store and retrieve sets of keystrokes that you can use to speed the development process. Many old geezers like Ted still have macros for some of their favorite WordStar commands like {SHIFT+END}{BACKSPACE} for Ctrl+K (clear to the end of the line), and {HOME}{SHIFT+END}{DEL}{DEL} for Ctrl+Y to erase the current line. Tamar has finally gotten around to creating a macro that replicates her favorite feature from a long-ago word processor—it switches the last two characters typed, so that you can quickly change MOID to MODI. The keystrokes you need are {SHIFT+LEFTARROW}{CTRL+X}{LEFTARROW}{CTRL+V}. Other clever ideas are to minimize the keystrokes you have to type for common sequences—for example, storing "CreateObject()"{RIGHTARROW} so you need only one key to get there. Play with the macro recording tool, available on the Tools menu, and check out the commands PLAY MACRO, SAVE MACROS and RESTORE MACROS for some ideas on what to do with these.

Along with macros, we would be remiss if we failed to mention CEE, the COB Editor Enhancement. We've been using this as long as we can remember, and it does much of what the built-in macro capabilities can do and more. You'll find CEE, a free product, on the CD.

Keep Exercising the Interface

We are all creatures of habit, to one extent or another, and we all tend to get into routines. Click here, drag there, call up the menu for this. And occasionally we'll gripe that it takes too many keystrokes to get some common task done. Inevitably, a co-worker will point out a button on a toolbar that does exactly what we need, without the clicking and dragging. Many developers use the Form Controls toolbar, but miss the Form Designer toolbar that gives you access to the Data environment, the Code Window, the Color Palette and many of the other tools you need to build forms.

Consider, too, developing your own toolbars or menu pads to provide the features you need. If you are constantly calling up a particular tool, consider creating a toolbar button for it. Add it to the Standard toolbar or write your own. This is your development environment—spiff it up to make your coding its most productive.

Productive Debugging

> Error is a hardy plant: it flourisheth in every soil.
>
> Martin Farquhar Tupper, *Proverbial Philosophy*

Our programs run correctly the first time, every time. Yeah, right—if you believe that one, we have a bridge in Brooklyn we'd like to sell you. We figure we spend at least as much time debugging our programs as we do writing them in the first place.

If your programs do run correctly the first time, every time, you can skip this part of the book. In fact, you should write a book and tell us how to do it. For the rest of you, we'll take a look at the kinds of errors that occur in programs, give you some ideas on how to root them out and show how VFP can aid your efforts.

"Whatever Can Go Wrong, Will"

> I will not steep my speech in lies; the test of any man lies in action.
>
> Pindar, *Olympian Odes IV*

Errors in programs fall into three broad categories. One of them is pretty easy to find, the second usually isn't too bad and the third is the one responsible for most of our gray hairs (at least a few of those have to be credited to our respective children).

The first group of errors, the easy ones, is the syntax errors. These are the ones that come up because you typed "REPORT FROM ..." or forgot the closing quote on a character string, and so on. These are easy because FoxPro will find them for you if you ask. (In fact, VFP 5 increased the strictness of syntax checking so even more of them than before can be found just for the asking.)

If you just start running the program, it crashes as soon as an error is found. Not bad, but you can do better. Use the COMPILE command or choose Compile from the Program menu and FoxPro checks the whole program for syntax errors and gives you an ERR file (with the same name as your program). One shot and you can get all of these. The Build option in the Project Manager gives you the same errors for all of the code within a project. We regularly select "Recompile All Files" as an easy "smoke test" for the project—just make sure to also check "Display Errors" to see the resulting ERR file.

The next group is a little more subtle. We call these "runtime errors" because they don't turn up until runtime. These errors result from comparing variables of different types, dividing by 0, passing parameters when none are expected, and so forth. They're things that FoxPro can't find until it actually runs the code, but then they're obvious. Again, your program crashes as soon as one of these turns up.

Because you have to tackle them one at a time and you have to actually execute a line of code to find an error in it, these are more time-consuming to deal with than syntax errors. But they're manageable. In VFP 5 and later, they're even more manageable because you can use assertions to test many of these things, so you can find them before VFP crashes. The task gets easier again in VFP 6 because the Coverage Profiler can help you figure out what's been tested, so you can test the rest.

The truly terrible, difficult errors are what we call "correctness errors." Somehow, even though you knew what the program was supposed to do and you carefully worked out the steps necessary to do it, it doesn't do what it should. These are the errors that try programmers' souls.

Tracking down correctness errors requires a planned, systematic, step-by-step attack. Many times, it also requires you to take a fresh perspective on the symptoms you're seeing—take a break or ask someone else to look at your code. (Tamar has solved countless correctness errors by talking them out with her non-programmer husband. Ted's favorite method is to try to explain the problem in a CompuServe message—invariably, two-thirds of the way through explaining it, the problem explains itself.)

Don't You Test Me, Young Man

> None but the well-bred man knows how to confess a fault, or acknowledge himself in an error.
>
> Benjamin Franklin, *Poor Richard's Almanac*, 1738

So now you can categorize your errors. So what? What you really want to know is how to get rid of them.

Let's start with a basic fact. You are the worst possible person to test your code. It's fine for you to track down syntax and runtime errors, but when it's time to see if it works, anyone else will do it better than you.

Why's that? Because you know how it's supposed to work. You're going to test the system the way it's meant to be used. No doubt after a little work, you'll get that part working just fine. But what about the way your users are really going to use the system? What happens when they push the wrong button? When they erase a critical file? When they enter the wrong data?

Understand we're not picking on you personally—we're just as bad at testing our own applications. The psychologists call it "confirmatory bias." Researchers find that a programmer is several times more likely to try to show that a program works than that it doesn't.

So how can we avoid the problem? The answer's obvious: Get someone else to test our code. That's what all the big companies do. They have whole testing departments whose job it is to break code. If you're not a big company, you could try what one of our friends used to do—he hired high school students to come in and break his code. We've been known to sit our spouses or kids down in front of an app and let them bang on it.

A second problem we've found is that clients are almost as bad at testing as we are. Not only do they have an investment in the success of the application, but very typically they hired you because they did not have the resources to develop the application—they won't find the resources to test it, either! The ideal situation is one in which the testing person's interest, motivation and job description is to find flaws in the program.

No matter who's testing the code, you need a structured approach to testing. Don't just sit down and start running the thing. Make a plan. Figure out what the inputs and outputs should look like (or should never look like!), then try it.

Here are some things you need to be sure to test (and it's easy to forget):

- Every single path through the program. You need to figure out all the different branches and make sure every single one gets tested. Change your system date if you have to, to test the end-of-decade reporting features or what happens on February 29, 2000.
- Bad inputs. What if the user enters a character string where a number is called for? What if he enters a negative invoice amount? What if she tries to run end-of-month processing on the 15th?
- Extreme values. What happens if the payment is due on January 1, 2001? What if someone's last name is "Schmidgruber-Foofnick-Schwartz"?
- Hitting the wrong key at the wrong time. We've seen applications that crash dead when you press ESC.

In larger projects, you should generate a set of test data right up front that handles all the various possibilities and use it for ongoing testing. It's easy to figure out the expected results once, then test for them repeatedly.

With large projects, it's also much more likely for a change in one place to cause problems in another. Plan for regression testing (making sure your working system hasn't re-exposed old buggy behavior due to changes) for these applications. Your test data really comes in handy here.

You need to test your error handler, too. The ERROR command makes it easy to check that it handles every case that can occur and does something sensible. When you design the error handler, keep in mind that every new version of FoxPro that's come along has introduced new error codes—be sure it's easy to add them.

Where the Bugs Are

> Truth lies within a little and certain compass, but error is immense.
>
> Henry St. John, Viscount Bolingbroke, *Reflections upon Exile*, 1716

Once you figure out that the program's broken, what next? How do you track down those nasty, insidious bugs that haunt your code?

FoxPro has always had some decent tools for the job, but starting in VFP 5 (that's getting to be a theme in this section, isn't it?), the task is much easier. We'll talk only about the Debugger introduced in that version. If you're using VFP 3, check out the *Hacker's Guide to Visual FoxPro 3.0* for suggestions on debugging using the older tools.

Assert Yourself

> Let me assert my firm belief that the only thing we have to fear is fear itself.
>
> Franklin D. Roosevelt

The way to start debugging is by keeping certain kinds of errors from happening in the first place. The ASSERT command lets you test, any time you want, whether any condition you want is met. Use assertions for any conditions that can be tested ahead of time and don't depend on user input or system conditions. If it can break at runtime even though it worked in testing, don't use an assertion. We use ASSERT the most to test parameters to ensure that they're the right type and contain appropriate data.

Give your assertions useful messages that help you hone right in on the problem. One trick is to begin the message with the name of the routine containing the assertion. A message like:

```
MyRoutine: Parameter "cInput" should be character.
```

is a lot more helpful than the default message:

```
Assertion failed on line 7 of procedure MyRoutine.
```

or, the worst, a custom message like:

```
Wrong parameter type.
```

Liberal use of assertions should let you get your code running faster and help to track down those nasty regression errors before they get to your clients.

Debugger De Better

> Error is the contradiction of Truth. Error is a belief without understanding. Error is unreal because untrue. It is that which seemeth to be and is not. If error were true, its truth would be error, and we should have a self-evident absurdity—namely, erroneous truth. Thus we should continue to lose the standard of Truth.
>
> Mary Baker Eddy, *Science and Health*, 1875

Before VFP 5, FoxPro could just barely be said to have a debugger. The Watch and Trace windows worked as advertised and gave you tools for seeing what was going on, but they were pretty limited. Fortunately, as so often happens with FoxPro, the development team heard our pleas and VFP 5 introduced "the new debugger," so called because it doesn't really have any other name.

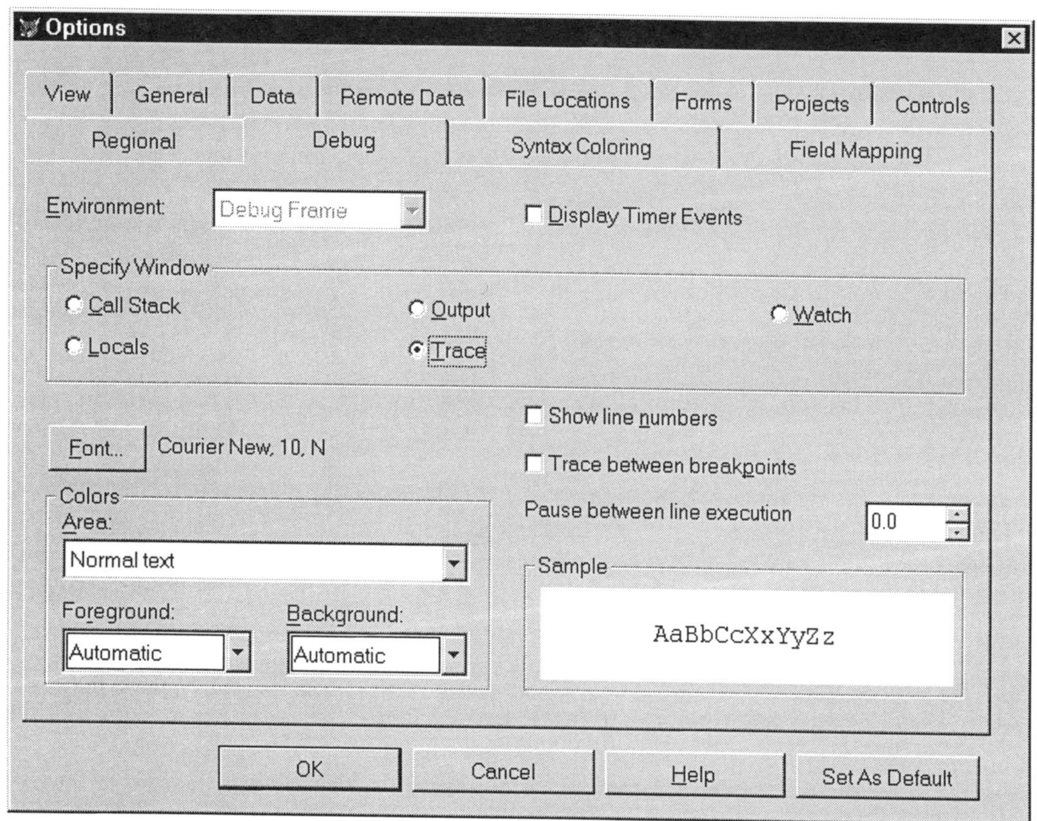

Figure 2-1: Tracing Paper—When the Trace window is chosen, you can specify whether to track between breaks and how long to wait between each line executed.

The debugger is composed of five windows and several other tools. It can run inside the VFP frame (meaning that the windows are contained in the main VFP window and are listed individually on the Tools menu) or in its own frame, with its own menu and its own entry on the taskbar. On the whole, we much prefer putting the debugger in its own frame. Then we can size and position both VFP and the debugger as we wish (someday we hope to have a monitor big enough to make them fit together nicely without compromises—perhaps our best hope is using two monitors side by side), minimize the debugger when we're not using it, and so forth. In addition, when the debugger has its own frame, tools like Event Tracking and Coverage Logging appear in the debugger's Tools menu. When the debugger lives in the FoxPro frame, those tools appear only on the debugging toolbar that opens when any of the debugger's windows are opened. We should point out that, even when in its own frame, the debugger is still not totally independent of VFP. It closes when VFP closes, and you can't get to it when you're in a dialog in VFP. (Well, actually, you can get to it by bringing it up from the taskbar, but you can't do anything there.)

The five main debugger windows are Trace, Watch, Locals, Output and Call Stack. Whichever frame you use, each of them is controlled individually.

You can open or close whichever windows are useful at the moment. Although we call them "windows," they're all actually toolbars and can be docked at will. In fact, these windows let you decide whether they can be docked. Right-click on any of them. If "Docking View" is checked, the window can be docked (by dragging or double-clicking). If "Docking View" is unchecked, double-clicking maximizes the window. Weird, but it's pretty cool to have that much control. It's interesting to note that Microsoft thinks debugging is so different from everything that goes on in the Windows platform that it can have unique window characteristics and nonstandard behavior. Or maybe this is the next interface paradigm coming down the road. We think not.

So what do these windows let you do? Trace and Watch are a lot like the old Trace and Debug windows, but with a lot more power. Locals saves on putting things into the Watch window—it lets you see all the variables that are in scope at the moment. Call Stack shows you the (nested) series of calls that got you to the current routine. Output, also known as Debug Output, holds the results of any DebugOut commands, as well as things you consciously send there, like events you're tracking. We'll take a look at each one, and point out some of the cooler things you can do.

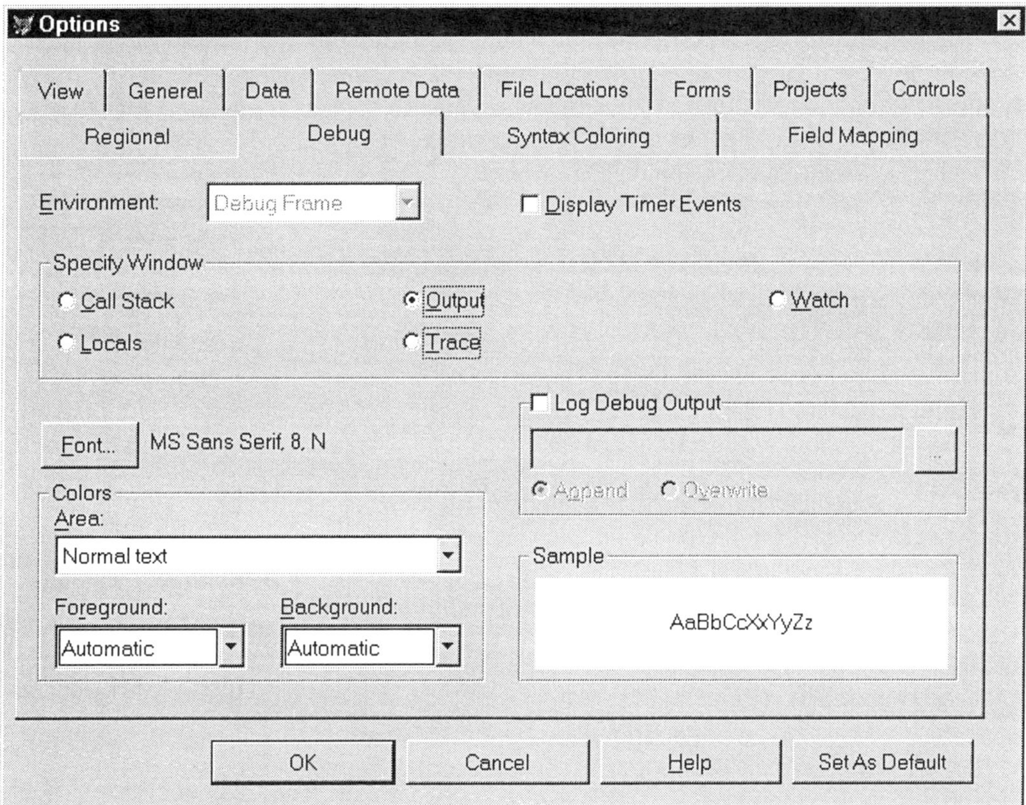

Figure 2-2: Putt-Putt Output—With the Output window chosen, you can indicate whether to store any output sent to that window to a file, and if so, where.

Before that, though, a quick look at the Debug page of the Tools-Options dialog. This is one of the strangest dialog pages we've ever encountered. Near the middle, it has a set of option buttons representing the different debugger windows. Choosing a different button changes the dialog, showing options appropriate only to that window. Figure 2-1 shows the dialog when the Trace window is chosen. Figure 2-2 shows the dialog when the Output window is chosen. Each window also has its own font and color settings.

One last general point: Since you're likely to be working on a number of programs and each probably has different debugging needs, you can save the debugger's current configuration and reload it later to pick up where you left off.

The Trace of My Tears

> Well had the boding tremblers learned to trace
> The day's disasters in his morning face.
>
> Oliver Goldsmith, *The Deserted Village*

The Trace window shows you code and lets you go through it at whatever pace you want. You can open programs ahead of time or wait until a Suspend in the code or a breakpoint stops execution. Once a program is open in the Trace window, you can set a breakpoint on any executable line. When you run the program, execution stops just before running that line.

In an application, the Trace window (together with the Call Stack window) gives you quick access to any program or object in the execution chain. You can also open up others and set breakpoints by choosing Open from the Debugger menu or using the Trace window's context menu.

Several commands let you execute a little bit of the program while still retaining control. Step Into executes the next command, even if it calls another routine. Step Out executes the rest of the current routine, stopping when it returns to the calling routine. Step Over executes an entire routine without stepping through the individual lines within; if you use it when you're on a line that's not a call to a subroutine, it's the same as choosing Step Into. Run to Cursor lets you position the cursor in the code, then execute all the code up to the cursor position. All of these options have menu shortcuts, so you can use a single keystroke (or a keystroke combination) to move on. (If some of the keystrokes don't work for you, check your development environment. Even if the debugger is running in its own frame, On Key Labels you've defined intervene and prevent keystrokes from executing debugger commands.)

When you run the Debugger in the FoxPro frame, the F7 (Run to Cursor) and Shift+F7 (Step Out) keystrokes don't work. They're fine when the Debugger lives in its own frame.

The Set Next Statement choice on the Debug menu is a little gem. While stepping through code, you can position the cursor, and then choose this one to skip over some code or go back and execute some again. This is probably one of the most overlooked options in all of VFP. Thanks to our friend Christof Lange for pointing it out to us.

The Pause between line execution option on the Trace portion of the debugger options (see Figure 2-1) is pretty cool. Sometimes you want to step through a program, but the simple act of doing so changes the results. This setting to the rescue—it lets you slow the program down (not one of our usual goals, but handy for debugging). Set it to a speed where you can see each line execute without growing a beard in between. Note that the dialog simply changes the system variable _THROTTLE.

Trace between breakpoints is also controlled from the Tools-Options dialog, as well as from the Trace window's context menu. It can make a big speed difference when you're trying to get to a particular trouble spot. It determines whether all code is echoed in the Trace window on the way to a breakpoint. If you turn it off, Trace stays the same until you reach a breakpoint, then the code there is updated—this can be a lot faster.

Opening a form in the Trace window is a pain. You can't just use File-Open as you can with a PRG. However, the new Breakpoints dialog makes it easy to set a breakpoint in a form, so you can stop execution quickly when you get there. See "Break It Up Out There" below.

Once a form is open, though, the Object and Procedure drop-downs let you get to the various methods in the form and set breakpoints as needed (or you can do it with the Breakpoints dialog).

Just Watch Me!

> Oh! death will find me long before I tire
> Of watching you.
>
> Rupert Brooke

The Watch window is the successor to the old Debug window. You put expressions in and you can see their values. But it does much more than that, too. You can set breakpoints (as you could in Debug) and you can change the values of variables, fields and properties on the fly.

Unlike the old Debug window, the Watch window lets you look at objects and arrays. Just put the object or array name in and it shows up with a "+" next to it to let you expand it and drill down. Very handy.

Watch out for ActiveX objects. Some of them don't interact so well with the Watch window and can hang VFP or make it play dead until you destroy the object. (Our tech editor also reports that he can crash VFP 5 under Windows 95 by putting a reference to a Word object in the Watch window.)

You can also drag and drop into the Watch window. If you want an expression that's almost the same as one that's already there, drag the one you have into the text box, edit it and hit Enter. You can drag from other windows as well, so you could drill down in the Locals window to find the property you want to watch, then drag it into the Watch window. When you do it that way, you don't even have to drop it in the text box first; just drop it right into the main part of the Watch window. You can do the same thing from the Trace window or even from VFP itself. No more typing long expressions and hoping you can get them right.

The Watch window lets you know what's changed recently. When the last command executed changed one of the items you're watching, the color in the Value column for that item changes. (Actually, it seems to stay changed for more than just the next command. We haven't figured out exactly when it changes back.)

To set a breakpoint in this window (as in the Trace window), click in the gray bar on the left. (As in the Trace window, a red dot appears next to the item with the breakpoint.) As soon as the value of that expression changes, program execution is suspended and you can get a look at the current state of affairs. (Note the difference between breakpoints in Trace, which happen before the marked line, and breakpoints in Watch, which happen after the value has changed.) With objects, you don't always know the name of the thing you want to look at. Say you want to see what's going on with a check box on a form. But the same form might be running several times. Instead of trying to figure out the name of the form, just refer to it via _Screen.ActiveForm—this expression always references the form that has the focus (unless it's a toolbar). Use _Screen.ActiveForm as a way of getting to the controls on the form. The nicest thing is that the Watch window is very forgiving—if the property or object you reference doesn't exist, no error is generated; you just have the message "(Expression could not be evaluated)" in the Value column for that expression. SYS(1270) is also a handy way to get a reference to an object so you can watch it. See that topic in the reference section for details.

Protected and Hidden properties are a special problem in the Watch window (and don't show up at all in the Locals window)—you can only see their values when you're in a method of the object. When you're executing other code (or even just sitting on a form), they show up as unable to be evaluated.

The columns in the Watch window can be resized. Just put the mouse over the divider between the columns. Voila, a sizer. We haven't yet found a good way to size things here so that we can always read everything that's showing, short of maximizing the debugger (and maybe the Watch window, too). But you can click into an item (click once on the line and again in the section you're interested in) and use the arrow, Home and End keys to see the hidden part.

Clicking into the Value section that way also lets you change the value, if it's possible. That is, you can change variable, field and property values, but you can't change the value of computed expressions. Very handy when you're 20 minutes into a complex test and you find you failed to initialize a counter to 0.

Local Hero

> The evil which assails us is not in the localities we inhabit but in ourselves.
>
> Seneca, *Moral Essays, "De Tranquillitate Animi" (On Tranquility of Mind)*

Just when you're convinced that the Watch window is the greatest thing since sliced bread, along comes the Locals window. This one cuts down dramatically on what you need to put into the Watch window. It shows you every variable that's in scope and, in fact, lets you choose the scope whose variables you want to see. Unlike the Watch window, you can't set breakpoints in Locals, but you can drill down in arrays and objects.

The context menu for this window gives you some control over which variables show up. The choices are a little strange, since they're not mutually exclusive. The Local and Public options do what they say—indicate whether variables declared as local and public, respectively, are shown. The Standard choice appears to really mean "private" and indicates whether private variables currently in scope are displayed, whether or not they were created by the current program. The Objects choice is independent of the other three and indicates whether variables holding object references are displayed, regardless of scope.

Call Me Anytime

> She was not quite what you would call refined. She was not quite what you would call unrefined. She was the kind of person that keeps a parrot.
>
> Mark Twain, *Pudd'nhead Wilson's New Calendar*, 1897

The Call Stack window lets you see where you are and where you've been. It shows the sequence of calls that got you to the current situation. However, it only shows call nesting—that is, if routine A calls routine B, which finishes, and then A calls C, which contains a breakpoint, the Call Stack window at the breakpoint shows only A and C. It doesn't show you that you visited B along the way.

Call Stack interacts with Locals and Trace. When you're stopped, you can click on any routine in the Call Stack window and the Locals window switches to show variables for that routine, while Trace shows the code for that routine.

At first glance, Call Stack isn't as useful as it should be, because it only works when Trace between breakpoints is on. Fortunately, though, as soon as you turn on Trace between breakpoints, the complete call stack does appear. Breakpoints also make the call stack appear. You can change the Trace between breakpoints setting with the context menu in the Trace window or the SET TRBETWEEN command, as well as in the Tools-Options dialog.

Here Comes Debug

We use the last of the Debugger windows a lot—it's the Debug Output window, and you can send all kinds of information there. By default, anything in a DebugOut command goes there, of course. The Event Tracker likes to send its output there, too.

Use the DebugOut command and the Debug Output window for the kinds of testing you've always done with WAIT WINDOWs or output sent to the screen. DebugOut interferes with your running program much less.

If you want to examine the output at your leisure, you can also redirect it to a file (either from Tools-Options or the SET DEBUGOUT command). If you forget to do so, the context menu for the window contains a Save As command. (You might want to think of it as a "save my bacon" command.)

Break It Up Out There

> A prince never lacks legitimate reasons to break his promise.
>
> Niccolò Machiavelli, *The Prince*, 1514

Breakpoints are one of the key weapons in the fight to make code work right. They let you stop where you want to see what's going on. As with so much else about debugging, breakpoints got much better in VFP 5.

In the old debugger, you could set breakpoints at a particular line of code or when a specified expression changed. With some creativity, you could stop pretty much anywhere, but it wasn't easy.

The new debugger makes it much simpler. First of all, you can set breakpoints while you're looking at the code in the development environment. The context menu for all the code editing windows includes a Set Breakpoint option.

Once you're working with the debugger, the breakpoint dialog is available from the Tools menu and has its own button on the Debugger toolbar. In addition to the same old choices, it also has options to stop at a specified line when a particular expression is true or after you've executed it a certain number of times. You can stop not only when an expression has changed, but also when an expression is true. Each breakpoint you specify can be turned on and off independently. Finally, breakpoints are among the things saved when you save the debugger configuration.

In an OOP world, it can be difficult to specify just where you want to put a breakpoint. What a pain to type in "_Screen.ActiveForm.grdMain.Columns[3].Text1.Valid". Fortunately, you don't have to. If you don't mind stopping at every Valid routine that contains code, just specify Valid. If you do mind stopping at all of them, maybe you don't mind stopping at each Valid in that form—specify Valid for the Location and the form's name (including the SCX extension) for the File. And so forth. And so on. Be creative and you'll get just what you want.

Some things are obvious candidates for breakpoints. If a variable is coming out with a value you don't understand, set a "Break when expression has changed" breakpoint on it. Similarly, if a setting is being changed and you can't figure out where, set the same kind of breakpoint on SET("whatever").

You can get even more clever than that. Wanna find out when a table is being closed? Set a breakpoint on USED("the alias"). When is a window being defined? Set a breakpoint on WEXIST("the window name").

You get the idea—you can set breakpoints on any change at all in program state as long as there's some way to express it in the language.

In fact, you can take advantage of this flexibility to set breakpoints in the Watch window as well. Put an expression like "CLICK"$PROGRAM() in the Watch window and set a breakpoint (by clicking in the left margin next to the item) to make VFP stop as soon as it reaches any Click method. You can use the same approach to set breakpoints on things like the line number executing. While the Breakpoint dialog gives you tremendously flexibility in describing your breakpoints, turning them on and off is much easier in the Watch window.

Boy, What an Event That Was

> Men nearly always follow the tracks made by others and proceed in their affairs by imitation, even though they cannot entirely keep to the tracks of others or emulate the prowess of their models.
>
> Niccolò Machiavelli, *The Prince*, 1514

One of the trickier aspects of working in an OOP language is that events just happen. For programmers used to controlling every aspect of an application's behavior, this can be disconcerting to say the least. Event Tracking is one way to calm your rapid breathing and get your blood pressure under control.

Like the breakpoint dialog, event tracking lives in the debugger's Tools menu and on the Debugger toolbar. It lets you choose whichever events you're interested in and have a message appear whenever that event fires (for any object at all). The messages go into the Debug Output window by default, but can also be sent to a file.

Be careful. Tracking an event like, say, MouseMove can generate a tremendous amount of output. Choose only the events you're really interested in, so the output is manageable.

One thing about event tracking is one of our least favorite aspects of the debugger. The button for it on the Debugger toolbar is a toggle. In fact, it's not really a button at all, it's a graphical check box. So, when you have event tracking in place, clicking the "button" doesn't bring up the dialog for you to change it—it turns it off. Then, when you click again to make changes, the check box in the dialog that actually controls tracking is unchecked. Yuck. This wouldn't be such an annoying problem except that there's no menu shortcut for event tracking, either. So you can't just hit a key combo to bring up the dialog. We sure hope someone at Microsoft notices how aggravating all this is soon. (We've told them.)

Cover Me, Will You?

> We gaze up at the same stars, the sky covers us all, the same universe compasses us. What does it matter what practical systems we adopt in our search for the truth. Not by one avenue only can we arrive at so tremendous a secret.
>
> Quintus Aurelius Symmachus, *Letter to the Christian Emperor Valentinian II*, 384

The last of the debugger's tools is Coverage Logging. This gadget creates a file (generally, voluminous) containing one line for each line of code that executes. It includes the filename, the routine name, the line number, the object containing the code, how long it took, and the nesting depth of the routine.

The file is comma-delimited, so it's easy to pull into a table. However, by itself, the file isn't terribly informative. Unfortunately, in VFP 5, that's all we had.

VFP 6 includes the Coverage Profiler, an application that analyzes coverage logs and gives you information such as how many times a given line was executed. If you point it to the right project, it'll tell you which files in that project were called and which ones weren't.

The Coverage Profiler that's provided is actually just a front end on an incredibly extensible coverage engine. You can enhance it in two different ways. The first is by specifying Add-Ins, similar to those you can specify for the Class Browser. The second alternative is to subclass the coverage class and define your own front end for it. We haven't had a chance yet to explore either of these, but we suspect there are a lot of possibilities.

The Coverage button on the Debugger toolbar has the same annoying behavior as the Event Tracking button, but we find it bothers us a lot less because we're far less likely to need to make changes and keep going. Also, all it takes to turn on Coverage Logging is a valid filename—there's no check box you have to remember to check.

Doing it the Old-Fashioned Way

You've set breakpoints, you've put everything you can think of in the Watch window, you tracked events until they're coming out of your ears, and you still can't figure out where it's going wrong. Time to step back and try another approach.

Grab a sheet of paper and a copy of the code (could be online or on paper). Now pretend you're the computer, and execute your program step by step. Use the paper to keep track of the current values of variables.

These days, we don't use this technique a lot, but when we do, it's invaluable. This systematic attack, or any method of logically proceeding through the possibilities, whether splitting the problem in half or bracketing it from input to output, is vastly superior to the panicked "change this, change that, change the other thing, try it again" mentality typical of amateurs. If you can't explain why it works, you haven't found the problem yet.

Staying Out of Trouble

> Nobody knows the trouble I've seen.
>
> *Anonymous Spiritual*

These are techniques we use to minimize our troubles. They're mostly pretty straightforward, once you know about them.

Get Me Outta Here

Always have an escape valve. Sometimes programs crash really badly and leave you with lots of redefined keys and all kinds of other trouble. Keep a cleanup program around, which at a minimum should include:

```
ON ERROR
ON KEY
SET SYSMENU TO DEFAULT
CLOSE ALL
CLEAR ALL
```

Give it a simple name like Kill.PRG and set some obscure key combination (like CTRL+Shift+F12) to DO this program. If your applications use an application object of some sort, put all the cleanup code in the app object's Destroy method and you'll cut way down on the number of times you need the escape hatch, since Destroy should run even if the application crashes.

Step By Step

Testing a whole application all at once is guaranteed to fail. Build it piece by piece and test each piece as you go. It's much easier to get a 20-line function working than a 20,000-line application. But if the 20,000-line app is made up of 20-line functions that work, it's a whole lot easier.

When you're testing, take it one thing at a time, too. For that 20-line function, see what happens if you forget the parameters, if you pass the wrong parameters, if you pass them in the wrong order. Once all that stuff is working, get to the heart of the thing and see if it works when you do hand it the right data. Try each endpoint; try typical data; try bizarre, but legal, data.

When building a complicated routine (especially parsing sorts of things), we've even been known to test one line at a time from the Command Window until we get it right, then plunk it into the routine. The added-in-VFP 5 ability to highlight several lines of code in the Command Window or a MODI COMM window and execute them makes this technique more valuable than ever.

You Deserve a Break

When your hair is all gone and you're pounding your bald head against the wall and you still can't see what's wrong, take a break. Go for a walk, talk to a friend, anything—just get away from your desk and let the other part of your brain kick in. The folk wisdom of "sleeping on it" really works for many difficult troubleshooting problems.

That's What Friends Are For

If a break doesn't work, ask somebody else. We've both worked alone (Tamar still does), but we're not afraid to pick up the phone and call a friend to say, "What am I doing wrong here?" If we don't need an instant answer, we'll post a message in the appropriate Fox forum on CompuServe—we've never failed to get some ideas there, even if no one knows the exact answer. (See "Back 'o Da Book" for some other places to get VFP help online.)

So What's Left?

> When you have eliminated the impossible, whatever remains,
> however improbable, must be the truth.
>
> Sir Arthur Conan Doyle, *The Sign of Four*, 1890

So, you're sure the file exists or that the variable is getting properly initialized. If you've tried everything else and you can't find the problem, question your assumptions. Go up a level and make sure things are as you expect when you get to the problem point. Sherlock Holmes knew what he was talking about.

Do It Right in the First Place

A lot of the things we mention elsewhere in this book will help to keep you from reaching the hair-pulling stage. It's a lot easier to realize you've initialized a variable incorrectly when you see something like:

```
cItem = 7
```

than when it's:

```
MyChosenItem = 7
```

Good documentation makes a difference, too. If you've declared cItem as LOCAL and commented that it contains "the name of the chosen item," you're not likely to make the mistake in the first place.

These are a Few of our Favorite Bugs

> Nothing is more damaging to a new truth than an old error.
>
> Johann Wolfgang von Goethe, *Sprüche in Prosa*

There are certain bugs we find ourselves fixing over and over and over again. Since we make these mistakes a lot, we figure other people do, too. (Check out "It's a Feature, Not a Bug" for more items along these lines.)

Is That "a AND NOT b" or "b AND NOT a"?

It's easy to mess up complicated logical expressions. Back to paper and pencil to get this one right. Make what logicians call a "truth table"—one column for each variable and one for the final result. Try all the possible combinations of .T. and .F. and see if you've got the right expression.

If the expression's really complex, break it into several pieces and check each one separately.

But I Changed That Already

> Change begets change. Nothing propagates so fast.
>
> Charles Dickens, *Martin Chuzzlewit*, 1844

You find a bug. You figure it out and fix the code. You run it again and nothing's different—the exact same problem you will swear you just fixed replays again and again. What gives? There are a couple of possibilities here.

One is that you're running an APP, and though you changed an individual routine, you didn't rebuild the APP file. Do.

Another is that you're not running the copy of the program you think you are. Check around for other copies in other directories and figure out which one you're actually running. Try deleting the FXP file, if you're dealing with a PRG. If you don't get a new FXP, you'll know you're not pointing at the program you think you are.

There's one more subtle case that can happen. FoxPro keeps stuff in memory to speed things up. In some situations, it doesn't do a good job of cleaning up when you need it to. If all else fails, try issuing CLEAR PROGRAM before you run again. Really desperate? QUIT and restart.

What is This?

In moving to object-oriented programming, we often forget to include the full reference needed to talk to an object. Writing FOR nCnt = 1 TO ControlCount doesn't do a bit of good—it needs to be This.ControlCount or ThisForm.ControlCount or This.Parent.ControlCount or something like that. We've found we're most likely to forget when dealing with array properties.

There are no easy solutions for this one—we all just have to learn to do it right.

I Really Do Value Your Input

Here's another one that you just have to learn, but it's pretty common for VFP newcomers and we still do it ourselves occasionally, especially when working with unfamiliar objects. The problem is referring to the object when you want one of its properties. Probably, this happens most with the Value property. Somehow, it seems appropriate that ThisForm.txtCity should contain the city that the user just typed in, but of course, it doesn't. You need ThisForm.txtCity.Value in this case.

Frequently Asked Power Tool Questions

Actually, some of these are frequently asked questions and others are "we expect these to be frequently asked" questions about things. There's a mix here of stuff we're tired of answering already (we hope putting it here will cut down on the number of times we're asked) and things we think will be like that.

If you don't see your question here, check out "It's a Feature, Not a Bug"—more of this kind of stuff is there. Some other items that might be on your "how do I" list are right in the text of this part of the book. And if you still don't see your question, try one of the public support forums for VFP. (See the appendix for a list of places where kind folks answer questions and chat about FoxPro.)

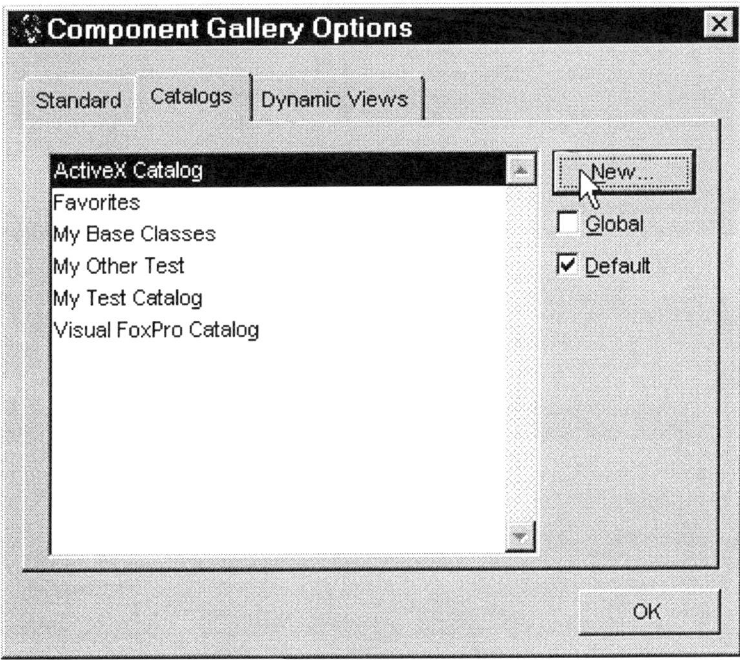

Figure 2-3: New Options for Old—Since when does creating a new one of anything belong in an options dialog?

Q: I'm using the Component Gallery to organize all my stuff. But the built-in catalogs don't really cover all the bases for me. I'd like to create some new catalogs. I've tried right-clicking everywhere I can think of and I can't find any way to make a brand new catalog.

A: We think the design of this particular feature is terrible. Like you, we figured we'd be able to right-click in the right pane of the CG (Component Gallery) while it displays the list of catalogs, and create a new one. But the Add Catalog option there doesn't let you create a new one, just add a catalog that already exists. There's a New option that appears sometimes, too, but it doesn't include catalogs.

Instead, you have to click the CG's Options button. Then choose the Catalogs page. That page has a New button that lets you create a new catalog. Click that button and specify a table to contain the information for the new catalog. If, like us, you're not big fans of embedded spaces in filenames, you can right-click the new catalog in the left pane and choose Rename to give it a useful name. The associated table retains the original name, but the CG shows the new name. Figure 2-3 shows the Options dialog with the New button.

Frankly, we can't think of a much worse way to handle this.

Q: At conferences, I've seen speakers grab a class from the Class Browser and drop it somewhere else to create an instance. But I can never make this work when I try it. What's the secret?

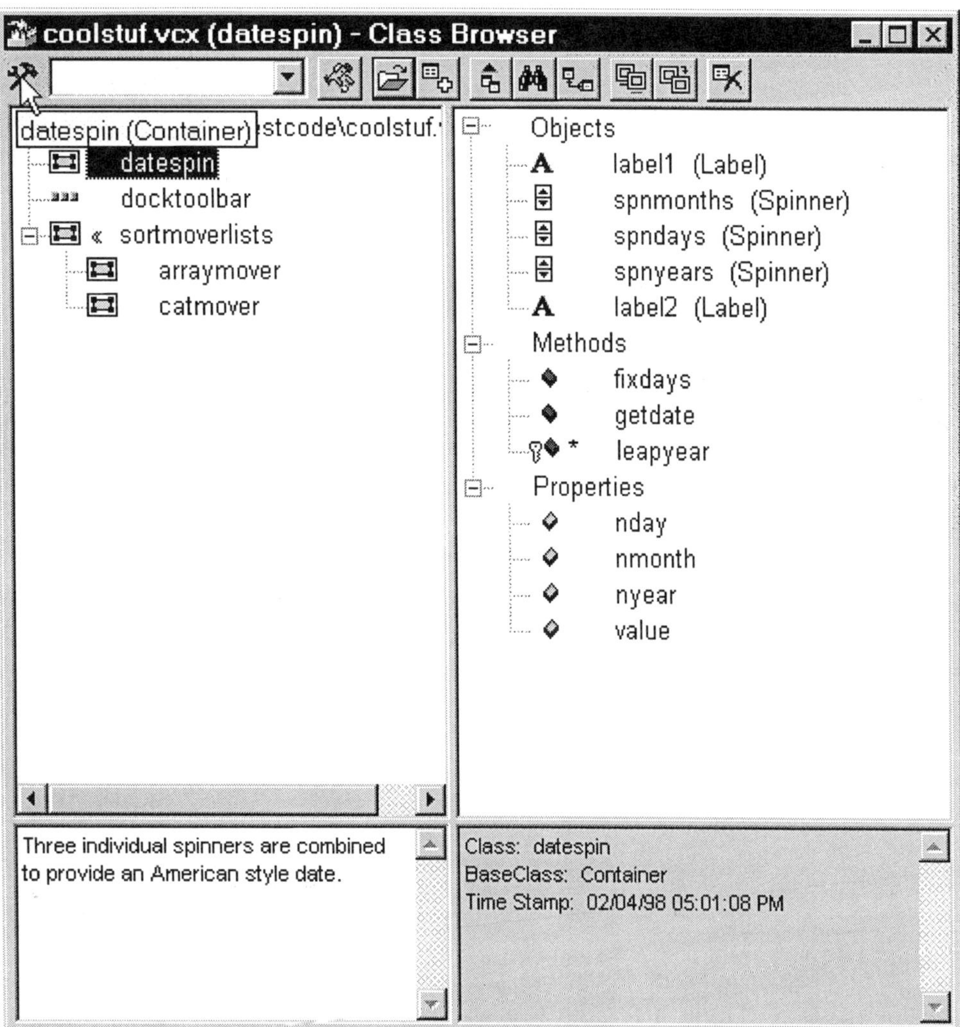

Figure 2-4: To drag an instance from the Class Browser, you have to choose the class, then drag the icon at the upper left. In this case, it's a hammer and wrench.

A: This is one of those things that demos really well, but is just complex enough to be hard to find on your own. It's really a two-step process. First, click the class you're interested in. Then, grab the icon that appears above the listview (just below the Browser's title bar). That's what you have to drag. The mouse pointer in Figure 2-4 is pointing at the appropriate icon.

Q: I want to add an array as a property of a class. But I can't figure out how to get FoxPro to understand that the property is an array.

A: In coded classes (which we hardly ever use), this one is very simple. Just put the DIMENSION statement in the class definition along with other properties. For example:

```
DEFINE CLASS Demo AS Custom

  DIMENSION aAnArray[7]
  cCharProperty = ""

  Name = "Demo Class"
ENDDEFINE
```

When you're creating classes in the Class Designer (or forms in the Form Designer), it's not really any harder—you use the New Property dialog. There are two ways to get there. The first works in all versions of Visual FoxPro. Use the New Property item on the Class menu (or the Form menu in the FD). In VFP 6 only, you can choose Edit Property/Method from the Class or Form menu, then choose New Property from that dialog. Once you reach the New Property dialog, when you enter the array name, be sure to follow it with brackets (our preference) or parentheses and the array dimensions. That's how FoxPro knows it's an array. Figure 2-5 shows the New Property dialog from VFP 6 with an array.

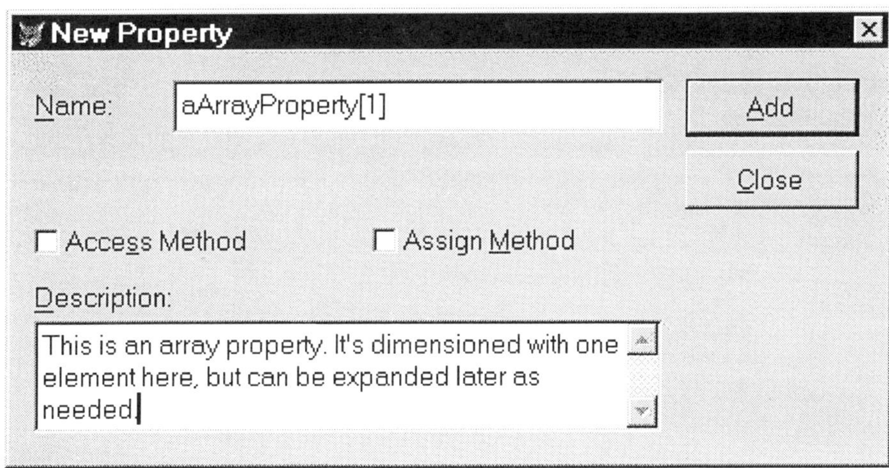

Figure 2-5: Adding an array property—don't forget the dimensions.

You can either specify the exact dimensions when you create the array property or you can redimension it in a method of the class. In forms, we often use array properties to hold the items for a list or combo box. In that case, we dimension the array as [1], then redimension and populate it with a query in the list or combo's Init method.

Properties you add to a class are listed on the Other tab of the Property Sheet. When you add an array property, you can see on the PropSheet that it's an array, but you can't specify an initial value (as you can with other properties you add). You have to do it in a method.

The thing we keep forgetting when dealing with array properties is that, like other properties, you can't just refer to them by name. You have to specify the containing object along with the property or use This or ThisForm. So, for example, if we use an array property of a form as the RowSource for a combo on that form, the assignment looks like:

```
* This would be in the combo's Init:
This.RowSource = "ThisForm.aComboContents"
```

Q: I've specified hotkeys for all my menu pads by preceding the hotkey in the prompt with "\<" (like "\<File"). But when my users press ALT+F, it doesn't activate the File menu.

A: Windows has two ways to let users press keys and make things happen in the menu. You're already using hotkeys, which let a user quickly choose an item when focus is already on the menu. The other approach is menu shortcuts, which can be pressed at almost any time to choose a menu item.

In VFP, hotkeys are specified by putting "\<" in front of the letter you want to choose the item. Pressing that letter chooses the item when the menu is already highlighted. Actually, it's a little more complicated—the exact effect of pressing any letter depends on whether any menu popups are open. (A hotkey for a menu pad works only if no other popups are open.)

Shortcuts work when focus isn't on the menu or when the popup containing the shortcut is open. Windows has a number of pretty standard menu shortcuts, like CTRL+C for copy and CTRL+Z for undo. ALT+underlined letter used to open a menu popup is also a shortcut (not a hotkey). It's pretty standard to use ALT+some key for menu pads and CTRL+some key for menu items.

In the Menu Builder, you specify shortcuts by clicking the Options button for an item. In the dialog that appears, there's a section labeled Shortcut. In the Key Label text box, press the key combination you want to use as a shortcut. Then, if necessary, tab to the other text box and type the description of the shortcut you want on the menu. Figure 2-6 shows you the Prompt Options dialog. For a menu pad, you may want to make the description empty, since no description appears anyway. For menu items, typically you use something like CTRL+A. (VFP is smarter about this than it used to be, and the default Key Text is usually what you want.)

One of the hardest tasks in an application can be finding enough unique, yet meaningful, key combinations for all the menu shortcuts.

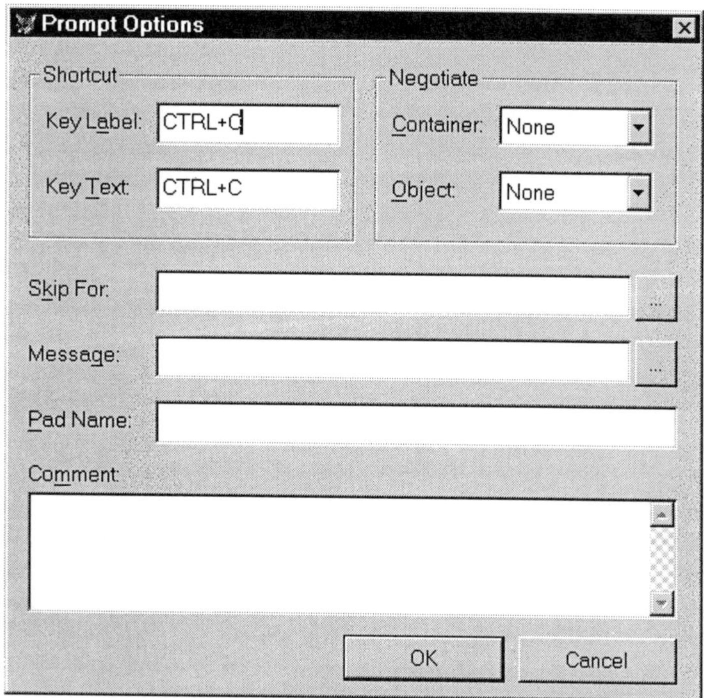

Figure 2-6: Specifying menu shortcuts—just click Options in the Menu Designer.

In code, you specify shortcuts with the KEY clause of the DEFINE PAD or DEFINE BAR command. (We had to look that one up because it's been years since we've defined a menu with code.)

Q: Whenever I try to add controls to a page of a page frame, they wind up on top of the page frame instead. I've been going to the property sheet and choosing the page I want first, but that's really tedious. There must be a better way to do this!

A: Your question can be generalized to a broader question: How do I edit the contents of a container and not just the container itself? It applies to page frames, grids and any other container objects.

As you've discovered, you can do it by brute force. Use the combo in the Property Sheet to select the object you want to edit. But, as you note, that's pretty tedious. We'd scream bloody murder if that were the only way to do it.

Right-click to the rescue. Right-click any container object and the menu that appears includes Edit as one of its options. Choose Edit and you have access to the items inside the container. Click on a page and it comes to the top. You can then drop controls on it.

With grids, it's a little more complicated. The Edit option doesn't even appear in the right-click menu unless ColumnCount has a value greater than 0. Once you choose Edit, you can click the header of a column to select the header, or anywhere else in the column to select the column.

You can tell when you have access to the items inside a container because there's a diagonally striped border around the container. Figure 2-7 shows a page frame with page 3 selected for editing.

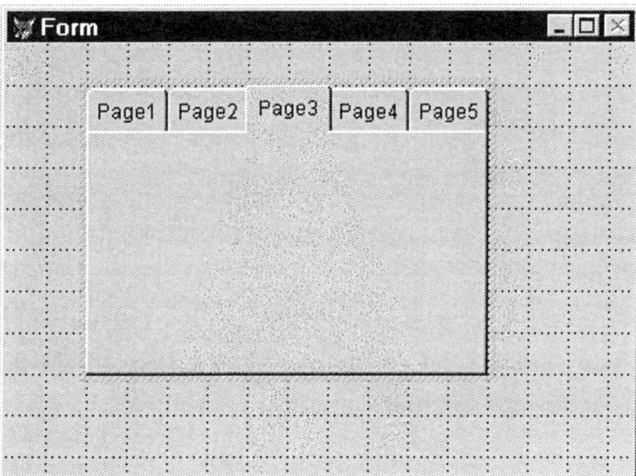

Figure 2-7: The striped border (reminds us of a college tie) indicates you're editing the contents of a container, not the container itself.

Q: If I change a property in the Property Sheet, then decide I didn't really mean it, how do I get rid of my change so that it inherits from the parent class again? When I delete the value I entered or put back the old value, I still see the property value in bold—that means I'm not inheriting, right?

A: Yep, boldface in the property sheet means you're getting a custom value, not the inherited value from the parent class. To get back to inheriting, choose the property in the PropSheet. Then right-click. The first option is "Reset to Default."

We think this is a really good item for the right-click menu. It's easy to find and use. But we think it's really dumb that right-click is the only way to get at this important item through the interface. What if your mouse isn't working? What if you have a handicap that makes it hard to use a mouse?

By the way, restoring a method to inherit is even easier than for a property. Just delete all the custom code for the method and it'll inherit from the parent class. One more "by the way"—you can restore defaults programmatically by calling the object's ResetToDefault method and passing the property or method you want to reset. For properties, it even works at runtime.

Q: When I create a grid, it has a text box in each column. When I add the control I really want in a column (say, a check box for a logical field), the default text box is still there. How do I get rid of it so I don't have the overhead of an extra control I'm not using?

A: This is one of those things that's pretty clumsy. We keep hoping the Microsofties will come up with something better.

In the Property Sheet, use the drop-down list to choose the control you want to delete. Then click on the *title bar* of the form or of the Form Designer. Be careful not to click on the form itself—that'll change the focus.

Now press Delete to remove the control you don't want.

Fortunately, adding a different control is much easier. Just right-click and choose Edit on the grid to get inside, then click the column to give it focus. Click the control you want in the Form Controls Toolbar and click in the column to drop it.

We were astonished to find that the Grid Builder doesn't handle this stuff automatically. If you specify a control other than a text box for a column in the Builder, the new control is added automatically. But the text box isn't removed. Why not? In our opinion, just plain bad design.

Q: How do you two know all this stuff?

A: We'd like to point out that it involves years of hard work, perseverance, perspiration and brilliance, but no one would believe us.

The Hacker's Guide itself is a labor of love that consumed nearly a year for each version, but we haven't mastered VFP by locking ourselves away in a cave. There are lots of people (we thank a lot of them in the Acknowledgements in the front of the book) who spend time online sharing their expertise with others. They have helped us or taught us many of the answers we share. CompuServe, Microsoft's newsgroups, Usenet newsgroups and hundreds of Internet resources are invaluable. In addition, we own many books on FoxPro, read a number of periodicals and a fair number of non-FoxPro-specific books on subjects from project management to user interface design (check out the Appendices for some recommendations). We regularly attend conferences to keep up with what's going on. We often resort to the Microsoft Knowledge Base (online or available on the TechNet and MSDN CD-ROMs) to find out the latest documented anomalies. So, while both of us have pretty good memories, we keep our resources (especially the *Hacker's Guide*) within reach so that we can answer those tough questions.

A Source is a Source, Of Course, Of Course

> Private information is practically the source of every large modern fortune.
>
> Oscar Wilde

Wait! Don't flip that page! Source code integration in Visual FoxPro is not just for team development! If you're a solo developer, or work in a group where each of you has your own project, source code control is for you, too.

Visual Studio 6 offers greater possibilities for tight integration of Visual FoxPro projects with the other tools supplied in the Visual Studio package. However, the integration with Visual SourceSafe started with Visual FoxPro 5.0, and SourceSafe has been a tool useful in coordination with FoxPro since before Microsoft bought either tool.

"Why Should I Bother with Source Control?"

> Integrity without knowledge is weak and useless, and knowledge without integrity is dangerous and dreadful.
>
> Samuel Johnson

Source code control can be a very useful tool to the solo developer as well as a key tool for multi-developer teams. For the solo developer, source code control provides backup facilities and the ability to perform a "grand undo" as well as retrieve early builds or versions. With a multiple-developer team, source code control can ensure that all members of the team work with the latest revision of source code, protect the members of the team from inadvertently overwriting each others' work, and can provide a simple method to keep track of multiple releases of the software to the same or different clients.

Source code control programs have been around for quite some time but, like difficult backup programs, programs that prove too hard to use are too easy to avoid. With the increasing complexity of projects and the improved accessibility of these products, they are tools worth the effort to learn. Integration of source code control directly into the development environment is a relatively recent feature that makes these programs easier to use.

Bear in mind that Visual SourceSafe, or any other source code control program, is a separate product and you must learn its terminology and operations to get the greatest benefit from it. While many operations can easily be performed from within the FoxPro interface, you should become familiar with the less frequently needed maintenance functions that may only be available within the program itself.

With SourceSafe, we'll caution you that many of the "features" are well hidden. SourceSafe, like FoxPro (and many other Microsoft products) was not created by the boys and girls of Redmond, but rather was purchased. The original product was developed primarily as a command line utility and supported clients on DOS, Macintosh, UNIX and Windows platforms. Many of the utility programs are only available from the command line. When you install SourceSafe as described below, make sure you check out the Administration tool and read through the both the user's and administrator's help files. The help file recommends that tools like Analyze, used to check the integrity of the SourceSafe data store, should be run on a weekly basis. We've worked with clients with gigabyte-sized data stores who weren't aware that the Analyze tool exists!

Visual Studio 97 Service Pack 2 causes "Invalid Page Faults" in VFP if you're using integrated SourceSafe projects! Avoid Service Pack 2. You can find Service Pack 3 for Visual Studio 97 on the Microsoft Web site.

This is a killer bug, because VSS crashes the machine about 10 minutes *after* you close a project that's under source code control. Uck.

(One of Ted's sessions on benchmarking at the 1997 DevCon included a close-up and personal demonstration of this bug.)

Getting SourceSafe Ready

> But their determination to banish fools foundered ultimately in the installation of absolute idiots.
>
> Basil Bunting

Follow the prompts of the Visual Studio 6 install (or the Visual SourceSafe install, if you purchased it separately) to install the full "server" installation of VSS to a section of your network where it can be accessed by all workstations. Each workstation that needs to access the shared SourceSafe install then needs to run NetSetup.EXE to install client software on the local machine. If you're installing on a stand-alone machine, you still need to go through these steps. The server install creates the data structures needed to store the SourceSafe information; the client install sets the Registry settings so VFP and other source-code control-enabled applications can recognize that the service is available.

A couple of additional settings need to be tweaked before the product is ready for use. In the Administrators tool, under Tools/Options, you should enable the multiple checkouts option (Figure 2-8) to allow all developers to jointly check out the PJM file that serves as the ASCII equivalent of the Project Manager. Some developers have reported success with leaving multiple checkouts disabled, and requiring each developer to individually and manually check out the PJM file (via the native VSS interface) in order to synchronize their project changes to the shared project. We haven't tried this, but suspect that a process that cumbersome is done less often than one that can just be picked from the VFP menu.

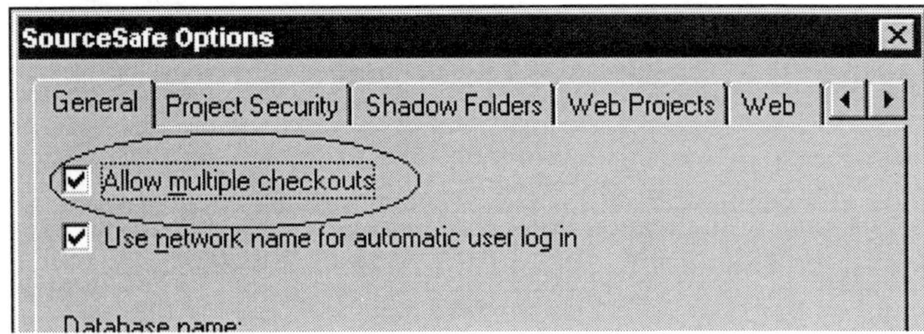

Figure 2-8: Administrator option for multiple checkouts must be turned on.

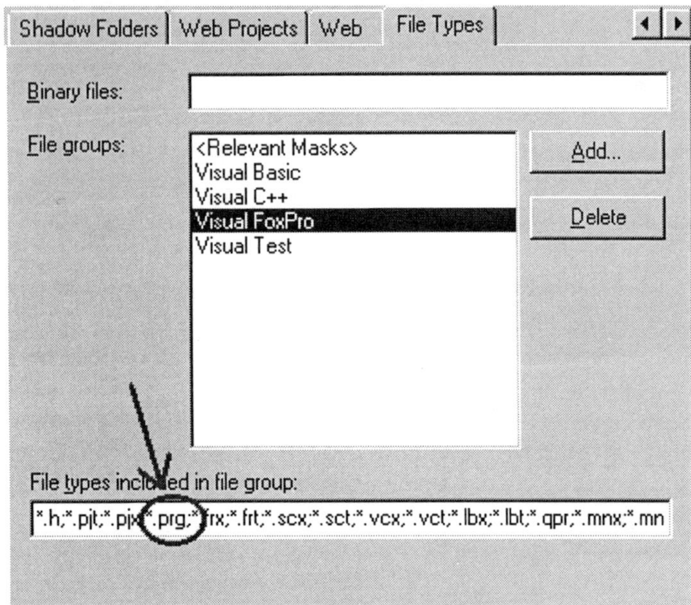

Figure 2-9: For VSS 5.0, you'll need to add the *.prg to VFP's File Types. They got it right in VSS 6.0.

If you're working with VSS 5.0, you also need to add .PRG to SourceSafe's list of file extensions for Visual FoxPro (Figure 2-9). Each workstation needs to turn on Visual SourceSafe from the Tools/Options dialog, using the Active source control provider drop-down (Figure 2-10). For the other options on the Projects tab, we've found that different developers are happier with them in different configurations. You'll need to experiment to determine which settings best fit your work style. Finally, note that the last SourceSafe option on the page is one for the text generation program. As we explain below, binary files are stored both in their native format and a text equivalent, to make comparisons easier. The source for the program that generates the text, SccText.PRG, is included with Visual FoxPro; you should consider modifying it to meet your needs if necessary.

The Intricate Dance of the Source and the Fox

> I do not know what the spirit of a philosopher could more wish to be than a good dancer. For the dance is his ideal, also his fine art, finally also the only kind of piety he knows, his "divine service."
>
> Friedrich Nietzsche, *The Gay Science*

Once VSS is installed, the developer who creates a project can select "Add Project to Source Control" (if he hasn't set things up to do this automatically via the Options dialog). All other developers can now access the project by selecting "Join Source Control Project" from their File menu.

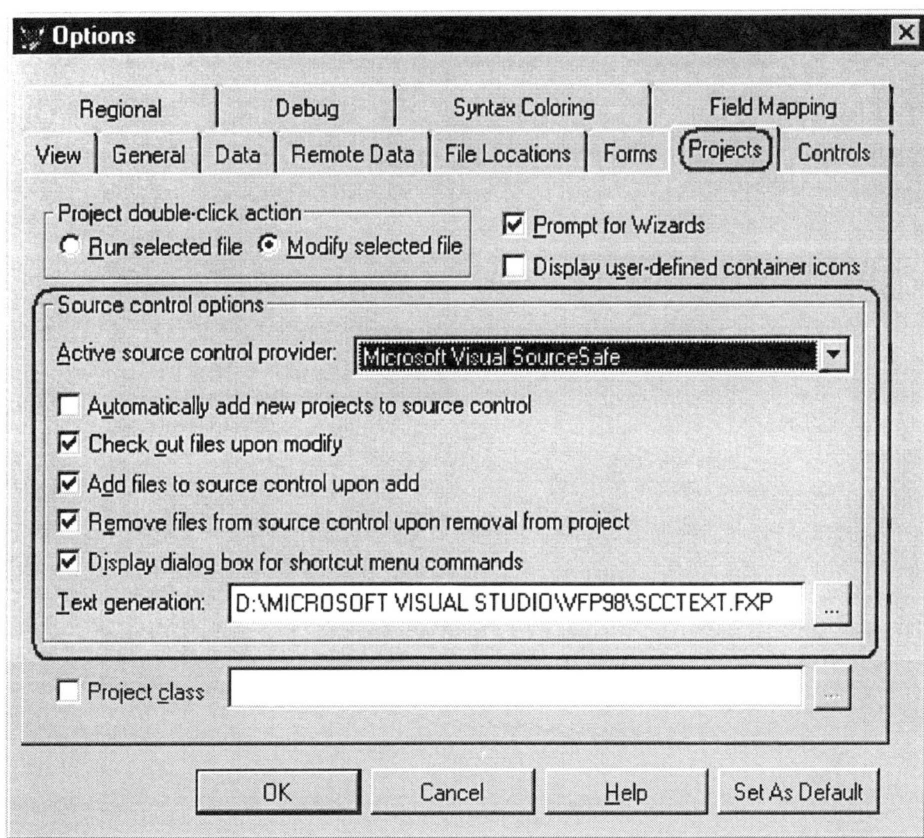

Figure 2-10: The Tools/Options/Project dialog provides SourceSafe options.

Integrated Source Code Control in Visual FoxPro

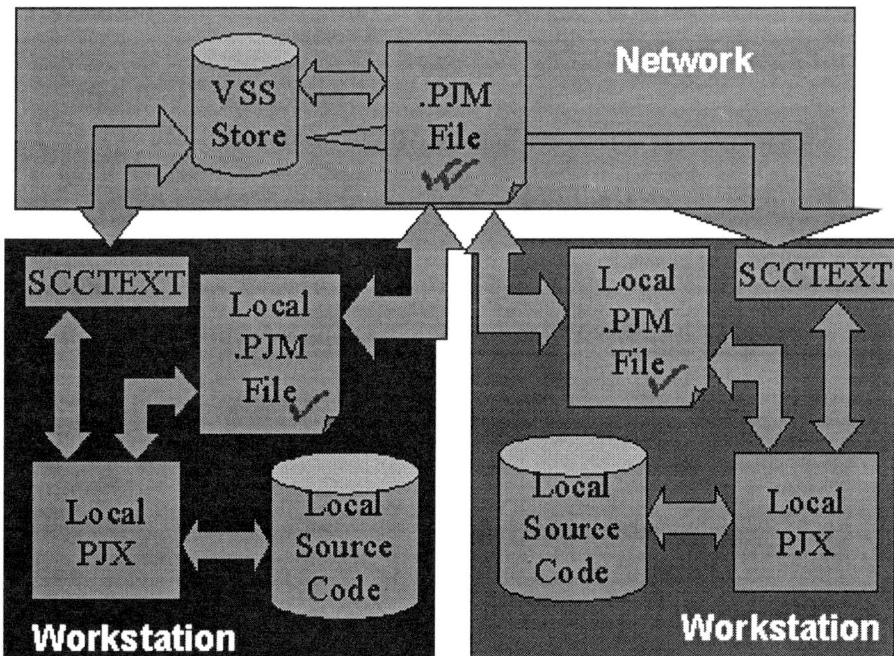

Figure 2-11: Source code control using VFP's Project Manager makes developers play nicely together.

Each developer maintains her own copy of the shared project, and each has a complete copy of all of the source code. By default, all of the source code is flagged read-only to prevent inadvertent code changes. After checking out an individual file, additions and modifications to the source code are made by each developer on his local machine. When the changes have been tested and are ready to be shared with the rest of the development team, the developer chooses "Update Project List" from the Source Control submenu of the Project menu. This option updates a text version of the project, a PJM file, with the changes this developer has made to her local project file. When other developers choose to update the shared project list, they see the changes made by this developer. Figure 2-11 shows the dance of files from place to place.

Source code control works best on text files, because differing versions of text files can be visually compared. Since FoxPro keeps a lot of its designs in table format (SCX, VCX, MNX), these files cannot be compared directly. Instead, the integrated source control creates an ASCII version of each of these files (with corresponding SCA, VCA and MNA extensions) so that changes can be "diffed" (checked for differences). The SccText.PRG program creates and interprets these ASCII files; this program can be modified (or replaced) to suit your needs.

Visual SourceSafe at Work

> You have a new source of doubt and apprehension.
>
> Charles Horton Cooley, *Human Nature and the Social Order*

When source control is in use, the Project Manager displays icons to show the status of each file (Figure 2-12).

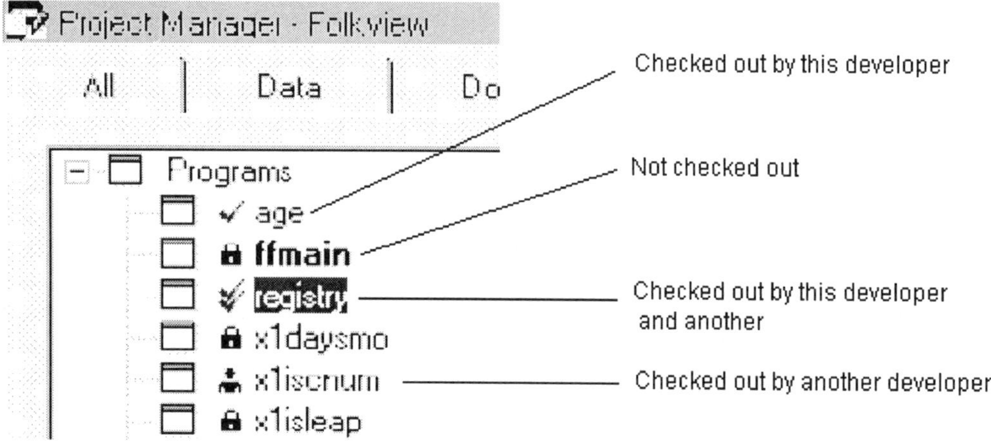

Figure 2-12: Icons within Project Manager tell us the status of each file. Even though a file might be available, there are no icons for "married," "single," or "just wants to be friends."

The PJ* Project files and database and table files should not be checked in. The project file is generated for each developer by the FoxPro-to-SourceSafe interface by reading the PJM file, which is checked out by each developer who joins the project. The PJM file contains the "header" information for the project—name, address, icon, generator options, and a line for each file within the project. Figure 2-13 shows a typical PJM file.

The Sourcerer's Apprentice

> In the world of knowledge, the essential Form of Good is the limit of our inquiries, and can barely be perceived; but, when perceived, we cannot help concluding that it is in every case the source of all that is bright and beautiful.
>
> Plato

Once you have succeeded in using Visual SourceSafe with the Visual FoxPro Project Manager, there are a number of ways in which the collaboration between the two products can be enhanced and your life, thus, made easier.

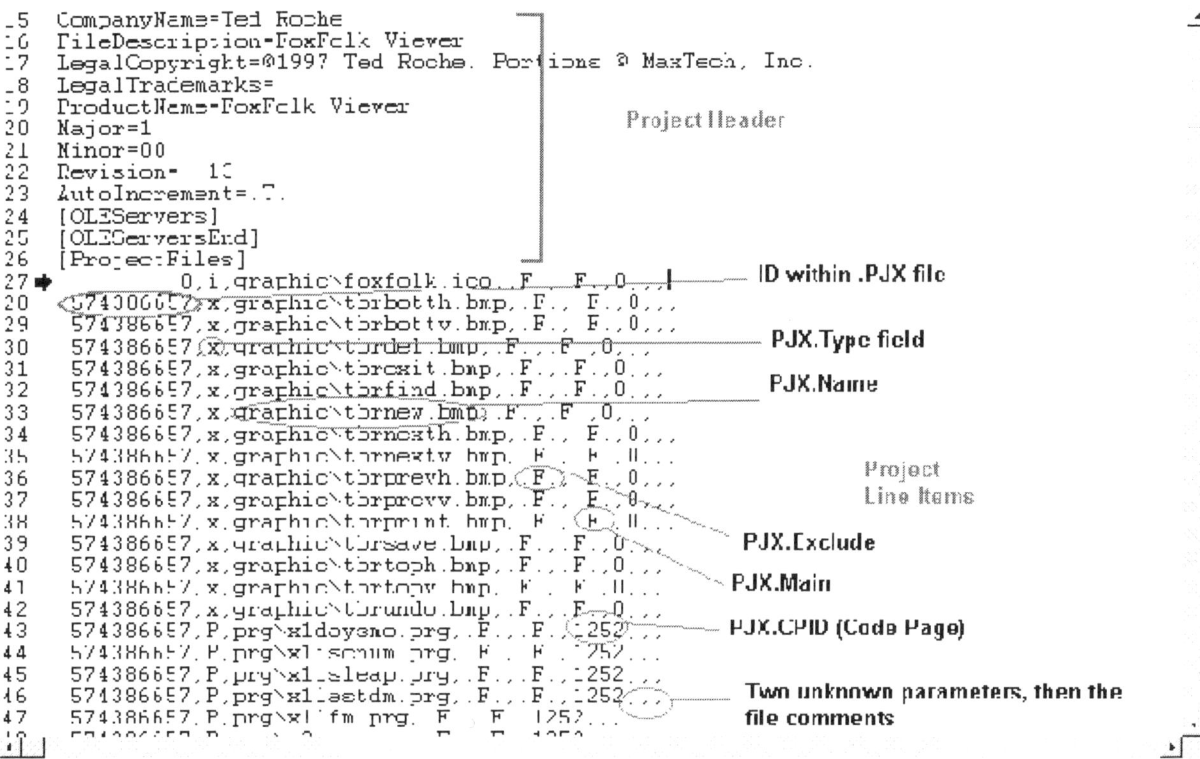

Figure 2-13: The PJM file is the text file equivalent of the Project Manager's PJX table. Not something we'd want to have to read regularly.

Automate It!

Rather than using the internal source code control mechanism, it is possible to control Visual SourceSafe using Automation directly from FoxPro. You can scan the contents of a project (PJX files are just data tables), or you can iterate through the files in a Project object and process the contents directly against the SourceSafe back end.

During the beta, we were amazed to discover that the documentation for SourceSafe 6.0 Automation was "expected to be available by the time the product ships." Now how the heck can anyone beta test undocumented methods? Guess at their name? We had better things to do with our time. Well, the documentation in this book was expected to be ready, too, but we *knew* we'd run late. And one week after Visual Studio's official launch? No docs. However, documentation for version 5.0 is available at http://www.microsoft.com/ssafe, Microsoft's site for VSS, and it appears to work correctly with VSS 6.0 as well. An extract of the object model is shown in Figure 2-14.

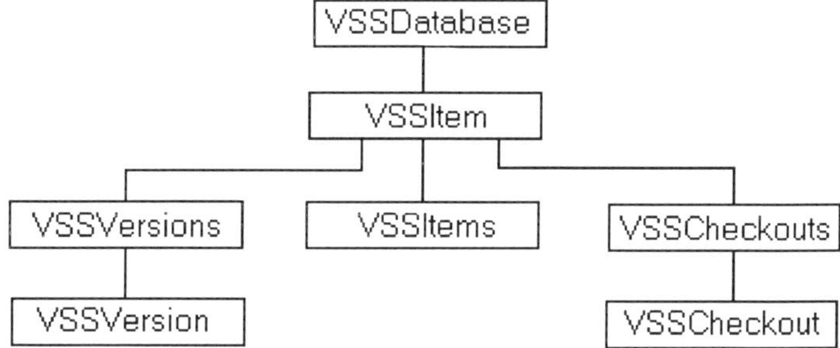

Figure 2-14: The Visual SourceSafe Object Model—Cindy Crawford is a lot more interesting to look at, but this one is informative.

The object model is pretty much like other OLE objects and collections (including the VFP Project, Server and

Files objects), only this time, the objects are files, *versions* of those files and records of checkouts. The objects are:

VSSDatabase: A SourceSafe database.

VSSItem: A project or file. Note there is also a VSSItems object that's a collection of all the children in one project.

VSSVersion: One way of representing a specific version of a file or project. VSSVersions is a collection of all the versions of a particular file or project.

VSSCheckout: A checkout record for a file. Note once again there's a collection, since one file may have many simultaneous checkouts.

Here's a routine that lists the files available along the path specified in a tree format:

```
*****************************************************************
* Program....: LISTTREE.PRG
* Abstract...: Recursively displays VSS tree
*****************************************************************
LPARAMETERS lcPath, lcPrefix, lcINIFile, lcUser, lcPassword
IF TYPE("lcPath") <> "C"
  lcPath = "$/"
ENDIF
IF VARTYPE(lcPrefix) <> "C"
  lcPrefix = SPACE(0)
ENDIF
IF VARTYPE(lcINIFile) <> "C" or EMPTY(lcINIFile)
  lcINIFile = "D:\VS98\Common\VSS\SrcSafe.INI"
ENDIF
IF VARTYPE(lcUser) <> "C" or EMPTY(lcUser)
  lcUser = "troche"  && substitute your own VSS login here
ENDIF
IF VARTYPE(lcPassword) <> "C"
  lcPassword = SPACE(0)
ENDIF
LOCAL loSSafe, loVSSItems, loRoot, loNode
loSSafe = CREATEOBJECT("SourceSafe")
loSSafe.Open(lcINIFile, lcUser, lcPassword)
loRoot = loSSafe.VSSItem(lcPath)
loVSSItems = loRoot.Items()
FOR EACH loNode IN loVSSItems
  ? lcPrefix + loNode.Name
  IF loNode.Type = 0  && project
    * Use recursion to drill down VSS tree
    do listtree with lcPath + loNode.Name + "/", ;
                     lcPrefix + "+", ;
                     lcINIFile, ;
                     lcUser, ;
                     lcPassword
  ENDIF

NEXT
RELEASE loNode, loVSSItems, loRoot, loSSafe
```

This second sample opens a database, displays a few properties and then checks out a specific file. Properties of the file are then displayed. Note this sample has the file paths, login information and filenames hard-coded for demonstration purposes; a general-purpose routine would accept these as parameters.

```
*****************************************************************
* Program....: TESTVSS1.PRG
* Abstract...: Demonstrate VSS Automation
* Changes....:
*****************************************************************
```

```
oSSafe = CREATEOBJECT("SourceSafe")

* Syntax is object.open(path to srcsafe.ini, username, password)
oSSafe.Open("D:\VS98\Common\VSS\SrcSafe.INI","troche","")

* The following lines show some of the object's properties
? oSSafe.UserName          && Troche, no surprise there
? oSSafe.CurrentProject    && $/simpserv, the last project opened
? oSSafe.SrcSafeINI        && the file and path above

* The next line assumes Sys2335 is a Visual SourceSafe project
* and Sys2335.PRG is a program of that
oFile = oSSafe.VSSItem("$/sys2335/Sys2335.PRG")
oFile.Checkout()
? oFile.IsCheckedOut = 2  && returns .T.
? oFile.Binary             && returns .F.
? oFile.IsDifferent        && returns .F.
? oFile.VersionNumber      && returns 1, 2, etc for your file
oFile.Checkin()
```

That Annoying SCC Window

Under Visual FoxPro 5.0, whenever a SourceSafe check-in, check-out, or "get latest" operation is attempted from within FoxPro, a top-level window appears to report any messages from SourceSafe, but more likely just blocks your access to the FoxPro application and occasionally intercepts keystrokes. Thanks to Christof Lange for pointing out that you can get rid of this annoying window with HIDE WINDOW "SOURCE" or HIDE WINDOW "Ergebnisse der Quellcode-Kontrolle", if you're using the German version of these tools.

This annoying behavior has been replaced in VFP 6.0 by the less annoying feature of echoing actions to the Command Window. We still wish we could just have the ability to turn this stuff off!

Files Outside of the Project Tree

SourceSafe doesn't allow you to include files outside the project directory tree; attempting to do so generates an error. There are several workarounds, depending on the situation. If the file is used in this application only, the simplest thing to do is just to move it into the directory structure. If the file is used in multiple projects, one alternative is to add it to a separate project within the SourceSafe native interface. Use sharing in VSS to add the file to the current project, and use "Get Latest Version" to copy a version to the appropriate project directory. Within FoxPro, add the shared file to the project, and when FoxPro protests that the file already exists under source code control, select "overwrite" to update the file to the (identical) most recent version.

Pinned to the Wall

While it's way beyond the basic introduction this section is meant to give you, SourceSafe can do some cool things. Look at sharing between projects to maintain control of common files (FoxTools, framework source code). Consider "pinning" to lock in versions for shared branches. A "pinned" file is a branch of the file versions that's locked at a particular revision until "unpinned." The idea is that common files can get updated, but the code you've shipped to a particular client doesn't reflect those changes until you open the safety pin.

Label Maker

Look at the labeling options within Visual SourceSafe to control and document versions sent to testing or released to clients. This is a big help when the client calls and reports some problem in their outer Mongolia office with code three revs back. With labeling on each released version, you can use the native SourceSafe interface to produce a snapshot of the code at that label point.

SccText.PRG—Sort Of Right

The October '97 issue of *FoxPro Advisor* has an excellent article by Mark Wilden with several suggestions for changes to SccText.PRG, the text generation program. One issue he identifies is that SCX and VCX files can jumble the order of methods each time they're saved. When SccText generates the method code to go in the corresponding SCA or VCA file, the methods are put in their order in the SCX or VCX and are not sorted. Since each version can have the methods in a different order, viewing differences in the files is difficult. Mark proposed a simple change to the SccText program to sort the methods before writing out the text file. Amazingly, Microsoft did not integrate these changes into the 6.0 version of SccText—it is byte-for-byte identical with the version that shipped with 5.0! If you ever find the need to compare versions of SCXs or VCXs, this change is well worth making.

Sharing Ought to Be Easier Than This

The Project/Source Control/Share option on the VFP Project menu allows you to add controlled files from any other project directly into your project. Unfortunately, there's no option to specify where these files are stored—all are dumped into the project root directory. You can move the file using the SourceSafe interface by dragging and dropping into the correct folder, and then deleting the file from the root. (Yes, this is how you have to do a "move"—copy and delete—there's no native move functionality in SourceSafe.) Finally, modify the PJM file directly to point to the new location of the file.

Source Control—It's Not Just for Code Anymore!

By default, the VFP-VSS interface doesn't put data files under source code control, nor does it include the database container. Consider adding data files that are more control files than end-user data. Take a look at the GenDBC program, included with Visual FoxPro in the Tools\GenDBC directory, to generate a program containing all of your database container properties and methods; once you create the program, put it under source control. Consider a tool like xCase or Stonefield Database Toolkit to generate the design metadata for preservation within SourceSafe.

The SourceSafe Web site also includes an add-on program for Microsoft Office 97 to add a SourceSafe menu to those products. Consider maintaining all project documentation under source code control as well.

Troubleshooting Speed Problems

Under some circumstances, the Project Manager takes *forever* to do anything with projects under source code control. Make sure you're using the latest version of FoxPro—5.0a had major speed improvements over 5.0, and each Service Pack (that hasn't crashed the system) has improved on that. Ensure your network is performing correctly by checking the configuration of your clients and server, monitoring performance at the server, or using a packet sniffer to watch network traffic. Use the SourceSafe admin tools like Analyze.EXE to test and correct problems with the SourceSafe data store. You'll also want to check the Microsoft Knowledge Base (see the "Back 'o Da Book" for details on the Knowledge Base) for updated information on this—we've heard of anecdotal cases, but haven't managed to chase down a cause yet.

Mother Said We Should Share

There's no concept in the SourceSafe model of "synching" between two SourceSafe repositories, nor is there significant support for remote sites or developers who want a separate SourceSafe installation for their laptop. The solutions at this point are manual: Check the files out from the "master" database and check them in to the "slaves." The process is arduous and requires close attention by the operators.

When duplicating SourceSafe-controlled projects between machines, a number of errors can be generated if the project's status, as stored in the PJX, doesn't match that of SourceSafe. For example, if you attempt to open a SourceSafe-controlled project on a machine connected to a different SourceSafe database, you can receive the error 'SCC API error "Project created" occurred. The project will be opened without source control.' This is proof positive that two wrongs don't make a right.

Two fields in the PJX table appear to determine how files are controlled within the project: the LOCAL field is a logical to determine whether the file is only used locally (.T.) or if it's controlled via source code control (.F.). In the project header record (the first record in the table), SCCDATA stores path names and SourceSafe control information. In the records for the individual files, the SCCDATA memo field appears to contain flags for the status of the associated file. Thanks to fellow MVP Christof Lange for hacking his way through this one: Bytes 260 and 261 (or 0x104 and 0x105) determine whether the file is checked in or out, by this developer or another, within this project or another project. These flags seem to be updated automatically by the Project Manager, but only if the LOCAL switch is set.

Give Me That Remote Control

There's no native support for remote access, and Visual SourceSafe over RAS is significantly slower than LAN speed. However, the VSS team worked hard at improving the performance of VSS over dial-up lines in the 6.0 product. Look for significant performance improvements. You should also consider alternatives such as using a shadow directory structure to allow developers to "get" all current source code without invoking VSS, using a store-and-forward process, like e-mail, to transfer files to and from remote users, or setting up an Automation server locally with a better remote interface.

Control That Source!

> There is no such source of error as the pursuit of absolute truth.
>
> Samuel Butler

Microsoft has provided us with hooks into the Project Manager and source code control to allow us to reliably maintain source code shared among multiple developers. A little time spent understanding how the mechanism works and how it can be used to your best advantage can pay off for the multi-developer team.

Section 3: Franz and Other Lists

To criticize is to appreciate, to appropriate, to take intellectual possession, to establish in fine a relation with the criticized thing and to make it one's own.

Henry James

Section 3 contains a bunch of stuff that didn't fit in anywhere else in the book. Most of it can be viewed as lists of one sort or another. You'll find our hardware recommendations, our opinionated list of useless commands to avoid, optimization tips, and a collection of weird items that make you think you've found a bug.

Hardware and Software Recommendations

(From a pair of hardware haters)

We hate hardware. Let's get that one fact out from the beginning. IRQs and memory locations, obscure settings and incompatibilities are the bane of our existence. We're FoxPro hackers, not wire weenies, and it saddens us that FoxPro requires any hardware at all—a virtual machine would be so much nicer to work on! However, this is the real world, and it's a fact.

In the three years since we first wrote this section for the *Hacker's Guide to Visual FoxPro 3*, much has changed, and yet much remains the same. Windows 95 did ship, with great fanfare, on August 24, 1995, and was the success we'd predicted. Windows 98 followed with much less to-do, and with many customers questioning whether it was worth the bother.

Hardware

"The faster and the bigger, the better" is a pretty good rule for FoxPro's use of hardware. More CPU power and faster clock speeds mean faster performance; swifter video performance makes FoxPro shine; and a well-tuned operating system is icing on the cake. However ...

> Moderation in all things.
>
> —Thornton Wilder, *Our Town*

A real fast processor isn't worth much if it's right only 98.997979% of the time. Blazing video performance that occasionally blazes into an inferno is useless. Whizzy new CD-ROMs ain't worth a darn if they sometimes spit out your still-spinning disk when you need to read them. (Ted had a "compatible" machine that actually did this.) They don't call it the "bleeding edge" for nothing. Unproven, version 1.0 technology is not the kind of thing that we bet the mortgage on, and you should probably consider these factors yourself. With proper backup and a consideration of the risks involved, investment in new technologies pays off for many hearty pioneers, but make sure when you're purchasing hardware that there is a conscious decision when to buy a workhorse and when to buy a new thoroughbred colt.

> It's always something.
>
> —Roseanne Rosannadanna

Our cut on things: read the books, read the magazines, ask online. Make sure that what you're purchasing is compatible, especially if a client is going to be running it.

At a minimum, Visual FoxPro claims it requires a 386 processor and 8 megabytes of RAM. Let's get real, folks—it is still theoretically possible to run Windows 95/98 on a 386 with 8 Mb of RAM, but not if you're running anything more strenuous than Paintbrush. Windows NT or any network drivers add to the burden. A Pentium or better is the minimum you want as a processor. As far as RAM goes, more is better. Since we recommend NT (see below), which recommends a laughable 16 Mb RAM on the box, we'll have to say 32 Mb minimum. But more is better.

Your users might be able to get away with less, but be careful cutting corners. Test your app on one of their machines regularly to ensure that the app will run acceptably on their hardware.

Hard disks

> You can never be too rich, too thin, or have too much hard drive space.
>
> —Anonymous

Hard disk space is an issue both for developers and end users. A full installation of Visual Studio requires an enormous amount of space. Even picking and choosing only those items you want directly related to FoxPro development can easily consume a half a gigabyte of space, an amount considered preposterous only a few years ago. Since disk space is priced at a few cents per megabyte, we can't see trading the inconvenience of trying to locate and load the CDs each time you need a component with the one-time hassle of getting the biggest drive you can afford.

One tip: If you're installing the common components onto a FAT drive, each file will take up a minimum of one disk cluster. Clusters are sized based on the total capacity of the partition divided by 65535. So the bigger the partition, the more space is wasted for the dinky bitmaps, cursors and icons supplied with the package. Consider formatting the partition as FAT32 if you are running Windows 98, or enabling compression under Windows NT to minimize the wasted space.

A second hard disk issue you need to be aware of is that Visual FoxPro's installation requires not only space on the volume where you want to install Visual FoxPro, but also free space on the drive where Windows is installed. Visual FoxPro comes with updated DLLs and Windows support files that will be installed in the main Windows and System subdirectories. These can take significant space. Obviously, overwriting these files will also require appropriate rights in the case of a network install.

In that same vein, check out the remarkably full-featured install program that comes with Visual Studio for options on portions of Visual FoxPro that may be reinstalled, deinstalled, or ignored. Dropping the (optional) ODBC support from an installation can save significant space—don't install it unless you need to. If you are installing workstation copies on multiple developers' machines, you might want only the network administrative copy to be a full copy, while each developer can get by with a smaller subset.

For end users, besides the space for your application and its data files, you need to plan on over 4 Mb for the runtime VFP 6*.* files.

Video

An accelerator card is a necessity for Visual FoxPro. What with dozens of toolbars, as well as property sheets, tabbed options dialogs, drop-downs, OLE objects, OCX Outline controls and what-have-you, a powerful video card can make an enormous difference in your productivity. 256 colors seems to have become the minimum, and 800 x 600 pixels is the minimum resolution we'd consider when running Visual FoxPro. Why 800 x 600, you ask? The following figures show the difference: Figure 3-1 shows a full-sized 640 x 480 form on a 1024 x 768 screen, with plenty of room to access the necessary tools. On the other hand (see Figure 3-2), the same form, brought up in 640 x 480 mode screen, cuts off some of the toolbars and prevents viewing the entire Property Sheet—you'll spend your life pushing scrollbars, moving dialog boxes, and cursing at Visual FoxPro. If you want to be able to interact with all parts of a 640 x 480 form while you're designing it, with the appropriate toolbars and property sheets also visible, "8 by 6" is the least you can consider, and 1024 x 768 may make even more sense. Stop me if you've heard this before—more is better.

While we're on the subject of video, the monitor is the other element that makes a huge difference. 1024 x 768 or greater resolution is impossible to read (at least with our aging eyes) on a small 14" or 15" monitor. Seventeen inches is the least we'll work on, and some of the new 19", 20" or even 21" monitors make viewing an absolute pleasure. You're going to spend an awful lot of your life in front of this tube—do yourself a favor and get the largest and clearest display you can afford.

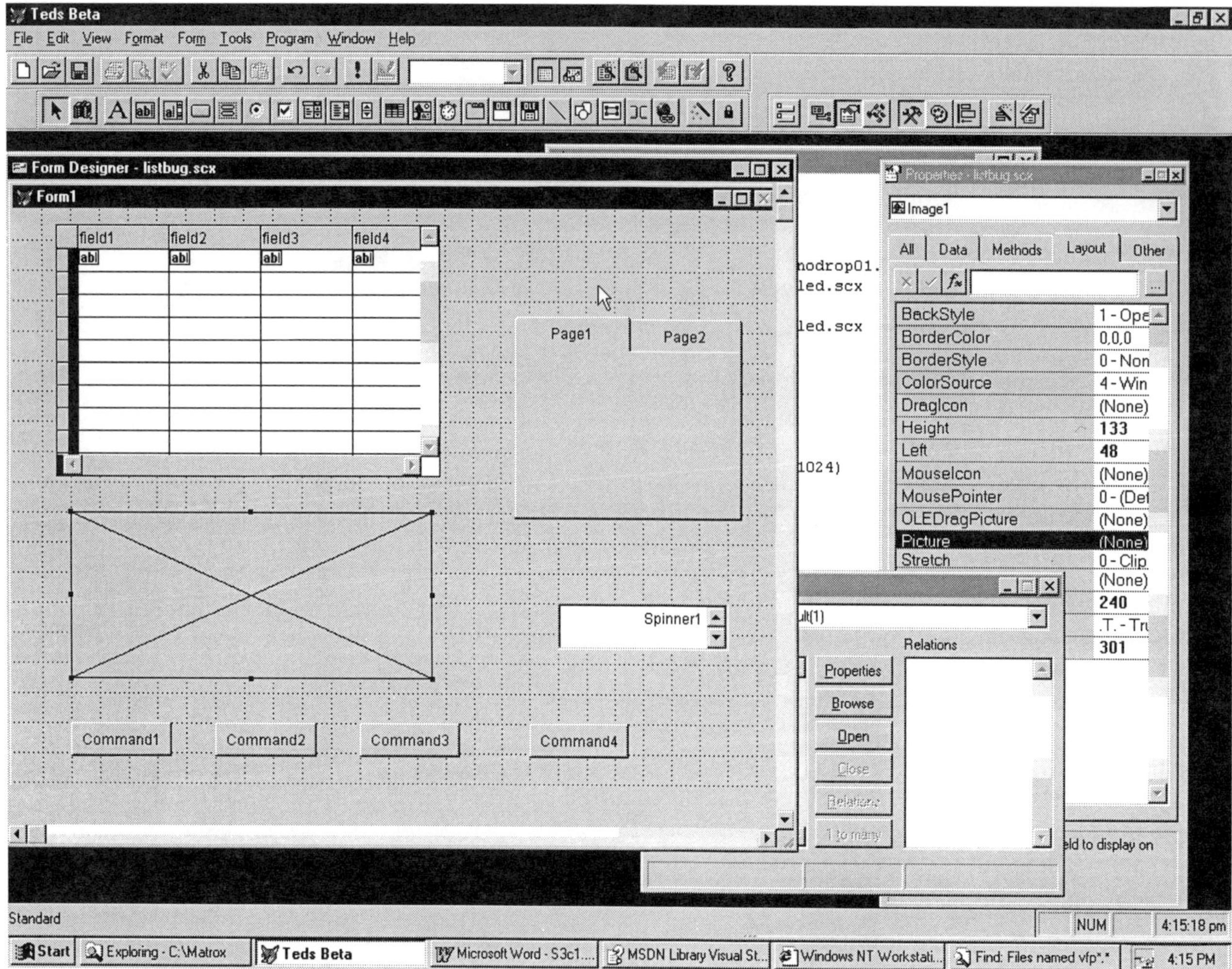

Figure 3-1: 1024 x 768 leaves plenty of room!

A caution, however. While we feel that justifying the costs of a large monitor is a no-brainer for a developer, it may not be as easy for dozens or hundreds of operators using your application. Just as with processing speed, make sure that you check out your application frequently on one of the lower-powered, lower-resolution machines it will run on, to ensure the interface is easy to use for the operators as well.

Operating systems

You have three choices for an operating system on which to run Visual FoxPro for Windows, and you shouldn't be surprised that they all have the name "Windows." Windows 95, Windows 98 or Windows NT. Here are our somewhat biased opinions.

Windows Ninety-X—the OS for the rest of us?

Microsoft released Windows 95 with the intention of eradicating Windows 3.1 from the face of the earth. Rather than trying to eliminate a competitor, we think their intention was to create a solid 32-bit platform for their own future products. And, overall, we think they succeeded marvelously. Windows 95 is compatible with nearly everything. Almost anything that ran in DOS or Win 3.1 runs under Win 95. Windows 95 supports networking natively, unlike the aging Win 3.1, and performs quite well on the vast majority of desktops.

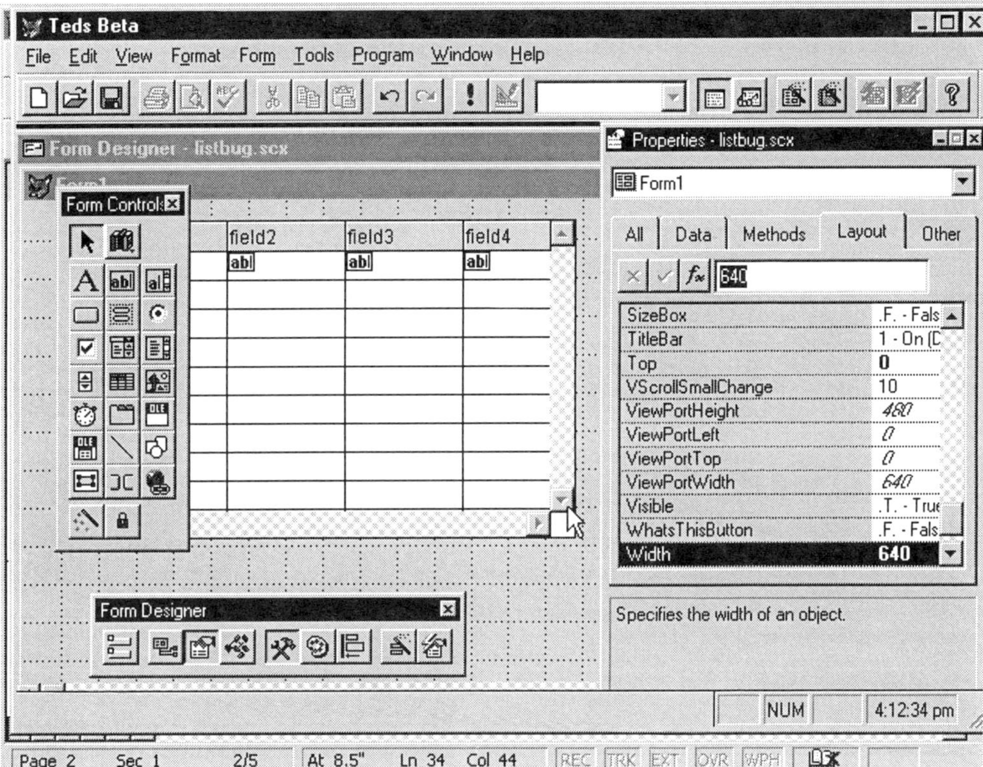

Figure 3-2 640 x 480: No way!!!

Microsoft nearly shot themselves in their collective foot with their continuing updates to the operating system. First there was Service Pack 1. The introduction of Internet Explorer 2.0 in the Plus! pack, followed by its widespread download from the Internet (with lots of slipstreamed OS files), led to more dissimilar desktops. Next, OSR-2, the OEM Service Release, was an updated version intended solely for Original Equipment Manufacturers, but found its way onto a lot of desktops. OSR-2.5 and/or the USB Update followed soon afterwards, leaving administrators in a position where nearly every Win 95 machine was unique unto itself.

Enter Windows 98. Win 98 did not arrive on the scene with as clear a mandate as Win 95, and we expect that its acceptance will be spotty. But it rolls together all of the little fixes and gotchas into one package and hopefully will standardize desktops again. At least for a while.

Windows NT—New Technology or Not Today?

You've probably read the advertising, seen the commercials, and read the reviews. We won't bore you by repeating all of that. We'll just share one anecdote. When Microsoft planned the FoxPro DevCon '95 in January, they hoped to show a late beta or perhaps even an early release copy of Visual FoxPro. Alas, a miracle did not come to pass, and instead they showed a late alpha/early beta copy of Visual FoxPro that crashed in nearly every session. But because they were running under NT, a simple double-click of the Visual FoxPro icon was all that was necessary to restart the app—NT cleaned up the mess very nicely, all by itself. That alone sold us.

Windows NT is solid, but that robustness comes at a price. Performance is comparable to Windows 95/98 only on the higher-end processors, and NT demands more RAM than 95/98. In addition, managing the Win NT domain model, setting up security or maintaining a large network does not come easy. For more than a few machines, the assistance of a Microsoft Certified System Engineer becomes less of a luxury and more of a necessity.

One caveat—ensure that your machine is *100%* NT compatible. The Hardware Compatibility List (HCL) is available from a number of Microsoft sources, and you should make sure that *all* of your peripherals are listed. Unlike DOS and earlier Windows incarnations, if it's not listed, it probably won't work. We've spent more than a few hours trying to shoehorn NT onto a machine that "should be" able to run NT, but some little part, perhaps a serial port or a video card, just wasn't compatible enough. Don't frustrate yourself. Get machines with NT preinstalled, if possible, and only attempt upgrading to NT if the machine is *really* compatible.

DOS, Windows 3.x, Warp-OS/2, Linux and the Mac OSes

No doubt, someone's out there, even as you read these words, oh, faithful reader, picking up their poison pen to write us a flaming, screaming, bombastic letter on how we have ignored the most powerful operating system in both the known and unknown universes: (fill in the blank). This next paragraph is for them. You can skip it.

We know. It's not our fault. VFP 5.0 and later run on 32-bit Windows and that's all. No dice. Sorry. Call Microsoft.

So, where should you want to go today?

We do call this section "Recommendations," so we should name our operating system of choice. Well, life is not always that easy.

Ted's notebook runs Win 98. He's constantly dragging it around to clients, plugging into strange networks, and messing with it. Win 98 gives him the Plug-and-Play features he needs, the best performance out of a too-soon-to-be-aging processor and the best use of limited memory. Tamar prefers Win NT for her notebook—an updated, faster machine with sufficient RAM. In his office LAN, Ted runs several Win NT machines to support Internet services, client-server work and his e-mail system. In his home office, a peer-to-peer LAN hosts a couple old clunkers running Win 95 to provide print and file services while a standalone NT server provides IIS and SQL Server. Tamar, on the other hand, likes the simplicity of running the same OS on both her machines and sticks with NT across the board.

So what should you choose? It depends on your situation. On older and less powerful machines, Win 98 will give you better performance. On newer, faster machines, Win NT will give you greater reliability with a minimal performance hit. Since your clients are likely to be running a mix of machines and operating systems, wherever feasible we recommend you run both (despite Tamar's stubbornness on the subject).

"Oil Change, tune-up and a Freemanize, please"

If you've run computers for a while, you recognize they need regular maintenance. The case needs to be opened yearly and the dust blown out. Backups should be done regularly to prevent loss in case of hardware failure. Hard disks need to be defragmented. Directories storing temp files should be purged. But here's one you may not have considered:

Format your hard drive regularly.

"What!?" you scream. "It took me days to install all this stuff and now you want me to blow it all away?"

Yup. The Freeman treatment (named in honor of Dan Freeman, a Prince Among Men, Microsoft MVP and guru extraordinaire) is the only reliable cure we've found for all those little aches and pains: The Registry that just doesn't seem right anymore. The weird DLLs with names you can't fathom. The bloat of the System directory to hundreds of megabytes.

Blow it all away.

Radical as the idea seemed to us at first, it does make some sense. Developers who install, test and remove a bunch of stuff from their machines are likely to get machines that bog down after a while. Downloading lots of goodies from the Internet and installing beta packages ensures that some "stuff" gets left lying around on your hard drive. Finally, the occasional misbehaving application will overwrite a key system file with an older or less stable one, and that's it—you're out of business.

Plan for the inevitable. Log the files you install on your machine. Keep a network directory available with the "goodies" you can't live without. Get a serious backup device for the stuff you need to restore regularly—digital tape, ZIP, Jaz and SysQuest are worth considering. Archive the CDs with your key development tools on them. And, of course, make lots of backups.

"It's a Feature, Not a Bug"

It's not surprising that a language with as many different roots as FoxPro has a number of odd behaviors—things that make you say "hmmm." Some of them, of course, are bugs. But this section is dedicated to those that really aren't bugs—the ones for which there's a legitimate explanation. You'll also find a number of these items in the Reference section. Often, you'll find a design icon next to them.

We'll Continue to Try

Comments and continued lines can get you in trouble. On the whole, the trouble isn't as severe as it used to be (before VFP 5), but you can still get yourself in trouble.

The problem comes up when you put the continuation ";" after a comment. The next line is still considered part of the comment, even if it doesn't start with a '*'. So, the following:

```
* This is the comment before the command ;
SELECT Something FROM SomeWhere INTO SomeOne
```

is actually treated as a comment. The query never executes.

Personally we like to put a "*" at the beginning of each line of a comment, but there is a situation in which we find the above behavior pretty handy. Sometimes, we need to comment out a command for testing purposes or because we've replaced it with a new version. If the command is continued onto multiple lines, it's sufficient to just stick a "*" in front of the first line. Of course, starting in VFP 5, it's easy enough to highlight, right-click, and choose Comment, too.

In VFP 3 and FoxPro 2.x, there's another situation where continuation can get you in trouble. You can't put in-line comments on a continued line. That is, lines like:

```
SELECT Something  ;  && here's the fields
   FROM SomeWhere ;  && and the table
   INTO SomeOne      && put it here
```

fail because FoxPro just drops the ";" and concatenates the whole thing into a single line. This behavior was changed in VFP 5 to our great relief.

But There Didn't Used to Be a Syntax Error There

When people started running existing applications in VFP 5, lots of them started seeing syntax errors in code that had been running for years. The code hadn't changed, so what was going on?

Way back in Xbase history days, someone decided that you should be able to put comments on the same line as the structured programming commands without having to use the comment indicator. That is, you could write:

```
IF x<3   Fewer than three remain
   ...
ENDIF
```

The rule applied to each of the components of the branching and looping commands (IF, DO CASE, DO WHILE, FOR and SCAN). In fact, we have little doubt it was really set up this way so you could write stuff like the following:

```
DO WHILE .NOT. EOF()
   * process records
ENDDO WHILE .NOT. EOF()
```

It looks real nice, but it turned out to cause a rather nasty, subtle problem. When FoxPro parsed one of these lines, it stopped as soon as it reached something syntactically incorrect. That's right, as soon as the parser found a syntax error, it figured it had a comment and gave up. Consider, for example:

```
IF x<3 .AND y>7
```

As far as versions of FoxPro through VFP 3 are concerned, that line only checks whether x is less than 3. The second part of the condition was totally ignored. (By the way, the dots used to be required around the Boolean logical operators .AND., .NOT. and .OR.)

VFP 5 changed the rules. You're still allowed to include comments without an indicator on lines that don't have any executable code (like ENDDO, ENDIF, DO CASE and so on), but if a line contains code (like IF or DO WHILE), the whole line is checked. Since we think the original design decision was terrible, we're delighted by the change. Anything to help root out stubborn hidden bugs.

By the way, the parser got stricter in other ways as well. Used to be that extra right parens at the end of an expression were ignored. No more. In general, from VFP 5 forward, the compiler does a better job of finding syntax errors and ensuring that you're running the code you think you're running.

The Single Letter Blues

On the whole, the designers of Visual FoxPro have done a tremendous job marrying object-orientation to Xbase. But there are places where the marriage seems a little rocky. The use of single-letter identifiers is one of them.

Traditionally, the letters A through J are alternate names for the first 10 work areas. (When the number of work areas went up to 25, Fox Software didn't extend this convention. It's just as well—they'd have a heckuva time finding 32,767 different characters to represent the work areas in Visual FoxPro.) In addition, the letter M was reserved to indicate that what followed was a memory variable.

None of this ever caused anyone any trouble because when the letters were used for work areas, they were always followed by either the pseudo-arrow notation "->" or a dot "." to indicate that what followed was a field name.

Enter OOP. Object-orientation uses the same dot to spell out the complete name of an object, like frmMyForm.grdMainGrid.colName.txtName. The dot lets you walk up and down the containership hierarchy.

So what's the problem? There is none, unless you try to use one of the letters A-J or M for the name of an object. For backward-compatibility reasons, you can't do that. Code like the following:

```
a=CreateObject("form")
a.Caption="My Form"
```

is doomed to failure. You can create the form, but the assignment blows up on you as VFP goes looking for a field named Caption in the first work area.

Of course, single-letter variable names are a lousy idea anyway (most of the time—we're still fond of x, y, z, and o for quick and dirty testing), so the workaround for this isn't terribly painful. It's like the old joke—"Doctor, it hurts when I do this." "Then don't do that." Use names longer than one character and you'll never run into this problem.

But Why Doesn't It Run?

Here's a behavior that drove people nuts in FoxPro 2.x and, even though the whole context surrounding it has changed in Visual FoxPro, it continues to drive people nuts.

Say your user is entering a new record and is sitting on a field that requires validation. After entering bad data for that field, but before moving focus to another field, the user clicks the Save button on your toolbar or chooses Save from the menu. Whoosh—the data is saved, including the bad data. What happened?

In VFP, as in FoxPro 2.x, the Valid routine for a text field doesn't execute until focus leaves that field. Clicking a button on a toolbar or picking a menu item doesn't change focus and therefore doesn't fire the Valid method or the LostFocus method, of course. (In fact, a toolbar never has focus, which lets you do pretty cool things.)

Why does it behave this way? Because we want it to. It feels wrong in this situation, but suppose the toolbar or menu item the user chose was Select All or Paste. We sure wouldn't want the focus to change (and the Valid and LostFocus methods to fire) in that case.

So how do we make sure the data gets validated? Simple—make sure focus changes. One way to do this is to reset focus to the same field:

```
_SCREEN.ActiveForm.ActiveControl.SetFocus()
```

Since menus and toolbars don't get the focus, _SCREEN.ActiveForm is still the same form as before. We just set the focus back to the object that had it, which triggers that control's Valid, LostFocus, When and GotFocus methods.

Print What Where?

Letting users choose the printer for a report at runtime and having it automatically adjust itself for that printer's settings ought to be a piece of cake. Isn't that one of the things Windows is supposed to handle for us? Unfortunately, VFP tries to be too smart and ends up making things a lot harder than they need to be.

When you create a report with the Report Designer, information about the currently selected printer and its settings is stored in the first record of the report table (FRX). When you print the report, VFP checks that information and uses it. If the selected printer was the Windows default, VFP is smart enough to use whatever printer the user chose. But if the selected printer was something else, VFP assumes that you meant it when you created the report with that printer chosen, and it expects to print to that printer.

Why does it behave this way? Well, we think the developers were trying to be helpful. They figured that, if you'd gone to the trouble of configuring a printer specially for the report, they ought to pay attention. The problem with this is that the people using your application probably don't even have the same printer you do. The other problem is that this is such a non-intuitive way of arranging for special settings that we can't imagine anyone doing it on purpose.

So how do you get VFP to print to the user's chosen printer and honor that printer's settings? Easy—throw out the stored settings. The information is in the Tag, Tag2 and Expr fields of the first record of the report. Just blank 'em out.

Our friend Brad Schulz, who knows more about printing from FoxPro than anyone else, suggests making a copy of the report at runtime, blanking the Tag, Tag2 and Expr fields of the copy, then stuffing the Expr field (which is plain text in an INI-file type format) with the settings you really want. Then, use the copy to run the report.

It Ran Okay in VFP 5!

Normally, the folks at Microsoft (and, before them, the folks at Fox Software) go out of their way to make sure that, whatever they change in a new version of FoxPro, code that ran in the old version will still run in the new one. But in VFP 6, they broke that rule. Not only that, they did it on purpose. Say what?!

With the year 2000 nearly upon us, the Fox team figured it was about time to really make FoxPro developers aware of the bugs lurking in their old code. So they added the SET STRICTDATE command to help us find problems and to keep us from making them in the first place. When you turn STRICTDATE on, VFP lets you know if any of your code contains ambiguous dates. Great, that sounds good.

But here's the catch. By default, it's set to moderate strictness in the development environment. That means that any date or datetime constants that don't use the long unambiguous format (that is, {^1958-9-28} rather than {9/28/58}) cause an error. (See the Reference section for the details.)

Well, it's nice that they can find our errors for us, but why they heck didn't they make the old way the default? Because if they had, we'd keep going along in our misguided belief that our old code was Y2K-compliant. They're forcing us to pay attention.

About now, you're probably wondering how you're supposed to upgrade your users to VFP 6 if all your dates are going to fail. That's easy. By default, STRICTDATE is set to 0 for them (that is, at runtime), but you'll want to set it to 2 on your development machine so you can catch and squash these bugs way before January 1, 2000.

Commands Never to Use

Our fellow developers amaze us. Never have a group of such clever people created so many amazing applications. And how they do it is equally stupendous, using commands or features of this remarkable language that we knew of only peripherally, or with capabilities we only suspected. However, there are a few commands whose use should only be relegated to legacy code. These commands have been replaced by better, newer or safer commands; have never really had a reason to exist in the first place; or they just plain break the machine.

We divide our list into two parts: commands that should never, ever be used, and commands that should only be used from the command window. Some commands are just useless, and we have a few favorites which we recommend you avoid altogether. But then, there are some commands that do useful things but have too many side effects to let us feel comfortable bringing them into a client's application.

Never, Ever Use These Commands:

ACCEPT, INPUT

These commands are two of the original Xbase commands. They were a pain to work with then, and they're a pain now. ACCEPT and INPUT have no place in our visually designed, event-driven applications. You can't assign picture clauses, valid routines or events to them. They're not objects, nor can they be subclassed. Leave 'em alone.

DEFINE BOX

An odd duck of a command to begin with, DEFINE BOX doesn't work in Visual FoxPro at all.

INSERT

Not to be confused with the very useful SQL INSERT INTO command, the INSERT command forces a record to be physically placed between two others, forcing FoxPro to rewrite the remainder of the table. Now, before you get out your poison pens and inform us that in order to run the XYZ Personal Information Manager, you must pass it a DBF sorted in physical order, think about some alternatives and whether you really need to rewrite all those records, which is asking for trouble from I/O errors or power interruptions. Consider using a SQL-SELECT with an ORDER BY clause to create an output file when needed, in a programmable order.

JOIN

JOIN creates a new table by merging two tables, potentially adding all of the records from the second table for each record in the first—a condition referred to as a "Cartesian join." Why would you want to do this? Beats us. Although you can control exactly which records of the second table are matched with which records of the first, there is a far easier way to do this—use a SQL SELECT. In addition to the advantage of working with more commonly understood syntax, SELECT offers many more capabilities in terms of the order of output records, the join conditions, and the form of output. This command is one for the bit bucket. Avoid it.

SET COMPATIBLE ON

This dangerous command is made much more so because it's accessible through the General tab of the Tools/Options dialog, represented by a check box labeled "dBASE Compatibility". Sounds innocuous enough. After all, we all just want to get along, right? Don't we want to be compatible?

But SET COMPATIBLE ON is an oxymoron, as we discuss in the reference section. Not only does it make the language less compatible with anything else out there, but it breaks code left and right in ways you can't even imagine. Originally, in the FoxBASE days, this was a way to have your cake and eat it, too: fast Fox code wrapped within an IF FOX....ENDIF routine, and compatibility if you needed to compile with other Xbase languages as well. But there are so many places where dBASE and FoxPro have parted company that this command should never make it into a production system.

SET DOHISTORY ON

This precursor to the Trace Window allowed you to record commands as they occurred for later dissection. Like core dumps, they were useful for dissection once the patient was well dead, but this forensic style of debugging has been replaced with the interactive real-time diagnostics tools of the Debugger—in particular, the Trace Window. Also, as we mention in the reference section, dumping this file can slow down performance to a crawl. Skip it.

SORT

Same deal as INSERT and JOIN. Fast and efficient indexing make the physical order of the database almost irrelevant. If you must create a table in a particular order for output, consider using SQL-SELECT to generate the table. Using a Rushmore-optimizable query, output will be far faster, and much less disk space will be consumed.

SYS(12), SYS(23), SYS(24), SYS(1001)

These functions provide a suite of memory-reporting functions. In MS-DOS days gone by, we needed to check to make sure that EMS memory was allocated and available, that we had the room to create our objects and that we weren't going to crash on creating the next object. Now, with the Win32 virtual memory system, this is far less likely, even on marginal machines, and these functions can, on the whole, be ignored.

UPDATE

UPDATE (not the SQL version, the Xbase one) is a close relative of the JOIN command, and works with a similar logic. This command updates the contents of one table based on the contents of a second. The logic is a bit loopy, and should your orders or indexes not match, really bad things can happen. There are too many commands that will let you avoid attempting this nightmare function to list them all, but let's give you an idea of a few. If you're updating multiple records interactively, set table buffering to update them all at once. Try SCATTER and GATHER and their cool ARRAY keyword to batch a group of records programmatically. Update from a cursor with a SCAN....ENDSCAN logical structure. See? Many work-arounds, and no need to use (or even to try to understand) this old behemoth of a command.

Commands for the Command Window, Never in an Application

Despite the section heading, a few of these might even belong in test code, not just in the Command Window. But, for sure, none of them belongs in an application.

These commands don't have as many poor side effects as the killers listed above, and sometimes they can speed the development process. As developers, we should be able to understand their bad or unintended side effects, and use them only in appropriate circumstances. For instance, ZAPping or PACKing test data can be more efficient for us, and if the files are lost, you should be able to easily re-create them from a test data generator or backup.

ZAP

The fastest way to blow away all the records in a table, ZAP fails to fire the delete trigger of tables contained within a database. With SET CONFIRM OFF, ZAP, to paraphrase the immortal words of a sneaker commercial, just does it, with no confirming dialog. There is no "undo" within the language to recover the lost records.

So what's wrong with using ZAP when you know what it is you mean to do? There are too many scenarios where some event can trigger a change to the current work area in such a way that ZAP can blow away your hard-earned data. For example, an ON KEY LABEL routine that changes work areas as part of its processing, and sloppily fails to change it back, can work under most circumstances within your system. If most of your data-manipulation routines check to make sure they are in the right area before performing their tasks, the OKL will probably work fine and could go undetected for years. But, if that OKL fires between the lines of code (ON KEY LABELs can occur between any two lines of code), say, SELECT TEMP and ZAP, well, we hope you have made good backups.

Use cursors for temporary data instead. Issuing a USE IN command closes the cursor, and VFP can handle cleaning up the disk space on its own.

PACK

The next worst thing to ZAPping your data, PACK has the remote potential for a complete loss of the data file, and is so easy to code by hand that using the internal function is unnecessary.

PACK works by copying all records not marked for deletion to a temporary file. It then renames the old file to a new name, the new file to the original name, and blows away the old file. Some gurus maintain that there exists some critical portion of time between the first rename and the second when a catastrophic system failure (such as the complete loss of power) could leave us with no data files whatsoever. While we have never seen this case ourselves, we feel due caution is wise, considering how painful such a loss could be.

As a work-around, we prefer instead to issue the equivalent commands ourselves. SELECT the data from the original table into a new table (hint: using ORDER BY at this point can reorder the data into the most commonly accessed order, speeding later I/O). RENAME the old table and RENAME the new table. DELETE the old table. Obviously, you will want to check along the way for sufficient disk space, to ensure the new file is created, checking that the new file has the expected number of records, and so forth. Most add-on application frameworks and data dictionary extensions come with a routine to perform this function. Considering the ease of the work-arounds, we can't see much advantage to using the function, except when the loss of a little test data to a developer would be minor.

APPEND

APPEND was intended primarily as an interactive command. APPEND gives you a raw view of a file, suitable for dumping data into a system. If you're testing from the command line and you just need to pop one record into the table with a negative balance, this is an easy way to do it. But this is not an end-user interface. It gives raw field names, no help on the status bar, no tooltips, and worst of all, no application logic ("save this record only if..."). APPEND is good for quick-and-dirty data entry by a programmer; it's unsuitable for end users.

BROWSE/EDIT/CHANGE

Interactively, these are a fast way to change your data on the fly and get back to troubleshooting. Database container rules and triggers keep you from shooting yourself in the foot too badly, but you don't have to endure the overhead of starting the entire app, logging in and getting going if all you want to do is test a routine for one condition in the data.

On the other hand, the same capabilities that make these functions attractive to us can make them a killer in the hands of an end user. BROWSE is not really an easily trappable part of the event loop (though we know many developers who have made it work), meaning that "On Selection" and "Upon Leaving" events are difficult to fire with reliability. Sequencing of data entry is not enforced—you can jump all over the BROWSE fields if you'd like.

These commands provide too many capabilities and too little control to hand to our end users. Use forms and grids in your application instead.

CREATE

We find it astounding that the Table Designer is available in applications distributed with the FoxPro runtime files. What on earth are they thinking up there in Redmond?

If your users want to be able to create tables on their own, guide them through their choices with your own dialogs (perhaps even a custom Wizard), then use one of the CREATE commands to make the table. Check to make sure they're not overwriting the main tables of your application—you can bet they won't check!

FIND

FIND was also intended more for interactive use, and is included "for backward compatibility." It locates the first record whose index value matches the parameter passed with the FIND command. It's really nice to be able to type FIND GATES in the Command Window, but use SEEK or LOCATE instead in your apps.

MODIFY STRUCTURE

This is as dumb as the CREATE command above. Why on earth do you think your users would be interested in learning all the rules of good table- and field-naming conventions? Don't include it in your apps. If tables need to be changed on the fly, use the ALTER TABLE command instead.

Faster Than a Speeding Bullet

Speed is where it's at. No client is going to pay you to make his app run slower. Fox Software's initial claim to fame was that FoxBASE (and later, FoxBASE+ and FoxPro) ran faster than its competitors. Fox's reputation for speed was well deserved. However, the speed gain has never been automatic. You have to do things right to make your code "run like the Fox."

The Rushmore optimization technology introduced in FoxPro 2.0 is based on indexes. Rushmore examines index files to determine which records meet the conditions for a particular command. So, in order to make things fast, it's important to create the right indexes and to write code that takes advantage of those indexes. The difference between the lightning-fast code your client uses to make crucial strategic decisions and the plodding code his competition uses might differ by no more than an operator or two, so listen up!

There are also some other tricks, not related to Rushmore, that can speed up your applications considerably. This section discusses both Rushmore and non-Rushmore optimization techniques.

Scared by a Mountain in South Dakota?

Fox Software always claimed that Rushmore was named after Dr. Fulton and the development team watched Hitchcock's *North by Northwest*. But we have no doubt the name caught on due to the phrase "rush" embedded in it. In fact, some of the FoxPro documentation and advertising used the phrase "RUSH me some MORE records."

As we mentioned above, the key to getting the most from Rushmore is to create the right indexes and take advantage of them. So how do you know which are the right indexes, and how do you take advantage of them?

Rushmore can optimize the SET FILTER command, and any command involving a FOR clause, as well as SELECT-SQL. The secret (not really a secret—it is documented) is to make the left-hand side of each expression in the filter, FOR or WHERE clause exactly match an existing index tag. For example, to optimize:

```
SUM OrderTotal FOR state="PA"
```

you need an index tag for state. If your tag is on UPPER(state), instead, you'd want to write the command as:

```
SUM OrderTotal FOR UPPER(state)="PA"
```

Suppose you want to find everyone named Miller in a table of Clients and that you have a tag on UPPER(cLastName+cFirstName) to put folks in alphabetical order. You optimize the BROWSE by writing it as:

```
BROWSE FOR UPPER(cLastName+cFirstName)="MILLER"
```

even though you're really interested only in the last name.

It's All in What You Index

We've answered the second question—how to take advantage of existing tags—but we still haven't tackled the first: What are the right indexes to create? That's because it's not always straightforward. There are a few clear-cut rules, but to a great extent, you'll need to use your judgment and test your theories against your data, on your hardware. Here are the rules:

- Create a tag for your primary key, the field that uniquely identifies the record. (Do this whether or not you define it as a primary key in the database.) You'll need it to look up particular records and for setting relations. (If your table is in a database, you'll want a tag for the primary key anyway for creating persistent relations.)
- Create a tag for any field or expression you expect to search on frequently.
- Create a tag for any field or expression you think you'll want to filter data on frequently. (This is to let Rushmore kick in.)
- Make sure the tags you create exactly match the conditions you'll need to search or filter on.
- Don't automatically create tags on every field. (That's called inverting the table.) It can make adding and updating records slower than necessary, especially if you have a lot of fields in your table. On the flip side, if you have a table, especially one that is rarely changed, and you do use every field in filters, then go ahead and invert the table.
- Do not create indexes with a NOT expression for Rushmore optimization. Rushmore ignores any tag whose expression contains NOT. If you need the NOT expression, say, for a filter, create both indexes, one with and one without the NOT.
- Don't filter your tags. That is, don't use the FOR clause of the INDEX command. Tags that are filtered are *ignored* by Rushmore. If you need a filtered tag for some reason, and you're likely to filter on that tag's index expression as well, create an unfiltered tag, too.

In general, you'll be trading off update speed for search speed. So, think about what you expect to do with this table. If it's going to have lots of additions but few searches, keep the number of tags to a minimum. If it'll be used for lots of searching, but rarely updated, create more tags.

But I Didn't Delete Any Records!

One of the optimization tips that fools lots of people has to do with SET DELETED. The typical conversation goes something like this:

"I have a query that's taking too long. How can I speed it up?"

"Create a tag on DELETED() for each table, if you have SET DELETED ON."

"But there are only a few deleted records. That shouldn't make much difference."

"Try it anyway."

(Later)

"You're right. It's much faster now. But there are only a few deleted records. How come it matters so much?"

What's going on here? In fact, you'll see the same speed-up even with NO deleted records. It's the setting of DELETED that matters.

Here's the point. Even in many complex queries and FOR clauses, Rushmore performs its magic almost entirely on the relatively small and compact CDX file, a file structured with nodes, branches and leaves to be searched efficiently. When DELETED is ON, FoxPro has to check each and every record in a result set (whether from a query, a filter, or FOR) to see if it's deleted—even if no records are actually deleted. This sequential reading of the entire cursor or file completely defeats the benefits of Rushmore. Don't do it!

By creating a tag on DELETED(), you let Rushmore do the checking instead of looking at each record sequentially, which makes the whole thing much faster. The larger the result set, the more speed-up you'll see.

Going Nowhere Fast

Another common problem goes like this. In troubleshooting sessions we attend, someone complains that a filter should be optimized, but it's dog slow. He's asked to show the filter and the tags. Everything looks good for Rushmore to optimize the filter. Puzzling.

Then he shows the code he's using. Typically, it looks something like this:

```
SET FILTER TO <something optimizable>
GO TOP    && put filter in effect
```

and the light goes on. GO TOP and GO BOTTOM are not optimizable commands. They move through the records sequentially, attempting to find the first record matching the filter.

Without a filter (and with SET DELETED OFF), this isn't generally a problem. Moving to the top or bottom of the current order is pretty quick. FoxPro can either locate the first or last record in the index or, if no tag is set, move directly to the beginning or end of the file.

But when a filter is set (or DELETED is ON, which is like having a filter set), once GO gets to the first or last record in the order, it has to search sequentially for the first record that matches the filter condition. This is what's so slow. Smart like a fox, eh? What a dumb idea! This is like you writing code to go to record 10 by issuing a SKIP, asking if this is RECNO()=10, and if not, SKIPping again.

What can you do about it? Don't use GO TOP and GO BOTTOM. How do you avoid them? By using a neat trick. It turns out that LOCATE with no FOR clause goes to the first record in the current order. So, for GO TOP, you just issue LOCATE, like this:

```
SET FILTER TO <optimizable condition>
LOCATE   && same as GO TOP
```

Okay, that works for finding the first record. What about the last record? You have to stand on your head for this. Well, almost. You really have to stand the table on its head. Try it like this:

```
SET FILTER TO <optimizable condition>

* reverse index order
lDescending=DESCENDING()
IF lDescending
   SET ORDER TO ORDER() ASCENDING
ELSE
   SET ORDER TO ORDER() DESCENDING
ENDIF
* now Top is Bottom and Bottom is Top
LOCATE  && same as GO TOP

IF lDescending
   SET ORDER TO ORDER() DESCENDING
ELSE
   SET ORDER TO ORDER() ASCENDING
ENDIF
```

After setting the filter (or with a filter already in effect), you turn the index upside down. If it was ascending, you make it descending; if it was descending, you make it ascending. Then, use LOCATE to go to the first record. Since you've reversed the order, that's the last record in the order you want. Then, reverse the order again. Voila! You're on the bottom record.

By the way, the code above works only if there is an index order set. If there might be no order, you have to check for that.

One more warning. Under particular circumstances, the work-around can be very slightly slower than just using

GO. In most cases, though, it tends to be an order of magnitude faster. We think it's worth it.

HAVING noWHERE Else To Go

SQL-SELECT has two clauses that filter data: WHERE and HAVING. A good grasp of the English language might lead us to believe that these are synonyms, but SQL is not English, and mixing these two indiscriminately is a sure-fire disaster in the making! It's not obvious where a particular condition should go at first glance. But getting it wrong can lead to a significant slowdown.

Here's why. The conditions in WHERE filter the original data. Wherever possible, existing index tags are used to speed things up. This produces an intermediate set of results. HAVING operates on the intermediate results, with no tags in sight. So, by definition, HAVING is slower than WHERE, if a query is otherwise constructed to be optimized.

So, when should you use HAVING? When you group data with GROUP BY and want to filter not on data from the original tables, but on "aggregate data" formed as the results of the grouping. For example, if you group customers by state, counting the number in each, and you're interested only in states with three or more customers, you'd put the condition COUNT(*)>=3 in the HAVING clause.

```
SELECT cState,COUNT(*) ;
       FROM Customer ;
       GROUP BY cState ;
       HAVING COUNT(*)>=3
```

A simple rule of thumb: Don't use HAVING unless you also have a GROUP BY. That doesn't cover all the cases, but it eliminates many mistakes. To make the rule complete, remember that a condition in HAVING should contain one of the aggregate functions (COUNT, SUM, AVG, MAX or MIN) or a field that was named with AS and uses an aggregate function.

The Only Good Header is No Header

FoxPro lets you store procedures and functions in a variety of places. But using the Project Manager gives you a strong incentive to put each routine in a separate PRG file. We generally agree with this choice.

But, if you're not careful, there's a nasty performance penalty for doing so. It turns out that having a PROCEDURE or FUNCTION statement at the beginning of a stand-alone PRG file increases the execution time by a factor of as much as 10!

You read that right. It can take 10 times as long to execute a PRG that begins with PROCEDURE or FUNCTION as one with no header. Hearing about this goodie (no, we didn't discover it ourselves), we tested a couple of other alternatives. It turns out that using DO <routine> IN <PRG file> cuts the penalty down some, but it's still twice as slow as simply eliminating or commenting out the header line.

SETting PROCEDURE TO the PRG, then calling the routine, speeds things up if you only have to do it once, but issuing SET PROCEDURE TO over and over again (as you'd need to for many different PRGs) is about 20 times slower than the slow way. That is, it's 200 times slower than omitting the header in the first place.

But wait, there's more. Not surprisingly, if the routine you're calling isn't in the current directory, but somewhere along a path you've set, it takes a little longer. For an ordinary routine with no header, the difference isn't much. Same thing if you're using SET PROCEDURE (which you shouldn't be, except for coded class libraries). However, the other two cases get a lot slower when they have to search a path. Using DO <routine> IN <PRG file> when the file isn't in the current directory is just about as slow as doing a SET PROCEDURE. But that's only the bad case. The horrible situation is calling a routine with a PROCEDURE or FUNCTION header directly—it can be as much as 1000 times slower than calling the same routine without the header!

The good news is that the path penalties go away as soon as you add the routines to a project and build an APP or EXE. That is, unless you're running in a very unusual setup, your users are unlikely to pay this price.

Bottom line. When you migrate a routine into a stand-alone PRG file, comment out the header line and just start with the code. It's easy and it'll speed up your applications considerably.

Loops Aren't Just for Belts

FoxPro offers three different ways to write a loop. Choosing the right one can make a big difference in your program. So can making sure you put only what you have to inside the loop.

Let's start with the second statement. Every command or function you put inside a loop gets executed every time through the loop. (Big surprise.) Put enough extra stuff in there and you can really slow a program down. The trick is to put each statement only where you need it. This is especially true when you've got nested loops—putting a command farther in than it has to be might mean it gets executed dozens more times than necessary.

Bottom line here: If the command doesn't depend on some characteristic of the loop (like the loop counter or the current record) and it doesn't change a variable that's changed elsewhere in the loop, it can probably go outside the loop.

Here's an example:

```
* Assume aRay is a 2-D array containing all numeric data
* We're looking for a row where the sum of the first three
* columns is greater than 100
lFound = .F.
nRowCnt = 1
DO WHILE NOT lFound AND nRowCnt<=ALEN(aRay,1)
   IF aRay[nRowCnt,1]+aRay[nRowCnt,2]+aRay[nRowCnt,3]>100
      lFound = .T.
   ELSE
      lFound = .F.
      nRowCnt=nRowCnt+1
   ENDIF
ENDDO
```

The version below eliminates repeated calls to ALEN() and the need for the lFound variable. Benchmarks with 10,000 records show that it's almost twice as fast as the original.

```
nNumofRows = ALEN(aRay,1)
DO WHILE aRay[nRowCnt,1]+aRay[nRowCnt,2]+aRay[nRowCnt,3] <= 100 ;
   AND nRowCnt < nNumofRows
  nRowCnt = nRowCnt + 1
ENDDO
```

We find we're most likely to make this particular mistake when we're dealing with nested loops, so scrutinize those especially.

What's This Good FOR?

In the case of loops that execute a fixed number of times, FOR is a better choice than DO WHILE. Because the counting and checking feature is built into FOR, it just plain goes faster than DO WHILE. In a simple test with a loop that did nothing at all except loop, FOR was more than 10 times faster than DO WHILE. Never write a loop like this:

```
nCnt = 1
DO WHILE nCnt <= nTopValue
   * do something here
   nCnt=nCnt+1
ENDDO
```

Always use this instead:

```
FOR nCnt = 1 TO nTopValue
   * do something here
ENDFOR
```

SCANning the Territory

Guess what? DO WHILE isn't the best choice for looping through records either. SCAN was designed to process a table efficiently and does it faster than DO WHILE. Our results show that SCAN is one-and-a-half to two times faster to simply go through an unordered table one record at a time. (This is where we have to come clean and admit that the phenomenal differences we reported in the original *Hacker's Guide* appear to have been flawed. We're seeing about the same results in VFP 3.0b and 5.0a as we are in 6.0.)

To give full disclosure, we did find that with some index orders, DO WHILE was as much as 20 percent faster. With other indexes, SCAN is faster, although it doesn't appear to have the same advantage as in an unordered table. (It's also worth noting that, with large tables, if the memory allocation to FoxPro isn't property tuned—see below—DO WHILE can be faster than SCAN.)

A word to the wise here: Don't just globally replace your DO WHILE loops with SCAN...ENDSCAN. SCAN has a built-in SKIP function—if your code already has logic to perform a SKIP within the loop, you can inadvertently skip over some records. Make sure to pull out those SKIPs.

To Wrap or Not to Wrap

One of the new capabilities that OOP gives us is "wrapper classes." These classes let us take a collection of related capabilities and put them all into a single class. The class gives us a more consistent interface to the functions involved and generally presents a tidy package.

The Connection Manager class described in the Reference section (see SQLConnect()) is pretty much a wrapper class, though it adds some capabilities. We've seen folks suggest wrapper classes for the FoxTools library (which desperately needs a consistent interface despite the addition of lots of its residents to the language). During the beta test for VFP 3, we played around on and off for months with a wrapper class for array functions that would let us stop worrying about things like the second parameter to ALEN().

On the whole, wrapper classes sound pretty attractive. Unfortunately, they also add a fair amount of overhead.

There's another way to do the same thing—just create an old-fashioned procedure file. Now that SET PROCEDURE has an ADDITIVE clause, it's no big deal to have lots of procedure libraries around. It turns out, of course, that procedure libraries also carry an overhead penalty.

Because the contents of the class or library matter so much, it's hard to produce benchmarks that give you hard and fast rules about this stuff. We tested with our embryonic array handler class, using only some of the simpler methods included (aIsArray, aElemCount, aRowCount, aColCount, aIs2D—all of which do exactly what their names suggest). We set it up as a class and as a procedure library. Then, we wrote a program that made a sample series of calls. We also wrote the same functionality in native code (ALEN() for aElemCount, ALEN(,1) for aRowCount and so on).

The sad result is that either a procedure library or a class is an order of magnitude slower than using the built-in functionality. In this example, the procedure library is faster than the class by about a third.

We also tested the same functions as stand-alone programs. The timing came out pretty much the same as the procedure library and the class. (The difference between this case and the timing reported in "The Only Good Header is No Header" is that a single SET PROCEDURE was used in this case rather than issuing SET PROCEDURE for each function call.)

Finally, we tested with everything (the test program, the stand-alone programs, the procedure file and the class definition) built into a single APP file. Using an APP improved the speed of each case a little, but didn't make a significant difference overall.

Our guess is that, as functionality becomes more complex, the overhead counts less. Given the other, overwhelming benefits of using modular code, we don't recommend you stop writing procedures. But, at this point, we can't recommend wrapper classes where a procedure library would do.

There are some benefits to a wrapper class, of course. The biggest benefit is the ability to sub-class to provide specialized behaviors. Where this is a possibility, it's worth the overhead.

What's in a Name?

You wouldn't think that a little thing like a name would matter so much. But it does. The name we're referring to is the Name property possessed by almost every object you can create in Visual FoxPro. (A few of the weird marriages of Xbase to OOP, like SCATTER NAME, produce objects without a Name property.)

When you CreateObject() an object whose class definition doesn't assign a value to the Name property, Visual FoxPro makes one up for you. That's nice. Except it insists on making it unique (usually, the class name or a variant thereof, followed by one or more digits, like Form3 or Text17). The problem is, as the number of objects of that class grows, making sure a name is unique takes longer and longer. The Microsoft folks say the time grows exponentially. We suspect that's an overstatement and that it's actually geometric. What it ain't is linear. What it really ain't is fast enough. (Before we go any further with this, we should point out that this applies only to code classes. All VCX-based classes have an implicit assignment of the Name property.)

We tested with a pair of very simple classes based on Custom. One contained nothing. The other contained an explicit assignment to Name. With 10 repetitions, the explicitly named class would instantiate so fast it couldn't be measured, but the nameless class was fast, too. By 100 repetitions, explicit naming was more than four times as fast. At 1,000 repetitions, the explicit version was eight to 10 times faster. At 5,000 of each class, explicit names are about 18 times faster than nameless objects to instantiate.

The moral of the story here is easy. Always assign a value to the Name property for any class you write in code.

Incidentally, it turns out that getting rid of all these objects once you instantiate is pretty expensive, too. Working with VCX-based classes, it took almost six times as long to destroy 5000 of the same object than to create them. With our explicitly named code class, destroying 5000 instances took two to three times as long as creating them.

Looks Can Be Deceiving

But, in this case, they're not. The form property LockScreen lets you make a series of changes to a form without the individual changes showing as you go. When you set LockScreen to .F., all the changes occur simultaneously. Visually, it's far more consistent.

We were all set to tell you that this is one of those times where the user's eyes will play tricks on him. He'll think the update is faster because he doesn't see the individual changes take place.

But guess what? The update really is faster this way. We tested a simple form with just a few controls. We changed only a few properties of the form (Height, Width, BackColor, ForeColor and Caption) once each. With LockScreen set to .T., the updates were about one-and-a half times faster. Surprise—the version that looks better is faster, too. We suspect it's because Windows only has to redraw the screen once.

What Type of Var are You?

Testing the type of a variable or field is one of those things we do a lot in our code. In VFP 6, it's something we can do faster than ever. The new VARTYPE() function is significantly faster than its predecessor, TYPE(). How much faster? With both variables and fields, we consistently find VARTYPE() three to four times as fast as TYPE().

One warning here. VARTYPE() is appropriate only for fields, variables, properties and the like. You can't use it with expressions to find out what type the result will be. In that case, you need TYPE(), which pseudo-evaluates the expression to find out the result type. VARTYPE() simply looks at what you pass it and tells you its type. So, VARTYPE("x+y") returns "C", regardless of the type of x and y, while TYPE("x+y") returns "N". So, don't throw

TYPE() out of your toolkit quite yet.

How to Create an Object and Other Mysteries of Life

VFP 6 also introduces a new way to create objects. The NewObject() function lets you instantiate objects without worrying about whether you've pointed to the class library ahead of time—instead, you just include the library name in the call. CreateObject(), of course, needs a Set ClassLib or SET PROCEDURE ahead of time.

So which way is faster? As usual, the answer is "it depends." With VCX-based classes, if you can issue Set ClassLib just once and then instantiate classes from that library repeatedly, CreateObject() is the way to go. It's anywhere from one-and-a-half to eight times faster than calling NewObject() with the class library. On the other hand, if you need to load the library each time, the Set ClassLib/CreateObject() pair is more than an order of magnitude slower than NewObject().

How about for classes written in code? In that case, issuing a single SET PROCEDURE and calling CreateObject() repeatedly is an order of magnitude faster than either NewObject() or the SET PROCEDURE/CreateObject() pair, which are pretty similar.

Oh, and one more—instantiating a coded class is a little faster than instantiating a VCX-based class. However, except in the case where you're setting the library each time (which you should never do), it's not enough faster to wipe out the benefits of developing classes visually.

We tested and found no performance penalty for having a lot of class libraries open, no matter where in the list the class you're instantiating is found. So the rule here is to think about how you're going to do things before you write the code and, if possible, just keep open the class libraries you use a lot. Then use NewObject() for the one-shots, the classes from libraries you need only once in a while.

Can You Have Too Much Memory?

It turns out that, in VFP, the answer is "yes." When you start VFP, it figures out how much memory it ought to be able to use, if it needs it. The number is generally about half as much as the machine actually has. Often, the amount that VFP picks is too much.

How can you have too much memory? Like this, according to our buddy Mac Rubel, who knows more about this topic than anyone else—more even, we suspect, than the folks who wrote VFP. However much memory VFP grabs, it assumes it has that much *physical* memory to work with. But, because it takes so much memory, it often doesn't—some of the memory it's working with is really disk space pretending to be memory, and that's slow. By decreasing the amount of memory VFP thinks it has available, you ensure that it only uses physical memory. VFP knows what to do when it needs more memory than it has available, and it's good at that. The last thing you want happening is the operating system swapping virtual (disk) memory for real memory while FoxPro thinks it is using RAM. So, as long as you restrict it to using physical memory, things are fast, fast, fast.

Okay, so how do you that? Use the SYS(3050) function. SYS(3050,1) controls foreground memory, the memory VFP has available when it's in charge. SYS(3050,2) is for background memory—how much memory FoxPro should have when you're off doing something else. In either case, you pass it a number and it rounds that down to a number it likes (multiples of 256) and that's how much memory it uses. It even tells you how much it really took.

We were really amazed how much of a difference this setting makes. On Tamar's machine with 64MB of RAM, VFP 6 takes 35,072 MB by default. Reducing it to just under 24,000 MB (by calling SYS(3050,1,24000000)) cut the time needed for one of the particularly slow tests in this section by a factor of 4! One disclaimer here: Tamar tends to operate with lots of applications open. A typical load while working on this book was six or seven apps running (not to mention those living in the system tray, like Dial-Up Networking and a virus checker). No doubt they all take some memory.

Practice, Practice, Practice

All of the tips we've given you here should speed up your code, but *your* application on *your* LAN with *your* data is the true test. Differences in network throughput, the architecture of your system, the design of your tables, your choice of indexes, the phase of the moon, what's on TV that night, and so forth all make significant differences in the performance you see. Our advice is always to examine and benchmark how a particular change affects your system. Keep in mind that a single test isn't conclusive unless it can be repeated, and you need to repeat tests with caution because FoxPro and the operating system and the network and even your disk controller might be caching information.

Section 4: Visual FoxPro Reference

"But 'glory' doesn't mean 'a nice knockdown argument'," Alice objected.
"When I use a word," Humpty Dumpty said, in rather a scornful tone, "it means just what I choose it to mean—neither more nor less."
"The question is," said Alice, "whether you can make words mean so many different things."
"The question is," said Humpty Dumpty, "which is to be master—that's all."

Lewis Carroll, *Through the Looking-Glass*, 1872

Section 4 is the meat of the book. You'll find a listing for every command, function, property, event, method and system variable. We've grouped them logically so that you can find several related topics in one place. There are cross-references, so you'll be pointed to the right topic even if you look up a related topic, and every item is listed alphabetically, even if it's only to say "See Flibbertigibbet."

For an explanation of the syntax we use for commands, see "How to Use This Book," back in the Introduction.

$ See At().

%, Mod()

The % operator and MOD() both compute the modulus of a pair of numbers. For those who never liked math in the first place, that's the remainder when you divide the first number by the second. (Actually, it is for the rest of us, too.) Another way to think of it is as the part you throw away when you apply FLOOR() to the quotient.

Usage

```
nRemainder = nDividend % nDivisor
nRemainder = MOD( nDividend, nDivisor )
```

Parameter	Value	Meaning
nDividend	Currency, Double, Integer, Numeric	The number being divided. (The number after "goes into".)
nDivisor	Currency, Double, Integer, Numeric	The number doing the dividing. (The number before "goes into".)
nRemainder	Number	The remainder when nDividend is divided by nDivisor.

MOD() and % are pretty straightforward when dealing with positive numbers, but they get interesting when one or both of the numbers is negative. The key to understanding the results is the following equation:

```
MOD(x,y) = x - (y * FLOOR(x/y))
```

Since the mathematical modulo operation isn't defined for negative numbers, it's a pleasure to see that the FoxPro definitions are mathematically consistent. However, they may be different from what you'd initially expect, so you may want to check for negative divisors or dividends.

A little testing (and the manuals) tells us that a positive divisor gives a positive result while a negative divisor gives a negative result.

MOD() is most useful when you want to set up intervals of some sort. For example, you might use it in a DynamicBackColor condition to get alternating colors in a grid.

Example

```
? 10%3          && returns 1
? MOD(22, 10)   && returns 2
? MOD(-7, 3)    && returns 2
? MOD(-7, -3)   && returns -1
? MOD(7, -3)    && returns -2
```

The type of the result depends on the divisor and the dividend. When you mix Currency and Numeric or Integer, the result is always currency. But when you mix Currency with Double, the divisor determines the result type, which is as it should be. The behavior of Currency with numbers feels like a bug to us. In any case, the various numeric types should all behave the same way.

See Also Ceiling(), Floor()

&, Evaluate(), ()

Sometimes you need to refer to a file without knowing its name or you need to build up an expression and then execute it. Think of & (macro expansion), EVALUATE() (better known as EVAL()) and () (called "indirect reference" or "name expression") as the guillotine that performs the execution. Hmmm, maybe that's not such a good analogy.

In any case, all three items are used to let you write code when you don't know exactly what should happen when the code is run. There are three levels, which correspond to the three choices.

Usage

```
(cName)
uResult = EVAL(cExpression)
&cString
```

First, perhaps you want to let a user select a report to run, or you'd like to use the same piece of code to open several different tables. Indirect reference lets you put a name in a variable and refer to the variable instead of giving the specific name. For example, if you write:

```
USE (m.cFileName)
```

FoxPro evaluates the variable cFileName and substitutes the name found there in the USE command.

Indirect reference works only when FoxPro expects a name. So you can't write something like:

```
BROWSE FOR (m.cExpression)
```

because FoxPro expects an expression there, not a name.

Which brings us neatly to the next level. When FoxPro expects an expression, you can use EVAL(), which tells FoxPro to evaluate the named variable, then use that result as part of the command. (Incidentally, TYPE() and EVAL() use exactly the same level of indirection. If you have trouble figuring out what parameter to pass to TYPE(), imagine that you're passing it to EVAL() to be evaluated.)

For example, in the BROWSE above, you could write:

```
BROWSE FOR EVAL(m.cExpression)
```

It turns out, though, that it's not a great idea to use EVAL() in a FOR clause. We'll explain why below. But here's a better example of EVAL():

```
STORE EVAL(cFieldName) TO SomeVar
```

EVAL() is essential in reports, where macro expansion doesn't work. You can use expressions like:

```
EVAL(FIELD(1))
```

to handle reporting on query results where the field names are unknown (such as in a crosstab). You can also use:

```
EVAL(cGroupExpr)
```

as a grouping expression to avoid designing separate reports where grouping is the only difference.

Finally, there are times when you want to build up whole pieces of code and then execute them. In this case, the string contains more than just an expression, perhaps even an entire command. Here, you need macro expansion. (These are "real" macros, not to be confused with the wimpy keyboard macros covered in SAVE MACROS, PLAY MACRO, and RESTORE MACRO. Keyboard macros are just a simplistic recording and playback of keystrokes. This macro expansion—arguably one of Fox's most powerful commands—tells Fox to interpret, compile and execute the code on the fly.) Macros are also used to substitute for reserved words. For example, you've probably written something like this:

```
cOldSafety=SET("SAFETY")
SET SAFETY OFF
* some code

SET SAFETY &cOldSafety
```

Here, the "ON" or "OFF" that was stored in cOldSafety is a character string, but the command SET SAFETY expects a keyword of ON or OFF. The & macro operator converts the string to a keyword.

Another common place for a macro is in queries. You might build up any of the field list, the table list or the WHERE clause in a string and then macro-expand it like this:

```
SELECT &cFieldList ;
    FROM &cTableList ;
    WHERE &cWhere
```

Macros are powerful and work almost everywhere (though not, as noted above, in reports). There are a couple of gotchas, though.

First, only variables can be macro expanded. You can't apply a macro to a field or property. So, you need two steps when the string to be expanded is in a field or property. Say the field cCmd contains an entire command to be executed by macro expansion. You have to do it like this:

```
cVar=cCmd
&cVar
```

The second gotcha is sort of a consequence of the first. When you macro-expand a variable, you can't use the "m." variable notation. This is okay because you can't macro-expand a field, so there's no ambiguity. But why does it work this way?

The "." is a terminator for macro expansion. (Boy, this is a gory topic. We've got "executed" commands and "terminators." Where's Arnold?) This means the string to be expanded ends as soon as you reach a period. This can be very convenient if you want to add something to the expanded string or expand several strings in sequence. Before the addition of indirect reference to the Fox language in 2.0, it was essential because you could write something like:

```
USE &cFileName..EXT
```

but now, with named expressions, it's better to write:

```
USE (cFileName+".EXT")
```

We still find uses for the double period in something like:

```
lcAlias = alias()
* more code in here
xx = &lcAlias..Field1
```

or:

```
ThisForm.pgfPageFrame.&PageName..Control.Property = .T.
```

though you could use EVAL(lcAlias+".Field1") in the first case.

The consequence of the period as terminator is what happens when you write something like:

```
&m.cVar
```

FoxPro sees this as "macro expand m, then tack the results onto 'cVar'." Since you don't usually have a character variable called "m", generally you get an error message when you do this. Even if there is a variable m, you certainly don't get what you wanted.

What about performance? We often see people going to great lengths to eliminate macros from their code. But the truth is that, in certain cases, macros are actually faster than EVAL(). Here are some guidelines:

Always use indirect reference rather than EVAL() or a macro. If FoxPro expects a name, indirect reference is the right choice.

In a command that will be executed repeatedly, it's generally better to use a macro than EVAL(). The macro is expanded once and substituted into the command while an EVAL() expression is evaluated each time the command executes. This is also true for scoped commands that apply to multiple records, like the BROWSE above. The macro is expanded once and the result used on each record; EVAL() is re-evaluated for each record. So, for the BROWSE above, you're better off issuing:

```
BROWSE FOR &cExpression
```

Macros that execute only once aren't really all that slow. The place to avoid macros is inside loops.

See Also Type()

=, Store

This operator and command let you assign a value to a memory variable. The results are the same, but STORE lets you save the same value to multiple variables. Both let you save a single value to all elements of an existing array.

Usage

```
Variable = uExpression
STORE uExpression TO Variable1 [, Variable2 [...] ]
```

STORE and = work only on variables and properties. A very common mistake (we can't tell you how often we've made it) is to try to use = to store a value in a field; it doesn't work. In fact, unlike most places in FoxPro, if you have a memvar and field with the same name, STORE and = assume you mean the memvar. (Most commands assume an unqualified, ambiguous reference is to a field.) Because of this, there's never a reason to use the "m." notation when assigning a value with = or STORE, and there's good reason not to—it turns out that assignment is faster without the "m."

Another way to save time with STORE is to use a single statement to initialize a bunch of variables:

```
STORE 0 to nOne, nTwo, nThree, nFour, nFive
```

is faster than:

```
nOne = 0
nTwo = 0
nThree = 0
nFour = 0
nFive = 0
```

STORE is also handy when you're writing generic code because it lets you use a name expression rather than a macro, typically a faster and less resource-intensive operation. That is, if cVarName contains the name of a variable, you can write:

```
STORE 0 TO (cVarName)
```

rather than:

```
&cVarName = 0
```

If the variable is an existing array and SET COMPATIBLE is OFF, the value of uExpression is stored in every element of the array. This is a quick way to initialize an array. With SET COMPATIBLE ON, the array is overwritten by a single memvar that gets the value of uExpression.

Objects change the game with = and STORE. You can use them with objects. What you get is a new reference to the same object, not a copy of the object. There isn't any easy way to create an exact copy of an object. We can think of some brute-force ways, but they're not pretty.

Example

```
dToday=DATE()
STORE 0 TO nTotal,nCount
DIMENSION aTotals[5]
aTotals=5
oObj1.SomeProperty="Old Value"
oObj2=oObj1
oObj1.SomeProperty="New Value"
? oObj2.SomeProperty          && Returns "New Value"
```

See Also Replace, Set Compatible

\, \\ See Set TextMerge.

* See Note.

@ Commands

These commands were among the most important commands in every version of FoxBase and FoxPro until VFP.

With the movement to control-based forms, the @ commands for controlling input and output move over to the "included for backward compatibility" category.

Don't write any new code in Visual FoxPro that uses the @ commands. As for converting older code, it's a hard call. So far, we're leaving our existing apps happily in 2.x and beginning only new projects or complete revisions in Visual FoxPro.

Nonetheless, you might have to move some old screens into Visual FoxPro. You have two choices: Maintain the screen in 2.x and use the generated SPR in Visual FoxPro, or let the Converter start the transition toward object-oriented input. The Converter itself also offers two choices—Functional Conversion and Visual Conversion. Functional Conversion gives you something you can use immediately, but at the cost of pretty ugly internal structure. Visual Conversion leaves you with work to be done, but moves you farther along the path to true object orientation.

Since they supplied us with the code, we expect that eventually we could get the Converter to produce code we'd be willing to maintain at a client site years down the road, but with 9000 pretty abstruse lines of code to decipher in the Converter, we generally feel it is easier to start with a clean slate and develop new forms, leaving the @ ... SAYs and GETs behind in 2.x. Besides, hasn't the client always been complaining about one piece of functionality in this screen? And things that need to get moved in that one? And don't you really need to re-engineer the way that query gets built? See what we mean? Start from scratch and give your clients their money's worth.

After several years of watching people struggle to get their 2.x code to run in VFP, we feel even more strongly about not doing it. However, we also recognize that some people have humongous applications that need to move forward for one reason or another. Our best advice is to check out the incremental conversion methodology developed by MicroEndeavors, Inc. that lets you keep your app running while you slowly move it to VFP.

You can mix and match the @ commands with Visual FoxPro's controls, so a form could contain both a Visual FoxPro text box and an @...GET. But we can't think of any reason you'd actually want to do this. If you want to put stuff right on the form, use the form's drawing methods: Box, Circle, Line and Print.

The entries for the individual @ commands do not go into great detail because we don't think you should use them in Visual FoxPro. If you need more information, pick up one of the excellent references available for FoxPro 2.x—see "Resource File" for some suggestions.

@ ... Box, @ ... To, @ ... Clear, @ ... Fill

These @ commands all relate to drawing on a window. @ ... BOX and @ ... TO draw boxes, @ ... CLEAR clears a rectangular area (sort of the inverse of drawing a box, we guess) and @ ... FILL fills a rectangular area with color.

There's no reason to use these commands ever. Use Visual FoxPro's controls and drawing methods instead. They're more powerful and better behaved.

See Also @ Commands, Box, Circle, Cls, Line, Shape

@ ... Class

The @ ... Class command allows you to create objects programmatically on a form. We recommend using the Form Designer rather than this command.

Usage
```
@ nRow, nColumn CLASS cClassName NAME nObjName
```

Parameter	Value	Meaning
nRow	Numeric	Row on which the object should appear. Equivalent to objName.Top.
nColumn	Numeric	Column in which the object should appear. Equivalent to objName.Left.
cClassName	Character	Name of a FoxPro built-in class or a hand-coded class definition.
nObjName	Character	The name for the object. The object's properties, events and methods can be referenced using this name.

We think Microsoft supplied this command to offer a method of converting your code gradually into the OOP way of doing things without having to convert hand-coded interfaces into the visual Form Designer all at one time. By changing your code from @...SAY and @...GET to @...CLASS, they probably thought you could start to use the more intuitive properties, events and methods without having to learn all of the kinks of using Forms. This might be a good idea under some very specific circumstances, but generally we advocate skipping this command and going right for the Form Designer. The Form Designer offers far more capabilities, and will be more easily maintainable than this odd duck of a command. What Microsoft has supplied here is a command with its own, different kinks from those you're going to have to learn sooner or later, anyhow.

This command does require a READ command to activate the controls. Also, don't be surprised if the controls appear inside a Pageframe1, on a first (and only) Page1, automagically added to your form when you issue the @ ... CLASS command.

Example

```
ON KEY LABEL F11 CLEAR READ
oForm = CREATEOBJECT("Form")
oForm.Show()
@ 10,10 CLASS "TextBox" NAME txtMyTextBox
oForm.PageFrame1.Page1.txtMyTextBox.Value = "Ta-da!"
oForm.PageFrame1.Page1.txtMyTextBox.BackColor = 255
READ  && press F11 to get out of this weird READ
```

See Also Read

@ ... Clear **See @ ... Box.**

@ ... Edit

This is the old way to create an Edit box or at least something that looks more or less like an Edit box, but without the properties, events and methods. Why bother? Use an Edit box instead.

See Also @ Commands, Edit box

@ ... Fill **See @ ... Box.**

@ ... Get

The @ ... GET command, in its various forms, puts FoxPro 2.x-style controls on a form. A READ then activates these controls. This whole mechanism is obsolete in Visual FoxPro. Don't use it for anything new. Use the corresponding Visual FoxPro controls instead.

Some controls had their names changed in this transition. Here's a list showing old FoxSpeak and new MicrosoftSpeak:

FoxPro 2.x Control Name	VFP Control Name
@ ... GET	TextBox
@ ... EDIT	EditBox
Check Box	CheckBox
Invisible Button	CommandButton (hint: Style=2)
List or Scrollable List	ListBox
Popup or DropDown	ComboBox
Push Button	CommandButton
Push Button Set	CommandGroup
Radio Button	OptionButton
Radio Button Set	OptionGroup
Spinner	Spinner

See Also @ Commands, CheckBox, ComboBox, CommandButton, CommandGroup, EditBox, ListBox, OptionButton, OptionGroup, Spinner, TextBox

@ ... Menu, Read Menu

These commands make up one of three obsolete menu schemes that, somehow, continue to work in Visual FoxPro. A truly hot item back in FoxBase, these commands let you create a popup menu using an array to contain the commands. If you do things just right, you can probably combine these menus with the light-bar menus of @ ... PROMPT and get something that looks almost like a Windows-style menu. Why bother?

@ ... MENU and READ MENU have no place in Visual FoxPro applications. Use the Menu Designer and standard Windows menus.

See Also Menus

@ ... Prompt, Menu To

Back in the late '80s, the light-bar menus used in Lotus 1-2-3 were cool. Any application that had them was thoroughly modern. So, of course, our FoxBase applications could include light-bar menus.

This is the late '90s. Light bar menus aren't cool anymore. Use the Menu Designer.

See Also Menus

@ ... Say

This obsolete command can put text right on a form, collect input with its optional GET clause, or display bitmaps and other OLE objects. Use label controls for the text capability, text boxes for the GET portion, and Images, OLEBound controls and OLEContainer controls for bitmaps and OLE objects.

See Also @ Commands, Image, Label, OLEBound, OLEContainer, TextBox

@ ... Say-BMP and OLE Objects

This is a funny command. Most @ ... SAY commands are purely for passive output. This command combines the typical "display this field" command with the option of specifying actions for the OLE object to perform. Most of the functionality of this command has been replaced with OLEControls and OLEBoundControls and their DoVerb methods.

We can't see a reason for using this command in new code, rather than using the new OLEBoundControl, OLEControl or Image controls. Placement and sizing can be controlled in the visual design tools, or with the associated Top, Left, Width and Height properties. The STYLE keyword maps to the BackStyle property for Images. The CENTER, ISOMETRIC and STRETCH keywords are available through the Stretch property, and the VERB keyword has been replaced with the DoVerb method. We detail this functionality to aid you in transporting a 2.x application to Visual FoxPro, but will be surprised if you can find a use for this command in Visual FoxPro.

Example

```
@ 0,0 SAY smplgrph.myGraph VERB "Edit"
```

See Also DoVerb, Image, OLEBoundControl, OLEControl, Registration Database

@ ... Scroll

This command would be a cool one if it produced the magic scroll you need to get to the next level in the adventure game, perhaps with some cool window-shade-scrolling effects, but alas, it is another of the legacy commands, left over from a character-based world long, long ago, and best avoided like the plague.

Usage

```
@ nRow, nColumn SCROLL
   [ LEFT | RIGHT | UP | DOWN ]
   [ BY nIncrement ]
```

Although some interesting effects can be created with this command, generally we feel it is best left alone. Like the form's direct drawing methods (Box, Circle, Line, etc.), the scrolling that takes place is overwritten when the screen or page is refreshed, as underlying objects which are moved do not have their appropriate properties changed. Use the Top, Left, Height and Width properties of objects to move them around on a form.

Example

```
@ 5,5 to 10, 10 SCROLL UP by 2
```

See Also Move, Scroll

@ ... To See @ ... Box.

?, ??, Set Space, Set("Space")

These commands let you produce streaming output (as opposed to the line-oriented output of @ .. SAY). ? and ?? produce output. SET SPACE determines whether a space is used between output items.

Usage

```
? | ?? [ uExpr1 [ PICTURE cMask ]
              [ FUNCTION [ cCodes ] [ V nWidth ] ]
       [ AT nColumn ]
       [ FONT cFontName [, nFontSize ] [ STYLE cStyleCodes ] ]
       [ , eExpr2 [ ... ] ] ]
SET SPACE ON | OFF
cSpaceSetting = SET("SPACE")
```

Parameter	Value	Meaning
uExpr*n*	Expression	The *n*th expression to print.

Parameter	Value	Meaning
cMask	Character	Output mask using the same codes as the InputMask property.
cCodes	Character	Function codes using the same list as the Format property.
nWidth	Numeric	The number of columns to devote to this item.
nColumn	Numeric	Starting column for this item.
cFontName	Character	Font to use for this item.
nFontSize	Numeric	Font size to use for this item.
cStyleCodes	Character	List of style codes to use in the specified font.

? streams output including a carriage return and line feed, while ?? sends output without those characters. When we first learned Xbase, it took us the longest time to understand that ? sends the CR/LF pair before it prints. So, to send several items on one line followed by a new line, you use a series of ?? and then issue ?.

Over the years, ? and ?? have gotten more and more powerful, acquiring much of the functionality of @ .. SAY. We use these a lot more than @ .. SAY, though, because they're handy for sending output to the active window when you're testing. However, we rarely use either one in applications.

When you include several expressions in a single command, each can have its own font and position clauses. Be careful how you combine them, though, because the column you specify in the AT clause is computed based on that item's font. It's easy to overwrite one item with another.

??CHR(7) is the traditional way to sound the bell in FoxPro. It still works just fine with one warning. You'll probably want to specify a small font for it because it can (eventually) make the active window scroll up. Two-point Arial works just fine. (SET BELL controls the frequency and duration of the tone.)

By default, when you include multiple items with ? or ??, a single space appears between them. SET SPACE OFF to run them together.

Example

```
? $12345 PICTURE "999,999,999" FUNCTION "$"  && displays $12,345
USE Employee
? First_Name,Last_Name   && Looks good
SET SPACE OFF
? First_Name,Last_Name   && Looks awful
```

See Also @ ... Say, Format, InputMask, Set, Set Bell, Set Print

&& See Note.

:: See DoDefault().

???

This operator sends its operands directly to the printer ... sort of.

Usage `??? cCodes`

In FoxPro/DOS, this was an incredibly useful operator. In simple cases, we used it to send printer control codes so we didn't have to mess with FoxPro's complex printer driver system. Unlike characters sent with other commands, these don't change FoxPro's tracking of the position of the print head in PCOL().

In Visual FoxPro, however, ??? is useless. In order to actually send the characters, you have to issue SET PRINT TO (which terminates the print job and gets Print Manager to actually send something through). We don't think our users want us to waste a sheet of paper every time we want to send control codes. Even if you can get the characters through to the printer, the next thing you send (like a report) reinitializes the printer and your settings are lost. Forget it—just don't bother.

Besides, it's not the Windows way. Printer drivers are our friends (at least most of the time).

See Also ?, ??, PCol(), Set Print

Abs(), Sign()

These two functions let you take the sign off a number.

Usage

```
nAbsoluteValue = ABS( nValue )
nSign = SIGN( nValue )
```

ABS() returns the absolute value of the number, that is, the number without the sign. SIGN() does the reverse and returns the sign without the number—it uses 1, 0 and -1 to represent positive, zero and negative signs, respectively. ABS() and SIGN() work on all four number types: currency, double, integer and numeric.

Example

```
? ABS(37)       && returns 37
? ABS(-37)      && returns 37
? SIGN(37)      && returns 1
? SIGN(-37)     && returns -1
? SIGN(0)       && returns 0
```

ABS() and SIGN() both handle null values, returning .NULL.

See Also Int()

Accept, Input

These are antique, obsolete, dinosaurous ways to get user input. They date back to the very origins of Xbase. Don't use them.

Usage

```
ACCEPT [ cPrompt ] TO cVariable
INPUT [ cPrompt ] TO Variable
```

ACCEPT can be used only for character input. INPUT accepts characters, numbers, dates, datetimes, logicals and currency, but characters must be delimited by quotes or square brackets, logicals (and .NULL.) by periods, dates and datetimes by curly brackets, and currency preceded by your currency symbol.

Not only are these commands totally obscure, but the results are likely to be ugly. The prompt is displayed in the font of the window that contains it, while the user's input is always displayed in 9-point FoxFont. That's as good a reason as any to stay away from these commands.

Example

```
ACCEPT "Enter a String" TO cStr
INPUT "Enter a Number" TO nNum
```

See Also Form, Text box, Wait

Access, Assign

These methods, added in VFP 6, make it easier to write good OOP code. Every property of an object can have an Access method and an Assign method. The property's Access method fires whenever the property is read (accessed) while its Assign method fires whenever the property is changed (assigned).

Usage

```
PROCEDURE property_Access

PROCEDURE property_Assign
LPARAMETERS uNewValue
```

One of the key OOP themes is encapsulation, the idea that an object should know how to take care of itself. These methods take that idea one step further and let a *property* take care of itself.

Ordinarily, when a property value is used or changed, there's nothing we can do about it because no event fires. When properties are bound to controls, we can take advantage of the control's events to notice changes to the bound properties, but that still leaves us with no way to respond to the use of properties or to changes to properties not bound to controls. Similarly, if we know a property is being used or changed in code, we can write more code at that point to deal with the change. But it requires us to know that the property is used or changed and to make sure we remember to add the code every single time.

Access and Assign methods take a different point of view. They belong to the property and monitor everything that happens to that property. When anyone looks at the property's value, the property's Access method fires. When anyone saves a value to the property, the property's Assign method fires. This means we can respond immediately to both uses and changes of a property.

Why do we care? Ever had one property that should be updated whenever another one gets changed? Ever wanted to keep track of the number of times a value is read? Ever wanted to create a read-only public property? Until now, we've always had to handle these situations by writing code wherever the property gets changed or wherever it gets used. Now we can encapsulate that code with the property itself so that we don't have to remember to copy the right code or call the right routine every time.

Not only do Access and Assign methods give you new events to hook into, they also let you control what the outside world can see and do with a property. A property's Access method is called before the value is provided to the code using the property—you can jump in and change what gets returned. Specifically, the code that uses the property sees the return value of the Access method, not the actual value stored in the property. So you can do things like have a different internal representation of a property than what the world sees.

As for the Assign method, it too gets called before the operation actually occurs. The new value is passed as a parameter. It's up to you whether the value actually gets assigned to the property. You can do any validity checking you want (so only a limited set of values are accepted), ignore the new value altogether (creating a de facto read-only property), change the input, or whatever. When you add an Assign method for a property, it gets created with a line setting the property to the parameter value, but you can change it if you want.

Access and Assign methods don't just apply to properties; there's also a special This_Access method that fires at the object level. This can lead to some very, er, interesting and powerful behaviors, like the third example below. In that example, if a property of an object does not exist, when an attempt is made to access it, the object creates the property on the fly! This_Access even fires when a method of the object is called.

As with the property-specific Access and Assign methods, This_Access fires first. It returns an object reference—the actual behavior that was requested is applied to that object. That's right—you can redirect a method call or a request for a property value or an attempt to assign a value to an entirely different object than the one mentioned in the call. It seems to us that you'd want to do such a thing only very rarely. Littering your code with this kind of thing is the path to ravioli code (the OOP equivalent of spaghetti code—code that's impossible to trace and understand).

We suspect there's a fair amount of overhead in calling these methods, so don't create them indiscriminately. Save them for those properties where they really make a difference.

On to practical matters. You create Access and Assign methods through the New Property dialog or the Edit Property/Method dialog. Each contains check boxes for Access and Assign. Checking either one adds that method for that property. The name of the method is propertyname_Access or propertyname_Assign. You can also create Access and Assign methods using the New Method dialog. Just watch your spelling.

You can even create Access and Assign methods for built-in properties of classes. Use the Edit Property/Method dialog. To do this for forms (created with the Form Designer), you have to create the methods using New Method—the form's built-in properties don't show up in the Edit Property/Method dialog. That's probably because forms aren't really sure whether they're objects or classes.

Once you create the methods, they appear in the usual places for methods: the Methods tab of the property sheet, the drop-down list in the method-editing window, and so forth. Because they already contain code, though, they're always in the top group in the method editor.

Example

```
* Make BackColor read-only
PROCEDURE backcolor_assign
LPARAMETERS vNewVal
* Throw away the new value
RETURN

* Limit a custom property to values between 1 and 10
PROCEDURE myproperty_assign
LPARAMETERS vNewVal

IF VARTYPE(vNewVal)<>"N"
   ERROR 1732  && "Data type invalid for this property"
ELSE
   IF BETWEEN(vNewVal,1,10)
      This.MyProperty = m.vNewVal
   ELSE
      ERROR 46  && "Expression evaluated to an illegal value"
   ENDIF
ENDIF
RETURN

* Make sure a property contains the right value when it's used.
* In this case, perimeter is meant to be the perimeter of a
* quadrilateral, so it should always be the sum of the
* four sides.
PROCEDURE perimeter_access

This.Perimeter = This.Side1 + This.Side2 + ;
                 This.Side3 + This.Side4
RETURN This.Perimeter

* Demonstration of on-the-fly property creation using
* This_Access

oDear = CreateObject("cusTestAA")

? oDear.False  && displays .F. for the newly-created property
oDear.BackColor = RGB(255,255,255)
? oDear.BackColor  && shows the numeric equivalent of white
release oDear

return

DEFINE CLASS cusTestAA as Custom
  PROCEDURE This_Access
  LPARAMETERS cMember
  * Determine if the member already exists
  IF PemStatus(This, cMember, 5)  && already exists, okay
  ELSE
    This.AddProperty(cMember)
  ENDIF
  RETURN This
ENDDEFINE
```

Access(), Call(), Catalog(), CError(), Change(), Clear Screen, Close Printer, Completed(), Convert, DExport, DGen(), Display History, Id(), IsMarked(), List History, LkSys(), Network(), Protect, Reset, Run(), Set Catalog, Set DBTrap, Set Design, Set IBlock, Set Instruct, Set LdCheck, Set MBlock, Set Precision, Set SQL, Set Trap, User()

What these commands and functions have in common is that they're all listed in the VFP Help (one version or another) as unsupported and coming from dBase IV. However, they can actually be divided into three groups: those that give errors, those that are simply ignored but don't give errors, and those that actually do something.

The first group, the ones that generate errors, includes CALL(), CATALOG(), CERROR(), CONVERT, DEXPORT, DGEN(), ISMARKED(), LKSYS(), PROTECT, RESET, RUN() and USER(). If you're converting dBase code that uses these items, you'll have to change it to get it to run.

The next group is a lot more benign, though likely to need changes, too. These items run without error, but either do nothing or do nothing useful. The members of this group are ACCESS(), CHANGE(), CLEAR SCREEN, COMPLETED(), DISPLAY HISTORY, LIST HISTORY, NETWORK() and all the SET commands listed, except for SET MBLOCK. If you're counting on one of these commands to change something, or on one of these functions to return a meaningful value, think again. (Incidentally, all the SET commands here have SET() counterparts that always return their hard-coded values.) The exact behavior of each of these items is listed in Help (search for "Unsupported dBASE IV Commands, Functions, and Clauses"), so we won't get into it here.

Finally, three of these supposedly unsupported commands actually do something. CLOSE PRINTER is equivalent to SET PRINTER TO—that is, it turns off the printer and restores the default printer setting.

SET MBLOCK is a little more interesting. This is a cousin to FoxPro's SET BLOCKSIZE command. It lets you specify the size of the chunks allocated for memo fields. However, it works a little differently (albeit more simply). The number you specify is multiplied by 64 to give the blocksize. SET("MBLOCK") returns the current setting, in the same scale.

ID() may be the most intriguing of the bunch. It returns the machine identification, including information about the current user. Help says the second part is the network machine number or 1, if there's no network, but that's not what we're seeing. On Tamar's desk machine (which has a network card, but is not attached to a network), ID() returns "TAMAR'S DELL # Tamar", exactly the same thing as SYS(0).

Example

```
? SET("BLOCK")   && 64, by default
? SET("MBLOCK")  && 1
SET MBLOCK TO 2
? SET("BLOCK")   && 128
```

See Also Set BlockSize, Set Printer

AClass()

AClass() lets you take an object and find out its entire lineage. An object is based on a class. That class may be a sub-class of another class, which may be a sub-class of another, and so on and so forth. AClass() stuffs the entire class hierarchy for the object into an array.

Usage `nLevels = ACLASS( ArrayName, oObject )`

Parameter	Value	Meaning
ArrayName	Name	Array to hold class hierarchy for oObject.

Parameter	Value	Meaning
oObject	Object	The object for which to trace the class hierarchy.
nLevels	Positive number	The number of rows in the array, which is the number of levels in the class hierarchy.
	0	ArrayName can't be created.

The class on which oObject is based goes in the first array element. That class' parent class goes in the second element and so forth. The last array element holds the name of the Visual FoxPro base class on which the entire hierarchy is based.

Because the function gives an error if oObject isn't an object or you pass too many or too few parameters, we haven't been able to find a case where AClass() returns 0. Nonetheless, it's good to know that the FoxPro development team has coded for all the oddball situations.

Example

```
oForm = CREATEOBJECT("Form") && create a new form
= AClass(aFormHier, oForm)   && creates a one-element array
                             && containing "FORM"

SET CLASSLIB TO \VFP\WIZARDS\WIZSTYLE  && wizard classes
oBoxFld = CREATEOBJECT("BoxField")
= AClass(aBoxHier, oBoxFld) && in VFP 6, creates a three-
                            && element array, with "BOXFIELD" in
                            && 1st element, "BOXBASE in 2nd
                            && and "CONTAINER" in 3rd.
```

See Also AInstance(), AMembers(), Array Manipulation, CreateObject(), Define Class

ACopy()

This function copies data from one array to another. Sounds simple, doesn't it? But it's not because ACOPY() doesn't require a one-to-one correspondence between the two arrays. You can copy from any consecutive set of elements in the source array to consecutive positions anywhere in the destination array. You can even copy data from one place to another in the same array! As with many array functions, ACOPY() doesn't care if the arrays you hand it are one-dimensional or two-dimensional; it treats them as one-dimensional. You supply a starting element and number of elements to copy from the source array and a starting element in the destination array.

Usage

```
nNumberCopied = ACOPY(SourceArray, DestArray [, nSourceStart
                       [, nSourceLength [, nDestStart ] ] ] )
```

Parameter	Value	Meaning
SourceArray	Array Name	The array containing the data to be copied. It can be one- or two-dimensional, but must exist.
DestArray	Array Name	The array to which data is copied. If it doesn't exist, Visual FoxPro creates it and makes it identical in dimensions to SourceArray. If it's too small to hold the number of elements copied, as many elements as fit are copied and then an error is generated. If DestArray is larger than the number of items copied, extra array elements are left alone. If DestArray has a different shape, elements are simply copied in order and the array is *not* reshaped to match the source.
nSourceStart	Numeric	The first element of SourceArray to be copied. This is always an element number, even if SourceArray is two-dimensional.

Parameter	Value	Meaning
nSourceStart	Omitted	All elements in SourceArray are copied.
nSourceLength	Numeric	The number of elements copied.
	Omitted	All elements from nSourceStart to the end of the array are copied.
nDestStart	Numeric	The first element of DestArray where copied data is placed. Copying continues from that element toward the end of the array.
	Omitted	Data is placed in DestArray beginning at the first element.
nNumberCopied	Numeric	The number of items copied.

As with other array functions, one of the tricks to understanding ACOPY() is the dual nature of FoxPro's two-dimensional arrays. Much of FoxPro's internal processing treats two-dimensional arrays as if they were one-dimensional, assigning each element an "element number" by going across each row in turn. (For example, the first item in the third row of a 3x2 array is element 5.) The two starting values in ACOPY(), nSourceStart and nDestStart, use this element notation.

Example

```
DIMENSION aSample[3,2]
* fill the array
FOR nCnt = 1 TO 6
    aSample[nCnt]=nCnt
ENDFOR
* copy the whole array
= ACOPY(aSample, aNew)
DISPLAY MEMORY LIKE A*  && shows new array
                        && identical to the original
* copy the last row
= ACOPY(aSample, aOneRow, 5)
DISPLAY MEMORY LIKE A*  && shows new array
                        && with one row filled in
* copy the second row
= ACOPY(aSample, aSecond, 3, 2)
DISPLAY MEMORY LIKE A*  && shows new array
                        && again one row filled in
* create a large, one-dimensional array
DIMENSION aLarge[50]
* copy the entire first array positioning at item 11
= ACOPY(aSample, aLarge, 1, 6, 11)
DISPLAY MEMORY LIKE A*  && show result
* now copy last 3 elements positioning at item 25
= ACOPY(aSample, aLarge, 4, 3, 25)
DISPLAY MEMORY  && show result
```

The examples show one really weird behavior of ACOPY(). When the destination array doesn't exist, FoxPro creates it and makes it match the source array. Sounds sensible, except for one thing. It does it even when copying only a subset of the element in the source. Take a look again at what happens when you copy only one row of the source to aOneRow—the new array is still 3x2 even though only the first row contains data. This behavior is documented, but we can't see why it was designed this way.

By now, you may have noticed that while ACOPY() is great for copying all the elements in an array or copying a group of rows, it's totally useless if you want to copy one or more columns. That's because of the way FoxPro handles two-dimensional arrays. Since we get asked about this a lot, here's a function that copies the data from one or more columns. Unlike ACOPY(), you do have to create the second array before you call the function in order to pass it (by reference) as a parameter. If the array is too small, aColCopy() redimensions it to the appropriate size to hold the copied data in the specified position. (If you pass a variable that's not an array, it gets turned into an appropriate array.) aColCopy() does require you to pass the number of the first column to copy since there's no reason to use it to copy a whole array.

```
FUNCTION aColCopy
* Copy one or more columns from a source array to a destination array.

LPARAMETERS aSource, aDest, nStartCol, nColCount, nDestCol
  * aSource = array to be copied
  * aDest = destination array
  * nStartCol = first column to copy - required
  * nColCount = number of columns to copy - optional.
  *             Go to end of aSource, if omitted
  * nDestCol = first column of destination to receive copied data - optional
  *            1 if omitted

LOCAL nRetVal,nOldRows,nOldCols,nOldCount,nItem
  * nRetVal = return value, number of columns copied.
  *         = -1, if can't copy

* Check source array
IF TYPE("aSource[1]")="U" OR ALEN(aSource,2)=0
  * not a 2-d array, can't do it
  RETURN -1
ENDIF

* Check for starting column
IF TYPE("nStartCol")<>"N"
  RETURN -1
ENDIF

* Check number of columns. Compute if necessary
IF TYPE("nColCount")<>"N" OR nStartCol+nColCount>ALEN(aSource,2)
  nColCount=ALEN(aSource,2)-nStartCol+1
ENDIF

* Check destination column.
IF TYPE("nDestCol")<>"N"
  nDestCol=1
ENDIF

* Check destination array for size. It must exist to be passed in.
* First, make sure it's an array.
* Then, see if it's shaped right for all the data.
* Two cases - if enough cols, but not enough rows, can just add
* If not enough cols, have to move data around.
IF TYPE("aDest[1]")="U"
  DIMENSION aDest[ALEN(aSource,1),nColCount+nDestCol-1]
ELSE
  IF ALEN(aDest,2)>=nColCount+nDestCol-1  && enough columns
    IF ALEN(aDest,1)<ALEN(aSource,1)   && not enough rows
      DIMENSION aDest[ALEN(aSource,1),ALEN(aDest,2)]  && add some
    ENDIF
  ELSE
    * now the hard one
    * not enough columns, so need to add more (and maybe rows, too)
    nOldRows=ALEN(aDest,1)
    nOldCols=ALEN(aDest,2)
    nOldCount=ALEN(aDest)
    DIMENSION aDest[MAX(nOldRows,ALEN(aSource,1)),nColCount+nDestCol-1]

    * DIMENSION doesn't preserve data location, so we need to adjust the data
    * We go backward from the end of the array toward the front, moving data
    * down, so we don't overwrite any data by accident

    FOR nItem=nOldCount TO 2 STEP -1
```

```
      * Use new item number and old dimensions to determine
      * new item number for each element
      IF nOldCols<>0
        nRow=CEILING(nItem/nOldCols)
        nCol=MOD(nItem,nOldCols)
        IF nCol=0
          nCol=1
        ENDIF
      ELSE
        nRow=nItem
        nCol=1
      ENDIF

      aDest[nRow,nCol]=aDest[nItem]
    ENDFOR
  ENDIF
ENDIF

* finally ready to start copying
FOR nCol=1 TO nColCount
  FOR nRow=1 TO ALEN(aSource,1)
    aDest[nRow,nDestCol+nCol-1]=aSource[nRow,nStartCol+nCol-1]
  ENDFOR
ENDFOR

RETURN nColCount*ALEN(aSource,1)
```

For example, suppose you want just the filenames from an ADIR() listing. You could use aColCopy() like this:

```
=ADIR(aFiles)
DIMENSION aNames[1]
=aColCopy(@aFiles,@aNames,1,1)
```

See Also ADel(), AElement(), AIns(), Array Manipulation, ASubscript(), Copy To Array, Dimension

ACos() See Cos().

Activate, Deactivate

These events fire when forms and pages become active or inactive.

Usage `PROCEDURE oObject.Activate | oObject.Deactivate`

Forms, formsets, toolbars and pages all have these events, and their behavior feels a little different for each. Let's start with toolbars because they're the simplest. A toolbar's Activate fires when you Show the toolbar. Its Deactivate fires when you Hide it. Period. End of story—even if the toolbar has a control on it that can gain focus. It doesn't matter—Activate doesn't fire even when you land on that control.

Pages next. A page's Activate fires in two situations—when that page comes to the top of the page frame (that is, when you change pages) and when focus on a form is on the page and the form is activated. (A page is not refreshed when it comes to the top; check out Refresh for details and UIEnable for a solution.) A page's Deactivate fires only when a different page in the page frame comes to the top. We can't figure out why the page behaves differently when the form is activated than when it's deactivated. We could argue this one either way—that is, we'd be comfortable with either the page's Activate and Deactivate firing when the form loses focus, or not firing when the form loses focus. But why are they different?

A form's Activate fires whenever that form comes to the top (conceptually—it may not be physically "on top"). Normally this happens because the user clicks on the form while another form has focus or because the tab sequence brings focus to a control on the form. A form's Deactivate fires whenever another form gets focus. Show and Hide fire Activate and Deactivate respectively, too.

Finally, the formset's Activate fires whenever any form in the set is activated. That's right, the formset's Activate fires when a different form comes to the top. In fact, the formset's Activate fires after the Deactivate of the old form and before the new form's Activate. The formset's Deactivate fires only when you Hide the formset or focus moves out of the formset.

Destroying an object does not fire its Deactivate event.

Example

```
* Only the active page in a pageframe is refreshed by
* the PageFrame's Refresh method. So, when you move a page
* to the top, it's generally a good idea to refresh it.
* You'd do that in the page's Activate method:
This.Refresh()
```

See Also Activate Window, Deactivate Window, Hide, Show, UIEnable

Activate Menu, Deactivate Menu, Activate Popup, Deactivate Popup

These commands do exactly what their names suggest. They turn on and off menu bars and menu popups. You're unlikely to ever need to issue the MENU versions of these commands—the Menu Designer handles all that. You might use the POPUP versions for context menus, but even there, mostly the Menu Designer takes care of this stuff.

Usage

```
ACTIVATE MENU MenuName [ NOWAIT ] [ PAD PadName ]
ACTIVATE POPUP PopupName [ AT nRow, nColumn ]
         [ BAR nMenuItemNumber ]
         [ NOWAIT ] [ REST ]
DEACTIVATE MENU MenuList | ALL
DEACTIVATE POPUP PopupList | ALL
```

The ACTIVATE commands here start a wait state (unless you include NOWAIT). When the corresponding DEACTIVATE is issued, control returns to the line following the ACTIVATE. With NOWAIT, it doesn't work that way. Instead, execution continues after the ACTIVATE, and the DEACTIVATE simply deactivates the thing and doesn't send control anywhere else.

The AT clause of DEFINE POPUP is a key to defining context menus. The row and column coordinates are specified in foxels. If your form's ScaleMode is pixels (as it should be), you'll need to do some conversion to place the popup where you want it. However, you shouldn't need to do this, except in VFP3. In later versions, the Menu Designer can handle all this for you.

The BAR clause lets you decide which item in the popup is initially highlighted. It doesn't work for system menu popups, only for those you define yourself. That's okay because, except in demos, it's not the Windows way to choose a bar for the user.

Example

```
* We wouldn't really do this in VFP though we did things
* like it all the time in FoxPro 2.x.
USE Employee
DEFINE POPUP EmpPop PROMPT FIELD ;
   TRIM(First_Name) + " " + TRIM(Last_Name)
ON SELECTION POPUP EmpPop DO Whozat
ACTIVATE POPUP EmpPop AT 0,10
RELEASE POPUP EmpPop

PROCEDURE Whozat
WAIT WINDOW "You picked " + PROMPT()
DEACT POPUP EmpPop
RETURN
```

See Also Define Menu, Define Popup, Menus, On Selection Menu, On Selection Popup, Release Menus, Release Popups

Activate Screen

By default, output from many commands goes to the active window. ACTIVATE SCREEN lets you direct it to the main Visual FoxPro window instead.

Usage `ACTIVATE SCREEN`

When a user-defined window (including one containing a form) is active, issuing a command like DISPLAY MEMORY or ? sends the output to the window. That's not usually what you want. It sure isn't when we do it. Issue ACTIVATE SCREEN before the DISPLAY whatever or ?, and the output goes to the main window instead.

Example

```
DEFINE WINDOW Test AT 0,0 SIZE 10,100
ACTIVATE WINDOW Test
* Now all output goes to window Test - prove it
DISPLAY MEMORY
* That's no good - try again
ACTIVATE SCREEN
DISPLAY MEMORY      && much better
RELEASE WINDOW Test && clean up
```

See Also Activate Window, _Screen

Activate Window See Define Window.

ActivateCell

This method lets you change the focus in a grid.

Usage `grdGrid.ActivateCell( nRelativeRow, nRelativeColumn )`

As the parameters indicate, this method operates relative to the visible portion of the grid. You can't use it to simply choose any record or field to gain focus. Parameters of (1,1) refer to the cell displayed in the upper left corner of the grid.

This method is weird. You can activate a cell in any column that's visible or to the right of the visible portion. You can only activate a cell in a row if at least part of that row is visible. No matter what, you can't go backward from the visible portion of the grid. A negative number is ignored for either parameter.

To set focus to a particular record, consider instead setting the record pointer to it with GO, LOCATE or SEEK. To move to a particular column, you can also use its SetFocus method. (You can do so even if the grid was created with ColumnCount = -1. The columns exist anyway as Column1, Column2, etc.)

Example

```
* This fails to find the first field of the first record
* if the leftmost column or topmost record
* has been scrolled off of the visible area:
Thisform.grdMyGrid.ActivateCell(1,1)
* On the other hand, this should work in all cases
LOCATE   && the better GO TOP
Thisform.grdMyGrid.Column1.SetFocus()
```

See Also ActiveColumn, ActiveRow, Go, Grid, Locate, Seek, SetFocus

ActiveColumn, ActiveRow

These grid properties tell you which column and row of a grid contain the focus. They're useful only when the grid has focus.

Usage
```
nCurrentColumn = grdGrid.ActiveColumn
nCurrentRow = grdGrid.ActiveRow
```

These properties return an absolute number measured from the first cell of the grid, regardless of what portion is visible now. ActiveColumn's value is based, however, on the visible order of the columns reflected by their ColumnOrder, not on the creation order that the Columns collection uses. What does this all mean? It means you'll never want to look at Columns[ActiveColumn], because it's meaningless.

You can't change the active cell with these properties. Use the ActivateCell method instead (though it works with relative rows and columns, not the absolute ones of these properties).

ActiveRow counts from the top of the grid. If you're looking at a table in natural, unfiltered order (SET ORDER TO 0 and SET DELETED OFF), ActiveRow is the same as RECNO(). As soon as you SET ORDER TO something or apply a filter, though, the two part company.

Accessing ActiveRow can be slow when dealing with large tables—in our tests in VFP 6, a loop through all the records in a grid took about four times as long to assign ActiveRow to a variable as to assign RECNO() to the variable.

Example
```
IF This.ActiveColumn = 3
  * Take an appropriate action
  WAIT WINDOW "Hey, we're in the third column"
ENDIF
```

See Also ActivateCell, Column, Columns, Grid, RelativeColumn, RelativeRow

ActiveControl See ActiveForm.

ActiveDoc

"Active" seems to be Microsoft's word for the end of the 1990s. We have ActiveX, Active Controls, Active Desktops, and now Active Documents. ActiveDoc is a new base class in VFP 6 that lets you run regular VFP apps in a browser. Frankly, we're not sure what's so "active" about these. In fact, "active doc" sounds to us like a physician who's always on the go, and doesn't make us think of browsers or applications or any of that.

Let's talk about the "how?" first and we'll address the "why?" (not to mention the "why not?") later on.

ActiveDoc is a shell into which you stuff your application. It handles all the interactions with the browser (called a "host" in the documentation, with the implication that there are lots of choices out there) and allows the application to run just as it always did. That's true to some extent, except, of course, that the interface you design for an app running under VFP probably isn't the same as what you'd design for a browser-based app. (We know, we said "why?" would come later, but it's hard not to say it now.)

The pieces all seem to work. The ActiveDoc gets things off and running and hands control over to a combination of the browser and the application. The browser talks to the active doc object, which in turn talks to the other portions of the app; there's even some chance for communication in the other direction.

Okay, we can't wait any more. What's wrong with this picture? The biggest issue is that the user has to have the VFP runtime available in order to run the app. That's right, you can't deploy an active doc application on the Web. You could use it on an intranet, but why bother? If every user needs the VFP runtime, why not just run a native VFP application? We haven't heard any satisfactory answers to that question, so we're not running out to turn all our apps into active doc apps.

But wait, there's more. Active doc apps are about the least stable thing we've encountered in VFP. We crashed VFP more testing active docs than any other portion of the product (okay, we crashed a late beta, but it was remarkably stable otherwise). We suspect the problems were related not to VFP itself, nor to IE 4 (which is the browser we tested with), but to the interactions between the two. Among the issues we encountered was finding abandoned, invisible VFP sessions when we shut down after working with active docs.

So is there any point to ActiveDocs at all, or is it just one of those features Microsoft added to the product so that they could claim VFP builds Web apps? We think the venue of ActiveDocs is going to be quite limited. This isn't the one-step solution for turning your networked VFP app into a Web app, but we're sure that clever VFP developers can come up with some hybridized applications taking advantage of VFP, DHTML and the IE scripting engine to create a solution that can't be created in any other way. We're looking forward to what the community can produce.

Despite all this, the design itself of the ActiveDoc object is fairly elegant. It has events that fire at appropriate times, including a couple that offer very sophisticated interaction with the browser.

Property	Value	Purpose
ContainerReleaseType	Numeric	Determines what happens when the browser releases the application.

Event	Purpose
CommandTargetExec	Fires when an action occurs in the browser that's not under the application's control, and gives the active doc a chance to modify or respond to the action.
CommandTargetQuery	Fires when there's a chance of browser action and lets the active doc decide what actions it wants to respond to.
ContainerRelease	Fires when something happens in the browser (like it gets shut down or the user navigates elsewhere) that means the application can't live there any more.
HideDoc	Fires when the user navigates away from the application.
Run	Fires when the application has been properly installed in the host (browser or VFP). This is the place to start things running.
ShowDoc	Fires when the user navigates to the active doc application and when the application first starts up.

See Also CommandTargetExec, CommandTargetQuery, ContainerRelease, ContainerReleaseType, HideDoc, Run, ShowDoc

ActiveForm, ActiveControl

When it comes to debugging, these may the two most important properties around. They give you a hook into whatever's going on at the moment. Both provide object references. ActiveForm points you to the form that contains the focus in a formset, or even just the form with focus without regard to formsets. ActiveControl points you to the control that has focus on a form.

Usage

```
frmCurrentForm = frsFormSet.ActiveForm
frmCurrentForm = _SCREEN.ActiveForm
oCurrentControl = frmForm.ActiveControl
```

Although these properties are themselves read-only (that's why the syntax goes only one way), you'll usually use them on the left-hand side of the "=" as part of a reference to a property of a form or a control on it. You can both test and change properties this way.

For debugging, the combination you'll use the most is _SCREEN.ActiveForm, which lets you touch the form that has focus. (You can also use _VFP.ActiveForm, but we suspect that, when you're working inside VFP, the _SCREEN format is cheaper.) You can put expressions like _SCREEN.ActiveForm.Height (or even _SCREEN.ActiveForm.pgfAbout.pagMemory.txtFreeMemory.Value) in the Watch window or in DebugOut commands and watch them change as you manipulate the form. You can also use similar expressions in the Command Window and assign new values to the properties to see how the changes affect the form. We use this technique extensively to cut down the design-test-design-test cycle. Just try things out on a live form. If you like it, incorporate it; otherwise, go on and try something else.

Utterly annoying, however, is that when you switch focus to the Debugger, ActiveControl no longer works. Even if the Debugger is sitting in its own frame. Since even our humongous monitors make it hard for us to position both VFP and the Debugger so that each is fully visible, this is truly a pain. Now that we have a really good debugger, among the things this complicates is drilling down into the control with focus. We have to go to the form level, find the right control (but how do we know which one it is when ActiveControl no longer tells us!), and start from there.

Because toolbars never get focus, ActiveForm and ActiveControl are useful in methods of the controls on toolbars. You can figure out where the user was before he or she clicked on the toolbar and take appropriate action. This simplifies sharing a toolbar among multiple forms.

When the focus is in a grid, ActiveControl always points to the grid rather than to the individual control within the grid which actually has focus. Thanks to our friend Drew Speedie, we have a way to climb down the containment hierarchy and find out which control is really is in control here, but it ain't pretty:

```
local lcActiveControl, lcJunk
loControl = _SCREEN.ActiveForm.ActiveControl
IF UPPER(ALLTRIM(loControl.BaseClass)) = "GRID"
  *  Name of the real ActiveControl:
  lcActiveControl = ;
  loControl.Columns[loControl.ActiveColumn].CurrentControl
  *  object reference to ActiveColumn:
  loControl = loControl.Columns[loControl.ActiveColumn]
  *  text string representing ActiveControl reference:
  lcJunk = "loControl." + lcActiveControl
  *  object reference to the real ActiveControl:
  loControl = &lcJunk
ENDIF
```

Example

```
* With a form running, you can change its
* title from the Command Window like this:
_SCREEN.ActiveForm.Caption = "Look what I can do!"

* To see the name of the control with focus:
? _SCREEN.ActiveForm.ActiveControl.Name

* To call a method of the active form from
* a button on a toolbar, put something like this
* in the button's Click:
_SCREEN.ActiveForm.Save()
```

See Also Form, FormSet, _SCREEN

ActivePage

This page frame property tells you which page is currently on top. Unlike similar properties for grids, this one lets you change things as well as find out what's going on.

Usage

```
pgfPageFrame.ActivePage = nWhichPage
nWhichPage = pgfPageFrame.ActivePage
```

ActivePage is based on the display order of the pages, not their creation order. That is, the page frame's ActivePage equals PageOrder for the page that's on top.

Unfortunately, the Pages collection uses creation order, so Pages[ActivePage] is meaningless. The only way to get from the number ActivePage returns to the actual object that is the current page is brute force—loop through all the pages until you find one whose PageOrder matches the PageOrder of the active page. (Of course, in a method of the page itself, you can use This.)

If you create an Assign method for ActivePage, it doesn't fire when you change pages by clicking on the new page. It does fire when you change pages using the keyboard or programmatically.

Example

```
* Find the active page in a page frame.
* Assume this is a pageframe method.
LOCAL nCurOrder, oCurPage, oActivePage

nCurOrder = This.ActivePage
FOR EACH oPage IN This.Pages
   IF oPage.PageOrder = nCurOrder
      oActivePage = oPage
      EXIT
   ENDIF
ENDFOR
* Now, act on oActivePage to manipulate the Active Page
```

See Also Page, Pages, Pageframe, PageOrder

ActiveProject

This property of the application object gives you access to the most recently used open project.

Usage

```
oProject = appApplication.ActiveProject
appApplication.ActiveProject.Property = uValue
uValue = appApplication.ActiveProject.Property
appApplication.ActiveProject.Method()
```

In VFP 6, you can manipulate projects programmatically. This property lets you figure out which one is on top so you can work with it. You access it through the _VFP variable or the Application object.

Beware. If no projects are open, accessing this property triggers an OLE error. Be sure to test with TYPE() (not VARTYPE()) or _VFP.Projects.Count > 0 before using it unless you know there's an open project.

Example

```
* Get a reference to the current project
oCurrentProj = Application.ActiveProject

* Display the name and last build date of the current project
?Application.ActiveProject.Name
?Application.ActiveProject.BuildDateTime
```

See Also Application, Project, Projects, _VFP

ActiveRow **See ActiveColumn.**

ADataBases()

This function fills an array with the list of open databases. It gives you both the name and the path for each database.

Usage

```
nCount = ADATABASES( aDatabaseArray )
```

Like the other array manipulation functions, ADATABASES() returns the number of rows in the array created. Similarly, if there are no open databases, ADATABASES() returns 0 and doesn't create or change (if it already exists) the specified array.

The function does not honor the setting of SET FULLPATH, but we think that's good. No matter what, the second column contains the full path to the database.

Example

```
CLOSE DATA ALL           && make sure no databases are open
? ADATABASES(aDbs)       && returns 0
OPEN DATA (_SAMPLES+"TasTrade\Data\TasTrade")
? ADATABASES(aDbs)       && returns 1
```

See Also ADBObjects(), Array Manipulation, AUsed(), Open Database

ADBObjects()

This function is really a whole bunch of different functions in one. It creates an array containing information about a database, but there are four different types of information that can be put in the array: tables, views, connections or relations. Unlike other functions returning status information, ADBObjects() only works on the current database; you can't tell it which database to look at.

Usage

```
nObjectCount = ADBOBJECTS( ArrayName, cInfoType )
```

Parameter	Value	Meaning
ArrayName	Name	The array into which database information is dumped.
cInfoType	"TABLE"	Put a list of tables in the database into the array.
	"VIEW"	Put a list of views in the database into the array.
	"CONNECTION"	Put a list of named connections in the database into the array.
	"RELATION"	Put a list of persistent relations in the database into the array.
nObjectCount	Positive number	The number of rows in the array (= the number of items of the specified type).
	0	No items of the specified type were found.

Unlike most other FoxPro keywords, cInfoType cannot be abbreviated. You must spell out "table", "view", "connection" or "relation." It's not case-sensitive, however; any combination of uppercase and lowercase will do.

When cInfoType is "TABLE", "VIEW" or "CONNECTION", the resulting array is one-dimensional and contains a list of the items of the specified type in the database. For "RELATION", a five-column array is created:

Column	Meaning
1	Child table.
2	Parent table.
3	The tag the relation is based on in the child table.
4	The tag the relation is based on in the parent table.

Column	Meaning
5	The referential integrity constraints on the relation in the order Update, Delete, Insert. For each type of integrity, there are three possible values: C = cascade R = restrict I = ignore If no referential integrity of a type was defined, that position is empty.

The possible values in the fifth column (referential integrity) depend on the trigger. The Insert trigger supports only Restrict and Ignore (and applies to the child table), while the other two accept all three choices.

Using ADBObjects() together with ADatabases() and AFIELDS(), you can create a pretty good picture of what your environment looks like at any time. Details about the tables, view and connections found with ADBObjects() are available using DBGetProp().

Example

```
OPEN DATABASE TasTrade
* create arrays of tables, views, connections, and relations
nTableCount = ADBObjects(aTables,"Table")
nViewCount = ADBObjects(aViews,"View")
nConnCount = ADBObjects(aConns,"Connection")
nRelCount = ADBObjects(aRels,"Relation")
* now look at all the info
DISPLAY MEMORY LIKE a*
```

See Also ADatabases(), Array Manipulation, DBGetProp(), Key(), Open Database, Relation(), Set Database, Tag(), Target()

Add

This method of the Files collection lets you add files to a project.

Usage `oAddedFile = oFiles.Add( cFileName )`

Although Add adds to a project, it's actually a method of the Files collection of the project, not of the project itself. The corresponding Remove method belongs to the File object rather than the Files collection. It makes sense in terms of what they do, but it is a little confusing at first glance.

You pass Add the name of the file you want to add, and it puts that file in the project. Then, it returns an object reference to the file object created, so that you can continue to manipulate it.

You have to include the extension as part of the filename, since you can add all kinds of files to a project. In fact, if you add a file with an extension that VFP doesn't recognize as a project component, it puts it into "Other Files" rather than choking. Nice job. If you add a table that's bound into a database, the whole database is added to the project.

If the file isn't in the current directory, you need to include the path to it (even if it's in the current SET PATH list).

In tools, you're probably better off using the Files collection of the project than depending on the reference returned by Add, although everything seemed to behave as long as we didn't get too tricky.

Example

```
MODI PROJ MyProject
oProj = Application.ActiveProject
oProj.Files.Add("MyNewProg.PRG")
```

See Also File, Files, Name, Project, Remove

Add Class See Create ClassLib.

Add Object See Define Class.

Add Table, Remove Table

These commands provide a programmatic way to control what tables are in a database. ADD TABLE adds an existing table to the current database, while REMOVE TABLE removes a table from the database, leaving it a free table.

Usage

```
ADD TABLE TableName | ?
        [ NAME LongName ]
```

TableName is the filename of the table (DBF) to add to the current database. If you specify ? instead, the standard Open File dialog appears and you can choose a table to add. (Choosing a file other than a table leads to an error message.)

The table being added must not be open. Presumably, this is because the "backlink" to the DBC must be added to the table header, and this kind of change requires exclusive access. (See "DBC, DBF, FPT, CDX—Hike!" for more on this.)

Only Visual FoxPro tables can be added to a database. FoxPro 2.x tables aren't eligible. If the specified table is not a Visual FoxPro table, you're prompted to permit conversion. If you don't allow it, the table isn't added. Even SET SAFETY OFF doesn't dispense with this dialog, so be sure you've got Visual FoxPro tables if you're adding to a database in an application. (You can open the files and test them with the SYS(2029).) The dialog that appears is sure to result in support calls otherwise.

The NAME clause lets you specify a "long name" for the table. This is a more readable and possibly longer than eight-character name by which the table can be referenced. You can even use names with spaces embedded if you want, but if you do so, you'll have to surround the name with quotes every time you refer to it. We don't recommend using embedded blanks.

The database must be open. There's no way to automatically open it or to be prompted as part of this command. If more than one database is open, the table is added to the current database (either the last opened or the one most recently chosen with SET DATABASE, whichever comes last).

Example

```
OPEN DATABASE Test
ADD TABLE Test1
ADD TABLE ?
```

Usage

```
REMOVE TABLE TableName | ?
        [ DELETE ]
```

TableName is the table to be removed from the database. If the table has a long name, you must use it in the REMOVE TABLE command. The DBF name is not recognized. If the long name has embedded blanks, you need to surround it with quotes.

If you specify ? instead, you're prompted with a list of tables in the database and can choose one to delete.

The specified table must not be open to remove it. Again, this is probably because the header must be changed. Once the table is removed, it's a free table and can be added to another database (unless you add the DELETE clause, discussed below).

If SAFETY is ON, a warning dialog appears, reminding you that removing a table from its database loses all long names. Oddly, though, you're not warned about all the other stuff you lose, such as rules, triggers, persistent relations and so forth. Frankly, we think they're far more important than long names. On the other hand, because indexes involving long field names don't get fixed either, and that makes it impossible to open the table, we can sort of see why they point it out. On the whole, though, we'd prefer a warning that points out all the problems rather than just picking on one.

A table that's the "one" side of a one-to-many persistent relationship can't be removed from a database. First you must delete the relationship (using ALTER TABLE or the Database Designer).

The DELETE clause lets you remove the table and discard it in one step. If you specify DELETE, the table is deleted from the disk as well.

See Also Alter Table, Create, Create Database, Sys(2029)

AddBS(), DefaultExt(), ForceExt(), ForcePath(), JustDrive(), JustExt(), JustFName(), JustPath(), JustStem()

If these functions, new to VFP 6, sound familiar, that's because they've existed in FoxTools.FLL (and DOS's FPATH.PLB) for a long time. Now they've been integrated into the native language, reducing the need for FoxTools to be loaded. See the FoxTools section, in the File Functions sub-section, for details on calling each of the functions.

If you're still working with an older version of FoxPro, you won't miss much by not having these functions. You can load FoxTools, or, if you have access to FoxPro 2.x, you can find many of these functions in code in the GenMenu and GenScrn programs. None of these functions is rocket science; most could be rewritten in an IIF() statement or two.

A word of caution: Since most modern operating systems support long filenames, including periods within the filename, you'll want to be careful using these functions. They assume that any characters after the first period are part of the file extension.

Example

```
? addbs("fred")                               && returns "fred\"
? defaultext("c:\test","txt")                 && "c:\test.txt"
? defaultext("c:\test.doc","txt")             && "c:\test.doc"
? defaultext("c:\test.document","txt")        && "c:\test.document"
? forceext("c:\test.document","txt")          && "c:\test.txt"
? forcepath("c:\test.document","c:\temp")
* returns "C:\Temp\test.document"
? forcepath("c:\test.document","xxx")         && "xxx\test.document
? justdrive("c:\test.document")               && "C:"
? drivetype(justdrive("c:\test.document"))    && 3 (see drivetype)
? justext("c:\test.document")                 && "document"
? justfname("c:\test.document")               && "test.document"
? justpath("c:\test.document")                && "c:\" - note slash
? justpath("c:\temp\test.document")           && "c:\temp" - no slash
? justpath("c:\Program Files\test.document")
* "c:\Program Files"
? juststem("c:\Program Files\test.document")  && "test"
```

See Also FoxTools

AddColumn, DeleteColumn

These methods let you add and remove columns from a grid on the fly. They're more powerful than simply changing ColumnCount because they let you put the new column wherever you want it.

Usage

```
grdGrid.AddColumn( nColumnPosition )
grdGrid.DeleteColumn( [ nColumnPosition ] )
```

The column position passed to these methods refers to ColumnOrder (the visible position), not position in the Columns collection (which is based on creation order). When you DeleteColumn, the columns after that one move up in the Columns collection. Added columns always go at the end of the collection, regardless of their ColumnOrder.

Help says DeleteColumn removes the active column if you don't pass the parameter. Tain't so. If you omit the nColumnPosition parameter, DeleteColumn tosses out the last column in ColumnOrder regardless of ActiveColumn.

Example

```
This.DeleteColumn(2)               && Remove 2nd Column
Thisform.grdMyGrid.AddColumn(3)  && Add a column, make it third
```

See Also AddObject, ColumnCount, ColumnOrder, Columns, RemoveObject

AddItem, AddListItem, Clear, RemoveItem, RemoveListItem

These methods let you populate and depopulate combo boxes and list boxes whose RowSourceType is set to 0 (for None) or 1 (for Value). The two Add methods add new items to the combo or list. The Remove methods take individual items out of the list. The Clear method removes all items from the list. Understanding the differences between the two pairs of add and remove commands could drive a person to drink. Luckily, Tamar's a teetotaler.

Usage

```
oObject.AddItem( cValue [, nIndex [, nColumn ] ] )
oObject.AddListItem( cValue [, nItemId [, nColumn ] ] )
oObject.Clear()
oObject.RemoveItem( nIndex )
oObject.RemoveListItem( nItemId )
```

Parameter	Value	Meaning
cValue	Character	The text of the item to be added to the list.
nIndex	Numeric	The position in the list of the item to be added or removed.
nItemId	Numeric	The unique identification number of the item to be added or removed.
nColumn	Numeric	The column in which the newly added item is to be placed.

Let's start with Clear. It's simple and does what it's supposed to. It removes all the items from a combo or list box. That's it. When you want to make a new start, call Clear.

Now on to the confusing stuff. The key to understanding the difference between the "item" and the "listitem" or "itemid" methods (not just Add and Remove, but a bunch of others, too) is to understand that Microsoft thought they were doing us a favor (and they were) in providing the two different numbering systems used for elements of a list or combo box.

The first numbering system is based on the "what you see is what you get" school of thinking. Each item is assigned a number based on its physical position in the list. This is called the item's ListIndex (or, more briefly, Index). As new items are added or old items are removed, an item's ListIndex can change. Changing the Sorted property also can change an item's ListIndex. So can moving items around with the mover bars. Fundamentally, a ListIndex is a fleeting thing.

The other numbering scheme is more permanent. When an item is added, it's assigned a unique ID number called ItemId. That item keeps that ItemId as long as it's in the list. No other item in the list will ever have that ItemId.

That's probably enough for you to distinguish between RemoveItem and RemoveListItem. RemoveItem accepts an Index and deletes the item that currently has that Index. RemoveListItem takes an ItemId and deletes the item that has (now and forever) that ItemId. (Actually, not quite forever. After you delete the item with a particular ItemId, you can add a new one with the same ItemId.) Reasonably straightforward, once you know the secret.

Unfortunately, adding items is even more complex. When the list or combo has only one column, it's not too bad, though. In that case, AddItem with no nIndex parameter inserts a new item. If Sorted is .F., it goes at the end of the list and simply gets the next Index (and, of course, a new unique ItemId). If Sorted is .T., it gets inserted at the appropriate location and is assigned the appropriate Index for that location. The Indexes of all the items after the new one go up by one, in the appropriate order.

Still with us? Okay, what if you pass a value for nIndex? If Sorted is .T., the value you pass is ignored and the new item goes into the correct alphabetical position. That's easy enough. If Sorted is .F., the new item is inserted at the position you passed and all the items following it move down one (their Indexes increase by 1).

The key fact to remember about AddItem is that it always adds a new row to the list or combo. Accepting this now will make it easier to understand the discussion about multi-column lists and combos below.

On to AddListItem. This method has a different point of view, but the simplest case is pretty much the same as the simplest case of AddItem. If you don't pass a value for nItemId, the new item is assigned a unique ID number and is either added at the end of the list or, if Sorted is .T., goes into its rightful position.

What if you do pass a value? It depends whether an item already exists with that ItemId. If not, a new item is added to the list and its ItemId is the one you passed. However, if there's already an item with that ItemId, its text changes to cValue. In other words, AddListItem doesn't always add a new item to the list—sometimes, it just changes an existing item. Again, keep this in mind as we tackle multi-column lists.

Take a deep breath. Here we go. When ColumnCount is more than 1, each item in the list has multiple columns. This is where AddItem and AddListItem really part company. AddItem is incapable of populating a multi-column list or combo box with data in more than one column for each row. Go back three paragraphs to see the reason why—AddItem always adds a new row.

What does this mean in practice? First, that the nColumn parameter of AddItem, while not meaningless (it does do what it says it does), is worthless. We have yet to want a list or combo where each row contains data in only one column.

Second, and more important, it means that the right way to fill a multi-column list or combo box is to use AddListItem. The unfortunate part of this is it means you have to keep track of which ItemIds have been used so you don't accidentally overwrite some data. Take a look at NewItemId—it's a big help in this process.

To fill one row of a multi-column list, you pass the same value of ItemId for each column and the appropriate value for nColumn for each data item.

We should note that you can also populate a list or combo by simply putting the desired data in the List or ListItem array property. In fact, you can avoid AddItem and AddListItem entirely if you want, unless you need to assign particular ItemIds. In that case, your best bet is probably to use AddListItem for the first column, then assign directly to ListItem for other columns.

A final note. We were very surprised to find that these methods work with RowSourceType = 1. We'd figured that type was pretty brain-dead—meant mostly for those cases where the list of items was truly fixed. Help is silent on whether this is meant to work or not, so don't assume that everything that works for RowSourceType=0 also works for RowSourceType=1. Also, be aware that an undocumented capability like this may just disappear down the road. All in all, our take is that you should just stick with RowSourceType 0 if you think the list may need to be changed, and save type 1 for really, really fixed items.

Example

```
* Fill a list box with the names and titles from Employee
* This code might be in the Init method of the list box
This.ColumnCount = 3
This.ColumnWidths = "75,60,150"

LOCAL nRow

SELECT Employee
nRow=1  && See NewItemId for a better way
```

```
SCAN
   This.AddListItem(Last_Name, nRow, 1)
   This.AddListItem(First_Name, nRow, 2)
   This.AddListItem(Title, nRow, 3)
   nRow=nRow+1
ENDSCAN

* To see them in alpha order, add
This.Sorted=.T.
```

See Also ComboBox, List, ListBox, ListCount, ListIndex, ListItem, ListItemId, NewIndex, NewItemId

AddObject, NewObject, RemoveObject

These methods let you add and remove objects from containers, both at design time and at runtime. You can add controls to a form or page or column, columns to a grid, pages to a page frame, buttons to a button group, and so on. And, of course, you can remove the ones that are already there.

Usage

```
oObject.AddObject( cName, cClass [, cOLEClass ]
                   [, uParamList ] )
oObject.NewObject( cName, cClass [, cClassLib [, cLibInApp
                   [, uParamList ] ] ] )
oObject.RemoveObject( cName )
```

Parameter	Value	Meaning
cName	Character	The name of the object to be added or removed.
cClass	Character	The class of the object to be added.
cOLEClass	Character	If cClass is "OLEControl", specifies the type of OLE object to add.
uParamList	List of expressions	Parameters to be passed to the Init method of the new object.
cClassLib	Character	The name of the file containing the class definition for cClass.
	Omitted	Either cClass is a VFP base class or the class library has already been opened with SET CLASSLIB or SET PROCEDURE.
cLibInApp	Character	The name (including extension) of an APP or EXE file containing cClassLib.

AddObject and NewObject (added in VFP 6) are similar, but NewObject doesn't require SET CLASSLIB or SET PROCEDURE first. The difference between these two is quite similar to the difference between CreateObject() and NewObject(). We suspect, as in that case, that we'll find ourselves using NewObject() more and more, once we remember to do so.

NewObject() also offers the opportunity to add objects based on classes built into APP or EXE files, without having to have the library available as a separate VCX or PRG.

At runtime, the object added to the container always has Visible set to .F., even if you explicitly set it in the object's Init. This lets you do all the fiddling around you need with the new object before it becomes visible, so the user doesn't see what's happening. To ensure the display does not update until all changes are made, you can also toggle the form's LockScreen property.

Because these methods work at design time as well as runtime, they're extremely useful in Builders. You can get the user's input, add the appropriate objects and set them up the way the user wants. For more on Builders, see "Builders and Wizards and Bears, Oh My!" on the book's CD.

Don't confuse these methods with the ones used to add items to a list or combo box.

Example

```
oForm = CreateObject('Form')
oForm.Show()
* Choose one of the next two method calls.
* This version assumes that the library file is in the
* search path.
oForm.AddObject('cmdClose',"CloseButton")
* or you could avoid the issue this way:
oForm.NewObject('cmdClose',"CloseButton","Buttons")

oForm.cmdClose.Top = 100
oForm.cmdClose.Left = 50
oForm.cmdClose.Visible = .T.

* Assume you have the equivalent of this definition in a
* visual class in a file called Buttons.VCX
DEFINE CLASS CloseButton AS CommandButton

   Caption = "Close"

   PROCEDURE Click

   ThisForm.Release()

   ENDPROC
ENDDEFINE
```

See Also AddItem, AddListItem, CreateObject, Define Class, Init, LockScreen, RemoveItem, RemoveListItem, Visible

AddProperty

This new method lets you add properties to objects both at design time and at runtime.

Usage

```
oObject.AddProperty( cNewProp [, eInitialValue ] )
```

Though it's not good OOP, sometimes you really just need one more property in an object after you've instantiated it. Maybe it deals with a rare situation. Maybe you're working with someone else's class library (with no source available) and don't want to add another level of subclassing.

Paul Bienick of Flash Creative Management wrote an AddProp.FLL in October of 1995 to add properties to existing objects, but there was no native language support for this technique until VFP 6. This new method lets you break the rules and add a property on the fly without the need for an outside library.

AddProperty works at design time, too, where we think it's a far better idea. Like several other additions in this version, it makes builders even easier to build. In combination with Access and Assign methods, this can make adding properties "on demand" a reality.

The best reason we've heard to use AddProperty at runtime is to create classes to represent records. You can add a property for each field, then handle tables just like other objects. Another really good reason is to create a parameter object to pass multiple parameters. An object like this is especially useful when you need more than one return value from a method. Create an object, use AddProperty to create a property for each item that needs to be passed and then pass just the object reference into the method. The method can modify the properties for whatever it needs to return.

Example

```
* Assume you have an abstract Record class.
* At runtime, add properties to represent the fields.
* Assumes table is open in current work area.
oData = CreateObject("Record")
FOR nFld = 1 TO FCOUNT()
   oData.AddProperty(FIELD(nFld))
ENDFOR
```

See Also Access, Assign, ReadExpression, ReadMethod, WriteExpression, WriteMethod

AddToSCC, RemoveFromSCC

These two methods of the File object allow an individual file to come under, or be freed from, source code control.

Usage

```
lResult = filFile.AddToSCC()
lResult = filFile.RemoveFromSCC()
```

Use these two methods to add a file to your source code control system or remove it.

Like the other SCC methods, these commands suffer from confirmation dialogs getting in the way of the processing. This means that you can't entirely automate things—you'll have to manually click in these dialogs. Since they aren't part of Fox's interface, even a risky maneuver like KEYBOARDing values won't work.

Example

```
* Clear all the files in a project out of SCC
oProject = _VFP.ActiveProject
FOR EACH oFile IN oProject.Files
  IF oFile.ReadOnly  && if .T., it is under SCC
    oFile.RemoveFromSCC()
  ENDIF
ENDFOR
```

See Also CheckIn, CheckOut, File, GetLatestVersion, Project, UndoCheckout

ADel() See AIns().

ADir()

This function creates an array containing information about files in a specified directory. Read it as "Array from directory" and it makes perfect sense.

Usage

```
nCount = ADIR( ArrayName [, cFileSpec [, cAttributes
               [, cCreatorType ] ] ] )
```

Parameter	Value	Meaning
ArrayName	Array Name	The array into which directory information is dumped. It's created or resized if necessary.
cFileSpec	Character	Only files matching cFileSpec are included. Wildcards * and ? can be used. cFileSpec can include a drive and directory as well.
	Empty	When used with a combination of D, H, and S attributes, limits results to files matching specified attributes.
	Omitted	Include all files from current drive and directory.
cAttributes (string may contain none, any or all of these four)	Omitted	Include only filenames, excluding directories and hidden and system files.
	D	Include information on sub-directories of the specified directory.
	H	Include information on hidden files.

Parameter	Value	Meaning
cAttributes (string may contain none, any or all of these four)	S	Include information on system files.
	V	Include only the volume information for the specified drive. You don't need to specify the root directory for this to work. Other attributes are ignored if "V" is included.
cCreatorType	Character	Mac file creator type—ignored in Windows.
nCount	Numeric	The number of rows in the resulting array; that is, the number of directory entries (files, directories and volume names) for which information was collected.
	0	No matching files were found.

The D, H and S attributes can be combined into a single attribute string. These interact with the file specification provided to select a subset of files and/or directories. To get a list of all sub-directories, pass the empty string for cFileSpec and "D" for cAttributes.

If the volume name is requested, a single element character array is created, containing the volume name. In all other cases, the array created has five columns, as follows:

Column	Meaning
1	File name—character.
2	File size in bytes—numeric.
3	Date file was last written—date.
4	Time file was last written—character.
5	File Attributes—a single five-character string. Each position represents one attribute. If the file has that attribute, the corresponding letter is there; if not, a "." is found in that location. The attributes are: R—read-only A—archive bit is set S—system file H—hidden file D—directory For example, "R...." means a read-only file, while ".A.H." means a hidden file needing to be archived.

We received a note from someone who read the original edition of this book and wondered what ADIR() returns if it can't create the array. We haven't quite figured out how to test that one. We think the only situation in which that could happen is if there are so many files in the directory that there's not enough memory to hold the resulting array. Seems to us that the directory structure would probably give out long before you could put enough files there to stress memory that way.

Example

```
? ADIR(aFiles)              && creates an array of all files in
                            && current directory
? ADIR(aDirect, "", "D")    && creates an array of all
                            && subdirectories of current directory
```

```
? ADIR(aDBFs, "*.DBF")      && fills array with list of tables
? ADIR(aDBFs, "DATA\*.DBF") && fills array with list of tables in
                            && DATA directory
```

See Also AFields(), Array Manipulation, Dir, Directory(), FDate(), FTime(), SYS(2000)

AElement(), ASubscript()

These two functions convert between the two numbering schemes for array elements: continuous element numbering and row/column numbering. Because some array functions use one form and others need the other form, these functions are pretty useful.

AELEMENT() takes an array, a row and, optionally, a column and returns the corresponding element number. ASUBSCRIPT() takes an array and an element number and returns either the row or the column.

Usage `nElement = AELEMENT( ArrayName, nRow [, nCol ] )`

Parameter	Value	Meaning
ArrayName	Array Name	The array in which you want to convert from row, column notation to element notation. It's necessary to specify the array because the shape of the array determines the conversion.
nRow	Numeric	The row number of the item for which the element number is desired.
nCol	Numeric	The column number of the item for which the element number is desired.
	Omitted	Treat ArrayName as a one-dimensional array and return nRow.
nElement	Numeric	The element number of the specified element. If the array is one-dimensional or nCol is omitted, nRow is returned.

Example

```
DIMENSION aTest[5], a2DTest[4,2]
? AELEMENT(aTest, 3)         && returns 3
? AELEMENT(a2DTest, 3)       && returns 3
? AELEMENT(a2DTest, 3, 2)    && returns 6
```

Usage `nSubscript = ASUBSCRIPT( ArrayName, nElement, nSubscript )`

Parameter	Value	Meaning
ArrayName	Array Name	The array in which you want to convert from element notation to row, column notation. It's necessary to specify the array because the shape of the array determines the conversion.
nElement	Numeric	The element number of the item for which either the row or column number is desired.
nSubscript	1	Return the row subscript of the element. In a one-dimensional array, this is the same as the element number.
	2	Return the column subscript of the element. In a one-dimensional array, gives an error message.

ASUBSCRIPT() is particularly useful when working with ASCAN(), which returns an element number. We often want to get a particular element out of the same row of the array as the element found by ASCAN(). ASUBSCRIPT() gives us the row number, which we can then use to grab the relevant item.

Watch out for one thing. When nElement isn't a valid element number for the array, you get an error. Frankly, we think we'd prefer if ASUBSCRIPT() returned 0 in that case and let us deal with it.

Example

```
DIMENSION aTest[5],a2DTest[4,2]
? ASUBSCRIPT(aTest, 3, 1)    && returns 3
? ASUBSCRIPT(a2DTest, 3, 1) && returns 2
? ASUBSCRIPT(a2DTest, 3, 2) && returns 1
* The next example assumes SearchItem has a value
* that can be found in the array.
? ASUBSCRIPT(a2DTest, ASCAN(a2DTest, SearchItem), 1)
```

See Also ALen(), Array Manipulation, AScan()

AError()

This function, new in VFP 3, makes error handling a little easier than in FoxPro 2.x. Instead of remembering the names of a bunch of different functions that return bits and pieces of information when an error occurs, you can use this function to put all the necessary information into a single array. Best of all, AERROR() can even be used to find out about errors that occur when Visual FoxPro talks to the rest of the world via OLE or ODBC.

Usage

```
nRows = AError( ErrorInfo )
```

The function returns the number of rows in ErrorInfo, usually one. The docs say that ODBC errors sometimes return multiple rows because multiple errors occur; we haven't been able to make that happen, but we're not client-server wizards.

The interpretation of the data varies depending whether it's a FoxPro, OLE or ODBC error. In each case, the first element is the error number and the next two spell out the error message. The charts in the online Help do a pretty good job of explaining each element, so we'll just mention a couple of things that aren't so clear.

Some FoxPro errors (like error 12, "Variable not found") also include the name of the item that caused the problem (with error 12, the variable name). In this case, the third element of the array contains the name of that item.

When an error is triggered because a field validation rule fires, the third column should get the name of the field. However, in VFP 6 and VFP 5, instead the third column contains the validation message (as does SYS(2018), the function this column is meant to replace). In VFP 5.0a and VFP 6, the fifth column contains the field number, so there is some way to get at the information, but we sure wish they'd fix this one instead of telling us it's "by design."

For OLE, help says the first element always contains 1427 or 1429. We've been able to generate 1426 as an OLE error and the list of error messages implies that 1428 is also a valid OLE error.

ODBC errors behave differently than the others. The SQL functions generally return a value to indicate their success or failure. (A negative value represents failure.) But the failure doesn't fire the application's error handler—you have to handle the error yourself. Even though the error handler isn't called, AERROR() still can pick up the error information. In the example below, we check for the error and call our error handler explicitly.

We're really pleased to have AERROR(). It definitely makes it easier to write error handlers.

Example

```
ON ERROR DO Handler
* Now force some errors
XYZ
USE NoSuchTable
oWord = CREATEOBJECT("Word.Basic")
oWord.FileOpen("NoSuchFile")
```

```
RELEASE oWord
* Substitute the name of a data source that exists
* on your system in the next line
nHandle = SQLCONNECT("Access With ODBC 2.0")
IF SQLEXEC(nHandle, "SELECT * FROM NoSuchTable") < 1
   DO Handler
ENDIF
= SQLDISCONNECT(nHandle)
ON ERROR

PROCEDURE Handler
* Handle errors that occur
* In this case, we'll just figure out which kind they are
* then save the information to a file

LOCAL aErrData[1]

= AERROR(aErrData)
DO CASE
CASE aErrData[1,1] = 1526
   * ODBC Error
   WAIT WINDOW "ODBC Error Occurred" NOWAIT
CASE BETWEEN(aErrData[1,1], 1426, 1429)
   * OLE Error
   WAIT WINDOW "OLE Error Occurred" NOWAIT
OTHERWISE
   * FoxPro error
   WAIT WINDOW "FoxPro Error Occurred" NOWAIT
ENDCASE

LIST MEMORY TO FILE ErrInfo.TXT ADDITIVE NOCONSOLE

RETURN
```

See Also Error, On Error

AFields()

This function puts information about table structure into an array. Read it as "Array from fields." In Visual FoxPro, this function returns a lot more information than in previous FoxPro versions.

Usage `nFieldCount = AFIELDS( ArrayName [, cAlias | nWorkarea ] )`

Parameter	Value	Meaning
ArrayName	Array Name	The array to hold table structure information.
cAlias	Character	The alias of the table whose structure information is placed in ArrayName.
	Omitted	If nWorkarea is also omitted, use current work area.
nWorkarea	Numeric	The number of the work area containing the table whose structure information is placed in ArrayName.
	Omitted	If cAlias is also omitted, use current work area.
nFieldCount	Positive number	The number of rows in the array, which is the number of fields in the specified table.

In VFP 6 and VFP 5, the resulting array has 16 columns. In VFP 3, the array has only the first 11 of these columns.

Column	Type	Meaning
1	Character	Field name.
2	Single Character	Field type (see TYPE() for a list of field types).
3	Numeric	Field size.
4	Numeric	Decimal places.
5	Logical	Nulls allowed?
6	Logical	Code page translation NOT allowed?
7	Character	Field Validation rule (from DBC).
8	Character	Field Validation text (from DBC).
9	Character	Field Default value (from DBC).
10	Character	Table Validation rule (from DBC).
11	Character	Table Validation text (from DBC).
12	Character	Long table name (from DBC).
13	Character	Insert Trigger expression (from DBC).
14	Character	Update Trigger expression (from DBC).
15	Character	Delete Trigger expression (from DBC).
16	Character	Table Comment (from DBC).

The sixth column indicates whether code page translation is allowed, but it uses a sort of double negative. In other words, this column is .T. if the field has the NOCPTRANS attribute, which happens if you define it as Character (binary) or Memo (binary). TYPE() doesn't supply this information, so you need to use either AFIELDS(), COPY STRUCTURE EXTENDED or SET("NOCPTRANS") to find out which fields have this attribute. All the columns from 10 to the end contain table-level information and are filled in only for the first field of the table (the first array row). We're not really sure why this information is returned by AFIELDS() at all. DBGetProp() returns the information, so it's already available, though not in array form. We guess it's to make it possible to use AFIELDS(), followed by CREATE TABLE with the FROM ARRAY clause.

As discussed in "DBF, FPT, CDX, DBC—Hike!," tables that contain nullable fields also have a hidden system field called _NullFlags. Note that this field is not returned by AFIELDS() (it wouldn't be very well hidden if it was, now, would it?) and therefore routines that think they can add the values returned from AFIELDS() to calculate the size of a DBF will break. Check out RecSize() instead.

The same array is created for a free table as for a table contained in a database, but the table-level columns are empty, in that case.

Example

```
SELECT Customer
= AFIELDS(aCustFlds)   && structure array for Customer
USE MyTable IN 0
```

```
= AFIELDS(aMyStruc, "MyTable")  && structure array for MyTable
```

See Also ADatabases(), ADBObjects(), ADir(), Array Manipulation, Copy Structure Extended, Create Table, DBGetProp(), FCount(), FSize(), RecSize()

AFont()

This function asks Windows for font information and creates an array containing the results. It's a maddeningly schizophrenic function: the format of the array changes depending on how many parameters you pass. You can ask for a list of fonts, for font sizes for a particular font, or whether a particular font and size is installed. In each case, the form of the answer is different.

Usage `lReturnValue = AFONT( FontArray [, cFontName [, nFontSize ] ])`

Parameter	Value	Meaning
FontArray	Array Name	The array to contain the font information.
cFontName	Omitted	Create a list of all installed fonts.
	Character	Get information for the specified font.
nFontSize	Omitted	Get all font sizes available for cFontName; if cFontName is scalable, create a single row containing -1.
	Numeric	Determine if cFontName is available in nFontSize. If so, create a single row containing .T.
lReturnValue	.T.	The array was created containing the specified information.
	.F.	The specified font/size combination doesn't exist and no array was created.

There are several strange things about AFONT(). First, unlike all the other array functions that get information and stuff it in an array, this one returns a logical value. The rest return the number of rows in the resulting array (or 0, if they fail).

The contents of the array created depend on the parameters passed. If cFontName and nFontSize are both omitted, the array contains as many items as installed fonts, with each element containing one font name.

If cFontName is specified, but nFontSize is omitted, the array elements are numeric. For scalable fonts, a single element is created with a value of -1. For non-scalable fonts, the array contains one row for each size of cFontName available. If there is no such font, the array doesn't get created.

If both parameters are specified, the array contains a single logical element (set to .T.) if cFontName is available in nFontSize. If not, the array doesn't get created at all. If the font isn't available in the specified size and the array already exists, it's not resized, but the first element is changed to .F.

We think this design is horribly confusing. It would be better either to return results in the same format regardless, or to have several different functions for this task. This setup ensures that we have to look up this function every time we use it.

Example

```
? AFONT(aFonts)  && Create a list of all available fonts
? AFONT(aCourier, "Courier")  && Check sizes for Courier
? AFONT(aAvailable, "MS Sans Serif",8)  && Check for particular
                                         && font/size combination
```

See Also Array Manipulation, GetFont()

AfterBuild See BeforeBuild.

AfterCloseTables See BeforeOpenTables.

AfterDock See BeforeDock.

AfterRowColChange See BeforeRowColChange.

AGetClass(), AVCXClasses()

These two functions are aimed more at tool builders than application builders. AGetClass() displays the Class Open dialog and returns information about the class chosen. AVCXClasses() fills an array with information about all the classes in a class library.

Usage

```
lChoseOne = AGetClass( ClassInfo [, cClassLib [, cClass
                       [, cDialogCaption [, cFileNameCaption
                       [, cButtonCaption ] ] ] ] ])
nClassCount = AVCXClasses( ClassInfo, cClassLib )
```

Parameter	Value	Meaning
ClassInfo	Array Name	An array containing the requested information. For AGetClass(), the array has two elements in a single row—the class library and class name chosen. For AVCXClasses(), the array has one row for each class in the library, with 11 columns containing information about the class.
cClassLib	Character	For AGetClass(), the name of the class library to highlight initially. For AVCXClasses(), the name of the class library whose class information goes into the array.
cClass	Character	The class to highlight initially.
cDialogCaption	Character	The caption to put on the Open dialog.
	Omitted or ""	The dialog caption is "Open".
cFileNameCaption	Character	The string to display next to the File Name prompt.
	Omitted or ""	"File Name:" is displayed.
cButtonCaption	Character	The caption for the OK button.
	Omitted or ""	The button says "OK".
lChoseOne	.T.	The user chose a class.
	.F.	The user chose Cancel or ESC.
nClassCount	Numeric	The number of classes in the class library chosen.

AGetClass() lets you prompt a user (who's probably a developer) to choose a class and provides the class library and class as a result. The various parameters let you customize the dialog to a great extent. Note that you can't skip over the earlier parameters to just provide the later ones (for instance, =AGetClass(aCl,,,"Chose a Class") gives the error "Function argument value, type or count is invalid"). But you can pass the empty string for any parameter except the class library and VFP behaves as if you'd stopped before you got there. So, = AGetClass(aCl,"controls.vcx","","Choose a Class") works just fine. However, if you pass "" for cClassLib, VFP yells.

AVCXClasses() lets you find out what's out there, a really handy trick when you're building developer tools. Not only does it give you the list of classes in the class library, but it tells you a great deal about them, including the base class and parent class, the name of the #INCLUDE file, and more.

One warning: The classes aren't put in the array in any particular order. To be more accurate, they're in the order of their records in the class library, which isn't likely to be a useful order.

Example

```
* Start in the FFC subdirectory
lGotOne = AGetClass(aClassInfo,"_base.vcx")
* To find out what classes are in the library
* containing the class just selected
nClassCount = AVCXClasses(aClassList, aClassInfo[1,1])
```

See Also AClass(), AMembers()

AGetFileVersion()

This function, new in VFP 6, lets you check on the version information built into a file. It's a native replacement for the GetFileVersion() function that was added to FoxTools in VFP 5.

Usage

```
nRows = AGetFileVersion( VersionArray, cFileName )
```

If the specified file has version information, VersionArray is created (or resized) with 15 rows and the function returns 15. (No doubt the exact number will change in future versions.) The contents of the rows are documented in Help.

If the file doesn't exist or doesn't have version information, the array isn't created (or is unchanged if it already existed) and the function returns 0.

AGetFileVersion() gives us three pieces of information we could not get with VFP 5.0 and the FoxTool's GetFileVersion(). The lucky 13th element of the array tells us whether the file is capable of OLE Self-Registration, an important item when installing new ActiveX services on a machine or troubleshooting the ones that are there. The 14th and 15th elements give us the string and hexadecimal descriptions of the language in which this file was localized.

Oh, you're wondering how to give a file version information. From the Build Options dialog, click Version and you can fill it in. Programmatically, you use the various File properties whose names begin with "Version."

This function works on all kinds of executable files, not just those you create with VFP. You can go poking around all kinds of places to see what's out there.

Example

```
? AGetFileVersion(aFileVer, home()+"VFP6.exe")  && Returns 15
```

See Also Build, VersionComments, VersionCompany, VersionCopyright, VersionDescription, VersionLanguage, VersionNumber, VersionProduct, VersionTrademarks

AIns(), ADel()

These two functions add and remove elements from an array, respectively. Their names, which imply insert and delete, are somewhat misleading because they don't affect the size of the array, only its contents. AINS() pushes extra data out the end of the array, while ADEL() leaves empty cells at the end. What makes these functions so useful is that they adjust the elements that follow the insertion or deletion point. That is, when you AINS(), the items from the insertion point on get pushed toward the end of the array. With ADEL(), items from the deletion point on get moved toward the beginning of the array.

Usage `nReturn = AINS( ArrayName, nPos [, nRowOrCol ] )`

Parameter	Value	Meaning
ArrayName	Array Name	The array to have an element, row or column inserted. If ArrayName is one-dimensional, a single element is inserted. If ArrayName is two-dimensional, either a row or column is inserted. The newly inserted element or elements are initialized to .F.
nPos	Numeric	The position at which the new element, row or column is inserted. All items from that position to the end of the array get pushed further out into the array. The data from the last element, row or column is lost. For a one-dimensional array, nPos is the element number. (See "DBF, FPT, CDX, DBC—Hike!" for an explanation of element numbers.) For a two-dimensional array, nPos is the row or column number where insertion takes place.
nRowOrCol	2	Insert a column into a two-dimensional array. This is the only documented third parameter, but see the next entry.
	Omitted or 1, 0 or negative number	Insert an element into a one-dimensional array or a row into a two-dimensional array. The documentation says 2 is the only third parameter you can pass, but passing a number less than or equal to 1 is identical to omitting the parameter.

As far as we can tell, AINS() always returns 1 except when an error occurs; then it doesn't return anything.

Example

```
DIMENSION aTest[3]
aTest[1] = 1
aTest[2] = 2
aTest[3] = 3
? AINS(aTest, 2)   && Insert a new 2nd element - returns 1
? aTest[1]         && 1
? aTest[2]         && .F.
? aTest[3]         && 2

DIMENSION a2DTest[3,2]
FOR nCnt = 1 TO 6
   a2DTest[nCnt] = nCnt
ENDFOR
? AINS(a2DTest, 2)  && Insert a new 2nd Row
DISPLAY MEMORY      && Shows 1 and 2 in first row, .F. in both
                    && elements of 2nd row and 3 and 4 in third
                    && row

* reinitialize
FOR nCnt=1 TO 6
    a2Dtest[nCnt] = nCnt
ENDFOR
? AINS(a2DTest, 1, 2)   && Insert a new 1st Column
DISPLAY MEMORY          && Shows first column as all .F.,
                        && 1, 3, 5 in second column
```

Because AINS() throws data away, you'll typically want to redimension the array before using it. Add the new element, row or column, then insert it in the right place.

```
* add a new third row to an existing array
DIMENSION aArray[ ALEN(aArray, 1) + 1, ALEN(aArray, 2) ]
=AINS(aArray, 3)
```

Unfortunately, adding a new column this way isn't so easy. AINS() handles column insertion neatly, pushing the items in the last column out into the bit bucket. But redimensioning an array to have an additional column isn't as well behaved. Data stays in the element with the same element number, which is not the same (row,column) position. Take a look at the aColCopy() function under ACOPY() to see how to work around this problem.

Usage `nReturn = ADEL( ArrayName, nPos [, nRowOrCol ] )`

Parameter	Value	Meaning
ArrayName	Array Name	The array to have an element, row or column deleted. If ArrayName is one-dimensional, a single element is deleted. If ArrayName is two-dimensional, either a row or column is deleted.
nPos	Numeric	The position from which the new element, row or column is deleted. All items from that position to the end of the array get moved forward to fill the beginning of the array. The last element, row or column is filled with .F. For a one-dimensional array, nPos is the element number. (See "DBC, DBF,FPT—Hike!" for an explanation of element numbers.) For a two-dimensional array, nPos is the row or column number.
nRowOrCol	2	Delete a column in a two-dimensional array. This is the only documented third parameter, but see the next entry.
	Omitted or 1, 0 or negative number	Delete an element in a one-dimensional array or a row in a two-dimensional array. The documentation says 2 is the only third parameter you can pass, but passing a number less than or equal to 1 is identical to omitting the parameter.

As with AINS(), it appears that ADEL() always returns 1 unless it fails.

Example

```
DIMENSION aTest[3]
aTest[1] = 1
aTest[2] = 2
aTest[3] = 3
? ADEL(aTest, 2)  && delete 2nd element
? aTest[1]        && 1
? aTest[2]        && 3
? aTest[3]        && .F.

DIMENSION a2DTest[3,2]
FOR nCnt = 1 TO 6
    a2Dtest[nCnt] = nCnt
ENDFOR
? ADEL(a2DTest,2)    && delete 2nd row
DISPLAY MEMORY       && shows 1 and 2 in first row,
                     && 5 and 6 in second row, and .F. in 3rd row

* reinitialize
FOR nCnt=1 TO 6
    a2Dtest[nCnt] = nCnt
ENDFOR
? ADEL(a2DTest,1,2)   && delete 1st column
DISPLAY MEMORY        && shows 2, 4, 6 in first column,
                      && .F. in 2nd column
```

With ADEL(), you'll usually want to redimension the array afterward. Remove the data, leaving empty cells at the end, then redimension to get rid of the empties.

```
* remove the 4th element of array and resize
=ADEL(aArray, 4)
DIMENSION aArray[ ALEN(aArray) - 1 ]
```

As with AINS(), redimensioning following deletion of a column is messy. You have to move data around to avoid losing it or having it in the wrong place.

See Also AElement(), ALen(), Array Manipulation, ASubscript(), Dimension

AInstance()

This function lets you find all the instances of any class. It puts the list in an array. Because you can instantiate a class as many times as you want, it seems like it would be convenient to be able to find all the instances. However, we have yet to actually use this function other than to test it.

Usage `nInstanceCount = AInstance( ArrayName, cClassName )`

Parameter	Value	Meaning
ArrayName	Array Name	The array to hold the instance references.
cClassName	Character	The name of the class for which to find instances. Both VFP base classes and user-defined classes can be specified.
nInstanceCount	Positive Number	The number of items in the array, which equals the number of references to cClassName found.
	0	No instances of cClassName were found.

Unlike the similar ASELOBJ() function, each element of the array holds the name of an object, not an object reference to the object. Using indirect variable references or macro substitution, you can operate on the objects themselves.

Example

```
oForm1 = CREATEOBJECT("Form")  && create a few forms
oForm2 = CREATEOBJECT("Form")
oForm3 = CREATEOBJECT("Form")
* now collect instances
nInstanceCnt = AInstance(aForms, "form")

* could loop through and do something
* In VFP 5 and VFP 6, the loop can use FOR EACH instead.
FOR nCnt = 1 TO nInstanceCnt
   cCaption = "Instance # " + LTRIM(STR(nCnt))
   STORE cCaption to (aForms[nCnt] + ".Caption")
ENDFOR
```

Although you can do something like the previous example, there's a much easier way to deal with a collection of objects. Simply use an array to hold the object references in the first place. Visual FoxPro allows you to do something like this:

```
DIMENSION aForms[3]

FOR nCnt = 1 TO 3
   aForm[nCnt] = CREATEOBJECT('form')
ENDFOR
```

Watch out for one thing with AINSTANCE(). If several variables refer to the same object, you still get one array item for each variable. So, if you're using the references to change all objects of the class, you may hit some of them more than once. On the other hand, this feature makes AINSTANCE() ideal for ensuring that you actually release an object when you want to.

Note that AINSTANCE() shares the same first four letters as AINSERT(); therefore you must use at least five letters for AINSTANCE().

AINSTANCE() may be helpful when you're dealing with cases where you haven't created the objects yourself, but you need to find out what's out there—for example, in a Builder or a handler of some sort.

Note that AINSTANCE() can't be used to find out about OLE classes such as Project and File. However, the application object offers collections that let you check on those as needed.

See Also AClass(), AMembers(), Application, Array Manipulation, ASelObj(), CreateObject()

ALen()

This function returns the number of elements, rows or columns in an array. For one-dimensional arrays, it returns the number of elements. For two-dimensional arrays, a parameter determines whether it returns elements, rows or columns. We often forget to include the parameter when asking for rows and end up with elements by accident. A better approach is to always pass 1 for the second parameter unless you specifically want the number of columns. With a one-d array, you still get the number of elements, but for a two-d array, you'll get rows, which is what we almost always want.

Usage `nReturnValue = ALEN( ArrayName [, nElemRowOrCol ] )`

Parameter	Value	Meaning
ArrayName	Array Name	The array whose elements, rows or columns are to be counted. Can be either one- or two-dimensional.
nElemRowOrCol	0 or Omitted	Returns the number of elements in the array.
	1	Returns the number of rows in a two-dimensional array. For a one-dimensional array, returns the number of elements.
	2	Returns the number of columns in a two-dimensional array. Returns 0 for a one-dimensional array.
nReturnValue	Numeric	The number of elements, rows or columns in ArrayName.

Example

```
USE Employee
COPY TO ARRAY aEmps FIELDS Last_Name, First_Name
nCount = ALEN(aEmps,1)

* check if an array is two-dimensional
IF ALEN(MyArray, 2) = 0
   * one-dimensional
ELSE
   * two-dimensional
ENDIF
```

Also, see the function aColCopy() under ACopy() for examples of ALEN() in use.

See Also ACopy(), AElement(), Array Manipulation, ASubscript(), Dimension

Alias, Exclusive, Filter, Order, ReadOnly

These are all properties of a cursor in the Data environment of a form, report or label. They let you indicate how the table or view the cursor refers to is to be opened.

These properties affect a table or view only if it is opened by the data environment, either because AutoOpenTables is .T. or by explicitly calling the OpenTables method. If the table or view is opened in other code, it uses the settings in the USE command and the current SET settings.

ReadOnly also applies to several controls and to the Project's File object.

Usage
```
frmForm.DataEnvironment.crsCursor.Alias = cAlias
cAlias = frmForm.DataEnvironment.crsCursor.Alias
```

Alias determines the alias assigned to the table or view. By default, the alias is the name of the table or view. If the name has embedded blanks, the default alias replaces them with underscores (for example, the view "Supplier Listing" becomes "supplier_listing").

Usage
```
frmForm.DataEnvironment.crsCursor.Exclusive = lIsExclusive
lIsExclusive = frmForm.DataEnvironment.crsCursor.Exclusive
```

Exclusive determines whether the table is opened exclusively or shared. In VFP 6 and VFP 5, Exclusive is read-only for views and set permanently to .T. In VFP 3, you can change Exclusive for views, but when you test ISEXCLUSIVE(), it returns .T. anyway. None of this really matters because views are always sharable. Every user can open the same view (unless offline views are involved).

The tables opened behind the scenes to populate a view are always opened shared, regardless of the view's Exclusive setting or the current value of SET("EXCLUSIVE"). On the whole, we think this isn't awful, though we'd rather have control over it. If you want to be sure these tables are opened the way you want them, add them to the data environment before the views that need them and set Exclusive the way you want it for each, or open them explicitly in the BeforeOpenTables or OpenTables method.

Usage
```
frmForm.DataEnvironment.crsCursor.Filter = cFilterString
cFilterString = frmForm.DataEnvironment.crsCursor.Filter
```

Filter determines the filter applied to the table or view. You can change the cursor's filter while the form is running and the visible set of records is updated.

In VFP 3, there's no way to turn the filter off entirely. That is, there's no equivalent to SET FILTER TO. This means to make all records visible, you have to resort to a trick like using ".T." for cFilterString. The problem with this is that you may end up with a filter that isn't Rushmore optimizable.

In VFP 5 and VFP 6, use the ResetToDefault method to clear the filter or set it to "".

Usage
```
frmForm.DataEnvironment.crsCursor.Order = cTagName
cTagName = frmForm.DataEnvironment.crsCursor.Order
```

Order determines the index in effect for the table or view. Like Filter, you can change Order while a form is running.

There's no way to turn off index order. That is, you can't restore the table to natural order by modifying the Order property. We can't even think of a work-around that restores natural record order—ResetToDefault doesn't work. (In fact, you can't reset Order to default in the property sheet, either. How odd!)

Okay, so we lied. We can think of a way to restore natural record order, but the cure may be worse than the disease. You can SET ORDER TO and the table is displayed in natural order. However, the cursor's Order property still reflects the last order you specified. (Fortunately, ORDER() does correctly return the empty string.)

Bottom line: If you need to work with records in natural order, you may want to stay away from the Order property in code. Use it in the property sheet to set the initial table order, but make all your changes with SET

ORDER and do all your testing with ORDER(). (Of course, the main reason to use natural order is because it's faster for some operations.)

We should probably explain why we say that Order affects views. Although views can't have index tags stored for them, you can index a view once it's open. One clever trick is to force OpenTables to open the tables and views prematurely (see DoDefault() for details), then create some index tags for your views. Once you've created them, you can set Order just as you can for a table (though you can't set Order in the property sheet—that value gets called on too soon).

Usage

```
frmForm.DataEnvironment.crsCursor.ReadOnly = lIsReadOnly
lIsReadOnly = frmForm.DataEnvironment.crsCursor.ReadOnly
```

For a cursor, ReadOnly determines whether the table or view is opened in read-only mode. If so, it can't be changed by the user or in code.

For a control (grid, column, text box, edit box, spinner, check box or combo box), ReadOnly determines whether the user can change the data displayed in the control. Even when ReadOnly is .T., the user can navigate in the control. To disable a control completely, use the Enabled property.

For the file object, ReadOnly is related to source control and indicates whether or not you can change the file at this moment.

Example

```
* The following assumes you've added the TasTrade
* Customer table to the DE of a form as the first table,
* so the corresponding object is named "Cursor1".
* You'd normally set these properties in the Form Designer,
* but here's the code:
ThisForm.DataEnvironment.Cursor1.Alias="Cust"
ThisForm.DataEnvironment.Cursor1.Exclusive=.T.
ThisForm.DataEnvironment.Cursor1.Filter="country='USA'"
ThisForm.DataEnvironment.Cursor1.Order="company_na"
ThisForm.DataEnvironment.Cursor1.ReadOnly=.F.
```

You need to set most of these properties at design time. Otherwise, your changes occur after the tables have been opened, which is too late. You can't change the cursor properties before opening tables at runtime because the cursor's Init doesn't fire until after the tables have been auto-opened. If you really need to, you can change these properties in the BeforeOpenTables or OpenTables methods.

See Also Alias(), Cursor, DataEnvironment, DoDefault(), Enabled, File, Filter(), IsExclusive(), IsReadOnly(), Order(), Set Exclusive, Set Filter, Set Order, Use

Alias(), DBF(), Select(), Used()

These functions return an assortment of information about work areas and the tables in use in them. (Why does this sound like the promo for a trashy talk show? "Work areas and the tables that use them—next Geraldo!")

Several of these functions have an optional parameter that can be either cAlias or nWorkarea. If either is passed, the function returns information about the table in use in the specified work area (the one where cAlias is the alias or the one numbered nWorkarea). When this parameter is omitted, these functions return information about the current work area.

Usage

```
cAliasUsed = ALIAS( [ cAlias | nWorkArea ] )
```

ALIAS() tells you the alias of the table open in the specified work area. We find it hard to imagine why anyone would ever pass cAlias to ALIAS(). If you already know the alias for the work area, why are you asking? However, it does mean you can write something like ?ALIAS(ALIAS()), which at least provides comic relief.

If there's no table in use in the specified work area, ALIAS() returns the empty string.

Example
```
cInUse = ALIAS()
```

Usage
```
cFileName = DBF( [ cAlias | nWorkArea ] )
```

DBF() tells you the name of the table open in the specified work area. In this case, specifying an alias makes lots of sense. You provide the alias and DBF() tells you what table it's an alias for. If no table is in use in the specified work area, you get the empty string.

DBF() is sensitive to SET FULLPATH. When FULLPATH is ON, DBF() returns a fully qualified path and filename. With FULLPATH OFF, DBF() returns just a drive and filename.

DBF() provides a way of distinguishing "real" cursors from those that are just filters of the original table. When FoxPro can get away with it, the cursor created by a SELECT-SQL is simply a filter of the table in the FROM clause. (You can prevent this behavior with the NOFILTER clause.) In that case, DBF("the cursor alias") returns the name of the original table. When a query creates a real cursor, DBF() returns the name of a temp file—a bunch of digits with a TMP extension.

Example
```
IF RIGHT(DBF(),3)="TMP"
   * it's a "real" cursor
ELSE
   * it's a filter
ENDIF
```

It's most important to distinguish between a real cursor and a filter when you want to use APPEND FROM to add the records in a cursor to another table. You have to APPEND FROM DBF("the cursor"). If the cursor is really just a filter, doing so adds all the records of the original rather than just the selected records. Be aware, however, that just because DBF() returns a .TMP name, the file does not actually have to be on the disk. VFP often buffers the contents of a small result set in memory and never writes them to disk. Consider COPY TO if you need to have data with a disk presence.

Usage
```
nWorkArea = SELECT( [ nDoWhat | cAlias ] )
```

Parameter	Value	Meaning
nDoWhat	0	Return the number of the current work area.
	Omitted	If cAlias is also omitted, return the number of the current work area.
	1	Return the number of the highest available work area.
	Anything else	Return 0.
cAlias	Character	Return the number of the work area where cAlias is open.
	Omitted	If nDoWhat is also omitted, return the number of the current work area.

SELECT() is a somewhat confused function—it has three related, yet quite different meanings. It can tell you the number of the current work area, or the work area where a table is open, or it can find an unused work area for you.

The 0 value for nDoWhat is unnecessary; omitting the parameter altogether has the same result.

SELECT(1) isn't all that useful anymore since SELECT 0 lets you find an available work area and USE ... IN 0 opens a table in an available area. We haven't found any reasons to want the highest rather than the lowest available work area—except, perhaps, to show off the 32,767 areas available in each data session.

SELECT() is especially useful when you need to change work areas in a black-box function. You can save the current work area, go do what you need to, then restore the work area before leaving the function. Other than this, we don't have any use for SELECT(), since we don't want to know what work area a table uses.

Example

```
LOCAL nSelect
* Save the work area
nSelect=SELECT()
* Now go to another
SELECT 0
USE SomeTable
* Do something
USE
* Return to original work area
SELECT (nSelect)
```

Usage

```
lInUse = USED( [ cAlias | nWorkArea ] )
```

USED() tells you whether a particular work area or alias is in use. With no parameter, it tells you whether there's a table open in the current work area. With nWorkarea, it tells whether the specified work area is in use.

When you pass an alias, it tells you whether any table is open with that alias. Notice that this is not the same as asking if a particular table is in use—this command checks aliases, not tables.

USED() is most handy to see whether you've already opened a particular table (and given it a particular alias). For example, you might use it to check whether a lookup table has already been opened.

Example

```
IF USED('lookups')
   SELECT lookups
ELSE
   SELECT 0
   USE lookups
ENDIF
```

See Also Alias, DBC(), DBUsed(), InDBC(), Select, Set Database, Set FullPath, Use

Align

Align is supposedly a property of OLE Controls (the holders for OCXs) that controls the position of their contents on the form. The documentation claims that it applies only to some OLE controls. We don't think that this is a VFP property at all, but rather a property of OCXs that appears in the VFP property sheet when available.

Usage

```
oleContainer.Align = nAlign
nAlign = oleContainer.Align
```

OLE controls are weird. If you put an OLE control on a form, you'll see some of the properties of the OCX appear on the VFP property sheet. We sure wish they'd given us a clue exactly which controls have an Align property; we haven't found any yet. But, in any case, we don't think the documentation for this property belongs in the VFP help file at all.

Example

```
frmForm.OLEControl.Align = 4
```

See Also OLEControl

Alignment

This is a property of many controls. Most of the time, it determines where the Caption or Value of the control appears. Whether Alignment applies to Caption or Value depends on the control. For controls that let you type into them (text box, edit box, combo box, spinner), Alignment is about Values. For other controls (check box, option button, header, label), Alignment is about Captions.

For grid columns, Alignment determines the position of the data shown in the column when the contained control doesn't have focus, and provides a default alignment for the contained control. In this case, it offers a lot more choices than for the other controls.

Usage

```
oObject.Alignment = nAlignment
nAlignment = oObject.Alignment
```

Parameter	Value	Meaning
nAlignment	0	Left—this is the default for most controls. For columns, this value means "middle left"—flush left and vertically centered.
	1	Right—this is the default for spinners and for a number of controls in the Middle Eastern version of Windows (in other words, for languages written right-to-left). For columns, this is "middle right"—flush right and vertically centered.
	2	Center—doesn't apply to some controls. For columns, this is "middle center."
	3	Automatic—applies only to text boxes and columns and is their default. It lets them adjust automatically based on whether the Value is character (left-justified) or numeric (right-justified).
	4	Top Left—applies to columns and headers only.
	5	Top Right—applies to columns and headers only.
	6	Top Center—applies to columns and headers only.
	7	Bottom Left—applies to columns and headers only.
	8	Bottom Right—applies to columns and headers only.
	9	Bottom Center—applies to columns and headers only.

First, be aware that, for those controls where Alignment affects Caption rather than Value (check boxes and the like), the meaning of Alignment is backwards from our instinctive reaction. Alignment here controls the position of the *control*, not the caption. That is, setting a check box to have left alignment means that the box appears to the left and the caption to the right.

Alignment has a whole collection of weird behaviors. With text boxes and spinners, if you use something other than the default alignment, the text or number bounces around when it receives and loses focus. Frankly, we think this is a bug, though it's in the "annoying" category rather than the "keeps you from getting something done" category.

In VFP 3, using Right alignment with option buttons causes a problem with the focus rectangle. When focus lands on a right-aligned check box or option button, the left-hand side of the focus rectangle is missing. This bug is fixed in VFP 5 and VFP 6.

Right-aligned option buttons have another problem as well. Each option button has its own Alignment property. So, some buttons in a group may be left-aligned while the others are right-aligned. We can't imagine why anyone would want to do this.

But wait, it gets better. When you right-align option buttons, by default, they're still lined up within the group based on their left edges. That is, the little circles don't line up. To solve the problem, you have to select the individual buttons and use the Layout toolbar or the Format menu to align the right edges.

Alignment and AutoSize have a strange relationship. For labels, setting AutoSize to .T. means that the value of Alignment is irrelevant. For check boxes and option buttons, you may want AutoSize set to .T. so that the entire caption shows—actually this isn't particularly related to Alignment, but the problem looks much stranger when using right-alignment than with left.

Alignments other than Left are a mess in combo boxes. When you use Center or Right alignment, the value in the combo disappears entirely in VFP 3. In VFP 5 and VFP 6, the value doesn't get aligned properly until you leave the combo. As long as it still has focus, the value is too far to the left.

For grid columns and headers, Alignment has a lot more choices than in the other cases. You can specify not just the horizontal alignment of the item, but its vertical alignment, too. For these controls, Automatic means centered vertically, but with horizontal alignment determined by the data type.

Non-Sparse columns don't pick up their vertical alignment immediately. When you start the form, the data is at the top. As soon as you click into the column, the data moves to the correct vertical position. You have to tab or click into each cell or do some scrolling to get all the data where it should be. Yuck!

Columns containing check boxes don't let you use any of the center alignments to center the check box itself in the column. In addition, check boxes in grids ignore the vertical alignment you specify (unless it's middle).

As far as we can tell, Alignment does work properly for headers and labels. That's a start.

Example

```
oForm = CREATE("Form")
oForm.Show()
oForm.AddObject("MyCheck", "CheckBox")
oForm.MyCheck.Visible = .T.
oForm.MyCheck.AutoSize = .T.
oForm.MyCheck.Caption = "Checker"
oForm.MyCheck.Alignment = 1  && Right
```

See Also AutoSize, Caption, DynamicAlignment, Value

_Alignment, _Indent, _LMargin, _RMargin, _Tabs

These variables are vestiges of the printer control system introduced in FoxPro 1.0. Like so much in FoxPro, it seemed like a good idea at the time, but has been superseded several times since.

These variables control aspects of individual lines produced by ? and ??. Except for _TABS, they're only effective when _WRAP is .T.

Usage

```
_ALIGNMENT = "LEFT" | "CENTER" | "RIGHT"
```

No, this variable doesn't determine the political affiliation of the end user. It indicates how text output with ? or ?? should be lined up. Best of all, it works as advertised.

Usage

```
_INDENT = nCharsToIndent
```

This one, on the other hand, is flaky. It works, sort of, when applied to memo fields, but not the rest of the time. We say "sort of" because it moves all lines of the memo out to the specified indent, not just the first line. Consider it a "block indent" rather than a "first line indent" and it makes some sense. This, no doubt, ties in with FoxPro's "automatic indent" capability which is so handy when writing code, but it keeps happening even when automatic indent is turned off.

Usage

```
_LMARGIN = nLeftMargin
_RMARGIN = nRightMargin
```

These variables let you set left and right margins for the print area. Both are measured from the left edge, in character columns of the current output font.

Usage

```
_TABS = cListOfTabStops
```

cListOfTabStops is a comma-delimited list of columns. Any CHR(9) in the text being output moves you to the next tab stop.

All in all, this is a nice set of pretty functional variables. It is remarkable that they work correctly with both proportional and non-proportional fonts. The only problem is they work with ? and ??. We don't use those much anymore, except to sound the bell, where margins and the like aren't particularly relevant.

Example

```
_LMARGIN = 5
_RMARGIN = 75
_WRAP = .T.
_TABS = "15,25,35"
? "Look"+CHR(9)+"I can"+CHR(9)+"Make"+CHR(9)+"Columns"
? "This is the beginning of a long line that will eventually "+;
 "wrap, showing how the margins work. In fact, showing THAT "+;
 "the margins work."
```

See Also ?, ??, _Wrap

ALines()

This new function lets you take character or memo data and dump it into an array, one line per array element. It's faster and easier than using MLINE() and _MLINE for the task. Each of the two approaches has advantages and disadvantages.

Usage

```
nLineCount = ALINES( DestArray, mField | cString [, lTrimIt ] )
```

Parameter	Value	Meaning
DestArray	Array Name	The array to contain the character or memo data.
mField, cString	Memo or Character	The string to be broken into lines. Can be a character or memo field or any character expression.
lTrimIt	.T.	Remove leading and trailing blanks from each line.
	.F. or Omitted	Leave leading and trailing blanks on lines.
nLineCount	Numeric	The number of lines in mField or cString, which is the same as the number of rows created in DestArray.

There are all kinds of times when we want to take a multi-line string and break it into its constituent lines for processing. We've had the ability to do so using the MLINE() function and its helper variable, _MLINE, for many versions of FoxPro. But it's always required a bunch of code—and putting the results into an array, which we often want to do, calls for even more code. Enter ALINES(), one function call to do the whole job.

ALINES() breaks up strings based on explicit line-break characters (either CHR(13) or CHR(10) or a combination of the two). It doesn't handle breaking long lines into reasonable lengths as MLINE() does and doesn't pay any attention to the MEMOWIDTH setting. This is both a good thing and a bad thing. When the string is VFP code that you want to execute one line at a time or text from another application that you're processing, not adding line breaks based on MEMOWIDTH is great. When the string is a message that you're trying to make printable, it's a pain. We wish they'd given us an optional line-length parameter (though it would undoubtedly slow the function down).

There's one other significant difference between ALINES() and MLINE(). MLINE() strips trailing blanks from each line it creates. By default, ALINES() doesn't. If you need those blanks, this is a big deal.

Example

```
* Assume mField is a memo field.
= ALINES(aAllLines, mField, .T.)

* Or use this with a string
nLines = ALINES(aAllLines, "Here is a string composed of " + ;
                "several lines."+ ;
                CHR(13)+"Here's the second line." + ;
                CHR(10)+"Here's the third line."+ ;
                CHR(13)+CHR(10)+"Notice that it doesn't "+ ;
                "matter which line break character you use.")
```

See Also MemLines(), MLine(), _MLine, Set MemoWidth

AllowAddNew

This property, added in VFP 5, gives you control over whether users can add new records to a grid by moving down out of the last item.

Usage

```
grdGrid.AllowAddNew = lLetUserAdd
lLetUserAdd = grdGrid.AllowAddNew
```

A lot of users view a grid as being pretty much the same thing as a word processor table or a spreadsheet, and expect to be able to add new records on the fly by moving out of the last record. This property controls that ability. When AllowAddNew is .T., pressing the down arrow in any field of the last record in a grid adds a new record to the RecordSource of the grid.

We're glad they added this property, but there's still not enough control over this capability. As programmers, we want an event that fires when a new record is added this way, so we can respond appropriately. The feature our users want is the one that tables in Word have—when you tab out of the last item in table, a new row is added to the table. You can do this in VFP, but you have to write an awful lot of code to make it work.

You can add records to the grid's RecordSource programmatically (APPEND BLANK or INSERT INTO) regardless of the setting of this property. This just controls the grid's interface.

AllowAddNew respects a table's read-only status. However, when the table is read-only for any reason (the table's or the grid's ReadOnly property is set to .T., the table was explicitly opened read-only with USE NOUPDATE or was created by a SELECT), attempting to add a record by pressing the down arrow gives you the error message "Cannot update selected cursor." We think this is terrible behavior—the down-arrow press should be ignored, just as it would be if AllowAddNew were set to .F.

Example

```
* You might let the user know that she can
* add records.
IF This.AllowAddNew

   * Make a label visible and set its caption
   ThisForm.lblAddMsg.Caption = ;
      "Add items by pressing down-arrow"
```

```
   ThisForm.lblAddMsg.Visible = .T.
ENDIF
```

See Also Append, Insert-SQL, ReadOnly

AllowHeaderSizing, AllowRowSizing

These two grid properties help to give you control over whether users can change the grids you so carefully set up. They determine whether the user can change the size of the header and the size of each row, respectively.

Usage

```
grdGrid.AllowHeaderSizing = lLetUserResizeHeader
lLetUserResizeHeader =  grdGrid.AllowHeaderSizing
grdGrid.AllowRowSizing = lLetUserResizeRows
lLetUserResizeRows =  grdGrid.AllowRowSizing
```

All rows in a grid have the same size, so AllowRowSizing indicates whether the user can resize all rows. There's no way to resize a single row.

The technique for resizing both headers and rows is somewhat restricted. To resize a grid header, you have to position your mouse near the left edge of the grid near the area where the header and the first row meet. The width of the area that gives you a resize cursor is the size of the record mark and delete mark columns, even if you've turned them off. Resizing rows works the same way—you have to have the mouse in the area where the record mark and delete mark columns belong. In addition, you only get a resize cursor at the bottom of the first visible row.

Example

```
IF This.AllowRowSizing
   WAIT WINDOW "You can make rows bigger or smaller by dragging"
ENDIF
```

See Also DeleteMark, RecordMark

AllowTabs

This property determines how Tabs behave in an edit box.

Usage

```
edtEditBox.AllowTabs = lAllowTabs
lAllowTabs = edtEditBox.AllowTabs
```

If AllowTabs is .F., which is the default, pressing Tab moves to the next control. If it's .T., the tab is added to the text; in this case, of course, Tab doesn't move you to the next control. But, in either case, you can use Ctrl+Tab to move forward and Ctrl+Shift+Tab to move backward. Our cut on this: Unless you design your user interface so that tabs are not needed anywhere else in the system, don't expect your users to remember when they can Tab and when they can't. Leave this one alone. If you really need Tabs in an edit box, include a note on the form telling the user how to move out of the box. If you need to allow input of formatted text, consider using the RichText control.

Example

```
* You might want to tell the user about CTRL+TAB
* to move on. You could set a label's caption:
ThisForm.lblCtrlTab.Caption = ;
    IIF(ThisForm.edtEditBox.AllowTabs, ;
        "CTRL+TAB when done ", "")
```

See Also EditBox

AllTrim(), LTrim(), RTrim(), Trim()

The functions in this group are used for removing spaces from the beginning or end of character strings. Let's clear up one thing right away: RTRIM() and TRIM() are identical. So, to paraphrase George Carlin, why are there two? Yep, it's another Xbase history thing. Way back when, the only function in this group was TRIM(), which removes trailing blanks from a string. Then LTRIM() was added to remove leading blanks. We figured the "L" stood for "Leading," but somehow people started thinking of it as "Left TRIM." Well, if there's a "Left TRIM," there must be a "Right TRIM," so RTRIM() was added to be complementary to LTRIM(). Another case of useless dBloat.

Technically, ALLTRIM(), which removes leading and trailing blanks, isn't really necessary either. You can do the same thing with LTRIM(TRIM(<a string>)). Even with a million or so iterations, the ALLTRIM() version is only slightly faster than the nested call, so it's not speed. We suppose it is a little easier to code it with ALLTRIM().

Usage

```
cReturnValue = ALLTRIM(cString)
cReturnValue = LTRIM(cString)
cReturnValue = RTRIM(cString)
cReturnValue = TRIM(cString)
```

The trim functions are particularly useful in two places. First is when dealing with character fields that may not be full, especially if you want to measure their length. LEN(<a field>) gives you the defined length of the field, not the amount of data it actually contains. To get that, you need:

```
LEN(TRIM(<a field>))
```

or, if there may be leading blanks:

```
LEN(ALLTRIM(<a field>))
```

The second place where trimming is particularly handy is in dealing with user input. If you want to search based on an input string, it's best to trim leading and trailing blanks. Users have a tendency not to worry too much about where the cursor is when they start typing or whether they've added extra spaces at the end. Say you're looking for a particular company in TasTrade's Customer table. If the name entered by the user is in m.cCompany, it's best to:

```
SET ORDER TO Company_Na
SEEK UPPER(ALLTRIM(m.cCompany))
```

Finally, notice that even ALLTRIM() doesn't remove all blanks from a string, just those at the beginning and end. Embedded blanks aren't touched—take a look at STUFF(), STRTRAN() and CHRTRAN() for that sort of thing.

Example

```
* If cFirstName and cLastName are fields,
* return a person's full name in the usual format
* For example: Herman Munster
?ALLTRIM(cFirstName)+" "+ALLTRIM(cLastName)
```

See Also ChrTran(), Len(), PadC(), PadL(), PadR(),StrTran(), Stuff()

Alter Table

We've been waiting for this command for years. Finally, we can change the structure of a table without resorting to all kinds of tricks. ALTER TABLE lets you add and remove fields, change a field, or change defaults and rules. ALTER TABLE works not only on tables, but on cursors built with CREATE CURSOR, though some clauses aren't relevant for cursors.

Usage

```
ALTER TABLE TableName
      ADD | ALTER [ COLUMN ] FieldName
            FieldType [ ( nFieldWidth [ ,nDecimals ] ) ]
            [ NULL | NOT NULL ]
            [ CHECK lFieldRule [ ERROR cFieldRuleMessage ] ]
            [ DEFAULT uDefaultExpression ]
            [ PRIMARY KEY | UNIQUE ]
            [ REFERENCES ReferencedTable
                     [ TAG ReferencedTag ] ]
            [ NOCPTRANS ]
      [ NOVALIDATE ]
ALTER TABLE TableName
      ALTER [ COLUMN ] FieldName
            [ NULL | NOT NULL ]
            [ SET DEFAULT uDefaultExpression]
            [ SET CHECK lFieldRule [ ERROR cFieldRuleMessage ] ]
            [ DROP DEFAULT ]
            [ DROP CHECK ]
      [ NOVALIDATE ]
```

```
ALTER TABLE TableName
      [ DROP [ COLUMN ] FieldName ]
      [ SET CHECK lTableRule [ ERROR cTableRuleMessage ] ]
      [ DROP CHECK ]
      [ ADD PRIMARY KEY uPrimaryKeyExpression
            TAG PrimaryKeyTag [ FOR lPrimaryKeyFilter ] ]
      [ DROP PRIMARY KEY ]
      [ ADD UNIQUE uUniqueKeyExpression [ TAG UniqueKeyTag1 ]
            [ FOR lUniqueKeyFilter ] ]
      [ DROP UNIQUE TAG UniqueKeyTag2 ]
      [ ADD FOREIGN KEY [ uForeignKeyExpression ]
            TAG ForeignKeyTag1 [ FOR lForeignKeyFilter ]
        REFERENCES ReferencedTable [ TAG ReferencedTag ] ]
      [ DROP FOREIGN KEY TAG ForeignKeyTag2 [ SAVE ] ]
      [ RENAME COLUMN OldFieldName TO NewFieldName ]
      [ NOVALIDATE ]
```

Parameter	Value	Meaning
FieldName	Name	The name of the field in the table to be added, changed or deleted. Long names can be used for tables in a database.
FieldType	Single character	The type to use for the field. Valid types are: C – Character D – Date T – DateTime N – Numeric F – Float (same as numeric) I – Integer B – Double Y – Currency L – Logical M – Memo G – General P – Picture
nFieldWidth	Numeric	The width of the field. For many types, the width is fixed and nFieldWidth should be omitted. For Double fields, nFieldWidth must be omitted.
nDecimals	Numeric	The number of decimal places for the field. Relevant only for some of the numeric types. For Double fields, nDecimals may be included, even though nFieldWidth is omitted.
lFieldRule	Logical	An expression that provides the field-level rule. Can call a function.
cFieldRuleMessage	Character	The error message to display when the field rule is violated.
uDefaultExpression	Same type as specified by FieldType	An expression that provides a default value for the field.
ReferencedTable	Name	The name of the table for which the field or expression is a foreign key. A regular index tag is created for this field or expression.

ReferencedTag	Name	The name of the tag in ReferencedTable to which the field or expression refers.
	Omitted	The field or expression refers to the primary key in ReferencedTable.
lTableRule	Logical	An expression that provides the table-level rule. Functions can be called. In VFP 3, table-level rules may not change the data in the table.
cTableRuleMessage	Character	The error message to display when the table-level rule is violated.
uPrimaryKeyExpression	Any type but Memo, General	An expression that forms the primary key for this table.
PrimaryKeyTag	Name	The name to assign the tag created for the primary key.
lPrimaryKeyFilter	Logical	An expression that filters the records in the primary key index. Only records for which the expression is true are included in the index. Don't do this—see below for the reason.
uUniqueKeyExpression	Any type	An expression that forms a candidate key for this table.
UniqueKeyTag1	Name	The name to assign the candidate key tag created.
lUniqueKeyFilter	Logical	An expression that filters the records in the candidate key index. Only records for which the expression is true are included in the index. Don't do this either, although we don't feel quite as strongly about this one.
UniqueKeyTag2	Name	The name of a candidate key to be deleted.
uForeignKeyExpression	Any type	An expression that is a foreign key into another table. A regular index tag is created for this expression.
ForeignKeyTag1	Name	The name of the tag to be created for uForeignKeyExpression.
lForeignKeyFilter	Logical	An expression that filters the records in the foreign key index. Only records for which the expression is true are included in the index. Need we say it again—don't do this.
ForeignKeyTag2	Name	The name of the tag that is part of a persistent relation to be removed. If SAVE is included, the tag is retained—only the relation is removed. If SAVE is omitted, the tag is also deleted.
OldFieldName	Name	The name of a field to be renamed.
NewFieldName	Name	The new name of the field.

There are three fundamental ways to use ALTER TABLE: you can add a field ("column" as this command calls it), change a field or change the table as a whole. Adding a field offers all the same bells and whistles as in CREATE TABLE. Changing a field can mean changing either its basic attributes, like type and size, or changing its database attributes, like default and rule. There are all kinds of ways to change the table itself, including changing its rule, removing fields, and changing indexes.

The three main ways to change a table, however, don't exactly map to the three forms of the command. The first form lets you both add and change fields. The second form is for field changes that don't involve the basic attributes, and the third form is for table changes. We're not sure why three forms are necessary, but we suspect it boils down to conforming with ANSI SQL. Fair enough. Of course, the FOR clauses added in VFP 6 surely are a violation of the ANSI standard for SQL.

ALTER TABLE requires exclusive use of the table. In VFP 3, if the table is in a database, the database has to be open exclusively as well. In VFP 5 or later, the database must not be opened NOUPDATE; SHARED or EXCLUSIVE will work.

There are many ways in which changes can go wrong. For example, when you add a rule, all existing records are checked to be sure they meet the new criteria. If not, the changes fail. Because one problem can cause the entire command to fail, you don't want to issue massive ALTER TABLEs that affect lots of things at once. Instead, take it one step at time, issuing a series of ALTER TABLE commands. (In fact, only some clauses can be combined or repeated.)

NOVALIDATE tells FoxPro to change the structure of the table without checking that all existing records meet all the new criteria. It's dangerous. While it can be helpful in some situations, it also can leave you with invalid data. In that case, the rules don't get checked until you actually change a field affected by a rule—passing through the field isn't sufficient. You may want to follow an ALTER TABLE NOVALIDATE with a loop that REPLACEs things and traps the errors so you can deal with them.

When you use ALTER COLUMN to specify a new type or size for an existing field, be sure to specify all the information for that field. ALTER TABLE treats this operation as if you'd deleted the field, then added it back. So, the settings for NULL and NOCPTRANS are lost, as are the default value and rule. You may want to use AFIELDS() to collect the information first, so you can reapply it.

When you use the second form of the command, though, giving only the name of the field, FoxPro understands that you're making changes to the field and changes only those items you specify.

If you want to remove a field that's part of a primary or candidate key, you have to explicitly DROP that tag as well as the field. You can do this in one ALTER TABLE command, but failing to DROP the tag generates an error.

RENAME COLUMN, on the other hand, won't let you shoot yourself in the foot too badly (unless you use NOVALIDATE, of course). If you try to rename a field that's used in a rule or a key expression, you get an error. Of course, you might have referenced the field elsewhere, so you still have to be careful.

DROP FOREIGN KEY is confusing because it can do two different things. Its main role is to remove persistent relations—it deletes the relation of which the named tag forms the many side. If you don't specify SAVE, the tag itself is also deleted.

One of the Xbase things that the SQL table handling commands haven't allowed is filtering an index tag; that is, specifying that only certain records should appear when a certain tag is in use. VFP 6 lets you add filters to keys with ALTER TABLE. On the whole, we suggest you stay away from filtered indexes. Rushmore doesn't use them and they're likely to cause confusion. The one situation where we can see the point is if you're recycling deleted records—in that case, you may want to filter your primary key on DELETED() so you don't run into uniqueness problems. If you do so, be sure to create a regular, unfiltered index tag for that field, too, so Rushmore can help you out.

Example

```
OPEN DATABASE Testing
CREATE TABLE Test1 (cId C(3), cName c(20) UNIQUE)
CREATE TABLE Test2 (cTest1Id C(3), dDate D)
ALTER TABLE Test1 ADD COLUMN nTotal N(4)
ALTER TABLE Test1 ALTER COLUMN cId C(3) PRIMARY KEY ;
      DEFAULT GetId("Test1")
ALTER TABLE Test1 ALTER COLUMN cName SET CHECK NOT EMPTY(cName)
ALTER TABLE Test1 DROP UNIQUE TAG cName
```

```
ALTER TABLE Test2 ADD FOREIGN KEY cTest1Id TAG cTest1Id ;
      REFERENCES Test1
```

See Also Create Cursor, Create Table, Index, Modify Structure

AlwaysOnBottom

This property lets you create forms that insist on staying underneath everything else.

Usage

```
frmForm.AlwaysOnBottom = lBottomDweller
lBottomDweller = frmForm.AlwaysOnBottom
```

Our initial reaction to this property was "Why the heck would you want to do that?" But a conversation with a member of the Microsoft VFP team, followed by an incredible demo at the 1998 FoxPro DevCon from super-guru Ken Levy, drove the point home. What this property lets you do is replace the VFP desktop with your own custom desktop, one with all the capabilities of a form. Ken's demonstration used a form with the Web Browser control on it, so inside VFP, while running other forms, he could navigate to Web sites, keep up-to-date on the weather, download files, and so forth. We're not at all sure we'd want to run our development environment that way, but we get it.

AlwaysOnBottom is also useful in an ActiveDoc environment, where it lets you set up the background for your application. We suspect that was the original intention of adding this property, but like many things Fox, it may find uses far beyond its original design.

We're pleased to find that this property behaves fairly sensibly (not to mention as documented). For example, if you turn on both AlwaysOnTop and AlwaysOnBottom, VFP is smart enough to ignore you and only keep the form on top.

Example

```
* If this window is in the background, add a label
IF This.AlwaysOnBottom
   This.AddObject("lblInfo","label")
   This.lblInfo.AutoSize = .T.
   This.lblInfo.Top = 50
   This.lblInfo.Caption = "I'm right behind you"
   This.lblInfo.FontSize = 20
   This.lblInfo.Visible = .T.
ENDIF
```

See Also ActiveDoc, AlwaysOnTop, Form

AlwaysOnTop, AutoCenter

These form properties control whether the form stays on top of other displayed forms and whether the form is automatically centered when it opens.

Usage

```
frmForm.AlwaysOnTop = lIsAlwaysOnTop
lIsAlwaysOnTop = frmForm.AlwaysOnTop
frmForm.AutoCenter = lStartsCentered
lStartsCentered = frmForm.AutoCenter
```

Forms with AlwaysOnTop set to .T. can't go beneath forms where that property is set to .F., even if the second one is the active form. If you have multiple AlwaysOnTop windows, though, they can go over each other. (To see how an AlwaysOnTop form behaves, right-click on the Property Sheet and make sure Always on Top is checked, or, in VFP 3, push the pushpin on the Property Sheet.) An AlwaysOnTop form doesn't prevent other forms from getting focus; it just makes it hard to use the other forms. Use the form's WindowType property or Show method parameters to make the form modal and prevent others from getting focus.

Forms with AutoCenter set to .T. appear centered when they first start up. Setting AutoCenter to .T. when a form is running centers it on the spot, but setting AutoCenter to .F. doesn't change the form's position. AutoCenter doesn't keep the user from moving the form, either—use Movable for that.

AlwaysOnTop is ignored at design-time, but in VFP 3, AutoCenter is not. Since it's a pain to design a form that's centered, if you're working in VFP 3 you'll probably want to set AutoCenter in the form's Init method rather than in the PropSheet.

Example

```
* Form Init might contain:
This.AlwaysOnTop = .T.
This.AutoCenter = .T.
```

See Also Form, Movable, Show, WindowType

AMembers()

This function gives you access to all the stuff inside an object. The parameters you pass it determine whether the array it creates contains all the properties of an object, all the properties, methods and contained objects, or just the contained objects. AMEMBERS() is particularly useful for writing black-box code like Builders.

Usage

```
nMemberCount = AMembers( ArrayName, oObject | cClass
                         [, nInfoType ] )
```

Parameter	Value	Meaning
ArrayName	Array Name	The array to hold the information about oObject.
oObject	Object	The object whose members are stored in ArrayName.
cClass	Character	The class whose members are stored in ArrayName.
nInfoType	Omitted	Put only a list of oObject's properties in ArrayName. In this case, ArrayName is one-dimensional.
	1	Put a complete list of oObject's properties, methods, and member objects in ArrayName. ArrayName is two-dimensional with names in the first column and either "Property", "Method" or "Object" in the second column.
	2	Put only a list of oObject's member objects in ArrayName. ArrayName is one-dimensional.
nMemberCount	Positive number	The number of elements in ArrayName if nInfoType is omitted or 2. If nInfoType is 1, the number of rows in ArrayName. In all cases, this is the number of members found.
	0	There are no members of the type specified. As far as we can tell, this can only occur with nInfoType=2.

When oObject doesn't exist, AMEMBERS() generates an error. That's good. What's not good is that it also goes ahead and creates ArrayName if it doesn't already exist. This is different than the other array-handling functions and appears to be a bug.

AMEMBERS() only works for native FoxPro objects. Attempting to get the members of an ActiveX server through this function will only result in frustration.

Example

```
oForm = CREATEOBJECT("Form")                && create a form
nPropCnt = AMembers(aProps, oForm)          && properties only
nMembCnt = AMembers(aMembs, oForm, 1)       && all members
nChildCnt = AMembers(aKids, oForm, 2)       && contained objects only
                                            && returns zero in this case
```

```
* now add some objects
oForm.AddObject("lblName", "Label")
oForm.AddObject("chkPresent", "Checkbox")

nChildCnt = AMembers(aKids, oForm, 2) && now returns two

* Do it for a class
nProps = AMembers(aProps, "Form")  && gets properties of a form

* Try an ActiveX Server
oWord = CREATEOBJECT("Word.Basic")
? AMembers(laMember, oWord)        && returns zero
```

See Also AClass(), AInstance(), Array Manipulation, CreateObject()

AMouseObj()

This function, new in VFP 6, gives you information about the current position of the mouse pointer.

Usage `nFoundSomething = AMouseObj( Info [, nRelativeToForm ] )`

Parameter	Value	Meaning
Info	Array Name	Name of the array to hold the results of the function.
nRelativeToForm	Omitted	Return information about the mouse position relative to the container of the object over which the mouse is positioned.
	1 (or any other value)	Return information about the mouse position relative to the containing form.
nFoundSomething	4	The mouse is positioned over an object and the array has been filled with the information.
	0	The mouse is positioned over something that's not an object in the sense of this function and the array is unchanged.

There are two confusing parts about this function. The first is what objects it recognizes. Any VFP form or control is recognized, as are some parts of the development environment. If the mouse is outside VFP or over one of the unrecognized objects, the function returns 0 and leaves the array alone. For no reason we can think of, Browses are among the unrecognized objects even though they're really grids internally.

The second confusing thing needs some background. The function fills the first two array elements with object references to the object itself and the object's container. The third and fourth elements contain the coordinates (in pixels) of the mouse position relative to the container. However (and this is the part we found confusing—with any luck, we've explained it so clearly, you won't be confused), if the optional second parameter is passed, the second element gets a reference to the containing form, no matter how deep in the hierarchy the control is. In that case, the point returned in the third and fourth elements is instead relative to the form.

To make matters even more confusing, the function doesn't handle grids properly. When you call AMouseObj() with the mouse over a grid column (either the header or the control in the grid) and omit the second parameter, both object references point to the column. Sounds like somebody can't decide how deep to drill here. The new GridHitTest method should help you work around this one.

You need to release the array (or at least null the first two elements) before you can release the form. Otherwise, the references in the array prevent the form from being destroyed.

Like SYS(1270), this function tells you about the mouse position without requiring a click. Because it's available at design time as well as runtime (as is SYS(1270)), we suspect it'll see a lot of use in builders.

Example

```
* Find out if we're over a particular form
IF AMouseObj(aWhereAreWe) = 4
   * Got something
   IF aWhereAreWe[1] = oSomeObject && note that we can now
                                   && compare objects directly
      * Do something
   ELSE
      * Do something different
   ENDIF
ENDIF
```

See Also ASelObj(), GridHitTest, Sys(1270)

ANetResources()

ANetResources() returns an array of the file or printer shares available.

Usage

```
nCount = ANetResources( ArrayName, cServer, nFileOrPrint )
```

Parameter	Value	Meaning
ArrayName	Array name	The array to be filled with the requested information. The usual VFP array behavior occurs: If no resources are found, the array isn't created if it doesn't exist, and isn't redimensioned if it already exists. If the resources do exist, the array is created if necessary, and is redimensioned to a one-column array with the proper number of rows if it does exist.
cServer	Character	The name of the network resource to query.
nFileOrPrint	1	Return file resources.
	2	Return print resources.
nCount	Numeric	The number of resources found. 0 if no resources are shared or the server can't be contacted.

A share is a directory or printing device on another computer on the network that has been made available for use by the network users. They are named using the Universal Naming Convention (UNC) as a string of the form "\\ServerName\ResourceName" and can be accessed through the Explorer, the DOS command line (NET USE for Windows, MAP for Netware) or within FoxPro by functions that support the UNC means of access—we're pleased to note that more and more functions and commands in VFP 6.0 seem to support this. Use ANetResources() to get a list of these file or printer shares. You might want to use this list to display options to the operator on where files might be found or saved, or to choose which print device to use. You do need to know the name of the server providing the service in advance—this isn't a tool to broadcast a request for services available. Look at the second column of the array created by APrinters() to get some server names.

Example

```
* Get the names of printer shares from Prometheus
? ANETRESOURCES(laNet, "\\Prometheus", 2)
```

See Also APrinters(), Directory(), File(), PrtInfo()

ANSIToOEM() See OEMToANSI().

Append

APPEND lets you add individual records to a table, either interactively or behind the scenes. It's also first cousin to the APPEND FROM and APPEND FROM ARRAY commands that add batches of records. They're discussed elsewhere.

Usage
```
APPEND [ BLANK ] [ IN nWorkArea | cAlias ] [ NOMENU ]
```

Used alone, APPEND opens a window for adding new records to the current table. The window displays records in the EDIT format (as opposed to BROWSE format). Each time you add data to the current new record, a template for another new record is added. The new record isn't committed to the table, however, until you actually put some data in it. This form of APPEND is really another variation of BROWSE. Notice that the same menu pad (Table) appears for APPEND as for BROWSE or EDIT, and the View menu pad displays the options for EDIT or BROWSE views.

APPEND BLANK adds a record with no interaction. All fields are blank (that is, ISBLANK() is true for each field in the added record). APPEND BLANK has had an up-and-down history. Prior to FoxPro 2, it was a very important command as the primary programmatic way to add new records. Then, INSERT-SQL stole the show because it has some advantages when editing memory variables—it's faster to INSERT a record than to APPEND BLANK and GATHER. With the addition of buffering in Visual FoxPro, APPEND BLANK has undergone a renaissance as a good way to work in data input forms. When you're working with buffered data, APPEND BLANK is the only way to add a blank record without rules firing. If your rules prohibit some columns from being empty, you need APPEND BLANK to give the user an empty record to fill.

The IN clause lets you add a record in a work area other than the current work area. Watch out for one documented, but nonetheless weird, behavior. When you APPEND BLANK IN another work area, everything behaves the way you'd expect—the record is added and you're left in the same work area you started in. But when you issue APPEND IN another work area, that work area becomes current.

NOMENU suppresses the Table pad and the Browse-related options on the View pad.

APPEND without BLANK respects SET CARRY.

Example
```
USE TestData
APPEND          && Now add data interactively

* This code might appear in the Click event of a Save button
* for a data entry screen that's in "continuous add" mode
= TABLEUPDATE()
APPEND BLANK
ThisForm.Refresh()
```

See Also Append From, Append From Array, Browse, Insert-SQL

Append From, Copy To, Import, Export

These commands let you move data in and out of DBF format. APPEND FROM and COPY TO also let you move data between tables.

Usage
```
APPEND FROM FileName | ?
        [ FIELDS FieldList ]
        [ FOR lCondition ]
        [ [ TYPE ] DELIMITED
          [ WITH Delimiter | WITH BLANK  | WITH TAB ]
```

```
            [ WITH CHARACTER Separator ]
           | DIF | FW2 | MOD | PDOX | RPD | SDF
           | SYLK | WK1 | WK3 | WKS | WR1 | WRK | XLS
           | XL5 [SHEET SheetName] | XL8 [SHEET SheetName ] ]
          [ AS nCodePage ]
IMPORT FROM FileName [ TYPE ] FW2 | MOD | PDOX | RPD | WK1
           | WK3 | WKS | WR1 | WRK | XLS
           | XL5 [ SHEET cSheetName ] | XL8 [SHEET cSheetName ]
          [ AS nCodePage ]
```

APPEND FROM and IMPORT bring in data in a foreign format and put it in a FoxPro table. The difference is that APPEND FROM adds data to an existing table, while IMPORT creates a new table, figuring out what fields it should have. (In some cases, the new table's field names are distinctly stupid.) In addition, APPEND FROM lets you specify the mapping of data to fields and lets you omit some of the incoming data.

APPEND FROM adds the data to the table open in the current work area. IMPORT creates and opens a table, giving it the same name as the source file, but with a DBF extension.

APPEND FROM deals with more file formats than IMPORT. In addition to all the foreign formats, you can use it to move data between two FoxPro tables or from text files into a table. (If you omit the TYPE clause entirely, data is appended from one FoxPro table to another.)

Don't count on a COPY TO and APPEND FROM pair returning the original file in all configurations. SYLK is limited to 9,999 records while APPENDing. COPYing to most of the spreadsheet formats, like DIF and MOD, introduces a header that may create a blank first record while importing. WK1, WKS, WR1 and WRK formats are limited to 8,192 rows. Note that for several of the formats, like WK3's, you can use APPEND, but not COPY TO.

We figure if you have data with one of the listed extensions, you know where it came from and what it looks like, so we won't get into details like "PDOX is paradox data." If you really want to know, Help has a complete list.

Instead, let's look at the ones that don't correspond to foreign file formats: DELIMITED and SDF. SDF is simpler—it stands for "system data format" and refers to a file where each field takes up a fixed amount of space corresponding to its length. Even if APPEND FROM didn't support SDF files, these are pretty easy to read in and parse.

DELIMITED is for files that contain data with delimiters and separators. There's a lot of confusion about those two, particularly since the command itself mixes them up. Delimiters are characters that surround the data in a field. For example, the word "snazzlefritz" is delimited by quote marks in this sentence. Separators come between two data items. For example, the following list of colors uses commas as separators: "chartreuse, lavender, fuchsia, taupe, teal." A delimited file normally contains both delimiters and separators. Here's an example (generated from the Labels.DBF that comes with VFP):

```
"DATAW","LABELLYT","Avery 4143",F,4869,/  /
"DATAW","LABELLYT","Avery 4144",F,39266,/  /
"DATAW","LABELLYT","Avery 4145",F,24620,/  /
"DATAW","LABELLYT","Avery 4146",F,32961,/  /
```

Each character field is surrounded by quotes (the delimiters), and fields are separated by commas. This is the default format for a delimited file.

TYPE DELIMITED can handle several other options; each is a little different. DELIMITED WITH BLANK uses no delimiters, and fields are separated by spaces. In DELIMITED WITH TAB, fields are actually delimited with quotes and separated by tabs. DELIMITED WITH Delimiter lets you specify the delimiter—fields are separated by commas.

VFP 5 introduced the DELIMITED WITH CHARACTER clause that lets you specify the separator. So DELIMITED WITH CHARACTER ! means that there's an exclamation point between each pair of fields. We can't see why they couldn't have improved the situation here by giving this option a useful name like SEPARATED BY. Nonetheless, we're very grateful to have this option because it increases the number of files we can handle without having to break out the low-level file functions.

You can combine DELIMITED WITH and DELIMITED WITH CHARACTER to specify both the delimiter and the separator.

On the whole, the choices are quite a mess. If you're still confused by this, we suggest you do what we did to figure all this out. Try COPY TO with each option on a small data sample.

The FOR clause of APPEND FROM looks at each record as if it had already been added to the table in question and evaluates the condition in that situation. In older versions of FoxPro, this was a big issue because the deleted flag of a record didn't come along on an APPEND, so it could be very difficult to copy all the deleted or all the undeleted records. Starting in VFP 3, the deleted flag comes along, so this issue just doesn't come up very often. The time you're most likely to run into this is if the table you're copying from has a logical field indicating that it should be copied, but the field doesn't exist in the destination. Say there's an lArchive field in the source indicating that the record is ready to be archived. When you issue a command like:

```
USE Archive
APPEND FROM Source FOR Source.lArchive
```

the lArchive field is evaluated only for the first record of the source, not for each one in turn. So either all records or no records are copied.

Finally, the AS clause of both commands lets you specify the code page of the original data so it can be translated on the way in.

Example

```
USE MyTable
APPEND FROM MyOtherTable FOR nAmount>500

IMPORT FROM MailList.XLS TYPE XLS
```

Usage

```
COPY TO FileName
        [ DATABASE DBCName [ NAME LongTableName ] ]
        [ FIELDS FieldList
         | FIELDS LIKE Skeleton
         | FIELDS EXCEPT Skeleton ]
        [ Scope ] [ FOR lForCondition ]
        [ WHILE lWhileCondition ]
        [ [ WITH ] CDX | [ WITH ] PRODUCTION ]
        [ NOOPTIMIZE ]
        [ [ TYPE ] FOXPLUS | FOX2X | DIF | MOD | SDF | SYLK
         | WK1 | WKS | WR1 | WRK | XLS | XL5 | XL8
         | DELIMITED [ WITH Delimiter | WITH BLANK
         | WITH TAB ] [ WITH CHARACTER Separator ] ]
        [ AS nCodePage ]
EXPORT TO FileName [ FIELDS FieldList ]
        [ Scope ] [ FOR lForCondition ]
        [ WHILE lWhileCondition ]
        [ NOOPTIMIZE ]
        [ TYPE ] | DIF | MOD | SYLK | WK1 | WKS | WR1 | WRK
         | XLS | XL5 | XL8
        [ AS nCodePage ]
```

Both COPY TO and EXPORT copy selected data to another file. We can't see much reason to use EXPORT, since COPY TO can do everything it does and more. (In fact, we're fairly convinced EXPORT exists only because IMPORT does.) Both create a brand-new file containing the specified data.

Because the original source for COPY TO and EXPORT is a table, you have more options as to which records are involved. The usual Scope, FOR and WHILE clauses let you pick and choose among the records. Unlike APPEND FROM, in COPY TO the clauses are evaluated before the data is copied. And, just in case you like to slow things down, there's NOOPTIMIZE.

See the discussion above for an explanation of SDF and DELIMITED files. COPY TO also includes the FOXPLUS and FOX2X options that let you create tables that are compatible with older Fox products. A

FOXPLUS table is really a dBase III Plus table and is compatible with just about everything around.

When you're copying to another Visual FoxPro table, you can make various choices. You can create either a free table or a table that's contained in a database. If you chose to put it into a database, you can specify a long name for it. You can also decide whether to copy the structural CDX file—that's what WITH is all about.

The AS clause lets you create the new file with a different code page than the original.

Example

```
USE Labels
* Check out some of the options.
COPY TO LabelPlus TYPE FOXPLUS
COPY TO Label2x TYPE FOX2X
COPY TO Label.Txt FIELDS Type, Id, Name, CkVal ;
   TYPE DELIMITED
COPY TO Label.Txt FIELDS Type, Id, Name, CkVal;
   TYPE DELIMITED WITH BLANK
COPY TO Label.Txt FIELDS Type, Id, Name, CkVal;
   TYPE DELIMITED WITH TAB
COPY TO Label.Txt FIELDS Type, Id, Name, CkVal;
   TYPE DELIMITED WITH ~
COPY TO Label.Txt FIELDS Type, Id, Name, CkVal;
   TYPE DELIMITED WITH CHARACTER #
COPY TO Label.Txt FIELDS Type, Id, Name, CkVal;
   TYPE DELIMITED WITH ~ WITH CHARACTER #
```

Take a look at the file created for each of the last six examples to understand the different DELIMITED options.

COPY TO is also our command of choice for eliminating deleted records in a file. We use it instead of PACK. See DELETE for a code sample.

See Also Append From Array, Copy File, Delete, Pack, Set Optimize

Append From Array, Copy To Array

These commands let you move data between tables and arrays. APPEND FROM ARRAY adds data to a table from an array, while COPY TO ARRAY moves table data into an array.

Usage

```
APPEND FROM ARRAY ArrayName
         [ FIELDS FieldList
          | LIKE IncludeList | EXCEPT ExcludeList ]
         [ FOR lExpr ]
COPY TO ARRAY ArrayName
         [ FIELDS FieldList
          | LIKE IncludeList | EXCEPT ExcludeList ]
         [ Scope ] [ FOR lExpr1 ] [ WHILE lExpr2 ]
         [ NOOPTIMIZE ]
```

APPEND FROM ARRAY and COPY TO ARRAY use the table open in the current work area. With COPY TO, if the array doesn't already exist, it's created as a two-dimensional array.

Many folks don't realize that these commands behave differently depending on whether ArrayName is one-dimensional or two-dimensional. With a one-dimensional array, these commands operate on a single record of the current table. With a two-dimensional array, they operate on multiple records. This behavior often trips people up when they want to copy a single field from multiple records. They create a one-dimensional array with as many items as records to be copied, but when they COPY TO ARRAY, they get just one field. Instead, either make sure the array doesn't already exist (so it gets created) or dimension it as a two-dimensional array with a single column.

```
USE Employee
DIMENSION aCity[RECCOUNT(), 1]
COPY TO ARRAY aCity FIELDS City
```

The FIELDS clause lets you specify which field or fields are involved. With APPEND FROM ARRAY, when no field list is specified, data is copied from the array into fields starting with the first until either all fields get a value or all columns have been used. With COPY TO, you get one column of the array for each field of the table. When a field list is specified for either command, columns are matched to the fields in the order they're listed. Starting in FoxPro 2.6, you can give either a specific list of fields to include or you can provide skeletons for field names to include and exclude. Both include and exclude skeletons can be used, and they work together to generate the complete result. For example, to get all character information from a table that precedes character fields with "c", but omit phone numbers, use:

```
USE TheTable
COPY TO ARRAY aMyData FIELDS LIKE c* EXCEPT cPhone
```

Incredibly, you can use LIKE and EXCEPT with APPEND FROM ARRAY as well to copy array data into specific fields. What you can't do in either APPEND FROM ARRAY or COPY TO ARRAY is combine a list of specific fields with inclusion and exclusion. Too bad. It would be very cool to be able to write something like:

```
USE TheTable
COPY TO ARRAY aMyData FIELDS cFirstName, cLastName LIKE n*
```

and end up with the name and all numeric fields.

The FOR clause of APPEND FROM ARRAY evaluates each row as if it had already been added to the table. If it doesn't pass the test, it's not added, however. This is the same way that other flavors of APPEND operate; it goes way back in Xbase history.

The Scope, FOR and WHILE clauses of COPY TO ARRAY determine which records get copied to the array. See "Scope, FOR, WHILE and Santa Clauses" in "Xbase Xplained" for an explanation.

You can probably ignore NOOPTIMIZE. See SET OPTIMIZE if you don't want to.

Actually, you can probably ignore the whole command. We don't find much use for COPY TO ARRAY. SELECT-SQL can do everything COPY TO ARRAY does and more.

Example

```
* copy everyone in Sales to array
USE Employee
COPY TO ARRAY aSales FOR UPPER(Title) = "SALES"

* now add them to some other table
SELECT SalesStaff
APPEND FROM ARRAY aSales
```

See Also Append From, Copy To, Dimension, Select-SQL, Set Optimize

Append General, Modify General

These two commands work with a table's ActiveX-based general fields. APPEND allows the addition of new data or the erasure of a field. MODIFY displays the field for editing or viewing.

Usage

```
APPEND GENERAL FieldName
        [ FROM FileName | FROM MEMO MemoField ]
        [ DATA cDataString ]
        [ LINK ]
        [ CLASS cClassName ]
```

Parameter	Value	Meaning
FieldName	Name	Name of the general field where the data is placed.
FileName	Name	Source of the data, if data is added from disk.
MemoField	Name	VFP 3/Mac only: imports picture fields into general fields.

Parameter	Value	Meaning
cDataString	Character	An initial data string (like PARAMETERS in FoxPro) to send to the application. Many OLE servers accept CF_TEXT formatted strings and use them as their initial data.
cClassName	Character	The OLE Class name, as listed in the Registry.

It's a little-known fact that APPEND GENERAL FieldName with no further arguments erases the data contained inside the general field.

The DATA keyword allows your application to squirt a little data into the general field. The most typical format for this data is called the CF_TEXT format, which is similar to the tab-delimited text format of the EXPORT and COPY commands: individual fields are separated with tabs, individual records with a carriage return and line feed pair. The example below demonstrates the creation of a simple graph with data preformatted in this fashion.

The CLASS keyword allows you to specify programmatically which OLE object is to be inserted into the general field. You can choose from the same items available from the "Insert Object" menu pad when working interactively. The trick to getting the right item is to determine what the class should be called. You can find these in your documentation or in the Registry under HKEY_CLASSES_ROOT. This clause can be used to override the default ActiveX server if more than one is installed on your system (for example, if you work with several programs that edit BMP files) or if the extension of the file is not the standard extension (such as DOC for word processing documents) used for the ActiveX server.

The LINK keyword is used to determine if the data should be embedded within the general field or linked to it. The advantage of embedding is that no link to the original file is retained, and changes made to the object are retained only within the copy in the table. The disadvantage of this method is that those changes cannot be shared with other applications. For example, the company logo bitmap might be modified in a paint program; if the copies stored in tables are linked, they too will immediately display the changed image. More information on general fields is located in "DBF, FPT, CDX, DBC—Hike!"

Usage

```
MODIFY GENERAL FieldName1 [, FieldName2... ]
        [ NOMODIFY ]
        [ NOWAIT ]
        [ WINDOW DefinitionWindow ]
        [ IN WINDOW ContainerWindow] | IN SCREEN
         | IN MACDESKTOP ]
```

Parameter	Value	Meaning
FieldName*n*	Name	Specifies the field name(s) to be displayed.
DefinitionWindow	Name	Specifies the window whose characteristics (size, color scheme, close box, whether it floats) are duplicated in the window created to display the general field.
ContainerWindow	Name	Names the window in which the general field editing window is created and in which editing takes place.

MODIFY GENERAL is very similar to the MODIFY MEMO command, except the data to be edited is visual rather than textual. In general, we feel we'll be avoiding this command in applications, since we can do most of the same things, and with finer control, with an OLEBoundControl placed on a form. From the command line, it's a handy way to view or edit the contents of a general field.

More information on OLE, COM and ActiveX is located in the "Active-Something" section in the back of the book.

Example

```
#DEFINE tab CHR(09)
#DEFINE crlf CHR(13)+CHR(10)
LOCAL cTestData
cTestdata = ""          + tab + "X-Axis" + crlf + ;
            "Command"  + tab + "431"    + crlf + ;
            "Function" + tab + "332"    + crlf + ;
            "Property" + tab + "211"    + crlf + ;
            "Method"   + tab + "43"     + crlf
CREATE TABLE SmplGrph (mygraph G)
APPEND BLANK
APPEND GENERAL MyGraph CLASS "MSGraph" DATA cTestdata
MODIFY GENERAL MyGraph NOMODIFY
```

See Also @ ... SAY-BMPs & OLE Objects, OLEBoundControl, OLEControl, Registration Database

Append Memo, Copy Memo

These commands let you move data between files and memo fields. Though Help implies that only text files can be manipulated this way, in fact these commands are also good for moving binary files in and out of memo files. You might, for example, store a compiled program in a memo field, then copy it to a file and run it when you need it. Memos can also store bitmaps, to be displayed when needed, if the resource overhead of OLE is too much for your targeted audience.

Usage

```
APPEND MEMO MemoField FROM FileName
        [ OVERWRITE ]
        [ AS nCodePage ]
COPY MEMO MemoField TO FileName
        [ ADDITIVE ]
        [ AS nCodePage ]
```

Parameter	Value	Meaning
MemoField	Name	The memo field into or out of which data is to be copied.
FileName	Name	The file from or into which the data is copied.
nCodePage	Numeric	The code page of the file.

At first glance, it seems odd that APPEND MEMO has OVERWRITE as an optional keyword while COPY MEMO has the inverse ADDITIVE. But all the APPEND commands add to existing data rather than replacing it, by default. On the other hand, COPY commands in FoxPro all default to replacing existing data. So, while these two are mutually inconsistent, they're each consistent with other commands. Guess we can't complain about that too much, except to wonder who made the initial decision way back when that APPEND and COPY should behave differently.

The optional AS clause lets you deal with the case that the text file uses a different code page than the table. You can specify the file's current code page and the data is translated on the way in. If you don't specify, the data is copied as-is (which is what you probably want in the case of, say, object code). In that case, you'll probably also want to mark the memo field as NOCPTRANS.

Example

```
* Store a compiled program in a memo field
APPEND MEMO mProgram FROM MyProgram.FXP OVERWRITE
* Now you can save it out and run it later
cProgramFile = SYS(3) + ".FXP"
COPY MEMO mProgram TO (cProgramFile)
DO (cProgramFile)
```

See Also Alter Table, Append From, Copy File, Copy To, Create Table, Set NoCPTrans

Append Procedures, Copy Procedures

These commands let you move code between the stored procedures of a database and text files. APPEND PROCEDURES adds the contents of a file to the current database's stored procedures, while COPY PROCEDURES lets you save the stored procedures in a file.

Usage

```
APPEND PROCEDURES FROM FileName
      [ AS nCodePage ]
      [ OVERWRITE ]
COPY PROCEDURES TO FileName
      [ AS nCodePage ]
      [ ADDITIVE ]
```

As with other APPEND/COPY pairs, the default for APPEND is additive, while the default for COPY is destructive. Hence, APPEND PROCEDURES has an optional OVERWRITE keyword that lets you replace what's already there, while COPY PROCEDURES' optional ADDITIVE clause lets you keep what's already there and add to it.

The AS codepage in each command specifies a codepage for the text file. On the way in, FoxPro converts from that codepage to the database's codepage. On the way out, the reverse happens.

COPY PROCEDURES assumes an extension of TXT (rather than PRG, as we'd expect). APPEND PROCEDURES, on the other hand, is even less sensible—if you don't give it an extension, it assumes you don't want one. So APPEND PROCEDURES FROM MyProc doesn't look for MyProc.PRG or even MyProc.TXT, but just plain old MyProc. The upshot of all this is that you should always include the extension with these commands.

In VFP 3, when the stored procedures already contain RI code generated by the RI builder, there's no final return. When you APPEND PROCEDURES, the first line of the text file ends up on the same line as the final RI-generated line. Leaving things that way is guaranteed to cause trouble down the road, so you'll want to make sure the extra return gets in there somehow, whether by manually inserting it or by making sure the first line of the appended file contains just a return. In VFP 5 and VFP 6, RI code does have a final return, so this is a non-issue.

APPEND PROCEDURES only works when the full VFP environment is available, since it needs to be able to compile the procedures.

Example

```
OPEN DATA MyTestData
APPEND PROCEDURES FROM GetId.PRG
COPY PROCEDURES TO TestProc.PRG
```

See Also Display Procedures, Modify Procedure

Application, _VFP

We considered putting "Application" twice in the heading above because Application is one of the many FoxPro keywords with more than one meaning. It's both a property and an object. Both refer to a VFP automation server, though. _VFP is a system variable that provides a reference to the automation server.

Usage

```
Application.Property = uValue
_VFP.Property = uValue
uValue = Application.Property
uValue = _VFP.Property
Application.Method()
_VFP.Method()
```

Since VFP 5, VFP is an automation server and has the ability to create custom automation servers. What this means is that other applications can call on VFP and the servers you build with it, and tell them to do things. The Application object and the _VFP system variable both provide an object reference to the server object, letting you address it from within VFP.

In the development environment, we don't need to use these two too much. When we do, we tend to use _VFP rather than Application, because it's so much shorter to type. Most often these days, we use _VFP to grab the ActiveProject so we can check out all the new capabilities on that front. Another item you might want to mess with is _VFP.StatusBar, which controls the text on the status bar.

In custom servers, these references are more important because they let you tailor the VFP environment in which the server lives.

Example
```
oProj = _VFP.ActiveProject   && grab a reference
Application.Top = 35         && position VFP
Application.Height = 100     && and size it
```

Usage `oApp = oObject.Application`

Application is also a property of every VFP base class. It contains a reference to the VFP application object that holds the object.

Example
```
o = CreateObject("Form") && create a form
? o.Application.Name     && returns "Microsoft Visual FoxPro"
```

See Also ActiveForm, ActiveProject, AutoYield, Caption, DataToClip, DefaultFilePath, DoCmd, Eval, Forms, FullName, Height, Help, Left, Name, OLERequestPendingTimeout, OLEServerBusyRaiseError, OLEServerBusyTimeout, Projects, Quit, RequestData, _Screen, SetVar, StartMode, StatusBar, Top, Version, Visible, Width

APrinters()

This function asks Windows about installed printers and stores the results in an array.

Usage `nPrinterCount = APrinters( PrinterArray )`

Parameter	Value	Meaning
PrinterArray	Name	Array in which to place printer information.
nPrinterCount	Positive Number	The number of rows in the array, which equals the number of installed printers.
	0	No printers are installed.

The array that is created has two columns. The first column contains the name of the printer (as shown in the Printers applet in the Control Panel) while the second contains the name of the port for which the printer is installed. Both columns are character.

Using APRINTERS() doesn't guarantee that a printer is actually connected and available, only that it was once installed in Windows. You still have to cope with broken, missing, or off-line printers.

Example `? APrinters(aPrint)`

See Also Array Manipulation, ANetResources(), GetPrinter(), PrintStatus(), PrtInfo(), Set Printer, Sys(13), Sys(1037)

Array Manipulation

FoxPro has quite a few functions for working with arrays; all of them begin with the letter "A" (we don't think it's scarlet, though). These functions can be loosely divided into various groups.

The first group is simply for working with an array itself. This group includes ACOPY(), ADEL(), AELEMENT(), AINS(), ALEN(), ASCAN(), ASORT() and ASUBSCRIPT().

Next, we have functions that collect information about the general environment and store it in an array. These are ADIR(), AError(), AGetFileVersion(), AFONT(), AMouseObj() and APrinters().

The third group gathers information about the data environment and stores it in an array. These functions are ADatabases(), ADBObjects(), AFIELDS() and AUsed().

The last group is a set of functions that put information about objects (the OOP kind of objects) into an array. In this group, we find AClass(), AGetClass(), AInstance(), AMembers(), ASelObj(), and AVCXClasses().

Finally, we have one function that doesn't fit into any of the other groups—ALines().

Here's a list of the various array functions with a quick description of each so you can figure out which one to go look up.

Function	Description
AClass()	Fills array with class hierarchy for object.
ACOPY()	Copies from one array to another.
ADatabases()	Fills array with list of open databases.
ADBObjects()	Fills array with contents of database.
ADEL()	Deletes items from array.
ADIR()	Fills array with list of files.
AELEMENT()	Converts (row, column) format to element format.
AError()	Fills array with error information.
AFIELDS()	Fills array with field list.
AFONT()	Fills array with font information.
AGetClass()	Lets the user choose a class and returns info about the class in an array.
AGetFileVersion()	Fills array with version information for an EXE or DLL.
AINS()	Inserts items into array.
AInstance()	Fills array with instances of object.
ALEN()	Computes size of array.
ALines()	Fills array with the lines of a character string.
AMembers()	Fills array with members of object.
AMouseObj()	Fills array with information about mouse position.

Function	Description
APrinters()	Fills array with list of printers.
ASCAN()	Finds item in array.
ASelObj()	Fills array with selected objects.
ASORT()	Sorts array.
ASUBSCRIPT()	Converts element format to (row, column) format.
AUsed()	Fills array with list of tables in use.
AVCXClasses()	Fills array with information about classes in a class library.

All the functions except the first group have a lot in common. They all go out, find something out, and stick the results into an array. They all handle the array similarly. If it doesn't exist, they create it. If it does exist and it's the wrong size, they resize it. If the array exists and the function doesn't return anything for some reason, they leave the array as it was. Almost all of these functions return the number of rows in the resulting array.

For information about the structure of FoxPro's arrays, see "DBC, DBF, FPT, CDX—Hike!" in "Wow, What a Concept!" Creating and resizing arrays is discussed under DIMENSION.

Although FoxPro's implementation of arrays is pretty good and works reasonably fast, do keep in mind that this is, after all, a database management system, and that in many cases, it just makes more sense to use a table or cursor. Also, some operations are much easier with a spreadsheet than with any DBMS. Nonetheless, we do think arrays are pretty cool and we use them a fair amount.

Asc(), Chr()

This pair of functions converts between numbers and the ASCII character set. ASC(a character) returns the ASCII code number for that character, while CHR(a number) returns the character whose ASCII number you pass. Note that ASC() can take a whole character string as a parameter, but it returns the ASCII code of the first character in the string.

Usage

```
nNumber = ASC( cString )
cChar = CHR( nNumber )
```

Since the ASCII character set has 256 items in it, numbered from 0 to 255, that's the range of these functions. CHR() chokes if you hand it a number less than 0 or greater than 255.

Be aware that the appearance of the results of CHR() depends on the display font. Most Windows fonts don't use the ASCII character set. You're generally pretty safe with the numbers that correspond to the English alphabet, punctuation and digits (though some fonts, like Wingdings, mess with those, too), but outside that range, especially above character 127, you'll see very different results as you change fonts.

CHR() was much more useful before FoxPro gained the capability to refer to many of the special characters using the curly brace notation. We used to write things like this:

```
KEYBOARD CHR(13)
```

But it's much more readable as:

```
KEYBOARD "{ENTER}"
```

so we switched.

ASC() is a handy hacker's tool for use in dissecting binary data. ASC() gives you the ability to convert a single character to numeric format. You can then use that number to perform binary math, splice and dice bits for calculations like timestamps, or add it to other numbers for multi-byte numeric conversion.

While ASC() is valuable if the character is unknown, we don't use ASC() to check expected values. It's handy once in a while when you want to check a string for a special character that you can't write in curly brace notation, but it's just as easy to write:

```
IF LEFT(cString,1)=CHR(<some value>)
```

as

```
IF ASC(cString)=<some value>
```

and somehow, the first form seems more readable, so ASC() doesn't get much use.

See Also Str(), Val()

AScan()

This function searches for a specified value in an array. It returns the element number if the value is found and 0 otherwise.

Usage `nElement = ASCAN( ArrayName, uExpression [, nStart [, nNumElems ] ]`

Parameter	Value	Meaning
ArrayName	Array Name	The array in which to search.
uExpression	Any type except Memo, General, Screen or Object	The item for which to search.
nStart	Numeric	The element with which to start searching.
	Omitted	Search the entire array.
nNumElems	Numeric	The number of elements starting with nStart to search.
	Omitted	Search all elements beginning with nStart.
nElement	Positive number	The element number of the first element (starting from nStart) where uExpression can be found.
	0	uExpression can't be found in the specified part of ArrayName.

As with ASORT(), to specify the number of elements, you also specify the starting element. nStart is an element number—use AELEMENT() to convert from row, column format.

Example

```
DIMENSION a2DTest[5, 3]
* fill array with nums 101 to 115
FOR nCnt = 1 TO 15
    a2DTest[ nCnt ] = nCnt + 100
ENDFOR

? ASCAN(a2DTest, 105)     && returns 5
? ASCAN(a2DTest, 100)     && returns 0
? ASCAN(a2DTest, 102, 4)  && returns 0 because 102 doesn't appear
                          && when starting from element 4
? ASCAN(a2DTest, 107, 4, 5)  && returns 7
```

Using nStart and nNumElems, it's easy to search a single row of an array for a particular item. Searching for an item in a specified column is much harder. You have to search for the item, then check if it's in the right column. AColScan() below takes an array, an item and a column number, and returns the row in which the specified item appears in the specified column. If the item doesn't appear in that column, AColScan() returns 0. If any of the parameters is no good, AColScan() returns -1. Another approach to the problem is to loop down the relevant column and compare the elements to the item you're searching for. We assumed this approach would be much faster in a large array with lots of columns. In fact, which version is better does depend on the structure of the array. If you have lots more rows than columns (as most of our arrays do), the code here is many times faster than a version that loops through. If you have an array with very few rows and lots and lots of columns (our test case had 20 rows and 1000 columns), the looping approach is faster. When rows and columns are about even, the ASCAN() version is still faster. Because we think people tend to use a lot more long, narrow arrays than short, fat ones, the ASCAN() version is shown here.

```
*FUNCTION aColScan
* Search a specified column of an array for a particular value.
* Return the row number of the first occurrence. Return 0 if not found.
* Return -1 if any parameter is no good.

LPARAMETERS aArray, eElement, nColumn
    * aArray = the array in which to search - must be passed by reference
    * eElement = the item to search for. It can be any scalar type
    * nColumn = the column in which to search

LOCAL lFoundIt,nStartPos,nFoundElem,nRetVal

* check parameters
IF TYPE("aArray[1]")="U"
    RETURN -1
ENDIF

IF TYPE("nColumn")<>"N" OR NOT BETWEEN(nColumn,1,ALEN(aArray,2))
    RETURN -1
ENDIF

* ready to go
lFoundIt=.F.
nStartPos=1
DO WHILE NOT lFoundIt AND nStartPos<=ALEN(aArray)
    nFoundElem=ASCAN(aArray,eElement,nStartPos)
    IF nFoundElem>0
        IF ASUBSCRIPT(aArray,nFoundElem,2)=nColumn
            lFoundIt=.T.
        ELSE
            nStartPos=nFoundElem+1
        ENDIF
    ELSE
        nStartPos=ALEN(aArray)+1
    ENDIF
ENDDO

IF nStartPos>ALEN(aArray)
   nRetVal=0
ELSE
   nRetVal=ASUBSCRIPT(aArray,nFoundElem,1)
ENDIF

RETURN nRetVal
```

See Also AElement(), Array Manipulation, ASort()

_ASCIICols, _ASCIIRows

These system variables control the layout when you use the ASCII clause of REPORT FORM. _ASCIICOLS has logical, intelligent behavior, while _ASCIIROWS, by behaving the same way, is incredibly silly.

Usage
```
_ASCIICOLS = nColumns
nCurrentColumns = _ASCIICOLS
_ASCIIROWS = nRows
nCurrentRows = _ASCIIROWS
```

The defaults for _ASCIICOLS and _ASCIIROWS are 80 and 63, respectively, the appropriate size for a U.S. standard portrait page. As you change _ASCIICOLS, the width of the columns in the report and the amount of space between them changes. Be forewarned that some data may be cut off as the number of columns decreases.

Foolishly, _ASCIIROWS acts pretty much like _ASCIICOLS. As _ASCIIROWS increases, more space is left between rows. As _ASCIIROWS decreases, the rows are put closer together. We think this is incredibly stupid. If you increase _ASCIIROWS, it's because you want more data on the page, not more space between the data.

Our diligent technical editor comments that he doesn't like the way _ASCIICOLS behaves, either. Having extra spaces between columns is a pain when you want to process the text file afterward. He finds that he needs to set _ASCIICOLS to the exact number of columns in the report to get what he needs.

Unfortunately, Microsoft doesn't see it this way and says the present behavior is correct. Their view is that _ASCIIROWS controls the amount of space taken up by a single row of the detail band. If you make _ASCIIROWS bigger, therefore, it means you want that row to take up more space. Because a row in an ASCII file takes a fixed amount of space, they resolve this by adding blank lines between rows and between repetitions of the detail band.

We can't imagine why anyone would want this behavior, and hope Microsoft comes to its senses soon. However, since it's been there for three versions already, we're starting to get the hint.

Example
```
_ASCIICOLS=105   && Landscape width
_ASCIIROWS=48    && Landscape height
REPORT FORM MyReport TO FILE Landscap.txt ASCII
```

See Also Report

ASelObj()

ASELOBJ() tells you which objects are selected in the Form or Class Designer. With these references, you can determine and/or change an object's properties. In addition, ASELOBJ() allows you to reach "through" an object to determine the object's container or the containing form's data environment.

Usage
```
nSelCount = ASelObj( ArrayName [, nContainer ] )
```

Parameter	Value	Meaning
ArrayName	Name	The array to contain the object references.
nContainer	Omitted	Get a reference to each selected object.
	1	Get a reference to the containing object of the selected objects.
	2	Get a reference to the data environment of the form.

nSelCount	Positive number	The number of elements in the array, which is the number of selected objects (or 1 for a container or data environment).
	0	No objects were selected, or in the case of nContainer = 2, the object(s) selected is not on a form. The array is not created in this case.

ASELOBJ() is a key to writing Builders. It lets you determine what control or controls are selected when the user runs a Builder. The object references in the array let you modify the properties and methods of the selected objects based on user input.

SYS(1270) is a first cousin to ASELOBJ(). It returns a reference to the object currently under the mouse and doesn't require that the object be selected.

Example

```
* Before typing the code below in the Command Window,
* open the Form Designer and place a few labels on the form.
* Select at least three labels.

= ASelObj(aObjects)

aObjects[1].Caption = "First Label"
aObjects[2].Caption = "Second Label"
aObjects[3].BackColor = RGB(255,0,255)
aObjects[3].ForeColor = RGB(0,255,0)
```

In a Builder, you can make this sort of change in code based on user input. With references to the form and data environment, you can make changes to those as well—for example, resizing the form to fit the controls it contains.

See Also Create Form, Sys(1270)

ASin() See Cos().

ASort()

This function sorts the elements in an array. You can sort the entire array or a consecutive subset. In a two-dimensional array, sorting can be based on any column. Either ascending or descending order can be specified.

Usage

```
nSuccess = ASORT( ArrayName [, nStartPos [, nNumElems
                  [, nSortOrder ] ] ] )
```

Parameter	Value	Meaning
ArrayName	Name	The array to be sorted.
nStartPos	Omitted	Sort the entire array.
	Numeric	Begin sorting at the specified element. In a two-dimensional array, sort based on the column containing nStartPos.
nNumElems	0, Negative number, or Omitted	Sort from nStartPos to the end of the array. Note that inclusion of any value other than –1 for this purpose is undocumented.
	Positive number	For a one-dimensional array, sort the number of elements specified. For a two-dimensional array, sort the number of rows specified.

Parameter	Value	Meaning
nSortOrder	0, Negative number, or Omitted	Sort in ascending order.
	Positive number	Sort in descending order.
nSuccess	1	Sort successful.
	-1	Sort unsuccessful. We've never seen this result.

There's a bug involving the nSortOrder parameter. According to the documentation, any non-zero value results in descending order. Nope, positive numbers give descending order; negative numbers result in ascending order. Confusing as heck, and we have a pretty good idea what the flawed line of code looks like.

In order to specify sort order, you have to provide the starting element and number of elements or rows to sort. Starting element isn't so hard, since it's usually 1, but providing the number of elements is a pain—ALEN() can be handy here. Fortunately, you can also specify –1 (or 0 or any other negative number) to indicate all elements.

Similarly, you have to specify the starting element in order to indicate the number of elements or rows to sort. This one makes sense, though, since the two are related.

With two-dimensional arrays, it's a little tricky to specify the starting element sometimes. The key is that it should be the element in the column you want to sort on, in the row where you want to start sorting. Say you have a 5x3 array and you want to sort the first three rows based on the second column. The starting element is 2. If you want to sort the last three rows based on the second column, the starting element is 12. AELEMENT() can give you a hand here.

FoxPro does not perform what's known in math as a "stable sort." In a stable sort, when two items have the same value in the column you're sorting on, they retain the same relative position they had before the sort. So, for example, if you have a two-column array containing last names and first names, a stable sort would allow you to sort them on first name, then on last name, and know they were completely ordered. FoxPro doesn't do this. We suspect it's because unstable sorts are much faster. Use a cursor and index it if you need to sort on multiple columns.

Example

```
= ADIR(aFiles, "*.DBF")      && Get a list of DBFs
= ASORT(aFiles)              && Put in name order
= ASORT(aFiles, 1, -1, 1)   && Put in descending name order
= ASORT(aFiles, 2)           && Put in size order
= ASORT(aFiles, 3, 3)        && Put the first 3 rows in date order
= ASORT(aFiles, 18, 5)       && Put the 4th through 8th rows
                             && in date order
```

See Also AElement(), ALen(), Array Manipulation, AScan()

Assert, Set Asserts, Set("Asserts")

This cool command lets you test conditions during development, such as verifying proper parameters sent to a function, without slowing down the runtime behavior of your application.

Usage

```
ASSERT lCondition [ MESSAGE cMessage ]
SET ASSERTS ON | OFF
lAreWeAsserting = SET("ASSERTS")
```

Assertions have been available in some languages for a long time. One of the most persuasive arguments for using assertions is in the wonderful book *Code Complete* (see bibliography), and we were pleased to see this addition to version 5.0. Assertions let you test situations during development without bogging down the runtime environment with a lot of testing. The idea is that your Quality Assurance process should catch these situations. Using assertions is equivalent to setting a global "glTesting" variable and then having blocks of code run only if glTesting is true. But another nice feature of assertions is that you don't have to worry about forgetting to turn them off! A note of caution here: because ASSERTs are tested only during development, conditions that could occur in the runtime environment (such as validating user-supplied parameters) still need to be tested the old-fashioned way.

When the assertion expression evaluates to .F., a dialog box pops up with your optional message (or a generic message citing the line number and name of the program containing the failed assertion) and presents these options: Debug, Cancel, Ignore or Ignore All. Debug suspends the application and brings the debugging windows forward. Cancel halts program execution. Ignore allows the procedure to continue. Ignore All both continues the procedure and SETs ASSERTS OFF until it is set ON again programmatically.

SET("ASSERTS") returns .T. at runtime if SET ASSERTS is ON, but assertions aren't tested, and users don't see the assertion-failure dialog box.

Example

```
ASSERT VARTYPE(toParameter) = "O" MESSAGE "Procedure " + ;
          PROGRAM() + " did not" + " get object parameter."
```

See Also Debug

Assign See Access.

Assist, _Assist

At first glance, ASSIST is a totally useless command; it appears to do nothing. In fact, ASSIST and _ASSIST are a set of very useful hooks that can give you quick access to whatever you'd like.

Usage

```
ASSIST
_ASSIST = cFileName
```

ASSIST and _ASSIST were added in FoxPro 2.6 for dBASE compatibility. They provided access to the Catalog Manager. Well, CatMan's gone in Visual FoxPro. The enhanced Project Manager includes the functionality of both the old Project Manager and Catalog Manager.

So what good are ASSIST and _ASSIST? Like many other system variables, _ASSIST lets you specify a program to run under particular circumstances—in this case, when the ASSIST command executes. The key is that it can be any program at all, and unlike other such variables (say, _GENMENU), there's no built-in time when _ASSIST is executed. It only runs when you tell it by issuing ASSIST.

For instance, we have several files (tables and text) we need to open each time we start to work on this book. But we're also using VFP for testing as we go. So, it's really handy to have a program that opens all the files we need and sets them up the way we want. By hooking this program to _ASSIST, resetting things is as simple as issuing ASSIST. Using a system variable means the setting doesn't go away when we issue CLEAR ALL to clean up from some disaster.

Example

```
_ASSIST = "HackSet.PRG"
ASSIST  && runs the program
```

ASubscript() See AElement().

At(), AtC(), RAt(), $

Did you ever need to know whether a string contains a particular substring? Say you have a memo field containing notes about a phone conversation and you want to see whether you discussed the "Super Duper Pooper Scooper." Enter this group of functions.

Technically, $ is an operator, while AT(), ATC() and RAT() are functions. But all of them are used to find a substring within a string. $ simply indicates whether or not the substring is there. The others all return the position where the string was found.

Usage

```
lIsItInThere = cSearchFor $ cSearchIn
nFoundPos = AT( cSearchFor, cSearchIn [ ,nOccurrence ])
nFoundPos = ATC( cSearchFor, cSearchIn [ ,nOccurrence ])
nFoundPos = RAT( cSearchFor, cSearchIn [ ,nOccurrence ])
```

AT() and RAT() are case-sensitive; ATC() is not (the "C" stands for "case," which seems backward to us, but at least the function exists). AT() and ATC() begin their search at the left-hand side of the string, while RAT() begins at the right (you can read it as "Right AT").

Watch out for one thing with RAT(). Even though it searches from the right, the position it returns is measured from the left. We guess that's the "RAT trap."

All three functions take an optional parameter indicating which instance of the string to search for, so you can find, say, the third use of "Super Duper Pooper Scooper" rather than the first or last.

You can use these functions together with LEFT(), RIGHT() and SUBSTR() to parse a string into its component parts. This is often useful when you inherit data that hasn't been properly normalized. For example, you might need to convert a single name field into first and last name fields or to pull apart an address field into street address, city, state and zip code.

Be aware that these functions can't be optimized by Rushmore (unless you have some pretty unusual and not terribly useful index tags), so you won't want to use them heavily for lookups. For example, don't store several codes in a single field and plan to use $ to see if a specific code is present; normalize the data instead.

Example

```
lFoundIt = "Super Duper Pooper Scooper" $ mNotes
nStartPos = AT("Super Duper Pooper Scooper", mNotes)
nStartPos = ATC("Super Duper Pooper Scooper", mNotes)
nLastOne = RAT("Super Duper Pooper Scooper", mNotes)

* Here's a more useful example which shows how you'd take apart
* a field containing city, state and zip code to create separate
* fields. You'd call this routine like this:
STORE "" TO cCity, cState, cZip
DO PARSADDR WITH cCityStZip, cCity, cState, cZip

* parsaddr.prg
* Parse single address variable into city, state and zip
* Assumes parameter cAddress has structure:
*    City, ST Zip
* Zip can be either 5 or 10 digit

LPARAMETERS cAddress, cCity, cState, cZip

LOCAL nStartZip, nStartState

nStartZip = RAT(" ",TRIM(cAddress))
cZip = TRIM(SUBSTR(cAddress, nStartZip+1))

nStartState = AT(",", cAddress)
cState = ALLTRIM(SUBSTR(cAddress, nStartState+1, ;
                 nStartZip-nStartState-1))

cCity = ALLTRIM(LEFT(cAddress, nStartState-1))

RETURN
```

VFP 3.0b added double-byte versions of the functions in this group: At_C(), AtCC(), RAtC(). They're the ones to use when you're working in a language with double-byte characters or if there's a chance your application will go international.

See Also AllTrim(), AtLine(), AtCLine(), At_C(), AtCC(), Left(), Occurs(), RatC(), RatLine(), Right(), Substr(), Trim(), Upper()

ATan() See Cos().

AtCC() See At_C().

AtCLine() See AtLine().

AtLine(), AtCLine(), RAtLine()

These functions are first cousins to AT(), ATC() and RAT(). Like their cousins, they also find occurrences of a specified string in another string, but these check line by line and return the line number where the string can be found. Line numbers are determined by line-break characters and the current value of SET MEMOWIDTH.

ATLINE() and company are handy for searching in memo fields, but like many of the memo field-related functions, they work perfectly well on character fields, too.

Usage

```
nLineFound = ATLINE( cSearchString, cWhereToSearch )
nLineFound = ATCLINE( cSearchString, cWhereToSearch )
nLineFound = RATLINE( cSearchString, cWhereToSearch )
```

Parameter	Value	Meaning
cSearchString	Character	The string to look for.
cWhereToSearch	Character or Memo	The string in which to look for cSearchString.
nLineFound	0	cSearchString doesn't occur in cWhereToSearch.
	Numeric	For ATLINE() and ATCLINE(), the first line of cWhereToSearch containing cSearchString. For RATLINE(), the last line of cWhereToSearch containing cSearchString

As with AT(), RAT() and ATC(), ATLINE() and RATLINE() are case-sensitive while ATCLINE() is not. RATLINE() searches from the last line of cWhereToSearch toward the beginning. Also, like the AT() family, there's no case-insensitive way to search backward.

Once you identify the line you want, MLINE() is handy for extracting it.

Unlike the AT() family, the ATLINE() functions don't have an optional parameter to specify which occurrence you want, so you have to track this yourself if you need it.

Example

```
* Find the beginning of notes for 2/1/95
nItemLine = ATLINE("2/1/95", Notes)

* Find the first line referencing "freezer", regardless of case
nFreezerLine = ATCLINE("freezer", Description)

* Find the last line referencing "degree"
nLastDegree = RATLINE("degree", LOWER(Education))
```

See Also ALines(), At(), AtC(), RAt(), MLine(), Set MemoWidth

ATn2() See Cos().

At_C(), AtCC(), RAtC()

These functions were added in version 3.0b. They perform the same role for double-byte (or mixed) character data that AT(), ATC() and RAT(), respectively, do for single-byte characters.

Usage

```
nFoundPos = AT_C( cString1, cString2 [ , nOccurrence ] )
nFoundPos = ATCC( cString1, cString2 [ , nOccurrence ] )
nFoundPos = RATC( cString1, cString2 [ , nOccurrence ] )
```

We're not equipped to test double-byte characters, so we can't say whether they work in that setting. They do work as expected on single-byte data.

There's actually a fairly good argument that you should use these functions all the time and forget the single-byte versions. That way, your apps need less work if you need them to operate in a double-byte environment. We haven't actually managed to change our habits yet, but we keep trying to convince ourselves.

See Also At(), AtC(), Double-Byte Character Sets, OS(), RAt()

AUsed()

With 32,767 work areas per data session, knowing what table is open in which work area is a significant task. AUSED() makes it simple by filling an array with a list of aliases and work areas for the current (or a specified) data session.

Usage

```
nUsedCount = AUSED( ArrayName [, nDataSession ] )
```

Parameter	Value	Meaning
ArrayName	Name	The array to be filled with alias and work area information.
nDataSession	Omitted	Get aliases and work areas for the current data session.
	Positive Number	Get aliases and work areas for the specified data session.
nUsedCount	Positive Number	The number of rows in the array, equal to the number of work areas in use in the data session or the number of open databases.
	0	No work areas in use.

The aliases appear in the array in the same order as they're displayed in the View window. It appears to be the reverse of the order in which they were opened. The array has two columns. The first column contains the alias, while the second contains the work area number.

Example

```
? AUSED(aAliases)        && create an array with aliases for the
                         && current data session
? AUSED(aAliases, 3)     && create an array with aliases for data
                         && data session 3
```

SELECT-SQL has a nasty habit of leaving open any tables it opens to perform a query. (If it finds a table open, it reopens it in another work area, like an internal USE AGAIN, but it cleans up after itself in that case.) In FoxPro 2.x, cleaning up after a query meant being sure to always use work areas in sequence (with SELECT 0), then making a note of the next available work area before the query, then looping through from that work area out to the end (225), closing whatever had been opened, while of course being sure not to close the cursor or table created by the query. All in all, a real pain and totally out of the question with 32K work areas to deal with.

AUSED() makes this job much simpler. We can simply get the list of open tables before and after the query and close the ones that were opened. We do still have to watch out for the newly created cursor or table. The code can be structured like this:

```
* get "Before" listing
nBeforeCnt = AUSED(aBefore)
* do the query here

* hold work area for result
nResultArea = SELECT()
* get "After" listing
nAfterCnt = AUSED(aAfter)

* now loop through changes, if any
IF nAfterCnt > nBeforeCnt
  FOR nPointer = 1 TO nAfterCnt-nBeforeCnt
     * Start from 1 because most recently opened
     * come first
     IF aAfter[nPointer,2] <> nResultArea
        USE IN aAfter[nPointer,2]
     ENDIF
  ENDFOR
ENDIF
```

See Also ADatabases(), Array Manipulation, Select-SQL, Set DataSession, Use, Used()

AutoActivate, AutoVerbMenu, DoVerb

AutoActivate determines the circumstances under which an ActiveX control should start to run. AutoVerbMenu enables a context-sensitive menu that, when invoked, displays actions the control knows how to take, such as Open, Edit or Play. DoVerb is a method for activating, editing or playing ActiveX objects.

Usage

```
oOLEObject.AutoActivate = nValue
nValue = oOLEObjectAutoActivate
```

Parameter	Value	Meaning
nValue	0	Manual. The object will not activate on a form, unless programmatically called with the DoVerb method.
	1	GotFocus. Activation takes place when the object receives the focus.
	2	DblClick. Object is activated when double-clicked or when Enter is pressed. This is the default.
	3	Automatic. The Help file claims this setting will determine when to activate the object based upon the "object's normal method of activation." Double-click seems to be the method of choice for all the ActiveX objects we've tried.

Different objects react differently to these settings, depending on the way they were designed. If the default verb of an object is "Play," as it might be for a sound or other multimedia data, activating the object causes it to play. Most objects have the default verb of "Edit," which brings forth their editing interface when they are activated.

Setting AutoActivate to 1 (GotFocus) on a really fast machine with lots of RAM has the cool effect of immediately displaying context-sensitive menus and toolbars for embedded objects that support Visual Editing—it looks very slick. On the other hand, if you might be dealing with objects that don't support the in-place editing feature, or that might be sluggish in updating the interface, you'll probably want to let the user choose to activate the property only when it needs to be, by setting AutoActivate to 2 (DblClick). Remember, the operator is in charge, and leaving him helpless and clueless that processes are starting on his machine is very bad user-interface diplomacy.

Set AutoActivate to 0 for those situations where you never want the object activated, or if it should be activated only under programmatic control. We haven't found a use for the Automatic (3) option for this property yet.

Example
```
ThisForm.OLEBoundControl.AutoActivate = 1  && GotFocus
```

Usage
```
oOLEObject.DoVerb( [ nVerb ] )
```

Parameter	Value	Meaning
nVerb	1, 2, 3...n	The specialized verbs for this object, stored in the Registry.
	0	The default action for this object, typically "Play" for multimedia objects and "Edit" for text-based and graphic objects.
	-1	Activate the object in edit mode, as in-place activation if supported by the object.
	-2	Activate the object in a separate window.
	-3	The Help file states that this verb "hides the creator application for an embedded object." We suspect this may be useful in manipulating an application via DDE or Automation while the application is hidden. The application does not run.
	-4	Activate the object for an in-place editing session only if the object can support in-place editing; otherwise generate error 1426—"OLE error code 0x..." with such informative error messages as "Invalid verb for OLE object," "The server threw an exception" (our favorite) and "Unexpected failure." (So what's an "expected failure"?). You'll want to trap for errors if you use this verb.
	-5	This setting should allow an object to be edited in its own window, if it supports single-click activation. We haven't found one yet.
	-6	This parameter should flush all "undo" information. Again, we haven't yet found OLE servers supporting this feature.

There are several cautions when working with ActiveX objects that bear repeating here. You cannot assume that ActiveX servers registered on one machine will be registered on them all. A new machine can be added to an office, or a catastrophe can easily destroy the Registration File information necessary for manipulating the servers. Check for the availability of OLE servers and specific verbs before attempting to use them. The error messages returned when these functions are unavailable, as we mentioned above, can be particularly uninformative.

Another thing to be wary of is that ActiveX services are typically not identical over the different Windows platforms. The server for WAV files in Win31 installations is a different one than that used in Win95, and an object embedded on one platform may not be accessible on another. In VFP 3, the sample code shown below works in Win31 with OLETypeAllowed as either 0 or 1, but Win95 seems to require 0. In addition, Win31 plays the sound automatically with verbs -1 and -2, while Win95 does not. Under VFP 5 and Windows NT, verb 3 produced "Catastrophic failure" messages when OLETypeAllowed was set to 1, and the far milder "The parameter is incorrect" when set to 0. Really! Someone ought to teach Microsoft that error messages should contain information! As always, we strongly encourage you to test on every platform.

Example
```
* OLESamp - activation of an OLE sound sample with varied verbs
LOCAL oForm
oForm = CREATEOBJECT("Form")
```

```
oForm.AddObject("oleSound","myOLEControl")
oForm.Show()
oForm.oleSound.Visible = .T.
FOR i = 3 TO -3 STEP - 1
  oForm.OleSound.DoVerb(i)
  WAIT WINDOW "DoVerb of " + LTRIM(STR(i)) + CHR(13) + ;
              "Press any key to continue..."
NEXT
RETURN

DEFINE CLASS myOLEControl AS OLEControl
  Height = 20
  OLETypeAllowed = 1
  DocumentFile = "c:\windows\chimes.wav"
  * "c:\winnt40\media\chimes.wav" for Win NT
ENDDEFINE
```

Usage

```
oObject.AutoVerbMenu = lShowMenu
lShowMenu = oObject.AutoVerbMenu
```

This setting determines whether calling up a context menu (by right-mouse-clicking or Shift+F10 when the object has focus) displays the verbs associated with the OLE object. If this is set .F., no automatic context menu appears, although you could fire your own from the RightClick event. Each object has verbs according to its type and what servers are installed on the machine. If no verbs are available, no menu appears.

Example

```
* An extension of the form above, this one has
* AutoVerbMenu turned on so that you can call up the
* context menu, and a close button to support the needed
* READ EVENTS.

LOCAL oForm
oForm = CREATEOBJECT("Form")
oForm.AddObject("oleSound","myOLEControl")
oForm.AddObject("cmdClose","cmdClose")
WITH oForm.cmdClose
  .TOP = oForm.Height - (.Height + 10)
  .Left = 0.5 * (oForm.Width - .Width)
  .Visible = .T.
ENDWITH
oForm.Show()
oForm.oleSound.Visible = .T.
read events
RETURN

DEFINE CLASS myOLEControl AS OLEControl
  Height = 20
  OLETypeAllowed = 1
  DocumentFile = "c:\winnt40\media\chimes.wav" && for Win NT
  AutoVerbMenu = .T.
ENDDEFINE

Define class cmdClose as CommandButton
  AutoSize = .T.
  Caption = "Close"
  Procedure Click
    ThisForm.Release()
    Clear Events
  EndProc
EndDefine
```

See Also OLEBoundControl, OLEControl, OLETypeAllowed, Registration File

AutoCenter See AlwaysOnTop.

AutoCloseTables See AutoOpenTables.

AutoIncrement

This property determines whether the version number of a project is automatically incremented each time you build an EXE or DLL from the project. It corresponds to the Auto Increment check box in the Version dialog of the Project Manager (accessed through the Build dialog).

Usage

```
lIncrementIt = prjProject.AutoIncrement
prjProject.AutoIncrement = lIncrementIt
```

Since VFP 5, we've had the ability to brand executables with a three-part version number (in the form 9999.9999.9999). Not only that, but we could set it up so that each time we build the project, the version number increases. This property gives us programmatic access to that decision.

There's only one minor glitch here. Setting AutoIncrement to .T. affects only the last section of the version number (the rightmost group). If you run out of room in that group (that is, it reaches 9999), your version numbers stop incrementing. Frankly, we hope we don't do 10,000 builds to EXE of any project we're working on any time soon, but Microsoft may. We've noticed several of their EXEs and DLLs with revision numbers in the seven and eight thousand range. It's intriguing to guess what they'll do for these files in a few years.

Example

```
Application.ActiveProject.AutoIncrement = .T.
```

See Also Build, Build DLL, Build EXE, Project, VersionNumber

AutoOpenTables, AutoCloseTables, OpenViews

AutoOpenTables and AutoCloseTables determine whether or not the items listed in the Data environment open and close when the object (form, formset, report, label) opens and closes. OpenViews, added in VFP 5, determines what kind of views get opened by OpenTables.

Usage

```
lValue = oObject.AutoOpenTables
lValue = oObject.AutoCloseTables
```

These properties are read-only at runtime, so you need to set them appropriately at design-time—that is, through the Form Designer, Report Designer or Label Designer. There is actually one way to set them programmatically. You can write code that subclasses the DataEnvironment base class. In the subclass definition, you can set these properties the way you want them. But, using a subclassed data environment is not for the faint of heart.

AutoOpenTables and AutoCloseTables interact with OpenTables and CloseTables. OpenTables and CloseTables are methods of the base DataEnvironment class. Their default behavior is to open and close, respectively, all tables and views listed in the DE. You can override or enhance them with your own code if you want.

When AutoOpenTables is .T., OpenTables is called automatically as part of the startup process for the object (form or whatever). Similarly, when AutoCloseTables is .T., CloseTables is called as part of the shutdown sequence. When either AutoOpenTables or AutoCloseTables is .F., the corresponding method is not called automatically.

See OpenTables for a situation where you'd want to turn off AutoOpenTables.

Usage

```
nValue = oObject.OpenViews
```

Parameter	Valuc	Meaning
nValue	0	Open both local and remote views.

Parameter	Value	Meaning
nValue	1	Open local views only.
	2	Open remote views only.
	3	Don't open any views.

You usually do want tables in the Data environment to be opened automatically, but views are another story. Depending on the data source and the situation, you may need more control over views, especially in a form. This property gives you some control.

This setting affects not just what happens when OpenTables runs automatically because AutoOpenTables is .T., but also what happens when OpenTables is called explicitly.

See Also AfterCloseTables, BeforeOpenTables, CloseTables, OpenTables

AutoRelease See Release.

AutoSize

This property determines whether controls stretch to fit their contents.

Usage

```
oObject.AutoSize = lFitSizeToContents
lFitSizeToContents = oObject.AutoSize
```

For about half of the affected controls, Caption determines the size when AutoSize is .T. This is the case for labels, both kinds of buttons and check boxes. For option buttons and check boxes, AutoSize interacts with Alignment. The control grows or shrinks on the side it's aligned on—that is, when you set AutoSize to .T. and Alignment to Left for a check box, it's the left edge of the check box that moves when the Caption changes.

For the other controls affected by AutoSize, generally it's their contents that determine their size.

Don't turn on AutoSize for button groups until you've positioned the buttons where you want them. Trying to move buttons around inside a group that keeps resizing itself as you go is kind of like trying to swat a fly. It keeps moving and you're always one step behind.

You can set AutoSize on for individual buttons in a group without having it on for the button group as a whole. This can lead to weird results. Normally, you'll want AutoSize on for individual buttons only when it's on for the group. What good is a button that's stretched to fit its entire caption if the button doesn't fit inside its container? Actually, there is one situation where you do want that combination. You can make the button group *larger* than the buttons within, so you can make other controls look as if they're inside the border of the group. For example, a button choosing "output to file" might have a text box next to it to specify the filename.

For OLE controls (both OLE Container and OLE Bound), AutoSize interacts with the Sizable property. If both are true, when the OLE control is activated, dragging the shaded border of the OLE object changes the amount of space the OLE control takes up on the form. Since a clever user could use this "windowshade" effect to hide the OK/Cancel buttons, we use these properties only if the user really needs to be able to enlarge the object.

Example

```
* Normally, you'll set this property at design time, but
* here's the runtime equivalent.
ThisForm.opgChoices.AutoSize = .T.
ThisForm.opgChoices.optChoice1.AutoSize = .T.
ThisForm.opgChoices.optChoice1.Caption = "Boy, is this long"
```

See Also Alignment, Left, Sizable, Width

AutoVerbMenu See AutoActivate.

AutoYield, DoEvents

This property and its related command control the interaction between VFP and ActiveX controls.

Usage

```
appApplication.AutoYield = lYield
lYield = appApplication.AutoYield
DoEvents
```

Parameter	Value	Meaning
lYield	.T.	This is the default setting, and the mode of Visual FoxPro 3. Windows events are processed as they are received, meaning the operator can interrupt your code.
	.F.	Use this setting if ActiveX controls on your forms need to run your custom code.

The challenge of working with ActiveX controls is that, at times, they seem to have a mind of their own. When AutoYield is left at the default setting, clicking on an ActiveX control sends that click directly to the control and it responds with its native behavior. If your code happens to be in the middle of doing something else, well, too bad.

In Visual FoxPro 5.0, Microsoft introduced the AutoYield property and corresponding DoEvents command to solve this problem. When you have a form with an ActiveX control, set the application's AutoYield property to .F. and process the messages received by the control by issuing DoEvents when you're ready to handle them.

DoEvents is also handy when you're executing processes that are normally not interruptible. For example, if a long loop is running, normally a button-click isn't processed until the loop is completed. Putting DoEvents in the loop tells FoxPro to go check for interface events, so that if the user is desperately clicking the Cancel button, you can find out. On the other hand, issuing DoEvents frequently is hazardous to your application's performance, by an order of magnitude in some cases. Since even a single DoEvents is pretty time-consuming, our Tech Editor recommends setting up a Cancel button, using your loop to test for MDOWN() over your button (detected with SYS(1270)), and only then invoking DoEvents. MDOWN() is efficient enough that you can check it every time through the loop and be more responsive to the user's click, while not bogging down the processing too badly.

Example

```
_VFP.AutoYield = .F.

FOR nCount = 1 TO nSomeInsanelyLargeNumber
   * do the normal processing for this loop
   * now check for user events
   IF MOD(nCount,100) = 0
      DoEvents
      * If user cancelled, get out
      IF LASTKEY()=27
         EXIT
      ENDIF
   ENDIF
ENDFOR
```

See Also SYS(2333)

AVCXClasses() See AGetClass().

Average, Calculate, Count, Sum

These commands all do calculations with data from a table. AVERAGE, COUNT and SUM, as their names suggest, compute averages, count records and compute totals, respectively. CALCULATE can do all of that as well as compute minimum and maximum values, standard deviations and variances, and net present value.

For all these commands, if TALK is ON, the number of records involved is displayed in the status bar, and for SUM, AVERAGE and CALCULATE, the result is displayed to the screen. If TALK is OFF, there's no visible display.

Usage

```
AVERAGE [ nExpr1 [, nExpr2 [, ... ] ] ]
        [ Scope ]
        [ FOR lForCondition ]
        [ WHILE lWhileCondition ]
        [ TO nResult1 [, nResult2 [ , ... ] ]
          | TO ARRAY Result ]
        [ NOOPTIMIZE ]
COUNT   [ Scope ]
        [ FOR lForCondition ]
        [ WHILE lWhileCondition ]
        [ TO nResult ]
        [ NOOPTIMIZE ]
SUM     [ nExpr1 [, nExpr2 [, ... ] ] ]
        [ Scope ]
        [ FOR lForCondition ]
        [ WHILE lWhileCondition ]
        [ TO nResult1 [, nResult2 [ , ... ] ]
          | TO ARRAY Result ]
        [ NOOPTIMIZE ]
```

Parameter	Value	Meaning
nExpr1, nExpr2, ...	Any numeric type	The expression (involving one or more fields) to be summed or averaged.
nResult1, nResult2, ...	Numeric	Variables to hold the averages, counts or sums.
Result	Numeric Array	Array to hold the averages or sums. A one-dimensional array is created if it doesn't exist. The array is expanded if it's too small.

COUNT simply counts the number of records included by the Scope, FOR and WHILE clauses. AVERAGE and SUM perform the specified calculation on each expression listed.

AVERAGE and SUM omit records containing null values in any field listed in the expression. Each expression is considered separately. If no expressions are supplied for SUM and AVERAGE, the sum or average is computed for every numeric field in the current table.

If nExpr*x* includes any Currency values, the result is Currency. Otherwise, it's Numeric.

Example

```
USE Customer    && TasTrade Customer table
COUNT FOR Country = "UK"   && number in the UK
* See whether UK customers are big spenders
AVERAGE Max_order_Amt FOR Country = "UK"

USE Order_Line_Items ORDER Order_Id
* compute order total
SEEK cOrderId  && cOrderId holds an order number
SUM quantity*unit_price WHILE order_id=cOrderId TO nOrderTotal
```

The last example shows how SEEK and WHILE can be combined to rapidly access all the records related to a particular item.

Usage

```
CALCULATE Func() [ , Func() [ , ... ] ]
          [ Scope ]
          [ FOR lForCondition ]
          [ WHILE lWhileCondition ]
          [ TO eResult1 [ , eResult2 [ , ... ] ]
            | TO ARRAY Result ]
          [ NOOPTIMIZE ]
```

Parameter	Value	Meaning
Func	AVG(nExpr)	Computes the average of the non-null values of the enclosed numeric expression.
	CNT([nExpr])	Counts the number of records that match the conditions. If nExpr is specified, counts the number of records meeting the conditions for which nExpr isn't null. Note the use of nExpr here is undocumented.
	MAX(eExpr)	Finds the maximum of the non-null values for the specified expression. The expression may be Character, Date, Datetime or any numeric type.
	MIN(eExpr)	Finds the minimum of the non-null values for the specified expression. The expression may be Character, Date, Datetime or any numeric type.
	NPV(nExpr1, nExpr2 [, nExpr3])	Computes the net present value of a series of cash flows. See below for more explanation.
	STD(nExpr)	Computes the standard deviation of the non-null values of the enclosed numeric expression.
	SUM(nExpr)	Computes the total of the enclosed numeric expression.
	VAR(nExpr)	Computes the variance of the non-null values of the enclosed numeric expression.
uResult1, uResult2, ...	Same type as passed expression	Variables to hold the results.
Result	Array	Array to hold the results. A one-dimensional array is created if it doesn't exist. The array is expanded if it's too small.

Unlike the commands above, which can perform only their particular operation (count, sum or average), CALCULATE can do a collection of different computations at once. This means you could compute, say, the total, average, minimum and maximum of some field (or expression) in one pass through a table. You are restricted to the functions provided—you can't just put in any old FoxPro function. However, the expression passed to the function can be any valid numeric expression.

NPV() differs from the other functions used in CALCULATE. Since neither of us knows beans about net present values (whaddaya want from a couple of math majors, anyway?), we'll assume you know what a net present value is if you're interested in this function. NPV() takes two or three parameters. The first is the interest rate per period expressed as a decimal. Remember to divide an annual rate by 12 if you're computing monthly values. The second expression is the periodic cash flow; this is normally a field and can be negative or positive. Negative values represent expenses; positive values represent income. The optional third parameter is initial investment. If you don't specify one, the first value of the second parameter is used and investment is assumed to occur at the end of the first period. The field value should be negative to indicate cash expended.

CALCULATE ignores null values in the function parameter.

The Scope, FOR and WHILE clauses of all four commands determine which records are included in the result.

(For more on these clauses, see "Scope, FOR, WHILE and Santa Clauses" in "Wow, What a Concept!".)

The system variable _TALLY receives the number of records involved in the calculation (the same number that appears in the status bar). Records including nulls are counted for this purpose, even if their null values have been ignored.

COUNT is faster than CALCULATE CNT(), but CALCULATE SUM() and CALCULATE AVG() appear to be slightly faster than SUM and AVERAGE, respectively, in VFP 6. As always, your mileage may vary, so test on your hardware and under conditions similar to your final system for the authoritative answer.

NOOPTIMIZE can usually be ignored. If you think you need it, see SET OPTIMIZE.

Example

```
USE Products  && from TasTrade
* Display number, average unit price,
* highest unit price, lowest unit price
* for those that are available
CALCULATE CNT(),AVG(Unit_Price), ;
          MIN(Unit_Price),MAX(Unit_Price) FOR ;
   NOT Discontinued
```

See Also Payment(), PV(), Select-SQL, Set Optimize

BackColor, ForeColor

These properties control the color of objects. Big surprise. BackColor is the background (or "paper") color, while ForeColor is the foreground (or "ink") color. For some objects, one or the other is irrelevant. For example, CommandButtons don't have a BackColor, while CommandGroups don't have a ForeColor.

Usage

```
oObject.BackColor = nColor
nColor = oObject.BackColor
oObject.ForeColor = nColor
nColor = oObject.ForeColor
```

nColor is a color number in the range 0 to 16777215. Since we don't have all 16 million colors at our fingertips, we generally use the predefined colors in FoxPro.H, RGB() (if we know the right red-green-blue trio) or GETCOLOR() to set these properties.

Changes to BackColor and ForeColor take place right away. However, text and graphics that have been drawn on a form (either through traditional Xbase commands like ?, DISPLAY, and so forth, or through the form's graphic methods like Line and Circle) don't change color when the form's ForeColor changes. You have to redraw them to change their color.

If a control's BackStyle is Transparent, its BackColor is ignored and the form's BackColor or an underlying object shows instead.

Well, almost. In VFP 5 and VFP 6, when a text box or edit box with BackStyle set to Transparent gets focus, the control's BackColor shows anyway.

Be aware that the actual colors you see are affected by factors like video card and resolution. For example, under some circumstances, with certain choices for a form's (or _SCREEN's) BackColor, we see some weird effects with text drawn to the form. Rather than being transparent, there's a box of another color around the text. To see if this is an issue for you, try setting your display to 256 colors, set _SCREEN.BackColor to Magenta (8388863) and then issue DISPLAY MEMORY. We see purple boxes around the DISP MEMO information.

Example

```
* You could let the user set a form's colors by putting
* a couple of buttons on the form. The Click code for the
* "Background Color" button might be:
```

```
ThisForm.BackColor = GETCOLOR()
* The "Foreground Color" button would have similar code.
```

See Also BackStyle, ColorScheme, ColorSource, DisabledBackColor, DisabledForeColor, FillColor, FillStyle, GetColor(), #Include, RGB(), SelectedBackColor, SelectedForeColor

BackStyle

Peek-a-boo! I see you.

Traditional Children's Game

This property determines whether or not you can see through controls. The default is 1 for Opaque, meaning that the control hides whatever's behind it.

Usage

```
oObject.BackStyle = nBackStyle
nBackStyle = oObject.BackStyle
```

Parameter	Value	Meaning
nBackStyle	0	The object is Transparent, meaning that whatever's behind it on the form is visible.
	1	The object is Opaque, meaning that whatever's behind it on the form is hidden.

Several controls, including lists and combo boxes, don't have a BackStyle property and always hide things behind them.

In an OptionGroup, there's a BackStyle property for the group as a whole, plus individual BackStyles for the buttons in the group. You can actually create some pretty cool effects this way. (Imagine alternating Transparent and Opaque for the option buttons in the group.)

The help says (correctly) that BackStyle is read-only for Pages in a Page frame where Tabs is set to .T. What it doesn't say is that you can set the Page frame's Tabs property to .F., set the Pages to Transparent, then set Tabs to .T., and voila, you've got transparent tabbed pages. We hope this isn't considered a bug because the Transparent page frame looks pretty cool (though some of the 3-D effects are a little strange). Even though the pages let the form's BackColor show through, stuff from the individual pages is kept segregated.

Example

```
* Make all labels on current form transparent
_Screen.ActiveForm.SetAll("BackStyle", 0, "Label")
```

See Also BackColor, FillColor, ForeColor, Tabs

Bar(), Menu(), Pad(), Popup(), Prompt()

These functions tell you about your most recent menu choice. The first four indicate which bar, menu, pad or popup you picked. PROMPT() returns the text for the chosen item. POPUP() can also tell you if a particular popup has been defined.

Usage

```
nChosenBar = BAR()
cChosenMenu = MENU()
cChosenPad = PAD()
cChosenPopup = POPUP()
lPopupExists = POPUP( PopupName )
cChosenPrompt = PROMPT()
```

The timing for retrieving these items can be tricky. Your best bet is to pass them to the processing routine you set up with ON SELECTION, so you're sure you get the right value.

These functions are set only when there are ON SELECTION commands for the items in question. For an item with no action set or with just an ON command, these functions don't change.

For an interesting exercise in what changes when, add some pads with ON EXIT conditions at various levels to the system menu. Put the five functions here in the Debug window and make some choices. Watch when the various functions have values and when they're empty. Putting WAIT WINDOWs in the ON EXIT conditions makes it particularly easy to see what's going on. As FoxPro works its way down to the chosen item, the status functions reflect the level currently being processed.

Example

```
ON SELECTION POPUP MyPop ;
   DO ProcessPopup WITH POPUP(), BAR(), PROMPT()
```

See Also Define Bar, Define Menu, Define Pad, Define Popup, Menus, On Exit Bar, On Exit Menu, On Exit Pad, On Exit Popup, On Selection Bar, On Selection Menu, On Selection Pad, On Selection Popup

BarCount(), CntBar(), CntPad()

These functions tell you how many bars are on a popup or how many pads are on a menu.

Usage

```
nBars = BarCount( [ cPopupName ] )
nBars = CntBar( [ cPopupName ] )
nPads = CntPad( cMenuName )
```

These functions expect a character string. Don't forget the quotes around the name of the item. BARCOUNT() and CNTBAR() do the same thing—BARCOUNT() is one of the functions added in FoxPro 2.6 for dBase compatibility. When you omit the popup name, they both return information about the active popup. We had trouble getting that value to show up in the Debugger—if we put CNTBAR() in the Watch window, then activated a popup, the value wasn't updated until we chose one of the items in the popup.

See Menus for an explanation of the different components of a menu.

Example

```
? BarCount("_MFILE")   && Returns 23 in VFP 6
? CntPad("_MSYSMENU")  && Returns 8 with default setup
```

See Also Define Bar, Define Pad, Menus

BarPrompt(), PrmBar(), PrmPad()

These functions look up the prompt of a particular bar or pad.

Usage

```
cPrompt = BarPrompt( nBar, cPopupName )
cPrompt = PrmBar( cPopupName, nBar )
cPrompt = PrmPad( cMenuName, cPadName )
```

Like the bar and pad-counting functions, these expect character strings for the names of menu components.

Although their parameter lists are reversed, BarPrompt() and PrmBar() share the same weird behavior with the built-in system menu bars. Ask for PrmBar("_MFile",1) and you get an error message instead of "New...". To get your hands on those prompts, you have to refer to the bars using their names, not their positions. Try PrmBar("_MFile",_MFi_New) instead. Note that you use the bar name without quotes. In fact, the bar names appear to be defined constants for a bunch of very negative numbers.

? STR(_MFi_New) yields -24064 in VFP 6, and PrmBar("_MFile", -24064) also returns "New...".

This behavior means that to build a list of bars in a system popup, you need to first use GetBar() to find the actual bar numbers, then use PrmBar() to look up the prompts.

Example
```
? PRMPAD("_MSysMenu", "_MSM_Edit")  && Returns "Edit"
```

See Also Define Bar, Define Pad, GetBar(), GetPad(), Menus, Sys(2013)

BaseClass, Class, ParentClass

These properties give you the pedigree of an object. They tell what class it's based on (Class), what class that class was derived from (ParentClass) and which of Visual FoxPro's base classes this whole inheritance chain derives from (BaseClass). Don't confuse ParentClass with Parent, which tells you what object contains the current object.

Usage
```
cClass = oObject.BaseClass
cClass = oObject.Class
cClass = oObject.ParentClass
```

These properties trace the class hierarchy, the family tree where one class derives behavior from another. They don't trace the object hierarchy, in which one object contains another.

Every class created in Visual FoxPro must originate from one of the built-in base classes. (See "Base Clef" in "OOP Is Not an Accident" for a list.) The BaseClass property contains the name of the Visual FoxPro base class that is the ultimate ancestor of this branch of the family tree.

Every object is based on a particular class, which is used as a template to create it. This is the class named in the CREATEOBJECT() function or in the ADD OBJECT clause of DEFINE CLASS or in the AddObject method used to add this object to another. The Class property tells us which one it is.

Finally, the class on which an object is based may be based on another class. That is, the class may be a subclass of another. This is the ParentClass of the object—the class from which its Class was derived. Microsoft introduced a lot of confusion here by calling this property "parentclass"—many OOP languages refer to it as "superclass" instead. The "superclass" terminology is somewhat less confusing because it matches "subclass." Nonetheless, if you visualize the family tree, you can see that the ParentClass of a class is the class one level up.

When an object is based directly on one of the FoxPro base classes, ParentClass is empty. That's because there's nothing one level up the class hierarchy.

You can't change any of these properties. Once you create an object, its class derivation is fixed. This is one reason we (along with the other experts) recommend you create subclasses of all the FoxPro base classes and subclass all your own classes from those. The Class Browser's Redefine button does let you change the class an object is based on, but it can't fix up all the things such a change affects.

Occasionally, you want to know more of the hierarchy than these properties give you. The ACLASS() function is handy in that case.

Example
```
oTest = CREATEOBJECT('Form')
? oTest.Class           && returns "Form"
? oTest.ParentClass     && returns ""
? oTest.BaseClass       && returns "Form"

* put the following in a program and run it
oParent = CREATEOBJECT("testParent")
oParent.ShowYourRoots()

oChild = CREATEOBJECT("testChild")
oChild.ShowYourRoots()

oSibling = CREATEOBJECT("testSibling")
oSibling.ShowYourRoots()

oGrandChild = CREATEOBJECT("testGrandchild")
oGrandChild.ShowYourRoots()

DEFINE CLASS testParent AS custom
```

```
   caption="My first class"

PROCEDURE ShowYourRoots
   WAIT WINDOW "Object = "+This.Name+CHR(13)+ ;
            "Class = "+This.Class+CHR(13)+ ;
            "ParentClass = "+This.ParentClass+CHR(13)+ ;
            "BaseClass = "+This.BaseClass
ENDPROC

ENDDEFINE

DEFINE CLASS testChild AS testParent
   caption="My second class"
ENDDEFINE

DEFINE CLASS testSibling AS testParent
   caption="Sibling rivalry"
ENDDEFINE

DEFINE CLASS testGrandchild AS testChild
   caption="My last class"
ENDDEFINE
```

Each object in the example shows for Class the name of the class you passed to CREATEOBJECT(). For ParentClass, it's the class named in the AS clause of the DEFINE CLASS command. Note that oChild and oSibling have the same ParentClass because the classes they're based on (testChild and testSibling, respectively) are both derived from testParent. Finally, the BaseClass for all of them is Custom because the first class we create in this hierarchy (testParent) is based on Custom.

See Also AClass(), CreateObject(), Define Class, Parent

_Beautify, _Browser, _Builder, _Converter, _FoxDoc, _FoxGraph, _Gallery, _GenGraph, _GenHTML, _GenMenu, _GenScrn, _GenXTab, _GetExpr, _SCCText, _SpellChk, _Transport, _Wizard

These system variables are all hooks. They let you specify a program or application that should run under specific circumstances. A number of them are unused in Visual FoxPro.

The table below shows the purpose of each hook and its default value. You can change the value of any of these in several ways: assign it a new value in a program or the Command Window, assign it a value in your Config.FPW file, or, for several of them, set it in the Tools-Options dialog.

Variable	Default value	Purpose
_BEAUTIFY	HOME() + "BEAUTIFY.APP"	Points to the Documenting Wizard that's used to produce formatted code and other documentation, like a cross-reference. Unused in VFP 3.
_BROWSER	HOME() + "BROWSER.APP"	Called when you choose Class Browser from the Tools menu. Don't confuse this variable with the _OBROWSER variable created by running the Browser. That one isn't a system variable and can be released. In VFP 3, available only in the Professional edition.

Variable	Default value	Purpose
_BUILDER	HOME() + "BUILDER.APP"	Called when you run a builder from any location.
_CONVERTER	HOME() + "CONVERT.APP"	Called when you open a FoxPro 2.x (or older) Project, Form or Report. In VFP 5 and VFP 6, also called when you open a VFP 3 project.
_FOXDOC	""	In FoxPro 2.x, called when you choose FoxDoc from the Program menu. Unused in VFP.
_FOXGRAPH	""	In FoxPro/DOS, provided a hook to a graphing package. Unused in VFP.
_GALLERY	HOME() + "GALLERY.APP"	New in VFP 6. Called when you choose Component Gallery from the Tools menu.
_GENGRAPH	HOME() + "WIZARDS\WZGRAPH.APP"	Points to the graphing wizard, which provides an interface to MS Graph.
_GENHTML	HOME() + "GENHTML.PRG"	New in VFP 6. Called when you choose Save As HTML from the File menu.
_GENMENU	HOME() + "GENMENU.FXP" or HOME() + "GENMENU.PRG"	Called when you choose Menu-Generate from inside the Menu Designer and when you build a project including a menu.
_GENSCRN	""	In FoxPro 2.x, called to convert SCX screen files into SPR screen programs. Unused in VFP.
_GENXTAB	HOME() + "VFPXTAB.PRG"	Called by programs created in the Query Designer with the CrossTab checkbox checked.
_GETEXPR	""	New in VFP 6. This variable may be one of the coolest additions in VFP 6. It lets you specify your own substitute for the Expression Builder. Whatever you specify is called by GETEXPR.
_SCCTEXT	HOME() + "SCCTEXT.PRG"	Added in VFP 5, called to convert forms, classes and other non-text files to a textual format for storage in a source control provider.
_SPELLCHK	HOME() + "SPELLCHK.APP"	Called when you choose Spelling from the Tools menu.
_TRANSPORT	""	In FoxPro 2.x, called when you open a project, form, report or label on a platform other than the one on which it was last edited. Unused in VFP—it uses _CONVERTER, above, instead.
_WIZARD	HOME() + "WIZARD.APP"	Called when you choose any wizard from any location.

Note that some of these variables (like _BEAUTIFY) just give you a reference to the program in use—changing these variables doesn't affect what happens when you call the appropriate tool from the menu. Others specify the program that's actually called—changing one of these means that, when you call that tool from the menu, the newly specified program is executed, not the default. In the table, the ones that simply provide a reference use the term "points to," while the others say "called."

In addition to the automatic ways in which the hooked programs are called, you can run them yourself using DO (_variable). In many cases, you'll need to pass appropriate parameters. See "Builders and Wizards (and Bears, Oh My!)" on the CD for the necessary parameters in those cases. Read the source code for VFPXTab and SCCTEXT, and the help file for BROWSER.APP.

You may also want to consider overriding the default setting of these variables with your own, improved code.

The unused variables provide a place to store permanent information. Unlike variables you create, nothing you can do releases these variables. They're as persistent as they come. You might use them to store vital information. You might also use them as hooks into things you're interested in. See _ASSIST for an example.

Example

```
* Run a crosstab
DO (_GENXTAB) WITH "Result"
```

See Also _Assist, _Coverage, _GenPD, GetExpr, _Startup

BeforeBuild, AfterBuild

These project hook events, as their names imply, fire before and after the project's Build method is called, whether the call comes from the interface or in code.

Usage

```
phkProjectHook.BeforeBuild( [ cResultFile ] [, nBuildType ]
                            [, lRebuildAll ] [, lShowErrors ]
                            [, lRegenerateIds ] )
phkProjectHook.AfterBuild( nError )
```

BeforeBuild receives exactly the same parameters as Build, with one difference. BeforeBuild gets them by reference and can change them. The changed values are what actually get passed on to Build. This means a project hook can totally hijack the build process and do whatever it wants, regardless of what the developer-user does interactively. (Of course, generally, changing a user's actions behind the scenes is frowned upon, except when it protects the user from himself.)

AfterBuild is a lot simpler and a lot less powerful. It receives a single parameter, indicating whether or not an error occurred that prevented the build from completing. We're not sure where the error numbers come from, though.

As with the other project hook events, you can use these either to log actions or to change them. NODEFAULT in BeforeBuild prevents the project from being built. NODEFAULT in AfterBuild is pointless—there is no default behavior.

Example

```
* We might use BeforeBuild to check whether there
* seems to be enough room for whatever we're building.
PROCEDURE BeforeBuild
LPARAMETERS cOutputName, nBuildAction, lRebuildAll, ;
            lShowErrors, lBuildNewGuids

LOCAL cOutDrive, nSpace, nProjSize, nSizeNeeded
cOutDrive = JustDrive(cOutputName)
nSpace = DISKSPACE(cOutDrive)

* Perhaps base expected need on project size.
* For project size, we'll use rough justice based on the number
* of files in the project. The average file size of 10000 is
* picked at random and needs to be tuned. You could scan the
* Project object's File collection and supply the File's Name
* to ADIR() and sum them up. Don't forget to add in the runtime!
```

```
* The next line assumes that the project hook's Init method
* grabs a reference to the project and stores it in
* a property called oProject.

nProjSize = This.oProject.Files.Count * 10000
IF nSpace < nProjSize

   LOCAL cBuildType, nResult

   * Figure out the type of build
   DO CASE
   CASE nBuildAction = 0
      cBuildType = "Project"
   CASE nBuildAction = 1
      cBuildType = "App"
   CASE nBuildAction = 2
      cBuildType = "Exe"
   CASE nBuildAction = 3
      cBuildType = "DLL"
   ENDCASE

   nResult = MESSAGEBOX("Drive " + cOutDrive + ;
                " doesn't appear to have enough free space " + ;
                " to build this project. Proceed anyway?", ;
                MB_YESNO + MB_ICONQUESTION + MB_DEFBUTTON2, ;
                "Build "+cBuildType)
   IF nResult = IDNO
      NODEFAULT
   ENDIF
ENDIF

RETURN
```

See Also Build, Project, ProjectHook

BeforeDock, AfterDock, Undock

These events fire as part of the docking or undocking sequence of a toolbar. BeforeDock fires whenever the toolbar is docked or undocked. AfterDock fires when a toolbar is completely docked (except in one case—see below). Undock fires when a toolbar is undocked, but before it reappears. (And HickoryDickoryDock fires when the mouse runs up the clock.)

Usage

```
PROCEDURE BeforeDock
LPARAMETERS [ nIndex , ] nLocation

PROCEDURE AfterDock
[ LPARAMETERS nIndex ]

PROCEDURE Undock
[LPARAMETERS nIndex ]
```

The nIndex parameter for all three is relevant only when the toolbar is contained in a control array. Then, it identifies the element of the array that fired the event.

The nLocation parameter to BeforeDock uses the same values as DockPosition. It lets you know where the toolbar will be docked. This lets you do things like remove or resize controls that don't dock well in that position. (For example, textual check boxes don't dock well at the sides.) It would be very cool if you could even bail out of the docking here, but you can't. Neither NoDefault nor Dock(-1) does anything in BeforeDock.

AfterDock is supposed to fire once the toolbar has settled into its new location. Most of the time, that's what happens. But in VFP 5, if you call Dock and pass the optional x and y coordinates to specify the exact docking position, AfterDock fires after the base bar has been laid down, but before the toolbar actually appears. In VFP 3, AfterDock always fires after the base bar has been laid down and before the controls appear.

In VFP 3, when a toolbar is moved from one docked location to another with the mouse, only BeforeDock and AfterDock fire. When you use Dock to move the toolbar from one docked position to another, BeforeDock fires, then Undock (for the old position), then BeforeDock and AfterDock fire. In VFP 5 and VFP 6, only BeforeDock and AfterDock fire, no matter which way you dock the toolbar. We suspect the later versions have it right and the original was doing just a little too much for us.

When you release a docked toolbar, Undock and BeforeDock fire after the toolbar's Destroy method. (In VFP 3, it's the other way around—BeforeDock, then Undock.) Our guess is that, for some internal reasons, FoxPro can't release a docked toolbar, so it has to undock it first. Because of this, you'll want to check for the existence of the contained objects before you start to manipulate them within these methods—otherwise, you'll end up with the dreaded "Unknown member" error.

Example

```
* Handle the case where a control doesn't fit for side docking
* Making the control invisible solves the problem

PROCEDURE BeforeDock
LPARAMETERS nLocation
IF INLIST(nLocation,1,2)
   * dock to side, so remove checkbox
   This.chkMyCheck.Visible = .F.
ELSE
   * see if we need to put it back
   IF INLIST(This.DockPosition,1,2)
      This.chkMyCheck.Visible = .T.
   ENDIF
ENDIF
```

See Also Dock, Docked, DockPosition, Toolbar

BeforeOpenTables, AfterCloseTables

These two events (and their associated methods) relate to the Data environment of forms, reports and labels. These events give you the opportunity to take actions before the tables are opened and after the tables close.

Usage

```
PROCEDURE DataEnvironment.BeforeOpenTables
PROCEDURE DataEnvironment.AfterCloseTables
```

As its name suggests, BeforeOpenTables happens before tables are opened, which is very early in the firing sequence. This makes it a good place to do anything you want to happen right away. We've been known to put some environmental settings (such as SET DELETED ON) in there.

AfterCloseTables isn't the last event. The Destroy events of the Data environment and the objects it contains happen later.

When we started testing this stuff, we got a real shock. BeforeOpenTables does not fire before the OpenTables method. That's because BeforeOpenTables is misnamed. A better (though terribly unwieldy) name would be BeforeAutoOpenTables because this event fires right before tables are opened automatically. If there's custom code in OpenTables, that code executes, then BeforeOpenTables fires, then the tables are automatically opened. (Of course, this behavior means there's not much use for BeforeOpenTables. Almost anything you'd want to put there could just as soon go in the OpenTables method.)

Example

```
* This might be a report's BeforeOpenTables method
* where the DE contains a view, so you need to set
* things up so the view's query gets the right results
PROCEDURE BeforeOpenTables

SET DELETED ON
SET ANSI ON
```

See Also AutoCloseTables, AutoOpenTables, CloseTables, OpenTables

BeforeRowColChange, AfterRowColChange

These grid events occur when their names say—before changing row or column and after changing row or column. They give you the opportunity to prevent the change or to take some action because of it.

Usage

```
PROCEDURE BeforeRowColChange | AfterRowColChange
LPARAMETERS nColIndex
```

In BeforeRowColChange, nColIndex is the number of the column you're leaving. In AfterRowColChange, it's the number of the column you've entered. Since these events fire on both row and column changes, we're baffled as to why there's a column parameter but no row parameter. Especially since you can get the same information from the grid's ActiveColumn property. Now, if they passed the reverse—the column you're headed for in BeforeRowColChange and the one you just left in AfterRowColChange—that would be handy. Of course, the same information would be useful for rows, too.

You can prevent the change by using NODEFAULT in BeforeRowColChange. Putting NODEFAULT in AfterRowColChange appears to have no effect at all. The docs indicate that BeforeRowColChange fires before the Valid of the control you're leaving and AfterRowColChange fires after the When of the control you're entering. Both are correct, but what they don't tell you is what happens if one of those controls returns .F. Fortunately, both behaviors are reasonably sensible. Returning .F. from the Valid leaves you in the same row and column you were in—AfterRowColChange doesn't fire. Returning .F. from the When sends FoxPro scurrying for a column that will accept the focus, if you got there with a keystroke. If you clicked into the cell that won't accept focus, you get a sort of false focus. The focus rectangle is there, but you can't type anything in. In either case, AfterRowColChange does fire for the cell that ends up with focus.

BeforeRowColChange fires when focus leaves the grid, and AfterRowColChange fires when the grid gets focus.

Example

```
PROCEDURE BeforeRowColChange
LPARAMETERS nColIndex

* Decide whether to allow the change
* This is a silly example designed to drive users nuts
IF MOD(INT(SECONDS()),4)=0
   NODEFAULT
ENDIF

RETURN
```

See Also ActivateCell, ActiveColumn, ActiveRow, Grid

Begin Transaction, End Transaction, Rollback, TxnLevel()

The transaction commands let you combine updates to a group of tables into a single process so all the changes either happen or don't happen. Transactions can be nested—TXNLEVEL() lets you find out how deep you are.

Usage

```
BEGIN TRANSACTION
END TRANSACTION
ROLLBACK
nCurrentLevel = TXNLEVEL()
```

One of the biggest complaints about FoxPro over the years has been the lack of transaction processing. It was possible to save an invoice header, then have a problem saving the detail records and have no clean way out. If power failed in the middle, you could get incomplete records. No more ... sort of.

When you need to make updates to multiple tables and it's an all-or-nothing deal (like invoice headers and details), wrap the whole process in a transaction. BEGIN the TRANSACTION, then go through each table attempting to update it. If you succeed in updating all the tables, END the TRANSACTION and go on with your life. If you can't update one of the tables, ROLLBACK the transaction, and either figure out and solve the problem or revert all the tables to their original state. (You may even want to wrap single table updates in a transaction if they involve updates to multiple records.)

So why do we say "sort of?" Because there's still a small window of time where a system crash or a power outage could leave you with messed-up data. Don't throw out those uninterruptable power supplies just yet. Nonetheless, with transactions, the window's much smaller than before.

Each record the transaction affects is locked at the time it becomes part of the transaction. (In fact, not only are these records locked, but they can't even be read by other workstations, so you want to keep transactions as short as possible.) END TRANSACTION and ROLLBACK unlock all the affected records.

You can nest one transaction inside another. This might happen when, say, an order entry branches off to add a new customer. If both the customer and order entry save routines use transactions, and the order entry save routine calls the customer save routine, the order can't be saved unless the customer save is successful.

The limit for nesting is five levels—shades of the READ levels of old. Just as read levels could be checked with RDLEVEL(), transaction levels can be checked with TXNLEVEL().

Transactions apply only to tables (and views) contained in databases. You can't use them on free tables. To be more specific, you can do things to free tables when a transaction is in progress, but the changes can't be rolled back. For remote views, consider using the backend data source's transaction capabilities through SQLSetProp(), SQLCommit() and SQLRollback().

Example

```
* Save invoice header and details in a transaction.
* This is only a sketch of the real code, which would
* probably include various error checking and handling.
BEGIN TRANSACTION

lGoOn = .T.

SELECT header
IF NOT TABLEUPDATE()
   lGoOn = .F.
ENDIF

IF lGoOn
   SELECT detail

   IF NOT TABLEUPDATE(.t.,.t.)
      lGoOn = .F.
   ENDIF
ENDIF

IF lGoOn
   END TRANSACTION
ELSE
   ROLLBACK
   =TABLEREVERT(.f.,"header")
   =TABLEREVERT(.t.,"detail")
ENDIF
```

You may be confused by the calls to TableRevert() after the Rollback—we were at first, too. What's going on here is that updating is normally a two-step process. The user updates the buffers by making changes (through whatever interface you provide). Then, calls to TableUpdate() copy the changes from the buffers to the actual tables. When you use transactions, you add another layer to that. TableUpdate() copies the changes from the buffers to another set of buffers (call them "transaction buffers") and END TRANSACTION copies from those buffers to the actual tables.

When you issue ROLLBACK, the changes are cleared from the transaction buffers, but the original buffers still contain the changed data. The TableRevert() calls discard those changes. In a real application, you probably wouldn't just give up and revert your changes like that, but would try to solve whatever problems prevented the save, and try again.

See Also Buffering, SQLCommit(), SQLSetProp(), SQLRollback(), TableRevert(), TableUpdate()

Between()

This function determines whether the value of one expression is between the values of two others. Both boundaries are included in the range—it's an "inclusive" test. BETWEEN() works on almost every field type in Visual FoxPro; only General is excluded.

Usage `lResult = BETWEEN( uExpression, eLower, eUpper )`

Parameter	Value	Meaning
uExpression	Character, Currency, Date, DateTime, Double, Integer, Logical, Memo, Numeric	The value to be compared to the specified boundaries.
uLower	Same or similar type as uExpression	The lower boundary.
uUpper	Same or similar type as uExpression	The upper boundary.
lResult	.T.	uExpression is between uLower and uUpper.
	.F.	uExpression is not between uLower and uUpper.

BETWEEN() does some conversion between related data types. If any of the three expressions is DateTime, dates are converted to DateTime by adding a time of "12:00:00 AM" (midnight). Watch out if you do this—if the lower boundary is DateTime (and doesn't have a time of midnight) and uExpression is Date and has the same date as the lower boundary, BETWEEN() returns .F., because uExpression gets the default time of midnight.

Numeric, currency, integer and double values can be mixed with BETWEEN() without problem. So can character data and memo fields holding characters.

BETWEEN() is Rushmore-optimizable. Our tests show that, with variables, BETWEEN() is between 25% and 40% faster than using the comparison operators. That is:

```
?BETWEEN(x,y,z)
```

is 25–40% faster than:

```
?x>=y AND x<=z
```

For Rushmore-optimizable record operations, the improvement isn't as great—our tests show BETWEEN() can be as much 6% to 7% faster than performing two comparisons, but not in every case. In some of our tests, the two forms were about even. In queries, we didn't see any significant differences between the SQL BETWEEN clause and the BETWEEN() function. Our inclination is to use the SQL BETWEEN there because it's part of the SQL standard.

If eExpression is null, BETWEEN() returns .NULL. If either boundary is null, BETWEEN() uses some smarts about the notion of lower and upper boundaries. If the lower boundary is null, but eExpression is greater than the upper boundary, the function returns false. Similarly, if eUpper is null, but eExpression is less than the lower boundary, BETWEEN() returns .F. because the result must be false. When BETWEEN() can't tell because of a null boundary, it returns .NULL.

Example

```
? BETWEEN(27, 12, 50)    && returns .T.
? BETWEEN(27, 27, 30)    && returns .T.
? BETWEEN("foxpro", "flocks", "sheep")  && returns .T.
? BETWEEN(DATE(), DATETIME(), DATE()+1) && returns .F.
```

See Also InList(), Max(), Min(), Select-SQL

BinToC(), CToBin()

These two functions let you change between integers and a character representation of their values. Their *raison d'etre* is to allow more efficient indexing.

Usage

```
cCharValue = BinToC( nInteger [, nChars] )
nInteger = CToBin( cCharValue )
```

Parameter	Value	Meaning
nInteger	Numeric	The number to be converted to character or the result of the conversion.
cCharValue	Character	The character-string representation of nInteger.
nChars	1	Use one character to represent nInteger.
	2	Use two characters to represent nInteger.
	4 or omitted	Use four characters to represent nInteger.

The character set we use has 256 characters. Internally, they're represented by the numbers from 0 to 255. The number system we use has only 10 characters, the digits from 0 to 9. If we use characters to represent numbers (as opposed to the other way around, which is how we usually think of things), we can represent large numbers using fewer characters than digits. That is, a single character can represent up to 256 different numbers, while a one-digit number can have only 10 different values. In essence, representing numbers using the character set lets us work in base 256.

These functions convert between numbers and their character representations—that is, converting to and from base 256. We can choose to use one, two or four characters to represent a single number. However, the range of values is restricted based on the number of characters used. This makes sense, since one character has only 256 distinct values, while two characters give us 256^2 and four offer 256^4.

To confuse matters, though, instead of mapping directly (number 0 to CHR(0), number 1 to CHR(1), and so forth), these functions can work with both positive and negative values. So a string of CHR(0)'s is used for the smallest number in the range, and the largest number in the range is converted to a string of CHR(255)'s. With one character, this means that CHR(0) represents -128 and CHR(255) represents 127. This means, among other things, that using these functions for converting between hex and decimal is, at best, complicated. Why would we want to do this? For space efficiency. It takes a lot less space to store large numbers in base 256 than in base 10 (used for most numeric types). The obvious place to apply this efficiency is in indexing of large tables. Our friend Mac Rubel has done extensive testing in this area, and finds that not only do indexes created with BINTOC() take up less storage space than characters, but they're actually faster to create and to work with. (The big winner in his testing, though, was Integers. For the best overall performance, go with Integer keys.)

Example

```
? BINTOC( -128, 1)  && returns CHR(0)
? BINTOC(127,1)      && returns CHR(255)
? CTOBIN("zzzz")     && returns -92636550
* Suppose you have an integer primary key field, iPKey
INDEX ON BINTOC(iPKey) TAG iPKey
```

See Also Asc(),Chr(), Transform()

BitAnd(), BitClear(), BitLShift(), BitNot(), BitOr(), BitRShift(), BitSet(), BitTest(), BitXor()

All these functions manipulate a bit value as a 4-byte signed integer. Visual FoxPro has the full complement of AND, OR, NOT and XOR operations. In addition, we have simple and accessible SET, CLEAR, TEST as well as Left and Right SHIFT commands.

For those of you who haven't had to slice and dice bits since school, a little base number review is in order here. Base 10, the decimal system, is the most common way of counting. From right to left, the digits are the ones place, the tens place, and the hundreds place. These can also be expressed as 10 to the zeroth power, 10 to the first power, and 10 to the second power. Base 2, or binary math, works the same way. The first place is the ones place, 2 to the zeroth. The second place (from the right) is the twos place, two to the first. The progression continues—third place is four, two squared; fourth place is eight, two to the third. Let's try to make this into a table and see what happens:

Binary Place→	7	6	5	4	3	2	1	0
Holds the value→	128	64	32	16	8	4	2	1
Decimal Value↓	Represented in Binary							
1	0	0	0	0	0	0	0	1
2	0	0	0	0	0	0	1	0
3	0	0	0	0	0	0	1	1
4	0	0	0	0	0	1	0	0
16	0	0	0	1	0	0	0	0
127	0	1	1	1	1	1	1	1
128	1	0	0	0	0	0	0	0
255	1	1	1	1	1	1	1	1

Table 1-1: How decimal values (left column) are represented in binary.

It's hard to fit more than eight bits across the page in a table, which makes sense—check out the sample Num2Bit.PRG, below, for a full 32-bit display.

So when we're talking about the value 128, our computer is really thinking 10000000. And 127, not very different to us, is very different to the computer, which represents it internally as 01111111. So why would any human being in his right mind want to play with all these ones and zeroes? This was the question we asked our algebra teachers, and hardly ever received a satisfactory answer. Well, here, finally, we have an answer.

Space. The final frontier. Uh, no, not that kind of space—space of the hard disk kind of space. What if you had to store six yes/no answers in a table? You could create a character field of four spaces, storing "Yes," "No," "Ya," "Nein," and "Nyet," but parsing and case-testing would probably be far too time-consuming. A logical field seems more efficient. But six logical fields take six bytes, perhaps not a major amount with gigabyte hard drives in the hundreds of dollars, but millions of these bytes clog the lines of communication. Multiply these by a few dozen fields in the more complex tables and you have the formula for bogging down whatever system you choose in wasted I/O, sloshing padding characters around.

In order to save space, many functions use individual bits within a byte to store simple yes/no information. For example, DBF headers store information on whether or not the file uses CDXs, memo fields, and whether the file is a DBC or not—all in byte 28. Divining this information is far easier thanks to the BIT functions. Other places where bit-splitting comes in handy are in deciphering the buttons pressed and modifier keys in MouseDown, MouseMove and related events, or in hacking SCX datestamp fields. Obviously, Microsoft has had these functions available to them internally for quite some time—it is great that they exposed them for us to use as well.

A little terminology primer is needed here. If a bit contains a 1, it is said to be "set" or "on." If a 0 instead occupies that place, the location is said to be "cleared" or "off." The operations of setting these bits can therefore be referred to as "setting" and "clearing."

All BIT functions operate on numbers in the range from 0 to ±(2^31-1), using 31 bits in a total of four bytes. The 32nd bit (bit 31, remember, we started counting at zero) is reserved for the negative flag. If bit 31 is set on, the value is considered negative, and the value of the following bits is different from what they mean for positive values. Negative 1 is expressed as 32 bits set to 1, negative two as 31 one-bits followed by a zero, negative three as 30 one-bits followed by zero-one, and negative four as 30 one-bits followed by two zeroes. We seem to remember this as "two's complement math," but we've been out of school way too long to think this way. This must make some sense to the computer, but little to us. Our advice: Use caution when manipulating bit 31 or shifting bits left, which could change the sign of the number. Combining BIT functions with addition or subtraction under these conditions can lead to inaccurate results.

Usage

```
nRetVal = BitAnd( nFirstArg, nSecondArg )
nRetVal = BitNot( nFirstArg )
nRetVal = BitOr( nFirstArg, nSecondArg )
nRetVal = BitXOr( nFirstArg, nSecondArg )
```

Parameter	Value	Meaning
nFirstArg	Numeric	First numeric value to process, ranging from 0 to ±(2^32-1).
nSecondArg	Numeric	Value to process against the first, restricted to the same range.

These fundamental functions perform bit mathematics. They allow the changing of one or more bits at the same time. BITAND() may be used with a "mask" as the second argument to allow through only selected bits. BITAND() returns a 1 in a bit position if and only if both arguments have a 1 in that position. For example, in the TimeStamp field illustrated in the Stamp2DT.PRG below, the hours field is stored in the five bits in positions 11, 12, 13, 14 and 15, and those individual bits can be isolated with a mask with only those bits set. BITNOT() reverses all the bits of the supplied number from 1 to 0 and 0 to 1. BITOR() can be used to ensure that some bits are turned on by supplying a mask with those bits turned on. BITXOR() matches two values to the most severe test—that a bit is set in one value and is not set in the other. BITXOR() returns a bit set if only one of the two numbers had that bit set, and zero if either both numbers do not have the bit set or both numbers do have the bit set. In other words, BITXOR() tests for a match in corresponding positions and sets a bit only if the two numbers do not match.

Usage

```
nRetVal = BitClear( nValue, nBitPos )
nRetVal = BitSet( nValue, nBitPos )
lRetVal = BitTest( nValue, nBitPos )
```

Parameter	Value	Meaning
nValue	Numeric	Value to process, ranging from 0 to ±(2^32-1).
nBitPos	Numeric	Bit position to modify or test. Ranges from 0 to 31.
nRetVal	Numeric	The result is the numeric value of taking the supplied nValue and SETting or CLEARing the specified bit.
lRetVal	.T.	Position nBitPos is set in nValue.
	.F.	Position nBitPos is clear in nValue.

These three handy functions allow access to a single bit to either clear it (set it to 0), set it (to 1) or query its current value (return .T. if the bit is 1 and .F. it it's 0). nBitPos must be in the range 0 to 31—numbers outside this range (or null) return error 11, "Invalid function argument value, type or count."

Example

```
* Num2Bit - return character representation of numeric bitmap

PARAMETER number
LOCAL I
LOCAL lcRetString
IF TYPE('number') <> "N" OR ABS(number) > 2^32
   lcRetString = "Must be number -2^32 to +2^32"
ELSE
  lcRetString = ""
  FOR I = 31 TO 0 STEP -1
    lcRetString = lcRetString + IIF(BITTEST(number,I),"1","0")
  NEXT
ENDIF
RETURN lcRetString
```

Usage

```
nRetVal = BitRShift( nValue, nAmt2Shift )
nRetVal = BitLShift( nValue, nAmt2Shift )
```

Parameter	Value	Meaning
nValue	Numeric	Value to shift, ranging from 0 to ±(2^32-1).
nAmt2Shift	Numeric	Number of bits to shift, positive or negative.
nRetVal	Numeric	The numeric value from taking the supplied number and shifting the bitmap the specified amount to the right or left.

The SHIFT functions return the result of moving all the bits a specified number of bit places to the right or left. For example, shifting the binary value 0110 one to the right results in 0011, to the left 1100. What happens to the values that fall off the right or left end of the value? They're gone—dumped into the bit-bucket, never to return. Zeroes are always used to fill in the newly created "holes" on the other end. These functions allow you to grab a specified range of bits and process them as a separate value. In combination with BITAND() and the other functions above, a value can be masked and those selected bits moved to the right or left to isolate a set of bits and calculate their value. This function hacks SCX/VCX timestamps and returns the correct datetime value for the record.

```
*********************************************************************
* Program....: STAMP2T6.PRG
* Version....: 1.0
* Author.....: Ted Roche
* Date.......: May 31, 1998
* Notice.....: Copyright © 1998 Ted Roche, All Rights Reserved.
```

```
* Compiler...: Visual FoxPro 06.00.8093.00 for Windows
* Abstract...: VERSION SIX ONLY!!!
* ...........: Simpler version of Stamp2DT written for HackFox3 and
* ...........: also published in FoxPro Advisor magazine
* Changes....:
*********************************************************************

parameter tnStamp

#DEFINE SecondsMask 15  && 00001111
#DEFINE MinutesMask 63  && 00111111
#DEFINE HoursMask   31  && 00011111
#DEFINE DaysMask    31  && 00011111
#DEFINE MonthsMask  15  && 00001111
#DEFINE YearsMask   63  && 00111111

#DEFINE SecondsOffset 1  && Note this is a LEFT shift, not RIGHT
#DEFINE MinutesOffset 5
#DEFINE HoursOffset   11
#DEFINE DaysOffset    16
#DEFINE MonthsOffset  21
#DEFINE YearsOffset   25

#DEFINE fMonth       BITAND(bitrshift(tnStamp,MONTHSOFFSET ),MONTHSMASK)
#DEFINE fDay         BITAND(bitrshift(tnStamp,DAYSOFFSET   ),DAYSMASK)
#DEFINE fYear   1980+BITAND(bitrshift(tnStamp,YEARSOFFSET  ),YEARSMASK)
#DEFINE fHour        BITAND(bitrshift(tnStamp,HOURSOFFSET  ),HOURSMASK)
#DEFINE fMinute      BITAND(bitrshift(tnStamp,MINUTESOFFSET),MINUTESMASK)
#DEFINE fSecond      BITAND(bitLshift(tnStamp,SECONDSOFFSET),SECONDSMASK)

IF TYPE("VERSION(5)") = "U"
  = MESSAGEBOX("This routine only works with Visual FoxPro 6.x or later.")
  RETURN .F.
ENDIF

LOCAL ltReturn
ltReturn = IIF(tnStamp = 0, {//::}, ;
               DATETIME(fYear, fMonth, fDay, fHour, fMinute, fSecond))
return ltReturn
```

This is a really handy function to check the last date that form elements were modified. Open up an SCX file and issue the command:

```
browse fields platform, uniqueid, timestamp, realtime=stamp2t6(timestamp),;
              classname=left(class,20), namebaseclass=left(baseclass,20)
```

This example requires some explanation. The TIMESTAMP field in SCX's and VCX's is composed of bitmaps of the year, month, day, hour, minute and second. In order to compress all this information into the smallest amount of space, the designers examined each of the values above, and calculated the amount of space each would take, in bits. The seconds field was trimmed on the right (using a BitRShift()) so the precision of this field is within two seconds, probably close enough. Then these values are mapped into a continuous range of 30 bits:

Value	Range	Number of bits required	Starting Position
Years since 1980	0 – 64	6	25
Months	1 – 12	4	21
Day	1 – 31	5	16
Hours	0 – 23	5	11
Minutes	0 – 59	6	5

Value	Range	Number of bits required	Starting Position
Seconds	even 0 – 58	5	0

Parsing out these values is a matter of masking out all other values, and then shifting the value of interest to the right. For example, if we wish to determine the hours setting of the value 510494257, first we BitRShift() this value 11 places to the right, and then mask all but the rightmost five bits to get our final value of 16—this screen element was last modified at 4 PM.

Note that this function has been updated for the *Hacker's Guide* VFP 6.0 edition—with the new parameters to pass to DateTime(), we no longer have to fool around with various SET("DATE") cases. Another win for unambiguous dates!

By the way, this method of storing datetimes is archaic—the datetime data type will store the same amount of information in 20 percent less space, while providing a far better clue to the hapless programmer trying to decode the TIMESTAMP field. We hope we'll see the change to using datetime fields in a future VFP version.

See Also ASC(), Val()

Blank

Duke: And what's her history?
Viola: A blank, my lord.

—William Shakespeare, *Twelfth Night*

BLANK was added to FoxPro in version 2.6 as part of Microsoft's attempt to woo dBASE users. It's part of an approach that's sort of halfway to nulls.

Usage

```
BLANK [ FIELDS FieldList ]
      [ Scope ]
      [ FOR lForExpression ]
      [ WHILE lWhileExpression ]
      [ NOOPTIMIZE ]
```

When records are first added to a table, fields that aren't assigned values (as with INSERT-SQL's VALUE clause) are "blank." What this really means is that, rather than containing an empty value of the field's specified type, all the fields contain spaces (CHR(32)). This is why sometimes an empty, noncharacter field shows up as totally blank in a Browse, while at other times it shows the empty value for its type (0 for numeric, .F. for logical, and so on).

Because the empty string isn't a legal value for most field types, somebody wised up along the way and realized that you could test for this. That's what ISBLANK() does. Well, if you can test for it and you'd like to distinguish between this kind of empty field and the kind that contains the usual empty value for the data type, you probably want to be able to re-create that situation. Enter BLANK. It populates the specified fields (or all fields if you don't specify) with CHR(32). When you apply ISBLANK() to the BLANKed fields, it returns .T.

BLANK is moderately useful for numerics and logical fields, but doesn't help at all with character or the date types, where CHR(32) is the normal empty value. Despite its limitations, there are a few places where BLANK seems useful—for example, when recycling deleted records, or for clearing several fields at a time. On the whole, though, with true nulls supported in Visual FoxPro, your best bet is to ignore BLANK and ISBLANK(). The one place we thought we might use blanks was a project in which we collected survey data. The varied answers seem to fit these new capabilities, since you can now store four states in a logical field—True, False, Blank and Null—as Yes, No, Don't Know, and Refused to Answer. However, unlike nulls, blanks do not remove themselves from calculations, still appearing as a logical false unless ISBLANK() is tested. The additional coding needed to check for this every time made it obvious that a much better solution was a single character status field.

If you insist on using this command, you'll find information on Scope and the FOR and WHILE clauses in "Xbase Xplained." As for NOOPTIMIZE, it's generally a bad idea—see SET OPTIMIZE for all the reasons.

Example
```
BLANK nTotal FOR lExpired
```

See Also Empty(), IsBlank(), Set Null

BOF(), EOF()

She was a phantom of delight
When first she gleamed upon my sight;

William Wordsworth, *She Was a Phantom of Delight,* 1807

These functions stand for Beginning Of File and End Of File, respectively. They tell you whether the record pointer is at the start or end of a table or cursor.

Usage
```
lReturnValue = BOF( [cAlias | nWorkArea] )
lReturnValue = EOF( [cAlias | nWorkArea] )
```

Parameter	Value	Meaning
cAlias	Character	Check the table whose alias is cAlias.
	Omitted	If nWorkArea is also omitted, check the table in the current work area.
nWorkArea	Numeric	Check the table currently open in nWorkArea.
	Omitted	If cAlias is also omitted, check the table in the current work area.
lReturnValue	.T.	The specified table is at the beginning or end of file, based on the current order.
	.F.	The specified table is not at the beginning or end of file.

BOF() and EOF() are not complementary as their names imply. Instead, we have one of those little inconsistencies that drive us all nuts. BOF() means *at* the beginning of the file; EOF() means *beyond* the end of the file. BOF() becomes true when you skip backward from the first record (in the current order), but the record pointer remains on the first record. However, every Xbase table has a "phantom" record at the end. EOF() is true when the record pointer is pointing to the phantom record, not to the last real record in the table. So the mechanism for getting to BOF() and EOF() is the same—skip backward or forward from the first or last record—but the results are not.

EOF() is useful when a relation has been set between two tables. If you move the record pointer in the parent table, and there are no matching records in the child table, EOF() becomes true for the child table. This is an easy way to check for matching records. Incidentally, you can do the same thing by checking FOUND() in the child area.

Besides a lack of relatives, various things can set the record pointer to EOF(). The simplest is to issue SKIP when you're already on the last record. Other things that leave the pointer on EOF() are a SEEK or SEEK() (with SET NEAR OFF) that doesn't find a match, a LOCATE that doesn't locate any matching records, and any of the scoped commands (like REPLACE or COUNT) issued with ALL or REST, and no WHILE clause to stop them sooner.

We recommend strongly that you never use work area numbers as parameters to BOF() and EOF() (or just about any other time, actually). While it's always been better to avoid them, this is even more true in Visual FoxPro, since the visual interface no longer provides a way to choose work areas by number.

Example

```
USE Customer
? RECNO()    && 1
? BOF()      && .F.
* make BOF() true
SKIP -1
? BOF()      && .T.
? RECNO()    && Still 1

* now go to the bottom
GO BOTTOM
? EOF()       && .F.
? RECNO()

* go to phantom record
SKIP
? EOF()      && .T.
? RECNO()    && Not the same as above;
             && one more than RECCOUNT()

* check for related records
USE Parent IN 0
USE Child IN 0 ORDER ParentId

SELECT Parent
SET RELATION TO ParentId INTO Child

* Browse child-less parents
BROWSE FOR EOF("Child")
* Another way to do this is:
BROWSE FOR NOT FOUND("Child")
```

See Also Go, Locate, Seek, Seek(), Set Near, Set Relation, Skip

BorderColor, BorderStyle, BorderWidth

These properties control the borders of objects that have changeable borders. But some of the results are pretty strange.

Usage

```
oObject.BorderColor = nColor
nColor = oObject.BorderColor
oObject.BorderStyle = nStyle
nStyle = oObject.BorderStyle
oObject.BorderWidth = nWidth
nWidth = oObject.BorderWidth
```

BorderColor is available for a bunch of controls, but on most of them has no effect unless you set SpecialEffect to 1 (Plain). With 3-D effects, BorderColor is ignored.

BorderColor determines the only color of a Line and the outside color of a Shape (the inner color comes from FillColor).

As with DrawStyle and DrawWidth, there's a strange relationship between BorderStyle and BorderWidth. Settings of BorderStyle other than None or Single work only when BorderWidth is 1. When you use a wider border, it doesn't matter what value you give BorderStyle—you still get a single-line border.

In VFP 5 and VFP 6, when a line or shape has a BorderWidth of 1, certain BorderColors show up wrong. The problem seems to occur with colors where the RGB values are some permutation of 0, 128, and 255. The same problem also occurs when BorderWidth of a line is greater than 1 and BorderStyle is set to 2, 3, 4 or 5.

For forms, BorderStyle controls more than appearance. Unless you use the default of 3 (Sizable), the form can't be resized using the mouse either at design-time or runtime. Although there are times you want to present fixed-size forms to users, it does make design a little difficult. We recommend you set BorderStyle in the Form's Init method if you need something other than the default.

Borderless forms are finicky. Setting BorderStyle to 0 (None) isn't good enough. You have to also turn off all the stuff that appears along the top of the window. In VFP 6, you can do that just by setting TitleBar to .F. In the older versions, Closable, ControlBox, MaxButton, MinButton and Movable must all be .F., and Caption has to be "", the empty string. If you miss any of those, you get a single-line border. It isn't until you turn off all those things that you can really see the difference between the three BorderStyles, other than 3-Sizable.

As with DrawStyle, we can't make much sense of the "Inside Solid" border style.

Example

```
* Make a very un-Windows kind of form - maybe for an alert
* Assume we have a reference, oForm, to the form
oForm.BorderStyle=1
oForm.Closable=.F.
oForm.ControlBox=.F.
oForm.MaxButton=.F.
oForm.MinButton=.F.
oForm.Movable=.F.

* Border stuff is fun with lines and shapes
* First, create a form
oForm=CREATEOBJECT("Form")
oForm.Show()

oForm.AddObject("CoolLine","Line")
oForm.CoolLine.Visible=.T.
oForm.CoolLine.Left=25
oForm.CoolLine.Top=25
oForm.CoolLine.Width=100
oForm.CoolLine.Height=150
oForm.CoolLine.BorderColor=GETCOLOR()  && Choose your favorite
oForm.CoolLine.BorderWidth=10

oForm.AddObject("DottyLine","Line")
oForm.DottyLine.Visible=.T.
oForm.DottyLine.Left=150
oForm.DottyLine.Top=40
oForm.DottyLine.Width=40
oForm.DottyLine.Height=25
oForm.DottyLine.BorderColor=GETCOLOR()  && Choose your favorite
oForm.DottyLine.BorderStyle=5
oForm.DottyLine.LineSlant="/"

oForm.AddObject("CoolShape","Shape")
oForm.CoolShape.Visible=.T.
oForm.CoolShape.Left=25
oForm.CoolShape.Top=100
oForm.CoolShape.Width=60
oForm.CoolShape.Height=50
oForm.CoolShape.BorderColor=GETCOLOR()  && Choose your favorite
oForm.CoolShape.BorderWidth=5
```

See Also BackColor, DrawStyle, DrawWidth, FillColor, FillStyle, ForeColor, SpecialEffect, TitleBar

Bound

This column property determines whether the control in a column uses the column's ControlSource or can have its own. Based on our tests, this is one property you shouldn't change, even though you can.

Usage

```
colColumn.Bound = lBoundToColumn
lBoundToColumn = colColumn.Bound
```

There are actually four possible setups for the ControlSource for a control in a grid column. The simplest is no ControlSource at all, either at the column or the control level. In that case, with Bound set to .T., there's a sort of automatic binding to the appropriate column of the RecordSource. That is, you don't really need to specify a ControlSource for either the column or the control.

If Bound is .T. and there's no ControlSource specified for the Column, you can indicate a ControlSource for the control, despite what it says in Help. (In some early versions of VFP, doing this led to a form that couldn't be opened. You had to go in and edit the SCX directly to fix the form, removing the ControlSource = "" line from the Properties memo field.)

In VFP 3, when Bound is .T., if you specify a ControlSource for the column, it's automatically propagated to the control in the column. You can't change it in the control, though the Property Sheet makes it seem like you can. Later versions don't propagate the ControlSource down to the column, though you can do so yourself without harm.

When Bound is .F., the column's behavior depends on the setting of Sparse and on whether you specify a ControlSource. If Sparse is .F. and no ControlSource is specified, things get really weird. You see nothing in the column until you start typing. After that, the Value propagates between rows. That is, whatever you type in the first row appears in the second row when you get there, and vice versa.

To confuse matters more, if Bound is .F., Sparse is .T. and there's no ControlSource, each cell shows the value of the appropriate column of the appropriate row in the table the grid is based on (despite the lack of binding). But, the value you type still propagates from cell to cell (though it's not stored in the underlying table), making it look like whatever you're typing is simply following you around. Specifying a ControlSource in this case gives you the exact same behavior. We can't see any reason to use either of these combinations of settings.

On the whole, as far as we can tell, you'll never want to set Bound to .F. The results are just too strange.

Example

```
* Normally, you'll set this up in the Property Sheet. You might
* use the following settings in a grid of Employee. The examples
* here are meant to be a guide to setting up the grid in the
* Form Designer, not commands to type in. Better yet, just drag
* the whole table or the fields you want from the DE.
Column1.Bound = .T.
Column1.ControlSource = "Employee.Last_Name"
Column2.Bound = .T.
Column2.ControlSource = "Employee.First_Name"
```

See Also Column, ControlSource, Sparse, Value

BoundColumn, DisplayValue

These properties relate to multi-column list boxes and combo boxes. BoundColumn determines which column is used to fill the Value property and the ControlSource. DisplayValue contains the value of the first column of the current item or the row number of the current item, or, in a drop-down combo, the text typed in by the user.

These properties, although a little tricky to understand, are among those that make lists and combos much easier to manipulate in Visual FoxPro than they were in FoxPro 2.x.

Usage

```
oObject.BoundColumn = nColumn
nColumn = oObject.BoundColumn
oObject.DisplayValue = cFirstColumnValue | cNewValue | nRow
nRow = oObject.DisplayValue
cFirstColumnValue = oObject.DisplayValue
cNewValue = oObject.DisplayValue
```

In Visual FoxPro, unlike FoxPro 2.x, you can have true multi-column list and combo boxes. With many of the options for populating these controls (see RowSourceType for the list), it's as simple as setting ColumnCount to something other than 1.

Once you have multiple columns, the question is "which column do we return?" In FoxPro 2.x, you had to write code for this—either parsing the item or looking up the return value in an array or table. In Visual FoxPro, just set BoundColumn to the desired column. If you have a list box containing, say, an employee's name and ID, in that order, set BoundColumn to 2 and the list box's Value contains the ID of the currently selected employee.

You can even bind the combo's or list's value to a column that isn't displayed. Just set ColumnWidths so the column in question has a width of 0, and set BoundColumn to that column. Using this approach, you can, for example, display the employee name and department, but return the employee ID from the list or combo.

With some RowSourceTypes, you can even bind to a column that isn't specified as part of the list or combo. For example, with 2-Alias, you can bind to columns beyond ColumnCount. Same thing for arrays.

DisplayValue, though tricky, is the key to making drop-down combos useful. Like a combo or list's Value, it can be either numeric or character, but unlike Value, you'll rarely want to make DisplayValue numeric. If it's numeric, it references a row of the list or combo. If it's character, it contains the contents of the first column of the currently selected row. On the whole, we recommend you stay away from the numeric version, except when BoundTo is set to .T. In fact, DisplayValue is always character by default—you have to go out of your way to make it numeric.

For the moment, let's look at character DisplayValues. In this case, whatever item is highlighted in the combo or list, DisplayValue holds the contents of the first column for that item. In a combo box, this is the part of the value that you see when the combo isn't dropped down—in other words, it's the value that's displayed. (Hey, DisplayValue—the value that's displayed.)

More importantly, when a user of a drop-down combo (Style = 0) types in a string that isn't in the list, that string is stored in DisplayValue and not in Value. You can tell whether the user has typed something in by either comparing DisplayValue to Value (if BoundColumn is 1) or by checking whether Value is empty, in the combo's Valid. If so, you need to do something with DisplayValue. The user's entry is *not* automatically added to the combo's list. You can do so with code (for appropriate RowSourceTypes)—see the example.

As for numeric DisplayValues, you get them only when you set DisplayValue to a number in the first place. If BoundTo is .F. (the default), DisplayValue contains the number of the row that's currently highlighted. If BoundTo is .T., DisplayValue contains the first column of the highlighted row whether or not it's numeric, but if that column is numeric, DisplayValue contains the value as a number in this case. (If you leave DisplayValue alone, it contains the value as a string.)

In a multi-select list box, both DisplayValue and Value reflect the last item selected. (Interestingly, this is true even when that selection actually de-selects the item.)

Example

```
* If you have a drop-down combo with RowSourceType = 0
* you might do this in Valid
IF EMPTY(This.Value)
   * The user typed in a new item. Add it
   This.AddItem(This.DisplayValue)
   This.ListIndex = This.NewIndex
ENDIF
```

See Also BoundTo, ColumnCount, ColumnWidths, ComboBox, ListBox, MultiSelect, RowSource, RowSourceType, Style, Value

BoundTo

This property was one of the most welcome additions to VFP 5. It lets you determine whether a numeric ControlSource for a combo or list contains the position of the selected item or the value of the item.

Usage `lBindToNumericValue = oObject.BoundTo`

As in FoxPro 2.x, the Value of combos and lists in Visual FoxPro can be either numeric or character. In 2.x, using a character variable for a list or popup filled that variable with the contents of the chosen item, while a numeric variable received the position of the chosen item in the list. In 2.x, this made a lot of sense. Lists usually drew their data from either an array (where knowing the position is helpful) or a table (whose record pointer was moved as you moved in the list). There was no way to display data from one field but bind the variable to a different field. So, it didn't matter much that, if the list data happened to be numeric, there was no direct way to grab it.

In VFP, where you can bind a field right to a control and the bound field doesn't have to be the first field displayed, the 2.x behavior is a pain. When the Value of a list or combo is initialized to a number or the ControlSource is numeric, by default, the position (Index) of the chosen item is stored. Even if the BoundColumn contains numeric data, it's the Index that gets stored.

Enter BoundTo. If this property is set to .T., the actual numeric data is stored if both Value/ControlSource and the column referenced by BoundColumn are numeric. Leave BoundTo at .F. and you get the Index. If the column referenced by BoundColumn isn't numeric, but Value/ControlSource are, the Index is stored. If Value/ControlSource are character, then the content of the bound column is stored, as usual.

Note that you have to make up your mind ahead of time on this one. It's read-only at runtime.

Changes to BoundTo are not compatible with setting Value in the property sheet. If BoundTo is set to anything but the default (that is, shows bold in the property sheet), any value saved to the Value property is lost (though Value shows as non-default).

There's also a problem when BoundTo is set to .T. and the combo is bound to a numeric property of an ActiveX control (or at least some ActiveX controls). If we set BoundTo to .T. and set ControlSource to the ChartTitle.Orientation property of an MS Graph object in the property sheet, VFP bombs when we try to run the form. If we wait and assign the ControlSource in code, the form runs and the binding takes, but the current value of the combo doesn't display when the combo is closed.

Example

```
oForm = CREATEOBJECT("Form")
* Add a list with character data in the first column
* and numeric in the second, which is the bound column.
OForm.AddObject("lstTwoCol","ListBox")
WITH oForm.lstTwoCol
   .Visible = .T.
   .RowSourceType = 1    && Value
   .RowSource = "Fred,17,Ethel,31,Lucy,2,Ricky,49"
   .ColumnCount = 2
   .ColumnWidths = "50,30"
   .BoundColumn = 2
   .BoundTo = .T.      && Treat column 2 as numbers
ENDWITH
oForm.Show()
```

See Also BoundColumn, ComboBox, ControlSource, ListBox, Value

_Box **See Define Box.**

Box, Circle, Line, Cls

These form methods let you draw rectangles, circles and ellipses, and lines on forms, and then get rid of them.

Usage

```
frmForm.Box( [ nLeft, nTop, ] nRight, nBottom )
frmForm.Circle( nRadius [, nCenterX, nCenterY
```

```
                         [, nAspectRatio ] ] )
        frmForm.Line( [ nLeft, nTop, ] nRight, nBottom )
```

The position and radius are measured in the form's Scalemode. If you omit nLeft and nTop for a Box or Line, the current position of the cursor indicated by the CurrentX and CurrentY properties is used. This makes sense, though we think it's kind of odd to have the first two parameters be optional. Similarly, if the center point of the circle is omitted, CurrentX and CurrentY are used.

nAspectRatio determines whether Circle draws a circle or an ellipse. The aspect ratio is the ratio of the vertical "radius" to the horizontal "radius". A value of 1 gives a circle. Larger values of nAspectRatio lead to an ellipse that is taller than it is wide. Smaller values of nAspectRatio give an ellipse wider than it is tall.

Circle does weird things with negative aspect ratios. For absolute values up to 1, negative and positive aspect ratios give the same results. But, with an absolute value greater than 1, a negative aspect ratio results in an ellipse larger than one with the same positive aspect ratio. Frankly, the whole thing smells like a bug. Circle shouldn't even accept a negative aspect ratio.

These items are drawn in the form's ForeColor and respect the settings of DrawMode, DrawStyle, DrawWidth, FillColor and FillStyle.

Shapes created in this way are different than those created with the Shape control. These are just images on the form, like the SAY commands of years gone by. They don't have properties, events or methods. In addition, while the shapes are initially drawn on top of any controls, they can fall behind other objects when the display is refreshed or that control gets focus.

Example

```
ThisForm.Box(50, 50, 100, 100)
ThisForm.Circle(25, 100, 100)
ThisForm.Circle(40, 20, 70, .5)
ThisForm.Line(100, 200)
```

Usage `frmForm.CLS()`

The CLS (for "CLear Screen") method clears away the stuff you draw with Box, Circle, Line, Print and PSet. It doesn't affect actual controls.

Don't confuse CLS with either the CLEAR command (which visually removes everything from a window, controls and all—the controls come back if you land on them) or the Clear method, which is used with list boxes and combo boxes.

See Also @ ... Box, @ ... To, Clear, CurrentX, CurrentY, DrawMode, DrawStyle, DrawWidth, FillColor, FillStyle, ForeColor, Print, PSet, ScaleMode, Shape

Browse, Change, Edit, Set BrStatus

> The desire of power in excess caused the angels to fall; the desire of knowledge in excess caused man to fall.
>
> Francis Bacon, *Of Goodness and Goodness of Nature*, 1625

What can we say about BROWSE? It's a contender for the most complex and powerful command in the language. It's also a contender for the most dangerous—handing an unknowing user a BROWSE without appropriate safeguards is like giving a toddler a magnet and your backup tapes.

CHANGE and EDIT are just other names for BROWSE. They present the same data in a different format. SET BRSTATUS determines if you get a status bar when you're in a BROWSE, even if you've turned the status bar off.

Usage

```
BROWSE [FIELDS FieldList]
       [ NAME ObjectName ]
       [ FOR lForExpr [ REST ] ]
       [ KEY eLowKeyValue [ , eHighKeyValue ] ]
       [ LAST | NOINIT ] [ PREFERENCE PreferenceName ]
       [ NORMAL ]
       [ FREEZE FieldName ]
       [ PARTITION nColumnNumber [ LEDIT ] [ REDIT ] ]
       [ LPARTITION ] [ LOCK nNumberOfFields ]
       [ NOLGRID ] [ NORGRID ] [ NOLINK ]
       [ NOAPPEND ] [ NODELETE ] [ NOEDIT | NOMODIFY ]
       [ NOMENU ] [ NOOPTIMIZE ] [ NOREFRESH ]
       [ NOWAIT ] [ SAVE ] [ TIMEOUT nSeconds ]
       [ WHEN lWhenExpr ]
       [ VALID [ :F ] lValidExpr [ ERROR cErrorMessage ] ]
       [ [ WINDOW DefinitionWindow ]
       [ IN [ WINDOW ] ContainingWindow | IN SCREEN
        | IN MACDESKTOP ] ]
       [ TITLE cTitleText ]
       [ FONT cFontName [, nFontSize ] ] [ STYLE cStyleCodes ]
       [ COLOR SCHEME nScheme | COLOR ColorPairList ]
       [ WIDTH nFieldWidth ]
       [ NOCLEAR ] [ FORMAT ]
```

BROWSE has no place in applications. In FoxPro 2.x, you could make some argument for it because there were no good alternatives. You either used BROWSE or lived without its row-at-a-time view of data. In Visual FoxPro, you can use a grid for that view and ignore BROWSE except as a powerful, interactive tool for you, the developer. As for CHANGE/EDIT, it's been obsolete for a long time.

BROWSE does have one new clause in Visual FoxPro worth learning. A BROWSE is really just a grid, although you can't find a BROWSE's Parent. The NAME clause lets you manipulate the grid with its PEMs, instead of relying on the same old confusing, complex clauses. The table below maps BROWSE's clauses to the grid and column properties, events and methods that give you the same (or often better) functionality.

Clause	PEM	Purpose
FIELDS	ColumnCount, Columns' ControlSource	Determine which fields appear.
FREEZE	Columns' ReadOnly	Keep fields from being edited. FREEZE specifies a single editable field. ReadOnly lets you decide for each field.
PARTITION, LOCK	Partition	Split the BROWSE/grid into two panes.
LEDIT, REDIT	View	Determine the editing mode for each pane.
LPARTITION	Panel	Determine which pane has focus.
NOLGRID, NORGRID	GridLines	Determine whether the grid (or a single pane) has lines dividing rows and columns.
NOLINK	PanelLink	Determine whether the two panes are linked together.
NODELETE	DeleteMark	NODELETE prevents the user from deleting records. DeleteMark determines whether a deletion column shows at all. Without it, records can't be deleted.

Clause	PEM	Purpose
NOEDIT, NOMODIFY	ReadOnly	Prevent the user from making any changes to data in a grid.
WHEN	When, AfterRowColChange	Determine whether you can enter grid or cell.
VALID	Valid, BeforeRowColChange	Test record for validity as you leave.
FONT	FontName, FontSize	Determine the font used for the BROWSE/grid.
STYLE	FontBold, FontItalic, FontStrikeThru, FontUnderline	Determine the characteristics of the font.
COLORSCHEME, COLOR	BackColor, ForeColor, GridLineColor	Determine the colors used.
WIDTH	Columns' ColumnWidth	Determine the width of individual columns in the grid.

While not every clause has a corresponding property or event, enough of them do to reduce what you have to do with BROWSE itself to pretty minimal—a good thing.

One item here is worth noting. Despite the fact that it's not even documented for VFP 6, the IN MACDESKTOP clause creates a free-floating browse window with its own entry on the taskbar.

Example

```
* BROWSE is great when you're working interactively.
USE Customer
BROWSE FIELDS Company_Name,Contact_Name,Phone
```

Usage

```
SET BRSTATUS ON | OFF
cBrStatus = SET("BRSTATUS")
```

This one's an antique dating back before Windows and its status bar. It determines what happens when you open a BROWSE and there's no visible status bar. If BRSTATUS is ON, the Xbase-style status bar appears.

See Also Grid

_Browser **See _Beautify.**

Buffering

One of the loudest religious arguments in FoxPro 2.x and older versions was whether to edit fields directly or edit memory variables and then commit the changes to the fields. The proponents for each side could produce all sorts of arguments for why their approach was The Right Way. We're glad to report that the argument is over, and neither side wins. Or maybe both sides win. We definitely win.

Built-in buffering is one of many cool features of Visual FoxPro. Now, you can write code that appears to edit fields directly, but really works on copies of the fields. When you turn buffering on (either through form properties or with CursorSetProp()), FoxPro maintains several buffers containing the data in its different states. No more SCATTER MEMVAR or GATHER MEMVAR.

Your code looks like it addresses the fields, but in fact it's really talking to one of these buffers. When the user makes up his mind whether to save or discard his changes, you can either commit the changes to the real table or throw away the buffered changes. One function call (either TableUpdate() or TableRevert()) does the trick in either case.

FoxPro not only gives you a copy of the data to work on, but it keeps a copy of the original data and the current status of the data, in case someone else changes it while you're working. No more making an extra copy to compare with the network.

Visual FoxPro has two buffering modes, each of which can be used in two different ways. The two modes are optimistic and pessimistic, referring to the locking scheme used. With the pessimistic approach, a record is locked as soon as you make any change. That way, no one else can change it until you release the lock by committing or reverting the buffer. With optimistic locking, the record isn't locked until you attempt to commit the changes. You run the risk that someone else will make changes at the same time, but records are kept out of circulation for the shortest possible time. There's no need for a religious war over buffering modes because each has its place. Use pessimistic locking for sensitive changes that must go through. Use optimistic locking for everything else. (Views always use optimistic buffering.)

The other buffering choice is whether to buffer individual records or entire tables. Again, this isn't all-or-nothing. You can use row buffering for some tables and table buffering for others. If you don't specify otherwise, Visual FoxPro uses table buffering when you use a grid for a table, and row buffering for all other tables.

With a buffered table, you can examine the current value of a field, the value it had when you started working with it (OldVal()—actually, the last time you committed it) and the value it has now on the network (CurVal()). You can also get information (GetFldState()) about the status of any field: Have you changed it? Have you deleted the record it belongs to? Is this a new record? And so forth. You can also find all the records that have changed using GetNextModified().

Using the various functions that control all this, you can write code that makes intelligent choices when conflicts arise, and only bothers the user if it doesn't know what to do.

In addition to buffering, Visual FoxPro lets you wrap updates (both local and remote) in transactions. With a transaction, everything you do is tentative. If one part of an update can't be completed, you can roll the whole thing back. No more worrying about adding the invoice header without the details. Wrap it in a transaction, and you save header and details or nothing at all.

See Also Begin Transaction, BufferMode, BufferModeOverride, CursorGetProp(), CursorSetProp(), CurVal(), End Transaction, GetFldState(), GetNextModified(), OldVal(), Rollback, SetFldState(), TableRevert(), TableUpdate()

BufferMode, BufferModeOverride

These properties determine the type of buffering used for tables and views in a form or formset. BufferMode sets a default for the whole form or formset. BufferModeOverride lets you do something different for an individual table or view.

Usage

```
oObject.BufferMode = nBufferMode
nBufferMode = oObject.BufferMode
crsCursor.BufferModeOverride = nBufferOverride
nBufferOverride = crsCursor.BufferModeOverride
```

These two similar properties use different numbering schemes. Check the lists in Help carefully.

For a form or formset's BufferMode, you have only three choices: no buffering, optimistic buffering or pessimistic buffering. If you choose either type of buffering, FoxPro automatically uses table buffering for any table in a grid and row buffering for the rest.

If you don't want the default for a particular cursor, use the cursor's BufferModeOverride. You get six choices there. One is to use the form default. Another is no buffering. The other four are the possible combinations of optimistic/pessimistic with row/table.

You can change both of these properties at runtime. However, the changes don't take effect until you call

CloseTables and OpenTables. Changing BufferModeOverride triggers a message to that effect.

See Also Buffering, CursorGetProp(), CursorSetProp(), DataSession, Set Multilocks

Build

This project method lets you build your project.

Usage

```
lSuccess = prjProject.Build( [ cResultFile ] [, nBuildType ]
                             [, lRebuildAll ] [, lShowErrors ]
                             [, lRegenerateIds ] )
```

Parameter	Value	Meaning
cResultFile	Character	The file in which to store the built application. You can include a path to put the result in a different directory.
	Omitted	Use the project name plus the appropriate extension.
nBuildType	1 or Omitted	Rebuild the project, but don't build an APP, EXE or DLL.
	2	Build an APP.
	3	Build an EXE.
	4	Build a DLL. This only works if you have at least one OLE Public class in the project.
lRebuildAll	Logical	Should every item in the project be rebuilt or only those that have changed?
lShowErrors	Logical	Should an edit window open up after the build to display an error message? Either way, any errors are stored in a file with an ERR extension.
lRegenerateIds	Logical	If you're building a DLL, should new component IDs be created? Typically, you would do this only if you have changed the interface of the DLL, because COM requires that the interface of an existing component never change.
lSuccess	.T.	The build was completed.
	.F.	The build was not completed. The only time we've seen this result is when we canceled in mid-build (after a missing file message appeared). If we build a project that has errors in it, but we let it run to completion, Build returns .T.

This method lets you do the things you'd normally do by clicking the Build button in the Project Manager or by issuing BUILD APP, BUILD EXE or BUILD DLL.

Help says you can mismatch cFileName and nBuildAction. Not so. If you specify, say, "Test.EXE" for cFileName and 2 (App) for nBuildAction, no output file is created. But the method returns .T. anyway.

Example

```
* Build an APP, using the project name for the output file
_VFP.ActiveProject.Build(,2)
```

See Also ActiveProject, AfterBuild, BeforeBuild, Build APP, Build DLL, Build EXE, Project

Build Project, Build App, Build EXE, Build DLL, External

We don't use the BUILD commands very often, though they represent some of our most frequent operations. These are command equivalents to the various Build options of the Project Manager—we almost always do it from there.

EXTERNAL tells the Project Manager that certain components are defined elsewhere and shouldn't be considered missing in action.

Usage

```
BUILD PROJECT ProjectName FROM FileNameList [ RECOMPILE ]
BUILD APP AppName FROM ProjectName [ RECOMPILE ]
BUILD EXE ExeName FROM ProjectName [ RECOMPILE ]
     [ STANDALONE | EXTENDED ]
BUILD DLL DLLName FROM ProjectName [ RECOMPILE ]
```

BUILD PROJECT is the same as creating a project, sticking one or more items (programs, forms, menus, reports, etc.) in it and then choosing Build, Rebuild Project. It treats the first item you hand it as the main program and works from there. All file objects explicitly referenced in any item in the project are added to the project. That is, if one program calls another, the second program is added to the project. Then, if that program calls two forms, those forms are added, and so forth.

Items referenced only on lines containing macro substitution are not added to the project. It doesn't matter whether the substitution involves the item name or not—if the program line contains a macro, BUILD PROJECT doesn't check it out for references. Similarly, items referenced indirectly aren't added. See EXTERNAL below for the solution in both cases.

BUILD APP and BUILD EXE take a project and create an executable program from it. BUILD APP makes a FoxPro APP file—to run it, you need a copy of Visual FoxPro. BUILD EXE makes a "compact" executable file that can be run from inside Visual FoxPro or using the Visual FoxPro support files (see Help for your VFP version to see what those files are).

There's not a huge difference between the contents of an APP or a compact EXE, except that you can run the EXE directly. There are some pretty cool things you can do, if you want. For example, your EXE might contain only the code to DO MyApp.APP, then the bulk of your application could live in an APP file. You could in fact have a generic EXE file called, say FOXR.EXE, which accepts a single parameter—the name of your APP file—and runs it.

The STANDALONE and EXTENDED keywords of BUILD EXE go back to FoxPro/DOS, where they did something. They're not accepted in VFP (and, in fact, cause errors), so you can just ignore them.

BUILD APP and BUILD EXE have a weird relationship. If you already have a file of one type for a particular project, and you build the other type, the one you have is deleted without warning. For example, if you have a project called MyProj and you've created MyProj.APP, issuing BUILD EXE MyProj FROM MyProj erases MyProj.APP. The setting of SAFETY doesn't matter—the file is gone, gone, gone.

BUILD EXE can also be used to build an Active Document application. To do so, the project must contain a class based on the ActiveDoc base class, and that class must be marked as the Main program.

BUILD DLL is part of the brave new world of components. It's for creating a custom automation server from your project—it corresponds to the Build OLE DLL choice in the Build dialog. To do this, at least one class in the project must be marked as OLE Public. The result of this command is a dynamic link library from which appropriate classes can be instantiated.

The RECOMPILE keyword indicates that all the individual components of the project should be recompiled before the appropriate result is built. This is the same as checking the Recompile All Files check box in the Build dialog. We sure wish the other options from that dialog were available in the command version. Well, okay, maybe we don't need Display Errors—after all, we're building the thing in code, but what about the options to run after building and to regenerate OLE Server IDs?

Example

```
BUILD PROJECT MyProj FROM MyProgram
BUILD APP MyProj FROM MyProj
BUILD DLL MyOLEProj FROM MyOLEProj RECOMPILE
```

Usage

```
EXTERNAL FILE FileList | ARRAY ArrayList | CLASS ClassList
         | FORM FormList | LABEL LabelList | LIBRARY LibraryList
         | MENU MenuList | PROCEDURE ProcList | QUERY QueryList
         | REPORT ReportList | SCREEN FormList | TABLE TableList
```

EXTERNAL's role in life is to tell the Project Manager about things. In most cases, you use it to trick the PM into including a file in a project when you haven't directly referenced it. This is useful when a particular item is called only via a macro or indirect reference. Without the EXTERNAL statement, it doesn't get added to the project or built into your APP or EXE. Pretty embarrassing to install at the client's site and have a "File does not exist" error pop up.

Because EXTERNAL doesn't take the complete path to the file in question (it simply ignores the paths you provide in the filename and uses only the path you've SET), you may need to point VFP to the specified files the first time you build the project after adding EXTERNAL declarations.

For arrays, EXTERNAL serves a slightly different role. When you pass an array as a parameter, it's listed just like any other variable in the parameter list. FoxPro has no clue that it's really an array. So, when you use that variable as an array in the routine, the compiler yells at you. Putting EXTERNAL ARRAY in the routine with the array parameter clues the compiler in.

Example

```
FUNCTION aIsArray

LPARAMETER aTestArray      && We know it's an array
EXTERNAL ARRAY aTestArray  && Now the compiler knows
```

See Also ActiveDoc, Compile, Create Project, Do, Modify Project, Parameters

BuildDateTime

This property of the Project object tells you when the project was last built.

Usage

```
tLastBuild = prjProject.BuildDateTime
```

BuildDateTime gives you a programmatic way to find out when a project was last built. It shows you the same information that's in the Project Info dialog for "Last Built:". The value returned is a datetime. If the project has never been built, you get the empty datetime ({ / / : : }).

Example

```
IF TTOD(Application.ActiveProject.BuildDateTime) < DATE()
   WAIT WINDOW "Haven't built this project today" NOWAIT
ENDIF
```

See Also ActiveProject, Build, Project, Projects

_Builder See _Beautify.

Buttons, ButtonCount

Let me take you a button-hole lower.

William Shakespeare, *Love's Labour's Lost*

These properties tell you about the buttons in a button group, whether they're option buttons or command buttons. ButtonCount tells you how many are in the group, while Buttons gives you access to the PEMs of the individual buttons.

Usage

```
oObject.ButtonCount = nNumberOfButtons
nNumberOfButtons = oObject.ButtonCount
oButton = oObject.Buttons( nButtonNumber )
```

You can change the number of buttons in a group by changing ButtonCount. If you lower ButtonCount, any extra buttons disappear into oblivion.

The Buttons collection lets you get at the individual buttons within a button group without worrying about their names. You can look up or change properties or invoke buttons' methods by accessing the button through Buttons.

To change properties of all the buttons in a group, use the button group's SetAll method instead.

Example

```
* Look for the button whose caption is "My Favorite Button"
* Assume we're in a method of the button group
LOCAL nButton, lFoundIt
nButton = 1
lFoundIt = .F.
DO WHILE nButton <= This.ButtonCount AND NOT lFoundIt
   IF This.Buttons[nButton].Caption = "My Favorite Button"
      lFoundIt = .T.
   ELSE
      nButton = nButton + 1
   ENDIF
ENDDO
IF lFoundIt
   WAIT WINDOW "My Favorite Button is "+LTRIM(STR(nButton))
ELSE
   WAIT WINDOW "My Favorite Button is missing"
ENDIF
```

See Also ControlCount, Controls, SetAll

_CalcMem **See Calculator.**

Calculate **See Average.**

Calculator, _CalcMem, _CalcValue

One of FoxPro's built-in tools plus two system memory variables that track the numbers stored in the calculator—the first stored in the calculator's memory and the second displayed.

The calculator is a desk-accessory-like utility included with Visual FoxPro, similar to the Calendar/Diary. Microsoft is discouraging its use by removing it from the visual interface of Visual FoxPro and making no effort to improve its awkward appearance, interface or features. The calculator can be invoked by issuing the command ACTIVATE WINDOW CALCULATOR. You can make it available on an as-needed basis by adding the menu pad _MST_CALCU to your custom menu.

The calculator can be operated completely from the keyboard. For those trivia buffs in the audience, here are the keystrokes that perform the equivalent button functions when the calculator has the focus:

Keystroke	Button Label	Effect
A	M+	Adds the current value to that stored in memory.
C	C	Press once to erase the current value displayed, twice to erase the calculation in process.
N	±	Reverses the sign of the current value.
Q	√	Returns the square root of the current calculator value.
R	MR	Recalls the value stored in memory.
Z	MC	Clears (zeroes) the value in memory.
S	M-	Subtracts the current value from that in memory.

The calculator takes advantage of a resource file, if one is in use, to store its most recent position. A "Properties" menu option is also available under the standard Edit menu that allows you to store preferences for automatically toggling the NumLock and determining the precision in which numbers are displayed.

Unless Microsoft begins to show more support for these rather cool little features, we think it might be best for you to consider alternatives like ActiveX controls, or coding your own, to ensure that you have control of the object's behavior now and in future versions.

Usage

```
nValue = _CALCMEM
nValue = _CALCVALUE
_CALCMEM = nValue
_CALCVALUE = nValue
```

_CALCMEM stores the value of the calculator memory (what's been stored there), while _CALCVALUE is the current value displayed in the calculator window.

If you assign values to _CALCVALUE and _CALCMEM, they appear to take. When you activate the Calculator, however, you'll find the values displayed as rounded integers—no decimal places are displayed. You can read a value with decimal places just fine from the calculator, but you can't place one there. This bug appears to be in all versions of Visual FoxPro.

Example

```
STORE PI() TO _CALCMEM
_CALCVALUE = 2.123
ACTIVATE WINDOW CALCULATOR    && You'll see "2" displayed and
                              && pressing MR displays "3"
```

See Also Calendar/Diary, Desk Accessories, Filer, Puzzle

Calendar/Diary, _DiaryDate

A Mac-like desktop accessory kept in Visual FoxPro for "backward compatibility," but hidden within the product, ignored.

Usage

```
ACTIVATE WINDOW CALENDAR
DEFINE BAR _MST_DIARY OF _MSYSTEM
               PROMPT "CALENDAR/D\<IARY"
```

Having only one application with the ability to do a slew of stuff was handy in the 640K, 20MB hard drive days. Now, with the ability to have many programs running at once in the Windows environment and multi-gigabyte drives considered standard equipment, the idea of a built-in calendar applet seems a little dated. Outlook, Microsoft's personal information manager in the Office package, and Outlook Express, included with Internet

Explorer, far exceed the capabilities of this "mini-app."

But this application has some neat features, and we are disappointed that Microsoft has chosen to ignore Calendar. The Calendar/Diary option has disappeared from the menu, and you need to dredge through the help file for the example code for the _DiaryDate variable to see how it can be called up programmatically. The fact that a system menu bar is defined for this function appears to be completely undocumented.

Figure 4-1: The Calendar / Diary interface in Visual FoxPro 3.0 and...

Figure 4-2: The same interface in Visual FoxPro 6: Bolding of characters is gone.

The interface for using the Calendar / Diary is pretty straightforward. The calendar is displayed on the left-hand side, and buttons across the bottom can be used to change the display to a specific month and year. Note also that there is a "Diary" menu that appears when the Calendar is activated, displaying keyboard shortcuts for many of these functions. In versions before VFP 6, a date with a diary entry associated with it is shown in a bolder font (see figure 4-1); the month and year are displayed in bold when the calendar is active, and in plain text when the diary is active. In VFP 6, all bolding effects are gone (see figure 4-2). Diary entries are stored in the currently active resource file. If no resource file is available, a dialog box appears when the calendar is activated for the first time, informing the user he/she will be unable to save diary entries. The entry is stored with a TYPE of "Data," an ID of "DIARYDATA," a NAME of the date in DTOS() format ("YYYYMMDD"), the actual entry in the memo field DATA, and a SYS(2007)-generated checksum in the CHKVAL field.

Since Microsoft hasn't updated the really ugly interface of this item, we can predict it will probably continue to receive minimal support, perhaps even disappearing in a future release. Using the calendar can be problematic in an application. Storage of diary data in the resource file can cause problems. Because the calendar is a built-in system window, it does not have all of the characteristics or programmability that we may want to integrate into our own application windows, causing difficulties including it within our event handlers. While it may be a handy utility for developers to use, we suggest you consider other sources for supplying a calendar to your users. Several intrepid users have developed all-FoxPro-coded versions of the calendars, available through many of the FoxPro magazines and online services. A second source you might want to consider is the rapidly developing ActiveX control market, where several vendors are developing and testing sophisticated calendar interfaces.

Usage
```
dDiaryDate = _DIARYDATE
_DIARYDATE = dDateToBeSet
```

_DIARYDATE is a system memory variable that stores the last date selected in the Calendar/Diary, or the present date if the Calendar has not been used.

Example
```
STORE {04/11/2000} to _DIARYDATE
? _DIARYDATE
```

See Also Calculator, Desk Accessories, DToS(), Filer, Puzzle, Set Resource, Sys(2007)

Call See Load.

Call() See Access().

Cancel, Suspend, Resume, Retry

CANCEL, SUSPEND and RESUME are all handy debugging commands. RETRY is a cousin to RETURN and is useful in error handlers.

Usage
```
CANCEL
SUSPEND
RESUME
RETRY
```

CANCEL kills program execution on the spot. We use it most when we're in the middle of debugging and figure out what the problem is. We cancel the program, go fix the bug and try again. Some folks use it to end applications, but it's not a particularly graceful exit—use RETURN instead.

SUSPEND and RESUME let you stop and restart a program. We haven't used SUSPEND much since the Trace window came along, but, once in a while, it's handy to be able to arrange for execution to stop at a particular point. RESUME we use a lot, though it's often from the Debugger menu. Actually, we're far more likely to press F5 or click on the green Resume button than to type the command or choose it from the menu. Regardless of how you issue it, though, RESUME picks up execution where you left off.

RETRY is an interesting command. It works like RETURN, except that it goes back to the command that got you there instead of the one after it. Using RETRY where you shouldn't is a quick ticket to an infinite loop.

However, in an error handler, RETRY is worth a million bucks. You can return to the statement that caused the error and try the operation again. This is useful for things like failed locks. You can also use it for situations where you've fixed the problem in the meantime (say, by re-creating a missing file).

Example
```
* This program lets you test these commands

WAIT WINDOW "In program. Press a key."
WAIT WINDOW "Type RESUME to go on" NOWAIT
SUSPEND

WAIT WINDOW "Back in program"

DO sub1

WAIT WINDOW "Back from sub1"

RETURN

PROC sub1
* See the difference between Return or Retry
* Enter "E" for Retry or something other than
* "R" to get out immediately.

WAIT WINDOW "(R)eturn or R(e)try" TO cGoOn
```

```
DO CASE
CASE UPPER(cGoOn)="R"
   RETURN
CASE UPPER(cGoOn)="E"
   RETRY
OTHERWISE
   CANCEL
ENDCASE

RETURN
```

See Also Return

Cancel, Default

These two button properties let you make things easier for keyboard users by designating cancel (or "escape") and default buttons in a form. When a button is designated as the cancel button, pressing Escape is the same as clicking that button. Pressing Enter is like clicking the default button (unless focus is on another button). These properties correspond to the "\?" and "\!" designators for buttons in FoxPro 2.x.

Usage

```
cmdButton.Cancel = lIsItCancel
lIsItCancel = cmdButton.Cancel
cmdButton.Default = lIsItDefault
lIsItDefault = cmdButton.Default
```

There are two strange things associated with these two properties. One is really a Windows thing. That's the relationship between default buttons and the Enter key. Some controls, like edit boxes, accept the Enter key. Unless focus is on one of those controls, pressing Enter chooses the default button. You can specify the default button for any form. But Enter selects the default only when focus isn't on a different command button. As soon as any other button gets focus, pressing Enter chooses that button. When focus moves to a control other than a command button, the button you specified again is the recipient of any Enter.

The reason for this weird behavior is that the Enter key is seriously overloaded. Enter is one of the ways to press a button when it has focus. Enter is also the keystroke for choosing the default button. The only way to merge these two behaviors is for a button with focus to be the default button. (FoxPro/DOS solves the problem by requiring Ctrl+Enter to choose the default button. FoxPro/Mac doesn't have the problem because buttons don't get focus.)

The second problem feels like a bug. A form set can have only one cancel button and one default button at a time. But Visual FoxPro isn't consistent about what to do if you mess up and specify more than one. When you change the Default property of any button in a form set to .T., the Default property for every other command button in the form set is set to .F. on the spot. When you set Cancel to .T., any other buttons' Cancel properties don't change. When you run the form, the first button created with Cancel=.T. wins, if it's enabled.

When the user clicks a cancel button, CHR(27), which is ESC, gets put in the keyboard buffer. This makes it possible to test for LASTKEY()=27 in Valid events to see if the user is trying to escape. In that case, you probably want to skip validation of the current field.

And finally, to answer the question you haven't asked yet, yes, a single button can be both the cancel and the default button at the same time.

Example

```
* Make the OK button be the default and the Cancel
* button be the cancel button
ThisForm.cmdOK.Default=.T.
ThisForm.cmdCancel.Cancel=.T.
```

See Also @ ... Get, CommandButton, Valid

Candidate(), Primary(), Descending(), For(), Sys(2021), Key(), Sys(14), Tag(), Unique()

These functions give you information about an index, either a stand-alone index or a tag. DESCENDING(), FOR() and, to a lesser extent, UNIQUE(), were welcome additions in FoxPro 2.6. CANDIDATE() and PRIMARY() were added in VFP 3. This group of functions tells you everything you'd need to know about an index in order to re-create it (except, of course, for the shortcomings we point out below).

These functions can all give information about indexes for the current work area or for another work area. For the specified work area, most let you get index information for the current master index or another index. Some of them let you specify a particular CDX file, as well.

The indexes open for any table are numbered based on the type of index and the order in which it was opened, with a catch. The order of indexes is:

- Stand-alone IDX files, in the order they were opened;
- Tags in the structural CDX file in their internal order;
- Tags in any other CDX files in their internal order, with the CDX's in the order they were opened.

This holds true even if you list a CDX before an IDX in the USE command.

So what's the catch? If you open additional indexes with SET INDEX, the order may change because stand-alone IDX files always get the lowest numbers.

All these functions take their parameters more or less from the following group, though some functions have more parameters than others.

Parameter	Value	Meaning
cIndexName	Character	The name of a compound CDX file or a stand-alone IDX file, about which to return information.
	Omitted	Return information about the nIndexNumber-th index among all open indexes.
nIndexNumber	Numeric	The relative position of the index about which to return information.
	Omitted	Return information about the master tag in the specified work area.
nWorkArea	Numeric	Return information about the specified index for the table open in work area nWorkArea.
	Omitted	If cAlias is also omitted, return information about the specified index for the table open in the current work area.
cAlias	Character	Return information about the specified index for the table open with alias cAlias.
	Omitted	If nWorkArea is also omitted, return information about the specified index for the table open in the current work area.

Usage

```
lIsCandidate = CANDIDATE( [ nIndexNumber
                            [, nWorkArea | cAlias ] ] )
lIsPrimary = PRIMARY( [ nIndexNumber
                        [, nWorkArea | cAlias ] ] )
```

These two functions tell you whether the specified index is either a candidate or primary index. Primary indexes can be defined only for tables contained in a database; candidate indexes can be defined for any Visual FoxPro table. Candidate indexes are defined with the ADD UNIQUE clause of ALTER TABLE, the UNIQUE clause of CREATE TABLE, or the CANDIDATE (not the UNIQUE!) keyword of INDEX. Primary indexes are defined with the ADD PRIMARY clause of ALTER TABLE or the PRIMARY KEY clause of CREATE TABLE. Although candidate and primary indexes have a lot in common, a given tag is one or the other. So, for any given tag, at most one of these two functions returns .T.

Only index tags in a compound index file (CDX) can be primary or candidate keys, so these functions always return .F. for stand-alone indexes (IDX). If you omit nIndexNumber, these functions return information about the master index tag (the one you SET ORDER TO).

Example

```
OPEN DATA TasTrade
USE Customer
* This table has two tags, Company_Na, a regular index
* and Customer_I, the primary index
? CANDIDATE(1)   && Returns .F.
? CANDIDATE(2)   && Returns .F.
? PRIMARY(1)     && Returns .F.
? PRIMARY(2)     && Returns .T.
```

Usage

```
lIsDescending = DESCENDING( [ cIndexName, ] nIndexNumber
                            [, nWorkArea | cAlias ] )
```

It used to be hard to find out if an index was in ascending or descending order. You had to get SET("ORDER") and parse for the string "DESCENDING". If it was there, you had a descending index; if not, it was ascending. Plus, you could only ask about the master index in the current work area. DESCENDING() was added in FoxPro 2.6 and makes life much simpler.

There's one ugly twist with both SET("ORDER") and DESCENDING(), though. They don't tell how an index *was* defined; they tell how it is *now*. There's no way to be absolutely sure whether an index was defined as ascending or descending except to close the table in every work area where it's in use, then open it and test the appropriate index immediately.

Example

```
USE Customer
DISPLAY STATUS  && shows two tags: Company_Na and Customer_I
? DESCENDING(1)  && returns .F.
? DESCENDING(2)  && returns .F.
SET ORDER TO Company_Na DESCENDING  && reverse name order
? DESCENDING(1)  && returns .T.

* now for the complication
SELECT 0
USE Customer AGAIN ALIAS MoreCust
? DESCENDING(1)  && returns .T.!
? DESCENDING(2)  && returns .F.
```

The example shows the problem. When you USE a table AGAIN, it picks up the current direction of any indexes opened with it. (It also can close some open indexes, but that has nothing to do with DESCENDING()—see USE for a discussion of that bug.)

In spite of this problem, DESCENDING() is a handy function and we're really glad it finally made it to the language.

Usage

```
cFilter = FOR( [ nIndexNumber [, nWorkArea | cAlias ] ] )
cFilter = SYS( 2021, nIndexNumber [, nWorkArea | cAlias ] )
```

These two functions are almost identical. FOR() is another of the FoxPro 2.6 enhancements. The Help file says that FOR() is there for dBASE compatibility—it lies. We think it's far better to use FOR() in a program than SYS(2021). Someone reading your program will understand what FOR() does; SYS(2021) will send them running to the manual. The only difference between them is that, despite the documentation to the contrary, if you omit the nIndexNumber parameter, FOR() tells you about the master index while SYS(2021) generates an error. FOR() looks better all the time. You can only use this feature (omitting the index number) in the current work area. For information about a filter in another work area, you have to pass the index number as well as the work area or alias.

So what do these functions do, anyway? They return the filter expression for a filtered index. That is, if your original INDEX command included a FOR clause, these functions return the expression you placed in the FOR clause. If the index isn't filtered, the functions return the empty string. Of course, Rushmore can't use filtered indexes, so most of the time they're not worth having.

FOR() returns the filter expression in all caps. This is no big deal, except for one thing. Even a string enclosed in quotes in the filter expression is returned in capital letters. That means that you can't necessarily re-create the index using the results of this function. Because SYS(2021) is smart enough to not to capitalize quoted strings, we suppose we have to change our minds and our advice and tell you to use SYS(2021) even though FOR() is more readable.

Example

```
USE Customer
* create a filtered index
INDEX ON UPPER(Company_Name) ;
      FOR Country = "France" ;
      TAG FrComps
? FOR()  && The new index is the master index
         && This returns the filter expression:
         && COUNTRY="FRANCE"
? SYS(2021,3) && Returns: COUNTRY = "France"
? FOR(1) && Returns "" since the first tag, Company_Na
         && has no filter.
* don't forget to delete this tag
```

Usage

```
cKey = KEY( [ [ cIndexName, ] nIndexNumber
            [, nWorkArea | cAlias ] ] )
cKey = SYS( 14, nIndexNumber [, nWorkArea | cAlias ] )
```

These two functions are also almost identical, but KEY() is more capable. Both return the key expression for the specified index. KEY() allows you to name a particular compound index (CDX) file, while SYS(14) requires an index number from the full set of open indexes. Also, like FOR(), with no nIndexName parameter, KEY() returns information about the master index. In the same circumstances, SYS(14) gives an error. For both of these reasons as well as readability, we recommend you use KEY().

Both functions return the key expression in all caps. If you go too far and there aren't as many indexes as nIndexNumber, they return the empty string. Very handy for looping through index information.

Example

```
USE Customer
* Customer has two index tags, Company_Na and Customer_I
? KEY(1)      && Returns "UPPER(COMPANY_NAME)"
? SYS(14,2)   && Returns "CUSTOMER_ID"
SELECT 0      && go to another work area
? KEY(2,"Customer")  && Returns "CUSTOMER_ID"
```

Usage

```
cTagName = TAG( [ [ cIndexName, ] nIndexNumber
                [, nWorkArea | cAlias ] ] )
```

This function tells you the name of an index. Despite the function name, it also returns names for stand-alone indexes. The name of the tag or the name portion of the IDX filename is returned in all caps.

If you omit nIndexNumber, TAG() returns the name of the master index (the same result as ORDER()).

Example

```
USE Customer
? TAG(1) && Returns "COMPANY_NA"
? TAG(2) && Returns "CUSTOMER_I"
```

Usage

```
lIsUnique = UNIQUE( [ [ cIndexName, ] nIndexNumber
                    [, nWorkArea | cAlias ] ] )
```

This function tells you whether the index was created with an Xbase unique index. This is not the same at all as the ADD UNIQUE clause of ALTER TABLE or the UNIQUE keyword of CREATE TABLE. Unique indexes in

Xbase are a disaster waiting to happen, and we recommend you run like the wind from them. (For details, see INDEX.)

UNIQUE() returns .T. if the specified index was created with the UNIQUE keyword of INDEX or with SET UNIQUE ON. If nIndexNumber is omitted, UNIQUE() tells you about the master index.

Example

```
USE Customer ORDER Company_Na
? UNIQUE()    && Returns .F.
? UNIQUE(2)   && Returns .F.
```

One of our favorite functions is AFIELDS(), which takes a table and returns an array containing a list of the table's fields and their characteristics. There's no corresponding function for indexes and we've always wanted one, so we used this group of functions to write our own. It's not quite as capable as AFIELDS() because you do have to create the array before calling it. Also, it only returns information about open indexes for a table—there's no way to know that a particular IDX or CDX is for a particular table unless it's open.

```
* aindexes.prg
* Fills an array with index information for a table
* Returns: the number of indexes found, if successful
*           0 if the table has no indexes
*          -1 if no parameters are passed
*          -2 if the first parameter is not an array
*          -3 if no alias is passed and there's no table open
*          -4 if the passed alias doesn't exist
*
* Call: nIndexCount = AINDEXES(@aIndexArray [, cAliasName ] )

PARAMETERS aIndexInfo, cAlias
* aIndexInfo = array to place index information
*    If there are any indexes, the array returns 9 columns:
*       1 - index type: "I" or "C"
*       2 - index (tag) name
*       3 - index file name
*       4 - index key
*       5 - index filter
*       6 - descending?
*       7 - unique in the Xbase sense?
*       8 - primary key?
*       9 - candidate key?
* cAlias = alias about which to return index information
*         if omitted, report on current work area

LOCAL nParams, nOldArea, nIDXCount, nCDXCount, nTagCount, nTotalCount

nParams = PARAMETERS()

IF nParams = 0
* no array specified
   RETURN -1
ELSE
   IF TYPE("aIndexInfo[1]") = "U"
      RETURN -2
   ENDIF
ENDIF

IF nParams = 1
* use current work area
   IF EMPTY(ALIAS())
   * no table in use
      RETURN -3
   ENDIF
ELSE
   IF TYPE('cAlias') <> "C" OR NOT USED(cAlias)
      RETURN -4
   ENDIF
ENDIF
```

```
nOldArea = SELECT()
IF nParams > 1
   SELECT (cAlias)
ENDIF

* ready to start going through indexes
* do IDX files first
nTotalCount = 0
nIDXCount = 1

DO WHILE NOT EMPTY(NDX(nIDXCount))
   nTotalCount = nTotalCount + 1
   DIMENSION aIndexInfo[nTotalCount, 9]
   aIndexInfo[nTotalCount, 1] = "I"
   aIndexInfo[nTotalCount, 2] = TAG(nIDXCount)
   aIndexInfo[nTotalCount, 3] = NDX(nIDXCount)
   aIndexInfo[nTotalCount, 4] = KEY(nIDXCount)
   aIndexInfo[nTotalCount, 5] = FOR(nIDXCount)
   aIndexInfo[nTotalCount, 6] = DESCENDING(nIDXCount)
   aIndexInfo[nTotalCount, 7] = UNIQUE(nIDXCount)
   aIndexInfo[nTotalCount, 8] = .F.
   aIndexInfo[nTotalCount, 9] = .F.

   nIDXCount = nIDXCount + 1
ENDDO

* now CDX's one by one
nCDXCount = 1
DO WHILE NOT EMPTY(CDX(nCDXCount))
   nTagCount = 1
   cCDXName = CDX(nCDXCount)
   DO WHILE NOT EMPTY(TAG(cCDXName, nTagCount))
      nTotalCount = nTotalCount + 1
      DIMENSION aIndexInfo[nTotalCount, 9]
      aIndexInfo[nTotalCount, 1] = "C"
      aIndexInfo[nTotalCount, 2] = TAG(cCDXName, nTagCount)
      aIndexInfo[nTotalCount, 3] = cCDXName
      aIndexInfo[nTotalCount, 4] = KEY(cCDXNAME, nTagCount)
      aIndexInfo[nTotalCount, 5] = FOR(nTotalCount)
      aIndexInfo[nTotalCount, 6] = DESCENDING(cCDXName, nTagCount)
      aIndexInfo[nTotalCount, 7] = UNIQUE(cCDXName, nTagCount)
      aIndexInfo[nTotalCount, 8] = PRIMARY(nTotalCount)
      aIndexInfo[nTotalCount, 9] = CANDIDATE(nTotalCount)

      nTagCount = nTagCount + 1
   ENDDO

   nCDXCount = nCDXCount + 1
ENDDO

* now clean up
SELECT (nOldArea)

RETURN nTotalCount
```

See Also Alter Table, Create Table, Index, Order(), Set Index, Set Order, TagCount(), TagNo(), Use

CapsLock(), InsMode(), NumLock()

These functions are really cool because they let you change the state of the user's keyboard programmatically. That's right—these functions let you turn the Caps Lock and Num Lock keys on and off and change from insert to overwrite mode and back. They also tell you the state of those items before you changed it.

Usage

```
lReturnValue = CAPSLOCK( [ lNewState ] )
lReturnValue = INSMODE( [ lNewState ] )
lReturnValue = NUMLOCK( [ lNewState ] )
```

Parameter	Value	Meaning
lNewState	.T.	Turn the setting on.
	.F.	Turn the setting off.
	Omitted	Don't change the setting.
lReturnValue	.T.	The setting was on before calling the function.
	.F.	The setting was off before calling the function.

Perhaps most cool of all is that you can actually see the light on the keyboard go on or off for CAPSLOCK() and NUMLOCK().

Example

```
* Switch to uppercase
lOldCaps = CAPSLOCK(.T.)
* now have user perform uppercase entry
* now reset it
CAPSLOCK(lOldCaps)

* reverse the insert setting
INSMODE(.NOT. INSMODE())
```

The only problem with the example is there's nothing to stop the user from pressing the Caps Lock key himself and turning caps off.

Now, there are right ways and wrong ways to toggle these settings. The wrong way, used by Ted's remote control package, is to switch off the Num Lock, not inform the operator, and leave it off when the package completes. Wrong, wrong, wrong. The entire idea behind the PC Revolution (just in case you're too young to remember) was empowerment of the end users. We cannot take back control of the horizontal and vertical, folks, they're gone and they ain't comin' back no more. The right way to change these settings is to let the user know, either through a status bar message or icon, or a message box, that you've switched off their Caps Lock because you knew it was what they wanted you to do, with the option to turn it right back on again. Give the user options to save preferences to a file, so the poor user who doesn't have a separate cursor control panel can have his Num Lock off, while you don't pester everyone else.

See Also Format, Lower(), Upper()

Caption

This property is a true example of polymorphism at work. It contains a user-definable string for every control that has a Caption, but the exact use of the string varies rather a lot from one control to the next.

Usage

```
oObject.Caption = cCaptionString
cCaptionString = oObject.Caption
```

Forms put their Caption in the title bar. Pages in a page frame put theirs in the tab (if there is one—if not, Caption is ignored). For labels and column headers in a grid, Caption is pretty much all there is. For the rest of the objects that have Captions, it's the text that identifies the object so the user knows which one to choose—the label on a command button or next to an option button or check box. Command groups and option groups can put the Caption from their contained buttons in their Value to indicate which button in the group was chosen.

The Caption of an object is not the same as the Name of the object, though they might contain the same string. The Name is the one you use to refer to the object; Caption's just a pretty face.

For those objects that can receive focus, you can set a hotkey in the Caption by putting "\<" in front of the hotkey letter. Labels can also have hotkeys—when you press the hotkey, focus moves to the first object after the label that can receive focus. (Pretty neat—you can give the label next to a text box or edit box a hotkey. When the user presses the hotkey, focus lands on the text or edit box.) Hotkeys on the tabs of a page frame work only when focus is already on the page frame, but hotkeys on controls in a page of a page frame work as long as the page is on top.

Headers can't handle hotkeys. That's okay—we're not totally sure what they'd mean there anyway. What's not okay is that when you type the hotkey characters "\<" into the Caption of a header, it leaves them there. That is, not only don't they get replaced with an underline, but they don't get removed from the string.

Keep in mind that SET KEYCOMP affects the use of hotkeys—with KEYCOMP set to DOS, hotkeys don't always work. (However, there's really no reason to SET KEYCOMP TO DOS anymore, since there's no DOS version of VFP.)

In check boxes, option buttons and command buttons, you can combine the caption with a picture. However, there's no way to specify their relative position. The picture always goes over the caption. In the rare cases where we have needed a bitmap with a caption next to, or on top of, the bitmap, we've cheated by using an empty Caption and placing the text in the bitmap itself.

In VFP 3 and VFP 5, to create a completely borderless form, Caption needs to be empty. (See BorderStyle for a complete list of settings needed for borderless forms.) In VFP 6, TitleBar makes this a lot easier and messing with Caption is unnecessary.

Example

```
ThisForm.Caption = "Favorite Things"

* You can change the title on the main Visual FoxPro window:
_SCREEN.Caption = "Visual FoxPro is Best!"

* Here's a button with a hotkey
ThisForm.cmdClose.Caption = "\<Close"
```

See Also Alignment, AutoSize, BorderStyle, Name, Picture, Set KeyComp, Style, TitleBar

Catalog() See Access().

CD, ChDir, MD, MkDir, RD, RmDir, Set Default, Set("Default"), DefaultFilePath

CD, MD and RD may have been our favorite new commands in Visual FoxPro (they were certainly the easiest to learn!). They do the same thing as in DOS (change directories, create a new directory, and delete a directory, respectively), but you don't have to shell out to DOS to do it. SET DEFAULT is the traditional FoxPro equivalent of CD. DefaultFilePath is the automation server equivalent of SET DEFAULT—it lets you set the default directory and find out what it is.

Usage

```
CD | CHDIR [ ? | cPath ]
MD | MKDIR cPath
RD | RMDIR cPath
SET DEFAULT TO [ cPath ]
cDrive = SET( "DEFAULT" )
appApplication.DefaultFilePath = cPath
cPath = appApplication.DefaultFilePath
```

We can't see any reason to use the long versions of these names, so it's CD, MD and RD from here on out.

CD is almost equivalent to SET DEFAULT. Both change FoxPro's default directory. That's where anything you create gets saved unless you specify otherwise. Unlike the same-named DOS command, FoxPro's CD can handle a drive as well as a directory. In FoxPro/DOS, there's a bug where changing the drive with SET DEFAULT doesn't remember to tell DOS about the change. This can lead to some rather nasty consequences. Fortunately, neither FoxPro 2.x for Windows nor Visual FoxPro shares this bug.

Our favorite form of CD is CD ?, which lets us find the directory we want, then change to it. (In fact, you can even shorten it to CD? if you want.)

Both CD and SET DEFAULT can't see directories with the System attribute. Attempting to change to such a directory generates an "Invalid path or file name" error. Oddly, though, all of these commands can deal with directories below a system directory in the tree. So, you can create a subdirectory of a system directory and move to that subdirectory, but while you're there, you can't issue CD .. to go to the parent. How odd!

The difference between CD and SET DEFAULT comes when you don't pass a path. In that case, CD returns the current default directory, though in a different form than either SYS(2003) or CURDIR(). The path includes the drive, is in all lowercase and does not include a final "\". The output goes to the active window, so be careful with this one. We use it all the time in development, but would never put it in an app.

With no path, however, the behavior of SET DEFAULT TO depends on whether you're currently on the drive containing the VFP startup directory. If so, the command doesn't do anything at all. If you're on a different drive, you're changed to the root directory of the drive containing the VFP startup directory. Weird!

For some reason, SET("DEFAULT") has never been enhanced to keep up with the times. It still returns just the drive with no path. No extra parameters or anything to let you find the path. Of course, CURDIR() does the trick.

DefaultFilePath is the automation-server version of SET DEFAULT. It lets you find out and set the default directory when you're addressing VFP as a server.

MD and RD are the really big wins here. CD is nice, but we always had SET DEFAULT. Now, you can create and destroy directories from within your application. What power! Your application can create the directories it needs to store data, create temporary directories and then clean up, and so on.

The same rules apply as in DOS, so the directory you're removing must be empty and you can't be parked there.

By the way, we've always thought that the person who named CD and MD must have majored in confusion. It took us years to remember they stood for "change directory" and "make directory" rather than "create directory" and "move to directory."

Example

```
MD TEST  && create a TEST subdirectory of current directory
CD TEST  && change to it
* do some work
* then delete the files
* then
CD ..
RD TEST  && get rid of it

* change to the directory I want to work in
CD H:\HACKER
? _VFP.DefaultFilePath  && Returns h:\hacker
```

CD and SET DEFAULT have a bug under the 32-bit versions of Windows (which, of course, means it always shows up in VFP 5 and VFP 6). In FoxPro 2.x and older versions, SET DEFAULT allowed you to change drives without changing directories. That is, you could SET DEFAULT TO <drive letter> and it didn't change the current directory on that drive. In VFP 3 under the 16-bit versions of Windows, you can do the same thing with either SET

DEFAULT or CD. However, under Windows 95 and NT, if you change to a subdirectory, then change to another drive, then back to the first drive, you're no longer in the subdirectory on that drive.

Here's an example that'll give you different results in Windows 95 and NT than in Win 3.1 and Windows for Workgroups:

```
CD D:
CD \VFP\SAMPLES
CD C:
CD D:
* now where are we
? CURDIR()       && "D:\" on 95 and NT; "D:\VFP\SAMPLES" on 3.1 and 3.11
```

Regardless of the platform, both MD and RD have a problem with relative addressing on another drive. (We suspect this is related to the previous bug, however.) If you try to create a new directory as a subdirectory of the current directory on another drive, it gets created at the root anyway. For example:

```
* This example only demonstrates the bug under 3.1 and 3.11,
* but it exists in 95 and NT, too.
CD H:\HACKER    && set default on other drive
CD F:           && back to work
? CURDIR("H:")   && returns "\HACKER\"
MD H:SHOWBUG    && should be a sub-directory of Hacker
CD H:SHOWBUG    && but it's not. This doesn't work, you need:
CD H:\SHOWBUG   && this works
```

The new directory created in the example is H:\SHOWBUG instead of H:\HACKER\SHOWBUG. The workaround is to explicitly reference the full path:

```
MD ("H:\HACKER\SHOWBUG")
```

What a pain! We hope they fix it soon, but we're not holding our breath.

See Also CurDir(), GetDir(), Run, Set Default, Sys(5), Sys(2003)

CDoW(), CMonth(), Day(), Month(), Year()

These functions return the character and numeric equivalents of the date or datetime supplied.

Usage

```
cRetVal = CDOW( dDate | tDateTime )
cRetVal = CMONTH( dDate | tDateTime )
nRetVal = DAY( dDate | tDateTime )
nRetVal = MONTH( dDate | tDateTime )
nRetVal = YEAR( dDate | tDateTime )
```

CDoW() and CMonth() display the current day ("Saturday") and month ("December"). The return values are always in Proper format: capitalized first letter, lowercase for the remainder. Use these functions for output only, and not for internal business logic, if your application will be used in multi-lingual settings where one man's Thursday can be another's Donnerstag.

Day(), Month() and Year() return the numeric equivalents of the day of the month, month, and year, based on the date or datetime supplied. They are absolute—they are based on the Gregorian calendar, a generally agreed-upon standard. Year() always returns the full year, including century, regardless of the setting of CENTURY. Two other similar functions, DoW() and Week(), are discussed in their own section, as they depend on the system settings of the "first week of the year" and the "first day of the week."

Example

```
? CDOW(DATE())              && the equivalent of "What day is it?"
? CMONTH(DATETIME())        && and "What month is it?"
SET DATE MDY
? DAY({06/15/95})           && returns 15
? MONTH({06/15/95})         && returns 6
? YEAR({06/15/95})          && returns 1995
```

See Also DoW(), Date(), DMY(), MDY(), GoMonth(), Set Century, Set Date, Set FDoW, Set FWeek, Set Mark, Week()

Cdx(), Mdx(), Ndx()

These functions give you the names of index files. CDX() and MDX() are identical. Both return the name of a compound index file; MDX() is included only for compatibility with dBASE. NDX() returns the name of a stand-alone index file.

Usage

```
cIndexFile = CDX( nWhichIndex [, nWorkArea | cAlias] )
cIndexFile = MDX( nWhichIndex [, nWorkArea | cAlias] )
cIndexFile = NDX( nWhichIndex [, nWorkArea | cAlias] )
```

Parameter	Value	Meaning
nWhichIndex	Numeric	Determines which open index file has its name returned.
nWorkArea	Numeric	Return index information about the table open in work area nWorkArea.
	Omitted	If cAlias is also omitted, return index information about the table in the current work area.
cAlias	Character	Return index information about the table open with alias cAlias.
	Omitted	If nWorkArea is also omitted, return index information about the table in the current work area.
cIndexFile	Character	The name of the specified index file.
	Empty	There is no such index file.

When multiple index files are opened for a table, they're assigned positions based on the order in which they're specified. For example, if you:

```
USE MyTable INDEX AnIndex, AnotherIndex
```

AnIndex is index 1 and AnotherIndex is index 2. The parameter nWhichIndex is based on this ordering. For CDX() and MDX(), a structural index file is always index 1, if it exists. Any CDX files explicitly opened come after the structural index.

We don't use these functions often, but when we do, it's usually CDX() and it's because some of the other index functions (like TAGNO() and TAGCOUNT()) need the name of the index file when you pass them an alias.

These functions have one very friendly behavior. If you pass a value for nWhichIndex larger than the number of index files of that type that are open, they return the empty string. This makes these functions ideal for writing code to find all the open indexes.

Example

```
* create an array containing all CDX files for current work area
LOCAL cCDX, nCDXCnt

DIMENSION aCDX[1]
aCDX[1]=""
```

```
nCDXCnt=1
DO WHILE NOT EMPTY(CDX(nCDXCnt))
   DIMENSION aCDX[nCDXCnt]
   aCDX[nCDXCnt]=CDX(nCDXCnt)
   nCDXCnt=nCDXCnt+1
ENDDO

* get the name of the third open stand-alone index file
* for MyOldTable
? NDX(3, "MyOldTable")
```

All three functions respect the current setting of SET FULLPATH. With SET FULLPATH ON, they return a fully qualified file name; when SET FULLPATH is OFF, they return only the drive and index name.

As with other functions that let you pass an alias or work area number, we strongly recommend you don't use work area numbers. Always refer to tables by their aliases.

See Also Index, Key(), Order(), Set FullPath, Set Index, Sys(14), Tag(), TagNo(), TagCount(), Use

Ceiling(), Floor()

These two functions have nothing to do with architecture, despite their names. They implement the mathematical concept of ceiling and floor, traditionally written with the symbols "⌈" and "⌊". The ceiling of a number is the next integer greater than or equal to the number, while the floor is the next integer less than or equal to the number. So, the ceiling or floor of an integer is the number itself. CEILING() and FLOOR() work on all the numeric types.

Usage

```
nResult = CEILING( nValue )
nResult = FLOOR( nValue )
```

Be careful when applying these functions to negative numbers. You may find the results a little counter-intuitive. For positive numbers, FLOOR() and INT() are the same. For negative numbers, CEILING() and INT() are the same. CEILING() and FLOOR() both return .NULL. when handed a null value.

Example

```
? CEILING(3.14159)   && 4
? FLOOR(3.14159)     && 3
? CEILING(-17.385)   && -17
? FLOOR(-17.385)     && -18
```

See Also Int(), Max(), Min(), Mod(), Round()

Century See Set Date.

CError() See Access().

Change See Browse.

Change() See Access().

ChDir See CD.

CheckBox

This control is the computer equivalent of all those little "Check All that Apply" spaces on paper forms. It's useful for items that have two states—"it is" or "it ain't."

Use check boxes for items that fit the this is/this isn't division. If you can't think of a word or short phrase that can be preceded by "is" or "is not" to indicate the state of the check box, then it's probably not the right control. For example, a check box is great for distinguishing between Active and Inactive ("is active"/"is not active" makes sense), but lousy for specifying gender ("is male"/"is not male" sounds weird). For those cases where a check box won't do, consider an option group instead.

Having said that, we now have to tell you that check boxes in Visual FoxPro have three possible values. In the immortal words of George Carlin, "Why are there three?"

Actually, it's for a pretty good reason. There are cases where the answer to the "is/is not" question is "I dunno." With Visual FoxPro, you can actually handle that case. (However, the only way for the user to actually enter an "I don't know" value is by pressing CTRL+0. Not only is this totally non-intuitive, but pressing CTRL+0 on a field that doesn't accept nulls generates an error.)

"I don't know" is the layman's term for null, which is one of the nicer additions in Visual FoxPro. The Value of a check box can be .F., .T. or .NULL. (or, if you have a C background, 0, 1, or 2).

Property	Value	Purpose
Alignment	Numeric	Determines which side of the caption the actual box is on.
AutoSize	Logical	Determines whether the check box resizes itself to the size of its caption and picture.
Caption	Character	The text that appears next to the check box.
Picture, DownPicture, DisabledPicture	Character	The filenames of pictures that appear on a graphical check box. Picture is used when the box is unchecked. DownPicture is used when the box is checked. DisabledPicture is used when the check box is disabled. If DownPicture or DisabledPicture is omitted, Picture is used for those states as well.
Style	Numeric	Determines whether the check box is textual or graphical. A graphical check box shows both the picture and the caption.

Another pleasant, though somewhat confusing, addition in Visual FoxPro is graphical check boxes. These things look like buttons, but when you click them, they stay down. (The buttons on the main VFP toolbar for the Command Window and Data Session Window are really check boxes.)

Example

```
* Set up a CheckBox subclass that's
* right-aligned and autosized and
* displays a message when clicked.
DEFINE CLASS RightCheck AS CheckBox

   Alignment = 1
   AutoSize = .T.

   PROCEDURE Click
      WAIT WINDOW "You called?" NOWAIT
   ENDPROC
ENDDEFINE
```

See Also Alignment, AutoSize, Caption, DisabledPicture, DownPicture, OptionGroup, Picture, Style

CheckIn, CheckOut, GetLatestVersion, UndoCheckOut

These methods allow you to move files in the Files collection into or out of your source code control provider.

Usage

```
lResult = filFile.CheckIn()
lResult = filFile.CheckOut()
lResult = filFile.GetLatestVersion()
lResult = filFile.UndoCheckOut()
```

All of these methods perform the exact same function as their like-named equivalents on the Project's context menu. Provided you have set up a source code control provider, and added this project to source code control, each of these methods tries its best to perform its function and returns .T. if successful or .F. if it fails. If source control is not set up or established for this project, the methods all return .F.

CheckOut registers a file with the source code control system as yours to modify, retrieves the most recent version, and flags the local file read-write, if necessary. CheckIn reverses the process, copying your changes to the central repository and freeing the file for others to modify while locking your local copy as read-only. GetLatestVersion retrieves the latest file, but doesn't lock it for your changes—use this to make sure you're working on the latest source code before a build or a test run. UndoCheckOut lets you just give up on all of those changes you've tried that didn't work, free the program for others to work on, and retrieve a local, read-only copy of the last version checked in.

In our configuration, using Visual SourceSafe, each of these methods brings up confirmation dialogs, despite the fact that the Tools-Options-Projects check box that says "Display dialog box for shortcut menu commands" is unchecked. This ruins the entire point of manipulating these things programmatically, in our opinion. We hope Microsoft will look at this and consider a more developer-friendly interface.

Example

```
* Here's a routine to check out, modify a file and check in
oProject = _VFP.ActiveProject
oFile = oProject.Files[1]
IF oFile.ReadOnly  && the file must be checked in
  oFile.CheckOut()
  oFile.Modify()  && make your changes
  oFile.CheckIn()
ENDIF

* Scan a project and get the latest version of all the files
FOR EACH oFile in oProject.Files
  oFile.GetLatestVersion()
NEXT
```

See Also Project, File, ReadOnly

ChildAlias, ChildOrder, OneToMany, ParentAlias, RelationalExpr

These are properties of a relation in the data environment of a form, label or report. They indicate, respectively, the alias and order of the child table in the relation, whether the relation is one-to-many, the alias of the parent table in the relation, and the expression from the parent that controls the relation.

When you drag a field from one table onto a tag of another, a relation is created with the first table's field for RelationalExpr and the second table's tag as ChildOrder. ChildAlias and ParentAlias are filled in automatically and can't be changed.

ChildOrder and RelationalExpr also apply to grids that are the "many" side of a one-to-many setup. If the tables involved have the appropriate relation, you don't need to set these properties at the grid level. When the tables don't have the relation, set it up for the grid.

Usage

```
cChildAlias = frmForm.DataEnvironment.relRelation.ChildAlias
cParentAlias = frmForm.DataEnvironment.relRelation.ParentAlias
```

These two properties are filled in when you create a relation in the data environment. They cannot be changed in the property sheet or in code. Changing the aliases of the cursors involved automatically changes these properties.

Usage

```
frmForm.DataEnvironment.relRelation.ChildOrder = cTagname
cTagName = frmForm.DataEnvironment.relRelation.ChildOrder
```

ChildOrder determines the order of the child table in the relation. ChildOrder supersedes the Order property of the cursor for the child table.

Usage

```
frmForm.DataEnvironment.relRelation.OneToMany = lIsOneToMany
lIsOneToMany = frmForm.DataEnvironment.relRelation.OneToMany
```

OneToMany indicates whether the relation is one-to-many. Even when a one-to-many persistent relation is used as the basis for the relation, this property doesn't get set automatically. You have to set it yourself. At first glance, this may seem odd, but it's been our experience that we don't actually use one-to-many relations in our forms that often. Back in 2.x, how frequently did you SET SKIP in a screen? (Reports, of course, are another story.)

Usage

```
frmForm.DataEnvironment.relRelation.RelationalExpr = cExpr
cExpr = frmForm.DataEnvironment.relRelation.RelationalExpr
```

RelationalExpr is the expression in the parent table on which the relation is based. In other words, it's the TO part of the equivalent SET RELATION.

Example

```
* These properties are normally set in the property sheet
* Assume you've put TasTrade's Customer and Orders tables
* in the Data Environment of a form. To have a one-to-many
* relation between them, properties are set as follows:
ThisForm.DataEnvironment.Relation1.ChildOrder="customer_i"
ThisForm.DataEnvironment.Relation1.RelationalExpr="Customer_id"
ThisForm.DataEnvironment.Relation1.OneToMany=.T.
```

Although ChildOrder, OneToMany and RelationalExpr can be changed in a running form, the changes you make don't take effect immediately. You need to CloseTables, then OpenTables. (In fact, it's better to CloseTables, make your changes, then OpenTables. Otherwise, there's an ugly information message for each change of this sort you make.)

See Also LinkMaster, Set Order, Set Relation, Set Skip

Chr() See Asc().

ChrSaw(), InKey(), LastKey()

These functions are all concerned with the keyboard buffer. CHRSAW() and INKEY() let you check if there's anything there, while LASTKEY() tells you what used to be there.

Usage

```
lKeyPressed = CHRSAW( [ nSeconds ] )
nKeyValue = INKEY( [ nSeconds ] [ , ] [ cFlags ] )
```

Parameter	Value	Meaning
nSeconds	Numeric	How long should we wait for a keystroke or click?
cFlags	"M"	Pay attention to the left mouse button, too.
	"E"	Expand keyboard macro and return a keystroke from it.
	"H"	Hide the cursor while we wait.
	"S"	Show the cursor while we wait.
lKeyPressed	.T.	There's something in the keyboard buffer.
	.F.	There's nothing in the keyboard buffer.
	0	There's nothing in the keyboard buffer.
	151	The user clicked the left mouse button.

Parameter	Value	Meaning
nKeyValue	Other numbers	The code for the key pressed by the user. See Help.

CHRSAW() and INKEY() are two variations on the same theme. They look at the keyboard buffer, and wait for a specified length of time to see what happens. CHRSAW() is the nonintrusive one—it just tells you whether any keystrokes appeared in the buffer in that time. INKEY() actually grabs the first keystroke, clears it from the buffer and gives you a code for it. They both quit waiting as soon as they see a keystroke.

CHRSAW() is handy when you want to know if the user did anything at all. Use INKEY() if you want to know what the user did or if you need to eat a keystroke. (See the discussion of LASTKEY() below for a work-around that uses INKEY() to eat a keystroke.)

INKEY() is also mouse-sensitive, if you want it to be. Before we had Visual FoxPro's DblClick event, INKEY() was an important part of detecting double-clicks. INKEY()'s mouse-detecting parameter is a little unusual, as the syntax above shows. Either a timeout value or a character flag can be passed to the function. Only in the case of passing both is a comma required.

The "E" flag, added in VFP 5, makes it easier to deal with the possibility that the keystroke pressed is actually shorthand for something longer. If the keystroke in the buffer has a macro defined, including the "E" tells INKEY() to return successive keys from the macro rather than just the original keystroke.

CHRSAW() is sensitive to SET TYPEAHEAD. If you turn off type-ahead, the function can't see the incoming keystrokes.

With events like KeyPress, Click and DblClick around, we don't expect to be using these functions much anymore.

Example

```
IF NOT CHRSAW(5)          && wait 5 seconds
   WAIT WINDOW "C'mon, buddy, DO something!"
ENDIF
```

Usage `nCode = LASTKEY()`

LASTKEY() tells you the code for the key most recently processed. Beware—checking LASTKEY() doesn't change its value. The old value stays there until another keystroke is processed. If you're checking LASTKEY() for certain keystrokes to, say, terminate an activity, you'll want to stuff it with a new value once you've checked it. (Use KEYBOARD and INKEY() to stuff LASTKEY() with any value you want.)

One place to use LASTKEY() is in dealing with users bailing out. As in FoxPro 2.x, a Valid routine can't look ahead to see what user action triggered the Valid. If the user clicks a Cancel button, we don't usually want to validate the field he was on before that. In our apps, Cancel buttons have their Cancel property set to .T., so the user can press Esc or click on them. Clicking a button with its Cancel property set to .T. stuffs LASTKEY() with 27 (just as if the user had actually pressed Esc). So the Valid routine can check for LASTKEY()=27 and bail out. See the example.

Example

```
* This is the beginning of a Valid method. It lets you bail
* out when the user chooses the Cancel button.
* We'll also stuff the keyboard with something innocuous so
* we don't trigger canceling of another Valid by accident.
IF LASTKEY()=27
   KEYBOARD CHR(255)
   =INKEY()  && eat the character we just keyboarded
   RETURN .T.
ENDIF
* now perform the actual validation
```

See Also Cancel, Click, DblClick, KeyPreview, KeyPress, Set TypeAhead

ChrTran(), StrTran(), Stuff(), Sys(15), Sys(20)

These five methods of manipulating strings are great for translation and some cool effects.

Usage

```
cRetVal = CHRTRAN( cSource, cCharsToReplace, cReplacements )
cRetVal = STRTRAN( cSource, cStringToReplace
                  [, cReplacementString ]
                  [ [, nStartOccurrence ]
                  [, nHowMany ] ] )
cRetVal = STUFF( cSource, nWhereToStart, nLong,
                 cReplacementString )
cRetVal = SYS( 15, cSource, cTransTable )
cRetVal = SYS( 20, cSource, nLength )
```

Parameter	Value	Meaning
cSource	Character	The original string to be manipulated.
cCharsToReplace	Character	The individual characters to be replaced.
cReplacements	Character	The new characters to replace those of cCharsToReplace, mapped one-to-one to the originals.
cStringToReplace	Character	The exact, case-sensitive string to locate and replace in cSource.
cReplacementString	Character	The new string to be substituted for cStringToReplace.
	Omitted	cStringToReplace is cut from the text.
nStartOccurence	Numeric	Optionally specify at which occurrence the replacement starts.
	Omitted	Replacement starts at the first occurrence.
nHowMany	Numeric	How many of the occurrences to replace.
	Omitted	All occurrences are replaced.
nWhereToStart	Numeric	Starting location for string replacement.
nLong	Numeric	Number of characters to be discarded from the original string.
	0	Preserve all existing characters while inserting new text.
cTransTable	Character	A string of up to 255 characters; replaces original characters based on position in string and ASCII value of original.
nLength	Numeric	The number of characters of cSource to process.

CHRTRAN() and SYS(15) are search-and-replace functions that operate on a single character at a time. Use CHRTRAN() to eliminate or translate one or a few characters, and SYS(15) if you need to translate all characters.

STRTRAN() is a similar search-and-replace function for entire words and phrases at one time. Use STRTRAN() to replace one word or phrase with another. STUFF() is more of an Insert function, optionally either overwriting existing characters or pushing them out of the way as it inserts new text. STUFF() may be more efficient at combining character strings than the + append operator, depending on the environment in which you are running and the tasks you must perform.

SYS(15) and SYS(20) were originally intended as methods of providing indexes to European users. SYS(15) worked by stripping accents from characters. SYS(20) worked by creating a longer string with binary values that would create a proper German phonebook order. SET COLLATE does a far better job of properly weighting these characters, rather than discarding them, and therefore should be used instead. However, SYS(15) does provide a universal translation mechanism that can be useful for other purposes, as shown in the last example below.

```
Example    ? CHRTRAN("ABCDE","ACE","XYZ")           && yields "XBYDZ"
           ? CHRTRAN("ABCDE","ACE","")              && yields "BD"
           ? CHRTRAN("ABCDE","ACE","X")             && yields "XBD"
           ? STRTRAN("The brown fox","brown","red") && "The red fox"
           ? STRTRAN("1a2a3a4a5a6a7a",'a','b',3,2)  && "1a2a3b4b5a6a7a"
           ? STUFF("5 pound sack", 1, 7, "10 pounds of potatoes in")
           * results in "10 pounds of potatoes in sack"
```

In the first example, CHRTRAN() is used to replace the characters A, C and E with X, Y and Z, respectively. In the second example, a blank string of replacements leads to the elimination of all letters listed as the second parameter. In the third example, a combination of the two above is shown where X is substituted for A, and C and E are eliminated completely. Our fourth and fifth examples show the word-replacement capabilities of STRTRAN(), in the latter case replacing only some specified occurrences within the source string. Finally, the last example shows the STUFF() function in action, inserting and replacing portions of a string. Here's an example of the power of SYS(15), an example we've found helpful when we discover we've left the CAPS LOCK on after a few pages of witty prose:

```
* Invert - return string with case reversed
LPARAMETER tcString
LOCAL i, cTransStr  && counter and string
cTransStr = ""
FOR i = 1 TO 255
  DO CASE
    CASE NOT ISALPHA(CHR(I))  && not a letter - don't change!
      cTransStr = cTransStr + CHR(i)
    CASE ISLOWER(CHR(I))    && lower case
      cTransStr = cTransStr + UPPER(CHR(i))
    CASE ISUPPER(CHR(I))    && upper case
      cTransStr = cTransStr + LOWER(CHR(i))
  ENDCASE
NEXT
RETURN SYS(15,cTransStr,tcString)
```

Applying this function to any block of text returns the original string, but with all uppercase characters changed to lower and all lowercase changed to upper.

See Also Chr(), Set Collate, SubStr()

ChrTranC(), StuffC()

These are double-byte equivalents of CHRTRAN() and STUFF(), added in version 3.0b. They appear to work, though we've been unable to test substitution of double-byte characters for single-byte and vice versa.

Usage

```
cRetVal = CHRTRANC( cSource, cCharsToReplace, cReplacements )
cRetVal = STUFFC( cSource, nWhereToStart, nLong,
                  cReplacementString )
```

See Also ChrTran(), Double-Byte Character Sets, Stuff()

Circle See Box.

Class See BaseClass.

ClassLibrary

This property contains the name of the class library (VCX) containing the class definition that an object is based on. It's the library containing the definition for the object's Class.

Usage `cClassLibrary = oObject.ClassLibrary`

You can look, but you can't touch. This one is read-only all the time. Intrepid hackers may think that diddling with this field at the SCX or VCX level is the only way to directly switch an object from one class hierarchy to another. We prefer not messing with the underlying power tool tables directly whenever possible (and then only with lots of backups!).

We suggest two alternatives. First, you can use the Class Browser's Redefine function to do this sort of thing. The other alternative is to query an existing object at design time and create a matching object with appropriate properties, events and methods, then delete the original object. A perfect job for a Builder! See "Builders and Wizards (and Bears, Oh My!)" on the CD.

ClassLibrary contains the full path to the library.

Example

```
IF cmdQuit.ClassLibrary = cmdSave.ClassLibrary
   WAIT WINDOW "Hey, we're brothers!"
ENDIF
```

See Also Class, Set ClassLib

CleanUp

This project method corresponds to the Clean Up Project option on the Project menu, but goes it one better. It packs the project table and, optionally, removes compiled code to force it to be recompiled.

Usage `prjProject.CleanUp( [ lDeleteObjectCode ] )`

Parameter	Value	Meaning
lDeleteObjectCode	.F. or omitted	Leave the compiled code in the project alone.
	.T.	Remove the compiled code from the Object memo field.

Over time, as you work on a project, lots of debris accumulates in the project file, including records marked as deleted because components were removed and memo fields bloating as code is recompiled and so forth. CleanUp throws away all that debris, leaving you with a nice, clean, smaller project file. This effect is the same as if you were to use the PJX file as a table and issue the command PACK.

However, the method has capabilities beyond what you can do with a mere PACK. The optional parameter lets you decide whether to clean out the Object field of the project as well. The Object field contains compiled code for programs, menus and queries. If you throw it out, the source gets recompiled the next time you build the project.

Example `_VFP.ActiveProject.CleanUp()`

See Also Pack, Project

Clear

This simplest of the Clear commands erases a window or clears the main screen.

Usage `CLEAR`

When you apply CLEAR to a form, the controls disappear but they're not destroyed. The form's Refresh method brings some of them back. Giving the form focus brings back some more. Clicking somewhere on the form brings back any controls at that location. Items drawn with the form's drawing methods don't come back (which is as it should be). In reality, CLEAR isn't really meant for forms. Use RemoveObject to get rid of controls and Cls to erase drawing objects.

If you use the Picture property of _SCREEN to create a backdrop for your application, like the background-tiled images on the Web, you may find that after a while, the top quarter or fifth of the screen stops clearing correctly and starts accumulating bitmap garbage. Force the screen to clear with:

```
LOCAL llLockScreen, lcPicture
llLockScreen = _SCREEN.LockScreen
_Screen.LockScreen = .T.
lcPicture =_SCREEN.Picture
_SCREEN.Picture=""
_SCREEN.Picture =lcPicture
_Screen.LockScreen = llLockScreen
```

Example

```
ACTIVATE SCREEN
CLEAR
```

See Also Cls, Refresh, RemoveObject

Clear See AddItem.

Clear All

This one does all kinds of things. It releases variables, menus and their components, and DLL functions, closes and releases windows, closes tables, sweeps the kitchen floor, plows the north 40 and curls your hair overnight.

Usage

```
CLEAR ALL
```

Of course, CLEAR ALL doesn't do everything. It doesn't release class libraries, procedure files or external API libraries. It doesn't close system windows or databases. It doesn't clear the system program buffer or the main window.

Nonetheless, we use it all the time. Our minimal "clean up after we've been messing around" sequence is CLOSE ALL, CLEAR ALL.

See Also Clear DLLs, Clear Memory, Close Tables, Release, Relcase Bar, Release Menus, Release Pad, Release Popup, Release Windows, Use

Clear Class, Clear Classlib

These two commands remove individual classes and entire class libraries from memory.

Usage

```
CLEAR CLASS ClassName
CLEAR CLASSLIB ClassLibName
```

In order to create instances of a class, you have to load the class definition into memory. Even after you destroy the instances, FoxPro keeps the definitions in memory in case you want to make more. These commands free up that memory ... except for one thing.

Neither of these commands works. When you issue either one correctly, you don't see any error messages, but the class or class library is not removed from memory. Use SET CLASSLIB TO without a class library to clear class libraries instead.

Example

```
SET CLASSLIB TO Connect
oConn = CreateObject('ConnMgr')
```

```
* Now work with the Connection Manager
* When you're done, you should be able to do:
CLEAR CLASSLIB Connect
* But nothing happens. You can still
oConn2 = CreateObject('ConnMgr')
```

With the addition of NewObject() in VFP 6, we think we don't really care whether these commands ever work. We no longer have to use precious memory (maybe not so precious any more, anyway) to load whole class libraries in order to instantiate things. We can just specify the class library on the fly.

See Also CreateObject(), NewObject(), Release Classlib, Set ClassLib

Clear DLLs

This one is supposed to remove all declared DLL functions from memory. Surprise, it works.

Usage `CLEAR DLLS`

We have mixed feelings over this one. First, DLL Declares are supposed to take up a really small amount of memory, so clearing them doesn't make much sense from that standpoint. Second, if you are dealing with any objects that DECLARE the DLLs in their Inits, and then ASSuMe that these declarations will be around later to play with, blam, you just blew them out of the water. Finally, our real issue is that there is no simple way to search for, nor delete, individual declares with language constructs like IsDLL(functionname) or Release DLL [ALL | LIKE]. While the circumstances in which you would need or want it are rare, we'd like to have the capability within the language, so CLEAR DLLS just doesn't cut it for us.

See Also Declare - DLL

Clear Events See Read Events.

Clear Fields

This old command (he played one) combines SET FIELDS TO with SET FIELDS OFF, and applies it to all work areas. It's relevant only if you're using SET FIELDS in the first place.

Usage `CLEAR FIELDS`

Example

```
USE OneTable
SET FIELDS TO First, Second
SELECT 0
USE Another
SET FIELDS TO Two, Night
CLEAR FIELDS
```

See Also Set Fields

Clear Gets, Clear Read

These are obsolete. They're part of the whole @ ... GET/READ mechanism that's been superseded by forms.

Just in case you have to support old code, here's the short form of what these functions do. CLEAR GETS releases the "pending" status of @ ... GETs without erasing them. CLEAR READ closes a READ, releases all its @ ... GETs and goes back to the read level above. CLEAR READ ALL closes all nested READs and fires the Valid clause of the foundation read.

See Also @ ... Get, Read

Clear Macros, Restore Macros, Save Macros, Play Macro, Set MacKey, Set("MacKey")

Maybe it's because there's always been a whole programming language to play with, but keyboard macros have never been a big thing in FoxPro. Other than the defaults that used to be set up on the function keys (you know, like F7 for DISPLAY MEMORY), we rarely record and use macros in FoxPro (though our technical editor tells us he has several macros he uses to this day). We never include macros in our applications.

The most important command in this group is CLEAR MACROS, which lets you get rid of any defined macros—until VFP 5, it was usually the defaults on the function keys we were clearing. We used RESTORE MACROS occasionally, too, to get the defaults back. PLAY MACRO executes a macro by name, while SAVE MACROS lets you store a group of macros. Finally, SET MACKEY specifies which key starts recording a macro.

Usage

```
CLEAR MACROS
```

This command should be part of the startup routine of any VFP 3 or FoxPro 2.x application. That way, when the user drops his pen or his cat on the keyboard, he won't end up with records full of "SET" and "DISPLAY STRUCTURE." It doesn't hurt in VFP 5 and VFP 6, either, though there are no defaults in there.

Usage

```
RESTORE MACROS [ FROM MacroFile | FROM MEMO MemoField ]
SAVE MACROS TO MacroFile | TO MEMO MemoField
```

Macros can be stored in either of two places: a special macro file (with an FKY for "function key" extension) or in a memo field. In either case, they're stored in a special format where two bytes are stored for each character. One byte stores bit flags for the special modifier keys—Alt, Ctrl and Shift—while the second character stores the keystroke. You can open an FKY file or a memo field containing macros and see the commands, but there's a lot more stuff in there, too. Check out the help topic "Macro File Format (.FKY)" for the underlying format. Hacking one of these files could lead to some cool applications, based on replaying macro files, such as testing data-entry portions of apps automatically.

RESTORE MACROS by itself loads the macros from a special file called DEFAULT.FKY. If you don't have that file, it restores the (nonexistent since VFP 5) default function key assignments.

Usage

```
PLAY MACRO MacroName [ TIME nDelay ]
```

As the name suggests, this command plays an existing macro. The TIME clause is pretty cool—it lets you slow the thing down in case there are places where you need to wait for FoxPro to catch up. It's good for debugging macros, too. You can see what's going on.

Like KEYBOARD (often a good alternative), PLAY MACRO doesn't actually make anything happen immediately. It stores the name of the macro to be played back when the program reaches a wait state (like BROWSE or READ EVENTS).

This command's behavior when you issue it more than once is yet another reason we don't use macros in applications. If several PLAY MACROs have been issued before a wait state, when the program finally reaches a wait state, the macros are played in reverse order. The last macro you played executes first. Bleh.

Usage

```
SET MACKEY TO [ KeyLabel ]
cKeyLabel = SET("MACKEY")
```

Through VFP 3, Shift+F10 brought up the Record Macro dialog. Starting in VFP 5, Shift+F10 was taken over by the context menus and there's no keystroke assigned for Record Macro—you have to use the menu (from the Tools menu, choose Macros, then Record). SET MACKEY lets you assign a key (or a different key, in VFP 3 and FoxPro 2.x) for the task. SET("MACKEY") tells you the current setting. If you SET MACKEY TO without a key label, it restores the default setting—no shortcut key in VFP 5 and VFP 6, Shift+F10 in earlier versions.

Example

```
RESTORE MACROS FROM MyMacros
PLAY MACRO ThisCoolMacro
```

```
CLEAR MACROS
```

See Also On Key Label, Set

Clear Memory

What do you know? The name actually describes what the command does. CLEAR MEMORY releases all memory variables, except system variables.

Usage
```
CLEAR MEMORY
```

Be careful how you use this command. Using it at the wrong time can really mess up your programs.

See Also Clear All, Release

Clear Menus, Clear Popups

These two commands each release different menu components from memory.

Usage
```
CLEAR MENUS
CLEAR POPUPS
```

CLEAR MENUS discards menus (the menu bar itself) and their associated pads. CLEAR POPUPS releases popups and their associated bars (that is, items—isn't term overloading fun?).

We never use either of these because we always build our menus with the Menu Designer and base them on the system menu.

Example
```
DEFINE MENU mymenu
DEFINE PAD one OF mymenu PROMPT "first"
DEFINE PAD two OF mymenu PROMPT "second"
ON PAD one OF mymenu ACTIVATE POPUP three
ON PAD two OF mymenu ACTIVATE POPUP four

DEFINE POPUP three
DEFINE BAR 1 OF three PROMPT "subitem 1"
DEFINE BAR 2 OF three PROMPT "subitem 2"
DEFINE POPUP four
DEFINE BAR 1 OF four PROMPT "item 1"
DEFINE BAR 2 OF four PROMPT "item 2"
DEFINE BAR 3 OF four PROMPT "item 3"

DISPLAY MEMORY  && to see what's defined
CLEAR MENUS
DISPLAY MEMORY  && note that only menu and pads are gone
CLEAR POPUPS
DISPLAY MEMORY  && now it's all cleaned up
```

See Also Release Bar, Release Menu, Release Pad, Release Popups, Set Sysmenu

Clear Program

This command does not refer to having lots of empty space on your Day-Timer®. It removes compiled programs from memory.

Usage
```
CLEAR PROGRAM
```

FoxPro caches programs to improve execution speed. Normally, it does a good job of noticing when you change a program and dumping the old version in favor of the new. However, under some circumstances, it messes up and runs the old version. That's when CLEAR PROGRAM is called for.

See Also Compile, Set Development

Clear Prompt

This command is so obsolete, we'd forgotten it ever existed. It releases menus built with the @ ... PROMPT command.

See Also @ ... Prompt, Menu To

Clear Read See Clear Gets.

Clear Resources

This command does two things for you. First, it lets your applications see changes to graphics and fonts. Second, it makes VFP give up some of the memory it likes to grab.

Usage
```
CLEAR RESOURCES [ cResourceFile ]
```

Parameter	Value	Meaning
cResourceFile	Filename	Clear the specified item from the cache so that a newer version can be seen. Also releases the memory used by the item.
	Omitted	Clear all cached items and release the memory they were using.

One of the tricks VFP uses for doing things fast is to keep the stuff it's using handy. When a form that involves a bitmap or other picture closes, rather than forgetting about that picture, VFP sticks it in a cache so it'll be available quickly the next time you need it. (This is much the same as what Internet Explorer does, so that going back to a page is faster than navigating to it in the first place.)

Most of the time, this is what we want. But there are two catches. The obvious one is that saving all that stuff uses up memory space (kind of like all that stuff we have in our houses because "it's too good to throw out and I might find a use for it"). Eventually, the cache might be taking up more space than you're willing to give it. CLEAR RESOURCES lets you clean it out (and it's a heckuva lot easier than cleaning out our closets and desks). You can clear out the cache entirely by issuing the command without a filename, or just get a specific file out of the way by naming it.

The second issue is more subtle. Suppose you run a form that contains an icon. Then you modify the icon. If the old version is still in the cache, when you run the form again it still shows the old one. (FoxPro does this sort of thing in other places, too. Programs are also cached and sometimes you have to really push to get it to see the latest version.) Again, CLEAR RESOURCES saves the day. Just specify the file you've changed, and it gets dropped from the cache so the new version can be seen.

Example
```
CLEAR RESOURCES MyFigure.BMP  && Clear away a picture to show
                              && the latest version.
```

See Also Image, Sys(1016)

Clear Screen See Access().

Clear TypeAhead

This command empties out the type-ahead buffer, throwing away any keystrokes the user has entered in advance.

Usage `CLEAR TYPEAHEAD`

Once in a while, you have a sensitive input item where you want to be sure the user knows what he's doing. You don't want mindless keyboarding to result in a disaster. When that's the case, you can CLEAR TYPEAHEAD just before entering the field in question. CLEAR TYPEAHEAD just before displaying a WAIT WINDOW, or any WAIT command where you really want some time to pass. CLEAR TYPEAHEAD affects MessageBox() calls as well.

See Also InKey(), MessageBox(), Set TypeAhead, Wait

Clear Windows

The last in the long list of Clear commands releases all user-defined windows from memory. It takes form windows as well as those defined with DEFINE WINDOW.

Usage `CLEAR WINDOWS`

When form windows are released with CLEAR WINDOWS, the variables that reference them are not released—instead, they become .NULL.

See Also Release, Release Window

ClearData, GetData, SetData

These are all methods of the DataObject, a COM object that provides access to data being dragged with OLE drag and drop. ClearData removes all data from the data object. GetData retrieves data, and SetData puts data into the data object.

Usage

```
oDataObject.ClearData()
uResult = oDataObject.GetData( [ nFormat | cFormat ]
                               [, @aHoldData ] )
oDataObject.SetData( uData | @aData [, nFormat | cFormat ] )
```

Parameter	Value	Meaning
nFormat	1, 7 or 13	Retrieve or place textual data in ASCII, OEM or Unicode format, respectively. As far as we can tell, in the U.S. Windows version of VFP, no native controls automatically supply either OEM or Unicode format data, though other applications might, and you can provide data in one of those formats.
	15	Retrieve or place a list of files.
	16	Documented (for SetData only) as providing a handle to the locale identifier for text on the clipboard, but we haven't been able to retrieve any data in this format.
	Any other number	Retrieve or place data in a custom format.
	Omitted	If cFormat is also omitted, place scalar data in the data object in the text (1) and "OLE Variant" formats, or place array data in the "OLE Variant Array" format.

Parameter	Value	Meaning
cFormat	"OLE Variant Array"	Retrieve or place multiple data items in their original format. Use this one to drag a whole array of data.
	"OLE Variant"	Retrieve or place data in its original type. For example, data from a spinner is treated as numeric, using this format.
	"VFP Source Object"	Retrieve a reference to the data source for this drag. By default, all VFP controls make this format available. Data cannot be placed in the data object in this format.
	Any other string	Retrieve or place data in a custom format.
	Omitted	If nFormat is also omitted, place scalar data in the data object in the text (1) and "OLE Variant" formats or place array data in the "OLE Variant Array" format.
aHoldData	Array name	The name of an array holding the data retrieved from the data object. Relevant only for some data formats.
uResult	.T.	Data in one of the array formats was successfully retrieved.
	.F.	The data object doesn't contain any data in the specified format.
	Other	The data retrieved from the data object.
uData	Expression	The data to be placed in the data object for one of the single-valued formats.
aData	Array name	The name of the array holding the data to be placed in the data object. Relevant only for the multi-valued formats.

The more we look at OLE drag and drop, the more we are impressed with its richness and depth. These methods (and, in fact, the whole idea of the data object) are among the things that make OLE drag and drop really powerful.

When you start dragging, the data object is created and data is put into it, based on what you're dragging and from where. For any given drag source, the data object can contain data in several different formats, and a drop target might choose to accept any one (or none) of those formats.

Left to its own devices, VFP (and Windows, as a whole) makes some pretty good decisions about what to do when you drop data. But sometimes you want to go a little further than that. These methods let you do so.

SetData lets you store data in the data object in whatever format you need at the moment, rather than just using the default for this particular pair of objects (the drag source and the drop target). Consider using the format constants in FoxPro.H to make your code easier to read. You can call SetData to stuff data into the data object in the drag source's OLEStartDrag or OLESetData methods. (Despite documentation to the contrary, OLESetData is called right after any custom code in the drop target's OLEDragDrop—that is, before the data is actually dropped.)

You can put just about any kind of data into the data object with SetData, but making sure it'll work is a little trickier. If you're retrieving the data yourself (with GetData), the precise format doesn't matter. But if you want to be able to drag into other applications, you need to get it right, so those apps find what they expect.

For example, with format 15, which provides a list of files, you must be sure each file in your list has a complete path, including drive designator. You can stuff a list of files collected with ADIR(), for example, into the data object, but if you don't add the drive and path, Explorer chokes when you drop them.

GetData is the other end of the process. It lets you pull out the data in whichever format you need at the moment. If you specify a nonexistent format, VFP ignores you and does whatever it would have done if you hadn't spoken up in the first place.

The formats provided actually cover a pretty wide range, so most of the time you won't need to create a custom format. When you do, be aware that the only data you can put there is character data or specially formatted character data created with CreateBinary(). You can't stick numbers or an array or anything fancy like that into a custom data format.

The "VFP Source Object" data type is particularly powerful because it gives you a reference to the object containing the dragged data. You can then do anything you want with that object, including referencing or changing its properties and calling its methods.

ClearData is the easy one to understand here. It pricks a data object and lets out all the air. That is, it removes all the data and all the formats and leaves an empty shell of an object. You can then fill it in with whatever you want. We haven't actually found a reason to use this method yet, other than to test it, but we're sure we will eventually.

Example

```
* If the data being dragged is a list of files, put
* the contents of the first file into the receiving
* edit box's Value. This code would go in the edit box's
* DragDrop method.
LPARAMETERS oDataObject, nEffect, nButton, nShift, ;
            nXCoord, nYCoord

#INCLUDE FOXPRO.H

LOCAL lHasFiles, FileArray[1]

IF oDataObject.GetFormat(CF_FILES)
   lHasFiles = oDataObject.GetData(CF_FILES, @FileArray)
   This.Value = FileToStr(FileArray[1])
ENDIF
```

See Also CreateBinary(), DataObject, GetFormat, OLE drag and drop, OLEDragDrop, OLESetData, OLEStartDrag, SetFormat

Click, RightClick, MiddleClick, DblClick

These events let you do something when the user clicks or double-clicks on an object. They also fire under a bunch of other circumstances. The Click method is likely to contain code more often than almost any other, especially for button objects.

Usage

```
PROCEDURE oObject.Click | oObject.RightClick
         | oObject.MiddleClick | oObject.DblClick
[ LPARAMETERS nIndex ]
```

The nIndex parameter is relevant only when working with control arrays, an occurrence we consider unlikely in most cases.

Although the names of these events are quite explicit, in fact, both Click and DblClick are fired by quite a number of occurrences other than the ones their names imply. Check Help for a complete list of things that fire Click and DblClick.

Basically, Click is fired by a mouse click on an object or by anything that's equivalent to that mouse click. So, for example, choosing a Default button on a form by pressing Enter fires that button's Click. So does pressing Spacebar on a button or check box. As for DblClick, it's the same idea—it's fired by double-clicks and by anything that's equivalent to a double-click from the control's point of view.

Since we can distinguish between mouse actions and keyboard actions with events like KeyPress and MouseDown, we're generally happy about the overloading of Click and DblClick. It would be a pain to have to call a button's Click method from some other method every time the user chose a button by pressing Spacebar or Enter.

One firing sequence is strange enough to warrant comment. In a list, using the arrow keys to move through the data fires both the When and Click events for the list. However, moving with the PgUp, PgDn, Home or End keys fires only the When.

It's nearly impossible to get a grid's Click to fire—normally the mouse events are routed to the headers or the controls in the grid. To get the grid's mouse events to fire, you have to click in an area on the inside of the grid that's unoccupied by a record—that is, below the last record or to the right of the last column.

In VFP 6 and VFP 5, clicking on the current page of a page frame in an area containing no control fires just the page's Click, while clicking on the tab of a page sometimes fires first the page frame's Click, then the form's Click, and finally the page's Click. In VFP 3, the sequence is the same, except that, in the second case, the form's Click doesn't fire. We can't see any reason why the form's Click fires in the later versions.

Clicking the mouse is not a single event. Before Click fires, both MouseDown and MouseUp fire. You can prevent Click events from occurring by putting NoDefault in MouseUp.

Putting NoDefault in MouseUp doesn't prevent the click events in Grids or Headers. We see different behavior in different versions as to what events NoDefault prevents in what controls. On the whole, we think a NoDefault in either MouseUp or MouseDown should prevent all the click events from firing in every control, and we're sure not seeing that.

If you want to be sure you're suppressing a particular click event, test your specific case.

RightClick is important mostly for attaching context menus (also known as shortcut menus or right-click menus) to objects.

MiddleClick was added in VFP 5 to accommodate three-button mouses (mice? rodents?). The introduction of Microsoft's IntelliMouse gave us a chance to test this one out—the mouse wheel can be pressed to produce a middle-click.

The wheel goes down, the wheel goes up and presto! The MouseUp and MiddleClick events fire. But what about MouseDown? No such luck. We can't get MouseDown to work for the middle button.

In general, it's best not to assume that your users have a middle-button-capable device unless you're coding for a very small, well-known audience. (Of course, in general, it's not a good idea to assume that users have a mouse. We've both had the experience of working on a machine with a dead mouse. The best applications let us work anyway.)

Example

```
* Typical Click code processes the user's action
* A command button labeled Save might have:
ThisForm.SaveRecord()
```

See Also Define Class, Mouse, MouseDown, MouseUp, MouseWheel, _DblClick

ClipControls

This property controls how Visual FoxPro redraws the form and its contents when controls moving around or appearing and disappearing cause new areas to be exposed, or when Refresh or another event causes Paint to fire—this could happen by changing the size of a control, moving it, or changing the Z-order to move controls around from front to back.

Usage
```
oObject.ClipControls = lSlowerVideo
lSlowerVideo = oObject.ClipControls
```

Parameter	Value	Meaning
lSlowerVideo	.T.	The form is repainted in a slower, more reliable mode, where all objects are fully repainted. This is the default.
	.F.	Screen objects revealed are repainted quickly, redrawing only those portions of the object newly revealed.

In highly unscientific tests here at Hacker Labs, consuming most of an otherwise perfectly fine summer afternoon, we were not able to see any significant difference in the speed of repainting text-based controls, graphics drawn with the graphics methods, graphic controls, or just about anything else we could throw on a form. We suspect that may be due to the blazingly fast hardware we were running on, where everything is just too blindingly fast to matter (NOT!). You ought to do your own testing on your own platforms if object redraw seems too slow.

Example
```
frmForm.ClipControls = .T.
```

See Also Box, Circle, Line, Move, Paint, Resize, ZOrder

_ClipText

This is a very cool system variable. It contains the contents of the clipboard. What makes it cool is that you can give it a new value, and doing so puts that value on the clipboard.

Usage
```
_CLIPTEXT = cExpr
cExpr = _CLIPTEXT
```

In Visual FoxPro for Windows (and FoxPro 2.x for Windows), FoxPro shares the Windows text clipboard. So, not only can you stuff strings into the clipboard to paste into your FoxPro app, you can stuff the clipboard in FoxPro and access that information in other Windows apps. You can also put information in the clipboard in other applications (like CharMap, to get those weird symbol characters) and access it through _CLIPTEXT in FoxPro applications.

Far more sophisticated use of the clipboard to pass data and more complex structures can be accomplished using the functions exposed in FoxTools or by using an Automation server's DataToClip() method. See those sections for details.

You can't put memo data directly into _CLIPTEXT, but apply any character function to it and you're in business. TRIM() usually does the trick.

Example
```
* Stuff the clipboard with the date
_CLIPTEXT = DTOC(DATE())
* Now you can insert the date by pressing CTRL+V

* Search a help DBF for the text copied by the user
SET TOPIC TO _CLIPTEXT
HELP
```

See Also DataToClip, FoxTools

CloneObject

This cool method lets you create an exact (well, almost exact) duplicate of an object. The only difference between the two is the name you assign the new one. The only bad thing we have to say about CloneObject is that it's available only at design time—we can think of all kinds of cool things we could do with it at runtime.

Usage
```
oObject.CloneObject( cNewName )
```

The newly cloned object becomes a member of the same container the original object is in. That is, if you clone a label on a form, the new label is added to the same form.

All the properties and methods of the original are copied to the clone.

Example
```
* Assume the Form Designer is open and a single object (that
* sits right on the form) is selected.
= ASELOBJ(aObject)      && Get a reference to the selected object
= ASELOBJ(oContainer, 1)      && Get a reference to the form
aObject[1].CloneObject( "NewOne" )
* Now we can reference it through the container
? oContainer[1].NewOne.Name  && Returns "NewOne"
```

See Also AddObject, AddProperty, ASelObj()

Closable, Movable

For a form, these two properties determine whether the control menu contains entries for Close and Move. Without those entries, the user can't close the form by double-clicking in the corner and can't grab the form and move it. In Windows 95 and NT, setting Closable to .F. also causes the close ("X") button in the upper-right corner to be disabled.

Movable also applies to grid columns and toolbars, and determines whether the user can move them around.

Usage
```
frmForm.Closable = lIsClosable
lIsClosable = frmForm.Closable
oObject.Movable = lIsMovable
lIsMovable = oObject.Movable
```

In VFP 3 and VFP 5, Closable and Movable both need to be .F. (as do a bunch of other items) in order to generate a form that has no border. See BorderStyle for the complete list. (In VFP 6, TitleBar offers a faster way.)

Movable controls only whether the user can move the object with the mouse. The object's position can be changed in code regardless of the setting of Movable.

In a grid, if some columns are Movable and others aren't, moving the ones that can be moved may have the effect of moving the columns that are supposedly immovable objects. Guess this constitutes an irresistible force.

If a toolbar's Movable property is set to .F., the only way to dock and undock it is to double-click it. Frankly, we can't think of any reasons you'd ever want a toolbar to be immovable.

Example
```
ThisForm.Closable = .F.
ThisForm.Grid1.Column1.Movable = .F.
```

See Also BorderStyle, ControlBox, MaxButton, MinButton, Sizable, TitleBar

Close All

CLOSE ALL is a kitchen sink command. It closes databases, tables and their indexes, and any files opened via the low-level file functions. It also closes certain system windows, but not user-defined windows. It closes alternate files, format files, procedure files and class libraries. Basically, it does everything the individual CLOSE commands do, plus a little more.

Usage `CLOSE ALL`

Example
```
USE MyTable IN 0
OPEN DATA TasTrade
CLOSE ALL
```

See Also Close Alternate, Close Databases, Close Format, Close Indexes, Close Procedure, Close Tables, Deactivate Window, Release Classlib, Use

Close Alternate

CLOSE ALTERNATE combines SET ALTERNATE OFF and SET ALTERNATE TO into a single command.

Usage `CLOSE ALTERNATE`

Example
```
SET ALTERNATE TO Test.TXT
SET ALTERNATE ON
USE Employee
DISPLAY NEXT 5
CLOSE ALTERNATE
```

See Also Set Alternate

Close Databases See Open Database.

Close Debugger See Debug.

Close Format

This version of CLOSE closes an open format file.

Usage `CLOSE FORMAT`

See Also Set Format

Close Indexes

They ought to call this one "Close Most Indexes." It closes stand-alone and non-structural compound indexes for the table in the current work area, but fortunately has no effect on the structural index file.

Usage `CLOSE INDEXES`

This command is pretty much obsolete since you should rarely, if ever, use any index files other than the structural index file.

See Also Set Index, Use

Close Memo See Modify Memo.

Close Printer See Access().

Close Procedure

This is an alternative way to close open procedure files. It does exactly the same thing as SET PROCEDURE TO without a filename.

Usage `CLOSE PROCEDURE`

See Also Release Procedure, Set Procedure

Close Tables

This command closes open tables. Big surprise. Except that sometimes it closes free tables and sometimes it doesn't.

Usage `CLOSE TABLES [ ALL ]`

When a database is current, CLOSE TABLES closes all the open tables that belong to that database. With no current database, CLOSE TABLES closes all free tables. Add ALL to close all open tables, regardless of the current state of affairs or the origins of the tables. As with CLOSE DATABASES, work area 1 is selected.

From the point of view of this command (and pretty much everywhere else), views are considered tables in the database that owns them, while cursors created with SELECT or CREATE CURSOR are free tables.

Example

```
OPEN DATA TasTrade
USE Customer IN 0
USE Employee IN 0
USE Orders IN 0

* Now one that's not in the database
USE FoxUser
* Now one from another database
USE TestData!Customer

SET DATABASE TO TasTrade
CLOSE TABLES      && Closes all tables from TasTrade
CLOSE TABLES ALL  && Closes FoxUser and TestData!Customer.
                  && Both TasTrade and TestData are left open.
```

See Also Close Databases, Open Database, Use

CloseTables See OpenTables.

Cls See Box.

CLSID

The CLSID (read "class ID") of a Server object is that ugly string of letters and numbers inside squiggly braces that OLE seems to love.

Usage `cClassID = oObject.CLSID`

The Class ID is the "magic number" that distinguishes your OLE class definition from all others. This 16-byte number is (like all geeks, we can't resist saying this) "unique across space and time" due to the GUID (Globally Unique IDentifier) algorithm used to generate it. Most introductory books on COM, ActiveX or OLE (whatever it's called this week) can give you a good introduction to GUIDs.

So who cares? Well, the ID of your class becomes the link through which all other programs locate the information they need to know about your class in the Registry. The object's class ID is registered on the target machine when you install your ActiveX control or server on that machine; you need to use the CLSID to go spelunking through the Registry while troubleshooting. VFP displays this number as a string, with each byte expressed in hexadecimal format.

You'll see a second CLSID in this context—the unique identifier for the type library, rather non-polymorphically referred to within VFP as the TypeLibCLSID. While similar in format, it serves a different purpose. Check the Reference section for that one for more details.

Example

```
MODIFY PROJECT SYS2335 NOWAIT  && one of Ted's test projects
oProject = _VFP.ActiveProject
? oProject.Servers.Count  && displays the servers available, 1
oProject.Servers[1].CLSID  && display the Class ID for it
* In this case, {6F2ED0B5-087E-11D2-AD72-00C04FA30529}
* Let us know if one of your servers has the same CLSID
```

See Also Project, Server, Servers, TypeLibCLSID

CMonth() See CDoW().

CntBar(), CntPad() See BarCount().

CodePage

This property contains the codepage assigned to a file.

Usage

```
nCodePage = filFile.CodePage
```

The codepage associated with a file indicates its underlying character set. This property lets you find out which one it is.

You can't set a file's codepage by changing this property, which sort of makes sense to us, because the project doesn't own the file. The same file might be part of dozens of projects and must have the same codepage regardless of project. If you want to set a file's codepage, check out COPY TO. On the other hand, you can change the codepage of files other than DBFs through the Project Manager interface, and the same arguments apply there. So we're confused about the disparity.

Example

```
? oProj.Files[3].CodePage
```

See Also Copy To, CPDBF(), CPCurrent(), File, Project

Col() See Row().

ColorScheme

This control property is provided mostly to aid in converting screens where the objects have color schemes assigned to them. It works only sporadically.

Usage

```
oObject.ColorScheme = nColorScheme
nColorScheme = oObject.ColorScheme
```

The old FoxPro/DOS coloring system includes 24 color schemes in each color set. Each scheme is meant to handle a different aspect of the interface. For details on this, see Create Color Set.

This property, together with ColorSource, is meant to let you apply those color schemes to controls in your forms. But it only works when it feels like it. First, you have to set ColorSource to 2 before FoxPro pays any attention at all to ColorScheme—that's documented. (In VFP 6, only the ColorSource Help has this information; the ColorScheme help says, in essence, "don't do that.")

Not only that, but if BackColor or ForeColor is changed for the object, it totally ignores the ColorScheme you've set and uses those colors.

We suggest you stay away from this property except in converted 2.x screen sets.

Example `This.ColorScheme = 3`

See Also BackColor, ColorSource, Create Color Set, ForeColor

ColorSource

This property lets you tell a control where to find the colors it uses. It combines a lot of backward-compatibility options with two choices that are the ones you should use almost all the time.

Usage
```
oObject.ColorSource = nColorSource
nColorSource = oObject.ColorSource
```

Parameter	Value	Meaning
nColorSource	0	Use the colors specified in the object's various color properties (ForeColor, BackColor, etc.).
	1	Use the color scheme used by the form containing the control. Because you can't control which color scheme the form uses, it's always scheme 1.
	2	Use the color scheme specified in the object's ColorScheme property.
	3	Use the default color scheme for this object based on the color set/color scheme system of coloring.
	4	Use the 3-D settings from the Windows Control Panel. This is the right choice for dialogs.
	5	Use the Window setting from the Windows Control Panel. This is the right choice for data-entry forms.

Until the last two options (nColorSource = 4 or 5) were added in VFP 5, this property could be relegated to backward compatibility. Options 1, 2 and 3 are all related to the complex color-scheme system created for FoxPro/DOS. If you need to figure this out, see Create Color Set.

Option 0 seems redundant to us because, regardless of the setting of ColorSource, if you change BackColor and ForeColor from their defaults, the colors you specify are used.

The really helpful choices here are 4 and 5. They tell a control or form to go to the Windows Control Panel (where the user gets to set colors for her entire system) and find out what the user has chosen and apply it here. Setting ColorSource to 4 says that the form we're on is a dialog and should use the settings for 3-D objects. ColorSource = 5 means the form is a document and should use the "window" colors. In Windows default color schemes, the main difference between those two is that dialogs have a gray background while documents have a white background. (We think it's ironic, at the least, that now that most users have color monitors, the industry trend is to use less color in applications.) Choose the right settings for your forms and they'll obey the user—very cool! This is one of the ways you let your user feel that your application is responsive.

Example `This.ColorSource = 5  && it's a data entry form`

See Also BackColor, ColorScheme, Create Color Set, ForeColor, Set Color Of Scheme, Set Color Set

Column **See Grid.**

ColumnCount **See Columns.**

ColumnLines

At last! Simple vertical lines between columns in a ListBox or ComboBox!

Usage

```
oObject.ColumnLines = lShowLines
lShowLines = oObject.ColumnLines
```

Years ago, we spent quite a bit of time, as did nearly everyone else, trying to find ways to simulate multiple columns in list boxes. Visual FoxPro makes it easy! ColumnLines allows us to determine whether or not vertical lines appear between the columns. By default it is set .T. to show lines. In order to have your lines appear as single solid lines running down the list or combo, you'll need to change the control's font to a fixed-width font (bleh!—lousy idea, and leads to a nonstandard, awkward interface) or diddle with the ColumnWidths property.

Column lines are an all-or-nothing deal. You have them either between every column or no columns. You can't specify which ones you want.

Example

```
lboListBox.ColumnLines = .T.
```

See Also ColumnCount, ColumnWidths, ComboBox, ListBox

ColumnOrder, PageOrder

These properties determine the position of columns in a grid and pages in a page frame, respectively. They affect the display, but not the underlying structure. They also affect some other properties, leading to a total mishmash for accessing individual columns or pages.

Usage

```
colColumn.ColumnOrder = nWhatPosition
nWhatPosition = colColumn.ColumnOrder
pagPage.PageOrder = nWhatPosition
nWhatPosition = pagPage.PageOrder
```

Regardless of the ColumnOrder or PageOrder you specify, the drop-down list in the Property Sheet and the appropriate collection property (Columns or Pages) show the columns or pages in their original creation order.

But other properties reflect the current order. When you reduce the number of columns or pages, the ones discarded are the ones with the highest ColumnOrder or PageOrder. ActiveColumn and ActivePage are also based on the current ordering, not the underlying order.

This last business is a real problem, since this means you can't use ActiveColumn or ActivePage as an index into Columns or Pages. The only way (other than using This) to get a handle on the active page or column is to use brute force to loop through the pages or columns to match the active one. What would be really nice here is a dual structure like the one used for lists and combos that gives you access both by creation order and by current display order.

When you change the order of one page or column, others may change as well. Oddly, the way they change differs. For pages, the new PageOrder must be between 1 and PageCount. (Actually, 0 is accepted, but it's treated just like 1.) The pages between the new position and the end all get pushed to the right.

Columns are different. First, the property sheet has a unique way of rejecting values out of bounds. If you type a value that's not between 1 and ColumnCount, it's summarily rejected and replaced with the column's current ColumnOrder. At runtime, values out of range are simply ignored, as if you didn't even issue the command. When you change ColumnOrder to something acceptable, that column and the one that already had the specified ColumnOrder change places. That is, if you take the column with ColumnOrder=4 and change its ColumnOrder to 7, it becomes the seventh column (visually), and the column that was seventh moves to fourth. What this means is that it's a heckuva lot easier to rearrange the columns with your mouse than by manipulating ColumnOrder.

Example

```
ThisForm.grdEmployee.colFirstName.ColumnOrder = 1
```

See Also ActiveColumn, ActivePage, Column, Columns, Grid, Page, Page frame, Pages

Columns, ColumnCount

These properties provide access to the columns in a grid. ColumnCount tells how many there are and Columns lets you actually touch the individual columns.

ColumnCount also applies to combo boxes and list boxes, where it tells how many columns are displayed in the list or combo, but lists and combos don't have a matching Columns collection. (Use the List or ListItem collection instead.)

Usage

```
colColumn = grdGrid.Columns( nColumnNumber )
oObject.ColumnCount = nNumberOfColumns
nNumberOfColumns = oObject.ColumnCount
```

Lists and combos with a RowSourceType of 8-Structure sort of ignore the setting of ColumnCount because there's only one column's worth of information to display. They show the structure data in the first column and leave any other columns empty.

On the other hand, lists and combos with a RowSourceType of 7-Files should ignore ColumnCount and don't. With ColumnCount more than 1, you end up with multiple, identical columns. Be sure to set ColumnCount to 1 or the default, 0, if you use this RowSourceType. (Of course, there are better ways to let the user choose a file, including the Common Dialogs control, so we sure don't plan to use a lot of lists and combos with RowSourceType = 7.)

The default of 0 for combos and list boxes seems to be the same as specifying 1. For grids, the default of -1 is smart—it includes all fields of the table.

As in FoxPro 2.x, getting columns in a multi-column list box or combo box to line up isn't automatic. However, it's much easier in Visual FoxPro. Set the ColumnWidths property appropriately.

The Columns collection lets you access the columns of a grid without knowing their names. Be aware that the order in Columns is creation order, not the display order reflected by the ColumnOrder property.

Example

```
* Set up a multi-column list box. Assume we're in the
* Init of the list.
This.ColumnCount = 3
This.ColumnWidths = "100,100,100"
This.RowSourceType = 2  && Alias
This.RowSource = "Customer"
```

See Also ColumnOrder, ColumnWidths, List, ListItem, RowSource, RowSourceType

ColumnWidths

The ColumnWidths property allows you to specify the widths of each column in a ComboBox or ListBox to force the columns to line up, even when using proportional fonts.

Usage

```
lboListBox.ColumnWidths = cWidthsExpr
cWidthsExpr = lboListBox.ColumnWidths
```

By default, each row in a list box or combo box has a width based on the contents and the font in which they're rendered—a visual disaster, as shown in Figure 4-3. Adding the setting of ColumnWidths brings these rogue columns under control, as in the right-hand part of the figure.

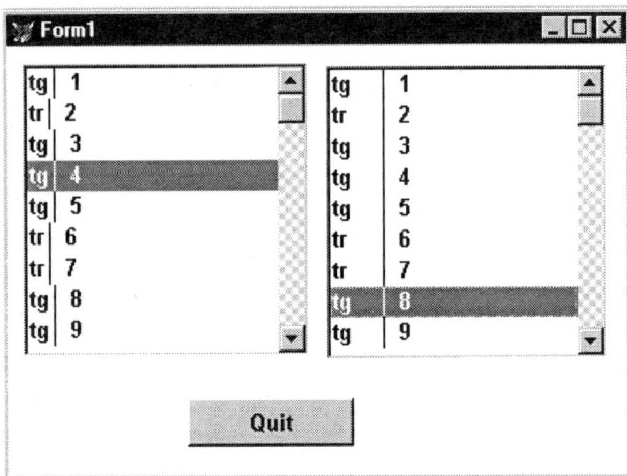

Figure 4-3: ListBoxes without and with the ColumnWidths property set.

Specify ColumnWidths as a character string containing a comma-delimited list of the widths of each column, in the current ScaleMode of the form, as in the example shown below. To calculate these widths, consider using TxtWidth() and FontMetric() to get the values you need.

In VFP 6, ColumnWidths doesn't work if the form's ScaleMode has been set to 3-Foxels. All columns get set to the width of the first column, whether you set this in the property sheet or in code.We generally think that using foxels is a bad idea, as the geometry of the form depends on a font that may not even be used, so you shouldn't run into this one very often.

The individual column widths may be separated by spaces for ease in reading, or packed tight if that is your preferred style—Visual FoxPro seems to read either with ease. If you want to leave your last column to take up as much space as it needs—say, for free-form text descriptions, just don't specify the last column width, and it will display all data in that column.

Example
```
lstListBox.ColumnWidths = "40, 20, 60, 80"
```

See Also ColumnCount, ComboBox, FontMetric(), ListBox, ScaleMode, TxtWidth()

COMArray()

This function controls how arrays are passed to COM objects. FoxPro's internal array handling is funky enough, but we have to support even more variations to successfully communicate with COM objects. This function lets us get there.

Usage
```
nCurrentType = COMArray( oObject [, nArrayType ] )
```

Parameter	Value	Meaning
oObject	**Object**	A reference to an object whose array-passing behavior you want to query or set.
nArrayType	Omitted	Returns the current setting for passing arrays for this object.
	0	Pass a zero-based array by value.
	1	Pass a one-based array by value. This is the default and the backward-compatible setting.

Parameter	Value	Meaning
nArrayType	10	Pass a zero-based array by reference.
	11	Pass a one-based array by reference.
nCurrentType	Integer	If nArrayType is omitted, contains the current setting for the specified object. If nArrayType is passed, contains that value. (That's because, by then, it is the current setting.)

In "Pass the Parameters, Please" in "Wow, What a Concept!" we talk about the trickiness involved in passing arrays from one FoxPro routine to another. The trick to remember is that UDFPARMS is set to Value (and that's a Good Thing), so to send an entire array to a function you need to precede the array name with an @ to pass it by reference.

It gets trickier when passing arrays out from FoxPro to a COM object. There are two separate gotchas involved, each addressed by this function. First, a COM object might expect things to be passed either by value or by reference. Second, the COM object might enumerate arrays by counting from 1, the way we humans do it, or by starting at 0, which is a little more efficient from the computer's view of things, though confusing as all get out to us.

You need to know which format the object is looking for, and set the settings here. There doesn't seem to be a way to sniff this out in advance. From what we've been able to tell with FoxPro acting as both client and recipient, Fox seems to be unaffected by this setting. But if your OLE server is from another source—say, VB, VC++ or Delphi—check with the vendor of the component for the right way to set this one.

Example

```
oDear = CreateObject("TestServer.cusServer")
? COMArray(oDear)        && returns the default 1
? COMArray(oDear,0)      && displays 0
? COMArray(oDear)        && still displays 0
? COMArray(oDear,10)     && now it says 10
? COMArray(oDear,11)     && and now 11
```

See Also Set UDFParms

ComboBox, ListBox

These two controls let a user choose one item from a specified, generally scrollable, list. In addition, combo boxes can be configured to let the user enter a new item as well (hence the name combo—it's a combination of a text box and a drop-down). List boxes, not to be outdone, optionally support multiple selection. Both controls have far more in common than different, though.

These are incredibly versatile, powerful controls, far more than the 2.x equivalents, the drop-down and the scrollable list. Some days, we might even argue that combos and lists are more powerful than grids.

Property	Value	Purpose
BoundTo	Logical	Determines whether a numeric Value indicates the row to highlight or the numeric data to highlight.
ColumnCount	Numeric	The number of columns displayed in a list or in the drop-down portion of a combo.
ColumnLines	Logical	Determines whether the lines between columns are visible.

Property	Value	Purpose
ColumnWidths	Character	A comma-delimited list of the widths for the columns. Required with proportional fonts to make straight columns.
DisabledItemBackColor, DisabledItemForeColor	Numeric	The colors used to represent disabled items in the list or combo.
DisplayCount	Numeric	Combo only. Determines how many items are displayed when you drop the combo open.
DisplayValue	Character or Numeric	Determines which item in a combo is displayed when the combo is closed (and displays first on the list when it opens). Contains text typed in by the user in a drop-down combo. For lists, indicates which item is highlighted.
FirstElement, NumberOfElements	Numeric	Determine which column of an array is displayed (one-column list or combo only) and which rows of the array are included.
IncrementalSearch	Logical	Determines whether the list or combo uses FoxPro's smart incremental search technique or Windows (3.1's) dumb one.
ItemBackColor, ItemForeColor	Numeric	The colors used for the items in the list or combo. For a combo, affects only the drop-down portion.
ItemData, ItemIdData	Array containing numeric	Can contain numeric data matched to the items in a list or combo.
List, ListItem	Array containing character	Contain the actual data from the list or combo.
ListCount	Numeric	The number of items in the list or combo.
ListIndex, ListItemId	Numeric	The position of the currently selected item in the list or combo.
MoverBars	Logical	List only. Determines whether the list has mover buttons that let the user reorganize the items.
MultiSelect	Logical	List only. Determines whether multiple items can be selected at the same time.
NewIndex, NewItemId	Numeric	The position of the most recently added item in the list or combo.
RowSource	Character	The data in the list or combo, or a pointer to it. RowSourceType determines the actual meaning.
RowSourceType	Numeric	The form of the data. Determines the interpretation of RowSource.
Selected, SelectedId	Array containing logical	Indicates, for each item, whether it's currently highlighted.

Property	Value	Purpose
SelectedItemBackColor, SelectedItemForeColor	Numeric	The colors used for highlighted items.
SelLength, SelStart	Numeric	Combo only. The length and starting position of highlighted text in the text box portion of the combo.
SelText	Character	Combo only. The highlighted text in the text box portion of the combo.
Sorted	Logical	Determines whether the items in the list or combo are sorted alphabetically.
Style	Numeric	Combo only. Specifies either combo box or drop-down list box.
TopIndex, TopItemId	Numeric	The position of the first item displayed in the list or combo.

Event	Purpose
DownClick	Supposed to fire when user clicks the down arrow on the scrollbar. Doesn't fire for lists, only for combos.
DropDown	Fires after user clicks down arrow to open combo, but before combo opens. (In early versions, fired late.)
InteractiveChange	Fires each time the user moves in the list. Also fires for each character the user types.
ProgrammaticChange	Fires when DisplayValue or Value is changed via code.
UpClick	Supposed to fire when user clicks the up arrow on the scrollbar. Doesn't fire for lists, only for combos.
When	In a combo, fires when focus is headed for the combo. In a list, fires whenever the list highlight moves.
Valid	In a combo, fires whenever the user closes the combo (except with ESC) or, in a drop-down list, when the user types enough to choose a value. In a list, fires when the user leaves.

Method	Purpose
AddItem, AddListItem	Add a new item to the list or combo.
Clear	Remove all items from the list or combo.
IndexToItemId, ItemIdToIndex	Convert between the two numbering schemes for items.
RemoveItem, RemoveListItem	Remove an item from the list or combo.

Method	Purpose
Requery	Refresh the list or combo to include the latest data from the RowSource.

You've probably noticed that many of the properties and methods come in pairs. This is because there are two ways to address each item in a list or combo. The "Index" properties address items by their current position in the list. The "ItemId" properties address the items by a unique, permanent ID number assigned when the item is added to the list. See ListIndex for more on this.

The behavior of lists and combos with numeric data confuses people. (Actually, it was confusing in FoxPro 2.x, too.) The key point is that, even when we think we're seeing numbers in a combo or list, we're actually seeing characters. Combos and lists cannot show numeric data. If you specify a RowSource that's numeric, FoxPro internally converts the data to character before displaying it.

The Value of a list or combo (and, therefore, the ControlSource it's bound to) can be either character or numeric. If the Value is character, it contains the text of the currently highlighted item. If the Value is numeric, by default it contains the index of that item. Before VFP 5, there was no way to get numeric data out of a list or combo. The BoundTo property lets you tell VFP to convert a numeric character string to a number before sticking it into Value or DisplayValue.

Example

```
* This code creates a subclass of ListBox
* that is, by default, based on an array called aItems
* that is a property of the list itself.
* The list is multi-select and displays
* a message whenever an item is highlighted.
DEFINE ArrayList AS ListBox

  DIMENSION aItems[1]

  RowSourceType = 5
  RowSource = "This.aItems"
  MultiSelect = .T.

  PROCEDURE InteractiveChange

  WAIT WINDOW "Got one!"

  ENDPROC
ENDDEFINE
```

See Also AddItem, AddListItem, BoundTo, Clear, ColumnCount, ColumnLines, ColumnWidths, DisabledItemBackColor, DisabledItemForeColor, DisplayCount, DisplayValue, DownClick, DropDown, FirstElement, IncrementalSearch, IndexToItemId, InteractiveChange, ItemBackColor, ItemData, ItemForeColor, ItemIdData, ItemIdToIndex, List, ListCount, ListIndex, ListItem, ListItemId, MoverBars, MultiSelect, NewIndex, NewItemId, NumberOfElements, RemoveItem, RemoveListItem, Requery, RowSource, RowSourceType, Selected, SelectedId, SelectedItemBackColor, SelectedItemForeColor, SelLength, SelStart, SelText, Sorted, Style, TopIndex, TopItemId, UpClick, Valid

COMClassInfo()

This function returns information on OLE or COM classes.

Usage

```
cRetVal = COMClassInfo( oObject [ , nInfoType ] )
```

Parameter	Value	Meaning
oObject	Object	The object to report on.
nInfoType	Omitted or 1	Return the object's ProgID.
	2	Return the object's VersionIndependentProgID.
	3	Return the object's friendly name.
	4	Return the object's CLSID.
cRetVal	Character	The value requested above.
	Empty string	The object specified was not a COM or OLE object.

This function lets you explore some of the properties of a COM object handed to you. We expect to use this function mainly in black-box routines that need to work with what they are passed.

Example

```
oGraph = CREATEOBJECT("MSGraph.Application")
* Determine which version is installed:
? COMClassInfo(oGraph,1)  && "MSGraph.Application.8"
* Grab the friendly name, perhaps to use as a caption
lcCaption = COMClassInfo(oGraph,3)
? lcCaption  && "Microsoft Graph 97 Application"
```

See Also VarType()

CommandButton, CommandGroup

Command buttons are what we used to call "push buttons" in FoxPro 2.x. Normally, they make something happen. Perhaps the most common command buttons are the ones labeled "OK" and "Cancel" that appear in dozens of dialogs throughout Windows.

In Visual FoxPro, command buttons can be used both singly and in groups. CommandGroups have a Value property that indicates which button in the group was last chosen. The Value can be either character or numeric. When character, it contains the Caption of the button last chosen. When numeric, it's the position of that button in the group.

Command buttons can contain text or a bitmap or both. In addition, command buttons can be invisible. Of course, in that case, the bitmap and the caption don't do you much good. Invisible buttons are one way to put a "hot spot" on a form. A command group can contain any combination of textual, graphical and invisible buttons.

CommandButton

Property	Value	Purpose
AutoSize	Logical	Should this button be resized automatically to fit the caption?
Cancel	Logical	Should this button be chosen when the Esc key is pressed?
Caption	Character	The message that appears on the button.
Default	Logical	Should this be the default button, chosen by pressing Enter?
Picture, DownPicture,	Character	The names (including path) of graphic files to appear on the

Property	Value	Purpose
DisabledPicture		button. Picture appears when the button is enabled and not pressed. DownPicture appears when the button is pressed. DisabledPicture appears when the button is disabled.
Style	Numeric	Determines whether the button is visible (0) or invisible (1).
Event	**Purpose**	
Click	Fires when the button is "pressed," using either the mouse or the keyboard.	

CommandGroup

Property	Value	Purpose
AutoSize	Logical	Should the group be resized to completely contain all of its buttons?
BackStyle	Numeric	Should the group let objects behind it show through or not? Objects behind the buttons themselves do not show through regardless, unless the button's Style is set to invisible.
BorderColor	Numeric	Color used for the border around the group.
BorderStyle	Numeric	Determines whether or not there is a border around the group.
ButtonCount	Numeric	The number of buttons in the group.
Buttons	Collection	References to the buttons in the group.
TabIndex	Numeric	The tab order of the button within the group.
Value	Numeric or Character	Which button in the group was chosen last?
Event	**Purpose**	
Click	Fires when a button in the group is "pressed," and doesn't have any Click code of its own.	
InteractiveChange	Fires when any button in the group is chosen because the group's Value changes.	

The relationship between a command group and the buttons in it is different than most of the container/contained object relationships in FoxPro. Normally, if an object doesn't have code in a particular event anywhere in its class hierarchy, no code runs when that event fires. For command buttons in a command group (and option buttons in an option group), 'tain't so. If a button has no Click code, for example, the group's Click code executes. If the button doesn't have anything in MouseDown, the group's MouseDown fires. Pretty cool. In fact, this is what control arrays were supposed to be all about.

However, for properties, the behavior propagates downward, but not the property values. That is, setting Enabled to .F. for a control group disables all the buttons in the group, but they're not dimmed and their individual Enabled properties remain .T. We've got mixed feelings on this one. We can see why it's nice to maintain the individual values—when you re-enable the group, it's good that buttons that were disabled before are still disabled. But the lack of a visual cue means we can't take advantage of this behavior. (Our assiduous tech editor points out that in VFP 6, you can use an Assign method for the group's Enabled to change the Enabled property of the individual buttons in the group. This does raise the issue of remembering what was enabled before the change to the group.)

Since command buttons have a separate existence, there's no problem subclassing them visually. However, there's no way visually to tell a subclass of CommandGroup to use your CommandButton subclass.

Like OptionButtons and OptionGroups, the interaction between the AutoSize properties of CommandButtons and CommandGroups is strange. You can have autosized buttons inside a non-autosized group with the result that the group's border clips the button itself.

Example

```
* Perhaps the most common button of all.
* Of course, we'd do this in the Class Designer.
DEFINE CLASS CloseButton AS CommandButton

   Caption = "\<Close"
   ToolTipText = "Close this form"

   PROCEDURE Click
      IF EMPTY(ThisForm.PARENT)  && a standalone form
         ThisForm.Release()
      ELSE
         ThisFormSet.Release()   && a formset
      ENDIF
   ENDPROC
ENDDEFINE
```

See Also AutoSize, BackStyle, BorderColor, BorderStyle, ButtonCount, Buttons, Cancel, Caption, Click, Default, DisabledPicture, DownPicture, InteractiveChange, OptionButton, OptionGroup, Picture, ProgrammaticChange, Style, TabIndex, Value

CommandTargetQuery, CommandTargetExec

These two events are the primary communication channels between an active document and its host (browser). CommandTargetQuery lets the active document tell the host what commands it's interested in. CommandTargetExec fires when the user does something in the host that the active doc might want to respond to.

Usage

```
PROCEDURE acdActiveDoc.CommandTargetQuery
LPARAMETERS aCommands, nCommandTextFlag, cCommandTextOut

PROCEDURE acdActiveDoc.CommandTargetExec
LPARAMETERS nCommandID, nExecOption, uArgIn, uArgOut
```

Parameter	Value	Meaning
aCommands	Array	A two-column array listing the commands (using a set of numeric values documented in the Help for CommandTargetExec) that the host thinks might happen soon. The active document can fill in the second column to indicate whether or not each command is permitted.
nCommandTextFlag	Numeric	A numeric value indicating what extra information the host wants back from the active document.
cCommandTextOut	Character	A parameter passed by reference to receive the extra information requested.

Parameter	Value	Meaning
nCommandID	Numeric	The command triggered by the user or host to which the active document can respond. The list of values is documented in Help.
nExecOption	Numeric	A value (documented in Help) indicating the normal reaction to the specified command.
uArgIn	Numeric (perhaps other)	An additional value passed with some commands to provide the active document with more information.
uArgOut	Expression	A parameter passed by reference to let the active document return information to the host.

These are two of the most obscure events we've had to decipher. Here's the deal. An active document is a special kind of application designed to let you run a regular VFP app inside a browser. (Don't ask us why you'd want to do that. Okay, do ask. You'll find our thoughts in the ActiveDoc section.)

When you put your application inside a browser, things can happen that your application doesn't know about. Things like the user navigating to a Web site or choosing a menu item from the browser's menu that isn't under the app's control. The Help for CommandTargetExec has a whole list of the kind of things that can happen and, in fact, shows the number assigned to each of those to identify it.

These two events give your app control over what happens when one of those things occurs. When one or more of those actions is possible, CommandTargetQuery fires and lets you decide whether the user should even be allowed to trigger one of those actions. It receives a two-column array as a parameter. The first column contains a list of all the actions that might happen. (For example, when the user clicks the browser's File menu, the array contains the codes for the items located on the File menu.) Code in the active doc fills in the second column to indicate whether the active doc wants the opportunity to respond to this action. Like so many things in VFP, the choices are additive. You can include more than one by adding the values together.

CommandTargetExec can fire when one of the actions actually occurs. Whether it fires or not, though, depends on the choices made in CommandTargetQuery. If the action was enabled, CommandTargetExec fires, giving the active doc the chance to respond, and passing the action code as well as some information about the usual way of handling that action (like whether the user is customarily prompted before proceeding). However, the active doc can treat the action however it wants (including doing something totally unrelated). Then, the active doc returns a value to the host indicating whether or not the action has been taken care of. If the active doc hasn't taken care of it, the host performs the normal default action.

Both of these events have a couple of extra parameters to allow additional data to be passed back and forth. For CommandTargetQuery, the host can request localized information about the command (nCommandTextFlag) and the active doc can return the information in cCommandTextOut, but only for the first action in the array. We thought this might let us customize the status bar text for host menu items when an active doc is running, but it appears that the host ignores the value in cCommandTextOut unless it asked for it. (Actually, since we haven't encountered a case where the host asks, and Help implies we shouldn't expect to any time soon, for all we know, it's always ignored.)

The additional parameters to CommandTargetExec aren't so esoteric. They're simply a mechanism for any of the actions to pass some additional information to the active doc and to get additional information back. For each of them, Help lists only one case where it's used—we confirmed that they behave as expected in those cases.

Example

```
* Running an active doc application in IE 4,
* when IE's File menu is dropped open,
* CommandTargetQuery receives a 6-row array. The
* code here shows how you might respond to a couple
* of those items.
```

```
* This code goes in CommandTargetQuery
FOR n = 1 TO ALEN(aCommands, 1)
   DO CASE
   CASE aCommands[n, 1] = 6 && Print
      aCommands[n, 2] = 2   && Enabled
   CASE aCommands[n, 1] = 4 && SaveAs
      aCommands[n, 2] = 2   && Enabled
   ENDCASE
ENDFOR

* Then suppose we want to subvert the behavior of those
* two actions. Put this code in CommandTargetExec.
* This.oForm is a custom property referencing a form in the app.
* We don't recommend reacting to these menu choices
* like this in real apps, but the Print action could,
* for example, run a report.

DO CASE
CASE nCommandID = 6 && Print
   This.oForm.Caption = "Printed"

CASE nCommandID = 4 && SaveAs
   CLEAR EVENTS

ENDCASE
```

See Also ActiveDoc

Comment, Tag

These two properties are there for you when you need them. Both of them let you store any character string you want and use it however you'd like.

Usage

```
oObject.Comment = cValue
cValue = oObject.Comment
oObject.Tag = cValue
cValue = oObject.Tag
```

Don't let the name Tag fool you. It has nothing to do with indexes. It's a carryover from Visual Basic, where it means a tag like the one you find in your shirt. It's just a place to put identification information.

We've been tempted occasionally to use one of these properties to hold the value of another property temporarily, so we can change it in one method and restore it in another. (Otherwise, we have to add a custom property to the object to hold the value.) We haven't done it because we're concerned that someone else might do the same thing and clobber our saved value. The right way to do this is to preserve whatever values you might find in Tag, and append your value to the end of the Tag. Wrap your values in delimiters that (you hope) no one else would duplicate. This is similar to the method FoxPro uses in its generated RI code.

At design time, both of these properties are limited to 255 characters. However, at runtime they appear to hold unlimited text. (We've tested them up to 100,000 characters, far more than we'd ever be likely to store there.)

Example

```
This.Comment = "This is my whiz-bang fancy spinner sample"

oObject.Tag = oObject.Tag + CHR(13) +"*** Tamar's Add-On ***"+;
              AddOn.Value + "*** EOF Tamar's Add-On ***"+CHR(13)
```

Compile, Set LogErrors, Set("LogErrors")

COMPILE converts your source code into executable object code, checking for errors along the way. SET LOGERRORS determines whether a log file containing the errors is created.

Usage

```
COMPILE FileSkel [ ENCRYPT ] [ NODEBUG ] [ AS nCodePage ]
SET LOGERRORS ON | OFF
lLogOn = SET("LOGERRORS")
```

If you're like us, you'll rarely issue the COMPILE command. Between its being on the menu and the Project Manager's doing it for us, it's pretty rare for either of us to actually type COMPILE in the Command Window. But, once in a while, there's a reason to compile a particular file or a group of files. The ENCRYPT and NODEBUG clauses correspond to the Encrypted and Debug Info check boxes in the Project Information dialog (though the latter is negative in the command and positive in the dialog).

By default, when you compile a program and errors are found, an ERR file is created containing information about the errors. If you SET LOGERRORS OFF, no such file is created. We can't imagine why anyone would ever turn that setting off.

Example

```
COMPILE *.PRG
```

See Also Build App, Build EXE, Build Project, Compile Classlib, Compile Database, Compile Form, Compile Label, Compile Report

Compile Database, Compile Form, Compile ClassLib, Compile Label, Compile Report

These are commands you won't normally need to use. They compile the code stored in a class library, database, form, label or report—an operation that usually happens automatically. However, if you go in and make changes (say, by operating directly on the underlying table), the updated code isn't compiled. In addition, when you move things back and forth between VFP 3 and later versions, they need to be recompiled (though moving from VFP 3 to the later versions generally causes an automatic compile). So these commands let you deal with that kind of situation.

Usage

```
COMPILE DATABASE DBCFileSpec | ?
COMPILE FORM SCXFileSpec | ? [ ALL ]
COMPILE CLASSLIB VCXFileSpec | ?
COMPILE LABEL LBXFileSpec | ?
COMPILE REPORT FRXFileSpec | ?
```

Databases contain code in stored procedures. Forms and class libraries contain code in methods. Reports and labels have code in the methods of their data environments and band events.

All of these commands let you compile a bunch of whichever object at once by specifying a name, including wildcards.

The docs say that COMPILE DATABASE can only handle one database at a time. Not so in VFP 6, though it used to be true.

The keyword ALL in COMPILE FORM says to compile the code for all VFP platforms. If you're in VFP 5 or VFP 6, Windows is all there is, so you're not likely to use ALL much, except in VFP 3. The newer additions to this group of commands (CLASSLIB, LABEL and REPORT) don't reject the ALL keyword, but we have no way of figuring out if they actually do anything.

COMPILE FORM can also be used to compile class libraries. While this is a moot point in VFP 5 and later, it's pretty handy in VFP 3, since COMPILE CLASSLIB doesn't exist there.

A count of the errors found while compiling can be displayed on the status bar. The actual errors are stored in a file of the same name as the object being compiled with an ERR file suffix.

To compile a database, you need to have exclusive access to it. That's not so bad because you'll probably want exclusive access for the kinds of changes that lead to compiling it anyway. Interestingly, you can compile a database whether it's open or closed, as long as you can get exclusive use.

These versions of the COMPILE command don't offer equivalents to the NODEBUG or ENCRYPT options available in a basic COMPILE. Even compiling forms within a project with these options turned on doesn't change the object code. Although we have hardly ever used them, this may cause some heartache for folks with security concerns.

Example

```
USE MyForm.SCX
MODIFY MEMO Methods
* Now change some of the code there and save it
USE
COMPILE FORM MyForm
```

See Also Compile, Create Classlib, Create Form, Create Label, Create Report, Modify Class, Modify Form, Modify Label, Modify Procedure, Modify Report

Completed() See Access().

CompObj()

This function compares two objects and tells you if they're identical. It does not tell you if they're really the same object.

Usage

```
lMatch = COMPOBJ( oObject1, oObject2 )
```

Parameter	Value	Meaning
oObject1	Object	A reference to the first object to be compared.
oObject2	Object	A reference to the second object to be compared.
lMatch	.T.	The two objects have the same list of properties and each property has the same value in the two objects.
	.F.	The two objects do not completely match.

This function confuses people. It takes two object references and compares the objects they point to. If the objects have exactly the same list of properties and the properties all have exactly the same values (the comparison is case-sensitive), the function returns .T.

So what's the problem? Many people want to use COMPOBJ() to see if two object variables point to the same object, but it only tells you if they don't. That is, if COMPOBJ() returns .F., you know you have two different objects, but if it returns .T., you don't know one way or the other. In VFP 6, checking whether two object references refer to the same object is as simple as comparing them with =, but in older versions, it's trickier. The example demonstrates the problem with COMPOBJ(), as well as showing the new and old ways to find out if you have two references to a single object.

Example

```
* Create two forms
o1 = CREATEOBJECT("Form")
o2 = CREATEOBJECT("Form")
? COMPOBJ(o1, o2) && Returns .F. - No surprise since
                  && their captions and names are different
? COMPOBJ(o1, o1) && Returns .T. - Again, no surprise
* make another reference to o1
o3 = o1
? COMPOBJ(o1, o3) && Returns .T. - Good
```

```
* Now watch this
o2.Caption = o1.Caption
o2.Name = o1.Name
? COMPOBJ(o1, o2) && Surprise - Returns .T.

* So how do we find out if they point to the same object.
* In VFP 6, do it like this:
? o1 = o2
* Thanks to Ken Levy for the basic idea here,
* useful in VFP 3 and VFP 5:
cHoldCaption = o1.Caption
o1.Caption = "XXX"
? COMPOBJ(o1, o3) && Still returns .T. - they're the same object
? COMPOBJ(o1, o2) && Returns .F. - they're different objects
o1.Caption = cHoldCaption
```

The trick in the older versions is to change a property of one object. If the other object changes, too, then they're really references to the same object. If the other object doesn't change, they're references to different objects that happen to be identical. This test is a good candidate for a generalized black-box function.

See Also CreateObject(), NewObject()

COMReturnError()

You know those obnoxious error messages you get that say "OLE IDispatch exception code blah, blah, blah?" Well, now you don't just have to be the poor hapless recipient of them—you can create your own and share the fun with others!

Usage `COMReturnError( cServerName, cErrorDescription )`

Parameter	Value	Meaning
cServerName	Character	This string is returned in the error message and should describe your software.
cErrorDescription	Character	This string is returned in the error message after cServerName.

Use this function to generate errors in your custom COM servers. The function works only within COM components, and generates a "Feature not available" error if executed in normal code or from the Command Window. The error generated is always error 1429, and if no error handler is in place, the error is displayed as "OLE IDispatch exception code 0 from *cServerName*: *cErrorDescription.*" If you do have an error handler in place, you can use the AError() function to get more information in order to handle the error appropriately.

AError() returns seven values for an OLE Error 1429, but this command lets us set only two of them. It sure would be nice in a future version if Microsoft would consider letting us set the error code to something other than the suspicious-looking zero. Even better, it would be nice to be able to set *all* of the values.

Error 1429 is documented as returning the sixth element of AError as either character or null. In our tests, it always came back as a numeric 0. If you're writing a generic error handler, look out for these type inconsistencies!

Example `COMError("MyServer","MyErrorGenerator")`

See Also AError(), Error, On Error

Configuration Files

There are a number of configuration files that you can take advantage of to customize Visual FoxPro, either in your development environment or in your users' runtime environments, but sometimes not both. Here we'll review some of the rules and hazards involved in that.

Registry

The Windows registration database is Microsoft's solution to the complaints that thousands of INI files crowd the Windows subdirectory. INI files, as we discuss below, are text files, easily edited by any end user with Notepad. To minimize multiple files, add a little bit of security, and also to allow remote maintenance of these settings, Microsoft has placed everything in the Registry. Unfortunately, we don't think Microsoft went far enough.

The developer environment stores dozens of settings in the Registry, but runtime environments do not, by default, read these same settings. This puts the developer in the situation where she may develop and test an app in an artificial environment that may be different from the user's environment. See "Registration Database" for more details.

Tools-Options dialog

The tabbed dialog available under the Tools-Options menu has a slew of settings for the developer. This is an easy, and safe, window into the Registry. The Installation Guide that comes with Visual FoxPro, under "Configuring Visual FoxPro," goes into these settings in great depth, so we won't repeat the list here.

Hold down the SHIFT key while clicking the OK button within the Options dialog and all the settings that have corresponding SET commands are echoed to the command window!

Config.FPW

Config.FPW stores a number of SET commands, as well as some special options available only in this file. How Visual FoxPro determines which Config.FPW file to use is a bit tricky. In the development environment, Visual FoxPro first checks to see if Visual FoxPro has been started up with the command line -c startup switch. If you've modified the shortcut's properties, or created a command line, such as:

```
D:\VFP\VFP.EXE -CD:\PROJECTS\CONFIG.VFP
```

Visual FoxPro uses the specified file. Next, Visual FoxPro checks for a DOS environment variable named FOXPROWCFG. If this exists, the file it points to is used. If not, Visual FoxPro searches the current directory, and then the DOS path for a file named Config.FPW. VFP uses the DOS path only, because the FoxPro path has not yet been established.

The runtime environment operates a little differently. For an APP or an EXE, besides using the methods above, you may include a file named Config.FPW in the project, using the Other-Text Files section. Visual FoxPro uses this file before starting the same sequence as the development environment.

SYS(2019) returns the path and filename of the current configuration file.

FoxPro.INI

In FoxPro for Windows and Visual FoxPro 3.0, FoxPro.INI stored the desktop settings to use on startup: the position and zoomed status, as well as the default desktop and printer font name, size and style. The file is in the main Windows directory. Visual FoxPro 3 settings are stored in a section cleverly named FoxPro 3. Typical settings look like the following:

```
[FoxPro 3]
Zoomed=1
```

```
Row=-4
Column=-4
Height=580
Width=808
FontName=Courier New
FontStyle=1
FontSize=9
PrtFontName=FoxPrint
PrtFontStyle=0
PrtFontSize=10
```

See the entry on "INI files" for information on manipulating these entries programmatically.

In Visual FoxPro 5.0 and later, these settings are stored on an individual user basis in the Registry under the key HKEY_CURRENT_USER\Software\Microsoft\VisualFoxPro\ {version} \Desktop, where {version} is 5.0 or 6.0.

In an application, you will probably want to start with SCREEN=OFF in your Config.FPW file, then set the settings of initial position and fonts based either on your application's requirements or on settings you have preserved from the last run of the program.

FOXUSER.DBF—The Resource File

Within FOXUSER, settings are stored for even more stuff. Earlier versions of FoxPro stored many other pieces of information, such as printer settings, which used to bloat this file. Now its primary purpose is to store the position and size of windows, toolbars and design surfaces you've worked with, restoring them to their previous positions when they are called up again. If you misplace a toolbar, somehow managing to position it off-screen, perhaps by changing your screen resolution, delete the associated record in the resource file to bring it back to its default. SYS(2005) returns the current file used as a resource file; SET RESOURCE turns it on or off or points it to a different file.

Command Line Switches

We often hear of people running into problems that sound like something confused in the Registry. Use the –A command line switch to start FoxPro without reading the current Config.FPW and Registry switches. Use –R to re-establish the associations that Visual FoxPro has with file extensions in Explorer and File Manager.

See Also INI Files, Registration Database, Set, Set Resource, Sys(2005), Sys(2019)

Container, Control

These two base classes with the incredibly confusing names are really just empty shells. The difference between them is that Container's shell is transparent, while Control's is opaque. (We'll handle the name conflict by referring to these classes with capital "C" and to the similarly named concepts with small "c".)

Both of these classes are containers (note the small "c" here) that let you combine other controls (small "c" here, too) into a unified whole. Container gives you access to the individual objects inside, while Control hides those objects from others. Essentially, Control protects the objects inside from meddlers. In either case, though, you can access the PEMs of the resulting object.

You'll use these classes as the foundation for building things you wish were in the product in the first place. For example, the date spinner class DateSpin in the CoolStuf library on the CD is really a sub-class of Container. Now that we've done the work for you, though, you can just drop a date spinner onto any form and use it as if it were a native control.

There's a third similar base class, Custom, which lets you construct non-visual objects. Like Container, it gives you access to the things inside.

Container and Control have few PEMs of their own because there's not much there until you put it there. With these base classes, you're definitely likely to add custom properties and methods when you sub-class.

Property	Value	Purpose
ControlCount	Numeric	The number of controls inside.
Controls	Collection	References to the controls inside.
Picture	Character	Name of a bitmap file that is tiled to produce "wallpaper" for the control.
Method	**Purpose**	
AddObject, RemoveObject	Container only. These methods let you add and remove objects from the container at runtime. Control doesn't support them because you can't do this, since the controls are not exposed.	

The different behavior of Container and Control carries through to subclassing as well. When you subclass something based on Container, you can change the things inside the original Container. When you subclass an object based on Control, the objects inside don't even show up in the property sheet. The class is truly a black box.

Example

```
* See the DateSpin example on the CD.
* Here's the beginning of the definition
* (as output by the Class Browser
*  and prettied up just a little).

DEFINE CLASS datespin AS container

   Width = 176
   Height = 31
   BackStyle = 0
   BorderWidth = 1
   *-- Currently chosen month
   nMonth = 1
   *-- Currently Chosen Day
   nDay = 1
   *-- Currently Chosen Year
   nYear = 1900
   Name = "datespin"

   *-- Contain the date currently displayed
   Value = .F.

ADD OBJECT label1 AS label WITH ;
      Comment = "/", ;
      FontBold = .F., ;
      FontSize = 24, ;
      BackStyle = 0, ;
      Caption = "/", ;
      Height = 18, ;
      Left = 48, ;
      Top = 5, ;
      Width = 13, ;
      Name = "Label1"
```

See Also AddObject, ControlCount, Controls, Custom, Picture, RemoveObject

ContainerReleaseType, ContainerRelease

This property and event let you indicate what to do when the user of an ActiveDoc application navigates away from it.

Usage

```
acdActiveDoc.ContainerReleaseType = nLiveOrDie
nLiveOrDie = acdActiveDoc.ContainerReleaseType
PROCEDURE acdActiveDoc.ContainerRelease
```

Parameter	Value	Meaning
nLiveOrDie	0	When the host releases the application, open an instance of the VFP runtime and continue running there.
	1	When the host releases the application, shut it down.

When you run an application in a browser, you face a unique problem. The user can abandon your application and move on to something else without explicitly quitting. This pair of members helps you solve that problem.

ContainerReleaseType lets you decide whether the application should be shut down or should keep running in the VFP runtime when the user navigates away from it. (Actually, if your browser has a cache like IE 3, this stuff doesn't happen until the application falls out of the cache.) When the user does leave, ContainerRelease fires so you can take appropriate action.

Example

```
PROCEDURE ContainerRelease

* Clean up if the app is shutting down
IF This.ContainerReleaseType = 1
   This.CleanUp()  && a custom method
ENDIF

RETURN
```

See Also ActiveDoc, HideDoc

Continue See Locate.

ContinuousScroll

This form property determines whether the form is updated as you move the scrollbar's thumb.

Usage

```
lRefreshWhileScrolling = frmForm.ContinuousScroll
frmForm.ContinuousScroll = lRefreshWhileScrolling
```

You know that little box on a scrollbar that shows you about where you are in the document, the one that you can grab and move to quickly scroll? It's called the "thumb." (Rumor has it that it got that name because it's modeled after a thumbwheel, literally a wheel moved by the thumb, on a bombsight.)

ContinuousScroll determines how a form behaves when you move the thumb of one of its scrollbars. When it's .T., the form is updated as the thumb moves. This is the way MODIFY COMMAND windows behave. When ContinuousScroll is .F., the form doesn't get refreshed until you stop dragging and release the mouse button. This is how Browses act.

On the whole, we're inclined to leave this one .T. and change it only if the form has so much complex stuff on it that refreshing continuously overtaxes the system. Since this one can be changed at runtime, you could let the user be in charge.

Like the xScrollSmallChange properties, we're not sure why grids and edit boxes don't have this property, too.

Example

```
* Turn it off
ThisForm.ContinuousScroll = .F.
```

See Also Form, HScrollSmallChange, Scrollbars, VScrollSmallChange

Control See Container.

Control Arrays

The documentation for just about every event includes an optional nIndex parameter that "uniquely identifies a control if it is in a control array." There's even a brief definition of "control array" in Help. But the docs give you no clue why you'd ever want to do this or how to make it work.

Our take is that control arrays were part of the original design of the object model to let you do things like group command buttons. The idea is that each element of an array is a reference to a different object. You can define methods for the array and apply them to the individual members. This would let you, for example, have one Click method that responds to a click on any object referenced in the array. The nIndex parameter tells you which one.

Sounds pretty neat, and it is similar to things we tried when simulating toolbars in FoxPro 2.x. But the CommandGroup and OptionGroup base classes do pretty much the same thing (though slightly differently).

We suspect that once the design team made it easy to group buttons, control arrays didn't seem quite so urgent, because the team never really finished implementing them. You can create control arrays in coded classes, but not in the Class Designer. The way you have to do things to make them work feels really kludgy. (See the example.)

Not only are control arrays hard to set up and hard to use, but they don't always work. For at least some of the base classes and some of the events, a control array's events don't fire when they should unless you bend over backward to help them. In those cases, unless the class on which a particular control in the array is based has code for the particular method, the array's method doesn't fire. Don't worry if this doesn't make sense to you—it doesn't make any sense to us, either.

Among the events affected in various versions of VFP are When, Valid, ErrorMessage and Message. Affected controls include text boxes, edit boxes and spinners. Because we consider control arrays pretty much useless, we haven't compiled an exhaustive list of event/control/version combinations that suffer from this malady.

In addition to all that, as far as we can tell, the Destroy event never fires for control arrays. Destroy fires for the contained objects, but never for the array itself.

Actually, only half the functionality of control arrays seems useless to us. We do expect to store object references in array properties. What we don't plan to do is define methods for the array—we'll rely on the methods of the underlying objects.

Example

```
* In order to define event methods for a control array, you
* have to define the form in code. As part of the form class
* definition, you can write methods for the array.
* In this example, the array holds a command button and a
* text box. The Click event has code.

DEFINE CLASS TestForm AS FORM
   * define the control array
   DIMENSION aControls[2]

   PROCEDURE Init
   * Here's where we can add the controls to the array

   This.AddObject("aControls[1]", "CommandButton")
   This.AddObject("aControls[2]", "TextBox")
   This.aControls[1].Visible = .T.
   This.aControls[2].Visible = .T.
   This.aControls[2].Top = 25

   ENDPROC
```

```
      PROCEDURE aControls.Click
      * Here's the click method that fires for any object
      * in the array
      LPARAMETERS nIndex

      WAIT WINDOW "You clicked on " + This.Name + ;
                  "["+PADL(nIndex,2)+"]"

      ENDPROC

   ENDDEFINE
```

See Also CommandGroup, Container, Control, OptionGroup

ControlBox

This property determines whether forms and toolbars have a control menu available in the upper left corner.

Usage

```
oObject.ControlBox = lHasControlMenu
lHasControlMenu = oObject.ControlBox
```

For forms (and _SCREEN), the contents of the control menu, if it's there, are determined by other properties. MaxButton and MinButton control the Maximize and Minimize items, respectively. Movable controls the Move item. Closable controls the Close item. BorderStyle, of all things, controls the Size item—sizing is available only when BorderStyle=3.

Setting ControlBox to .F. also disables the Minimize, Maximize and Close buttons on the title bar.

The new-in-VFP 6 TitleBar property overrides the setting of ControlBox. If TitleBar is 0, there's no control menu or any of the other stuff that normally resides on the title bar—that's because there's no title bar.

For toolbars, ControlBox determines whether you get a close button. Before you turn this one off, think hard about it. In most applications, the user should decide whether a particular toolbar is available or not. While we recognize that there are some specialized applications where keeping a toolbar alive is essential, in the average data entry app, it shouldn't be.

Example

```
_SCREEN.ActiveForm.ControlBox = .F.   && turn off control menu
```

See Also BorderStyle, Closable, Maximize, Minimize, Movable, TitleBar

Controls, ControlCount

These properties let you access all the controls in a container without knowing what they are. ControlCount tells you how many there are, while Controls is an array where each element contains a reference to one control. Controls is also referred to as a collection. (Other collections in Visual FoxPro include Forms and Pages.)

Usage

```
nControls = oObject.ControlCount
oControl = oObject.Controls( nControlNumber )
oObject.Controls( nControlNumber ).Property = uPropertyValue
uPropertyValue = oObject.Controls( nControlNumber ).Property
oObject.Controls(nControlNumber).Method()
```

ControlCount can't be changed. It's just a way for you to find out how many controls there are.

Controls, on the other hand, is a handle—it lets you grab the controls in a container and look at them, manipulate them, or do whatever you like to them. Be careful, though—different controls have different properties and methods, and you can't just loop through, doing the same thing to every control. Also, remember that Controls only gets you to the top level. If the control you're looking at is a container itself (like a command group or page frame), you still may have to dig down into that container to get at everything on the form. Fortunately, each container type either has a unique collection of its own (like Buttons or Pages) or has its own Controls collection (Column or Page, for example).

It's often easier to manipulate properties with the SetAll method than to loop through Controls. In fact, SetAll is more thorough. It digs down through multiple layers of containment. With the Controls collection, you get just the ones at the top level and you have to drill down manually. The example below shows one piece of the manual operation.

We expect to use SetAll whenever we want to make global changes and save the Controls collection for cases where we don't want to drill down or when we need to examine properties of the objects, not just change them, or when we need to call methods.

Beginning in VFP 5, most containers also have an Objects collection, despite documentation to the contrary. This is an ActiveX collection (that is, it uses Windows ActiveX capabilities) rather than a native VFP collection. It provides a handle to each of the contained objects of whichever object you're looking at. Be aware, however, that not every Objects collection in VFP has a Count property to tell you how many there are.

Example

```
* In VFP 5 and VFP 6, FOR EACH can be used to loop
* through the collection. This avoids the need for the
* nCounter variable and means you don't need to check
* ControlCount.
LOCAL nCounter
FOR nCounter = 1 TO ThisForm.ControlCount
   * Make sure the property you're interested in exists before
   * changing it.
   IF TYPE("ThisForm.Controls[nCounter].BackColor") = "N"
      ThisForm.Controls[nCounter].BackColor = RGB(255,0,0)
   ENDIF

   * If it's an option button group, dig down and do the
   * contained buttons, too.
   IF UPPER(ThisForm.Controls[nCounter].BaseClass) = ;
      "OPTIONGROUP"
      ThisForm.Controls[nCounter].SetAll("BackColor", ;
          RGB(255,0,0))
   ENDIF
ENDFOR

* SetAll does everything above and more.
ThisForm.SetAll("BackColor", RGB(255,0,0))
```

See Also ButtonCount, Buttons, ColumnCount, Columns, FormCount, Forms, Objects, PageCount, Pages, SetAll

ControlSource

This property lets you link (bind) a variable, field, or another property to a control's Value.

Usage

```
oObject.ControlSource = cSource
cSource = oObject.ControlSource
```

Back in FoxPro 2.x, every control had to have what we called an "underlying variable"—something to hold the control's value. Now that controls have their own Value property, that's no longer necessary. You only have to bind something to a control when you want to. That's what ControlSource is about.

Most of the controls have a couple of choices for data type. (For example, a check box's Value can be either numeric or logical.) With these controls, the type of the item named in ControlSource determines the type of Value. Bind a logical field to a check box, and that check box's Value is logical. Bind a numeric field, and the check box's Value is numeric.

For lists and combos, ControlSource can be either character or numeric. When the ControlSource is numeric, its interpretation is determined by the control's BoundTo property. With the default .F. for BoundTo, Value (and the ControlSource) contains the position (or ListIndex) of the chosen item. To have a numeric value from the list's data stored in Value and the ControlSource, you have to set BoundTo to .T.

Although the ControlSource is bound to the control's Value, the item named in ControlSource doesn't get updated until after the control's InteractiveChange is finished. Don't test the value of a ControlSource until you reach the Valid event—if you need to test sooner, test the control's Value. In fact, it's better OOP to refer only to the control's Value in its methods and not mention the ControlSource by name. If you reference the actual object named in ControlSource, the code is no longer well encapsulated and the control is no longer as easily reusable.

Example

```
This.ControlSource = "Employee.Last_Name"
```

See Also BoundTo, InteractiveChange, ListIndex, Valid, Value

Convert See Access().

_Converter See _Beautify.

Copy File, Delete File, Erase, Rename

These commands let you do file maintenance without leaving FoxPro. They all do what their names suggest. Delete File and Erase do the same thing—get rid of an existing file.

Usage

```
COPY FILE SourceFile TO DestFile
DELETE FILE [ FileName | ? ] [ RECYCLE ]
ERASE [ FileName | ? ] [ RECYCLE ]
RENAME OldFileName TO NewFileName
```

As with any potentially destructive command, be careful when you use these, especially across drives or directories. Starting in VFP 5, DELETE FILE and ERASE have the potential to be very destructive, in fact, since they accept DOS wildcards and let you delete multiple files at once. In addition, they ignore the setting of SET SAFETY—once you issue the command, the file is history. Invoking these commands with the "?" or blank parameter brings up a standard "Select file" dialog. Watch out for this in applications, because the latest incarnations of that dialog give users an awful lot of power via the right-click menu.

COPY FILE respects SET SAFETY. RENAME ignores SET SAFETY, but it won't let you give a file the name of an existing file. Neither of these commands accepts the "?" to let the user choose a file. However, COPY FILE doesn't scream if you specify ? for the DestFile; it also doesn't do anything.

DELETE FILE and ERASE don't care whether the file you specify exists. If you give them a nonexistent filename, they just do nothing and go merrily on their way. This is a trap waiting to catch you because it means a typo in a program might keep a file from being deleted with you none the wiser. (Actually, with TALK ON, you do get some feedback to the status bar, but that doesn't help much in a program.)

Help warns you about renaming tables contained in a database with RENAME. Heed this warning—you'll only create trouble for yourself if you don't. This is what RENAME TABLE is for.

Example

```
* Copy a file to make a backup
COPY README.TXT TO README.BAK

* Change the current transaction file into
* a history file.
cHistFile = "XACT"+TRANSFORM(YEAR(DATE()),"9999")
RENAME XActions.DBF TO (cHistFile+".DBF")

* Clean up a temp file. Either of the following will do
DELETE FILE TEMP.TXT
ERASE TEMP.TXT
```

See Also ADir(), Copy To, Delete, File(), Filer, Rename Table, Set Safety

Copy Indexes, Copy Tag

These two commands let you convert between stand-alone IDX files and compound indexes. They seem most useful when converting an older application or when you need to maintain compatibility with other Xbase varieties.

Usage

```
COPY INDEXES IndexesToCopy | ALL [ TO CDXName ]
COPY TAG TagToCopy [ OF ContainingCDX ] TO IndexName
```

COPY INDEXES copies one or more IDX indexes into a single compound index file. By default, the result is the structural index for the table, but you can specify a different CDX file. Each new tag is named for the IDX file where it originated. Use ALL to copy all open IDX indexes.

COPY TAG takes a single tag and makes a stand-alone IDX for it. You need the OF clause only when you have multiple tags with the same name and you want to copy one that's not from the structural CDX.

We haven't used COPY INDEXES since we were converting FoxBase and FoxPro 1.x applications to FoxPro 2.0. We've never used COPY TAG.

Example

```
USE Customer
COPY TAG Company_Na TO MyComp    && Create a stand-alone MYCOMP.IDX
COPY TAG Customer_I to Id        && Create a stand-alone ID.IDX
* re-open with the IDXs
USE Customer INDEX MyComp,id
COPY INDEXES ALL TO MoreTags     && Create a new CDX
```

See Also Copy File, Index, Set Index, Set Order

Copy Memo See Append Memo.

Copy Procedures See Append Procedures.

Copy Structure, Copy Structure Extended, Create From

These commands let you duplicate the structure of an existing table, or create a similar but not identically structured table. They used to be extremely important commands, but newer commands do all the same things more easily.

Usage

```
COPY STRUCTURE TO cTable
        [ DATABASE DatabaseName [ NAME LongTableName ] ]
        [ FIELDS cFieldList ]
        [ [ WITH ] CDX | PRODUCTION ]
```

COPY STRUCTURE creates a new table with a structure identical to the table open in the current work area. If the optional field list is included, only the listed fields are included in the new table. The newly created table is not opened. Including the optional CDX or PRODUCTION clause, with or without the keyword WITH, also duplicates the structural compound index file for the table. The undocumented DATABASE and NAME clauses let you put the new table in an existing database and give it a long name.

COPY STRUCTURE loses the rules, triggers, and so on that are associated with the new table. Null and code page information is preserved. In VFP3, the information was lost because you couldn't put the new table in a database.

COPY STRUCTURE is probably the most useful command in this group because we do occasionally find that we need to create an exact clone of an existing table.

Example

```
USE Orders
* create a table to create archives
COPY STRUCTURE TO OldOrders
```

Usage

```
COPY STRUCTURE EXTENDED TO cStructureTable
         [ DATABASE DatabaseName [ NAME LongTableName ] ]
         [ FIELDS cFieldList ]
```

COPY STRUCTURE EXTENDED creates a new table containing information about the table open in the current work area. It contains 16 fields representing the 16 types of information needed to create a table in a DBC. The list of fields created is identical to the columns created by AFIELDS().

Column	Type	Meaning
FIELD_NAME	Character	Field name
FIELD_TYPE	Single Character	Field type—see CREATE TABLE for a list
FIELD_LEN	Numeric	Field width
FIELD_DEC	Numeric	Number of decimals
FIELD_NULL	Logical	Does the field accept nulls?
FIELD_NOCP	Logical	Do not allow code page translation?
FIELD_DEFA	Memo	Default value for field
FIELD_RULE	Memo	Field validation rule
FIELD_ERR	Memo	Field validation text
TABLE_RULE	Memo	Table validation rule
TABLE_ERR	Memo	Table validation text
TABLE_NAME	Character	Long name for the table
INS_TRIG	Memo	Insert trigger code
UPD_TRIG	Memo	Update trigger code
DEL_TRIG	Memo	Delete trigger code
TABLE_CMT	Memo	Table comment

If the FIELDS clause is included, records are created only for the listed fields. The table-level information (the last seven fields) appears only in the first record of the new table.

You can indicate that the table is to be added to a database and even give it a long name in that database. We're not quite sure why you'd want to do this—maybe for some kind of data dictionary.

COPY STRUCTURE EXTENDED used to be the standard way to modify the structure of an existing table. You'd create this table, then modify it as needed (since it was a table after all), then you could use CREATE FROM to create a new table and copy the data from the old. Rename the new table and you were on your way. Beginning in FoxPro 2, though, better ways came along. Either a combination of AFIELDS() and CREATE TABLE or a simple SELECT-SQL was generally simpler. In Visual FoxPro, you don't need to go to any of these extremes. To modify the structure of an existing table, you can simply ALTER TABLE.

In addition to ALTER TABLE being a better way to modify an existing table, COPY STRUCTURE EXTENDED simply doesn't get enough information to let you re-create a table. (Neither does AFIELDS().) Field captions are omitted. In VFP3, table triggers were omitted as well.

Usage

```
CREATE cTable [ DATABASE DatabaseName NAME LongTableName ]
       FROM cStructureTable
```

CREATE FROM creates a new table, taking structure information from a table like the ones created by COPY STRUCTURE EXTENDED. The structure table can have the same 16 columns shown in the table above, but you can actually get away with only the first four or the first 11. Using any other set of the columns generates a "Structure is invalid" error in VFP 6.

Keep in mind that there is a limit of 255 fields per table. If you hand CREATE FROM a table with more 255 records, there's no guaranteeing what it'll do. In some cases, VFP does something reasonably intelligent under the circumstances, but in others it gets downright weird.

Like the other versions of CREATE, CREATE FROM leaves the new table open in the current work area. You can indicate that the new table is to be added to a database and given a long table name. In VFP3, if a database is open when you issue CREATE FROM, the new table is added to the database.

CREATE FROM doesn't ignore deleted records in the structure table. This means if you COPY STRUCTURE EXTENDED, then modify the table by deleting some of the records (that is, remove fields from the listing), you need to PACK the structure table before issuing CREATE FROM. Otherwise, your new table will have the fields you tried to remove. This bug is nothing new—older versions do the same thing.

Given the various problems and peculiarities of these commands and the fact that there are better ways to do everything they do, we recommend you stay away from these.

See Also AFields(), Alter Table, Copy To, Create Cursor, Create Table, Select-SQL

Copy Tag See Copy Indexes.

Copy To See Append From.

Copy To Array See Append From Array.

Cos(), Sin(), Tan(), ACos(), ASin(), ATan(), ATn2(), DToR(), RToD(), Pi()

Sines, sines,
everywhere there's sines,
breakin' up the scenery,
blowin' my mind
—with apologies to Five Man Electric Band

Okay, everyone remembers their high school trigonometry, right? No? We don't blame you. With any luck, you will never be called upon to write an app requiring these functions, but it's nice to know they're available should you need them.

All the functions describe angle in terms of radians, a unit of measure. (You might remember there are 2 times pi radian units in a circle, just as 360 degrees describes the circle.) If you need to convert your angles back and forth between the two numbering systems, the DTOR() and RTOD() functions allow you to switch back and forth between the units of measure. All functions properly respect nulls, returning null if any of their supplied parameters are null.

Usage

```
nRetValue = COS( nAngle )
nRetValue = SIN( nAngle )
nRetValue = TAN( nAngle )
```

Parameter	Value	Meaning
nAngle	Numeric	The angle to calculate, expressed in radians.
nRetValue	Numeric	The trigonometric value of the specified angle.

These three functions—sine, cosine and tangent—return the equivalent trigonometric functions.

Example

```
? COS(PI()/3)    && returns 0.50
? SIN(PI()/3)    && returns 0.87
? TAN(PI()/3)    && returns 1.73
```

Usage

```
nRetValue = ACOS( nTrigValue )
nRetValue = ASIN( nTrigValue )
nRetValue = ATAN( nTrigValue )
nRetValue = ATN2( nXValue, nYValue )
```

Parameter	Value	Meaning
nTrigValue	Numeric	The value returned from the trigonometric function.
nXValue, nYValue	Numeric	The X and Y coordinates of a point in any of the four quadrants describing a line through the origin. This line and the line y=0 form the angle returned by ATN2().
nRetValue	Numeric	The angle, in radians, whose trigonometric value is supplied to the function.

The "arc" functions (arcsine, arccosine and arctangent are inverse trigonometric functions) return what angle must have been supplied to their matching trigonometric functions (sine, cosine and tangent) to return the value supplied to them as a parameter. There are two arctangent functions—cleverly named ATAN() and ATN2()—to allow for two different ways of supplying the parameters: either the value of the tangent function, or the equivalent X and Y coordinates of the angle.

Example

```
? ACOS(.5)       && returns 1.047, or PI/3
```

Usage

```
nAngleInRadians = DTOR( nAngleInDegrees )
nAngleInDegrees = RTOD( nAngleInRadians )
```

Parameter	Value	Meaning
nAngleInDegrees	Numeric	The angle expressed in degrees.
nAngleInRadians	Numeric	The angle expressed in radians.

DTOR() and RTOD() convert degrees to radians and vice versa.

Example

```
? DTOR( 90 )          && returns 1.57, or PI/2
? RTOD( PI() / 2 )    && returns 90
```

Usage

```
nRetValue = PI()
```

PI() returns the static value 3.1415...

Example

```
? PI()  && displays 3.1415...etc., depending on SET(DECIMALS)
```

Count See Average.

Count

This is a property of each of the OLE collections that are part of VFP. In each case, it tells you how many objects are in that collection.

Usage `nCount = colCollection.Count`

Chalk one up for polymorphism. VFP's native collections, like Forms and Controls, each have their own corresponding count property with a distinct name, such as FormCount and ControlCount. The WhateverCount property belongs to the same object that owns the collection. For example, forms have a Controls collection and a ControlCount property.

But the developers got smarter. The new OLE collections, like Projects and Objects, own their own count and they all use the same name for it.

Of course, we don't need the count for a collection as much as we used to because FOR EACH lets us loop through all the members without worrying about how many there are.

Example

```
* How many projects are open?
? Application.Projects.Count
```

See Also Files, For Each, Objects, Projects, Servers

_Coverage See Set Coverage.

CPConvert(), CPCurrent(), CPDBF(), IDXCollate(), Set Collate, Set("Collate"), Set NoCPTrans

This slew of functions allows Visual FoxPro to manipulate variables, tables and indexes in a multiple-code-page environment.

Usage `cResult = CPConvert( cFromCP, cToCP, cText )`

Parameter	Value	Meaning
cFromCP	Integer	Original code page from which cText is to be translated.
cToCP	Integer	Destination code page for result.
cText	Character or memo	Text to be translated.
cResult	Character	Text after translation.

CPConvert() is not often needed. It accesses the underlying code page translation engine in Visual FoxPro to allow translation of individual phrases. Use this when you have code page-dependent information entered into a table with the incorrect code page for the table.

Example `WAIT WINDOW CPCONVERT(437,1252,"Jos"+CHR(130))`

Usage `nCodePage = CPCurrent( nWhichOne )`

Parameter	Value	Meaning
nWhichOne	Omitted or 1	In Windows, the Windows code page; in other FoxPro platforms, the operating system's code page.
	2	In Windows, the underlying (MS-DOS) code page. In the other platforms, this should return the same as 1.
nCodePage	Numeric	Number of the code page requested.

This function would be far simpler were it not for the idiosyncratic way in which IBM and Microsoft implemented their systems. MS-DOS was here first, and it uses the ASCII code set to produce symbols like the line and box-drawing characters. Windows, on the other hand, chose to base its character sets on the far more widely accepted ANSI characters. Since Windows is merely a thin veneer on top of MS-DOS, programmers on that platform need to be able to detect both code pages and deal with them.

Example

```
? CPCURRENT(2)  && what's the MS-DOS code page?
```

Usage

```
nCodePage = CPDBF( [ cAlias | nWorkArea ] )
```

Parameter	Value	Meaning
cAlias	Character	Alias of the table whose code page is to be returned.
	Omitted	If nWorkArea is also omitted, use the table in the current work area.
nWorkArea	Integer	Work area number of the table whose code page is to be returned.
	Omitted	If cAlias is also omitted, use the table in the current work area.
nCodePage	Numeric	Number of the code page requested.

Use this function to detect the current code page assigned to a table. To change or zero out the code page, use the CPZERO.PRG, located in VFP\TOOLS\CPZERO. To accomplish the same thing in your program, use the GETCP() dialog to determine the correct code page, and then call the CPZERO.PRG, which you can include within your application, to change the code page.

Example

```
* The Wizard table should be flagged for US Windows codepage
DO CPZERO WITH HOME()+"\Wizards\Wizard.DBF",1252
USE Wizard.DBF IN 0 ALIAS DaWiz
? CPDBF("DaWiz")  && should return 1252
```

Usage

```
cCollation = IDXCollate( [cCDXName, ] nIndexNumber
                         [, cAlias | nWorkArea ] )
```

Parameter	Value	Meaning
cCDXName	Character	The name of the compound index file to examine. If no file is specified, IDXCollate() works on currently open indexes.
nIndexNumber	Integer	As is typical of index functions, this refers to a number assigned to each open stand-alone index, in the order they were opened, then the tags of the structural index, then any other compound indexes open, with each tag enumerated in the order created.

Parameter	Value	Meaning
cAlias	Character	Alias of the table whose index collation is to be returned.
	Omitted	If nWorkArea is also omitted, use the table in the current work area.
nWorkArea	Integer	Work area number of the table whose index collation is to be returned.
	Omitted	If cAlias is also omitted, use the table in the current work area.
cCollation	Empty string	The number of the index specified exceeds the number of open indexes, or the work area number specified has no open file.
	Character	The collation sequence which applies to this index.

A collation sequence is the set of rules that determine the order in which values within the index will be presented. The most familiar (and the default) is MACHINE, which is a straight binary ordering of the values stored within the index. See Set Collate below for more details on this.

Example

```
USE HOME() + "\Wizards\BuilderD.DBF"
? IDXCOLLATE(1)  && returns "MACHINE"
```

Usage

```
SET COLLATE TO cSequence
cSequence = SET( "COLLATE" )
```

Parameter	Value	Meaning
cSequence	Character	Specifies the sequence in which items should be sorted.

We Americans do not appreciate some of the conveniences of computing using the English language. Unfortunately, in being English-centric, many of the early developers of computers made data interchange between different languages a real challenge. Sort order is one very good example of this. In both Germanic and many Romance languages, the sort order is dictated not just by the individual value or weight of each character, but also the values of its nearby characters or the addition of diacritical marks or ligatures to those characters. A straight sort by the binary value of individual characters, even when correctly translated by code page into the correct alphabetic sequence, won't do it.

A caution: Recently we've run into a few cases where the performance of FoxPro's queries is far slower than we'd expect. In some cases, joins between tables where one table is lacking the proper index results in missing records. In all of these cases, the problem was that the indexes were created with a non-Machine collation. Our thumbrule: Always create index tags with the Machine sequence if they are to be used in Select statements.

Each collation sequence has specific ordering rules, needed for a specific purpose. For example, to list an alphabetical sequence of names in German, SET COLLATE TO "GERMAN". A handy ordering sequence for case-insensitive sorts is the GENERAL sorting order.

All collation sequences except Machine use 2 bytes per key so the maximum size of a key expression is only 120 bytes, not 240 as Help states.

Example

```
SET COLLATE TO "GENERAL"
```

Usage
```
SET NOCPTRANS to cFieldList
cFieldList = SET( "NOCPTRANS" )
```

SET NOCPTRANS is a relic from the 2.x days, where a field that should be treated as containing binary data, and not translated from one code page to another, was flagged by explicitly issuing the SET NOCPTRANS command each and every time it was open. Needless to say, somewhere in their code, nearly everyone forgot to issue the command, and binary data got translated into garbage left and right. Visual FoxPro solves the entire problem by allowing data to be specified as "Binary" within the Table Designer and with the NOCPTRANS keywords of the CREATE TABLE and ALTER TABLE commands.

See Also GetCP(), Index, Set CPCompile, Set CPDialog

Create, Modify Structure

These two commands are for interactively creating and modifying tables. Although they can be used in programs, you'd rarely want to do so since they bring up the Table Designer. You probably don't want to give an application's users access to that dialog.

Usage
```
CREATE [ cTableName | ? ]
```

Omitting the table parameter is the same as passing the "?"; both bring up the Save As dialog (customized to the CREATE command) to let you specify a name for the new table. Once a table name has been specified, the Table Designer appears. For ideas on working with the Table Designer, see "DBF, CDX, FPT, CDX—Hike!" and "What Power Tools? in the front of the book."

Example
```
CREATE MyNewTable
```

Usage
```
MODIFY STRUCTURE
```

MODIFY STRUCTURE, or, as most FoxPro people write it, MODI STRU, also brings up the Table Designer. In this case, though, it shows the structure for the table open in the current work area. If no table is open there, the Open dialog appears to let you choose one.

Back in the dark ages, we toyed with the idea of changing a table's structure in a program by playing a macro against the old version of the Table Designer. But with Visual FoxPro's inclusion of ALTER TABLE, there's no reason to even think about this anymore.

The Table page of the Table Designer shows a total length for the record. Unfortunately, for records that accept nulls in any field, it's wrong. It's one less than the correct value returned by RECSIZE().

See Also AFields(), Alter Table, Create Cursor, Create Database, Create Table, Display and List, RecSize()

Create Class, Modify Class

These commands open the Class Designer (CD).

Usage
```
CREATE CLASS [ ClassName | ? ]
         [ OF ClassLibraryName | ? ]
         [ AS ParentClassName [ FROM ParentClassLibrary ] ]
         [ NOWAIT ]
MODIFY CLASS [ ClassName | ? ]
         [ OF ClassLibraryName | ? ]
         [ AS ParentClassName [ FROM ParentClassLibrary ] ]
         [ METHOD cMethodname ] [ NOWAIT ] [ SAVE ]
```

When you create a class, you need to specify at least three pieces of information: the name to assign the new class, a library (VCX) in which to store the new class, and the class on which the new class is based. If it's based on a user-defined class, you may need to specify the library containing that class, too. MODIFY CLASS doesn't need quite as much information—just the name of the class to edit and the class library where it can be found.

The two commands behave differently when you don't provide all the necessary information. Not surprisingly, CREATE CLASS assumes you want to create a new class and displays a dialog labeled "New Class" that lets you specify the name of the new class, the base class, and the library in which to store the new class. An incomplete MODIFY CLASS, on the other hand, brings up a special form of the File-Open dialog that lets you look inside existing class libraries and choose one of those to edit. In fact, we often use MODIFY CLASS just to see what's out there.

We were really surprised to find that MODIFY CLASS includes the AS and FROM clauses, so we checked it out. If you use AS and specify a different parent class than the one on which the one you want to edit was originally based, you get prompted to overwrite the old definition with a new one. (That is, if you say MODIFY CLASS MyObject AS Check box and you'd originally defined it as Spinner, the old definition gets discarded in favor of the new one.) The setting of SAFETY doesn't matter in this case—you always get prompted. Good thing.

The METHOD clause is a cool one—one added with developers in mind. Issuing this command from the command window brings you right into the code window with the method you specify ready for editing. When we're in the middle of the code-test-debug cycle, having this command to scroll up to in the command window and re-run is so much faster!

NOWAIT and SAVE let you use these commands in a program and have the CD behave sensibly. With NOWAIT, program execution continues, leaving the CD open and available. SAVE lets you click outside the CD without having it shut down abruptly. You only need SAVE if you don't have NOWAIT.

Example
```
CREATE CLASS MySpinner AS Spinner OF Controls
```

See Also Create ClassLib, Define Class

Create ClassLib, Add Class, Remove Class, Rename Class

These commands let you maintain class libraries (VCX) in code.

Usage
```
CREATE CLASSLIB LibFileName
```

This command creates a new, empty class library. By default, it has an extension of VCX. You can specify a different extension, but we don't recommend it—the memo portion gets an FPT extension and the whole thing is pretty confusing. Go with the flow and use VCX/VCT.

Actually, in VFP 6, you *can't* specify a different extension. No matter what filename you give to CREATE CLASSLIB, the file is created with a VCX extension and the corresponding memo file gets a VCT extension. Even if you surround the filename with quotes, the VCX extension is added at the end.

You can't abbreviate the "classlib" portion of CREATE CLASSLIB to the first four letters because it conflicts with CREATE CLASS. You need at least CREA CLASSL.

SET SAFETY determines whether you get a dialog confirming you want to overwrite the class library if the library already exists.

Example
```
CREATE CLASSLIB MyStuf
```

Usage
```
ADD CLASS ClassName [ OF CurrentLibrary ] TO NewLibrary
    [ OVERWRITE ]
REMOVE CLASS ClassName OF LibFileName
```

These two commands add and remove existing classes. ADD CLASS lets you copy a class from one library to another. REMOVE CLASS, not surprisingly, deletes a class from a library. Be careful about removing classes—if other classes are based on the one you remove, they're orphaned and unusable. (You may not see this effect right away. Until the class library is packed, the deleted class can be found.)

You need the OF clause in ADD CLASS only when the library containing the class you want to copy isn't among the current set of libraries (set with SET CLASSLIB).

Think twice before you copy a class from one library to another. Normally, you don't want to keep multiple copies of a class around because that defeats the whole purpose of OOP—reducing your maintenance burden. Think of ADD CLASS as something you do when you want to send only some of the classes in a library to someone else or when you want to move a class from one library to another, but not as something you do regularly. Ordinarily, you'll subclass rather than copy.

Example
```
ADD CLASS DateSpin OF CoolStuf TO MyStuf
REMOVE CLASS DateSpin OF CoolStuf
```

Usage
```
RENAME CLASS OldClassName OF ClassLib TO NewClassName
```

As its name suggests, this command lets you change the name of a class in a class library. As with REMOVE CLASS, use this command with caution because it can result in orphaned classes. Subclasses based on the class do not get updated with the new name. Use the Class Browser's Rename button instead to rename a class and any subclasses contained in the same library or another library open in the Browser. The Browser's Redefine button lets you clean up afterward if you mess up and rename a class that has offspring.

Example
```
RENAME CLASS DateSpin OF MyStuf TO DateSpinner
```

See Also Create Class, Modify Class, Set Classlib

Create Color Set

This command lets you save a named color set to the resource file. It's part of the FoxPro for DOS color system, but does work in Visual FoxPro. Since colors are really the user's domain in a Windows application, and there are simpler ways to handle colors in VFP if you want to break the rules, the only reason to work with this system is to maintain old code.

Usage
```
CREATE COLOR SET ColorSetName
```

FoxPro for DOS includes an incredibly complex, yet somehow elegant, scheme for specifying colors for the various visible components of an application. The elegant part is that you have tremendous control over colors. The complex part is the implementation.

A color set consists of 24 color schemes. Each scheme is composed of 10 color pairs and each pair has (surprise) two colors: foreground and background. A color pair can be specified either by specially designated characters (see the list under Colors Overview in Help) or by using a special form of RGB() that accepts six values—the first three are foreground, the last three are background.

In FoxPro for DOS, each element of the user interface is controlled by one of the color schemes. Within the schemes, each color pair is used for certain aspects of those elements. For example, in many schemes, color pair 4 controls active titles while color pair 5 controls inactive titles. Color pairs 1 and 2 usually control disabled and enabled text.

FoxPro for DOS uses only about half of the 24 color schemes for its own interface, leaving the rest available for custom coloring. The whole system, while hard to grasp initially, makes it easy both to stick with standard system colors and to branch out and use other setups.

Naturally, it's different in Visual FoxPro. The biggest difference is that, instead of the wide range of colors used by the FoxPro for DOS interface, Visual FoxPro (and FoxPro for Windows before it) uses very few colors. Almost everything in the interface is white, black or gray. Even if you choose one of the more outlandish Windows color schemes (in Windows 3.1, "Hot Dog Stand" was always a good choice for seeing what would shake out—the newer Windows versions don't come with anything quite so loud), you still see lots of black and gray in VFP.

In fact, choosing a different Windows color scheme points out that Visual FoxPro borrows a lot of its colors from Windows. But once you start fiddling (using SET COLOR OF SCHEME), the connection to the Windows colors is broken.

In addition, some aspects of the interface (like the system menu bar) aren't controlled by FoxPro's color schemes. No matter how much you try, you just can't change them.

If all that explanation hasn't scared you off , you're ready for CREATE COLOR SET. It's actually a simple command. It saves the current values for all 24 color schemes to the resource file under a name you specify. As in FoxPro 2.x for Windows, there's no tool to help you set up the schemes. Use SET COLOR OF SCHEME.

Example

```
* Save the current set of color schemes in the resource file
CREATE COLOR SET MyFavoriteColors
```

See Also ColorSource, RGB(), RGBScheme(), Set Color Of Scheme, Set Color Set, Set Resource

Create Connection, Modify Connection, Rename Connection, Delete Connection

These commands let you maintain connections to remote data sources as part of a database.

Usage

```
CREATE CONNECTION [ ConnectionName | ? ]
      [ DATASOURCE cDataSource
       [ USERID cUserId ] [ PASSWORD cPassWord ]
       [ DATABASE cDatabase ] ]
      | CONNSTRING cConnectionString ]
MODIFY CONNECTION [ ConnectionName | ? ]
DELETE CONNECTION [ ConnectionName ]
RENAME CONNECTION OldName TO NewName
```

CREATE CONNECTION lets you either create a connection totally in code or start the Connection Designer. If you include a connection name and either the DATASOURCE or CONNSTRING clause, the connection is created and stored without opening the Designer. Including DATASOURCE or CONNSTRING without a name brings up a Save dialog to specify a name. Any less than that brings up the Connection Designer. Named connections can be used both in views and in establishing SQL pass-through connections. See "Your Server Will Be With You in a Moment" for more information about connections.

MODIFY CONNECTION opens the Connection Designer and lets you edit the specified connection.

DELETE and RENAME CONNECTION are for maintenance of connections in a database. They do what their names say.

Example

```
CREATE CONNECTION MyAccessConnection ;
  DATASOURCE "MS Access 7.0"
MODIFY CONNECTION MyAccessConnection
RENAME CONNECTION MyAccessConnection TO MoreDignifiedConnection
DELETE CONNECTION MoreDignifiedConnection
```

See Also Create SQL View, DBGetProp(), Display Connections

Create Cursor

This command lets you create a temporary table. Cursors created this way are read-write (like those created for views, but unlike those created by SELECT-SQL). Cursors are not part of a database, but can have several features normally found only in database-contained tables.

Usage

```
CREATE CURSOR Alias
        ( Fieldname1 Fieldtype1 [( nSize1 [ , nDecimals1 ] )
           [ NULL | NOT NULL ]
          [ CHECK lFieldRule1 [ ERROR cRuleText1 ] ]
          [ DEFAULT eDefault1 ]
          [ UNIQUE ]
          [ NOCPTRANS ] ]
          [ , Fieldname2 ... ] )
        | FROM ARRAY aFieldArray
```

Parameter	Value	Meaning
Alias	Name	The alias to assign to the newly created cursor. This is not a filename and does not have to be unique across users.
Fieldname*x*	Name	The name of the *x*th field in the cursor.
Fieldtype*x*	Single letter	The letter denoting the type of the *x*th field in the cursor. See the help file for a list.
nSize*x*	Numeric	The size of the *x*th field.
nDecimals*x*	Numeric	The number of decimal places in the *x*th field.
lFieldRule*x*	Logical	The field-level rule for the *x*th field.
cRuleText*x*	Character	The error message to use when the field-level rule for the *x*th field is violated.
eDefault*x*	Expression	An expression that evaluates to the default value for the *x*th field.
aFieldArray	Array	An array containing definition information for the cursor.

Cursors are really handy when you just need to work with some data temporarily, then throw it out. You don't have to worry about unique names or about erasing files. Create the cursor, populate it, use it, and then close it, at which point it goes away as if it had never been. Unlike cursors created with SELECT-SQL, you can change the data in cursors created with CREATE CURSOR, so they're good for tasks like grabbing a set of records and letting a user mark those to be printed. The original data is left untouched, but you get what you need.

The clauses of CREATE CURSOR are a subset of those for CREATE TABLE and are explained in detail there. (CREATE TABLE has some other clauses not mirrored in CREATE CURSOR.)

There are a few interesting things about this command. First, the name you give the cursor is an alias (like in the ALIAS clause of USE). There's no reason to create a unique name for it. In fact, you can't use a name generated with SYS(3) because, starting with FoxPro 2.5, aliases beginning with digits don't work. CREATE CURSOR does support long names both for the alias and for the field names.

Like other cursors, the ones you create with this command disappear when you close them.

Most interesting about cursors in Visual FoxPro is that they accept some of the database-related clauses. We'd expect CHECK, ERROR and DEFAULT to be restricted to tables that are part of a DBC and, in fact, when working with tables rather than cursors, they are. But there's some special mechanism that lets you use these clauses with cursors.

In VFP3.0 and 3.0b, when you use the UNIQUE clause to create a compound index (CDX) for a cursor, closing the cursor doesn't clean up the CDX. Instead, the CDX file is left behind in the directory specified for temporary files. You can identify it there by the all-digit name followed by a CDX extension. This bug is fixed in later versions.

We're particularly fond of the FROM ARRAY form of CREATE CURSOR and, in programs, are more likely to use that than the form listing all the fields explicitly. One handy trick is to use AFIELDS() to create an array with field information from an existing table or cursor, modify the array as needed, then CREATE CURSOR (or TABLE) FROM ARRAY.

Beware of the number of fields in the cursor you are trying to create. CREATE CURSOR FROM ARRAY crashes Visual FoxPro 3.x with an Invalid Page Fault if there are more than 316 rows (that is, fields to be created), and generates a "Function argument value, type or count is invalid" for 313 to 315 fields listed. Weirdly enough, it can create up to 312 fields. VFP 5.0 crashes with an Invalid Page Fault at 256 fields. VFP 6 finally gets it right with either "Array dimensions are invalid" for 5-column arrays or "Too many columns" for 5+ column arrays if the array contains 256 or more rows. The bottom line is that no version of FoxPro supports any more than 255 fields. We wouldn't count on creating these nonstandard cursors.

If any of the fields support NULL, you are limited to 254 columns because of the hidden "_NullFlags" column (see "Nulls" in "DBF, FPT, CDX, DBC—Hike!")

Once you CREATE a cursor, you can pretty much treat it like a table, as long as you're careful not to close it. This means that you can use table and row buffering with cursors—an advantage in designing forms since you needn't worry about whether the actual data resides in a table, a view or a cursor.

Interestingly, CURSORGETPROP() doesn't distinguish between CREATEd cursors and tables. In both cases, it returns 3 ("table") for SourceType. You can tell if you're working on a cursor by checking DBF() or CURSORGETPROP("SourceName")—for a cursor, you'll get a temporary filename composed of digits and a TMP extension.

Example

```
CREATE CURSOR Temp (CharFld C(10) UNIQUE, ;
                    NumFld N(3) CHECK NumFld>25, ;
                    DateFld D DEFAULT DATE())

* create a cursor identical to the Customer table
USE Customer
=AFIELDS(aFieldList)
CREATE CURSOR NewCust FROM ARRAY aFieldList
```

See Also AFields(), Create, Create Table, CursorGetProp(), Select - SQL, Use

Create Database, Delete Database

These commands create and destroy databases, respectively. A database is a collection of tables, views, connections, and other stuff. See "DBC, DBF, FPT, CDX—Hike!" for more on what constitutes a database in Visual FoxPro.

Usage

```
CREATE DATABASE [ Name | ? ]
```

If you omit Name, whether or not you include the "?", the Open dialog appears with a default name of

DATAn.DBC, where *n* is the number of times you've used the Open dialog to name a new database in this session. It doesn't matter whether or not you assign a name other than the default. If you use the Open dialog, the counter on the end goes up. Try this:

```
CREATE DATABASE ?
* change the name to Fred and choose OK
CREATE DATABASE ?
* note that new database name offered is DATA2.DBC
```

Weird, but it doesn't really matter, since you'd never want to use the default name.

Creating a database opens it (exclusively). Unlike tables, databases don't use anything like work areas, so opening one doesn't close any others that are already open. The newly created database is empty. You have to use commands or the Database Designer to put stuff in it.

When a database is open and current, creating a new table automatically puts it in the open database.

Be careful about database names. Because the database is stored as a file, you only get as many characters as the Windows version allows. Using VFP 3 in Windows 3.1, you can CREATE DATABASE AVeryLongName, but it's stored as AVeryLon.DBC.

Example `CREATE DATABASE MyImportantData`

Usage `DELETE DATABASE Name | ? [ DELETETABLES ] [ RECYCLE ]`

DELETE DATABASE is the right way to get rid of a database. It does all the necessary cleanup, including freeing all the tables in the database. Deleting the DBC, DCT and DCX files any other way orphans the tables in the database, which leaves them unusable until you issue the FREE TABLE command.

Unlike CREATE DATABASE, you must specify either a name or the ? with DELETE DATABASE. The ? brings up the Open dialog to choose a database to delete, bizarre as that sounds. (In fact, despite its title, the Open dialog is the one that has the right functionality.)

Specifying DELETETABLES means that Visual FoxPro should delete all the tables in the database along with the database itself. This is pretty drastic, but can be handy when working with test data.

Add the RECYCLE keyword to send the database files to the purgatory of the Windows recycle bin. Without it, they're gone, gone, gone.

Not surprisingly, restoration of a database from the recycle bin doesn't work very well. When you open the restored database, it appears to contain what it did before, but the tables still think they're free tables, if you specified not to delete them as well. You have to let VFP correct the backlinks before the database works right.

A database must be closed in order to delete it.

DELETE DATABASE respects the setting of SAFETY.

See Also Add Table, Close Database, Create, Create SQL View, Create Table, DBGetProp(), DBSetProp(), Modify Database, Open Database, Pack Database, Set Database, Set Safety, Validate Database

Create Form, Modify Form, Create Screen, Modify Screen

These commands open the Form Designer.

Usage

```
CREATE FORM | SCREEN [ FormName | ? ]
        [ AS ClassName FROM ClassLib ]
        [ NOWAIT ] [ SAVE ] [ DEFAULT ]
```

```
        [ WINDOW DefinitionWindow ]
        [ IN [ WINDOW ] ContainerWindow | IN SCREEN ]
MODIFY FORM | SCREEN [ FormName | ? ]
        [ METHOD MethodName ]
        [ NOENVIRONMENT ] [ NOWAIT ] [ SAVE ]
        [ WINDOW DefinitionWindow ]
        [ IN [ WINDOW ] ContainerWindow | IN SCREEN ]
```

You can specify a form to open, specify ? to be prompted or omit the form name entirely. With CREATE, omitting FormName opens the Form Designer with a default name, while ? brings up a special form of the Save As dialog. With MODIFY, either omitting the name or using ? brings up the File-Open dialog.

If you use CREATE FORM with a file that already exists and SAFETY is set on, a dialog lets you know the file already exists. You can either throw it out (by choosing "Yes") or open it (by choosing "No"). With SAFETY set off, the same command simply opens the existing form.

MODIFY FORM with a nonexistent file name behaves like CREATE FORM—it opens the Form Designer with an empty form.

DEFAULT is a really neat clause, though we don't use it much. You can (and should) specify a form template class in the Tools-Options dialog. Normally, every new form you create is based on the specified template. But if, for some reason, you want to base a form on FoxPro's Form base class, specify DEFAULT in the CREATE FORM command.

In VFP 6, we finally have the clause we really want in CREATE FORM. The new AS ClassName FROM ClassLib clause lets us specify the base class for a new form on the fly. It works the same way here as in CREATE CLASS. If, for some reason (we can't think of one), you include both AS and DEFAULT clauses, the DEFAULT clause wins and the form is based on the VFP base form class.

The METHOD clause of MODIFY FORM was added in VFP 5. It lets you open a form and, at the same time, open a method-editing window to a particular method. It doesn't matter whether or not the specified method has code in it, which is very cool.

WINDOW DefinitionWindow specifies an existing window from which the Form Designer borrows size and position. Unlike some other commands with WINDOW clauses, other characteristics of DefinitionWindow (such as its title) are ignored.

IN WINDOW works here pretty much as it does elsewhere, letting you imprison the Form Designer in ContainerWindow. As far as we can tell, IN SCREEN makes no difference whatsoever and can safely be ignored.

As with other CREATE and MODIFY commands, NOWAIT lets you open an editing window in a program and leave it there while you go on to other tasks. SAVE, as elsewhere, is unnecessary as long as you have NOWAIT. In a program, without NOWAIT or SAVE, clicking on another window that's not part of the Form Designer closes it.

The NOENVIRONMENT clause, included for backward compatibility, doesn't do anything.

The SCREEN versions of these commands (CREATE SCREEN and MODIFY SCREEN) are included for backward compatibility as is the "quick screen" version of CREATE SCREEN (its syntax isn't shown above). In FoxPro 2.x, the optional FROM clause let you create a new screen programmatically without the Screen Builder even appearing. This clause and its other options are ignored in Visual FoxPro—this form of the command opens the Form Designer, just like any other version. (You can create forms programmatically in Visual FoxPro, but you'd probably do it with a Builder. The Builder could use CreateObject() to create the initial form, then manipulate the form properties and contents, and finally use the SaveAs method to store the newly populated form.)

Example

```
* Open the FD, specifying the base class for a form.
CREATE FORM MyNewForm AS MyBaseForm FROM MyClasses
* Open the FD in a program, prompting for a form to edit
```

```
MODIFY FORM ? NOWAIT
```

See Also Compile Form, Do Form

Create From See Copy Structure.

Create Label, Modify Label, Create Report, Modify Report

These commands open the Label and Report Designers. There's also a special form of CREATE REPORT that lets you set up a report without opening the Report Designer.

Usage

```
CREATE LABEL | REPORT [ FileName | ? ]
        [ WINDOW DefinitionWindow ]
        [ IN [ WINDOW ] ContainerWindow | IN SCREEN
         | IN MACDESKTOP ]
        [ NOWAIT ] [ SAVE ]
MODIFY LABEL | REPORT [ FileName | ? ]
        [ WINDOW DefinitionWindow ]
        [ IN [ WINDOW ] ContainerWindow | IN SCREEN
         | IN MACDESKTOP ]
        [ NOWAIT ] [ SAVE ]
        [ NOENVIRONMENT ]
```

See CREATE FORM for explanations of the various clauses in the ordinary form of these commands. There's also a unique form of CREATE REPORT described below.

Example

```
CREATE LABEL MyLabel
CREATE REPORT MyReport
```

Usage

```
CREATE REPORT FileName | ? FROM TableName
        [ FORM | COLUMN ] [ FIELDS FieldList ] [ ALIAS ]
        [ WIDTH nColumns ] [ NOOVERWRITE ]
```

This is a pretty cool command. It lets you create a report programmatically without having to actually mess with the FRX table. The reports it creates aren't nice enough to actually use for anything, but they do provide a good starting point. With a little help from SET FIELDS, they can also be good enough for a client who wants some very simple ad hoc reporting capabilities. Basically, this form is a command version of the Quick Report option on the Report menu.

There are two types of quick reports. A FORM report has one row per field—it looks like APPEND or EDIT. A COLUMN report has one row per record with a column for each field—it looks like a BROWSE.

There are times when you really need fields in a report to be aliased and other situations where the alias gets in the way. The ALIAS keyword lets *you* decide which case you have. Including it adds the table's name to each field in the report. Regardless of whether you specify ALIAS, the named table is placed in the report's Data environment.

NOOVERWRITE protects you from yourself. If you already have a file with the specified filename, nothing happens. Really, nothing happens—no error message, no new report. Without this clause, but with SAFETY ON, you get prompted if the file exists.

The WIDTH clause is ignored. No matter what value you pass, FoxPro does its own thing and uses as many columns as it thinks you need or as many as fit the current page setup. To control the report's width, you'll have to limit the field list.

See Also Compile Form, Compile Label, Compile Report, Create Form, Label, Report

Create Menu, Modify Menu

These two commands open the Menu Designer. They share many of their clauses with other Create/Modify pairs.

Usage

```
CREATE | MODIFY MENU [ MenuName | ? ]
         [ WINDOW DefinitionWindow ]
         [ IN [ WINDOW ] ContainerWindow | IN SCREEN
          | IN MACDESKTOP ]
         [ NOWAIT ] [ SAVE ]
```

See Create Form for explanations of the various clauses of these commands.

The Menu Designer creates Windows-type menus, using DEFINE MENU et al. Beginning with VFP 5, it can also be used to create shortcut menus (also known as right-click or context menus).

Example

```
CREATE MENU AppMenu
```

See Also Create Form, Define Bar, Define Menu, Define Pad, Define Popup, Set SysMenu

Create Project, Modify Project

These two commands open the Project Manager. Both can be used whether or not the project already exists. Their behavior differs in how they handle that situation and in what they do when you don't tell them what project to open.

Usage

```
CREATE | MODIFY PROJECT [ ProjectName | ? ]
         [ NOWAIT ] [ SAVE ]
         [ WINDOW TemplateWindow ]
         [ IN [ WINDOW ] ContainerWindow | SCREEN ]
         [ NOSHOW ]
         [ NOPROJECTHOOK ]
```

Both CREATE PROJECT and MODIFY PROJECT have one very neat capability. If you use either one to start a new project, then decide to bag it before you put anything in the project, a dialog appears asking whether to delete the empty project from the disk. Having a choice here is really nice. We can think of two very different scenarios. Scenario 1 is the more common one—you've mistyped the name of the project you want to work on or you're in the wrong directory. In that case, you press Esc to get out and you can get rid of the misnamed project. In scenario 2, you want for some reason to create an empty project—you can do it.

The WINDOW and IN WINDOW clauses are meant to give you flexibility in where and how the Project Manager appears, similar to what you get with MODIFY COMMAND or BROWSE. However, they don't work. Frankly, we're not sure why you'd want these clauses for these commands anyway.

NOWAIT, on the other hand, is useful. If you MODIFY PROJECT in a program, it lets you continue the program, leaving the project open. SAVE keeps the project window open when you open it programmatically and the user then makes another window active.

The bottom line is that these are commands you'll use a lot from the Command Window in their most basic form. Before VFP 6, you were very unlikely to put them in programs. However, the new ability to address a project as an object and the project hook base class means that we expect to do a lot more manipulation of projects programmatically. So perhaps these commands will get more programmatic use.

The NOSHOW and NOPROJECTHOOK keywords are new in VFP 6 and, while not directly related to each other, they're really both related to the addition of project hooks. NOPROJECTHOOK is sort of obvious—when you use it, the project is opened without creating an associated project hook object. That means, of course, that you can't do all the things with the project that you can when you have a project hook.

So how does NOSHOW relate to project hooks? Well, until we had them, there wasn't much reason to want to open a project without showing the Project Manager. Now you might want to open a project and have all kinds of things going on in code without anything being visible.

Example `CREATE PROJECT MyCoolProject`

See Also Build App, Build Exe, Build Project, Project, ProjectHook, Projects

Create Query, Modify Query

These two commands open the Query Designer, for a new or existing query, respectively, sort of.

Usage

```
CREATE QUERY [ cFileName | ? ]
        [ NOWAIT ] [ SAVE ]
        [ AS nCodePage ]
        [ WINDOW cDefiningWindow ]
        [ IN [ WINDOW ] cContainingWindow |
          IN SCREEN | IN MACDESKTOP ]
MODIFY QUERY [ cFileName | ? ]
        [ NOWAIT ] [ SAVE ]
        [ AS nCodePage ]
        [ WINDOW cDefiningWindow ]
        [ IN [ WINDOW ] cContainingWindow |
          IN SCREEN | IN MACDESKTOP ]
```

Specifying the ? in CREATE QUERY brings up the Save As dialog, so you can specify a name for the new query. Unlike some of the other CREATE commands, omitting the parameter in CREATE QUERY doesn't display the Save As dialog—instead you see Query1 (or whatever number you're up to) and you can name it on the way out. With MODIFY QUERY, either ? or omitting the file name entirely brings up the Open dialog.

For CREATE QUERY, the Query Designer opens with the Add Table dialog in front of it. This lets you add the first table to the query on the way in. (You can skip that step by pressing ESC or clicking Cancel.)

These commands include a bunch of optional clauses (many of them undocumented) generally relevant only in programs. Since you can't include the Query Designer in a distributed application, issuing these commands in a program isn't terribly useful, unless you are in one of those unusual installations that has purchased the development version of Visual FoxPro for each desk. Even if you could distribute the Query Designer, it's not a very good tool for end users. It's both too restrictive and too low-level. Get FoxFire! or another add-on query creation tool instead.

If you really think you need one of the optional clauses, check out MODIFY COMMAND, which supports them and where they're actually useful. For more information on using the Query Designer, see "These Are Not Your Father's Power Tools."

And what about that "sort of" in the introduction above? Turns out if you CREATE QUERY AnExistingQuery (with SET SAFETY ON), you get asked if you want to overwrite it. If you say no, it opens up just as if you'd issued MODIFY QUERY. If SAFETY is OFF, CREATE QUERY AnExistingQuery just opens it up. Stupidly, in either case, the Choose Table dialog appears as if it were a new query. If you MODIFY QUERY ANewQuery, it behaves like CREATE QUERY. Frankly, we like this behavior because it means we can just use MODIFY QUERY all the time and forget that CREATE QUERY exists.

A typical interactive session for us involves lots of typing from the command window, and we like just cursoring up a few lines and hitting return to repeat a previously entered command. We expect that FoxPro will "do what we mean, not what we say," and past versions have allowed us this luxury. CREATE FORM myNewForm means "create a new one" the first time we issue it, but it means "drag up the old one" if we say it again. If we really mean to create a new form, then we'll see that there's already one by the name we chose, and we'll close it and use a new name. We can't remember the last time we chose to overwrite an existing form. This is the behavior in the current product for the CREATE FORM command, and we expect the same for the CREATE QUERY.

It turns out we have different habits here. One of us habitually uses MODIFY for these tasks while the other prefers CREATE. If you want to use CREATE, you'll want SAFETY OFF, so you don't have to keep telling VFP not to overwrite existing queries (or forms or whatever).

Beware. If you issue MODIFY QUERY for an existing QPR and the Query Designer can't figure out how to parse the query (most likely because you changed it by hand), the Query Designer opens with less than your entire query represented. What you actually see depends on the query. The QD parses what it can and plonks those items in the right places, but anything it doesn't understand (and even some things that it should understand) gets dumped. The View Designer, which is really just another face for the Query Designer, behaves pretty much the same way.

Example

```
CREATE QUERY MyNewQuery
```

See Also Create SQL View, Modify Command, Modify View, Select-SQL

Create Report See Create Label.

Create Screen See Create Form.

Create SQL View, Delete View

These commands add and remove both local and remote views from a database. CREATE SQL VIEW is rather long-winded, but it must be, because CREATE VIEW is an old (useless) Xbase command.

Usage

```
CREATE SQL VIEW [ ViewAlias ] [ REMOTE ]
        [ CONNECTION Connection [ SHARE ]
         | CONNECTION DataSource ]
        [ AS SQLSelect ]
```

Parameter	Value	Meaning
ViewAlias	Name	The name to assign the new view.
	Omitted	If the AS clause is also omitted, open the View Designer for a new view. Otherwise, prompt for a name for the new view.
Connection	Name	The name of an existing connection in the database that should be used to access remote data.
DataSource	Name	The name of an existing ODBC data source that should be used to access remote data.
SQLSelect	Included	Define the view to use the specified query.
	Omitted (along with the AS keyword)	Open the View Designer for a new view.

This command has two modes. In one, it opens the View Designer so you can specify the view visually. In the other, it lets you define a view programmatically (and invisibly). There are so many other ways to open the View Designer, and CREATE SQL VIEW is such a long command (15 characters, counting embedded blanks) that we think its importance lies in programmatic use. Behind the scenes, you can specify either a local or remote view and have it added to the open database.

Omitting both the REMOTE keyword and the CONNECTION clause results in a local view. Including either gives you a remote view. You can specify CONNECTION without REMOTE and still keep it behind the scenes. If you specify REMOTE and don't indicate a connection, you'll be prompted to choose one.

SQLSelect can be any valid query. It doesn't get an INTO clause, though, because view data is put in a cursor automatically. Don't wrap the query in quotes. Strange as it seems to us, too, you explicitly issue the query as part of this command.

One warning on queries for remote views: Because they'll be interpreted by the server, make sure you use only standard SQL syntax, not VFP's extensions.

The View Designer actually does more than CREATE SQL VIEW. To specify the items on the Update Criteria tab of the View Designer, use DBSETPROP().

Don't confuse CREATE SQL VIEW with the lame Xbase CREATE VIEW, which attempts to save all current environmental settings to a VUE file.

One of the really cool things about Visual FoxPro is parameterized views. A parameter is simply a variable that belongs to the view. You can use it in the WHERE clause of the query that defines the view—just precede it with "?" to make it a parameter. If the variable exists when you USE (or REQUERY()) the view, its current value is substituted. If the variable doesn't exist, the user is prompted (with a pretty decent looking dialog) to supply a value.

Coolest of all, if you change the parameter's value and REQUERY(), the view is re-created with the records that now match the condition. Parameterized views let you write a query once, but use it for a wide range of conditions.

Example

```
CREATE SQL VIEW EmployeesByBirthDate ;
   AS SELECT * FROM TasTrade!Employee ;
         WHERE Birth_Date >= ?Birthdate
```

The example creates a parameterized view called EmployeesByBirthDate that chooses employees from TasTrade's employee table who were born on or after a specified date. When you open the view with USE EmployeesByBirthDate, if the variable Birthdate exists, its current value is substituted into the query. If it doesn't exist, a dialog appears, prompting for a value.

This one's really cool. When you use a parameterized view as the source for a control in a form (say, a grid or list), the parameter can be something like "ThisForm.SomeProperty." You can set up the view just as you want it on the form and not have to use a separate variable for the parameter. When you open the view outside the form, you get prompted for the parameter just as you do in any other case. This is the only place we know of in Visual FoxPro where you can use ThisForm notation in something other than method code or a property definition. Here's an example, letting you filter Employee on country.

```
CREATE SQL VIEW EmpsByCountry AS ;
   SELECT First_Name,Last_Name FROM TasTrade!Employee ;
      WHERE Country = ?ThisForm.Country
```

In the form that displays this view, you'd create a Country property and, perhaps, have a combo box with Country for a ControlSource. The combo's InteractiveChange method could REQUERY() the view and Refresh the form.

Usage `DELETE VIEW [ ViewName ]`

This command is just what it sounds like. It removes an existing view from a database. Although Help says otherwise, you can omit ViewName and you're prompted with a list of views in the current database.

Example `DELETE VIEW EmployeesByBirthDate`

See Also Create Connection, Create Database, Create View, CursorSetProp(), DBSetProp(), Select-SQL

Create Table

This is a case of practically a whole language in a single command. This command, which lets you define tables programmatically, has been tremendously enhanced in Visual FoxPro. Since it was introduced in FoxPro 2.0, CREATE TABLE has made life a lot simpler for developers. Before that, creating a table meant you had to have something to start with—usually another table with the same or similar structure to the one you wanted to create. Then you could apply COPY STRUCTURE or the pair COPY STRUCTURE EXTENDED and CREATE TABLE FROM. CREATE TABLE freed us from that nonsense.

In Visual FoxPro, CREATE TABLE has whole new aspects. Not only can it create the table itself, but it can also create index tags and persistent relations. In addition, it lets you set both field-level and row-level rules and establish default values.

Usage

```
CREATE TABLE | DBF TableName [ NAME LongTableName ] [ FREE ]
           ( FieldName1 FieldType1
              [ ( nFieldWidth1 [, nDecimals1 ] ) ]
              [ NULL | NOT NULL ]
              [ CHECK lFieldRule1 [ ERROR cFieldRuleMessage1 ] ]
              [ DEFAULT eDefaultExpression1 ]
              [ PRIMARY KEY | UNIQUE ]
              [ REFERENCES ReferencedTable1
                     [ TAG ReferencedTag1 ] ]
              [ NOCPTRANS ]
            [, FieldName2 ... ]
            [, PRIMARY KEY ePrimaryKeyExpression
                    TAG PrimaryKeyTag ]
            [, UNIQUE eUniqueKeyExpression1 TAG UniqueKeyTag1
              [, UNIQUE eUniqueKeyExpression2 ... ] ]
            [, FOREIGN KEY eForeignKeyExpression1
                   TAG ForeignKeyTag1 [ NODUP ]
               REFERENCES ReferencedTable2
                   [ TAG ReferencedTag2 ]
                [, FOREIGN KEY eForeignKeyExpression2 ... ] ]
            [, CHECK lTableRule [ ERROR cTableRuleMessage] ] )
            | FROM ARRAY ArrayName
```

Parameter	Value	Meaning
TableName	Name	The filename for the new table.
LongTableName	Name	The long name to give the table in the open database (128 characters max).
FieldName*x*	Name	The name of the *x*th field in the table. Long names can be used for fields of tables in databases.
FieldType*x*	Single character	The type to use for the *x*th field in the table. Valid types are: C – Character D – Date T – DateTime N – Numeric F – Float (same as Numeric) I – Integer B – Double Y – Currency L – Logical M – Memo G – General

Parameter	Value	Meaning
FieldType*x*		Designate the Character (Binary) and Memo (Binary) field types seen in the Table Designer with the NOCPTRANS keyword, as shown above.
nFieldWidth*x*	Numeric	The width of the *x*th field in the table. For many types, the width is fixed and nFieldWidth should be omitted. Only Character, Numeric, and Float require field width. Cannot be specified for Double.
nDecimals*x*	Numeric	The number of decimal places for the *x*th field in the table. Relevant only for Numeric, Float and Double.
lFieldRule*x*	Logical	A logical expression that provides the field-level rule for the *x*th field in the table. Can call a function.
cFieldRuleMessage*x*	Character	The error message to display when the field rule for the *x*th field is violated.
eDefaultExpression*x*	Same type as specified by FieldType*x*	An expression that provides a default value for the *x*th field in the table.
ReferencedTable*x*	Name	The name of the table for which the field or expression is a foreign key. A regular index tag is created for this field or expression.
ReferencedTag*x*	Name	The name of the tag in ReferencedTable*x* to which the field or expression refers.
	Omitted	The field or expression refers to the primary key in ReferencedTable*x*.
ePrimaryKeyExpression	Any type	An expression that forms the primary key for this table. Normally used when the primary key is a composite of several fields.
PrimaryKeyTag	Name	The name to assign the tag created for the primary key.
eUniqueKeyExpression*x*	Any type	An expression that forms a candidate key for this table. Normally used for composite keys.
UniqueKeyTag*x*	Name	The name to assign the *x*th candidate key tag created.
eForeignKeyExpression*x*	Any type	An expression that is a foreign key into another table. A regular index tag is created for this expression. Normally used for composite keys.
ForeignKeyTag*x*	Name	The name of the tag to be created for eForeignKeyExpression*x*.
lTableRule	Logical	A logical expression that provides the table-level rule. Functions can be called.
cTableRuleMessage	Character	The error message to display when the table-level rule is violated.

There's so much going on in this one command that you could (and we did!) spend days testing all the combinations. Let's try to break it down into logical components instead.

The first thing is to note that there's information at two levels: table and field. The initial part of the command until the opening parenthesis applies to the table, as does everything following the field list. (In the syntax diagram, that's everything from the second PRIMARY KEY to the end.)

Many of the clauses appear to be repeated. That's because you can specify a number of things at both levels. Within the field list, for example, CHECK indicates a field-level rule. After the field list, it indicates a table-level rule.

In addition, some items can appear more than once. Of course, the whole field listing is available for each field. In addition, at the table level, you can specify multiple candidate keys (with the UNIQUE clause) and multiple foreign keys.

Types of Tables

You can create two different types of tables: free tables and tables that belong to a database. Many clauses apply only when you're adding a table to a database. They are NAME, CHECK (and ERROR), DEFAULT, PRIMARY KEY, FOREIGN KEY and REFERENCES (and TAG), at all levels where they appear. The attributes created by these clauses apply only to tables in a database.

The FREE keyword is needed only if there's a database set and you don't want the new table to belong to it. With no database set, free tables are created automatically.

In VFP 3, to add tables to a database, the database had to be open exclusively. In VFP 5 and VFP 6, you can add tables to a shared database. Regardless, the new table is opened exclusively in an available work area.

Field Information

For each field, we start out with the same information we've always had—a field name, type, and size. But there's so much more here now. CREATE TABLE rightfully rejects certain VFP reserved words as field names, things like PRIMARY and FOREIGN that are just too confusing for it to deal with. Unfortunately, the Table Designer isn't as discriminating and lets you use these keywords as field names. If you're stuck with a such a table and need to re-create it with code, the solution is to surround the offending field names with quotes. Of course, it would be even better if the Table Designer wouldn't let you shoot yourself in the foot this way.

Fields can accept or reject nulls (poor nulls, being rejected all the time). Generally, we recommend you allow nulls only where they're meaningful—dealing with them is a pain, so don't have more than you need. SET NULL determines whether any field accepts null, unless you specify NULL or NOT NULL. Like every good rule, there's one exception: If you omit both NULL and NOT NULL, but include PRIMARY KEY or UNIQUE, the field doesn't accept nulls.

NOCPTRANS determines whether codepage translation affects the field. Some kinds of data (for example, binary keys) are damaged when translated to another codepage—you can indicate which fields are badly affected. When the table is opened under another codepage, those fields are unchanged.

Indexes

Several kinds of indexes can be created right along with the table. As expected, the PRIMARY KEY clause establishes a primary key for the table—one to a customer, please.

The UNIQUE clause that appears at both the field and table levels has nothing to do with Xbase's traditional (and not really) unique indexes—the ones you create by SETting UNIQUE ON or adding the UNIQUE keyword to INDEX. UNIQUE in CREATE TABLE produces what's called a "candidate key"—like a primary key, no duplicates are allowed. The main difference between a primary key and a candidate key is that we've indicated that the primary key is primary. The other difference is that free tables can have candidate keys, but not primary keys.

You can't specify primary or candidate keys at the field level for fields using long names. When you try, you get the error message "Tag name is too long." That actually makes sense because the field name is used as the tag name, and tag names are still limited to 10 characters. In fact, maybe that limit is the real bug here.

The REFERENCES clause at the field level and the FOREIGN KEY clause at the table level let you create regular indexes that are related to other tables in the database. (Include NODUP to make it a candidate rather than a regular index.) You specify an expression in this table (at the field level, it's the field itself) that relates to an existing tag in another table. The REFERENCES portion mentions the other table and the tag you're relating to there.

You can, of course, create additional indexes with the INDEX command.

Rules

Tables in a database can have rules at both the field and table levels—that's the CHECK clause. Rules are your opportunity to make sure newly entered data is good enough for the field or table. In VFP 3, rules were not permitted to change the record. In VFP 5 and VFP 6, you can change fields of the current record in rule code. Be careful—it's your responsibility to make sure that the changes don't result in an infinite sequence of calls to the rule code.

Hip, Hip, Array!

There's an alternative to listing out all the fields with all their information. Put the data into an array (with the same structure as the ones created by AFIELDS()) and just base the table on the array. This is a great choice when you want a table that's similar, but not identical, to an existing table. Use AFIELDS() on the first table, modify the array, then CREATE TABLE from it.

However, index information doesn't come along this way. When you CREATE TABLE from an array, all you get is the field structure (including rules, defaults and so forth) and the table-level rules.

Triggers

CREATE TABLE doesn't let you create the triggers for the table. You do that with the CREATE TRIGGER command.

Example

```
* Create a near duplicate of an existing table
USE Original
nFldCount=AFIELDS(aStruc)
DIMENSION aStruc(nFldCount+1,ALEN(aStruc,2))
aStruc[nFldCount+1,1]="cMyNewField"  && Name
aStruc[nFldCount+1,2]="C"            && Type
aStruc[nFldCount+1,3]=5              && Size
aStruc[nFldCount+1,4]=0              && Decimals
aStruc[nFldCount+1,5]=.F.            && Nulls
aStruc[nFldCount+1,9]="JUNK"         && Default
CREATE TABLE NewOne FROM ARRAY aStruc

* Create a database from scratch
CREATE DATABASE Clients
CREATE TABLE Client ;
   (cClientId C(6) DEFAULT GetId("Client") ;
                   PRIMARY KEY NOCPTRANS, ;
    cLastName C(20) CHECK NOT EMPTY(cLastName) ;
                    ERROR "Must provide last name", ;
    cFirstName C(15), ;
    mStreetAddress M, ;
    cCity C(20), ;
```

```
         cState C(2) CHECK EMPTY(cState) OR ;
                           LookUpState(cState) ;
                     ERROR "Unknown State", ;
         cZip C(9), ;
         CHECK NOT (EMPTY(cState) AND NOT EMPTY(cCity)) ;
        )
     CREATE TABLE Meetings ;
        (cMeetingId C(6) DEFAULT GetId("Meetings") ;
                         PRIMARY KEY NOCPTRANS, ;
         dMeetingDate D, ;
         cClientId C(6) REFERENCES Client, ;
         nMeetingLength N(3) ;
        )
```

In the first example, we add a field to the list from an existing table and create a new table. In the second example, we create a database with two tables. Each has a primary key (as all good tables should) and each has a default value that calls a routine that generates a new key. There's a persistent relation between the cClientId fields of the two tables. Several fields have rules. The rule for cState lets you leave it empty, but if it's not empty, you better be able to find it by looking it up. Clients has a table-level rule, too, which says that if you fill in the city, you have to fill in the state.

See Also AFields(), Alter Table, Create Cursor, Create Trigger, INDEX, Set NoCPTrans, Set Null

Create Trigger, Delete Trigger

These two commands let you add and remove triggers for tables in a database.

Usage

```
CREATE TRIGGER ON TableName
     FOR INSERT | UPDATE | DELETE AS lTrigger
DELETE TRIGGER ON TableName
     FOR INSERT | UPDATE | DELETE
```

A trigger is a piece of code that runs under certain conditions. Visual FoxPro supports three kinds of triggers: Insert, Update and Delete. The Insert trigger for a table fires when you append a record and when you RECALL a deleted record. The Update trigger fires when you modify a record, and the Delete trigger fires when you delete a record. Buffering postpones triggers until you do something that attempts to commit the change.

Although lTrigger can be a simple expression, usually it's a call to a routine (in fact, most often a stored procedure) that returns either .T. or .F. If a trigger returns .F., the current error handler (yours or FoxPro's) is called.

When a trigger returns .F. in a Browse or grid, it bypasses any custom error handler, and FoxPro's default "Trigger failed" message appears.

Triggers cannot change data in the table they belong to. They can (and often do) change data in other tables in the same database.

The RI builder uses triggers to enforce referential integrity. It generates code that is saved with the database's stored procedures and sets the tables' triggers to appropriate calls to that code. (These routines are one example of trigger code that changes other tables.)

The Delete trigger doesn't fire when you ZAP a table. Although we think using ZAP is a terrible mistake, except on your own test data, this is an absolute violation of the integrity of the database. It leaves a huge landmine in the path of any user who knows enough to be dangerous.

Example

```
CREATE TRIGGER ON MyTable FOR INSERT AS MyTrigger

* And here's the trigger code
PROCEDURE MyTrigger

WAIT WINDOW "New record added. Total is now " + ;
            LTRIM(STR(RECCOUNT()))
RETURN .T.
```

See Also Create Database, Create Table, Modify Database, _TriggerLevel

Create View, Set View, Set

Here's a pair of commands you should avoid, plus one we use all the time. We can't figure out why CREATE VIEW and SET VIEW aren't marked "for backward compatibility only"—they should be. Actually, even in backward times, views of this sort weren't such a good idea. SET by itself, though, is handy when you're developing—it opens the View window.

CREATE VIEW creates a "view file" with the extension VUE that contains information about the current FoxPro environment. SET VIEW reads the information in a VUE file and re-establishes that environment.

Usage

```
CREATE VIEW ViewFileName
SET VIEW TO ViewFileName | ?
SET VIEW ON | OFF
SET
```

Sounds pretty good, so what's our complaint? First of all, views have never contained all the information needed to make them really useful. For example, they include the open tables and indexes, but not the record pointers for those tables. To really save the environment, try reduce, reuse, recycle.

Second and far more serious, VUE files (like MEM files) are a mysterious format. You can't open them up and mess around, except using the low-level file functions. It makes far more sense to create your own status table—you can use the various status-tracking functions to get the information you need and store it all in a nice, readable format.

Don't confuse this CREATE VIEW command with CREATE SQL VIEW, which lets you define views of remote and local data. Those views have nothing to do with these views.

The help file lists all the things that get stored in a view, so we won't repeat them here. We did find a couple of oddities in SET VIEW's behavior, which we will share.

Although the current default directory is stored as part of the view, in VFP 3 it wasn't restored. But the paths to open tables were stored relative to the default directory. So, if you SET VIEW from a different directory than you CREATEd it, VFP 3 couldn't open the tables. VFP 5 and VFP 6 are better behaved in this regard—they set default to the stored default directory.

In the "that's interesting, but when will I ever use this?" category, Visual FoxPro's updated View window (now called the Data Session window) tends to show open tables in reverse work area order. If you use the View window to open tables or you habitually issue SELECT 0 before USEing a table, you'll normally see the tables in reverse work area order. When SET VIEW restores the open tables, they turn up in work area order in the View window. (We don't know when you'll ever use this piece of information, either.)

SET VIEW ON or OFF is something completely different. It controls the View window. SET VIEW ON makes it appear, and SET VIEW OFF makes it disappear. We've never seen any reason to type that many characters, because using SET, by itself, opens the view window; pressing ESC while it has focus closes it.

See Also AUsed(), Create SQL View, Relation(), Set, Set Alternate, Set Default, Set Fields, Set Filter, Set Format, Set Help, Set Path, Set Procedure, Set Resource, Set Skip, Set Status Bar, Used()

CreateBinary()

This function converts a string containing binary data to a format that can be recognized by an OLE object.

Usage

```
cOutString = CreateBinary( cInString )
```

Parameter	Value	Meaning
cInString	Character	Binary characters to be converted.
cOutString	Character	String flagged internally by VFP as containing binary data.

When working exclusively in Visual FoxPro, this function is not necessary. It is used for passing information back and forth to OLE objects and controls. Visual FoxPro actually does a lot of translation behind the scenes when interacting with OLE objects, and this is one of those cases where we have to give it a hint. When passing character variables to an OLE object, VFP translates them into the OLE type string. OLE strings, however, can only hold text, and not the binary data that Visual FoxPro is capable of storing in character variables. CREATEBINARY() flags a variable as containing binary information, so that FoxPro's built-in translation mechanisms know how to convert it before sending it to the OLE control.

Note that you can only abbreviate the function to CreateB(), due to the other functions CreateObject() and CreateOffline().

Example

```
lcString1 = CHR(01) + CHR(02) + CHR(03)
lcString2 = CreateBinary( lcString1 )
? lcString2 == lcString1  && .T., identical within VFP
oObject.Method(lcString1)  && OLE Error
oObject.Method(lcString2)  && works
```

See Also CreateObject, OLEBoundControl, OLEControl

CreateObject(), NewObject()

These functions instantiate objects based on a specified class. The class may be one of the FoxPro base classes, a user-defined class, or a class from a registered OLE server.

Usage

```
oObject = CREATEOBJECT( cClassName
                        [, uParam1 [, uParam2 [, ...] ] ] )
oObject = NEWOBJECT( cClassName [, cClassLib [, cLibInApp
                     [, uParam1 [, uParam2 [, ... ] ] ] ] ] )
```

Parameter	Value	Meaning
cClassName	FoxPro class name	Create an object of the specified FoxPro class.
	COM Object class name	Start the COM Object, if it's not running, and either create or get a handle to an object of the specified class.
uParam1, uParam2, ...	Any expressions	Parameters to pass to the Init method of the class.
cClassLib	Character	The path and filename of the library, program or application containing cClassName. An extension of VCX is assumed, if you omit it.

Parameter	Value	Meaning
cLibInApp	Character	The path and filename (including extension) of the application containing cClassLib.
oObject	Object	A reference to the newly created object.

NewObject() was added in VFP 6 and lets you instantiate things without having to issue SET CLASSLIB or SET PROCEDURE first. Instead, you can incorporate the information about where to find the relevant class into the command. Because you can omit the class information if you want, and then NewObject() behaves just like CreateObject(), we suspect we'll be using NewObject() all the time, if we can only retrain our fingers from typing o=CREA("whatever").

NewObject() even lets you deal with classes whose definition exists only in an application (APP or EXE or whatever). You don't have to have the actual class library available. Just point to the class library and the application:

```
o = NewObject("MyClass", "MyClassLib", "MyApp.APP")
```

and VFP is able to dig through the app file and find the class definition.

We think this is really cool stuff. It'll make it much easier for people to distribute class libraries without having to distribute the source.

For automation objects, cClassName consists of the application name followed by the class name. For example, to open Word 97, you use:

```
oWord = CreateObject("Word.Application")
```

See "It Was Automation, You Know" for more on Automation.

Almost every object has an Init method that fires when the object is created. (The few that don't are those created in oddball ways, such as SCATTER NAME.) You can pass parameters to the Init method of FoxPro objects by including them in CreateObject() or NewObject(). Beware, though: When container objects are instantiated, the Init methods of the contained objects execute before the Init of the container. For example, the Inits from all the controls in a form fire before the Init for the form.

Passing parameters to Init is a good way to set properties of an object at creation time. In the Init method, assign the values of the passed parameters to the appropriate properties.

Example

```
oMine1 = CREATEOBJECT("MyClass", 37, "Mustang")
? oMine1.Flivver   && Returns 37
? oMine1.Giblet    && Returns "Mustang"

oMine2 = CREATEOBJECT("MyClass")
? oMine2.Flivver   && Returns 0
? oMine2.Giblet    && Returns ""

oMine3 = CREATEOBJECT("MyClass", 14)
? oMine3.Flivver   && Returns 14
? oMine3.Giblet    && Returns ""

DEFINE CLASS MyClass AS CUSTOM

   * add some properties
   Flivver = 0
   Giblet = ""

PROCEDURE Init

   LPARAMETERS nFlivver, cGiblet
```

```
      IF NOT EMPTY(nFlivver)
         This.Flivver = nFlivver
      ENDIF
      IF NOT EMPTY(cGiblet)
         This.Giblet = cGiblet
      ENDIF
   ENDPROC

   ENDDEFINE

   * If the definition above is stored in MyClass.PRG
   * you could also:
   oMine4 = NewObject("MyClass","MyClass.PRG")
```

See Also AddObject, Define Class, Do Form, GetObject(), Init, NewObject

CreateObjectEx()

Distributed computing arrives at last! This function lets you create objects *external* to the machine you're working on.

Usage

```
oHandle = CreateObjectEx( cCLSID
                          | cProgID [ , cComputer ] )
```

Parameter	**Value**	**Meaning**
cCLSID	Character	The class identifier of the object you're trying to create, typically in the form returned by the CLSID property ({HhHhHhHh-HhHh-HhHh-HhHh-HhHhHhHhHhHh}, where each "Hh" is a hexadecimal representation of one byte).
cProgID	Character	The programmatic identifier for the class. This is the "friendly name" of the COM server, as stored in the Registry. For example, "Word.Application".
cComputer	Character	The name of the computer on which this object is created. The name can be in Universal Naming Convention (UNC) format, as in "\\ServerName," or in another format that can be resolved to an individual machine name, such as a TCP/IP address or domain name. Services to resolve the addresses must be available to the machine.
	Omitted	Create the object on the local machine.
oHandle	Object	Returns a handle to the object if created successfully. In our experience, failure to create the object typically brings up the error handler.

If you've been following the adventures of Microsoft and the idea of running portions of your application on other machines, you know they introduced the idea of Remote Automation in the VFP 3 timeframe. Remote Automation required that a separate Automation Manager run on the server machine to support communications between the two machines. It was awkward to set up, and it wasn't terribly stable. Not long after that came the similar idea of Distributed COM, where the COM model itself works with remote components by presenting a proxy object on the local machine that imitates the interface of the remote object, and DCOM itself handles the communication between machines. (Microsoft refers to this as "remoting an object." We've learned that in English every noun verbs, but this is the first time we've seen an adjective verb.) CreateObjectEx() is another step along the way.

With CreateObjectEx(), there are two ways to work with a remote object. First, if the class ID of the object itself is known, it can be called directly from any client machine, without the need to pre-install any software on those clients. This is ideal for those situations where you don't have control over the configuration of the client machines. An example might be over the Web or a WAN. This lets you invoke a remote object without messing with the client's Registry. The second calling format, using the ProgID (the English language version of the COM object's name, such as "MyServer.MyObject") has the advantage of much more readable code, but the disadvantage of having to be pre-registered on each client machine.

So what's the advantage of this over the earlier versions of DCOM? The real payoff comes in the last parameter, where the name of the computer on which to create the object is specified. Since this is a string parameter, it can be programmatically assigned at runtime. This gives you the option of creating load-balancing schemes or strategies of pooling computers to perform intensive tasks, and then finding the most available machine at runtime.

Example

```
oProj = _vfp.ActiveProject          && get a handle to the project
cCLSID = oProj.Servers[1].CLSID     && Get 1st server's class id
oWow = CreateObjectEx(cCLSID,"")    && Create the object locally
```

See Also CLSID, CreateObject(), ProgID

CreateOffline(), DropOffline()

These functions, added in VFP 5, let you create and destroy offline views.

Usage

```
lSuccess = CreateOffline( cViewName [, cPathAndFile ] )
lSuccess = DropOffline( cViewName )
```

Parameter	Value	Meaning
cViewName	Character	The name in the database of the view for which to create or drop an offline view.
cPathAndFile	Character	The path and filename for the table to be created to hold the offline view. Be careful to include the filename here. If you don't, you're likely to end up with a file that has the directory name you intended and is one directory level higher than you expect.
	Omitted	The table is created in the current directory using the view name as the filename.
lSuccess	.T.	The view was successfully taken offline or brought back online.
	.F.	The view could not be taken offline or brought online.

First things first. Because CreateOffline() has its first seven letters in common with CreateObject(), you need at least CreateOf() for VFP to know what you mean. On the other hand, Drop() is sufficient for DropOffline().

Offline views are one of those things that seemed like such a good idea when they were added to the product, but we don't actually know anyone who's using them in production applications. They're VFP's version of replication and, in typical FoxPro fashion, you have control over what happens, but the price is that you have to write a lot of code. (For the most part, it's the same conflict resolution code you normally use. See GetFldState() for a simple version of conflict resolution code.)

When you take a view offline, you get a physical copy of the data in the specified location. The original view is marked as read-only in the database, so anyone opening it actually gets the newly created table, not an on-the-spot query. If the offline view is created on or moved to a different drive, then no one else can touch that view . When you're ready, you open the view online, resolve conflicts and save the changed data. Then, you can bring the view back online (or drop the offline view) to make it behave like a regular view.

When would you use this strategy? Consider a sales force that's mostly on the road at client sites. They need to be able to update data for their clients on the fly, without having to dial into a server or any such thing. When they come back, or maybe even when they get back to the hotel at night, they need to send the updated data to the server.

So what's the problem? First, note that part about the original view being marked read-only. To make offline views work in this scenario, you have to provide each salesman with his own set of views for the relevant tables. Second, there's that "resolve conflicts" part—it's no easier in this setting than anywhere else. It still requires a bunch of good, solid code.

Nonetheless, we're not exactly sure why no one's using this technique. All the pieces seem to work, and there are settings where it seems just the ticket.

So, on to these two functions, which along with a couple of clauses in the USE command, are the key to offline views. As with so much of the good data-handling stuff in Visual FoxPro, SET MULTILOCKS must be ON to either create or drop an offline view.

CreateOffline() doesn't actually create a new view. It takes an existing view, copies the data to the specified location, and tells the database about it.

A few complications. First, as we mentioned above, be careful to provide a path and filename, not just a path. We've ended up with a table called Offline.DBF more times than we care to admit while testing this.

If the view you specify is parameterized, VFP behaves as it normally does when you open a parameterized view. That is, if the parameter already exists, it just does the job. If the parameter doesn't exist, you're prompted for it.

Taking a view offline doesn't leave it open, though it does leave the tables on which the view is based open.

When a view is offline, it's really offline. The original, online version cannot be opened for viewing or maintenance, let alone to make changes. Attempts to open it actually open the offline view itself, if it's physically present. (You can tell the difference by checking DBF() for the view.) On the whole, it's better to define one set of views for offline work and a separate set for ongoing business, though that does increase the likelihood of conflicts to be resolved down the road.

Watch out for this one. In all versions of VFP 5, if CreateOffline() fails, DBSetProp() still returns .T. for the Offline property.

On to DropOffline(). This one tells the database that its wandering view is home again. It deletes the table containing the offline view and updates the database so it knows to use the original, online version. The view must be closed before you can take it online.

DropOffline() expects the original name of the view as a parameter, not the name of the table you stored it in. While this surprised us at first, in fact it does make sense. The view name is the database's way of keeping track of the view; the name of the physical table in which it's stored is incidental.

If you want to keep your changes, be sure to USE the view ONLINE, and issue appropriate TableUpdate() calls before you drop the offline view. Once you drop it, it's gone, gone, gone.

Example

```
* Take a view from Tastrade offline.
* Give it a short file name
? CreateOffline("Order History","OfflineViews\OrdHist")

* Now work with the offline view
USE "Order History" ALIAS OrdHist
* Make changes as desired

* When you're done:
USE "Order History" ONLINE
* Commit changes
```

```
? TableUpdate(.T.)
USE

* Put it away
? DropOffline("Order History")
```

See Also Create SQL View, TableUpdate(), Use

CToBin() See BinToC().

CToD(), DToC(), DToS()

These functions convert character strings to dates, dates to characters, and dates to character strings in system (YYYYMMDD) format, respectively. All the functions respect the settings of CENTURY, DATE and MARK, so make no assumptions about the placement of particular characters or the exact delimiters used, unless you explicitly SET them first.

Usage

```
dRetVal = CTOD( cDate )
cRetVal = DTOC( dDate | tDateTime [, 1 ] )
cRetVal = DTOS( dDate | tDateTime )
```

CTOD() converts a character expression to a date. CTOD() lets you omit zeros before numbers and translates any of the common delimiters (/, -, .) regardless of the current setting of DATE or MARK.

DTOC() converts a date or datetime to a character string, using the current DATE, MARK and CENTURY format. The optional 1 in the second parameter (actually, any parameter will do—logical, numeric, string, or even .NULL.!) outputs the string in DTOS() format (see below) rather than the current default. Only the date portion of a datetime variable is returned—see TTOC() to get the full datetime value in character form. Without the second parameter, the return value of DTOC() can vary from 8 to 10 characters, depending on the settings of CENTURY. DTOS() converts a date or datetime to a character string of the format YYYYMMDD. This is a format handy for creating indexes, since all dates get listed chronologically. Only the date portion of a datetime variable is returned—see TTOC() to get the full datetime value in character form.

Example

```
cSetDate = SET("DATE")
SET DATE MDY
dRetVal = CTOD(ltrim(str(nMonth))+"/01/1900")
SET DATE &cSetDate

cRetVal = DTOC(datetime())
cRetVal = DTOS(DATE())
```

See Also CDoW(), CMonth(), DoW(), Date(), DMY(), MDY(), GoMonth(), Set Century, Set Date, Set Mark, TToC()

CToT(), DToT(), TToC(), TToD()

These functions convert between dates and characters, and datetimes. Like their predecessor functions DTOC() and CTOD(), each can be read as "something TO something." For example, DTOT() can be understood if said as "Date TO dateTime". CTOT() converts a Character string TO a dateTime.

Usage

```
tReturnValue = CTOT( cString )
tReturnValue = DTOT( dDate )
cReturnValue = TTOC( tDateTime )
dReturnValue = TTOD( tDateTime )
```

CTOT() is pretty smart. If anything less than a full time string is specified, it does its best to figure out what you mean, but it does need some help from you. In particular, in VFP 3.x, CTOT() is unable to parse the time segment without at least one colon. This was fixed in VFP 5.0. Here is what it does under a variety of conditions:

```
? CTOT("7/4/1976")            && 07-04-1976 12:00:00 AM
? CTOT("7/4/1976 ")           && 07-04-1976 12:00:00 AM
? CTOT("7/4/1976 1")          && in VFP 3, empty datetime variable
                              && 07-04-1976 01:00:00 AM in 5 and 6
```

```
? CTOT("7/4/1976 12")          && in VFP 3, empty datetime variable
                               && 07-04-1976 12:00:00 PM in 5 & 6
? CTOT("7/4/1976 12:")         && 07-04-1976 12:00:00 PM
? CTOT("7/4/1976 12:1")        && 07-04-1976 12:01:00 PM
? CTOT("7/4/1976 12:11")       && 07-04-1976 12:11:00 PM
? CTOT("7/4/1976 12:11:")      && 07-04-1976 12:11:00 PM
? CTOT("7/4/1976 12:11:1")     && 07-04-1976 12:11:01 PM
? CTOT("7/4/1976 12:11:11")    && 07-04-1976 12:11:11 PM
```

DTOT() converts date to datetime values by setting the datetime variable to the same date and setting the time to midnight. TTOC() returns a character string, which respects the setting of SET CENTURY, SET SECONDS and SET HOUR, so your return value can vary from 14 to 21 characters in length. TTOD() converts a datetime to a date by truncating the time portion.

The two functions for converting characters to date and datetimes are a potential source of ambiguous dates. Because the interpretation of the string takes place at runtime, the settings in place at that time for DATE and CENTURY can affect the interpretation of the string. If a routine is called from more than one place, it is possible for the same line of code to yield two different date values. For these reasons, SET STRICTDATE has a special setting (2) just for detecting the CTOD() and CTOT() functions in code, and flagging them as places where the potential for ambiguous dates exists. See the section on SET STRICTDATE for details.

Example

```
? DTOT({04/01/95})
* returns 04/01/1995 12:00:00am

? TTOC({04/01/1995 12:00:00am})
* returns "04/01/1995 12:00:00am"

? TTOD({04/01/1995 12:34:56 am})
* returns 04/01/1995
```

There's one conversion many folks feel is missing. There's no function to convert a date and a time to a new datetime variable. There are two possibilities, both pretty simple. If the time is in the format returned by SECONDS(), as the number of seconds since midnight, just add the numeric seconds since midnight to the converted date-to-datetime.

```
tNewDateTime = DTOT(dOldDate) + nTimeInSeconds
```

On the other hand, if you've stored the time in an Hour:Minute:Second character string format, the following expression should take care of your needs:

```
tNewDateTime = CTOT(DTOC(dOldDate) + ' ' + cTimeInSeconds)
```

See Also Date(), DateTime(), Day(), DoW(), DMY(), GoMonth(), MDY(), Month(), Set Century, Set Date, Set Hour, Set Mark, Set Seconds, Set StrictDate, Year()

CurDir(), Sys(2003), Sys(5)

Where am I? That's the question these three functions answer. CURDIR() and SYS(2003) give you the default directory, while SYS(5) provides the default drive. CURDIR() also can tell you the current directory on other drives.

Usage

```
cCurrentDirectory = CURDIR( [ cDriveDesignator ] )
cCurrentDirectory = SYS( 2003 )
```

Without CURDIR()'s optional parameter, the two functions return exactly the same thing. Except that CURDIR() includes the final "\" while SYS(2003) omits it. Go figure.

Pass a drive designator (like "C:") to CURDIR() to find out the current directory on that drive.

This isn't really a bug with CURDIR(), but it's worth pointing out here. When you use CD or SET DEFAULT to change drives, it resets the current directory on the drive you were in to the root. So CURDIR("another drive") always returns "\". How useful.

We used to use CURDIR() all the time to figure out where we were. We still do, in applications, but interactively, CD all by itself is six fewer characters to type. Actually, it's seven fewer because you have to put a "?" in front of CURDIR() to get results. We never use SYS(2003) since we can never remember which SYS() function it is.

Usage
```
cCurrentDrive = SYS(5)
```

SYS(5) (and the equivalent SET("DEFAULT")) give you the current drive designator. Put it together with CURDIR() to find out exactly where you are right now.

Example
```
CD F:\VFP\SAMPLES
* Where are we?
? CURDIR()          && Returns "\VFP\SAMPLES\"
? SYS(2003)         && Returns "\VFP\SAMPLES"
? SYS(5)             && Returns "F:"
CD H:\HACKER
? SYS(5) + CURDIR() && Returns "H:\HACKER\"
? CURDIR("F:")     && Should return "\VFP\SAMPLES\", but returns
                   && "\" because changing to H: changed the
                   && default on F:
```

See Also ChDir, Set Default

_CurObj See ObjNum().

CurrentControl, DynamicCurrentControl, Sparse

These properties (together with the actual objects in the column) determine what control you see in any particular grid cell. If a column has more than one control specified, CurrentControl indicates which should appear, unless DynamicCurrentControl has a value. In that case, the expression specified for DynamicCurrentControl determines which control shows up.

Sparse specifies whether the current control (whichever property determines it) appears all the time in every row for that column or only when that cell has focus.

Usage
```
grcColumn.CurrentControl = cControl
cControl = grcColumn.CurrentControl
grcColumn.DynamicCurrentControl = cExpr
cExpr = grcColumn.DynamicCurrentControl
```

A grid column can contain as many controls as you like to allow different modes of displaying or entering the same information. These two properties determine which of the multitudes the user actually sees.

Like the other Dynamic... properties, DynamicCurrentControl expects a character string containing an expression. The expression itself should evaluate to the name of a control as a character string. (This is yet another place where we're glad FoxPro offers multiple sets of string delimiters.)

If DynamicCurrentControl evaluates to a control the column actually contains, that value supersedes any value in CurrentControl. Although DynamicCurrentControl is pretty dynamic, fortunately it's not so dynamic that the control actually changes while you're sitting on it, even if the expression's value changes.

Our tests indicate that you can't use "This" in the expression to refer to the grid column. We're not too surprised, since the expression gets evaluated not in a method of the column, but at the grid or form level. You need to use ThisForm.TheGridsName.TheColumn, instead.

Example
```
* Say a particular column has a ControlSource of nFld. You can
* put a textbox and a spinner in the column and show the user
* the textbox for odd values and the spinner for even values.
* Why? Why not?
ThisForm.grdMyGrid.grcNFld.DynamicCurrentControl= ;
   "IIF(MOD(nfld,2)=0,'spnNFld','txtNFld')"

* If, on the other hand, we'd just like to have the user see the
* spinner every time:
ThisForm.grdMyGrid.grcNFld.CurrentControl = "spnNFld"
```

Usage
```
grcColumn.Sparse = lHideControl
lHideControl = grcColumn.Sparse
```

One of the coolest features of Visual FoxPro is putting any control you want in a grid. However, looking at a grid full of combo boxes and spinners and check boxes could drive someone nuts. That's where Sparse comes in. When you set Sparse to .T. (the default), the current control for a column shows only when a cell of that column has focus and shows only for the cell with focus. In many cases, it's a lot nicer to look at only the value as text until you're ready to edit it. Then, you want to see the combo or check box or whatever.

When CurrentControl for a cell is a check box bound to a logical field and Sparse is .T., nothing at all shows when the cell doesn't have focus. It's empty. Since check boxes aren't too ugly, your best bet is probably to set Sparse .F. for those columns.

The control that shows when Sparse is .T. and a cell doesn't have focus is a text box. But you don't have any control over it at all. It's not the default text box that gets put in the column when you create the grid. It's a different text box, internal to FoxPro.

Why do you care? Because, even if the control you're using for a column is a text box, when Sparse is .T., things you specify for that text box apply only to the current cell. By "things," we mean properties like InputMask and Format that you might want to see all the time. Fortunately, in VFP 5 and VFP 6, columns have Format and InputMask properties that apply when Sparse is .T. and the cell doesn't have focus. Columns also have their own BackColor and ForeColor that apply in the same circumstances. These colors also propagate down to the contained controls, unless those controls have their own.

If you need more control than that (or you're in VFP 3), forget about Sparse. Instead, put both the control you want and a text box in the column. Format the text box the way you want it and set DynamicCurrentControl to an expression that chooses the text box when the cell doesn't have focus and the other control when it does. You need to compare ActiveColumn for the grid to the particular column's ColumnOrder and check ActiveRow against the record number (if you're working with records in natural order). Our example below shows how to do this.

Example
```
* In the same grid as above, here's the DynamicCurrentControl
* expression to use the spinner when the cell has focus and the
* textbox the rest of the time:
IIF(ThisForm.grdMyGrid.ActiveColumn = ;
    ThisForm.grdMyGrid.grcNFld.ColumnOrder AND ;
    ThisForm.grdMyGrid.ActiveRow = RECNO(),"spnNFld","txtNFld")
* and, of course, we'll need:
ThisForm.grdMyGrid.grcNFld.Sparse = .F.
```

See Also Column, Grid

CurrentX, CurrentY

A number of form methods draw right on the form. These two properties track the position of the drawing pen.

Usage
```
frmForm.CurrentX = nXPosition
nXPosition = frmForm.CurrentX
frmForm.CurrentY = nYPosition
nYPosition = frmForm.CurrentY
```

Several of the drawing methods use CurrentX and CurrentY as defaults if you omit position parameters. All the drawing methods change the value of CurrentX and CurrentY. Like all drawing routines, units are expressed based on the current ScaleMode setting.

Example

```
? _SCREEN.CurrentX, _SCREEN.CurrentY
_SCREEN.Box(100, 100, 200, 250)
? _SCREEN.CurrentX, _SCREEN.CurrentY
_SCREEN.CLS
? _SCREEN.CurrentX, _SCREEN.CurrentY
_SCREEN.DrawWidth = 10
_SCREEN.PSet()
? _SCREEN.CurrentX, _SCREEN.CurrentY
```

See Also Box, Circle, Cls, Line, Print, PSet, ScaleMode

Cursor, Relation

These two classes are members of the Data environment. Cursor represents an individual table or view (but we'll say only "table" below unless something is relevant only to views) that's been added to the DE. Relation contains information about a relation between two cursors in the DE.

Each time you add a table to the Data environment, a new Cursor object is added. It points to the table and lets you set properties (like Alias and Order) used when the table is opened by the DE, either automatically because AutoOpenTables is .T. or by explicitly calling OpenTables.

When you add a table to the DE and that table has a persistent relation with a table already in the DE, a Relation is added. (If the new table has persistent relations with multiple tables, multiple relation objects are added.) The new relations reflect the structure of the persistent relation—in a one-to-many persistent relation, the "one" side becomes the parent and the "many" side becomes the child. Order is automatically set appropriately in the child (via the Relation's ChildOrder property, not the Cursor's Order property).

However, the OneToMany property of the relation is never set to .T. automatically—you have to do that yourself. We originally had mixed feelings about this one. After all, we've already told FoxPro it's a one-to-many relationship. However, we rarely end up setting OneToMany ourselves—it just doesn't seem that important. Besides, with a grid for the "many" side, you can see all the children for the current parent anyway.

You can also add relations by "drawing" them in the Data environment Designer. Drag from a field of one table to a field or index of another. (If there's no index for the field you specify on the child side, you're prompted to let Visual FoxPro create it for you.) Notice that the technique for setting up relations in the DE is different than in the Database Designer. That's because the relations here are temporary relations (the SET RELATION TO kind), not persistent relations.

Cursor

Property	Value	Purpose
Alias	Character	The alias to use for this table or view in the form.
BufferModeOverride	Numeric	Indicates the type of buffering to use for this cursor.
CursorSource	Character	The name of the table or view the cursor is based on. For free tables, includes the full path.
Database	Character	The name of the database containing this table or view.
Exclusive	Logical	Indicates whether or not to open the table exclusively.

Property	Value	Purpose
Filter	Character	The filter expression to apply to the cursor.
NoDataOnLoad	Logical	View only. Indicates whether the data for the view is loaded initially or waits until REQUERY() is executed.
Order	Character	The name of a tag to apply to the cursor.
ReadOnly	Logical	Determines whether the table or view is opened in read-only mode.

Relation

Property	Value	Purpose
ChildAlias	Character	The alias for the child cursor (the INTO part of SET RELATION).
ChildOrder	Character	The tag used to order the child so the relation can be applied. Should correspond to RelationalExpr.
OneToMany	Logical	Determines whether a one-to-many relation is established.
ParentAlias	Character	The alias for the parent cursor.
RelationalExpr	Character	The expression to use to set the relation. Equivalent to the "TO" clause of SET RELATION.

Only the Filter and Order properties of cursors (and the Name, Comment and Tag properties of both cursors and relations) can be changed at runtime with equanimity. To change any other property of a cursor or relation, you should first use CloseTables to close all the tables in the DE. Then, make your changes and call OpenTables to reopen the tables with the new settings. If you change things without closing the tables first, you get an error message and the change isn't effective until you CloseTables and OpenTables anyway.

Like other contained classes, these can be subclassed only in code. There's no way, though, to get the Data Environment Designer to use your subclasses.

Example

```
* You'll normally set this stuff only in the Properties Sheet
* In fact, most of it happens automatically. Here are some
* items you might actually set.
* Assume the PropSheet is pointing at a cursor for Employee.
Filter = "NOT EMPTY(Sales_Region)"
Order = "Last_Name"

* At runtime, you might:
ThisForm.DataEnvironment.Cursor1.Order = "Name"
```

See Also Alias, BufferMode, BufferModeOverride, ChildAlias, ChildOrder, CursorSource, Database, DataEnvironment, Exclusive, Filter, NoDataOnLoad, OneToMany, Order, ParentAlias, ReadOnly, RelationalExpr, Set Relation

CursorGetProp(), CursorSetProp()

These functions let you inspect and change properties of open tables and views. The changes you make affect the table or view only as long as it's open. For permanent changes, use DBSetProp().

For tables, the only property that can be changed is Buffering.

Usage

```
uPropValue = CURSORGETPROP( cProperty [, nWorkArea | cAlias ] )
lSuccess = CURSORSETPROP( cProperty [, uNewValue ]
                          [, nWorkArea | cAlias ] )
```

Parameter	Value	Meaning
cProperty	Character	The name of the cursor property to look up or change.
uNewValue	Character, Numeric or Logical	The new value to assign to the specified property. The value must be of the appropriate type for the property.
nWorkArea	Numeric	The work area containing the cursor.
	Omitted	If cAlias is also omitted, use the current work area.
cAlias	Character	The alias for the cursor.
	Omitted	If nWorkArea is also omitted, use the current work area.
uPropValue	Character, Numeric or Logical	The current value of cProperty.
lSuccess	.T.	The change was successful.
	.F.	The change was unsuccessful.

The complete property list is in Help, reasonably well documented. We'll go over the errors and omissions here, as well as mention one property that deserves a little light.

Three kinds of "cursors" are affected by these commands: FoxPro tables, local views and remote views. Remote views have all the properties listed in Help. Local views have all the properties except ConnectHandle and ConnectName. FoxPro tables have only four of the listed properties: Buffering, Database, SourceName and SourceType. Checking or changing a property that a particular cursor doesn't have brings up an error message.

The descriptions for UpdatableFieldList and UpdateNameList in Help are backward. UpdatableFieldList contains a comma-delimited list of fields that can be updated in the view. If you use the View Designer, it contains the names of the items with check marks in the "pencil" column. UpdateNameList is sort of like SELECT's AS clause—it matches field names in the result cursor with the source field names. The result field name comes first, followed by a space, followed by the aliased field name in the original source. It, too, is set automatically if you use the View Designer.

Help also says that issuing CURSORSETPROP() without uNewValue resets the property to its default value. Our tests show that to be mostly true, but in each version, some items don't reset as documented. For example, in every version we tested, FetchMemo resets to .T. when the value is omitted, not to .F. Be sure to either always specify a value or make sure that the property resets to what you think it does before you count on this behavior.

The SourceName property isn't well-known but is extremely handy for dealing with tables and views with spaces in their names (not something we recommend, of course). The problem is that when you open such a table or view, VFP substitutes spaces for underscores in the alias. If you then try to use some generic code with something like DBGetProp(ALIAS(), ...), it'll bomb because the alias isn't the same as the name. Instead, use something like:

```
lcSource = CursorGetProp("SourceName")
DBGetProp(lcSource, ...)
```

Example

```
USE Employee
? CURSORGETPROP("Buffering")     && Returns 1
? CURSORGETPROP("SourceName")    && Returns Employee
? CURSORGETPROP("SourceType")    && Returns 3

CREATE DATA Test
CREATE SQL VIEW MyEmps AS ;
    SELECT EmployeeId, First_Name, Last_Name ;
       FROM Employee WHERE Region = ?Region
USE MyEmps
? CURSORGETPROP("Buffering")     && Returns 3
* Set updating properties
? CURSORSETPROP("KeyFieldList", "Employee_Id")
  && Employee_Id is primary key
? CURSORSETPROP("UpdateNameList", ;
 "first_name Employee.first_name,last_name Employee.last_name")
? CURSORSETPROP("SendUpdates", .T.)
? CURSORSETPROP("Tables", "Employee")
? CURSORSETPROP("UpdatableFieldList", "First_Name,Last_Name")
* Now the view is updatable
```

In the second example, we make the view updatable for just this one time. To make it updatable permanently, use DBSETPROP() to set the corresponding properties.

See Also DBGetProp(), DBSetProp(), SQLGetProp(), SQLSetProp()

CursorSource, Database

These two properties belong to cursors in the DataEnvironment. They determine what table or view the cursor references. CursorSource contains some version of the name of the table or view—the name used depends on whether it's a table or view and, for tables, whether it's free or contained in a database. (See Help for the details.) Database contains the full path to the database containing the table or view, if the cursor isn't a free table.

Usage

```
curCursor.CursorSource = cName
cName = curCursor.CursorSource
curCursor.Database = cFullyPathedFileName
cFullyPathedFileName = curCursor.Database
```

Being able to change these properties, especially Database, at runtime is important. By changing Database, you can change a form from using last year's data to this year's, or from using one client's to another's, or from using local data to remote. Changing CursorSource seems less common to us.

You can make these changes in the DataEnvironment's OpenTables method. To our pleasant surprise, although the objects involved haven't been Init-ed yet, the changes stick and do affect the initial automatic opening of tables. Keep in mind that doing it in OpenTables means it'll happen every time you call that method.

Don't change these while the tables are open—you'll get an error. Instead, call CloscTables to close them, make the changes, and then call OpenTables to reopen them.

If you want to choose a database based on a parameter to the form, you can't use all of the automatic table-opening features of the form. That's because OpenTables occurs before all other events (even Form.Load and more importantly, Form.Init, which receives parameters), when AutoOpenTables is .T. In this case, you can set AutoOpenTables to .F., and, in the form's Init, set Database for each cursor (think SetAll), then call OpenTables. Unfortunately, this means you can't bind controls to the table data at design time. Our esteemed technical editor suggests using a "global" property, such as oApp.cDataDirectory, to point to the data. Then you can set the Database property of cursors in the form's Load

Example

```
* Point a cursor to the already open and current database
ThisForm.DataEnvironment.curCustomer.Database = DBC()
```

See Also Alias, BeforeOpenTables, Cursor, DataEnvironment, OpenTables

CurVal(), OldVal()

These functions give you access to the extra buffers that FoxPro maintains for buffered records and tables. CURVAL() tells you the current value of a field on disk, while OLDVAL() tells you the value a field had the last time you retrieved it from disk.

Usage

```
uValue = CURVAL( cExpr [ , cAlias | nWorkArea ] )
uValue = OLDVAL( cExpr [ , cAlias | nWorkArea ] )
```

These two functions let you figure out what's going on so you can save your changes without clobbering somebody else's. For tables, CURVAL() keeps its finger on the pulse of the actual data that's sitting on the disk. For views, CURVAL() contains the data value sitting in the buffers—you may need to REFRESH() the view before CURVAL() is up to date. OLDVAL() looks at a copy of the data that's originally created when you open the table buffered, and gets updated whenever you issue TABLEUPDATE() or TABLEREVERT().

You can use these functions in two ways, which correspond to the optimistic and pessimistic views of the world. You can try to TABLEUPDATE() and, if it fails, combine GETFLDSTATE() with these two to figure out what items are causing the failure. Or, if your glass is half empty, you can go through the data first and use these functions to identify and resolve conflicts, then update the table. The catch we see with this second technique is that, unless you explicitly lock the record, another user could still make changes to the data after you had checked it but before you committed your changes. This means that followers of this second technique would still need to incorporate the code of the first method, above. Too much work for us, we think.

You're not restricted to passing a single field name to these functions. They actually can return information about an expression. Whatever you pass, note that they expect a character string, not a name.

Example

```
USE Employee
SET MULTILOCKS ON
? CURSORSETPROP("Buffering", 3)
* Make some changes to a record
* Now see what happened to Last_Name field
* Note that there are two cases which are NOT mutually exclusive
IF Last_Name <> OLDVAL("Last_Name")
   WAIT WINDOW "You changed the last name"
ENDIF
IF OLDVAL("Last_Name") <> CURVAL("Last_Name")
   WAIT WINDOW "Someone else changed last name"
ENDIF
```

See Also Buffering, CursorSetProp(), GetFldState(), TableRevert(), TableUpdate()

Curvature

A property of a shape that describes how rounded its corners are, from square to circle.

Usage

```
shpShape.Curvature = nCurves
nCurves = shpShape.Curvature
```

Parameter	Value	Meaning
nCurves	0	No curvature; right-angle corners form a square or rectangle.
	1 through 98	Increasing curvature, forming ovals.
	99	Ultimate curvature, forming a circle or ellipse.

Curvature can be used to dynamically change the shape of the object as conditions change. We haven't found a lot of use for this in our data-based applications, but it can be used for great special effects.

Example
```
frmForm1.shpShape1.Curvature = 99   && draws a circle,
                                    && if height=width
```

See Also FillColor, FillStyle, Height, Shape, Width

Custom

This base class is the building block for non-visual objects. It's similar to the Container class, except that it can't be seen. Like the other classes that are meant primarily as building blocks (Container and Control), Custom's name is somewhat overloaded. We'll use capital "C" when we mean the class.

Subclass Custom for most classes that don't need to appear on a form (though Timer, ActiveDoc and HyperLink are better when you need their specific abilities). Although Custom-based classes have no visual appearance, you can and should build them in the Class Designer rather than in code.

Custom has only a few PEMs, the ones that are shared by every class like Name, Class, Init and Destroy, and the ones that all containers have, like AddObject and RemoveObject.

If you don't need the container capabilities of this class, but are just using it as a convenient place to hang a few custom methods and properties, consider using some of the other base classes. Several are even simpler and may consume fewer resources than Custom. One area where this is especially true is instantiation time, if you need a slew of them. Contributor Steven Black has suggested Line and Relation as "ultralightweight" classes.

Property	Value	Purpose
Picture	Character	A picture used to represent the class in the Form and Class Designers.

Example
```
* See SQLConnect() for a class based on Custom
```

See Also Container, Control, SQLConnect()

Database See CursorSource.

DataEnvironment

This class lets forms and reports handle their own data—it's another step on the way to full encapsulation. Unfortunately, it has some basic weaknesses that make it far less useful than it should be. Don't confuse this base class with the nonexistent, but nonetheless documented, DataEnvironment property.

Every form created in the Form Designer has a data environment (DE) object added automatically. It just happens when you create the form. The data environment itself contains two kinds of objects, cursors and relations. Cursors are a general-purpose way of handling tables and views (from a form's standpoint, the two are identical). Relations are descriptions of temporary relations to be established between cursors.

You set up the data environment in the Data Environment Designer (available via a myriad of techniques in the Form Designer, including the form's context menu, the Form Designer toolbar, and the View menu when focus is on the form in the Designer). Each time you add a table in the DE Designer, a cursor object is added to the data environment. If the table has a persistent relationship with another table already in the DE, a relation object is created, too. You can add other relations by dragging from a field of one table to a tag of another.

The DE can be set to automatically open the tables and establish the relations when you run the form (or report). Even if you don't do it automatically, you can explicitly open things with the DE's OpenTables method. Whether or not you let the DE open and close things automatically, the ability to store all the data information needed for a form or report as an intelligent part of that object is terrific.

Weaknesses—did we say weaknesses? Yeah, we did. One of them is really a flaw of forms rather than of the DE itself. When you create form classes (that is, subclasses of the form base class), you can't store a DE with them. So, you can't do your data settings once and then inherit them over and over.

The other big flaw is that the data environment is another of Visual FoxPro's "half-classed" objects. You can subclass it, but not visually, and like many other contained objects, you can't visually add coded subclasses to the container—in this case, a form. We know a number of people (and at least one of the popular commercial frameworks) who are subclassing the DE anyway and swapping their custom DE class into forms at runtime.

Property	**Value**	**Purpose**
AutoCloseTables	Logical	Determines whether tables and views in the DE are automatically closed when the form shuts down.
AutoOpenTables	Logical	Determines whether tables and views in the DE are automatically opened when the form starts.
InitialSelectedAlias	Character	Determines which cursor in the DE is selected after the DE is fully initialized.
OpenViews	Numeric	Determines which kinds of views are automatically opened when the form starts.
Event	**Purpose**	
AfterCloseTables	Fires immediately after the tables are closed by CloseTables.	
BeforeOpenTables	Fires just before the tables are opened by OpenTables.	
Method	**Purpose**	
CloseTables	Closes the tables listed in the DE.	
OpenTables	Opens the tables and establishes the relations listed in the DE.	

The relationship among BeforeOpenTables, OpenTables and AutoOpenTables is complex. Check those topics for an explanation.

Example

```
* Data Environment settings are always established
* in the Properties Sheet, not at runtime.
* You might set:
AutoOpenTables = .T.     && Open them up automatically
AutoCloseTables = .F.    && Leave 'em open
```

See Also AfterCloseTables, AutoCloseTables, AutoOpenTables, BeforeOpenTables, CloseTables, Cursor, DataEnvironment Property, InitialSelectedAlias, OpenTables, OpenViews, Relation

DataEnvironment Property

This form property doesn't exist. Help says it provides a reference to a form's data environment. It doesn't. If you use the default name for the data environment ("DataEnvironment"), it looks like there's a DataEnvironment property. But, as soon as you change the data environment's name, it becomes apparent that you were simply walking down the containership hierarchy.

See Also DataEnvironment

DataObject

This COM class is one of the keys to the power of OLE drag and drop. It contains the data being dragged in various formats. Because this is not a native VFP class, it can't be subclassed in VFP. The object exposes only methods, no properties, and has no events of its own. Let's point out right up front, too, that data objects appear only in OLE drag and drop operations, not in native VFP drag and drop. That means, among other things, that any references to "drag source" or "drop target" or any of the other drag and drop terms below mean OLE drag and drop. None of this stuff applies to the native drag and drop.

When an OLE drag and drop operation begins, a data object is created. Information about the source data is put into the data object, which is then passed to a number of the OLE drag and drop methods. You can both access and modify the data in the data object. You can even populate it with your own custom data.

The data object accepts data in many different formats. For any one drag and drop operation, it can contain the same data in more than one format. One common, easy-to-understand format is text. If you highlight some text in a control and start dragging, the data object contains that text in its format numbered 1 (which means "text"). If the drag source is a VFP control, the data object also contains data in the "VFP Source Object" format. That one offers you a reference to the drag source. A number of other formats are built in to handle things like lists of files, non-character data, and so forth.

However, if none of the formats is what you need, you can also create your own and put whatever data you want into it, even if it has nothing whatsoever to do with the drag source. (Actually, you can do that with the built-in formats, too. Want to confound your user? Set up a drag source that automatically replaces its text data with the string "Sorry, Charlie!")

The data object exists only for the length of the drag and drop operation. As soon as the mouse button comes up and any drop is processed, the data object self-destructs.

You can't watch the data object in the debugger. That's partly because it's a COM object, but much more because there's no way to get to the debugger while the various methods that let you touch the data object are running. You can't put breakpoints in them or use SUSPEND (well, you can, but it doesn't work). Even if an error occurs in those methods, you can't get to the debugger.

There are only a few methods available for working with the data object, but they give you everything you need to do the job.

Method	Purpose
ClearData	Remove all data and formats from the data object.
GetData	Retrieve data in a specified format from the data object.
GetFormat	Determine whether the data object contains data in a specified format.
SetData	Place data in a specified format into the data object.
SetFormat	Indicate that the data object contains data in a specified format.

Example

```
* See the various OLE drag and drop methods, as well as
* the methods listed above for examples of using the data object
```

See Also ClearData, GetData, GetFormat, OLE drag and drop, OLEDragDrop, OLEDragOver, OLESetData, OLEStartDrag, SetData, SetFormat

DataSession, DataSessionID, Set DataSession, Set("DataSession")

These functions determine whether a Form, FormSet or Toolbar shares the same data environment as other objects in the application or has its own private session.

Usage

```
oObject.DataSession = nDataSessionType
nDataSessionType = oObject.DataSession
nID = oObject.DataSessionID
oObject.DataSessionId = nID
nID = SET( "DataSession" )
Set DataSession to nID
```

Parameter	Value	Meaning
nDataSessionType	1	Use the same default data session that other objects may be using.
	2	Use a private data session unique to this object.
nID	Integer	Reports the individual data session if the object's datasession is set to 2 (Private). Otherwise, reports 1, the default data session.

Set an object's DataSession to 2 to keep it private. This allows multiple instances of the same object to be running at the same time without interfering with each other. Each form has its own DataSessionID, its own set of work areas, its own record pointers and its own set of aliases. This last is really cool. With a private data session, you can use the same alias every time, something you can't do with USE AGAIN. You can use the SET DATASESSION command to switch to that private data session. You might want to do this to examine it for debugging. You would also do it anytime you are running generic black-box code that needs to affect the underlying data tables, such as a "Skip" button's Click procedure in a toolbar. Just make sure to preserve the original DataSessionID if you issue a SET DATASESSION TO in a black box, so that you can restore the original DataSessionID again on the way out.

We doubt we would use SET DATASESSION within an application form—it's hard to picture a need for a user to jump from one to another data session within the same form. We've also heard that data session-jumping can lead to unstable apps even without data-bound controls, and we're not surprised. However, switching data sessions from a common toolbar or utility program not only makes sense, it is probably the only way to perform some common functions.

You can see which data sessions are active at the moment with the Data Session window's "Current Session:" drop-down list. Picking a different data session from the list issues a SET DATASESSION command—use it with caution!

Realize that a form's selection of "Default Data Session (1)" for the data session is NOT the same as selecting the *Public* (number 1) data session. A default data session is the one that was open when the form was called—if you call a form set to the default data session from a form with a private data session, they share that "private" session. So forms can share a private data session—a nice feature when you need a follow-on dialog within your form. Be aware that once the called form closes, the calling form's data session appears as "Unknown" in the Data Session dialog; this seems to be a harmless side-effect, though.

A number of SET commands are scoped to a single data session. This is a great way to ensure that your different forms don't interfere with each other. The SET commands scoped this way are listed in the SET reference.

The DataSession property is read-only at runtime, with the idea that you can't change your mind after starting a form. The DataSessionID property is initially assigned by FoxPro but can be changed from one data session to another, even to the default data session (1). However, data-bound controls can get awfully confused when you slip the data out from under them.

Example `Thisform.DataSession = 2`

See Also Set

DataToClip See DoCmd.

Date(), DateTime(), Time()

Date(), DateTime() and Time() return values for the present. New to VFP 6.0, Date() and DateTime() can now be used to return any specified date or datetime in a Year-2000-compliant format.

Usage
```
ldDate = DATE( [ nYear, nMonth, nDay ] )
ltDateAndTime = DATETIME([ nYear, nMonth, nDay
                     [, nHours [, nMinutes [, nSeconds  ] ] ] ])
lcTheTime = TIME( [ uShowFractions ] )
```

Parameter	Value	Meaning
nYear	100 - 9999	The year of the date variable to create. Note that dates in the years 1753 and before could cause problems, because the Gregorian calendar wasn't standardized until then.
nMonth	1 – 12	The month of the variable to create.
nDay	1 – 31	The day of the variable to create.
nHours	0 – 23	Unlike the "strict date" format, this function accepts 24-hour based time. That makes sense — it would be a pain to have to pass two parameters.
hMinutes	0 – 59	The number of minutes to assign to the datetime return value.
nSeconds	0 – 59	The number of seconds in the return value.
uShowFractions	Any type will do	Display the time with tenths and hundredths of a second.

The format of the return values of Date() and DateTime() is affected by a number of SET commands. The sequence of month-day-year is determined by SET DATE, the separators between the numbers by SET MARK, and the number of digits shown for the year by SET CENTURY. In addition, SET HOURS changes the time display to 24-hour or 12-hour (with trailing "AM" or "PM") format. SET SECONDS ON | OFF determines whether the seconds portion of the value is displayed. None of these affects what is actually stored in a field, only what is displayed.

As part of the effort to ensure that VFP developers can write Year-2000-compliant code, Microsoft extended the Date() and DateTime() functions so they accept all the date and time components as numbers, always returning the correct date or datetime value regardless of the settings of DATE and CENTURY. DATE and CENTURY, especially the ROLLOVER clause, make the resolution of dates by the CTOD() and CTOT() functions unpredictable, and thus these functions were extended.

TIME() always returns a character string in the form “HH:MM:SS” in 24-hour format, with no regard to the SET HOURS setting. It always displays seconds, regardless of the SET SECONDS command (which was added for datetime variables). We think it should respect both. If a parameter is passed (any number, character, null, anything will do), the time is displayed with tenths and hundredths of seconds—impressive, but probably not entirely accurate. In early versions, we calculated actual accuracy around .054 seconds (one-eighteenth of a second). So does anyone really know what time it is? Does anyone really care?

Example

```
? "TODAY IS ", DATE()  && returns "04/15/1998"
* Calculate the date of the next New Years Day
ldNewYears = DATE(1+YEAR(DATE()),1,1)
? DATETIME()           && returns "04/15/1998 23:15:22"
? TIME()               && returns "23:15:22"
? TIME(1)              && returns "23:15:22.15"
```

See Also CToD(), CToT(), Day(), DoW(),DMY(), DToC(), DToT(), GoMonth(), Hour(), MDY(), Minute(), Month(), Sec(), Seconds(), Set Century, Set Date, Set Hours, Set Mark, Set Seconds, Set StrictDate, Set SysFormat, SYS(2), TToC(), TToD(), Year()

DateFormat, DateMark See Set Date.

Day() See CDoW().

DBC() See Set Database.

DBF() See Alias().

DBGetProp(), DBSetProp()

These functions let you check and change properties of a database and its contents.

Usage

```
uPropertyValue = DBGETPROP( cItem, cItemType, cProperty )
lSuccess = DBSETPROP( cItem, cItemType, cProperty, uNewValue )
```

Parameter	Value	Meaning
cItem	Character	The name of the database element whose property is being inspected or modified.
cItemType	Character	The type of database element. Legal values are "CONNECTION", "DATABASE", "FIELD", "TABLE", "VIEW"
cProperty	Character	The name of the property to inspect or change.
uNewValue	Character, Numeric or Logical	The new value for cProperty. Must be the appropriate type.
uPropertyValue	Character, Numeric or Logical	The current value of cProperty.
lSuccess	.T.	The change was made. If the change fails, FoxPro generates an error.

Visual FoxPro has three sets of SetProp()/GetProp() functions. Each serves a slightly different role. SQLSetProp() and SQLGetProp() let you inquire about and change open connections to remote data and set up the defaults for new connections. CursorSetProp() and CursorGetProp() serve a similar role for open tables and views.

DBGetProp() and DBSetProp() are a little different than the other two pairs. They operate on a database itself and let you ask about and modify the contents of the database. Not the data, of course, but the description of the data known as the metadata. (We never met a data we didn't like.) With these functions, you talk about the database itself, its stored connections, tables and views, and the fields of the tables and views. This is where you can determine that a particular view is always updateable or that a certain connection is asynchronous. The information stored in the database is then used when the connection, table or view is opened. Think of these properties as the defaults for the database members. In OOP terminology, DBGetProp() and DBSetProp() operate on the class, while the other GetProp()/SetProp() functions operate on instances of the class. (Of course, this isn't really an OOP situation, but the analogy is handy.)

DBGetProp() and DBSetProp() handle a lot more cases than the others. So, you have to indicate whether the object of interest is a database, connection, table, view or field. You also have to tell what object you're interested in. When you're looking at properties of a field, you have to add the table's alias to the field name in the functions. For example, to see the caption for the LastName field of Customer, you'd write:

```
? DBGetProp("Customer.LastName", "Field", "Caption")
```

Unlike the other SetProp() functions, you can't omit the new value to reset these properties to their defaults. Since that feature doesn't always work as expected in the other cases, maybe it's just as well.

It's pretty easy to figure out which properties are read-only and which are read-write. If there's another command in the language that lets you set a property, it's read-only here. For example, the field property DefaultValue is read-only because you set it with CREATE TABLE or ALTER TABLE. On the other hand, the Comment property of each object, which can only be set through menu choices, is read-write.

The Help file contains a complete list of each type of property.

In all versions of VFP before VFP 6 (that is, through 5.0a), you can't successfully clear the value of field properties of views using DBSetProp(). To get rid of the values there, you have to set them to a single blank. But, when you do so, opening the view gives you an error message, although you can proceed.

The Tables property of views is a little confusing. Its purpose is to list all the tables that can be updated by the view. In essence, it's the FROM clause of the SQL UPDATE command you need to send changes back to the source (if SQL UPDATE could handle multiple tables, anyway).

The database has to be current to apply these functions, even for the database-level properties (which include the database name in the function call). Having the database open, but not current, isn't enough! To use DBSetProp() in VFP 3, you need exclusive access to the database; that restriction has been removed in VFP 5 and VFP 6.

Example

```
OPEN DATA TasTrade
? DBGETPROP("customer", "table", "comment")
* Returns "Customer Information"
? DBGETPROP("customer.discount", "field", "defaultvalue")
* Returns 0
```

See Also Add Table, Alter Table, Create Connection, Create Database, Create SQL View, Create Table, CursorGetProp(), CursorSetProp(), DBC(), Display Database, Set Database, SQLGetProp(), SQLSetProp()

DblClick See Click.

_DblClick

This system variable determines how long the user can pause between mouse clicks and still have it considered a double-click. It also determines the speed for incremental search in list and combo boxes.

Usage

```
_DBLCLICK = nSeconds
```

nSeconds can range from .05 (1/20th of a second—we don't know anybody who can double-click that fast) to 5.5 (handy for someone with a physical disability that makes double-clicking difficult). Because the ability to double-click varies widely from one person to the next, you'll make your users really happy if you let them set this through your application.

Of course, we and our users would be even happier if this setting were controlled by the similar setting in the Windows Control Panel. We can't figure why the initial setting doesn't come from there, but you could poke around in the Registry to find it and set it yourself (the setting seems to vary with the driver; on Tamar's machine, the item is HKEY_CURRENT_USER\ControlPanel\Mouse\DoubleClickSpeed; on Ted's, it's HKEY_CURRENT_USER\ControlPanel\Microsoft Input Devices\Mouse\DoubleClickTime).

The second use of this variable surprises most people. After all, this is _Dbl*CLICK*. What does the speed at which you type into a combo or list have to do with clicking? This was a bad call when it was set up this way; Microsoft really ought to bite the bullet and add a new variable to control incremental search speed, backward compatibility notwithstanding.

Example
```
_DBLCLICK = 1    && 1 second delay
```

See Also ComboBox, ListBox, Set Mouse

DBSetProp() See DBGetProp().

DBUsed()

This function tells you whether a specified database is open. It's the equivalent of USED() for database containers.

Usage
```
lInUse = DBUSED( cDatabase )
```

Unlike many other functions, this one doesn't have a default result if you omit the parameter. Calling DBUSED() without a parameter results in an error message.

We haven't found a whole lot of uses for this function. We suspect it's more useful in developer tools, where you want to manipulate a particular database, than in client applications. One use in both situations, though, is to double-check that a particular database is still open before you try to SET DATABASE TO it.

Example
```
CLOSE ALL
? DBUSED("TasTrade")   && Returns .F.
OPEN DATA TasTrade
? DBUSED("TasTrade")   && Returns .T.
CLOSE DATA
USE Customer           && Automatically opens database
? DBUSED("TasTrade")   && Returns .T.
```

See Also ADatabases(), DBC(), Open Database, Used()

DDEInitiate(),DDETerminate(), DDEAbortTrans(), DDEPoke(), DDERequest(), DDEExecute(), DDELastError(), DDESetOption(), DDEAdvise(), DDEEnabled(), DDESetService(), DDESetTopic()

Despite all the hoopla you've heard about the wonders of OLE, COM and ActiveX, Dynamic Data Exchange—one of COM's forebears—is not yet dead. Getting on in years, yes. Dead, no, not just yet.

In most cases, we prefer to use the new Active technologies when developing communications between applications. ActiveX communications are more robust, support richer data types, and are more easily integrated into an OOP environment. But it takes two to tango. If the application on the other end of the phone only speaks DDE, then that is the language FoxPro must speak, too. Visual FoxPro supports the whole complement of DDE commands, providing capability as a client or a server.

In case you're new to the DDE scene, let's do a brief overview of the ways in which DDE can be used. DDE is often described as similar to a phone conversation. One party initiates the phone call, the two parties exchange information, and the parties terminate the call.

If VFP is the calling application—if we're driving the conversation—we first DDEInitiate() the conversation with the other party. This other application is commonly referred to as the server, confusing the situation with client-server database technology (as well as with Web technology). The client in DDE is the one running the show, running the code, and the server is the application that responds. DDERequest() and DDEPoke() provide the verbs to get and set variable values. DDEExecute() passes a command to the server. DDETerminate() completes the conversation.

DDELastError() is the function used to get the details when things go wrong.

It may be that we don't want to talk with the server as much as register an interest in the values it has in a particular document, and ask to be advised if these change. DDEAdvise() is the trick for this. Again, you DDEInitiate() and DDETerminate() a conversation, with the request for DDEAdvise() in the middle.

Finally, if your application must play the server and be called upon by other applications, DDESetService() defines the services available, DDESetTopic() sets (surprise!) the topics of the conversations, and DDEEnable() allows the server to toggle on and off DDE services while processing.

DDE is never our first choice for interprocess communication mechanisms. Automation is far more powerful (and, we think, easier to code). DDE is less reliable, not uniformly implemented and not rock stable. But for those applications that support only DDE, or in situations of limited resources, Visual FoxPro is up to the task of communicating well using DDE. Visual FoxPro can carry on a variety of conversations, working as a client with cold, warm and hot links, as well as working as a DDE server.

If you're really interested in the DDE server stuff, a trip down memory lane is required. The FoxPro development environment itself is not a DDE server, but rather the interface is in place for you to hook up your own application as a DDE server. Not much is documented in this version, but Mike Taylor of MicroMega wrote a cool application, FoxData, as a FoxPro DDE server. It was included with the sample code for FoxPro 2.x, and it demonstrated some neat little nooks and crannies in getting FoxPro to work. In addition, several excellent magazine articles and at least one book (listed in the references in the appendices) get into DDE in some depth.

Usage

```
nChannel = DDEInitiate( cAppDDEName, cTopic )
lReturn = DDETerminate( nChannel | cAppDDEName )
```

Parameter	Value	Meaning
cAppDDEName	Character	Also known as a "service name," this is the handle an application uses to identify itself via DDE, like the CB chatter. Visual FoxPro uses "FoxPro" contrary to the Help file. Excel uses "Excel." Word uses "WinWord." Ain't standards wonderful? If cAppDDEName is supplied with DDETerminate, all channels with this server are closed at once.
cTopic	Character	The topic of your conversation. "System" is often a good ice-breaker for speaking with an application you're trying to get acquainted with.
nChannel	-1	Indicates DDEInitiate could not establish a channel. Use DDELastError to determine why.
	Positive Integer	The channel number that uniquely identifies this conversation for use with the other DDE functions.

Parameter	Value	Meaning
lReturn	.F.	Indicates DDETerminate could not close a channel. The other application may have already terminated, or an invalid channel number might have been passed. Use DDELastError to determine why.
	.T.	Successful termination.

DDEInitiate() is used to start a conversation between two applications, and DDETerminate() to finish it. Negative or false returns from these functions (and the ones below) are indicative of errors that should be checked out with DDELastError().

DDEInitiate() attempts to start a conversation with another application by searching the list of DDE servers available in memory. By default, if the server isn't running, FoxPro offers to start the server by popping a dialog up on the screen. Typically, this is an option you will not want to offer the end user. You probably want to start the application if it isn't running. Use DDESetOption() and the Run command to do this, as shown in the second example below.

Most of the tricks to using DDE involve finding out the names of the services and topics available, and the commands and syntax the application recognizes. Far too often these are poorly documented, if they're documented at all.

Example

```
? DDEInitiate("WinWord","Document1")

= DDESetOption("Safety",.F.)  && Turn off dialogs
nChannel = -1
nTries = 0
DO WHILE nChannel = -1 and nTries < 3
  nChannel = DDEINITIATE("WinWord","System")
  IF nChannel = -1  && command failed
    IF DDELASTERROR() = 16  && Connect failure
      nTries = nTries + 1
      RUN /N7 WINWORD.EXE
      LOOP
    ENDIF
  ELSE
  ... error handling here...
  ENDIF
ENDDO
IF nTries = 3  && three tries and you're out...
  ... error handling here, too...
```

Usage

```
lResult = DDEAbortTrans( nChannel )
uResult = DDEPoke( nChannel, cItemName, cData
                  [ , cFormat [ , cAsynchUDF ] ] )
uValue = DDERequest( nChannel, cItemName
                    [ , cFormat [ , cAsynchUDF ] ] )
```

Parameter	Value	Meaning
nChannel	Integer	Identifies the particular DDE conversation, set by DDEInitiate().
lResult	.T.	The attempt to abort the transaction succeeded.
	.F.	Unable to abort the transaction. We haven't been able to produce this at will, but we suspect it would occur only when connection with the other party in the DDE conversation was lost.

Parameter	Value	Meaning
cItemName	Character	The item whose data is either being requested or changed. For Excel, this could be a row/column address such as "R2C3".
cData	Character	The data to be placed in cItemName. All data must be passed as a character string and the receiving application must translate it to numeric, if necessary.
cFormat	Character	Dictates the format the data appears in, most usually CF_TEXT, which is tab-separated fields.
cASynchUDF	Character	If an asynchronous connection is desired (usually because the answer might take some time), this parameter supplies the name of the function to run when the data is ready. The six pieces of data this function receives are spelled out in the Help file.
uResult	Logical	Reports whether the data was accepted by the application. Use DDELastError() to get information on the error if lResult is .F.
	Integer	If an asynchronous transaction is selected, DDEPoke() returns the unique transaction number, which is the last parameter to the cAsynchUDF when the transaction is finished.
uValue	Character	The result of querying cItemName.
	Integer	The transaction number, which is the last parameter to the cAsynchUDF when the transaction is finished.

DDERequest() and DDEPoke() are the read and write equivalents of transactions via DDE. DDERequest() requests a value from another application and DDEPoke() places a value in it.

In some cases, poking or requesting a value might cause the server application to have to go off and do some number crunching or other time-consuming processing. In this case, an "asynchronous" connection can be made, whereby the server app "calls back" Visual FoxPro when the deed is done, and passes back results by starting a User-Defined Function (UDF) within FoxPro and passing it several parameters. It is up to your application to monitor an asynchronous transaction, because the DDESetOption("Timeout") value does not apply. If an excessively long time has passed or other conditions make the transaction no longer necessary, the transaction can be halted with DDEAbortTrans().

Example

```
* get the value of cell 2,3
nValue = VAL(DDERequest(nExcel,"R2C3"))
```

Usage

```
lResult = DDEExecute( nChannel, cCommand )
nResult = DDEExecute( nChannel, cCommand, cAsynchUDF )
```

Parameter	Value	Meaning
nChannel	Integer	Identifies the particular DDE conversation, set by DDEInitiate().
cCommand	Character	The command for the server to execute. Each DDE server is unique in the commands, syntax and format it understands.

Parameter	Value	Meaning
cAsynchUDF	Character	If an asynchronous connection is desired (usually because the answer might take some time), this parameter supplies the name of the function to run when the data is ready. The six pieces of data this function receives are spelled out in the Help file.
lResult	.T.	Synchronous command completed successfully.
	.F.	Synchronous command failed. Test using DDELastError().
nResult	-1	Asynchronous command failed. Test using DDELastError().
	Integer	The transaction number to be returned as the last parameter of the cAsynchUDF specified above.

DDEExecute() allows Visual FoxPro to pass commands to the DDE Server, which the server then executes.

Example

```
* Send the command to WinWord to print the current document
=DDEExecute(nWord,"[FilePrint]")
```

Usage

```
nValue = DDELastError()
```

Parameter	Value	Meaning
nValue	0	Last command did not generate an error.
	Integer	See table of errors in Help.

Use DDELastError() to detect problems that DDE is having. Rather than firing the global error handler set in ON ERROR, this function gives you the option of handling the error locally.

Example

```
IF DDELastError() = 0  && no error, continue processing
```

Usage

```
lValue = DDESetOption( "Safety" [, lSafetyOn ] )
lValue | nValue  = DDESetOption( "Timeout" [, nTimeout ] )
```

Parameter	Value	Meaning
lSafetyOn	Logical	Determines if warning dialogs appear (.T.) or not (.F.). See example in DDEInitiate(), above.
	Omitted	Returns present setting of safety in lValue.
lValue	.T.	Function completed successfully.
	.F.	Function failed.
nTimeout	Numeric	Amount of time FoxPro waits for a response from the other end of a DDE conversation, expressed in milliseconds. Default is 2 seconds. Legal values from 1 to 594 billion or so—too long for us to wait!
	Omitted	Returns current timeout setting in nValue.

Parameter	Value	Meaning
nValue	Numeric	Current setting for timeout.

This function is the DDE equivalent of the SET command and matching SET() function. Without the second parameter, it returns the present setting; with the second parameter, it sets the specified setting to the passed values. With Safety set to .F., our recommended setting, you will need to do more error checking, but your users will not be presented with dialogs allowing them to mangle the DDE portion of your application. As for Timeout, we expect that you might need to raise it for slower systems or systems with a lot going on, but we've never had to mess with the settings ourselves.

Example
```
? DDESetService("Timeout")  && display the current timeout
```

Usage
```
lValue = DDEAdvise( nChannel, cItemName, cUDFName, nTypeLink)
```

Parameter	Value	Meaning
nChannel	Integer	Identifies the particular DDE conversation, set by DDEInitiate().
cItemName	Character	The name of the item the application is to monitor. The server alerts Visual FoxPro if the data changes. For Excel, this might be a cell address.
cUDFName	Character	The name of the routine to run when a change is made to the item identified above.
nTypeLink	0	Manual or "cold" link. Turns off a warm or hot link.
	1	Notify or "warm" link.
	2	Automatic or "hot" link.
lValue	.T.	Function completed successfully.
	.F.	Function failed.

This function allows the creation of "warm" and "hot" links between Visual FoxPro and another application. Both cause a Visual FoxPro routine to run when a change occurs in their environment. The difference between the two link types is that the warm link only notifies Visual FoxPro of the change, while the hot link passes the changed data as well.

The routine you indicate receives six items, similar to the AsynchUDF in DDEPoke() and DDERequest() above. Your Visual FoxPro application can then determine what action to take based on this new data.

Example
```
* This command sets up a hot link between an open Excel DDE
* conversation and FoxPro. If the operator or a function
* changes the value of the contents of row 2, column 2, the
* FoxPro routine will run.
= DDEAdvise(nExcel,"R2C2", "MyUDF", 2)
```

Usage
```
lValue = DDEEnabled( [ nChannel , ]  [ lOnOff ] )
```

Parameter	Value	Meaning
nChannel	Integer	Identifies the particular DDE conversation, set by DDEInitiate().
	Omitted	If no channel is specified, the command applies globally to all channels.
lOnOff	Logical	Turns on or off either the specified channel or all channels of DDE while processing a time-critical function.
	Omitted	Reports whether the specified channel or all channels currently have DDE enabled.
lValue	.T.	Indicates either that a channel or global DDE processing is enabled, or that the last change to the status was accepted, depending on parameters supplied.
	.F.	Channel or global DDE processing is disabled, or the function failed to complete successfully.

DDEEnabled() applies only when FoxPro is working as a server. DDE, by default, is turned on globally, but is not enabled for individual channels until the channels are initialized. DDETerminate() also disables the local channel. When the channel is enabled, it's possible for incoming DDE traffic to disrupt the middle of a process, so use DDEEnabled() to "mute" the channel for a few moments until the function can complete.

Example
```
=DDEEnable( 5, .T. )  && re-enable DDE channel 5
```

Usage
```
lResult = DDESetService( cName, cAction [, cFormat | lSwitch ] )
```

Parameter	Value	Meaning
cName	Character	Name of the service to maintain.
cAction	"Advise"	Switch to set notification of changes on or off. The server side of warm and hot links, like DDEAdvise().
	"Define"	Defines the name of a new service.
	"Execute"	Switch to enable or disable the execution of commands by the service.
	"Formats"	Specifies which formats data may be transferred in.
	"Poke"	Enables or disables a client's ability to poke data to this service.
	"Release"	Releases this service name.
	"Request"	Enables or disables DDERequest() messages.
cFormat	Character	Specifies the format in which data can be transferred, using Microsoft shorthand like CF_TEXT (tab-delimited ASCII).

Parameter	Value	Meaning
lSwitch	Logical	For Advise, Execute, Poke and Request above, determines if the feature should be enabled.
	Omitted	If both cFormat and lSwitch are omitted, returns the current state of the specified action.
lResult	.T.	If requesting the status of a feature, it's enabled. If attempting to change an item, the change was successful.
	.F.	If requesting the status of a feature, it's disabled. If attempting to change an item, the change failed.

Did you ever wonder how DDE servers got their service names? This is how: A good server, like FoxPro, has the ability to programmatically set its own service names and change them on the fly. This is a one-stop-does-it-all command for using FoxPro as a DDE server—it defines all of the service names, the functions they support, and the formats they accept.

Example

```
* Create a new service, called Queries, which only
* accepts requests, and transfers all data as tab-delimited text
= DDESetService( "Queries", "Define" )
= DDESetService( "Queries", "Advise", .F. )
= DDESetService( "Queries", "Execute", .F. )
= DDESetService( "Queries", "Poke", .F. )
= DDESetService( "Queries", "Request", .T. )
= DDESetService( "Queries", "Formats", "CF_TEXT" )
```

Usage `lValue = DDESetTopic( cService, cTopic [, cUDFtoRun ] )`

Parameter	Value	Meaning
cService	Character	A service name, defined with DDESetService(), above.
cTopic	Character	A name for the individual topic.
	Empty string	Indicates that the UDF name that follows should be run for all topic names that don't have a UDF defined for them.
cUDFtoRun	Character	The name of the routine to be run when this service and topic are accessed. This UDF receives six parameters, as described in the Help, to indicate what it is to do.
	Omitted	If no UDF is specified, the topic name is released.
lValue	.T.	Topic name successfully created or released.
	.F.	Command failed. Use DDELastError() to determine why.

DDESetTopic sets the individual topics within the services, and defines which routines should run when a DDE client accesses a topic.

Example

```
* Define a topic Tables under the Queries service name
* which runs the procedure TablProc when called.
=DDESetTopic( "Queries", "Tables", "TablProc" )
```

See Also GetObject(), OLEControl, OLEBoundControl

Deactivate See Activate.

Deactivate Menu, Deactivate Popup See Activate Menu.

Deactivate Window See Define Window.

Debug, Close Debugger

These two commands start up and shut down the VFP debugger, respectively.

Usage

```
DEBUG
CLOSE DEBUGGER
```

These commands are the easy part. Learning to use the new (to 5.0) debugger effectively is not. (See "Productive Debugging" in Section 2 for more on that subject.) When you've set the debugger to its own frame, issuing DEBUG is the same as choosing Debugger from the Tools menu. When the debugger is sharing the FoxPro frame, DEBUG opens the Trace and Watch windows. You have to open the others yourself, either from the menu or with ACTIVATE WINDOW commands. (Hint: the name for each window is the caption that it displays. For the debug output window, you need quotes: ACTI WIND "debug output".)

CLOSE DEBUGGER is a pretty smart bugger. It closes whichever debugger windows are open.

Example

```
DEBUG
* Do some testing
CLOSE DEBUGGER
```

See Also DebugOut, Set Debug, Set Step, Set TrBetween

Debug, Encrypted

These properties of the Project object correspond to the Debug Info and Encrypted check boxes in the Project Information dialog. They determine whether or not debugging information is stored with the application and whether the object code is encrypted.

Usage

```
prjProject.Debug = lAddDebuggingInfo
lAddDebuggingInfo = prjProject.Debug
prjProject.Encrypted = lEncryptObjectCode
lEncryptObjectCode = prjProject.Encrypted
```

When the Debug property is .T., VFP adds information to the compiled code that allows you to see the source code in the Debugger. Without that information, you get the "Source is not available" or "Source is out of date" message in the Trace window, and you can't set breakpoints. (Well, you can set them, but they don't do anything.) Normally, you'll want to leave this one set to .T. until you have the thing working. Then, you might consider turning it off to save space and to make it a little more difficult to hack your application.

The Encrypted property determines whether or not the compiled code is run through an encryption algorithm. The idea is to give you one more line of defense against the evildoers who want to reverse-engineer your code. However, for true security, you probably need to use one of the various third-party tools around.

These properties also have counterparts in the COMPILE command. To control debugging information there, you use NODEBUG to turn it off; otherwise, it's on. The keyword for encryption there is ENCRYPT. Guess it's too much to ask for consistency.

Example

```
* These lines might be part of a program
* that documents an open project.
?"Debugging info is " + IIF(oProj.Debug,"on","off")+"."
?"Object code is " + IIF(oProj.Encrypted,"","not ")+"encrypted."
```

See Also ActiveProject, Build, Compile, Project, Projects

DebugOut, Set DebugOut, Set("DebugOut")

So how do you figure out what's going on in a particularly knotty piece of code when it doesn't do what you want? You might step through it, but sometimes the mere act of stepping through code changes the results. Often, you sprinkle it with messages that tell you what's going on at various points in the code so you can see what's happening without changing the results. These commands make that task much easier.

Usage

```
DEBUGOUT uExpression
SET DEBUGOUT TO  [ FileName [ ADDITIVE ] ]
cDebugOutFile = SET("DEBUGOUT")
```

DEBUGOUT lets you send any message you want from your code to the Debug Output window of the debugger. You can pass it data of any printable type, even memo fields, and it handles it correctly. DEBUGOUT is a much better choice than the WAIT WINDOWs we're all accustomed to using. By its very nature, WAIT can change the timing of activities in your code. The only thing DEBUGOUT does is take a tiny, tiny chunk of time to send the data you pass it along. Best of all, you don't even really have to pull DEBUGOUT statements out of your code. If the Debug Output window isn't available (either because it's closed or because you're running the runtime), the output just goes into the bit bucket.

SET DEBUGOUT lets you send the output to a file as well as the Debug Output window. (Actually, if the debugger is closed, the redirected output goes only to a file.) Just specify a filename and VFP happily sends anything that's going to the Debug Output window to that file as well. Include ADDITIVE to continue an existing file. Issue SET DEBUGOUT TO with no filename to close the current output file.

One warning here: VFP empties the specified file as soon as you issue SET DEBUGOUT, not the first time you put something in. So make sure you have the right filename before you press Enter.

SET("DEBUGOUT"), of course, tells you the name of the current debug output file.

There's one other point worth noting. The Debug Output window actually receives more than just DEBUGOUT statements. Assertion messages and any events being tracked land there, too, and are placed in the specified file, as well.

Example

```
SET DEBUGOUT TO Whatgives.Txt
DEBUGOUT "See, this goes to the window and the file"
ASSERT .F. MESSAGE "Yuck!"
DEBUGOUT "You can send any type like this:"
DEBUGOUT DATE()
DEBUGOUT TIME()
DEBUGOUT 42
```

See Also Assert, Debug, Set EventTracking, Wait

Declare See Dimension.

Declare-DLL

This command offers a very cool method for integrating commands from external DLLs directly into Visual FoxPro.

Usage

```
DECLARE SHORT | INTEGER | SINGLE | DOUBLE | LONG | STRING
        APIFunctionName IN DLLName [ AS YourFunctionName ]
        [ SHORT | INTEGER | SINGLE | DOUBLE | LONG | STRING
          [ @ ] [ Param1Name ]
        [, SHORT | INTEGER | SINGLE | DOUBLE | LONG | STRING
          [ @ ] [ Param2Name ]
        [, SHORT | INTEGER | SINGLE | DOUBLE | LONG | STRING
          [ @ ] [ ParamnName ] ] ] ]
```

Parameter	Value	Meaning
APIFunctionName	Name	The case-sensitive name of the function within the DLL.
DLLName	Name	The DLL within which the function is located. If the function is one of the standard Win32 functions, you may specify WIN32API instead of needing to determine the version-correct name for the DLL.
YourFunctionName	Name	Optionally, you may alias the function to a name more easily remembered or more in keeping with your naming standards.
@	Literal	Specifies that this parameter is passed by reference and not by value, the default.
Param*n*Name	Name	Optional parameter name—we strongly suggest you always use this as a bit of in-line documentation: What is this value and why is it here?

Dynamic Link Libraries (DLLs for short) are the Windows equivalent of procedure files—collections of useful functions compiled into a single file. It is through DLLs that we can access most of the functionality available to programmers within the Windows Application Programming Interface (commonly referred to as the Win32 API), as well as access functions provided by third-party vendors. Before you can use a function in a DLL, you must tell FoxPro about it—providing the function's name, the library that contains it and a list of the parameter types it expects.

Note that the VFP documentation is a bit misleading in not showing the parameter name as an optional element, but we think it should always be added anyway.

This is the preferred method of accessing DLLs, and we recommend it over using FoxTools or FLL manipulation whenever possible, just because it involves fewer intermediaries, and hence is less likely to go wrong. However, the DECLARE method is only available for 32-bit DLLs; older DLLs will have to settle for either the RegFn() function built into FoxTools, or a 32-bit FLL wrapper.

Unlike almost everything in Visual FoxPro, the mechanism for registering API calls is case-sensitive. Make sure you type the name as it appears in your documentation. If you get the message "Cannot find entry point BlahBlahBlah in the DLL," check your use of case.

A common complaint we hear is that VFP is limited in the types of parameters it can pass and is therefore unable to use DLL functions that require pointers or structures to be passed to them. In a great many cases, this is untrue. Most functions that require a pointer to a string will be just as happy if passed the string itself. Rather than declaring the function as requiring a DOUBLE to point to the string, modify your declaration to STRING and the function is likely to work fine. As for structures, it is true that Visual FoxPro does not support the idea of structures internally, as a memory type, but structures can be created programmatically and passed to the functions that require them. The second example below illustrates the technique required.

There is a 32-bit version of RegFn(), cleverly called RegFn32(), built into FoxTools as well. We haven't run into a case where using that function is preferable over the DECLARE method.

Example

```
* Display the Windows System Directory:
DECLARE INTEGER GetSystemDirectory ;
        in Win32api ;
        STRING @cWinDir, ;
        INTEGER nWinDirLength
lcWinDir = SPACE(255)
nWinDirLength = getSystemDirectory(@lcWinDir,len(lcWinDir))
```

```
? LEFT(lcWindir,nWinDirLength)

* This excerpt from a routine uses WinAPI calls
* to create a memory space ("heap"), and copy
* a string to it, then pass a pointer to that
* memory location to a function.
Declare Integer StartDoc in Win32Api ;
       Integer, String
Declare Integer HeapCreate in Win32Api ;
       Integer, Integer, Integer
Declare Integer HeapAlloc in Win32Api ;
       Integer, Integer, Integer
Declare lstrcpy in Win32Api Integer, String

LPARAMETER tcDocName
* Create a true string w/ pointer for the name
This.lnHeap = HeapCreate(0, 8192, 8192)
This.lnDoc = HeapAlloc(This.lnHeap, 0, Len(tcDocName)+1 )
lstrcpy(This.lnDoc, tcDocName )

* Create a structure
lcStruct = CHR(12) + REPLCATE(CHR(0),3) + ;
           This.ToInt(IIF(EMPTY(tcDocName),0,This.lnDoc)) + ;
           REPLICATE(CHR(0),4)

* Call the Win API function
StartDoc( tnHDC, lcStruct )
```

See Also FoxTools, Set Library

Default See Cancel.

DefaultExt() See AddBS().

DefaultFilePath See CD.

#Define, #UnDef, #If, #EndIf, #IfDef, #IfNDef, #Include, _Include

Visual FoxPro 3.0 introduced many new concepts to FoxPro programmers, and the ability to manage constants, like the other "real" languages, was a most welcome feature. Visual FoxPro supports the ability to insert defined constants into program, form and class code, as well as the ability to conditionally test and undefine these constants as required.

These are not FoxPro commands, but rather preprocessor directives. If you include one of these as a string and attempt to macro-expand it within FoxPro, you get the error message "Syntax error." That's because these commands are not intended to be run by the FoxPro interpreter, but are directed to the preprocessor, which produces the pseudo-object code ("p-code"), which the Visual FoxPro interpreter then runs. To distinguish them from FoxPro commands, we often refer to them as "compiler directives," even though, strictly speaking, FoxPro lacks a true compiler.

Here's the inside scoop. Within the development version of FoxPro, source code can be compiled at various times. When saving a method of a form, the code is compiled during the save process. When running a program whose compiled version is older than its source (with SET DEVELOPMENT ON), the source is recompiled. Finally, source is recompiled when you explicitly tell it to—either by selecting Compile from the Program menu or by building a project. When the preprocessor is called into play, it scans the source code for preprocessor directives, all of which begin with the # symbol. If it finds any of these, it performs the action specified by the command. If this command introduces more preprocessor directives (such as #INCLUDEing another file) these directives are completed, too, until all directives have been performed. At that point, FoxPro source code is converted into the p-code the interpreter (and runtime) will be able to run. Let's review the various commands, and see what they can do.

Usage

```
#DEFINE cName eExpression
#UNDEF cName
```

#DEFINE declares a placeholder cName, which is to be replaced at compile time with the expression eExpression defined in the statement. #DEFINE statements work as in-line search-and-replace commands, replacing any occurrence of a specified phrase with an expression. This search and replace occurs in any command line anywhere a command keyword (or even a command itself) can appear. #DEFINE does not affect a literal string set off from the commands with quotation marks, but it does work within square brackets. The example below shows how you might want to take advantage of this.

#DEFINE is in effect only for the single program that contains the command or the current event or method procedure within a form or class. This is because this is the largest amount of code the preprocessor sees at one time—form methods are each compiled individually. A #DEFINE can be narrowed in scope even further with the addition of an "undefine" (#UNDEF) statement—only code between the #DEFINE and #UNDEF has the substitution performed.

Example

```
#DEFINE c_nVERSION_NO   "1.23"
* The following inserts the literal TTOC() expression
* into the source, rather than the date & time
#DEFINE c_tVERSION_BUILT TTOC(DATETIME())
* 1st example: evaluate both outside of quotes
WAIT WINDOW "Version "+ c_nVERSION_NO + ;
           ", built "+c_tVERSION_BUILT
* 2nd example: Constants evaluated inside square brackets
WAIT WINDOW [Version c_nVERSION_NO , built c_tVERSION_BUILT]
* 3rd example: Constant substitution doesn't take place
* within single or double quotes
WAIT WINDOW 'Version c_nVERSION_NO , built c_tVERSION_BUILT'
```

Usage

```
#IF eExpression
#ENDIF
```

This pair of statements tests a condition at compile time, and if it's true, the code within the IF...ENDIF pair is included in the source code to be compiled. This lets you include lots of code in your application while developing—tracing and debugging routines, special function key definitions that can pause and single-step the code, routines to provide "backdoors" into certain parts of the application—and prevent the code from even being included in the final version you install at a client site. What a relief not to worry that some data entry clerk will find that "Ctrl+Alt+Shift+F12" routine you used to test the end-of-the-year closeout routine in July!

#IF directives can also be used to include or exclude platform- or version-specific code. In VFP 3.0 and earlier, slightly different commands or functions are needed on the different platforms to support platform-specific functions. When the new version on the new platform is released, the commands or functions are not recognized on the older software of other platforms, generating compiler errors and defeating the cross-platform compatibility trademark of FoxPro. This new code can be "wrapped" in the #IF...#ENDIF test so that it's included only on the new platform, as the second example below illustrates.

Example

```
#IF C_DEBUGGING
  do DeBugLog with Program(), Pcount()
#ENDIF

* Use the new, faster VARTYPE() if
* compiling under VFP 6

#IF "FOXPRO 06" $ UPPER(VERSION(1))
  IF VARTYPE(toObject) <> "O"
#ELSE
  IF TYPE("toObject") # "O" or ISNULL(toObject)
#ENDIF
    RETURN .F.
  ENDIF
```

Usage
```
#IFDEF cConstantName
#ENDIF
```

This pair of statements tests for the existence of a predefined constant, declared with the #DEFINE statement above, at compile time, and if it's defined, the code within the IFDEF...ENDIF pair is included in the source code to be compiled.

Example
```
#IFDEF cAuditing  && Auditing functions to be included
  IF cAuditing
    DO AuditTrail with ...
  ELSE
.... more code
#ENDIF
```

Usage
```
#IFNDEF cConstantName
#ENDIF
```

This pair of statements is the reverse of the above, the equivalent of NOT in the IF portion of the test. If a predefined constant is not in effect, either through the lack of a #DEFINE statement or the removal of the definition using an #UNDEF, the code within the IFNDEF...ENDIF pair is included in the source code to be compiled.

Example
```
#IFNDEF C_DEBUGGING
  SET DEVELOPMENT OFF
  SET TRBETWEEN OFF
#ENDIF
```

Usage
```
#INCLUDE cFileName
_INCLUDE = eFileAndPathName
```

#INCLUDE inserts a second file into the first file, in memory, just before performing the compile. This allows you to keep a set of handy #DEFINEs around, written in just one place, and stick them into all of your programs. A couple of caveats apply, of course:

One very neat thing is that a file that's #INCLUDEd can have any or all of the preprocessor directive statements within it, and these, too, are processed by the preprocessor. Our suggestion: Break constant files into bite-sized chunks and create a STANDARD.H file that #INCLUDEs them all. That way, if a specific set of definitions must be maintained, they can be located most easily. Breaking them up by function (display, I/O, security) can make it easier to swap out a set when replacing or upgrading a subsystem. An alternative is to have a "common" set of definitions in a COMMON.H and include that in "subsystem" include files.

Rather than using this function in every method of a form or class, check out the "Include File..." option on the Form or Class menu. This makes the #INCLUDEd material available to each and every method within the form or class.

In VFP version 3.x, compiling a file that #INCLUDE's other files doesn't return any error messages if the #INCLUDEd file is not located or cannot be opened because it is in use. This one trips us up all the time: If you open FOXPRO.H to see what they called a constant, and then compile and run a program using that file without closing the editing window, you'll get stupid errors like "Variable 'COLOR_RED' is not found." In VFP 5.0 and later, a dialog appears, informing you the file can't be opened, and generates an .ERR file if you choose "Ignore" to continue compiling. Way to go, Fox Team!

We've mentioned FOXPRO.H in a few places throughout the book, and thought we should clue you in on this file. This file contains predefined sets of constants for many of the more difficult-to-remember functions, such as color numbers, low-level file routines, PRTINFO() types, parameters to MessageBox() and so forth. This file is worth browsing and using. We far prefer to see code using these constants, because it's much easier to read and, therefore, to maintain.

_INCLUDE is a new system memory variable introduced in VFP 6. _INCLUDE is supposed to be set to (HOME()+"FOXPRO.H") on startup, according to the documentation, but in fact, it's blank unless we set the preferences in Tools | Options | File Locations. When _INCLUDE is set to a header file, this file is automatically included in the compilation of all forms and classes. This is a wonderful way to ensure that your constants are available throughout your projects. We wish, however, they would have considered making _INCLUDE available for *all* compilation—programs, menu code, whatever—for consistency.

Example

```
* STANDARD.H
#INCLUDE FOXPRO.H
#INCLUDE MyVars.H

* Much easier-to-read code
#INCLUDE FOXPRO.H
IF MESSAGEBOX("Question",;
              MB_YESNO + MB_ICONQUESTION + MB_DEFBUTTON2, ;
              "Title") = IDYES
* than:
IF MESSAGEBOX("Question", 292, "Title") = 6  && what's 292? 6?

_INCLUDE = LOCFILE(HOME()+"FOXPRO.H","H")
```

See Also DrawMode, DrawStyle, FillStyle, FontMetric(), MessageBox(), MousePointer, PrtInfo(), SysMetric(), Type()

Define Bar See Define Menu.

Define Box, _Box

DEFINE BOX is one of those commands you should forget you ever noticed. What it's supposed to do is draw a box around output data. In FoxPro/DOS, this command worked more or less as intended.

As far as we can tell, it doesn't work at all for printed output in Visual FoxPro (nor did it work in FoxPro/Windows); and it works badly when you SET PRINT TO a file.

_BOX determines whether DEFINE BOX actually draws a box or not. For output to file, it appears to work as advertised.

Don't use DEFINE BOX! Use the Report Designer to create output and take advantage of its box-drawing tool. Use the form's built-in Box() method to draw simple boxes on forms, or the new Shape control if finer control is needed, but avoid this mess at all costs!

See Also ?, ??, @ ... Box, @ ... To

Define Class

This command is the code-based method for defining new classes based on existing ones (including the Visual FoxPro base classes). You define a class "as" an existing class, then spell out the differences between the new class and the old one. Visual class design offers all of the capabilities of this command, with greater flexibility, but there are a few classes that can't be subclassed visually.

Usage

```
DEFINE CLASS ClassName AS ParentClass [ OLEPUBLIC ]
        [ PROTECTED ProtectedPropertyList ]
        [ HIDDEN HiddenPropertyList ]
        [ Property = uExpr ]
        [ ADD OBJECT [ PROTECTED ] ObjectName AS ObjectClass
          [ NOINIT ]
          [ WITH PropertyList ] ]
```

```
        [ [ PROTECTED | HIDDEN ] PROCEDURE | FUNCTION MethodName
          Commands
          [ ENDPROC | ENDFUNC ] ]
ENDDEFINE
```

Parameter	Value	Meaning
ClassName	Name	The name to assign the new class.
ParentClass	Class Name	The existing class on which the new class is based.
ProtectedPropertyList	List of Names	Names of properties that can be seen only within the class and its subclasses.
HiddenPropertyList	List of Names	Names of properties that can be seen only in this class.
Property	Name	A property to receive an initial value. It can be one listed in ProtectedPropertyList or HiddenPropertyList, a new property to add, or a property inherited from ParentClass.
uExpr	Expression	The value to assign to Property.
ObjectName	Name	The name to give an object to be added to this class as a member. Only container classes can contain object members.
ObjectClass	Class Name	The class on which the object ObjectName is based. It must be derived from a base class that can be a member of this type of container class.
PropertyList		A list of initial assignments to properties of ObjectName in the form: Property = uExpr
MethodName	Name	A valid procedure or function name. The method may be a new one or one inherited from ParentClass.
Commands		The code to execute for method MethodName. May include the special NoDefault designator that indicates that the base system behavior for this method should not be executed and the DoDefault() function that calls up the class hierarchy.

The property assignment, ADD OBJECT and method definition sections can be repeated. A single class definition can contain many of each.

Let's look at each part of a class definition. Start with the DEFINE CLASS line. You can't create classes out of nothing. Every new class is derived from an existing class. Ultimately, all classes can trace their heritage back to one of the Visual FoxPro base classes. (See "Base Clef" in "OOP is Not an Accident" for a list.)

When creating a class, you base it on the class that's closest in appearance and behavior to what you want to end up with. That way, you minimize the amount of work you have to do to get what you want.

Basing one class on another means that the new class starts out with all the properties, events and methods of the ParentClass, and that changes to the ParentClass will usually be passed along to the new class. (That's inheritance.) This is a Good Thing, since it lowers your maintenance burden. In fact, it's one of the main points of OOP.

Adding the OLEPUBLIC keyword defines this class as a custom Automation server that can be instantiated from other applications. You have to BUILD DLL or BUILD EXE to use such classes as servers. (You can also use these classes inside a single VFP session, but we're not sure why you'd want to. Maybe for testing.)

Protection, in the OOP sense, has nothing to do with paying off the local mobster. A protected property, member or method can't be seen outside the object itself (except that its subclasses can see it, too). This is how you keep other objects from messing around with this one. If outside objects need to know or change the value of a protected property, you can provide a method to allow this.

Hidden properties and methods are even more protected than protected ones. Not only can't other objects see them, even subclasses can't see them. Unfortunately, hidden properties and methods can't even be used by methods that are themselves called via :: or DoDefault(). This means that hidden is pretty much useless.

The property assignments serve a couple of purposes. First, you can use them to assign values to properties that already belong to the class, including those you just defined as protected or hidden. (See "Faster than a Speeding Bullet" to learn why you should always assign a value to the Name property.) Second, you create new properties this way. If you don't know what values you want for them yet (perhaps they'll be assigned in the class's Init method), just give them empty values of the appropriate type.

When the class you're defining is derived from a container class (like Form, Container, and so forth), you can add member objects in the definition. In some cases, you're restricted to members of certain classes—see "Not Quite All There" in "OOP is Not an Accident."

When you add objects this way, you can set some of their properties up front using the WITH clause. The OOP experts recommend that you don't do this because it's tantamount to subclassing the thing on the fly. It's better to either create a subclass that has the properties you need or to make the changes in the container's Init method.

The NOINIT clause says that the object should be added to this class without running its Init method. We haven't yet run into a case where this is useful, but we're sure it's there for a reason.

Finally, you can define methods. Again, these can be new definitions for existing methods inherited from ParentClass or its ancestors, or brand-new methods that belong only to this class. Just about any FoxPro command is valid inside method code.

There are two special things you can do in method code. Each of them relates to dealing with inherited behavior. First, you can explicitly call methods belonging to the parent class (or even its ancestors) by using the :: operator or the DoDefault() function. Second, you can suppress the default system behavior of an event by including the NoDefault keyword. For more information on both of these, see "OOP is Not an Accident."

Now that we've gone through all this, we're honor-bound to tell you that we don't think you should do it this way very often. There are greater benefits to defining your classes visually using the Class Designer: drag and drop, builders, manipulation in the Class Browser and Component Gallery, and more. You get a lot more flexibility with visual design. Sometimes, when we are trying out some ideas for a new class, we'll code the class from the keyboard, because it's quick and easy to make repeated changes to get the behavior we want. Then, when the rough building is done, we'll convert the class definition into a visual one to give us access to the richer tools.

Example

```
DEFINE CLASS EasyForm AS FORM
* Here's a pretty basic form that auto-centers, has a Close
* button and lets you pass it a background color and a window
* caption.

   AutoCenter = .T.

   ADD OBJECT cmdClose AS CloseButton

   PROCEDURE Init(nBackColor, cCaption)

      IF TYPE("nBackColor") = "N"
         This.BackColor = nBackColor
      ENDIF
```

```
      IF TYPE("cCaption") = "C"
         This.Caption = cCaption
      ENDIF

      This.cmdClose.Left = (This.Width - This.cmdClose.Width) /2
      This.cmdClose.Top = This.Height - This.cmdClose.Height - 10
   ENDPROC
ENDDEFINE

DEFINE CLASS PassForm AS EasyForm
* This is a subclass of our basic form above. It insists on
* being passed a built-in password or you can't create it. Not
* exactly user-friendly, is it?

   PROTECTED cPassWord
   cPassWord = "Yowza!"

   PROCEDURE Init(nBackColor, cCaption, cPass)

      IF TYPE("cPass") = "C" AND cPass = This.cPassWord
         DoDefault(nBackColor, cCaption)
      ELSE
         RETURN .F.
      ENDIF
   ENDPROC

ENDDEFINE

DEFINE CLASS CloseButton AS CommandButton
* Standard Close button. Caption is "Close" and it releases the
* form when clicked.

   Name = "cmdClose"
   Caption = "Close"
   Height = 40
   Width = 60

   PROCEDURE Click

      ThisForm.Release()
   ENDPROC

ENDDEFINE
```

The example defines two form classes, one derived from the other, and a button class. The form classes have one member object, a Close button. The password property in PassForm is not an example of how to put a password on a form—just a demonstration of the kind of thing you might want to protect. To check out these classes, put all this code in a program file. Then, use code like the following:

```
SET PROCEDURE TO <the program you created>
oForm = CREATEOBJECT("PassForm", RGB(255,0,255), "Showing Off", "Yowza!")
oForm.SHOW()
```

In VFP 6, you can use NewObject() instead of CreateObject() and skip the SET PROCEDURE line. If you do so, be sure to include both the filename containing the definition and the empty string for the application parameter before the values to pass to the form's Init method. You need a line like this:

```
oForm = NewObject("PassForm","MyForm.prg","",RGB(255,128,128),;
                  "Why not?","Yowza!")
```

See Also ::, Create Class, CreateObject(), DoDefault(), Modify Class, NewObject(), Set ClassLib, Set Procedure

Define Menu, Define Pad, Define Popup, Define Bar, Release Menus, Release Pad, Release Popups, Release Bar

These commands create and destroy the components of a Windows-style menu. See Menus for an explanation of the various components.

Because the Menu Designer generates the DEFINE commands for you and the RELEASEs aren't needed when you're dealing with the system menu bar, you'll rarely write these commands yourself. (The exception is using DEFINE POPUP and DEFINE BAR to create right-click menus, but, starting in VFP 5, the Menu Designer can do that for you, too.)

Usage

```
DEFINE MENU MenuBarName
        [ BAR [ AT LINE nRow ] ]
        [ IN [ WINDOW ] ContainingWindow | IN SCREEN ]
        [ FONT cFontName [, nFontSize ] ] [ STYLE cStyleCodes ]
        [ KEY KeyLabel ] [ MARK cMarkCharacter ]
        [ MESSAGE cMessageText ] [ NOMARGIN ]
        [ COLOR SCHEME nScheme | COLOR ColorPairList ]
RELEASE MENUS [ MenuBarList [ EXTENDED ] ]

DEFINE PAD PadName1 OF MenuBarName PROMPT cPadText
        [ AT nRow, nColumn ]
        [ BEFORE PadName2 | AFTER PadName3 ]
        [ NEGOTIATE PositionInVFP [, PositionInActiveDoc ] ]
        [ FONT cFontName [, nFontSize ] ] [ STYLE cStyleCodes ]
        [ KEY KeyLabel [, cKeyText ] ] [ MARK cMarkCharacter ]
        [ SKIP [ FOR lExpression ] ] [ MESSAGE cMessageText ]
        [ COLOR SCHEME nScheme | COLOR ColorPairList ]
RELEASE PAD PadName | ALL OF MenuBarName

DEFINE POPUP PopupName
        [ FROM nTop, nLeft ] [ TO nBottom, nRight ]
        [ IN [ WINDOW ] ContainingWindow | IN SCREEN ]
        [ FONT cFontName [, nFontSize ] ] [ STYLE cStyleCodes ]
        [ PROMPT FIELD FieldName
         | PROMPT FILES [ LIKE FileSkeleton ]
             | PROMPT STRUCTURE ]
        [ TITLE cMenuTitleText ] [ FOOTER cFooterText ]
        [ KEY KeyLabel ] [ MESSAGE cMessageText ]
        [ MARGIN ] [ MARK cMarkCharacter ]
        [ MOVER ] [ MULTISELECT ] [ SCROLL ]
        [ SHORTCUT ]
        [ RELATIVE ] [ SHADOW ]
        [ COLOR SCHEME nScheme | COLOR ColorPairList ]
RELEASE POPUPS [ PopupList [ EXTENDED ] ]

DEFINE BAR nBarNumber1 | SystemItemName OF PopupName
        PROMPT cBarText
        [ BEFORE nBarNumber2 | AFTER nBarNumber3 ]
        [ FONT cFontName [, nFontSize ] ] [ STYLE cStyleCodes ]
        [ KEY KeyLabel [, cKeyText ] ] [ MARK cMarkCharacter ]
        [ MESSAGE cMessageText ] [ SKIP [FOR lExpression ] ]
        [ COLOR SCHEME nScheme | COLOR ColorPairList ]
RELEASE BAR nBarNumber | SystemItemName | ALL OF PopupName
```

The DEFINE commands create the objects and leave them in memory. You need an ACTIVATE command or SYSMENU set appropriately to actually use these things. The RELEASE commands remove the definitions from memory.

There are a few things here that are different from FoxPro 2.x, as well as a few that are just plain confusing. Let's take a look.

The FONT and STYLE clauses at each level were added in VFP 3. These clauses let you decide what font to use when you're not working with the system menu. The system menu picks up its font settings from the Registry and ignores any fonts you specify.

Like so many other menu components, fonts propagate from container to contained item. That is, the font you specify for a menu is used for the pads of that menu, unless they include the FONT clause. The font you specify for a popup applies to all bars in that popup that don't have their own font definition.

These clauses give you the ability to create menus as ugly as some of the flyers we receive for social events. Just because you can use lots of different fonts doesn't mean you should.

We ranted in the original *Hacker's Guide* about the inability to set fonts for the system menu. Since then, however, we've come to see the user-interface light and realized that menus really should be based on system-wide settings and that coding specific fonts and sizes into your application's menus is likely to annoy your users.

The MARK clause is ignored. No matter what you specify, you get the checkmark character.

DEFINE PAD's NEGOTIATE clause controls what happens to a pad when your application works with another application. How the pad behaves for OLE in-place editing is dictated by the PositionInVFP keyword; how it behaves in an active document is determined by the PositionInActiveDoc. The choices are NONE, LEFT, RIGHT and MIDDLE. NONE means the pad doesn't appear in that case. The exact meaning of MIDDLE seems to vary depending on which application is taking over. For active documents, RIGHT means "put the item on the Help menu." Weird behavior, but it is documented that way.

The PROMPT clause of DEFINE POPUP lets you create a popup without having to define individual bars. You can automatically fill it with a list of files, the fields of a table, or, the most useful, the value of an expression for each record in a table. These popups are pretty restricted in what else they can do—no multiselect and no mover bars are the most serious restrictions.

The SHORTCUT keyword of DEFINE POPUP was added in VFP 5 to make it easier to create context (or shortcut) menus. When you add the SHORTCUT keyword, the generated popup has the substantial 3-D look of Windows' context menus. Without it, the popup is a pretty sad-looking thing.

Some of the other common clauses are discussed under Menus.

Example

```
DEFINE MENU MyMenu FONT "Arial",14 STYLE "I"
DEFINE PAD MyFirst OF MyMenu PROMPT "First"
DEFINE PAD MySecond OF MyMenu PROMPT "Second"

DEFINE POPUP MyPop1
DEFINE BAR 1 OF MyPop1 PROMPT "Item 1"
DEFINE BAR 2 OF MyPop1 PROMPT "Item 2"

DEFINE POPUP MyPop2
DEFINE BAR 1 OF MyPop2 PROMPT "Other 1" FONT "Courier New",12
DEFINE BAR 2 OF MyPop2 PROMPT "Other 2"
DEFINE BAR 3 OF MyPop2 PROMPT "Other 3"

ON PAD MyFirst OF MyMenu ACTIVATE POPUP MyPop1
ON PAD MySecond OF MyMenu ACTIVATE POPUP MyPop2

ON SELECTION BAR 1 OF MyPop1 ?"Item 1 chosen"
ON SELECTION BAR 2 OF MyPop1 ?"Item 2 chosen"
ON SELECTION POPUP MyPop2 ?"Item from Popup2"
ON SELECTION BAR 3 OF MyPop2 ?"But I'm different"

ACTIVATE MENU MyMenu
```

See Also Activate Menu, Activate Popup, Deactivate Menu, Deactivate Popup, Menus, On Bar, On Pad, On Selection Bar, On Selection Menu, On Selection Pad, On Selection Popup

Define Window, Release Windows, Activate Window, Deactivate Window, Hide Window, Show Window, Move Window, Modify Window

This group of commands lets you work with windows the Xbase way. Many of their capabilities have been superseded by use of properties and methods, though some still require these commands.

Usage

```
DEFINE WINDOW WindowName
         FROM nTop, nLeft TO nBottom, nRight
         | AT nTop, nLeft SIZE nHeight, nWidth
         [ IN [ WINDOW ] ContainerWindow | IN SCREEN
           | IN DESKTOP | IN MACDESKTOP ]
         [ NAME ObjectName ]
         [ FONT cFontName [, nFontSize ] ] [ STYLE cFontStyle ]
         [ TITLE cWindowTitle ] [ FOOTER cWindowFooter ]
         [ HALFHEIGHT ]
         [ DOUBLE | PANEL | SYSTEM | NONE ]
         [ CLOSE | NOCLOSE ] [ GROW | NOGROW ]
         [ FLOAT | NOFLOAT ] [ MDI | NOMDI ]
         [ MINIMIZE | NOMINIMIZE ] [ ZOOM | NOZOOM ]
         [ SHADOW | NOSHADOW ]
         [ FILL cFillChar | FILL FILE FillFileName ]
         [ ICON FILE IconFileName ]
         [ COLOR SCHEME nColorScheme | COLOR PAIR ColorPairs ]
```

Out of all that mess, only one clause is new in Visual FoxPro—the NAME clause. It's the key to making user-defined windows easy to work with. NAME lets you turn the window into a form object. Once you do that, you can manipulate its properties directly and avoid working with the other commands in this group. There are properties corresponding to almost all the clauses above that actually work. (A fair number of the clauses are included only for backward compatibility and are ignored in Visual FoxPro.) Get in the habit of creating forms and manipulating their properties that way, and your code will be far easier to read and maintain than trying to decipher this behemoth of a command.

You have two options for specifying the initial size of a window. The AT - SIZE option is more in tune with the Visual FoxPro way, since its parameters map directly onto the Top, Left, Height and Width properties.

The table below shows the mapping of DEFINE WINDOW clauses to form properties.

Clause	Property	Meaning
FROM - TO, AT - SIZE	Top, Left, Height, Width	The size of the window.
FONT	FontName, FontSize	The font and size for the window.
STYLE	FontBold, FontItalic, FontOutline, FontShadow, FontStrikethru, FontUnderline	Font attributes for the window.
TITLE	Caption	The caption that appears in the window's title bar.
HALFHEIGHT	HalfHeightCaption	Should the window have a half-height title bar?
DOUBLE, PANEL, SYSTEM, NONE	BorderStyle, BorderWidth	The type and size of the window border.
CLOSE, NOCLOSE	Closable	Can the window be closed by double-clicking in the Close box?

Clause	Property	Meaning
GROW, NOGROW	BorderStyle	Can the window be resized?
FLOAT, NOFLOAT	Movable	Can the window be moved?
MDI, NOMDI	MDIForm	Does the window behave like an MDI window?
MINIMIZE, NOMINIMIZE	MinButton	Can the user minimize the window?
ZOOM, NOZOOM	MaxButton	Can the user maximize the window?
FILL FILE	Picture	The bitmap used as wallpaper.
ICON FILE	Icon	The icon to use when the window is minimized.
COLOR SCHEME, COLOR	BackColor, ForeColor	The colors for the window.

There are a few clauses that work but don't have exact parallels among the form's properties. The various IN clauses that specify the container of a particular window can't be duplicated in the object model.

In addition, ForeColor and BackColor don't provide the same degree of control offered by the COLOR SCHEME and COLOR clauses.

Usage
```
RELEASE WINDOWS WindowList | SCREEN
```

This command undefines one or more windows. If you use the NAME clause when you define the window, you can do this by calling the window's Release method instead.

RELEASE WINDOWS also lets you deactivate system windows and toolbars.

Watch out for the SCREEN clause—RELEASE WINDOW SCREEN attempts to shut down VFP, even if it's issued in a top-level form.

Usage
```
ACTIVATE WINDOW WindowNameList | ALL | SCREEN
        [ IN [ WINDOW ] ContainerWindow | IN SCREEN
          | IN MACDESKTOP ]
        [ BOTTOM | TOP | SAME ]
        [ NOSHOW ]
DEACTIVATE WINDOW WindowNameList | ALL
SHOW | HIDE WINDOW WindowNameList | ALL | SCREEN
        [ IN [ WINDOW ] ContainerWindow | IN SCREEN
          | IN MACDESKTOP ]
        [ BOTTOM | TOP | SAME ]
        [ SAVE ] [ REFRESH ]
```

These commands turn windows on and off. A window must already be defined to be ACTIVATEd or SHOWn and DEACTIVATEing or HIDEing a window doesn't undefine it. The difference between ACTIVATE and SHOW and between DEACTIVATE and HIDE is subtle. SHOWing a window makes it visible, while ACTIVATEing a window both makes it visible (unless you specify the NOSHOW clause) and gives it the focus. HIDEing a window makes it invisible, while DEACTIVATEing a window both makes it invisible and clears out its contents.

When you work with window objects (via DEFINE WINDOW's NAME clause), these distinctions are handled differently. The Show method activates a window and gives it focus, like ACTIVATE WINDOW. But the Hide method behaves like HIDE WINDOW, making the window invisible without clearing it. If the window doesn't contain any objects, the Cls method clears it. However, if you use AddObject to put objects in the window, you have to RemoveObject each object to clear it out.

The Show method can't handle the various IN clauses or the positioning clauses BOTTOM, TOP and SAME. Show also doesn't offer an equivalent to ACTIVATE's NOSHOW clause, which lets you activate a window without making it visible—you can SHOW WINDOW later. FoxPro 2.x's GENSCRN uses NOSHOW in the screens it generates to keep users from seeing all the controls being drawn. (This is something of a non-issue because controls added with AddObject are invisible until you explicitly make them visible, and you don't have to activate a form window to put controls in it.)

The SCREEN clause applies only to ACTIVATE WINDOW and SHOW WINDOW, and appears to be most relevant when you have windows that are defined IN DESKTOP. Then, the SCREEN clause lets you reactivate the main VFP window.

The REFRESH clause of SHOW WINDOW updates a Browse with the most recent data.

The SAVE clause of HIDE WINDOW and SHOW WINDOW is ignored—it's a relic from FoxPro/DOS.

Usage

```
MOVE WINDOW WindowName
        TO nNewTop, nNewLeft | BY nRows, nCols | CENTER
MODIFY WINDOW WindowName | SCREEN
        [ FROM nTop, nLeft [ TO nBottom, nRight ]
           | AT nTop, nLeft [ SIZE nHeight, nWidth ] ]
        [ FONT cFontName [, nFontSize ] ] [ STYLE cFontStyle ]
        [ TITLE cWindowTitle ] [ HALFHEIGHT ]
        [ DOUBLE | PANEL | SYSTEM | NONE ]
        [ CLOSE | NOCLOSE ] [ GROW | NOGROW ]
        [ FLOAT | NOFLOAT ]
        [ MINIMIZE | NOMINIMIZE ] [ ZOOM | NOZOOM ]
        [ SHADOW | NOSHADOW ]
        [ FILL FILE FillFileName ]
        [ ICON FILE IconFileName ]
        [ COLOR SCHEME nColorScheme | COLOR PAIR ColorPairs ]
```

It's when you get to these two commands that the ability to make a window into an object really shines. Instead of issuing the verb-oriented MOVE WINDOW or MODIFY WINDOW commands, we can simply tweak the properties of an object to get it to do what we want. The table above shows which properties to change for which clauses. (Use AutoCenter to get the effect of MOVE WINDOW CENTER.)

As in the other commands, the SCREEN clause addresses the main Visual FoxPro window (which you can also reference via the system variable _SCREEN). We do occasionally use MODIFY WINDOW SCREEN with no arguments to restore the defaults without having to remember what we've changed. One caveat—MODIFY WINDOW SCREEN clears the screen as well as resetting its properties.

Example

```
* Let's try doing things the old way and the OOP way
DEFINE WINDOW test FROM 5,5 TO 15,50 DOUBLE ;
   TITLE "Test Window" FLOAT GROW ZOOM MINIMIZE CLOSE
ACTIVATE WINDOW test
* now change some attributes
MODIFY WINDOW test NOFLOAT NOCLOSE TITLE "Whaddaya think?"
MOVE WINDOW test TO 10,8
RELEASE WINDOW Test

* Here's the OOP way
DEFINE WINDOW test FROM 5,5 TO 15,50 DOUBLE ;
   TITLE "Test Window" FLOAT GROW ZOOM MINIMIZE CLOSE ;
   NAME oTest
oTest.Show()
* now change some attributes
```

```
oTest.Movable = .F.
oTest.Closable = .F.
oTest.Caption = "Whaddaya Think?"
oTest.Top = 10
oTest.Left = 8
oTest.Release()
```

Although the second version takes more lines, we find it much easier to follow. In fact, we'll only be using DEFINE WINDOW with its multitude of clauses when we can't avoid it.

Beware: The two versions aren't exactly identical. The measurement schemes used for the old way and the Xbase way are different. MOVE WINDOW measures in rows and columns, while Top and Left are measured in either foxels or pixels, depending on the window's ScaleMode.

See Also AutoCenter, BackColor, BorderStyle, BorderWidth, Caption, Clear Windows, Closable, ColorScheme, FontBold, FontItalic, FontName, FontOutline, FontShadow, FontSize, FontStrikethru, FontUnderline, ForeColor, Form, HalfHeightCaption, Height, Hide, Icon, Left, MaxButton, MDIForm, MinButton, Movable, Release, ScaleMode, _Screen, Show, Top, Visible, Width

DefOLELcID, OLELcID

These two properties were added in the 3.0b revision of Visual FoxPro to support multilingual applications. Along with SYS(3004) and SYS(3005), they determine the locale ID used for the user interface of OLE Controls sensitive to this property.

Usage

```
frmForm.DefOLELcID = nLocale
nLocale = frmForm.DefOLELcID
nLocale  = oleControl.OLELcID
```

Parameter	Value	Meaning
nLocale	0	Use the default OLE Locale ID of the form, or the system default determined with SYS(3004).
	Other	See the documentation for SYS(3005) for a partial list of acceptable values, or the Windows SDK documentation for more thorough coverage.

The DefOLELcID and OLELcID properties affect the language used for the user interface of OLE controls; the OLE Automation commands are unaffected (use SYS(3005) to change the OLE Automation commands). DefOLELcID properties apply to a form or the main Visual FoxPro _SCREEN. This property can be set or read. The read-only OLELcID property can be queried for individual controls.

We think Microsoft went out of its way to make this property hard to decipher—why didn't they take out all the vowels while they were at it? "DefaultOLELocale" would not have been that much longer, and far easier to comprehend. We suspect it was one of those other languages, or perhaps the OLE team itself, that created this funky term, and the Fox team was just forced to go along with the joke.

Example

```
* Set a form's DefOLELcID to 1036 (French) or 1031 (German).
* Add an Outline OCX to the form.
* Right-click on the OCX and select 'Properties...'
* Note the 'General' tab is labeled 'Général' or 'Allgemein'
* Note, too, that everything else here is in English!

* In an international app, store the language properties
* in a global application status property, and set the
* language of each form on startup.
Procedure Form.Load
thisform.DefOLELcID = oApp.GlobalSets.DefOLELcID
```

Changing a form's DefOLELcID doesn't change the display in the property window for any of the OLELcIDs. Hacking the SCX reveals that this "property" is never even stored for the OCX, but just reflects the setting of the form. Our theory is that this isn't truly a property of controls at all, but only the form's property exposed at this level at runtime. This is contrary to the Help file, but probably makes more sense—how many times do you want a form where each OLE control speaks a different dialect?

See Also SYS(3004), SYS(3005)

Delete, Deleted(), Pack, Recall, Set Deleted, Set("Deleted")

These commands and functions control deletion of records from a table. Deleting a record in FoxPro (and in any other Xbase language) is a dance—a two-step—because it takes two steps to really and truly make a record go away. First, you "mark" the record for deletion. You can permanently throw away all the marked records when you want. Until you do so, you can "unmark" the record. It's like file deletion in Windows 95 where you put a file in the Recycle Bin, but it's not really deleted from the disk until you empty the bin. Come to think of it, it's not so different from real life. You put something in the trash, but you can retrieve it (and uncrumple it) until the trash can is emptied.

The first byte of every record in each table is a deletion flag. That's why the total length shown in the Table Designer is always at least one more than the sum of the field lengths (null fields can further increase the record length; see "Nulls" in "DBF, FPT, CDX, DBC—Hike!") This flag field contains an asterisk ("*") when the record is marked for deletion and a space when it's not marked. You can see this by opening up a table using a hex editor—that's how we figured it out.

Usage

```
DELETE [ Scope ]
       [ FOR lForExpression ]
       [ WHILE lWhileExpression ]
       [ IN cAlias | nWorkArea ]
       [ NOOPTIMIZE ]
RECALL [ Scope ]
       [ FOR lForExpression ]
       [ WHILE lWhileExpression ]
       [ IN cAlias | nWorkArea ]
       [ NOOPTIMIZE ]
```

DELETE marks one or more records for deletion. The command accepts a Scope, a FOR and a WHILE. Its default scope is NEXT 1. (Good choice for a destructive command. It limits the damage if you make a mistake.) RECALL unmarks one or more records. Again, the default scope is NEXT 1.

Both DELETE and RECALL allow you to specify another work area using IN. Don't! These are destructive commands—definite belt-and-suspenders territory. Always SELECT the work area you want to work in and DELETE the fewest records that make sense. In many cases, you should ask the user to confirm the deletion at least once; in extreme cases, maybe even twice depending on the reason for the deletion. DELETE and RECALL both accept the NOOPTIMIZE keyword, but we've never been able to think of a reason to use it. If you really think you need it, see SET OPTIMIZE.

With Visual FoxPro's Referential Integrity builder, you'll need to write a lot less deletion code than before. If you set deletion to Cascade in appropriate one-to-many relationships, you need to delete only the record on the one side, and the RI code handles all the many records.

Visual FoxPro actually offers two ways to delete records (though only one to recall them). DELETE-SQL has pretty much the same functionality as the traditional Xbase DELETE. However, Xbase's DELETE pays attention to the current deletion status of records and therefore seems to be faster when some records are already deleted.

Example

```
* this might be in the Click event of a Delete button
#INCLUDE FoxPro.H
IF MESSAGEBOX("Do you really want to delete this record",;
     MB_YESNO + MB_ICONQUESTION + MB_DEFBUTTON2, ;
     "Delete current record?") = ID_YES
```

```
        DELETE NEXT 1
    ENDIF
```

Usage `PACK [ MEMO ] [ DBF ]`

PACK permanently removes all marked records. What it actually does is copy all the unmarked records into a new file and then rename the new file. (The table is also reindexed.) Because PACK does this behind the scenes, there is a small chance for data loss if your system crashes during a PACK.

Use PACK with caution. Before VFP, the standard advice was to do the same steps yourself, using COPY TO, DELETE FILE and RENAME. That's still your best bet for free tables. Either way, you need exclusive access to the file to perform this maintenance. Also, in either case, you should SET ORDER TO the tag you use most often before starting the process. That way, the records in the resulting file will be in the order in which they are most often accessed, resulting in better performance. Here's an example to get you started:

```
USE MyTable ORDER BestOrder EXCLUSIVE
COPY TO MyNewTable FOR NOT DELETED()

IF FILE("MyNewTable.DBF") AND FILE("MyNewTable.FPT")
   * only go on if the new version was created
   USE
   DELETE FILE MyTable.DBF
   DELETE FILE MyTable.FPT
   DELETE FILE MyTable.CDX
   RENAME MyNewTable.DBF TO MyTable.DBF
   RENAME MyNewTable.FPT TO MyTable.FPT

   * Now re-create the indexes
ELSE
   WAIT WINDOW "Trouble in Paradise" NOWAIT
ENDIF
```

For tables in a database, things are a little more difficult. Using the COPY TO approach, you lose all the database information for the table. In particular, your relations get trashed. Your best bet is to get a good database maintenance tool (like Stonefield Database Toolkit) to handle these chores.

Memo files (FPT) can accumulate a lot of wasted space because replacement of existing data doesn't reuse the same disk space. Over time, this can really add up, especially if those humongous general field OLE objects are used and edited. PACK MEMO cleans up this wasted space without removing the records marked for deletion. There's also a PACK DBF version, but it's another of those items that seems to have been added for completeness, not because it was useful. (If you find a reason to use it, let us know.)

Usage `lIsDeleted = DELETED( [ cAlias | nWorkArea ] )`

DELETED() tells you if a record has been marked for deletion. If so, it returns .T. By default, DELETED() refers to the current work area, but you can pass it an alias or work area number to check the status of the current record in another work area.

DELETED() can be very handy in FOR clauses, letting you do things like:

```
BROWSE FOR NOT DELETED()
```

to see all the current records in a table.

Usage
```
SET DELETED ON | OFF
cDeletedSetting = SET("DELETED")
```

The final members of this group are the most confusing. SET DELETED is extremely useful, but equally counter-intuitive. This command tells other commands whether or not to pay attention to records marked for deletion. SET DELETED ON indicates that marked records should be ignored (that is, turn off the deleted records). SET DELETED OFF says to include the marked records (that is, turn them on). It's only recently that we've been able to use this command without looking it up first. (Even the Microsoft/Fox technical writers have trouble with this one. The FoxPro 2.5 Language Reference contained an error that made both options sound like SET DELETED ON.)

Setting DELETED ON is similar to setting a filter. It's as if the deleted records don't exist. You can issue commands with a scope of ALL and have the deleted records ignored. Many applications operate with DELETED ON all the time.

If you choose to SET DELETED ON, every table should have an index tag with a key of DELETED(). Rushmore uses the tag to optimize elimination of deleted records. Otherwise, result sets have to be checked sequentially for records marked for deletion. It doesn't matter whether or not any records are actually deleted. Only the SET DELETED choice matters. (See "Faster than a Speeding Bullet" for more on this.)

SET("DELETED") returns either "ON" or "OFF" to indicate the current setting. It's handy for saving the old setting when you need to change it.

Example

```
cOldDeleted=SET("DELETED")
SET DELETED OFF
* find a deleted record, perhaps to recycle it
LOCATE FOR DELETED()
RECALL NEXT 1
* stuff some data into it
GATHER MEMVAR
* now clean up
SET DELETED &cOldDeleted
```

See Also Delete-SQL, Reindex, Set, Set Optimize

Delete Connection **See Create Connection.**

Delete Database **See Create Database.**

Delete File **See Copy File.**

Delete Tag **See Index.**

Delete Trigger **See Create Trigger.**

Delete View **See Create SQL View.**

Delete-SQL

This is the "other DELETE." Like the Xbase DELETE, it lets you mark one or more records in a table for deletion. The records aren't physically deleted until you PACK the table.

Usage

```
DELETE FROM [ Database! ] Table
     [ WHERE lCondition ]
```

Parameter	Value	Meaning
Database	Name	Name of database containing the table from which records are to be deleted.
	Omitted	Delete records from a free table or the named table in the current database.

Parameter	Value	Meaning
Table	Name	Table from which to delete records.
lCondition	Logical	Determines which records are deleted.
	Omitted	All records in cTable are deleted.

Be careful with this command. Unlike the Xbase DELETE, the default for DELETE-SQL is to delete all records in the table.

Even when there's a tag on DELETED(), DELETE-SQL doesn't check the tag unless you include the clause NOT DELETED() in the WHERE clause. Amazing. If the clause is included, you get a Rushmore-ized delete.

Because the two-step delete is an Xbase concept, there's no SQL equivalent to RECALL. You have to use the Xbase RECALL command.

Despite its SQL antecedents, DELETE-SQL only lets you delete records in a single table. Because you can list only one table in the FROM clause, there's no way to create a join condition with another table. However, you can use a sub-query in the WHERE clause to base the deletion decision on information from other tables. Functionally, DELETE-SQL doesn't provide anything that Xbase DELETE doesn't already have. The only slight advantage it offers is that the table doesn't need to be open initially, but it leaves it open afterward anyway.

You might think it would be better to use DELETE-SQL when dealing with remote data. But the truth is that you'll always be working on a view of that data, and Xbase DELETE works just as well. We're willing to have our opinion changed, but right now we can't see a whole lot of reasons to use DELETE-SQL.

Example

```
* delete all orders for a specified customer
DELETE FROM TasTrade!Orders WHERE customer_id="WOLZA"

* delete all orders for the current customer record
* assumes Customer is open
DELETE FROM TasTrade!Orders ;
   WHERE Customer_id=Customer.Customer_id

* Get rid of customers who've never bothered to place an order
DELETE FROM TasTrade!Customer ;
   WHERE Customer_id NOT IN ;
         (SELECT Customer_ID FROM Orders)
```

See Also Delete, Deleted(), Recall, Sys(3054)

DeleteColumn See AddColumn.

Deleted

This event fires when you click on the delete mark column in a grid.

Usage

```
PROCEDURE grdGrid.Deleted
LPARAMETERS nRecNo
```

The name Deleted is a little misleading, because the event fires whenever you click in the delete mark column, whether you're deleting or recalling the record. The record number of the record affected is passed to nRecNo.

Help says Deleted fires when the DELETE command is used to delete a record, too. It's wrong. None of Xbase DELETE, DELETE-SQL or RECALL fire Deleted. Only clicks in the delete mark column do it.

Use NODEFAULT in the method to prevent the deletion or recall. Better yet, set DeleteMark to .F. and the user can't delete records in the grid at all.

Example

```
PROCEDURE Deleted
* Confirm the deletion
LPARAMETERS nRecNo

LOCAL nResult
* In this example, the message uses the record number.
* In an application, you'd use data from the record.
nResult = MESSAGEBOX("Do you really want to delete record" ;
          + LTRIM(STR(nRecNo)), MB_YESNO + MB_ICONQUESTION)
IF nResult = IDNO
   NODEFAULT
ENDIF

ENDPROC
```

See Also DeleteMark, Grid

DeleteMark See RecordMark.

Descending() See Candidate().

Description

This property contains the description of a file or server in a project.

Usage

```
cDescription = oObject.Description
oObject.Description = cDescription
```

This is a property of both the File and Server objects. For files, it contains the description you see at the bottom of the Project Manager when the file is highlighted. You can edit it interactively by choosing Edit Description from the context menu or the Project Menu. Note that you can only access descriptions for files through this property. Classes, although their descriptions are visually edited the same way, can't be accessed programmatically with this technique, though descriptions for class libraries can.

For ActiveX server classes, Description contains the description from the Servers page of the Project Info dialog. However, you have to build an EXE or DLL from the project before anything shows up on that page. (And, if you add a new OLE public class, you have to build again before the new class is available.) So, you can't set this property when you first create the class.

Description accepts any valid characters. However, we don't recommend using CHR(13) and CHR(10) to write multi-line descriptions. You can't see anything but the first line in the Project Manager or the Edit Description dialog. Description is limited to 255 characters. If you assign 256 characters to Description, it is reset to an empty string.

Example

```
oProj.Files[1].Description = "The main program for this app."
```

See Also File, Files, Name, Project

Desk Accessories

A collection of "mini-apps" included within Visual FoxPro. These utilities vary in usefulness. Ignored by Microsoft for several releases, once kept grudgingly in the product for "backward compatibility," these are being phased out.

Usage

```
ACTIVATE WINDOW cWindowName
DEFINE BAR cBarName OF _MSYSTEM PROMPT cPrompt
```

Parameter	Value	Meaning
cWindowName	CALENDAR	The Calendar/Diary applet.
	CALCULATOR	The Calculator applet.
	FILER	The Filer applet. FP 2.x only.
	PUZZLE	The Puzzle game. VFP 3.x and earlier.
cBarName	_MST_DIARY	The Calendar/Diary applet.
	_MST_CALCU	The Calculator applet.
	_MST_FILER	The Filer applet.
	_MST_PUZZL	The Puzzle game.

See the individual entries for details on how each applet works.

In FoxPro 2.0 days, the idea that more than one application could run at the same time was a novel idea. As a DOS-based application, the desk accessories were a boon to productivity. Now, with the ability to have many programs running at once in the Windows environment, the idea seems a little dated. It would seem sensible that these applications could be retired. However, each of them brings some unique capabilities to Visual FoxPro that we think the product would be poorer without.

It seems that Microsoft would be just as happy if these applications went away. There has been little or no effort to update the apps' interfaces. Documentation on how to use these functions is scanty, at best. Mention of the ability to use these functions from the predefined system menus, if it is in the documentation, has completely eluded us. Filer was eliminated in the move to Visual FoxPro, although it's back as a VFP-COM tool—see the Filer entry for details. Puzzle was eliminated after VFP 3. We suspect the Calendar and Calculator's days are numbered as well.

We're not sure these applets are appropriate for inclusion in a completed application (except the Puzzle, of course—a terrific time-sink). But we do encourage you to add them to your arsenal of development tools.

Example

```
ACTIVATE WINDOW FILER
```

See Also _CalcMem, _CalcValue, _DiaryDate, Calculator, Calendar/Diary, Filer, Puzzle

Desktop

This property determines whether or not a form is constrained by the main Visual FoxPro window. When Desktop is .T., the form can move around independently.

Usage

```
lContained = frmForm.Desktop
```

You set this one at design time and live with it. Makes sense to us—this isn't something you'd want to mess around with at runtime.

When a form has Desktop = .F., moving it beyond the bounds of the main window clips off portions of the window. With Desktop = .T., the whole window shows.

Even when a form has Desktop set to .T., it still belongs to the main Visual FoxPro window. Minimizing the main window makes the form disappear, and you can't keep the form around after you shut down VFP. To create a window that's not a child of the main VFP window, use the ShowWindow property.

Example

```
IF This.Desktop
   This.Caption = "Look at me. I float free"
ENDIF
```

See Also AlwaysOnTop, AutoCenter, MaxHeight, ShowWindow

Destroy See Init.

DExport, DGen() See Access().

_DiaryDate See Calendar/Diary.

Difference() See Soundex().

Dimension, Declare

These two identical commands create new arrays or change the size of existing ones.

Usage

```
DIMENSION | DECLARE ArrayName( nRows [, nCols ] )
                    [, aArray2( nRows2 [, nCols2 ] )
                     ...]
```

FoxPro supports both one- and two-dimensional arrays. If only nRows is specified, a one-dimensional array is created. If both nRows and nCols are specified, you get a two-dimensional array. However, any two-dimensional array in FoxPro can be treated like a one-dimensional array at any time. See "DBF, FPT, CDX, DBC—Hike!" for more information on FoxPro's weird (but convenient) array handling.

DIMENSION scopes arrays as private. The commands PUBLIC [ARRAY] and LOCAL [ARRAY] use the same arguments to create arrays of global and local scope, respectively. A classic example of dBloat. Either a new command PRIVATE [ARRAY], dropping the DIMENSION/DECLARE syntax, or DIMENSION [PUBLIC | PRIVATE | LOCAL] (our preference) would make more sense to us.

Arrays in FoxPro can use either parentheses (as shown above) or square brackets to enclose their row and column information. We recommend square brackets to avoid confusion with functions. (We only used parentheses in the syntax above because we've been using square brackets to indicate optional clauses.)

If ArrayName exists when you issue DIMENSION or DECLARE, it's reshaped to match the new dimensions specified. Data is moved to the cell with the same element number as its original location (see AELEMENT() for an explanation of element numbers). Any new elements get a value of .F. Take a look at the aColCopy function under ACopy() to see how to put the data back where it belongs when you add columns.

Example

```
DIMENSION aMyArray[3], aMyOtherArray[10,17]

* Add to an existing array
SELECT category FROM masterlist INTO ARRAY aCategory
DIMENSION aCategory[ ALEN(aCategory, 1) + 1 ]
aCategory[ ALEN(aCategory, 1) ] = "Other"
```

See Also ACopy(), AElement(), ALen(), Array Manipulation, Local, Public

Directory, Display Files, List Files

Three nearly synonymous commands to list files meeting specified file skeletons, similar to the DOS DIR equivalent, but with Visual FoxPro-specific extensions.

Usage
```
DIRECTORY | DISPLAY FILES | LIST FILES
      [ ON cDriveLtr ]
      [ [ LIKE ] [ cPath ] [ cFileSkeleton ] ]
      [ TO PRINTER [ PROMPT ] | TO FILE cFileName [ ADDITIVE ] ]
```

Following the rule in Visual FoxPro that every rule has an exception (including this one), the DIRECTORY command is one of the few (perhaps the only) that can be abbreviated to three letters (DIR) rather than the usual (but not always true) four.

If no file skeleton is specified, Visual FoxPro lists only DBF files, and includes information on the number of records in the file, the file size, and also a comment if the file is a FoxBase 2-style file. If a skeleton is supplied, only the names of the specified files are listed, similar to the wide-listing format of the DOS DIR command.

Although the command has the same name, this is not DOS. Note that the syntax above has the drive letter and the path as separate arguments. It appears that everything after the first letter in the drive parameter is ignored. DIR D:\EXAMPLES is likely to give you different results than DIR ON D\EXAMPLES\. This can be confusing. Our advice: skip the ON parameter, forget passing the LIKE optional keyword, and pass the path just like DOS, as in DIR D:\EXAMPLES or DIR *.PRG

Unlike all the other DISPLAY/LIST commands, the FILES list lacks a NOCONSOLE option.

The output options, TO PRINTER and TO FILE, work similarly to the remainder of the DISPLAY and LIST commands. The DISPLAY and LIST versions have the usual differences. DIR works like DISPLAY FILES.

Example
```
DISPLAY FILES ON C LIKE \VFP\SAMPLES\MAINSAMP\DATA  && this is the same
DIR C:\VFP\SAMPLES\MAINSAMP\DATA                    && as this
```

See Also ADir(), Directory(), Display and List, File()

Directory() See File().

DisabledBackColor, DisabledForeColor

These properties determine the appearance of a control when it's disabled (that is, when its Enabled property is .F.).

Usage
```
oObject.DisabledBackColor = nColor
nColor = oObject.DisabledBackColor
oObject.DisabledForeColor = nColor
nColor = oObject.DisabledForeColor
```

The docs say both disabled forecolors and backcolors colors are dithered with gray, but as far as we can tell, this doesn't apply at all to backcolors and applies to forecolors only for some controls.

Example
```
* match an object's disabled colors to its regular colors
* with the dithering of the forecolor, this should result
* in the back remaining the same and the lettering dimming
* for those controls so affected.
This.DisabledBackColor = This.BackColor
This.DisabledForeColor = This.ForeColor
```

See Also BackColor, DisabledItemBackColor, DisabledItemForeColor, ForeColor, GetColor(), RGB()

DisabledItemBackColor, DisabledItemForeColor

These properties control the colors used for disabled items in a list or combo box.

Usage

```
oObject.DisabledItemBackColor = nBackColor
nBackColor = oObject.DisabledItemBackColor
oObject.DisabledItemForeColor = nForeColor
nForeColor = oObject.DisabledItemForeColor
```

We've come up with only two situations where these properties come into play.

When the RowSourceType for a list or combo is an array or explicit list, you can disable individual items by preceding the text with "\". So, an array item containing "\Zowie" is disabled in a list or combo.

The only other time an item is disabled is when RowSourceType=7 (Files). In that case, there's an entry that represents the current directory. It's disabled. It shows up in these colors. The separator bar that divides the top portion of the file list from the main body uses DisabledItemBackColor, but its ForeColor is black no matter what.

Because the normal dithering makes disabled items look different than enabled items, we suggest you go with the flow and just let these be the same as ItemBackColor and ItemForeColor.

See Also ComboBox, DisabledBackColor, DisabledForeColor, ItemBackColor, ItemForeColor, ListBox, RowSourceType

DisabledPicture See Picture.

DiskSpace(), Sys(2020), Sys(2022), Sys(2006), IsColor(), Sys(17), Sys(2010)

These functions all return information about the hardware or system configuration. Several of them don't provide accurate information.

Usage

```
nSpaceAvailable = DISKSPACE( [ cDrive ] )
cTotalSpace = SYS(2020)
cClusterSize = SYS(2022 [, cDrive ])
```

These three functions provide information about the default disk drive. As the name implies, DISKSPACE() tells you how much room is currently available. It's handy when you want to copy a file to a disk. SYS(2020) tells you the total size of the disk and SYS(2022) returns the number of bytes per cluster. These can also be useful when figuring out what's going to fit on a disk. There can be a maximum of 65,535 disk clusters on each volume under DOS or other FAT-based systems. On large volumes, these clusters can assume whopping sizes—16K or even 32K or larger! If you will be installing scads of dinky little files (like Visual FoxPro's BMPs and ICOs), you may want to consider warning the operator about how much space your files could waste!

You'll want to test for reasonableness in the return values of SYS(2022), and watch for differences between the versions of VFP. Ted's CD-ROM had a perfectly acceptable 32,768 bytes per sector—as long as there was a disk in the drive. Remove the disk, and the same function under VFP 3 returns 14,988,640 bytes per sector—a bit too high to be likely! VFP 5 reported DISKSPACE() of -1 and SYS(2020) of 0 and SYS(2022) generated error 1907, "Drive specifier is invalid." VFP 6 returns similar results, with an error 1002, "Input Output failure," under Windows NT 4. Check out the Windows API or FoxTools function DRIVETYPE() to warn of a removable drive.

The parameter cDrive was introduced in VFP 5 to save us the trouble of having to SET DEFAULT TO every drive we want to test. It would have been nicer if they had added it for all the drive functions, though—SYS(2020) still only reports on the default drive. DISKSPACE() accepts the cDrive parameter as "X", "X:" or

) still only reports on the default drive. DISKSPACE() accepts the cDrive parameter as "X", "X:" or "X:\" but any other format confuses it. SYS(2022), on the other hand, ignores all characters beyond the first letter, and will happily report the cluster size of "Chihuahua" versus "Dalmatian."

Example

```
SET DEFAULT TO A:          && a 3 1/2 drive
? SYS(2020)                && Returns "1457664"
? SYS(2022)                && Returns "512"
? DISKSPACE()              && Might return 854016.000
```

Usage

```
cGraphicsCard = SYS(2006)
lColorCapable = IsColor()
```

These two return information about the graphics and color capabilities of the system. They are hangovers from the DOS days when monochrome monitors and EGA cards might mean you'd need to make some changes in your displays. SYS(2006) returns the type of graphics card and monitor in use. However, it appears it can't recognize anything more advanced than VGA in VFP 3, and just returns "Color/Color" in VFP 5 and VFP 6. ISCOLOR() returns .T. if the system is color-capable. Under Windows, we let Windows take care of most of this stuff, but we can query SYSMETRIC() for far more detailed information if necessary.

Usage

```
cProcessor = SYS(17)
```

SYS(17) returns, as a string, the processor type.

On the 32-bit versions of Windows, SYS(17) works just fine (at least until the next processor upgrade comes along). In VFP 3 under 16-bit Windows, SYS(17) on a Pentium returns "80486"—not what the client who just spent megabucks for a new machine wants to see. It's not FoxPro's fault, though—it's a Windows thing.

Usage

```
nFiles = SYS(2010)
```

This function returns 255. In FoxPro/DOS, it returns the files setting from CONFIG.SYS, but someone decided that, in Windows, you didn't need to know. Under Windows 3.1 or later, you always have 255 file handles available.

Example

```
? SYS(2006)         && Might return "Color/Color"
? ISCOLOR()         && Might return .T.
? SYS(17)           && Might return "Pentium"
? SYS(2010)         && Returns 255
```

See Also GetEnv(), Set Default, Set Display, SysMetric()

Display and List

These two commands do more than Jack-of-all-trades. They have so many variations, it's hard to keep track of them. But fundamentally, they all come down to showing you some information about the current state of FoxPro.

The various forms of these commands are described in the pages that follow. Before we get to that, let's take a look at what's the same throughout.

By default, all the forms of both DISPLAY and LIST send output to the active window. All support optional TO PRINT and TO FILE clauses that let you send output somewhere else as well, and a NOCONSOLE clause that lets you suppress output to the active window. Unfortunately, there's no TO SCREEN clause that lets you redirect output to the main FoxPro window, so you may need to issue ACTIVATE SCREEN before a DISPLAY or LIST command.

Interestingly, the FILE keyword of TO FILE appears to be optional. Issuing DISPLAY STRUCTURE TO SCREEN results in a file called SCREEN.TXT, containing the structure of the open table. The FILE clause of these commands has an optional, undocumented ADDITIVE option to add the new listing to an existing file.

As with other commands supporting TO PRINT, there's an optional PROMPT clause that brings up the Print Setup dialog.

There are two differences between DISPLAY and LIST. DISPLAY stops when the screen (or window) is full of information and waits for a keypress to continue. LIST scrolls the output. When using the most basic form of DISPLAY or LIST, the one that simply shows data from an open table, DISPLAY has a default scope of NEXT 1 while LIST has a default scope of ALL. These differences mean that DISPLAY is a better choice for on-screen output and LIST is better for output to a printer or file.

See Also Display, Display Connections, Display Database, Display DLLs, Display Files, Display Memory, Display Objects, Display Procedures, Display Status, Display Structure, Display Tables, Display Views, List, List Connections, List Database, List DLLs, List Files, List Memory, List Objects, List Procedures, List Status, List Structure, List Tables, List Views

Display, List

This form of DISPLAY and LIST shows data from the table open in the current work area.

Usage

```
DISPLAY | LIST [ FIELDS ] uExpressionList
         [ Scope ] [ FOR lForExpression ] [ WHILE lWhileExpression ]
         [ OFF ]
         [ TO PRINT [ PROMPT ] | TO [ FILE ] cFileName ]
         [ NOCONSOLE ]
         [ NOOPTIMIZE ]
```

These are very old commands. They've added a few new clauses along the way, but the basics date back to the beginnings of Xbase history.

These are most useful for checking out data interactively. When you're trying to figure out what went wrong or you need a quick-and-dirty list to send someone, DISPLAY and LIST give you a fast way to get the information.

uExpressionList can contain any expression at all. Most typically, you have either fields of the current table or expressions based on those fields. If the current table is the parent of a temporal relation, you might also include fields from the related table. (If you specify fields in unrelated tables, you'll see the same values for fields in the non-selected table for each record in the selected table, because there is nothing within this command to move the record pointer in the unselected table.) Similarly, a constant or UDF can be used in the expression list to produce an output column not available from the source table.

By default, these commands include the record number as the first item in the listing. OFF gets rid of the record number. SET HEADING controls the field and function names at the top of the list.

It's hard to imagine a situation where NOOPTIMIZE would be relevant to DISPLAY or LIST, but since they do have a FOR clause and they are sensitive to SET FILTER, we guess NOOPTIMIZE was needed for completeness. Check out SET OPTIMIZE if you care.

Example

```
USE Customer
DISPLAY Customer_Id, Company_Name
LIST Customer_Id, Company_Name TO PRINT OFF
```

See Also ?, ??, Display and List, Set Heading, Set Optimize

Display Connections, List Connections

These commands provide a list of named connections in a database. The name of the connection and the data source or connection string is listed.

Usage

```
DISPLAY | LIST CONNECTIONS
         [ TO PRINTER [ PROMPT ] |
           TO [ FILE ] cFileName [ ADDITIVE ] ]
         [ NOCONSOLE ]
```

The same information is available using ADBOBJECTS() and DBGETPROP().

A database must be open and current before issuing the command.

Example

```
USE MyTestDBC
CREATE CONNECTION TestConnection ;
        DATASOURCE "MS Access 7.0 Databases"
DISPLAY CONNECTIONS
```

See Also ADBObjects(), Create Connection, DBGetProp(), Display and List, Modify Connection

Display Database, List Database

These commands show you the contents of the current database, listing all tables and views, their fields, indexes, relations, and other properties, but not stored procedures.

Usage

```
DISPLAY | LIST DATABASE
        [ TO PRINTER [ PROMPT ]
          | TO [ FILE ] cFileName [ ADDITIVE ] ]
        [ NOCONSOLE ]
```

Most of the information shown in the listing is available from either ADBOBJECTS() or DBGETPROP(). However, the index information can only be extracted by opening the individual tables and using the TAG(), KEY() and other index functions.

This means there's one case where you'll want to parse the output of LIST DATABASE—when a table is trashed and you can't open it to find index information. Even then, it doesn't give you everything you need, just the tag name and whether or not it's a candidate key. A better solution is to use the GENDBC utility provided with Visual FoxPro in the first place—it creates a program which, when run, re-creates your database. We recommend you make a habit of running it against a database every time you change its structure. Call it insurance. (Be forewarned: In VFP 3 and VFP 5, we know of at least one case where GENDBC can't provide you a perfect replica. Adding a FOR condition to a primary key is reasonably complex and GENDBC doesn't handle it right.)

These commands are fairly forgiving. If you issue them without an open database, you're prompted to choose one.

In VFP 3, the query that produces a view sometimes gets cut off in the listing produced by this command. You can see the problem by opening the TasTrade sample database and issuing DISPLAY DATABASE. Then, check the *SQL lines for the views. The problem appears to be fixed in later versions.

Example

```
OPEN DATA TasTrade
LIST DATABASE TO DATLIST.OUT NOCONSOLE
MODI COMM DATLIST.Out  && leave wordwrap off
ERASE DATLIST.Out
```

See Also ADBObjects(), Candidate(), DBGetProp(), Descending(), Display and List, For(), Key(), Primary(), Relation(), Tag(), Target()

Display DLLs, List DLLs

These two commands show the dynamic link library calls that have been declared in the current sessions.

Usage

```
DISPLAY DLLS [TO [ FILE ] Filename [ ADDITIVE ]
              | TO PRINTER [PROMPT]]
             [ NOCONSOLE ]
LIST DLLS    [TO [ FILE ] Filename [ADDITIVE ]
              | TO PRINTER [PROMPT]]
             [ NOCONSOLE ]
```

These commands are typically used during development and debugging to determine if DLLs have been declared. They probably aren't things you'd want to leave around in a program. If you need to test whether a DLL has been declared in a program, the best bet is to test TYPE("MyDLLFunctionCall(param, param, param)"), but realize that this test actually calls and runs the function. You wouldn't want to do this with any function that causes undesirable side effects, like shutting down Windows. Since issuing the DECLARE function again does not seem to cause any harm, we prefer to do that than to risk unintentional side effects with this trick.

Each DLL is listed with its name, alias (if assigned), and the path of the target DLL.

Example

```
LIST DLLS TO PRINT PROMPT NOCONSOLE
DISPLAY DLLS
```

See Also Declare-DLL

Display Files See Directory.

Display History See Access().

Display Memory, List Memory

These commands list memory variables.

Usage

```
DISPLAY | LIST MEMORY [ LIKE cFieldSkeleton ]
         [ TO PRINTER [ PROMPT ] ]
           | [ TO [ FILE ] cFileName [ ADDITIVE ] ]
         [ NOCONSOLE ]
```

This command lists all memory variables, along with their scope, type, and value. While this can be useful for debugging, it can also be awfully wordy. We think it might be handier if we got to narrow down our list with options such as LIST MEMORY LOCAL or LIST MEMORY DATETIME.

In addition, and looking like an afterthought, at the end of the list comes a listing of other objects taking up memory: menu, pad, popup and window definitions. Although these are informative, we think they deserve their own commands, or at least keywords as above to separate them from the rest of the display.

Like most DISPLAY/LIST commands, the output can go to the screen, the active output window, or a file. For a few variables, it isn't too bad to ACTIVATE SCREEN, LIST MEMO LIKE btn* and then press the Ctrl, Alt and Shift keys together to display the results. However, if a lot of variables need to be listed and values compared against each other, this method quickly proves tiresome. When developing in Visual FoxPro, it can be awfully hard to find the screen, an alternate output window is always too small for the long list, and you can't scroll backward through the list. So, you could consider DISPLAYing TO FILE, and put up with the fact that the TEMP file directory has one more file in it, using the ListMemo program below.

Example

```
LIST MEMO LIKE LA*

* ListMemo.PRG - windowed List Memory viewer
LIST MEMORY TO FILE (SYS(2023)+ "\TEMPLIST.TXT") NOCONSOLE
MODI FILE (SYS(2023)+ "\TEMPLIST.TXT") NOWAIT
```

See Also Display and List, Type()

Display Objects, List Objects

These commands show information about the structure and content of all instantiated objects.

Usage

```
DISPLAY | LIST OBJECTS
         [ TO PRINTER [ PROMPT ]
           | TO [ FILE ] cFileName [ ADDITIVE ] ]
         [ NOCONSOLE ]
```

Be prepared for a lot of output from this command. For each object, it shows the class hierarchy, a complete list of properties and their values, a list of member objects, and a list of methods and events.

You can get most of the information in the listing using AINSTANCE() and AMEMBERS(), but the only other way we've found to get a list of existing objects is with DISPLAY/LIST MEMORY.

These commands show information about each named object. This leads to a subtle and annoying bug. When you run a form with DO FORM, unless you add the NAME clause, the object created has the same name as the form itself. If you run the same form several times without the NAME clause, all the objects are referenced through the same variable. Visual FoxPro somehow keeps things straight internally, but DISPLAY and LIST OBJECTS show you only one instance of the form. (Of course, when you create multiple instances of a single form, you should give each a unique name.)

Example

```
o1=CREATEOBJECT("form")
LIST OBJECTS TO FILE object.txt NOCONSOLE
```

See Also AInstance(), AMembers(), CreateObject(), Display and List, Do Form

Display Procedures, List Procedures

These two commands tell you about stored procedures in a database.

Usage

```
DISPLAY | LIST PROCEDURES
          [ TO PRINT [ PROMPT ]
           | TO [ FILE ] cFileName [ ADDITIVE ] ]
          [ NOCONSOLE ]
```

The names of the procedures are listed in the order in which they're stored in the database. Note that this is not the same order you see in the Project Manager. The PM lists stored procedures alphabetically.

This listing includes those procedures added automatically by the Referential Integrity Builder. Note that DISPLAY/LIST PROCEDURES show you only the names of the procedures, not their contents.

A database has to be open and set as current before you issue these commands.

When you DISPLAY or LIST PROCEDURES to a file, the indentation of the procedure names is strange. We can't see any rhyme or reason to it. Even stranger, the listing that appears in the file and the one you see on the screen if you don't include NOCONSOLE have different indentation. Bizarre. If you're planning to parse this file, make sure to use LTRIM() on the results so the indentation doesn't matter.

Example

```
OPEN DATABASE TasTrade
LIST PROCEDURES TO FILE TTProcs.TXT
```

See Also Copy Procedures, Display and List, Display Database

Display Status, List Status

A command suitable for use only during development, which can let the bewildered developer answer the question, "Where the heck are we?"

Usage

```
DISPLAY | LIST STATUS
         [ TO PRINTER [ PROMPT ]
           | TO [ FILE ] cFileName [ ADDITIVE ] ]
         [NOCONSOLE]
```

This can be a great command to help a developer understand what's going on in an application, because it lists a ton of information—some of it far more difficult to access programmatically. It's arranged pretty sensibly, although there are obviously a few spots where information was "tacked on" through several versions of the Fox product line. The basic status of all work areas, which is the current database, where record locks are in use, which indexes are in effect, are all covered. A slew of SET commands are shown, as are low-level file handles, text merge settings and external DLL declarations. We'd like to see this expanded to include more information on which database containers are open, as well.

All of the information displayed should be available using functions listed under See Also, below, but a few are not. Which functions have been declared in external DLLs, for example, is a bit of information displayed by this command, but unavailable elsewhere.

Example
```
DISPLAY STATUS TO MyStat  && creates MyStat.TXT
```

See Also Alias(), CDX(), Display and List, DBF(), Tag()

Display Structure, List Structure

This variation on the theme tells you the structure of the table open in the current or a specified work area.

Usage
```
DISPLAY | LIST STRUCTURE
         [ IN nWorkArea | cAlias ]
         [ TO PRINTER [ PROMPT ]
           | TO [ FILE ] cFileName [ ADDITIVE ] ]
         [ NOCONSOLE ]
```

The listing shows the name, type and size (plus decimals) of the field, as well as whether it accepts nulls, whether its tag (if it has one) is ascending or descending, and the collation sequence used. The heading of the listing includes the complete filename and path, the number of records in the table, the date of the last update (the value returned by LUPDATE()) and the table's code page.

Before VFP, DISPLAY STRUCTURE listings generally fit nicely onto the screen, unless you were using a really big font. In VFP, to accommodate long field names, the whole display got wider and, unless your monitor is humongous and your font is terribly small, the thing wraps and is generally much harder to read than it used to be. Fortunately, this is a design-time tool, not something users ever see, and we find we mostly want to look at field names and types, which are pretty easy to pick out regardless. Still, at least for free tables, it would be helpful to be able to have the nice little display we used to get.

You can put all the same information plus some more into an array using AFields().

Example
```
USE MyTable
DISP STRU  && does anyone ever type out the whole command?
```

See Also AFields(), Create, Display and List, LUpdate()

Display Tables, List Tables

These two commands produce a list of the tables in a database. Each is listed with both its internal name and its complete path and file name.

Usage
```
DISPLAY | LIST TABLES
         [ TO PRINT [ PROMPT ]
           | TO [ FILE ] cFileName [ ADDITIVE ] ]
         [ NOCONSOLE ]
```

Like the other commands that list database components, these insist you open the database and make it current before using them.

The information displayed is more or less available from a combination of ADBObjects() and DBGetProp().

Example
```
OPEN DATA TasTrade
LIST TABLES TO PRINT
```

See Also ADBObjects(), DBGetProp(), Display and List

Display Views, List Views

These two commands provide a list of views in the current database. Each shows the name of the view and whether it's local or remote. Views that have been taken offline also include a notation to that effect.

Usage
```
DISPLAY | LIST VIEWS
        [ TO PRINTER [ PROMPT ]
          | TO [ FILE ] cFileName [ ADDITIVE ] ]
        [ NOCONSOLE ]
```

You can get the same information using a combination of ADBObject() and DBGetProp().

A database needs to be open and current before issuing these commands.

Example
```
OPEN DATA TasTrade
LIST VIEWS TO PRINTER
```

See Also ADBObjects(), Create SQL View, DBGetProp(), Display and List, Modify View

DisplayCount

At last! This property, new in VFP 6, lets you determine how many items show up when you open a combo box.

Usage
```
cboCombo.DisplayCount = nHowManyItems
nHowManyItems = cboCombo.DisplayCount
```

By default, when you drop a combo open, seven items show up. If there are fewer than seven items in the list, of course, only that many show. If there are more than seven, you get scroll bars. DisplayCount lets you change all that. Well, actually, not all that—just the magic number.

Why would you want to change DisplayCount? We can think of a few reasons. When the number of items in a combo is large, seven just isn't very many to show at a time. (Of course, combos aren't meant for huge lists—asking a user to scroll through hundreds or thousands of items isn't very good interface design.)

Sometimes, you have a small, fixed list, with more than seven items in the list. Why should a user have to scroll when there are only nine or 10 choices? (Consider the drop-down for RowSourceType in the property sheet, for example.)

Finally, in situations where form real estate is scarce, you may want to limit the number of items that appear at once in order not to obscure some other fields while the user is choosing.

DisplayCount isn't choosy enough about what values it accepts. It'll let you specify 0 or a negative number, though fortunately, in that case, it ignores you and just displays seven items. More seriously, when you make DisplayCount big, the list doesn't even show up when you drop the combo open. On Tamar's system, things start getting weird once DisplayCount gets over 50 and, by 130, the list doesn't even show up. In between, there are some other weird behaviors. The moral of the story is to choose reasonable values for DisplayCount.

Example
```
ThisForm.cboChoices.DisplayCount = 12
```

See Also ComboBox

DisplayValue See BoundColumn.

DMY(), MDY()

DMY() returns a character string in the form day-month-year, and MDY returns month-day-year, when supplied with a date or datetime variable.

Usage
```
lcDateToDisplay = DMY( dDate | tDateTime )
lcDateToDisplay = MDY( dDate | tDateTime )
```

Neither of these two functions has much going in the user-friendly department. Both DMY() and MDY() precede a single-digit day with a zero, and both display two-digit years if CENTURY is set OFF. We would typically use these functions to display a date on a report, and both fall short of our standards for that task.

The following function produces a much prettier version of DMY(), always returning a four-digit year field and not preceding single-digit values with a zero:

```
* GoodDmy.PRG - return a prettier DMY value
* Parameter: tdDate - a date or datetime value
*            default - today's date
* Returns: String of form DD Mmmmmm YYYY
PARAMETER tdDate
IF EMPTY(tdDate) OR NOT INLIST(type('tdDate'),"D","T")
  tdDate = DATE()
ENDIF
RETURN PADL(DAY(tdDate),2) + " " + ;
       CMONTH(tdDate) + " " + ;
       STR(YEAR(tdDate),4)
```

MDY() returns a character string in the form MMM DD, YY (or YYYY, depending on SET CENTURY). Like the DMY() function, this one isn't too smart, preceding single-digit dates with a zero, and displaying years as two-digit numbers if CENTURY is set OFF. A better version is:

```
* GoodMDY.PRG - return a prettier MDY value
* Parameter: tDate - a date or datetime value
*            default - today's date
* Returns: String of form Mmmmmm DD, YYYY
PARAMETER tdDate
IF EMPTY(tdDate) OR NOT INLIST(TYPE('tdDate'),"D","T")
  tdDate = DATE()
ENDIF
RETURN CMONTH(tdDate) + " " + ;
       LTRIM(STR(DAY(tdDate))) + ", " + ;
       STR(YEAR(tdDate),4)
```

Example

```
? DMY({03/18/1954})  && returns "18 March 1954"
? DMY({01/01/01})    && returns "01 January 01" with CENTURY OFF
? MDY({03/18/1954})  && returns "March 18, 1954"
```

See Also Day(), Dow(), Date(), DateTime(), GoMonth(), Month(), Set Century, Set Date, Set Mark, Year()

Do

This command runs a routine as a procedure (as opposed to a function).

Usage `DO ProcName [ WITH ParameterList ] [ IN FileName ]`

Parameter	Value	Meaning
ProcName	Name	The procedure to execute.
ParameterList	List of expressions	The actual parameters to pass to the procedure.
FileName	Name	The name of a file containing the procedure.

Parameters to a procedure are passed by reference, except in three cases. The first is if the actual parameter is an expression rather than a variable or field. The second is if you put parentheses around the actual parameter (which, in effect, turns the item into an expression). Finally, properties are always passed by value rather than by reference. When variables are passed by reference, they must exist before the DO. See "Xbase Xplained" for more on parameter passing.

You can omit parameters in the call. Parameters at the end of the parameter list can be simply left off. Parameters in the middle can be omitted by placing nothing between the commas separating parameters. When a parameter is omitted, Visual FoxPro passes .F.

Using the IN clause can be pretty slow. See "Faster Than a Speeding Bullet" for speed comparisons of the different ways of calling a routine.

Example

```
DO MyRtn WITH a,b,c               && all passed by reference
DO MyRtn WITH 3*x,(b),DATE()      && all passed by value
DO MyRtn WITH a,,c                && omitted parameter
```

See Also Procedure, Return

Do Case

This control structure lets you choose among multiple, mutually exclusive alternatives. You lay out the choices and exactly one is chosen. When you only have two choices, IF is more appropriate. To choose among alternatives in expressions, use IIF().

Usage

```
DO CASE
CASE lCondition1
     Commands
[ CASE lCondition2
     Commands
[ CASE lCondition3
     Commands
[ ... ] ] ]
[ OTHERWISE
     Commands ]
ENDCASE
```

The conditions are evaluated in sequence. As soon as VFP finds a case whose condition evaluates to true, the commands following that case are executed. Execution then continues following the ENDCASE. If there's an OTHERWISE clause and no case before it has a true condition, the commands following OTHERWISE are executed.

Because the conditions are evaluated in order, you can assume previous conditions have failed in writing conditions for later cases. The following code displays a message about an employee based on his or her age.

Example

```
nThisYear = YEAR(DATE())
DO CASE
CASE nThisYear - YEAR(Birth_Date) >= 70
   ? 'Golden Oldie'
CASE nThisYear - YEAR(Birth_Date) >= 60
   ? 'SixtySomething'
CASE nThisYear - YEAR(Birth_Date) >= 50
   ? 'FiftySomething'
CASE nThisYear - YEAR(Birth_Date) >= 40
   ? 'FortySomething'
CASE nThisYear - YEAR(Birth_Date) >= 30
   ? 'ThirtySomething'
CASE nThisYear - YEAR(Birth_Date) >= 20
   ? 'Babe in the Woods'
OTHERWISE
   ? 'Wunderkind'
ENDCASE
```

Each case after the first in the example assumes the failure of the previous cases and doesn't bother to check whether the age is less than the upper limit for the group.

We suggest you always include an OTHERWISE case. Without OTHERWISE, if none of the cases test true, execution continues on the line following the ENDCASE, with no error message. After you have coded all the possible cases and none could ever, ever be left, code an OTHERWISE as an error trap. You'll be surprised how often they come up!

Remember that even though DO CASE looks like it can handle multiple records, it's just a branching command. It executes only once unless you put it inside a loop.

See Also If, IIf()

Do Form

This command runs a form or formset from its SCX file.

Usage
```
DO FORM FormName | ?
       [ NAME oName ] [ LINKED ]
       [ WITH ParameterList ] [ TO uResult ]
       [ NOREAD ] [ NOSHOW ]
```

When you run a form or formset, FoxPro automatically creates an object variable to give you access to it. By default, the variable's name is the name of the form or formset (the filename up to, but not including, the SCX extension). The NAME clause lets you specify the name instead. The variable can even be an array element. In fact, many application frameworks store references to active forms in an array that's a property of an application object. Whether you supply the name or use the default, you can access the form's PEMs using the reference.

But there's a catch. The variable created is an additional reference to the form, supplementing an internal reference of some sort. When you release the variable (or it goes out of scope), the form still exists—unless you include the LINKED keyword. LINKED says the form's existence is tied to the variable itself. When the variable is destroyed, the form should be, too.

WITH passes parameters to the form. For forms you create with Visual FoxPro, parameters are passed to the Init method, even though it's not the first to execute. Forms converted from FoxPro 2.x receive parameters in the Load method instead. The parameters are scoped to the method that receives them, so you either need to process them there or store them in a custom property of the form or formset.

One of our favorite tricks in FoxPro 2.x was to turn a screen into a function and have it return a value. Visual FoxPro forms aren't quite as versatile in this way. You can't call them as functions. But, if you make the form modal, it can return a value. You set this up by RETURNing the desired value in the Unload method of the form or formset. The value you return gets put in the variable listed in the TO clause. One warning: You can't directly return the value of a property from a control because the controls get destroyed before Unload. If you want to return a property value, you have to save it to a form property before you start shutting things down.

The NOREAD clause is supposed to replace the #NOREAD generator directive of FoxPro 2.x. That directive told the screen-generator program to create code to paint the screen, but not to include the READ that activated the controls. In our tests, DO FORM whatever NOREAD (where *whatever* is a converted FoxPro 2.x screen) errors out because the variables for the controls don't get created at the right time. With the NOREAD clause, events fire in a really weird order.

NOSHOW lets you create a form without making it visible. You can then do some manipulation of the form object before you show it to the user. To make a NOSHOW form visible, call its Show method or set its Visible property to .T. There's a small difference between the two methods of making it visible. When you call the Show method, the form gets focus; setting Visible to .T. displays it, but doesn't give it the focus.

Example
```
DO FORM MyForm NAME oApp.aActiveForms[nFormCnt]
```

See Also Create Form, Do

Do While

This is the granddaddy of loop commands. It's been in Xbase almost from the beginning. It lets you execute a group of commands when some condition exists until that condition fails. Over the years, most of the uses for it have been superseded by more specialized commands, but it still comes in handy now and then.

Usage

```
DO WHILE lCondition
   Commands
   [ LOOP ]
   [ EXIT ]
ENDDO
```

lCondition is an expression. It's evaluated only at the beginning of each pass through the loop. So, once you get in, you complete that pass regardless of changes to lCondition inside.

It is important to provide some way of exiting the loop. Generally, you do this by changing a variable that's used in lCondition. Forgetting to provide a way out results in what's known as an "infinite loop"—it's not a pretty sight. A very good reason for leaving SET ESCAPE ON when developing.

LOOP and EXIT are escape routes from the loop. LOOP shortcuts the current execution of the loop, proceeding directly to re-evaluation of lCondition. EXIT ends the loop entirely.

We know people who routinely write loops like this:

```
DO WHILE .T.
   * some processing
   IF <something or other>
      EXIT
   ENDIF
ENDDO
```

We think this is bad practice. It hides the structure of the loop and makes it much harder to understand what's going on. We avoid both LOOP and EXIT and recommend you do the same.

Try something like this instead:

```
lcNextFile = SYS(2000,"*.DBF")
DO WHILE NOT EMPTY(lcNextFile)
  * process the file
  lcNextFile = SYS(2000,"*.DBF",1)
ENDDO
```

If you need to do something a certain number of times, use a FOR loop instead. To touch every element of an array or collection, use FOR EACH. To process a series of records in a table, use SCAN instead.

Our good technical editor points out that, once in a while, you may want to combine DO WHILE with SCAN for a nested loop. You'd use this in the case where you want to look at records in some order and do something to all the records that, say, have the same key. The structure of this sort of loop is shown in the first example below.

DO WHILE works better than SCAN for the outer loop because it doesn't automatically skip a record each time. The SCAN WHILE loop leaves the record pointer on the first record that doesn't match the current, which is right where we want to start the next pass.

Example

```
* Process through a cursor, using the inner SCAN to
* make some change to the records. The outer DO ... WHILE
* doesn't move the record pointer
GO TOP
DO WHILE NOT EOF()
  lcKey = KeyField
  SCAN WHILE KeyField = lcKey
    * do something with the set of records having this key in
    * common
  ENDSCAN
ENDDO

* generate a unique filename
* working around non-uniqueness of SYS(3)
cFileName = SYS(3) + ".TMP"
DO WHILE FILE(cFileName)
  cFileName = SYS(3) + ".TMP"
ENDDO
```

See Also Exit, For, For Each, Loop, Scan

Dock

This method lets you dock or undock a toolbar programmatically. You pass the appropriate position.

Usage `tbrToolBar.Dock( nDockPosition [, nXPosition, nYPosition ] )`

Parameter	Value	Meaning
nDockPosition	-1	Undock the toolbar.
	0	Dock the toolbar at the top.
	1	Dock the toolbar at the left.
	2	Dock the toolbar at the right.
	3	Dock the toolbar at the bottom.
nXPosition, nYPosition	Omitted	Put the toolbar at the next available position on the specified side. For undocking, return the toolbar to its last undocked location.
	Numeric	Position the toolbar at the specified location. For each dock position, only one of the two coordinates is used (nXPosition for top and bottom, nYPosition for the sides). For undocking, put the toolbar at the specified location.

When you don't specify a position, VFP's interpretation of the "next available position" may not be the same as yours. In particular, the position chosen depends on where the toolbar's been docked before and where it's coming from.

Dock fires several events, depending on the value of nDockPosition. The exact firing sequence is different in different versions of VFP. In VFP 6, BeforeDock fires first, then AfterDock fires, except when nDockPosition is -1. In that case, Undock fires first, followed by BeforeDock. If the toolbar is visible, Dock updates both Docked and DockPosition. If the toolbar isn't yet visible, those properties aren't updated until the toolbar is SHOWn. In VFP 3, using Dock to move from one docked position to another fires BeforeDock, Undock, then BeforeDock and AfterDock. This is a different sequence than you see when you move from one docked position to another with the mouse. In that case, only BeforeDock and AfterDock fire. In VFP 5 and VFP 6, no matter how you dock the toolbar, only BeforeDock and AfterDock fire.

It is, of course, frustrating to have firing sequences change along the way and, to be honest, we're not convinced that they've got it right quite yet. BeforeDock, followed by AfterDock, feels right for docking, regardless of whether you're initially docking the thing or moving it from one position to another (though we could argue for a call to Undock first in the latter case). But, why does BeforeDock fire when you *undock* a toolbar?

Example

```
* Dock a toolbar at the bottom
ThisFormSet.tbrNavButtons.Dock(3)

* Undock a toolbar and put in at a specific position
ThisFormSet.tbrStandard.Dock(-1,100,100)
```

See Also AfterDock, BeforeDock, Docked, DockPosition, Toolbar, Undock

Docked, DockPosition

These properties tell whether a toolbar is docked and, if so, where. We can't see why there are two properties for this, since DockPosition contains all the information you need. Our guess is that Docked was originally planned, but Microsoft found that people needed more information, so they added DockPosition. Don't know why they didn't ditch Docked at the same time. Now we're stuck with another case of dBloat.

Usage

```
lIsDocked = tbrToolBar.Docked
nPosition = tbrToolBar.DockPosition
```

Parameter	Value	Meaning
nPosition	-1	Toolbar is not docked.
	0	Toolbar is docked at top.
	1	Toolbar is docked at left.
	2	Toolbar is docked at right.
	3	Toolbar is docked at bottom.

Toolbars can be docked by the user or programmatically using the Dock method. In either case, these properties get updated. However, if you use the Dock method to position a toolbar before it becomes visible, Docked and DockPosition don't reflect the new status until the toolbar is SHOWn.

You can't change DockPosition directly. Use the Dock method instead. This means you can't preset the docking position for a toolbar in the Form Designer (or in the Class Designer). Use code like the example instead.

Example

```
* Pre-dock a toolbar at the top so it's ready when it appears
* This could go in the toolbar's Init event
This.Dock(0)
```

See Also AfterDock, BeforeDock, Dock, Toolbar, Undock

DoCmd, Eval, SetVar, DataToClip, RequestData

These methods all let you drive VFP from a distance. They're methods of the VFP automation server. DoCmd, Eval and SetVar let you execute various VFP commands and functions. DataToClip and RequestData take data from an open table and put it on the clipboard or in an array. You can use these methods from within VFP (referencing them through the _VFP object), but they're far more useful when you've created an instance of the VFP Automation Server from some other application.

These functions are typically not used from within a FoxPro program, but rather within the code of another application that calls VFP as an automation server. Just as we can call Word or Excel to perform their magic for us, we can call on FoxPro from these languages.

Usage

```
cEmptyString = oApp.DoCmd( cVFPCommand )
uResult = oApp.Eval( cExpr )
cEmptyString = oApp.SetVar( cVarName, uValue )
```

DoCmd, Eval and SetVar let you issue VFP commands, evaluate expressions and set variables, respectively. The only really tricky thing here is figuring out when you need quotes and when you don't.

DoCmd accepts any legal VFP command and executes it. (At least, we haven't yet found one it wouldn't take.) Use it to set paths, open tables, move record pointers, and so forth. It *is* sort of like using a voice-dictation system and having to remember to switch from dictation mode to command mode, but it works.

Eval evaluates whatever expression you pass it and returns the result. It's smart enough to return whatever type you come up with, so you don't have to do a lot of conversion from character to what you really need. Beware: you pass the expression as a string.

SetVar lets you transfer data that belongs to the client application to the server. You pass it the name of a variable as a string, plus a value. The value is assigned to the variable. If the value is an expression, it's evaluated by the local client before it's passed to the VFP automation server.

We were fairly confused about SetVar for a long time. It seemed to us that you could do the same thing with DoCmd by passing a STORE command. The key difference is that, when you pass a STORE command to DoCmd, the VFP Automation Server evaluates the new value. When you use SetVar, the client application does the evaluation. So each has its place.

Example

```
oVFP = createobject("visualfoxpro.application")
oVFP.Visible = .T.  && so we can see it
* Change the background so we can tell the two apart.
oVFP.DoCmd("_SCREEN.BackColor = RGB(64,128,128)")
oVFP.DoCmd("USE [C:\Program Files\DevStudio\" + ;
           "VFP\Samples\Data\Customer]")
? oVFP.Eval("DATE()")  && returns DATETIME()! not date
oVFP.SetVar("lnRecCount",oVFP.Eval([RECCOUNT("CUSTOMER")]))
? oVFP.Eval("lnRecCount")  && shows 92 records
```

Usage

```
uResult = oApp.DataToClip( [ cAlias | nWorkArea ]
                           [, nNumberOfRecords ]
                           [, nDataFormat ])
aArray = oApp.RequestData( [ cAlias | nWorkarea ]
                           [, nNumberOfRecords ] )
```

Parameter	Value	Meaning
cAlias	Character	The alias from which to gather data.
	Omitted	If nWorkArea is also omitted, gather data from the current work area.
nWorkArea	Numeric	The work area from which to gather data.
	Omitted	If cAlias is also omitted, gather data from the current work area.
nNumberOfRecords	Numeric	The number of records to place on the clipboard or in the array.
	Omitted	Put one record on the clipboard or in the array.
nDataFormat	1 (or 2) or omitted	Separate fields with spaces.
	3	Separate fields with tabs.
aArray	Array	An array to hold the specified records.
uResult	Numeric	The number of records returned.
	Character	The empty string. Returned only when the specified cAlias is not used or nWorkArea has no table open.

These two methods are quite similar. They both grab one or more records from an open table and do something with them. DataToClip puts them on the clipboard, while RequestData stores them in an array. In both cases, though, you're left with data that you can manipulate from within another application.

Both methods have one confusing piece of syntax. Although all their parameters are optional, you still need placeholders to omit them. That is, even if you want to use the current work area, you need to put in the comma that precedes the number of records—otherwise, the number is interpreted as a work area number.

DataToClip gives you a choice of output format. Omitting the format or specifying 1 (or the undocumented 2) pads each field with spaces to its full size. Giving a format of 3 pads the fields as needed, then puts a tab between each pair of fields.

Example

```
* Continuing from the example above
? oVFP.DataToClip()  && shows 92 records copied
aData = oVFP.RequestData()  && Loads aData with records
? ALEN(aData)    && 1104 elements
? ALEN(aData,1)  && 92 rows
? ALEN(aData,2)  && 12 fields each
```

See Also Application, Evaluate(), _VFP

DoCreate

This may be the most mysterious property we've encountered. It's documented only as a reserved word, appears in just about every form we've come across, but can't be accessed at runtime and doesn't seem to do much of anything.

Usage

```
frmForm.DoCreate = lLogicalValue
```

Though we've shown the value as accepting either logical value, in practice we've only ever encountered .T.

By now, you may be wondering why you've never run across this property. (We're beginning to wish we hadn't.) It's not hard to miss it. It doesn't appear in either the property sheet or the debugger and you can't refer to it in code either at design time or runtime.

So where *did* we find this one? One of the nice things the Class Browser can do for you is provide you a list of what your class or form would look like (more or less) if you wrote it in code instead of using the appropriate designer. When we ask the Browser to show us the code for pretty much any form we create, the opening section includes the line:

```
DoCreate = .T.
```

According to one of our sources, that line tells VFP when to create the object. However, we've tried changing the value to .F. and eliminating the line altogether and our forms still run happily. We thought maybe it was something special about SCX-based forms, but the line appears in our form classes, too.

So, we're sorry to say that we at Hacker Labs have failed to crack this case. We know a lot more about DoCreate than we did before, but we still have no idea why it's there.

See Also Forms

DocumentFile, HostName

DocumentFile is a property of OLE bound and unbound controls. It allows you to query or, under limited circumstances, set the linked file. HostName allows you to specify your application's name as you wish it to appear when editing OLE objects.

Usage

```
cFileName = oleObject.DocumentFile
oleObject.DocumentFile = cFileName
cHostName = oleObject.HostName
oleObject.HostName = cHostName
```

DocumentFile returns the name of the file associated with a linked object—either an OLEBoundControl or an unbound OLEControl. It's blank for an object with embedded data. This is the only way we know of to tell the difference. DocumentFile is read-only at runtime, but may be set for an OLEControl only in a class definition. We're a bit surprised at how restrictive this is. You can't place an embedded or linked OLE control on a form without specifying the name of the document. We would think you could at least change this property on the property sheet in design mode.

HostName is a setting for purely cosmetic purposes. In FoxPro 2.x, a number of users (well, at least two) complained that "FoxPro" was prominently displayed when editing OLE objects in their server application (equivalent to OLE servers which don't support in-place editing in version 3.x). When saving an application, a dialog appeared, prompting "Do you want to save changes to FoxPro..." and, finally, the menu prompt under the file pad offers the option "Exit and return to FoxPro." HostName allows you to replace the text in all of these places with your own application's name.

In some OLE servers, leaving HostName blank leads to some funny dialogs, such as "Do you want to save changes to ?" and menu prompts "Exit and Return to." This is a lack of grace on their part, and not necessarily FoxPro's fault. Similarly, some applications do not respect the case of the HostName string supplied, instead displaying lowercase only. If you have an application or company name where the case is significant, you'll find this to be a real inconvenience. But don't blame the fox for this one.

Example

```
* Creates a form with a sound player olecontrol
* and a close button. Double-click the olecontrol
* to play the sounds.
* AutoVerbMenu provides a context menu to the control
* Right-mouse-click and select 'Edit' to bring up the
* Sound Player. Note the File menu has the option
* "Exit and Return to <your version of FoxPro>"
* and the Sound Player title bar shows the HostName
oForm = CREATEOBJECT("frmSound")
oForm.Show()
READ EVENTS
RETURN

DEFINE CLASS frmSound AS form
  ADD OBJECT cmdClose AS CommandButton
  ADD OBJECT oleSound AS OleControl ;
    WITH DocumentFile = "C:\WinNT40\Media\Chimes.WAV"
  Procedure Init
    WITH This.oleSound
      .AutoVerbMenu = .T.
      .HostName = VERSION()
      * Center the oleControl
      .Height = 2 * .Height
      .Top = 0.5 * (ThisForm.Height - .Height)
      .Left = 0.5 * (ThisForm.Width - .Width)
    ENDWITH
    WITH This.cmdClose
      * Center the Close button on the form bottom
      .Caption = "Close"
      .Top = ThisForm.Height - (.Height+5)
      .Left = 0.5 * (ThisForm.Width - .Width)
    ENDWITH
  EndProc
  Procedure cmdClose.Click
    CLEAR EVENTS
  EndProc
ENDDEFINE
```

See Also OLEBoundControl, OLEControl

DoDefault(), ::

This function and the operator composed of two colons (called the "Scope Resolution" operator by the docs) let you call methods higher up in the class hierarchy. You use them most often when you want to augment a method to do everything the parent class's method does, plus some more.

Usage

```
uReturn = DoDefault( [ uParmList ] )
uReturn = ClassName::Method( [ uParmList ] )
```

Parameter	Value	Meaning
uParmList	List of expressions	Parameters to pass to the method being called.
ClassName	Name	The name of the class whose method you want to call.
Method	Name	The name of the method to be called.
uReturn		The value returned by the method called.

DoDefault(), added in VFP 5, calls directly up the class hierarchy. That is, it can only call the parent class's version of the method you're in. The :: operator gives you more flexibility than that, but most often, you use it the same way. You can, in fact, call any method that's in the class's inheritance tree. You can't call a method that belongs to a class the current class doesn't inherit from.

Despite the fact that :: is more flexible, it's better to use DoDefault() when you can because it doesn't tie your code to a particular class or method name. Your code is more reusable if you allow the DoDefault() to find the appropriate class hierarchy for the method it finds itself in.

The initial release of VFP 5 had a bug in DoDefault() that caused a problem when there was a method in the hierarchy that didn't have any code. If you issued DoDefault() in a method and the same method in the parent class was empty, the method in the parent class's parent class executed twice. The bug is fixed in VFP 5.0a and VFP 6.

VFP 5 and VFP 6 have a truly insidious bug as well (pointed out to us by our assiduous tech editor). It occurs if you use DoDefault() in a method that automatically calls the same method of other objects (for example, a form Refresh, which automatically calls Refresh of member objects, or KeyPress when KeyPreview is .T., which automatically forwards the keypress to the object with focus) and there's no code in the same method of the parent class of the original object (the form, in the examples). In that case, the keyword This in the other methods of the contained object(s) (the member objects in the Refresh example, the object with focus in the KeyPress example) doesn't refer to the object whose code is being executed but to the original object whose code had the DoDefault() (the form, in the examples). This is a truly ugly bug and we hope it gets exterminated very soon.

Example

```
DEFINE CLASS CloseButton AS CommandButton
   * set appropriate properties up here
   * including
   Caption = "Close"

   PROCEDURE Click
      ThisForm.Release
   ENDPROC

ENDDEFINE

DEFINE CLASS ConfirmCloseButton AS CloseButton

   PROCEDURE Click
      LOCAL nResult
      nResult = MESSAGEBOX("Closing Form",33)
      IF nResult = 1    && OK
         DoDefault()
```

```
            * or, in VFP 3
            * CloseButton::Click
         ENDIF
      ENDPROC

   ENDDEFINE
```

See Also Class, Parent, ParentClass, This

DoEvents See AutoYield.

_Dos, _Mac, _Unix, _Windows

These system variables tell you which platform FoxPro is running on. In Visual FoxPro for Windows, _WINDOWS is true and the rest are false. In VFP/Mac, _MAC is .T. If we ever see Visual FoxPro for the other platforms, we expect we'll see the matching system variables set true, but we're not holding our breath.

Usage

```
lIsDos = _DOS
lIsMac = _MAC
lIsUnix = _UNIX
lIsWindows = _WINDOWS
```

Back when cross-platform meant more than Windows 95 and Windows NT, these variables were useful for cross-platform development. They allowed you to bracket platform-specific code so it didn't cause errors on the other platforms.

Example

```
DO CASE
CASE _WINDOWS
   MODIFY WINDOW screen FONT "Arial",10
CASE _MAC
   HIDE WINDOW screen
ENDCASE
```

See Also OS()

DoScroll

DoScroll is a method to scroll a grid horizontally and vertically as the user would with the scrollbars. It was introduced with grids in VFP 3, so we were really surprised this method was not extended to forms when forms gained scrollbars in VFP 6.

Usage `grdGrid.DoScroll( nDirection )`

Parameter	Value	Meaning
nDirection	0	Simulates a click on the scrollbar up arrow.
	1	Simulates a click on the scrollbar down arrow.
	2	Simulates a page-up click—clicking in the space above the thumb and below the scroll arrow.
	3	Simulates a page-down click—clicking in the space below the thumb and above the scroll arrow.
	4	Simulates a click on the left scrollbar arrow.
	5	Simulates a click on the right scrollbar arrow.

Parameter	Value	Meaning
nDirection	6	Simulates a form-left click—clicking in the space to the left of the thumb and the right of the scroll arrow.
	7	Simulates a form-right click—clicking in the space to the right of the thumb and the left of the scroll arrow.
	Omitted or any other number	Ignored.

A useful alternative to including scrollbars on the grid itself, DoScroll can be used to cause the same effect without all the visual interference, or with an alternative user interface. The Scrolled event fires after DoScroll is called, and receives a parameter for direction matching that is set by this method.

Example `grdGrid.DoScroll(0)`

See Also Grid, Scrollbars, Scrolled

Double-Byte Character Sets

Western languages are based on a set of sounds. Words are built from letters, each of which makes a particular sound. (Well, in English, it's a little more complicated because some letters make different sounds in different situations—or even the same situation. Take "read", for example. But the key point holds. Words are built from sounds.) As a result, Western languages can be represented with relatively few characters. English has 26 characters; other Western languages have similar quantities.

In the Far East, words are built from ideas, not from sounds. Languages like Chinese and Japanese use a system of pictographs, where a particular symbol represents an idea and symbols are combined to make words or phrases. These languages have far more characters than Western languages.

Representing the Eastern languages on a computer has always been a challenge. The standard character set on Western computers uses eight bits (one byte) to represent a character. That provides 256 choices, far more than are needed for the alphabetic characters, the digits and common punctuation marks. Several sets of these characters are available, in the form of code pages, to support the various diacritical marks (accents and so forth) of the different European languages. But 256 doesn't even come close to enough for Eastern languages.

The solution is to use two bytes (16 bits) per character. That provides more than 65,000 variations. Such character sets are called "double-byte character sets."

Beginning with version 3.0b, Visual FoxPro provides support for double-byte character sets (DBCS). You can write an application using the English version of Visual FoxPro (but a Japanese or Chinese version of Windows) and it can be used in the Far East. Obviously, the interface elements—menu names, text box captions and message box prompts—need to be "localized" for the target language, but the code should run as is.

There are a host of functions to support DBCS. Many of them duplicate longstanding FoxPro functions (like AT() and SUBSTR()), while a few add necessary new functionality.

Because we don't use any of the Far East versions of Windows, we haven't been able to bang on these new functions as much as we'd like. They all appear to work in our single-byte versions of Windows.

See Also At_C(), AtCC(), ChrTranC(), IsLeadByte(), IMEStatus(), LeftC(), LenC(), LikeC(), RatC(), RightC(), StrConv(), StuffC(), SubStrC()

DoVerb **See AutoActivate.**

DoW(), Week()

Returns the numeric values of the day of the week and week of the year, based on the date or datetime supplied. You can optionally specify a starting point as well.

```
Usage  nDayOfWeek = DOW( dDate | tDateTime [, nFirstDayofWeek ] )
       nWeekOfYear = WEEK( dDate | tDateTime [, nFirstWeek ]
                           [, nFirstDayOfWeek ] )
```

Parameter	Value	Meaning
dDate | tDateTime	Date or DateTime	The date or datetime value from which to calculate the day of the week or week of the year.
nFirstDayofWeek	Omitted	Use Sunday as the first day. This is for compatibility with older versions of FoxPro.
	0	Use the current setting of FDOW.
	1 - 7	Use days Sunday - Saturday as the first day.
nFirstWeek	Omitted or 1	The first week includes January 1.
	0	Use the current setting of FWEEK.
	2	The first week of the new year has four or more days.
	3	The first week of the new year falls entirely within the new year.
nDayOfWeek	1 - 7	Indicates which day of the week dDate | tDateTime is.
nWeekOfYear	1 - 53	Indicates which week of the year dDate | tDateTime is.

These functions return the day and week for the supplied date or datetime. The parameters nFirstDayOfWeek and nFirstWeek can be confusing if you haven't worked with them before, and can give less than intuitive results.

Let's try an example to see if your confusion can lead to total befuddlement, er, enlightenment. January 1, 1998 is a Thursday, and your client tells you that they never start a new workweek with two or fewer days, so Thursday and Friday count as the last week of 1997. The WEEK() function, with a parameter of 2, gives you a return value of 53, for the 53rd week of 1997, for January 1st and 2nd.

```
? WEEK({^1998-01-01},2) && returns 53, the last week of 1997
```

On the other hand, if your client tells you they always start the new year on a full seven-day week (a good idea if they track production per week), you could use the parameter of 3 so that January 1st and 2nd fall into the 52nd full week of 1997.

```
? WEEK({^1998-01-01},3)  && returns 52, the 52nd and last full
                         && 7-day week of 1997
```

If your client's company starts their weeks on Monday, or Thursday, or Saturday, you can adjust that, too, with the nFirstDayofWeek parameter.

It is possible to set the "first day of week" and "first week of year" settings on the Tools-Options dialog, under the Regional tab (see Figure 4-4), but the settings you make apply only to the development version—runtime versions do not check the Options stored in the Registration Database. For runtime situations, you might want to set these in the Config.FPW file with FDOW= and FWEEK=, or programmatically with the equivalent SET FDOW TO and SET FWEEK TO. However, for those folks really into spelunking the depths and messing with what Microsoft has handed us, check out the registration database to see where all the native settings are stored. In either NT or Win 95, search for the key:

```
MyComputer\HKEY_CURRENT_USER\Software\Microsoft\VisualFoxPro\6.0\Options
```

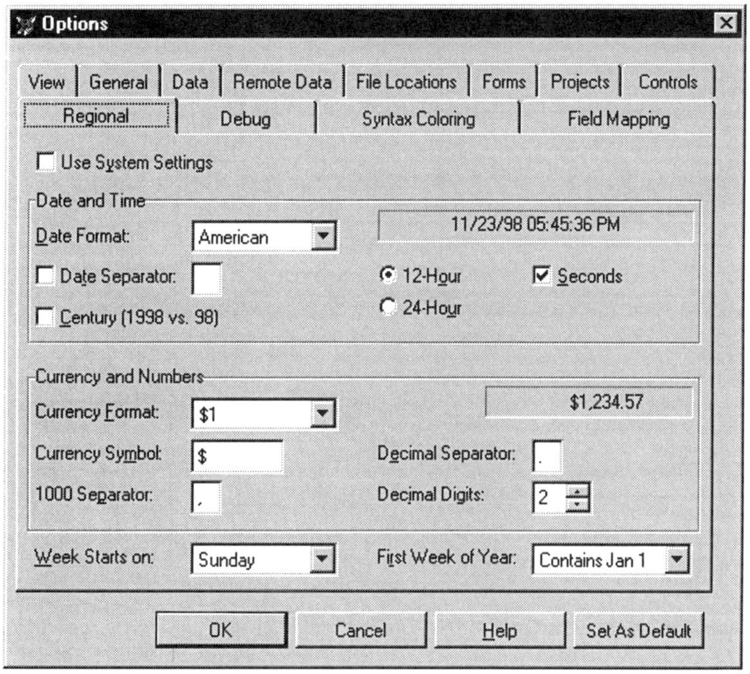

Figure 4-4: The Regional tab of the Tools-Options dialog includes First Day of Week and First Week of Year.

Example

```
? DOW({^1982/4/11})    && returns 1, since 4/11/82 was a Sunday
? DOW({^1982 4 11},2)  && returns 7, the week starts on Monday
? WEEK({^2001.01.01})  && returns 1, the first week
                       && of the new millennium
```

See Also Date(), Day(), DMY(), GoMonth(), MDY(), Month(), Registration Database, Set Century, Set Date, Set FDow, Set FWeek, Set Mark, Year()

DownClick See UpClick.

DownPicture See Picture.

Drag, DragMode, DragIcon, DragOver, DragDrop

These properties, events and method allow you to put drag-and-drop with VFP objects in your applications. It's astonishingly easy to get simple drag-and-drop to work, but making it look smooth and elegant is another story. Drag-and-drop with other applications or ActiveX controls uses a collection of properties and methods whose names start with OLEDrag or OLEDrop.

Usage

```
oObject.DragMode = nDragMode
nDragMode = oObject.DragMode
oObject.Drag( [ nDragAction ] )
```

Parameter	Value	Meaning
nDragMode	0	Use manual dragging.
	1	Enable automatic dragging.
nDragAction	0	Cancel dragging.

Parameter	Value	Meaning
nDragAction	1 or Omitted	Start dragging.
	2	Stop dragging.

Any draggable object can have dragging enabled in either of two ways. The object's DragMode can be set for automatic dragging. In that case, when the user presses the left mouse button on that object, dragging begins immediately.

Most people prefer manual dragging for the additional control it provides. In that case, you leave DragMode set to 0 and call the object's Drag method to turn dragging on when you're ready. Usually, Drag(1) is called in the object's MouseDown method—you can test to make sure it's a good time for drag-and-drop. MouseMove is another good place to start dragging. You can check whether the mouse has moved far enough to indicate dragging, in case the user's hand simply twitched.

Regardless of which way you start, when you're dragging, the object doesn't recognize mouse events—even the MouseUp that ends the drag. In fact, with manual dragging, you stay in the method that started the drag until the mouse button is released. (This is an intricate bit of cooperation between Windows itself that provides the drag features and FoxPro. We guess technically you're in the Drag method all that time and return to the method that started the drag when you stop dragging.)

Normally, a drag ends when the user releases the mouse button. The other two values for nDragAction let you put an abrupt stop to dragging. With 0 (cancel), that's the end of it. With 2 (stop), the DragDrop event of the object you're over at the time fires. We can come up with some silly examples for this, but truly useful cases are harder to think of.

In VFP 3, timers and drag-and-drop don't mix very well. Timer events get backed up until you stop dragging. The problem is gone in VFP 5 and VFP 6.

Usage

```
oObject.DragIcon = cCursorFile
cCursorFile = oObject.DragIcon
```

This property lets you specify an icon to be used for the object while you're dragging it. If you don't specify one, you drag a hazy outline of the object itself.

You can change DragIcon dynamically. The DragOver event of another object can change the dragged object's DragIcon to indicate valid actions. Most often, you see this in the form of the international "no" symbol when dropping isn't valid. But, you can indicate all kinds of things—use a down arrow for "please drop here" or a magnifying glass to indicate that dropping zooms in.

DragIcon expects a CUR cursor file—not, as its name suggests, an ICO. VFP can be picky about its cursors, too, but VFP 5 and VFP 6 seem to be a lot more flexible about this than VFP 3. (In VFP 3, you must have a VGA-Mono 2-Color 32 x 32 format cursor or things get weird. Naturally, lots of the cursors that came with VFP 3 weren't in that format.) A bunch of cursors get installed in Visual FoxPro's samples (check the directory HOME(4)). In VFP 6, you can use the GETPICT() function, which is a specialized File-Open dialog for pictures, to look at them. In earlier versions of VFP, GETPICT() can't read CUR files! In VFP 5, however, any version of the File-Open dialog shows you the picture next to the filename. In VFP 3, you can use the Imagedit application that's installed by the Professional edition to look at exploded versions of them.

Usage

```
PROCEDURE oObject.DragOver
LPARAMETERS [ nIndex, ] oSource, nXCoord, nYCoord, nState

PROCEDURE oObject.DragDrop
LPARAMETERS [ nIndex, ] oSource, nXCoord, nYCoord
```

Parameter	Value	Meaning
nIndex	Numeric	This object is part of a control array. nIndex is the item number within the array.
	Omitted	The object is not part of a control array.
oSource	Object	A reference to the object being dragged.
nXCoord, nYCoord	Numeric	The mouse coordinates relative to the form when the event fires.
nState	0	The dragged object is just entering this object's space.
	1	The dragged object is now leaving this object's space.
	2	The dragged object remains over this object's space.

These two events belong not to the object being dragged, but to the target—the object over which you're dragging or onto which you're dropping. When you drag an object over another object (even over a form itself), the DragOver event of the latter object fires. An easy way to see this happening is to put WAIT WINDOW "Dragging over "+This.Name NOWAIT in the DragOver event of everything under the sun. When you drop an object, the DragDrop event of the target object fires.

Both events give you access to the object being dragged via the oSource parameter. It's very cool—you can change the object you're dragging based on where it is or where you drop it.

Use the nState parameter of DragOver to make decisions about what to do—the most common is to change DragIcon of the dragged object. A typical setup is to have your code for nState=0 save the object's old icon and set a new one, then the code nState=1 can reset DragIcon to the old value. Two caveats. First, you'll have to save the old icon to a property somewhere (a property of the dragged object makes the most sense to us). You can't use a local variable in the DragOver method because you don't stay in DragOver—it gets called repeatedly. The more serious problem is restoring the icon. If you drag over the object so the icon gets changed, but then drop without leaving that object, the old icon is never restored. Next time you drag this object, it's still set to the replacement icon. Be sure to restore it after the drop or before you start dragging again.

If an object is small enough, it's possible to drag another object over it without firing the first object's DragOver method. When dragging slowly, DragOver always fires, but if you drag quickly across a narrow object, DragOver may fail to fire.

Example

```
* This form is on the disk as Dragger.SCX.
* The object we want to drag is a textbox. Put it in the
* middle of the form. In the prop sheet:
DragIcon = HOME(4) + "CURSORS\DRAGPICT.CUR"

* In the textbox's MouseDown event:
This.Drag(1)
This.DragIcon = HOME(4)+"CURSORS\DRAGPICT.CUR"

* The form contains 4 other objects: a button, a shape and
* two vertical lines. Position one vertical line near the left
* edge of the form and put this code in its DragOver:
oSource.Drag(0)   && Cancel drag

* Put the other line near the right edge of the form.
* In its DragOver, put:
oSource.Drag(2)   && End drag
```

```
* In this line's DragDrop method, put:
WAIT WINDOW "Ouch, that hurts!" NOWAIT

* Put the button and the shape between the two lines, but not
* on top of the textbox. In the button's DragOver method, put:
DO CASE
CASE nState = 0
   oSource.DragIcon = HOME(4) + "CURSORS\NODROP01.CUR"
CASE nState = 1
   oSource.DragIcon = HOME(4) + "CURSORS\DRAGPICT.CUR"
ENDCASE

* In the shape's DragOver method, put:
DO CASE
CASE nState = 0
   oSource.DragIcon = HOME(4) + "CURSORS\BULLSEYE.CUR"
CASE nState = 1
   oSource.DragIcon = HOME(4) + "CURSORS\DRAGPICT.CUR"
ENDCASE

In the shape's DragDrop method, put:
WAIT WINDOW "Right on target!"

In the form's DragDrop method, put:
oSource.Left = nXCoord
oSource.Top = nYCoord
```

See Also MouseDown, MouseMove, OLE drag and drop, OLEDrag, OLEDragDrop, OLEDragMode, OLEDragOver, OLEDragPicture

Draw, Paint

So what's the difference between drawing and painting? Seems to us you use brushes to paint, but you hold the colors in your hands to draw, like with a pencil or crayon.

Wait a minute, not that kind of draw and paint. The FoxPro kind. Draw is a method you can call on to have a form redisplayed. Paint is an event that fires every time the form needs to be redisplayed because of changes. Toolbars also have a Paint event, but not a Draw method.

Usage `PROCEDURE frmForm.Draw | oObject.Paint`

Draw is similar to Refresh, but doesn't update the data in controls—it only redraws them. We really can't see when we'd use Draw, but we're sure someone will find a clever way to exploit it.

Paint is more interesting. It gets called a lot. Paint fires anytime a visual aspect of the form or toolbar changes, except for a control being used as intended. For example, Paint fires when focus changes because the focus rectangle has to be redrawn. Paint fires when the form loses focus because the title bar color changes. Paint fires when resizing uncovers part of a control.

For a toolbar, Paint fires when you resize, dock or undock it and when you click on it to use it (we're not sure why on that last one).

Paint fires often enough that you don't want to put too much in there because it can bog things down. As with Draw, we're not clear yet on when we'd want to use Paint, but we're certain the time will come when we're glad it's there.

Example

```
* You can see what fires Paint by putting the following in the
* Paint method
DEBUGOUT "Paint fired - "+This.Name
```

See Also ClipControl, Hide, Refresh, Show

DrawMode, DrawStyle, DrawWidth

These three properties affect the way drawing occurs on a form (including the main FoxPro window, _SCREEN). DrawMode also affects the drawing of Shape and Line controls.

Usage
```
oObject.DrawMode = nDrawMode
nDrawMode = oObject.DrawMode
```

DrawMode determines the way colors are mixed. For shape controls, BorderColor and FillColor specify colors for the outside edge and interior, respectively. The BorderColor of a line control determines its color (and it has no interior, of course). For shapes drawn with the Box, Circle and Line methods, the outside edge is based on the form's ForeColor, while the form's FillColor specifies the interior.

Normally, the appropriate colors are used directly, regardless of the BackColor of the form or any other considerations. It turns out, though, that this "normal" behavior is actually something called "copy mode," which means "copy the color of the object onto the form." That's DrawMode 13. Visual FoxPro supports 15 other drawing modes as well. The other modes perform various kinds of mixing of the object's specified drawing color with the form's BackColor. For example, DrawMode 15 ("Merge") combines the object's specified color with the form's BackColor (kind of like painting one color over another while the bottom color is still wet).

The names given for the values of DrawMode are totally mystifying, with a few exceptions. Blackness (DrawMode 1) and Whiteness (DrawMode 16) are pretty clear (or opaque). Regardless of the specified color, they draw black and white, respectively. Mode 11 (NOP, meaning "no operation") is pretty simple, too. It doesn't actually draw anything, thus making your object invisible.

Many of the other modes are based on the idea that colors have inverses (remember the color wheel you learned in elementary school?). You get the inverse of a color by subtracting each of its red, green and blue values (that's the "R", "G" and "B" in RGB()) from 255, so the inverse color of RGB(128,0,0)—a deep red—is RGB(127,255,255)—light blue-green.

DrawMode 6 (Invert) draws using the inverse of the form's BackColor. DrawMode 4 (Not Copy) uses the inverse of the specified color for the object.

Another interesting pair is modes 7 and 10 (XOR—"exclusive OR"—and Not XOR). These two modes look at the foreground and background colors bitwise and are interested only in bits turned on in one of the two colors, but not both. Mode 7 uses the color this produces. Mode 10 uses the inverse of mode 7.

The remainder of the draw modes use combinations and variations of these techniques.

Usage
```
frmForm.DrawStyle = nDrawStyle
nDrawStyle = frmForm.DrawStyle
```

DrawStyle applies only to forms, and determines the type of line used for the outside border of things drawn with the Box, Circle and Line methods. The default (0) is a solid line—there are six other choices.

Styles 1 through 4 are all variations of dots and dashes, and apply only when DrawWidth for the form is 1. As soon as you use a wider line, the dots and dashes blend together and you get solid lines again.

Style 5 is transparent, meaning that though the item is drawn, you can't see it. This appears to be the way to get borderless objects from the drawing methods.

Finally, Style 6 is labeled as "inside solid," but we can't get it to do anything at all. No matter what settings we specify for related properties, nothing happens. If there's already something there, it stays there. If there's nothing there, nothing appears. We're not sure what this one is supposed to do, but this can't be it.

Usage

```
frmForm.DrawWidth = nDrawWidth
nDrawWidth = frmForm.DrawWidth
```

DrawWidth determines how wide (in pixels) the border lines are for the Box, Circle and Line methods. The default is 1. You can go all the way up to 32,767, but we can't imagine why you'd want to. Actually, you can specify any number at all, but anything less than 1 is treated like 1. We suppose anything over 32767 is treated as 32767 (we haven't figured out how to test that, even in 1280x1048 video).

DrawWidth interacts with DrawStyle, as noted above.

Figure 4-5 shows a form that lets you play with the settings of DrawMode, DrawStyle, FillStyle, FillColor and BackColor. When you click the "Change it" button, the current values from the lists and the colors chosen by pressing the Form Color and Fill Color buttons are applied to the Shape (top) and box (lower) on the left of the form. You'll find this form as TestDraw.SCX on the disk.

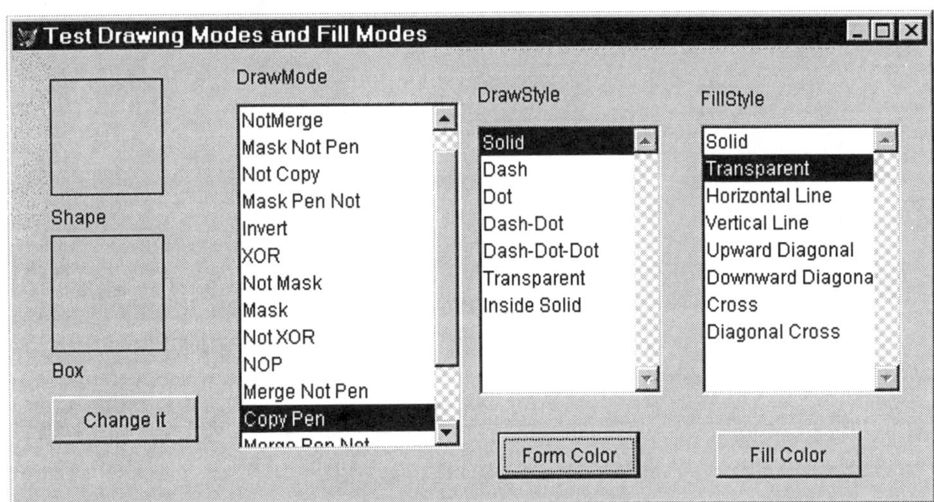

Figure 4-5: Testing drawing parameters

Example

```
* The "Change it" button in the form shown has all
* the interesting code in its Click method.
* nFormColor and nFillColor are custom properties
* of the form that get set by the appropriate buttons.
ThisForm.BackColor = ThisForm.nFormColor
ThisForm.Shape1.DrawMode = ThisForm.lstMode.ListItemId
ThisForm.Shape1.FillColor = ThisForm.nFillColor
ThisForm.Shape1.BorderColor = ThisForm.nFillColor
ThisForm.Shape1.FillStyle = ThisForm.lstFillStyle.ListItemId-1
ThisForm.DrawMode = ThisForm.lstMode.ListItemId
ThisForm.DrawStyle = ThisForm.lstDrawStyle.ListItemId-1
ThisForm.FillColor = ThisForm.nFillColor
ThisForm.FillStyle = ThisForm.lstFillStyle.ListItemId-1

* Redraw the box to see the new effects
ThisForm.Box(ThisForm.Shape1.Left, ;
             ThisForm.Shape1.Top + ThisForm.Shape1.Height + 10,;
             ThisForm.Shape1.Left + ThisForm.Shape1.Width, ;
             ThisForm.Shape1.Top + ;
             (2 * ThisForm.Shape1.Height) + 10)
```

See Also BackColor, Box, Circle, FillColor, FillStyle, ForeColor, Line

DriveType()

This function reports the type of drive specified, reading only the first letter of the supplied parameter. It duplicates, with one exception, the DriveType() function of FoxTools, which itself is just a wrapper around the

Win32 GetDriveType().

Usage `nType = DriveType( cDriveLetter )`

Parameter	Value	Meaning
cDrive	A - Z	The drive whose type is to be checked.
nType	0	Under VFP 3.x and 5.x, no such drive.
	1	In VFP 6.0, no such drive.
	2	Floppy drive.
	3	Hard disk.
	4	Removable or network drive.
	5	CD-ROM.
	6	RAM disk.

This function is handy to have, but we don't understand why we have it built into our database management language. It is easy enough to access it directly from the underlying Win32 API, as shown in the second example below. Just dBloat, as far as we can tell…

Take the answers provided with a grain of salt. Depending on how vendors have designed their drivers to interact with the operating system, your results may vary. For example, Iomega Jaz and ZIP drives respond as floppies (type 2) under Win95 and Win NT, but if the operator uses the supplied Iomega software to make the disk "non-removable," the drive shows as a hard disk (type 3). Use DiskSpace(), SYS(2020) and SYS(2022) to determine what kind of drive you're working with.

VFP 3.x and 5.x with FoxTools reports 0 for unknown drives. VFP 6.0 reports 1 instead.

And, of course, it doesn't always work. DriveType() doesn't work with UNC paths, returning 0 or 1 for an unknown drive.

Example

```
* Returns 2 for most folks
? DriveType("A")
* This code provides the same functionality for VFP 3 or 5
* on any Win32 Platform
LPARAMETERS tcDrive
DECLARE Integer GetDriveType ;
  IN WIN32API ;
  AS WGDT ;
  STRING DriveLetter
RETURN WGDT(LEFT(tcDrive,1) + ":")

* Z: is mapped as a Zip drive on the network
? DriveType("\\Orion\ZIPDrive")  && 1: unknown
? DriveType("Z")                 && 4: removable/network drive
* On the local machine, this drive displays type 2 - floppy
```

```
SET DEFAULT TO Z
? SYS(2020)                         && 100431872 - 95.8 Mb
? SYS(2022, "Z")                    && 2048 - 2K cluster size
```

See Also DiskSpace(), FoxTools, Sys(2020), Sys(2022)

Drop Table, Drop View

These two commands let you remove tables and views from a database, as well as delete free tables. We could do all of this before with other commands, but DROP is the ANSI-standard keyword for removing things.

Usage

```
DROP TABLE TableName | FileName | ? [ RECYCLE ]
DROP VIEW ViewName
```

The syntax for DROP TABLE reminds us of George Carlin's immortal question, "Why are there three?" The answer is that you can delete a table that's contained in a database by simply giving the table's name, or delete a free table by specifying its path and name or avoid having to remember names by specifying ?.

DROP TABLE changes its behavior depending on whether there's a current database. If a database is set, it assumes you're handing it the name of a table in the database (or want to choose one, if you put ?). If you specify a free table in that case, you get an error message, even if you give its complete path and file name. The command just isn't smart enough to understand that you couldn't care less about the open database.

When you issue DROP TABLE ?, if there's a database set, you get a little dialog box that lets you choose a table from the database. If no database is current, you get the standard Windows Save dialog with a caption of "Delete" and the list limited to tables. Pretty smart. Of course, it would be even nicer if you could switch from database-container tables to free tables or choose a database and then see its tables.

The RECYCLE clause gives you the chance to go back again, sort of. If you add it, the table (and its associated index and memo files) lands in the Recycle Bin rather than going off into file heaven. You can restore them in the usual way. However, the result is as if you'd removed the table from the database with the REMOVE TABLE command—all the stuff that applies only to database tables (like rules and triggers and format and InputMask, and so forth) is lost.

In VFP 5, if the table you specify is the parent of a persistent relation, VFP's reaction to DROP TABLE depends on the case you use in the command, of all things. If you specify the table in all lowercase, instead of removing it from the database and deleting it, VFP gives you an error telling you it's "referenced" in a relation. Yeah, so what? But wait, it gets better. If you include even one uppercase letter in the name, the DROP TABLE command works. The table and relation are removed from the database, and the table is deleted. In VFP 6, the situation is much simpler. It just doesn't let you drop a table that's referenced in a relation. We're not sure if that's a good thing or a bad thing, but we know for sure that it's not a documented thing.

DROP VIEW is a lot easier to deal with. Give it a view name in the current database and it removes the view from the database. There's no RECYCLE clause here, and unlike choosing a view and pressing Delete in the Database Designer, there's no confirmation dialog, so be careful.

Help says DROP VIEW is just another name for DELETE VIEW. So why doesn't DROP VIEW accept ? to let us choose a view to delete? DELETE VIEW does.

Example

```
* Careful - these commands will remove data from the sample applications -
* try this on a copy!
OPEN DATABASE TasTrade
DROP TABLE Setup
SET DATA TO
```

```
DROP TABLE \MyData\MyTable
SET DATA TO TasTrade
DROP VIEW top25cust
```

See Also Add Table, Create SQL View, Delete File, Delete View, Erase, Remove Table

DropDown

This event fires when the list portion of a combo box drops open.

Usage

```
PROCEDURE cboCombo.DropDown
[ LPARAMETERS nControlIndex ]
```

As with many other events, the nControlIndex parameter is relevant only when the combo is one of a group of controls contained in an array. In that case, the parameter is passed to tell you which member of that group triggered the event.

This event fires before the list drops down to give you a last chance to change the contents of the list.

Except in VFP 3. There, the list drops first, then the event fires. We were very pleased to see this bug among the fixes in VFP 5.

Example

```
PROCEDURE cboState.DropDown
   IF ThisForm.lAllowNoChoice
      This.AddItem("None of the above")
   ENDIF
ENDPROC
```

See Also ComboBox, DownClick

DropOffline() See CreateOffline().

DToC() See CToD().

DToR() See Cos().

DToS() See CToD().

DToT() See CToT().

DynamicAlignment

This column property determines how contained controls should be aligned.

Usage

```
grcColumn.DynamicAlignment = cExpression
cExpression = grcColumn.DynamicAlignment
```

By supplying a character expression to the DynamicAlignment property, the contents of displayed cells can be aligned to the right, center or left of a column within a grid based on their content or other runtime conditions. This property could be used in combination with the DynamicColor properties to make unusual or out-of-bounds values stand out from the remainder of the display. DynamicAlignment is different from plain ol' Alignment in that it is evaluated individually for each cell in the column, so that cells meeting certain criteria can be differentiated from all the other cells in that column—Alignment applies to all the cells in a column.

Sometimes DynamicAlignment is too dynamic. When moving up or down a column of cells where alignment changes from cell to cell, the current cell can occasionally be seen to "jump" to one of the other alignments when the cursor key is pressed to move into a cell with different alignment. We suspect that the DynamicAlignment is being evaluated for the cell about to receive the focus, but inadvertently is applied to the current cell. As soon as the new cell receives the focus, the older cell is redrawn correctly, but the momentary wiggle is distracting. We've seen similar problems with simple, non-dynamic Alignment as well—see that section for details.

Example

```
grcColumn.DynamicAlignment = "iif(nValue<nThreshold,0,1)"
```

See Also Alignment, Column, DynamicBackColor, DynamicForeColor, Grid

DynamicBackColor, DynamicForeColor

These properties are among the things that make grids so cool. Using these properties, you can specify conditions for each column of a grid to base its colors on anything you want (though you'll usually base them on data in the grid). So, you can show negative balances in red, or color a grid like a checkerboard, or show sales on Sunday in purple on white. In fact, you can even drive your users to distraction by basing a column's colors on things like the day of the week or the time of day.

Usage

```
colColumn.DynamicBackColor = cColorExpression
cColorExpression = colColumn.DynamicBackColor
colColumn.DynamicForeColor = cColorExpression
cColorExpression = colColumn.DynamicForeColor
```

These properties have a level of indirection that BackColor and ForeColor don't. You don't specify a particular color—you give a string containing an expression that, when evaluated, returns a color. Our experience is that, most often, the expression involves IIF(). However, any valid character string that evaluates to a number in the appropriate range will do. You can, for example, add a method to the form that figures out what color you want and call that routine. The most important thing is to remember to enclose the expression in quotes so it gets evaluated at runtime—not when you specify it.

The specified expressions are re-evaluated for each visible row each time the column is refreshed. Be careful how much computation you include, since too much can bog the system down.

Example

```
* Suppose you have a form containing a grid showing the
* TasTrade Products table. Some products are discontinued.
* Rather than having a separate column to indicate that,
* you could show those products in reverse video.
* For each column, the DynamicBackColor would be set as:
This.DynamicBackColor = "IIF(Products.Discontinued, ;
                             This.ForeColor, This.BackColor)"
* DynamicForeColor is set as:
This.DynamicForeColor = "IIF(Products.Discontinued, ;
                             This.BackColor, This.ForeColor)"
```

See Also BackColor, DynamicAlignment, DynamicFontBold, DynamicFontItalic, DynamicFontName,DynamicFontOutline, DynamicFontShadow, DynamicFontSize, DynamicFontStrikeThru, DynamicFontUnderline, DynamicFontStyle, DynamicInputMask, ForeColor, RGB()

DynamicCurrentControl See CurrentControl.

DynamicFontBold, DynamicFontItalic, DynamicFontName, DynamicFontSize, DynamicFontStrikeThru, DynamicFontUnderline, DynamicFontOutline, DynamicFontShadow

The first six of these properties let you control the font characteristics of individual cells in a column of a grid. Like the dynamic color properties, these are very cool. The last two properties don't do anything in VFP/Windows, but can be used in VFP/Mac.

Usage

```
colColumn.DynamicFontBold = cBoldExpression
cBoldExpression = colColumn.DynamicFontBold
colColumn.DynamicFontItalic = cItalicExpression
cItalicExpression = colColumn.DynamicFontItalic
colColumn.DynamicFontName = cNameExpression
cNameExpression = colColumn.DynamicFontName
colColumn.DynamicFontSize = cSizeExpression
cSizeExpression = colColumn.DynamicFontSize
colColumn.DynamicFontStrikeThru = cStrikeThruExpression
cStrikeThruExpression = colColumn.DynamicFontStrikeThru
colColumn.DynamicFontUnderline = cUnderlineExpression
cUnderlineExpression = colColumn.DynamicFontUnderline
```

Each of these properties accepts a character expression that evaluates to a legal value of the font property in question. That is, the expressions for DynamicFontBold, DynamicItalic, DynamicFontStrikeThru and DynamicFontUnderline should evaluate to logical values, while the expression for DynamicFontName should result in a character value (a font name) and for DynamicFontSize, the expression should yield numeric results.

The key, though, is that the value of the DynamicWhatever properties is the character expression itself. It shouldn't be evaluated until the form is actually executing.

Most of the time, the expressions involve IIF() and values in the table the grid is based on. Of course, you can use anything at all and can do really weird stuff if you choose. You're limited only by your imagination, which, judging by FoxPro programmers we know, is a really scary thing.

Example

```
* In the grid described under DynamicBackColor, imagine that we
* want to highlight expensive products. We'll set some columns
* to use italics for any product with a unit_price more than $50

* For each column you want italicized, set:
This.DynamicFontItalic = "IIF(Product.Unit_Price>50,.T.,.F.)
```

DynamicFontOutline and DynamicFontShadow don't do anything in Visual FoxPro for Windows, since it doesn't support outline and shadow fonts (and that's because Windows doesn't support them). These two do work in Visual FoxPro for Mac.

See Also AFont(), DynamicAlignment, DynamicBackColor, DynamicForeColor, DynamicInputMask, FontBold, FontItalic, FontName, FontOutline, FontShadow, FontSize, FontStrikeThru, FontUnderline

DynamicForeColor See DynamicBackColor.

DynamicInputMask

This is the newest addition to the Dynamic... property group for columns. Like the others, it lets you specify an expression that's evaluated at runtime for each row in the grid. In this case, the result of the expression provides an InputMask for the column.

Usage

```
colColumn.DynamicInputMask = cInputMaskExpression
cInputMaskExpression = colColumn.DynamicInputMask
```

This property finally lets us do something we've been wanting to do since FoxPro 2.x—use an appropriate input mask (PICTURE clause) for the expected input in different rows. You provide an expression that results in a valid InputMask and VFP does the rest. Most often, you'll use either IIF() or a custom function to figure out the right mask. One thing that often trips us up: Make sure that when setting the value, you specify DynamicInputMask as a string, with beginning and ending string delimiters. Otherwise, you can spend quite a while chasing down "Expression is invalid" messages at runtime.

Example

```
* Specify an InputMask for PostalCode based on the Country.
* This is the short version.
This.DynamicInputMask = "IIF(UPPER(Country) = 'USA'," + ;
   "'99999-9999',IIF(UPPER(Country)='CANADA'," + ;
   "'A9A 9A9','XXXXXXXXXX'))"
```

See Also DynamicBackColor, DynamicForeColor, Format, InputMask

Edit See Browse.

EditBox

The EditBox is Visual FoxPro's answer to the @ ... EDIT of Xbase-gone-by. It provides an area for freeform text editing, complete with scrolling, tabs and so forth.

An edit box can be based on a memo field, a character field or variable, or just a literal character string.

Property	Value	Purpose
AllowTabs	Logical	Indicates whether Tabs can be entered.
Format	Character	Specifies Xbase-style formatting functions.
HideSelection	Logical	Indicates whether selected text retains its highlight when focus moves to another control.
MaxLength	Numeric	Specifies the maximum number of characters that can be entered.
ScrollBars	Numeric	Indicates whether the edit box has scrollbars.
SelStart, SelLength	Numeric	Indicate the starting position and length of the selected text.
SelText	Character	The currently selected text.

Example

```
* Set an edit box (Edit1) to have no scroll bars,
* to accept tabs and to accept no more than 50 characters
ThisForm.Edit1.ScrollBars = 0
ThisForm.Edit1.AllowTabs = .T.
ThisForm.Edit1.MaxLength = 50
```

If you need to format the text within the edit box, allowing things like italics or bold, consider using the RichText ActiveX control instead.

See Also AllowTabs, Format, HideSelection, MaxLength, ScrollBars, SelLength, SelStart, SelText, Text box

Eject, Eject Page, On Page

EJECT and EJECT PAGE both send ejects to the printer, but clean up from it differently. EJECT is intended for use with @...SAY output, while EJECT PAGE is meant to work with ? and ?? streaming output. ON PAGE lets you establish an event handler for reaching the end of the page (or a specified line) in streaming output.

Usage

```
EJECT
EJECT PAGE
```

EJECT sends a formfeed to the printer. But it doesn't take effect until you SET PRINT TO to finish the print job. EJECT PAGE also sends a formfeed, but it resets a bunch of the printer variables, as well. It's a better choice in a program using streaming output.

Usage `ON PAGE [ AT LINE nTriggerLine ] [ Command ]`

ON PAGE is an event handler. In streamed output, when you reach the end of the page, the specified command is executed. If you include the AT clause, the command is executed when you reach that line. The ON PAGE handler lets you leave top and bottom margins and include a header or footer.

Be sure to turn off the ON PAGE handler (by issuing ON PAGE with nothing following) before you SET PRINT OFF. If you're redirecting output to a file and don't do so, you end up sending a blank page to the printer.

When you issue EJECT PAGE inside an ON PAGE handler, it uses linefeeds to complete the page regardless of the setting of _PADVANCE.

We haven't used these commands since FoxBase days and we don't expect to start doing so now. Use the Report Designer or a third-party reporting tool.

Example

```
SET PRINT TO test.txt
SET PRINT ON
_PAGENO = 1
_PLENGTH = 15
ON PAGE AT LINE 12 DO footer

FOR ncnt=1 TO 3
   ?"Page "+PADL(_pageno,2)
   FOR ncnt2 = 1 TO 20
      _PCOLNO = 2*ncnt2
      ??"Line "+PADL(ncnt2,2)
      ?
   ENDFOR
ENDFOR
ON PAGE
SET PRINT OFF
SET PRINT TO

PROCEDURE footer

?"This is the end of the page"
EJECT PAGE

ENDPROC
```

See Also ?, ??, _PageNo, _PLength

Empty()

This function tells you whether an item is empty—that is, devoid of content. It has two major uses: checking whether a string is totally blank without having to worry about SET EXACT and checking if a variable or field is uninitialized without worrying about its type. Both of these are important enough that EMPTY() appears frequently in our code.

Usage `lIsItEmpty = EMPTY( eExpr )`

Parameter	Value	Meaning
eExpr	Character	Check whether eExpr is composed only of spaces, tabs (CHR(09)), line feeds (CHR(10)) and carriage returns (CHR(13)).

Parameter	Value	Meaning
eExpr	Any numeric type	Check whether eExpr is 0 or blank.
	Logical	Check whether eExpr is .F.
	Date	Check whether eExpr contains the empty date { / / }
	DateTime	Check whether eExpr contains the empty datetime { / / : : }
	Memo or General	Check whether eExpr is completely empty—that is, has no contents at all.
	Screen	Gives a "Data Type Mismatch" error.
lIsItEmpty	.T.	eExpr is empty according to the definition for the type.
	.F.	eExpr is not empty.

Until nulls were added, EMPTY() had only one confusing behavior—that a character variable or field containing only blanks (CHR(32)) is considered empty, while a memo field containing blanks is not. Nulls add to the confusion a little - EMPTY(.NULL.) returns .F. That's because nulls are special and indicate unknown data. Being null is not the same thing as being empty. Use ISNULL() to test for .NULL.

EMPTY() behaves strangely when presented with an object reference variable. If the variable actually contains an object reference, EMPTY() generates error 11, "Function argument value, type or count is invalid" which we disagree with—if it's an object reference, it's not empty. If the variable is .NULL., EMPTY correctly returns .F. You have to test VARTYPE(var) or TYPE('var') before checking for EMPTY() to avoid this bug.

Example

```
? EMPTY(cLastName)

IF EMPTY(nUserInput)
   WAIT WINDOW "Enter a numeric value"
ENDIF
```

See Also IsBlank(), IsNull(), Set Exact, Type(), VarType()

Enabled

This property determines whether a control or form can get focus. It's Visual FoxPro's equivalent to FoxPro 2.x's SHOW GET ENABLE | DISABLE.

Usage

```
oObject.Enabled = lValue
lValue = oObject.Enabled
```

When Enabled is .F., the object is dimmed. In addition, you can't click on the object. Okay, you can click on it, but nothing happens. You can't tab to it, either.

Grids behave a little differently than other controls in this regard. If you disable the control in a column of a grid, then click on that control, the grid cell itself receives "focus" of some sort. You can't use the control, but the cell is highlighted. You still can't tab into that control.

Disable controls when they don't make sense. By selectively enabling and disabling controls based on the responses of the user, you can both encourage and shepherd the users along the path of "normal" choices and prevent them from choosing inappropriate or nonsensical choices.

There's one potential gotcha with Enabled. When you disable a container (like a form), the objects in that container (like controls) are inaccessible, but they don't get dimmed, so there's no visual cue to the user. We like the fact that disabling the container keeps users away from the contents—it would be a pain to have to cycle through the contents and disable them individually. We just wish there were an easy way to get a visual cue. Our best suggestion is to create a custom method for the container EnableIt(), which accepts .T. or .F., then issues SetAll(Enabled, <the passed value>), followed by This.Enabled = <the passed value>. Use the custom method instead of simply setting Enabled for the container. In VFP 6, you can use an Assign method of the Enabled property of a container to do this.

Example

```
* You may want to enable the Save button of a dialog
* as soon as the user makes a change to a particular field.
* You could put something like this in the InteractiveChange
* method of that field:
ThisForm.btnSave.Enabled=.T.
```

See Also ReadOnly, Show Get, Show Gets, Visible

Encrypted **See Debug.**

End Transaction **See Begin Transaction.**

EndCase **See Do Case.**

EndDo **See Do While.**

EndFor **See For.**

EndFunc **See Function.**

EndIf **See If.**

#EndIf **See #Define.**

EndPrintJob **See PrintJob ... EndPrintJob.**

EndProc **See Function.**

EndText **See Text ... EndText.**

EOF() **See BOF().**

Erase **See Copy File.**

ErasePage, ReleaseErase, ReleaseWindows

Here are three properties you might have some difficulty finding in the reference books (except this one, of course) when you have trouble with them in a program. They are used in "READ-compatibility" mode only, and ought to be avoided like the plague.

Usage

```
frmForm.ErasePage = lEraseOrNot
lEraseOrNot = frmForm.ErasePage
frmForm.ReleaseErase = lEraseOnRelease
lEraseOnRelease = frmForm.ReleaseErase
frmForm.ReleaseWindows = lRelease
```

```
lRelease = frmForm.ReleaseWindows
```

Parameter	Value	Meaning
lEraseOrNot	Logical	Determines whether one page is erased when a child READ level is called, or whether the image is preserved for the return from the nested READ.
lEraseOnRelease	Logical	Determines whether a control's image should be saved on the screen after the control has been released or the READ has terminated.
lRelease	Logical	The equivalent to the Release Windows check box in the generator options of converted forms, this determines whether the images of windows are preserved after the READ that created them has been terminated. This trick was used with great success in Y. Alan Griver's "CodeBook" series for FoxPro 2.x, but VFP's event and form models make it unnecessary.

In *Hacker's Guide for Visual FoxPro 3.0*, we speculated that these properties were last-minute additions to the READ-compatibility model, since they are not documented in the printed materials, the Help file, or even the Readme file. Microsoft has had numerous opportunities to correct this, if it was truly an oversight. We've concluded that Microsoft just didn't want us messing with them. And they're probably right.

We're willing to go along with that idea for these properties. While they do provide a better level of compatibility with code written for the old READ model, we don't plan to run any forms in compatibility mode, except under the most dire of circumstances. Nested READs and READ SAVE tricks were nice features to be able to try in the 2.x model, but they are not part of the main-form management scheme, and trying to integrate them into a true VFP product will certainly cause trouble.

These properties are not native properties of the base class Form, but are added to the form in Convert.PRG (check it out in the subdirectory HOME()+\TOOLS\CONVERT).

See Also _Converter, READ, WindowType

Error, Error(), LineNo(), Message(), On Error, On("Error"), On Escape, On("Escape"), On ReadError, On("ReadError"), Sys(2018)

These handy functions and commands provide some key debugging facilities to the Visual FoxPro development environment. ERROR(), LINENO(), MESSAGE() and SYS(2018) can provide details about what went wrong, while you can use the ON ERROR, ON ESCAPE and ON READERROR event handlers to control the flow of events and to determine what to do now. We think the ON techniques are mostly relics of bygone Xbase days, but have some suggestions on how to handle errors in Visual FoxPro. ERROR is a cool command that lets you test all the error-handling functions once you have them in place.

Usage `ERROR nNumber [, cMoreInfo ] | cCustomMessage`

Parameter	Value	Meaning
nNumber	Integer	The value of a valid error message—most seem to be in the range of 1 to 1999, although more than a few in that range are still open. Passing a bad error number results (surprise!) in an error—1941, to be precise: "Error code is not valid." Sheesh!

Parameter	Value	Meaning
cMoreInfo	Character	If the error message can provide specific information, you can pass that information to the error handler here. This is the equivalent of the information passed back by SYS(2018), and is displayed in the help file listing as "<name>", as in "File <name> not found."
cCustomMessage	Character	You know those advertisements and billboards that say "Your message could be here?" Well, never to be left out, Visual FoxPro provides this opportunity for you, too, to write error messages. All generate error 1098, the "User-defined error," but with your message. There is no way we can see to supply the equivalent of SYS(2018), however.

This command allows you to do many things: You can pass on an error condition that you don't want to handle locally, or you can create your own error. You can test your error-handling routines by generating errors 1 through 1999. Or you can use the built-in facilities to display your own error messages, using the new Error 1098, a custom user-defined error and message.

We'd like to be able to use ERROR in an object's ERROR method to invoke the global error handler. Unfortunately, it doesn't work. It calls the default Cancel/Suspend/Ignore dialog. See the entry for the Error method for our thoughts on this one.

Example

```
ERROR 1767, "its child"
* Produces the error message "Parent object will not ;
* allow this property setting for its child" - try to say
* that with a straight face <g>.

ERROR "TILT!"  && generates error 1098
```

Usage

```
nError = ERROR()
cErrorMessage = MESSAGE()
cCode = MESSAGE(1)
cMoreInfo = SYS(2018)
```

The ERROR() function returns the last error, if an ON ERROR trap is in place. If there have been no errors, or the error handler is not in place, ERROR() returns zero. ERROR() is also reset by a RETURN or RETRY command, so the very act of finishing the ON ERROR routine clears the error code. Preserve this value within your ON ERROR routine, if needed. ERROR() does not detect low-level or DDE errors; use FERROR() or DDELastError() for those sub-languages.

The two values of the MESSAGE() function preserve the error message and the code of the offending line. The error message hangs around forever, until the next error overwrites it. MESSAGE(1) is a funny function. When you're running the interactive version of VFP, sometimes it returns the original line of code even if the program file is specifically compiled with the encrypt option! Sometimes, rather than displaying the entire line of code, the error handler translates the tokenized FoxPro command into its original form, and displays it with an ellipsis if additional information was included in the command. The Help claims this occurs when "the source code is unavailable." We've usually found that to mean when the source file is not in the current directory or on the path. Finally, in the runtime version, MESSAGE(1) returns the same error message that's displayed with MESSAGE().

SYS(2018) returns the parameter or additional information supplied to a command that may have caused the error to occur. This might be the name of a file or memory variable that does not exist. This value is used internally by the error handler to display specific error messages, such as "File <name> does not exist." SYS(2018) returns the <name> portion of the error, if one exists.

Field validation errors got harder to process after VFP 3. In VFP 3, inserting data into a table that violated the field rule always generated error 1582, and populated the MESSAGE() function with "Field <fieldname> validation rule is violated" and the SYS(2018) value with the fieldname. That SYS(2018) value made it easy for us to know which field had the problem, perhaps to set focus back to that control. In VFP 5, SYS(2018) contains the field's RuleText if it's been filled in, or an all-uppercase version of MESSAGE(). There's no easy way to find the fieldname—you need to parse it out of the MESSAGE() text, which is localized differently for different languages, or scan the DBC for a field with a matching message. They had it right to begin with. Bogus.

Example

```
ON ERROR WAIT WINDOW "Error " + LTRIM(STR(ERROR())) ;
                     + CHR(13)+;
                     "Message()  " + MESSAGE() + CHR(13) + ;
                     "Message(1) " + MESSAGE(1) + CHR(13) + ;
                     "SYS(2018) " + SYS(2018)
DO LUNCH  && file does not exist, and displays:
* ERROR()     1
* Message()   File 'lunch.prg' does not exist.
* Message(1)  "do lunch  && file does not exist, and displays:"
* SYS(2018)   LUNCH.PRG
```

Usage

```
ON ERROR [ Command ]
ON ESCAPE [ Command ]
ON READERROR [ Command ]
cCommand = ON( "Error" )
cCommand = ON( "Escape" )
cCommand = ON( "ReadError" )
```

The ON ERROR event handler still has a place within the workings of Visual FoxPro. ON ESCAPE can have some applicability under some circumstances. ON READERROR is old and should be allowed to expire quietly.

ON ERROR is the last resort for errors that have stumped the local Error method, or occur in a place where those procedures do not have control. There are a huge number of errors, but most fall into a small number of categories: catastrophic, and worse. Our general feeling is that the error handler should record as much information about the error as possible (storing such values as LINENO(), PROGRAM() and lots of SYS() values to a text file or memo field) and then shut down the operation.

ON ESCAPE can be better replaced in forms with KeyPress events, but it may still have a place in areas where the user input is limited and the event model weak, such as in the running of reports. If you create a UDF() within a report to pause and present a "Cancel/Resume" dialog to the user, you could trigger this with the ESCAPE key with an ON ESCAPE trap, as in the example which follows. Trigger a variable to change values when the escape key is pressed, then test for that value change in a UDF within the report processing. To minimize the time consumed in firing and testing the UDF, you should probably place it in the group band or page bands of the report, so it doesn't fire for every record.

The ON READERROR command is one of the two or three in the language that your authors have never used. The intent of the command is to define a routine to be triggered when an invalid entry is made in a input control that's part of a READ—an invalid date, a number outside an acceptable range, or an item that failed its VALID test. We were surprised to find it worked within the VFP event model at all. But, even in FoxPro 2.x, there are usually better ways to handle these cases. There is one case we know of, though, where ON READERROR is worth its weight in gold. An "Invalid Date" error fires before any associated Valid code, and doesn't let the user out of the entry until the date has been corrected. In the case of two-digit date entry, where the user may be entering a valid date for another century, an ON READERROR routine can process the keystrokes entered and "fix" the date to a valid entry, solving the Year 2000 problem for some legacy applications. Credit for this idea goes to our friend Christof Lange.

Example

```
* See the ON ERROR example above

cOldEscape = ON("ESCAPE")  && preserve the old value
lStopReport = .F.
ON ESCAPE lStopReport = .T.
REPORT FORM MyReport

* Within MyReport, call the UDF TestStop(), which follows:
* TestStop().PRG
* If Escape has been pressed, present an "OK/Cancel" dialog
* to the user. If they choose to cancel printing, force the
* report to end by jumping to the bottom of the table.
* Otherwise, reset the flag to show Escape had been
* pressed and resume.

IF lStopReport
  IF MESSAGEBOX(17,"Continue Printing?","Report Paused") = 2
    GO BOTTOM
  ELSE
    lStopReport = .F.
  ENDIF
ENDIF
RETURN
```

See Also AError(), DDELastError(), Error, FError(), KeyPress, MessageBox(), On Key, Retry, Return, Set Reprocess

Error

You could write a book about error handling in Visual FoxPro. In fact, we wish someone would. There are multiple ways to tackle the issues involved. The Error event is one part of the picture—it fires when an error occurs in any method of an object.

Usage

```
PROCEDURE oObject.Error
LPARAMETERS [ nIndex, ] nError, cMethod, nLine
```

Parameter	Value	Meaning
nIndex	Numeric	If the object is a control array, which item in the array fired the event?
nError	Numeric	The error number.
cMethod	Character	Which method caused the error?
nLine	Numeric	The line number on which the error occurred.

The Error event lets you handle errors locally, but should you? Our technical editor has proposed the most elegant error handling scheme we've seen. (He insists that we point out that his scheme is based on ideas he heard from Mac Rubel and Lisa Slater Nicholls.) Each object handles what it can and passes what it can't up the class hierarchy. If nothing in that hierarchy can deal with the error, it goes up the containership hierarchy (traveling up the class hierarchy of each container along the way). Finally, if you reach the ultimate parent of all parents and still haven't dealt with the error, a global error handler kicks in.

So when does Error fire, anyway? It fires when something in a method of the object causes an error. If you mess up the call to an object's method, though, it's not the called object whose error handler fires, it's the calling object. For example, if a method of cmdDoIt calls the AddItem method of lstMyList, but messes up the call as lstMyList.AddItm, cmdDoIt's Error event fires because it can't find the called method.

If there's no code at all in the Error method (and nothing in the Error methods all the way up the object's class hierarchy), an object's errors get passed on to the current error handler set up with ON ERROR. That's good.

The bad news is what happens if an error occurs in the Error method. Does it call your ON ERROR handler? Nope, you get the usual FoxPro Cancel/Suspend/Ignore dialog. Better debug those Error methods really well before you send them out to users.

Error 1116, "Too many windows are open," does not invoke the error method, nor does it fire the ON ERROR handler.

You can accidentally mess yourself up as well. If all the code in the Error method is commented out, you get no indication of the error. Your ON ERROR handler isn't called in this case because Error contains code, even if it is commented out. This isn't a bug, but it is confusing.

Don't call the ERROR command in your Error method, either. This is the same as having a real bug in your Error code and calls the C/S/I dialog.

In VFP 6, it appears that every base class has an Error method. In VFP 5, Separator does not, and in VFP 3, neither do Column and Header. An error in the code of these events always invokes the global ON ERROR handler—not, as you might suspect, the error handler for the container objects.

Example

```
* For an OLE control, we might trap OLE errors locally
PROCEDURE oleMyGeneral.Error

LPARAMETERS nError, cMethod, nLine

IF nError = 1427 or nError = 1429   && OLE errors
   LOCAL ARRAY aErrInfo[1]
   = AERROR(aErrInfo)
   * now figure out how to handle this OLE error
ELSE
   * call the application's error handler
   oApp.HandleError(This.Name,nError,cMethod,nLine)
ENDIF

RETURN
```

See Also AError(), Error, Error(), On Error

ErrorMessage, Message

Unlike Error, ErrorMessage shouldn't be part of anyone's error-handling strategy in new applications. Like Message, it's a backward-compatibility method included to make it possible to port FoxPro 2.x code to Visual FoxPro.

ErrorMessage fires when an object's Valid returns .F. If you return a string, it gets displayed in a WAIT WINDOW. Message is similar. It fires when you land on an object, and places the returned string in the Windows-style status bar (or at the bottom of the screen, if you're not using the status bar).

Usage

```
PROCEDURE oObject.ErrorMessage | oObject.Message
[ LPARAMETERS nIndex ]
```

ErrorMessage and Message share a weird bug with When and Valid. When you define an ErrorMessage method or a Message method for a control array, it doesn't always fire when it should. For some types of controls, the class the control is based on must include a definition for the same method or FoxPro can't find the one for the control array. You don't have to actually put anything in the method, just define it. Very strange. Of course, it's also fairly irrelevant because we can't think of any reason to use control arrays.

ErrorMessage is the Visual FoxPro replacement for the ERROR clause of @ ... GET. You can actually put anything you want in the method, but whatever you return is displayed in a WAIT WINDOW (if NOTIFY is ON). A better choice is to present whatever message you need in the control's Valid (using WAIT WINDOW or MessageBox) and then return 0 from the Valid.

Message replaces the MESSAGE clause of @ ... GET. It works the same as ErrorMessage except the returned text appears in the status bar. StatusBarText does the same thing and isn't labeled "For Backward Compatibility."

Example

```
PROCEDURE spnMonth.ErrorMessage
RETURN "Choose a month between 1 and 12"
```

See Also Error, StatusBarText, Valid, When

Eval See DoCmd.

Evaluate() See &.

Exclude

This property indicates whether a file gets built into a project or is simply listed there for reference.

Usage

```
lExcluded = filFile.Exclude
filFile.Exclude = lExcluded
```

Projects are not just a container to let you see what files are used in a project. When you build a project into an APP, EXE or DLL, the files in the project become part of that result file. That is, they do unless they're excluded from the project. You can recognize excluded files because they have the international "not" symbol next to them in the Project Manager.

Why would you exclude a file? The most common reason is because it's a data file. Files included in the application are read-only. Because you generally do want users to be able to modify the data in your tables, it's wise to exclude tables from the project. But why bother putting them in the project at all, just to mark them as excluded? Because it gives you quick access to them when you're working on the project.

You should exclude certain other files from a project as well, including libraries. By default, data files and libraries are excluded when they're added to a project.

Exclude lets you find out whether a file is excluded and gives you a programmatic way to change the setting. You can include or exclude any file except whichever file is set as the main file for the project. Not surprisingly, VFP insists that that one be included.

Example

```
* Check the Exclude status of all files in the project
FOR EACH oFile IN _VFP.ActiveProject.Files
   ?oFile.Name+" is "+IIF(oFile.Exclude,"not ","")+"included."
ENDFOR
```

See Also File, Files, MainFile, Project

Exclusive See Alias.

Exit

This command works only within a loop. It immediately exits the loop and continues the program with the statement following the loop-closing command (ENDDO, ENDFOR/NEXT, or ENDSCAN).

We don't use EXIT except in a few closely controlled circumstances because it makes code too hard to maintain. This is a "Beam me up, Scotty" command which can lead to spaghetti code.

See Also Do While, For, For Each, Loop, Scan

Exp(), Log(), Log10()

These functions are FoxPro's contribution to transcendental computing (which has nothing to do with transcendental meditation). EXP() stands for "e to the power," while LOG() and LOG10() compute logarithms for base e and base 10, respectively.

Usage
```
nResultValue = EXP( nPower )
```

EXP() raises the constant e to the specified power, as in e^{nPower}. You probably last saw this in college. Until now, so did we.

nPower can be any of the numeric types, but EXP() returns Numeric regardless.

Example
```
?EXP(1)       && Returns 2.72 with default SET DECIMALS TO 2
SET DECIMALS TO 4
?EXP(1)       && Returns 2.7183
?EXP(-1)      && Returns 0.3679
?EXP(.5)      && Returns 1.6487
```

Usage
```
nResultValue = LOG( nValue )
nResultValue = LOG10( nValue )
```

These two functions compute logarithms—no need for log tables or interpolation (another couple of things you probably haven't thought about since college).

If you're like us, whenever you see something like $y = \log_{10}x$, you have to stop and say "Oh yeah, that means that 10 to the y is x" and then it makes sense again. On the other hand, if you're a normal human being, and not a math nerd like us, you'll probably swear that you never saw this stuff before in your life—it's okay, it's really not that bad! LOG() computes natural logarithms; that is, logs with a base of e. LOG10() computes logs with a base of 10. LOG() and EXP() are inverse functions, so LOG(EXP(nValue))=nValue.

As with EXP(), nValue can be any numeric type, but both functions return Numerics.

Example
```
?LOG(1)       && Returns 0
?LOG(100)     && Returns 4.6052
?LOG10(1)     && Returns 0
?LOG10(100)   && Returns 2 - hey, this makes sense!
```

Export See Append From.

External See Build Project.

FChsize(), FClose() See Low-Level File Functions.

FCount(), Field(), FSize()

FCOUNT() returns the number of fields in a table. FIELD() returns the name of a specified field in a table. FSIZE() is confused: it is two different functions, depending on the setting of—ugh! —SET COMPATIBLE. Generally speaking, we avoid these commands altogether, and let AFIELDS() give us all the information at once.

Usage
```
nFieldCount = FCOUNT( [ cAlias | nWorkarea ] )
cFieldName = FIELD( nField, [ cAlias | nWorkarea ] )
* With SET COMPATIBLE OFF:
nFieldSize = FSIZE( cFieldName, [ cAlias | nWorkarea ] )
* with SET COMPATIBLE ON:
nFileSize = FSIZE( cFileName )
```

Parameter	Value	Meaning
cAlias	Character	The alias of the table about which information is returned.
	Omitted	If nWorkarea is also omitted, use current work area.
nWorkarea	Numeric	The number of the work area containing the table about which information is returned.
	Omitted	If cAlias is also omitted, use current work area.
nFieldCount	Numeric	Number of fields in specified table.
nField	Numeric	Number of the field to return, based on physical order of the table.
cFieldName	Character	The field's name.
nFieldSize	Numeric	Size of the field (SET COMPATIBLE OFF).
cFileName	Character	The name of the file.
nFileSize	Numeric	Size of the file (SET COMPATIBLE ON).

FCOUNT() does not report on hidden, system fields (see "DBF, FPT, CDX, DBC—Hike!"). If you use FCOUNT() and FSIZE() to try to calculate the size of a table, you'll come out with the wrong number if any of the fields are nullable. You need to use RECSIZE() or AFIELDS() to test for this, and while you're at it, you can use the return value of AFIELDS() for a better FCOUNT() and the sum of the AFIELDS() size values for a better FSIZE().

FIELD() returns the name of the field based on its order within the table. Because fields within a table can be rearranged quite easily, you'll not want to hardcode field-order numbers into your code. Instead, FIELD() could prove valuable in a black-box looping structure where you're scanning for certain field names. However, AFIELDS() provides a lot more information in an easily manipulated array and tends to be the function we prefer to use.

FSIZE() is a horror show. Fox Software and Ashton-Tate each went its own way with this function—it's one of the few that is affected by the dreaded SET COMPATIBLE command. If SET COMPATIBLE is OFF or FOXPLUS, FSIZE() returns the field size of the specified field. If FSIZE() is called with SET COMPATIBLE STUPID, er, we mean, ON or DB4, it returns the size of the specified file. Our advice: leave COMPATIBLE SMART (FoxPlus) and use ADIR() to get file sizes.

Example

```
SET COMPATIBLE FOXPLUS
USE HOME() + "LABELS"
nFieldSize = FSIZE("Name", "Labels")  && returns 24
SET COMPATIBLE DB4
nFileSize = FSIZE(HOME()+"Labels")   && returns 6622
? FCOUNT("LABELS")                   && seven
? FIELD(3, "LABELS")                 && returns "NAME"
```

See Also ADir(), AFields(), ALen(), RecSize(), Set Compatible

FCreate() **See Low-Level File Functions.**

FDate(), FTime()

These functions return the date and time a file was last updated, according to the operating system.

Usage

```
dLastDate = FDATE( cFileName )
cLastTime = FTIME( cFileName )
```

cFileName may include a path. If not, FoxPro looks first in the default directory, then along the FoxPro path.

Example

```
? FDATE("WinWord.EXE")  && Returns 7/11/97 for Word 97 SR-1
? FTIME("WinWord.EXE")  && Returns 12:00:00 AM for Word 97 SR-1
```

Now that we have DateTime data, it would be nice to return the file date and time as a single string. On the other hand, adding FDateTime() to the language would be another case of unnecessary dBloat. It's easy enough to write your own using the conversion shown under CTOT(). Or you could just use ADIR(), which not only returns both date and time, but is well-behaved if the file doesn't exist.

See Also ADir(), CToT(), FSize(), LUpdate()

FEof(), FError(), FFlush(), FGets() See Low-Level File Functions.

Field() See FCount().

File

This object is the building block for projects. Every project contains a Files collection composed of File objects. Each File object represents one file (or group of files, like a form) in the project.

Property	Value	Purpose
CodePage	Numeric	The codepage for this file.
Description	Character	The description saved for this file. The description appears in the bottom panel of the Project Manager when the file has focus.
Exclude	Logical	Indicates whether the file is to be included in an APP or EXE built from the project. Actually, indicates whether it should be *excluded.*
FileClass, FileClassLibrary	Character	If the file is a form, these two indicate the name and library of the class it's based on. If the file is not a form, each contains an empty string.
LastModified	DateTime	The date and time at which the file was last changed.
Name	Character	The filename, including the path.
ReadOnly	Logical	This property tells you if the file can be edited. ReadOnly is .T. if the file is checked in under source code control or if it is flagged Read-Only. ReadOnly cannot be directly changed—you need to either check out the file or clear the Read-Only attribute to toggle this property.
SCCStatus	Numeric	Indicates the file's status with the project's source control provider. If there is no source control provider, contains 0.
Type	Single character	Indicates what kind of file this is.

Method	Purpose
AddToSCC	Adds the file to the project's source control provider.
CheckIn	Checks the file into the source control provider.
CheckOut	Checks the file out of the source control provider.
GetLatestVersion	Brings a read-only copy of the file in its current state to the local drive.
Modify	Opens the file in its native editing tool.
Remove	Removes the file from the project, optionally deleting it from the disk as well.
RemoveFromSCC	Removes the file from source control.
Run	Runs the file. For reports, previews the file.
UndoCheckOut	Changes the file's source control status to checked in, discarding any changes since checkout.

It might seem that there's a method missing from the list—Add. But you can't apply Add to a file object because there is no such object at the time you're adding the file. So Add is a Files collection method.

File, like Project, is a COM class, not a native VFP class. This means, among other things, that it has no events. It also means we can't subclass it, because we have no control over the creation of File objects. It happens automatically when a project is opened or when a file is added to a project.

Example

```
* See what's in a project
FOR EACH oFile IN _VFP.ActiveProject.Files
   ? oFile.Name, oFile.Type
ENDFOR
```

See Also AddToSCC, CheckIn, CheckOut, CodePage, Description, Exclude, FileClass, FileClassLibrary, Files, GetLatestVersion, LastModified, Modify, Name, Project, ReadOnly, Remove, RemoveFromSCC, Run, SCCStatus, Type, UndoCheckOut

File(), Directory()

These two handy functions check if a file or directory exists. If there's any doubt in your mind before trying to open a file, or if you want to make sure there isn't an output file by that name and offer the user the option of supplying a new name or overwriting, these are the functions for you.

Usage

```
lFileExists = FILE( cFilePath )
lDirExists = DIRECTORY( cDirectory )
```

FILE() returns a logical value if the filename specified exists in the specified directory. So far, so good.

If no directory is specified, in addition to the current directory, FoxPro also searches the FoxPro PATH (not the DOS path) set with the SET PATH statement, and returns .T. if the file is found anywhere along that path. It can be argued that "It's a feature, not a bug," as we might in the section by that name, but this one trips us up often. To specify that FILE() only search the current directory, you must explicitly specify at least the directory path name, starting at the root of the drive. So you'll probably want to type this command as FILE(CURDIR() + cFileName) in most cases.

DIRECTORY() tells us if a directory exists. The parameter can be a relative path ("..\MyDir") or explicit from the root of the drive (" C:\MyDir\MySubDir") and isn't required to end with a slash. If one is there, it's ignored. DIRECTORY() does not support UNC names.

Example
```
lOutFileHere = FILE( "OutPut.PRN" )
lDirExists = DIRECTORY( "C:\Temp" )
```

See Also ADir(), Set Path

FileClass, FileClassLibrary

These properties indicate the name of the class on which a form is based and the class library containing that class. They apply to File objects.

Usage
```
cClass = filFile.FileClass
cClassLib = filFile.FileClassLibrary
```

Forms contain information about their class and class library in the Class and ClassLibrary properties. (Big surprise.) But that information is available only when the form is open. When you're working on a project and want to know the provenance of its forms, use FileClass and FileClassLibrary. (Seems to us this is most useful for documentation tools.)

These properties contain the empty string for files other than screens.

Example
```
FOR EACH oFile IN oProj.Files
   IF NOT EMPTY(oFile.FileClass)
      ?oFile.Name + " is based on class: " + oFile.FileClass + ;
       " from classlib: " + oFile.FileClassLibrary
   ENDIF
ENDFOR
```

See Also Class, ClassLibrary, File, Files, Project

Filer

Alas, poor Filer, we knew it well. Issuing this command in VFP 5 or later results in "Unrecognized command verb." Not so much as a decent sendoff.

The good news, even though the command itself has been removed from the language, is that the Filer utility lives on. In the Tools/Filer subdirectory of your main VFP directory is a Filer form. It uses a Filer.DLL to do the heavy lifting of searching through the directory structures. The DLL is a COM object available to any COM hosting tool, like VFP.

The form supplied is just a sample of what can be done. The tool itself is a weak imitation of the power we used to have in Filer itself, but the code is clear and there are at least a few comments. Consider modifying and enhancing the sample form, or perhaps even using the DLL within your own forms for browsing and manipulating files.

Example
```
DO FORM LOCFILE(HOME()+"\tools\filer\filer.scx")
```

See Also ADir(), Dir, Display Files

Files

This collection contains one item for each file in a project. It's part of the VFP 6 scheme for handling projects and their contents programmatically.

Usage
```
prjProject.Files.Method()
prjProject.Files[ nIndex ].Method()
uValue = prjProject.Files[ nIndex ].Property
prjProject.Files[ nIndex ].Property = uValue
```

The Files collection gives you access to all the items in a project. It's an array in which each element is a File object. The collection has only one property of its own, Count, which tells how many files there are. There are a couple of methods that operate on the collection as a whole. Add adds a new file to the project. Item gives you access to an individual file. We can't see why you need Item—you can do the same thing simply by referencing Files[nSomeItem]. It's probably an OLE thing. Like Projects, Files is an ActiveX, rather than a native, collection. Most of the time, this isn't an issue, but it probably does have an effect on system resources. For sure, the error messages you get when you mess up on this stuff are OLE errors, not native VFP errors.

Also, like Projects, the collection itself has a Count property that tells you how many there are.

Example

```
* List all the files in the active project
FOR EACH oFile IN Application.ActiveProject.Files
   ?oFile.Name
ENDFOR
```

See Also Add, Count, File, Item, Project

FileToStr(), StrToFile()

This pair of functions makes it much easier to move text in and out of files. They don't actually add new capabilities to the language, but they replace large chunks of code to set up files and copy strings in and out of them.

Usage

```
cFileContents = FileToStr( cFileName )
nCharsWritten = StrToFile( cFileContents, cFileName
                           [ , lAdditive ] )
```

Parameter	Value	Meaning
cFileContents	Character	The string read from or written to a text file.
cFileName	Character	The name of the text file to be read or written.
lAdditive	.T.	Add cFileContents to an existing text file.
	.F.	Overwrite cFileName with cFileContents, if it already exists. If SAFETY is ON and the file exists, the user is prompted before overwriting.
nCharsWritten	Numeric	The number of characters (bytes) written to the text file.

FileToStr() reads the data in a file and turns it into a single string, which you can then process using whichever of VFP's string handling tools you prefer. StrToFile() takes a string you hand it and saves it in a file, giving you a little bit of control over handling overwriting of an existing file.

If you specify an existing file in StrToFile, but answer "No" to the Overwrite dialog, the function returns cFileContents, instead of something sensible like zero. (The function is smart enough to return 0 if the file you specify is read-only, though, but not smart enough to check whether it's read-only before prompting you to overwrite it.)

You can move data in and out of files other than text files with these functions, if you're careful. For example, you can copy an entire table to a single string variable and even write it back out to create a new table, as long as it doesn't include any of the field types that need an FPT file (such as memo or general). We expect to use these functions most, though, for parsing tasks. In fact, we used FileToStr() to help write this book—we read in and parsed information from the Help file to create a table of all the language elements we needed to write about.

Example

```
* Here's an unusual way of copying a whole table
cData = FileToStr("MyTable.DBF")
=StrToFile(cData,"MyNewTable.DBF")
```

See Also \|\\, Low-Level File Functions

FillColor

This property determines the color used to fill in graphic objects and shapes.

Usage

```
oObject.FillColor = nColor
nColor = oObject.FillColor
```

The FillColor property of a form specifies the color used to fill in rectangles, circles and ellipses drawn with the form's Box and Circle methods. (_SCREEN is considered a form for this purpose.) A shape's FillColor determines its interior.

FillColor matters only when FillStyle is something other than the default 1 (Transparent).

See DrawMode for a form that demonstrates the effects of FillColor and FillStyle.

Example

```
_Screen.FillColor = RGB(128,0,0)   && deep red
_Screen.FillStyle = 6              && checks - country style
_Screen.Box(0, 0, 100, 100)
```

See Also BackColor, DrawMode, DrawStyle, FillStyle

FillStyle

This property determines the pattern used to fill graphic objects and shapes. A form's FillStyle applies to items drawn with the form's Box and Circle methods. A shape has its own FillStyle property.

Usage

```
oObject.FillStyle = nFillStyle
nFillStyle = oObject.FillStyle
```

The default FillStyle is 1 for Transparent. In this case, the object's FillColor is ignored. For the other seven fill styles (which range from solid through variously oriented lines to straight or diagonal cross-hatching), FillColor determines the color of the interior. The settings for FillStyle are included in FoxPro.H.

See DrawMode for a cool form that demonstrates the effects of FillStyle.

Example

```
* Create a form
oForm = CREATEOBJECT("Form")
oForm.AddObject("MyShape", "Shape")
oForm.MyShape.Visible = .T.
oForm.Show()
oForm.MyShape.FillStyle = 0                && Solid
oForm.MyShape.FillColor = RGB(0,0,255)   && Blue
oForm.MyShape.FillStyle = 4                && Diagonal, still blue
```

FillStyle offers two diagonal styles—4 and 5—labeled "upward diagonal" and "downward diagonal." For no reason we can fathom, these are interpreted differently for shapes than for graphic objects drawn with Box and Circle. We think shapes are getting it right and that graphics are confused. Regardless, it's pretty strange when you have two objects with the same FillStyle and the lines go one way in one and the other way in the other.

See Also DrawMode, DrawStyle, FillColor, Shape

Filter See Alias.

Filter() See Set Filter.

Find See Seek.

FirstElement, NumberOfElements

These properties mimic one of the coolest (and most underused) features of FoxPro 2.x. When a combo or list box is based on an array, you can control which column of the array and which sequence of rows appear.

Usage

```
oObject.FirstElement = nFirstElementToShow
nFirstElementToShow = oObject.FirstElement
oObject.NumberOfElements = nNumberToShow
nNumberToShow = oObject.NumberOfElements
```

These properties apply only when the list or combo has RowSourceType set to 5 (Array) and only when ColumnCount is set to 1. (The latter limit was not documented in earlier versions of VFP, but is correct in the VFP 6 Help file. We're quite grateful since we're very tired of telling people that these properties won't do what they wanted them to—let them choose a rectangular portion of the array to go into the list.)

In any case, under the right circumstances, what these properties do is pretty cool. Imagine that you have a multi-column array and you want to show the contents of the third column in a list. You could set ColumnCount to 3 and then set ColumnWidths so that the first two don't show up at all, but why bother? If you only need the one column, just set FirstElement to 3 and only the third column appears.

There's a more complex way to use FirstElement. The items in an array are numbered in what's officially known as row-major order. This means you go all the way across one row numbering, then move to the next row. If the value you give FirstElement isn't in the first row of the array, then not only does it determine which column appears, but it also indicates that the list or combo starts with the specified row. That is, with a three-column array, FirstElement=8 means to show the second column, starting with the third row.

NumberOfElements is pretty simple. It indicates how many rows are included in the list or combo.

It's at this point that we get a tad disappointed that they didn't make this work for multi-column lists and combos. We could imagine wanting multiple columns but limiting the display to a subset of the array. Oh well, it's not that hard to ACOPY() the relevant rows to another array and use that, or to set RowSourceType to 0 and AddItem the elements into the list or combo.

Example

```
* This example sets up a combo to show last names
* of Employees. It can be set to show only those from
* a specified country.

* This code goes in the form's Load
* and assumes you've added a property to the form
* aEmp[1].
* It creates an array of Employees ordered by country
SELECT Employee_Id, First_Name, Last_Name, Country ;
   FROM Employee ;
   ORDER BY Country ;
   INTO ARRAY ThisForm.aEmp

* Now set a combo's properties in the combo's Init as follows
* to show only the last name column (or make equivalent
* settings in the property sheet):
This.RowSourceType = 5
This.RowSource = "ThisForm.aEmp"
This.FirstElement=3

* In a method on the form, you can change
* the combo to include only Employees from a
* specified Country (cCountry), as follows:
LOCAL nFirst, nFirstRow, nCount
nFirst = ASCAN(ThisForm.aEmp, cCountry)
nFirstRow = ASUBSCRIPT(ThisForm.aEmp, nFirst, 1)
IF nFirst > 0
```

```
      nCount = 1
      DO WHILE nFirstRow + nCount <= ALEN(ThisForm.aEmp,1) ;
               AND ThisForm.aEmp[nFirstRow + nCount, 4] = cCountry
         nCount=nCount+1
      ENDDO
   ENDIF
   * Now set combo properties.
   * FirstElement is first occurrence of cCountry - 1
   * to get last name
   ThisForm.cboEmps.FirstElement = nFirst-1
   ThisForm.cboEmps.NumberOfElements = nCount
```

See Also ACopy(), AddItem, ColumnCount, ColumnWidth, ComboBox, ListBox, RowSource, RowSourceType

FkMax(), FkLabel(), Set Function

These functions and command are one way to use the function keys. FKMAX() and FKLABEL() tell you how many and what function keys are available. SET FUNCTION lets you define a keyboard macro and assign it to a function key.

Usage

```
nKeyTotal = FKMAX()
cKeyName = FKLABEL( nKey )
```

FKMAX() simply counts the number of function keys and returns the count. Unless ... you SET COMPATIBLE ON, in which case it also counts the number of Ctrl and Shift combinations available and returns the total. You'd think it would be three times the number of function keys (or even more if you can use things like Ctrl+Shift+key), but in this mode, FoxPro doesn't see the F11 and F12 keys. Plus, Shift+F10, which used to bring up the macro definition dialog, doesn't get counted. It's considered unavailable. Missing F11 and F12 strikes us as carrying compatibility a little too far. Is it really necessary to duplicate the competition's bugs, too?

FKLABEL() lets you translate the number of keys into the actual labels of the keys, which you can then use in SET FUNCTION or ON KEY LABEL. With SET COMPATIBLE ON, you get all the valid combinations, too. For reasons we don't understand, the values of nKey you can pass to FKLABEL() begin with 0, not 1. So FKLABEL(0) is "F1" and so forth. Must be C programmers at work.

Example

```
PROCEDURE DispFKey
* Display a list of all the valid function keys
* Pass "ON" or "OFF" to determine COMPATIBLE setting
LPARAMETER cSetCompat
   * cSetCompat determines setting for SET COMPATIBLE
   * Default to current setting

LOCAL cOldCompat, nCnt
COldCompat = SET("COMPATIBLE")

IF TYPE('cSetCompat')="C" AND ;
        INLIST(UPPER(cSetCompat),"ON","OFF")
   SET COMPATIBLE &cSetCompat
ENDIF

FOR nCnt = 1 TO FKMAX()
   ?FKLABEL(nCnt-1)
ENDFOR

SET COMPATIBLE &cOldCompat
RETURN
```

Usage

```
SET FUNCTION nKeyNumber | cKeyLabel TO [ cCharSequence ]
```

SET FUNCTION assigns the specified function key a keyboard macro of the same sort you can create with the Tools/Macros dialog. (It didn't always work this way, but it's a sensible choice.) Once you assign such a macro, whenever you press that function key, FoxPro behaves as if you'd typed in the specified key sequence wherever the focus rests.

nKeyNumber corresponds not to the numbers you pass to FKLABEL(), which start with 0, but to the actual number on the function key. That is, SET FUNCTION 2 TO something-or-other is the same as SET FUNCTION F2 to something-or-other. With COMPATIBLE ON, SET FUNCTION 12 is the same as SET FUNCTION CTRL+F2.

The sequence of characters is specified as a string and must be enclosed in quotes (unless you store it to a variable first). Use ";" to indicate a return. If you're putting a command in, you need that semicolon or the command just sits there and waits.

Before VFP 5, by default, functions F2 through F9 had keyboard macros set up when you started FoxPro. Several of these were quite useful during development. F5 executed DISPLAY STRUCTURE, F6 was DISPLAY STATUS and F7 was DISPLAY MEMORY. Tamar used these all the time. (Ted has a cat who likes to run across the keyboard.) On the other hand, we hardly ever remembered that F9 was APPEND and we had to look up F8 to find out that it was DISPLAY. By now, you're catching on that these assignments go back to the very beginnings of Xbase history. None of them belongs in any application. However, we know that lots of people don't turn them off by the frequency with which we hear complaints about SET or APPEND turning up in people's data. CLEAR MACROS turns off these macros as well as any others you've defined or loaded. RESTORE MACROS restores either this default set or any other set you've stored away.

The new debugger added in VFP 5 has its own uses for the function keys, so the default assignments were removed. Tamar was aggravated, but she's gotten used to it. Ted never noticed because of his cat.

There is no way to determine what is stored to a function key macro programmatically. Ted's favorite macro, one to place a comment with his initials and today's date at the end of the current line of code, has to be programmed via the Record Macro dialog each day, because you cannot set macros containing control-key sequences in code.

Example

```
* Give the user a shortcut for entering today's data
SET FUNCTION F9 TO "KEYBOARD DTOC(DATE());"
```

See Also Clear Macros, On Key Label, Restore Macros, Save Macros, Set, Set Compatible

FldList() See Set Fields.

FLock(), IsFLocked(), IsRLocked(), Sys(2011)

FLOCK() locks all records in a table, preventing any other user from obtaining a lock on the file. Records are still visible for others to view, browse and report on. SYS(2011) can be used to detect the status of the current record, without attempting to actually place a lock on the record. The Is?Locked() functions return a logical rather than SYS(2011)'s localizable string, for easier internationalization.

Usage

```
lResult = FLOCK( [ nWorkArea | cAlias ] )
```

Parameter	Value	Meaning
nWorkArea	Integer	Specifies the work area of the table to be locked.
	Omitted	If cAlias is also omitted, the file lock is attempted in the current work area.
cAlias	Character	Specifies the alias of the table to be locked.

Parameter	Value	Meaning
cAlias	Omitted	If nWorkArea is also omitted, the file lock is attempted in the current work area.
lResult	.T.	The lock was placed successfully.
	.F.	No lock was placed, either because others have locks on the table, or because there's no table open in the specified area or with the supplied alias.

You can use FLOCK() to ensure that changes to all records will be performed, say, before issuing a REPLACE ALL command. We try to avoid using this command, unless all records must be locked, since it must be manually released with UNLOCK ALL and doesn't scale well into client-server environments. Instead, we try to use table buffering and multi-locks to lock only those records we want to affect. Use BEGIN TRANSACTION, ROLLBACK and END TRANSACTION to ensure that all or none of the updates are made to the tables.

Example

```
? FLOCK("Customer")
```

Usage

```
cReturn = SYS(2011)
lLock = ISFLOCKED( [ nWorkArea | cAlias ] )
lLock = ISRLOCKED( [ nRecNo, [ nWorkArea | cAlias ]  ])
```

Parameter	Value	Meaning
cReturn	"Exclusive"	The current table is opened exclusively.
	"Record Unlocked"	The current record is not locked by this workstation.
	"Record Locked"	The current record is locked by this workstation.
	Empty String	There is no table open in the current work area.
nRecno	Integer	The record number whose lock is tested.
lLock	.T.	The file or record is already locked.
	.F.	The file or record is not locked, or, if you specified a work area, no table is open in that work area.

SYS(2011) has confused a number of developers, who think this function tells them whether or not they will be able to lock the record. It doesn't. This function just reports whether the local FoxPro application has the record locked. In order to determine if someone else has the record or file locked, the application must attempt to lock the record. This function is missing a second, optional parameter, allowing the developer to specify the alias or work area of the record of concern. It is notable by its absence. Like all SYS() functions, SYS(2011) won't give you an error if you supply too many parameters, so don't think that SYS(2011, lcAlias) is actually working on the alias you specify. SYS(2011) returns the localized lock status as text, such as "File Locked," "Exclusive," "Record Locked" or "Record Unlocked." This is almost useless in an application that might run on several different localized runtimes. So, in VFP 5, Microsoft introduced the two IS functions, which return a logical result, regardless of the language in use. Unlike SYS(2011), however, you may not get the whole picture. If a table is open exclusively, ISFLOCKED() reports .T., while ISRLOCKED() reports .F. So, to get the full story on whether a REPLACE can be sure to work, you need to check ISEXCLUSIVE() OR ISFLOCKED() OR ISRLOCKED().

Even more confusing, the IS functions return .F. if the work area you specify has no table open. If, on the other hand, you supply a bogus alias, you get the error "Alias not found." These functions should consistently do one or the other.

Example

```
? SYS(2011)
lSafeToSave = ISEXCLUSIVE() OR ISFLOCKED() OR ISRLOCKED()
```

See Also Begin Transaction, CursorSetProp(), IsExclusive(), Lock, Unlock

Floor() See Ceiling().

Flush, Set Autosave, Set("Autosave")

No, this is not the command to let you do what you'd like with that last guy's code. FLUSH forces cached writes of data to the disk. SET AUTOSAVE permits you to determine how often the automated flush will occur. Both are less necessary than they were with earlier versions of the software and less reliable hardware of the past.

Usage

```
FLUSH
```

FLUSH empties all buffers of data to be written to disk. Buffers are automatically flushed when the table is closed or a record is unlocked.

In rare cases, the loss of a computer or the network before all disk writes are completed can result in the loss of data within a record, or even the corruption of a table header, leading to the dreaded "Not a table" error message. Visual FoxPro and its immediate predecessors seem to be better at this than the bad old days of dBASE III and FoxBase, but we're not sure how much of this is due to improvements in the product and how much is due to more reliable hardware and much more common UPSes. Also, new logic was added into the process of opening a file in VFP, so that if it detects the header is "one off" from the actual record count, it just increments the header count, invisibly and silently, and continues the file open process. In addition, because releasing record and file locks automatically flushes the data (although not the file headers), the increased popularity of rapid lock-update-unlock techniques has probably also contributed to the overall reliability of our systems. Row- and table-buffering techniques that also commit data to disk as rapidly as possible alleviate most of the need for this command.

Our ever-astute technical editor has had more practical experience with this than we have, and he reports that buffering seems to update the data records, but not always the table and memo headers. Even an explicit FLUSH may not be the solution—Doug reports that FLUSH updates the table and memo file headers but not the CDX header. Closing a file, issuing an explicit FLUSH, or waiting for the timeout for automatic flushing (we think that that is five minutes, set internally and inaccessible to us) may still not be sufficient for the most paranoid. Realistically, the command is a FoxPro solution for something that is not a FoxPro problem—the problem is the environment in which you are asking FoxPro to perform. If your network suffers frequent crashes, fix it. Until you can, consider FLUSHes as a Band-aid to lower the frequency, but not necessarily eliminate, file corruption. If the crashing can't be stopped, consider a more robust data storage technique like client-server instead of the direct writing to ISAM files of the FoxPro DBF model.

Forcing a FLUSH defeats the automated caching of Visual FoxPro and leads to degraded performance. Because writes are performed automatically upon the release of locks, the only situations in which FLUSH is likely to save more data is where tables are being bulk-updated in an exclusive or file-locked situation.

Bottom line: If you're losing a lot of data, you can use FLUSH to improve the situation a little. But improving the online reliability of your system will be a far better long-term investment. We don't use this command much at all.

Usage

```
SET AUTOSAVE ON | OFF
cOnOrOff = SET( "AUTOSAVE" )
```

This is a second opportunity for you to force disk writes more often. Setting AUTOSAVE ON forces updates to be written when READs are exited or control returns to the Command Window. While it is not documented as doing so, we suspect that setting AUTOSAVE ON also flushes buffers as each form is closed, since it does have a data session scoping. If you need to do a lot of updating to your system interactively or from the Command Window and have problems with the system staying up long enough for your changes to be written to disk, SET AUTOSAVE ON. The tradeoff might be slightly slower performance. As we mentioned above, in most cases it is much better to make the system more reliable than to drag down performance with commands such as these.

See Also Clear, Close, CursorSetProp(), FFlush(), Set MultiLocks, Set Reprocess, Use

FontBold, FontItalic, FontName, FontSize, FontStrikeThru, FontUnderline, FontOutline, FontShadow

These properties control the font characteristics of forms and controls. FontBold, FontItalic, FontStrikeThru and FontUnderline are all logical—.T. means the control's text should use that font characteristic. FontOutline and FontShadow don't do anything in VFP/Windows, though they control the specified font characteristics in VFP/Mac.

Usage

```
oObject.FontBold = lBoldValue
lBoldValue = oObject.FontBold
oObject.FontItalic = lItalicValue
lItalicValue = oObject.FontItalic
oObject.FontName = cNameValue
cNameValue = oObject.FontName
oObject.FontSize = nSizeValue
nSizeValue = oObject.FontSize
oObject.FontStrikeThru = lStrikeThruValue
lStrikeThruValue = oObject.FontStrikeThru
oObject.FontUnderline = lUnderlineValue
lUnderlineValue = oObject.FontUnderline
```

The docs say FontSize can go up to 2048 points, but we haven't been able to get past 127 without an error message. This isn't terribly limiting—at 127 points, you can get about five characters across a 640x480 screen. We can't imagine wanting anything much bigger than that.

The controls on a form do not inherit their font characteristics from the form. The form's Font properties affect only text written directly on the form—for example, with the form's Print method or sent directly to the form by various output commands when the form is active.

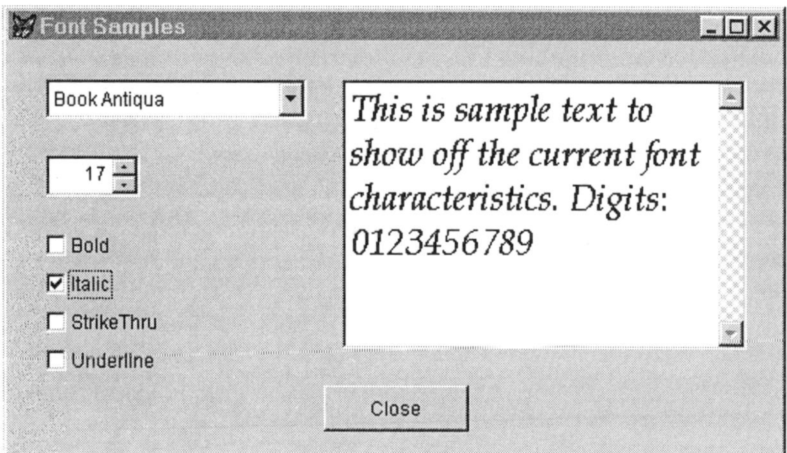

Figure 4 – 6: Font Characteristics Form

The CD contains a form that lets you play with font characteristics. The form is shown in Figure 4-6. The ControlSource for each of the controls other than the edit box is set to the appropriate font characteristic of the edit box. For example, the ControlSource for the Bold check box is:

```
ThisForm.edtSample.FontBold
```

There's only one complication on this form. Spinners don't update their ControlSource until you leave, so instead the InteractiveChange method of the spinner contains the following line:

```
ThisForm.edtSample.FontSize=this.Value
```

which updates the sample right away.

Example

```
* Set an object to use 12-point Courier New Italic
This.FontName="Courier New"
This.FontSize=12
This.FontBold=.F.
This.FontItalic=.T.
This.FontStrikeThru=.F.
This.FontUnderline=.F.
```

See Also AFont(), DynamicFontBold, DynamicFontItalic, DynamicFontName, DynamicFontOutline, DynamicFontShadow, DynamicFontSize, DynamicFontStrikeThru, DynamicFontUnderline, GetFont()

FontCondense, FontExtend

Another pair of do-nothing properties. These were added in version 3.0b in preparation for the Macintosh version of Visual FoxPro, where they control condensed and extended fonts. In VFP for Windows, they're ignored.

See Also FontName, FontOutline, FontShadow

FontItalic **See FontBold.**

FontMetric(), SysMetric()

Everything you ever wanted to know about your fonts and the display subsystem, dredged right out of the heart of the Windows API.

Usage

```
nResult = FONTMETRIC( nFontAttribute
                      [, cFontName, nFontSize [, cFontStyle ] ] )
nResult = SYSMETRIC( nScreenAttribute )
```

Parameter	Value	Meaning
nFontAttribute	Numeric, 1 – 20	An index to the specific attribute of the font you want returned. See the Help file for the list.
cFontName	Character	Name of the font to be examined.
	Omitted	Uses the current font in the active window.
nFontSize	Numeric	Size in points of the font to be examined.
	Omitted	May only be omitted if cFontName, above, is also omitted. Uses the current font in the active window.
cFontStyle	Character	Font Style—see the Help file for the entire list.
	Omitted	If all of the optional parameters are omitted, uses the font style of the active window. If a font name and size are specified, uses the Normal style of the specified font.
nScreenAttribute	Numeric, 1 – 32	Returns information on the screen's measurements.

Use these functions to determine the characteristics of fonts and of the display in order to place your output most precisely. These functions are, for all practical purposes, identical to their Windows API counterparts, FontMetric() and GetSystemMetric(). These functions only deal with pixels, rather than the foxel measurement system available through the ScaleMode property.

Example

```
WAIT WINDOW "Current screen resolution is " + ;
        LTRIM(STR(SYSMETRIC(1))) + " by " + ;
        LTRIM(STR(SYSMETRIC(2)))

? FONTMETRIC(7,"Times New Roman",10,"B")  && 17 pixels
```

See Also AFont(), FontBold, FontItalic, FontName, FontOutline, FontShadow, FontSize, FontStrikethru, FontUnderline, GetFont(), ScaleMode, TextWidth, TextHeight, TxtWidth(), WFont()

FontName, FontOutline, FontShadow, FontSize, FontStrikeThru, FontUnderline See FontBold.

FOpen() See Low-Level File Functions.

For

This command creates a counted loop. The commands inside the loop are executed a set number of times. Don't confuse this command with the FOR clause that's permitted on many commands. (See "Scope, FOR, WHILE and Santa Clauses" for more on that one.)

Usage

```
FOR CounterName = nStart TO nStop [ STEP nIncrement ]
    [Commands]
    [EXIT]
    [LOOP]
ENDFOR | NEXT
```

Parameter	Value	Meaning
CounterName	Numeric	The loop counter. It's initially assigned nStart, then changed by nIncrement each time through until it passes nStop. Created if it doesn't exist.
nStart	Numeric	The starting point of the loop.
nStop	Numeric	The ending point of the loop.
nIncrement	Omitted	Increase CounterName by 1 each time through the loop.
	Numeric	Indicates how much CounterName changes by each time through the loop.
Commands	Any Visual FoxPro commands	The command(s) to be executed each time through the loop.

nIncrement can be positive or negative. It doesn't have to be an integer, so you can increment by .5 or 2.7395, if that's what you need. If nIncrement is negative, nStart is normally larger than nStop. The loop ends when CounterName passes nStop (in the direction determined by nIncrement)—CounterName doesn't ever have to exactly equal nStop.

Watch out for one subtle point. If nStart and nStop are equal, the commands inside the loop execute exactly once. If nStart is greater than nStop and nIncrement is positive, or nStart is less than nStop and nIncrement is negative, the commands don't execute at all.

Any of nStart, nStop and nIncrement can be expressions. But the expression is evaluated only once—when you first reach the loop. The boundaries and the increment are "burned in" and don't change, no matter what you do to the variables involved inside the loop.

You can change the value of CounterName inside the loop, but we don't recommend it. It's the road to a maintenance nightmare.

LOOP and EXIT allow you to short-circuit the loop. LOOP bails out of the current pass through the loop, and goes back to increment the counter and try again. EXIT bails out of the loop entirely, continuing with the next command after ENDFOR.

Structured programming theory says that every construct in a program should have one entrance and one exit. Both LOOP and EXIT violate this rule. Since neither one is necessary (you can always set a logical flag and use IF to skip any commands you want to), we recommend you use them very sparingly. We avoid LOOP entirely; EXIT is useful because it allows some loops to be written as FOR loops rather than DO WHILE. There's an example of this below.

It's a little-known fact that you can end a FOR loop with NEXT rather than ENDFOR. Unlike Basic's NEXT, you don't repeat the loop counter, though, as in NEXT X.

VFP 5 added the FOR EACH command, which lets you loop through all the elements of a collection or array without using a counter. It's a good alternative to FOR in a number of situations.

Example

```
* Get a list of tables
nDBFCount = ADIR(aDBFs,"*.dbf")

* Now print them out
FOR nCnt = 1 TO nDBFCount
    ? aDBFs[nCnt, 1]
ENDFOR

* Since the array created by ADIR() has 5 columns, the STEP
* clause provides an alternate way to write the loop above.
* Since the output of ADIR() could change in future versions,
* the code above is preferred, though
FOR nCnt = 1 TO ALEN(aDBFs) STEP 5
    ? aDBFs[nCnt]
ENDFOR

* Add up values in an array (aValues) until you top 1000
* This example can be done with FOR or DO WHILE.
* Both versions are here.

* FOR version
nTotal = 0
FOR nCnt = 1 TO ALEN(aValues)
    nTotal = nTotal + aValues[nCnt]
    IF nTotal > 1000
        EXIT
    ENDIF
ENDFOR

* DO WHILE version
nTotal = 0
nCnt = 1
DO WHILE nCnt <= ALEN(aValues) AND nTotal <= 1000
    nTotal = nTotal + aValues[nCnt]
ENDDO
```

See Also Do While, Exit, For Each, If, Loop, Scan

For Each

This command, introduced in VFP 5, is a variation on the traditional counted FOR loop. It lets you go through all the elements in an array or collection without having to figure out up front how many there are. Unlike a regular FOR loop, FOR EACH can handle some changes in the size of the array or collection inside the loop.

Usage

```
FOR EACH uRef IN aGroup
    [ Commands ]
    [ EXIT ]
    [ LOOP ]
ENDFOR | NEXT
```

Parameter	Value	Meaning
uRef	Variable	A variable that takes on the value of each element of the array or collection in turn.
aGroup	Array or Collection	The array or collection to be processed.
Commands	Any Visual FoxPro commands	The command(s) to be executed each time through the loop.

One annoying feature of a FOR loop is that you have to figure out ahead of time where it ends. For arrays, this often means using ALEN(). The flip side of this is that the endpoint is calculated once, on the way into the loop, and if the array's size changes inside the loop, either the loop bombs (because the array got shorter) or it simply doesn't process the new items. FOR EACH is the solution to this problem. Rather than using an explicit counter, you tell it to process every member of an array or collection. The loop continues until each element has been touched, even if the array grows or shrinks inside the loop.

Beware, though—FOR EACH processes the elements in order. If you insert new items into the middle of an array, and the loop has already passed that point, the new elements are not processed and some old elements may be handled more than once. Similarly, if you remove items in the middle of a loop (using ADEL() or by removing items from a collection), some items may not get processed. Although *you* don't have to keep a counter, FOR EACH uses one internally and does process each element in order.

The variable uRef takes on the value of each item of the array in turn. This is especially handy when you're processing a collection; in that case, uRef gives you an object reference to a member of the collection. For example, if you use a FOR EACH loop on a form's Controls collection, uRef provides an object reference to each control in the collection in turn, and you can manipulate that object's properties and call its methods using the reference.

Be careful, however, when you're processing an array that doesn't contain object references. uRef gets the value of the element, not a pointer to it. This means that changes to uRef do *not* affect the array itself. Also, uRef is created as a private variable if it has not already been explictly declared. Good programming practices dictate you should always be declaring your variables and their scope. This is one of those situations where a LOCAL or PUBLIC declaration could prove essential.

LOOP and EXIT behave here the same as they do for regular FOR loops—they let you jump out from the middle. LOOP sends you on to the next item, while EXIT ends the loop altogether.

Example

```
* Get a list of all the open forms in the main VFP window and
* minimize those that are maximized
ACTIVATE SCREEN
FOR EACH oForm IN _SCREEN.Forms
   ? oForm.Caption
   IF oForm.WindowState = 2
```

```
        oFormWindowState = 1
    ENDIF
ENDFOR
```

See Also For, Local

For() See Candidate().

ForceExt(), ForcePath() See AddBS().

ForeColor See BackColor.

Form, Formset

Forms and formsets are container classes that, from one point of view, put the "visual" in Visual FoxPro. Formsets contain forms and toolbars. Forms contain controls.

Form

Property	Value	Meaning
ActiveControl	Object	A reference to the control on the form that currently has focus.
AlwaysOnBottom	Logical	Determines whether this form always stays underneath other windows, like a kind of wallpaper.
AlwaysOnTop	Logical	Determines whether this form stays on top of other windows, even when it doesn't have focus.
AutoCenter	Logical	Determines whether the form automatically centers itself when it first appears. Also allows you to center a form at any time.
BorderStyle	Numeric	Determines the type of border of the form. Also determines whether the form can be resized.
BufferMode	Numeric	Determines the type of buffering used for cursors in the form's data environment, unless the cursors override this setting individually.
Caption	Character	The title that appears in the form's border.
ClipControls	Logical	Determines what gets redrawn when the form is resized or controls are moved about.
Closable	Logical	Determines whether the form can be closed by the operator with the mouse and Ctrl+F4.
ContinuousScroll	Logical	Determines how the form behaves when you use the scrollbars.
ControlBox	Logical	Determines whether the form has a Windows standard control menu.
ControlCount	Numeric	The number of controls currently on the form.

Property	Value	Meaning
Controls	Collection	References to the controls currently on the form.
CurrentX, CurrentY	Numeric	The position of the drawing cursor on the form.
DataSession	Numeric	Determines whether the form has its own private data session.
DataSessionId	Numeric	The data session being used by the form.
DefOLELCId	Numeric	Indicates the default locale ID (language) for OLE objects used in the form.
Desktop	Logical	Determines whether the form is contained in the main Visual FoxPro window.
DrawMode	Numeric	Determines the way colors work in drawing methods.
DrawStyle	Numeric	The type of lines drawn by drawing methods.
DrawWidth	Numeric	The width of lines drawn by drawing methods.
FillColor	Numeric	The color used to fill figures drawn with drawing methods.
FillStyle	Numeric	The pattern used to fill figures drawn with drawing methods.
HalfHeightCaption	Logical	Determines whether the title bar uses a FoxPro/DOS compatibility style or the standard Windows style. Although the two choices are nearly indistinguishable visually, there are functional differences. Keep this property set to .F.
HScrollSmallChange	Numeric	Determines how far the form scrolls on a single click on a horizontal scroll arrow.
Icon	Character	The icon file used in the form's title bar.
KeyPreview	Logical	Determines whose KeyPress event fires when the user presses a key—the form's or the control's.
LockScreen	Logical	Determines whether the form is visually updated immediately when some kinds of changes are made to the form or its controls.
MaxButton, MinButton	Logical	Determines whether the form has maximize and minimize buttons.
MaxHeight, MaxWidth	Numeric	The largest size to which the user can resize the form.
MaxLeft, MaxTop	Numeric	The position at which the form appears when maximized.
MDIForm	Logical	Determines whether the form behaves like an MDI (multiple document interface) form.
MinHeight, MinWidth	Numeric	The smallest size to which the user can resize the form.

Property	Value	Meaning
Movable	Logical	Determines whether the user can move the form.
Picture	Character	Filename of a picture to be tiled as wallpaper on the form.
ReleaseType	Numeric	Indicates how the form was released.
ScaleMode	Numeric	The measurement system used for the form.
ScrollBars	Numeric	Determines what kind of scrollbars, if any, the form has.
ShowTips	Logical	Determines whether tooltips are displayed.
ShowWindow	Numeric	Determines whether the form is a child of the VFP window, a top-level form itself, or a child of a top-level form.
TitleBar	Numeric	Determines whether the form has a title bar.
ViewPortHeight, ViewPortWidth	Numeric	Indicate the size of the viewport into the form, that is, the size of the visible area.
ViewPortLeft, ViewPortTop	Numeric	Indicate the top left corner of the portion of the form currently visible.
VScrollSmallChange	Numeric	Determines how far the form scrolls on a single click on a vertical scroll arrow.
WindowState	Numeric	Is the form normal size, maximized or minimized?
WindowType	Numeric	Indicates whether the form is modal or modeless. Also used to indicate READ compatibility.

Event	Purpose
Activate, Deactivate	Fire when the form gains or loses focus.
Load, Unload	First and last events to fire.
Moved	Fires when the form is moved.
Paint	Fires when part of the form is exposed and has to be redrawn.
QueryUnload	Fires when the form is released. Issue NODEFAULT in this method to prevent the form from being destroyed.
Resize	Fires when the form is resized.
Scrolled	Fires when the form's scrollbars are used.

Method	Purpose
Box, Circle, Line	Drawing methods that put figures on the form.

Method	Purpose
Box, Circle, Line	Drawing methods that put figures on the form.
Cls	Drawing method that clears figures and text from the form.
Draw	Repaints the form.
Point	Returns the color of a particular point.
Print	Drawing method that puts text on the form.
Pset	Sets the color of a particular point.
Release	Destroys the form.
SaveAs	Creates a new SCX based on the currently displayed form.
SaveAsClass	Creates a new class in a VCX based on the currently displayed form.
SetViewPort	Sets the ViewPortLeft and ViewPortTop properties to determine which portion of the form is visible.
Show, Hide	Make the form visible and invisible. Show also activates the form initially.
TextHeight, TextWidth	Return the height and width of a specified string in the current form's font.

FormSet

Property	Value	Meaning
ActiveForm	Object	Reference to the form in the set that has focus.
AutoRelease	Logical	Indicates whether the formset object should be released when all the forms in the set have been released.
BufferMode	Numeric	Determines the type of buffering used by default for cursors in the formset.
DataSession	Numeric	Determines whether the formset has its own private data session.
DataSessionId	Numeric	The data session being used by the formset.
FormCount	Numeric	The number of forms in the set.
Forms	Collection	References to the forms in the set.
ReadCycle, ReadLock, ReadMouse, ReadObject, ReadSave, ReadTimeOut, WindowList	Various	Special properties used only in forms converted from FoxPro 2.x screens. They correspond to various READ clauses.

Property	Value	Meaning
WindowType	Numeric	Indicates whether the formset is modal or modeless. Also used to indicate READ compatibility.
Event	**Purpose**	
Activate, Deactivate	Fire when the formset gains or loses focus.	
Load, Unload	First and last events to fire in the formset.	
ReadActivate, ReadDeactivate, ReadShow, ReadValid, ReadWhen	Events to model FoxPro 2.x READ clauses. Used only for forms converted from FoxPro 2.x screens.	
Method	**Purpose**	
Release	Destroys the formset.	
Show, Hide	Makes the formset visible and invisible. Show also activates the formset initially.	

Forms and formsets are different from other objects in Visual FoxPro for several reasons. First, there are two different ways to create and activate them. Like other objects, they can be stored as classes, then instantiated with CreateObject() or NewObject(). However, individual form and formset instances can also be stored in SCX files and executed with Do Form. (Note that form and formset classes stored in VCX libraries do not include a data environment, while forms stored in SCXs do.)

The second difference is that forms and formsets have Load and Unload methods that fire before Init and after Destroy, respectively. Load lets you open databases and tables before the controls in a form are instantiated and initialized, so you can bind controls to fields. Similarly, the controls need to be destroyed before you can close the tables—Unload (which follows the Destroys for the controls) gives you that opportunity. (You use Load and Unload for table handling only if you're not letting the data environment automatically open and close tables. Since you can't save a data environment with a form or formset class, there are some good reasons to use Load and Unload this way.)

The firing sequence is confusing, though, because parameters to a form or formset are normally passed to the Init method, just like other controls, even though other events fire first. (For forms converted from 2.x, parameters go to the Load method.)

It took us awhile to catch on that windows you create with DEFINE WINDOW are really forms, too. In fact, there's no reason ever to define a window again. Just instantiate a form and you can put whatever you want in it. There's nothing to keep you from putting a Browse in an instantiated form, for example (not that we use Browse anything but interactively in Visual FoxPro).

Example

```
DEFINE CLASS HackForm AS Form
   Caption = "Hacker's Example Form"
   BackColor = RGB(0,0,255)
   ForeColor = RGB(255,255,255)

   PROCEDURE Resize
      LOCAL cMessage
      cMessage = "Hey, watch it buster!"
      This.Cls
      This.CurrentX = (This.Width-This.TextWidth(cMessage))/2
      This.CurrentY = This.Height/2
      This.Print(cMessage)
```

```
      ENDPROC

      PROCEDURE Moved
         LOCAL cMessage
         cMessage = "Who do you think you're moving?"
         This.Cls
         This.FillColor = RGB(255,0,0)
         This.FillStyle = 0
         This.Box(This.Width/4, This.Height/4,;
                  3*This.Width/4,3*This.Height/4 )
         This.CurrentY = This.Height/2
         This.CurrentX = This.Width/4 + 2
         This.Print(cMessage)
      ENDPROC
   ENDDEFINE
```

See Also Activate, ActiveControl, ActiveForm, AlwaysOnBottom, AlwaysOnTop, AutoCenter, AutoRelease, BorderStyle, Box, BufferMode, Caption, Circle, ClipControls, Closable, Cls, ContinuousScroll, ControlBox, ControlCount, Controls, Create Form, CreateObject(), CurrentX, CurrentY, DataEnvironment, DataSession, DataSessionId, Deactivate, Define Window, DefOLELCId, Desktop, Do Form, Draw, DrawMode, DrawStyle, FillColor, FillStyle, FormCount, Forms, HalfHeightCaption, Hide, HScrollSmallChange, Icon, KeyPreview, Line, Load, LockScreen, MaxButton, MaxHeight, MaxLeft, MaxTop, MaxWidth, MDIForm, MinButton, MinHeight, MinWidth, Movable, Moved, NewObject(), Paint, Picture, Point, Print, PSet, QueryUnload, ReadActivate, ReadCycle, ReadDeactivate, ReadLock, ReadMouse, ReadObject, ReadSave, ReadShow, ReadTimeOut, ReadValid, ReadWhen, Release, ReleaseType, Resize, SaveAs, SaveAsClass, ScaleMode, ScrollBars, Scrolled, SetViewPort, Show, ShowTips, ShowWindow, TextWidth, TextHeight, TitleBar, Unload, ViewPortHeight, ViewPortLeft, ViewPortTop, ViewPortWidth, VScrollSmallChange, WindowList, WindowState, WindowType

Format

Format describes the rules for acceptable characters that can be entered by the user, or the rules used to display fields or memory variables for output. It is the controls' equivalent of the FORMAT clause used with @... GET input, and recognizes the same options:

Format character	Meaning
A	Alphabetic characters only.
B	Left-justifies numeric data.
D	Display in the current date format. Used primarily with date variables, but it works with strings and datetimes. No built-in validation for character strings.
E	Use British date format: month-day-year, separators determined by SET MARK TO, century display by SET CENTURY. Same behavior as "D" format.
I	Center text within the field (try this, if you must, only with non-proportional fonts!).
J	Right-justifies text within field.
K	Select entire control on entry to field. This one's here for backward compatibility—use the SelectOnEntry property instead
L	Display leading zeroes. Useful only with numeric values.

Format character	Meaning
M*list*	Multiple-choice box. While a neat idea, we recommend you stay away from this one, and try listboxes and drop-down lists instead. List consists of comma-delimited explicit text, rather than the variables or data-driven lists possible with other controls. Bad things happen if the variable is undefined or of the wrong type.
R	Specifies that characters in the InputMask that do not have special meaning (see InputMask) serve as placeholders in the format mask and are not returned as values to the field.
Sn	Scrolling region of n characters. A handy way to squeeze too much text into too little space. Use with the SIZE clause to limit the size of the text box. An edit box is recommended as a better and more intuitive alternative.
T	Trim both leading and trailing spaces before returning values to field.
YS	Display a date using the Short format from the Control Panel.
YL	Display a date using the Control Panel's Long format.
Z	Display zeroes as blanks.
!	Convert alphabetic to uppercase.
^	Display numbers in scientific notation. Lousy for input—it does not allow typing mantissa nor exponent, only a whole number and decimal place. Use for display only.
$	Display the currency symbols specified with SET CURRENCY.

The FORMAT property needs to be specified only once and applies to the entire field. This is a "global" format for the field, differing from the InputMask property, which is specified on a character-by-character basis. Because Format and InputMask share many of the same letters, this often leads to confusion. When expressed in a single command, such as an @...SAY clause or a TRANSFORM() function, FORMAT properties are distinguished by being preceded with an @ symbol.

Example

```
@ 5,5 get lcSSN picture "@R 999-99-9999"  && Social Security #
? TRANSFORM(12345.67, "@$ 999,999.99")  && yields $ 12,345.67
* Depending on your Control Panel Regional Settings,
* you may see a different output:
? Transform({^1999-06-02},"@YL")
* yields "Wednesday, June 2, 1999"

* The equivalent of the first example above for a VFP control
ThisForm.txtSSN.Format = "R"
ThisForm.txtSSN.Picture = "999-99-999"
```

See Also @ ... Get, InputMask, SelectOnEntry, Set Currency, Set Mark, Set Point, Set Separator, Transform()

Forms, FormCount

Forms is a collection property—it's an array containing one entry for each form in a form set. FormCount tells you how many forms there are, but, in VFP 3, it gets confused by toolbars.

Usage

```
frmForm = frsFormSet.Forms ( nIndex )
nFormCount = frsFormSet.FormCount
```

You can't change either of these properties directly. They're there for reference only.

For a form set, Forms shows you the forms in the set in creation order. Any toolbars in the set are included in the collection, whether they're docked or not.

When you apply Forms to _SCREEN, it gets a little more complicated. Every form displayed on the screen is listed, but the order in which they're listed changes based on which form is active. Then, there are toolbars. Custom toolbars that are displayed get included in _SCREEN's Forms collection. But in VFP 3.0, they disappear from Forms when you dock them. Visual FoxPro's built-in toolbars never appear in Forms.

In VFP 3, FormCount forgets to count toolbars at all, whether or not they're listed in Forms at that moment. Unless you're checking _SCREEN's FormCount. Then, it counts undocked toolbars, but not docked toolbars. (The behavior we describe here is in VFP 3.0b. We think it may have been different in 3.0.) These bugs are fixed in VFP 5 and VFP 6.

To add to the misery, you can't apply ALEN() to Forms to find out how many there really are. (In fact, even though the collection properties look like arrays, you can't apply any of the array functions to them.) And the FOR EACH loop that keeps you from needing ALEN() isn't available in VFP 3, where the bugs occur.

In VFP 5 and VFP 6, the Objects collection also gives you access to all the forms in a form set. For the _VFP application variable, Objects gives you access to all the active forms or form sets. But note that form sets get a single entry in Objects, not one for each form. You can then drill down to find the individual forms.

Example

```
* Check if a particular form is in a given formset
FOR nCount = 1 TO ThisFormSet.FormCount
   IF Forms[nCount].Name = cName
      WAIT WINDOW "Found It"
      EXIT
   ENDIF
ENDFOR
```

See Also ControlCount, Controls, Objects, _SCREEN, _VFP

Found()

This function reports on the success of various search commands. It's affected by LOCATE, CONTINUE, SEEK, SEEK(), INDEXSEEK(), relations and the antique FIND command.

Usage `lFoundMatch = FOUND( [ cAlias | nWorkArea ] )`

FOUND() is maintained separately for each work area and always reflects the most recent search there. If you need to hang on to the result, it's wise to store it to a variable before proceeding.

LOCATE, CONTINUE, SEEK, SEEK(), INDEXSEEK() and FIND all affect FOUND() pretty much the same way. You issue one of those commands, and FOUND() returns .T. if the command was successful and .F. otherwise. (Interestingly, KEYMATCH() doesn't update FOUND().) On the whole, we think it's a better choice to check IF FOUND() after a search than to use IF EOF(), as many folks who've been using Xbase for a long time do. Not only is IF FOUND() easier to read and understand, but it also avoids any possible issues with a search using SET NEAR or one that's limited in some way and, therefore, doesn't move the record pointer to end-of-file. The subtle case is using FOUND() with a relation. When a temporal relation has been established (with SET RELATION), you can check FOUND("the child alias") to determine whether a parent record has any children. If it does, FOUND("the child alias") returns .T. You can use this in a filter or FOR clause to affect only parents with child records.

Example

```
USE Employee ORDER Last_Name
SEEK "FULLER"
? FOUND()        && Returns .T.
SEEK "HOSSENPFEFFER"
? FOUND()        && Returns .F.
```

```
USE Customer
USE Orders IN 0 ORDER Customer_I
SET RELATION TO Customer_Id INTO Orders
* look at all customers without orders
BROW FOR NOT FOUND("Orders")
```

See Also Continue, Find, IndexSeek(), KeyMatch(), Locate, Seek, Seek(), Set Near, Set Relation

Fox, FoxPro

Two variables that don't exist until you declare them, and then they're immediately .T., these were added in an era when generic Xbase code could bracket functions that should run only under the Fox languages.

Usage

```
PUBLIC FOX | FOXPRO
lRunningWithTheFox = FOX | FOXPRO
```

Parameter	Value	Meaning
lRunningWithTheFox	.T.	When you're running in a Fox product, FOXPRO is true in FoxPro 1.x or later, while FOX is true in FoxBase and later.
	.F.	Running under some other language.

In days long past, it wasn't unusual for a developer to write an application in his favorite development environment, run the code for testing in another, and compile the code into a compact little EXE for distribution with a third product. In that case, the code would need to be able to detect which language it was running in before it tried to use any language-specific code. These two variables were the means of detecting the Fox Software FoxBase and FoxPro products.

Normally, declaring variables public initializes them as .F. These two are the exception.

Example

```
RELEASE FOXPRO
PUBLIC FOXPRO
IF FOXPRO
  * do it right…
ENDIF
```

See Also _DOS, _MAC, _UNIX, _WINDOWS

_FoxDoc, _FoxGraph See _Beautify.

FoxTools

FoxTools.FLL is a dynamic link library (DLL) that has been specially compiled with the Visual FoxPro Library Construction Kit (now built into the Professional Edition) so it works with FoxPro. It includes some useful utility functions. Check out HOME() + "\TOOLS\FOXTOOLS.CHM" for additional details.

In Visual FoxPro 6.0, many of these functions have been incorporated directly into the language and no longer require the FLL to be loaded. These include: AddBS(), DefaultExt(), DriveType(), ForceExt(), ForcePath(), and the entire set of Just* functions. However, FoxTools still contains several functions that make it useful, and we include this reference as an aid to those functions as well as to developers unfamiliar with FoxTools who need to maintain code from an older version. The functions included directly within VFP 6.0 are marked with an asterisk.

Registering and Using DLL Functions: RegFn(), RegFn32(), CallFn()

Two functions within FoxTools allow Visual FoxPro applications to access and call functions built into dynamic link libraries (DLLs). The functions called this way may be part of the Windows native API, or they may be supplied by a third party. Any function that can operate when supplied with character and numeric parameters (structures cannot be created and passed from Visual FoxPro) can be run from FoxPro.

Usage

```
nFuncHandle = RegFn( cFuncName, cParamTypes,
                     cRetType, cLocation )
nFuncHandle = RegFn32( cFuncName, cParamTypes,
                       cRetType, cLocation )
```

Parameter	Value	Meaning
cFuncName	Character	The name of the function. Note that many function names are case-sensitive.
cParamTypes	Character	A list of the type of parameters accepted by the function, in the order they must be supplied. Parameters which are to be passed by reference need to be preceded with an '@' symbol. Acceptable types are: C = Character string D = Double-precision floating number F = Floating point I = Integer L = Long S = Short integer
cRetType	Character	A single character, describing the type of the return value of the function.
cLocation	Character	The name of the DLL containing the function. If the function is built into the core Windows API, WIN32API can be specified instead, which allows the same code to run on different Windows installations.

The ability to access DLL functionality using FoxTools was important when introduced in FoxPro 2.5, but it has been superceded somewhat by the addition of the DECLARE-DLL command. However, DECLARE accesses only those DLLs that have been recompiled to work within the 32-bit environment in which Visual FoxPro lives. Older, 16-bit applications are accessible only through the RegFn()-CallFn() sequence.

Registering DLLs works the same way whether they are 16- or 32-bit. First the function must be "registered" with FoxPro: FoxPro must be told the name of the function, its location, what parameters it accepts and what it returns.

In VFP 3 on Win 3.1 installations, RegFn() calls 16-bit DLLs; on 32-bit installations (WinNT and Win 95), RegFn() can also access 32-bit DLLs. RegFN32() always uses 32-bit DLLs. We recommend the use of DECLARE-DLL if you can be sure you're accessing a 32-bit DLL, and RegFn() otherwise.

One last note: If you'll be calling 16-bit functions using RegFn() from the 32-bit platforms, make sure Ddereg.EXE is included in your distribution disks, because this provides the mechanism to communicate with 16-bit DLLs. For VFP 3 running under Win32s, you'll need to include the file Fll32_16.DLL instead.

Usage

```
RetVal = CallFn( nFuncHandle, Param1, Param2, ... )
```

Now that you've gone to all the trouble of declaring the function, invoking it is pretty straightforward. Use the function handle returned to you from the RegFn() function as the first parameter to tell CallFn() which function it should be accessing, then pass the number and type of parameters specified in the RegFn() function. The return value you receive should be of the type specified.

Example

```
* Resource. PRG - Displays free system resources
SET LIBRARY TO home()+"FOXTOOLS" ADDITIVE
nGFSR = RegFn('GetFreeSystemResources', "I", "I", "USER")
? "System Resources ", CallFn(nGFSR,0)
```

```
? "GDI Resources", CallFn(nGFSR,1)
? "User Resources", CallFn(nGFSR,2)
```

File Functions

These functions modify a supplied drive, path, filename and extension to return only a portion of the supplied information or force a specific format. Almost all of these functions have been added to the language in VFP 6.

Function	Parameters	Purpose
AddBS*	cPathAndFile	Returns the string with an ending backslash, if one isn't already present.
CleanPath	cPathAndFile	Makes a best guess at the correct path and filename, removing invalid characters.
DefaultExt*	cPathAndFile, cExt	Appends file extension cExt to cPathAndFile, if no extension is present.
ForceExt*	cPathAndFile, cExt	Forces (appends or replaces) the specified extension onto the filename.
ForcePath*	cPathAndFile, cPath	Forces (prepends or replaces) the specified path onto the filename.
JustDrive*	cPathAndFile	Returns just the drive letter.
JustExt*	cPathAndFile	Returns just the extension.
JustFName*	cPathAndFile	Returns the filename with extension.
JustPath*	cPathAndFile	Returns the path, with drive if supplied.
JustStem*	cPathAndFile	Returns the filename without a path or extension.
ValidPath	cPathAndFile	Determines whether a drive, path, filename and extension could be valid, following the rules of DOS file and path naming restrictions. Does not test for the existence of the path or file. Does not work with operating systems that support spaces in path names.

Clipboard Functions

These functions provide access to the Windows clipboard, to determine the format of the information saved there and manipulate it. Use these functions to examine the contents of the clipboard and request the data in a specific format, or to register the format your application uses to post data onto the clipboard. These can be handy especially if you are using Fpole.DLL to transfer data to and from your application.

Function	Parameters	Purpose
CloseClip	none	Closes the handle opened with OpenClip().
CountClipF	none	Returns the number of different formats in which the information on the clipboard may be requested.
EmptyClip	none	Empties the clipboard.

Function	Parameters	Purpose
EnumClipFm	nIndex	Returns a number corresponding to the format in which the clipboard contents may be requested. See the Windows SDK documentation (WinUser.h) for details.
GetClipDat	nFormat	Retrieves a handle to the current clipboard data in the format specified by nFormat.
GetClipFmt	nFormat	This is supposed to retrieve a custom clipboard format name, but it is way too deep into the weird Windows way for us to follow. If you really need to use this function, we recommend you plow through the Win32 SDK for help.
IsClipFmt	nFormat	Returns a logical response to the query of whether the clipboard contents can be rendered in the specified format.
OpenClip	nWndHandle	Opens the clipboard for manipulation by the other functions listed here. We recommend passing MainHwnd() as the argument.
RegClipFmt	cFormatName	Allows you to register a custom clipboard format, use it to render data into the clipboard and later extract it.
SetClipDat	nFormat, cData	Allows storage of data to the clipboard in the format specified.

String Functions

Functions for doing some useful things with string manipulation.

Function	Parameters	Purpose
NextWord	cText, nPosition [, cDelimiters]	Returns the first word or word fragment starting at position nPosition in the supplied character string or memo field, optionally ending at the specified word delimiters (in addition to space and tab).
Reduce	cString [, cCharacter]	This function is documented as a means to replace repeated occurrences of cCharacter in cString with a single occurrence. It will, as long as cCharacter is a space (or omitted and allowed to default to a space—also undocumented). If it is any other character, all occurrences of that character are obliterated and replaced with spaces. Blech. You can write better.
StrFilter	cString1, cString2	Removes all the characters from cString1 not in cString2. We can do the same thing with STRTRAN() or SYS(15), so we see no particular advantage to this function.
WordNum	cText, nIndex	Returns word number nIndex from supplied character string or memo field.
Words	cText	Returns the number of words in the supplied text.

FoxPro API Functions

These functions allow access to the internal editing and Windows functions of the Visual FoxPro editor. They start with _ED and _W and are documented, not in FoxTools' Help file, but rather in the main Help file supplied with FoxPro.

Miscellaneous Functions

A plethora of other functions got tossed into FoxTools, because someone needed them or asked for them.

Function	Parameters	Purpose
DriveType*	cDriveLetter	There's one difference between the native VFP 6.0 command and the FoxTools function for earlier VFP versions: If the drive does not exist, VFP 5.0 and earlier return 0. VFP 6.0 returns 1. In all other cases, both functions return the type of drive specified: 2=diskette, 3=hard drive, 4=network or removable, 5=CD-ROM, 6=RAM disk.
FoxToolVer	none	Returns the version of FoxTools, "3.12" for Visual FoxPro 3.0b, and "6.00" for VFP 6.0.
GetFileVersion	cFileName, @ArrayName	Introduced in VFP 5.0, superceded by the more useful and native AGETFILEVERSION() in VFP 6.0, this function returns the version information about a file.
GetProStrg	cSection, cEntry, cDefault, @cReturn, nRetLen	Equivalent of Windows API GetProfileString. See the entry DECLARE-DLL for a detailed study of this function.
MainHwnd	none	Returns the window handle of the main FoxPro window required by many Windows API functions.
MkDir	cDirectory	Creates a directory. "Included for backward compatibility"—use the Visual FoxPro MD command instead.
MsgBox	*numerous*	See the FoxTools documentation for all the parameter variations. See also the MessageBox() entry for an explanation of when to use this function rather than MessageBox(), and the undocumented SYSTEMMODAL option.
PutProStrg	cSection, cEntry, cValue	Writes an entry to Win.INI in the format cEntry=cValue. See the discussion in DECLARE-DLL for good reasons not to use this function.
RGBComp	nRGBNumber, @nRedColor, @nGreenColor, @nBlueColor	Returns the values of the three Red, Green and Blue colors from a single color number you get back from a function like GETCOLOR().
RmDir	cDirectory	Removes a directory. "Included for backward compatibility"—use the Visual FoxPro RD command instead.

Many of the functions have been included within FoxTools because they are used in the programs that come with Visual FoxPro—programs such as AddLabel.App, Browser.App, Builder.App and Convert.App. These functions can be included within your own programs, provided that you bundle FoxTools with your application. Note that FoxTools.FLL must actually be included on the disk, and not bound into your APP or EXE, in order to be used.

Example

```
? FoxToolVer()     && returns "6.0"

* Throw some text into the clipboard and see what formats
* it can be pasted into another application
_CLIPTEXT = "Hey!"

NOTE: The results you see will vary by platform, but these ;
      should give you an idea of what to expect.
? OpenClip(0)      && returns .T.
? CountClipF()     && returns 3 (formats)
? EnumClipFm(0)    && returns 1 (CF_TEXT)
? EnumClipFm(1)    && returns 16 (CF_LOCALE)
? EnumClipFm(16)   && returns 7 (CF_OEMTEXT)
? CloseClip()      && returns T.

* Word counting functions:
? words("Four score and seven years ago")         && returns 6
? wordnum("Four score and seven years ago",4)     && "seven"
? nextword("Four score and seven years ago",5)    && "score"


? Reduce("1   2   3")  && returns "1 2 3" (single spaces)
```

See Also AddBS(), AGetFileVersion(), Declare - DLL, DefaultExt(), DriveType(), ForceExt(), ForcePath(), GetColor(), JustDrive(), JustExt(), JustFName(), JustPath(), JustStem(), MD, MessageBox(), RD, Set Library, StrTran, Sys(15)

FPuts(), FRead() See Low-Level File Functions.

Free Table

> No one can be perfectly free till all are free.
>
> Herbert Spencer, *Social Statics*, 1851

This command is designed to save your skin. If you've somehow lost a database (accidentally deleted it, trashed it, or something), it lets you rescue the poor trapped tables within.

Usage `FREE TABLE TableName`

When you add a table to a database, a backlink is added to the table header, pointing at the database (see " DBF, FPT, CDX, DBC—Hike!" for more on this). This is why you can open a table in a database and have the database open up, too. (Of course, it's also one of the primary reasons Visual FoxPro tables aren't backward-compatible.)

If the database can't be found, Visual FoxPro has a quandary. FREE TABLE is the solution to that puzzle. It clears the backlink and turns the table back into a "free table" once again. Don't confuse this command with REMOVE TABLE—that's the one to use for taking a table out of a healthy database. FREE TABLE is for emergencies.

The help for FREE TABLE contains dire warnings about what happens if you free a table and the database is still around. Actually, Visual FoxPro seems to handle this pretty well, offering to re-create the backlink when you try to access the table from within the database. You can, of course, confuse the heck out of FoxPro if you add the table to another database, then try to access it from the first. Each time you try to access it from the one that doesn't own it at the moment, you get prompted to create the backlink. Shades of infinite loops.

The interface also handles the case of a table whose database can't be found. You're prompted to free the table. Since we don't see any of this as the sort of thing you'd put in an application, you may rarely need this command—most of the time, you'll handle these problems through the interface. FREE TABLE will be reserved for times when you have a whole bunch of enslaved tables to emancipate.

Example `FREE TABLE MyTable`

See Also Add Table, Open Database, Remove Table, Validate Database

FSeek() See Low-Level File Functions.

FSize() See FCount().

FTime() See FDate().

FullName See Home().

FullPath(), Sys(2014)

These two functions let you retrieve file paths. FULLPATH() gives you the complete path to a file while SYS(2014) lets you find a relative path between a file and a directory. Both return spurious information about nonexistent files, so you have to check up on them.

Usage

```
cAbsolutePath = FULLPATH( cFileName
                          [, nUseDOSPath | cBaseFile ] )
cRelativePath = SYS( 2014, cFileName [, cBasePath ] )
```

Parameter	Value	Meaning
cFileName	Character	The name of the file whose path you want.
nUseDOSPath	Numeric	Look all along the DOS path to find cFileName.
	Omitted	If cBaseFile is also omitted, look all along the FoxPro path to find cFileName.
cBaseFile	Character	Use the location of cBaseFile as the location from which to do relative addressing.
	Omitted	If nUseDOSPath is also omitted, look all along the FoxPro path to find cFileName.
cBasePath	Character	Find the minimum path to cFileName from cBasePath.
	Omitted	Find the minimum path to cFileName from the default directory.

These two functions do related, yet nearly opposite, things. FULLPATH() takes a pathless or relatively pathed file and returns the absolute path to it. SYS(2014) takes a pathless or absolutely pathed file and returns a relative path to it.

What do we mean by absolute and relative paths? An absolute path is one where the exact directory names are hard-coded—for example, C:\WINDOWS\SYSTEM. A relative path uses the DOS directory shortcuts (especially ".." for "parent of current directory") to provide directions from one place to another. For example, if you're in Visual FoxPro's TOOLS\ADDLABEL directory, you can find Filer.DLL in ..\FILER. It doesn't matter what the name of the Visual FoxPro directory is or on what drive. As long as the directory tree is the one FoxPro installed, the relative path above will find the Filer library.

Within an application, you generally want to use relative paths, so you can install the application in any directory and still have it find its files. Most of Visual FoxPro's meta-data tables (SCX, PJX, and so on) store relative paths whenever possible. But there are times (like for reporting) when you need to know the absolute path to a file. That's where FULLPATH() comes in. Similarly, when you're writing developer tools and other things that store paths, you'll want to convert from an absolute path to a relative path—enter SYS(2014).

If you pass FULLPATH() only cFileName, FoxPro searches the current FoxPro path (created with FoxPro's SET PATH) and returns an absolute reference to the named file. If you pass the optional numeric parameter, it does the same thing, except it uses the DOS path (set in DOS' PATH environment variable) rather than the FoxPro path.

If cFileName includes relative references, they're converted to absolute. When you add the optional character parameter, things get interesting. The relative references are converted with respect to the file you pass.

SYS(2014) goes the other way. Hand it a filename and a directory and it returns the shortest path from that directory to the file. Whenever possible, it makes the references relative, using the .. notation.

Be careful with the second parameter. If you omit the final "\", FoxPro assumes you've simply added a filename at the end and works from a directory one level higher than you meant.

Under Win32s, FoxPro gets horribly confused if you omit the third parameter to SYS(2014) and specify an absolute path on the current drive for the file. The path returned includes far too many references to the parent directory. You could climb all the way to the root and then some. Of course, this is only a problem for VFP 3 running under Windows 3.1, since VFP 5 and VFP 6 don't run in Win32s.

Both these functions will mislead you if you specify a file that doesn't exist. They return a path to the specified filename and don't bother to tell you it's not really there. With FULLPATH(), you're safe as long as the file exists somewhere on the path (either FoxPro or DOS, depending on the second parameter). SYS(2014) gives back really weird paths, but they amount to pointing to the nonexistent file in the current directory. The bottom line is that you can't count on either of these to make sure the file is there. Check with FILE() before you try to use it.

Example

```
* Assume Visual FoxPro is installed in F:\VFP
CD F:\VFP\SAMPLES
SET PATH TO TASTRADE, TASTRADE\DATA
* Search on FoxPro path
? FULLPATH("TasTrade.DBC")
* Returns "F:\VFP\SAMPLES\TASTRADE\DATA\TASTRADE.DBC"

* Search DOS path
? FULLPATH("Win.ini",1)&& Returns "C:\WINDOWS\WIN.INI"

* You can use FULLPATH() to find the location of a table
* in a DBC (which ADBOBJECTS() doesn't give you)
OPEN DATA TasTrade
? FULLPATH(DBGETPROP("customer","table","path"),DBC())
* Returns "F:\VFP\SAMPLES\TASTRADE\DATA\CUSTOMER.DBF"

SET PATH TO

* Use SYS(2014) for relative paths
CD F:\VFP\SAMPLES\TASTRADE
? SYS(2014,"\VFP\VFP.EXE",CURDIR()) && Returns "..\..\VFP.EXE"
? SYS(2014,"F:\VFP\TOOLS\FOXTOOLS.CHM",
     "F:\VFP\GALLERY\FAVORITES.DBF"
* Returns "..\TOOLS\FOXTOOLS.CHM"

* Now here's the absurd case demonstrating the bug in Win32s
* This example only gives these results in VFP3 under Win3.1
? SYS(2014,"\VFP\SAMPLES\CONTROLS\CANCEL.BMP")
* Returns "..\..\..\..\CONTROLS\CANCEL.BMP"
```

See Also ChDir, CurDir(), Set Default, Set Path

Function, Procedure, Return, EndFunc, EndProc

FUNCTION and PROCEDURE indicate that what follows is a subroutine. RETURN indicates that control should return from a subroutine and may include a value to pass back to the calling program.

Usage

```
FUNCTION RoutineName [ ( LocalParameterList) ]
PROCEDURE RoutineName [ ( LocalParameterList ) ]
```

RoutineName is the name of the subroutine. It follows the usual naming rules for FoxPro (which are laid out in Help).

Although the help for both FUNCTION and PROCEDURE fails to mention it, you can specify parameters for a routine by putting them in the header line as shown above. Parameters specified this way are local, which is our preferred scope anyway.

On the other hand, the help does explain clearly where Visual FoxPro looks for a routine when you call one and which one gets used, if there are several with the same name.

It doesn't matter whether you call a routine a function or a procedure in the header line. They're identical and, in fact, often you don't need either one. If a routine lives by itself in a PRG, it'll run faster without either a FUNCTION or a PROCEDURE declaration. (If you really feel the need to put one there, comment it out.) See "Faster than a Speeding Bullet" in "Franz and Other Lists" for more on this subject.

As for functions and procedures being identical, of course they're not. But it's not *what* you call a routine that determines whether it's a function or a procedure, it's *how* you call it. When you use the DO RoutineName syntax, the routine is called as a procedure. When you use the RoutineName() version, it's called as a function. The one key difference between the two is that procedures can change the value of passed variables ("by reference") where functions usually only receive their value ("by value"). We say "usually" because, like most things in FoxPro, you can change this if you want. Read up on the SET UDFPARMS command and "Just Some Routine Inquiries, Ma'am" in "Xbase Xplained" for more details.

We recommend you use FUNCTION or PROCEDURE to indicate how you expect the routine to be called.

Usage

```
RETURN [ eReturnValue ] [ TO MASTER ] [ TO FunctionName ]
ENDFUNC
ENDPROC
```

RETURN has two purposes in life. First, it indicates the end of execution of a routine and can be read there as "return control to whoever called this routine." In this context, RETURN can appear either at the end of a routine or within a routine. You can omit RETURN at the end of a routine if you don't need to return a value, and either the file ends there or the next line begins another function or procedure declaration, but we think you should put it there anyway to clearly indicate your intent.

RETURN's second purpose is to hand a value back to the caller. Given the dual nature of subroutines as both functions and procedures, returning a value could be very hairy. In fact, this part of FoxPro is quite well designed. If a routine has a return value and you call it as a procedure, the return value is ignominiously dumped in a bit bucket somewhere along the line, never used. On the other hand, if a routine doesn't have a return value and you call it as a function anyway, it returns .T. Finally, if a routine doesn't even have a RETURN statement and is called as a function, it also returns .T.

The TO clauses are a little more tricky, and we generally avoid them because they can violate good structured programming principles. RETURN TO MASTER blasts through the entire program stack, returning control to the topmost program. Any other code waiting to execute in the intervening routines is ignored. This has the potential of leaving your application in an unstable condition, and we typically use this only in dire situations, such as deep in an error handler.

RETURN TO FunctionName lets you do something almost as dangerous—leapfrog over the calling routines to a particular place in the calling stack. If you design your application exactly right, you may get away with this, but if you're expecting cleanup code to fire in the routines skipped over to restore the environment, you could be out of luck.

Be aware that RETURN TO expects a literal procedure name—you'll need to use &lcProcName to macro-expand a variable procedure name. For an object method, you need to use only the method name and not the object designation—RETURN TO ReadEvents works, but RETURN TO oApp.ReadEvents bombs. Far worse, RETURN TO anywhere or RETURN TO &lcProcName will perform a RETURN TO MASTER if "anywhere" hasn't been declared or if the lcProcName isn't in the calling stack. We'd expect a syntax error instead.

We generally agree it's best to have one and only one RETURN in each routine. Definitely, you should put RETURN at the end of the routine, whether you need it or not. It's also better to do all your calculations and store the return value in a variable, then have a single RETURN RetVal at the end of the routine. However, we've compromised this principle in the case of "short-circuiting" a routine. In many routines in this book, we test parameters and bail out if those tests fail. Once all the tests are passed, however, we have a single RETURN at the end of the real work. Our second example, the MakeName routine below, shows the compromise. If any parameter is no good, we give up and return the empty string. Once all the tests are passed, though, there's only one RETURN.

ENDFUNC and ENDPROC are weak cousins of RETURN. They were introduced into the language with the DEFINE CLASS command, but all three can be used interchangeably. ENDFUNC and ENDPROC, however, can't return values, nor do they support the TO clause.

Example

```
PROCEDURE CleanUp
* Clean up after a program dies
SET SYSMENU TO DEFAULT
CLOSE ALL
CLEAR ALL
ON KEY

RETURN

FUNCTION MakeName( cFirst, cMiddle, cLast)
* Combine a first name, middle name and last name to
* get one nicely, formatted name. cMiddle may be omitted.
* Sample call: ?MakeName("Tamar","E.","Granor")
*              ?MakeName("Ted",,"Roche")
LOCAL cFullName

IF TYPE("cFirst")<>"C" ;
   OR (TYPE("cMiddle")<>"C" AND TYPE("cMiddle")<>"L") ;
   OR TYPE("cLast")<>"C"
   RETURN ""
ENDIF

IF EMPTY(cMiddle)
   cFullName=TRIM(cFirst)+" "+TRIM(cLast)
ELSE
   cFullName=TRIM(cFirst)+" "+TRIM(cMiddle)+" "+TRIM(cLast)
ENDIF

RETURN cFullName
```

See Also Define Class, LParameters, Parameters

FV(), Payment(), PV()

These functions do computations for financial transactions. They return future value, payment amount, and present value, respectively.

Usage

```
nFutureValue = FV( nPayment, nPeriodicInterest, nPeriods )
nPresentValue = PV( nPayment, nPeriodicInterest, nPeriods )
```

Parameter	Value	Meaning
nPayment	Any numeric type	The amount paid or received at the end of each period. (For example, the amount paid into a retirement account each month.)
nPeriodicInterest	Any numeric type	The interest rate for one period. If payments are made monthly, this is the monthly interest rate.
nPeriods	Any numeric type	The number of periods involved. For example, if there are monthly payments for one year, nPeriods is 12.
nFutureValue	Numeric or Currency, depending on the type of nPayment	The future value of an investment.
nPresentValue	Numeric or Currency, depending on the type of nPayment	The amount that must be invested to end up with a specified amount at the end of a specified time.

Future Value is simply compounding of interest. It says, "If I put away so many dollars (or francs or whatever) every month (or year or whatever) at this interest rate, how much will I have after so many months (or years or whatever)?" nPayment is the "so many dollars," nPeriodicInterest is "this interest rate," and nPeriods is "so many months."

A positive nPayment indicates money being socked away. A negative nPayment indicates debt being incurred. It doesn't really matter which way you do this, though, because you get the same answer, except for the sign.

Present Value is more complicated. It translates to "If I want to have so many dollars at the end of so many months (or years or whatever), and I'm getting this much interest, how much do I have to set aside?" It's complicated because the "so many dollars" is the total of nPayment over nPeriods (that is, nPayment*nPeriods). The result is the amount you'd have to invest in a series of equal payments at that interest rate to end up with the desired total; you have to divide by nPeriods to figure out how much you need each period.

For example, if you want to end up with $1,200 after 12 months, you'd set nPayment to 100. You get back the amount you need to put away at nPeriodicInterest in order to end up with your $1,200. To figure your monthly payment, divide the result by 12.

As with FV(), whether nPayment is positive or negative doesn't make much difference in the result—only in how you explain it. If nPayment is positive, PV() represents the amount you need to save to end up with the desired result. If nPayment is negative, PV() is the amount you need to pay in order to pay off a debt, if the other person is giving you the specified interest rate.

Both PV() and FV() allow you to pass negative numbers for nPeriodicInterest and nPeriods, but the results don't change. That is, FV(100, .01, 12)=FV(100, -.01, 12). Clearly this is wrong. Either these functions should reject negative interest rates and periods or they should return appropriate results. These bugs have been there since time immemorial, so we've pretty much given up hope of their getting fixed.

If .NULL. is passed in any parameter of these functions, the result is null.

Example

```
* $100 a month at 12% for one year
?FV(100, .01, 12) && Future Value is 1268.25 - what you'll have
                  && after one year of this
?PV(100, .01, 12) && Present Value is 1125.51 - pay 1/12th each
                  && month to end up with $1200.
```

Usage `nPayment = PAYMENT( nPrincipal, nPeriodicInterest, nPeriods )`

Parameter	Value	Meaning
nPrincipal	Any numeric type	The amount of debt. For example, the amount of a mortgage.
nPeriodicInterest	Any numeric type	The interest rate for one period. If payments are made monthly, this is the monthly interest rate.
nPeriods	Any numeric type	The number of periods involved. For example, for a 30-year mortgage paid monthly, nPeriods is 360.
nPayment	Numeric or Currency, depending on nPrincipal	The monthly payment necessary to pay off nPrincipal at nPeriodicInterest in nPeriods.

PAYMENT() is the function that lets you compute your mortgage or car payments. It tells you the monthly payment needed to amortize a specified amount (nPrincipal) at a given interest rate (nPeriodicInterest) over a specified length of time (nPeriods).

Like PV() and FV(), you can specify a negative principal. This changes the sign of the result, giving a negative payment amount. If a .NULL. is passed in any parameter, the result is null.

PAYMENT() shares the bug of allowing, but ignoring, negative interest rates and number of periods.

In all these functions, don't forget to divide the annual interest rate by 12 if you're dealing with monthly periods or by 52 if you've got weeks. You'll get some really strange results otherwise. (For a $100,000 30-year loan, if you forget to divide the 8% interest rate by 12, you get to pay $8,000 a month instead of $733.76.)

Finally, be aware that these functions assume interest compounding every period. While this is common in the U.S., other places may have other customs.

Example

```
* $10,000 at 12% for 1 year, monthly payments
? PAYMENT(10000, .01, 12)       && Returns 888.49
* make it weekly payments
? PAYMENT(10000, .12/52, 52)    && Returns 204.30
* make one annual payment
? PAYMENT(10000, .12, 1)        && Returns 11200
```

See Also Calculate

FWrite() See Low-Level File Functions.

_Gallery See _Beautify.

Gather See Scatter.

_GenGraph, _GenHTML, _GenMenu See _Beautify.

_GenPD See Set PDSetup.

_GenScrn, _GenXTab See _Beautify.

GetBar(), GetPad()

These functions let you figure out what's what in a popup or menu that's been rearranged in some way, either by having items released or by using a mover. GETBAR() is so confusing, we've ended up testing it every time we've ever needed to use it (but we think we've got it nailed now).

Usage

```
nBarNumber = GETBAR( cPopupName, nBarPosition )
cPadName = GETPAD( cMenuName, nPadPosition )
```

What makes GETBAR() confusing is that menu bars are numbered rather than named like all the other menu components. So GETBAR() expects a number referring to the bar's position and returns the number that identifies the bar. At first, the two numbers are the same. But, if you release any bars or if the popup has mover capability and the bars get moved around, the numbers no longer match up—at which point it starts to get confusing.

GETPAD(), on the other hand, is straightforward. Hand it a menu name and a position and it tells you the name of the pad in that position. Use it together with PRMPAD() to get a list of all the prompts on a menu.

Both of these functions are mostly irrelevant in VFP apps where you're unlikely to code any of this stuff by yourself.

Example

```
* Get the prompts of all bars picked from a mover multi-select
* popup.
LOCAL nCnt, nThisBar
FOR nCnt = 1 TO CNTBAR()
   * first, get bar number of bar in current position
   nThisBar = GETBAR("MyPop", nCnt)
   * now, see if it's marked
   IF MRKBAR("MyPop", nThisBar)
      ? PRMBAR("MyPop", nThisBar) + " was chosen"
   ENDIF
ENDFOR

* Get the prompt of the third menu pad
? PRMPAD("_MSYSMENU", GETPAD("_MSYSMENU", 3))
```

See Also Define Bar, Define Pad, Menus, PrmBar(), PrmPad()

GetColor()

This function brings up the Windows Color Picker dialog and returns the color chosen.

Usage

```
nColor = GETCOLOR ( [ nDefaultColor ] )
```

Parameter	Value	Meaning
nDefaultColor	Numeric	A number from 0 to 16,777,215 representing the default color to be highlighted in the Color Picker.
nColor	-1	The user pressed Esc or clicked Cancel.

Parameter	Value	Meaning
nColor	0 - 16,777,215	The number of the color chosen by the user.

We found a number of nits to pick in the behavior of this dialog (in particular, when it's expanded to allow custom colors), but since this is a Windows common dialog, we can't blame the Visual FoxPro developers, so we won't yell too loud here. After all, this is a Visual FoxPro book, not a Windows book. But here's our laundry list of problems with GETCOLOR().

First, if the initial color is black, you'll notice that the RGB values shown in the expanded dialog are all 0. Click all you want in the big color rectangle and the RGB values don't change until you click somewhere in the narrow bar off to the right. You see a similar problem if the initial color is white. A Microsoftie tried to explain this to us as correct behavior, but it's just plain weird.

If you add a color to custom colors, then close the dialog, open it again, and add another color, it overwrites the first one. You have to remember to click the place you'd like the new color to land on the palette to avoid this, but then you have to go back and click the color you want to start with. All in all, adding custom colors is a usability nightmare.

Even without fiddling with custom colors, there's some pretty strange behavior. If you pass in a color that isn't in the palette, the dialog opens with the first color in the dialog highlighted, regardless of its relationship to the color you specified. (In Win 3.x, we're pretty sure it at least tried to approximate the color you wanted, but we don't have any 3.x machines left to test on.) If you then click OK, you get back the color value you passed instead of the highlighted color. Among other things, this means you see the same color highlighted, but get back an assortment of different values. Or, put another way, in any given call, you see one color highlighted, but the return value is a different color.

All in all, we think it's way past time the OS group got around to overhauling this dialog.

If you do pass a number in, remember that you can't just send three values between 0 and 255. Use RGB() to combine them into a single color value.

The number that GETCOLOR() returns is a single integer between -1 and 256^3. The procedure below lets the user choose a color, then returns separate red, green and blue values.

Example

```
* ParsColr.PRG
* Get a color and Parse it into its RGB components.
* Set all three to -1 if the user cancels.
* This is a native code alternative to the FoxTools
* RGBComp() function.
* Sample call:
*     STORE -1 TO nRed, nGreen, nBlue
*     DO ParsColr WITH nRed,nGreen,nBlue

LPARAMETERS nRed, nGreen, nBlue

LOCAL nColor

nColor = GETCOLOR()

IF nColor<>-1  && user didn't cancel
   nBlue  = INT(nColor/(256^2))
   nColor = MOD(nColor,(256^2))
   nGreen = INT(nColor/256)
   nRed   = MOD(nColor,256)
ELSE
   STORE -1 to nBlue, nGreen, nRed
ENDIF

RETURN
```

See Also FoxTools, RGB()

GetCP()

The GetCP() function calls up a dialog that allows the operator to pick a code page.

Usage
```
nCodePage = GETCP( [ nInitialCP [, cPrompt [, cTitle ] ] ] )
```

Parameter	Value	Meaning
nInitialCP	Integer	Displays the specified code page as selected in the list box. You must pass some value (even though it doesn't need to be a valid code page) if you pass a value for cPrompt or cTitle.
	Omitted	No code page is highlighted.
cPrompt	Character	The prompt to appear within the dialog box. Practically limited to around 200 characters, but more are accepted.
	Empty string or omitted	Prompt is "Please select a code page for cross-platform data sharing." Note that you must pass the empty string, and not just omit the parameter, if you pass the cTitle parameter.
cTitle	Character	The title to display in the dialog box title bar. If the title exceeds the space allowed, it is truncated with an ellipsis.
	Empty string or omitted	Dialog title is displayed as "Code Page."
nCodePage	0	User selected Cancel, Close from the control menu or pressed Escape.
	Integer	The code page selected by the user.

Use this dialog to allow your users to chose a code page for tagging a file, translating, or perhaps selecting which code page to use for generation. There appears to be no way to preset the option group on the left-hand side of the dialog to show anything but "All platforms." Check out the CpZero.PRG supplied with Visual FoxPro to modify the code page of an existing DBF.

Example
```
? GETCP( 1250, "Convert file to which code page?", ;
               "Code Page Conversion" )
```

See Also CPConvert(), Set CPDialog

GetData See ClearData.

GetDir(), GetFile(), LocFile(), PutFile()

Using these functions definitely comes under the category of not reinventing the wheel. They bring up various standard dialogs. GETDIR() displays the Select Directory dialog. GETFILE() shows the File-Open dialog. LOCFILE() tries to find the specified file first, but reverts to the File-Open dialog if it can't. PUTFILE() brings up the Save As dialog.

All these functions let you navigate through directories. There's some internal setting that remembers where you last navigated. Calling one of these functions without specifying an initial directory starts you where you left off—even if you call a different one of the functions. That's right—they all share this hidden setting. Fortunately, you can override FoxPro's memory by SETting DEFAULT or CDing to the directory you'd like to start in.

Lately, we use all the functions in this group (except GetDir()) a lot less than we used to. Instead, in our applications, we usually use the Common Dialogs control these days. The Common Dialogs offer more control over various settings than these functions do, and make our apps work more like other Windows apps. (The Common Dialogs control has its own aggravations, too, but for the most part, the advantages of using it outweigh the disadvantages.)

Usage
```
cDirName = GETDIR( [ cStartDir [, cCaption ] ] )
```

Parameter	Value	Meaning
cStartDir	Character	The directory that should be initially highlighted in the dialog.
	Omitted	Start from the last chosen directory or the default directory.
cCaption	Character	A message to display over the list of directories.
	Omitted	No message appears over the list.
cDirName	Character	The full path to the directory chosen.
	Empty	The user pressed Esc or chose Cancel.

Before VFP 5, we used GETDIR() a lot in development. CD GETDIR() was an easy way to change the default directory without having to remember where we are or where we're going. Since VFP 5, though, we can CD ? for the same effect.

GETDIR() (and CD) can't see directories that are flagged as "system." They simply don't appear. Fortunately, ADIR() can find them if you give it the right values ("DS") for the third parameter.

Example
```
cDataDir = GETDIR("AppDir\","Where's the data?")
```

Usage
```
cFilePath = GETFILE( [ cExtensions [, cTextCaption
                     [, cButtonCaption  [, nButtonChoice
                     [, cDialogTitle ] ] ] ] ] )
cFilePath = LOCFILE( cFileName [, cExtensions
                     [, cTextCaption ] ] )
```

Parameter	Value	Meaning
cExtensions	Character	A semicolon-delimited (;) or vertical bar-delimited (|) list of file extensions to display in the File-Open dialog. Can include DOS wildcards.
	Omitted	Show all files.
cTextCaption	Character	The caption to place next to the textbox that shows the name of the selected file. (In the older Windows interface, this caption appears over the list of files.)
	Omitted	Caption is "File Name:"

Parameter	Value	Meaning
cButtonCaption	Character	The caption to appear on the OK button.
	Omitted	Caption is "OK".
nButtonChoice	0 or omitted	Use OK and Cancel buttons.
	1	Use OK, New and Cancel buttons.
	2	Use OK, None and Cancel buttons.
cDialogTitle	Character	The caption to appear in the dialog's title bar. In VFP 3, this parameter was the Mac creator type.
	Omitted	The dialog caption is "Open".
cFileName	Character	The file to locate.
cFilePath	Character	The full path to the file chosen.
	Empty	The user pressed Esc or chose Cancel in GETFILE().

Use LOCFILE() when you're looking for a specific file and want to ask the user for help if you can't find it. (LOCFILE() checks the current directory first, then the FoxPro path.) Use GETFILE() to let the user choose any input file. We use GETFILE() a lot in developer tools where the user specifies a file to process.

These two functions handle Esc/Cancel differently. GETFILE() returns the empty string—good choice. LOCFILE(), since it was looking for a specific file, gives an error (#1—"File Does Not Exist").

The current incarnation of the File-Open dialog has a text box for the filename with a drop-down list underneath labeled "Files of Type". When you specify multiple extensions, the first extension in the list determines what appears as the current choice in the Files of Type drop-down. However, when you drop it open, you see all the extensions you specified, as well as an All Files choice. For any extension that's registered, the drop-down shows the natural language description rather than the actual extension.

No matter what you specify for nButtonChoice, there's a Help button on the dialog. In addition, when you set nButtonChoice to 0 (or omit this parameter), there is a disabled Code Page button. With the other choices, that position is occupied by either the New or None button. We haven't found a way to make the Code Page button come alive.

The cTextCaption parameter specifies a string that appears next to the text box for entering the filename. The space for this caption is pretty limited (much more so than in the older version of the dialog), so you need to keep this one short.

This one's really a Windows thing. Both these functions let you specify a nonexistent file. They don't create the file. They just hand you back the full path to some file that ain't there. Always use FILE() to check the result of GETFILE() and LOCFILE() for existence.

Example

```
cInpFile = GETFILE("PJX","Choose a Project","Choose")
IF FILE(cInpFile)
   * Process the project in some way
ELSE
   * Cancel because the user did
   DO CleanUp
```

```
   RETURN
ENDIF

* Find a particular file
cCustomer = LOCFILE("Customer.DBF","DBF","Customer")
IF FILE(cCustomer)
  ... process file here
ENDIF
```

Usage

```
cFilePath = PUTFILE( [ cTextCaption [, cFileName
                     [, cExtensions ] ] ] )
```

Parameter	Value	Meaning
cTextCaption	Character	The caption to appear next to the file textbox. In the old Windows interface, this appeared over the list of files.
	Omitted	Caption is "File Name:"
cFileName	Character	The default filename for the new file.
	Omitted	No default name is used. The Files of Type drop-down list shows "File".
cExtensions	Character	List of extensions (delimited with ";" or "|") for files displayed in file list. Can include DOS wildcards.
	Omitted	Files with no extension and those with TXT extension are displayed.
cFilePath	Character	The full path to the file chosen.
	Empty	The user pressed Esc or chose Cancel.

Use PUTFILE() to choose a file for output. It lets you pick an existing file or specify a new one. Regardless of the setting of SAFETY, if the user picks an existing file, he's prompted with an overwrite message. We haven't found any way to get rid of this message and substitute our own. The Files of Type drop-down behaves as described above for GETFILE().

PUTFILE() expects parameters in a very different order than the other functions. It's a real pain and means we always end up looking up the parameters for this whole group of functions. But we do see the point. In every case, the parameters are pretty much in the order of likelihood of their being used.

Example

```
cOutFile = PUTFILE("Result file:","Results.txt","TXT")
IF NOT EMPTY(cOutFile)
   REPORT FORM MyReport TO FILE (cOutFile) ASCII
ELSE
   WAIT WINDOW "Report Cancelled" NOWAIT
ENDIF
```

See Also ChDir, File(), Set Default

GetEnv()

This function returns the value of a DOS environment variable.

Usage

```
cValue = GETENV( cVarName )
```

Use GETENV() to find information like the DOS path, the directory in which Windows is installed, and so forth. On a network, there are likely to be variables containing information about the network configuration.

You can also create environment variables for your own purposes in AUTOEXEC.BAT and query them with GETENV(). You might set up your development machine with a variable, DEVMODE, set to "YES" and use that value to trigger certain behavior in your apps (debugging behaviors, for example).

When the variable you specify doesn't exist, GETENV() returns the empty string. This is both a good thing and a bad thing. It's good because it makes schemes like the one above work—your users don't have to have a DEVMODE variable. It's bad because it makes it easy to make typos. The moral of the story is that you need to double-check GETENV() calls—in fact, test them in the command window first.

Example

```
cCurDOSPath = GETENV("Path")
```

See Also OS()

GetExpr

GETEXPR is a cool little command that allows you to bring up the Expression Builder within your application.

Usage

```
GETEXPR [ cPrompt ] TO cRetVal
        [TYPE cVarType [ ; cErrorMsg ] ]
        [DEFAULT cExpr]
```

Parameter	Value	Meaning
cPrompt	Character	The message that appears within the Expression Builder as a prompt.
cVarType	Character	The variable type the Builder should verify, expressed as a single letter using the standard type abbreviations. Accepts D, L, C, I, N, T, F, Y, and B—everything but Memo, General and Picture.
cErrorMsg	Character	The text to appear in a message box if Visual FoxPro can't evaluate the supplied expression or it's not of type cVarType. The test occurs when the user chooses either Verify or OK. Note the strange syntax here: cErrorMsg must be included in the same string as cVarType, separated from it by a semicolon.
cExpr	Character	A default to be supplied to the user.
cRetVal	Character	The expression entered by the user, the default value if the user doesn't change it (whether he selects OK or Cancel), or an empty string if the user enters nothing and no default is supplied. If the return variable did not exist, it is created. If no default is specified, an empty string is returned.

The Expression Builder is called a Builder, but is different from all the other Builders available within Visual FoxPro. However, since this is the only Builder available within a runtime application, the end users shouldn't be confused by the terminology.

The display of system memory variables at first appears to be alphabetical (_Alignment, _Box, _Indent, _LMargin) but scrolling through the list reveals a jumble with the new 6.0 additions—_Gallery, _GetExpr, _Include, _GenHTML, _Samples) at the end. We think this list would make far more sense in alphabetical order.

The error dialog that appears with your cErrorMsg text has both OK and Help buttons; for the life of us, we couldn't find a way to bring up this function without the Help button being disabled. If they're gonna offer help, Microsoft ought to give us a ContextID to hook onto.

Note that the cVarType parameter does not control the type of the return variable—a string is always returned. If no entry is made, the string either contains the default or, if no default was supplied, is empty. You must check for an empty return before attempting to convert the variable (using VAL(), CTOD(), CTOT() or your own parsing routine) to the desired variable type.

The Builder is not what we would call a graceful example of user interface design, but it is a tool that can bring much power into the hands of your more capable users. All table fields are available and system memory variables may or may not be visible.

There is no way to determine if the user hit Cancel. In this case, the default value is returned.

If the user opens any of the drop-down lists (date, math, logical or string), then presses ESC, the drop-down list closes, as you'd expect, but the highlighted value in the popup is placed in the Expression edit box, anyway.

If any change has been made to the expression in the dialog before Cancel is pressed, a confirmation dialog appears: "Discard changes to expression?" In many cases where the option to cancel is non-destructive, we find this confirmation dialog to be intrusive, but there doesn't appear to be a way to turn it off—it shows up regardless of SET CONFIRM or SET SAFETY.

The Options button allows the end user to determine which variables and expressions she wants to see, and whether aliases should or should not be included in the resulting expression. The preferences selected in the Options dialog are stored in the current resource file, with a type of "PREFW" and an Id of "GETEXPR." Flagging this record as Read-Only and distributing your resource file with your application is a nice way to get a customized Expression Builder into your client's hands. Obviously, if no resource file is available, the options selected are not preserved from one session to another.

GETEXPR is a distinctive Xbase command. Unlike most language constructs within the system, GETEXPR is designed as a *command* and not a function, so even though it returns a value like GetPict() or GetDir(), it is written in a vein similar to Calculate, another Xbase oldie-but-goodie.

The new _GETEXPR system memory variable provides a hook to allow a developer to create her own dialog or modify some of the behaviors of the existing one. Whenever the GETEXPR command is found, FoxPro looks to the _GETEXPR variable and runs the code specified there instead.

Although this is a pretty cool feature, it has some rules you'll want to follow. Your replacement routine must accept four parameters, matching the dialog caption, return type, error message and default of the native command. If these settings are not specified in the call, VFP provides empty strings to your routine, so you don't need to validate the type of the supplied parameters. The native GETEXPR command accepts blank strings in any of these positions just as if that option had been omitted, and you will want your routine to do the same.

Using GETEXPR within a routine that has been designated as the _GETEXPR function causes a recursive call, eventually leading to the FoxPro error "Allowed DO nesting level exceeded." If you need the native functionality, save the _GETEXPR value and restore it after invoking the command.

Example

```
* GE.PRG - shell around GetExpr
* To use: STORE "YourPath\GE.PRG" to _GETEXPR
* GETEXPR <your arguments>

#DEFINE CR CHR(13)

LPARAMETERS cExpressionType, cErrorMessageText, ;
   cDefaultExpression, cCaptionText

wait window "Expression type:    " + cExpressionType + CR + ;
            "cErrorMessageText:  " + cErrorMessageText + CR + ;
            "cDefaultExpression: " + cDefaultExpression + CR + ;
            "cCaptionText:       " + cCaptionText ;
     nowait

LOCAL cParm2, lcGetExpr

* Here's where you can modify supplied parameters,
* choose to invoke your own custom forms, or
* default to the native functionality.

* Construct the second parameter
cParm2 = cExpressionType + ;
         IIF(NOT EMPTY(cErrorMessageText), ;
             ";" + cErrorMessageText, "")

* This routine is the GetExpr call, store off the value
lcGetExpr = _GETEXPR
_GETEXPR = SPACE(0)

* Invoke the native GetExpr
GETEXPR cCaptionText to lcRetVal ;
        TYPE cParm2 ;
        DEFAULT cDefaultExpression

_GETEXPR = lcGetExpr
RETURN lcRetVal
```

See Also Configuration Files, CToD(), CToT(), _GetExpr, Set Resource, Val()

_GetExpr See _Beautify.

GetFile() See GetDir().

GetFldState(), SetFldState()

This is an interesting pair of functions. GetFldState() is essential to any sensible strategy for dealing with conflicts when saving data. SetFldState() is strange—both in how it's supposed to behave and in how it actually behaves. They're both relevant only when you're dealing with buffered data.

Usage

```
uCodes = GetFldState( cField | nFieldCode
                      [, cAlias | nWorkarea ] )
lSuccess = SetFldState( cField | nFieldCode, nCode
                        [, cAlias | nWorkarea ] )
```

Parameter	Value	Meaning
cField	Character	The name of a field whose status is being queried or changed.
nFieldCode	-1	Query the status for all fields in the current record.
	0	Query or change the deleted status of the current record. Maybe this is because the deleted mark can sort of be seen as the "zeroth" field of any table.
	Positive	Query or change the nFieldCode-th field in the current record, based on the table's structure.
nCode	Numeric	The status to assign the specified field. See Help for a list.
cAlias	Character	The alias for the table whose status is being queried or changed.
	Omitted	If nWorkArea is also omitted, query or change the table in the current work area.
nWorkArea	Numeric	The work area containing the table to be queried or changed.
	Omitted	If cAlias is also omitted, query or change the table in the current work area.
uCodes	Numeric	Contains the status of a single field or the deleted status of the current record. See Help for meaning of status values.
	Character	Contains a string where the first character is the deleted status for the current record and each subsequent character is the changed status of a field. Fields are represented in definition order.
	.NULL.	Returned by GetFldState() when the record pointer is at end-of-file.
lSuccess	.T.	The field's change status or the record's deletion status was changed.
	.F.	Doesn't occur.

GetFldState() makes a lot of sense. It tells you whether a particular field has changed or if the record has been deleted. It also tells you if a record is new. Most of the conflict resolution strategies we've seen involve using GetFldState() to figure out which fields have changed, so you can see if someone else changed the same fields. (Would that human conflict resolution were so simple.)

When you add a new record and it has default values set, GetFldState() returns 4 for those fields, even if the user leaves the default values alone. If your framework checks for changes in order to figure out things like whether certain buttons should be enabled or disabled, at last you have a reason to use SetFldState(). Reset the state right after the append and your other code will still behave as you expect it to.

One warning here: GetFldState() doesn't get changed for a field until you've left the control it's bound to. If you make changes but don't leave the field, causing its Valid to fire, the changes don't get sent to the control's ControlSource and GetFldState() doesn't see them. This is consistent with controls not getting their Value changed until Valid is fired.

SetFldState() is another story. The docs say it changes the status of a field or record. That it does. But the docs also say that the change affects what FoxPro attempts to update—that is, by changing the status of a field from "changed" to "unchanged", you can keep FoxPro from updating the real record underneath. Doesn't work for us. We can SetFldState() all we want and FoxPro still updates the original table with all the changes we've made.

What does appear to work is the reverse—making a field or record look like it has been changed when it hasn't. We've seen a few people suggest this as part of various strategies, but haven't yet found a reason we'd want to do so.

Example

```
* You can prevent an update from failing by checking for
* conflicts ahead of time. Loop through all the fields and check
* whether other users have changed any that you changed.
* This example assumes you're dealing only with existing records
* and handles only a single record. Wrap it with a loop
* involving GetNextModified() to handle multiple records.
FOR nCnt = 1 TO FCOUNT()
   * Did you change this field?
   IF GetFldState(nCnt)<>1
      * Did anyone else change it?
      IF CurVal(FIELD(nCnt))<>OldVal(FIELD(nCnt))
         * Conflict. You changed it and so did someone else
         * Ask the user what to do?
         nNowWhat = MessageBox("Someone else changed "+ ;
                    FIELD(nCnt) + ", too. Save anyway?",
                    MB_YESNO+MB_ICONEXCLAMATION, ;
                    "Save Conflict")
         IF nNowWhat = IDNO
            * grab other user's value
            REPLACE (FIELD(nCnt)) WITH CurVal(FIELD(nCnt))
         ENDIF
      ENDIF
   ENDIF
ENDFOR
* Now you're ready to actually update the thing.
```

See Also Buffering, CurVal(), GetNextModified(), OldVal(), TableUpdate()

GetFont()

This function invokes FoxPro's font dialog and returns information about the chosen font.

Usage

```
cFontInfo = GETFONT( [ cFontName [, nFontSize
                     [, cFontStyle ] ] ] )
```

The developers of FoxPro faced a dilemma of sorts with this function. There are three pieces of information to return about a font—its name, its size and its style—but a function can return only one item. They couldn't just let you pass a parameter telling which one you want, because the value returned depends on user input. So they did the best they could and the function returns a single, comma-delimited string containing all three pieces of information.

GETFONT() offers the user a choice of all fonts installed on the machine, but does not display printer fonts (fonts installed only on the printer, also called "soft fonts").

If Cancel is selected instead, an empty string is returned; you can test for this case with EMPTY().

In VFP 6, you can prime the pump. Passing one or more of the parameters sets up the dialog with the items you pass initially highlighted. Very handy if you want to use "Beesknees ITC" (a font we really have installed, though we're not sure why), but aren't sure whether it's TrueType and, if not, what sizes and styles it allows. If you specify a font that doesn't exist, MS Sans Serif (one of our least favorite fonts of all time) is highlighted. If you specify a font, but no size, 10 point is highlighted. If you don't specify a style, Regular is highlighted.

GETFONT() can't handle the empty string for the first parameter. It coughs up an error message. This is particularly strange since it can deal with empty values for the other two parameters and stupid values for the font name.

Since every command we can think of that needs font information wants the three items separately, a routine to parse GETFONT()'s return value seems useful. That's the example below. The procedure calls GETFONT(), then sets its parameters to the three components of the return value.

Example

```
* ParsFont.PRG
* Call GETFONT() and parse the return value into its three
* components: name, size, style
* Sample Call:
*     DO ParsFont WITH cFontName, nFontSize, cFontStyle
* or:
*     ParsFont(@cFontName, @nFontSize, @cFontStyle)

LPARAMETERS cFontName, nFontSize, cFontStyle

LOCAL cFontInfo, nCommaPos1, nCommaPos2

* Call varies depending on parameters passed
DO CASE
CASE EMPTY(cFontName) OR TYPE("cFontName")<>"C"
   cFontInfo=GETFONT()
CASE TYPE("nFontSize")<>"N" OR nSize = 0
   cFontInfo = GETFONT(cFontName)
CASE EMPTY(cFontStyle) OR TYPE("cFontStyle")<>"C"
   cFontInfo = GETFONT(cFontName, nFontSize)
OTHERWISE
   cFontInfo = GETFONT(cFontName, nFontSize, cFontStyle)
ENDCASE

IF NOT EMPTY(cFontInfo)
   nCommaPos1 = AT(",", cFontInfo)
   cFontName = LEFT(cFontInfo, nCommaPos1 - 1)
   nCommaPos2 = AT(",", cFontInfo,2)
   nFontSize = VAL(SUBSTR(cFontInfo, nCommaPos1 + 1, ;
                          nCommaPos2 - nCommaPos1 - 1))
   cFontStyle = SUBSTR(cFontInfo, nCommaPos2 + 1)
ENDIF

RETURN
```

Be aware, too, that the Windows Common Dialogs control offers an alternative to this function.

See Also AFont(), FontMetric()

GetFormat, SetFormat

These are methods of the data object that contains data being dragged with OLE drag and drop. GetFormat tells you what kinds of data are available. SetFormat lets you expand that list.

Usage

```
lIsItThere = oDataObject.GetFormat( nFormat | cFormat )
oDataObject.SetFormat( nFormat | cFormat )
```

Parameter	Value	Meaning
lIsItThere	.T.	The data object contains data in the specified format.
	.F.	The data object doesn't contain any data in the specified format.

Parameter	Value	Meaning
nFormat	1, 7 or 13	The data object contains textual data in ASCII, OEM or Unicode format, respectively. As far as we can tell, no VFP controls automatically supply either OEM or Unicode format data (using the American English version of VFP and Windows), though other applications may and you can provide data in one of those formats.
	15	The data object contains a list of files.
	Any other number	The data object contains data in a custom format.
cFormat	"OLE Variant Array"	The data object contains multiple data items, in their original format. We haven't been able to find any drag source that automatically provides data in this format, but it can be used to drag the contents of an array without converting all the data into character.
	"OLE Variant"	The data object contains data in its original type. For example, data from a spinner is returned as numeric, using this format, while it's character with format 1.
	"VFP Source Object"	The data object contains a reference to the data source for this drag. This is always true when dragging from VFP objects.
	Any other string	The data object contains data in a custom format.

These methods are a little tricky. First, they belong to an object that isn't a VFP object. The data object is a COM object created when an OLE drag and drop operation begins, in order to hold the data being dragged. It's capable of holding many different kinds of data, and even of holding the same data in more than one form.

GetFormat lets you find out what kinds of data it's holding at the moment. SetFormat lets you tell the data object that it's capable of holding data in a specified format. Both methods are only relevant in the OLE drag and drop methods, because those are the only ones where a data object exists. (Actually, if the OLE drag and drop methods call other methods and pass the data object as a parameter, you can call its methods from there, too.)

For reasons known only to the folks who designed this stuff, formats can be either numbered or named. So both methods accept either a number or a string for the format parameter.

There are a handful of built-in formats, including one that seems to have been created just for VFP. In addition, you can create your own formats and stuff whatever data you want into the data object for that format. This lets you do very cool things, like dragging a picture onto a form and turning it into wallpaper, or one we saw demonstrated at DevCon, dragging data from VFP and turning it into a table in Word.

To create a format, you call SetFormat in the drag source's OLEStartDrag method and pass the name for your format. (You can pass a number, but we don't recommend it. It's a lot easier to remember "Tamar's Special Format" than 37.) Once you've created a format, you can stick data for your format into the data object using its SetData method. You can add the data in OLEStartDrag or wait until drop time, and call SetData from the source's OLESetData method.

You don't actually have to explicitly create new formats with SetFormat. You can just call SetData, passing both the data and the format.

Back to more regular operations. When a drop takes place, you can check what formats the drag source contains and then figure out what to do. For example (in fact, the example below), if data is dragged from a listbox into an edit box, you might choose to put a comma-delimited list of all the selected items into the edit box.

Any given drag source may support more than one format. In fact, most of the VFP controls do so. That's because the "VFP Source Object" format was specially created to give you access to the actual drag source, so all VFP controls support that one. In addition, many of them also support the text (1) and "OLE Variant" formats.

When data is available in multiple formats, you have to figure out which one to use at drop time. However, VFP's default behavior in this area seems logical to us. For the most part, the choices it makes are the ones we'd normally want. We can write code for the rest.

Example

```
* This code could go in an editbox's OLEDragDrop method.
* If the data dropped comes from a listbox, it creates a
* comma-delimited string of the selected items and assigns
* that string to the editbox.
LPARAMETERS oDataObject, nEffect, nButton, nShift, ;
            nXCoord, nYCoord
LOCAL oSource, cResult, nCount

IF oDataObject.GetFormat("VFP Source Object")
   * We have a VFP data source, so get a reference
   oSource = oDataObject.GetData("VFP Source Object")
   * Is it a list? If so, loop through
   IF UPPER(oSource.BaseClass) = "LISTBOX"
      cResult = ""
      FOR nCount = 1 TO oSource.ListCount
         IF oSource.Selected[ nCount ]
            cResult = cResult + oSource.List[ nCount ] + ","
         ENDIF
      ENDFOR
      * Strip trailing comma
      cResult = SUBSTR(cResult, 1, LEN(cResult)-1)
      This.Value = cResult
      * Prevent normal dragdrop behavior
      NODEFAULT
   ENDIF
ENDIF

* See OLEDrag for an example of creating a custom format.
```

See Also DataObject, GetData, OLE drag and drop, OLEDragDrop, OLESetData, OLEStartDrag, SetData

GetHost(), IsHosted()

Use these functions to manipulate the browser supporting your Active Document.

Usage

```
lIsOrIsnt = IsHosted()
oBrowser = GetHost()
```

Parameter	Value	Meaning
lIsOrIsnt	.T.	Current form is hosted within a browser.
	.F.	Form is not hosted in a browser.
oBrowser	Null	No browser object is available.
	Object	An object reference to the browser is acting as host.

Use the IsHosted() function to separate the logic that should run when your forms are running as ActiveDocuments from the logic that they should use as stand-alone forms. If running as ActiveDocuments, a call to GetHost returns an object reference to the hosting browser. Using this reference, you can determine the identity of the host, and then manipulate the object model of the host (such as turning off features or changing the navigation model) to properly host your application.

Example

```
IF IsHosted()
  loBrowser = GetHost()
  WAIT WINDOW "Hosted by " + loBrowser.Name
ELSE
  WAIT WINDOW "Not browsing"
  loBrowser = .NULL.
ENDIF
```

See Also ActiveDoc

GetLatestVersion See CheckIn.

GetNextModified()

Boy, do we wish this function had been around forever! It provides an easy way to find all the records that have changed in an editing session. It works only with table-buffered data. Pass it a record number and it finds the next record after that that has changed.

Usage

```
nNextChanged = GetNextModified( nStart [, cAlias | nWorkArea ] )
```

Parameter	Value	Meaning
nStart	0	Find the first changed record in the table.
	Positive number	Find the next changed record after record nStart.
cAlias	Character	Look for changed records in the table open as cAlias.
	Omitted	If nWorkArea is also omitted, look for changed records in the current work area.
nWorkArea	Numeric	Look for changed records in work area nWorkArea.
	Omitted	If cAlias is also omitted, look for changed records in the current work area.
nNextChanged	0	There are no changed records after record nStart.
	Positive number	The record number of the next changed record.
	Negative number	The temporary record number of a newly added record.

GetNextModified() uses the natural order of the table, not any index you might have in effect. So, GetNextModified(0) returns the lowest positive record number for a changed record. You proceed through all the previously existing records in record order, then get the negative record numbers for newly added records.

GetNextModified() is another piece of the strategy for avoiding and resolving conflicts. As with the other related functions, you can use it either proactively or reactively. That is, you can try the TableUpdate() and, if it fails, use GetNextModified() together with CurVal(), OldVal() and GetFldState() to figure out what happened. Or do all that first, resolve all the conflicts, then TableUpdate().

You can only use GetNextModified() when you're table buffering. Try it on a row-buffered table and you get an error.

Remember that "modified" means you touched it. FoxPro isn't smart enough yet to know if you changed it, then changed it back. Look at SetFldState() if you find yourself in that situation.

GetNextModified() has two weaknesses that make it more useful for figuring out why TableUpdate() doesn't work than for using it to see if TableUpdate() will work. First, if the user changes a field in a form but doesn't move off that field, GetNextModified() and GetFldState() don't see that field as changed. Also, because GetNextModified() moves the record pointer, it fires row rules whether you want it to or not. We think we'll be sticking to the optimistic approach to saving records.

Example

```
* Loop through an open table, finding all the changed records
nNextRec = GetNextModified(0)
DO WHILE nNextRec <> 0
   IF nNextRec > 0
      * This is an existing record. Check for conflicts.
      * Then save it
   ELSE
      * This is a new record. Save it.
   ENDIF
   nNextRec = GetNextModified(nNextRec)
ENDDO
```

See Also Buffering, CurVal(), GetFldState(), OldVal(), SetFldState(), TableRevert(), TableUpdate()

GetObject()

GetObject() opens an existing document or creates a new object handle to an Automation server application. Like many aspects of ActiveX, exactly how this is implemented and the necessary parameters for successful execution vary by application.

Usage

```
oObject = GetObject( cFileName [, cClassName ] )
```

Parameter	Value	Meaning
cFileName	Character	Name of an existing file, or (depending on the application) a blank or null value.
	Omitted	Return a handle to an existing application, for some Automation servers.
cClassName	Character	Name of a registered server class (you can look them up in the Registry).

Omitting the first parameter and passing "Excel.Application" for the second starts Excel if it is not running, or grabs another handle to the application if it is executing. We use this technique, followed by Excel's FileOpen() function, if we need to work with multiple spreadsheets.

The latest generation of office applications from Microsoft (Office 97 as we write this) is much better behaved than its earlier counterparts. Word, Excel and PowerPoint all seem to work much better as Automation servers.

Example

```
* Open the MySheet spreadsheet in Excel and get
* A handle to the application
oExcel = GetObject("MySheet.XLS","Excel.Application")
* Talk to the running Word application
oWord = GetObject(, "Word.Application")
```

See Also CreateObject()

GetPad() See GetBar().

GetPEM(), PEMStatus()

These two functions were added in version 3.0b. They let you ask questions about the properties, events and methods of objects and classes. Although these two are extremely useful, they have some problems.

Usage

```
uValue = GETPEM( oObject | cClass, cPEMName )
uResult = PEMStatus( oObject | cClass,
                     cPEMName | cObjectName, nAttribute )
```

Parameter	Value	Meaning
oObject	Object	The object about which PEM information is to be returned.
cClass	Character	The name of a class about which PEM information is to be returned.
cPEMName	Character	The name of the property, event or method about which information is to be returned.
cObjectName	Character	Name of a contained object of oObject or cClass.
nAttribute	0	Has the property changed?
	1	Is the property read-only?
	2	Is the PEM protected?
	3	Which is this: property, event, method or (contained) object?
	4	Is the PEM user-defined?
	5	Is there such a PEM?
	6	Is this PEM inherited from a class higher in the class hierarchy?
uValue	Character, Numeric, Currency, Date, DateTime, Logical	The current value of the specified PEM. If cPEMName refers to an event or method, uValue receives (as a character string) the code contained in the event or method.
uResult	Logical or Character	The value of the specified attribute for the specified PEM.

These functions let you poke around in an object or a class definition to see what's what. Used together with AMEMBERS(), you can put together quite a complete picture of an object or class.

GetPEM() might seem a little redundant for properties. After all, you can just check the property's value. But having one function that works on both properties and methods makes lots of coding easier. We suspect GetPEM() will find lots of use in builders and developer tools, though it doesn't replace the ReadExpression method. Even at design -time, GetPEM() evaluates the property value. If a property is defined with an expression (such as "=DATE()"), it doesn't return the expression, it returns the current value of the expression.

For methods, GetPEM() is equivalent to the ReadMethod method (sounds redundant, doesn't it?). Like ReadMethod, it works only at design time.

PEMStatus() provides a lot of useful information about classes and objects that lets you figure out who they are and where they came from. The last value for nAttribute, 6, which indicates whether the PEM was inherited or added at this level, is new in VFP 6. Also new in VFP 6 is the ability to ask about a member object by passing its name. We're a little puzzled by this one, frankly, since it doesn't seem to tell anything you couldn't find out elsewhere.

Although you can find out whether a property is protected, there's no way to check whether it's hidden. We suspect that Microsoft simply hasn't noticed yet that that's a useful piece of information.

Both functions have a nasty bug when working with classes at runtime. In order to use the function, the class definition has to be in memory. To get it there, you have to instantiate the class at least once. You can destroy the instance immediately, but you have to have done it.

Passing 0 for PEMStatus()'s third parameter is supposed to work only for properties. In fact, you can do it with methods of visual classes (though not code classes), too, but the results aren't quite what you'd expect. If the method has code at any level in the class hierarchy, PEMStatus() returns .T. While this is somewhat useful (and more than the docs would lead you to expect), it doesn't help you figure out if you've overridden a method in this particular subclass or instance.

And yet another bug, this one more serious than either of the others. In some situations, if an object calls PEMStatus() more than twice in the same line of code, the object can't be released. We've been unable to nail down exactly the combination of circumstances that causes this one. For sure, using PEMStatus(_SCREEN.ActiveForm,…,5) three or more times in a line is one way to do it. In general, if you have an object that won't go away, check for multiple use of PEMStatus().

Example

```
oForm = CreateObject("FORM")
oForm.Left = 20
? GetPEM(oForm, "Left")              && Returns 20
? PEMStatus(oForm, "Left", 0)        && Returns .T.
? PEMStatus(oForm, "BaseClass", 1)   && Returns .T.
? PEMStatus(oForm, "Init", 3)        && Returns "Event"

SET CLASSLIB TO CoolStuf             && from the included disk
oSpin = CreateObject("DateSpin")     && To work around bug
RELEASE oSpin
? GetPEM("DateSpin", "BackStyle")    && Returns 0
? PEMStatus("DateSpin", "nYear", 2)  && Returns .F.
? PEMStatus("DateSpin", "nYear", 4)  && Returns .T.
```

See Also ReadExpression, ReadMethod, Sys(1269), WriteExpression, WriteMethod

GetPict()

This function brings up a special version of the File-Open dialog designed to let you choose graphic files. Read the name as "Get Picture."

Usage

```
cPictureFile = GETPICT( [ cExtension [, cPrompt
                          [, cOpenCaption ] ] ] )
```

Parameter	Value	Meaning
cExtension	Character	A semicolon-delimited (;) or vertical bar-delimited (|) list of file extensions to display in the Open Picture dialog. Can include DOS wildcards. As with GETFILE(), each extension type is shown separately in the drop-down. The first one you list is the drop-down value when the dialog opens. While you're not restricted to graphic types, attempting to preview a file that isn't of one of the supported graphic formats displays the message "Preview not available" in the preview box. (That's actually acceptable behavior, in our view. Sure beats an error message.)
	Omitted	In VFP 6, show all supported graphics files. In VFP 3 and VFP 5, show bitmap and icon files. Lets you see them all at once or one category at a time. Note that some popular graphic formats (including TIF) are still not supported.
cPrompt	Character	The prompt to put next to the text box for the filename. (In VFP 3, the prompt goes over the file list.)
	Omitted	The prompt is "File Name:"
cOpenCaption	Character	The caption to appear on the first ("OK") button.
	Omitted	The button says "OK".
cPictureFile	Character	The fully qualified name of the selected file.
	Empty	The user exited the dialog without choosing a file.

There's nothing about this dialog that forces the user to choose a picture. It's just set up to make it easier to choose pictures. As with other Windows Open dialogs, the user can change the extension or choose from "All Files." Check the files returned to make sure they're the type you expect (or at least have the right extension).

In VFP 6, they fixed our biggest complaint about this function. In FoxPro 2.x, the dialog you used to choose a picture had an "automatic preview" capability. If you paused on a filename more than briefly, the picture appeared in the Preview window. In VFP 3 and VFP 5, to preview a picture, you had to push a button. VFP 6 finally gets it right. The dialog has a check box that lets you decide whether or not to show a preview. The preview seems to be quite fast, too—no waiting around until FoxPro feels like showing you the picture.

Another VFP 6 improvement is that the preview (and FoxPro itself) can handle a myriad of graphic types. In older versions, it was limited to bitmaps and icons.

Example

```
* Let the user choose an icon for the current form
cIcon = GETPICT("ICO","Choose an icon")
IF NOT EMPTY(cIcon) AND RIGHT(cIcon,3)="ICO"
   This.Icon = cIcon
ENDIF
```

See Also DisabledPicture, DownPicture, GetFile(), Icon, Picture

GetPrinter(), PrtInfo(), Sys(1037)

These three functions are a wonderful relief from the printing challenges of early FoxPro versions.

GETPRINTER() presents the Windows dialog to choose the printer for output, PRTINFO() allows the programmer to query all the details of the capabilities of the printer, and SYS(1037) puts up a decent Print Setup dialog.

Usage `cPrinterChosen = GETPRINTER( )`

Parameter	Value	Meaning
cPrinterChosen	Character	The name of the printer chosen.
	Empty String	User chose Cancel, or closed the dialog box any way other than selecting OK.

This is a weak-looking dialog, allowing the user only to select a printer, but not set other properties. We don't understand why we don't get the full dialog we see in REPORT FORM...TO PRINT PROMPT.

Example

```
cPrinter = GETPRINTER()
IF NOT EMPTY(cPrinter)
  SET PRINTER TO NAME (cPrinter)
ENDIF
```

Usage `nResult = PRTINFO( nIndex [, cPrinterName ] )`

Parameter	Value	Meaning
nIndex	1	Orientation.
	2	Paper size. If -1 is returned, use parameters 3 and 4 to determine the custom paper size.
	3	Paper length, in tenths of a millimeter.
	4	Paper width, in tenths of a millimeter.
	5	Scaling factor.
	6	Number of copies to print.
	7	Paper tray chosen as the default paper source.
	8	Print quality, expressed in dots per inch, if a positive number, or a relative scale (Draft, Low, Medium, High) if a negative number (-1 to -4, respectively).
	9	Color printing? 1=Color, 2=Single color.
	10	Printer duplexing (printing both sides of the page) mode.
	11	Vertical resolution, in dots per inch.
	12	Options for printing TrueType fonts.
	13	Whether or not output is collated.

Parameter	Value	Meaning
cPrinterName	Character	The name of the printer, as returned by GETPRINTER() and APRINTERS().
nResult	-1	With two exceptions noted above (paper size, number 2 and print quality, number 8), a negative return indicates the information is unavailable. Either this feature may not be implemented for this printer, or you may have specified a printer that doesn't exist.
	Integer	Result of querying the particular parameter above, as documented above and in the help file.

These return values can be used to very precisely plan out how output will appear on the page. This is tremendously useful if you are trying to generate reports on the fly, or trying to make a certain amount of material fit on a single page. Rather than trying to memorize the above 13 possible index values and what they're good for, use the Foxpro.H file and the easier to use constant names included there.

Example

```
* Note that the following must be compiled
* to include FoxPro.H and run properly
#INCLUDE \VFP\FOXPRO.H
? "Orientation: "
nResult = PRTINFO(PRT_ORIENTATION)
DO CASE
  CASE nResult = -1
    ?? "Not Available"
  CASE nResult = 0
    ?? "Portrait"
  CASE nResult = 1
    ?? "Landscape"
ENDCASE
```

Usage `cEmptyString = SYS( 1037 )`

The documentation claims that SYS(1037) brings forth a Page Setup dialog. Very confusingly, calling this function brings up a dialog labeled "Print Setup." But selecting the "Properties" button on the dialog does allow you to adjust the default paper size, orientation and other settings specific to your printer. These settings are overridden if you select "Page Setup" from the menu for a specific report. If you want to give the user the ability to use his SYS(1037) settings instead, you need to delete the stored settings from the report. They're in TAG and TAG2 of the first record of the FRX—you can use something like this:

```
SYS(1037)
SELECT * FROM MyReport.FRX INTO CURSOR TempReport
SELECT TempReport
BLANK FIELDS TAG, TAG2
REPORT FORM TempReport TO PRINT
```

There are few areas of the product that cause more confusion and grief than printing. Much of this is due to a lack of understanding of what the product can do, some to misleading documentation, and some to the fact that "everyone knows" Fox can't do something. Carefully examine the functionality and return values of each of these functions, and we think you'll find that Fox can do whatever printing task is needed.

To see a Page Setup dialog, call up a report in the Report Designer, and select—surprise!—Page Setup from the File menu. There are options for the number of columns, whether the print area occupies the whole page (or just the printable portions), the order in which labels should print (left to right, or up and down) and the margin to use. These would be some nice features to be able to call up while a user is trying to fit text on his labels, without having to call up the entire designer.

The help for FoxPro 2.6a claims that SYS(1037) only works for the Macintosh. Wrong. It also brings up the Print Setup dialog in version 2.6a for Windows. Where it does, finally, bring up the Page Setup dialog is on the Mac only. Page Setup on the Mac doesn't have the Page Layout options of the Report Writer, either, but the name of the dialog is, in fact, Page Setup. We suspect this is just a case of bad translation among the several platforms, but we sympathize with our poor fellow developers who spend time trying to get the right dialog box to come up.

Example
```
=SYS(1037)
```

See Also #INCLUDE, APrinters(), Set Printer

Go, GoTo, Skip

These are two of the original commands in the Xbase language, useful for jumping to specific records while working interactively, but other commands have replaced their utility within programs in most cases.

Usage
```
[ GO | GOTO ] [ RECORD ] nRecordNumber | TOP | BOTTOM
   [ IN nWorkArea | cAlias ]
```

Yes, you read the syntax diagram above correctly. This is the only command in the language where the command itself is optional. Type a record number all by itself into the command window, and the record pointer moves there. This trick only works with record numbers, and does not support the new IN syntax. Issuing just the record number works in programs, as well, but add the optional GO to keep from confusing people. Lines like:

```
&cRecNo
```

won't make sense to many people. The keywords TOP and BOTTOM go to the first and last records, respectively, in the current index order, or in the natural record order if the table doesn't have a current active index, obeying any filter in place. The IN clause allows you to move the record pointer in another area by specifying either the work area number or the alias of the table open in that area.

GO is not Rushmore-optimizable. Rather than using GO TOP or BOTTOM, use LOCATE instead—see the trick to it in "Faster Than a Speeding Bullet."

Many of us have used the trick of storing the record number to a memory variable, doing some processing, and then restoring the record pointer to its original position with GO. This still works fine in Visual FoxPro, but a common extension of the trick may not. If the record pointer was at the "phantom record," beyond the last true record in the file, issuing GO (nRecNo) would result in a "Record is out of range" error, so the trick was to store –1 as the record number if the record pointer was at the end of the file, and place the record pointer back there if so. This is a clever trick, but beware: If you are working on tables with table buffering enabled, Visual FoxPro actually does use negative record numbers for uncommitted buffered records. Consider using 0 (zero) instead.

Example
```
nRecNo() = IIF( EOF(), 0, RecNo() )
... do your processing here
CASE RECCOUNT() = 0
  * DO NOTHING
CASE  nRecNo = 0
  GO BOTTOM
  SKIP
OTHERWISE
  GO (nRecno)
ENDCASE
```

Usage
```
SKIP [ nHowMany ] [ IN nWorkArea | cAlias ]
```

SKIP is used to move the record pointer manually a specified number of records. Like many commands that depend on the actual physical ordering of records, this command used to be far more popular than it needs to be today. If your applications require you to do a lot of SKIPping around, you may need to review your database schema for design problems.

nHowMany can specify a positive or negative number, and the record pointer is moved by that many records.

Usually, this movement takes place in the current table and work area, but there are two situations under which it will occur in another area. The first is illustrated in the syntax diagram above, where a table alias or work area number is explicitly given. The second is the case where there is a SET SKIP in effect. SET SKIP defines a one-to-many relationship where skipping takes place in the child (many) side of the relation, and the parent record pointer is moved if necessary to match that of the child.

SKIP is not Rushmore-optimizable. Even in the case of large tables with complex indexes, FoxPro can usually buffer enough of the table that the slowdown is not obvious, but in repetitive processes, the deficit can become apparent. Use SCAN...ENDSCAN if a large number of records need to be processed, or even a LOCATE and CONTINUE pair of commands rather than slogging through the whole file.

Example

```
SKIP -2    && go back two records
```

See Also Locate, RecNo(), Scan, Set Skip

GoBack, GoForward

These commands instruct the current Active Document host to navigate back or forward through its history list.

Usage

```
oLink.GoBack()
oLink.GoForward()
```

The Go commands mean nothing when running in a VFP shell, and nothing happens. Only when the hyperlink object is in an ActiveDocument that is itself hosted in a browser supporting history do the GoBack() and GoForward() methods actually navigate the browser to another address.

Example

```
oLink.GoBack()
oLink.GoForward()
```

See Also Hyperlink, NavigateTo

GoMonth()

This function returns a date offset from the date or datetime supplied by the number of months indicated (positive or negative). It is limited to dates in the year 1753 or later, returning empty dates if that lower limit is exceeded. Watch out for the type change this function causes: GOMONTH() always returns a date, whether supplied with a date or a datetime.

Usage

```
dReturn = GOMONTH( dDate | tDateTime, nOffset )
```

Have you ever wondered how to keep track of Aunt Tilly's birthday? Without fail, I always think it's a May date in April and an April date in May. And which birthday is it, anyway? Is she 60? 75? 142? Well, the answer, of course, is to keep track of Tilly's date of birth in a database, specifically in a date field, and have your machine remind you when her birthday approaches. How do you know when her birthday is coming up? Date math, of course! Just subtract the date from today, and you'll get, er, 26,263 days. Nope, that's not right—because FoxPro calculates the entire date, including the year amount. What you'll need to do is to compare the dates after shifting them into the same year and sound an alarm when the date's within a week or two. An excellent application for the GOMONTH() function, as demonstrated in the DiffDate function below:

```
* DiffDate.PRG
* returns the absolute difference in number of days between 2 dates,
* ignoring year, i.e., 9/8/43 vs. 9/9/94 returns 1 and
* 7/6/12 vs. 7/5/83 returns 1
LPARAMETERS tdDate1, tdDate2
LOCAL ldNewDate, lnDifference
* Validate parameters, force to today's date if blank
tdDate1 = MakeItDate(tdDate1)
tdDate2 = MakeItDate(tdDate2)
* Use GOMONTH() function to bring dates into the same year, then
* subtract the difference
```

```
ldNewDate = GOMONTH(tdDate1, (year(tdDate2)-year(tdDate1))*12)
lnDifference = tdDate2 - ldNewDate
* If they're still too far apart, bump ldNewDate a year + / -
IF ABS(lnDifference) > 182
  ldNewDate = GOMONTH(ldNewDate, 12*SIGN(lnDifference))
  lnDifference = tdDate2 - ldNewDate
ENDIF
RETURN ABS(lnDifference)

FUNCTION MakeItDate (tdDate2Test)
* Validate the parameter is a legitimate date or
* default to today's date instead
RETURN IIF(EMPTY(tdDate2Test) OR ;
           NOT INLIST(TYPE("tdDate2Test"),"D","T"), ;
           DATE(), ;
           tdDate2Test)
```

Example

```
? GOMONTH({06/15/1958},70*12)   && returns "06/15/2028"
* A favorite of our tech editor, to calculate the last day
* of the current month
ldLastDay = GOMONTH(date(), 1) - day(date())
```

See Also CDoW(), CMonth(), Date(), Day(), DMY(), DoW(), MDY(), Month(), Set Century, Set Date, Set Mark, Year()

GotFocus, LostFocus

These events fire when an object gains or loses focus. They're similar to the When and Valid events, but don't include any testing to see whether the object can get or lose the focus. Also, unlike Valid, LostFocus fires every time focus leaves the control, whether or not the user has actually used the control.

Usage

```
PROCEDURE oObject.GotFocus | oObject.LostFocus
[ LPARAMETERS nIndex ]
```

The nIndex parameter is needed only if the method is for a control array.

GotFocus fires after When for the same object, and only if When returns .T. In other words, only if the object is actually allowed to have the focus.

LostFocus fires when you leave the object. For objects where Valid fires as you leave (text boxes and edit boxes, for example), Valid fires first. If Valid returns .T., allowing focus to leave, LostFocus fires. LostFocus is really useful, though, in controls that don't always fire Valid. You can still detect that the user is moving along and act accordingly. This ability was sorely lacking in FoxPro 2.x.

In the first edition of this book, we recommended against using the SetFocus method in either of these methods. At the time, we said that the results were odd and unpredictable, though we couldn't make anything disastrous happen. Since then, Microsoft has declared that you can't use SetFocus in the Valid method, meaning that LostFocus is really your only chance to decide where focus lands at runtime. We've heard a few stories about odd behavior and seen some mildly strange firing sequences with SetFocus in LostFocus, but we still haven't come across anything disastrous and haven't personally seen any behavior that gives us pause. So, at this point, we will cautiously retract the original warning, leaving it with just a "If you see something strange, check out interactions between LostFocus and SetFocus."

Example

```
* You might enable/disable certain options only when you're
* sitting on a particular control. In this case, we enable
* a button as we go in and disable it on the way out.
PROCEDURE edtDetails.GotFocus
* Enable the button to show more details
ThisForm.cmdBlowItUp.Enabled = .T.
ENDPROC

PROCEDURE edtDetails.LostFocus
* Disable the details button
```

```
ThisForm.cmdBlowItUp.Enabled = .F.
ENDPROC
```

See Also Activate, Deactivate, SetFocus, When, Valid

Grid, Column, Header

A grid is a "browse-in-a-read" or at least the VFP equivalent. Columns and Headers are the stuff that grids are made of.

A grid is a container object. It contains columns. Columns are also containers. They contain headers and controls. Each column has only one header, but can contain as many controls as you like. By default, each column starts out with a single text box.

Grids display table or cursor contents. Each row of the grid reflects a single record. When you access the control in a column, it's bound to the appropriate field of the current record (or an expression based on the current record).

Grid

Property	Value	Purpose
ActiveColumn, ActiveRow	Numeric	Contain the number of the column and row that have focus, respectively. Measured in absolute terms from the first row and column of the grid. Uses ColumnOrder for columns, not creation order.
ChildOrder	Character	When the grid is the "many" side of a one-to-many relation, can indicate the name of the index tag by which the table is ordered. ("Can" because you can also do this using Data Environment properties.)
ColumnCount	Numeric	The number of columns in the grid. Set it to -1 to have one column for each field in the current RecordSource.
Columns	Collection	References to the columns in the grid.
DeleteMark	Logical	Determines whether the grid has a "delete mark" column, allowing the user to click to delete or recall a record.
GridLineColor	Numeric	The color in which the grid lines appear.
GridLines	Numeric	Determines whether the grid has horizontal or vertical grid lines, neither or both.
GridLineWidth	Numeric	The thickness of the grid lines.
HeaderHeight	Numeric	The height of the headers in the grid.
Highlight	Logical	Determines whether the contents of the cell with focus are highlighted when you tab into the cell.
LeftColumn	Numeric	Contains the ColumnOrder of the left-most column currently visible in the grid.

Property	Value	Purpose
LinkMaster	Character	When the grid is the "many" side of a one-to-many relation, can indicate the alias of the "one" table.
Panel	Numeric	Determines which side of a split grid has the focus.
PanelLink	Logical	Determines whether the two sides of a split grid are linked.
Partition	Numeric	Determines where the divider for a split grid appears. When 0, the grid isn't split.
RecordMark	Logical	Determines whether the grid has a column (on the left border) that contains a pointer for the current record.
RecordSource	Character	The table name, alias or filename of the table or query that provides the data for the grid.
RecordSourceType	Numeric	The type of object that provides the data for the grid.
RelationalExpr	Character	When the grid is the "many" side of a one-to-many relation, can indicate the expression that links the two tables.
RelativeColumn, RelativeRow	Numeric	The column and row of the cell with focus, relative to the cell visible in the upper-left corner.
RowHeight	Numeric	The height of the rows in the grid.
Scrollbars	Numeric	Determines what scrollbars, if any, the grid has.

Event	Purpose
AfterRowColChange	Fires after focus has moved to a new cell.
BeforeRowColChange	Fires when the user attempts to move focus to a new cell.
Scrolled	Fires when the user uses the scrollbars.

Method	Purpose
ActivateCell	Sets focus to a particular cell in the grid.
AddColumn, RemoveColumn	Add and remove columns from the grid.
DoScroll	Scroll the grid in a specified direction.
GridHitTest	Returns information about the grid element at a specified point.

Column

Property	Value	Purpose
Bound	Logical	Determines whether the controls in the column are bound to the column's ControlSource or their own.
ColumnOrder	Numeric	Determines the display position of the column within the grid.
ControlCount	Numeric	The number of controls in the column.
Controls	Collection	References to the controls in the column, including the header.
CurrentControl	Character	The name of the control in the column that is presented to the user.
DynamicAlignment	Character	An expression that evaluates to a legal Alignment value and indicates the alignment for each cell in this column at this time.
DynamicBackColor, DynamicForeColor	Character	Expressions that evaluate to color values indicating the colors used for this column at this time. Evaluated individually for each cell in the column each time the cell is redrawn.
DynamicCurrentControl	Character	An expression that evaluates to the name of one of the column's controls. Indicates which control the user should see.
DynamicFontBold, DynamicFontItalic, DynamicFontName, DynamicFontSize, DynamicFontStrikeThru, DynamicFontUnderline	Character	Expressions that evaluate to appropriate font property values. Indicate which font characteristics the column should have at this time. Like other Dynamic... properties, evaluated each time the grid is refreshed.
DynamicFontOutline, DynamicFontShadow	Character	Do nothing except in VFP/Mac.
DynamicInputMask	Character	An expression that evaluates to a valid input mask, indicating the mask to be used for this column at this time. Evaluated each time the grid is refreshed.
Movable	Logical	Determines whether the user can move the column.
Resizable	Logical	Determines whether the user can resize the column.
SelectOnEntry	Logical	Determines whether the contents of the column are highlighted when the user tabs into it.
Sparse	Logical	Determines whether the current control for the column shows all the time or only when the cell has focus.

Header

Headers have no unique or unusual properties, events or methods, just the basic ones shared by many classes.

One of the trickiest issues with grids is figuring out which object in a grid receives events, especially mouse events. The grid receives these events only if nothing it contains is able to. If you click in a control of a column, the control's Click is executed. If you click on the header of a column, the header's Click fires. To fire the grid's Click, you have to click on a row after the last record, or on the record mark or delete mark.

Like other objects designed only to be contained in a particular container, columns and headers can't be subclasse5d in the Class Designer. (See Pageframe for the consequences of this.) A good builder can be useful here, as can putting some code in the grid class's Init method.

Aside from all other differences, you can build grids two different ways depending on the value of ColumnCount. When ColumnCount is -1, the grid contains one column for each field of the RecordSource. In this case, you can change column properties in code using the Columns collection, but you can't do it in the property sheet. When ColumnCount is positive, you can set up each specified column ahead of time.

Example

```
* Set up a grid as the child side of the relation between
* the TasTrade Orders and Order_Line_Items tables.
* Assume both tables are in the Data Environment, but that
* the relation between them has been removed. Usually, you
* wouldn't do it this way - you'd use the relation in the DE.
* Set these grid properties as shown:
RecordSource = "Order_Line_Items"
ChildOrder = "Order_Id"
LinkMaster = "Orders"
RelationalExpr = "Order_Id"

* Now let's put only the columns we want to see:
ColumnCount = 3

* Now switch to column properties.
* For column1.header1:
Caption = "Product Id"

* For column1:
ControlSource = "Order_Line_Items.Product_Id"

* For column2.header1:
Caption = "Unit Price"

* For column2:
ControlSource = "Order_Line_Items.Unit_Price"

* For column3.header1:
Caption = "Quantity"

* For column3:
ControlSource = "Order_Line_Items.Quantity"

* Now set the column up to use blue for any item where quantity
* is more than 10. For column3:
DynamicForeColor = "IIF(Order_Line_Items.Quantity>10, ;
   RGB(0,0,255),RGB(0,0,0))"

* You'll want to do more cosmetic stuff like resizing the
* columns and so forth.
```

See Also ActivateCell, ActiveColumn, ActiveRow, AddColumn, AfterRowColChange, BeforeRowColChange, Bound, ChildOrder, ColumnCount, Columns, ColumnOrder, Controls, ControlCount, CurrentControl, DeleteColumn, DeleteMark, DoScroll, DynamicAlignment, DynamicBackColor, DynamicCurrentControl, DynamicFontBold, DynamicFontItalic, DynamicFontName, DynamicFontOutline, DynamicFontShadow, DynamicFontSize, DynamicFontStrikeThru, DynamicFontUnderline, DynamicForeColor, DynamicInputMask, GridLineColor, GridLines, GridLineWidth, GridHitTest, HeaderHeight, Highlight, LeftColumn, LinkMaster, Movable, Panel, PanelLink, Partition, RecordMark, RecordSource, RecordSourceType, RelationalExpr, RelativeColumn, RelativeRow, Resizable, RowHeight,

Scrollbars, Scrolled, SelectOnEntry, Sparse

GridHitTest

This is a very cool method, added in VFP 6. It lets you figure out where you are in a grid. It is a little strange to use, though, because unlike any other method we can think of, it expects some parameters to be passed by reference.

Usage

```
lInGrid = grdGrid.GridHitTest( nXCoord, nYCoord
                   [, @nGridComponent [, @nRelativeRow
                   [, @nRelativeColumn [, @nGridPane ] ] ] ] )
```

Parameter	Value	Meaning
nXCoord, nYCoord	Numeric	The point to check to determine whether it's in the grid.
nGridComponent	Numeric	If the point is in the grid, receives a value indicating which part of the grid that point is in. Otherwise, receives 0.
nRelativeRow	Numeric	If the point is in the grid, receives the relative row in the grid where the point is found.
nRelativeColumn	Numeric	If the point is in the grid, receives the relative column in the grid where the point is found.
nGridPane	Numeric	If the point is in the grid, receives the pane of the grid where the point is found.
lInGrid	.T.	The point is in the grid. "In the grid" includes everything up to the very outside border of the grid.
	.F.	The point is not in the grid.

At any time, only one row of a grid is truly active. But there are times when we want to act upon cells other than those in the active row. GridHitTest makes this task much easier. It lets us pass a point and find out not only whether that point is in the grid's space (which we could do with a little arithmetic), but what part of the grid it's over. If the point is within the rows and columns, GridHitTest tells us which row and column the point is in. The row and column returned are relative, not absolute. That is, only visible rows and columns are counted. Last and probably least, this method also tells us which pane of the grid the point is in. This is relevant only when the grid is split, something we recommend only rarely.

As we noted above, the format of this method is unique. It's the only method we've encountered that really wants to be a procedure rather than a function. Be sure to precede the last four parameters with "@" so they can receive the appropriate return values.

Help suggests using GridHitTest for OLE drag and drop. In fact, it also helps with conventional drag and drop. Dragging and dropping into grid cells has always been a real pain, but this method makes it easy. When the grid's DragDrop method fires, use GridHitTest to determine whether you're over a cell and, if so, which one. Then, activate the cell and stuff the data into it. The example shows one way to do it.

Example

```
* Code for grid's DragDrop event to put data into cell
* There are some assumptions here, including that the control
* of interest is the second one. (The first is always the
* header.) More code could get rid of that assumption.
LPARAMETERS oSource, nXCoord, nYCoord

cData = oSource.Value
```

```
LOCAL nComp, nRow, nCol
IF This.GridHitTest(nXCoord,nYCoord,@nComp,@nRow,@nCol)
   IF nComp = 3
      This.SetFocus()
      This.ActivateCell(nRow,nCol)
      This.Columns[This.ActiveColumn].Controls[2].Value = cData
   ENDIF
ENDIF
```

See Also ActivateCell, DragDrop, Grid, MCol(), MRow(), OLEDragDrop

GridLineColor, GridLineWidth

These two properties, not surprisingly, determine the color and width of a grid's lines between cells.

Usage

```
grdGrid.GridLineColor = nRGBValue
nRGBValue = grdGrid.GridLineColor
grdGrid.GridLineWidth = nWidth
nWidth = grdGrid.GridLineWidth
```

The color setting for GridLineColor accepts the standard RGB color value, an integer in the range of 0 to 16,777,215, as returned by the RGB() function.

One neat trick to try with GridLineColor is to set the colors of the row and gridlines so the grid seems to disappear at some points. In our example below, a grid set up with white gridlines and the "green-bar paper" effect of every other line alternating green and white (through the use of DynamicForeColor settings) would appear to have white vertical gridlines only in the green rows.

The width setting for GridLineWidth is expressed in pixels and accepts a numeric value from 1 to 40. The decimal portion of the number is ignored. In VFP 3.0, a value of less than 1 causes the gridlines to nearly vanish, leaving all but a little remnant at the intersection of the horizontal and vertical gridlines. A value greater than one-half the height of the row hides the entire row.

GridLineWidth and GridLineColor do not affect the widths or colors of the RecordMark or DeleteMark columns, if they are included, nor do they affect the thickness or color of the lines between the headers. We think this takes away from the overall effect of having such fine control over the gridlines, and hope Microsoft considers extending the properties to cover the whole grid.

Example

```
* Green Column Headers grdGrid1.SetAll('BackColor',rgb(0,192,0),'Header')
* Alternating white and green rows within grid
* This version works only if the grid shows records in
* their physical order.
grdGrid1.SetAll('DynamicBackColor', ;
       "iif(recno()%2=1,rgb(255,255,255),rgb(0,192,0))", ;
       'Column')
grdGrid1.GridLineColor = RGB(255,255,255)  && White lines
grdGrid1.GridLineWidth = 1  && Single pixel width
grdGrid1.GridLines = 2  && Vertical lines only
```

See Also DeleteMark, Grid, GridLines, RecordMark, RGB()

GridLines

This property determines whether horizontal gridlines, vertical gridlines, or both should be displayed in a grid.

Usage

```
grdGrid.GridLines = nGridValue
nGridValue = grdGrid.GridLines
```

Parameter	Value	Meaning
nGridValue	0	Display no gridlines.

Parameter	Value	Meaning
nGridValue	1	Display only horizontal gridlines.
	2	Display only vertical gridlines.
	3	The default: Display both horizontal and vertical gridlines.

Horizontal and vertical gridlines can take up a lot of space on the grid and distract from what the client is there to see—the data. Turn off distracting gridlines if the form can still be read without them. Better yet, include a toggle so the viewer can turn them on and off as desired! Consider other ways of separating records, like DynamicBackColor, if grid lines don't work for you. You'll probably want to turn off RecordMark and DeleteMark while you're at it, too, but short of hiding the headers altogether, we haven't found a way to get the separator lines between them to disappear.

Example
```
frmFormOne.grdMyDataGrid.GridLines = 1  && horizontal only
```

See Also DeleteMark, DynamicBackColor, Grid, GridLineColor, GridLineWidth, RecordMark

GridLineWidth See GridLineColor.

HalfHeightCaption

This property lets you give a form a title bar that's a little different than the regular one.

Usage
```
frmForm.HalfHeightCaption = lHasHalfHeight
lHasHalfHeight = frmForm.HalfHeightCaption
```

In VFP 3 under Win 3.x, the title bar created by this option really was half-height. We think it was for backward compatibility and conversion of FoxPro/DOS screens, because we couldn't see any reason why you'd want a half-height title bar. They're mucho ugly.

Under the modern versions of Windows, the size of the caption bar changes only very slightly. However, the size of the icon in the upper left corner changes noticeably. It's a little bigger with HalfHeightCaption set to .T.—as a side effect of that, the buttons on the right-hand end of the title bar are a little closer together. In addition, the form's control menu loses its "sticky" property. When you click on it, once you release the mouse button, the menu closes.

Given the minimal changes this property induces and the oddball behavior of the control menu, we can't think of any reason at all to touch it anymore.

Example
```
ThisForm.HalfHeightCaption = .T.
```

See Also BorderStyle, Caption, TitleBar

Header See Grid.

Header()

This function tells you the size of a table header. The header contains definition information for the table.

Usage
```
nHeaderSize = HEADER( [ cAlias | nWorkArea ] )
```

You can get the header size of any open table by passing the alias or work area. Visual FoxPro tables have much larger headers than tables from older versions of FoxPro. For details on header contents, see "DBF, FPT, CDX,

DBC—Hike!"

You can combine the result of HEADER() with record size information from RECSIZE() and the record count from RECCOUNT() to determine the space requirements of a table.

Example

```
CREATE TABLE Test (CharFld C(1),NumFld N(1))
? HEADER()       && Returns 360

* determine space requirements for Customer:
* Header length plus the size of one record, times
* the number of records, plus one byte for a
* terminating Ctrl+Z (only if records exist)
USE Customer
nSpaceNeeded = HEADER() + RECCOUNT() * RECSIZE() + 1
```

See Also AFields(), FCount(), FSize(), RecCount(), RecSize()

HeaderHeight

This property specifies the height, in pixels, of a grid's column headers.

Usage

```
grdGrid.HeaderHeight = nHeight
nHeight = grdGrid.HeaderHeight
```

Why "HeaderHeight" instead of just "Height?" At first, we felt that this was a slip-up by the development team, the anti-polymorphic urge to name every variable in an application differently. "This property really should be Height, just like in all the other objects," we thought. But look at its scope—HeaderHeight is defined at the Grid level of containership, not for each individual column, since all Headers must share the same height property, so it is HeaderHeight. We still feel that it is somehow "out of scope" and violating encapsulation for a header's property to be stored outside the object in its grid container, but headers, columns and grids share a special relationship—the contained objects, like goldfish in a bowl, can exist only inside the container, so this dependence, while not truly Pure Object Oriented Programming (POOP), works. 'Nuff said.

Example

```
ThisForm.Grid1.HeaderHeight = 20
```

See Also Column, Grid, Header

Height, Width

These properties, not surprisingly, control the height and width of visual objects, including forms and controls.

Usage

```
oObject.Height = nValue
nValue = oObject.Height
oObject.Width = nValue
nValue = oObject.Width
```

The size of an object is measured in the current ScaleMode.

Height and Width are measured differently from each other and differently for different objects. For forms, Height and Width exclude borders and titles. For controls, Height includes the border, but Width is measured from the center of the border. According to the docs, measuring a control's width this way makes it easier to line up controls with different borders. We're not sure we see the point.

You can change the size of an object by modifying Height and Width. However, controls contained in grid columns can't be resized.

Example

```
frmMyForm = CREATEOBJECT("form")
frmMyForm.SHOW()
frmMyForm.Height = frmMyForm.Height + 20
frmMyForm.Width = frmMyForm.Width * 1.5
```

The example demonstrates that you can make changes relative to existing values. You can use this ability to size contained objects to fit inside the container—for example, making sure a certain set of controls fits into a form.

Example

```
* Resize Demo

frmResizeDemo = CREATEOBJECT("ResizeForm")
frmResizeDemo.Show()
READ EVENTS

DEFINE CLASS ResizeForm as Form
  ScaleMode = 0  && Note that this is foxels for simplicity
  MinHeight = 10
  Add Object edtNote as Speech
  Add Object btnQuit as QuitButton

  * Custom Properties
  nQuitBtnMargin = 3
  nEdtBoxMargin = 5
  PROCEDURE Init
    This.ReSize()
  ENDPROC

  Procedure ReSize
    ThisForm.btnQuit.Top = ThisForm.Height - This.nQuitBtnMargin
    ThisForm.btnQuit.Left = (ThisForm.Width - ;
                             ThisForm.btnQuit.Width ) / 2
    ThisForm.edtNote.Height = ThisForm.Height - ;
                              ThisForm.nEdtBoxMargin
    ThisForm.edtNote.Width  = ThisForm.Width - ;
                              2*ThisForm.edtNote.Left
  ENDPROC

  PROCEDURE Destroy
    CLEAR EVENTS
  ENDPROC
ENDDEFINE

DEFINE CLASS QuitButton AS CommandButton
  Caption="Quit"
  HEIGHT = 2
  PROCEDURE Click
    CLEAR EVENTS
  ENDPROC
ENDDEFINE

DEFINE CLASS Speech AS EditBox
  Left = 3
  Value = "Four score and seven years ago " + ;
          "our fathers brought forth on " + ;
          "this continent a new nation, conceived " + ;
          "in liberty and dedicated to the proposition " + ;
          "that all men are created equal."
ENDDEFINE
```

For a form, Height and Width are constrained by MaxHeight, MinHeight, MaxWidth and MinWidth. Regardless of the values you assign, the Height and Width will never go beyond those boundaries.

See Also Left, Top, MaxHeight, MaxWidth, MinHeight, MinWidth, ScaleMode

Help, Set Help, Set("Help"), Set HelpFilter, Set Topic, Set Topic ID

Visual FoxPro is unusual in having not one, not two, but three help engines built in: one for cross-platform-compatible DBF-based help, one for interfacing to the native "legacy" Windows HLP engine, and one for the new compressed HTML Help CHM files. These flexible commands allow you to use the best features of each.

Usage

```
SET HELP ON | OFF | TO cHelpFileName
cOnOrOff = SET( "HELP" )
cHelpFileName = SET( "HELP",1 )
```

```
HELP [ cTopic | ID nHelpContextID ] [ NOWAIT ]
   [ IN [ WINDOW ] winName | IN [ WINDOW ] SCREEN ]
```

Three help engines! What pandemonium! What to do? Here's our take.

The DBF Help is "included for backward compatibility" and produces the world's ugliest help screens. We think it could be the basis for an awesome tool for generating help, but we wouldn't consider actually showing an application with DBF-based help to a client. The "classic" WinHelp engine is a pretty decent help engine, and if you already have substantial investment in tools to create HLP files, don't abandon them just yet. Microsoft will be shipping the WinHelp engine as part of the operating system for some time yet, so plan a transition to HTML Help when it makes sense for you.

Finally HTML Help. We think this is a pretty cool new tool, but it's fairly new—version 1.1 as we write this—and has undergone fairly tumultuous changes in its short life. You will notice that the CD accompanying the book has the entire Hacker's Guide in HTML Help format. We're impressed with what we can do with this, and think we're going to like it. HTML Help provides all of the capabilities of WinHelp (except one) and is easier to write (HTML is much prettier than RTF, in our opinion) and test.

The one gotcha that might keep you using WinHelp for a while is that HTML Help does not work with the "WhatsThisHelp" feature of dialogs. Since there are other ways of presenting that information, such as having a Help button on the form, or using ToolTips to pass information to the client, we don't think this is a big loss.

Most of the Help commands and optional clauses are based on Fox Software's original DOS Help engine, and don't apply to, or don't make sense in most VFP applications. For applications using either of the newer Windows engines, SET HELP TO your help file, set the HelpContextIDs of the forms and controls that can supply help, and sit back and let the engine do its thing.

You may want to SET HELP OFF if you are allowing the user to edit or modify the DBF form of the file, to avoid a "File is in use" error. Otherwise, plan to leave Help ON the rest of the time.

SET HELP TO accepts a path and file name. If the filename specified has an HLP extension, FoxPro uses the WinHelp engine; with a DBF extension it attempts to use the built-in DBF engine. A file with a CHM extension runs the HTML Help engine. If you try something completely different, different versions react in different ways, but you usually end up with an error message. In VFP 6, the DBF engine fires first and reports "Not a table." In VFP 3 and 5, we got "Not a Windows Help file." In the next version, we're betting we get an HTML Help engine error, just so they keep firing differently. Sheesh.

For DOS-based Help, the WINDOW | IN WINDOW clauses are the same as those described in the MODIFY MEMO topic, so we won't drag you through the syntax again.

Pass the cTopic string or numeric HelpContextID to bring up a specific topic. Items in the Visual FoxPro interface have HelpContextIDs assigned—use SYS(1023) to sniff them out. You will need to assign HelpContextIDs to the controls and forms you create. Pass nothing to get the main contents screen.

HELP NOWAIT really is only applicable for the DBF form of help, as the WinHelp HLP format is by nature NOWAIT. DBF Help could be a pain to manage inside a Foundation Read in 2.x, but allowing it to NOWAIT while other processing goes on seems more natural in VFP.

DBF Help needs a character field for the topic name and a memo field for the details as the first two fields in the table. SET HELP to any table that lacks the proper structure and kablooie! Fatal Errors or Invalid Page Faults left and right! How rude! We would expect an "I'm sorry, this is not a valid Help file format," not a crash-and-burn scene! Unsatisfactory.

If your DBF Help has the right structure, but no records, VFP 6 displays a new error—2036—with the message "The current Help file is empty" with an OK and a Help button—think about that one. Versions of VFP before 6.0 would crash, so this is an improvement.

The DBF form of Help is U G L Y, and Microsoft did nothing to improve the interface in VFP 3.0, 5.0, or 6.0. They could have jazzed it up a little, thrown in some 3-D effects, beveled a few angles, moved the buttons around, but, no, nothing. Pitiful. If DBF help is their Mac-Windows cross-platform solution, Microsoft needs to introduce ugly as a new standard. Come to think of it, maybe they already have.

Many people seem to be unaware of it, but there is a another method of invoking help, besides pressing F1 or issuing the help command, and that's Shift+F1. Similar to the "What's This?" option introduced in the Windows 95 interface, Shift+F1 turns the cursor to a combined question mark and pointer arrow and provides the Help file with the ContextID of the item clicked on by the user, whether it is a form, a button or even a menu selection. This form of "safe" exploring of an interface lets users determine what actions will occur upon selection of unfamiliar options and is a great way for them to learn the product non-destructively. This is a technique that should be encouraged, we think!

In addition, in combination with SYS(1023), it is a nice way of determining the HelpContextIDs of the built-in gadgets (like a GETFONT dialog) that your application's help file needs to support.

Example

```
SET HELP TO \VFP\FOXHELP.DBF
SET HELP ON
? SET("HELP") && "ON"
? SET("HELP",1) && "C:\VFP\FOXHELP.DBF"

HELP WhatsThisButton  && brings up help on WhatsThisButton
HELP ID 1075708407    && brings up help on the standard toolbar
```

Usage

```
SET HELPFILTER [ AUTOMATIC ] TO lExpression
SET TOPIC TO [ cTopic ] | [ ID nHelpContextID ] [ lExpression ]
```

HELPFILTER is the equivalent of SET FILTER, and applies only to the DBF form of Help. lExpression can be any expression that evaluates to a logical true or false value for each record. The AUTOMATIC keyword causes the filter to be cleared after Help has been called up and closed. Several folks came up with clever schemes to add additional fields onto the basic ones supplied with the DBF-style help and use these fields to supply more screen-sensitive help than just a single entry. Pressing the Topics button in DBF-style help while a HELPFILTER is in effect shows only those records that pass the filter criteria.

SET TOPIC TO allows the Help file to be pointed to a particular entry before Help is invoked. SET TOPIC TO does not change the position of either Help file unless the Help command is executed again. Both forms, the character-based Topic and the numeric ContextID, can be used with either the DBF or WinHelp engines; however, there are some slight differences in behavior. For a specific topic to be displayed, Windows Help requires the entire topic title to be entered, whereas the DBF format will locate the first topic that matches the supplied string.

The logical expression only makes sense for DBF Help. You should also be able to supply a logical expression to SET TOPIC, similar to that used in SET HELPFILTER. It worked in 2.6. It doesn't in 3.0, nor does it work in 5.0. It is no longer documented in 6.0.

SET TOPIC doesn't work at all with HTML Help.

With most controls and forms, you don't need to set their topics programmatically. Use their HelpContextID property instead.

Example

```
* Using a custom DBF with fields cFIELD and cScreen
* This should work in 3.0, but doesn't
SET TOPIC TO cField = This.Name or cScreen = ThisForm.Name
* This form does work with FOXHELP.DBF and HLP
SET TOPIC TO "Sample"
* As does this:
SET TOPIC ID TO 1895825500

SET HELPFILTER TO HelpFile.Screen = WONTOP() or ;
                  HelpFile.Screen = "GENERAL"
* New topics in Help, not covered in the docs
SET HELPFILTER TO TOPIC = "Changes"
```

See Also HelpContextID, Modify Memo, Set Filter, Sys(1023)

Help

This method of the VFP Automation server calls Help. Big surprise.

Usage

```
oVFP.Help( [ cHelpFile ] [, nContextId | ,, cTopic ] )
```

Parameter	Value	Meaning
cHelpFile	Character	The name (including path) of the help file to open.
	Omitted	Open the current help file (as specified with SET HELP).
nContextId	Numeric	Position help on the topic with the specified HelpContextId.
	Omitted	If cTopic is also omitted, position help on the first topic.
cTopic	Character	Position help on the specified topic. If cTopic doesn't uniquely specify a single topic, show the Help index positioned on the closest match.
	Omitted	If nContextId is also omitted, position help on the first topic.

This is the Automation server equivalent to the native HELP command, except that it actually combines the functionality of both HELP and SET HELP. It's fairly smart and fairly well-behaved (except for the glaring omission below). If the right help file is already open, this method doesn't open it again—it just brings the help window to the top. The method also interacts appropriately with SYS(1023) and SYS(1024), which let you find out the context IDs for dialogs and so forth. Once you call SYS(1023), calls to the Help method are intercepted, as if you'd invoked Help from the interface.

Although you can include both a context ID and a topic, only the context ID is processed in that case. If there's no topic with that ID, it doesn't matter whether or not the topic is valid—you get an error message.

Watch out when you want to specify only a topic. You do need the extra comma for the missing context ID.

This method doesn't know about HTML Help. If you invoke _VFP.Help from the VFP 6 Command Window, you get an error message. Given that Microsoft has decreed that HTML Help is the future, this is a pretty big mistake.

On the other hand, this method handles a wide variety of Windows Help files, bringing up the right version of Help.

Example

```
* Open VFP 5 help from VFP 6
_VFP.Help("\vfp5\foxhelp.hlp")

* Position the currently open help to the ASSERT command
_VFP.Help(,,"assert")

* Open VFP 5 help to the topic with context id 536875079
_VFP.Help("\vfp5\foxhelp.hlp",536875079)
```

See Also Application, Help, Set Help, Sys(1023), Sys(1024)

HelpContextID

HelpContextID is a property of all of the controls that can gain focus, and it provides the link between the control and its matching Help topic for context-sensitive help. All three of the help engines—DOS, WinHelp and HTML Help—recognize and use the context IDs.

Usage

```
nID = Object.HelpContextID
oObject.HelpContextID = nID
```

The HelpContextID property is one of the more common among objects, belonging to everything from _SCREEN to option buttons. Use the SYS(1023) and SYS(1024) functions to determine the HelpContextIDs of the forms and buttons on built-in dialogs you want to include in your application.

Menus lack a facility for adding HelpContextIDs to developer-created pads and bars.

Some, but not all, of the built-in pads lose their context IDs as well. Create a quick menu and run it. Press Shift+F1 and select Edit-Paste from the menu, and Help is gone. SET SYSMENU TO DEFAULT and repeat the steps, and it's back. We suspected at first that only pads relevant to the runtime would have their HelpContextIDs preserved, but that doesn't seem to be the case, either. As we mention in the menu sections, this part of the Visual FoxPro is in serious need of an overhaul.

HelpContextIDs offer a great opportunity for an enterprising third-party developer. Someone could write Builders and Wizards for quick data entry of context-sensitive help from within the design surfaces, scanning and auditing programs to ensure help file coverage, and automating generation of IDs by scanning projects and their associated files.

HelpContextIDs seem to be limited in range to ±2,147,483,647, but we think that 2^32 separate help topics should be enough for most of our systems.

Example

```
* We've created a help file where we want a standard
* "this is what happens if you select quit" help topic.
* We've assigned that topic HelpContextID 37 in the HLP file.
* In each of the forms where we want that help, we
* assign the topic to the associated buttons:
oForm.btnQuit.HelpContextID = 37  && standard 'Quit'  help
* Actually, we can do this just once if we make it part of a
* quit button class.
```

See Also Activate Menu, Help, Sys(1023), Sys(1024)

Hide See Show.

Hide Menu, Show Menu, Hide Popup, Show Popup, Move Popup, Size Popup

These commands date back before the Windows menu revolution, when you could set your own standards for how the menus and popups in your application behaved. In those days, it was okay to have menus disappear and reappear and to move popups around on the screen. These days, we don't do that—it violates the Window interface guidelines and, more important, confuses the heck out of users.

Usage

```
HIDE MENU MenuList | ALL [ SAVE ]
SHOW MENU MenuList | ALL [ PAD PadName ] [ SAVE ]
HIDE POPUP PopupList | ALL [ SAVE ]
SHOW POPUP PopupList | ALL [ SAVE ]
```

The SAVE clause in each command leaves an image of the thing around so the user thinks it's still there. But the image is brain-dead—it just takes up real estate.

These commands have no place in a Windows application.

Usage

```
MOVE POPUP PopupName TO nRow, nCol | BY nRows, nCols
SIZE POPUP PopupName TO nRows, nCols | BY nRows, nCols
```

These commands, which can take absolute values (with TO) or relative values (with BY), might have some place in Visual FoxPro applications. Since popups are the key to right-click menus, there are cases where you might want to move or resize a popup dynamically.

Example

```
* Make popup wider and shorter
SIZE POPUP MyPopup BY 5,-10
```

See Also Define Menu, Define Popup, Menus

Hide Window See Define Window.

HideDoc See ShowDoc.

HideSelection

This property determines whether selected text remains highlighted when focus moves to another control. The default is for the highlight to disappear when focus changes.

Usage

```
oObject.HideSelection = lHideIt
lHideIt = oObject.HideSelection
```

The controls that support selection of text are text boxes, edit boxes, spinners and combo boxes (only in combo mode—not as drop-downs). For some reason, combo boxes didn't have a HideSelection property in VFP 3, but that was remedied in VFP 5.

HideSelection doesn't affect spinners at all. That's because spinners don't remember their selection properly as soon as they lose focus. See SelLength for the details on this bug.

You'll usually want to leave HideSelection set to .T. Things get confusing when too many highlights appear. Setting HideSelection to .F. (that is, letting all the highlights show) seems most useful when you want to perform some operation on the selected text.

Example
```
ThisForm.Edit1.HideSelection = .F.
```

See Also ComboBox, Edit box, SelLength, SelStart, SelText, Spinner, Text box

Highlight, HighlightRow

These two properties, along with the SelectOnEntry property of the controls within a grid's cells, determine whether cell contents in a grid are highlighted when you move into the cell. The effects you can create with them are a little strange.

Usage
```
grdGrid.HighlightRow = lColoredBorder
lColoredBorder = grdGrid.HighlightRow
grdGrid.Highlight = lAllowHighlights
lAllowHighlights = grdGrid.Highlight
```

There are two kinds of highlighting for each cell in a grid. First, there's a focus highlight that indicates which cell has focus—the border of the cell is colored. This highlight is controlled by HighlightRow, which was added in VFP 5. When you turn this one off, you don't actually get rid of the focus highlight—it just changes from colored and noticeable to a just barely visible thickening of the cell border. It appears that the non-highlight is always a pale gray, though, no matter what color your grid lines are.

In addition to this highlight, normally when you tab into a grid cell, the text there is selected (highlighted). Two properties can change this. Highlight changes it for the whole grid. By default, it's True, setting highlighting on for all columns of the grid. We'd be inclined to turn highlighting off when a grid is read-only. The highlight confuses people in that case.

The other property that controls highlighting is the column's SelectOnEntry. Once you turn highlighting on for the grid, you can then control each column individually.

We should point out that, even with all the relevant settings turned on, you don't get the whole row highlighted the way you do in lists. Grids are not lists, and you would have to do some more tricks, including setting DynamicBackColor for every column. Christof Lange published a very complete solution to the problem in the Ask Advisor column in the October '98 issue of *FoxPro Advisor*.

When HighlightRow is .F., but Highlight is .T., the highlighting of individual cells looks pretty strange.

For a good laugh, read the Help entry for Highlight, paying specific attention to the descriptions of the settings. Amazingly, it's been this way since VFP 3.

Example
```
ThisForm.grdReference.HighlightRow = .F.   && No focus highlight
ThisForm.grdReference.Highlight = .F.      && No highlight of contents, either
```

See Also GridLines, SelectOnEntry

Home(), Sys(2004), FullName

Until VFP 6, the first two functions here were identical. With no parameters (or no additional parameters for SYS(2004)), they both return the directory from which Visual FoxPro was started. Obviously, the mnemonic HOME() is a better choice than the mysterious SYS(2004) (despite the fact that SYS(2004) is burned on our brains). VFP 6 added a number of alternate uses for HOME() to let us find various other directories.

FullName is the Automation Server version of the same information—it gives you both the full path to the directory and the name of the executable that started the VFP session in question.

Usage
```
cHomeDirectory = HOME( [ nWhichDir ] )
cHomeDirectory = SYS(2004)
cStartingEXE = appApplication.FullName
```

Parameter	Value	Meaning
nWhichDir	Omitted	Return the directory from which VFP was started. For the development environment, this is the location of VFP.EXE; for a runtime application, it's the location of the runtime files.
	1	Return the root directory of the VFP directory tree, in other words, the directory into which VFP was installed.
	2	Return the directory to which the VFP samples were installed. Same as _SAMPLES.
	3	Return the Common subdirectory of the Visual Studio installation.
	4	Return the Common\Graphics subdirectory of the Visual Studio installation.
	5	Return the samples directory of the Visual Studio/MSDN installation. Probably one level above HOME(2).
	6	Return the Common\Tools directory of the Visual Studio installation.

First, be aware that HOME() and SYS(2004) always include the final backslash. (So does FullName, but that's because it's separating the path from the filename.)

Many of us have gotten in the habit of assuming that HOME() and SYS(2004) always refer to the main FoxPro directory. We shouldn't have. The functions actually return the directory containing the necessary Visual FoxPro libraries. When you run an EXE from outside Visual FoxPro, this is the directory containing the various support libraries. Most often, that directory is the Windows system directory (C:\WINDOWS\SYSTEM\ for Win9x, C:\WINNT\SYSTEM32 for WinNT), not the one containing our EXE file. On the whole, this means we're using these functions a lot less than we did in FoxPro 2.x.

To find the directory containing your application, you'll have to parse SYS(16,1) to find everything before the last backslash. See the example below.

FullName is a property of the VFP application object. It tells you both the full path to the instance of VFP that's running and the name of the executable that's operating as a server. Since the application object also has a version property, we suspect we're far more likely to just grab the path here than to try to figure out which version is running by looking at the EXE name.

The VFP 6 additions to HOME() make it easier to write code that uses the various common elements provided with Visual Studio and, for that matter, to write about those common elements or find them during development. It also makes the development team's job easier because they no longer have to worry about moving things around. We just have to remember to write our code using the various permutations of HOME() rather than assuming, for example, that the VFP samples are always in a \SAMPLES subdirectory or that bitmaps are in a \GOODIES\GRAPHICS\BITMAPS directory. Since HOME(2) or HOME(4) is shorter anyway, we're happy. Now we just have to use these enough to remember them.

Example

```
WAIT WINDOW "Support files are in " + HOME()
WAIT WINDOW "This app is running from " + ;
            JustPath(SYS(16,1))
* Find out about the application object in the current session
* though it's far more likely you'll be doing this in another
* automation client.
? _VFP.FullName
```

```
* Use a bitmap file
_SCREEN.Picture = HOME(4)+"BITMAPS\ASSORTED\BALLOON.BMP"
```

See Also FoxTools, JustPath(), Sys(16), Version, _Samples

HomeDir

This project property contains the home directory of the project. In the Project Info dialog, it shows as "Home:". The home directory of a project is used as the base for relative paths stored with the project's files.

Usage

```
prjProject.HomeDir = cPath
cPath = prjProject.HomeDir
```

The name of each file in a project (available via the Name property of the File object) includes the path to the file. Any file that comes from the same drive as the project is stored with a relative path (though it's displayed with an absolute path). When the project is processed in any way, those paths are considered to be relative to the home directory. (That is, the path uses the . and .. notations to show how you get from the home directory to the directory containing this file. Files on other drives have absolute paths containing the drive and full directory hierarchy down to the file.) This means that you mess with HomeDir at your own risk, since changing it is likely to wreak havoc on your next build.

Example

```
* Report the home directory of the current project
? "Home directory = ",Application.ActiveProject.HomeDir
```

See Also File, Name, Project

HostName See DocumentFile.

Hour(), Minute(), Sec()

These functions extract the hour, minute and second portions of a datetime value. Backward compatibility with previously existing functions makes for some funny, non-intuitive abbreviation rules.

Usage

```
nHours = HOUR( tDateTime )
nMinute = MINUTE( tDateTime )
nSeconds = SEC( tDateTime )
```

Hour() always returns the number of hours since midnight, regardless of the setting of SET HOUR. Minute() returns a numeric value from 0 to 59. No surprises here. Minute() may be abbreviated as short as Minu(), but realize that MIN() is the Minimum function, something completely different. Though confusing, it fits the general rule that you can abbreviate commands and functions to four characters or more. Sec() returns a numeric value from 0 to 59. In the opposite logic to Minute(), Sec() must be just the three characters—anything from Seco() up to Seconds() causes Visual FoxPro to return the number of seconds since midnight, or squawk if a parameter is passed.

Example

```
? "The time is now " + LTRIM(STR(HOUR(DATETIME()))) + ;
  " hours, " + LTRIM(STR(MINUTE(DATETIME()))) + ;
  " minutes and "  + LTRIM(STR(MINUTE(DATETIME()))) + ;
  " seconds past midnight"
```

See Also Date(), DateTime(), Min(), Seconds(), Set Hour

Hours See Set Hours.

HScrollSmallChange, VScrollSmallChange

These two properties control how much a form scrolls each time you click on one of the arrow keys of a scrollbar.

Usage

```
frmForm.HScrollSmallChange = nHorizontalAmount
nHorizontalAmount = frmForm.HScrollSmallChange
frmForm.VScrollSmallChange = nVerticalAmount
nVerticalAmount = frmForm.VScrollSmallChange
```

Did you ever wonder how applications decided how much to scroll when you use the arrows on the scrollbars? Us neither, but now we know anyway.

The default for these properties is 10 pixels, but you can set it as high or low as you want. You can even change it dynamically. This seems most appropriate when the amount of information changes dramatically, or if you want to provide the feeling of acceleration on a *really* long form.

Note that only forms have these properties, even though edit boxes, grids and some other controls can have scrollbars, too. Sounds like control discrimination to us.

Example
```
ThisForm.HScrollSmallChange = 30
```

See Also ContinuousScroll, Form, Scrollbars

Hyperlink

The Hyperlink object allows you to include links to the World Wide Web as native controls within your FoxPro forms. These links work within stand-alone FoxPro applications and in Active Documents.

Method	Purpose
GoBack	Moves to the previous link in the history list.
GoForward	Moves to the next link in the history list.
NavigateTo	Navigates to the specified link. Starts a browser if used in a stand-alone FoxPro application.

The hyperlink object is a nonvisual class with the usual class properties and methods. But its main purpose in life is hosting the three methods above, providing the ability to navigate to hyperlinks.

Navigating to a hyperlink is not just a matter of issuing a RUN /N "MyLink.HTML" call. The hyperlink object shields us from the steps needed to locate the program charged with hosting HTML files, invoking it, and passing it the correct address. In addition, when the hyperlink is within a container supporting browsing history (typically when you're hosting an Active Document in Internet Explorer), the GoForward and GoBack methods allow you to programmatically move through the history list.

Example
```
* In a stand-alone app, you can invoke a browser with:
oLink = CREATEOBJECT("hyperlink")
oLink.NavigateTo("http://www.microsoft.com/vfoxpro")
* You don't need to be limited to the World Wide Wait
* Browsers can also host other documents, if their
* associated viewer applications are installed:
oLink.NavigateTo("d:\My Documents\MyLetter.DOC")
```

See Also GoForward, GoBack, NavigateTo

Icon

This property has two similar, but slightly different, meanings. For forms (and _SCREEN), it specifies the icon in the corner of the title bar. In that case, it's the OOP equivalent to the old ICON clause of DEFINE WINDOW. For projects, it indicates the icon that's used for an EXE built from the project. In that meaning, it's the same as what you specify through the Attach Icon check box in the Project Information dialog.

Usage
```
frmForm.Icon = cIconFile
cIconFile = frmForm.Icon
prjProject.Icon = cIconFile
cIconFile = prjProject.Icon
```

The file specified by cIconFile needs to be an ICO file, not a BMP or other graphic. Visual FoxPro 6 includes some ICO files in the Gallery\Graphics, and Visual Studio offers a bunch more under the Common\Graphics\Icons directory. (You can avoid hard-coding those paths by taking advantage of the new parameters to HOME().) Be sure to include the icons used by your forms when you distribute your application. You should build them into the APP or EXE so you don't forget. Once you do so, you don't need to distribute the icon files separately.

Example

```
* Choose a new icon for the main FoxPro window
_Screen.Icon = GETPICT()

* Specify the icon for a form from within a method of that form
This.Icon = "F:\VFP\GALLERY\GRAPHICS\MUSIC.ICO"
```

See Also Define Window, Home(), Modify Window, Picture, Project, _Screen

Id() See Access().

IDXCollate() See CPConvert().

#If See #Define.

If

This is the original branching command. It lets you choose between two paths of action based on a condition. If the condition is true, you follow the first path. If it's not true, you take the second path. IF can only be used in programmatic code. To have conditional code in an expression, use IIF().

Usage

```
IF lCondition [ THEN ]
     Commands
[ ELSE
     Commands ]
ENDIF
```

If lCondition is true, the commands on the lines immediately after the IF are executed. There are two possibilities for what happens if the condition isn't true. If an ELSE clause appears, the commands following ELSE are executed. If there's no ELSE, no commands are executed and we continue after the ENDIF.

Visual FoxPro introduced a new wrinkle in IF. Conditions can no longer be divided into true or false—they might be null. If lCondition is null, the ELSE branch is taken.

The optional THEN keyword was added in VFP 5 … sort of. Until VFP 5, FoxPro read IF lines until it found something that didn't seem to be valid code. At that point, it assumed the rest of the line was a comment, even without a comment indicator. (See NOTE for more on this topic.) When VFP 5 limited that ability to lines containing only keywords, people who'd always included THEN after an IF were left out in the cold. Microsoft took pity on them and made the THEN keyword legal at the end of the IF line.

Example

```
* move forward, but don't end up at EOF
SKIP
IF EOF()
   GO BOTTOM
ENDIF

* print one message for kids - another for adults
IF YEAR(DATE()) - YEAR(dBirthdate) < 21
   ? "Come see our incredibly cool new gizmos"
ELSE
   ? "Come in now for amazing bargains"
ENDIF
```

FoxPro uses a "short circuit" way of evaluating lCondition. As soon as it's clear what the final result will be, FoxPro stops evaluating. This can be a handy shortcut, but it's a double-edged sword. You'll run into trouble if you depend on anything after the first portion of an IF to be evaluated. Here's an example of the good side of this behavior:

```
SELECT Transactions
IF NOT EOF() AND Transactions.lPrint
   * Print out this record
ENDIF
```

In this example, we count on the NOT EOF() test being passed before we check the field lPrint. Now the down side:

```
IF lCondition AND MyUDF()
   * do something
ENDIF
```

In this example, we have to keep in mind that MyUDF() is called only when lCondition is true, so we shouldn't be counting on something to happen in MyUDF() every time we execute the IF. Similarly, when testing your code, make sure you test all combinations of conditions. If you've tested your code when the first few conditions always cause a branch, you may not detect problems at the end of your test:

```
IF MyUDF() OR HerUDF() OR TheirUDF() OR Syntax Error
   * do something
ENDIF
```

The code above will work fine until the first three functions each return .F.

IFs can be nested one inside another. If you find yourself nesting a whole series of Ifs, though, take a look at DO CASE—it may be more appropriate for the situation.

See Also Do Case, IIf()

#IfDef, #IfNDef See #Define.

IIf()

This is one of the most versatile and useful functions in FoxPro. It allows you to put the equivalent of an IF-ELSE-ENDIF right in the middle of any expression.

Usage `uResult = IIF( lCondition, uThenResult, uElseResult )`

Parameter	Value	Meaning
lCondition	.T.	Returns the value of uThenResult.
	.F. or .NULL.	Returns the value of uElseResult.
uThenResult	Anything except General	If lCondition is true, returns the value of this expression.
uElseResult	Anything except General	If lCondition is not true, returns the value of this expression.
uResult	Anything except General	The value of either uThenResult or uElseResult.

This function got more complicated with the addition of nulls. It used to be simple—if lCondition is true, return uThenResult; if lCondition is false, return uElseResult. But now there's the chance that lCondition is null. In that case, IIF() returns uElseResult.

IIF() is useful whenever you need to specify an expression and can't use IF-ELSE-ENDIF. We use it a lot in reports and queries.

Example

```
? IIF(x>y, "larger", "smaller")
IIF(paid, "X", " ")
```

The second example might appear in a report. It prints an "X" for those who've paid and leaves an empty space for those who haven't.

When combined with the aggregate functions, IIF() can do some pretty powerful things in a query. This example counts how many TasTrade employees are 30 and over (should we trust them?) and how many are under 30.

```
SELECT SUM(IIF(YEAR(Birth_Date)+30 <= YEAR(DATE()),1,0)) AS Over30, ;
       SUM(IIF(YEAR(Birth_Date)+30 > YEAR(DATE()),1,0)) AS Under30;
  FROM TasTrade!Employee ;
  INTO CURSOR AgeCount
```

IIF()'s can be nested, just like IF...ELSE...ENDIF structures, and execute with nearly the speed of a single command. Down this path leads madness, or at least "cryptocode," as our friend Mac Rubel calls it. Try to avoid having to debug lines of code that are indecipherable even to their author:

```
lReturnValue=IIF(CDOW(dDate)="Tuesday","Yes",IIF(CMONTH(dDate)="March", ;
"Maybe",IIF(YEAR(dDate)%4=0 and YEAR(dDate)%100 <> 0, "No","Idunno")))
```

Yuck. Keep It Simple, Stupid.

See Also Do Case, If

Image

The Image control is used to place bitmaps on a form. Images, unlike bitmaps in 2.x versions of FoxPro, may also participate in events.

Property	**Value**	**Meaning**
BackStyle	0	Transparent: objects behind the picture should be visible.
	1	Opaque, the default: objects behind the image are obscured.
Stretch	0	Clipped: the image is shown actual size. If the image exceeds the size of the control's width and height, the remainder of the image is cropped.
	1	Isometric: the image is stretched or shrunken to fit the area of the Image control, without distorting the image's proportions.
	2	Stretch: The image is distorted to fill the entire width and height of the Image control.
Picture	Character	The path and filename of the picture to be displayed. Visual FoxPro 3.x and 5.x display only BMPs and ICOs natively, and an OLE server is needed for other formats. VFP 6 supports GIFs and JPGs as well as BMPs, ICOs, CURs and ANIs.

The Image control contains the usual Top, Left, Height and Width properties, and the usual suspects for methods: MouseUp, MouseDown, Click, DragOver, DragDrop, and so on. Although an image can be used as a pushbutton, or a hot area or "invisible button" in 2.x terminology, we prefer to use CommandButtons and Check boxes for these tasks, due to their richer capabilities: Buttons have DownPicture and DisablePicture properties as well as When, Valid and InteractiveChange events.

While it isn't documented, Image controls can display cursors (CUR) and animated cursors (ANI) as well. Images don't allow their pictures to be edited—use an OLEControl or OLEBoundControl for that.

Example
```
oForm.AddObject("imgPicture","Image")
oForm.imgPicture.Picture = GETPICT() && handy dialog new to 3.x!
oForm.imgPicture.Visible = .T.
```

See Also OLEBoundControl, OLEControl

IMEMode, IMEStatus()

This pair is for writing applications that deal with double-byte character sets, in particular, Japanese and Korean language applications. They let you indicate how a special tool called an Input Method Editor behaves when you enter a field or open a Browse or other editing window.

Usage
```
oObject.IMEMode = 0 | 1
nIMEMode = oObject.IMEMode
nIMEStatus = IMEStatus( [ 0 | 1 ] )
```

IMEMode is a property of several controls that accept text. IMEStatus() is a function that both tells you what's going on and lets you change it. They're both ignored unless you're running a Far Eastern version of Windows.

In Far Eastern languages, it takes two bytes to represent each character because they're based on pictographs rather than sounds. Entering these two-byte characters is a challenge—you certainly don't want a keyboard with 65,000 items on it. The solution is a special application that lets you choose the appropriate pictograph; such an application is called an Input Method Editor (IME).

IMEMode indicates what should happen with the IME when the control gets focus. You can set it to open the IME, close the IME or simply do whatever the operating system is set for. IMEStatus() does two jobs—it lets you turn the IME window on and off, and it tells you the current IME setting.

It seemed a little extreme to install a Far Eastern version of Windows just to test this stuff, so all we've done is make sure they don't crash in the U.S. version of Windows.

Example
```
This.IMEMode = 1   && Have IME Window open
```

See Also Double-Byte Character Sets

Import See Append From.

#Include, _Include See #Define.

Increment

This property applies to spinners and determines how much the spinner changes each time you click one of the arrows.

Usage
```
spnSpinner.Increment = nValue
nValue = spnSpinner.Increment
```

Increment can be either positive or negative. With a negative increment, clicking the up arrow (or pressing the up arrow key) decreases the displayed number, while clicking the down arrow increases it. Weird, but we guess you might want to do it when dealing with dates or times where up could mean further back in time and down could mean more recent.

Increment can be changed while a form is active. For example, you might relate the increment to the magnitude of the spinner value. For instance, increment by 2 until you reach 100, then go by 5 until 200, then by 10. Like the other spinner properties, you can't set the property itself to change dynamically, but you can change the property programmatically while the form is running. The example shows the code.

Example

```
* Update spinner increment to be based on the spinner value
* The following code goes in the spinner's InteractiveChange
* method, so the increment is checked each time the spinner
* value changes.
DO CASE
CASE This.Value < 100
   This.Increment = 2
CASE This.Value < 200
   This.Increment = 5
OTHERWISE
   This.Increment = 10
ENDCASE
```

If the program changes the spinner value in code, too, you'd need to do the same thing in the spinner's ProgrammaticChange method.

See Also KeyboardHighValue, KeyboardLowValue, SpinnerHighValue, SpinnerLowValue

IncrementalSearch

This property of combo boxes and list boxes determines whether typing a series of keystrokes accumulates the characters or jumps to a series of different items while searching.

Usage

```
oObject.IncrementalSearch = lIsIncremental
lIsIncremental = oObject.IncrementalSearch
```

When IncrementalSearch is off (.F.), each time you type a character, the list or combo jumps to an item beginning with that character. This is the Windows way (well, the Windows 3.1 way—the Windows 95 interface is smarter than that) and we've always hated it.

In the FoxPro (and Windows 95) way, each character you type is added to a search string and gets you closer and closer to the item you're looking for. This feature is called "Incremental Search" because you get a little bit closer to the one you want with each keystroke. Setting IncrementalSearch to .T. gives you this behavior and is the default.

Of course, eventually you'd like to be able to start over. How long this takes is controlled by, of all things, the system variable _DBLCLICK (which also controls the amount of time between clicks to have two clicks considered a double-click, hence its name). If the length of time specified by _DBLCLICK elapses, the search string is discarded and you start over. We recommend you give your users control over the "incremental search clear" setting because some people type fast and others need longer. Since there's no reason why your users should want this tied to double-click speed, your best bet is probably to change _DBLCLICK in the GotFocus of combos and lists, and reset it in LostFocus. It will, of course, affect double-clicking while those controls have focus, but it's the best we can do until (or is that unless?) Microsoft decides to give us independent control over this one.

When a combo box is set to Style 2 (drop-down), IncrementalSearch also applies to the "keyboard steering" feature that lets you move through the list without opening the drop-down.

Example

```
ThisForm.cboMyCombo.IncrementalSearch = .T.
```

See Also ComboBox, _DblClick, ListBox, Sorted

InDBC()

This function tells you whether a specified object is in the current database.

Usage

```
lItsInThere = INDBC( cObjectName, cObjectType )
```

Parameter	Value	Meaning
cObjectName	Character	The name of the item to look for in the database.
cObjectType	"Table"	Check for a table called cObjectName in the database.
	"Field"	Check for a field called cObjectName in the database. cObjectName must contain the alias and field name.
	"Index"	Check for an index called cObjectName in the database. cObjectName must contain the alias and the tag name.
	"View"	Check for a view called cObjectName in the database.
	"Connection"	Check for a connection called cObjectName in the database.

INDBC() works only for the current database and only if you know the name of the object you're interested in. To find out what tables, views and connections are in the database, use ADBObjects(). For fields, use AFIELDS(). For indexes, use the AINDEXES() function shown under CANDIDATE() (and on the CD).

Example

```
OPEN DATA TasTrade
? INDBC("Customer","Table")                  && Returns .T.
? INDBC("Fred","Table")                      && Returns .F.
? INDBC("Customer.Company_name","Field")     && Returns .T.
? INDBC("Supplier Listing","View")           && Returns .T.
? INDBC("Furshlugginer","Connection")        && Returns .F.
? INDBC("Customer.Company_Na","Index")       && Returns .T.
? INDBC("Company_Na","Index")                && Returns .F.
```

See Also ADBObjects(), AFields(), Candidate(), DBC(), DBGetProp()

_Indent See _Alignment.

Index, Reindex, Delete Tag, Set Unique, Set("Unique")

These commands all relate to the care and feeding of indexes. INDEX lets you create regular, unique and candidate indexes. REINDEX re-creates existing indexes. DELETE TAG lets you remove index tags from a compound index file. SET UNIQUE determines whether newly created indexes are regular or unique—leave it set to OFF all the time.

Usage

```
INDEX ON eKeyExpr
      TO IDXFile | TAG TagName [ OF CDXFile ]
      [ FOR lFilter ]
      [ COMPACT ]
      [ ASCENDING | DESCENDING ]
      [ UNIQUE | CANDIDATE ]
      [ ADDITIVE ]
```

Parameter	Value	Meaning
eKeyExpr	Expression	The index key.
IDXFile	Name	A stand-alone index file to contain this index.
TagName	Name	The name to assign this tag.
CDXFile	Name	A compound index file to contain this tag.

Parameter	Value	Meaning
CDXFile	Omitted	Store this tag in the structural compound index file for this table.
lFilter	Logical	An expression that determines whether a particular record is included in this index.

FoxPro's indexes can be divided up several ways. The first distinction is in how and where they're stored. There are two kinds of index files: stand-alone and compound. As the names suggest, a stand-alone index holds data for a single key, while a compound index can hold multiple keys.

By default, stand-alone indexes are stored with an extension of IDX. These are compatible with all versions of FoxPro going back to FoxBase. Stand-alone indexes can also have the COMPACT attribute, which reduces their storage requirements. Since compact stand-alone indexes were introduced at the same time as compound indexes, there's not much reason to use them. In fact, the only reason to use stand-alone indexes at all is to maintain compatibility with other products or older versions that can't read compound index files.

Compound indexes use a default extension of CDX. Each index in the file is called a tag and has a name that identifies it. Within a single CDX, each tag's name must be unique, but a table can have several tags of the same name in different compound index files.

Every table may have a structural CDX file. That's a compound index file that has the same name as the table—only the extension is different. If a table has a structural CDX, it's automatically opened whenever the table is opened, and closed whenever the table is closed. We strongly suggest you use the structural CDX for every index you plan to maintain. Use other compound index files or stand-alone indexes only for infrequent, on-the-fly operations. That way, you're sure that your indexes are always kept up-to-date.

The next question is what goes into the index. There are several choices here.

A regular index contains a key for each record in the table.

A candidate index contains a key for each record in the table and prohibits duplicates in the key expression—attempting to add a record with an existing key generates an error. Candidate indexes can also be created with CREATE TABLE and ALTER TABLE. Those two commands also let you create a primary index—that's a candidate index that you've designed as the primary key for the table. Only tables in a database can have primary indexes. You can't create primary indexes with INDEX.

"Unique" indexes are misnamed. (In fact, candidate indexes are unique. These are not.) We're not sure how they ever got into the language, but we are sure you shouldn't use them. Ever. A so-called unique index contains a key only for the first record that has a particular key value. That is, once a key value occurs, no other records with that key value get added to the index. There's no mechanism to enforce uniqueness here, just a way to find one of each. However, unique indexes are not properly maintained. If you delete a record that's represented in the index, FoxPro does not add the next record in the table that has the same key value. Don't ever use "unique" indexes—there's always a better way to do it.

Each of the index types can be filtered by adding the FOR clause. In that case, only the records meeting lFilter are added to the index. Filtered indexes are properly maintained—as records change, the index is updated to include those that now qualify. However, any index that's filtered in this way is ignored by Rushmore when it attempts to optimize commands, so use these cautiously. (Don't be misled by the VFP 6 Help, which seems to imply that filtered tags are used by Rushmore. In fact, what it's really saying is that Rushmore will optimize the INDEX command itself if appropriate tags exist.)

In VFP 3 and VFP 5, the only way to filter a primary key is through the visual tools. A new clause of ALTER TABLE in VFP 6 lets you create filtered primary keys directly.

Indexes can be created in either ascending or descending order. Regardless of how you create them, you can use them in either order as well by specifying ASCENDING or DESCENDING in the SET ORDER command. The only advantage of creating an index in descending order is that the first time you SET ORDER TO it, if you don't specify, it's descending. We don't think that's enough of an advantage to make it worth worrying about whether an index is ascending or descending. Create all indexes in ascending order and use them as needed. As we mention in SET ORDER TO, you only need to use the ASCENDING/DESCENDING keyword the first time you open an index in a session. Once you do so, it's opened in that orientation until it's explicitly set the other way. In fact, if a table is open more than once using the same tag for ordering, all the copies are either ascending or descending. You can't SET ORDER TO ATag ASCENDING in one work area and SET ORDER TO ATag DESCENDING in another at the same time. An index key can be simply a single field, or it can be any valid FoxPro expression (though it normally contains a field of the table). For character fields, it's almost always a good idea to use UPPER() in the index key so you can search without worrying about case. For example, the Company Name tag for TasTrade's Customer table is UPPER(COMPANY_NAME).

When indexing on fields of different types, the best bet is generally to convert them all to strings and concatenate the strings. For example, a key involving a string and a date normally uses DTOS() to put the date in character format and in true date order (including the year).

Occasionally, you need an index that uses two fields in different orders. For example, you might want to index an orders table in customer-number order with each customer's orders in reverse date order. To do this sort of thing requires a trick—subtract the field you want in descending order from a suitably large number or date. Date math lets you use the trick with both numbers and dates. There's an example below.

VFP lets you specify an index key that doesn't have a fixed length (like ALLTRIM(cLastName)). However, internally, it pads the index back to a standard length. Most often, we've seen people do this when combining fields (as in ALLTRIM(cLastName)+ALLTRIM(cFirstName)). This is a bad idea and can actually put the records in the wrong order. Well, wrong as in you didn't mean that one; VFP is just doing what you told it. Since index keys always have fixed length anyway, there's no reason to trim them.

FoxPro lets you create indexes whose keys reference another table. Don't! Just like mama told you, just because you can doesn't always mean you should. Like "unique" indexes, indexes with foreign fields are not automatically maintained. There's always another way to do it either by setting a relation or using SELECT-SQL. In the same vein, user-defined functions can be used as part of an index expression. Don't do it—performance can be slowed by several orders of magnitude; and loss of, or change to, the UDF code can wreak havoc with your data design.

Finally, the ADDITIVE clause. This is one we haven't used for years. When you're working with non-structural indexes, opening one index closes others. Creating an index is the same as opening one from this point of view. ADDITIVE lets you create a new stand-alone or non-structural compound index without closing other stand-alone or non-structural compound indexes.

You should have exclusive use of a table before you start creating indexes. A stand-alone index or the first tag of a compound structural index can be created with only shared use of a table, but additional tags cannot be added to the structural index. We think that if you are doing system-wide maintenance like indexing, it is always a good idea to own the table exclusively.

Example

```
USE Orders
INDEX ON Order_Id TAG Order_Id CANDIDATE && Prevent duplicates
INDEX ON UPPER(Ship_To_Country) TAG ShipCtry
* This one's in customer order, then reverse date order
INDEX ON UPPER(Customer_Id)+STR({12/31/2099}-Order_Date) TAG CustDate
* Create an index in date order, only for records with
* some notes.
INDEX ON Order_Date FOR NOT EMPTY(Notes)
```

Usage `REINDEX [ COMPACT ]`

This command regenerates all open indexes in the current work area. It sounds like a really useful command and we've been known to use it occasionally. But it has no place in an application. If the index header information is damaged, REINDEX leaves the damage there—it doesn't fix it. It's much better to delete all the tags and re-create them from scratch. (But see our comments below.)

The COMPACT keyword converts stand-alone indexes to compact, stand-alone indexes. We've never used that one.

Usage

```
DELETE TAG TagName1 [ OF CDXFile1 ] [, TagName2 [ OF CDXFile2 ] [, ... ] ]
DELETE TAG ALL [ OF CDXFile3 ]
```

As the name suggests, DELETE TAG removes a single index from a compound index file. When specifying individual tags, you only need the OF clause if there are multiple tags with the same name.

Since the introduction of compound index files, DELETE TAG ALL has been a key component of just about every file maintenance system. Dozens of books and articles tell you to DELETE TAG ALL, then use INDEX to rebuild your indexes. In fact, we've told people to do that many times. In addition to avoiding the problems of REINDEX, it does a nice job of cleaning out the CDX file, throwing away any residual garbage that might be lurking there. (That's because it makes the CDX file disappear. Deleting all the tags in a CDX, either one by one or with DELETE TAG ALL, actually deletes the file.)

Unfortunately, for tables in a database, just deleting tags creates all kinds of trouble. Like PACK, this is another case where a good database maintenance tool like Stonefield Database Toolkit is worth its weight in gold.

Example

```
* To clean up a free table's indexes, you can do something like:
USE MyTable
DELETE TAG ALL
INDEX ON UPPER(cLastName+cFirstName) TAG Name
INDEX ON DateField TAG DateField
```

Usage

```
SET UNIQUE ON | OFF
cUniqueSetting = SET( "UNIQUE" )
```

This setting determines whether indexes are "unique" by default. Don't use it. In fact, we suggest you don't use so-called unique indexes at all. But, if you insist on doing so, use the UNIQUE keyword of INDEX. Don't mess with this system-wide (actually, now it's data session-wide) setting. The corresponding and undocumented SET("UNIQUE") tells you the current setting.

See Also Alter Table, Create Table, Descending(), For(), Key(), Seek, Set Order, Tag(), TagCount(), TagNo(), Unique()

IndexSeek() See Seek.

IndexToItemId, ItemIdToIndex

These methods convert between the two numbering schemes for items in list and combo boxes.

Usage

```
FUNCTION IndexToItemId
LPARAMETERS nIndex

FUNCTION ItemIdToIndex
LPARAMETERS nItemId
```

Each item added to a list or combo has two numbers assigned to it. ItemId is a unique, unchanging number. Index is based on the item's current position in the list, and changes as items are added and removed, and when the Sorted property changes. (See AddItem for a complete explanation of the two numbering systems.)

These methods convert between ItemIds and Indexes. They're not needed often, since pretty much everything for handling lists and combos comes in two forms—one for Indexes and one for ItemIds. The only thing we can think of that doesn't offer both approaches is Picture, which uses only the indexes. However, the conversion functions are also handy when the list has mover bars and is based on or related to an array. The functions let you process items in the order they appear, but still connect to your outside arrays based on the ItemID.

Example

```
* Convert the currently selected index to an item id
nItemId = IndexToItemId( ListIndex )
```

See Also AddItem, AddListItem, ComboBox, ListBox, ListIndex, ListItemId, RowSourceType

INI Files

INI files are nothing more than text files used to store settings. INI files come in two flavors: public and private. The public INI file is Win.INI; all applications are supposed to share this file politely. Private INI files are specific to an application. This section discusses how you can read and write to both.

Doing it in Public: Win.INI

Win.INI is a throwback to Windows 3.1 and is currently supported only for compatibility with 16-bit applications. Do not trust entries in Win.INI to be at all accurate (such as which files are associated with which extension, which printer is currently selected as the default, what other printers are available, international settings for currency, date and time, and other vital information like what wallpaper background is in use).

However, in the current incarnations of Win32 (Windows 9x and NT 4.0), Microsoft has modified the Windows API so calls to read and write the Win.INI actually talk to the Windows Registry. Don't be surprised to find that your SetProfileString call doesn't seem to affect the Win.INI text, but works anyway. (For the hackers who just really have to know, the mappings are stored in HKEY_LOCAL_MACHINE\Software\Microsoft\Windows NT\CurrentVersion\IniFileMapping\win.ini under NT; we haven't figured out exactly how Win9x does it.) Since the Win.INI and its Registry equivalent are public information available to all applications, you may want to read the settings there.

The Windows API GetProfileString() function returns the specified value, or a default string passed to it if it is unable to locate the entry. Following is a simple routine to use this function:

```
* ReadWini - read the WIN.INI file
* Returns a WIN.INI entry 'cEntry' from section 'cSection'
* or blank if not found
PARAMETERS cSection, cEntry
LOCAL cDefault, cRetVal, nRetLen
cDefault = ""
cRetVal = SPACE(255)
nRetLen = LEN(cRetVal)
DECLARE INTEGER GetProfileString IN WIN32API ;
                STRING cSection, ;
                STRING cEntry, ;
                STRING cDefault, ;
                STRING @cRetVal, ;
                INTEGER nRetLen
nRetLen = GetProfileString(cSection, ;
                           cEntry, ;
                           cDefault, ;
                           @cRetVal, ;
                           nRetLen)
RETURN LEFT(cRetVal,nRetLen)
```

Some of our favorite parameters to send to READWINI:

Section Parameter	Entry Parameter	Returns:
.NULL. or 0	.NULL. or 0	List of all section names, each separated by CHR(0). This seems to work reliably under Windows NT, but it returns empty strings under Windows 95.

Section Parameter	Entry Parameter	Returns:
{any section name}	.NULL. or 0	List of all entries in that section, each separated by CHR(0).
"Ports"	.NULL. or 0	Returns a CHR(0)-delimited list of all ports defined on the machine.
"Ports"	Port name returned above	Returns a string of settings for that port.

Microsoft has made it a little easier with the addition in Visual FoxPro 3.0b of two new functions to FoxTools.FLL, GetProStrg() and PutProStrg(), to read and write these "public" profile strings.

Example

```
SET LIBRARY TO HOME()+"FOXTOOLS.FLL" ADDITIVE
LcBuffer = SPACE(1000)
* The function fills lcBuffer with the WIN.INI section
* names out of the Registry, each separated with CHR(0)
lnLen = GetProStrg(0,0,"Empty", @lcBuffer, LEN(lcBuffer)
? LEFT(lcBuffer, lnLen)
* Typical sections include Ports, Devices, etc.
* Let's look at one

lcBuffer = SPACE(1000)  && reset the buffer
lnLen = GetProStrg("PrinterPorts", 0, "Empty", ;
             @lcBuffer, LEN(lcBuffer))
? LEFT(lcBuffer, lnLen)
* lcBuffer should now contain a list of printers

lcBuffer = SPACE(1000)  && reset the buffer
lnLen = GetProStrg("PrinterPorts", "Epson Stylus Color 500",;
                   "Empty", @lcBuffer, LEN(lcBuffer))
? LEFT(lcBuffer, lnLen)
* lcBuffer should now have the settings for your printer,
* in this case, "winspool, Ne00:, 15, 45"
```

Private INI files

> Private information is practically the source of every large modern fortune.
>
> Oscar Wilde

A private INI file is just a text file, and it is something that every Tom, Dick and Harry can open and mess with using Notepad. That's the bad news, but also the good news. If we have to dial into a client site and view a set of preferences, an INI file is easy. If we have to coach a client through rebuilding one over the phone (heaven forbid starting with the COPY CON command!), it is far easier to create a few lines of an INI file than it is to rebuild the Registry (see "Registration Database" for more information on the Registry). On the other hand, the Registry does include some nice features, like automatic system backup, that our poor little INI file will be without.

The Win32 SDK documentation is pretty firm about these commands existing for "backwards compatibility," and insisting that real 32-bit apps use the Registry instead. We sympathize with Microsoft wanting everyone to play with their new toy, and agree that the Registry does offer wonderful features of security, reliability, multi-user support, and remote administration, but the use of INI files is so darned easy, it will be a while until they disappear. Even Microsoft continues to use INI files, although not for as sweeping a purpose as in Windows 3.1. Check your Windows directory for *.INI—there are still a few there.

The two routines that follow, to read and write private INI files, look an awful lot like the code above. Note that the API functions are not case sensitive—they locate the appropriate sections and settings regardless of the case. READPINI() reads a specified section and entry from a private INI file. Specify the full path of the INI file, unless you want the file stored in the Windows directory.

```
* ReadPini - read a private .INI file
* Returns the .INI entry 'cEntry' from section 'cSection'
* or blank if not found
PARAMETERS cSection, cEntry, cINIFile
LOCAL cDefault, cRetVal, nRetLen
cDefault = ""
cRetVal = space(255)
nRetLen = LEN(cRetVal)
DECLARE integer GetPrivateProfileString IN WIN32API ;
                STRING cSection, ;
                String cEntry, ;
                STRING cDefault, ;
                STRING @cRetVal, ;
                INTEGER nRetLen, ;
                STRING cINIFile
nRetLen = GetPrivateProfileString(cSection,;
                                  cEntry, ;
                                  cDefault, ;
                                  @cRetVal, ;
                                  nRetLen, ;
                                  cINIFile)
return left(cRetVal,nRetLen)
```

RITEPINI() writes out a new value to an INI file, and returns a logical value for the success of the operation.

```
* RitePini - Write an entry in a private .INI file
* returns .T. if successful, .F. if not
PARAMETERS cSection, cEntry, cValue, cINIFile
LOCAL nRetVal
DECLARE Integer WritePrivateProfileString IN WIN32API ;
                STRING cSection, ;
                STRING cEntry, ;
                STRING cValue, ;
                STRING cINIFile
nRetVal = WritePrivateProfileString(cSection, ;
                                    cEntry, ;
                                    cValue, ;
                                    cINIFile)
RETURN nRetVal=1
```

Example

```
* Determine whether the VFP ODBC driver is installed:
? ReadPini("ODBC 32 bit Drivers", ;
           "Microsoft Visual FoxPro Driver (32 bit)", ;
           "ODBCINST.INI")
```

See Also Configuration files, Declare-DLL, Registration Database, Set, Set Resource, Sys(2005), Sys(2019)

Init, Destroy

These events fire when an object is created and when it's released, respectively. They're similar to the constructor and destructor methods of other OOP languages, but differ from those because they don't actually perform the construction or destruction themselves.

Usage

```
PROCEDURE oObject.Init
[ LPARAMETERS [ nIndex , ] [ ParamList ] ]

PROCEDURE oObject.Destroy
```

For all objects except forms and formsets, Init and Destroy are the first and last events to fire. Forms and formsets also have Load and Unload events that bracket the others and let you handle opening of tables and the like. If the data environment is used, some of its events fire even before and after Load and Unload, respectively.

Init is a good place to do things that can't be done at design-time, but need to happen right away. It's also a good time to send messages to an object's members, especially if they're based on parameters passed to the container.

Init lets you short-circuit creation of an object. Returning .F. from Init creates the object reference, but sets it to .Null. Canceling creation of one object in a container doesn't prevent the container from being created, however.

When dealing with containers, the Inits for the contained objects fire first (from the inside out) and the Init of the container fires last. On a form, this means that all the controls' Inits fire before the form's Init.

Destroy happens in the other order. The container's Destroy fires first and it takes all the others with it, from the outside in.

This one's a documentation bug, not a product bug, we think. Like many other events, when the control that triggered it is a member of a control array (an array property holding references to objects), Init accepts a numeric parameter indicating which member of the array fired the event. Help doesn't show the nIndex parameter for Init.

Destroy, on the other hand, is documented as accepting an nIndex parameter, but it's really hard to tell because it never fires at all.

Init is also the method to which you can pass parameters when you create an object. For all objects except forms and formsets, this makes a great deal of sense since Init fires first. With forms and formsets, it's somewhat inconvenient because a lot of things happen before you reach the Init. But, we're pleased by the consistency anyway.

There is one case where Load, rather than Init, receives parameters. When you're dealing with a formset converted from FoxPro 2.6 (with WindowType = 2 or 3), parameters go to the Load event, not to Init.

You'll often want to hold onto the parameters passed to the Init method. Since the actual parameters themselves are released when the Init method ends, the trick is to create properties of the object and use Init to save the parameter values to the properties. Our example shows how.

Example

```
* This Init might be for a button
PROCEDURE Init
LPARAMETERS cCaption, nTop

This.Caption = cCaption
This.Top = nTop

ENDPROC
```

See Also Load, Unload

InitialSelectedAlias

This property of the DataEnvironment determines which table is selected after the tables in the data environment have been opened.

Usage

```
frmForm.DataEnvironment.InitialSelectedAlias = cAlias
cAlias = frmForm.DataEnvironment.InitialSelectedAlias
```

InitialSelectedAlias means you don't have to worry about the order in which you add things to the data environment. Just specify which one should be current when everything's open and set up.

There's one gotcha, though. The alias you specify is selected at the end of the OpenTables method (the internal part that you have no control over). If a method that fires later (like a control's Init) changes the work area, it isn't restored. For example, if a listbox is based on a query, the query is executed as part of the listbox's Init and the work area containing the query result becomes current. If you want to make sure a particular alias is current whenever you enter a particular form, use the form's Activate method to SELECT it. If you want it selected when the form first opens, put it in the form's Init (if there's only one form) or the formset's Init (when you have multiple forms).

Keep in mind that both the DataEnvironment's Init and the Form's Load come after OpenTables.

Example

```
* You'll normally set this one in the Property sheet
* To bring up the propsheet for the DE, open the
* DE window, then right-click on it and choose
* Properties. Then, you can find the InitialSelectedAlias
* property of the Data Environment and put something like:
Customer
```

See Also Activate, Init, Load, OpenTables, Select

InKey() See ChrSaw().

InList()

This function determines whether the value of the first expression is in the list of values supplied. INLIST() works on almost every field type in Visual FoxPro—only General is excluded.

Usage `lIsItThere = INLIST( eExpression, eList1, eList2, ...)`

Parameter	Value	Meaning
eExpression	Character, Memo, Currency, Date, DateTime, Double, Integer, Logical, Numeric	The value to search for in the list.
eListn	Same as eExpression	Valid values.
lIsItThere	.T.	The matching item was found in the list.
	.F.	The matching item was not found in the list.

INLIST() does some conversion between related data types. If any one of the expressions is DateTime, dates are converted to DateTime by adding a time of "12:00:00 AM" (midnight). This can be a subtle gotcha—if your dates are converted to DateTimes by one rogue DateTime variable, the comparison must be exact, in date and time. Numeric, float, currency, integer and double values can be mixed with INLIST() without problem, as can character data and memo fields holding characters. Consistent with the rule that NULLs are propagated through functions, INLIST(.NULL., list,...) returns .NULL., and a .NULL. contained within the list results in a .NULL. return, if the value you're trying to match is not in the list.

INLIST() is limited to 25 arguments in the list, or 26 parameters total. This is consistent with the limits of the MIN() and MAX() functions, but inconsistent with the UDF limit of 27 parameters. As we state below, if a list gets to this size, you probably should be using another method of storage besides hard-coding the list. INLIST() is case-sensitive, as shown in the third example below. There is no case-insensitive version as with AT() and ATC().

It is your authors' feeling that while this is a nice function to use interactively, hard-coding acceptable values for a test may not always be the wisest path. Designing your system so additional cases may be added without changes to your program code can make your system easier to maintain and enhance. Storing the information you wish to compare in a table also opens up options of loading an array and using the ASCAN() function or performing the comparison with a Rushmore-optimized SEEK() or SQL SELECT WHERE...IN clause.

Example

```
? INLIST(27, 12, 27, 50)                    && returns .T.
? INLIST("one", "two", "three", "one")  && returns .T.
? INLIST("one", "two", "three", "ONE")  && returns .F.
```

See Also AScan(), Between(), Seek(), Select-SQL

Input See Accept.

InputMask

InputMask describes the acceptable characters that can be entered by the user, or formats fields and memory variables for output. It is the controls' equivalent of the PICTURE clause used with @... GET input, and recognizes the same options:

InputMask character	Meaning
A	Alphabetic characters only
L	Logical: Allows and displays uppercase and lowercase characters T, F, Y and N
N	Alphabetic and numeric digits only
X	Any character—alphabetic, numeric, symbols
Y	Allows Y,y,N,n for logicals; displays uppercase only
#	Allow digits, signs and spaces
9	For character data: only allow entry of digits. For numeric entry: same as #, above
!	Converts alphabetic to uppercase
$	Displays dollar sign
$$	Floating dollar sign, flush against number
.	Displays correct SET POINT value separating whole number from decimal
,	Displays correct SET SEPARATOR value used to separate thousands

InputMask defines each character of a field; if you want three uppercase characters, you must specify "!!!" This is in contrast to the Format property, which need only be specified once and applies to the entire field. Because Format and InputMask share many of the same letters, this often leads to confusion. When expressed in a single command, such as a SAY clause or a TRANSFORM() function, FORMAT properties are distinguished by being preceded with an @ symbol.

Currency formatting is very handy, but sometimes confusing. The picture clauses to display currency use the USA-specific dollar sign, point and comma, which might cause you to think these were only good for U.S. currency. But, no, Visual FoxPro is an international application—surely Microsoft wouldn't be so America-centric! Well, yes and no. The point and comma are placeholders for the correct currency symbols in your application, as defined with SET POINT and SET SEPARATOR. But the dollar sign is, well, just a dollar sign. To get the proper currency formatting (as specified with SET CURRENCY), you need to use the "$" Format property, not the "$" InputMask.

Example

```
SET POINT TO ","
SET SEPARATOR TO "."
SET CURRENCY TO " mk"
SET CURRENCY RIGHT
* The next line displays "$ 12.345,00" wrong!
? TRANSFORM(12345, "$ 999,999.99")
* This next example works correctly using the $ Format
? TRANSFORM(12345, "@$ 999,999.99")  && DISPLAYS "12.345,00 mk"

* An input field Social Security numbers, and the variable only
* stores 9 digits, saving the space wasted with the hyphens
ThisForm.txtSSN.Format = "R"
ThisForm.txtSSN.Picture = "999-99-999"
```

See Also @ ... Get, Format, Transform(), Set Currency, Set Point, Set Separator

Insert

INSERT adds records to the current table at the current record pointer position. INSERT is almost always a bad idea. This command is part of FoxPro's Xbase legacy and generally leads to bad code. In all our experience, we've only found one situation where using INSERT was a good idea—more on that below.

Don't confuse this INSERT command with the SQL INSERT command, which is very useful.

Usage

```
INSERT [ BLANK ] [ BEFORE ]
```

Used by itself, INSERT is much like APPEND by itself, but requires exclusive access. It adds a record and brings up an EDIT-type window to fill in the fields. The fly in the ointment is that the new record is physically inserted immediately following the current record. This means that every record following that position has to be physically moved to make room. On a large table, INSERT is a spectacularly bad choice.

Adding the BLANK keyword is like using the BLANK keyword of APPEND. The new record is added behind the scenes and there's no interaction.

The BEFORE keyword indicates that the new record should precede rather than follow the current record.

If the table has any open indexes (even if order is set to 0), the new record is added at the end, whether or not you specify BEFORE. This actually makes it a better command than it is otherwise, but also makes it obsolete since you can do the same thing with APPEND.

INSERT can't be used with most of the cool stuff in Visual FoxPro. You can't INSERT in a buffered table, or in one that has rules, triggers, primary keys or candidate keys.

INSERT respects SET CARRY, bringing forward values from specified fields when CARRY is ON.

So, what about the one time we've found INSERT useful? The situation was a very small table (never more than a couple of hundred records), which was to be copied out to an SDF file, from which it would be sent to the printer. The record order was essential to the reporting process. Because the result might be more than one page, we needed to insert a record containing a page feed character after every 54 records. INSERT was just the ticket. The moral, though, is the situation has to be pretty unusual before it's worth using INSERT.

See Also Append, Insert-SQL, Set Carry

Insert-SQL

This form of INSERT is actually useful—unlike the Xbase version. It adds one or more records to a specified table, filling in fields at the same time.

Usage

```
INSERT INTO cFileName [ ( cFieldList ) ] VALUES  ( uValueList )
INSERT INTO cFileName FROM ARRAY aValueArray | MEMVAR
```

Parameter	Value	Meaning
cFileName	Character	The name of the table getting new records.
cFieldList	Character	A comma-delimited list of fields for which values are specified.
	Omitted	Values are specified for all fields.
uValueList	Assorted	A comma-delimited list of values to place in the new record.
aValueArray	Array	An array containing values to place in the new record.

You can't mix and match the two forms of INSERT. You can either specify a field list and then list individual values, or you can insert all values from an array or from corresponding memory variables. This is an item we'd really like to see improved. Well, actually, you can limit the fields in the second form if you use SET FIELDS, but it leads to the kind of code that gives us nightmares. If you want to go that route, put the SET FIELDS command as close as possible to the INSERT and make sure you've added clear comments. Be sure to turn off SET FIELDS as soon as you're done, too. In the first form, if cFieldList is omitted, uValueList must contain one item for each field in cFileName, in field order. Any fewer results in an error message, "Must specify additional parameters." Any greater results in "Syntax Error." If cFieldList is included, uValueList must match it, item by item.

In the second form, using FROM, you can omit fields, but the exact ability varies with the two sources for the data. With FROM ARRAY, values are placed in fields by taking the array elements in order until you run out of either fields or elements. If the array is two-dimensional, a new record is added for each row.

With FROM MEMVAR, values are placed in any field for which there is a correspondingly named memory variable. This version is great when you've issued SCATTER MEMVAR—you can collect the variable values back up into a new record.

If cFileName isn't already open, INSERT opens it in an available work area and leaves it open. The work area containing cFileName becomes the current work area.

Because it updates the table only once, INSERT INTO is a better choice than APPEND BLANK, GATHER MEMVAR, which updates twice. Index entries and field values are written only once, speeding I/O.

However, INSERT isn't very good for adding new, empty records to be populated by the user. If the table has any field-level rules that prohibit empty fields, INSERT fires the rules right away (regardless of the buffering mode) and you get an error. With table-level rules, you can INSERT empty records as long as you fill the required fields before moving to the another record. Given all this complication, you're better off using APPEND BLANK to add empty records. (You'll still need to be buffered if there are field-level rules.) Save INSERT for cases where you've already got the data in hand.

Watch out when you want to insert data from one table into another. The INSERT command changes work areas behind the scenes *before* it evaluates the new field values, so you need to add the alias to fields from other tables. Similarly, if you have a variable with the same name as a field in the table to which you're adding a record, be sure to use the m. notation.

Example

```
* Add a record to Customer
INSERT INTO Customer (Customer_Id, Company_name, Contact_name) ;
             VALUES ("MSFT","Microsoft","Bill Gates")

* Create and save a new record
USE SomeTable
```

```
SCATTER MEMVAR BLANK
* Let the user edit the record
INSERT INTO SomeTable FROM MEMVAR
```

The second example is typical of code written in FoxPro 2.x to create a new record. The SCATTER would take place in a screen's Setup snippet (and again after a Save or Cancel) and the INSERT would be in the Valid code for a Save button. With Visual FoxPro's buffering, there are fewer reasons to edit memory variables, and code like the example has become outdated.

See Also Append, Gather, Insert, Replace, Set Fields

InsMode() See CapsLock().

Instancing

A property of all COM servers, accessible via the Server object, this one is documented incorrectly in both Help and FoxPro.H.

Usage

```
oServer.Instancing = nInstancing
nInstancing = oServer.Instancing
```

Parameter	Value	Meaning
nInstancing	0	Not creatable.
	1	Single use.
	2	Multiple use.

A server's instancing describes how it is used. Let's start with the simple case—a single-use server is created when an application requests it, and is released when the application releases it. That's easy. A multi-use server can be used by more than one application at the same time. Non-creatable instancing is the most confusing. We've read the documentation for several development languages and still don't have a really good explanation for why you would want to do this. Perhaps these servers are ones that should only be turned on programmatically, but we haven't run across a case yet.

Last time we checked, the values above are correct and those in FoxPro.H wrong. You'll want to correct them there or avoid using the file.

Example

```
oProject.Servers.Item[1].Instancing = 2
```

See Also Project, Server, Servers

Int(), Round()

These two functions are for losing precision. INT() removes the decimal portion of a number. ROUND() lets you specify the desired precision and then it rounds more or less according to the usual rounding rules.

Usage

```
nNoDecimals = INT( nNumber )
nRounded = ROUND( nNumToRound, nPlaces )
```

Parameter	Value	Meaning
nNumber or nNumToRound	Numeric, Float, Integer, Double or Currency	Number to be processed.

Parameter	Value	Meaning
nPlaces	0	Rounds to the nearest integer.
	Positive	Rounds to the specified number of decimal places.
	Negative	Rounds to the specified power of 10. For example, passing nPlaces=-2 rounds to the nearest hundred.

We were taught that when the first digit being dropped is 5, you look at the digit to its left—if it's even, you round down; if it's odd, you round up. ROUND() doesn't do it that way—it always rounds up on a 5. Beware of this if you're doing statistical or engineering calculations where such things matter.

For positive numbers, INT() and FLOOR() are the same. For negative numbers, INT() is the same as CEILING().

Example

```
? INT(37.2738)            && Returns 37
? ROUND(37.2738,0)        && Returns 37
? ROUND(37.2738,1)        && Returns 37.3
? ROUND(37.2738,2)        && Returns 37.27
? ROUND(37.2738,3)        && Returns 37.274
? ROUND(37.2738,-1)       && Returns 40
? ROUND(37.2738,-2)       && Returns 0
? ROUND(-11.92,0)         && Returns -12
? ROUND(-11.92,1)         && Returns -11.9
? ROUND(-11.92,-1)        && Returns -10
```

See Also Ceiling(), Floor(), Min(), Max()

IntegralHeight

This is one of those properties that makes you look good to your users—or maybe we should say, without it, you don't look so good. It lets you indicate that the height of a list box, edit box or text box should be adjusted so that it fits an exact number of lines and doesn't leave any partial lines showing.

Usage

```
lWholeLinesOnly = oObject.IntegralHeight
```

For edit boxes and list boxes, IntegralHeight moves up the visible bottom of the control to cut off any partial lines. For text boxes, the visible bottom is moved up to show exactly one line of text. In this case, the actual height of the control isn't changed, but part of it isn't shown.

For edit boxes and text boxes, if the box is too small for even a single line of text, the actual Height of the box is increased to accommodate one line.

If a list box is too small for one line, however, setting IntegralHeight to .T. makes the display so small you can't see even a partial line of text.

Although you can't change IntegralHeight at runtime, the controls are smart enough to resize themselves if something like the font size changes. However, with a list, if you make the font big enough that not even one whole item fits in the original height, the list shrinks to show a single line of pixels. We think this one's a bug, too, and we have some pretty good ideas about what needs to be fixed in the internal code.

Example

```
* A builder might set IntegralHeight for all * the relevant controls on a form.
ASELOBJ(aForm,1)
aForm[1].SetAll("IntegralHeight",.t.)
```

See Also Height

InteractiveChange, ProgrammaticChange

Where have these events been all our lives? Well, all our professional lives, anyway. With InteractiveChange and ProgrammaticChange, we finally have the kind of control we've always wanted over changes in a form. InteractiveChange fires when a control's Value changes due to a user action. ProgrammaticChange fires when the Value changes because of something in code.

Usage

```
PROCEDURE InteractiveChange | ProgrammaticChange
[ LPARAMETERS nIndex ]
```

As with other events, nIndex is relevant only when a control array is involved, which is practically never.

In the text-based controls, InteractiveChange fires every time the user presses a key. It's handy to do things like enabling a button as soon as there's a value, but use Valid if you want to validate the complete user input rather than each individual character. (You can do many of the same things in KeyPress, too.)

These events are tied to the Value property of the control. When Value changes, the appropriate event fires. For combos and lists, changing DisplayValue programmatically also fires ProgrammaticChange. That's because changes to DisplayValue also affect Value.

For most controls, InteractiveChange doesn't fire when you re-choose the same item you just chose. For example, clicking the OptionButton that's already chosen in a group doesn't fire InteractiveChange for the OptionGroup. (Most of the time, this makes sense to us, since the Value of the control hasn't changed.) CommandGroups are the exception. Pressing a button in a CommandGroup always fires InteractiveChange for the group.

The place where the lack of firing is most counter-intuitive is with multi-select list boxes. If you click an item to select it, then Ctrl+click it to deselect it, InteractiveChange fires only the first time. Again, it's because Value hasn't changed, but, with multi-select, somehow it seems as if something must have changed. If this doesn't fire InteractiveChange, how about giving us an event it does fire?

In VFP 5.0a and earlier, changes to a combo's or list's Selected property do not fire ProgrammaticChange, even if doing so changes the object's Value. This is a bug, plain and simple. Fortunately, it's fixed in VFP 6.

Example

```
PROCEDURE InteractiveChange
* This might be the InteractiveChange procedure for a textbox
* that is the only required input in a dialog.
* Once the user has entered a value, we enable the OK button.
ThisForm.cmdOK.Enabled = .T.
RETURN
```

See Also Valid, Value

Interval

The Timer control's Interval property determines the length of time between Timer events firing.

Usage

```
nInterval = tmrTimer.Interval
tmrTimer.Interval = nInterval
```

The Interval property specifies how much time (in milliseconds) elapses between each firing of the Timer's Timer event. Timers are turned off by setting the Enabled property .F. or by setting the Interval to zero. In earlier versions, we found that zeroing out the Interval and restoring its value can be more efficient than the time-consuming toggling of Enabled when the interval is very small. You'll need to test the two alternatives in your environment to see which works best for you.

Example

```
frmForm.Timer1.Interval = 1500  && One and a half seconds
? frmForm.Timer1.Interval
```

See Also Timer Control, Timer, Reset Method

IsAlpha(), IsDigit(), IsLower(), IsUpper()

These functions all tell you about the state of a character. ISALPHA() returns .T. if the character is alphabetic while ISDIGIT() returns .T. if it's a numeric digit. ISLOWER() and ISUPPER() check the case of a character and return .F. if it's the wrong case or not alphabetic.

Usage

```
lIsItAlphabetic = ISALPHA( cString )
lIsItADigit = ISDIGIT( cString )
lIsItLower = ISLOWER( cString )
lIsItUpper = ISUPPER( cString )
```

Although you can pass an entire character string to these functions, they only look at the first character, so:

```
?ISDIGIT("1abc")
```

returns .T., as does:

```
?ISUPPER("Smith")
```

Use these functions in parsing and in validating user input. For example, you might check all the characters of a supposedly numeric string before applying VAL() to it. However, if you need all uppercase or all lowercase letters for an operation, it's easier to just apply UPPER() or LOWER().

Note that Windows and its ANSI font standard has a different interpretation of which characters constitute the alphabet from DOS and its ASCII basis. ISALPHA() is true for many of the high-order characters (like *ƒ*, Š, and Ñ), which Windows/ANSI maps to non-English alphabets, while FoxPro/DOS reported .F. for anything other than A through Z, uppercase and lowercase.

Example

```
? ISALPHA("\WINWORD")    && returns .F.
? ISDIGIT("Age 7")       && returns .F.
? ISLOWER("lower case")  && returns .T.
? ISUPPER("\WINWORD")    && returns .F.
```

See Also Lower(), Upper()

IsBlank()

ISBLANK() indicates whether a passed expression is blank, as distinguished from empty.

Usage

```
lReturnValue = ISBLANK( eExpression )
```

This function was added in FoxPro 2.6 for dBASE compatibility. It represents an approach that's sort of halfway to real nulls.

Blank is that pristine condition you see for numbers or logicals in a Browse until you actually store some data in that field. Blanks are of limited utility because they can't be distinguished from emptiness for character and date types. With the addition of true nulls in Visual FoxPro, we can't see any reason to use blanks anymore. Even if the possibility of using a four-state logical field is attractive at first, you'll find coding and processing blanks to be far more work than it is worth.

The BLANK command lets you reset fields to blank.

Example

```
CREATE TABLE Test (cfld C(3), dfld D, nfld N(3), lfld L)
* add a record
APPEND BLANK
? ISBLANK(cfld)    && returns .T.
? ISBLANK(dfld)    && returns .T.
? ISBLANK(nfld)    && returns .T.
? ISBLANK(lfld)    && returns .T.
```

```
* now store empty values in it
REPLACE cfld WITH "", ;
    dfld WITH {}, ;
    nfld WITH 0, ;
    lfld WITH .f.

? ISBLANK(cfld)    && returns .T.
? ISBLANK(dfld)    && returns .T.
? ISBLANK(nfld)    && returns .F.
? ISBLANK(lfld)    && returns .F.
```

See Also Blank, Empty(), IsNull()

IsColor() See DiskSpace().

IsDigit() See IsAlpha().

IsExclusive(), IsReadOnly()

These two functions tell you what kind of access you have to a table or database.

Usage

```
lExclusive = ISEXCLUSIVE( [ cAlias | nWorkArea | cDatabase [, nType ] ] )
lReadOnly = ISREADONLY( [ cAlias | nWorkArea ] )
```

Parameter	Value	Meaning
cAlias	Character	Tell whether the specified alias was opened for exclusive access or read-only.
	Omitted	If nWorkArea and cDatabase are also omitted, tell whether the table open in the current work area was opened exclusively or read-only.
nWorkArea	Numeric	Tell whether the table open in the specified work area was opened for exclusive access or read-only.
	Omitted	If cAlias and cDatabase are also omitted, tell whether the table open in the current work area was opened exclusively or read-only.
cDatabase	Character	Tell whether the specified database (DBC) was opened for exclusive access.
	Omitted	If cAlias and nWorkArea are also omitted, tell whether the table open in the current work area was opened exclusively.
nType	1 or Omitted	Return information about a table.
	2	Return information about a database.
lExclusive	.T.	The table or database was opened for exclusive access.
	.F.	The table or database was opened for shared access.
lReadOnly	.T.	The table was opened for read-only access.
	.F.	The table was opened for read-write access.

Before Visual FoxPro, you had to mess with SYS(2011) to figure out if a table was open exclusively. ISEXCLUSIVE() is much more intuitively named, and since it returns a logical, it's easy to incorporate in code and doesn't depend on the language you're using.

ISREADONLY() indicates whether the specified table is open in read-only mode. This function was on many developers' "most wanted" list for a long time. It makes it easier to write black-box routines that might process either tables or cursors. (Cursors created by SQL-SELECT are read-only.) This function only accepts table aliases, not database containers, which is a shame since a DBC can be opened read-only. Now that you don't need exclusive access to be able to modify a DBC, not being able to tell whether it's read-only is a bit of a pain.

Example

```
SET EXCLUSIVE ON
USE Customer
? ISEXCLUSIVE()  && Returns .T.
USE Customer SHARED
? ISEXCLUSIVE()  && Returns .F.
SET EXCLUSIVE OFF
USE Customer
? ISEXCLUSIVE()  && Returns .F.
USE Customer EXCLUSIVE
? ISEXCLUSIVE()  && Returns .T.
? ISEXCLUSIVE("TasTrade",2)  && Returns .T.
USE Customer NOUPDATE
? ISREADONLY()            && Returns .T.
USE Customer
? ISREADONLY()            && Returns .F.
SELECT Last_Name,First_Name FROM Employee INTO CURSOR Names
? ISREADONLY()            && Returns .T.
? ISREADONLY("Employee")  && Returns .F.
```

See Also Set Exclusive, SYS(2011), Use

IsFLocked() See FLock().

IsHosted() See GetHost().

IsLeadByte()

This function (added in version 3.0b) lets you determine whether a string is double-byte or single-byte. It tells you whether the first byte in the string is a "lead byte" (the first half of a double-byte character). We've confirmed that it returns .F. for single-byte characters, but can't test the other case.

Usage

```
lDoubleByte = ISLEADBYTE( cString )
```

See Also Double-Byte Character Sets

IsLower() See IsAlpha().

IsMarked() See Access().

IsMouse()

A function to determine whether or not a mouse is present—but it hasn't worked since FoxPro 2.x!

Usage

```
lMouseHere = ISMOUSE()
```

It is possible to run most Windows functions using nothing but the keyboard. Some people prefer using the keyboard. Other users, particularly those in high-speed, "heads-down" data entry, find keyboard entry far faster. Still others, such as those with vision or motor limitations, may require it. Plan to develop interfaces that support full keyboard functionality, even when the underlying controls (such as switching pages on a page frame) don't support a keyboard method natively.

We find that we tend to design interfaces similar to those we use. This is a natural tendency, and one that, in theory, is a benefit of the Macintosh and Windows GUIs. However, there are items in Visual FoxPro's interface that are best left there, and not disseminated in our applications. Forcing users to switch from keyboard to mouse, rather than offering them the option, is the sign of a poorly designed interface. Before shipping your application, consider ripping the mouse out of the back of your machine and verifying that all the functionality is available from the keyboard.

By designing our systems to work with either interface, a test for the presence of a mouse becomes unnecessary. This is one test we don't anticipate installing in our startup routines, but if your client has systems without mice and will pay you to program it, here's the function to do it.

Except, of course, it doesn't work. ISMOUSE() seems to always return .T. under Visual FoxPro, whether or not the hardware is present, whether or not drivers are installed for the mouse.

Example

```
IF ISMOUSE()  && good, there's a mouse,...
```

See Also IsColor()

IsNull(), NVL()

These two functions let you handle null values that appear in data. IsNull() tells whether an expression is null, while NVL() lets you substitute for null values.

Usage

```
lIsItNull = ISNULL( uExpr )
```

uExpr can be an expression of any type. If its value is .NULL., IsNull() returns .T.

You need IsNull() because .NULL. is never equal to any value, even itself. Nor is it unequal to other values. That is,

```
.NULL.=.NULL.
```

returns .NULL. and so does:

```
.NULL.<>.NULL.
```

The only way to find out if you have a null value is to test with IsNull(). Because many operators and functions propagate nulls, it's important to catch them in any situations where they have the potential of propagating through your code, wreaking havoc. As we say in "DBF, FPT, CDX, DBC—Hike!", the decision to use nulls has some pretty severe consequences for your code.

In VFP 3 and VFP 5, probably the most common place to use IsNull() was in code like IF TYPE('oObject') = "O" AND NOT IsNull(oObject). This checks first whether a supposed object variable is, in fact, an object—in case, say, you haven't instantiated it yet. Okay, that makes sense, but why the IsNull() check? Because when an object is destroyed, the variable referencing it retains its type ("O"), but is assigned the null value. So you need both tests to make sure you have a reference to an object, not just to an object-type variable. VFP 6 makes the test much easier. You can now use IF VARTYPE(oObject) = "O", because VARTYPE() returns "X" for any variable with a null value.

Example

```
IF NOT ISNULL(dBirthdate)
   * compute age
ENDIF
```

Usage `UNonNullValue = NVL( uTestExpr, uSubstituteValue )`

NVL() provides a way to keep nulls from propagating without having to use IsNull(). uTestExpr is tested. If it's not null, its value is returned. If uTestExpr is null, the value of uSubstituteValue is returned.

Think of NVL(x,y) as shorthand for:

```
IIF(ISNULL(x), y, x)
```

With a fairly simple text expression, the NVL() version is about 25 percent faster. Presumably, the more complex uTestExpr is, the more time you save with NVL() because it only has to evaluate the expression once, while the IIF() version has to evaluate it twice. As with many such situations, though, unless you're dealing with an extremely complex expression or performing the computation repeatedly, the times involved are quite small. So, use the more readable version. Fortunately, in this case, we think NVL() is easier to read and less error-prone, too.

Note that built-in functions which are designed to work with groups of records (AVERAGE, SQL SELECT's aggregate functions, SUM and CALCULATE) usually do not need to use NVL() functions, because these functions, by default, skip .NULL. values in their calculations.

Example

```
* Say you're totaling the values in an array
* and some of them might be null. If you include them
* in the total, the result will be null. Use NVL() instead
nTotal = 0
FOR nCnt = 1 TO ALEN(aArray)
   nTotal = nTotal + NVL(aArray[nCnt], 0)
ENDFOR
```

See Also Empty(), IsBlank(), Set Null, VarType()

IsReadOnly() See IsExclusive().

IsRLocked() See FLock().

IsUpper() See IsAlpha().

Item

This is a method that behaves more like a property or collection. It belongs to the various ActiveX collections available in VFP 6 and lets you grab an individual member of those collections.

Usage `oItem = Application.oCollection.Item( uIndex )`

VFP has a number of ActiveX collections, including Projects, Files, Servers and so forth. These are array-like objects that contain references to multiple objects of the same type. Item is a way to get your hands on one member of a collection.

Inside VFP, it doesn't seem very important to have this method. It's easier to write _VFP.Projects[1] than _VFP.Projects.Item(1). However, we suspect that when you're driving VFP from another application, the first notation may not be available. In addition, we also suspect that, like the Count property of the collections, Item is a fairly standard method in the ActiveX world, so it's better for VFP's collections to have it than not. (In fact, we're pretty sure these collections are implemented using some standard classes, and that Count and Item have simply come along for the ride.) Bottom line—we don't see ourselves using the Item method in our VFP code.

As you'd expect, you can pass a numeric index to Item. That's no big deal. However, you can also pass the name of the item you want. That's cool! This eliminates the need to iterate through all members of a collection, looking for the one you want—instead, you just specify it by name. Even more cool is that this notation works even with the shortcut version. That is, you can use either _VFP.Projects.Item("Test.PJX") or just

_VFP.Projects("Test.PJX"). In some of their VBA documentation, Microsoft explains this by saying that Item is the default method of collections.

Notice that when you're referring to a file (as with the Projects or Files collections), you need the whole filename, including the extension, but not the path.

One interesting note: Although Item is labeled a method with a single parameter, you can use square brackets instead of parens to pass the parameter. Makes us think that maybe Item is really just another collection.

Example

```
* One way to loop through the open project and display names
FOR nCount = 1 TO _VFP.Projects.Count
   ? _VFP.Projects.Item[nCount].Name
ENDFOR

* Here's how we'd really do this
FOR EACH oProject IN _VFP.Projects
   ? oProject.Name
ENDFOR
```

See Also Count, Files, Projects, Servers

ItemBackColor, ItemForeColor

These properties determine the color of items in a list box or combo box.

Usage

```
oObject.ItemBackColor = nBackColor
nBackColor = oObject.ItemBackColor
oObject.ItemForeColor = nForeColor
nForeColor = oObject.ItemForeColor
```

In a combo box, these properties determine colors only for the items in the drop-down part of the combo. The color of the text box part that's always visible is determined by BackColor and ForeColor (and SelectedBackColor and SelectedForeColor, when some text is highlighted).

For both combos and lists, SelectedItemBackColor and SelectedItemForeColor determine the color of the highlighted item or items.

Example

```
ThisForm.cboMyCombo.ItemBackColor = RGB(255,0,255)
ThisForm.cboMyCombo.ItemForeColor = RGB(255,255,255)
```

See Also BackColor, ForeColor, DisabledItemBackColor, DisabledItemForeColor, SelectedItemBackColor, SelectedItemForeColor

ItemData, ItemIdData

These two array properties let you associate a number with each item in a list or combo box.

Usage

```
oObject.ItemData( nIndex ) = nValue
nValue = oObject.ItemData( nIndex )
oObject.ItemIdData( nItemId ) = nValue
nValue = oObject.ItemIdData( nItemId )
```

There are two properties here where it seems one would do. Like List and ListItem, these are really just two names for the same array. The difference is in how you access them. ItemData keeps things in order by the item's Index, while ItemIdData is ordered by the item's unique ItemId. (See AddItem for an explanation of Index vs. ItemId.)

What does this dual-named array actually hold? By default, nothing. The elements get created as the list items are added, but there's nothing there. You get to fill them up.

The docs say that these properties only work right up to 60 items. They're partly right. In VFP 3, there were a number of problems with lists containing more than 60 items, but those got fixed in VFP 5. Of course, that's the version where the limit was first documented. Oops. We've tested with lists containing up to 10,000 items (despite our feeling that that's at least 9,000 more items than we think should be in any list box), and ItemData and ItemIdData had no problem keeping up.

At first glance, we thought these would be pretty cool. We could imagine sticking, say, employee names in the list and putting their IDs in ItemData/ItemIdData. But you can only put numbers in these, not other types. While that works if you're using Integers for surrogate IDs, you can also just put the IDs into the list and not show them. And, in fact, if your list is based on an array or a table, all the data is available through the List and ListItem collections anyway.

We have come up with one case where ItemData/ItemIdData seems useful. Suppose you have an array or table and you want to put some (but not all) of the items in a list. You can use AddItem or AddListItem to put the items you want in the list and then use this array to hold the row number in the original array or the record number (or primary key) of the item. Then, when the user picks an item, you can look up the row or record number and get right back to the original data.

Of course, there are other ways to handle this situation, but we'll never turn down a gift horse. Bottom line—we have yet to use these properties, other than for testing.

Example

```
* Fill a list with only those Employees that have a
* sales region listed. Set up ItemData to hold the
* recno() for each such employee.
SELECT Employee
SCAN
   IF NOT EMPTY(Sales_region)
      This.AddItem(Last_Name)
      This.ItemData[ This.NewIndex ] = RECNO()
   ENDIF
ENDSCAN
```

See Also AddItem, ComboBox, List, ListBox, ListIndex, ListItemId, NewIndex, NewItemId

ItemForeColor See ItemBackColor.

ItemIdToIndex See IndexToItemId.

ItemTips

ItemTips are cool. They're tooltip-like windows that appear for items in a list that are too wide for the list box. Like tooltips, they appear when you pause the mouse over the item. No more making a list wide enough to accommodate the widest item. Just turn on ItemTips and choose a reasonable width.

Usage

```
lstList.ItemTips = lUseItemTips
lUseItemTips = lstList.ItemTips
```

Surprisingly, ItemTips can be changed at runtime. We find it hard to imagine a situation in which that would be good interface design—except, perhaps, for applications in which the user controls whether lists have item tips.

In VFP 5 (both the original version and 5.0a), item tips and private data sessions don't mix. When ItemTips is on in a form with a private data session, moving the mouse over the list gives the error "Cannot access selected table." The bug is fixed in VFP 6.

ItemTips don't mix very well with multi-column lists, either. In VFP 5 (including 5.0a), the value of ItemTips is simply ignored in multi-column lists. No item tips appear. In VFP 6, item tips appear only for the first column and only for items that would show an item tip if the whole width of the list were devoted to the first column. Microsoft says this is by design, but we think it's just stupid.

Example

```
* Create a form.
* Add the TasTrade customer table to the DE.
* Drop a list on a form and set properties as follows:
RowSourceType = 6 - Fields
RowSource = Customer.Company_Name
ItemTips = .T.
* Run the form and move the mouse over the items in the list
```

See Also ListBox, ShowTips, ToolTipText

Join, Total, Update

As long as we've been using Xbase, we've heard that these three commands should be avoided. At least as far back as FoxBase+, the manuals warn that JOIN may be very slow and can overrun available disk space.

As a result of these dire warnings, we never looked very hard at these commands (though we've occasionally been called on to maintain code that uses them). Now that we've done so, we've decided it's just as well. They're hard to use, limited in capability, and can be extremely slow.

Usage

```
JOIN WITH cAlias | nWorkArea TO cTable
        FOR lForExpression
        [ FIELDS cFieldList ]
        NOOPTIMIZE
```

JOIN is sort of a limited version of SELECT-SQL. It matches up records in a pair of tables based on some condition and creates a new table (cTable) containing fields from both the original tables. One table must be open in the current work area; the other must be open in another work area. The FOR clause determines how the records are joined. You can limit the fields in the result using the FIELDS clause, but JOIN can't handle memo or general fields and you can't use expressions in the field list.

For very small data sets, JOIN can be competitive in speed with SELECT, but as soon as you get beyond a handful of records, it bogs down. The thought of throwing NOOPTIMIZE into the mix is really frightening.

JOIN has a bug when dealing with long field names. In the newly created table, all field names are truncated to 10 characters or less. This makes some sense since the table is created as a free table.

Frankly, we can't see any reason to use JOIN ever. Anything you can do with it, you can do more easily with SELECT-SQL.

Example

```
* Here's an example involving very small tables so you
* can see the result in this lifetime. It fails in VFP 6
* and VFP 5, but does work in VFP 3.
USE category
SELECT 0
USE products
JOIN WITH category TO temp FOR category_id=category.category_id

* Here's the SELECT-SQL equivalent
SELECT * FROM category, products ;
   WHERE category.category_id=products.category_id ;
   INTO TABLE temp
```

Usage

```
TOTAL TO cTable ON uField
        [ FIELDS nNumericFieldList ]
        [ Scope ]
        [ FOR lForExpression ]
        [ WHILE lWhileExpression ]
        [ NOOPTIMIZE ]
```

TOTAL is similar to working with GROUP BY in SELECT-SQL, but far more limited. It groups records from the table open in the current work area based on the listed field (uField) and totals the numeric fields listed in nNumericFieldList. If FIELDS is omitted, all numeric fields are totaled. A new table is created to hold the result. All fields from the original table are included in the result. You can limit the records included in the computation using the Scope, FOR and WHILE clauses.

So what else is wrong with TOTAL? The new table created has the same structure as the original. If the total for a field is too big to fit, you lose precision. Also, since all fields are carried along, you get random results for fields that aren't either totaled or listed in the ON clause. (Actually, this is the same thing that happens when you include extraneous fields in a GROUPed query, but at least there you have a chance to omit them.) TOTAL is limited to working with a single table—you can't match up records from multiple tables. Finally, you can't compute expressions, only sum existing fields, so you can't do things like total quantity*unit price to get an invoice total.

Bottom line: Like JOIN, we can't see a lot of reasons to use TOTAL.

Example

```
* We couldn't find a way to use TOTAL with the sample
* TasTrade database that comes with Visual FoxPro.
* The table in this example is from the Tutorial
* data that shipped with earlier versions of FoxPro.
USE Detail       && Invoice detail lines
* compute invoice totals
TOTAL ON ino TO InvTotal FIELDS Ltotal
```

Usage

```
UPDATE ON uJoinFieldName FROM cTable
        REPLACE uFieldName1 WITH eExpression1
        [ , uFieldName2 WITH eExpression2 [ , ... ] ]
        [ RANDOM ]
```

UPDATE is a sort of early way of creating a relation between two tables and using it to modify data. The table in the current work area gets updated based on establishing a relation between it and another open table. The relation is based only on a single identically named field (uJoinFieldName) in the two tables. The current table must be ordered on the common field either with an index or the natural order of the records. The other table (cTable) should also be ordered on the common field. If not, you must include the RANDOM keyword.

For each matching record found in cTable, each listed field is updated as specified in the REPLACE clause. The expression eExpression*n* can reference fields from both tables (actually, we suppose, from any open tables).

Got all that? It took us a while. This is an incredibly complicated command to do something that there are much easier ways to do. UPDATE-SQL lets you do similar things a lot more simply since you can specify the relationship explicitly in its WHERE clause. But, even in FoxPro 2.x, you could do this sort of thing by setting a relation and then using REPLACE.

In addition to the difficulty of using it, in a properly normalized database, there aren't likely to be a lot of places where you'd want to do this sort of computation. The only thing we can think of is updating a table from a copy, and that's often easier in Visual FoxPro just by using the built-in buffering techniques.

We just can't see any reason to use UPDATE.

Example

```
* Again, we can't see a way to use UPDATE with
* the nicely normalized TasTrade database.
* The example uses the old, less normalized,
* Tutorial data.
SELECT 0
USE Detail
SELECT 0
USE Invoices

* Clear out existing invoice totals
REPLACE ALL iTotal WITH 0

* Now recompute
UPDATE ON ino FROM Detail ;
   REPLACE iTotal WITH iTotal+Detail.Qty*Detail.Price
```

See Also Replace, Select-SQL, Update-SQL

JustDrive(), JustExt(), JustFName(), JustPath(), JustStem() See AddBS().

Key() See Candidate().

Keyboard

This command gives your program the ability to type. You can treat a string as if it had been typed at the keyboard.

Usage
```
KEYBOARD cString [ PLAIN ] [ CLEAR ]
```

KEYBOARD is handy for self-running demos and the like. But it's also useful when you want to force a particular menu choice or some other action.

The trickiest aspect of KEYBOARD is that the keyboarded characters aren't processed until the program reaches a wait state. They simply sit in the keyboard buffer, just as keystrokes typed by a user would. For example, if you KEYBOARD something in a control's method, the keystrokes aren't processed until the method finishes and control returns to the form. When the form is again waiting for input, the keyboarded keystrokes are removed from the buffer and processed in the order they were entered.

FoxPro uses a special notation to allow you to refer to key combinations as well as the special keys on the keyboard (Home, End, and so forth). You enclose the key name in curly braces, like {ALT+F3}. Check out the online help file under ON KEY LABEL for a list of special keys.

The PLAIN clause is handy when you've redefined a key but still need to keyboard it just as a character. PLAIN means that FoxPro should process the key simply as a character rather than checking for an ON KEY LABEL or macro for that keystroke. PLAIN is especially useful if you've redefined keys like Tab, Spacebar or Enter.

CLEAR is useful when your users have a habit of hitting keys when they shouldn't. It clears out the keyboard buffer before inserting the specified characters. This gives you better control over the exact sequence of events.

We KEYBOARD a lot less in Visual FoxPro than we did in FoxPro 2.x because the ability to call methods of other objects directly, together with access to so many system and user events, simply eliminates much of the need. Rather than building KEYBOARD into our applications, nowadays we tend to use it more in test scripts, which allows us to repeat a standard sequence of keystrokes to set up a system in a particular way for testing.

Example
```
* force a "copy" from the menu
KEYBOARD "{CTRL+C}"
```

See Also Inkey(), Lastkey(), On Key Label, Sys(1500)

KeyboardHighValue, KeyboardLowValue, SpinnerHighValue, SpinnerLowValue

These properties determine what values you can enter in a spinner using either the keyboard or the arrow buttons.

Usage
```
spnSpinner.KeyboardHighValue = nValue
nValue = spnSpinner.KeyboardHighValue
spnSpinner.KeyboardLowValue = nValue
nValue = spnSpinner.KeyboardLowValue
spnSpinner.SpinnerHighValue = nValue
nValue = spnSpinner.SpinnerHighValue
spnSpinner.SpinnerLowValue = nValue
nValue = spnSpinner.SpinnerLowValue
```

KeyboardHighValue and KeyboardLowValue correspond to the Range clause of FoxPro 2.x's spinners. The spinner cannot lose focus unless its value is between KeyboardLowValue and KeyboardHighValue, which leads to a gotcha—if you assign these in the wrong order (put the higher value in KeyboardLowValue and vice versa), you can't leave the spinner at all. There is a way out, but it's a pain—don't do it! (The only way we could find involved using the mouse to create a new program that changes one of the bounds, then using the mouse to run that program.)

SpinnerHighValue and SpinnerLowValue, on the other hand, control only how high and low you can go using the spinner's arrows. Messing up these values just means that the arrows behave strangely. You can still use the spinner from the keyboard.

Note also that using up and down arrow keys to change the spinner isn't keyboarding—it's just like clicking on the arrows themselves.

Spinners in Visual FoxPro are much better than those in FoxPro 2.x. You can change any of these properties (as well as Increment) on the fly, so a spinner's range can change during a program. The only thing you can't do, to our regret, is set up what we guess should be called DynamicSpinnerHighValue, and so forth. That is, you can't assign a variable to one of these properties and have it changed dynamically—when the variable changes, you need to reassign the spinner property.

Figure 4-7 shows a form containing a date spinner class, DateSpin, based on the Container class. The range for the day spinner (the one in the middle—this uses American dates) changes based on the month and year chosen with the other spinners.

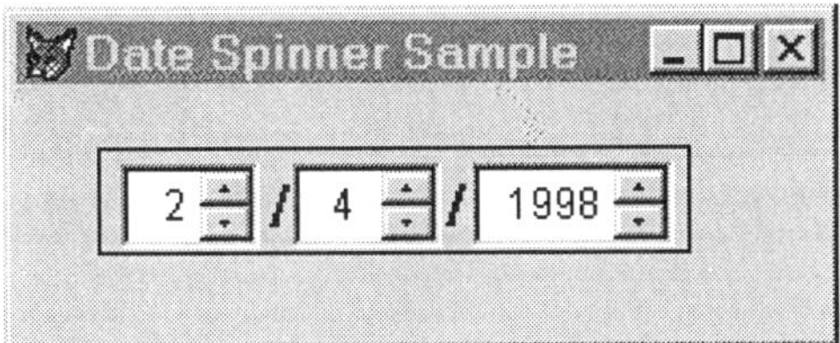

Figure 4-7: Date Spinner—One spinner controls another

The LostFocus methods for the month and year spinners each call a custom method of the container, FixDays, to update the day spinner's properties, as follows:

Example

```
* FixDays
DO CASE
CASE INLIST(This.nMonth, 1, 3, 5, 7, 8, 10, 12)
   This.spnDays.SpinnerHighValue = 31
   This.spnDays.KeyboardHighValue = 31
CASE INLIST(This.nMonth, 4, 6, 9, 11)
   This.spnDays.SpinnerHighValue = 30
   This.spnDays.KeyboardHighValue = 30
CASE This.nMonth = 2
   IF This.LeapYear(This.nYear)
      This.spnDays.SpinnerHighValue = 29
      This.spnDays.KeyboardHighValue = 29
   ELSE
      This.spnDays.SpinnerHighValue = 28
      This.spnDays.KeyboardHighValue = 28
   ENDIF
ENDCASE

IF This.nDay > This.spnDays.SpinnerHighValue
   This.nDay = This.spnDays.SpinnerHighValue
ENDIF
```

LeapYear is also a custom method of the DateSpin class. It returns .T. when the year passed to it is a leap year, and .F. otherwise.

DateSpin is in the CoolStuf class library on the CD.

See Also Increment, RangeHigh, RangeLow

KeyMatch()

This function lets you check whether a particular key value already exists in an index. It's sort of a manual way to do what primary and candidate indexes do automatically. KEYMATCH() was one of the functions added for dBASE compatibility in FoxPro 2.6 that's actually somewhat useful.

Usage

```
lIsItThere = KEYMATCH( uKeyValue [, nWhichKey
                       [, nWorkArea | cAlias ] ] )
```

Parameter	Value	Meaning
uKeyValue	Expression	The value to check for.
nWhichKey	Numeric	The index to check. See Candidate() for an explanation of index numbers.
nWorkArea	Numeric	Check the key for the table open in the specified work area.
	Omitted	If cAlias is also omitted, check in the table open in the current work area.
cAlias	Character	Check the key for the table open with the specified alias.
	Omitted	If nWorkArea is also omitted, check in the table open in the current work area.
lIsItThere	.T.	A record exists with the specified key value for the specified index.
	.F.	No record has the specified key value for the specified index.

This function actually sounds more useful than it is. Two factors keep it from being something we use all the time.

First, you have to specify tags by number, not by name. We don't want to know the number of an index—the name of the tag is enough for us. This isn't as limiting as it seems, since you can use TagNo() to convert from tag name to tag number, but it's just one more step.

The second factor is the really important one. Though it sounds like it shouldn't, KEYMATCH() moves the record pointer. The record pointer is restored to the original position at the end of the function call, but the fact that it moves at all makes KEYMATCH() useless in the situation where we want to use it—to check in a row-buffered cursor whether a particular item has been entered already. The movement of the record pointer commits the record we're adding—definitely not what we want to have happen. Fortunately, VFP 6's new INDEXSEEK() function does exactly what we want. In older versions, we'll stick to USEing the table again in another work area to check for duplicates.

Example

```
USE Employee ORDER Last_Name
? KEYMATCH("KING")                              && Returns .T.
? KEYMATCH("     10", TAGNO("Employee_I"))  && Returns .T.
SET ORDER TO
? KEYMATCH("KING", 2)                           && Returns .T.
? KEYMATCH("GATES", 2)                          && Returns .F.
```

See Also IndexSeek(), Locate, LookUp(), Seek, Seek(), TagNo()

KeyPress, KeyPreview

The KeyPress event lets you take action as soon as a user presses a key. When combined with the KeyPreview property, you can act at the form level when a key is pressed on any control.

Usage

```
PROCEDURE oObject.KeyPress
LPARAMETERS [ nControlIndex, ] nKeyPressed, nModifiers
```

Parameter	Value	Meaning
nControlIndex	Numeric	When a control is a member of a control array, nControlIndex is passed, indicating which control in the array received the keypress.
	Omitted	The control receiving the keypress is not a member of a control array.
nKeyPressed	Numeric	The code for the key that was pressed. The codes passed by KeyPress are the same as those returned by INKEY().
nModifiers	Numeric	A code indicating whether any of Shift, Ctrl, or Alt were held down when the key was pressed. Each modifier has a value (Shift=1, Ctrl=2, Alt=4). nModifiers is the sum of the values for whichever of the modifier keys were held down.

Your KeyPress method code must accept these parameters. You only need the nControlIndex parameter in the KeyPress code if the method is for a group of controls contained in a control array. In that case, nControlIndex indicates which element of the array triggered the event (which of the controls received a key press).

In many cases, the value of nKeyPressed already reflects the modifier keys pressed, but there are a few keys that return the same value with at least some of the modifiers. The arrow keys, for instance, don't distinguish between shifted and unshifted.

The really big plus of nModifiers is that it lets you know if multiple modifier keys are pressed. When you use more than one of Shift, Alt, and Ctrl, you may be surprised by the value of nKeyPressed. If Alt is included, you always get the keycode for the Alt version of the key, regardless of the condition of Ctrl and Shift. If Alt isn't used, but Ctrl is (with or without Shift), you get the code for the Ctrl version of the key. Only when Shift and a key are used without either Alt or Ctrl do you get back the value for the shifted key. Finally, you get the unshifted key value only when the key is used without any of the modifiers.

This means that code which checks the character pressed must look like this:

```
IF INLIST(nKeyCode, 98, 66, 2, 48)  && Check for a "b"
```

Frankly, we think it would make more sense to always pass the unshifted value and let you figure it out with nModifiers. But this does make KeyPress work more like INKEY(), so it was probably done this way to make the transition to KeyPress easier.

KeyPress doesn't catch keystrokes that are valid menu shortcuts. For example, with the default system menu, pressing CTRL+A in a text box selects all the text in the box and doesn't fire the KeyPress event.

Example

```
* To see how KeyPress works, try the following:
* Create a form in the Form Designer
* Add a textbox to the form
* Put the following code in the KeyPress event of the textbox
WAIT WINDOW "Key = " + ALLTRIM(STR(nKeyCode)) + CHR(13) + ;
          "Modifier = " + ALLTRIM(STR(nShiftAltCtrl))
* Run the form and try typing different keys and key
* combinations into the textbox
```

Usage
```
oForm.KeyPreview = lValue
lValue = oForm.KeyPreview
```

KeyPreview is a form property that indicates whether all key presses should be routed to the form's KeyPress method before the KeyPress method for the individual controls. When KeyPreview is true, the form's KeyPress method is triggered whenever a key is pressed. This allows you to perform actions at the form level based on the keys pressed. Once the form's KeyPress method finishes, the KeyPress method for the specific control fires.

Our favorite use for KeyPreview is to set a custom form property indicating that data has changed since the last save. The Save button can be enabled and disabled based on the custom property (and can reset the property after each save). Similarly, when the form is closed, you can display a message indicating data has changed if the property is true. While this technique isn't foolproof (it doesn't catch changes made with the mouse only), it is useful in forms where all data is entered from the keyboard and other controls are used only to perform actions on the data (save, cancel, etc.).

Our tech editor points out another handy use for turning on KeyPreview. You can test for an Esc press and exit the form without having to have a Close button marked as the Cancel button. Just check for nKeyCode = 27.

Example
```
* The form should have a property lChanged
* Set KeyPreview=.t.
* The form level KeyPress contains:
IF UPPER(this.ActiveControl.BaseClass) $ "TEXTBOX,EDITBOX" ;
   AND NOT INLIST(nKeyCode, 9, 13, 15, 271)
   * We're only interested in input keystrokes,
   * not keystrokes on buttons, etc.
   * We also only want to recognize "data" keystrokes,
   * so we omit Tabs, Returns, etc.
   * The list to omit could also include arrow keys and
   * other navigation keys.
   this.lChanged=.T.
ENDIF

* Now, the form's QueryUnload method
* can contain code like:
LOCAL nChoice
IF thisform.lChanged
   * prompt the user to save changes
   nChoice = MESSAGEBOX("Save changes", ;
             MB_YESNOCANCEL + MB_ICONQUESTION + MB_DEFBUTTON1)
   DO CASE
   CASE nChoice = IDYES
      * save the current record
   CASE nChoice = IDCANCEL
      * kill the form close
      NODEFAULT
   ENDCASE
ENDIF
```

See Also InKey()

Label See Report.

Label

The Label control is a more modern version of the @ ... SAY command, with added features that allow its participation in the event loop.

Property	Value	Purpose
AutoSize	Numeric	Tells the Label control to resize itself automatically to fit the text specified with Caption.
Caption	Character	Up to 256 characters to be displayed. Preceding a character with "\<" causes that character to act as an "access" or "hot" key, moving focus to the next control beyond the label in tab order. This is a neat solution for providing accelerator keys to those controls lacking a Caption.
WordWrap	Numeric	Causes the Caption text to be wrapped onto multiple lines with a fixed Width property. Even with AutoSize set .T., the Height of the Label control does not change to accommodate the wrapped text.

While similar to the @ ... SAYs of old, the label is a full participant in the event loop with MouseMove, MouseUp, MouseDown, Click and Drag-related events. Like most text-based controls, it has a whole slew of properties that can be modified at runtime, including a bunch of Font properties: FontName, FontSize, FontOutline, FontStrikeThru, FontThis and FontThat. Unlike the @ ...SAYs of old, it does not require a nuclear physicist to calculate the location of the old text, erase it, and place new text in its place at runtime—just change the value of Caption, and the control handles it automatically.

Label does lack some features it might be nice to have in a read-only control, such as the ability to bind to an underlying data source. Most solutions we've seen involve using Text boxes with their colors tweaked and Enabled set to .F.

Example

```
oForm.AddObject("lblMyText","Label")
WITH oForm.lblMyText
  .Top = 20
  .AutoSize = .T.
  .FontName = "Times New Roman"
  .FontSize = 18
  .FontItalic = .T.
  .Caption = "Hello, World!"
  .ForeColor = 4259584
  .Visible = .T.
ENDWITH
```

See Also Textbox

LastKey() See ChrSaw().

LastModified

This property belongs to files in a project and indicates when the file was last changed. Not surprisingly, it's read-only.

Usage

```
tLastChanged = filFile.LastModified
```

To get to this information through the interface, you have to go to the Files page of the Project Info dialog. On the whole, we think accessing this property may be easier.

Example

```
* See whether file is recent
IF oFile.LastModified < DATE()-30
  WAIT WINDOW "You should check for an updated version of " + ;
              oFile.Name
ENDIF
```

See Also File

Left, Top

These two properties together indicate the location of an object.

Usage

```
oObject.Left = nPosition
nPosition = oObject.Left
oObject.Top = nPosition
nPosition = oObject.Top
```

Left is the position of the left-hand edge of a form or control, while Top is the location of the top of the object. Both are measured in the current ScaleMode and are relative to the containing object. That is, Left for a control in a form is the distance from the left edge of the form.

You can move an object by changing its Left and/or Top values, except for controls contained in columns of a grid.

If you're like us, you might expect MaxLeft and MaxTop to provide limits for the values of Left and Top. In fact, they don't. They're about the position of the form when it's maximized.

Example

```
frmMyForm = CREATEOBJECT("FORM")
frmMyForm.Show()
frmMyForm.AddObject("chkMyCheck", "Checkbox")
frmMyForm.chkMyCheck.Visible = .t.
frmMyForm.chkMyCheck.Left = 10
frmMyForm.chkMyCheck.Top = 20
* now add another object under the first
frmMyForm.AddObject("chkMyOtherCheck", "Checkbox")
frmMyForm.chkMyOtherCheck.visible = .t.
frmMyForm.chkMyOtherCheck.Left = frmMyForm.chkMyCheck.Left
frmMyForm.chkMyOtherCheck.Top = ;
   frmMyForm.chkMyCheck.Top + 20
```

See Also Height, MaxLeft, MaxTop, ObjToClient(), ScaleMode, Width

Left(), Right(), SubStr()

These functions let you pull apart character strings. LEFT() grabs a specified number of characters from the beginning; RIGHT() takes the specified number from the end. SUBSTR() is the most general, but also the most difficult to use; it lets you extract a consecutive string of characters from anywhere in the original string.

You can combine these functions with AT() (or similar search functions) to parse a string.

Usage

```
cReturnValue = LEFT( cString, nCharacters )
```

LEFT() returns the first nCharacters characters of cString.

Example

```
?LEFT("Hacker's Guide", 8)    && returns "Hacker's"
```

Usage

```
cReturnValue = RIGHT( cString, nCharacters )
```

RIGHT() returns the last nCharacters of cString. But watch out for trailing blanks. RIGHT() uses the string you give it and doesn't remove trailing blanks. You'll probably want to TRIM() the string before you apply RIGHT().

Example

```
?RIGHT("Hacker's Guide",5)    && returns "Guide"
?RIGHT("This string has 2 trailing blanks  ",2) && returns "  "
```

Usage

```
cReturnValue = SUBSTR( cString, nStart [ , nLength ] )
```

Parameter	Value	Meaning
cString	Character	The string from which a portion is to be extracted.
nStart	Numeric	The position of the first character to extract.
nLength	Numeric	The number of characters to extract. If there are fewer than nLength characters from nStart to the end of the string, all remaining characters are returned.
	Omitted	All characters from nStart to the end of the string are extracted.

In versions of VFP through 5.0a, SUBSTR() does one truly odd thing. Its behavior if nStart is greater than the length of the string depends on the current value of SET TALK. Really! With SET TALK OFF, you simply get the empty string. But with SET TALK ON, attempting to start a SUBSTR() after the end of the character string gives an error message of "Beyond String." Try the following:

```
SET TALK OFF
?SUBSTR('abc',4)
SET TALK ON
?SUBSTR('abc',4)
```

Why two different behaviors? The folks at Microsoft say it's an attempt to be forgiving. If TALK is OFF, you're probably in a program and don't want it to crash it. But if TALK is ON, you're probably working interactively and need to know where you went wrong. Nice try, but we'd prefer consistency and apparently, finally, so does Microsoft. In VFP 6, SUBSTR() accepts a value of nStart beyond the end of cString regardless of the setting of TALK.

Example

```
?SUBSTR("Visual FoxPro",9,2)    && returns "ox"
?SUBSTR("Visual FoxPro",8)      && returns "FoxPro"
* line below returns "Fox"
?SUBSTR("Visual FoxPro",AT(" ","Visual FoxPro")+1,3)
```

All three of these functions have double-byte counterparts for working in languages like Chinese: LeftC(), RightC(), and SubStrC().

See Also At(), AtC(), LeftC(), Occurs(), RAt(), RightC(), SubstrC()

LeftC(), RightC(), SubStrC()

These are the double-byte (and mixed) versions of LEFT(), RIGHT() and SUBSTR(), respectively, added in version 3.0b. As with the other double-byte functions, we can't test these thoroughly since we're not running in a double-byte environment. However, they do work properly with single-byte data.

Usage

```
cReturnValue = LEFTC( cString, nCharacters )
cReturnValue = RIGHTC( cString, nCharacters )
cReturnValue = SUBSTRC( cString, nStart, nLength )
```

See Also Double-Byte Character Sets, Left(), Right(), SubStr()

LeftColumn

This property helps you figure out which columns of a grid are displayed. It always contains the ColumnOrder of the leftmost column currently showing.

Usage

```
nLeftmostColumn = grdGrid.LeftColumn
```

There's no corresponding RightColumn property, nor is there a NumberOfColumnsDisplayed. The only way we can see to figure out exactly which columns are displayed is to start with LeftColumn and then look at ColumnWidths and the grid's Width and figure it out the hard way.

You can't change this property directly. Use the DoScroll method to change which columns are displayed.

Example

```
* Scroll if necessary to make sure Column2 is visible
IF This.LeftColumn>2
   LOCAL nCnt
   FOR nCnt = 1 TO This.LeftColumn - 2
      This.DoScroll(4)
   ENDFOR
ENDIF
```

See Also ActiveColumn, ColumnOrder, DoScroll, RelativeColumn

Len()

This function tells you how long a string is.

Usage

```
nStringLength = LEN( cString )
```

That's it, just the length of the string you pass it.

Except for one thing. There's a gotcha when you use LEN() on a character field (it works fine on memo fields). Fields in FoxPro are fixed-length, so strings that don't fill the allocated space get filled with trailing blanks. When you apply LEN() to a character field, you get back the defined size of the field, not the size of the actual contents. Apply TRIM() or ALLTRIM() before LEN() if you want to know how many characters you've actually put in a field.

Like most of the string-handling functions, LEN() has a double-byte alternative, LENC(), useful for handling strings in languages that have larger character sets.

Example

```
? LEN("abcdef")         && returns 6
? LEN(LastName)         && returns defined length of LastName field
? LEN(TRIM(LastName))  && returns length of LastName for
                        && current record
```

See Also AllTrim(), FSize(), LenC(), Trim()

LenC()

Added in VFP 3.0b, this function tells you the length of a string and whether it's single-byte, double-byte or mixed. It's the double-byte equivalent of LEN(). We haven't tested in a double-byte situation.

Usage

```
nLengthInCharacters = LENC( cString )
```

See Also Double-Byte Character Sets, Len()

Like()

This function compares a string to a template string that may contain wildcards.

Usage

```
lMatch = LIKE( cWildcardString, cCompareString )
```

Parameter	Value	Meaning
cWildcardString	Character	The template string. It may contain the wildcards "*" (0 or more characters) and "?" (one character).

Parameter	Value	Meaning
cCompareString	Character	The string to check against the template.
lMatch	.T.	cCompareString matches the form of cWildcardString.
	.F.	cCompareString does not fit the form of cWildcardString.

We've never actually used this function, so we asked around before writing this section and couldn't find anyone who'd ever used this function. However, in playing with it, it turns out to be fairly neat.

Unlike the DOS wildcards, "*" and "?" may appear multiple times in cWildcardString, and the "*" isn't restricted to the end of the string. So, for example, you could use "*X*" to check for a string containing at least one "X." Note that these are not the same wildcards as the LIKE clause of SQL-SELECT, even though they do behave the same way.

One use we can imagine for LIKE() is to check user input to see if it forms a valid name of the type needed for an operation. One trap here is that LIKE() is case-sensitive, so you must remember to compare items in the same case or use UPPER().

For some reason, LIKE() doesn't use SET EXACT to determine the significance of trailing blanks. Instead, it's controlled by SET COMPATIBLE. The Fox version (OFF or FOXPLUS) considers trailing blanks, while the dBASE version (ON or DB4) ignores them.

Example

```
? LIKE("T*", "Tamar")                && Returns .T.
? LIKE("T*", "Ted")                  && Returns .T.
? LIKE("T*", "Cherry Tomato")        && Returns .F.
? LIKE("*.DBF", UPPER(cFileName))  && Is it a table name?
```

See Also Difference(), Select-SQL, Set Compatible, Set Exact, Soundex()

LikeC()

This one is the double-byte version of LIKE(). It appears to work properly with single-byte data, and we don't have double-byte data to test on. Like the other "C" functions, it was added in version 3.0b.

Usage

```
lMatch = LIKEC( cWildcardString, cCompareString )
```

See Also Double-Byte Character Sets, Like()

Line See Box.

Line

The Line control is an improved version of the feeble lines we could place on 2.x screens, but it does appear strange at large widths. This is a full partner in the event loop, with its own properties, events and methods.

Property	Value	Purpose
BorderWidth	Numeric	The width of the linc drawn, in pixels. Note that lines with a BorderWidth of 6 or more start to take on an oblong shape.
LineSlant	"\"	Line slants from the upper left to lower right corner.
	"/"	Line slants from the upper right to lower left corner.

Property	Value	Purpose
LineSlant	Any other character	Ignored.

This control puts a line into a rectangle described by its Top, Left, Height and Width properties, and responds to the usual stimuli of MouseClicks and DragDrop events. We doubt we'll use its events for much, however, because it is a pretty limited input device. It's not obvious by looking at Line's properties, but you create a horizontal line by setting its Height to 0 or a vertical line with Width of 0.

Don't assume the Width of a Line control is its actual width, nor that the control's Height is its real height. BorderWidth plays a tricky part here. Visual FoxPro attempts to create a line of width BorderWidth by drawing half the thickness above the line and half below, a reasonable algorithm. But this principle is taken too far, including the endpoints, creating a half-circle of one half of the BorderWidth around each. This is not only ugly, but inconsistent with other controls whose visual appearance is cropped at the rectangle described by their Top, Left, Height and Width properties.

So, the real "top" and "left" of a line control is its Top or Left minus one-half its BorderWidth, and its real "width" and "height" is its Width and Height plus BorderWidth.

Example

```
* A simple line control on a form, showing the oblong shape
oForm = CREATEOBJECT("form")
oForm.Show()
oForm.AddObject("linMine", "Line")
WITH oForm.LinMine
   .Top = 30
   .Left = 30
   .BorderWidth = 20
   .Height = 0
   .Visible = .T.
ENDWITH
```

See Also LineSlant

LineNo() See Error.

LineSlant

This property determines if the Line control slants from the upper-left to the lower-right corners, or from the lower-left to the upper-right corners of the rectangle described by the Line's Height, Width, Top and Left properties.

Usage

```
linLine.LineSlant = cWhichWay
cWhichWay = linLine.LineSlant
```

You have two choices for the cWhichWay property—the slash "/" and the backslash "\". But, you say, what if you want a vertical line—can't you supply a bar or pipe character "|" or, for a horizontal line, a hyphen, dash or underscore? Nope. Any other character other than the two slashes is either ignored or generates an error.

To create a vertical or horizontal line, change the Height or Width property to zero and then adjust the other settings to place the line where you'd like it.

Example

```
linLine1.LineSlant = "/"
```

See Also Line

LinkMaster

LinkMaster lets you specify the parent table that should drive the contents of a grid. You'll normally use it together with ChildOrder and RelationalExpr.

Usage

```
grdGrid.LinkMaster = cParentAlias
cParentAlias = grdGrid.LinkMaster
```

The folks who designed Visual FoxPro think you'll most often use a grid as the "many" side of a one-to-many relationship. They're probably right.

As a result, grids have a bunch of properties aimed at making it easy to set up that situation. Most of these properties are shared with the data environment's Relation object. LinkMaster isn't one of those—it belongs only to grids.

There are actually two ways to set up a one-to-many grid. You can do it either by establishing the correct relation in the data environment or by setting the grid's properties directly. If you specify a one-to-many relationship between two cursors in the data environment and then put the child (many) table in a grid, you'll always see only the child records that relate to the current parent (one) record (even if no fields from the parent appear in the form).

The alternative approach is to specify everything at the grid level. When you do that, LinkMaster contains the alias for the parent table. Set ChildOrder and RelationalExpr to complete the relationship.

Although LinkMaster can be changed at runtime, we haven't been able to actually make changing it do anything useful. Generally, you'll need to change ChildOrder as well, and that's tricky when you're working in a grid.

Example

```
* You'll normally set this one in the Property Sheet, but the
* code would look like:
This.LinkMaster = "OrdItems"
```

See Also ChildOrder, RecordSource, Relation, RelationalExpr

List See Display.

List Connections See Display Connections.

List Database See Display Database.

List DLLs See Display DLLs.

List Files See Directory.

List History See Access().

List Memory See Display Memory.

List Objects See Display Objects.

List Procedures See Display Procedures.

List, ListItem

These two properties are arrays that give you access to the data in a list or combo box. These are very, very cool properties. They not only let you look up the information, but also let you change it when appropriate.

Usage

```
oObject.List( nIndex [, nColumn ] ) = cValue
cValue = oObject.List( nIndex [, nColumn ] )
oObject.ListItem( nItemId [, nColumn ] ) = cValue
cValue = oObject.ListItem( nItemId [, nColumn ] )
```

To paraphrase George Carlin, "Why are there two?". Like everything else to do with list boxes and combo boxes, it's because there are two ways to enumerate the items there. The Index approach is based on the current position of items in the list. An item's Index can change for all kinds of reasons. List contains the items in Index order.

An item's ItemId, however, is fixed. Once it's assigned, it never changes. The item's contents might change (see AddListItem), but the ItemId stays the same. ListItem contains the items in order by ItemId.

To find the currently selected item, you use List[ListIndex] or ListItem[ListItemId]. Of course, you have to prefix each of them with all the right OOP stuff, so it's more likely to look like:

```
This.List[ This.ListIndex ]
```

or even

```
ThisForm.lstMyList.ListItem[ ThisForm.lstMyList.ListItemId ]
```

On to what we think is pretty cool stuff. See that nColumn parameter? It works not only in a multi-column list, but any time the RowSource for the list has multiple columns. If your RowSourceType is 2 (Alias), you can access every column of the table or view the list is based on by specifying an appropriate value for nColumn. Same thing for a SQL statement (RowSourceType=3) or a Query (RowSourceType=4) or an Array (RowSourceType=5).

What about changing items using these properties? You can do this only for lists or combos with RowSourceType set to 0 or 1. In other words, changes work only when the list of items really belongs to the control, not when it's based on some outside data. That's okay with us—in the other cases, we can just change the underlying data (and then call Requery to update the list).

Amazingly, you can even add items by simply assigning a value for an item that didn't exist before. Given how hard it is to figure out AddItem and AddListItem, directly manipulating List or ListItem may be a viable alternative.

Example

```
* Set a variable to the currently selected item
cCurValue = This.List[ This.ListIndex ]
```

See Also AddItem, AddListItem, ComboBox, ItemData, ItemIdData, ListBox, ListCount, ListIndex, ListItemId, Requery

List Status See Display Status.

List Structure See Display Structure.

List Tables See Display Tables.

List Views See Display Views.

ListBox See ComboBox.

ListCount

This property tells you how many items are in a list or combo box. To our pleasant surprise, it works regardless of the method used for filling the list or combo.

Usage `nItems = oObject.ListCount`

As the help says, ListCount is a read-only property. You can look, but you can't touch. It's most useful for traversing the List or ListItem collection (or any of the collections associated with lists and combos, actually). Of course, in VFP 5 and VFP 6, you can use FOR EACH to do that, so you don't have to know how many items there are.

Example

```
* tell the user how many choices there are
WAIT WINDOW "You have " + ;
            LTRIM(STR(ThisForm.lstMyList.ListCount)) + ;
            "choices." NOWAIT
```

See Also ComboBox, For Each, ListBox, List, ListItem

ListIndex, ListItemId

These properties provide two different ways to identify the currently selected item in a list or combo box.

Usage

```
oObject.ListIndex = nSelectItem
nSelectItem = oObject.ListIndex
oObject.ListItemId = nSelectItem
nSelectItem = oObject.ListItemId
```

Each item in a list or combo box gets a unique ID number (ItemId) that it keeps no matter how the list changes. In addition, each item can be accessed based on its visible position (or Index) in the list. (For a complete explanation of the two ways of looking at a list, see AddItem.)

ListItemId returns the unique ID number for the currently selected item in the list or combo. ListIndex returns the visible position of the currently selected item. The ItemId of an entry never changes; its Index changes as items are added and removed, if the Sorted property changes, and when items are moved around with the mover bars.

ListItemId can be used as an index into the ListItem, ItemIdData and SelectedId array properties. ListIndex can be used with the List, ItemData and Selected array properties. (List and ListItem contain the actual data shown in the list or combo box. ItemData and ItemIdData are auxiliary arrays you can use to store additional data related to the list items. Selected and SelectedId indicate which items are currently highlighted.)

Example

```
* Find the contents of the selected item
cCurItem = cboMyCombo.List[ ListIndex ]
* or
cCurItem = cboMyCombo.ListItem[ ListItemId ]

* Remove the currently selected item
lstMyList.RemoveItem[ ListIndex ]
* or
lstMyList.RemoveListItem[ ListItemId ]
```

See Also AddItem, AddListItem, ComboBox, IndexToItemId, ItemData, ItemIdData, ItemIdToIndex, List, ListBox, ListItem, RowSourceType, Selected, SelectedId

LkSys() See Access().

_LMargin See _Alignment.

Load, Call, Release Module

These are the commands to load, run and release BIN files, the oldest form of extension to the dBASE API, and remarkably, they are not supported in Visual FoxPro. They'll be missed, because there were some cool BIN files that could do neat things in 25 bytes, and they didn't suffer from the inconvenience of needing to be recompiled when each new version of FoxPro came along.

Issuing LOAD yields error 1001, "Feature is not available." The CALL command is ignored. RELEASE MODULE generates the same error 1001.

See Also Set Library

Load, Unload

These events are the first and last to fire for a form or formset (though DataEnvironment events occur before Load and after Unload).

Usage

```
PROCEDURE oObject.Load
PROCEDURE oObject.Unload
```

In VFP 3, despite documentation to the contrary, Load and Unload do not receive the optional nIndex parameter when the form or formset is contained in an array. In VFP 5 and VFP 6, Load does receive the nIndex parameter, but Unload does not. Go figure. (None of this is a big deal since there's no reason ever to use control arrays.)

When dealing with contained objects, the Init of the inner objects fires before the Init of the container. This means, for forms, the controls within the form fire their Init before the form itself and that the form's Init runs before the formset's. This presents a problem for data-bound controls. Opening tables in the form's Init is too late. The controls need the tables open earlier.

One solution is to use the form's data environment and let it handle all the table opening, relations, SETs and so forth. However, form classes don't have a Data environment and it's complicated to get SCX-based forms to use your own DataEnvironment subclass. So, some people avoid the data environment entirely and handle table management themselves.

Enter Load. It fires before the control's Inits and lets you open tables, establish relations, and so forth, so the controls have access to the data they need. You can also handle form-wide settings in Load. Remember that many of the SET commands are scoped to individual data sessions, so things like SET TALK OFF need to occur in every form that uses a private data session. (We suggest having the Load method of your master form class call a custom method to take care of this stuff. Then, all your other forms can inherit from that class.)

Unload serves the same role at the end of the form. The form's Destroy fires before the Destroys for the individual controls, so tables can't be closed there. You can do it in Unload (or in the Data environment.)

In forms created by converting FoxPro 2.x screens, the Load method is the one that accepts parameters. (These are forms with WindowType = 2 or 3.) Any parameter statement in the Setup snippet of the 2.x screen is moved to the Load method automatically in a functional conversion.

The Unload method also is the place to return a value from a modal form. If you put a RETURN statement in Unload and call the form with DO FORM whatever TO variable, the returned value ends up in the specified variable. One warning here—by the time Unload fires, the controls on the form have been destroyed and their properties don't exist anymore. You can't return the Value of some control, for example. Instead, in that control's Destroy event, save the Value to a form property, then return the form property in Unload.

Example

```
PROCEDURE Load
* Set things up
SET DELETED ON
SET TALK OFF

RETURN
```

See Also DataEnvironment, Destroy, Form, FormSet, Init

LoadPicture(), SavePicture()

These two functions let you manipulate graphic images in a format compatible with ActiveX controls.

Usage

```
oPicture = LoadPicture( cPathAndFileName )
lSuccess = SavePicture( oPicture, cPathAndFileName )
```

Parameter	Value	Meaning
oPicture	Object	An object reference to a loaded graphic resource that can be used with an ActiveX control.
cPathAndFileName	Character	A character expression specifying the file to load or save, respectively.
lSuccess	.T.	The file was saved successfully.
	.F.	We couldn't ever make this happen. If the drive or path doesn't exist, or the disk wasn't inserted, we got an error rather than a return value of .F.

SAVEPICTURE() has a fatal flaw. Attempting to save to a completely full diskette locks VFP 6 without an error message.

LoadPicture() gives an "illegal file descriptor" (VFP 5) or an "Unknown COM Status code 0x800a01e1" (VFP 6) error if you try to load a file that's included in the running APP or EXE. It does so even if the file *also* physically exists on disk. This is a biggie: It means you can't include image files in the EXE but must ship them as separate files. The bitmaps can be listed in the project manager as long as they're marked as Excluded.

These two functions are intended for use with ActiveX controls, such as the ImageList, that require graphic resources to display. Rather than accepting filenames, these controls need object handles. These functions supply that handle and can save the resulting file if passed a handle. The object created is a curious one, lacking the usual VFP object properties of Class, BaseClass and Name, because it is more of an OLE object than a VFP one. This object does have several properties worth examining:

Property	Value	Meaning
Height, Width	Numeric	The picture's dimensions, measured in twips. Twips are 1/20th of a point, which is 1/72nd of an inch.
Type	Numeric	The source of the picture: 1—bitmap (BMP, JPG, GIF) 2—metafile (WMF) 3—icon (ICO) 4—enhanced metafile (EMF)
hPal	Binary Numeric	A handle to the associated palette.

The FoxhWnd control, first included with VFP 5.0, allows the display of GIF and JPG bitmaps within the VFP 5.0 environment if you pass it an object reference created with LOADPICTURE(). LOADPICTURE() also works with Windows metafiles (WMF), enhanced metafiles (EMF) and icons.

Example

```
oPicture = LoadPicture(HOME()+"fox.BMP")
lSuccess = SavePicture(oPicture, HOME()+"newfox.bmp")
```

See Also GetPict(), PutFile()

Local, Private, Public

These three commands let you specify the scope of variables. FoxPro has had PRIVATE and PUBLIC for a long time, but LOCAL was added in Visual FoxPro. In the words of an ad, this changes everything.

Usage

```
LOCAL [ ARRAY ] Variable1 [ , Variable2 [ , ... ] ]
PUBLIC [ ARRAY ] Variable1 [ , Variable2 [ , ... ] ]
PRIVATE Variable1 [ , Variable2 [ , ... ] ]
PRIVATE ALL [ LIKE FileSkel | EXCEPT FileSkel ]
```

In addition to the distinction between the three scopes (discussed below), there's a big difference between what LOCAL and PUBLIC do and what PRIVATE does. LOCAL and PUBLIC actually create variables—once you issue them, the variables actually exist. PRIVATE doesn't create variables—it reserves names—so if and when you create the variable, it becomes private. This difference has been tripping people up for years.

Though the syntax diagram above doesn't show it, to declare local or public arrays, whether or not you include the ARRAY keyword, you need to specify the array dimensions.

Okay, on to scope. We'll start with PUBLIC because it's easy. If you make a variable public, it can be seen in any routine at all. It continues to exist until you explicitly RELEASE it. You can hide a public variable by declaring a private or local variable of the same name.

All variables you create in the Command Window are public.

You can't make an existing variable public. If you try, you'll get an error message. You have to release the variable first, then declare it public.

Except when working in the Command Window, there's very little reason ever to create a public variable anymore. Public variables are dangerous—they're hard to keep track of and are more likely to cause problems in your applications than any others.

There are better ways of making a value available globally. If a login name needs to be accessed and used throughout an application, rather than declaring it public (and available for any program to manipulate, fold, spindle and mutilate), consider crafting a "Security" or "Application" object whose protected properties contain these previously global variables. Use custom methods within this object to return the values when they're needed. Though it seems like a lot of work to set up, this technique can make it easier in the long run to extend the functionality of your application.

PRIVATE is a little tricky. Private variables are visible in the routine where you create them and in all routines called by that routine, unless those routines have their own private or local variables with the same names. When the routine that created the variable finishes executing, it's automatically released. (You can, of course, release it yourself first.)

Got that? We didn't think so. Think of it this way: When you create a private variable, you can see it until the routine that created it ends (or you explicitly release it). If that routine calls another routine, it too can see your variable unless it declares a variable of its own with the same name.

Because no routine should have to know what variables are used by the routine that called it (or the one that called that one or the one that called that one), in FoxPro 2.x, good programmers began every routine with a PRIVATE declaration for every variable they intended to use or a PRIVATE ALL LIKE something, which reserved a set of variable names for the routine. This protected the variables of the calling routine. Otherwise, a variable used but not declared explicitly in a routine could clobber the value of the same-named variable in a routine higher in the calling chain.

Fortunately, there's a better way. Local variables can be seen only in the routine that creates them. It doesn't matter what else you call—nothing outside the one routine can see a local variable.

Local is the way to go. Pretend you're working in Pascal and declare every variable right up front (or right before you use it). Use LOCAL every time unless you have a very specific reason not to. Then, document that reason. If a subroutine needs to know the value of a variable in your calling routine, pass it explicitly as a parameter. This good programming practice is referred to as "loose coupling," and results in better documented, easier to maintain code.

Example

```
PUBLIC cUserName     && But don't really do this
PRIVATE ALL LIKE j*  && Variables beginning with j are private
LOCAL nCnt, cName
```

See Also Dimension, External, Parameters

Locate, Continue

These commands let you look for data in a record. You can search based on as many fields as you want. Unlike SEEK, you don't need an index on the field or fields of interest. But if the right indexes exist, Rushmore can make this command as fast as greased lightning.

Usage

```
LOCATE [ FOR lForCondition ]
       [ Scope ]
       [ WHILE lWhileCondition ]
       [ NOOPTIMIZE ]
CONTINUE
```

For several generations of Xbase, LOCATE was one of those commands you never wanted to use. It was slooooow. Then, along came Rushmore and suddenly, not only was LOCATE usable again, it was cool.

With no Scope or WHILE clause, LOCATE finds the first record in the table that meets lForCondition. When Scope is included, only the records in the specified scope are searched and the record pointer lands up on the first matching record in the scope. WHILE behaves as it always does, short-circuiting the command as soon as a nonmatching record is found.

In spite of the documentation, the FOR clause is optional. Issuing a bare LOCATE moves the record pointer to the first visible record—that is, the first record that meets the current filter conditions. This is a much faster way of moving to the first record than issuing GO TOP when there's a filter in use or DELETED is on.

CONTINUE continues the search—that is, it finds the next matching record.

When a match is found, FOUND() becomes .T. If no match is found, FOUND() returns .F. If no Scope or WHILE is included and SET NEAR is OFF, a failed search also leaves the record pointer at end-of-file and EOF() set to .T.

Example

```
USE Customer
* Find all customers in Germany for whom we have a fax number
LOCATE FOR UPPER(Country) = "GERMANY" AND NOT EMPTY(Fax)
DO WHILE FOUND()
   * do something with the record
   CONTINUE
ENDDO
```

As mentioned above, LOCATE is Rushmore optimizable. The example is optimized only if there are index tags for UPPER(Country) and Fax. (You can replace the LOCATE/DO WHILE/CONTINUE loop in this example with a SCAN WHILE loop, which is optimizable under the same conditions.)

Don't use LOCATE in applications unless the condition is optimizable, at least partially, or the table or cursor has relatively few records. Consider adding indexes to take advantage of Rushmore. Otherwise, without Rushmore, LOCATE examines every single record in turn.

See Also EOF(), Found(), Go, Seek, Seek(), Set Filter

LocFile() See GetDir().

Lock(), RLock(), Set MultiLocks, Set("MultiLocks"), Unlock

These functions and commands allow locking and unlocking of one or more records. It is only by locking a record that the application can be sure that it is viewing the actual data on disk. MULTILOCKS allow more than one record in a table to be locked at one time; this is essential for table buffering. With the introduction of buffering in Visual FoxPro, explicit record locking is needed far less frequently.

Usage

```
lSuccess = RLOCK | LOCK ( [ [ cRecordList, ]
                             nWorkArea | cAlias ] )
```

Parameter	Value	Meaning
cRecordList	Character	A comma-separated list of the record numbers to be locked.
nWorkArea	Numeric	Specifies the work area in which the lock should be placed.
	Omitted	If cAlias is also omitted, place the lock in the current work area.
cAlias	Character	Specifies the alias of the table receiving the lock.
	Omitted	If cAlias is also omitted, the lock takes place on the current table.
lSuccess	.T.	Lock(s) were successfully placed.
	.F.	The lock(s) failed because another user has the record or table locked, or the work area has no table open, or the record numbers do not exist. If the alias is not valid, the error "Alias not found" is generated.

LOCK() and RLOCK() are exactly the same. RLOCK() stands for Record Lock, to differentiate it from FLOCK(), the File Lock function. The LOCK() function was inherited from another Xbase dialect, but functions exactly the same as RLOCK().

RLOCK() locks a record, flagging it as available for update only by this workstation. Other workstations can view the record or display the record's values in reports, but they cannot change the record. A record lock will fail if another workstation has already locked that record, or locked the file.

This is termed an "explicit" record lock, where you actually issue a lock command in code. Implicit record locks are created by the system and released automatically when a command that must change a record is issued against an unlocked record. These commands include APPEND, DELETE, GATHER, INSERT and REPLACE, as well as table-locking commands such as REPLACE ALL, UPDATE and ALTER TABLE. We prefer to issue explicit locks as much as possible, so we can handle locking problems locally. An alternative to consider in your system's design is to handle these locking issues globally, with a combination of the ON ERROR command and SET REPROCESS settings. Transactions and both optimistic and pessimistic locking work as implicit lock commands, and can be handled using the ON ERROR and SET REPROCESS methods as well.

RLOCK() can lock multiple records with a single command. Strangely, this option requires that you specify the alias or work area where the locks should be placed. This is another of those unusual commands where the optional arguments come *before* the others, so it takes a little study to get it right. Unlike an individual RLOCK(), throwing multiple locks with this command does not assume you mean the current work area. We usually just tack on ALIAS() as the second parameter when we want the locks applied to the current work area.

Issuing RLOCK() with a list of multiple records to lock returns .T. if the locks can be placed—even if MULTILOCKS is set OFF! But only the last record ends up locked—each is locked in sequence, as if you had issued separate RLOCK()s for each record, and then each is unlocked automatically as the next record is locked. This is dumb! RLOCK() should always return .F. if a list of records is supplied, and MULTILOCKS is not ON.

Specifying the record number 0 (zero) locks the table header without locking any individual records. We've never done this, and aren't sure why this would be preferable to an FLOCK(). Locking the table header prevents other users from adding records, because the number of records is stored in the header, but it does allow individual record locks on existing records. So why might you want to do this? One of the few scenarios we can imagine is if you want to run a report off the table, and don't want records added in the middle of the report to throw off your count or totals. By SETting LOCK ON, you can read the current values of individually locked records, and get the most accurate report on the state of the table with the least inconvenience to other users on the network. However, if you choose this method, be aware that your technique for adding records must be able to gracefully handle the possibility that records cannot always be added to a table. SYS(2011) reports condition as "Header Locked."

Example

```
? RLOCK("82,93,75",ALIAS()) && locks 3 records
```

Usage

```
SET MULTILOCKS ON | OFF
cOnOrOff = SET( "MULTILOCKS" )
```

MULTILOCKS is required in order to be able to lock more than one record at a time. MULTILOCKS actually uses a different technology than the older single-lock-per-table technique. Because it doesn't seem to make an extraordinary demand on resources, we recommend you leave MULTILOCKS ON all the time. MULTILOCKS is required for row and table buffering, and is scoped to each data session.

Contrary to the Help file, setting MULTILOCKS OFF unlocks all records in the table, if more than one record is locked, but leaves an individual lock if only one is in place. It also leaves individual locks in place in other work areas, although it does clear multiple locks on those tables.

Usage

```
UNLOCK [ RECORD nRecord ] [ IN nWorkArea | cAlias ] | [ ALL ]
```

Parameter	Value	Meaning
nRecord	0	Unlocks the table header.
	Integer	Unlocks the specified record number.
nWorkArea	Integer	Specifies the work area in which lock(s) are to be released.
	Omitted	In cAlias is also omitted, unlocks records in the current work area.
cAlias	Character	The alias of the table whose locks are to be released.
	Omitted	If nWorkArea is also omitted, unlocks records in the current work area.

UNLOCK releases previously set locks on one record, all records, or a table header. UNLOCK with no further arguments releases all file and record locks in the current work area. UNLOCK RECORD 0 releases a table header lock. UNLOCK ALL releases all record and file locks in all work areas in the current data session.

UNLOCK and its relative RLOCK() show some distinctive inconsistencies—you lock records with a function, but unlock them with a command. You can specify multiple records to lock with a character string, comma-separated list, but you can unlock only an individual record or all of them—not a specified subset. While we're not campaigning for the ability to specify lists of records to unlock—we've never needed the function much—we do find the inconsistencies worth noting.

Example

```
UNLOCK ALL
```

See Also CursorSetProp(), CurVal(), FLock(), GetFldState(), IsFLocked(), IsRLocked(), OldVal(), On Error, Set DataSession, Set Lock, Set Refresh, Set Reprocess, SetFldState(), Sys(2011), TableUpdate()

LockScreen

This property lets you make a bunch of changes to a form at once without the user seeing each change as it happens. Not only that, it speeds up the process. However, be careful because it can make it look like the system is hung.

Usage

```
frmForm.LockScreen = lBatchChanges
lBatchChanges = frmForm.LockScreen
```

Some changes aren't batched, even when LockScreen is .T. It appears that the ones that affect the form window itself, like the form's Caption, BorderStyle, MaxButton, MinButton, ControlBox, and the like, and the ones controlling the form's position, like Left and Top, happen anyway. Changes that affect the interior of the form appear to be batched.

Don't change WindowState while LockScreen is .T. The borders change, but the interior doesn't get repainted.

Setting LockScreen can speed up the process of making changes because the form is repainted only once instead of multiple times. Even if wasn't really faster, it would probably look faster because the changes "snap" into place instead of being executed one at a time. (However, we should add that we've heard a few people argue that LockScreen actually slows things down. So, as always, test in your application for definitive answers.)

OLE Controls typically are not affected by LockScreen because, even though we consider them to be "on" our forms, they are actually individual Windows windows, and they don't know from LockScreen. To make changes more quickly to some OLE Controls, turn LockScreen on for the form, then move the OLE Control to a position off-screen, say, -1000, -1000. Make the changes to the OLE Control, then put it back where it was. Set LockScreen to .F. and the form repaints. This trick can speed up the process of making a lot of changes to an OLE Control, in cases where each change normally would cause the entire control to repaint. A smart control recognizes that it is not in the visible area of the display, and doesn't bother with the relatively slow repainting.

To make your heart stop, try setting LockScreen .T. for the active form, then Alt+Tab over to another application and back to Visual FoxPro. See how the box identifying Visual FoxPro doesn't go away? Imagine this happening to your user. How long would it take her to hit Ctrl+Alt+Delete? Make sure you don't leave LockScreen .T. for too long.

Example

```
ThisForm.LockScreen = .T.
ThisForm.BackColor = RGB(0,0,255)
ThisForm.Text1.Left = ThisForm.Text1.Left+10
ThisForm.SetAll("FontName", "Arial")
ThisForm.LockScreen = .F.
```

See Also Paint, Refresh

Log(), Log10() See Exp().

LookUp()

LOOKUP() is a very cool, but very complex, way to pull information out of a table. It lets you look up information based on one field or tag, but return information from a different field. It's kind of like many of the lists and combo boxes we set up, where the user chooses based on one piece of data, but we store a different data item behind the scenes.

Usage

```
uResult = LOOKUP( FieldToReturn, uSearchExpr, SearchField [, cSearchTag ] )
```

Parameter	Value	Meaning
FieldToReturn	Name	The name of the field whose value is returned.
uSearchExpr	Expression	The value to search for.
SearchField	Name	The field in which to search for uSearchExpr unless cSearchTag is included. Ignored if cSearchTag is included; see below.
cSearchTag	Character	The name of an index tag that should be used to search for uSearchExpr.
	Omitted	Search for uSearchExpr in the field SearchField.
uResult	Anything except empty value	The search expression was found, so the value of FieldToReturn for that record is returned.
	Empty	No record was found with the specified value.

LOOKUP() actually provides two different ways to search, either in a particular field or using a particular tag. If you specify a tag, it doesn't matter what you pass for SearchField as long as it's a valid field name in the table. If you don't pass a tag name, FoxPro searches for the value in SearchField. If there's a tag on SearchField, it's used to speed up the search. Otherwise, each record in turn is checked.

Notice also that both field names (the one to return and the one to search) are specified as names while the tag name is specified as a string. Weird.

In addition to returning the specified field, LOOKUP() moves the record pointer to the matching record. When LOOKUP() uses a tag to perform the search, and there's more than one matching record, you get the first one in that index. If there's no tag for that search, you get the first matching record in physical order, even if order is currently set. If no match is found, the record pointer moves to the end of the file (that is, EOF() is .T.).

The value returned by LOOKUP() is always of the same type as FieldToReturn. If no match is found, you get an empty value of the specified type.

We don't use LOOKUP() a lot because it's complex and because SEEK and SEEK() let us do the same thing. Although they require more code, the code itself is easier to understand.

Example

```
USE Employee
* No index used for this one
? LOOKUP(Birth_Date, "Laura", First_Name)  && Returns {1/9/58}
* Use name index. Specification of Last_Name is ignored, but
* aids in readability
? LOOKUP(Home_Phone, "FULLER", Last_Name, "Last_Name")
  && Returns "(206) 555-9482"
* Since there's an index on Employee_Id, it's used automatically
? LOOKUP(Last_Name, "   10", Employee_Id)  && Returns "Martin"
```

See Also KeyMatch(), Locate, Seek, Seek()

Loop

This command ends the current pass in a loop, taking control directly to the loop-ending command (ENDDO, ENDFOR/NEXT, ENDSCAN). Then, the loop condition is evaluated and execution proceeds normally.

Don't use LOOP. It creates spaghetti code and makes maintenance much harder. LOOP can always be replaced by an IF that skips the remaining code in the loop.

See Also Do While, Exit, For, For Each, Scan

LostFocus See GotFocus.

Low-Level File Functions

Low-level file functions (LLFFs) are cool. They can be a hacker's best friends, and are certainly essential tools in our toolbox. With LLFFs, you can open and read all those nasty binary files that the operating system and manufacturers would prefer you didn't take apart. With LLFFs, it's possible to translate a Windows Cardfile into a .DBF, read and rewrite a FoxPro macro file, translate the Screen memory variable stored in a .MEM file, or study and perhaps rearrange the FoxPro codepage sort logic (FOXPRO.INT).

See the disk for the result of a few hours of taking apart the .FKY keyboard macro function file and analyzing the results: PeekFKY.PRG dumps the contents of a macro file to the screen. Check out the topics SAVE MACROS and RESTORE MACROS, and think about what you could do with keyboard macros being updated programmatically.

Low-level file functions follow a logic that will be familiar to users of other languages, but may be a little different for FoxPro devotees. Rather than referring to a file by its alias, a file "handle" number is created using FOPEN() or FCREATE(). A file pointer, like a record number, determines where the next bytes are read or written to. The FSEEK() function allows us to move this file, repositioning the pointer relative to the current position or to the top or bottom of the file. FREAD() or FGETS() reads data from the file, either byte-by-byte or by lines, and FWRITE() or FPUTS() matches the reading functions with their equivalent outputs. Finally, a few miscellaneous functions allow flushing (FFLUSH()), end-of-file testing (FEOF()) and error checking (FERROR()).

Low-level file functions were the most common ways to manipulate files that were not in DBF format, but there are several other techniques, some new to Visual FoxPro. These techniques may have advantages over LLFFs for your task, and bear consideration. If you are working with ASCII text, consider sticking the file in a memo field with APPEND MEMO and using the memo field functions MLINE() and MEMLINES() to hack it apart, or an APPEND FROM TYPE SDF to pull it into multiple records. If the text files are in the Windows INI format, consider the WinAPI calls described in "INI Files." New to VFP 6 are the StrToFile() and FileToStr() functions to load an entire file into one character variable in one swoop.

If you'll be writing out a text file, consider SET ALTERNATE and SET TEXTMERGE as well as using LLFFs.

But for hacking binary formatted data, there's nothing better than the low-level file functions. Let's see what they can do.

FChSize()

FCHSIZE() modifies the size of a file on disk. This command can increase, decrease or zero-out the size of a file.

Usage `nNewSize = FCHSIZE( nFileHandle, nSize )`

Parameter	Value	Meaning
nFileHandle	Integer	The file handle created with FOPEN() or FCREATE().
nSize	Numeric	Final desired size.
nNewSize	–1	An error has occurred; see FERROR() for more information. Check for disk space, file opened with write access, or network rights issues.
	Numeric	The new size of the file.

Example `lnRetVal = FCHSIZE(8, 0)`

The above example zeroes out the length of the file opened with file handle 8.

FClose()

FClose() closes a file opened with low-level file functions.

Usage `lSuccess = FCLOSE( nFileHandle )`

Parameter	Value	Meaning
nFileHandle	Integer	The file handle created with FOPEN() or FCREATE().
lSuccess	.F.	An error has occurred; see FERROR() for more information. Check for the correct file handle, network rights.
	.T.	File successfully closed.

Note that issuing the CLOSE ALL command closes all files opened with the low-level file functions.

Example

```
* Close the file opened with file handle 8.
llRetVal = FCLOSE(8)
```

FCreate()

FCREATE() creates a file on disk, and returns a "handle"—a numeric value that other low-level file functions must have to refer to the same file.

Usage `nHandle = FOPEN( cFilename [, nAttribute ] )`

Parameter	Value	Meaning
cFilename	Character string	The full path and filename of the file to be opened.
nAttribute	0 or omitted	Read-Write. Any option other than the default 0 parameter prevents FoxPro from writing to the file.
	1	Read-only.
	2	Hidden.

Parameter	Value	Meaning
nAttribute	3	Read-only and hidden.
	4	System.
	5	Read-only and System.
	6	System and Hidden.
	7	Read-only, Hidden and System.
nHandle	–1	An error has occurred; see FERROR() for more information.
	Positive integer	File successfully opened.

Example
```
* Create the AUTOEXEC.BAT files to be read/write.
lnHandle = FCREATE("C:\AUTOEXEC.BAT", 0)
```

If you create a file and forget the handle number, such as by issuing the command =FCREATE("test",0), you can determine the file handle of all open files with the DISPLAY STATUS command.

No warning is given to overwriting an existing file, even if SAFETY is SET ON!

FEOF()

FEOF() tests for end-of-file on a file opened with low-level file functions.

Usage `lAtEof = FEOF( nFileHandle )`

Parameter	Value	Meaning
nFileHandle	Integer	The file handle created with FOPEN() or FCREATE().
lAtEof	.F.	Not at end-of-file.
	.T.	At end-of-file.

Example
```
* Check for end-of-file for the file opened with file handle 8.
llRetVal = FEOF(8)
```

FEOF() returns .T. if passed an invalid file handle. Neither a FoxPro error condition (like error 1113: "no file is opened in that area, stupid") nor a low-level file error (see FERROR(), for example 6: "Invalid file handle") is generated.

FError ()

Low-Level File Functions error-handling is funny but useful. Rather than use FoxPro's built-in error generation and the language's error-handling capability, LLFFs set an error condition detectable by FERROR(). This allows local testing of the success or failure of LLFF execution, where a global error-handling method may not be appropriate. No arguments are accepted.

Usage `nErrNum = FERROR()`

Error Number	Meaning
2	File not found.
4	Too many files open (limited by file handles).
5	Access denied.
6	Invalid file handle given.
8	Out of memory.
25	Seek error (usually top of file).
29	Disk full.
31	Error opening file.

Example

```
nFileHand = FOPEN("NUL:")
if nFileHand < 0  && negative means error
do case
  case FERROR() = 2  && File Not Found...
```

FFlush ()

FFLUSH() flushes data to disk.

Usage `lSuccess = FFLUSH( nFilehandle )`

Parameter	Value	Meaning
nFilehandle	Integer	The file handle created with FOPEN() or FCREATE().
lSuccess	.T.	FLUSH successful.
	.F.	Error.

Example `llRetVal = FFLUSH(8)`

The above example flushes all data to disk for the file opened with file handle 8.

FGetS()

FGETS() reads data from a low-level file. FGETS reads characters until it reaches the first of these three limits: the number of characters specified in the second parameter, the first (next) occurrence of a carriage return, or the end of the file.

Usage `cString = FGETS( nFileHandle [, nBytes ] )`

Parameter	Value	Meaning
nFileHandle	Integer	The file handle created with FOPEN() or FCREATE().
nBytes	Numeric	Maximum number of bytes to read; defaults to 254 if not specified.

Parameter	Value	Meaning
cString	Character string	Characters read.

Example `lcRetVal = FGETS(8,400)`

The above example reads characters from file handle 8, starting at the current file position, and ending at the first occurrence of a carriage return, the specified number of bytes, or the end-of-file (hint: test FEOF()).

FOpen ()

FOPEN() opens a file on disk for reading and/or writing, and returns a "handle"—a numeric value that other low-level file functions (LLFFs) must have to refer to the same file. While it may be theoretically possible to open other DOS devices, such as "LPT1:" or "COM1:" with this command, results under Windows are less than 100 percent predictable (and get less predictable under Win98 and NT!). A far better solution to serial port manipulation is to use the Win API function calls (i.e., OpenComm()) or a third-party library specially designed for serial-port work.

Usage `nHandle = FOPEN( cFilename [, nMode ] )`

Parameter	Value	Meaning
cFilename	Character string	The full path and filename of the file to be opened.
nMode	0 or omitted	Read-only, buffered.
	1	Write-only, buffered.
	2	Read/write, buffered.
	10	Read-only, unbuffered.
	11	Write-only, unbuffered.
	12	Read/write, unbuffered.
nHandle	–1	An error has occurred; see FERROR() for more information.
	Positive integer	File successfully opened.

Example `nHandle = FOPEN("C:\AUTOEXEC.BAT", 0)`

The above example opens the AUTOEXEC.BAT files to be read, with buffering turned on. Buffering is normally the preferred method of access.

FPutS()

FPUTS() writes data to an opened low-level file. FPUTS writes characters until it reaches the smaller of these two limits: the number specified in the third parameter, or the total length of the string supplied.

Usage `nRetVal = FPUTS( nFileHandle, cString [, nBytes ] )`

Parameter	Value	Meaning
nFileHandle	Integer	The file handle created with FOPEN() or FCREATE().
cString	Character	Character string to be written to file.
nBytes	Numeric	Maximum number of bytes to write; defaults to the length of the string supplied plus an ending carriage return-line feed pair.
nRetVal	0	An error occurred. Test with FERROR(), check for correct file handle, file rights.
	Integer	The number of bytes written.

Example

```
* Write characters to file handle 8,
* starting at the current file position,
* ending at the end of the string or
* the specified number of bytes
lnRetVal = FPUTS(8,MyTestStr,127)
```

The return, lnRetVal, reflects the number of characters written, including a final carriage return (CHR(13)) and line feed (CHR(10)).

FRead()

FREAD() reads data from a low-level file. Unlike FGETS(), FREAD() just reads the number of characters specified, ignoring the value of those characters. (FGETS() is sensitive to carriage returns and line feed characters.) FREAD() stops after reading the number specified in the second parameter, or encountering the end-of-file.

Usage `cString = FREAD( nFileHandle, nBytes )`

Parameter	Value	Meaning
nFileHandle	Integer	The file handle created with FOPEN() or FCREATE().
nBytes	Numeric	Maximum number of bytes to read.
cString	Character string	Characters read.

Example

```
* Read characters from file handle 8,
* starting at the current file position,
* ending at the specified number of bytes, or the end-of-file
*(hint: test FEOF())
lcRetVal = FREAD(8,400)
```

FSeek()

FSEEK() repositions the file pointer within a low-level file. This is sort of the low-level file function equivalent of the GO command for DBFs.

Usage `nPosition = FSEEK( nFileHandle, nLocation [, nRelativeTo ] )`

Parameter	Value	Meaning
nFileHandle	Integer	The file handle created with FOPEN() or FCREATE().

Parameter	Value	Meaning
nLocation	Numeric	Location at which to position the file pointer.
nRelativeTo	0 or omitted	Measure nLocation from the beginning of the file.
	1	Measure nLocation from the current file pointer position.
	2	Measure nLocation from the end of the file; that is, start at the end and move nLocation characters toward the beginning.
nPosition	Integer	The new position within the file, expressed as the number of bytes offset from the beginning.

Example

```
* Moves the file pointer to a position 400 characters
* from the beginning of the file
lcRetVal = FSEEK(8,400)
=FSEEK(8,0,0)  && GO TOP
=FSEEK(8,0,2)  && GO BOTTOM
lnWhereAmI = FSEEK(8,0,1)  && return current file position
```

FWrite()

FWRITE() writes data to a low-level file. Unlike FPUTS(), FWRITE() writes exactly what you specify, without appending any characters (such as carriage returns or line feeds). Use FWRITE() when you are trying to write data out to a very specific file format, such as Windows CardFile, FOXPRO.INT or another binary format.

Usage

```
nRetVal = FWRITE( nFileHandle, cString [, nBytes ] )
```

Parameter	Value	Meaning
nFileHandle	Integer	The file handle created with FOPEN() or FCREATE().
cString	Character	The data to be written to the file.
numBytes	Numeric	Maximum number of bytes to write.
nRetVal	0	An error has occurred. Check for correct file handle, string, disk space and rights.
	Integer	The number of characters actually written.

Example

```
nRetVal = FWRITE(8,REPLICATE("Fred",200),400)
```

The above example writes 400 characters to file handle 8, starting at the current file position.

See Also Append Memo, Close All, FileToStr(), MemLines(), MLine(), Set Alternate, Set TextMerge, StrToFile()

Lower(), Proper(), Upper()

It's a funny thing. These three functions do very similar things, yet UPPER() and LOWER() are among the most important functions in FoxPro, while PROPER() is one of the most useless. All three take a character string and return a string with the case of the letters modified—UPPER() converts them all to uppercase, LOWER() makes them all lowercase, and PROPER() supposedly makes proper names out of them (with a capital letter at the beginning of each word).

Usage

```
cResult = LOWER( cString )
cResult = PROPER( cString )
cResult = UPPER( cString )
```

In many comparisons and searches, using either UPPER() or LOWER() is essential, so the operation is case-insensitive. You don't want to worry about whether the user has entered "Smith", "smith", "SMITH", or "sMiTH". So you apply UPPER() or LOWER() to both sides of the comparison or to both the search string and the target of the search. For example, if a user has filled in variables cLastName and cFirstName, you could search for a matching record like this:

```
LOCATE FOR UPPER(LastName) = UPPER(cLastName) AND ;
           UPPER(FirstName) = UPPER(cFirstName)
```

The same logic applies when creating indexes based on character strings. If case is irrelevant (which is true more often than not), apply UPPER() to the data being indexed and then always be sure to SEEK using UPPER(the search string). For example, to re-create the company name index for TasTrade's Customer table, you use:

```
INDEX ON UPPER(Company_Name) TAG Company_Na
```

Then, to search for QUICK-Stop, you'd:

```
SET ORDER TO TAG Company_na
SEEK "QUICK-STOP"
```

To search for the company whose name is contained in m.cCompany, use:

```
SEEK UPPER(m.cCompany)
```

Actually, if m.cCompany comes from user input, you should probably trim it first to get rid of any leading or trailing blanks that might have crept in:

```
SEEK UPPER(ALLTRIM(m.cCompany))
```

You can use LOWER() exactly the same way as UPPER() in searches and comparisons. Just pick one or the other and always use it, so you know what to expect. Harking back to our mainframe days, we both tend to use UPPER(), but LOWER() is more readable, the ergonomists tell us; we just haven't lowered ourselves to using LOWER() yet.

PROPER() is one of those great ideas that just didn't work out. Its purpose is to let folks enter names without worrying about capitalization. Then, you can come along later and apply PROPER() to fix it up. Unfortunately, names just aren't that simple. While PROPER() is great for run-of-the-mill names (like Granor or Roche), it falls apart when you hand it stuff like O'Hara or MacNeill.

Fundamentally, PROPER() is too simple-minded to do the job. It takes whatever you hand it and returns it with the first character of each word capitalized. If that's not appropriate, too bad. Fortunately, there are plenty of smart Fox programmers out there. The code on the CD includes an alternative for PROPER() called UL(), written by our friend Sue Cunningham.

See Also IsLower(), IsUpper()

LParameters, Parameters, Set UdfParms, Set("UdfParms")

PARAMETERS and LPARAMETERS specify the formal parameters for a procedure or function. SET UDFPARMS determines whether the default for parameters sent to functions is passing by value or by reference. (For basics on parameter passing, see "Pass the Parameters, Please" in "Xbase Xplained.")

Usage

```
LPARAMETERS ParameterList
PARAMETERS ParameterList
```

ParameterList is a comma-delimited list of variable names that receive the parameters when the routine is called. These variables are also known as "formal parameters." (The values passed by the calling routine are known as "actual parameters.")

LPARAMETERS or PARAMETERS must be the first executable statement in the routine. This means the only things that can be put between the FUNCTION or PROCEDURE line and the parameter declaration are comments and compile-time directives, such as #INCLUDE and #DEFINE.

LPARAMETERS creates the parameters as local variables, while PARAMETERS makes them private. We strongly recommend you use LPARAMETERS unless you have a specific reason not to. You can only use one or the other in a given routine. As soon as FoxPro finds a parameter declaration, it rejects any other.

You can also list parameters as part of the function or procedure heading. Parameters created that way are local. See the comments in the example below for an example of how to do this.

Example

```
FUNCTION OneName
* Take a first name and last name and return one name
* If either parameter is missing or wrong type,
* return the empty string
* The heading could be:
*    FUNCTION OneName(cFirst, cLast)
* instead, and the LPARAMETERS lines omitted,
* with the same effect.

LPARAMETERS cFirst, cLast

* Test parameters
IF PCOUNT() < 2
   RETURN ""
ENDIF

IF TYPE("cFirst") <> "C"
   RETURN ""
ENDIF

IF TYPE("cLast") <> "C"
   RETURN ""
ENDIF

RETURN TRIM(cFirst) + " " + TRIM(cLast)
```

Usage

```
SET UDFPARMS TO REFERENCE | VALUE
cParmSetting = SET( "UDFPARMS" )
```

Parameters can be passed either by reference or by value. When passed by reference, changes to the formal parameter also change the actual parameter passed. When parameters are passed by value, changes to the formal parameter in the routine do not affect the actual parameter. Another way to look at this is that a parameter by reference means that the parameter is not a separate memory variable, but just a placeholder (sort of an alias) within the routine, and all use of that parameter within the procedure refers back to the original variable. When passing parameters by value, on the other hand, the original memory variable is shielded, and only the value is transferred to the new routine, which must create a new memory variable to hold this value.

In order to pass the entire contents of an array (rather than just the first element), it must be passed by reference.

In FoxPro, by default, parameters are passed to procedures by reference and to functions by value. (But it's the call that determines whether you have a procedure or function, not the routine's definition.)

SET UDFPARMS lets you change the default, and muck up your system worse than you ever anticipated. If you set UDFPARMS to REFERENCE, all parameters are passed to functions by reference. Don't do that!

You can always pass a parameter to a function by reference by putting an "@" in front of it in the function call. This is a local, readable solution to the problem. Changing UDFPARMS can have all kinds of unforeseen effects on your code and on other people's code that you use.

Not surprisingly, SET("UDFPARMS") returns either "VALUE" or "REFERENCE". If you must change the setting of UDFPARMS, be sure to save and restore the old setting.

See Also Function, Local, Parameters(), PCount(), Private, Procedure, Set

LTrim() See AllTrim().

LUpdate() See RecSize().

_Mac See _Dos.

MacDesktop

This property doesn't do anything in the Windows version of Visual FoxPro. In the Mac version, it controls whether or not a form is a child of the main Visual FoxPro window. Use ShowWindow to control this in the Windows version.

See Also Desktop, MDIForm, ShowWindow

MainFile, MainClass, SetMain

These properties and method indicate and control the main file in a project—that is, the one that gets executed first when the project is run. MainFile and MainClass tell you what the main file is, while SetMain lets you set it programmatically. MainFile and MainClass correspond to the bolded entry in the Project Manager; SetMain is the equivalent of the Set Main option on the Project menu.

Usage

```
cMainFile = prjProject.MainFile
cMainClass = prjProject.MainClass
lMainChanged = prjProject.SetMain([ cMainFile [, cMainClass ]])
```

Parameter	Value	Meaning
cMainFile	Filename including extension	The starting program or form of a project, or the class library containing the starting ActiveDoc.
	Empty string	No main file is designated for this project.
cMainClass	Class name	The starting Active Document class of a project.
	Omitted	Either the main file is a program or no main file is designated for this project.
lMainChanged	.T.	The main file was changed.
	.F.	The main file was not changed.

MainFile contains the name of the file marked as main. If the main object in the project is an active document, MainFile contains the class library while MainClass contains the actual name of the ActiveDoc class. If you pass a class name but no class library, VFP sets the project to have no main file (as if you'd passed only the empty string).

Since the main program for a project can actually be a program, a form or a class, SetMain requires the extension. However, the path to the file is not required, although you can include it. On the other hand, MainFile always reports the complete path.

The return value of SetMain is weird. The method returns .T. only if you actually change the main file. So if you call SetMain with the current main file, it returns .F. We were misled into thinking that a call didn't work for quite a while until we caught on.

Example

```
* Assume the active project contains an active document
* class named 'acdFred' in a classlib called 'MyActiveDocs'
Application.ActiveProject.SetMain("MyActiveDocs.VCX","acdFred")

* Find out about the main program of a project referenced
* by the variable oProj.
?oProj.MainFile, oProj.MainClass
```

See Also ActiveDoc, Project, Projects

Margin

This property of all the text-based controls lets you specify a margin that's left empty around the inside of the input area.

Usage

```
oObject.Margin = nMarginInPixels
nMarginInPixels = oObject.Margin
```

Note that the margin is measured in pixels regardless of the form's ScaleMode. Not so unreasonable, since we can't imagine wanting a margin large enough to measure in foxels.

The margin goes around all four sides of the input area. It's the part that doesn't get highlighted when you select all the text in the control.

Be careful not to make the margin too big. The control's contents disappear with no warning if the margin covers the entire area. (Keep in mind that you're actually getting twice as many pixels as you specify in each dimension, since the margin applies at both top and bottom and both right and left.)

Example

```
MyForm.edtNotes.Margin = 4
```

See Also BorderWidth, ComboBox, Editbox, ScaleMode, Spinner, Textbox

Max(), Min()

These two functions take a list of values and return either the largest or smallest value in the list. Any of the numeric types (Numeric, Float, Integer, Currency, Double) can be used, as well as character, memo, date and datetime expressions. The result of numeric comparisons is Numeric unless all the values passed in are Currency, in which case the result is Currency. If Dates and Datetimes are mixed, Datetime is the result. All Memo and Character comparisons return type Character. General, Screen and Object variables yield an "Operator/operand type mismatch" or "Data type mismatch," as you might expect.

Usage

```
nReturnValue = MAX( nExpr1, nExpr2 [, nExpr3 ... ] )
nReturnValue = MIN( nExpr1, nExpr2 [, nExpr3 ... ] )
```

Like the other numeric functions, MAX() and MIN() propagate nulls. This means if one of the values passed in is .NULL., you get back .NULL. If you need the minimum or maximum of the non-null values, use CALCULATE or SELECT-SQL instead. Of course, you'll need to put the values in a table to use those commands, but with CREATE CURSOR and INSERT INTO around, that's not such a big deal.

MAX() and MIN() are limited to 26 expressions per call. The official explanation is that you're allowed to pass 24 more than the required number, which is two; go figure. We don't think we've actually ever passed more than three, so the limit doesn't seem like much of a big deal.

Example

```
? MAX(27,39,-203)    && Returns 39
? MIN(27,39,-203)    && Returns -203

nHighValue = MAX(nUser1,nUser2,nUser3)
```

See Also Calculate, Select-SQL

MaxButton, MinButton

These properties determine whether a form contains the Windows standard Maximize and Minimize buttons.

Usage
```
frmForm.MaxButton = lHasMax
lHasMax = frmForm.MaxButton
frmForm.MinButton = lHasMin
lHasMin = frmForm.MinButton
```

Setting either of these properties to .F. leaves the corresponding option off the form's control menu and ignores double-clicks on the form's title bar, meaning that the user can't maximize or minimize the form.

However, as with a number of other properties (like Movable), you can still change the form in code. Regardless of MaxButton and MinButton, you can maximize or minimize a form by setting its WindowState appropriately (or with the old ZOOM WINDOW command).

Be careful about programmatically minimizing windows with MinButton set to .F. The only way for the user to restore the window in that situation is by choosing it from the Window menu. Be even more careful about programmatically maximizing a window with no MaxButton. There doesn't seem to be any way for the user to restore that one.

Although you can control these properties individually, visually they're linked at the hip. If either property is set to .T., both buttons appear, though one of them is disabled. However, Help is wrong when it says that an MDI child form always has a minimize button. If MinButton and MaxButton are both .F., the setting of MDIForm doesn't matter—there are no buttons.

MaxButton and MinButton are among the properties that must be .F. in order to have a truly borderless form in VFP 3 and VFP 5. See BorderStyle for the complete list. (In VFP 6, you can do it with just TitleBar and BorderStyle.)

Example
```
ThisForm.MaxButton = .F.   && user can't maximize
ThisForm.WindowState = 2   && but you can
```

See Also BorderStyle, TitleBar, WindowState, Zoom Window

MaxHeight, MaxLeft, MaxTop, MaxWidth, MinHeight, MinWidth

Specifies how large or small a form window can be sized and where it can be placed.

Usage
```
nHowTall = objForm.MaxHeight
nHowWide = objForm.MaxWidth
nHowShort = objForm.MinHeight
nHowThin = objForm.MinWidth
objForm.MaxHeight = nHowTall
objForm.MaxWidth = nHowWide
objForm.MinHeight = nHowShort
objForm.MinWidth = nHowThin
```

The MaxHeight and MaxWidth properties specify the maximum dimensions to which a form can be stretched. This stretching can occur via operator action by resizing the window with mouse or keyboard, or programmatically (using ZOOM WINDOW, or by changing WindowState, Height or Width). MinHeight and MinWidth specify the minimum dimensions the form can assume. The "minimized" or "iconized" state is not affected by the Min-dimensions; only resizing using the mouse or keyboard, or by changing the form's Height and Width, is affected.

Usage
```
nColumn = objForm.MaxLeft
nRow = objForm.MaxTop
objForm.MaxLeft = nColumn
objForm.MaxTop = nRow
```

MaxLeft and MaxTop, on the other hand, specify the position a form should have when maximized. When the form is maximized, it is not movable, nor can it be resized using the mouse or keyboard. While all the other "Max" properties are the maximum value within a range of values that a particular property can have, the MaxTop and MaxLeft are the only values their properties can have when the form is maximized. We think this is an unfortunate overloading of the prefix, and bound to lead to confusion.

All of these properties respect, and are scaled to, the appropriate ScaleMode.

Example

```
oForm = CREATEOBJECT("TestForm")
oForm.Show()

DEFINE CLASS TestForm AS Form
  #INCLUDE FOXPRO.H
  ScaleMode = SCALEMODE_PIXELS
  Top = 10
  Left = 10
  Height = 100
  Width = 100
  MaxHeight = 200
  MaxWidth = 200
  MaxTop = 15
  MaxLeft = 15
  MinHeight = 50
  MinWidth = 50
ENDDEFINE
```

See Also Height, Left, ScaleMode, Top, Width, WindowState, Zoom Window

MaxLength

This property determines the maximum number of characters that can be entered in an edit box or text box.

Usage

```
oObject.MaxLength = nMaxChars
nMaxChars = oObject.MaxLength
```

To let the user enter an unlimited number of characters, set MaxLength to 0. When MaxLength is non-zero, additional characters are thrown away. Be careful when you bind controls to fields. If MaxLength is less than the field length (or the current length of a memo field), if you change the data at all, the characters beyond MaxLength may be discarded.

In VFP 3, this property applied only to edit boxes. It was added to text boxes in VFP 5.

Example

```
This.MaxLength = 400
```

See Also Editbox, Textbox

MaxTop, MaxWidth See MaxHeight.

MCol() See MRow().

MD See CD.

MDIForm

This property determines whether a form is MDI (Multiple Document Interface) compliant.

Usage

```
frmForm.MDIForm = lIsItMDI
lIsItMDI = frmForm.MDIForm
```

We have a lot of ambivalence about the MDI approach. We love being able to open multiple documents at once.

Sometimes we love it when maximizing one of those documents maximizes them all, but other times the same behavior makes us tear our hair out. We suspect most Windows users feel the same way.

Visual FoxPro's approach to this problem is actually a nice compromise. Windows you define have a choice. They can be MDI windows or not. Maximizing an MDI window takes only other MDI windows with it, not all open windows. This means you can make intelligent decisions about how any given window ought to behave. Turn MDIForm on for the ones that ought to work this way and leave it off for the others. Just make sure you're using some sensible criteria to decide which is which, or your users will be horribly confused.

Help for VFP 6 and VFP 5 says that MDIForm is for backward compatibility and that you should use ShowWindow instead. That's a typical Microsoft way of trying to push us into following their latest "standard." ShowWindow, while a very nice property, doesn't offer the same choices as MDIForm. They're both relevant.

Example
```
This.MDIForm = .T.
```

See Also Define Window, MaxButton, ShowWindow, WindowState, Zoom Window

MDown() See MRow().

Mdx() See Cdx().

MDY() See DMY().

MemLines(), MLine(), _MLine

The functions MEMLINES() and MLINE() and the system variable _MLINE let you pull apart a memo field or multi-line character string into its component lines. MEMLINES() tells you how many lines the field contains while MLINE() returns a specified line. _MLINE keeps track of how far into the field you've gone looking for lines.

Usage
```
nNumberOfLines = MEMLINES( mField | cString )
cResult = MLINE( mField | cString, nLine [ , nStartPos ] )
_MLINE = nStartPos
```

Parameter	Value	Meaning
mField, cString	Memo or Character	The string to be broken into lines.
nLine	Numeric	The line to return with MLINE().
nStartPos	Numeric	The offset from the beginning of the string to start looking for lines.
nNumberOfLines	Numeric	The number of lines in mField or cString (based on SET("MEMOWIDTH")).
cResult	Character	The nLine-th line of mField or cString, starting from nStartPos, based on SET("MEMOWIDTH"). This string is trimmed and doesn't include a carriage return or line feed at the end.

Both MEMLINES() and MLINE() base their results on the current setting of MEMOWIDTH. In addition, they both divide the string at a space, if possible. If the string doesn't have any spaces within SET("MEMOWIDTH") characters, the line ends after exactly that number. If the string contains any carriage-return characters (CHR(13)), those also indicate line breaks no matter how many characters precede them.

_MLINE lets you return successive lines without having to count as you go. Each call to MLINE() assigns _MLINE the place to start looking for the next line after the one returned. That is, if MLINE() returns a 23-character line from the beginning of a string, _MLINE gets set to 24 automatically. This means you can pass _MLINE for nStartPos and leave nLine set at 1 to return successive lines of a memo field or string. To do so, set _MLINE=0 before applying MLINE() the first time.

Using _MLINE to retrieve a series of lines has a spectacular effect on the speed in processing large strings. In the first code snippet, we try to read a string one line at a time by incrementing the line number:

```
FOR I = 1 TO MEMLINES()
  ? MLINE(myString,i)
NEXT
```

This second snippet doesn't appear much different:

```
_MLINE = 0
FOR I = 1 TO MEMLINES()
  ? MLINE(myString,1,_MLINE)
NEXT
```

However, the second code fragment can run circles around the first! Why? The reason is that, in the first example, Visual FoxPro has to read the file and break it into lines, one line at a time, until it gets to the line number you've specified. In the second example, you've already supplied the offset where the function must start counting, and told it just to return the first line—isn't that a lot easier?

One subtlety here is that _MLINE is an offset, not a position. That is, it's the number of characters to move from the first character to find the starting position. Huh? With an offset, you start at a given position and move the specified number of characters to the right. The one you land on is the place to start. This means that _MLINE is one less than the position of the first character to be considered.

If you think of _MLINE as a position, you'll run into trouble in one situation. The interaction between MLINE() and _MLINE is designed to remove the blank space between words when a line break occurs. That is, the space between two words doesn't become part of either line when that word break is used as a line break. So, _MLINE appears to point at the space.

However, if there are no spaces and MLINE() simply takes the maximum number of characters, _MLINE points at the last character in the first line. The second line properly starts with the next character. What all this means is that you can't count on _MLINE being the number of characters used so far.

Many folks miss the fact that this group of goodies can be applied to character strings just as well as to memo fields. They're very handy for dividing a message to be displayed into lines of the right length.

In VFP 6, the new ALines() function lets you do a lot of the same things you can do with MLINE() and _MLINE, but doesn't trim the result or rely on the setting of MEMOWIDTH, which may have advantages for some uses.

These functions should also be considered as replacements for low-level functions on text files. Low-level functions typically read a file one character or line at a time, process it, and then go back for more. If, instead of doing this, you plunk the whole file into a memo field, you can then run these functions on the result. Because Visual FoxPro will buffer as much of the memo file in memory as it can manage, the difference in performance can be impressive.

Example

```
* Take a message and divide it into appropriate length lines
nOldMemo = SET( "MEMOWIDTH" )
SET MEMOWIDTH TO 30

nNumLines = MEMLINES( cMessage )
DIMENSION aMessage[ nNumLines ]

_MLINE = 0
FOR nCnt = 1 TO nNumLines
```

```
    aMessage[nCnt] = MLINE(cMessage, 1 ,_MLINE)
ENDFOR

SET MEMOWIDTH TO nOldMemo
```

See Also ALines(), AtCLine(), AtLine(), Low-Level File Functions, RAtLine(), Set MemoWidth

Memory(), Sys(12), Sys(1001), Sys(1016), Sys(23), Sys(24)

These are all memory-related functions. In Visual FoxPro, only three of them return anything even remotely useful. SYS(1001) tells you the size of the virtual memory pool available to Visual FoxPro. SYS(1016) tells you how much memory is currently occupied by user-defined objects. The undocumented MEMORY(1) returns SYS(1001)/1024, that is, the virtual memory pool in KB.

Usage

```
nMemoryPool = SYS( 1001 )
nMemoryInUse = SYS( 1016 )
nMemoryPoolInKB = MEMORY( 1 )
```

Help says the number returned by SYS(1001) is about four times the physical memory of the machine. That seems about right; however, with some setups, our results were on the low side of that figure.

As for SYS(1016), we do wonder what's considered "user-defined" since we get a result of about a quarter of a megabyte when we first fire up VFP 6 before we get around to defining anything. Toolbars seem to count, since releasing them can lower the result. We suspect the system memory variables are taking up space in "user memory," too.

Example

```
? SYS(1001)   && Returns 266027008 on Tamar's 64-meg machine
? SYS(1016)   && Returns 272840 right after startup
              && on that machine with a fairly minimal CONFIG.FPW
? MEMORY(1)   && Returns 259792 on that machine.
```

The remaining memory functions don't return anything useful. MEMORY(), without the undocumented parameter, always says 640 (for 640 KB), while SYS(12) gives the same result in bytes—653360. SYS(23) and SYS(24) always return 0. (In fact, MEMORY(<any integer>) returns various values, some of which are recognizable, but none of which are documented.

See Also Sys(3050)

MemoWindow, OpenWindow

These properties are supposed to let you handle memo fields the same way you did way back before FoxPro even had the @...EDIT command, let alone all the goodies we have now. In those days, you used an @...GET for memos, and the user pressed Ctrl+PgDn to open an editing window. It was a major improvement in FoxPro 2.0 when you could specify a window of your own defining and have the memo window open up automatically, as soon as focus hit the @...GET. (@...EDIT was even more of an improvement, of course.) MemoWindow mimics the first piece—letting you specify the window. OpenWindow is supposed to provide the second, but it's broken. Since we can't see any reason to do things this way, we don't consider it a terrible problem. Nonetheless, read on.

Usage

```
txtTextBox.MemoWindow = cWindowName
cWindowName = txtTextBox.MemoWindow
txtTextBox.OpenWindow = lAutoOpen
lAutoOpen = txtTextBox.OpenWindow
```

MemoWindow seems to behave as expected. The memo field uses the specified window instead of the default.

OpenWindow doesn't do a blessed thing. Turn it on, turn it off, no matter. To open the memo window, whether the default or one you've defined, you have to press Ctrl+PgDn (or Ctrl+PgUp) or double-click on the text box.

Even if it worked, we'd recommend you don't use these properties. Users shouldn't have to know about the internal structure of their data, and showing them the term "memo" forces them to. Use an edit box for memo fields. We think that separate memo field windows may be needed in some circumstances, especially where the client is looking over long, narrative-type information and wants a full-screen view. We would probably design this as a small edit region on the form, with a Zoom button to go to a full-screen view. The full-screen view would really just be a modal, draggable, resizable black-box form with an edit box occupying all the form's real estate. This way, you can still have full control of the edit box's properties and events.

See Also Editbox, Modify Memo, Textbox

Menu

Patient: "Doctor, it hurts when I do this."
Doctor: "So don't do that."

Traditional Vaudeville Routine

MENU is one of a number of schemes created somewhere between the late Cretaceous and early Jurassic periods of Xbase. The fact that it is even supported at all in Visual FoxPro is a source of wonder to us, and a testament to the devotion Microsoft places on backward compatibility. But don't do that.

We put this section here just to tell you to use the Menu Designer. It can do all this command is capable of and more—like negotiating with OLE objects and browsers for menu placement, and pre- and post-generation processing by such cool utilities as GenMenuX. Use the Menu Designer instead.

Usage

```
Don't. (Okay, see the reference manuals-for an
older version-if you must know. They look OK.)
```

See Also Activate Menu, Create Menu, Modify Menu

Menu To See @ ... Prompt.

Menu() See Bar().

Menus

FoxPro has four—count 'em, four—different kinds of menus, not including those you might hand-build with a form (like putting up a series of buttons with choices). Why this embarrassment of riches? Historical reasons, of course. Each time a new type of menu became common, the next version of FoxBase/FoxPro included it. The number of menu commands in the language is staggering.

However, other than for testing purposes, we haven't actually written a menu command in years. We build our menus using the Menu Designer and let it generate all the code we need. With the addition of Andrew Ross MacNeill's GenMenuX, there's not much we can't do with generated menus. So, our first piece of advice is: Don't write menu code.

So what kinds of menus can you build, anyway? The antique varieties come in three flavors: Lotus-style lightbar menus, individual (somewhat ugly) menu popups, and an array-based precursor to Windows-type menus. They're all quirky and tedious to create and, most important, none of them fully conforms to the Windows interface standard. Don't use them.

The Real McCoy

So what's left? Component-style, Windows-type menus. Coincidentally, exactly the kind the Menu Designer lets you create.

Windows menus are built out of four types of components: menu bars, pads, popups and bars. That's right—the term "bar" has two different meanings in this context. (So what else is new?) The "menu bar" refers to the one line across the top of a window that contains the main options for that window or application. The term "bar" is used for individual items in a menu popup—things like "New" or "Open" or "Print." In between those two levels, we have pads—the items that appear on the menu bar—like "File," "Edit," and "Help"; and we have popups, which appear when you choose a menu pad. The popups contain the actual menu items (or bars) that you can choose to do something. Figure 4-8 shows the Visual FoxPro menu bar. It has eight pads at this point. The Window pad has been chosen, opening the window popup. The popup has 10 bars, including the three horizontal divider bars.

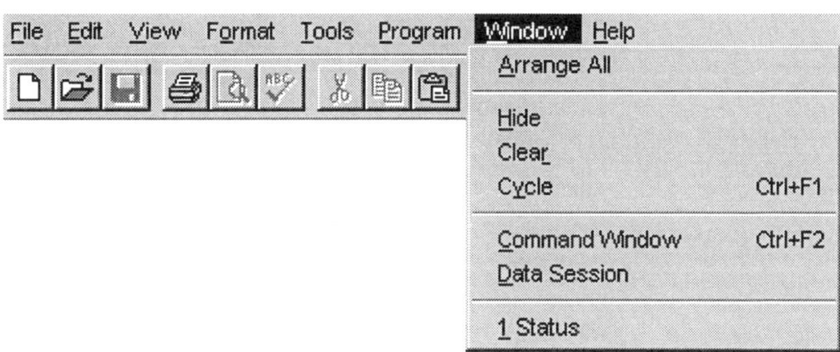

Figure 4-8: A Windows menu is composed of four types of components: a menu bar, pads, popups and bars. You shouldn't hang out in bars.

Component menus actually break down into two pairs of containers and contents. A menu bar without pads or a popup without bars is like an Oreo cookie without the cream.

A menu may have many, many levels, but there's always one menu bar with a collection of pads. Those pads have popups, each of which contains bars. The bars, however, may point to more popups, which in turn have more bars, and so forth and so on and scooby-dooby-dooby. Generally, it's not a good idea to have more than two levels of popups and bars. Users don't appreciate having to navigate down, down, down. It's very easy to get lost, and be unable to find a particular bar again without trolling through the entire menu structure. In addition, users with motor challenges will have a much harder time trying to keep all the menus open. If there are that many choices, call a dialog and let them make all the choices in parallel.

Are Shortcuts and Hot Keys Anything like Cold Cuts and Hotcakes?

Menu pads and bars (the contained objects) have a number of characteristics in common. Each has a prompt (the text that appears for it). The prompt can include a "hot key," a single letter that's underlined, which the user can press to choose that item when focus is on the container (the menu bar or popup). In addition, a keyboard shortcut, which chooses the item at any time, can be included. Each item may also have a message that appears in the status bar when the item is highlighted. A "skip for" condition may be specified, indicating that the item is disabled under certain conditions.

The difference between menu hot keys and menu shortcuts is a little subtle. Hot keys are available only when focus is already on the menu. You press just the underlined key. In Figure 4-8, hot keys are active only for the bars of the Window menu. "C" is the hot key for the Command Window.

Shortcuts are available when the menu doesn't have focus. They usually are either Alt or Ctrl plus a key or a function key. Typically, Alt plus a key is used for menu pad shortcuts, while Ctrl plus a key is used for menu bar shortcuts. In Figure 4-8, Ctrl+F2 is the shortcut for the Window-Command Window bar. Alt+F is the shortcut for the File pad.

When you specify a menu, either in code or in the Menu Designer, you have to specify hot keys and shortcuts separately. Hot keys are specified by preceding the letter with "\<" in the prompt. Shortcuts are specified with the KEY clause of the appropriate command or through the Options dialog in the Menu Designer.

In most applications, some menu options shouldn't be available some of the time. When an item isn't available, the user should be aware of it; usually, unavailable options are dimmed. FoxPro handles some of this automatically. When a modal form is active, almost all menu items are dimmed. (Only things like Edit-Copy are available.) Most of what needs to be done, though, is under your control. The SKIP FOR clause of the various menu commands or the SKIP FOR check box in the Options dialog of the Menu Designer lets you specify a condition for dimming the item. Pay attention to the name of this clause—it's SKIP FOR, not ALLOW FOR. That is, the condition you specify should be .T. when the item is to be dimmed. This is one of those counter-intuitive things, like SET DELETED, that makes FoxPro so, er, idiosyncratically lovable, and just has to be accepted because "it's always been that way."

The Font of Knowledge

Menus haven't changed much in Visual FoxPro. But there are two new features worth looking at. First, finally we have control over the font used for each menu component. Now we can make menus that look like ransom notes. Alternate fonts, however, are not available in menus that replace the system menu. Because this is the kind the Menu Designer is meant to build, you have no font choices there. (Besides, as with so many other items, the only person who should change the font for system menus is the user.)

Also, to accommodate various ActiveX issues, each menu pad can specify how it behaves when a different application takes over. Any pad can disappear or stick around in any of three specified locations. Similarly, each menu pad can indicate what happens to it when it's used in an ActiveDocument.

Handmade isn't Always Better

Building a menu in code is a tremendous undertaking. (If you don't believe us, open the Menu Designer, specify a Quick Menu, then Generate it. Take a look at the code.) You have to DEFINE each component with the appropriate command. Then, for each pad and bar, you have to specify the appropriate ON command to indicate what happens when the user chooses that item.

Menu DEFINE commands, though long-winded, are pretty straightforward. You indicate what item you're specifying, then provide each piece of information about it, such as the prompt, the message, the skip for condition, the shortcut, and so on.

The commands that indicate what happens when the user does something are more complex. They come in two flavors: ON and ON SELECTION. The ON commands are simpler—you use them to nest menus. Use ON PAD, for example, to indicate which popup to activate when the user chooses a particular menu pad.

The ON SELECTION version specifies a command to execute when the user chooses that item. These are cool because they propagate downward. That is, if you specify an ON SELECTION for a popup, it applies to any of that popup's bars that don't have actions of their own. This is particularly handy when you're first building an application. Specify something like WAIT WINDOW "Not implemented yet" at a high level, then fill in the individual items as you go.

Designer Menus

Almost everything you can do in code, you can do in the Menu Designer much more easily. Definitions go into the Prompt text box, plus a few of the Options items. For pads and bars, the ON vs. ON SELECTION choice is incorporated into the Result type drop-down list. A result type of "Submenu" corresponds to ON, while a result type of "Command or Procedure" is really ON SELECTION. (The final result type, "Pad Name" or "Bar #", lets you build components of Visual FoxPro's own menu right into your application menus.)

For the menu bar itself and menu popups, you can specify a routine to run ON SELECTION in the Menu Options dialog on the View menu.

Menus built in the Menu Designer are stored in tables with extensions of MNX/MNT. To turn a menu into something you can use, you have to generate the menu (either from Menu-Generate or through the Project Manager). This runs a program whose name is stored in _GENMENU, typically GENMENU.PRG, (written in

FoxPro) that reads the MNX table and uses textmerge to create the program, with an MPR extension, that implements your design. (The aforementioned GENMENUX uses the _GENMENU variable to hook itself into the process. You change _GENMENU to point to GENMENUX, then it calls GENMENU when it's ready to.)

Who's In Charge Here?

Once you have a menu defined, then what? You have to tell FoxPro to use your menu. There are a couple of ways to do this.

The Windows way (and the approach normally used by the Menu Designer) is to define your menu pads as belonging to _MSYSMENU, the system menu. Combined with SET SYSMENU AUTOMATIC, that's all it takes to let your menu replace FoxPro's.

Occasionally, you might have a reason to do it a different way (though we haven't in a long time). In that case, you use ACTIVATE MENU to start things rolling.

Shortcuts Again?

In the wonderful, but sometimes confusing, world of FoxPro, it's normal to have two meanings for the same or similar phrases. Menus include yet another example. As we said above, a menu shortcut is a key combination that executes a menu bar without navigating to it (like CTRL+C for Copy). In the last few years, shortcut menus have come into vogue. No, these aren't menu items that substitute for a key combination, as the phrase might make you think. Shortcut menus are also known as context menus or right-click menus. They're the popups that appear when you right-click somewhere.

In VFP 5 and VFP 6, you can create shortcut menus in the Menu Designer. Simply choose Shortcut from the dialog that appears when you CREATE MENU and you're on your way. The generated menu starts at the popup level and goes down from there. To hook it to right-clicks, put code like:

```
DO MyShortCut.MPR
```

in the RightClick event of the relevant object. If you want a context menu that appears on all right-clicks, not just on a particular object, use something like:

```
ON KEY LABEL RightMouse DO MyShortCut.MPR
```

Just like standard menus, the shortcut menus you create in the Menu Designer can use the system menu bars. So, for example, to put a copy item in a shortcut menu, you specify the result as "Bar #" and the action (ever noticed that column in the Menu Designer is unlabeled?) as "_MED_COPY". (Lose the quotes in both places.)

In VFP 3, you have to write your own DEFINE POPUP and DEFINE BAR code for shortcut menus. Then, in the RightClick event for whatever triggers the popup (or with ON KEY LABEL RightMouse), use ACTIVATE POPUP.

See Also @ ... Prompt, Activate Popup, Activate Menu, Create Menu, Define Bar, Define Menu, Define Pad, Define Popup, Menu, Menu To, _GenMenu, On Bar, On Exit Bar, On Exit Menu, On Exit Pad, On Exit Popup, On Pad, On Selection Bar, On Selection Menu, On Selection, Pad, On Selection Popup, Read Menu, Set SysMenu, Set TextMerge

Message **See ErrorMessage.**

Message() **See Error.**

MessageBox(), FoxTool's MsgBox()

Haven't you wondered how all those cool Windows programs display the same type of dialogs—with the same icons, text faces, and screen positioning? Perhaps it's a conspiracy. Nah. Maybe they all agreed on a convention and are actually sticking with it? Get real. The only reason those boxes all look the same is because they are all produced from the same function, and FoxPro programmers have access to that function as well.

MessageBox is a function introduced to the language in Visual FoxPro 3.0 that duplicates much of the functionality already available to FoxPro 2.x programmers in the FoxTools.FLL function MsgBox. (See FoxTools and SET LIBRARY TO for more information on FoxTools and libraries in general.) The big difference between using the two is that MessageBox() is built-in and doesn't require the use of any external libraries. The little difference is that the order of parameters differs between the two. Both functions return the same values to indicate the user's choice.

Usage

```
nReturnValue = MessageBox( cMessage, nIconButtons, cTitle )
nReturnValue = MsgBox( cMessage, cTitle, nIconButtons )    && FoxTools version
```

Parameter	Value	Meaning
cMessage	Character	A character string or expression to display in the body of the dialog box. Use CHR(13) to separate lines of text. Automatically word-wrapped.
nIconButtons:	0	No icon.
choose one icon:	16	Stop icon.
	32	Question mark.
	48	Exclamation point.
	64	Information (i).
add to that value	0	OK.
which button set	1	OK, Cancel.
to display:	2	Yes, No.
	3	Yes, No, Cancel.
	4	Abort, Retry, Ignore.
	5	Retry, Cancel.
and add to	0	First button has the focus.
that the default button:	256	Second button has the focus.
	512	Third button has the focus.
and if desperate:	4096	System modality: forces the messagebox to always be on top.
cTitle	Character	A character string or expression to display in the title bar of the box.
nReturnValue	1	OK
	2	Cancel

Parameter	Value	Meaning
nReturnValue	3	Abort
	4	Retry
	5	Ignore
	6	Yes
	7	No

The second numeric parameter is calculated by adding the three numeric values for the icon, types of buttons and default button, and passing that value as a single numeric parameter.

Example

```
* This example displays the dialog box shown in Figure 4-9
MessageBox("Your system appears to have been destroyed."+;
        chr(13)+"Purging all traces of your work..."+ ;
        "Press any key to continue...", 16,;
        "Monologue Box, not Dialog Box")
```

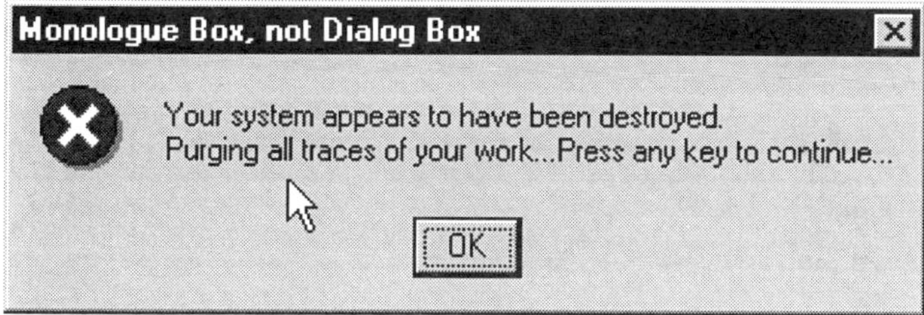

Figure 4-9: Sample dialog box

Figure 4-9 is a pretty sample, but a terrible user interface example. Remember, dialog boxes should allow you to have a *dialogue* with your users, your clients, the people who sign your paycheck. These are not opportunities to show how much smarter you are than they (you never know what you may prove!). Give the people who pay your salary intelligent, understandable options, not one-way, no-way-out warnings that Armageddon is around the corner. While we're on a tear, Figure 4-10 shows our second-least-favorite dialog:

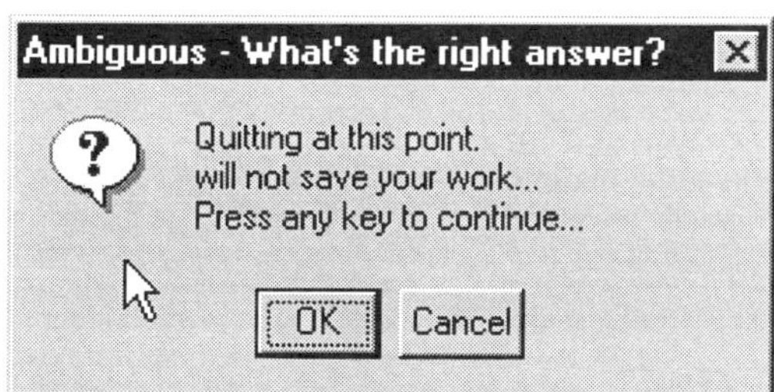

Figure 4-10: A really bad dialog box

Don't ever leave a dialog as confusing as this for your end users to mess with. You risk invoking the 50-50-90 law: If there's a 50-50 chance of your end users choosing a particular option, 90 percent of the time they'll choose the one that causes the most destruction.

You might be wondering how you can keep track of, and decode in the future, the obscure settings of the message functions' numeric parameter. Fortunately, Microsoft has taken care of this by letting you #INCLUDE any of the MessageBox parameter settings stored within the FoxPro.H file, an ASCII text file. By including this file, provided with FoxPro, code can be changed from this:

```
IF MessageBox("This is the message body", 21, ;
              "This is the title") = 1
```

to this:

```
#INCLUDE "FOXPRO.H"

IF MessageBox("This is the message body", ;
              MB_RETRYCANCEL + ;
              MB_ICONSTOP + ;
              MB_DEFBUTTON1, ;
              "This is the title") = IDOK
```

Add 4096 to the numeric parameter passed to the message function to invoke system modality. In Win31, this was a "last resort" style dialog, without all the features (nor did it consume all the resources) of its fancier siblings. The title was displayed as the first line of text within the box. Body text did not word-wrap. Icon settings were ignored and no icon was displayed. In VFP 5.0 and 6.0, now that FoxPro runs on Win32 platforms only, the System Modal setting is not that severe. In Windows 95 and 98, there seems to be no difference from an ordinary message box. In NT, the message box always stays on top, even if you switch applications underneath it. But it is not the potential system-locking-up monster it was under Windows 3.1. Good riddance!

The folks at Hacker Labs went to town on this function in VFP 3, and we documented several weird behaviors in that product in the *Hacker's Guide for Visual FoxPro 3.0*. In VFP 5 and 6, these loopholes seem to have been plugged.

See Also #Include, FoxTools, Set Library, Wait

MiddleClick See Click.

Min() See Max().

MinButton See MaxButton.

MinHeight See MaxHeight.

Minute() See Hour().

MinWidth See MaxHeight.

MkDir See CD.

_MLine, MLine() See MemLines().

Mod() See %.

Modify

This method belongs to the File object and lets you programmatically open a file from an open project for editing.

Usage `filFile.Modify( [ cClassName ] )`

For most of the files in a project, opening the appropriate editor is as simple as calling this method. Modify can even open another application to let you edit its files. For example, if you have a BMP in the project, calling its Modify method opens PaintBrush (or whatever application you have associated with BMP files).

Things are a little more complicated for classes, though. The file that belongs to the project is the class library, not the class itself. So, to edit a particular class, you call the Modify method on the class library and pass the name of the class to be edited. If you omit the class name, the special Open dialog for class libraries comes up to let you choose a class.

When Modify is called, the QueryModifyFile project hook method fires first, if there is one, to determine whether or not Modify should actually proceed. If QueryModifyFile issues NODEFAULT, the Modify is aborted.

Example

```
* Go through a project and open all the programs for editing
* Assume we have a reference to the project in oProj
FOR EACH oFile IN oProj.Files
   IF oFile.Type = "P"
      oFile.Modify()
   ENDIF
ENDFOR

* Open a particular class.
oProj.Files[3].Modify("frmBase")
```

See Also Add, File, Files, Modify Class, Modify Command, Modify Database, Modify File, Modify Form, Modify Label, Modify Menu, Modify Project, Modify Query, Modify Report, Modify Structure, Name, Project, QueryModifyFile, Remove, Type

Modify Class See Create Class.

Modify Command, Modify File

These two commands open a text editing window. Their default behaviors are designed so MODIFY COMMAND (or MODI COMM, as we usually type it) is better for editing program files, while MODIFY FILE (better known as MODI FILE) is better for free-form text.

Usage

```
MODIFY COMMAND | FILE [ FileName | FileSkel | ? ]
      [ NOEDIT | NOMODIFY ] [ NOMENU ]
      [ NOWAIT ] [ SAVE ]
      [ RANGE nStartChar, nEndChar ]
      [ WINDOW DefinitionWindow ]
      [ IN [ WINDOW ] ContainerWindow
        | IN SCREEN | IN MACDESKTOP ]
      [ SAME ]
      [ AS nCodePage ]
```

Most of the clauses for these two are the same as those for MODIFY MEMO. They're discussed there. These two have something else in common with MODIFY MEMO - unlike most of the MODIFY commands in FoxPro, they have no CREATE equivalent. To make a new one, you just specify a file that doesn't exist (not true for MODIFY MEMO, of course).

The AS nCodePage clause lets you indicate that the file was saved under a different code page and needs to be translated as it's opened.

If you pass a file skeleton (that is, a filename including the DOS wildcards "?" and "*"), all files matching that skeleton open for editing. Watch out—opening 100 programs for editing, although fun to watch, can eat an awful lot of memory. If you omit the filename entirely, an empty editing window opens. Beware! When you do that, you can't add any of the other clauses—they're interpreted as the filename. So MODI COMM NOEDIT opens the editor for a file named NOEDIT.PRG rather than giving you an empty, read-only edit window (a pretty stupid thing to do anyway).

MODIFY COMMAND assumes a PRG file unless you specify an extension. MODIFY FILE assumes TXT.

The various characteristics of different kinds of editing windows are controlled by a Properties dialog accessed from the Edit/Properties menu or the context menu of such windows. (In VFP 3, this information was provided in the Edit page of the Tools-Options dialog.) By default, MODI COMM windows don't word-wrap and do automatically indent to match the previous line, two of our favorite characteristics when writing code. MODIFY FILE has the opposite settings for those two, making it much better for, say, creating a README file.

MODI COMM's defaults make it great for displaying output text files. You get both horizontal and vertical scroll bars and you can see the actual format of the data.

Modifying a read-only file and then choosing to save it with File/SaveAs leaves the ridiculous " [read only]" appended to the name. This cropped up in VFP 5 and is still a problem with VFP 6.

You can change the characteristics for individual files or the default for an extension in the Properties dialog. We recommend you leave the defaults the way they are—lots of programs assume those two settings, especially the word-wrap setting.

Example
```
MODIFY COMMAND MyProg    && Opens MyProg.PRG
MODIFY FILE ReadMe       && Opens ReadMe.TXT
MODIFY COMMAND Output.TXT NOMODIFY     && Show output
```

See Also Do, Low-Level File Functions, Modify Memo, Set TextMerge

Modify Connection See Create Connection.

Modify Database

This command opens the Database Designer to let you interactively change the structure of a database (DBC).

Usage
```
MODIFY DATABASE [ Name | ? ] [ NOWAIT ] [ NOEDIT ]
```

If both Name and the "?" are omitted, the current database is opened. If there is no current database, the Open dialog lets you choose one. If Name isn't open, MODIFY DATABASE opens it, sets it as the current database, and brings up the Database Designer. Note that, in this case, the current setting of EXCLUSIVE determines whether you'll actually be able to make any changes.

Be careful what you assume with MODIFY DATABASE. When you USE a table that's part of a database, the database gets opened automatically, but does not become the current database. If you then MODIFY DATABASE <that database name>, you'd expect to see the open database. However, if you're in a different directory and the directory containing the database isn't in your FoxPro path, you'll actually be creating a new database in the current directory.

NOWAIT lets you open the Database Designer in a program and leave it waiting while you issue other commands.

NOEDIT allows you to view the database schema, but prevents you from inadvertently making changes to it. Be aware that the NOEDIT keyword isn't as strong as the NOUPDATE keyword of OPEN DATABASE. Although you can't visually add and remove things from the database, you can do so programmatically.

Example
```
MODIFY DATABASE MyData
```

See Also Create Database, Open Database, Set Database

Modify File See Modify Command.

Modify Form See Create Form.

Modify General See Append General.

Modify Label See Create Label.

Modify Memo, Close Memo, Set Window Of Memo

These commands give you programmatic control over the window used for editing a memo field. We haven't used any of them much since we got the ability to edit memo fields right in a form (@ .. EDIT in FoxPro 2.x and Edit box in VFP). These aren't even all that useful interactively because it's just as easy to set things up (say, in a Browse) the way we want them with the mouse.

MODIFY MEMO opens an editing window for the specified memo field. CLOSE MEMO closes the specified memo editing window. SET WINDOW OF MEMO lets you predefine a window for memo editing so it has the characteristics you want.

Usage

```
MODIFY MEMO MemoField1 [ , MemoField2 [ , ... ] ]
        [ NOEDIT | NOMODIFY ] [ NOMENU ] [ NOWAIT ]
        [ RANGE nStartPos, nEndPos ]
        [ [ WINDOW DefinitionWindow ]
          IN [ WINDOW ] ContainerWindow | IN SCREEN
          | IN MACDESKTOP ]
        [ SAME ]
        [ SAVE ]
```

Parameter	Value	Meaning
MemoField*n*	Name	A memo field for which an editing window should open.
nStartPos, nEndPos	Numeric	A range of characters in MemoField*n*, which are highlighted when the window opens.
DefinitionWindow	Name	The name of a window that provides the size, shape and characteristics for the editing window.
ContainerWindow	Name	The name of a window in which the memo editing window is placed.

We don't think we've ever used MODIFY MEMO on multiple fields at once. When you do, the memo windows all open in the same place, one on top of the other, unless you've previously opened them and moved them around. Some help!

There are several different ways that the position of the editing window can be specified. The command contains two different window-related clauses—WINDOW and IN WINDOW—which serve very different roles. WINDOW specifies a defined window that serves as a template for the editing window. The memo field isn't edited in DefinitionWindow, but it draws its characteristics from that window. If you look at the Window pull-down menu after using MODIFY MEMO WINDOW, you'll see two windows listed: DefinitionWindow and the memo window itself. (In fact, you can release DefinitionWindow once you've issued MODIFY MEMO and save the memory it's using.)

IN WINDOW is different. It specifies a parent or container window for the memo-editing window. The editing window is forced to stay inside ContainerWindow, which must be active for the editing window to appear. Moving the editing window beyond the bounds of ContainerWindow crops it.

You can combine WINDOW and IN WINDOW in a single MODIFY MEMO to specify both a template and a container.

IN SCREEN indicates that the memo-editing window should have the main Visual FoxPro window as its parent rather than a different window. This is an issue only if you've previously placed the editing window in another window.

IN MACDESKTOP creates a free-floating edit window that has an entry in the taskbar and can be moved around like any app. We're not sure when you'd use this, but it is interesting.

NOEDIT and its undocumented synonym, NOMODIFY, let you look, but you can't touch. (The NOMODIFY clause of the various MODIFY commands is one of our favorites because it lets us write oxymorons like MODIFY MEMO MyNote NOMODIFY. That's right up there with WAIT WINDOW MyMessage NOWAIT.)

NOMENU removes the Format pad from the menu or prevents it from appearing if it wasn't already there. Use this if you don't want the user to be able to change the font (not a very nice thing to do).

NOWAIT and SAVE let you open up a bunch of windows at once and then leave them open for the user. NOWAIT indicates that execution should continue once the editing window is displayed, rather than waiting for the user to close it. Supposedly, SAVE keeps the window from closing when another window is activated. It's needed in a program only when you don't use NOWAIT—in that case, it keeps your editing window alive until you close it.

SAME is another clause that doesn't really seem to do much of anything. Help says it lets you display the memo-editing window without it becoming active. We see that behavior only if the window's already displayed.

Example

```
USE Employee
MODIFY MEMO Notes

* Set up the window in advance
DEFINE WINDOW NotesMemo FROM 0,0 TO 10,70 PANEL
* Don't allow changes
MODIFY MEMO Notes WINDOW NotesMemo NOMODIFY
```

Usage

```
CLOSE MEMO MemoField1 [ , MemoField2 [ , ... ] ] | ALL
```

CLOSE MEMO closes the editing windows for the fields listed or for all memo fields, even if they're from different tables.

Usage

```
SET WINDOW OF MEMO TO [ DefinitionWindow ]
```

This command lets you specify a predefined window to use as a template whenever a memo-editing window is opened. This window functions like the one listed in the WINDOW clause of MODIFY MEMO—it provides characteristics for the memo window. The memo is actually edited in a different window based on DefinitionWindow. The template is used both for MODIFY MEMO and for editing triggered by a user from a Browse or a grid.

You can override SET WINDOW OF MEMO by including the WINDOW clause in MODIFY MEMO.

To find out the current DefinitionWindow, check SET("WINDOW").

Example

```
* Define a memo editing template window
DEFINE WINDOW WindMemo from 0,0 TO 10,70 PANEL
SET WINDOW OF MEMO TO WindMemo

* Now edit some memo fields
MODIFY MEMO Employee.Notes
MODIFY MEMO Category.Description

* Shut them down
CLOSE MEMO ALL
```

See Also Browse, Editbox

Modify Menu See Create Menu.

Modify Procedure

This command opens the program editor for the stored procedures of the current database. It's the same editor you get with MODIFY COMMAND and MODIFY FILE.

Usage
```
MODIFY PROCEDURE
```

Be careful when editing stored procedures. The RI Builder stores its results at the end of your hand-coded stored procedures, and you need to take care to make your changes/additions without disturbing the RI Builder-generated procedures at the end. You'll know when you've reached the beginning of the code generated by the RI Builder by the scary warning in the comment line.

Although we don't use these features every day, we're a little disappointed we didn't get clauses similar to the MODIFY COMMAND command—NOEDIT, NOMENU, NOWAIT, WINDOW, etc.—or some variation on the METHOD keyword introduced in VFP 5 for forms and classes. Being stuck with the FoxPro editor is bad enough, but this leaves us with little opportunity to expand on it.

Example
```
OPEN DATA TasTrade
MODIFY PROCEDURE
```

See Also Create Trigger, Display Procedures, Modify Database, Open Database

Modify Project See Create Project.

Modify Query See Create Query.

Modify Report See Create Label.

Modify Screen See Create Form.

Modify Structure See Create.

Modify View, Rename View

These commands let you perform maintenance on views. MODIFY VIEW opens the View Designer to edit an existing view (or create a new view). RENAME VIEW lets you change the name of an existing view.

Usage
```
MODIFY VIEW [ ? | ViewName [ REMOTE ] ]
RENAME VIEW OldName TO NewName
```

If you don't specify a view to modify, you're prompted with a list of all the views in the current database. The REMOTE keyword seems to be not only superfluous, but totally ignored. We can't find any situation where you'd need it.

As with other database maintenance, in VFP 3 you need exclusive use of the database to use these commands.

Be careful what views you open with MODIFY VIEW, or more precisely, what views you save once you've opened the View Designer. It can't handle any but the simplest views. In particular, the View Designer has problems with table relationships that involve what we like to call "unrelated siblings," that is, tables that are both children of the same parent but do not have an inherent relationship. (For example, the TasTrade orders table can be seen as parent to both the customer and shipper tables. But customer and shipper have no relationship.) In addition, if you've written a view by hand, there's a good chance the VD can't parse it correctly. When you open a view beyond its abilities, it makes it up as it goes. If you save the nonsense the View Designer comes up with, your view will be damaged. One basic rule—if you open a view with the View Designer and it looks funny, press ESC and get out without saving.

If you rename a view and other views are based on that view, the dependent views won't work anymore. You can't even open them up in the View Designer to fix the problem without losing the definition. You can fix things up by using DBSetProp() to gather and store all the relevant properties, and then redefine the view. The big problem, of course, is knowing that you have views dependent on a renamed view.

In all versions, the database containing the view must be current.

Example

```
MODIFY VIEW MyRemoteView
RENAME VIEW ShortName TO MuchLongerAndMoreExplicitName
```

See Also Create SQL View, Open Database, Set Database

Modify Window See Define Window.

Month() See CDoW().

Mouse

This command does for your resident rodent what KEYBOARD does for your keyboard—lets you make things happen automatically. Of course, just as using KEYBOARD doesn't actually depress the keys, MOUSE doesn't physically move or click your real mouse—it just makes it seem like you did.

Usage

```
MOUSE [ CLICK | DBLCLICK ] [ AT nRow, nCol ]
      [ DRAG TO nEndRow1, nEndCol2 [, nEndRow2, nEndCol2 ... ] ] [ PIXELS ]
      [ WINDOW WindowName ]
      [ LEFT | MIDDLE | RIGHT ] [ ALT ] [ CONTROL ] [ SHIFT ]
```

MOUSE is a pretty versatile command. You can use it to position the mouse, click or double-click either button, or drag the mouse. The syntax diagram doesn't make it clear, however, that you have to do at least one of those things. MOUSE, by itself, gives you a syntax error. You need to include one of the first three options (or two or all three of them).

If you include both AT and CLICK or DBLCLICK, the mouse is positioned at the specified point, then clicked. Similarly, AT with DRAG positions the mouse before dragging it. You can specify more than one point to drag to and sure enough, the mouse moves to each point in sequence. The only situation in which this makes sense is when you have things happening in DragOver events.

How does MOUSE know whose coordinate system to use for the points you specify? By default, it measures things based on the main Visual FoxPro window using foxels. Specify PIXELS to measure in pixels instead. Use the WINDOW clause to tell MOUSE to measure relative to a different window. One cool thing is to use WINDOW (WONTOP()) so things happen in the active window.

In VFP 3 and VFP 5, when you use the WINDOW clause, the title bar is included in the window, so (0,0) is not the first point inside the window, but something above and to the left of it. In VFP 6, the title bar no longer counts.

The last line of syntax let you specify which button is clicked and whether any of the modifier keys should be sent with the click. (Check out MouseDown and MouseUp to see what you can do with the keys.)

In VFP 3, two of the optional keywords are messed up. MIDDLE generates an error in that version. Since most users don't have three-button mice, MIDDLE is no big loss—we weren't planning any applications to use three buttons anyway. The second problem is only a documentation bug. The docs for VFP 3 say to use CTRL to have the CTRL button "pressed" with your click. Nope, it's CONTROL instead. Bad choice, since other parts of the language (KEYBOARD, in particular) use CTRL, and that's what it says on our keyboards. Both problems are fixed in later versions, but it would have been nicer if they'd used the same keyword as everywhere else.

So what do you do with this command, anyway? You make things happen. Its obvious application is self-running demos. MOUSE isn't quite as useful in that situation as you'd expect because it can't get to the menu, but it's still handy for clicking on items, dragging things and the like. MOUSE is also useful in builders, to let you bring things to the top or select a bunch of items, although the need for it decreases as more and more objects are exposed at design time.

Example

```
* Say we've selected some objects and used ASELOBJ() to
* store references to them in aObjs. Later, we can reselect
* them.
LOCAL nCnt, nTitleSpace, nBorderSpace

* We need to add space for the title bar of both the FD and the
* form itself vertically, and the borders of the FD
* horizontally, plus a little fudge factor to make sure we hit
* the object. In VFP 6, you don't need the fudge factors, but
* we think that's a bug.
nTitleSpace = 2 * SYSMETRIC(9)
nBorderSpace = 2 * SYSMETRIC(3)

MOUSE CLICK AT -1,-1 WINDOW (WONTOP())  && to clear selections
FOR nCnt = 1 TO ALEN(aObjs,1)
   MOUSE CLICK AT aObjs[nCnt].Top + nTitleSpace + 3, ;
                  aObjs[nCnt].Left + nBorderSpace + 3 ;
         WINDOW (WONTOP()) PIXELS SHIFT
ENDFOR
```

See Also Click, DblClick, Keyboard, MCol(), MiddleClick, MouseDown, MouseUp, MouseMove, MRow(), RightClick

MouseDown, MouseUp

These two events give you access to each of the components of a click. MouseDown fires when the user presses a mouse button, and MouseUp fires when the user releases the button. These even respond to up to three different mouse buttons and can tell you whether you're pressing any of the modifier keys (Shift, Ctrl, Alt) at the same time.

Usage

```
PROCEDURE oObject.MouseDown | oObject.MouseUp
LPARAMETERS [ nIndex , ] nButton, nKeys, nXCoord, nYCoord
```

Parameter	Value	Meaning
nIndex	Numeric	The member of a control array that fired the event.
	Omitted	The control is not in a control array.
nButton	1	Left button
	2	Right button
	4	Center button

Parameter	Value	Meaning
nKeys	0	No modifiers pressed
	1	Shift key pressed
	2	Ctrl key pressed
	3	Shift and Ctrl keys pressed
	4	Alt key pressed
	5	Shift and Alt keys pressed
	6	Ctrl and Alt keys pressed
	7	Shift, Ctrl and Alt keys pressed
nXCoord, nYCoord	Numeric	The coordinates of the mouse location in the form's ScaleMode.

MouseDown and MouseUp give you a chance to do something before a Click, RightClick, MiddleClick or DblClick actually occurs. In fact, putting NoDefault in these events can prevent clicks. See Click for more on that—there are some problems.

We're not sure why FoxPro can't detect pressing multiple buttons (like left and right together), but we're delighted by the fact that the right mouse button and even the middle button are full players here.

FoxPro uses the Ctrl+Alt+Shift combination to let you hide a bunch of windows to see what's behind them. We love this capability and use it all the time. However, it interferes with mouse events. When you press all three keys and then push a mouse button, none of the mouse events fire. If it's important to be able to Ctrl+Alt+Shift+Click, add the line OUTSHOW=OFF to your Config.FPW file.

You may have different keys pressed when MouseDown fires than when the corresponding MouseUp is executed. However, except in very weird circumstances (such as having a WAIT WINDOW without NOWAIT in a MouseDown event), you always get MouseUp for the same object that fired MouseDown, even if you've moved the mouse in between. However, nXCoord and nYCoord reflect the true position of the mouse at the time the button goes down or comes up, so you can test whether you're still over the same object. (Dragging the mouse off the control between MouseDown and MouseUp does prevent that control's Click from firing.)

Example

```
* MouseDown is a good place to initiate drag-and-drop
This.Drag(1)
```

See Also AMouseObj(), Click, DblClick, Drag, DragDrop, MiddleClick, MouseMove, RightClick

MouseIcon **See MousePointer.**

MouseMove

Have you ever wanted to do something just because the mouse moved over a particular point on the screen? We have (although providing tooltips, the thing we've most wanted to do, is built into Visual FoxPro). MouseMove is the key to reacting to the rodent's movements.

Usage

```
PROCEDURE oObject.MouseMove
LPARAMETERS [ nIndex , ] nButtons, nKeys, nXCoord, nYCoord
```

As with the other control events, we have the same, old, nearly useless, optional nIndex parameter. It's for the rare occasions when you use a control array.

The other parameters are neat. They tell you which mouse buttons and which modifier keys (Shift, Ctrl, Alt) are pressed as the mouse moves along. The last two tell you where you are. You can use the parameters to figure out how to respond to the mouse movement.

Example

```
PROCEDURE MouseMove
* Tell the user what's going on
LPARAMETERS nButton, nShift, nXCoord, nYCoord

DO CASE
CASE nButton = 0
   cButton = "No buttons"
CASE nButton = 1
   cButton = "Left"
CASE nButton = 2
   cButton = "Right"
CASE nButton = 3
   cButton = "Left and Right"
CASE nButton = 4
   cButton = "Center"
CASE nButton = 5
   cButton = "Left and Center"
CASE nButton = 6
   cButton = "Center and Right"
CASE nButton = 7
   cButton = "All three"
OTHERWISE
   cButton = "That's odd!"
ENDCASE

DO CASE
CASE nShift = 0
   cShift = "No keys"
CASE nShift = 1
   cShift = "Shift"
CASE nShift = 2
   cShift = "Ctrl"
CASE nShift = 3
   cShift = "Shift+Ctrl"
CASE nShift = 4
   cShift = "Alt"
CASE nShift = 5
   cShift = "Shift+Alt"
CASE nShift = 6
   cShift = "Ctrl+Alt"
CASE nShift = 7
   cShift = "All three"
OTHERWISE
   cShift = "That's odd!"
ENDCASE

DEBUGOUT "Moving over " + THIS.Name + ;
         " at " + LTRIM(STR(nXCoord)) + "," + ;
         LTRIM(STR(nYCoord)) + " with " + ;
         cButton + ", " + cShift NOWAIT

* A shorter, but less readable, way to test for the different
* conditions is to use BitTest as follows:
lLeft = BitTest(nButton,0)
lRight = BitTest(nButton,1)
lCenter = BitTest(nButton,2)
lShift = BitTest(nShift,0)
lCtrl = BitTest(nShift,1)
lAlt = BitTest(nShift,2)
```

As with the other mouse events that pass the nKeys parameter, you can't reliably detect nKeys=7 (Ctrl+Alt+Shift) unless you've set OUTSHOW=OFF in your Config.FPW file. (We've seen some cases where you can detect it temporarily, but then the form stops responding until you release at least one key.)

See Also Click, DblClick, DragOver, Mouse, MouseDown, MousePointer, MouseUp, MouseWheel

MousePointer, MouseIcon

These properties let you determine what kind of icon the mouse uses at any given time. You can use any icon you want. If it's in the set provided, you only need to set MousePointer. To use any other icon, you set MousePointer and MouseIcon.

Usage

```
oObject.MousePointer = nMousePointer
nMousePointer = oObject.MousePointer
oObject.MouseIcon = cIconFile
cIconFile = oObject.MouseIcon
```

A value of 0 for MousePointer uses the default for the object. A value between 1 and 14 (12 in VFP 3) chooses one of the standard mouse pointers. Both Help and FoxPro.H contain the list. Most of them are pretty familiar, including the various sizing pointers and the hourglass. A couple of them, though, we've never seen in any application we've used.

Sometimes, you need a pointer that isn't in the list. Fortunately, in VFP 5 and VFP 6, there's a way to get one. Set MousePointer to 99 and set MouseIcon to the file you want to use. ICO, CUR and ANI files work, but other kinds of graphics don't. (You can specify the others, but you won't see them. They're ignored.)

When an object is being dragged, its DragIcon takes precedence over the MousePointer or MouseIcon of any object you drag it over.

Example

```
This.MousePointer = 10

#INCLUDE FOXPRO.H
oObject.MousePointer = MOUSE_HOURGLASS

This.MousePointer = 99
This.MouseIcon = HOME(4)+"CURSORS\Bullseye.Cur"
```

See Also DragIcon, #Include, MouseMove

MouseUp See MouseDown.

MouseWheel

This event, introduced in Visual FoxPro 5.0, allows users of wheel-enabled devices to affect FoxPro controls.

Usage

```
Procedure Object.MouseWheel()
LPARAMETERS [nIndex, ] nDirection, nModifierKeys, nXCoord, nYCoord
```

Parameter	Value	Meaning
nIndex	Integer	Used in the rare case that the object is part of a control array.
nDirection	Numeric	Indicates the direction and magnitude of the mouse wheel movement. In VFP 5.0, the Help referred to this as "nDelta" and they changed it in the 6.0 Help to "nDirection." In either case, the parameter describes the direction with the sign of the variable—negative for backward, zero for no movement and positive for forward—and a multiple of a fixed number, dependent on the particular device, to describe the number of clicks forward or backward.

Parameter	Value	Meaning
nModifierKeys	Integer	A set of bit flags to indicate whether the Shift, Alt or Control keys are used. Shift sets the number to 1, Control to 2 and Alt to 4. If more than one of the keys is used, nModifierKeys is the sum of them.
nXCoord	Integer	The x-coordinate of the mouse, relative to the current form, in the current ScaleMode.
nYCoord	Integer	The y-coordinate of the mouse, relative to the current form, in the current ScaleMode.

Microsoft, Logitech and several other vendors have recently introduced wheel-bearing mice and trackballs. While the most common purpose of the wheel is to provide for scrolling in documents longer than the screen, most Microsoft software (including, of course, Visual FoxPro) supports additional functionality. Clicking the mouse wheel in an edit box or scrolling region can allow the user alternative scrolling modes. Check out all of the native behaviors before you decide to write your own.

With the information supplied in this event, you may choose to have your controls provide their own behaviors. Use the SIGN() function to determine the direction of motion. Have the user tune your application by capturing, in some "tune-up" dialog, just what his mouse driver returns for a single mouse-wheel click. Use BITTEST() to determine which modifier keys are in use.

Example

```
* Example code from a test toolbar
* Three command buttons display the RGB values
* One textbox shows the "nDirection" sign and magnitude
* Holding Shift, Control or Alt modifies the BackColor
* of the toolbar

LPARAMETERS nDirection, nShift, nXCoord, nYCoord
LOCAL lnIncrement

* && -1 for backward, +1 for forward
lnIncrement = SIGN(nDirection)

* Foxtools loaded in Init
LOCAL lnRed, lnGreen, lnBlue
* Foxtools function to return individual R, G, B values
=RGBComp(This.BackColor, @lnRed, @lnGreen, @lnBlue)

* nShift is, or contains, 1 - Shift
lnRed = lnRed + IIF(BITTEST(nShift,0), lnIncrement, 0)
* nShift is, or contains, 2 - Control
lnGreen = lnGreen + IIF(BITTEST(nShift,1), lnIncrement, 0)
* nShift is, or contains, 4, - Alt
lnBlue = lnBlue + IIF(BITTEST(nShift,2), lnIncrement, 0)

* Restrict the values to the range 0 - 255
lnRed = MAX(0,MIN(255,lnRed))
lnGreen = MAX(0,MIN(255,lnGreen))
lnBlue = MAX(0,MIN(255,lnBlue))

This.cmdRed.Caption = "R: " + PADL(lnRed,3,"0")
This.cmdGreen.Caption = "G: " + PADL(lnGreen,3,"0")
This.cmdBlue.Caption = "B: " + PADL(lnBlue,3,"0")

This.BackColor = RGB(lnRed, lnGreen, lnBlue)

* Display the nDirection
This.TEXT1.Value = nDirection
```

See Also BitTest(), Control Arrays, MiddleClick, MouseDown, MouseMove, ScaleMode

Movable See Closable.

Move

This method lets you move an object. You can resize it at the same time.

Usage `oObject.Move( nLeft [, nTop [, nWidth [, nHeight ] ] ] )`

The parameters are the new values for the specified properties. We can think of some fun things to do with movable controls. (Imagine a button that jumps away when the user clicks on it. Or don't just imagine it—see the example.)

Example

```
* This might be the Click for a command button.
This.Move(This.Left + This.Width/4, ;
          This.Top - 50, This.Width / 2, This.Height * 3 / 2)
=inkey(.1)  && stop and let the user see
This.Move(This.Left - This.Width / 2, ;
          This.Top + 50, This.Width * 2, This.Height * 2 / 3)
```

The example points out that moving an object relative to its position, or sizing it relative to its size, is something of a pain. For an object that needed to do this a lot, we'd be inclined to create a custom method RelativeMove that would understand its parameters as relative to current position and size. Here's the code:

```
* RelativeMove - a custom method
* Pass positive values to move right and down and to make object larger
* Pass negative values to move left and up and to make object smaller
LPARAMETERS nLeft, nTop, nWidth, nHeight
LOCAL nNewLeft, nNewTop, nNewWidth, nNewHeight

nNewLeft   = IIF( VARTYPE('nLeft')="N", This.Left + nLeft, This.Left)
nNewTop    = IIF( VARTYPE('nTop')="N", This.Top + nTop, This.Top)
nNewWidth  = IIF( VARTYPE('nWidth')="N", This.Width + nWidth, This.Width)
nNewHeight = IIF( VARTYPE('nHeight')="N", This.Height + nHeight, This.Height)

This.Move(nNewLeft, nNewTop, nNewWidth, nNewHeight)

ENDPROC
```

See Also Moved, Resize

Move Popup See Hide Menu.

Move Window See Define Window.

Moved

This event fires when an object is moved either by the user or in code.

Usage `PROCEDURE oObject.Moved`

Calling the Move method fires this event, but only if the object actually moves. If you pass the current values of nLeft and nTop to Move, Moved doesn't fire.

For a form, Moved also fires when the user moves the form and when the form is resized from the left or the top. That's right, pulling down the top of the form with the mouse fires Moved. That's because Moved fires whenever the value of Left or Top changes.

In situations where both Moved and Resize are fired (like resizing from the top or left), Moved executes first.

When you move columns around in a grid, Moved is called only for the column triggering the move, not for every column that changes position as a result.

Example

```
* In a formset, when one form is moved, you might move another
* to make sure it's still visible. Put code like this in the
* first form's Moved to keep the forms side by side.
* Of course, the user may not appreciate this, if he's trying
* to separate the forms.
nBorderWidth = SYSMETRIC(3)
IF This.Left + This.Width + ThisFormSet.form2.Width + ;
   4 * nBorderWidth <= _SCREEN.Width
   ThisFormSet.form2.Left = This.Left + This.Width + ;
     2 * nBorderWidth
ELSE
   ThisFormSet.form2.Left = ;
     This.Left - ThisFormSet.form2.Width - 2 * nBorderWidth
ENDIF
ThisFormSet.Form2.Top = This.Top
```

See Also Left, Move, Resize, SysMetric(), Top

MoverBars

This property determines whether or not a list has a little button at the side of each item that lets you slide the items around and change the list's order.

Usage

```
lstList.MoverBars = lHasMoverButtons
lHasMoverButtons = lstList.MoverBars
```

As the help indicates, MoverBars are relevant only when the RowSourceType for the list is either 0 or 1. That is, you can only move things around when the list "owns" the items. When the list is simply borrowing the items from another source, like a table or array, it can't change their order. (That's why Sorted applies only to some RowSourccTypes, too.)

When items are moved around in the list, their index changes. If an item is highlighted and you move it, the value of the list's ListIndex (index for the currently highlighted item) changes. The List property is the key to finding out what's where. It contains all the items in the order you're seeing them. In addition, InteractiveChange fires when items are moved.

In VFP 3, the interaction of moving items with multi-select is pretty nicely implemented. If you're careful and touch only the mover buttons, not the items themselves, the selection status of the items doesn't change. In other words, you can highlight a bunch of items, then move items around and still end up with the same items highlighted.

Unfortunately, they broke it. In VFP 5 and VFP 6, when you move items in a multi-select list, the highlight stays in the same position rather than moving with the items. That is, you have the items with the same set of indexes highlighted, rather than the items with the same itemids. This also means that ListIndex doesn't change when you move a highlighted item in a multi-select list.

Example `frmMyForm.lstSomeList.MoverBars = .T.`

See Also InteractiveChange, List, ListBox, ListIndex

MrkBar(), MrkPad() See Set Mark Of.

MRow(), MCol(), MWindow(), MDown()

These functions let you find out what's going on with the mouse. MROW() and MCOL() provide the current mouse position, while MWINDOW() tells you which window the mouse is in. MDOWN() tells you whether a mouse button is down at the moment.

You can get just about all the same information using various events including MouseMove and MouseDown.

Usage

```
nYCoord = MROW( [ cWindow ] )
nXCoord = MCOL( [ cWindow ] )
```

Parameter	Value	Meaning
cWindow	Character	Return coordinates relative to the specified window.
	Omitted	Return coordinates relative to the active window. If no user-defined window is active, return coordinates relative to the main Visual FoxPro window.

MROW() and MCOL() have interesting behavior. Their output is always relative to a particular window and is given in foxels. When a user-defined window is active, these functions are dynamic. You can watch them change in the Debugger. When no user-defined window is active, the Debugger values update only when you click somewhere. No doubt the difference is the presence of the MouseMove event of a form, which tracks the mouse position anyway.

When the mouse is positioned outside the specified window in either dimension, the function for that dimension returns –1. (For example, if the mouse is below the window, MROW() returns –1.)

When the Debugger is in its own frame, clicking into it evaluates these functions with respect to the position of the VFP frame. Kind of strange, but not terribly important since users aren't likely to run your apps with the Debugger open.

Usage

```
cWindow = MWINDOW()
lIsThisWindow = MWINDOW( cWindow )
```

MWINDOW() does two different things. By itself, it returns the name of the window the mouse is currently over (which is the form whose MouseMove would be triggered at the moment if it contained any code). Pass it a window name and it tells you whether the mouse is over that window.

Usage

```
lButtonDown = MDOWN()
```

MDOWN() lets you know if either left or right mouse button is currently pressed. It returns .T. as long as the button is down. MDOWN() has trouble keeping up when you're not in a window.

We used to use all of these functions in attempts to make event-driven applications in FoxPro 2.x. We really don't use them much in VFP because the enhanced event model provides these capabilities and much more, though we occasionally use MDOWN() to do manual drag-and-drop or something like the example.

Example

```
DO WHILE MDOWN()
   * increase a variable while the mouse button is down
   nCount = nCount+1
ENDDO
```

See Also Click, MiddleClick, MouseDown, MouseMove, MouseUp, RightClick, WOnTop(), WOutput()

MToN() See NToM().

MultiSelect

This property determines whether list boxes can have multiple items highlighted at once.

Usage
```
lstList.MultiSelect = lMultipleItems
lMultipleItems = lstList.MultiSelect
```

When MultiSelect is .T., you can use all the standard Windows methods for choosing one or more items. These include Shift+Clicking at the beginning and end of a range to highlight everything in between, and Ctrl+Click to select and deselect individual items. Shift+Spacebar and Ctrl+Spacebar perform the same functions, and Shift plus the cursor control keys can highlight a range to add.

In VFP 3, there is a limit of 60 selected items at once. You can put more than 60 items in the list and you can try to select them, but as you select more items, once you get past 60, your first selections get deselected. We weren't at all surprised that this bug was fixed fast. (It's there in VFP 3.0 and 3.0b, but fixed in 5.0 and later.)

You can find out which items are highlighted at any time by checking the Selected or SelectedId property. In fact, you can make items be highlighted by setting Selected to .T. for those items.

VFP 3 has another multi-select bug, too. When RowSourceType is 2, 3, 4 or 5 (that's Alias, SQL, Query and Array), a previously selected item doesn't always deselect when it should. Here's the simplest example. Run a form with a multi-select list of one of these types and a button. Click an item in the list. Now click the button. Now click a different list item. We see two highlighted items. This nasty bug was also fixed quickly.

Example
```
frmMyForm.lstMyList.MultiSelect = .T.
```

See Also ComboBox, ListBox, MoverBars, RowSourceType, Selected, SelectedId

MWindow() See MRow().

Name

This property is one of the keys to OOP. It's what you use to refer to an object so you can look at its properties, change them, or call a method.

Usage
```
oObject.Name = cName
cName = oObject.Name
```

Every object in Visual FoxPro has a Name property, except for those created in weird ways like using SCATTER NAME.

You can assign a name to an object in the Property Sheet when you add it to another class, or in its own Init method (or the container's Init method). Although you can change the Name of an object at runtime, it's usually not a good idea once you get past the Init method. If you have code that depends on an object's Name and you change Name, the code fails.

If you don't assign an object a Name, FoxPro does it for you. That's why the first text box you add to a form is Text1 and the next is Text2 and so on. With classes defined in code (rather than a VCX), there can be a tremendous performance penalty for letting FoxPro do it. See "Faster Than a Speeding Bullet."

Despite the warning above, in a code class, don't ever assign Name a value in the properties section *unless* it's the same as the class name. Instead, assign the new instance a Name in Init. When you do the assignment in the properties section, it changes the name of the class, not the name of instances of the class.

Although you usually use Name to refer to an object, you don't do that for the outermost object that gets created via either CreateObject() or Do Form. For that object, use the variable holding the object reference—then, you can drill down into the object using the Names of the various members.

Example

```
DEFINE CLASS MyTextBox AS TextBox

* Don't do this!
* Name = "anything"
* But do this for speed issues, if using a coded class
Name = "MyTextBox"

PROCEDURE Init

* Do it this way instead or class name changes
This.Name = "anything"

ENDPROC

ENDDEFINE
```

See Also Caption, Class, Scatter

NavigateTo

This method of the hyperlink object tells the associated browser to go to a particular address. If the hyperlink is on a stand-alone VFP form, a new instance of the default browser is invoked; if the hyperlink is on an Active Document, that browser host is redirected.

Usage

```
oHyperLink.NavigateTo(cLegalAddress)
```

Parameter	Value	Meaning
cLegalAddress	Character	Any legal address that could be accepted by a browser: http:, ftp:, news:, or a local file: address.

NavigateTo invokes a specified address. If the hyperlink object is within an Active Document hosted in a browser, that browser seeks the new address. If the hyperlink is in a VFP stand-alone application, the operating system is called to handle the hyperlink, typically starting the default browser and bringing up the specified link. On our systems, even if a browser is already open, the hyperlink call always starts a new browser. If this isn't the behavior you want, you'll probably have to look to Automation to get it working your way.

Example

```
oLink.NavigateTo("http://www.microsoft.com/vfoxpro")
oLink.NavigateTo("news://msnews.microsoft.com")
```

See Also Hyperlink, GoBack, GoForward

Ndx() See Cdx().

Network() See Access().

NewIndex, NewItemId

These properties tell you the index and itemid of the item you most recently added to a list or combo box.

Usage

```
nIndexAssigned = oObject.NewIndex
nItemIdAssigned = oObject.NewItemId
```

To understand the distinction between index and itemid, see the entries for AddItem and for ListIndex and ListItemId. These two have the same division of labor as those last two properties.

You're far more likely to need NewItemId than NewIndex. If you're adding a series of items to a multi-column list, NewItemId can be a big help. As long as you use it every time, you don't have to worry about finding unique itemids.

Example

```
* Use NewItemId to avoid counting as you add a series of items
* to a multi-column list.
* This is the same example as in the AddListItem entry,
* except that NewItemId is used instead of an explicit counter

* Fill a list box with the names and titles from Employee
* This code might be in the Init method of the list box
This.ColumnCount = 3
This.ColumnWidths = "75,60,150"

SELECT Employee
SCAN
   This.AddListItem(Last_Name)
   This.AddListItem(First_Name, This.NewItemId, 2)
   This.AddListItem(Title, This.NewItemId, 3)
ENDSCAN

* To see them in alpha order, add
This.Sorted=.T.
```

See Also AddItem, AddListItem, ComboBox, ListBox, ListCount, ListIndex, ListItemId

NewObject See AddObject.

NewObject() See CreateObject().

NoDataOnLoad

This cursor property helps forms involving views appear on the screen more quickly by deferring the actual population of the view until you ask for it.

Usage

```
crsCursor.NoDataOnLoad = lDontLoadIt
lDontLoadIt = crsCursor.NoDataOnLoad
```

NoDataOnLoad corresponds directly to the NODATA clause of USE. The point is to get the data source to build the structure of the view without bothering to send the data along.

When NoDataOnLoad is .T., FoxPro sends the view's query to the data source, but adds specific code to tell the data source not to return any records. With SQL Server, it uses the SET FMTONLY ON command; with other servers, it may resort to a trick such as "WHERE 1=0." Most remote data sources are smart and process a query like that one quickly. A few data sources are stupid and do a whole lot of work before they notice there are no records to return. You'll need to test against your planned server to find out how smart it is, in this case.

This property also affects local views. However, you might not see the difference unless the view is based on fairly large tables. With small tables, things happen so fast that this difference is negligible.

However, a good use of NoDataOnLoad is for parameterized views where the parameter may not be known until the remainder of the form is running, or even until the operator selects a value. A parameterized view with NoDataOnLoad set to .T. doesn't prompt for the parameter, but still returns the initial structure used to bind controls.

Example

```
* This property is pretty much always set in the property sheet
* but you can do it like this:
ThisForm.DataEnvironment.Cursor1.NoDataOnLoad = .T.
```

See Also Cursor, Use

NoDefault See Define Class.

Normalize()

We're hard-pressed to come up with an explanation of how this little gem got added to the language. Its purpose is to validate an expression as legitimate VFP syntax, and it does an okay "first pass" job of it, but testing TYPE() and EVAL() is just as accurate. Nonetheless, this is a cool function that makes it easier to compare user input to information you retrieve using FoxPro functions. NORMALIZE() takes a string and converts it to a standard format like that returned by many of FoxPro's built-in functions. FoxPro keywords get expanded to full length and converted to uppercase, and the "->" turns into a period. Plus, the syntax of the expression is checked.

Usage

```
cCleanExpr = NORMALIZE( cExpr )
```

Many FoxPro functions (like KEY(), FILTER() and so on) return expressions in a particular format. NORMALIZE() lets you convert other expressions to the same format, making comparisons much easier.

NORMALIZE() does some error checking of the expression. The key word here is "some." If the expression isn't syntactically valid, you get an error message. For example, if you pass "x and ", you get a "Missing Operand" error. (Make sure you've got an error handler in place to catch it.)

Don't expect NORMALIZE() to catch all the errors in input expressions, though. It only looks for the most basic syntax errors. The semantics of the expression aren't checked at all, so if you, say, compare a character field to a date field, NORMALIZE() won't yell about it. Even a flaw as simple as '"abc"=37' doesn't trigger an error message.

In addition, NORMALIZE() behaves like a number of FoxPro commands in ignoring anything following a valid expression. That is, NORMALIZE("x y") returns "X" rather than an error message. No doubt that's because, until VFP 5, you could compile and run:

```
IF X Y
```

without an error message. The "Y" was seen as a comment. We wish the developers had made NORMALIZE()'s test more stringent, though.

In spite of the error-checking weaknesses, we still think NORMALIZE() is pretty cool. Just don't count on it to find errors in input expressions. Even though it's cool, we can't see a lot of places we're going to actually use NORMALIZE()—let us know if you come up with some.

Example

```
? NORMALIZE('upper(Region)="PA" and allt(Last_Name)="Grant"')
* Above returns
* 'UPPER(REGION)="PA".AND.ALLTRIM(LAST_NAME)="Grant"'

? NORMALIZE('Employee->Birth_date > {01/01/65}')
* Above returns
* 'EMPLOYEE.BIRTH_DATE>{01/01/1965}'

* You can apply NORMALIZE() to Expression Builder results
GETEXPR "Enter Filter" TO cFilt
cFilt = NORMALIZE(cFilt)
IF cFilt = FILTER()
   * Do something
ELSE
   * Do something different
ENDIF
```

See Also Proper(), Upper()

Note, *, &&

All three of these symbols mark the beginning of a comment. NOTE and * can be used only at the beginning of a line (actually, as the first non-blank characters), while && can be used at any point in the line. Once && appears, the rest of the line is a comment.

Usage

```
NOTE cComment
* cComment
&& cComment
```

There's one big gotcha involving comments. Like other commands, comments can be continued with a semicolon. So, in the following example:

```
* This is a comment;
USE MyTable
```

the USE is never executed. This gotcha got even more gotcha-like with the addition of syntax coloring in VFP 5. Continuations of comments aren't colored like comments; they're colored like code. We sure wish Microsoft would bite the bullet and get this one right.

There's also a cool trick you can play on folks. Very few people are aware that NOTE starts a comment. Most people will be firmly convinced that the following will crash:

```
Note: This routine does absolutely nothing
FUNCTION DoNothing
RETURN
```

NOTE can be followed by non-alphabetic characters, like !@#$:, but not a letter, such as NOTES.

In certain places, you don't need a delimiter for a comment. As part of the Xbase legacy, comments can be added on lines containing some of the looping and branching commands, including ELSE, ENDIF, and ENDDO. You'll often see older Xbase code (or code written by those who've been using Xbase a long time) like this:

```
IF dDate>DATE()-30
   DO something
ENDIF dDate>DATE()-30
```

Be aware that you can't do this with ENDWITH—it doesn't like extraneous characters.

Until VFP 5, you could even put comments on the IF line, in that example. As soon as something was read that couldn't be parsed, VFP would assume it was a comment. This led to lots of code with subtle errors. To make matters worse, these items aren't colored as comments by Visual FoxPro, making them confusing to the developer reading the code.

Omitting the comment delimiters on lines like DO CASE and ENDDO and so forth doesn't seem to have the potential to do any harm down the road (unlike putting them on the DO WHILE or IF lines), but it just doesn't seem like such a big deal to us to type && before the comment, so we always do.

Example

```
NOTE This is a comment
* So is this
USE MyTable  && Open the table
```

NToM(), MToN()

NTOM() and its counterpart, MTON(), convert numeric values to currency and vice versa.

Usage

```
nNumeric = MTON( mCurrency )
mCurrency = NTOM( nNumeric )
```

Why the "M" in the function name, rather than a "C" for Currency? Well, "C" is already taken as the type for Character fields, so Microsoft chose "M" because it's one of the few letters that doesn't occur in the word "currency." No, actually, we suspect they chose it as shorthand for "Money." It's not intuitive, however, and violates the rules used to name other conversion functions, such as DTOT(), CTOD(), in that the type abbreviation for currency ("Y") isn't in the function name. Besides, we think that NTOY() and YTON() are cool names for functions.

These functions aren't always required. REPLACE converts one to the other automatically. A literal number can be expressed as currency by preceding it with the $ delimiter. However, if you are performing heavy mathematics like interest calculations, you'll want to convert your currency values to numeric if digits beyond four decimal places are important—they often are!

Example

```
REPLACE yMoneyField with NTOM(nNumerics)
nRatio = MTON(yDollars)/nNumeric
```

See Also CToD(), DToC(), Type()

NullDisplay, Set NullDisplay, Set("NullDisplay")

This property and command let you determine what the user sees when a displayed value is null. The function tells you the current setting.

Usage

```
oObject.NullDisplay = cNullString
cNullString = oObject.NullDisplay
SET NULLDISPLAY TO [ cNullString ]
cNullString = SET("NULLDISPLAY")
```

By default (in VFP 3, always), nulls are displayed as .NULL.—not very informative to the average user, is it? Starting in VFP 5, you can control what's shown. SET NULLDISPLAY is the global version—it affects all displays except those for which the NullDisplay property has been set. SET NULLDISPLAY affects all forms of output, not just controls used in forms. The NullDisplay property affects a single object.

Beware: Neither grids nor columns have their own NullDisplay property. Of course, the controls in the columns have NullDisplay, but when Sparse is .T. for a column, the control's NullDisplay is used when the cell has focus and the SET NULLDISPLAY setting applies when the cell doesn't have focus. This means that what you see for a given cell with a null value can change as you move in and out of the cell. Bottom line: When grids are involved, SET NULLDISPLAY and NullDisplay should be set the same (or leave NullDisplay empty to use the default value). In fact, that's usually the case.

Use something that means "I dunno" (like "???") for your null display string and your users will probably get it.

Example

```
SET NULLDISPLAY TO "???"
?.null.    && displays ???
```

See Also Set Null

NumberOfElements See FirstElement.

NumLock() See CapsLock().

NVL() See IsNull().

Object

This keyword lets you dig inside an OLE Container control to talk to the actual ActiveX control inside. Most of the time, though, you don't need it.

Usage

```
oleContainer.Object.Property = uValue
uValue = oleContainer.Object.Property
oObject = oleContainer.Object
oleContainer.Object.Method()
```

To put an ActiveX control (formerly known as an OLE control) on a form, you first drop an OLE Container control (one of the VFP base classes) onto the form, then choose the appropriate ActiveX control. If you prefer and you've registered the control with VFP, you can choose the control from the ActiveX controls toolbar, but it still brings an OLE Container with it. Both the OLE Container and the ActiveX control have properties and methods.

When you're writing code, you can almost always ignore the fact that there are two levels of objects here, and just refer to the ActiveX control's PEMs as if they belong to the OLE Container. However, in a few rare cases, this approach doesn't work—that's when you need the Object keyword. Stick it after the reference to the OLE Container to make sure you're addressing the ActiveX control, not its container.

The most obvious place that Object is needed is when you're actually trying to get an object reference to the ActiveX control. For example, the ActiveX TreeView control uses an ActiveX ImageList. You have to set the TreeView's ImageList property in code, giving it a reference to the ImageList you've already created. In this case, the Object keyword is required.

Example

```
* Say you've put an ImageList on the form and called its OLE Container
* oleImageList. To assign this ImageList to a Treeview in an
* OLE Container called oleTree, use:
ThisForm.oleTree.ImageList = ThisForm.oleImageList.Object
```

See Also OLEControl

Objects

This collection property gives you a handle to all the objects instantiated in an instance of VFP. It's convenient for writing generic tools and especially useful for Automation servers. It also lets you look inside most of the container classes.

Usage

```
oObject = oContainer.Objects[ nIndex | cName ]
```

For the application-level collection, you can access Objects either through the _VFP system variable that references the current VFP session or through the Application object. (Every control contains a property that points to the VFP instance that contains it.) Objects contains an element for each object that's been created in the VFP session in question. So what's an object in this context? Let's start with the easy stuff. Anything you create with CREATEOBJECT() or NEWOBJECT() counts as an object. So does any form you run with DO FORM. Then, it gets more interesting. Browses count because, behind the scenes, a browse is really a grid. Opening the Class Designer adds a formset object to the collection—we're not sure why it's a formset rather than an object of the class you're working on. Maybe it refers to the designer rather than the object being designed. Opening the Form Designer adds two objects to the collection: a data environment object and a formset object. Finally, opening the Report Designer or Label Designer adds only a data environment object to the collection, because there are no Report or Label objects.

You can manipulate at least some of the design-time objects that show up in the _VFP.Objects collection, but we've found that it's a dangerous game to play. We crashed or froze VFP more often in a couple of hours playing with the Objects collection than in weeks of doing other stuff.

All of VFP's container classes have their own collections to let you see what's inside. (For example, Form and Column both have Controls collections, while PageFrame has Pages.) However, as of VFP 5, those that have Controls also have a corresponding Objects collection; so do formsets—in that case, the Objects collection parallels the Forms collection. There actually is a rule here. Those objects that can contain objects of more than one type have an Objects collection in addition to their native collection. The objects that are limited to a single type of child (like OptionGroups, which are composed only of OptionButtons, or Grids, which are composed of Columns) have only their native collections.

Since we could already drill down into those objects with their native collections, why would we use Objects? Primarily for consistency. It keeps us from having to remember the name of the native collection (though that's not a big deal, since it's usually Controls). More importantly, though, Objects is a common collection in the Automation world. By including it, VFP makes things easier for programmers who want to talk to VFP but don't know it that well. Of course, the fact that some containers don't have Objects makes this a lot less useful than it could be.

The Objects collection has a Count property that tells you how many objects are in the collection at the moment. Objects also has an Item method that allows you to iterate through the collection by number or name. This is redundant in VFP, where we can just specify the index directly on the Objects collection, but we suspect it's a standard feature of COM objects like Objects.

Getting access to the Objects collection at runtime is flaky. As long as you're drilling down directly from the _VFP application object, all is well. But if you create an object reference to, say, a form, VFP can't see the Objects collection. That is,

```
? _VFP.Objects["frmMyForm"].Objects.Count
```

tells you the number of controls on the form. But:

```
oForm = _VFP.Objects["frmMyForm"]
? oForm.Objects.Count
```

gives an error message.

Example

```
* Find out what objects exist
FOR EACH oObj IN _VFP.Objects
   ? oObj.Name
ENDFOR
```

See Also Application, Buttons, ButtonCount, Columns, ColumnCount, Controls, ControlCount, Count, CreateObject(), Forms, FormCount, NewObject(), Pages, PageCount, _VFP

ObjNum(), ObjVar(), _CurObj

Here's another batch of stuff that was crucial in FoxPro 2.x and is obsolete in Visual FoxPro. In FoxPro 2.x, each item (@ ... GET or @ ... EDIT) on a screen was assigned a unique "object number." Within button groups, each button received its own number. These two functions and one system memory variable operated on those object numbers.

OBJNUM() takes a variable listed in @ ... GET or @ ... EDIT and returns its object number. OBJVAR() (added in version 2.6) takes an object number and returns the name of the variable associated with it. _CUROBJ controls the focus—it contains the number of the object with focus. Changing _CUROBJ changes the focus.

Visual FoxPro has alternative ways to accomplish these tasks, and the object-number system is only partly there. Visual FoxPro forms don't use it. Forms that include any @ ... GETs or @ ... EDITs do, but OBJNUM() and OBJVAR() don't recognize any Visual FoxPro controls on the form, only the GETs and EDITs.

The bottom line is: don't mix and match. Use Visual FoxPro's new form methodology. Refer to objects on the screen by their object hierarchy (Form.PageFrame.Page.Object) rather than a number, and move focus to the desired object by calling its SetFocus method. If you can't do this for some reason, then stick completely with the old @-based system.

See Also @ Commands, ActiveControl, SetFocus, This

ObjToClient()

The position properties of an object are always relative to the object's container. That is, when you put a text box on a page of a page frame, the text box's Left and Top tell you where it is on that page. Occasionally, what you really want to know is where the object is on the form. That's what OBJTOCLIENT() is all about. You hand it an object and it tells you something about that object with respect to the form that contains it.

Usage

```
nResult = OBJTOCLIENT( oObject, nMeasurement )
```

Parameter	Value	Meaning
oObject	Object	The object for which you want to know the position.
nMeasurement	1	Return the top of oObject relative to the form.
	2	Return the left edge of oObject relative to the form.
	3	Return the width of oObject in pixels.
	4	Return the height of oObject in pixels.

The only reason we can see for including height and width here is that OBJTOCLIENT() returns the information in pixels and your form might be using foxels. After all, height and width aren't relative to the container.

So why would you want to know this, anyway? Maybe you want to add something to the form at the same position as something else. Or maybe to use the MOUSE command to click on something. You also might use this function to figure out some of the metrics of built-in objects.

Example

```
? OBJTOCLIENT( ThisForm.PageFrame1.Page1.Checkbox1, 1 )
   * Returns distance in pixels from left edge of form to left
   * edge of checkbox
```

See Also Height, Left, Mouse, ScaleMode, Top, Width

ObjVar() See ObjNum().

Occurs()

It might be better if this function were called "occurrences" because that's what it counts. OCCURS() returns the number of times one string is contained in another. For example, if you want to know how many times "iss" occurs in "Mississippi", OCCURS() is just what you need.

Let's say (in spite of relational theory) you've stored a series of codes in a memo field, separated by spaces, and you want to know how many codes a given record has. Use OCCURS() to count the spaces, then add 1 to get the result.

Usage

```
nReturnValue = OCCURS( cSearchFor, cInString )
```

The return value is the number of times cSearchFor appears in cInString. OCCURS() is case-sensitive, so you may need to apply UPPER() to one or both strings.

Together, with AT() or RAT() and SUBSTR(), LEFT() or RIGHT(), OCCURS() is handy when you're parsing character strings. For instance, if you allow a user to enter a comma-delimited list of values to search for, and you need to break up that list into a series of individual items, you can do it like this:

Example

```
* cInput is the input string
* store the results in array aValues with one item per element
nItems=OCCURS(",",cInput)
DIMENSION aValues[nItems+1]

FOR nCnt=1 TO nItems
   * find the first comma
   nCommaPos=AT(",",cInput)

   * grab the string before it
   aValues[nCnt]=LEFT(cInput,nCommaPos-1)

   * shorten the string
```

```
      IF nCommaPos<>LEN(cInput)
         cInput=SUBSTR(cInput,nCommaPos+1)
      ELSE
         cInput=""
      ENDIF
   ENDFOR

   * now take last item
   * check just in case there was a trailing comma
   IF EMPTY(cInput)
      DIMENSION aValues[nItems]
   ELSE
      aValues[nItems+1]=cInput
   ENDIF
```

The example uses OCCURS() to figure out how many commas there are and then assumes that's one less than the number of items. It then loops through, lopping off one item at a time and shoving it into the array. At the end, it checks to make sure there really is an item after the last comma before grabbing what's left of the input.

See Also $, At(), InList(), Left(), RAt(), Right(), SubStr(), Upper()

OEMToANSI(), ANSIToOEM()

These functions convert text between the IBM character set and its closest equivalent in ANSI. Great way to forever and hopelessly mangle text. Use Code Pages instead. OEMTOANSI() was a great idea for U.S. translation of text from DOS to Windows before the code page support of FoxPro version 2.5a, but far better ways exist now. OEMTOANSI() converts characters 15, 20, 21 and those of values 128 and above from their values on the IBM-PC character set to their equivalents on the Windows platform, and ANSITOOEM() attempts to go the other way.

That's great, you say, but what about those characters, such as line and box drawing characters, that don't have a close equivalent? Mangled right into vertical bars and plus symbols, they are, matey. Since these characters lose their original value, you cannot run the opposite function back on them and hope to come out with the original string. Use the AS clauses of functions such as MODIFY FILE or the CPConvert() function for fields.

Usage

```
cRetVal = OEMTOANSI( cString )
cRetVal = ANSITOOEM( cString )
```

Example

```
@ $+1,0 say OEMtoANSI("Jos"+chr(130)) font "Times",9
@ $+1,0 say ANSItoOEM("José") font "FoxFont",9
```

These two examples show us the translation both ways. In the first example, we take "Jos" and CHR(130), which shows up as a black block in most Windows fonts, and translate it to the proper Windows characters to display "José." In the second example, we display this name in FoxFont, using the ANSITOOEM() function to map the accented letter to its correct equivalent in FoxFont.

In case you're curious, "OEM" stands for "Original Equipment Manufacturer" and was a code word for IBM's ASCII. This function doesn't translate all manufacturers' codes—just one. ASCII, if you're really dying to know, is the American Standard Code for Information Interchange—which it is not, being an IBM invention foisted on the world as a standard. Kind of like Windows. ANSI, on the other hand, stands for the American National Standards Institute; they really do make standards.

See Also Asc(), Chr(), CPConvert(), CPCurrent(), CPDBF(), Modify File, Modify Command

OldVal() See CurVal().

OLE drag and drop

When we first learned that VFP 6 would support OLE drag and drop, we thought, "That's nice. Now we'll be able to drag between ActiveX controls and native controls." Then we realized it applied to the development environment, too, and that we'd be able to drag from VFP to Word or drag files from Explorer into the Project Manager or the Command Window. Even better, but still nothing to write home about.

Then we started to actually play with the programmatic elements of OLE drag and drop. The farther we went, the closer our jaws got to the floor. This is cool stuff!

OLE drag and drop is, of course, not just a VFP thing. This is the model used throughout Windows to allow applications to share data through drag and drop. So what we use in VFP to move data from a calendar control to a text box is the same set of PEMs that the Windows programmers use to move files from one directory to another, or that Word and Excel use to drag data from one to the other.

The design of OLE drag and drop is truly elegant. It involves three objects, each with a job to do, and each with the appropriate tools to do it.

The first two objects are fairly obvious. First, there's the *drag source*, the control or application from which the data is being dragged. Second, there's the *drop target*, the control or application onto which the data might be dropped. So far, so good, but what's the third? The third is a COM object called the *data object*. It contains the data from the drag source in various formats, and makes that data available to the drop target upon request.

In VFP's native drag and drop, responsibilities are partitioned between the drag source and the drop target. The drag source starts things off and specifies the icon to be used; the drop target responds to the drag in a couple of events. But that's all there is.

OLE drag and drop is much more complex, but that complexity gives you much more control. With OLE drag and drop, it's possible that either the drag source or the drop target belongs to another application and thus isn't accessible to you programmatically. For example, if you drag files into VFP from Explorer, VFP owns only the drop target, not the drag source.

To deal with this, both the drag source and the drop target have a chance to respond every step of the way. For example, whenever the drop target's OLEDragOver event fires, indicating that data is passing over the object, it also fires the drag source's OLEGiveFeedback event, so the drag source can decide whether or not it likes the drop target and behave accordingly. Even if the drop target is outside VFP, a VFP drag source's OLEGiveFeedback event fires. Similarly, when the drag source comes from outside VFP, a VFP drop target's events fire as expected.

In addition to giving both participants a chance to react, the control over OLE drag and drop is finer than for native drag and drop. The drag source and drop target both can indicate not just whether a drop is possible, but whether a drop of this source onto this target produces a copy or a move. The drop target can also respond differently based on the mouse buttons that are used and whether any of the keyboard modifiers (Ctrl, Alt, Shift) are down.

As if all that weren't enough, OLE drag and drop also provides fine control over the actual data that is dropped. The data object is automatically filled with appropriate data (based on the drag source and any highlighting), but its methods let you inquire about what's there and, if you want, change it to meet your needs.

Data in the data object is stored in one or more of a set of formats. There are a number of built-in formats, but you can define your own as well, allowing you to store whatever data you want and process it as you desire when a drop occurs. With the built-in formats, you can replace the default data with your own data as well.

Debugging OLE drag and drop sequences is incredibly difficult. It's almost impossible to get to the debugger when an error occurs, and you can't set breakpoints successfully or use SUSPEND in the OLE drag and drop events. (If you try, you get the error "CANCEL or SUSPEND is not allowed" and, if that's not bad enough, the error dialog has Cancel, Suspend, Ignore and Help buttons.) In addition, you can put the data object in the Watch window, but you can't actually find out anything about it.

We actually sort of understand what the problem is here. As soon as you're in the debugger, your drag and drop operation ends, so you're not in the relevant method anymore and the data object no longer exists. Rather than deal with that issue, you simply can't stop there.

We've had some success using DEBUGOUT statements and the Event Tracker from OLE drag and drop methods to see what's going on, but it's certainly much harder than normal debugging.

Despite the debugging complications, the interactions among the three participants make it possible to do some very sophisticated manipulation using OLE drag and drop, certainly well beyond anything you could accomplish with VFP's native drag and drop. The beauty of the object model involved leads us to truly admire the folks who designed it.

See Also ClearData, DataObject, GetData, GetFormat, OLECompleteDrag, OLEDrag, OLEDragDrop, OLEDragMode, OLEDragOver, OLEDragPicture, OLEDropEffects, OLEDropHasData, OLEDropMode, OLEDropTextInsertion, OLEGiveFeedback, OLESetData, OLEStartDrag, SetData, SetFormat

OLEBoundControl, OLEControl

These controls are containers for all sorts of interesting objects—sounds, pictures, graphs, cartoons, video clips—whatever you can find an OLE Server to work with. They are very similar, with the major difference that the OLEBoundControl stores its data in a Visual FoxPro general field.

Property	Value	Purpose
AutoActivate	Numeric	Determines how the object can be activated: It can be set so the object can only be activated programmatically, or each time the object receives the focus. By default, the object is activated only if it's double-clicked.
AutoSize	Logical	Determines whether the container—the VFP portion of the control—resizes to fit the area the OLE Control wants to take up. By default, AutoSize is .F. and the developer specifies the size of the control on the form.
ControlSource (Bound control only)	Character	The field with which the control is associated. Must be a general field.
DocumentFile	Character	Contains the origin of the linked data. Blank if the data is embedded. Read-only.
HostName	Character	The window title to use when an object is edited in its own window. A character string you can supply with your own application's name rather than the feeble "Object from FoxPro 283839" message we had in 2.x.
Object	Object	An object reference to the contained object itself. Allows the properties and methods of the OLE Server to be accessed and manipulated.

Property	Value	Purpose
OLEClass	Character	The server the data belongs to. Read-only at runtime and design time, this can be specified only when the class is created in code or by using the APPEND GENERAL command on the underlying field.
OLETypeAllowed	Numeric (0,1, and 2)	This property tells whether there is any data associated with the OLE Control, and whether the associated object is an OCX, embedded data, or linked data.
Sizable	Logical	Determines whether the OLE object can be resized within the control. If the control's AutoSize is set to .T., the entire container and contents can be made a different size. If only this property is true, the view of the OLE object is magnified or shrunk within a fixed frame.
Event	**Purpose**	
DoVerb	Activates the object in a number of different ways.	

The two types of OLE controls are windows into other applications. We can use their properties to control the presentation and capabilities of that other application. The primary difference between the two is that the OLEBoundControl changes to reflect record-specific data, since the data is associated with a FoxPro field.

Example

```
* Create a general field record for a bound control
CREATE CURSOR temp (genlfield G)
APPEND BLANK
* Add a picture - the "class" to use depends on your
* Windows installation - this is for Win95
APPEND GENERAL genlfield ;
  FROM c:\windows\winlogo.bmp ;
  CLASS "Paint.Picture"
* Create a form with a bound control
oForm=CREATEOBJECT("form")
oForm.AddObject("olbPic","OLEBoundControl")
* Size the control to decent size
oForm.olbPic.Width = .9 * oForm.Width
oForm.olbPic.Height = .9 * oForm.Height
* Point it to the data source and display the form
oForm.olbPic.ControlSource = "Temp.GenlField"
oForm.olbPic.Visible = .t.
oForm.show()

* Create an unbound control, and manipulate it via
* OLE Automation
oForm = CREATEOBJECT("DemoForm")
oForm.AddObject("oleCalendar","oleCalendar")
oForm.oleCalendar.Resize()  && fill the form
oForm.oleCalendar.Visible = .T.  && display it
WITH oForm.oleCalendar.Object
   .ShowTitle = -1
   .TitleFontColor = RGB(128,0,128)
   .TitleFont.Name = "Times New Roman"
   .TitleFont.Size = 14
   .TitleFont.Italic = .T.
ENDWITH
oForm.Show()
READ EVENTS  && Wait here until form destroyed.

DEFINE CLASS DemoForm AS Form
```

```
  PROCEDURE DESTROY
    CLEAR EVENTS
  ENDPROC
ENDDEFINE

DEFINE CLASS oleCalendar AS OLEControl
  OLEClass = "MsCal.Calendar"
  PROCEDURE ReSize
    This.Width = ThisForm.Width * 0.9
    This.Height = ThisForm.Height * .9
  ENDPROC
ENDDEFINE
```

See Also Append General, AutoActivate, ControlSource, DocumentFile, DoVerb, HostName, Modify General, OLEClass, OLETypeAllowed

OLEClass

Specifies the name of the server that created and is responsible for the current OLE bound or unbound control.

Usage

```
cName = oControl.OLEClass
```

OLEClass contains the name of the server through which the OLEControl's data was created, and which will be called up again if the object needs to be redisplayed, edited or played. This name should exactly match a key entry in the Registry.

OLEClass is read-only once the object has been created. It would be nice to just move items around from server to server, but because each is responsible for its own methods of data storage, this isn't possible with current OLE technology. We think if a BMP is a BMP, just because it has been embedded or linked into a control by one app, we shouldn't be prevented from getting at it with any other BMP-compatible program. Maybe we'll see some improvement in OLE 3.0.

For OLEControls, OLEClass is specified during the creation process using the DEFINE CLASS command, or with the visual tools by selecting the data file to create or add to the control when placing it on a form. For OLEBoundControls, OLEClass is determined by the field to which it's bound. The field's OLE class, in turn, is set when it's populated with data using the APPEND GENERAL command

Example

```
DEFINE CLASS myPaint AS OLEControl
  OLEClass = "Paint.Picture"
ENDDEFINE

? oControl.OLEClass

APPEND GENERAL gData FROM "C:\WINDOWS\CANYON.MID"
* an OLEBoundControl associated with this field yields
? olbGData.OLEClass  && displays "midfile"
```

See Also Append General, Registration Database, OLEBoundControl, OLEControl

OLECompleteDrag See OLEDrag.

OLEControl See OLEBoundControl.

OLEDrag, OLEStartDrag, OLECompleteDrag

These methods all belong to the drag source of an OLE drag and drop. OLEDrag starts a drag and drop, while OLEStartDrag and OLECompleteDrag fire at the indicated times to let you take action.

Usage

```
PROCEDURE OLEDrag
LPARAMETERS lDetectDrag
```

```
PROCEDURE OLEStartDrag
LPARAMETERS oDataObject, nEffect

PROCEDURE OLECompleteDrag
LPARAMETERS nEffect
```

Parameter	Value	Meaning
lDetectDrag	.F.	Begin dragging as soon as OLEDrag is called. This choice makes it impossible to highlight some text in a control and drag only the highlighted text, but might be appropriate for non-textual controls.
	.T.	The drag doesn't begin until either the mouse moves some distance or some time has passed after the OLEDrag call. We went hunting to figure out how to change the distance or the time, but couldn't find anything. (We expected they'd be somewhere in the Control Panel, but we couldn't turn them up.) A look in the Registry didn't turn up anything promising either, so perhaps these settings really are fixed.
oDataObject	Object	An object reference to the data being dragged and to information about the data.
nEffect (Applicable values are added together)	0	For OLEStartDrag, the drag source doesn't allow any kind of dragging. For OLECompleteDrag, no drop was performed.
	1	For OLEStartDrag, the drag source allows its data to be copied. For OLECompleteDrag, data was copied to the drop target.
	2	For OLEStartDrag, the drag source allows its data to be moved. For OLECompleteDrag, data was moved to the drop target.
	4	For OLEStartDrag, the drag source allows its data to be linked. For OLECompleteDrag, data was linked to the drop target.

OLE drag and drop can be started either automatically by setting the drag source's OLEDragMode property to 1-Automatic or manually by calling the drag source's OLEDrag method. (We guess, technically, it's not the drag source until you do so, of course.) No matter which way you do it, the OLEStartDrag method fires, giving you a chance to take any action you'd like. OLECompleteDrag fires when the drag ends, whether or not it results in a drop.

Ever tried to highlight some text and had Windows start dragging instead? Then the lDetectDrag (which we'd rather call lWaitForDrag) parameter of OLEDrag is for you. When it's .F., the drag begins as soon as OLEDrag is called. When lDetectDrag is .T., VFP gets smart and waits to see whether you keep the mouse down a bit or start moving it—if so, dragging starts. Best of all, .T. is the default value, so that's what you get when you set OLEDragMode to 1-Automatic, too.

As far as we can tell, calling OLEDrag makes sense only from the MouseDown event. Using it in MouseMove (which is the solution to the dragging-too-soon problem for VFP's native drag and drop) gives you weird cursor and highlight behavior, but doesn't start dragging. A call to OLEDrag from any other method seems to be totally ignored.

Calling OLEDrag doesn't work in ActiveX controls, at least in any of the ones we tried. What makes this worse is that some of them don't have an OLEDragMode property or the equivalent, which means there's no way to drag out of them.

Dragging data from a spinner can be tricky. It's really hard to highlight the data you mean to highlight, so it can appear that you're not getting the results you wanted. We think this is related to a bug involving the Alignment property for spinners. You can read about that one under Alignment.

Like a number of the OLE drag and drop events, OLEStartDrag lets you change the nEffect parameter to change what follows. Setting nEffect to 0 prevents the drag. (Interestingly, issuing a NODEFAULT in OLEStartDrag doesn't prevent the drag.) Similarly, setting nEffect to 2 allows the data to be moved but not copied. While the whole arrangement of changing parameters that appear to be passed by value in order to change the operation strikes us as strange, the results are pretty cool.

In addition to indicating the operations available, you can do something far more complex in OLEStartDrag. The data that's dragged around and eventually dropped can come in various formats. Simple formats include text in various representations (ASCII, Unicode, etc.) and a list of files (for example, when you drag from Explorer). Some data is available in multiple formats, and you can request the appropriate format for the drop target in OLEDragDrop. (See DataObject and GetFormat for more on the built-in formats.)

However, you can also define your own formats, and OLEStartDrop is the place to do it. You call the data object's SetFormat method, giving it the name of your custom format. Then, call the data object's SetData method to tell it what to return when that format is requested. The examples include setting a custom format.

As for OLECompleteDrag, we haven't found a lot of use for it yet. Basically, it lets you know what really happened so you can act accordingly. We're not sure exactly what "act accordingly" means in this case, though.

Example

```
* Turn on dragging with instant gratification. You might do this
* for an object where highlighting is irrelevant.
This.OLEDrag(.f.)

* Create a custom data format for OLE drag and drop.
* This format is for dragging an Image object. When dropped,
* it supplies the name of the picture it contains.
* This code goes in the Image control's OLEStartDrag event:
oDataObject.SetFormat("Picture")
oDataObject.SetData(This.Picture,"Picture")

* To retrieve the picture's name, put code like this in the
* OLEDragDrop event of the target. In this case, it's a form
* and the form's wallpaper is set to the specified picture.
IF oDataObject.GetFormat("Picture")
   This.Picture = oDataObject.GetData("Picture")
ENDIF
```

See Also DataObject, GetData, GetFormat, OLE drag and drop, OLEDragMode, OLEDragDrop, SetData, SetFormat

OLEDragDrop See OLEDragOver.

OLEDragMode, OLEDropMode

These two properties determine whether, and in what way, a control plays OLE drag and drop.

Usage

```
nODragMode = oObject.OLEDragMode
oObject.OLEDragMode = nODragMode
```

```
nODropMode = oObject.OLEDropMode
oObject.OLEDropMode = nODropMode
```

Parameter	Value	Meaning
nODragMode	0	Default. Don't allow data from this object to be dragged.
	1	Allow data from this object to be dragged.
nODropMode	0	Default. Don't allow data to be dropped on this object.
	1	Allow data to be dropped on this object.
	2	If data is dropped on this object, pass it to the object's container.

OLEDragMode is easy. You either turn it on or off. If it's on (1), you can drag from that object. If it's off (0), you can't. That's all. Well, almost all. If OLEDragMode is off, you can still start dragging an object manually by putting a call to OLEDrag in an appropriate event, usually MouseDown or MouseMove.

OLEDropMode is a little more complex. Having it off (0) is simple. You can't drop on the object and, if you don't make something different happen, you see the "No drop" graphic over that object. On (1) isn't too complicated, either. You can drop on the object and various events fire when you do.

The interesting one is "Pass to Container" (2). In this case, when you drop on an object, rather than respond to it itself, if the object's container has OLEDropMode set to either 1 or 2, the container receives the drop and can respond accordingly. What makes this interesting is that there's a good chance that the container doesn't automatically accept the kind of data you're dropping, so you have to go in and mess with data formats and the like before the container will accept the drop. But it's very cool when you get it working. You can both drag and drop from the same object by setting both of these properties to non-zero values.

An object can use either VFP's native drag or OLE drag, but not both. If you set DragMode to 1 (Automatic), the value of OLEDragMode is ignored, and the object uses native dragging. However, an object can accept both native drops and OLE drops. Microsoft advises not mixing the two modes in one application, and we tend to agree that it could get confusing for the operator.

Example

```
* You'll usually set these properties at design time.
* But you might let a user decide whether to have drag
* and drop enabled, based on an application setting.
* So you might have code in the object's Init.
This.OLEDragMode = oApp.lDragAndDrop
```

See Also DragDrop, DragMode, GetData, GetFormat, OLE drag and drop, OLEDrag, OLEDragDrop, OLEDropEffects, OLEDropHasData

OLEDragOver, OLEDragDrop

As their names suggest, these two events fire when data is dragged over an object or dropped onto an object, using OLE drag and drop. They give you a chance to respond programmatically to the drag or the drop.

Usage

```
PROCEDURE oObject.OLEDragOver
LPARAMETERS oDataObject, nEffect, nButton,
            nShift, nXCoord, nYCoord, nState

PROCEDURE oObject.OLEDragDrop
LPARAMETERS oDataObject, nEffect, nButton,
            nShift, nXCoord, nYCoord
```

Parameter	Value	Meaning
oDataObject	Object	A reference to a DataObject containing the data being dragged and information about it.
nEffect (all applicable values are added together)	0	This target won't accept this drop.
	1	The drop results in a copy.
	2	The drop results in a move.
	4	The drop copies the dropped data into the target and creates a link between the original source and the target. Because of VFP's caching of resources, this isn't useful for drop targets in VFP.
nButton (all applicable values are added together)	1	The left button was used for the drag.
	2	The right button was used for the drag.
	4	The middle button was used for the drag.
nShift (all applicable values are added together)	1	The Shift key was held down.
	2	The Ctrl key was held down.
	4	The Alt key was held down.
nXCoord, nYCoord	Numeric	The mouse position in pixels, relative to the form, when the event fired.
nState	0	The mouse is entering the object.
	1	The mouse is leaving the object.
	2	The mouse is inside the object.

First, we think some of the parameter names are less than illuminating. We'd use nTargetReaction rather than nEffect, nModifierKeys rather than nShift, and nWhereAreWe instead of nState. However, since the parameter declarations are automatically placed in the methods, we show the official names in the table.

These events belong to the drop target in OLE drag and drop. That is, they fire for the object under the mouse to indicate that the user is either dragging something over the object (OLEDragOver) or attempting to drop something into the object (OLEDragDrop). The drag source has events that fire right after these: OLEGiveFeedback fires after OLEDragOver, while OLECompleteDrag fires after OLEDragDrop. However, if either the source or the target is not a VFP object, you don't have access to one set or the other of these methods.

These events fire only for objects whose OLEDropMode is set to 1-Enabled. If OLEDropMode is set to 2-Pass to Container, the container's OLEDragOver and OLEDragDrop events fire instead.

Several of the parameters are bit-math things. The value you see is the sum of all the choices that apply. So, for example, if the user holds down Shift and Alt, nModifierKeys contains 5.

Both nButton and nShift are unreliable when nState is 1; that is, when the mouse is leaving the object. Sometimes they contain the right value, but often they contain 0.

Some ActiveX controls don't fire these events, while others do. We can't blame this on the VFP team, of course, since they didn't write these controls. Bottom line here is that you need to test whether the control you're using pays attention. The simplest way to do so is to put WAIT WINDOW PROGRAM() NOWAIT in each of the relevant events on a test form and run it. We'd rather recommend DEBUGOUT, but we haven't found it to be reliable even in the controls that do fire these events. Sometimes we see a WAIT WINDOW when a DEBUGOUT in the same method produces no results. Frankly, we think the problem is with the controls, not with VFP, because some controls handle DEBUGOUT just fine.

So, what is it you use these events for? To take action based on the user's movements. You can inquire as to whether the data being dragged is available in a format this object can accept and set the target's properties accordingly. You can also reject a drop if you don't like its looks.

For OLEDragDrop, there are various default behaviors based on the objects involved and the buttons pressed. For example, dragging text from a text box to an edit box moves the highlighted text normally, but copies it if Ctrl is pressed.

You can change the results by writing appropriate code involving the DataObject's GetFormat and GetData methods, as well as, perhaps, checking the nButton and nShift values. However, the default behavior still occurs at the end of the method unless you also include NODEFAULT. In addition, the drag source's OLECompleteDrag is called at the end of OLEDragDrop. It receives as parameters the current value of nEffect, so if you do something different from what was indicated by the value received, you should give nEffect a new, appropriate value, so OLECompleteDrag can respond correctly.

Example

```
* You might put this code in a form's DragOver event
* to allow it to accept data passed from one of its controls
IF oDataObject.GetFormat(1)
   This.OleDropHasData = 1
   This.OLEDropEffects = 1
ENDIF

* Suppose I want a drop into an editbox to copy rather than
* move, despite the default. This code could go in OLEDragDrop
nEffect = 1  && reset nEffect so OLECompleteDrag knows the score
This.Value = oDataObject.GetData(1) && copy the data
NODEFAULT    && prevent the default behavior
```

See Also DataObject, GetData, GetFormat, NoDefault, OLE drag and drop, OLECompleteDrag, OLEDrag, OLEDropEffects, OLEDropHasData, OLEDropMode, OLEGiveFeedback, OLEStartDrag

OLEDragPicture, OLEGiveFeedback

This property and method give you control over what the user sees during OLE drag and drop. OLEDragPicture controls the image of what's being dragged. OLEGiveFeedback is a method that lets you change the cursor used for the drag, as well as take other actions if you want.

Usage

```
oObject.OLEDragPicture = cPictureFile
cPictureFile = oObject.OLEDragPicture
PROCEDURE oObject.OLEGiveFeedback
LPARAMETERS nEffect, eMouseCursor
```

Parameter	Value	Meaning
cPictureFile	Filename	The name of the file containing the graphic to show being dragged.
nEffect	Numeric	The reaction of the object currently under the mouse to OLE drag and drop. Indicates whether a drop is welcome and, if it is, what the result is.
eMouseCursor	0	Use the cursor specified by the drop target for nEffect. We have no control over what that cursor is, but most objects seem to make good choices.
	1-16	Specifies which of the built-in cursor graphics is currently being used or should be used.
	Numeric other than 0-16	Only the regular mouse pointer appears.
	Filename	The name of a graphic file containing the mouse pointer currently in use or the one that should be used.

It's always nice to let users know what's going on. With OLE drag and drop, there are two pieces of information you can provide.

The first is a picture of what's being dragged. For example, in Windows Explorer, if you drag a single file, you see its name and icon going with you; when you drag a group of files, you get an outline of a bunch of boxes that sort of look like filenames and icons. In VFP, OLEDragPicture provides this information. It belongs to the drag source (the object you're dragging from). Most often, we think, you'll set this one in the Property Sheet and leave it alone. In some cases, though, you might want to set it in OLEStartDrag based on what's actually highlighted and being dragged.

You can change OLEDragPicture on the fly, even while a drag is occurring, but the actual picture doesn't change until the current drag ends and you start another.

The second piece of information users want is what will happen if you drop at the current position. Rather than having a property that controls this, there's a method that fires and lets you specify what the user should see. OLEGiveFeedback fires each time you drag over something. (Free translation: this one fires a lot.) It tells you how the something will handle a drop if you release the mouse button, and what mouse cursor is currently in use. Unlike most events in VFP, though, the second parameter, eMouseCursor, is passed by reference, so you can change the cursor. You can set eMouseCursor to the name of a graphic cursor file (CUR or ANI). You can't use ICO files, however.

OLEGiveFeedback is a *drag source* event, so it fires even when you're dragging over objects outside VFP. That's right, you can drag data from VFP into other apps and still control the mouse cursor. Giving control to the drag source is generally an improvement over VFP's native drag and drop, where the target can tell the source what DragIcon to use, but the source can't do anything about it.

While the nEffect parameter lets us know what action a drop will bring, it doesn't tell us what object we're over. Seems to us that passing a reference to the potential drop target would be handy. The new AMouseObj() function to the rescue. You can find out not only the drop target itself, but its container as well.

Example

```
* Specify a cursor based on the potential drop action
* Most drop targets will provide the usual cursors anyway,
* so we'll do strange things here.
```

```
LPARAMETERS nEffect, eMouseCursor

DO CASE
CASE nEffect = 0 && Can't drop here
   eMouseCursor = 11  && Hourglass - that'll confuse 'em
CASE nEffect = 1 && Copy
   eMouseCursor = 5 && Sizer
OTHERWISE
   eMouseCursor = 3 && I-Beam, why not?
ENDCASE
```

See Also OLE drag and drop, OLEDragOver, OLEDropEffects

OLEDropHasData, OLEDropEffects

These properties give the drop target a chance to decide how to handle dropped data. OLEDropHasData indicates whether the drop target is compatible with the data being dragged. OLEDropEffects determines the actions the drop target supports.

Usage

```
oObject.OLEDropHasData = nIsItAcceptable
nIsItAcceptable = oObject.OLEDropHasData
oObject.OLEDropEffects = nActionsAccepted
nActionsAccepted = oObject.OLEDropEffects
```

Parameter	Value	Meaning
nIsItAcceptable	-1	Let VFP figure out whether this drop target can accept any of the data that's being dragged. This is the default.
	0	The drop target can't accept any of the data that's being dragged.
	1	The drop target can accept some form of the data being dragged.
nActionsAccepted (add all desired values together)	0	The drop target doesn't accept any drops.
	1	Data can be copied to this target.
	2	Data can be moved to this target.
	4	A link can be created between this object and source data. This option isn't relevant for native VFP objects because they don't have the capability of handling linked data.

These properties are both involved in deciding what a drop target does with a particular drop. OLEDropEffects indicates what kinds of drops are accepted. Like many of the OLE drag and drop properties, you add together all the values that apply. (Since 0 is always part of the result, doesn't that mean that no drops are ever accepted?)

OLEDropHasData goes farther. It says whether the particular data being dragged at this moment can be dropped on this target. As George Carlin (and we, elsewhere in this book) said, "Why are there three?" But this one makes sense (except for the actual values used). You can say "No, there's no relevant data," "Yes, there is useful data here" or "I dunno. Why don't you figure it out for yourself?"

OLEDropHasData is an unusual property—it can be changed only at runtime, not at design time. That's because you set it for a particular drag operation.

At first glance, it might be hard to see why you'd ever want to set OLEDropHasData to anything but -1. In fact, it might be hard even at second glance. After all, can't VFP just figure out whether there's relevant data and behave accordingly? But, in fact, OLEDropHasData is one of a set of properties and methods that make OLE drag and drop very cool. First, it lets you drop data onto things that wouldn't normally accept the drop. For example, you might allow a text string to be dropped on a form and set the form's caption to that string. (No, we don't know *why* you'd ever do this, but we did it, as we were working our way through understanding the subject.) To do that, you have to tell the form that, despite its feelings to the contrary, it can accept drops of textual data. (Then, in the form's OLEDragDrop method, you write some code that sets the Caption to the dropped string.)

Like most of the OLE drag and drop properties, these two have their constants included in FoxPro.H. Use the constants for much more readable code.

In addition, you can create your own data formats. In that case, there's no way that VFP can figure out whether a particular object can accept that data. You set OLEDropHasData to 1 if this target accepts your custom format. There's an example of this in the OLEDrag section.

Example

```
* Say, text dragged onto a form should be used
* to change the form's Caption. In the form's OLEDragOver
* method, put this code:
#INCLUDE FOXPRO.H
IF oDataObject.GetFormat(1)
   This.OLEDropHasData = 1
   * allow either move or copy
   This.OLEDropEffects = DROPEFFECT_COPY + DROPEFFECT_MOVE
ENDIF
```

See Also DataObject, GetFormat, OLE drag and drop, OLEDrag, OLEDragOver, OLEDragDrop

OLEDropMode See OLEDragMode.

OLEDropTextInsertion

This property determines whether an object lets you insert text into the middle of words with OLE drag and drop, or only at the ends of words.

Usage

```
oObject.OLEDropTextInsertion = nInsertionType
nInsertionType = oObject.OLEDropTextInsertion
```

Parameter	Value	Meaning
nInsertionType	0	This object lets you put dragged text anywhere.
	1	This object always puts dragged text at the beginning of a word.

Of all the OLE drag and drop properties, this might be the easiest to understand. It determines, for a drop target, whether text dropped on that target gets inserted exactly where the pointer is positioned or only at the beginning of a word. When you set the property to 1, no matter where the pointer is placed, the dragged text goes at the beginning of that word. When it's 0 (the default), text goes right where you put it. We can see the need for each choice for different situations, and, in fact, could even see this one as user-configurable.

The name of this property makes sense to us; so does its behavior. But somehow, we feel a slight mismatch between those two and the values it accepts. We're not sure exactly what we would use if it were up to us, though; .T. and .F. don't cut it, either. We do find the settings kind of backward. 0 feels like "off" to us, but putting dragged text anywhere seems like "on." We guess we'll get used to it eventually.

Example

```
* Set this property based on the user's choice
IF lPutTextAnywhere
   This.OLEDropTextInsertion = 0
ELSE
   This.OLEDropTextInsertion = 1
ENDIF
```

See Also OLE drag and drop

OLEGiveFeedback See OLEDragPicture.

OLELcID See DefOLELcID.

OLERequestPendingTimeout, OLEServerBusyRaiseError, OLEServerBusyTimeout

Microsoft certainly wasn't miserly with the letters when naming these jawbreakers! They all have to do with how you manage delays and timeouts within your OLE Server application.

Usage

```
nPendingTimeout = oApp.OLERequestPendingTimeout
oApp.OLERequestPendingTimeout = nPendingTimeout
nBusyTimeout = oApp.OLEServerBusyTimeout
oApp.OLEServerBusyTimeout = nBusyTimeout
lRaiseError = oApp.OLEServerBusyRaiseError
oApp.OLEServerBusyRaiseError = lRaiseError
```

Parameter	Value	Meaning
nPendingTimeout	Positive number	The amount of time in milliseconds to wait before displaying a message that the application is busy.
	Zero or negative	No message is displayed.
nBusyTimeout	Numeric	The amount of time to wait (in milliseconds) before raising an error if OLEServerBusyRaiseError is .T.
	Zero or negative	No error is raised.
lRaiseError	.T.	Create an error if an OLE request waits longer than the OLEServerBusyTimeout specified delay.
	.F.	Don't error if the request is not answered in time. Without an error message, your application appears to hang.

We find these settings a little confusing because their names don't make clear the differences between them. The Request setting dictates the response to a *user* request, like clicking on a button or form. The ServerBusy settings affect how VFP reacts if *program code* can't continue because a server is busy. Note, also, that both situations apply only if VFP is trying to work with a COM server in a separate process space—an EXE, not a DLL—and that you get no timeout errors if VFP is working with an in-process, DLL COM server.

OLERequestPendingTimeout is the amount of time delay after a mouse click or key is pressed before displaying "The action cannot be completed because the other program is busy. Choose 'Switch To' to activate the busy program and correct the problem." The default is 5 seconds. We think that failing to respond to a user request is a cardinal sin among UI no-no's, and we prefer to crank this down to 500 milliseconds or so.

OLEServerBusyTimeout and OLEServerBusyRaiseError work together to determine the behavior an application should take if a request to an OLE server is rejected because the server is busy. After the amount of time specified by the Timeout, VFP will raise an error if ...RaiseError is set to true, or not. This error is not in the form of a VFP error as we had hoped, nor an OLE error, but rather the same old "This action cannot be completed..." dialog. We think that's lame. If we need to create a COM server and expect sub-five-second response time, we want the process to fail and let us know we can't get it. That would give VFP control and developers the chance to do something about it.

Example

```
_VFP.OLERequestPendingTimeout = 500   && half a second
_VFP.OLEServerBusyTimeout = 5000      && five seconds
_VFP.OLEServerBusyRaiseError = .T.    && let operator know
```

OLESetData

This event is part of the set of PEMs that gives you total control over what actually gets dropped during OLE drag and drop. It lets you determine the data dropped, at the very last minute, just as it's needed.

Usage

```
PROCEDURE oObject.OLESetData
LPARAMETERS oDataObject, uFormat
```

Parameter	Value	Meaning
oDataObject	Object	An object reference to the data being dragged and information about it.
uFormat	Numeric or Character	The data format requested by the drop target.

OLESetData belongs to the drag source. When a drag operation ends with a drop, VFP looks for data that's compatible with the target and either copies or moves it to the target.

OLESetData gives you a chance to change that data. It fires after any custom code in OLEDragDrop, but before the drop actually takes place. It also fires if the data object's GetData method is called. (If you do that, be sure to add a NODEFAULT in OLEDragDrop or you end up with double your dropped data.)

Help says that OLESetData fires only when there's no data in the appropriate format. Not so. It fires whenever it contains code. We're hoping this one is a documentation bug, not a product bug, because we really like the idea of deciding what to drop at the very last minute.

Why would you want to replace the data to drop at the end? Good question. Help suggests that the main reason is to put the data into the DataObject only when it's needed. The implication is that, when you're dealing with a lot of data, carrying it around could eat resources.

We can think of times when we want to base the final decision of what to drop on other conditions at the time. You might want to populate the drop target with data fresh from the database by issuing a select when it's performed. It's possible the drop might even be the event that creates the data, so perhaps you'll populate the data object with the primary key. It seems to us that the main condition to check this way is the identity of the drop target. You might want to return different data depending on where it's going. (For drop targets in VFP, you can use AMouseObj() to find the drop target because, by definition, the mouse must be over the drop target at the time.)

The uFormat parameter indicates which format the target is looking for, so you can take different actions depending on what the target wants.

You might be puzzled by the choice of data types for uFormat. The older formats still retain the numeric values used for clipboard and DDE work, while some of the newer formats tend to have more descriptive text names. Check FoxPro.H for a list of the more common ones. Custom formats can also be assigned either a number or a string. (Because character strings tend to convey information while numbers generally don't, we recommend using them.)

We don't see ourselves using this event a lot, but we have a feeling that, on those rare occasions where we do need it, it will be invaluable.

Example

```
* The example for OLEStartDrag shows how to create
* a custom format and add to it. In that example,
* the data is added in OLEStartDrag. But, that line
* could instead occur in OLESetData:
oDataObject.SetData(This.Picture,"Picture")
```

See Also DataObject, GetData, GetFormat, OLE drag and drop, OLEDragDrop, SetData

OLEStartDrag See OLEDrag.

OLETypeAllowed

This property indicates whether an OLE control's data is embedded or linked.

Usage `nRetVal = oleObject.OLETypeAllowed`

Property	Value	Purpose
nRetVal	1	Data is embedded.
	0	Data is linked.
	-1	This is an OLEBoundControl and the bound General field is empty.
	-2	This is an OLE control (OCX).

OLETypeAllowed can be set for an OLEControl using the DEFINE CLASS command, but it is read-only in the visual design tools. It is always read-only at runtime. For an OLEBoundControl, this value changes as the APPEND GENERAL command or equivalent menu commands are used to change the contents of the control, or as you move through the table to records with different types of data in the General field.

Example `? ThisForm.OLEBoundControl1.OLETypeAllowed`

See Also OLEControl, OLEBoundControl

On AplAbout, On MacHelp, RunScript, Set AplAbout, Set MacDesktop, Set MacHelp, Set XcmdFile

Forget you ever saw these commands. They're only for compatibility with FoxPro/Mac and Visual FoxPro/Mac. In fact, as of VFP 5, they're not even documented in the VFP Help file.

The good news is that, except for RUNSCRIPT and SET("XCMDFILE"), they're all just ignored in Visual FoxPro. RUNSCRIPT, however, generates a "Feature Not Available" error, while SET("XCMDFILE") gives "Invalid argument used with the SET function."

On Bar, On Pad, On Selection Bar, On Selection Menu, On Selection Pad, On Selection Popup

These commands are the key to making your menus do something. The DEFINE commands set up the menus and the ACTIVATE commands turn them on, but without the ON and ON SELECTION commands, not much happens after that.

The ON BAR and ON PAD commands let one menu component activate another component. The ON SELECTION commands are much broader—they let you specify anything at all to happen when a particular item is chosen.

Usage

```
ON BAR nBar OF PopupName [ ACTIVATE POPUP SubPopupName |
        ACTIVATE MENU SubMenuName ]
ON PAD PadName OF MenuName [ ACTIVATE POPUP PopupName |
        ACTIVATE MENU SubMenuName ]
```

With hierarchical menus, choosing a pad of a menu generally opens a popup. Choosing a bar from a menu popup sometimes leads to another popup. That's what ON BAR and ON PAD are about. When a menu bar calls another popup, FoxPro takes care of putting in the little arrow that indicates a nested menu.

We've never used the ACTIVATE MENU alternative here and it violates every menu standard we know of, so we don't plan to start using it anytime soon.

Example

```
* From the system menu:
ON PAD _MSM_FILE OF _MSYSMENU ACTIVATE POPUP _MFILE
```

Usage

```
ON SELECTION BAR nBar OF PopupName [ Command ]
ON SELECTION MENU MenuName | ALL [ Command ]
ON SELECTION PAD PadName OF MenuName [ Command ]
ON SELECTION POPUP PopupName | ALL [ Command ]
```

The MENU and POPUP versions of these propagate down one level to their contained pads and bars. You can then override those choices for individual bars and pads.

ON PAD and ON BAR commands take precedence over ON SELECTION BAR and ON SELECTION PAD. That is, if you specify both for a bar or pad, the popup or menu you specified gets activated when the bar or pad is chosen. The code specified in ON SELECTION is ignored.

Example

```
USE Employee
DEFINE POPUP EmpPop ;
   PROMPT FIELDS TRIM(First_Name - (" " + Last_Name))
ON SELECTION POPUP EmpPop WAIT WINDOW "You picked "+PROMPT()
```

See Also Activate Menu, Activate Popup, Define Bar, Define Menu, Define Pad, Define Popup, Menus

On Error, On Escape See Error.

On Exit Bar, On Exit Menu, On Exit Pad, On Exit Popup

We have to thank the designers of dBASE for these cool commands. According to Help, they're in FoxPro only for dBASE compatibility. Like many of the other so-called compatibility commands, these actually do something useful.

Each command sets up an event handler for the specified item that fires when you leave that item. Like other menu event handlers, these propagate downward to fire when an item doesn't have its own handler.

Usage

```
ON EXIT BAR | PAD ItemName OF ContainerName [ Command ]
ON EXIT MENU | POPUP ItemName [ Command ]
```

These events behave differently on the system menu than they do in user-defined menus. In a user-defined menu, once an item gets focus its ON EXIT event fires as soon as it loses focus. We can think of situations where this would let us keep track of what's going on as a user works his way through, say, a right-click menu.

In the system menu, the events fire after the user chooses an item at the lowest level of the menu, but before the code associated with that item executes. For any given menu choicc, no matter how deep it is in the menu hierarchy, no more than two of these events fire—the one for the menu pad and the one for either the actual menu bar chosen or the popup containing that menu bar.

If a bar doesn't have an ON EXIT event, the ON EXIT event for the popup that contains it fires instead. If neither the bar nor the popup has an ON EXIT defined, only the pad's event fires.

We can't find anything that fires the ON EXIT event for the menu itself.

Since these fire before the code associated with the item, why do we care? Why not just do whatever it is in the code for the item?

We can think of at least one case where these events make things much simpler. Many folks like to have the menu reopen to the last choice after it finishes processing that choice. The simplest way to do this is to KEYBOARD all the hot keys that get you there, but setting up the KEYBOARD command is something of a pain. ON EXIT BAR is the perfect place to fill a global variable or an application property with the series of keystrokes needed. Then, a single command (KEYBOARD oApp.cStrokes) can reopen the menu for every choice.

Best of all would be to not have to change the saved keystrokes when the menu changes. The best hope for automating this process is a driver for GenMenuX (a tool that wraps around the menu-generation program and gives you the opportunity to change things—see "Back o' da Book" for more info). The driver could go through the MNX and figure out the appropriate keystrokes to save, then generate the ON EXIT BAR commands as part of the menu cleanup code. Let us know if you write one.

Realize, however, that this is a nonstandard way of using menus in Windows, and may cause some of your users to feel your app is somewhat more questionable or amateurish.

Example
```
ON EXIT BAR 1 OF MyPopup WAIT WINDOW "You chose Bar 1"
```

See Also Define Menu, On Bar, On Pad, On Selection Bar, On Selection Menu, On Selection Pad, On Selection Popup

On Key, On Key =, On Key Label, On("Key"), Pop Key, Push Key

These commands provide the ability to interrupt the flow of normal event processing by jumping immediately to a routine you've created. Similar to the dreaded GOTO command of the venerable BASIC language (and others), these can lead to code nearly impossible to debug.

Usage
```
ON KEY [ Command ]
cOnCommand = ON( "KEY" )
ON KEY = nKeyCode [ Command ]
ON KEY LABEL KeyLabel [ Command ]
cOKLCommand = ON( "KEY", cKeyLabel )
```

Parameter	Value	Meaning
Command	Literal command	The procedure to run, usually called with a DO command when a key is pressed.
nKeyCode	Numeric	See the Help for the complete listing of funky keys that can be detected, including Alt+Function Keys, Insert, End, and Del.
KeyLabel	Literal—see table in Help.	Provides coverage for both the regular alphanumeric keys and similar keys to nKeyCode, but provides far more readable code. For example, you can specify LEFTARROW instead of 331.
cOnCommand	Character	Returns the current setting of the ON KEY command.
cOKLCommand	Character	Returns the command associated with the specified ON KEY LABEL.
cKeyLabel	Character	Specify the key or key combination for which to get information.

These commands allow developers to trap a number of keystrokes and perform processing based on them.

Unfortunately, in order to make the ON KEYs work properly, the detection of these keystrokes is built right into the native event loop, and checking for these keystrokes occurs between each line of code processed. That means when a specified key is pressed, regardless of what process was in effect, control jumps immediately to the specified procedure. When the procedure is completed, control attempts to return to the line of code following the one last executed.

That's cool if you write perfect code that restores everything to the way it was before you started, and you never run timing-critical code while the ON KEYs are in effect. But if you ever forget to reselect the original work area, or reset a SET command, heaven help you. If the code that was in process before the ON KEY rudely interrupted depends on these settings, the code you've been running for weeks, months or years, the code you know works without a fault will crash and burn, and you will be left trying to explain how your code could have failed in this bizarre manner.

As you may surmise, we're not in favor of using ON KEYs. Although other alternatives might require a little more coding up front, they will provide a more stable final product. Use the KeyPress event to trap individual characters, or hot-key accelerators in the Captions of controls to switch focus to a new control. Use keyboard macros to stuff the keyboard.

Where ON KEY LABELS (OKLs, for short) do still have a place is in development. We prefer to use keyboard macros for events we would like to have occur only while the machine is in an "inputable" wait state, but sometimes you need to interrupt running procedures, and nothing will get you out of an infinite loop like an OKL along the lines of ON KEY LABEL F12 CANCEL. Ted likes to open the debugger with an OKL on F11 set to DEBUG.

Our advice: Avoid the ON KEY and ON KEY= commands and stick with the native event loop. Use ON KEY LABELs only in development situations where the native event loop must be overridden.

Example

```
ON KEY LABEL F3 DEBUG

* TestKeys - display the ASC() value of most keyboard keys
* Press Escape when done
SET ESCAPE ON
ON ESCAPE RETURN
DO WHILE .T.
  ON KEY WAIT WINDOW NOWAIT LTRIM(STR(INKEY()))
ENDDO
```

Usage

```
PUSH KEY [ CLEAR ]
POP KEY [ ALL ]
```

PUSH KEY stores the current ON KEY settings to a stack, and POP KEY brings these definitions back into effect. The CLEAR keyword clears all definitions that were in effect, until the POP KEY is used to restore them. The ALL keyword POPs all stored functions off the stack.

Use PUSH KEY CLEAR when entering a routine where you want no ON KEYs to be in effect, such as a modal form, or where you want to set a whole new batch of ON KEYs, or in the actual procedure called by the ON KEY routine. Use POP KEY ALL to clear all ON KEY LABELs. ON KEYs, on the other hand, must be cleared with an ON KEY command.

See Also KeyPress, On(), Set Function

On MacHelp See On AplAbout.

On Pad See On Bar.

On Page See Eject.

On ReadError See Error.

On Selection Bar, On Selection Menu, On Selection Pad, On Selection Popup See On Bar.

On ShutDown, On("ShutDown")

This clever event handler lets Visual FoxPro applications behave like other Windows applications and respond intelligently when the user closes them in any of a variety of ways, including shutting down Windows, choosing End Task from the Task Manager and closing the app's main window.

Usage

```
ON SHUTDOWN [ Command ]
cShutdown = ON("SHUTDOWN")
```

Back in FoxPro/DOS, we had total control over when and how our applications were closed. Those days are gone forever. In Windows, users can close an application in all kinds of ways. This command helps us get used to it.

Normally, the command you specify is a call to a routine that checks what's going on and takes appropriate action. For example, you might check for unsaved changes and let the user tell you what to do about them. (That's how most of the Windows apps we use behave, in fact.)

Omit the command to turn off the shutdown routine and restore the default behavior (which is to present a message, "Cannot Quit Visual FoxPro"). With some system dialogs running, you don't even get this message—your request to shut down FoxPro is simply ignored. Our impression is that this happens when the running dialog is actually a Windows dialog, not a FoxPro dialog.

ON SHUTDOWN is designed to assume that you are definitely going to go ahead and shut down the application. It's not always well-behaved when you try to return to your application. Our experience is that you need to be careful about what you put in the shutdown routine. You probably want to be careful out of respect for your users, too. When the user says, "Get me out of here," you should if you can. It's okay to stop and ask about saving unsaved work, but it's pretty obnoxious to ignore the user's request entirely.

You can use QueryUnload along with ON SHUTDOWN to check the active forms and figure out if you can shut them down before you actually do so. See QueryUnload for an idea of the kind of code you might use there. The example here shows what the shutdown routine might look like.

The ON SHUTDOWN routine can also be a method of an object, such as an application manager object. Then the ON SHUTDOWN call would look like:

```
ON SHUTDOWN oApp.OnShutDown()
```

Example

```
ON SHUTDOWN DO DownShut

PROCEDURE DownShut
* Here's an rough sketch of what you might do

LOCAL lShutDown
lShutDown = .T.

FOR nCnt = _SCREEN.FormCount TO 1 STEP -1
   * Backward because we're going to change things
   IF _SCREEN.Forms[nCnt].BaseClass = "Form"  && skip toolbars
      IF _SCREEN.Forms[nCnt].QueryUnload()
         _SCREEN.Forms[nCnt].Release()
      ELSE
         lShutDown = .F.
         EXIT
      ENDIF
   ENDIF
ENDFOR
```

```
IF lShutDown
   ON SHUTDOWN
   CLEAR EVENTS
ENDIF

RETURN
```

See Also QueryUnload, Quit

On()

On, Comet! On, Cupid! On Donder and Blitzen!
Clement Moore, *A Visit From St. Nick*, 1823

A number of commands in FoxPro let you set up "event handlers" using statements that begin with ON, then tell what the event is, and then contain a command to execute in that case. For example, ON ERROR DO ErrHand or ON KEY LABEL F1 HELP. This function lets you find out what those event handlers are. The most common reason to do so is to save the current value so you can replace it temporarily and then restore it.

Usage `cCurrentHandler = ON( cHandler [, cKeyName ] )`

Parameter	Value	Meaning
cHandler	Character	The second word of the ON command whose current setting should be returned. For example, "ERROR", "KEY". For ON KEY LABEL, use "KEY".
cKeyName	Character	For ON KEY LABEL, the key or key combination whose current setting should be returned.

For everything but ON KEY LABEL, using ON() is pretty straightforward. You just ask for ON("whatever"), like ON("ERROR"). For ON KEY LABEL, you have to specify which key you're interested in, like ON("KEY","F1").

The legitimate values for cHandler are: APLABOUT, ERROR, ESCAPE, KEY, MACHELP, PAGE, READERROR and SHUTDOWN. It turns out you can pass any character value at all without an error. If it's not a legitimate value for cHandler or if the specified handler hasn't been set, ON() returns the empty string.

There's a trap here because misspelling the value for cHandler can lead you to believe there isn't one in effect. For example, if you write ON("ERR"), you get back the empty string and you may think this means there's no error handler in effect. You need to specify ON("ERROR") to get the error handler. We can see why they did it this way. It's much more forgiving and probably easier to add to in the future if new handlers come along, but it means you need to double-check your use of ON().

Example

```
* Save then restore the current error handler
cHoldError = ON( "ERROR" )
ON ERROR DO MyNewErrorHandler
* do some processing
* now restore it
ON ERROR &cHoldError
```

See Also On AplAbout, On Error, On Escape, On Key, On Key Label, On MacHelp, On Page, On ReadError, On Shutdown

OneToMany See ChildAlias.

Open Database, Close Databases

These commands open and close databases, respectively. Opening a database does not open any of the tables in it, but closing a database does close all of its tables.

Usage

```
OPEN DATABASE [ Name | ? ]
              [ EXCLUSIVE | SHARED ]
              [ NOUPDATE ]
              [ VALIDATE ]
```

The EXCLUSIVE, SHARED, and NOUPDATE options behave the same way for the database as they do for an individual table opened with USE. However, the settings specified in OPEN DATABASE don't affect opening of tables in the database. That is, if you open a database shared, but have SET EXCLUSIVE ON, a USE for a table in the database is still exclusive. For NOUPDATE especially, this has important implications. Opening a database NOUPDATE is not sufficient to prevent changes to the data in the database; it prevents changes only to the contents of the database container: which tables are included, persistent relations and stored procedures. Fortunately, it also prevents changes to the structure of the individual tables in the database. Unfortunately, working interactively, you only find this out when you go to save your changes or if you have the Database Designer open and notice the "Read Only" in its title-bar.

The prevention of changes when the database is open NOUPDATE isn't complete. If you attempt to add an index to a table, even though the INDEX command gives you an error message, enough information gets stored that the database is considered invalid.

Also, if you open a database EXCLUSIVE or NOUPDATE, then reopen it without closing it first, it doesn't matter whether you specify the same keyword(s) again. The database retains the same characteristics. To change them, you have to close the database, then open it with different keywords.

The VALIDATE keyword lets you check a database for internal consistency. There are various ways a database can get messed up. (Deleting one of its tables or indexes with Explorer comes to mind as an obvious choice.) Unfortunately, OPEN DATABASE VALIDATE doesn't do anything about it if the database is invalid; it just reports an error and doesn't open the database. Consider it as "Open the database only if it is valid." You have to use VALIDATE DATABASE RECOVER to fix the problems. If you omit the VALIDATE keyword, you can open the database anyway and work with it for a while until the problem comes up to bite you. In fact, you have to open the database in order to apply VALIDATE DATABASE.

Example

```
OPEN DATABASE TasTrade
```

We suspect we won't actually be issuing OPEN DATABASE all that often because opening a table in a database opens the database as well. (Watch out, though—although opening a table opens the database, it doesn't make it the selected database.) Most of the time, that's all we'll need to do. The best reasons for explicitly opening the database are to add one of the optional keywords, to work on the structure of a database, or so that you don't have to remember the short filenames for the tables and can use only the long names you've assigned.

Usage

```
CLOSE DATABASES [ ALL ]
```

By itself, CLOSE DATABASES closes the current database and any of its tables or views that may be open. (See SET DATABASE for an explanation of "current database.") If no database is current, it closes all open free tables (sort of like what CLOSE DATABASES does in older versions of FoxPro).

One warning: If something else (like the Project Manager) is keeping a database open, CLOSE DATABASES doesn't close it, even if you include the ALL clause.

Adding the optional ALL keyword closes all open databases, their tables and views, plus all free tables. The venerable CLOSE ALL includes CLOSE DATABASES ALL among its functionality.

Example

```
CLOSE DATABASE
```

See Also Close, Create Database, DBC(), Delete Database, Modify Database, Set Database, Validate Database

OpenTables, CloseTables

These methods of the Data environment open and close the tables listed there.

Usage

```
PROCEDURE oDEObject.OpenTables
PROCEDURE oDEObject.CloseTables
```

By default, OpenTables opens all the tables and views listed in the Data environment and establishes the specified relations among them, while CloseTables closes them. You can override this behavior with your own code. However, opening and closing tables and views is part of the default behavior for these methods—that means they'll do it unless you put NODEFAULT in your version of the method.

OpenTables is sensitive to the value of OpenViews. That property determines whether OpenTables opens all views, no views, or just local or remote views.

If AutoOpenTables is .T., OpenTables is called implicitly at startup of the object (form, formset, report or label). Similarly, AutoCloseTables set to .T. means that CloseTables is called automatically.

You can also call OpenTables and CloseTables in code.

The firing order of OpenTables and BeforeOpenTables is seriously confusing. Any custom code in OpenTables fires first, then BeforeOpenTables fires, then the actual opening of tables that's the default behavior of OpenTables occurs. We think BeforeOpenTables is misnamed and should actually be called BeforeAutoOpenTables, but we do see that 20 characters is just a little long for a method name.

What's going on here is that OpenTables and CloseTables are really unique among all the events and methods of Visual FoxPro. Technically, they're methods, but in some ways they behave more like events. Having AutoOpenTables set to .T. causes the OpenTables method to fire automatically like an event and unlike any other methods. OpenTables and CloseTables need to be in a special category all by themselves.

The biggest consequence of the relationship between OpenTables and BeforeOpenTables is that there's not much reason ever to use BeforeOpenTables. You can put the same code in OpenTables and it'll run before the tables open.

You might wonder when you'd want to override the default behavior of these methods. The most important case is to use a single form with different databases. The Database property of a cursor in the Data environment has a hard-coded path. You have to change it at runtime if you want to refer to a different database than the one you used when you created the DE. You can do that in code. But, if the choice of database is based on something else in the form, say a parameter, you can't make the change until after the form is initialized. In that case, you can put code in OpenTables to change the database property of each cursor (either specifically or by looping to find them). In the Form's Init method, you can explicitly call OpenTables. Your code to change the database reference executes first, then the default of opening the tables occurs, using the newly specified database. (Of course, you may prefer to put this code in Init rather than OpenTables, so you can do it once in a form class and be done with it.)

Example

```
* In a very simple version of the case described above,
* the form's Init method might be:
PARAMETER cWhichDBC

* WhichDBC is a custom property of the form
This.WhichDBC=cWhichDBC
ThisForm.DataEnvironment.OpenTables()
```

```
* If there are two tables in the DE,
* the OpenTables method might look like:
This.Cursor1.Database=ThisForm.WhichDBC
This.Cursor2.Database=ThisForm.WhichDBC

* Be sure to set AutoOpenTables to .F. in the Property Sheet
```

OpenTables doesn't need to include the USE or SET RELATION commands because that happens automatically when the method is called. A form with this structure can even be called and told to use the open database by passing DBC() for the parameter.

In real code, you'd want to use AMEMBERS() and a loop to change the cursor's database properties, rather than hard-coding. Similarly, the Init would probably do some checking on the parameter to make sure it refers to a real DBC and perhaps even to ensure that the necessary tables exist in that DBC.

Another time to put code in OpenTables is to create indexes on the fly for views. You can set things up so that the tables and views open, and then you do some indexing. The code looks like this:

```
* First, make the tables and views open right away
NODEFAULT  && Prevent the table opening from running at the end of the method
DoDefault() && Make the table opening happen right now
SELECT SomeView
INDEX ON SomeField TAG SomeTag
```

You can use the same approach to do any other kind of thing that should happen as soon as the tables have opened.

See Also AfterCloseTables, AutoCloseTables, AutoOpenTables, BeforeOpenTables, OpenViews

OpenViews See AutoOpenTables.

OpenWindow See MemoWindow.

OptionButton, OptionGroup

Option button is the name for what we used to call a "radio button" back in FoxPro 2.x. They come in bunches where only one can be chosen at a time. Option buttons are good for sets of mutually exclusive options. (For example, groups of ages such as 0-12, 13-24, 25-49, 49-64, and 65 and above.)

Since options come only in sets, we can't create them individually. An OptionGroup is a container that holds option buttons. It's the group that has a Value, not the individual buttons. (Though, for some strange reason, individual option buttons do have ControlSource and Value—don't ask us why. We think they forgot to remove them when they added OptionGroups.)

Like check boxes, option buttons can be textual or graphical. With graphical option buttons, the currently selected button stays depressed. If the group's Value doesn't correspond to any of the buttons (which shouldn't really occur, but FoxPro lets you do this), none of the buttons is down.

OptionGroup

Property	Value	Purpose
AutoSize	Logical	Determines whether the group grows and shrinks to match the sizes of the buttons within.
ButtonCount	Numeric	The number of buttons in the group.

Property	Value	Purpose
Buttons	Collection	References to the individual buttons in the group.
Value	Numeric	The number of the currently chosen button in the group.
	Character	The caption of the currently chosen button in the group.

OptionButton

Property	Value	Purpose
Alignment	Numeric	Determines which side of the caption the button appears on.
AutoSize	Logical	Determines whether this button resizes itself when the caption changes.
Caption	Character	The text for the button.
Picture, DownPicture, DisabledPicture	Character	The names of graphics files used for a graphical option button. Picture is used when the button is not chosen. DownPicture is used when the button is chosen. DisabledPicture is used when the button is disabled. If either of DownPicture or DisabledPicture is not specified, Picture is used in that circumstance.
Style	Numeric	Determines whether the button is textual or graphical.
TabIndex	Numeric	The "tab" order of the button within the group.

Unlike 2.x radio buttons, option buttons can be organized any way you want within the group. You can line them up vertically or horizontally, put them in rows and columns, or arrange them totally randomly. Whatever arrangement you choose, we recommend you set the button's TabIndex to match it in some way.

Despite its name, TabIndex doesn't have much to do with the Tab key. With KEYCOMP set to Windows, you can't actually tab between buttons in a group. You have to use the arrow keys. TabIndex controls the order you see when you do that. (With KEYCOMP set to DOS, Tab does go through all the buttons in a group before moving on to the next control, but who sets KEYCOMP to DOS in a VFP app?)

Both individual buttons and the group as a whole have AutoSize properties. In some cases, the interaction of these is a little weird. If you set AutoSize on for the individual buttons, but not for the group as a whole, you may lose part of some captions. Same thing if you turn on AutoSize for the group, but not for the individual buttons. We think you'll usually want AutoSize on for both. The group's AutoSize is especially useful when you want the buttons arranged other than in the default column.

At first glance, it looks like subclassing option buttons and groups is a little easier than with other container-contained pairs. You can subclass both OptionButtons and OptionGroups in the Class Designer. But that's as far as it goes. You still can't tell your OptionGroup subclass to use your OptionButton subclass instead of the default. You can do all this in code, but it requires a lot of messing around.

When you do go ahead and subclass OptionGroup with the default OptionButtons, you run into a counting problem. You're stuck with however many buttons you put in the group. When you put your subclass in a form, you can't reduce the number of buttons and, if you increase ButtonCount, the new buttons don't have whatever special settings drove you to subclass the thing in the first place. If you create your subclass with no buttons, then all the buttons you add have to be set up appropriately. Your best bets are probably to create a group with no buttons and use AddObject to add your button subclass at runtime, or to use the default buttons, but do most of your work in the OptionGroup subclass and make liberal use of SetAll.

OptionGroups and OptionButtons share a behavior with CommandGroups and CommandButtons that has to do with the nearly symbiotic relationship between the buttons and the group. Unlike other container/container pairs, when an option button doesn't have code for a particular method, the group's code for that method fires. As far as we're concerned, this is just one more reason to write all your code in the OptionGroup and forget that OptionButtons have methods.

As with page frames, we're hoping for some great builders in this area.

Example

```
* Here's one possible approach to subclassing
* (except we'd really do this in the Class Designer, not code).
DEFINE CLASS MyOptionGroup AS OptionGroup

   ButtonCount = 0
   AutoSize = .T.

   PROCEDURE Init
   * Set up the buttons here. You won't see the
   * changes at design time, but they'll be
   * right at run-time

   This.Setall("Alignment", 1)
   This.Setall("AutoSize", .T.)

   ENDPROC
ENDDEFINE
```

See Also Alignment, AutoSize, ButtonCount, Buttons, Caption, DisabledPicture, DownPicture, Picture, Set KeyComp, Style, TabIndex, Value

Order See Alias.

Order(), Set Order, Set("Order"), Set Index, Set("Index"), Sys(21), Sys(22)

These commands and functions all relate to putting an index in control and finding out which one is currently in control. ORDER() and SET ORDER are the most up-to-date ways to do this stuff. SET ORDER lets you specify a tag or stand-alone index to control the table. ORDER() lets you find out which one it is. SET INDEX lets you open stand-alone indexes and non-structural compound indexes, as well as setting one of them in control. SYS(21) and SYS(22) are antique ways to find out which index is in charge. Don't use them because, like all the SYS() functions, their names give you no clue what they're about.

When tables or indexes are opened, each stand-alone index and tag is assigned a number, based on its position. Several of these commands use that number to refer to a particular index or tag. See CANDIDATE() for details on this numbering. Like work area numbers, we recommend you avoid these numbers whenever possible and refer to indexes by name.

Usage

```
cCurrentOrder = ORDER( [ cAlias | nWorkArea
                       [, nIncludePath ] ] )
```

Parameter	Value	Meaning
cAlias	Character	Return the current order in the work area whose alias is cAlias.
	Omitted	If nWorkArea is also omitted, returns information for the current work area.

Parameter	Value	Meaning
nWorkArea	Numeric	Return the current order for work area nWorkArea.
	Omitted	If cAlias is also omitted, return information for the current work area.
nIncludePath	Numeric	Include the full path to the index file.
	Omitted	Return just the index or tag name.
cCurrentOrder	Character	The name of the current index or tag. If nIncludePath is specified, includes the full path to the index file. For tags with nIncludePath, returns the name of the compound index file with its path rather than the tag.

ORDER() is the function to use when you want to save the current order before changing it. But it can give you much more information with the optional nIncludePath parameter. With two calls, you can find out both the tag in charge and the name and path of the index file containing that tag.

Usage

```
SET ORDER TO [ nIndexNumber | IndexFileName
         | [ TAG ] TagName [ OF CompoundIndexFile ]
         [ IN cAlias | nWorkArea ]
         [ ASCENDING | DESCENDING ] ]
SET INDEX TO [ IndexFileList | ?
         [ ORDER nIndexNumber | IndexFileName
           | [ TAG ] TagName [ OF CompoundIndexFile ]
           [ ASCENDING | DESCENDING ]
         [ ADDITIVE ] ]
```

Parameter	Value	Meaning
nIndexNumber	Numeric	The number for the index to put in charge.
IndexFileName	Name	The name of a stand-alone index to put in charge.
TagName	Name	The name of a compound index tag to put in charge.
CompoundIndexFile	Name	The name of the compound index file containing the specified tag. Can be omitted if the tag name is unique.
cAlias	Character	Set the current order in the work area whose alias is cAlias.
	Omitted	If nWorkArea is also omitted, set order for the current work area.
nWorkArea	Numeric	Set the current order for work area nWorkArea.
	Omitted	If cAlias is also omitted, set order for the current work area.
IndexFileList	List of Names	A list of index files to open.

SET INDEX TO lets you specify index files to open as well as the order to set. SET ORDER specifies just the new order. We don't use SET INDEX much anymore because we almost always keep all the indexes we need in a single, structural index file.

The ASCENDING/DESCENDING switch here is confusing because you can create indexes in either ascending or descending order and use them both ways as well. The key fact is that the terms "ascending" and "descending" keep their normal meanings and don't double up. That is, if you create a tag in descending order and then SET ORDER TO that tag DESCENDING, it doesn't get reversed to ascending. Two descendings don't make an ascending.

The other confusing thing is that the direction you create the tag only matters when you first open the table any given time. Once you SET ORDER TO that tag once, FoxPro remembers the last direction you used that tag in. If you omit ASCENDING and DESCENDING on a subsequent SET ORDER, you get the orientation you used last. (If you omit them initially, you get the creation direction for that tag.) This effect continues until you close and reopen the table.

Also, keep in mind that a table can't use the same index/tag in two different orders at the same time. That is, if you USE a table twice and SET ORDER in each to the same tag, you can't make one ascending and the other descending. The last one set wins.

Like so many other SET commands, issuing SET ORDER TO without a tag or index name clears the setting. In this case, it indicates that record-number order should be used. SET ORDER TO 0 does the same thing as does SET ORDER TO "". SET INDEX TO without any files closes open indexes except for the structural CDX.

Usage

```
cCurrentOrder = SET( "ORDER" )
cIndexList = SET( "INDEX" )
```

SET("ORDER") provides information in a different format than ORDER(). It gives the name of the current tag and the name of the index file that contains it. If order is currently descending, it also includes the word "DESCENDING." Until FoxPro 2.6 added the DESCENDING() function, this was the only way to find out if an index was being used in descending order. Since the information is available in other forms and parsing the string returned is something of a pain, we suggest you forget about SET("ORDER"), except for saving and restoring the current order, where it gives you exactly the information you need.

SET("INDEX") gives you a string that you can pass back to SET INDEX. It's a complete list of all the index files (with paths) open for the current table. It even includes the structural CDX. If an order is set, the ORDER clause is included, too. Oddly, SET("INDEX") uses lowercase for the information from your table while all the other functions in this group use uppercase.

Usage

```
nTagNumber = SYS( 21 [, nWorkArea ] )
cTagName = SYS( 22 [, nWorkArea ] )
```

Since you can get the same result as SYS(21) and SYS(22) with TAGNO() and ORDER(), we can't see any reason to use these obtusely named functions.

Example

```
USE Customer
SET ORDER TO Company_Na
? ORDER()                  && Returns "COMPANY_NA"
? ORDER("Customer", 1)          && Returns something like
* "H:\VFP5\SAMPLES\TASTRADE\DATA\CUSTOMER.CDX"
? SET("ORDER")                  && Returns something like
* "TAG COMPANY_NA OF H:\VFP5\SAMPLES\TASTRADE\DATA\CUSTOMER.CDX"
? SYS(21)                  && Returns 1
? SYS(22)                  && Returns "COMPANY_NA"
? SET("INDEX")                  && Returns something like:
* "h:\vfp5\samples\tastrade\data\customer.cdx ORDER TAG company_na OF
h:\vfp5\samples\tastrade\data\customer.cdx"
```

See Also Candidate(), Descending(), Index, TagNo()

OS(), Sys(9), Version(), Version

These three functions and one property give you information about your software setup. OS() provides DOS and Windows version information, while SYS(9), VERSION() and the application object's Version property provide

FoxPro version information.

Usage `cOpSys = OS( [ 1 | 2 ] )`

Without the optional parameter, OS() returns the underlying operating system and version. With a parameter of 1, you get the Windows version. However, these days, those two are generally the same thing. (In FoxPro for Windows 2.x, OS() gave us a DOS version, while OS(1) gave us a Windows version.)

Passing 2 to OS() tells you whether the operating system supports double-byte character sets, a handy thing to know if you're writing international applications. We can tell you that this option, new in VFP 6, works when you don't have a double-byte system, but neither of us is in a position to test whether it works when you do have double-byte characters.

Example

```
? OS()    && Returns Windows NT 4.00 on Tamar's system
? OS(1)   && Also returns Windows NT 4.00 on Tamar's system
? OS()    && Returns Windows 4.00 on Ted's Win95 system
? OS(2)   && Returns "" on both Tamar's and Ted's machines
```

Usage `cSerialNumber = SYS(9)`

From the truly useless information department, we bring you SYS(9). It returns your Visual FoxPro serial number. Now there's an item we use every day.

Usage

```
uVersionInfo = VERSION( nExpression )
cVersionNumber = appApplication.Version
```

Parameter	Value	Meaning
nExpression	Omitted	Return product name and version.
	1	Return product name, version, date and serial number.
	2	Return edition information:
		0 – Runtime
		1 – Standard
		2 – Professional
	3	Return localization information. See Help for the list of languages.
	4	Return the version number portion only, but complete with all the major and minor and build number info.
	5	Return just the version number, as a number, not a string. The first digit is the major version number, and the other two are the minor revision number.

VERSION() and Version, on the other hand, we use. We use them interactively to determine which build of the product we have for bug reporting or to ensure that an application will run. We also use them in our applications because there are some things we want to do differently when running an EXE than when running on our development systems, and things we want to handle differently depending on the version of the product. Version is particularly useful for custom automation servers, so they can figure out what version of VFP they're running in.

VERSION() was seriously enhanced in Visual FoxPro and gained more functionality (the 4 and 5 parameters) in

VFP 6. All the changes make it much easier to use in applications. We don't have to check for specific strings to figure out if we're in a distributed app; we just have to pass 2. The localization information makes it much easier to handle multilingual apps as well.

In one of the few stunningly dumb additions to Visual FoxPro, the type of the return value of this function depends on which parameter you pass it. None, 1, 3, or 4 returns a character string, but passing a parameter of 2 or 5 returns a numeric value. We would be just as happy testing VERSION(2) = "2" as = 2, and this would make the function more consistent.

Example

```
* At the end of an app, if we're in interactive VFP,
* we need to put some things back the way we found them.
IF VERSION(2)<>0
   SET HELP TO cOldHelp
   SET RESOURCE TO cOldResource
   MODIFY WINDOW SCREEN
ENDIF
```

See Also GetEnv(), StartMode

Otherwise See Do Case.

Pack See Delete.

Pack Database

Unlike its table-oriented counterpart, PACK, this command is actually useful. Information about a database is stored in an ordinary FoxPro table (well, okay, actually a Visual FoxPro table) with a special extension. Various operations on a database can leave deleted records behind. PACK DATABASE cleans up the deleted records, leaving the DBC file smaller and more manageable.

Usage `PACK DATABASE`

PACK DATABASE does for a DBC what PACK does for a DBF. The difference is that there are other (read: safer) ways to perform the same function on a DBF. When you PACK DATABASE, FoxPro not only throws away the garbage, it also reorganizes what remains. In particular, each record in a DBC has a unique object ID (cleverly named "objectid") always equal to the physical record number; PACK DATABASE reassigns the object IDs to keep them matching the record numbers.

To our pleasant surprise, opening the DBC with USE and issuing PACK also updates the objectid field. However, using COPY TO for a "safe PACK", of course, doesn't update the object IDs and results in a table that's not recognized by FoxPro as a database.

Our take: Always make a backup and then use PACK DATABASE if you need it, and don't risk destroying your database. Which isn't to say that there aren't times to open the DBC as a table and muck around—this just isn't one of them. Be aware that PACK DATABASE has the same risks as PACK. It's just that there isn't another way to get the job done. Be sure to back up your database before you pack if you care about keeping it intact.

The database must be opened EXCLUSIVE in order to pack it.

See Also Close Database, Modify Database, Open Database, Remove Table, Validate Database

Pad() See Bar().

PadC(), PadL(), PadR()

These functions pad strings with a specified character. The final letter of each function indicates where the padding occurs: C for center, L for left, and R for right.

Usage

```
cPaddedString = PADC( eExpr, nLength, cPadCharacter )
cPaddedString = PADL( eExpr, nLength, cPadCharacter )
cPaddedString = PADR( eExpr, nLength, cPadCharacter )
```

Parameter	Value	Meaning
eExpr	Character, Memo, Numeric, Float, Currency, Double, Integer, Date or DateTime	The item to be padded.
nLength	Numeric	The length the string should be after padding.
cPadCharacter	Character	The character to use for padding.
	Omitted	Spaces (CHR(32)) are used for padding.

Many folks don't notice the third parameter here and think these functions can only be used to pad with blanks. cPadCharacter can be any character at all, so you can use these functions to fill a money amount with "*"s or add a dot leader to an item in a report.

Another thing most folks miss is that you can pass more than just character strings to the PADx functions without first converting them. The conversion is automatic. The number, date or datetime is converted so that it occupies the minimum space possible, then padding is applied.

PADL() is particularly useful when dealing with character strings composed entirely of digits. With PADL(), it's easy to keep them right-justified so they sort properly. If numeric character strings are left-justified, they sort wrong. (For an example, take a look at the SYS() functions in the FoxPro Help index— they list as SYS(1), SYS(10), SYS(11), SYS(100), ... , SYS(2), and so forth.) It's easy to make them sort properly though—just use:

```
PADL(ALLTRIM(cNumber), LEN(cNumber))       && pads with blanks
```

or

```
PADL(ALLTRIM(cNumber), LEN(cNumber), "0")  && pads with zeroes
```

Either approach yields proper sorting.

PADC() is handy in reporting when you want to center an expression, but the expression length may vary. Apply PADC(), using the size of the allocated space as the length.

Example

```
PROCEDURE GetId(cTable)
* Get a new unique id for the specified table
* assumes next id for each table is stored in IdTable

LOCAL nOldWorkArea, cOldOrder, lWasUsed, cRetValue

nOldWorkArea = SELECT()
IF USED("IdTable")
   lWasUsed=.T.
   SELECT IdTable
   cOldOrder=ORDER()
ELSE
   lWasUsed=.F.
   SELECT 0
   USE IdTable
ENDIF

SET ORDER TO TableName

* Find this table
```

```
SEEK cTable

IF FOUND()
   * lock it, grab it and update it
   DO WHILE NOT RLOCK()
   ENDDO

   cRetValue=NextId
   REPLACE NextId WITH ;
           PADL(INT(VAL(cRetValue))+1,;
           LEN(NextId),"0")
   UNLOCK RECORD RECNO()
ELSE
   cRetValue="0000"
ENDIF

IF lWasUsed
   SET ORDER TO (cOldOrder)
ELSE
   USE IN IdTable
ENDIF

SELECT (nOldWorkArea)
ENDIF

RETURN cRetValue
```

The function shown here returns the next available ID for a specified table. It uses PADL() to ensure that the ID has the right number of digits. It assumes you have a table with two fields, TableName and NextId, with one record for each table in your application. It finds and locks the record for the specified table, grabs NextId, then computes the next NextId before unlocking the record.

There is one thing to watch out for with the PADx() functions. If nLength is less than the current length of cString, all three functions truncate the original string from the right. For example:

```
?PADL("Original",5)
```

returns

```
"Origi"
```

See Also Len(), Replicate()

_PAdvance

This used to be one of the most useful of the printer variables. It let you determine whether page breaks were made up of a single form-feed character (Ctrl+L or CHR(12)) or as many linefeeds (CHR(10)) as needed to get to the top of the next page. This one saved an awful lot of people with odd-sized paper.

But, as far as we can tell, it doesn't work with the Report Designer (though we're pretty sure it did in FoxPro 2.x). Since that's the way to go for reporting, _PADVANCE has become obsolete. (It does actually work with @SAY reports, but who wants to write those?)

Usage

```
_PADVANCE = "FORMFEED" | "LINEFEEDS"
```

Example

```
_PADVANCE = "FORMFEED"
SET DEVICE TO PRINT
SET PRINT TO TEST.TXT
FOR nBatch = 1 TO 20
   FOR nRow = 1 TO 10
      @nRow,1 SAY "Line "+PADL(nRow,2)
   ENDFOR
ENDFOR
SET PRINT TO
```

```
SET DEVICE TO SCREEN
* Check Test.Txt and you'll see the CHR(12)'s after each batch
```

See Also Eject, _PLength

Page, PageFrame

Multi-page tabbed dialogs were one of the hottest things around when VFP was introduced. Now it seems they're everywhere. Visual FoxPro's version is called a PageFrame. It's a container object that contains Pages. Pages are also containers and can contain any controls, even other PageFrames.

We do think page frames are pretty cool looking. We also think they're terribly overused. Like so many of the other widgets in Windows, page frames are useful in dialogs. The Tools-Options dialog is the prime example of this, but many builders also make good use of page frames (and those guys are all built in Visual FoxPro). However, you can go too far with this. A page frame is heavily mouse-oriented—it has no place in heads-down data entry. (Neither do a lot of the other fancy controls, but that's not what we're talking about here.)

Use page frames where they make the resulting form clearer. The builders are a good example of this—while everything in the builder is related, each page contains a set of items that are closely related to each other.

Although tabbed interfaces are all the rage, you can also make tabless page frames. We can imagine using them for some of the things we used to do with multi-screen sets where all the screens occupied the same location.

PageFrame

Property	Value	Purpose
ActivePage	Numeric	The number of the page currently on top. This number is based on PageOrder, not creation order.
PageCount	Numeric	The number of pages in the pageframe.
PageHeight, PageWidth	Numeric	The size of an individual page.
Pages	Collection	References to the individual pages in the pageframe.
Tabs	Logical	Determines whether the individual pages have tabs at the top.
TabStretch	Numeric	Determines whether multiple rows of tabs are used when the tabs don't fit in a single row.
TabStyle	Numeric	Determines whether all tabs are the same width or each is sized to accommodate its Caption.

Event	Purpose
Moved	Fires when the pageframe's position is changed programmatically.

Page

Property	Value	Purpose
ActiveControl	Object	Reference to the control on the page that has focus.
Caption	Character	The text on the page's tab. Can include a hotkey.

Property	Value	Purpose
ControlCount	Numeric	The number of controls on the page.
Controls	Collection	References to the individual controls on the page.
PageOrder	Numeric	The display position of this page in the pageframe.

The documentation for VFP 5 and VFP 6 says that Pages have the KeyPreview property. They did in VFP 3 (though it didn't do anything there). It was removed in VFP 5.

Page frames and pages refresh differently than other controls. When the Refresh method for a page frame is called, it calls only the Refresh method for the ActivePage. The other pages don't get visually refreshed.

We can see why the Refresh methods don't all fire up front—it could really bog things down. But why the heck don't they get refreshed when they come to the top? How are your changes supposed to filter through?

Under the circumstances, we don't see ourselves putting much code in the Refresh method for an individual page. We'll use the page's Activate method or the controls' UIEnable events instead for things we want to be sure happen. We'll also put This.Refresh() in each page's Activate method to make sure the controls get refreshed. (We'd love to handle all this with a nice subclass of PageFrame, but read on.)

Subclassing PageFrame is a real pain. You can create subclasses, but there are several nasty restrictions on them.

First, if you use the Class Designer, they always contain Pages—you can't subclass Page and stick your subclass in a page frame. Page is one of the "half-classed" objects discussed in "OOP is Not an Accident." In fact, you can create subclasses of Page in code, and even create subclasses of PageFrame that use your Page subclasses, but you can't do it visually. More important, when you add pages to the page frame by upping PageCount, the new ones are based on Page, not your subclass. There's no way to tell a page frame subclass to always use a particular Page subclass. This is a serious limitation. However, FoxPro programmers, always willing to go the extra mile, have found a solution. You can put code in the page frame class's Init method to remove the base class pages and substitute your custom pages. You can even set all the properties as they were in the base pages, so that you can do your design work in the Form Designer. Going this way, though, you lose the ability to add custom code to the individual pages, since there's no way to add code to an object at runtime.

Second, when you put your subclassed page frame in a form in the Form Designer, you can't reduce the number of pages—the only way to get rid of a page is to RemoveObject at runtime.

No big deal, you say. You'll just use a subclass with no pages and change PageCount in the Form Designer. But then you lose most of the benefits of subclassing in the first place—you can't define your default page and start out with it.

Next problem. If you leave the pages on the page frame, when you drop the class onto a form or create an instance, you can't change the names of the individual pages.

Fundamentally, there's no good way to create a single subclass of PageFrame and use it wherever page frames are called for. Your best choices are to put a lot of code in your page frame subclass to modify pages as they're instantiated or to subclass Page in code and use AddObject at runtime to add your subclass to the page frame. We're not thrilled with either choice, but it's looking more and more like Microsoft isn't going to get around to making Page a first-class citizen.

Early versions of VFP had some problems dealing with changes to a page's Name after you've started messing with it. All the code to set page properties is stored in the Properties memo of the page frame that contains it. In earlier versions, when you set some properties for the page, and then changed the page's name, some of the property assignments used the original default name (Page1 or whatever) while some used the new name.

Example

```
* All the changes shown here would be made
* in the Property Sheet.
* Set a PageFrame to have 3 pages.
* With the PageFrame selected:
PageCount = 3

* Set a page to have white on blue text
* and to have a tab of "Sky".
* With the page selected:
BackColor = RGB(0,0,255)
ForeColor = RGB(255,255,255)
Caption = "Sky"
```

See Also ActiveControl, ActivePage, Caption, ControlCount, Controls, KeyPreview, Moved, PageCount, PageHeight, PageOrder, Pages, PageWidth, Tabs, TabStretch, TabStyle, UIEnable

PageCount See Pages.

PageHeight, PageWidth

These two properties tell you the size of an individual page in a page frame. Because all pages must be the same size, they're properties of the page frame itself, not of the individual page.

Usage

```
nPageHeight = pgfPageFrame.PageHeight
nPageWidth = pgfPageFrame.PageWidth
```

As the syntax indicates, these are read-only properties. They're a function of the Height and Width of the page frame. In addition, PageHeight is affected by the presence or absence of tabs.

In VFP 3, changes to BorderWidth (which matter only when Tabs is .F.) have a delayed reaction in the Form Designer—you don't see them reflected in PageHeight until you set Tabs to .T., then set it back to .F. or close and reopen the form. As far as we can tell, changes to BorderWidth at runtime don't change PageHeight at all. Similarly, PageWidth isn't affected by BorderWidth under any circumstances.

In VFP 5 and VFP 6, both PageWidth and PageHeight are affected by changes to BorderWidth, both at design time and runtime.

The value of these properties is always given in the current ScaleMode for the containing form. In VFP 6, in the default pixels, our tests show that PageWidth is Width - 2*(BorderWidth+1). With no tabs, PageHeight is Height - 2*(BorderWidth+1). With unstacked tabs, it appears that PageHeight is always 30 pixels less than Height. Stacking the tabs changes Height, but PageHeight stays the same as with unstacked tabs.

Example

```
IF This.PageWidth>200
  * add something
  This.AddObject("NewButton", "CommandButton")
  * now set it up appropriately
ENDIF
```

See Also BorderWidth, Height, Page, PageFrame, ScaleMode, Tabs, TabStretch, Width

_PageNo

This variable is that rare bird—a system variable that works in the most up-to-date way of getting output, but not very well in the older, obsolete ways. It contains the current page number and can be used to put the page number on a report. Although you can use it with ? and ?? output, _PageNo's value there is based solely on the number of lines output and _PLength—it doesn't notice when you issue EJECT (though EJECT PAGE does properly update _PageNo). With @..SAY output, we can't get anything sensible from _PageNo.

Usage

```
_PAGENO = nPageNumber
```

Example

```
* You might put the following expression in a report:
"Page "+LTRIM(STR(_PAGENO))
```

See Also Eject Page, _PLength, Report

PageOrder See ColumnOrder.

Pages, PageCount

Pages is an array that gives you access to each page in a page frame without needing to know the page's name. PageCount tells you how many pages are in the page frame.

Usage

```
pgfPageFrame.PageCount = nNumberOfPages
nNumberOfPages = pgfPageFrame.PageCount
pagPage = pgfPageFrame.Pages[ nPageNumber ]
```

Pages is a collection property—an array that gives you access to all the objects in a container—in this case, pages in a page frame. PageCount tells the number of elements in Pages. You can change PageCount, which adds or removes pages in the page frame. Be careful about decreasing PageCount. The controls on the extra pages simply fall off into the bit bucket, never to be seen again.

You also need to be careful about which pages disappear when you make PageCount lower. This is controlled not by the page order in Pages, but by the PageOrder property. If you make PageCount smaller than the current number of pages, those pages whose PageOrder is greater than the new PageCount are discarded.

Page frames also don't have an Objects collection, as do many of the other container objects. Most containers in VFP seem to have an Objects collection. But those containers whose contents are restricted to members of a particular base class don't. So forms and columns do, but page frames and button groups don't.

Example

```
* Count the total number of controls in a PageFrame
* Assume the PageFrame is PageFrame1 on the current form
LOCAL nPage, nTotalControls
nTotalControls=0
FOR nPage = 1 TO ThisForm.PageFrame1.PageCount
   nTotalControls = nTotalControls + ;
      ThisForm.PageFrame1.Pages[nPage].ControlCount
ENDFOR

* In VFP 5 and 6, you can do this with a FOR EACH loop
* instead. Note that the code in the loop is more readable.
LOCAL nTotalControls, oPage
nTotalControls=0
FOR EACH oPage IN ThisForm.PageFrame1.Pages
   nTotalControls = nTotalControls + oPage.ControlCount
ENDFOR
```

See Also ControlCount, Controls, Objects, PageOrder

PageWidth See PageHeight.

Paint See Draw.

Panel, PanelLink, View

These grid properties hearken back to the days when people actually used split Browses for data entry. In the never-ending quest for backward compatibility, grids offer the same set of options for side-by-side panels, with each panel able to use either the one-row-per-record Browse mode or the one-row-per-field Edit/Change mode. It's far easier to set this stuff up in Visual FoxPro than it ever was before, though we don't see ourselves using it any more than we did—other than for the rare quick-and-dirty dBASE III data-entry situation. Although there are times where a split grid would be handy, given how hard it is to do it well with VFP's grid, we're much more inclined to use an ActiveX control in those cases.

Panel determines, in a split grid, which side has the focus. PanelLink determines whether the two sides are linked—that is, if you move to a new record on one side, do you move on the other side, too? View specifies which mode each side of the split uses or, if the grid is unsplit, which mode the whole grid uses.

Usage

```
grdGrid.Panel = nWhoHasFocus
nWhoHasFocus = grdGrid.Panel
grdGrid.PanelLink = lLinked
lLinked = grdGrid.PanelLink
```

These two are relevant only when Partition is positive—that is, when the grid is split into two panes (or panels). Use Panel to programmatically set focus to one side or the other, or to see where focus is.

PanelLink actually controls more than just what happens if you move the record pointer. A number of the visual properties can be applied either to both sides or to just the current side, depending on the value of PanelLink. (See Help for a list of the affected properties.) Fortunately, you can unlink the panels, make some changes, then relink them by manipulating PanelLink. Unfortunately, since you can see the properties of only one panel at a time, it's easy to get confused when you're doing this.

Usage

```
grdGrid.View = nModes
nModes = grdGrid.View
```

This misnamed setting has nothing to do with the window formerly known as View (now called Data Session), the kind of views you create with CREATE VIEW, or the views that are members of a database. They've overloaded the term yet again.

The value of View determines whether you see Browse mode or Edit/Change mode. If the grid is split, it determines the mode for each side. An unsplit grid is treated like the *right* panel, so you need to set View to 1 (Browse Change) or 3 (Change Change) to get record-at-a-time editing.

The design-time appearance of a grid (or panel) in Change mode is totally useless. You can't tell anything about it.

If you put controls other than text boxes in a grid, when you change the grid to use Change mode, it still uses your controls. (Of course, we haven't used a grid in Change mode yet.)

Example

```
* Split the grid
ThisForm.grdMyGrid.Partition = 100
* Now use Browse mode on the left, Edit/Change mode on the right
ThisForm.grdMyGrid.View = 1
* Unlink the two panels
ThisForm.grdMyGrid.PanelLink = .F.
* Set up each side the way you want it
ThisForm.grdMyGrid.Panel = 0   && Left
ThisForm.grdMyGrid.RowHeight = 30
ThisForm.grdMyGrid.GridLineColor = RGB(255,0,0)
ThisForm.grdMyGrid.Panel = 1   && Right
```

```
ThisForm.grdMyGrid.RowHeight = 25
ThisForm.grdMyGrid.GridLineColor = RGB(0,0,255)
```

See Also Grid, Partition

Parameters See LParameters.

Parameters(), PCount()

These functions tell you how many parameters were passed to a procedure or function, but there's a subtle difference between them.

Usage

```
nParmCount = PARAMETERS()
nParmCount = PCOUNT()
```

PARAMETERS(), the FoxPro version, tells you how many parameters were passed in the last function or procedure call. PCOUNT(), supposedly added only for dBASE compatibility and not even listed in the Help index before VFP 5, tells you how many parameters were passed to the routine you're now in. This time, we think dBASE got it right.

Using PARAMETERS() has always been a tricky thing. You have to be sure to grab the value as soon as you enter the routine and hope that no ON KEY LABEL or other interrupt occurs that could change the value before you get it.

PCOUNT(), on the other hand, gets that part right every time. We recommend you stick with PCOUNT() and avoid PARAMETERS().

Example

```
* Demonstrate the difference between PARAMETERS() and PCOUNT()
DO rtn1 WITH 1,2,3
DO rtn2 WITH 1,2,3

PROCEDURE rtn1

PARAMETERS a, b, c

? "Parameters() returns", PARAMETERS()      && 3
? "Now I'll use a function"
= myudf(a)
? "Now parameters() returns", PARAMETERS()  && 1!

RETURN

PROCEDURE rtn2

PARAMETERS a, b, c

? "Pcount() returns", PCOUNT()      && 3
? "Now I'll use a function"
= myudf(a)
? "Now pcount() returns", PCOUNT()  && still 3

RETURN

PROCEDURE myudf()

PARAM x

RETURN
```

One of Visual FoxPro's cool new capabilities introduced a gotcha in these two functions. You can leave parameters out of the list passed by just putting in a placeholder (","). These omitted parameters are filled in by Visual FoxPro as .F. values. But PARAMETERS() and PCOUNT() count the number of commas and add 1, rather than counting the actual number of parameters passed. In the example above, if you call the first routine with:

```
DO rtn1 WITH 1,,3
```

you still get 3 from both PARAMETERS() and PCOUNT().

The problem here is that, no matter which way this is handled, the ability to leave parameters out in the middle makes the whole business of parameter checking much harder. As it stands, there's no way to really check which parameters were passed and which were omitted. So you need to be extra careful to check each parameter for validity and not make assumptions about what was passed and what wasn't.

See Also Function, LParameters, Parameters, Procedure

Parent

This keyword has nothing to do with family trees, either yours or an object's. Parent points to the container object containing the specified object. It traces through the containership hierarchy, telling you which object contains the current object. Don't confuse it with ParentClass, which tells about the class hierarchy.

Usage

```
oParentObject = oObject.Parent
uValue = oObject.Parent.pProperty
oObject.Parent.pProperty = uValue
oObject.Parent.mMethod [ (uParams) ]
```

Some classes of objects are allowed to contain other objects. For example, forms contain controls, grids contain columns, and so forth. If an object is contained in another object, Parent gives you a reference to the containing object.

Parent is handy when you want to reference properties and methods of other, related, objects. For example, in a grid column, you might want to refer to a property of the grid. To do so, you can use This.Parent.<whatever>. You can even carry this further and walk down another part of the family tree (to a sibling, niece or nephew of the current object) with a notation like This.Parent.Column2.<whatever>.

Some controls may be buried several layers down in the object hierarchy. For example, consider a check box that's in a column of a grid, which in turn is on a page of a page frame. The check box's parent is the column. The column's parent is the grid. The grid's parent is the page. The page's parent is the page frame. Then, finally, the page frame's parent is the form.

Given the possibility of so many layers of nesting, and that you may not know how many layers are involved, in many cases it's better to use ThisForm or ThisFormSet when you can. The choice of whether to trace up and back down the hierarchy or just jump to the top and back in really depends on how closely related the objects are and how much you know about the setup. For example, to move from a control in one column of a grid to the control in another column of the same grid, it's probably best to use something like This.Parent.Parent.Column2.TheControl. But, to go from a control in a column of a grid to another control elsewhere on the form, ThisForm.OtherControl seems simpler and avoids the question of whether the grid is within another grid, or in a page frame, or anything else like that.

You can't change the Parent of an object; you can simply look it up and use it to refer to other objects.

We can't figure out whether Parent is actually a property of every base class or just an object reference keyword like This. In VFP 3, checking AMEMBERS() for an object doesn't turn up Parent, but in VFP 5 and VFP 6, it does. For that matter, Parent shows up in the debugger looking like a property. Objects created with SCATTER NAME don't have a Parent property, but then they don't have a Name property, either, so we're not sure we want to judge anything by them. We're not sure it really matters, but it would be nice to know for sure. This week, we're inclined to lean toward Parent being a property.

Example

```
* Use the SetAll method of a commandgroup to
* disable every button in the
* group when a particular button is pressed
```

```
* This line would appear in the Click event for
* the button that triggers the change.
This.Parent.SetAll("Enabled",.F.)
```

See Also ParentClass, This, ThisForm, ThisFormSet

ParentAlias See ChildAlias.

ParentClass See BaseClass.

Partition

Specifies where the grid's left and right panels split.

Usage

```
grdGrid.Partition = nWhere2Split
nWhere2Split = grdGrid.Partition
```

Parameter	Value	Meaning
nWhere2Split	Numeric	Specifies the pixel location where the left and right panels are split. This is always expressed in pixels and is not affected by ScaleMode.

The partition must have a value from 0 (for no split) to a value slightly less than the grid's Width property.

Graphically, you can drag the partition all the way to the right, where it takes a value 2 pixels less than the width. With one pixel each for the black lines on the left and right of the grid, that makes sense. Programmatically, you can't go as far. You start getting problems when you run into the vertical scrollbar. In the range of widths where the partition displays on top of the scrollbar, setting the partition width works, but it generates a beep and no error. Setting the partition to more than 2 pixels less than the width generates an error. We're sure the folks who tested this one were using a grid with no scrollbar!

To be able to set Partition to the full range of the grid, set Scrollbars to 0 and then restore it after setting Partition where you like. You can use SYSMETRIC(5) to determine the width of the scrollbars.

In VFP 3.0, there seems to be no way to turn off the partition completely. The SplitBar property was introduced in VFP 5. We've had more than a few clients confuse themselves terribly by messing with the partition and then being unable to make things right; it's great to be able to protect them from themselves. If SplitBar is set to .F., the setting of Partition is ignored.

In versions of FoxPro before 6.0, you can't even detect the partition being moved, except by trapping the value of Partition in MouseDown and checking it in each MouseUp. In 6.0, we thought of two new possibilities. You could test for the "SplitBar" value in GridHitTest. The only problem with this is that Partition is not assigned new values while the splitbar is being dragged, only when it stops, so you might as well stick with the MouseDown, MouseUp trick. The other idea we had was to add a Partition_Assign method to the grid.

Partition_Access does not fire when you drag the SplitBar gadget around, nor when you release it. Like many built-in properties, it seems like the changing of this value cannot be trapped with the Access method.

While we would hardly ever consider using a partitionable grid in an application, the fine control we have is reassuring.

Example

```
grdGrid1.Partition = 143
```

See Also Access, Assign, GridHitTest, Panel, PanelLink, ScrollBars, SplitBar

PasswordChar

I shall be as secret as the grave.

Miguel de Cervantes, *Don Quixote de la Mancha*

This property makes a task that used to be hard really easy. It lets you specify that a text box should display a particular character instead of the character input by the user. Use it to hide passwords while they're being input.

Usage

```
txtTextbox.PasswordChar = cChar
cChar = txtTextbox.PasswordChar
```

Using PasswordChar doesn't affect the Value of the text box. It simply hides it from the user. You'll probably want to combine PasswordChar with an InputMask to limit input to a fixed number of characters.

When you enter a value for PasswordChar in the Property Sheet, do not surround it with quotes. Just type the desired character. Otherwise, you'll end up with a quote as your PasswordChar.

A number of characters can't be used for PasswordChar. Assigning any of the prohibited characters sets PasswordChar to the empty string, which results in no masking of input.

Valid PasswordChars are CHR(33) – CHR(126), CHR(130) – CHR(140), CHR(145) – CHR(156), CHR(159), and CHR(161) – CHR(255). This includes all the letters and numbers and lots of punctuation marks. In some fonts, some of the valid characters may be invisible, which leaves the text box empty—not a good choice. In fact, most of the time, the best choice is to use the asterisk "*" (CHR(42)), which is something of a Windows standard for passwords.

You can change PasswordChar dynamically and characters already typed change to the new value. You might use this ability for some cool visual tricks.

Example

```
* Assume there's a variable cPassword
* containing the password for the current user.
*
* Create a form with a textbox and a button
* Using the property sheet, set the textbox as follows:
*    PasswordChar = "*"    && asterisks
*    InputMask = "AAAA"    && four alphabetic chars
*    Format = "K"          && select all on entry
* Set the button as follows:
*    Caption = "Check"
* In the Click method of the button, put:
IF ThisForm.Text1.Value == cPassword
   * They pass - close the form
   RELEASE ThisForm
ELSE
   * No good - tell the user
   WAIT WINDOW "Invalid Password. Try again"
   ThisForm.Text1.SetFocus
ENDIF
*
* Save the form and run it. When you type in a bad
* password and click Check, you get the message.
* When you type in the right password, the form
* closes.
```

Of course, in an application, you'd want to make this a lot more foolproof, and that can be tough, 'cause fools are so darned clever. You'd want a Cancel button to let the user give up. You'd keep the form from being closed except by a valid password or by Cancel. You'd probably have a limit on the number of tries and so forth. The example, though, gives you the basic structure for this kind of test.

See Also Chr(), InputMask, Text box

Payment() See FV().

_PBPage See PrintJob ... EndPrintJob.

PCol() See Row().

_PColNo

This variable indicates the current output column for output created with ? and ??. It's analogous to the PCOL() function used with @...SAY output.

Usage
```
_PColNo = nStartColumn
```

You can set _PCOLNO to start ?? output in a specified column.

Example
```
SET PRINT TO test.txt
SET PRINT ON

FOR ncnt = 1 TO 20
   _PCOLNO = 2*ncnt
   ?? "Line "+PADL(ncnt,2)
   ?
ENDFOR

SET PRINT OFF
SET PRINT TO
* now examine Test.Txt to see the effect of setting _PCOLNO
```

See Also ?, ??, PCol()

_PCopies See PrintJob ... EndPrintJob.

PCount() See Parameters().

_PDriver, _PDSetup See Set PDSetup.

_PECode, _PEject See PrintJob ... EndPrintJob.

PEMStatus() See GetPEM().

_PEPage See PrintJob ... EndPrintJob.

Pi() See Cos().

Picture, DownPicture, DisabledPicture

These properties let you associate images with various aspects of certain controls. The meaning of Picture varies according to the control—in fact, for a couple of controls, it's an array property.

Usage
```
oObject.Picture = cPictureFile
lstList.Picture( nIndex )= cPictureFile
cboCombo.Picture( nIndex )= cPictureFile
cPictureFile = oObject.Picture
                | lstList.Picture( nIndex ) | cboCombo.Picture( nIndex )
```

In VFP 3, these properties accept only BMP files. In VFP 5, ICO was added. In VFP 6, they're even more flexible, accepting those two types as well as GIFs and JPGs.

Picture is truly a case of polymorphism at work. The table below shows how to interpret Picture for each class that has it.

Class	Meaning
CheckBox, OptionButton	If Style is 1-Graphical, picture is displayed above caption. If Style is 0-Standard, Picture is ignored.
ComboBox, ListBox	Picture is an array property. Each element corresponds to one item in the list and is displayed next to that item. The array is indexed in ListIndex (not ListItemId) order.
CommandButton	Displayed above caption on button.
Custom	Displayed in Class Designer and Form Designer to identify object, invisible at runtime.
Form, Page, Container, Control	Picture is tiled to form wallpaper.
Image	Display picture in control.

The pictures for lists and combos can only be specified at runtime and are reset whenever the list or combo's Requery method is called. In addition, the pictures only "take" when you're using one of the RowSourceTypes where the list or combo really owns the data—0 (None), 1 (Value), 5 (Array), or surprisingly, 8 (Structure).

Example

```
* Let the user assign a picture to each item in a list.
* This code might be in the Init for the list. More
* realistically, the data might have pointers to the appropriate
* picture files. The user won't appreciate having to point to
* all the pictures.
LOCAL nCnt

FOR nCnt = 1 TO This.ListCount
   This.Picture[ nCnt ] = GETPICT("BMP;ICO;GIF;JPG", ;
                                  "Choose a picture")
ENDFOR
```

Usage

```
oObject.DownPicture = cPictureFile
oObject.DisabledPicture = cPictureFile
cPictureFile = oObject.DownPicture | oObject.DisabledPicture
```

Check boxes and both kinds of buttons have three states: enabled but not chosen, chosen (or down), and disabled. You can assign a separate bitmap for each state. Picture is the enabled, but not chosen, bitmap. DownPicture is used when the control is chosen. DisabledPicture appears on a disabled control.

Usually, you'll choose similar, but slightly different pictures for the three. DisabledPicture may be a gray version of Picture. DownPicture might indicate the result of the choice. For example, if Picture shows a book, DownPicture could be an open book.

Example

```
* Set up a graphical checkbox. The specified graphics
* were included with VFP 3.
This.Style = 1
This.Picture = "\VFP\SAMPLES\GRAPHICS\BMPS\OUTLINE\CLOSED.BMP"
This.DownPicture = "\VFP\SAMPLES\GRAPHICS\BMPS\OUTLINE\OPEN.BMP"
```

See Also Icon, ListIndex, Style

Play Macro See Clear Macros.

_PLength, _PLineNo

These variables are part of the printer control system for streamed output produced with ? and ??. _PLENGTH determines the length of a page, and _PLINENO determines the current line number.

None of this has anything to do with reports generated in the Report Designer.

Usage

```
_PLENGTH = nPageSizeInLines
nPageSizeInLines = _PLENGTH
_PLINENO = nNextLineToUse
nNextLineToUse = _PLINENO
```

_PLENGTH and _PLINENO interact with the ON PAGE command to determine when that command's event fires.

Setting _PLINENO doesn't change where the next line appears. It simply changes where the streaming output engine thinks it's printing.

Example

```
* See ON PAGE
```

See Also ?, ??, Eject Page, _LMargin, On Page

_PLOffset, Set Margin

This system variable and command do the same thing. They establish a left border for the printable page when using ? and ??.

Usage

```
_PLOFFSET = nLeftBorder
SET MARGIN TO nLeftBorder
nLeftBorder = _PLOFFSET
nLeftBorder = SET( "MARGIN" )
```

_PLOFFSET and SET MARGIN work only in the printed (or redirected to file) output produced. The echo that appears in the active window ignores them. If _LMARGIN is greater than 0, it gets added to nLeftBorder to produce the actual left margin.

Example

```
_PLOFFSET = 15
SET PRINT TO Test.Txt
SET PRINT ON
?"This is a text"
SET PRINT OFF
SET PRINT TO
MODI FILE test.txt&& note indentation
```

See Also ?, ??, _LMargin

Point See PSet.

Pop Key See On Key.

Pop Menu, Pop Popup See Push Menu.

Popup() See Bar().

_PPitch, _PQuality

These don't do anything. They may have been somewhat useful, a long time ago, in a galaxy far, far away.

_PreText See Set TextMerge.

Primary() See Candidate().

Print

This method lets you put text on a form (or the main Visual FoxPro window).

Usage `frmForm.Print( [ cTextToDisplay [ nHorizPos, nVertPos ] ] )`

The specified text is displayed on the form at the position of CurrentX and CurrentY using the form's ForeColor and Font settings. CurrentX and CurrentY are updated to the end of the string. If cTextToDisplay is omitted, CurrentY increases by the height of a line in the form's font.

The undocumented nHorizPos and nVertPos parameters let you decide where to put the string in VFP 6. They respect ScaleMode, so you can use either pixels or rows and columns.

Can you have a bug for an undocumented feature? We think so.

Although you can omit either of these parameters, the position of the string when you do is pretty strange. Sometimes, the CurrentX and/or CurrentY values seem to be used. At others, it appears that 0 is used. Yet, other times, it looks like the one value you pass is used for both parameters. Bottom line, either pass both or neither. It's not worth the aggravation to omit one.

You can give Print multi-line strings, but they're pretty badly behaved. The second and subsequent lines start at the left-hand edge of the form, regardless of the initial position of CurrentX. The help is either misleading or wrong (hard to tell which) about how multi-line strings affect CurrentX and CurrentY, too. As with single-line strings, CurrentX and CurrentY end up at the ending position of the string.

Strings that don't fit on the form wrap to the next line, kind of like multi-line strings.

On the whole, we'd say to stay away from Print, except for carefully controlled special cases.

Example

```
_SCREEN.CLS()
_SCREEN.Print("This is a test. ")
_SCREEN.Print("This is only a test.")
_SCREEN.Print()
_SCREEN.CurrentX=200
* The next line will print "Here's a multi-line string" starting
* at position 200, then put "See what happens" at the left-hand
* edge of the next line.
_SCREEN.Print("Here's a multi-line string"+chr(13)+;
              "See what happens")
* Try the undocumented position parameters
_SCREEN.Print("I'll position this where I want it",200,475)
```

See Also Cls, CurrentX, CurrentY, ForeColor, FontBold, FontItalic, FontName, FontSize, FontStrikeThru, FontUnderline, ScaleMode

PrintJob See PrintJob ... EndPrintJob.

PrintStatus(), Sys(13)

These commands are of no use in Visual FoxPro, because they always return the same value.

Usage

```
lRetValue = PRINTSTATUS( )
lcRetVal = SYS( 13 )
```

In FoxPro for MS-DOS, PrintStatus() usefully returns .T. or .F., and SYS(13) returns "READY" or "OFFLINE," depending on whether your printer is truly ready or not. Under DOS, you needed to have control of things like the printer status, to keep the dreaded "Abort, Retry, Ignore" messages from obnoxiously popping up and destroying your screen. Under Windows, we let Windows worry about these things. Using FoxPro 2.x Windows or Mac, and under Visual FoxPro for Windows, this function lies and returns .T. or "READY" for backward compatibility.

Example
```
IF PRINTSTATUS()        && okay to print...
IF SYS(13) = "READY"    && okay to print...
```

See Also APrinters(), GetPrinter(), PrtInfo(), Set Printer, Sys(1037)

Private See Local.

PrmBar(), PrmPad() See BarPrompt().

Procedure See Function.

ProgID

The Programmatic Identifier (known as ProgID) is the string you pass to CreateObject() or NewObject() to create a COM object. This property tells you what string to use for a particular COM object you're creating. The property is read-only.

Usage
```
cMyServername = oServer.ProgID
```

When you create a COM server as part of a VFP Project, the server's name is created in the form "Project.ClassName," where Project is the name of your project and ClassName is the name of the visual class or program that defines the server class. To create an instance of your object, pass this name to CreateObject(). The ProgID displays the name to pass.

You cannot change this name directly. You can change the first half by modifying the server name using the Project's ServerProject property, and the second half by renaming the class library or program that defines the object.

Example
```
* Ted's project for testing SYS(2335) was called SYS2335
* His test class was a program named Fred.PRG
? oProject.Servers[1].ProgID          && "SYS2335.fred"
oDear = CREATEOBJECT("SYS2335.Fred")  && creates the object
```

See Also CreateObject(), NewObject(), Project, Server, ServerProject

Program(), Sys(16)

These two functions tell you about the program currently executing and the execution chain. They're especially handy when you're debugging.

Usage
```
nProgDepth = PROGRAM( -1 )
cProgInChain = PROGRAM( [ nLevel ] )
cProgInChain = SYS( 16 [, nLevel ] )
```

PROGRAM() returns just the name of the program without any path information. SYS(16) provides the complete path. Neither pays any attention to the setting of FULLPATH. If the program is contained in another file (like a procedure file or a class library), SYS(16) specifies the name of that file as well.

nLevel traces the execution chain. Specifying either 0 or 1 returns the main program that started the whole thing. As nLevel increases, you get closer to the currently executing program. If nLevel is greater than the number of programs in the chain, both functions return the empty string. Omitting the nLevel parameter from either function returns the currently executing program.

PROGRAM(-1), new to VFP 6, tells you how deep you are in the program chain. Before that, you had to test for EMPTY(PROGRAM()) to know when you'd reached the end. Watch out for one thing here—PROGRAM(-1) is numeric, while passing any other value gives a character return.

Our technical editor reminds us that SYS(16) is incredibly useful for locating files in an interactive development environment. He often builds tools that need to open a table or access some other file that belongs to the tool. Although all these files are in the same directory, it isn't usually the current directory when the tool is running, so code like USE Table or LOADPICTURE(SomePicture) bombs out. To avoid hard-coding paths, he uses code like:

```
lcDir = LEFT(SYS(16), AT('\', SYS(16)))
&& or in VFP 6, lcDir = JustPath(SYS(16))
USE (lcDir + 'MYTABLE')
```

The example below is a function that traces the entire execution chain and fills an array with the results. You might call this function from an error handler to determine what was going on when the program failed.

Example

```
* AProgram.PRG
* Fill an array with the programs in use, except this one.
* Column 1 contains the program name returned by PROGRAM().
* Column 2 contains the detailed information returned by
* SYS(16).
* Return the size of the array
* If parameter isn't an array, return -1.

LPARAMETERS aProgs

* Check parameter
IF TYPE("aProgs[1]")="U"
   RETURN -1
ENDIF

* Trace the calling chain
LOCAL nLevel
FOR nLevel = 1 TO PROGRAM(-1)
   DIMENSION aProgs[nLevel,2]
   aProgs[nLevel,1] = PROGRAM(nLevel)
   aProgs[nLevel,2] = SYS(16,nLevel)
ENDFOR

* now remove last row which represents this program
DIMENSION aProgs[nLevel-2,2]

RETURN nLevel-2
```

See Also Do, On Error

ProgrammaticChange See InteractiveChange.

Project

This is one of the newly exposed Automation objects that give us programmatic access to projects and their contents. Every time a project opens, a corresponding project object is created. The Projects collection is composed of Project objects. (Doesn't that have a nice ring to it—"project object"?)

Property	Value	Purpose
AutoIncrement	Logical	Indicates whether the project's version number is incremented every time the project is built.
BuildDateTime	DateTime	Contains the date and time of the most recent build of the project.

Property	Value	Purpose
Debug	Logical	Indicates whether debugging information is stored with the project.
Encrypted	Logical	Indicates whether compiled source code in the project is encrypted to provide a measure of extra security.
HomeDir	Character	Contains the path to the home directory for the project.
Icon	Character	Contains the filename for the icon used for an EXE built from the project.
MainClass	Character	If an ActiveDoc is the main object for the project, contains the name of the ActiveDoc class.
MainFile	Character	If a form or program is the main object for the project, contains its filename. If an ActiveDoc is the main object, contains the name of the class library containing the ActiveDoc class.
Name	Character	Contains the path and filename for the project.
ProjectHook	Object	If a project hook has been created for the project, contains a reference to it.
ProjectHookClass, ProjectHookLibrary	Character	If the project has a project hook, contain the class name and class library name, respectively.
SCCProvider	Character	Contains the name of the source control provider for the project.
ServerHelpFile	Character	If the project contains server classes, contains the name of a help file for the type library for those classes.
ServerProject	Character	If the project contains server classes, contains the name assigned to the project for Automation purposes. This is used along with the actual class name to instantiate the server classes. By default, this is the same as the project name.
TypeLibCLSID	Character	If the project contains server classes, contains the unique ID created for registering the type library for those classes.
TypeLibDesc	Character	If the project contains server classes, the description for the type library for those classes.
TypeLibName	Character	If the project contains server classes, the name of the type library for those classes.
VersionComments	Character	The comments from the Version dialog.
VersionCompany	Character	The company name from the Version dialog.
VersionCopyright	Character	The legal copyright information from the Version dialog.

Property	Value	Purpose
VersionDescription	Character	The file description from the Version dialog.
VersionLanguage	Numeric	The language ID from the Version dialog.
VersionNumber	Character	The three-part version number from the Version dialog.
VersionProduct	Character	The product name from the Version dialog.
VersionTrademarks	Character	The legal trademarks from the Version dialog.

Method	Purpose
Build	Rebuilds the project or builds the project into an APP, EXE or DLL.
CleanUp	Packs a project file, optionally stripping the object code.
Close	Closes the project.
Refresh	Updates the visual display of the project and can update the source control status.
SetMain	Sets a file or class as the main object for the project.

Most of the property values for a project can be found somewhere in the Project Manager, though some are pretty well hidden. A lot of the information, including server information, is in the Project Info dialog. You get to the various VersionWhatever properties by pressing the Version button in the Build dialog. At runtime, all the version information is available by calling AGetFileVersion() in VFP 6 or FoxTool's GetFileVersion() in VFP 5.

See Also ActiveProject, AutoIncrement, Build, BuildDateTime, CleanUp, Close, Debug, Encrypted, File, Files, HomeDir, Icon, MainClass, MainFile, Name, ProjectHook, ProjectHookClass, ProjectHookLibrary, Refresh, SCCProvider, SetMain, ServerHelpFile, ServerProject, TypeLibCLSID, TypeLibDesc, TypeLibName, VersionComments, VersionCompany, VersionDescription, VersionLanguage, VersionNumber, VersionProduct, VersionTrademarks

ProjectHook Class

This is the base class for project hooks, a new tool you can attach to a project to let you make things happen while you're working with the project. Every time a project opens, it has the opportunity to create and attach a project hook.

Everything really interesting about project hooks happens in their event methods.

Event	Purpose
AfterBuild	Fires when a project's Build method has completed.
BeforeBuild	Fires when a project's Build method is called (whether it's called through the interface or programmatically). Allows you to both make sure certain things happen before the build and change the nature of the build by changing the parameters to Build. NODEFAULT halts the build process.

Event	Purpose
Destroy	Fires when the project is closed. Lets you turn out the lights as you leave. (Destroy also fires if you release the project hook without closing the project, of course.)
Init	Fires when the project is opened. Lets you do things on the way in. One good thing to do here is give the project hook a reference to the project. (Of course, Init fires if you create a project hook without having it attached to a project, too.)
QueryAddFile	Fires when a new file is added to the project. Can prevent the file from being added.
QueryModifyFile	Fires when any file in the project is opened for modification (before the appropriate editor opens). Can prevent the editor from opening.
QueryRemoveFile	Fires when any file is removed from the project. Can prevent the removal.
QueryRunFile	Fires when any file in the project is executed. For reports, read "previewed" for "executed". Can prevent the execution.

Each of these events fires in response to a particular method of the Project COM object. What's most cool is that they fire no matter how that method got called.

Except for AfterBuild, these methods all have the power to prevent the specified Project method from actually executing—issue NoDefault to do so.

Although you can create project hooks in code (rather than visual) classes, and instantiate and attach those project hooks to open projects, there's no way to make a code class the default project hook for a project. When you try to set ProjectHookLibrary to a PRG, VFP yells at you.

ProjectHooks do a fine job of trapping almost every manipulation of a project, but the design does miss one. There is no QueryNewFile where a developer tool could take care of things such as naming new files, inserting standard comment blocks, or rejecting a new file.

Example

```
* This simple project hook class simply provides you with
* feedback as you work.
* Set the Include file for the class as FoxPro.H (in the main
* VFP directory) to get access to the project constants used
* in BeforeBuild.
DEFINE CLASS prjshowme AS projecthook

   Name = "prjshowme"

   *-- A pointer to the project associated with this project
   *-- hook.
   oProject = .NULL.

   PROCEDURE AfterBuild
      LPARAMETERS nError
      WAIT WINDOW "Finished building project"
   ENDPROC

   PROCEDURE BeforeBuild

      LPARAMETERS cOutputName, nBuildAction, lRebuildAll, ;
```

```
            lShowErrors, lBuildNewGuids
      LOCAL cBuildType
      DO CASE
      CASE nBuildAction = BUILDACTION_REBUILD  && 1
         cBuildType = "rebuild project"
      CASE nBuildAction = BUILDACTION_BUILDAPP && 2
         cBuildType = "build APP"
      CASE nBuildAction = BUILDACTION_BUILDEXE && 3
         cBuildType = "build EXE"
      CASE nBuildAction = BUILDACTION_BUILDDLL && 4
         cBuildType = "build DLL"
      ENDCASE

      WAIT WINDOW "About to " + cBuildType + " " + ;
            cOutputName NOWAIT
   ENDPROC

   PROCEDURE QueryRunFile
      LPARAMETERS oFile
      WAIT WINDOW "Running file "+oFile.Name NOWAIT
   ENDPROC

   PROCEDURE QueryRemoveFile
      LPARAMETERS oFile, cClassName, lDeleteFile

      LOCAL cDelete
      IF lDeleteFile
         cDelete = "Deleting"
      ELSE
         cDelete = "Removing"
      ENDIF

      IF EMPTY(cClassName)
         WAIT WINDOW cDelete + " file " + oFile.Name NOWAIT
      ELSE
         WAIT WINDOW "Removing class " + cClassName + ;
                     " from " + oFile.Name NOWAIT
      ENDIF
   ENDPROC

   PROCEDURE QueryModifyFile
      LPARAMETERS oFile, cClassName

      IF EMPTY(cClassName)
         WAIT WINDOW "Modifying file " + oFile.Name NOWAIT
      ELSE
         WAIT WINDOW "Modifying class " + cClassName + ;
                     " of " + oFile.Name NOWAIT
      ENDIF
   ENDPROC

   PROCEDURE QueryAddFile
      LPARAMETERS cFileName
      WAIT WINDOW "Adding file "+cFileName NOWAIT
   ENDPROC

   PROCEDURE Init
      WAIT WINDOW "Opening project" NOWAIT
      IF VARTYPE(_VFP.ActiveProject )= "O"
        This.oProject = _VFP.ActiveProject
      ENDIF
   ENDPROC

   PROCEDURE Destroy
      WAIT WINDOW "Closing project" NOWAIT
   ENDPROC
ENDDEFINE
```

See Also AfterBuild, BeforeBuild, Destroy, Init, NoDefault, Project, ProjectHook Property, ProjectHookClass, ProjectHookLibrary, QueryAddFile, QueryModifyFile, QueryRemoveFile, QueryRunFile

ProjectHook Property

This property gives you an object reference to the current project hook for a project. Amazingly, you can change it on the fly.

Usage

```
prjProject.ProjectHook = phkProjectHook
phkProjectHook = prjProject.ProjectHook
```

A project hook is a VFP object associated with a project that lets you jump in and exercise some control as the project is processed. When a project is open, this property points you to its current project hook. We recommend you return the favor and give your project hooks a reference to their projects.

We were somewhat stunned to discover that you can change this property at runtime. Just create a project hook object and attach it. (In fact, the same project hook instance can be attached to more than one project.) The project hook stays attached only as long as the project is open, though—it doesn't become the default for the project. While we don't see ourselves taking advantage of this capability often, we can imagine that there might be some unusual tasks for which we might want to create a special project hook class, then open a series of projects in sequence, hook them up and do whatever it is. This is also the only way to attach a project hook to a project when that project hook is defined in code, rather than visually.

There are kinks you will need to look out for if you attach project hooks this way. Because the object needs to be instantiated before it's attached to the project, the Init code can't make assumptions that "its" project is _VFP.ActiveProject, or even that there's a project open. Overall, switching hooks on the fly is something we will probably leave to the third-party vendors and builders. But we can see some the possibility of some cool stuff possible this way.

Example

```
* Attach a project hook to the active project
_VFP.ActiveProject.ProjectHook = NewObject("phkHook","MyLibr")
```

See Also Project, ProjectHook Class, ProjectHookClass, ProjectHookLibrary

ProjectHookClass, ProjectHookLibrary

These properties tell you the pedigree of the default project hook for a given project.

Usage

```
cPHkClass = prjProject.ProjectHookClass
prjProject.ProjectHookClass = cPHkClass
cPHkLibrary = prjProject.ProjectHookLibrary
prjProjectHookLibrary = cPHkLibrary
```

Every project can have a project hook class associated with it, so that whenever the project is opened, a project hook of that class is created and linked to the open project. These properties tell you what that class is.

You can change these at runtime. However, you have to do it in the right order, which is library first, then class. When you change the class, VFP checks for a class of that name in the current ProjectHookLibrary. If there isn't one or it has the wrong base class, VFP complains. If the project has no current project hook class and library, specifying the class first brings up the class selection dialog.

Changing these properties doesn't change what project hook is associated with the project right now. If there's already a project hook, it stays there. If the project didn't have one, it still doesn't. The new class is used the next time the project is opened.

Change either property to an empty string to free the project from its project hook the next time it opens.

Example

```
* Change the project hook class and library for
* the active project
_VFP.ActiveProject.ProjectHookLibrary = "MyLibrary"
_VFP.ActiveProject.ProjectHookClass = "MyProjectHook"
```

See Also Project, ProjectHook Class, ProjectHook Property

Projects

Projects is a collection (an array property) that gives you access to all open projects. It's a property of the _VFP and Application objects.

Usage

```
oProject = appApplication.Projects[ nIndex ]
appApplication.Projects[ nIndex ].Property = uValue
appApplication.Projects[ nIndex ].Method()
```

One of the big changes in VFP 6 is the ability to access projects and their contents programmatically. This makes it easier to write all kinds of cool tools to manipulate projects. The Projects collection is the first step in the process. It contains one element for each open project. The items in the collection are Project objects (try saying that one 10 times fast). The collection's Count property tells you how many there are.

To access the Projects collection, you need to use either the _VFP variable or the Application object. Projects is an ActiveX collection, not quite fully native to VFP. In practice, this means that any errors you get are OLE errors rather than native VFP errors.

Beware: As you open projects, the ones that are already open get pushed farther and farther down in the collection. That is, the most recently opened project is Projects[1] while the first project you opened is at the end of the collection. However, bringing a project to the front doesn't change its place in the collection.

Example

```
* Open a few projects.
* Now to see what's open:
FOR EACH oProj IN Application.Projects
   ?oProj.Name
ENDFOR
* How many projects are open?
? Application.Projects.Count
```

See Also ActiveProject, Application, Count, Project, _VFP

Prompt() See Bar().

Proper() See Lower().

Protect See Access().

PRow() See Row().

PrtInfo() See GetPrinter().

_PSCode See PrintJob ... EndPrintJob.

PSet, Point

These two form methods give you fine control over colors. PSet lets you color an individual pixel. Point tells you the color of a specified pixel.

Usage

```
frmForm.PSet( [ nXCoord, nYCoord ] )
nColor = frmForm.Point( [ nXCoord, nYCoord ] )
```

Parameter	Value	Meaning
nXCoord, nYCoord	Numeric	The coordinates of the point of interest.
nColor	-1	The specified point is not in the form.
	0 - 16,777,215	The color of the specified point.

If the coordinates are omitted for either method, the values of CurrentX and CurrentY are used. PSet sets the specified point to the current ForeColor. PSet interacts with DrawWidth—if DrawWidth is more than one, multiple pixels get colored. (In fact, at the resolutions we work at, we can't even see the colored pixel when DrawWidth is 1. Either that or no pixel gets colored when DrawWidth is 1.) The docs say the colored pixels are centered on the specified point. That's wrong in VFP 3—in that version, the colored pixels use the specified point as the upper-left corner.

In VFP 5 and later, when DrawWidth is greater than 2, the point you specify doesn't actually get colored. Instead, as we said, you get a box centered on the specified point. The confusing thing is that applying Point to that point immediately after "painting" it with PSet gives you not the foreground color, but the background color. See the examples to see how this works. In fact, FillStyle and FillColor determine what color that point actually is. It's as if you called the Box method.

These methods are not affected by ScaleMode—they always address individual pixels.

Example

```
* Color a few points
_SCREEN.ForeColor = RGB(255, 0, 0)
_SCREEN.PSet(100, 100)     && It's red, but hard to see
? _SCREEN.Point()            && Returns 255
_SCREEN.Cls
_SCREEN.DrawWidth = 10
_SCREEN.PSet()             && Now you can see it
? _SCREEN.Point()          && Returns the value of BackColor
? _SCREEN.Point(100, 100)  && So does this
? _SCREEN.Point(95, 95)    && This, however, gives you 255
? _SCREEN.Point(95, 104)   && So does this and a number of others
? _SCREEN.Point(-10, -200)   && Returns -1
```

See Also Box, CurrentX, CurrentY, DrawWidth, FillColor, FillStyle, ForeColor, ScaleMode

_PSpacing

This system variable determines the line spacing for output generated with ? and ??.

Usage `_PSPACING = nLineSpacing`

You can set _PSpacing to anything you want, as long as it's between 1 and 3. Only the integer part of the value is significant—no line-and-a-half spacing allowed.

Example

```
SET PRINT TO test.txt
SET PRINT ON

_PSPACING = 2
FOR ncnt = 1 TO 20
   _PCOLNO = 2*ncnt
   ?? "Line "+PADL(ncnt,2)
   ?
ENDFOR
SET PRINT OFF
SET PRINT TO
* Note that the line spacing is doubled
```

See Also ?, ??

Public See Local.

Push Key See On Key.

Push Menu, Pop Menu, Push Popup, Pop Popup

These commands let you save and restore a defined menu or popup, so you can replace it with another, then return to it.

Usage
```
PUSH MENU MenuName
POP MENU MenuName [ TO MASTER ]
PUSH POPUP PopupName
POP POPUP PopupName
```

The PUSH and POP in these commands are the traditional operations of a stack—a last-in, first-out data structure that resembles our desks. You put things into a stack (or push them) one at a time. When you remove something (or pop it) from the stack, you get the last one you added first. (Calling and returning from procedures uses a stack, too—when you call a procedure, the one you're in gets pushed onto a stack. Each subsequent call adds another procedure to the stack. When you hit a return, the top item on the stack—the routine that called the one you're in—is popped.)

FoxPro gives us access to several stacks, including the two here, for menu and popup definitions. We rarely use the popup stack, but the menu stack is really handy. You can PUSH MENU _MSYSMENU to save the current system menu, then run a menu program (MPR) that makes some changes—maybe adds another pad or removes a few bars. When you're done with the operation, just POP MENU _MSYSMENU and you have the original menu back.

You can use the menu stack to make your menu work the way FoxPro's does. On the way into a particular form, you can add a menu pad specific to that form. When you leave the form, you can get rid of that pad. In an event-driven app, you'll probably want to do all this menu handling in the form's (or formset's) Activate and Deactivate events.

Example
```
* In a form's Activate event
PUSH MENU _MSYSMENU
DO MyForm.MPR

* In the form's Deactivate
POP MENU _MSYSMENU
```

See Also Define Menu, Define Popup, Menus

PutFile() See GetDir().

Puzzle

It's not FreeCell or Myst, but there's a simple little game built into Visual FoxPro 3.0 to help you pass the time waiting for a printout. Removed in VFP 5.0.

Usage
```
ACTIVATE WINDOW PUZZLE
```

Puzzle was introduced with the FoxPro 2.0 interface, as one of the Mac-like Desk Accessories. (In fact, it's a rip-off of the puzzle found on the Mac's apple menu.) It is not available from the menu interface in Visual FoxPro 3.0, but it's still in there. Add the menu bar _MST_PUZZLE to your custom menu, or issue the command above to make it appear. In later versions, the menu errors with "Feature not available," and the command complains, "Window 'PUZZLE' has not been defined."

See Also Calculator, Calendar/Diary, Desk Accessories, Filer

PV() See FV().

_PWait See PrintJob ... EndPrintJob.

QueryAddFile, QueryModifyFile, QueryRemoveFile, QueryRunFile

These events are among the things that make project hooks so powerful. They fire just before the indicated action occurs and give you a chance to meddle.

Usage

```
phkProjectHook.QueryAddFile( cFileName )
phkProjectHook.QueryModifyFile( filFile [, cClassName ] )
phkProjectHook.QueryRemoveFile( filFile [, cClassName | lDeleteIt ] )
phkProjectHook.QueryRunFile( filFile )
```

Parameter	Value	Meaning
cFileName	Character	The name of the file being added, including the path.
filFile	File Object	An object reference to the file affected.
cClassName	Character	The class to be modified or removed from the class library. Passed only if filFile is a class library and, for QueryRemoveFile, only if an individual class is selected for removal, not the whole class library.
lDeleteIt	Logical	Indicates whether the file is also being deleted from the disk.

These are some of the events that give project hooks their hook. You can do whatever you want before the specified action takes place, including prevent it. Among the things you might want to do are log the action or confirm it with the user (though we'd hate that, if it were us).

To prevent the action, put NODEFAULT in the code. If you're thinking of doing so, remember that a developer-user might be a little puzzled to click Modify and not have an editor open up, so save this one for when it really makes sense. When is that? One thing that comes to mind is when the developer chooses Run and the file really needs a lot of other stuff in place in order to run properly. Rather than running it and making a mess, you might want to tell the developer what needs to happen first and abort the run.

The other place where stopping an action in its tracks might make sense is when you're doing lots of project manipulation programmatically. You can call the project/file method to do something, and let the QueryWhateverFile method figure out whether it really ought to happen.

There's one Query-Action that we think is missing here—a QueryOnNew() event that would fire when a developer adds a new file to a project. This would give us the hooks we need to enforce security of a project, fully log what's going into a project, or invent our own source control routine. We can think of lots of cool things to add to this event, as a hook for our project builds. Maybe next version...

Example

```
* Log additions to a project
* Assume that the log table is open, perhaps opened
* by the project hook's Init event.
PROCEDURE QueryAddFile
LPARAMETERS cFileName

INSERT INTO Log VALUES ("Add",cFileName,DATETIME())
RETURN
```

See Also Add, AfterBuild, BeforeBuild, Modify, ProjectHook, Remove, Run

QueryUnload

> We ask and ask: Thou smilest and art still,
> Out-topping knowledge.
>
> Matthew Arnold, *Shakespeare*, 1849

This method is called when the user closes a form with the Close box or when code causes a form to close. It's the place to double-check that the user really wants to close the form and to give her a chance to save her work before closing.

Usage `PROCEDURE oForm.QueryUnload`

QueryUnload is called before the form's Destroy method and gives you a chance to abort the closure. Including NoDefault in QueryUnload prevents the form from closing.

QueryUnload is not called when a form's associated variable is released or when the form's Release method is called directly.

The ReleaseType property indicates how a form is being closed. It's set before QueryUnload triggers, so you can investigate in the QueryUnload method and take different actions based on the reason the form is closing.

Example

```
* Here's a typical QueryUnload method
LOCAL nchoice, lReturn

* assumes the form has #INCLUDEd "FoxPro.h"
nchoice = MESSAGEBOX("Save changes", ;
            MB_YESNOCANCEL + MB_ICONQUESTION + MB_DEFBUTTON1)

lReturn=.t.
DO CASE
CASE nchoice = IDYES
   WAIT WINDOW "Saving changes"
CASE nchoice = IDNO
   WAIT WINDOW "Exit without saving"
CASE nchoice = IDCANCEL
   NODEFAULT
   lReturn=.f.
ENDCASE

RETURN lReturn
```

You'll normally want to integrate QueryUnload for individual forms with an application's ON SHUTDOWN routine. That way, when a user closes your application by double-clicking in the main window, she'll get a chance to save her work in open windows.

The return value lReturn in the example lets you call QueryUnload from a Shutdown routine and determine whether or not the user allows the form to close. If so, you can call the form's Release method from the Shutdown routine to close the form. If not, you can abort the closing of the application.

See Also On ShutDown, Release, ReleaseType

Quit

This command closes Visual FoxPro. It's equivalent to choosing File-Exit from the main menu or double-clicking on the control menu.

Some folks use Quit to end their applications. We don't recommend it, because it shuts down FoxPro in the process, something you won't much appreciate when you're testing an app. Use RETURN instead. Reserve QUIT for those times, such as in an error handler when all hell has broken loose, that you really want your user out of FoxPro, and not just out of your app.

Usage `QUIT`

QUIT triggers the ON SHUTDOWN routine if there is one. Make sure that routine is available or you won't be able to quit.

The Help file includes a dire warning about being sure to issue QUIT when you exit VFP. For development mode, it's an excellent warning, but when your users are working in the runtime environment, terminating your application has the same effect, and QUIT is unnecessary.

See Also Cancel, Clear Events, On ShutDown, Return

Rand()

Ain't life Rand? This function returns random numbers. Actually, they're technically known as "pseudo-random" numbers. This means that you can produce the same sequence over and over. It's important because, when testing, you need the ability to work on the same data.

Usage `nReturnValue = RAND( [nSeed] )`

Parameter	Value	Meaning
nSeed	Any negative number or zero	Seeds the function with a value based on the system clock.
	Any positive number	Seeds the function with the passed value.
	Omitted	Seeds the function based on the last value returned by it. If this is the first call, the seed is 10001.

All random-number functions need a seed value based on which the function computes a random result. Passing the same number should (and does, in FoxPro) return the same "random" number. This ability allows you to test on the same data set.

To get the most random results, pass a negative number or zero as the initial seed. That seeds the function based on the system clock. On subsequent calls, omit the seed and FoxPro uses the previous number as a seed. You'll always get the same sequence if you start with the same value, but with a negative initial seed, that's very unlikely.

To mathematicians, a "random number" is always between 0 and 1, and that's what RAND() returns. Since you'll usually want a random integer in some range, you need to scale the result appropriately. The formula to convert the result to an integer between 0 and some boundary seems simple:

```
INT(nBoundary*RAND())
```

but things are seldom what they seem.

In all versions of FoxPro before VFP5, RAND() returns both 0 and 1, but very rarely. Using the formula above, you get many fewer occurrences of nBoundary from a sequence of calls to RAND() then any other number in the range. You can fix that by adding 1 to the result (INT(nBoundary*RAND())+1), but then you get too few zeroes. There's no good solution to the problem. The best solution is for RAND() to never return one or the other of the endpoints (that is, RAND() should either never return 0 or never return 1).

Good news. Starting in VFP5, that's exactly how it's done. RAND() never returns 1, so you can use INT(nBoundary * RAND()) to get values from 0 to nBoundary-1 or INT(nBoundary * RAND()) + 1 to go from 1 to nBoundary. No more ugly correction code that fouls up statistics.

One question you'd think we'd hear a lot is "How random are the results of RAND()?" There are various tests you can run to test the randomness of a sequence of random numbers. The CD contains two tests. Each generates a sequence of random numbers and then computes a statistic about it. The first is the Chi-Squared test. It returns a value you can look up in a table (try a statistics textbook, or check out Excel's CHIDIST() function) to see how random RAND() is. The second test is called the "Coupon Collectors" test. The return value is the average number of random numbers you have to generate in order to be sure you've gotten at least one of each value in a range.

Example

```
* Here's the right way to use RAND() in a program, if you
* want a truly random sequence.
* First, seed RAND() with -1 (or 0 or any other negative number)
RAND(-1)

* Then, use RAND() with no seed inside whatever loop
* you're performing.
FOR nCnt = 1 TO nIterations
  nRand = RAND()
  * Now do something with nRand
ENDFOR
```

RangeHigh, RangeLow

These events take the place of the old Range clause of @ ... GETs. For text boxes and spinners, they fire on the way out and ensure that the value is within the specified range. If not, focus stays on the current control.

Usage

```
PROCEDURE oObject.RangeHigh
[ LPARAMETERS nControlIndex ]
RETURN nRangeHigh

PROCEDURE oObject.RangeLow
[ LPARAMETERS nControlIndex ]
RETURN nRangeLow
```

As with other events, the parameter is relevant only if the object involved is a control array. Then, nControlIndex indicates which member of the array fired the event.

We were surprised as heck to find these as events, not properties, but then we thought about it. In FoxPro 2.x, the Range clause could actually call functions to compute the boundaries, so there is a history of involving code. The two Range events each fire, Low then High, when attempting to shift focus to another control. They fire before Valid and LostFocus, and both fire, even if the RangeLow event fails.

In any case, to have these events function like the old Range clause, just have each one return the appropriate boundary value. We don't recommend this, though, because if the test fails, the error message is the same old default WAIT WINDOW with a message like "Range: 0 to 20." Do your testing in the Valid clause (or the field-level rules) where you have more control over what happens next. For spinners, if you don't need code to compute the boundaries, you can store the range in the two property pairs SpinnerLowValue and SpinnerHighValue, and KeyboardLowValue and KeyboardHighValue. That'll do a good job of keeping the user from entering the wrong value.

If you do choose to use these events, ensure that your routines return a numeric value, or a nasty infinite loop can occur, with the stupid control insisting "Range: to .T." Ever tried to type a .T. into a spinner? It's not easy!
Incidentally, these controls are just as stupid if you reverse the High and Low values.

Help is incredibly misleading about the relationship of these events to combo and list boxes. It appears to be just bad documentation, though, not any bugs in the product.

In FoxPro 2.x, the "1st Element" and "# of Elements" conditions for lists and drop-downs were implemented through the Range clause. (Take a look at a generated SPR to see this.) When you convert a 2.x screen that contains procedures (rather than expressions) for those items, whatever you had there goes in the RangeLow and RangeHigh events. In that case, RangeLow and RangeHigh do fire on the way into the form.

Other than that situation, as far as we can tell, RangeHigh and RangeLow never fire for lists or combos. The code is there, but it never gets executed. It definitely doesn't specify which item in the control is initially selected, as the Help says. Try DisplayValue for that.

Example

```
* This method might be used for a textbox on a form where
* the lower bound is based on another value entered on the
* same form.
PROCEDURE txtGrade.RangeLow
RETURN ThisForm.nAge - 5
```

See Also DisplayValue, Valid

RAt() See At().

RAtC() See At_C().

RAtLine() See AtLine().

RD See CD.

RdLevel()

This function returns the current read level when using READs. It has no use with forms using the Visual FoxPro event model.

Usage

```
nCurrentReadLevel = RDLEVEL()
```

Example

```
IF RDLEVEL()=5  && or 10, in later versions
   WAIT WINDOW "Sorry, you're maxed out. No more READs for you"
ELSE
   DO Another.SPR
ENDIF
```

In FoxPro 2.x, we mostly used RDLEVEL() in menu SKIP FOR conditions to prevent some options from being available when other options were in use. With a foundation READ in place, giving a menu item a SKIP FOR condition of RDLEVEL()>1 prevents the user from choosing that item when any screen is active. This is useful in modal applications and for items that need to be the only thing running, like reindex routines.

See Also Read

Read

In all versions of FoxPro before Visual FoxPro (not to mention other assorted Xbase variants), READ was perhaps the most important command in the language. It activates input controls created with @ ... GET and @ ... EDIT. From FoxPro 2.0 forward, READ was also the prescribed method of keeping an application active, through the deservedly much maligned Foundation READ.

In Visual FoxPro, there's only one important form of READ: READ EVENTS, which is discussed below. All the rest are obsolete and should be used only in old code that hasn't been updated. Use the Form Designer and Visual FoxPro's controls instead of Screen Builder and @ ... GETs and @ ... EDITs.

If you need to know the ins and outs of READ (say, to maintain or update some old code), check out a good

FoxPro 2.x reference—you'll find several listed in the Appendix.

See Also @ Commands, Read Events

Read Events, Clear Events

These are the commands that hook your forms into the native event loop of Visual FoxPro, as we describe in "A Gala Event." Despite their inclusion in the READ and CLEAR help topics, these commands are best left by themselves, without the extra paraphernalia of the older READ model. READ EVENTS MODAL TIMEOUT 15, for example, while accepted by FoxPro as a valid command, does not time out and does not act modally.

The right way to use READ EVENTS is to issue the command after your application has started up and established its environment, custom menu and global settings. When your application is done, issue CLEAR EVENTS to release your code from the suspended animation of the READ EVENTS event loop, and then your code can proceed to close out all open forms, and close out your application.

Example

```
READ EVENTS  && start event loop processing
CLEAR EVENTS && end event loop processing
```

See Also Read, Clear

Read Menu See @ ... Menu.

ReadActivate, ReadDeactivate, ReadShow, ReadValid, ReadWhen

These formset events are descendants of the READ command's event-handling clauses, one event to a clause. They get populated when you apply Functional Conversion to a 2.x screen and fire at the appropriate times when you run the resulting formset.

These events fire only when WindowType is 2 or 3—the types reserved for READ compatibility. You have no reason to ever put code in one of these yourself.

Don't confuse ReadWhen and ReadValid with the useful, control-level When and Valid events. Note also that the ReadActivate, ReadDeactivate and ReadShow events don't replace the form and formset Activate, Deactivate and Show events. Those fire as well. The firing sequence is nicely documented in Help under the aptly named "Event Firing Sequence" in the "Overview of READ Compatibility Architecture."

See Also Read, ReadCycle

ReadBackColor, ReadForeColor

Help just barely lists these properties and indicates that they're used only for backward compatibility. We've looked everywhere we can think of and we can find neither hide nor hair of them. Seems like they got cut, but not fully removed from Help.

See Also BackColor, ForeColor, Set Intensity

ReadCycle, ReadLock, ReadMouse, ReadObject, ReadSave, ReadTimeOut

These formset properties map directly to clauses of the now-obsolete READ. They're used when the Visual FoxPro Converter translates 2.x screen sets into Visual FoxPro.

Except in formsets created by Functional Conversion, you don't even have access to these properties. Well, actually, you have access to them, but it doesn't matter what value you assign—they're ignored unless

WindowType is 2 or 3. And you can't create formsets with WindowType set to 2 or 3, except in code. More importantly, you have no reason to create formsets with WindowType set to 2 or 3.

If you must use functional conversion, let the Converter set these properties to match your 2.x screens. Better yet, stay away from functional conversion and the half-breed forms it creates.

ReadTimeOut is documented as holding seconds (at least in VFP 3—in later versions, it's just barely documented at all). In fact, it's measured in milliseconds. The Converter does properly detect a #READCLAUSES TimeOut and converts the number it finds to milliseconds.

See Also Read, ReadActivate, ReadDeactivate, ReadShow, ReadValid, ReadWhen

ReadDeactivate See ReadActivate.

ReadExpression, WriteExpression, ReadMethod, WriteMethod

These are the methods that make builders and wizards possible. ReadExpression and WriteExpression give you access to properties containing expressions (as opposed to values). ReadMethod and WriteMethod let you access and change method code.

Usage

```
cPropExpression = oObject.ReadExpression( cProperty )
lSuccess = oObject.WriteExpression( cProperty, cPropExpression )
cCode = oObject.ReadMethod( cMethod )
lSuccess = oObject.WriteMethod( cMethod, cCode )
```

Parameter	Value	Meaning
cProperty	Character	The name of the property whose expression is being accessed or changed.
cPropExpression	Character	An expression beginning with "=" that is assigned to cProperty. The expression is not evaluated in the WriteExpression call, but is stored to the property for evaluation at runtime.
cMethod	Character	The name of the method whose code is being accessed or changed.
cCode	Character	The code for cMethod. Lines are delimited with CHR(13).
lSuccess	Logical	Indicates whether the change was successful.

In VFP 3, all of these methods are available only at design time. In VFP 5 and 6, ReadExpression, WriteExpression and ReadMethod are available at runtime as well.

ReadExpression and ReadMethod return what they find in the specified property or method. WriteExpression and WriteMethod return .T. if they're successful. As far as we can tell, they never actually return .F. because they trigger errors instead.

ReadMethod and WriteMethod are pretty straightforward. They simply let you grab the code that's already in a method or put new code there. Be aware that WriteMethod overwrites any existing code. To add to what's already there, grab it first with ReadMethod and then concatenate the new code onto the end.

The property-related methods are a little more confusing. What's going on here is that they're meant for properties containing expressions rather than values. If Caption = "My Great Form," you can find that out without ReadExpression. But if Caption = "My Form - " + MDY(DATE()), you need ReadExpression to find it out. If you just look at Caption, you'll see something like "My Form - September 28, 1998"—not what you want to know.

Similarly, if you want to store an expression to a property, you can't just write the assignment. If you set Caption to "My Form - " + MDY(DATE()), the expression gets evaluated immediately and the result is stored in Caption. Again, not what you want. WriteExpression lets you store the expression itself, so it can be evaluated at runtime.

With the new AddProperty method in VFP 6, we suspect WriteExpression will be more useful than ever, since we can now create properties that can't be set up at design time, so we'll have more need to store expressions in properties at runtime.

You need to call these methods for the object you actually want to change. You can't pass a name that drills down into the object hierarchy (like "Form1.Grid1.Column1.BackColor") for cProperty or cMethod—you have to pass something like "BackColor" or "Click". At design time, you get your hands on the object you want by calling ASelObj() or SYS(1270).

Because you're dealing with strings here and they might need quotes inside, this is one place where having three sets of character delimiters really comes in handy. We've used all three ("", '', []) in a WriteExpression call.

Munging up the expression, by skipping or mismatching a pair of string delimiters, returns the informative "Unknown error code: " followed by a negative number. If you see this, try reworking your expression; something in there is confusing FoxPro.

You'll find more information on these methods in "Builders and Wizards (and Bears, Oh My!)" on the CD.

Example

```
* Set a form's caption to include today's date
* Get a reference with aSelObj()
= aSelObj(aSelect, 1)
* Now assign the property:
aSelect[1].WriteExpression("Caption", ;
   '= "My Form - " + MDY(DATE())')

* Set the DynamicForeColor property of a grid column
* First we put a reference to the grid in aSelect[1]
* Make sure the grid is selected, then:
= aSelObj(aSelect)
* Now we can work with it
aSelect[1].Column1.WriteExpression("DynamicForeColor", ;
   '= "IIF(balance<0, RGB(255,0,0), RGB(0,0,0)"')

* Hmm, maybe we want all columns to have that. Let's
* set the grid's Init to do it for all columns, but we
* don't want to lose anything already in the Init
cInitCode = aSelect[1].ReadMethod("Init")
aSelect[1].WriteMethod("Init", cInitCode + CHR(13) + ;
   [This.SetAll("DynamicForeColor", ;
   "IIF(balance<0, RGB(255,0,0), RGB(0,0,0))")])
```

See Also AddProperty, ASelObj(), Sys(1270)

ReadForeColor See ReadBackColor.

ReadKey()

We didn't use this function much in FoxPro 2.x. We don't use it at all in Visual FoxPro. It tells you how the last READ or full-screen editing command was exited.

Usage

```
nCode = READKEY( [ nReadOnly ] )
```

The optional parameter tells READKEY() to pay attention only to the last READ and indicate the cause for its death. Otherwise, the function returns information about the last full-screen editing command that ended—this includes Browse, Append, Read and a few others.

See Help for the list of codes returned if you have to maintain old code that includes this function. Don't write any new code using it.

See Also ReleaseType, TerminateRead

ReadLock **See ReadCycle.**

ReadMethod **See ReadExpression.**

ReadMouse, ReadObject **See ReadCycle.**

ReadOnly **See Alias.**

ReadSave **See ReadCycle.**

ReadShow **See ReadActivate.**

ReadTimeOut **See ReadCycle.**

ReadValid, ReadWhen **See ReadActivate.**

Recall **See Delete.**

RecCount() **See RecSize().**

RecNo()

This function returns the physical position number for a record. It also has an optional parameter that makes it part of FoxPro's "soft seek" process.

Usage `nReturnValue = RECNO( [ cAlias | nWorkArea  | nSoftSeek ] )`

Parameter	Value	Meaning
cAlias	Character	Return the record number in the table open as cAlias.
	Omitted	If nWorkArea is also omitted, return the record number in the current work area.
nWorkArea	Numeric	Return the record number in the table open in work area nWorkArea.
	Omitted	If cAlias is also omitted, return the record number in the current work area.
nSoftSeek	0	Return the record number of the closest match to the last SEEK.
	Omitted	Return the record number of the current record in the specified work area.

RECNO() has two totally different functions, one of which most FoxPro users are familiar with and the other far more obscure. When the nSoftSeek parameter is omitted, RECNO() finds the physical record number of the current record in the specified table.

When 0 is passed for nSoftSeek, RECNO() follows up on the last SEEK and returns the record number of the closest match found. If no match is found, RECNO(0) returns 0. Soft seek can be used only in the current work area—you can't specify an alias or work area number together with the zero. The definition of "closest match" is based on the normal string-matching scheme used in FoxPro. That is, start matching from the left and stop when you can't match anymore. Unlike a regular comparison, soft seek can ignore non-blanks after the matching portion of either string. For example, if you SEEK "Comfort", and there's no record for "Comfort", but there is one for "Compass", RECNO(0) points to the "Compass" record, even though "Compass" is never equal to "Comfort", regardless of the setting of SET EXACT. We can't remember ever actually using this information, though—on those rare occasions when we want to do a soft seek, we tend to use SET NEAR. Remember that the physical record number isn't terribly meaningful. The only place it's really useful is with GOTO. Pretty much the only time we ever use record numbers is when we need to keep track of the current record pointer position when we want to move it temporarily.

VFP's data buffering adds a new wrinkle to record numbers. When table buffering is on, new records are assigned temporary record numbers until they're committed to the table. The temporary record numbers are negative, starting with -1. Be careful when working with these record numbers. First, you need to be aware that some record numbers may be negative. Second, the record number for a particular record may change (usually when a previously added record is removed with TABLEREVERT()), so you can't just save a record number and assume that you'll be able to find that record again. All this is one more reason not to rely on record numbers.

And, if you need one more reason, be aware that using RECNO() in a query isn't reliable either, unless the query involves only a single table.

Example

```
USE Customer
? RECNO()           && returns 1
SKIP 5
? RECNO()           && returns 6

* now check out softseek
SET ORDER TO Company_Na
SEEK 'CAESAR'
? FOUND()  && returns .F.
? RECNO(0) && returns 13, which is "Centro comercial Moctezuma"

* hold pointer position and return
IF EOF()
   nCurrentRec=0
ELSE
   nCurrentRec=RECNO()
ENDIF
* do some processing
IF nCurrentRec=0
   GO BOTTOM
   SKIP
ELSE
   GO nCurrentRec
ENDIF
```

See Also GoTo, Seek, Set Near

RecordMark, DeleteMark

These two properties determine whether a grid has the two special columns at the left that contain a little record pointer and indicate deleted records, respectively.

Usage

```
grdGrid.RecordMark = lHasRecordMark
lHasRecordMark = grdGrid.RecordMark
grdGrid.DeleteMark = lHasDeleteMark
lHasDeleteMark = grdGrid.DeleteMark
```

Although we've shown both of these as needing logical values, you can actually specify 0 or 1 (for .F. and .T., respectively) as well. We can't figure why this is, since generally you can't use numerics for logicals in FoxPro. Guess some C guy got carried away.

If you set both of these to .F. (or zero), the left-hand border of the grid is pretty wimpy looking. So, even if you don't want delete markers (and you probably don't), you may want the RecordMark column. A grid with RecordMark = .T. and DeleteMark = .F. looks pretty nifty. The DeleteMark is pretty lame—it blacks out an entire box. We'd prefer an "X" or skull-and-crossbones, or even better, a column where we can put in our own controls and method calls—come to think of it, we can do that! And we think you should.

So why don't you want delete markers? When DelcteMark is .T., the user can delete a record by clicking on the delete mark for that row. At that point, triggers fire, the record needs to be locked and so forth. We don't think we'll be writing many applications in which deletion should be as easy as clicking in a grid. Generally, deletion is a pretty serious operation and you should control it in your app. We've also heard some stories about locking issues and the like when users delete records from parent-child grids or try to use a single click to both select and delete a record. Although we haven't been able to replicate these ourselves, we've heard enough of them to believe that allowing deletion in grids requires kid gloves.

A DeleteMarkReadOnly property to let our users look but not touch has been suggested by others, but we'd suggest you drop the DeleteMark altogether and add in a read-only check box.

Example

```
* Add a record mark to an existing grid
ThisForm.grdMyGrid.RecordMark = .T.
```

See Also ActiveRow, Delete, Deleted, Recall, RecNo()

RecordSource, RecordSourceType

These two properties determine what table or cursor provides the data for a grid. RecordSourceType, which tells the grid what kind of object to get its value from, offers the expected choices plus one really strange one. RecordSource identifies the particular item that provides the grid data.

Usage

```
grdGrid.RecordSource = cSource
cSource = grdGrid.RecordSource
grdGrid.RecordSourceType = nSourceType
nSourceType = grdGrid.RecordSourceType
```

A grid can be based on a table, an alias, a query, a SQL statement or a "prompt." The list should raise several questions. We'll answer them before you can ask.

The difference between "Table" and "Alias" is that "Table" opens the table automatically, while "Alias" expects to find it open.

"Query" takes a QPR file (such as created by the Query Designer) and fills the grid with the results. The file's extension must be QPR, regardless of whether you use the QD or write the code yourself. (This strikes us as poor design.) "SQL Statement," like the similar choice for combos and lists, lets you type a query directly into the RecordSource. This option was added in VFP 5. With both query choices, make sure the query results are directed somewhere (the easiest is into a junk cursor) or the default Browse pops up before the grid gets filled. The query choice for grids is much less flexible than that for combos and lists because grids have no Requery method. If you want to re-execute the query to refill the grid, you have to reset RecordSource to the file or command, but that throws away any changes you've made to the grid columns, including their ControlSources. (See below for more on this.) A better choice than either "Query" or "SQL Statement" is to create a view with the data you want and base the grid on that.

The final choice, "Prompt," is pretty odd. We suppose it's meant to give you the functionality you get when you issue a BROWSE and no table is open in the current work area. Since we generally do that only by accident, we can't see why grids need to do it. "Prompt" behaves differently depending on the situation. First, if there's a table open in the current work area, it's used as the grid's RecordSource and no dialog appears at all. This is the same behavior you get if you leave RecordSourceType set to 1-Alias and RecordSource blank.

With RecordSourceType set to 2-Prompt, if no table is open in the current work area you're prompted to choose one, but if the table you choose is already open in another work area, the grid doesn't get filled at all—it consists of just a thin black outline. We can't think of any situation in which that's the desired result.

If you get prompted and the table isn't already open, it's opened and used for the grid.

We were pleased by the addition of SQL Statement to the list, but we're still hoping the list of RecordSourceTypes will be enhanced down the road. The one we'd really like to see there is Array, but we bet the creative folks who gave us 10 choices for list and combo RowSourceType can come up with some more, too.

Once you've chosen a RecordSourceType, filling in RecordSource is pretty simple.

If you do something that closes the RecordSource of a grid (like rerun the query that created it), the grid clears out. All you have is a rectangle in the grid's BackColor. If you re-create the cursor or reopen the table, you have to reset RecordSource to the cursor (or SQL statement) to refill the grid, but any column-level changes you've made (like header captions or column widths or ColumnCount) are lost for good. This is another case where a view is a better choice.

There is a work-around (read: trick) you can use to prevent all your changes from being lost. Instead of just resetting RecordSource, first set it to the empty string, then do whatever table manipulation you need to do (close and reopen a table, run a query, whatever), then reset RecordSource to its original value. However, if you've set the ControlSources of the individual columns to something other than the default (that is, the same-numbered field in the table), you have to save the ControlSources and restore them afterward, too.

Example

```
This.RecordSourceType = 0 && Table
This.RecordSource = "Employee.DBF"
```

See Also Grid, RowSource, RowSourceType

RecSize(), LUpdate(), RecCount()

These three functions return status information on a specified table based on information stored in the table's header. If your tables start giving you wacky results, and you're an intrepid enough hacker to hex-edit the header to fix them (make a backup first!), here are some clues as to how they are stored. All three functions return an empty value—0 for the numeric functions, and an empty date for LUPDATE()—if no table is available, but complain if passed a bogus alias. When passed a null value, all three functions return error 17, "Invalid table number."

Usage

```
nRetVal = RECSIZE( [ cAlias | nWorkArea ] )
```

Parameter	Value	Meaning
cAlias	Character	The alias of the table whose record size is returned.
	Omitted	If nWorkArea is also omitted, use current work area.
nWorkArea	Numeric	The work area containing the table whose record size is returned.
	Omitted	If cAlias is also omitted, use current work area.

RECSIZE() reports the size of a single record. This information is stored in bytes 10 and 11 of the file header, in low-byte, high-byte binary format. Unlike FCOUNT() and AFIELDS(), RECSIZE() returns the true length of each record, including the first byte used as the deleted flag, and the bytes of the hidden _NullFlags field (see

"DBF, FPT, CDX, DBC—Hike!") if there are any nullable fields.

Example
```
CREATE TABLE sample (dDate D, ;
                     cTime C(6), ;
                     yCurrency Y, ;
                     nNumeric N(9,3), ;
                     mMemo M)
? RECSIZE()  && 36
COPY TO sample2 TYPE FOX2X
USE sample2
? RECSIZE()  && it took 54 characters to store in Fox 2.x!
```

Usage `dRetVal = LUPDATE( [ cAlias | nWorkArea ] )`

Here's a function we were pleased to see changed in VFP 6. In previous versions, LUPDATE() reports the date the file was last updated, using the same parameters and following the same rules as RECSIZE() above. For VFP 5 and earlier, this information is stored in bytes 1, 2 and 3 of the file header in binary format—one character each for year, month and day, in that order. We pointed out in the first *Hacker's Guide* that this was not Year 2000 compatible. Well, someone listened. VFP 6 ignores the bytes in the file header and reads the directory entry for the date last modified.

For Visual FoxPro 5 and earlier, only the last two digits of the year are stored within the DBF header—updating a file in 1900 or in 2000 both store CHR(00) to byte 1. While the former is unlikely, the latter will happen Real Soon Now, and you should consider several coding alternatives. If you're planning on having code last into the next century, you may need to test LUPDATE()'s return and add 100 to it if the current date is greater than 12/31/1999. Or write a roll-your-own type of ROLLOVER process. Or you could avoid this function altogether: consider the FDATE() function instead.

Example `? LUPDATE("Customer")  && displays date last updated`

Usage `nRetVal = RECCOUNT( [ cAlias | nWorkArea ] )`

RECCOUNT() returns the current number of records in the table, using the same parameters and following the same rules as RECSIZE() above. This information is stored in bytes 4, 5, 6 and 7 of the file header, in low-byte, high-byte binary format. Obviously, this limits the maximum table size to 2,147,483,648 records, but this isn't a limit most of us will be too concerned with. While DOS is limited to only 2 gigabytes per logical volume, most of the more recent operating systems can easily handle the raw size of such a table. Throughput and raw I/O limitations, however, encourage more reasonable sized tables. The few demigods who manipulate data of this size have found several strategies to work around the limits: segregate the data logically (A–M in one file, N–Z in a second), or partitioning by date or type.

Example `? RECCOUNT("Labels")  && 86 on our copies - yours may vary`

See Also ADir(), AFields(), Display, FCount(), FDate(), FSize(), List

Refresh

This method updates an object. It's the VFP equivalent of FoxPro 2.x's SHOW GET and SHOW GETS commands.

Usage `oObject.Refresh( [ lUpdateSourceControl ] )`

When a record pointer moves or you recalculate a value, you usually want to update the display right away. That's what Refresh is for. (Draw simply redraws what was already displayed.)

Refresh is also a method of the Project object, letting you refresh the visual display of the Project Manager after making changes. This is equivalent to selecting Refresh from the Project menu, or pressing F5 when the project has the focus. This isn't useful for solo developers, but is handy in situations where one person might add to a class library and another wants to see the changes.

The optional parameter applies to projects under source code control. It determines whether or not the source control status of each file in the project is updated at the same time as the display is refreshed. Since your teammates can change the status of files you might be interested in, this method call gives you an easy way to see what has changed.

Refresh drills down into contained objects except for Pages. Only the top page (the visible one) of a page frame is refreshed by calling the page frame's Refresh. Microsoft's stated reason is performance. Given the speed of form refreshes generally, it seems like a good choice to us. You can refresh an individual page in its Activate event.

Although Refresh looks at the data source for the control, it doesn't update the contents of lists and combos. Use the Requery method for that.

Example

```
* A simplified version of the Click code for a Next button is:
SKIP
ThisForm.Refresh()
```

See Also Activate, Draw, Project, Requery

Refresh(), Requery()

These functions let you update the data in views. Don't confuse them with the methods of the same names. REFRESH() updates one or more records in a view with the current data from the original data source. REQUERY() updates an entire view—if it's parameterized, it may prompt for new parameters as well.

Usage

```
nRefreshCount = REFRESH( [ nNumToRefresh [, nStartOffset
                        [, cAlias | nWorkArea ] ] ] )
```

Parameter	Value	Meaning
nNumToRefresh	Numeric	The number of records to be refreshed from the original.
nStartOffset	Positive	Back up the specified number of records (relative to the current record in the view) and start the refresh there.
	Omitted or 0 or Negative	Refresh records starting with the current record.
cAlias	Character	Refresh records in the work area containing cAlias.
	Omitted	If nWorkArea is also omitted, refresh records in the current work area.
nWorkArea	Numeric	Refresh records in the specified work area.
	Omitted	If cAlias is also omitted, refresh records in the current work area.
nRefreshCount	Numeric	The number of records actually refreshed. Might be less than nNumToRefresh if you're near end-of-file, for example.

REFRESH() lets you update just the records you're working on with the current data from the source tables. You can use it on both local and remote views. If nothing has changed in the view, you simply get updated data from the source for the specified records.

The interactions between changes made to the view and changes others make to the original data are tricky. If you've changed the data, the changes are sent to the source only if you're using row buffering (the default for views) and you refresh multiple records. In that case, it's actually the movement of the record pointer that sends the changes. The rest of the time, if you've changed the data, your changes are sent and changes in the original data don't update the view.

The second parameter nStartOffset is incredibly confusing. It behaves as we've documented it above (and, in VFP 5 and VFP 6, it's documented to behave that way)—we can't figure who designed it to be this way, though. Passing a negative value for nStartOffset makes it start with the current record. Passing a positive value makes it go backward that number (or to the beginning of the view) and start there. We suggest you don't use nStartOffset.

Example

```
* This code might be in the Click of an Edit button
* so the user sees the most current information
* before editing:
=REFRESH()
ThisForm.Refresh()
```

Usage

```
nResult = REQUERY( [ cAlias | nWorkArea ] )
```

Parameter	Value	Meaning
nResult	1	View was requeried successfully.
	0	Requery did not complete successfully.

REQUERY()'s role is also to update the data in a view, but it tackles the whole view at once. It also has a special role when dealing with parameterized views.

When you REQUERY() a parameterized view, you get a chance to change the parameters. If the parameters exist as variables, the new values are simply passed to the source and used in the query to determine which records to send along. If the parameters don't exist, the View Parameter dialog appears (once for each parameter), asking for a value.

As with REFRESH(), the handling of updated values differs based on the type of buffering used. With row buffering, the REQUERY() call moves the record pointer, sending changes to the source. With table buffering, you have to explicitly commit or revert changes before you can REQUERY(). Attempting to REQUERY() a view with changes in the buffer generates an error.

In both cases, changes to the source data are reflected in the view following REQUERY().

Example

```
* Assume you have a view of the TasTrade employee table
* parameterized on Title (job description) with a parameter
* called cTitle. To change the open view to look at all the
* Sales Reps, you could:
cTitle = "Sales Representative"
=REQUERY()
```

See Also Create SQL View, CursorSetProp(), Refresh, Requery, Use

Regional, #Region

Regional variables were a bizarre scoping technique in FoxPro 2.x. This approach is no longer supported in VFP 5 or VFP 6.

Usage

```
#REGION nRegionNumber
REGIONAL RegionalVar1 [, RegionalVar2 [ , ... ] ]
```

Okay, you've got down PUBLIC and PRIVATE variables, right? LOCALS are pretty straightforward. So now there's nothing left to figure out, right? Wrong. REGIONAL throws a curve ball at the scoping model.

Regional variables were created for FoxPro 2.x screen sets containing snippets from different screens that could contain the same variable names. When a variable conflict was detected, the Screen Generator would issue REGION commands. At compile time, FoxPro modifies the variable names to unique variable names. Each variable is padded to 10 characters with underscores, then the last few characters are replaced with the region number. Each of these newly created variables behaves as a private variable from here on in.

Since variables associated with forms are now properties of the form, the scoping of Form.Property eliminates the need for this method of variable renaming on the fly. We don't expect we will ever code a REGIONAL command ourselves (we haven't yet!), and we include the gory details of how REGIONAL works here purely for reference, should the reader need to convert older code. Otherwise, we suggest you stay away from this command.

REGIONAL is out of the range of typical application development. Expect trouble integrating third-party tools into your application if you choose to get into REGIONALs in a big way. Debugging can also be a little more challenging, since these variable names are generated at compile time and don't exist in your source code.

See Also Local, Private, Public

Registration Database

It's been a long, strange trip for the Registry. Under Windows 3.1, this odd little file was more of a curiosity than an important file. Now, under Windows 95, 98 or NT, it is probably the most critical set of files on your system. The Registry stores important information on the system's hardware, startup, configuration, network protocols and application characteristics. Perhaps most importantly from the perspective of application developers, the Registry is the primary repository of all things Active: ActiveX controls, keys to ActiveX servers and services, and anything and everything having to do with the classes and instantiating them. If the Registry is corrupt, there's not much chance any component-dependent application will function. If ever there was a reason to make reliable and regular backups of your system, the Registry is it.

The internal structure of the Registry is beyond us, but the interface that it presents through the API is pretty straightforward. The Registry is represented as a series of tree structures, or "hives," each with a particular purpose. Each hive branches from its root nodes into many branches, each of which, in turn, can also branch. The final leaf nodes of these keys contain one or more values, typically a single string, integer or binary value.

Each hive has a specific purpose. HKEY_CURRENT_USER, not surprisingly, is data about the logged-in client: files stored especially for him or settings he has personalized. HKEY_LOCAL_MACHINE deals with machine-specific settings and drivers, and HKEY_CLASSES_ROOT deal with software classes installed system-wide (rather than just for a specific user). The remaining hives, HKEY_USERS, HKEY_CURRENT_CONFIG, and HKEY_DYN_DATA, hold information far more useful to the system than to us as developers. You can examine the Registry by using the REGEDIT program supplied with the operating system—but be careful! A poorly considered change can make your system unbootable. Windows NT users also have the option to use Regedt32.EXE, which provides more options, such as opening another computer's Registry, or editing the security privileges for specified sets of keys.

The Solutions Sample that comes with Visual FoxPro provides three examples of manipulating the Registry from within FoxPro. The solutions sample also includes a great class library in Registry.PRG and, new to VFP 6, a visual class library version. These classes are based on an earlier version written by Randy Brown that appeared on the CD-ROM included with the *Hacker's Guide to Visual FoxPro 3.0*, and we're pleased that Microsoft chose to include this within its product. The program includes classes for basic Registry manipulation, as well as specific classes to read and write Registry settings for Visual FoxPro, ODBC, application extensions and INI files.

There are a couple situations when you will need to manipulate the Registry. The first is when you are installing software on a client's machine. Typically, Setup takes care of the registration issues for you. If you're using the Microsoft-supplied Setup Wizard, you just need to select the ActiveX check box for the items that need to be registered, and they're automatically added to the Registry as part of the install process.

Another time you'll want access to the Registry is when your application wants to read or write settings. Registry.VCX is great for providing this interface. If these are application-wide settings, such as the location of files on the network, set up a Registry key under HKEY_LOCAL_MACHINE. If the values are more appropriate to be customized to each user, such as screen colors or positions, use HKEY_CURRENT_USER instead. In either case, you'll want to follow the convention of storing your values in this format:

```
\Software\YourCompany\YourAppName\Version\YourKeys
```

This will give you the most flexibility in supporting multiple versions of your application, perhaps importing older settings into a newer version.

The third situation is the one we wish we were never in—troubleshooting a failed installation or an application that won't work. As we've said, the Registry is a complex database of branching structures and multiple values. If an errant program writes random information into the Registry, there's a good chance that nothing will work again. We usually take as methodical an approach as possible to troubleshooting. If the troubles seem isolated to a single component, attempt to unregister and reregister that component (issue the command RegSvr32 /? from the command line for the options available), uninstall and reinstall that component. If that doesn't cure the problem, sometimes removing and reinstalling the entire application might provide the cure.

The next step is to try to recover the Registry from a backup. Check your operating system for documentation on creating a rescue disk (RDISK) or emergency boot disk (EBD) as appropriate. Several commercial backup programs also support backup and restoration of the Registry.

If you're still in trouble, two options remain: trying a Registry-repair program or reinstalling the operating system and all applications. The first may be your only choice if you lack all the files needed for a full reinstall; the latter is assured of working, but with a high cost in terms of time and effort. We have had some luck in recovering systems using the RegClean tool from Microsoft (search their Web site for the most recent version; I wouldn't trust one over six months old!), but several commercial products are also out there. Check your favorite programming magazines or a good Web search engine for some ideas.

Run Regedit.EXE to browse through the Registry and get some idea of what your application may want to do. We encourage you to consider the Registry for configuration information, customizations for each user, and state information, such as the most-recently-used (MRU) files, databases, configurations, or sub-systems of your application. These items, if managed correctly and presented properly, give your application a professional look.

See Also Configuration Files, INI Files

Reindex **See Index.**

Relation **See Cursor.**

Relation(), Target()

These two functions tell you about temporary relations—the kind you set up with SET RELATION. RELATION() tells you the relational expression while TARGET() tells you what alias the relation is pointing at.

Usage

```
cRelationalExpr = RELATION( nRelationNumber [, cAlias | nWorkArea ] )
cTargetAlias = TARGET( nRelationNumber [, cAlias | nWorkArea ] )
```

Parameter	Value	Meaning
nRelationNumber	Numeric	Which relation of this parent are we interested in?
cAlias	Character	Provide information about relations for which cAlias is the parent.

Parameter	Value	Meaning
cAlias	Omitted	If nWorkArea is also omitted, provide information for relations in which the current work area is the parent.
nWorkArea	Numeric	Provide information about relations for which the table in nWorkArea is the parent.
	Omitted	If cAlias is also omitted, provide information about relations in which the current work area is the parent.

RELATION() and TARGET() provide information from the point of view of the parent table in a relationship. TARGET() gives the alias of the child table, while RELATION() returns the expression from the parent table that drives the relation.

Because a single table may be parent to a number of children, you must specify which relation from the parent you're interested in. Relations are numbered in the reverse order of creation. That is, both TARGET(1) and RELATION(1) return the information for the most recently established relation.

Both functions return the empty string if there is no relation nRelationNumber for the specified parent. This makes looping through all relations easy; just stop when you get an empty return value for either function.

There are two main reasons you'd use these functions. In both cases, the relative order of the relations isn't terribly important, since you'll be looping through the relations.

The first reason is to determine if a particular relation has already been established. In this case, you'd loop through TARGET() until you run out of relations or find the one you're looking for.

The second case is to store information on all existing relations. In this case, you'd want to loop through all the relations. (The example below shows a function, aRelns, that does this.) Interestingly, if you store the information in an array, then process the array from top to bottom, you end up reversing the order of the relations. Since each relation involves a single parent and a single child, this isn't terribly important.

Example

```
* arelns.prg
* Fill an array with all relations from a specified table.
* Return the number of relations
* If there's a problem with parameters, return -1

PARAMETERS aRelations,cAlias
* aRelations = array to hold relation info
* cAlias = alias of the parent. If omitted, current work area

LOCAL nParams, nRelCnt

nParams = PARAMETERS()

IF nParams = 0 OR TYPE('aRelations[1]') = "U"
   RETURN -1
ENDIF

IF nParams = 1
   * use current work area
   IF EMPTY(ALIAS())
      * no table in use
      RETURN -1
   ENDIF
ELSE
   IF TYPE('cAlias') <> "C" OR NOT USED(cAlias)
      RETURN -1
   ENDIF
```

```
ENDIF

nOldArea = SELECT()
IF nParams > 1
   SELECT (cAlias)
ENDIF

* now start processing relation information
nRelCnt = 1
DO WHILE NOT EMPTY(RELATION(nRelCnt))
   DIMENSION aRelations[nRelCnt, 2]
   aRelations[nRelCnt, 1] = RELATION(nRelCnt)
   aRelations[nRelCnt, 2] = TARGET(nRelCnt)
   nRelCnt = nRelCnt + 1
ENDDO

RETURN nRelCnt - 1
```

The function does not determine whether the relation is one-to-one or one-to-many. That information is available as a single result for the parent. Use SET("SKIP") to get the list of one-to-many relations for a parent.

See Also Set Relation, Set Skip

RelationalExpr See ChildAlias.

RelativeColumn See RelativeRow.

RelativeRow, RelativeColumn

These properties tell you which cell of a grid has focus relative to the current position of the data in the grid.

Usage

```
nRow = grdGrid.RelativeRow
nCol = grdGrid.RelativeColumn
```

The values in these properties are counted from the cell currently in the upper-left corner of the grid. Like ActiveRow and ActiveColumn, you can't change these (use ActivateCell instead); and they reflect ColumnOrder, not the underlying order in the Columns collection.

RelativeColumn can deal with the idea that the column with focus might get scrolled out of the visible part of the grid. If it scrolls off to the right, RelativeColumn just keeps getting bigger. If it scrolls off to the left, RelativeColumn gets negative.

RelativeRow, however, isn't that smart. If the current record isn't visible in the grid, RelativeRow becomes 0. (ActiveRow has the same behavior.)

The combination of RelativeColumn and LeftColumn (LeftColumn + RelativeColumn - 1) always tells you where you are in the grid. Of course, ActiveColumn gives you the same information.

Example

```
* You might check in the grid's Scrolled event to see if
* the current record has gone offscreen.
IF This.RelativeRow = 0
   * do something to move the record pointer so focus is
   * in the visible area
ENDIF
```

See Also ActivateCell, ActiveColumn, ActiveRow, Columns, ColumnCount, LeftColumn

Release

This command sends memory variables into oblivion, freeing up the memory they occupy.

Usage

```
RELEASE ALL [ EXTENDED | LIKE Skeleton | EXCEPT Skeleton ]
RELEASE MemvarList
```

You'll rarely use this command for private or local scalar (non-array) variables. They're automatically released when the routine that creates them finishes. It's a little more common to release local or private array variables so you can re-create them with new dimensions. Since you can do that with DIMENSION, usually you release an array only when you're using it with a command or function that doesn't automatically redimension its result, like COPY TO ARRAY.

Public variables are another story. They stick around until you explicitly release them. RELEASE ALL doesn't release public variables in programs (though it does from the Command Window). Use the EXTENDED clause to release public variables, as well as the others, in programs.

The EXTENDED, LIKE and EXCEPT clauses don't much like each other. Only the first one you specify is honored. You can't RELEASE ALL EXTENDED LIKE hack*. This limit doesn't bother us that much because we rarely, if ever, use public variables in programs.

This limit applies even when you're not dealing with public variables. You can't RELEASE ALL LIKE n* EXCEPT nCount, which is a shame.

However, it's not the behavior that really bothers us. After all, it is documented that way. What makes this a bug in our eyes is that it doesn't *tell* you it's ignoring you.

You should release a variable before you make it public—just in case. PUBLIC declarations trigger an error if a local or private variable already exists with that name in that scope.

Example

```
NOTE: This only works as a program, not if the commands ;
      are typed in from the command window.
LOCAL a1, a2, a3, b1, b2, c1, c2, c3, x
PUBLIC a4, b3
* Now do something with them
RELEASE ALL LIKE b*
DISPLAY MEMORY  && b1 and b2 are gone; b3 is not
RELEASE ALL EXTENDED
DISPLAY MEMORY  && all gone
```

See Also Clear All, Clear Memory, Local, Private, Public

Release Bar See Define Menu.

Release ClassLib See Set ClassLib.

Release Library See Set Procedure.

Release Menus See Define Menu.

Release, AutoRelease

The Release method lets you get rid of forms and form sets in an OOP way without needing to know the name of the variable that references the thing. AutoRelease determines whether a form set gets released when all its forms are gone.

Usage

```
oObject.Release()
frsFormSet.AutoRelease = lLetItGo
lLetItGo = frsFormSet.AutoRelease
```

Release exists because you need a way to shut down a form (or form set) when the user presses the OK (or Cancel or Close or whatever) button. Just put ThisForm.Release() in the Click method and you're set. This method of shutting down a form does not fire the form's QueryUnload method, so you may want to call QueryUnload explicitly and issue Release only if QueryUnload returns .T.

It's possible to close all the forms in a form set and still have the form set object hanging around in memory. AutoRelease lets you change that. If you set it to .T., the form set is released as soon as its last form member is gone. However, form sets created in the Form Designer are always released when their last form goes away, regardless of the setting of AutoRelease. Only form sets created as objects (using CreateObject() or NewObject()) can cling to life when they're empty.

Take a look at the example for ON SHUTDOWN for one approach to using Release.

Example

```
* Put this in a Close button's Click method.
ThisForm.Release()
```

See Also Destroy, On Shutdown, QueryUnload, ReleaseType, Unload

Release Module See Load.

Release Pad, Release Popups See Define Menu.

Release Procedure See Set Procedure.

Release Windows See Define Window.

ReleaseErase See ErasePage.

ReleaseType

This property sounds a lot more useful than we've found it. It tells you how a form was released so you can take different actions accordingly.

Usage

```
nReleaseType = frmForm.ReleaseType
```

ReleaseType gets set just before QueryUnload, so you can check it there or in the form's Destroy or Unload method.

The descriptions in Help of what each value means are pretty limited. You get a ReleaseType of 1 in lots of cases, not just by clicking Close on the control menu or using the Close box. CLEAR WINDOWS or RELEASE WINDOWS sets ReleaseType to 1, too. Shutting down Windows, though, sets ReleaseType to 2.

The other descriptions are closer to reality, although you don't have to actually release the variable referencing a form to get a ReleaseType of 0. Letting it go out of scope all by itself does the trick, too. Calling the form's Release method also sets ReleaseType to 0.

Example

```
* You might check whether you're leaving VFP entirely
* since some application actions are unnecessary in that case.
IF This.ReleaseType = 2
   WAIT WINDOW "Bye, now. Come again soon"
ENDIF
```

See Also Destroy, QueryUnload, Unload

ReleaseWindows See ErasePage.

Remove

This file method removes things from a project or, more technically, from the Files collection of a project.

Usage `filFile.Remove( [ lDeleteIt ] )`

Remove is part of the programmatic control of projects introduced in VFP 6. It lets you take files out of a project and, optionally, delete them as well.

Like the other project methods, Remove interacts with the project hook methods that let you insert custom code to occur around project actions. In this case, QueryRemoveFile is executed before the actual removal and can abort the process.

Example

```
* Remove the first file from the active project without deleting
_VFP.ActiveProject.Files[1].Remove()
```

See Also Add, File, Files, Modify, Project, QueryRemoveFile

Remove Class See Create ClassLib.

Remove Table See Add Table.

RemoveFromSCC See AddToSCC.

RemoveItem, RemoveListItem See AddItem.

RemoveObject See AddObject.

Rename See Copy File.

Rename Class See Create ClassLib.

Rename Connection See Create Connection.

Rename Table

This command lets you change the long name of a table in a database.

Usage `RENAME TABLE OldName TO NewName`

RENAME TABLE doesn't affect the actual DBF filename, only the long name stored in the database. All the necessary DBC data is updated to reflect the new name, and you don't have to redefine any of the indexes or relations. Only the database itself is updated, not things based on it, though. So you do have to modify your own code and forms, as well as any generated code, from tools like the RI Builder or GENDBC code.

As with other database maintenance, in VFP 3 the database must be open exclusively. VFP 5 and 6 remove this restriction, but no one else can have the table open when you make this change. We think that's probably a reasonable restriction.

Example `RENAME TABLE MyTable TO YourTable`

See Also Add Table, Open Database, Rename

Rename View See Modify View.

Replace

REPLACE puts data in fields. It's the table counterpart to STORE or =, which put data in variables, but have no effect on fields. (We can't tell you how often we've written code that uses = with fields and then had to figure out what was wrong with it.)

Usage

```
REPLACE uField1 WITH eExpr1 [ ADDITIVE ]
        [, uField2 WITH eExpr2 [ ADDITIVE ]
        [, ... ] ]
        [ Scope ] [ FOR lForExpression ]
        [ WHILE lWhileExpression ]
        [ IN cAlias | nWorkArea ]
        [ NOOPTIMIZE ]
```

Unless you tell it otherwise, REPLACE applies to the current record in the current work area.

eExpr*n* must be the same or a compatible type with uField*n*. Some type conversion occurs automatically (for example, since there really is only one numeric memory variable type, from numeric to double or currency), but other conversions need to be specified explicitly (for example, character to date).

ADDITIVE is permitted only when the destination field is a memo field. It indicates that eExpr*n* should be added to the end of the existing value of uField*n* rather than overwriting it.

The fields do not all have to be in the same table. However, there's a gotcha here. The Scope, FOR and WHILE clauses are applied to the controlling table (usually the current work area). If you reach EOF() in that table, no further replacements take place in any table. Despite much yelling by many Xbase programmers over the years, this really isn't a bug. It's supposed to work this way and it's as good a choice as any other behavior in this situation.

Here's the deal. REPLACE lets you change fields of multiple records in multiple tables at once. Suppose you've written a REPLACE that moves data into records from three different tables at once. Suppose further that the REPLACE has a scope clause of NEXT 5. What if you reach the end of one of those tables before you've hit five records? For simplicity's sake, the rule has always been that it's the current work area that counts. As long as you're not at EOF() in the current work area, the REPLACE continues (although some data may land in the bit bucket). As soon as you hit EOF() in the current work area, the REPLACE ends. No questions asked. (For explanations of Scope, FOR and WHILE, see "Xbase Xplained.")

Prior to Visual FoxPro, the work-around for the problem was to SELECT the desired work area before the REPLACE. The addition of transactions in VFP eliminates the need for a single REPLACE to modify records in multiple tables. Together with the IN clause, there's no reason to ever run into this problem. Use a series of REPLACE commands and have each one IN the right work area. Wrap the whole thing in a transaction and you can be pretty much assured you're saving all the data or none of it.

See "WHILE away the Hours" in "Xbase Xplained" for another gotcha involving the WHILE clause.

NOOPTIMIZE says to turn off Rushmore before doing the replacements. We've never needed to do so, but if you think you might, see SET OPTIMIZE.

Example

```
* Two ways to update a memo field
REPLACE notes WITH notes+chr(13)+ ;
                   dtoc(date())+" Called - line was busy"
REPLACE notes WITH chr(13)+dtoc(date())+ ;
                   "Called - line was busy" ADDITIVE

* Suppose the area code for a bunch of phone numbers
* changes. You need to update those records.
* Assume you've stored the exchanges that are changing
* in a table, EXCHANGES, with one field, Exchange, and
* a tag on that field.
* The old area code is stored in cOldCode.
```

```
* The new area code is stored in cNewCode.
USE PhoneList
USE Exchanges IN 0 ORDER Exchange
SET RELATION TO LEFT(Phone,3) INTO Exchanges
REPLACE AreaCode WITH cNewCode ;
   FOR AreaCode=cOldCode ;
   AND FOUND("Exchanges")
```

See Also Begin Transaction, Insert-SQL, Set Optimize, Store, Update-SQL

Replace From Array

This command is another FoxPro 2.6 addition. It's similar to GATHER, but lets you store array data in more than one table at a time. It also completes the set of commands that contains COPY TO ARRAY and APPEND FROM ARRAY, letting you copy data into an array, then store it back into the same records.

Beware—this is a powerful and dangerous command. It has the potential for great destruction if used carelessly. It can overwrite mounds of data in one line. Our general feeling is that you probably shouldn't be introducing this command into new development—generally we recommend using views for updating data. We've included it in the documentation here to help you understand 2.x code you may be called upon to update.

Usage

```
REPLACE FROM ARRAY ArrayName
      [ FIELDS FieldList ]
      [ Scope ]
      [ FOR lForExpression ]
      [ WHILE lWhileExpression ]
      [ NOOPTIMIZE ]
```

The fields in the fieldlist (or all the fields, if you omit the FIELDS clause) are filled one by one with elements of the array. Each row of the array corresponds to a record, but you have to include a Scope, FOR or WHILE clause to affect multiple records. (See "Xbase Xplained" for details on those clauses.)

If you use the FIELDS clause of REPLACE FROM ARRAY to update multiple records of multiple tables at once, make sure you've set a relation between the tables. Otherwise, you'll affect the same record over and over in tables other than the current work area.

Like REPLACE, if the table in the current work area is at end-of-file, this command doesn't do anything.

Array elements corresponding to memo or general fields are ignored. This makes sense since the corresponding COPY TO ARRAY creates elements for those fields, but populates them only with .F. There's no MEMO clause here to let you work with memo data.

You probably don't want NOOPTIMIZE. If you really think you do, check out SET OPTIMIZE.

Example

```
USE Customer
* Position on the record you want
COPY TO ARRAY aCust
* Now edit the array contents as desired
* When you're ready to update the record
REPLACE FROM ARRAY aCust
```

See Also Append From Array, Copy To Array, Replace, Set Optimize

Replicate()

This function lets you create a string composed of multiple copies of another string.

Usage

```
cNewString = REPLICATE( cString, nTimes )
```

Parameter	Value	Meaning
cString	Character	The string to be repeated to produce the result.
nTimes	Numeric	The number of times to repeat cString.
cNewString	Character	A string consisting of nTimes copies of cString.

REPLICATE() is handy for allowing you to use proportional fonts for input without ending up with too many characters. By specifying an InputMask (PICTURE clause in 2.x) of REPLICATE("X", LEN(<field>)), the user can't enter more characters than the field holds.

In the little-known-facts department, you can pass an entire string to REPLICATE(), not just a single character. We suspect many experienced Xbase programmers don't realize this.

Example

```
? REPLICATE("X", 30)   && Returns a string of 30 X's
? REPLICATE("Fox", 3)  && Returns "FoxFoxFox"
```

See Also ChrTran(), InputMask, Space(), StrTran(), Stuff()

Report, Label

These commands let you generate reports and labels created with the Report and Label Designers. They have a multitude of options—some pretty new, others as old as Xbase itself.

Usage

```
REPORT FORM ReportFileName | ?
       [ Scope ] [ FOR lForExpression ]
       [ WHILE lWhileExpression ]
       [ RANGE nStartPage [ , nEndPage ] ]
       [ PREVIEW [ [ WINDOW DefiningWindow ]
           [ IN  WINDOW ContainingWindow ]
           | IN SCREEN ]
         [ NOWAIT ]
         | TO FILE OutFileName [ ASCII ]
         | TO PRINTER [ PROMPT ] ]
       [ NOCONSOLE ] [ NOEJECT ]
       [ HEADING cHeadingText ] [ PLAIN ] [ SUMMARY ]
       [ ENVIRONMENT ] [ PDSETUP ]
       [ NOOPTIMIZE ]
       [ NAME ObjectName ]
LABEL [ FORM LabelFileName | FORM ? ]
       [ Scope ] [ FOR lForExpression ]
       [ WHILE lWhileExpression ]
       [ PREVIEW [ IN SCREEN ] [ NOWAIT ]
         | TO FILE OutFileName [ ASCII ]
         | TO PRINTER [ PROMPT ] ]
       [ NOCONSOLE ]
       [ ENVIRONMENT ] [ PDSETUP ] [ SAMPLE ]
       [ NOOPTIMIZE ]
       [ NAME ObjectName ]
```

The "FORM" in REPORT FORM and LABEL FORM stands for "format" and, in fact, you can still write it that way. More importantly, the term "format" makes it clear what these commands do—they produce a report or a label based on a specified format.

LABEL has a neat trick. If you just type LABEL without FORM, you're prompted to choose a label file. For both labels and reports, specifying ? does the same thing.

The Scope, FOR and WHILE clauses limit output to the records meeting those conditions. See "Xbase Xplained" for details.

Report and label output can be sent various places. By default, it appears in the active window. You can suppress that output with NOCONSOLE.

Specifying PREVIEW puts the output in the Print Preview window. Preview mode is much better in VFP than in FoxPro 2.x, with a dockable toolbar, an assortment of zoom ratios and a NOWAIT clause that lets you put up a report and then continue a program. Starting in VFP 5, you can also define a window for the Preview and give it a custom title and appearance (much as you can for a Browse). Then, you can use the WINDOW clause to put the preview in the custom window.

VFP 6 gives you even more options. First, the IN WINDOW option lets you confine the preview to a specified window. Second, when you have a top-level form, issuing PREVIEW without specifying a window puts the preview in that window—this is a major improvement over previous versions, which put the preview into the main VFP window. Finally, the new IN SCREEN clause is for those rare cases where you're working in a top-level window, but want the preview in the main VFP window. We can't quite imagine that situation, but we're sure it'll help someone, somewhere.

The LABEL command doesn't offer the WINDOW clause, but does now preview in a top-level window and supports the IN SCREEN clause, even though it's not documented.

The biggest remaining weakness in report previews is that you can only zoom up to 100%. We can think of plenty of situations where we'd like to zoom to 150% or 200% or even 400%—we sure do it in other applications.

There are two ways to send report or label output to a file. If you specify TO FILE without the ASCII clause, all the codes for the specified printer go with it. You can then send that file to the printer at your leisure.

The ASCII clause, on the other hand, lets you create a file that a human can read, instead of one filled with gobbledygook printer control. The output with ASCII is VFP's best guess of a character-based layout from a graphical one—this option is best for columnar reports without many fonts, sizes or multiple rows of information to line up. Not only that, it's fast—really fast. On the other *other* hand, the formatting you get with ASCII is pretty basic. Finally, you can send your report to the printer. Add the PROMPT clause to let the user choose a printer; otherwise, FoxPro uses the printer you specified in Page Setup or the Windows default, if you didn't change it. There are several problems with the PROMPT clause in VFP 5—they're documented in the Microsoft Knowledge Base, so we won't repeat them here.

The RANGE clause lets you indicate which pages of a report should be produced. It's ignored when you specify PREVIEW, but does affect output to the screen, printer or a file. Very handy for those times when one page of a 30-page report gets jammed in the printer.

NOEJECT and PDSETUP have something in common. They don't do anything with Visual FoxPro reports. Both have their origins in FoxPro for DOS, where they were very handy.

ENVIRONMENT is almost as useless. It applies only to reports converted from older versions of FoxPro, where you didn't have properties like AutoOpenTables available. With the ENVIRONMENT clause, the report's data environment is opened regardless of the setting of AutoOpenTables.

HEADING and PLAIN also date way, way back. HEADING was designed to let you specify a page heading for a report when you run it—it let you send things like "First Quarter 1995" and so forth, putting what you send on the last line of the Page Header band. HEADING still works, but it doesn't pay any attention to what's already on that line, clobbering any text already there. We recommend you avoid it and simply use expressions in your reports. PLAIN eliminates page headings from the report—note that you get no page headings at all, not even on the first page, as Help says.

SUMMARY omits the detail band. All the other bands appear. It's one way to get (surprise) summary information.

The SAMPLE clause of LABEL doesn't do a thing and, in fact, is no longer documented. In FoxPro/DOS, it let you print a test label to see if the labels were properly aligned in the printer. Microsoft doesn't believe anyone uses dot-matrix printers with Windows, so you can't do this. Instead, we recommend you run a test set in a loop with LABEL FORM MyLabel NEXT nHowManyToASheet until the operator is happy with the results.

NOOPTIMIZE slows down your report. See SET OPTIMIZE if you think you might need to use this.

Last, but by no means least, is the NAME clause. Although reports and labels are not objects (in the OOP sense), their data environments are. The NAME clause lets you assign a name to the DataEnvironment of a report or label. You can use that name in method code (which seems like a bad idea to us—use This instead) or from the command window or a program; with the NOWAIT clause of PREVIEW, your program can still be running while the preview is displayed. You can also reference the data environment from code running in the entry and exit events for the report's bands. We haven't ever actually used these abilities in an application, but it's nice to know they're there. By the way, if you don't include the NAME clause, you can still reference the data environment by using the report name.

Example

```
* Put a report preview in a specified window.
DEFINE WINDOW RepPreview FROM 0,0 to 50,100 title "Employees"
REPORT FORM Employees PREVIEW WINDOW RepPreview NOWAIT
LABEL FORM Customer TO PRINT
REPORT FORM Employees TO FILE emps.txt ASCII
REPORT FORM SaleHist TO PRINT RANGE 5,7
```

See Also _ASCIICols, _ASCIIRows, Compile Label, Compile Report, Create Label, Create Report, DataEnvironment, Modify Label, Modify Report

Requery

This method of list and combo boxes lets you update their contents when the underlying data source has changed.

Usage `oObject.Requery()`

Sometimes the data item on which a list or combo is based changes. For example, a list based on an array might contain all the Employees in a particular country. If another control on the form lets the user change countries, we need to refill the array (probably using SELECT), then update the list. The update part is done by calling the list's Requery method.

If the list or combo is based on a SQL Statement or Query, the Requery call is even more important. In that case, Requery both re-executes the query and repopulates the list.

In general, you need to call Requery any time something has happened in the application that might have changed the data that the list or combo is based on. Requery repopulates the list or combo and refreshes its display.

Most of the time, you won't put any code in the Requery method. (In fact, we find that we rarely put code in any method that isn't tied to an event.) But Requery has a cool feature. Say your list or combo is based on a query and the query has a macro, maybe for the ORDER BY or GROUP BY clause. You can't reference a property (like the Value of a combo box, perhaps) in a macro. Instead, in the Requery method, you can copy the property to a local variable, which is used by the macro. Since the custom code in Requery is executed before the default behavior of updating the list or combo, this works out neatly. In fact, in general, when a query needs to execute in order to refill a list or combo, we like to put the query in Requery, thus encapsulating the whole refresh in one method. That way, other controls don't have to know anything about the list or combo's RowSourceType.

Here's an example. Say your form has a list of Customers and a combo, called cboOrderBy, which lists the existing tags for Customer. (Yeah, in a real app, we'd make it more user-friendly.) The list could have RowSourceType = 3 (SQL Statement) with RowSource set to:

```
SELECT First_Name,Last_Name FROM Customer ORDER BY &cTag
```

Then, Requery would contain:

```
LOCAL cTag
cTag = ThisForm.cboOrderBy.Value
DODEFAULT()   && call any inherited behavior and perform the base behavior
              && of refilling the list
```

When you call the list's Requery method, the combo's value is copied to cTag and used in the ORDER BY clause.

Don't confuse this Requery method with the REQUERY() function used with views. While they have a similar function, they're independent of each other. (There are times, in fact, when you'll need to call REQUERY(), then follow it with a call to a control's Requery method.)

Example

```
* If lstEmployee shows all the Employees in cCountry, based on a
* SQL Statement,and cCountry is entered via cboCountry, put code
* like this in cboCountry's Valid method:

ThisForm.lstEmployee.Requery()
```

See Also ComboBox, ListBox, Requery()

Requery() See Refresh().

RequestData See DoCmd.

Reset See Access().

Reset

The Reset method of the Timer Control resets the Timer to start its countdown from the beginning.

Usage `tmrTimer.Reset()`

A Timer is a built-in FoxPro control that counts down a specified interval of time (cleverly specified by its Interval property) and then performs the code included in the Timer event. Reset causes it to start counting down again from the beginning. The Enabled property determines if the Timer is active. Setting the Interval property to zero also deactivates a Timer—the Timer event will not fire, even though the Enabled property is .T.

Example `TIMER1.Reset()`

See Also Timer Control, Timer, Interval

ResetToDefault

This method was added in version 3.0b, probably because people were so disappointed it wasn't the original version. It lets you do in code at either runtime or design time what the "Reset to Default" option on the right-click menu on the property sheet does—restore a property or method that's been changed so it inherits from its parent class.

Usage `oObject.ResetToDefault( cPEM )`

This method provides a programmatic way to restore a property or method to its default value. This is important because, otherwise, that PEM can't inherit from higher in the class hierarchy. Assigning the default value is *not* the same as restoring it.

For properties, ResetToDefault works at design time and runtime. The property is reset to the default for the class on which the object is based. At runtime, this means any changes that have occurred since the object was instantiated are discarded. At design time, it means going one level up the class hierarchy and restoring that value.

For methods, ResetToDefault works only at design time. This seems reasonable to us—since you can't change code at runtime, what would restoring the default mean?

This method makes writing builders and other developer tools much easier. One warning: If the object doesn't have the specified property, you get an error message. Use PEMStatus() first to ensure that the property applies to the specified object.

Example

```
IF PEMSTATUS(oObject, "BackColor", 5)
   * it exists
   oObject.ResetToDefault("BackColor")
ENDIF
```

See Also GetPEM(), PEMStatus()

Resizable

This property determines whether a column's width can be changed interactively.

Usage

```
grcColumn.Resizable = lResizable
lResizable = grcColumn.Resizable
```

It is possible that you will want to keep certain columns of a grid at a fixed width, in order to prevent data from being either hidden or exposed. This is the property to set to do that. However, keep in mind that if any columns have the Movable property set, it might be possible to move the column off the viewable area.

Example

```
ThisForm.Grid1.Column1.Resizable = .T.
```

See Also Grid, Movable, Width, Resize

Resize

This event fires each time an object is resized.

Usage

```
PROCEDURE oObject.Resize
[ LPARAMETERS nIndex ]
```

You can ignore the optional parameter to Resize unless you're using control arrays. If you are, read that section so we can convince you to stop.

A Resize event occurs each time a user resizes a container control whose properties allow resizing. A Resize event also occurs if the properties that control the size of a container (Height and Width) are changed programmatically. Classes based on any of the following "containing controls" have Resize events: Container, Control, Form, Grid, Column, OLEControl, OLEBoundControl, Pageframe and Toolbar. Different controls have different properties that determine if they can be resized interactively. For a column, the Resizable property has to be True. For a Form, BorderStyle must be set to 3. Sizable is the relevant property for the OLEControls. All the other objects must be resized programmatically for the Resize event to fire.

You might choose to refresh certain objects within a Resize event, such as ensuring that all buttons are still visible on a form, or shrinking text and label font sizes to fit a new column size. Resize events are a handy place for the code to resize or rearrange controls within a container. Check out the _resizable control that comes with the FoxPro Foundation Classes before trying to write your own.

One caution when resizing controls: Ensure that the container control hasn't been shrunk too small to hold a control before changing the contained control's properties, or an error could result. You might need to take advantage of the MinHeight and MinWidth properties of a form, or programmatically check limits for the other containers before manipulating contained objects.

Example

```
Procedure Form1.Resize
* Move the Quit button to 50 pixels from the bottom of the form
ThisForm.cmdQuit.Top = ThisForm.Height - 50
* Center the button horizontally
ThisForm.cmdQuit.Left = .5 * (ThisForm.Width - ThisForm.cmdQuit.Width)
*
* The form contains a custom edit box. It needs to take up all;
* space left to right except a margin and stretch itself to ;
* the height available on the form.
*
* Make the Width the form width less two margin widths
ThisForm.edtEditBox.width = ThisForm.Width - 2 * ThisForm.edtEditBox.Left
*
* Make the box height 108 pixels plus whatever room is ;
* available beyond the minimum form height
ThisForm.edtEditBox.Height = 108 + (ThisForm.Height - ThisForm.MinHeight)
```

See Also BorderStyle, Column, Container, Control, Control Arrays, Form, Grid, Height, MinHeight, MinWidth, OLEBoundControl, OLEControl, Pageframe, Resizable, Sizable, Toolbar, Width

Restore From, Save To

Allows the storage and retrieval of a series of memory variables to either a memo field or a file. Seems like a good idea, but has some limitations.

Usage

```
SAVE [ ALL LIKE VarSkeleton | ALL EXCEPT VarSkeleton ]
        TO FileName | MEMO MemoField
RESTORE FROM FileName | MEMO MemoField [ ADDITIVE ]
```

SAVE and RESTORE allow specified memory variables to be stored into a memo field or a MEM file (the default extension, which can be overridden). This can be used to store a series of state variables or settings that can be restored at will. However, a few limitations apply. First, all variables are restored with private scope, regardless of their initial scope. Secondly, failure to use the ADDITIVE keyword results in the obliteration of all variables in memory.

The worst limitation we see, though, is that MEM files are difficult to read. The files and memo fields are stored in a binary format, which is a pain in the neck (though possible) to parse. Fixing a broken MEM file is not for the weak of heart. In addition, it can be really difficult to troubleshoot a problem where a MEM file clobbers existing variables.

We prefer to either store our settings to a DBF with predefined fields for each setting or use an INI file or the Registry to store free-form settings.

Example

```
SAVE TO MYARRAYS.MEM ALL LIKE LA*
RESTORE FROM MYARRAYS ADDITIVE
```

See Also INI Files, Registration Database

Restore Macros See Clear Macros.

Restore Screen See Save Screen.

Restore Window, Save Window

One of the mutant branches of the Xbase evolution toward windows management that died a fitting death along the way. Retained in Visual FoxPro for "backward compatibility."

Usage

```
RESTORE WINDOW Window1 [,Window2 [, ... ] ] | ALL
        FROM MEMO MemoField | FileName
SAVE WINDOW Window1 [,Window2 [, ... ] ] | ALL
        TO MEMO MemoField | FileName
```

These commands let you save and restore a series of window definitions to either a file or a memo field. The definitions are stored in incomprehensible, undocumentable (and undocumented) binary format. The filename has a WIN extension, unless a different extension is specified. Although we could see the advantage of this method in order to allow users to customize their environment to meet their needs, we have never actually seen this method succeed in an application. With the fine control available in form events such as Resize and Move, we feel that custom methods to save and restore the Top, Left, Height and Width properties have far more chance of succeeding than the use of these commands.

Example

```
SAVE WINDOW Form1 to Form1
RESTORE WINDOW Form1 FROM Form1
```

See Also Move, Resize, Restore, Save

Resume, Retry See Cancel.

Return See Function.

RGB()

This function takes values for the red, green and blue components of a color and returns the unique number for that color. Because Visual FoxPro offers more than 16 million colors, RGB() is a lot more convenient than trying to remember individual color numbers.

Usage

```
nColorNumber = RGB( nRedValue, nGreenValue, nBlueValue )
```

Each of the three color values ranges from 0 to 255.

If you went to school (and we figure most of you did), you may wonder why we specify red, green and blue values. After all, the primary colors are red, yellow and blue.

The answer is that there are two different types of color around. The colors we all learned about in school are paint colors. With paint, mixing red, yellow and blue in appropriate proportions can make everything except white. Paint colors are subtractive—each color you add removes more of the visible color until you eventually end up with black, the absence of color.

Computers (and TVs and so forth) use light color, though. This is additive color in which each color you add increases the total color of the result until you end up with white (total color). In light colors, the primaries are red, green and blue.

The result of RGB() is a number between 0 and 16,777,215 (which is 256^3 less one). It sounds mysterious, but in fact, the formula used to compute the result is simply:

```
nBlueValue * (256^2) + nGreenValue * 256 + nRedValue
```

We can't figure why they did it backwards, but we suspect it wasn't the Visual FoxPro developers who made this choice.

The header file that ships with FoxPro, FoxPro.H, includes values for 16 colors—use those when you can. (COLOR_RED is a lot more readable than RGB(255,0,0) or 255.) When you need a color other than those 16, use RGB() unless you want the user to choose, in which case use GETCOLOR().

The SET COLOR OF SCHEME command uses a special version of RGB() that takes six numbers and converts them into a color pair—that's a foreground and a background color.

Example

```
ThisForm.BackColor = RGB(128,0,64)
```

See Also #Include, BackColor, FoxTools, ForeColor, GetColor(), RGBScheme(), Set Color Of Scheme

RGBScheme() See Set Color Set.

Right() See Left().

RightC() See LeftC().

RightClick See Click.

RightToLeft

This property determines whether text in a control runs from left to right (as in usual in Western languages) or right to left (as they do it in Middle Eastern languages).

Usage

```
oObject.RightToLeft = lReadRightToLeft
lReadRightToLeft = oObject.RightToLeft
```

This is another of those items that we can't really test properly. It only kicks in if you're using a Middle Eastern version of Windows. The basic idea is sound, though—in those languages where text is normally read from right to left, you want it to work that way, but not for every control. After all, even in those languages, numeric digits still run left to right. So this property lets you handle things at the individual control level.

In our U.S. English versions of Windows, changing it doesn't cause any weirdness; VFP simply ignores us. There is one strange behavior here. The property sheet shows .T. as the default value for this property, but behaves in all other ways as if .F. were the default. Doesn't seem to do any harm, though.

Note that this property has nothing to do with whether text is aligned to the left or to the right in a control. Use Alignment for that one.

Example

```
ThisForm.txtFirstName.RightToLeft = .T.
```

See Also Alignment

RLock() See Lock().

_RMargin See _Alignment.

RmDir See CD.

Rollback See Begin Transaction.

Round() See Int().

Row(), Col(), PRow(), PCol()

Back in FoxBase days, even early FoxPro days, we used these functions a lot. We can't remember the last time we used them, though. They return the cursor position on the screen and on the printer, respectively.

Usage

```
nCurScreenRow = ROW()
nCurScreenCol = COL()
nCurPrintRow = PROW()
nCurPrintCol = PCOL()
```

You can substitute $ for either ROW() or COL() in @ .. GET and @ .. SAY commands to specify the current location. ROW() and COL() do not respect the settings of ScaleMode, always reporting the row and column coordinates in foxels.

Example `@ROW(), COL()+1 SAY "Here's some information"`

See Also @ ... Get, @ ... Say, CurrentX, CurrentY

RowHeight

Specifies the height, in pixels, of the rows in a grid. All rows have the same height.

Usage
```
Grid.RowHeight = nHeight
nHeight = Grid.RowHeight
```

You can use this property to modify the row height of a grid. You might want to do this if you place controls other than text boxes within the grid. RowHeight is automatically changed if the Grid's FontName or FontSize is altered, so you'll want to make global font changes before manipulating the row's height. We generally prefer to set the font characteristics of each separate column (or even each control), rather than making the overall change, if there are any complex controls within the grid.

Setting RowHeight to -1 causes the grid to automatically resize to the proper height for the Grid's FontSize. This setting ignores any FontSize settings assigned in columns or text objects, so is appropriate only for a text-only grid with a single font style. Using this technique on a grid with carefully sized check boxes and spinners squashes everything.

Example `grdGrid1.RowHeight = 23`

See Also Grid, FontName, FontSize

RowSource, RowSourceType

These two properties combine to determine the contents of a list box or combo box. RowSourceType indicates the type of data contained, while RowSource contains either the actual data or a pointer to it.

Usage
```
oObject.RowSourceType = nSourceType
nSourceType = oObject.RowSourceType
oObject.RowSource = cSource
cSource = oObject.RowSource
```

There are 10 choices for nSourceType, from 0 to 9. The choice you make for RowSourceType determines the kind of value you specify for RowSource. This table shows the various options:

RowSourceType	Meaning	RowSource Contents
0	None	Nothing—combo or list data is added using either the AddItem or AddListItem methods or by directly populating List or ListItem.
1	Value	The actual items for the list or combo as a comma-separated list. If ColumnCount is more than 1, the items are distributed into all the columns going across one row at a time. Don't leave spaces after the commas; these are interpreted as the first character of the next item.
2	Alias	The alias for an open table whose data is used to populate the list or combo. If ColumnCount is greater than 0, the first ColumnCount fields are shown. If ColumnCount is 0, you see the first field only, just as if ColumnCount were 1.

RowSourceType	Meaning	RowSource Contents
3	SQL Statement	A SELECT-SQL statement, the results of which populate the list or combo. ColumnCount is treated as with RowSourceType=2. Be sure to do something with the query results—if there's no INTO clause, a Browse appears when the query executes on the way into the form.
4	Query	The name of a QPR file. The query is run and the results populate the list or combo. ColumnCount is treated as with RowSourceType=2. Again, make sure you do something with the results or you'll see the default Browse.
5	Array	The name of an array used to populate the list or combo. If the array is a property of the form, be sure to precede its name with "ThisForm." If ColumnCount is greater than 0, the first ColumnCount columns of the array are used.
6	Fields	A list of fields from a single table. Only the first field should be preceded by the alias of the table. Field names are comma-delimited. Normally, the number of fields in the list should equal ColumnCount.
7	Files	A file skeleton. The list or combo is populated with the names of files in the current directory matching the skeleton, plus items for navigating directories. Make sure ColumnCount = 1 or 0 or you'll get really weird results.
8	Structure	The alias of an open table. The list or combo is populated with the names of fields from the specified table. Field names occupy the first column. Any other columns are empty.
9	Popup	The name of a popup defined elsewhere. The popup's items are used to populate the list or combo.

The last three RowSourceTypes are really included only for compatibility with FoxPro 2.x. We can't see a whole lot of reasons to use any of them. For a file list, you're better off using GETFILE() or PUTFILE() or the Common Dialogs control. We didn't use structure popups or lists in our 2.x apps—we're not planning to start now. (The exception, of course, is for developers' tools.) As for lists or combos based on popups, there were reasons to do it in 2.x, but we think RowSourceType=0 is a far better alternative. The only good arguments we've seen for using RowSourceType = 9 are to allow each element in a list or combo to be colored separately, something that's occasionally useful, but not your run-of-the-mill technique, or to set up a combo with divider lines between groups of items, something that's fairly complex any other way.

Be careful with RowSourceTypes 2 and 6. They're connected right to the underlying tables, and moving the cursor in the list moves the record pointer. Among other things, this means that you should never set the RowSource and the ControlSource of a type 6 combo to the same field.

It's not just making a choice in a combo that moves the record pointer. Simply passing the mouse over an item in a dropped combo so that the item is highlighted is enough to position the record pointer on that item. The pointer doesn't go back where it came from if you close the combo without making a selection.

We find that we use RowSourceTypes 0, 3, 5 and 6 the most. RowSourceType 1 is handy for situations where you know the list of choices can't change.

Example

```
* This code in the Init for a list box populates
* an array that's a property of the form and
* sets the list to use the array.
SELECT Last_Name,First_Name,Employee_Id ;
  FROM Employee ;
  INTO ARRAY ThisForm.aEmps
This.RowSourceType = 5
This.RowSource = "ThisForm.aEmps"
This.ColumnCount = 2
This.ColumnWidths = "80,60"

* This code in the Init of a form
* populates a combo on that form
* with selected items from Customer.
* It assumes the combo's RowSourceType is
* set to the default 0.
ThisForm.cboFaxTo.ColumnCount=2
ThisForm.cboFaxTo.ColumnWidths="150,120"
SELECT Customer
SCAN FOR NOT EMPTY(Fax)
  WITH ThisForm.cboFaxTo
    .AddListItem(Company_Name,.NewItemId+1,1)
    .AddListItem(Contact_Name,.NewItemId,2)
  ENDWITH
ENDSCAN
```

See Also AddItem, AddListItem, ColumnCount, ComboBox, List, ListBox, ListItem

RToD() See Cos().

RTrim() See AllTrim().

Run, !

RUN, or its equivalent shorthand ! (often spoken as Bang!), allows Visual FoxPro to run other programs. In the Windows version, you can access both Windows and DOS programs.

Usage

```
RUN | ! [ /nFreeMemory [K] ] ProgramName    && DOS version
RUN | ! [Options] WinProgName               && Windows version
```

Parameter	Value	Meaning
nFreeMemory	Numeric	States the amount of memory required in kilobytes. FoxPro for DOS attempts to clear out this amount before invoking the specified program.
ProgramName	Name	The name of the DOS program for FoxPro for DOS to run.
Options	Omitted	Indicates that Visual FoxPro should start the specified program within a DOS box.
	/N or /N1	Means "NOWAIT," indicating that this is a Windows program. These settings run the Windows program, making the application active, running it in its "normal" size. "Normal" depends on the application. Many applications store the position they were in when they were last closed, and restore this setting under this "normal" condition. Others always open maximized, minimized, or somewhere in between.

Parameter	Value	Meaning
Options	/N2	Runs the Windows program as the active application, but minimized.
	/N3	Runs the Windows program as the active application, in its maximized format.
	/N4	Runs the Windows program, restoring its normal window size, but does not activate it.
	/N7	Runs the Windows program, leaving it inactive and minimized.
WinProgName	Name	The name of the program, either a DOS or Windows program, for Visual FoxPro for Windows to run.

We break our rule in the diagram above in showing both the DOS and Windows versions of this command, but for an awfully good reason. Microsoft, and Fox Software before them, hopelessly mangled the explanation of these commands, and we'd like to clear the air. FoxPro for DOS, and FoxPro for DOS only, allows the specification of how much memory is required. The documentation folks chose to show it as /n, where *n* stood for the memory required in kilobytes. Then, some clever programmer decided that "/N" should be used as shorthand for "NOWAIT" for Windows programs only. This is just too much for anyone to get the first time through. If you need to run WordStar.Exe, an application requiring 320 kilobytes of memory, from your FoxPro/DOS application, you would issue either of these commands:

```
RUN /320 wordstar.exe
RUN /320K wordstar.exe
```

Visual FoxPro for Windows can run either DOS or Windows applications. If an application is run without the "NOWAIT" option, a DOS application is assumed. If a file extension is not specified, Visual FoxPro first looks for a file with the same program name and the extension PIF. A PIF, or Program Information File, dictates several characteristics of how an application should run. We won't drag you through all the details—check out the Windows manuals or some of the better books in our bibliography for all the gory stuff. If a PIF cannot be found, Visual FoxPro runs FoxRun.PIF, normally located in the \VFP directory, or uses the default settings if this file cannot be found. It is FOXRUN.PIF that makes all of your DOS commands hang around, and your FoxPro session appear that it is locked up, but your alternative is to have your DIR or MEM commands appear and disappear too quickly to be seen. Consider making custom PIFs for commands you use often, and make sure to include them with your application if it needs to be distributed to others.

Running Windows programs is a pretty straightforward process. Select whether you would like the application you are running to take over the visual display and become active, or perhaps sit in the background, and set your /N settings appropriately. We often use /N7 to start applications we are going to converse with from FoxPro, using either Dynamic Data Exchange or Automation.

Example

```
* Start Excel in the background, minimized
RUN /N7 EXCEL.EXE
```

See Also Configuration Files, DDEInitiate

Run

This ambiguously named event is the main program for active documents.

Usage

```
PROCEDURE acdActiveDoc.Run
LPARAMETERS cHyperLinkTarget
```

Parameter	Value	Meaning
cHyperLinkTarget	Character	Additional information that can be appended to the address of your ActiveDoc and passed as a parameter. See the example below. Requires that the ActiveDoc be on a Web site and navigated to via HTTP.

When you run an ActiveDoc application, a bunch of things happen on the way in (like the Browser starting up, if it's appropriate). Once all that's done and the ActiveDoc object has been created and situated, this event fires. This is the place to do all those things that normally live in the main program of your application, or, if you prefer, just call the main program of your application. Normally, this method either contains READ EVENTS or calls a routine that does.

Example

```
* Here's a simple Run method that puts up one form
* and issues a READ EVENTS
DO FORM MyMainForm
READ EVENTS

* Three different sites might link to your ActiveDoc, and want
* to pass to the Run parameter their settings. Site 1 would have
* a link of :
http://www.yoursite.com/yourdoc.app#Site1Parameters
* site 2 might be
http://www.yoursite.com/yourdoc.app#Site2Parameters
```

See Also ActiveDoc

Run

Some keywords just plain have too many meanings in FoxPro. *Run* is definitely in this category. This version is a method of the File object. Not surprisingly, it executes the file.

Usage `filFile.Run`

Calling this method is just like clicking the Run button in the Project Manager. Programs, queries, forms, menus and applications run. For reports and labels, the Run method is like clicking the Preview button. Bizarre, but it makes sense since in the Project Manager, the Run button turns into a Preview button when a report has focus. In the same vein, tables get browsed. Other kinds of files do nothing. Regardless of what actually happens, the method returns .T.

Just like when you run things from the PM, there's no way to pass parameters to the called file. This could be a problem if what you're trying to do programmatically with your project is test it.

If the project has an associated project hook, the QueryRunFile event fires before the file runs. That gives you a chance to react to the call.

Example `_VFP.ActiveProject.Files[3].Run`

See Also File, Project, QueryRunFile

Run() See Access().

_RunActiveDoc, Sys(4204)

This system variable and function are related to getting active document applications to run. _RunActiveDoc contains the name of the program called by the Run Active Document option on the Tools menu. SYS(4204) controls active document-debugging mode.

Usage

```
cActiveDocLauncher = _RunActiveDoc
_RunActiveDoc = cActiveDocLauncher
Sys( 4204 [, nOnOrOff ] )
```

Parameter	Value	Meaning
cActiveDocLauncher	Character	The name of a program to run to launch active document applications. Defaults to "RunActD.FXP" in the VFP home directory.
nOnOrOff	0	Turn off debugging mode for active document applications.
	1 or omitted	Turn on debugging mode for active document applications.

Because active document applications can run in VFP itself or in a browser, testing and debugging them presents some special problems.

First, the code you need to run an active doc app is different depending on whether you want it to run in a browser, in the VFP runtime, or in the VFP development environment. Rather than force us to figure it all out, the VFP team has provided us with a clever little tool that offers a jumpstart. When you choose Tools-Run Active Document from the menu or issue DO (_RunActiveDoc), a little dialog appears that lets you choose an active doc application and indicate where it should run.

If you don't like the application provided, though, you can replace it with one of your own by changing the value of _RunActiveDoc. You can make the change either programmatically or through the File Locations page of the Tools-Options dialog. Press the Set As Default button on that page to save your preference to the Registry, whether you use the dialog to set it or do it programmatically. Otherwise, you'll have to reset it every time you start VFP.

Take a look at the PRG Microsoft supplies—there are some interesting routines for reading and writing configuration information to the resource file, as well as a glimpse of how Microsoft localizes its applications.

So much for letting us test our active doc apps. The second problem is debugging them. If your app is running in a browser, how can you use the debugger to see what's happening? That's what SYS(4204) is about. When you set it to 1, the debugger can see the app running in the browser and lets you check things out. When SYS(4204) is set to 0, the debugger doesn't know a thing about your browser-hosted app.

Unlike most of the SYS() functions, SYS(4204) doesn't return either the current or the new value. In fact, there's no way to determine the current value of this setting. You'd think, by now, Microsoft would know that for every setting, there should be an equal and opposite way to find the current setting.

Incidentally, the way the active doc launcher provides the Browser (Debugging) mode is by turning on SYS(4204). No magic.

Example

```
_RunActiveDoc = "MyGreatActiveDocLauncher"
SYS(4204,1)  && turn on debugger in browser mode
DO (_RunActiveDoc)
```

See Also ActiveDoc, Run Method

RunScript See On AplAbout.

_Samples

This system variable, new in VFP 6, contains the path to the sample code that comes with Visual FoxPro.

Usage `_SAMPLES = cPathToSamples`

Now that MSDN has taken over VFP's sample code, finding it isn't as simple as looking in HOME()+"\SAMPLES", especially since both VFP and MSDN can be installed wherever you want to put them. This variable makes it easier to find the samples when you want to look them over for ideas, or take advantage of some item located there in your own code.

HOME(2) contains the same value. In fact, changing _SAMPLES changes the return value of HOME(2). Of course, changing _SAMPLES doesn't move the samples, so think twice before you change the variable. The location of the samples is stored in the Registry and _SAMPLES gets its value from there, but changing _SAMPLES, then using Tools | Options and saving as default does store the new value.

Example

```
USE (_SAMPLES + "TasTrade\Data\customer" )
```

See Also Home()

Save Macros See Clear Macros.

Save Screen, Restore Screen

These obsolete commands let you save and restore an image of any window.

Usage

```
SAVE SCREEN [ TO VarName ]
RESTORE SCREEN [ FROM VarName ]
```

Back in the days before windows or Windows, there were times when you needed to overwrite part of the screen (for example, with a confirmation message) and then be able to get back to where you were. These commands sort of let you do that. SAVE SCREEN let you make a copy of the screen image, either in a special buffer or in a variable. RESTORE SCREEN let you put the image back.

The key word in all that is "image." The restored screen wasn't live any more. Any @ .. GETs in it didn't work when it was restored.

Nothing's changed. SAVE SCREEN still saves an image, though it can work on a window rather than the background screen. RESTORE SCREEN still doesn't make things live. However, it's easy to fool yourself into thinking these commands are smarter than they are. When you CLEAR a Visual FoxPro form, the controls are still there, alive, even if you can't see them. If you SAVE SCREEN a form, then CLEAR the form, then RESTORE SCREEN, it looks as though live controls have been restored. In fact, all that was restored was the image. The controls were live all along.

A word of caution: SAVE SCREEN TO creates a variable type unique unto itself—the type "S" variable. This one has some funny behaviors not seen elsewhere. An S variable cannot be passed to a routine as a parameter. While S variables in FoxPro/DOS stored two bytes per row/column cell (one for the character, one for the color), in Windows these files seem to grow enormously as they, we suspect, inefficiently store all the color characteristics for each pixel. This means that not only are the variables and files ridiculously large, they are also incompatible between platforms.

These are legacy commands. Avoid them in new code. Toggle Visible properties to make things go away and use Refresh methods to make objects redraw themselves. Stay away from this stuff.

Example

```
SAVE SCREEN TO sBackDrop
CLEAR
* Now display something else
CLEAR
RESTORE SCREEN FROM sBackDrop
```

See Also Clear

Save To See Restore From.

Save Window See Restore Window.

SaveAs, SaveAsClass

These two very cool methods let you create a form or object, make changes, then save the changed form or object (or some control on it) for future use. They're incredibly handy when you're trying to get something just right. These two methods work only on visual objects—one more argument for doing everything in VCXs rather than in code—though we hope that limit will go away eventually, leading to true "two-way tools."

Like many of the non-event methods, you're likely to simply use the built-in versions rather than replace or supplement them with your own code.

Usage

```
PROCEDURE oObject.SaveAs
LPARAMETERS cFileName [, oDEName ] )
```

SaveAs lets you take a running form or formset and, if you want, an existing data environment and save them together as a new form or formset. The original form or formset has to be based either on an existing SCX or VCX or have been instantiated directly from the Form or FormSet base class.

If the form or formset started out as an SCX, you have to RemoveObject its original data environment before you can save it with a new one. If the form or formset originated via CreateObject() or NewObject() (whether from a VCX or the base form or formset class), you can specify the data environment object without having to do that prep work.

Usage

```
PROCEDURE oObject.SaveAsClass
LPARAMETERS cClassLib, cClassName [, cDescription ]
```

SaveAsClass goes a step further, which makes it a lot more useful in our book. (Yeah, this is our book and we say SaveAsClass is a lot more useful than SaveAs.) With SaveAsClass, you can take pretty much any object and save it, as is, into a class library, from which you can instantiate to your heart's content.

SaveAs lets you subclass a form or formset on the fly. SaveAsClass lets you subclass just about anything on the fly and make it a class that you can use as needed. SaveAsClass works for any of the objects that can be subclassed visually. As with SaveAs, everything in the object you want to save has to have started out as a visual object. You can't start with a code class and end up with a visual class.

Note that the parameters are all character, though Help implies that they're names without quotes. We strongly recommend that you always include the optional cDescription parameter so you can remember later why you saved this class.

The class library you specify does not have to exist. It'll be created if it doesn't. Watch out, though—this means that a typo can lead to a new VCX. We find that we tend to expect the class name to come before the class library in the parameter list and get it wrong a lot of the time.

Example

```
* Execute these commands from the Command Window,
* substituting your form for MyForm
DO FORM MyForm
* Choose a new backcolor
WITH _SCREEN.ActiveForm
   .BackColor = GETCOLOR()
   .Caption = "Testing SaveAs"
   .SaveAs("MyNewForm")
ENDWITH

* If we want to add a new data environment, we need
* to remove the old one
_SCREEN.ActiveForm.RemoveObject("DataEnvironment")
* Now create a new one
```

```
oDE = CREATEOBJECT("DataEnvironment")
* Change its name just so we can see the difference
oDE.Name = "TestDE"
* Now save a new form
_SCREEN.ActiveForm.SaveAs("MyNewDEForm",oDE)

* Now save a class from this form
_SCREEN.ActiveForm.SaveAsClass("Test","MyNewForm", "Testing SaveAsClass")
* Now you can close the original form and
* check out the various clones
```

See Also ActiveForm, Create Class, Create ClassLib, CreateObject, Do Form, _Screen, Set ClassLib

SavePicture() See LoadPicture().

ScaleMode

This property determines whether a form or toolbar measures things in pixels or in foxels.

Usage

```
oObject.ScaleMode = nScaleMode
nScaleMode = oObject.ScaleMode
```

ScaleMode has only two possible values: 0 for foxels, 3 for pixels. Given the choice of values, we've sort of expected some other choices (points? inches? twips?) to turn up. Other values are used in other products, but we're pretty happy not having to do the pixel-to-twip conversion, ourselves.

A pixel (the term stands for "picture element") is the smallest addressable unit on the monitor. When you say a monitor supports 1024x768, you're saying it has at least 1024 pixels across and 768 up and down.

A foxel is a FoxPro invention created so that FoxPro developers wouldn't have to think in pixels in Windows, and rows and columns in DOS. After all, can you really tell whether an item is 200 pixels from the top or 201? (Actually, we can if one item is 200 pixels from the top and another is 201. But if they line up neatly at either position, that pixel doesn't matter much.) A foxel is more or less the size of a character in the current font. (Actually, foxels might not be a FoxPro invention, just a FoxPro name for the idea. Someone just told us about something called a "dialog box unit" that sounds an awful lot like a foxel. Microsoft uses dialog box units to specify many of the dimensions within their interface standards.)

By default, forms and toolbars use pixels. Since you don't have to actually specify values for anything (just do it visually), we generally agree with this choice and work in foxels only rarely. Windows is a pixel-based environment and you'll probably be much happier keeping ScaleMode=3 throughout your applications.

ScaleMode is part of what our tech editor refers to as an "obscure" bug. He's right—you have to do just the right set of things to trigger this one, but if you do, boom! VFP GPFs. (Hey, a whole sentence with no vowels. Cool!)

Here's the setup. If you're working in design mode and an object is selected, and you run a builder that removes the selected object from the form with RemoveObject, changing the form's ScaleMode afterward causes a crash. Weird. Even weirder is that if you omit any of the pieces (like removing a different object or executing the sequence from the Command Window), there's no crash.

Example

```
DO CASE
CASE ThisForm.ScaleMode = 3
   * Using pixels, move one character down
   This.Top = This.Top + FONTMETRIC(1)
CASE ThisForm.ScaleMode = 0
   * Using foxels, move one character down
   This.Top= This.Top + 1
ENDIF
```

See Also FontMetric(), SysMetric(), TxtWidth()

Scan

This loop command is designed for sequentially processing the records in a table. It automatically moves the record pointer forward each time through the loop and stops when it reaches the end of the table.

Usage

```
SCAN [ Scope ] [ FOR lForCondition ] [ WHILE lWhileCondition ]
     [ NOOPTIMIZE ]
        Commands
        [ LOOP ]
        [ EXIT ]
ENDSCAN
```

The default scope for SCAN is ALL, so if no other scope is specified and there's no WHILE clause, processing starts with the first record in the current order. When there's a WHILE clause, processing starts with the current record. (For an explanation of Scope, FOR and WHILE clauses, see "Scope, FOR, WHILE and Santa Clauses" in "Xbase Xplained.")

SCAN processes records in the current index order. With a FOR clause, you'll get better performance by setting ORDER TO 0 before the loop. There's also a gotcha involving loops and indexes. If you're processing records in an index order and you change the value of the index key in the loop, the record immediately moves to its new position in the index and you may process some records twice or some not at all. Bottom line is, don't change the key of the current index order inside a loop.

SCAN replaces any loop that looks like:

```
DO WHILE .NOT. EOF()
   * Do some processing
   SKIP
ENDDO
```

We tested empty loops, just going through a table from top to bottom, and found SCAN to be about twice as fast as the equivalent DO WHILE. Your mileage may vary.

SCAN always reselects the right work area (the one the loop started in) when it reaches ENDSCAN, so you don't need to reselect even if you've changed work areas inside the loop. We know a lot of people who do so anyway. There doesn't appear to be a performance penalty for this, so if you're the belt-and-suspenders type, go right ahead.

LOOP and EXIT let you duck out before the show ends. LOOP short-circuits the current pass through the loop, going directly to ENDSCAN without executing any commands in between. EXIT cuts out of the loop entirely, going on to the command after ENDSCAN. Since you can avoid LOOP with IF and you can add a WHILE condition to avoid EXIT, we can't see too many reasons for using either of these in a SCAN loop. Both LOOP and EXIT violate structured programming guidelines.

You can probably ignore NOOPTIMIZE. We've never found a use for it. But, if you really want to know about it, check out SET OPTIMIZE. NOOPTIMIZE is the local equivalent.

We don't use many SCAN loops because most of the table-processing commands accept Scope, FOR and WHILE clauses, which allow us to do the same thing in a single command. The best time to use a loop is when you have several things to do to each record or when you need to do something complex.

Example

```
USE Company
* Loop through, printing fax if available and phone
* number otherwise
SCAN
   IF EMPTY(Fax)
      ? Phone
   ELSE
      ? Fax
```

```
    ENDIF
ENDSCAN
```

See Also Do While, Exit, For, For Each, Loop, Set Optimize

Scatter, Gather

These commands were part of every application we wrote in FoxPro 2.x (and even in earlier versions). We don't use them the same way in Visual FoxPro because VFP's buffering capabilities make it unnecessary, but one VFP-only version of the commands can be useful.

SCATTER copies all or part of a record to an array, memory variables or an object. GATHER collects data from an array, variables or an object and sticks it in the current record.

Usage

```
SCATTER [ FIELDS FieldList |
        [ LIKE Skeleton1 ] [ EXCEPT Skeleton2 ] ]
        MEMVAR | TO ArrayName | NAME ObjectName
        [ MEMO ] [ BLANK ]
GATHER [ FIELDS FieldList |
        [ LIKE Skeleton1 ] [ EXCEPT Skeleton2 ] ]
        MEMVAR | FROM ArrayName | NAME ObjectName
        [ MEMO ]
```

Parameter	Value	Meaning
FieldList	List of fields	The fields to include in the command.
Skeleton1	Fieldname with wildcards	A specification for which fields to include in the command. Wildcards are * and ?.
Skeleton2	Fieldname with wildcards	A specification for which fields to exclude from the command. Wildcards are * and ?.
ArrayName	Name	An array to hold the scattered data or from which to get the gathered data. SCATTER creates or enlarges the array, as needed, but doesn't shrink it.
ObjectName	Name	An object that has a property corresponding to each specified field. SCATTER creates the object.

Both the LIKE and EXCEPT clauses can be included in a single command, but they can't be mixed with an explicit field list.

There are three forms of these commands that differ in where they put or get the data: MEMVAR, TO array and NAME. MEMVAR uses a set of memory variables with the same names as the fields. SCATTER MEMVAR creates the memory variables; GATHER MEMVAR collects data from them.

Using TO or FROM indicates that field data is stored in an array. SCATTER creates or redimensions the array, if necessary. GATHER collects data from the array, matching it element by element with the record.

The NAME clause lets you create an object that has a property for each specified field. SCATTER creates and populates the object. GATHER collects data from the object. Note that objects created this way differ from almost every other object you can create in Visual FoxPro. Unless the table being SCATTERed happens to have such fields, these objects have neither Name nor Class properties. They have no methods or events. Listing memory shows the object as type Object with class "EMPTY." These "lightweight" objects are ideal candidates to use as parameters, having no visible presence and no surprising behaviors.

The MEMO clause indicates that memo fields should be included in the command. Without it, memos are ignored. When you're working with arrays and omit MEMO, you need to be careful that you don't get mixed up about which column refers to which field, since memo fields are skipped. General fields are always skipped, so watch out for those, too.

BLANK says to create the memvars, array or object, but populate it with blank values of the appropriate type. In a FoxPro 2.x application, you'd typically SCATTER MEMVAR BLANK at the beginning of an Add operation, then APPEND BLANK and GATHER MEMVAR when the user asked to save.

Visual FoxPro appears to fix a "by design" bug in older versions. In FoxPro 2.x, if you SCATTER MEMVAR, then call a routine that makes one of the SCATTERed memvars private and GATHER in that routine, if the called routine contains no assignment to the private memvar, FoxPro would find the memvar in the calling routine and GATHER it even though the PRIVATE declaration should have hidden the memvar in the calling routine. Visual FoxPro respects the privacy of the variable. This change should only create a problem for you if you depended on the old behavior.

We don't use SCATTER and GATHER much in Visual FoxPro. Instead, we use row and table buffering and work with the fields directly. However, we do know people who use the NAME clause to create "record objects" so that they can write more OOP-y code.

Example

```
* Create an object corresponding to a Customer record
* Assumes the record pointer is on the relevant customer
SCATTER NAME oCust MEMO
* Now you can refer to the fields as properties of the object
? oCust.Company_Name
? oCust.Customer_Id
* After editing, you can:
GATHER NAME oCust
```

See Also Append From Array, Copy To Array, CursorSetProp()

SCCProvider

This property of the Project object tells you whether the project is under source code control, and if so, who the provider is.

Usage

```
cProvider = prjProject.SCCProvider
```

The SCCProvider property returns, as a string, the Registry key under HKEY_LOCAL_MACHINE that contains information about the source code control provider for this project. You can use this information to plunge into the Registry and get the settings for this particular provider. As we haven't played with anything other than Visual SourceSafe, we can't tell you much about what you can find there, but you'll probably want to fire up a good Registry editor and see what you can find.

Example

```
#DEFINE HKEY_LOCAL_MACHINE   0x80000002
lcProvider = oProject.SCCProvider
IF NOT EMPTY(lcProvider)
   oRegistry = NewObject("Registry", ;
                         HOME() + "FFC\Registry.vcx")
   cValue = space(255)
   oRegistry.GetRegKey("SCCServerName ", @cValue, ;
                    lcProvider, HKEY_LOCAL_MACHINE)
   ? "The project's database is controlled by " + cValue
ENDIF
```

See Also Project, Registration Database

SCCStatus

This property of the File object tells you the status of a file within the source code control system.

Usage `nStatus = filFile.SCCStatus`

Property	Value	Purpose
SCCStatus	0	File is not under source code control.
	1	File is checked in.
	2	File is checked out to you.
	3	File is checked out to someone else.
	4	File has a merge conflict.
	5	File has been merged.
	6	File is checked out to multiple users—watch out!

Use this property to determine whether a file is controlled in the source-code-control system (when the status returns a non-zero value) and what its status is.

Use the SCCFILE_* constants in FoxPro.H to write more readable code.

Example

```
#INCLUDE FOXPRO.H
oFile = oProject.Files[1]
IF oFile.SCCStatus = SCCFILE_CHECKEDOUTMU
  MessageBox(oFile.Name + " is checked out multiple times!"
ENDIF
```

See Also AddToSCC, CheckIn, CheckOut, File, RemoveFromSCC, SCCProvider

_SCCText See _Beautify.

Scheme() See Set Color Set.

SCols(), SRows()

These two functions tell you about the size of the main Visual FoxPro window with respect to the current font. You can find similar (sometimes the same) information using the system variable _SCREEN and its properties Height and Width.

Usage

```
nScreenCols = SCOLS()
nScreenRows = SROWS()
```

The functions return the number of columns and rows available in the main window using the current font. If you change the screen font, the results change. Of course, resizing the window (whether in code or interactively) changes the results. The values returned are in foxels, FoxPro's special unit of measure that corresponds roughly to a character. These functions are primarily included for backward compatibility with DOS applications that used to have to check for 43-line EGA screens and 50-line VGA screens.

The system variable _SCREEN is an object reference to the main window. You can both inquire about and change that window's characteristics by referencing the variable. The Height and Width properties tell you about the size of the window. By default, those properties use pixels, which are not sensitive to font changes. However, by changing _SCREEN.ScaleMode to 0, you can see the results in foxels. In that case, Height and Width are the same as SROWS() and SCOLS(), respectively.

Example

```
nRows=SROWS()
nCols=SCOLS()

? SROWS(),SCOLS()
_SCREEN.FontName="Courier New"
? SROWS(),SCOLS()
_SCREEN.FontSize=14
? SROWS(),SCOLS()
```

See Also FontBold, FontItalic, FontMetric(), FontName, FontSize, Height, Modify Window, ScaleMode, _Screen, SysMetric(), WFont(), Width

_Screen

This system variable makes it easy to manipulate the main Visual FoxPro window. It contains an object reference to the window that you can use to manipulate the window's properties.

Usage

```
_SCREEN.Property = uValue
uValue = _SCREEN.Property
_SCREEN.Method()
```

The screen object is a little strange. It contains some properties that apply to forms (like Controls and ControlCount) and others that apply to formsets (like Forms, FormCount and ActiveForm). It doesn't respond to any events, but it does have a small set of methods. The SaveAsClass method lets you create a visual class with the same characteristics as the window. However, it loses the formset properties en route and becomes a form-based class.

Some of the things you can do with _SCREEN, you can also do with MODIFY WINDOW. But it's much easier to change properties using _SCREEN and far more of them are available. However, after you've made a whole lot of changes, it's hard to remember how you found things. You can restore the main window to just about the condition you found it in by issuing MODIFY WINDOW SCREEN with no arguments.

There are a few items that aren't restored by this—one that we know of is DrawWidth. Some items are restored in practice, but _SCREEN's properties are wrong. BackColor is one like that.

One of the most common uses we find for _SCREEN is getting access to the currently active form through the ActiveForm property. This property contains an object reference to the form that has focus. Since toolbars are never ActiveForm, they can use _SCREEN.ActiveForm to call methods of the current form. _SCREEN.ActiveForm is also handy in the Debugger to figure out what's going on.

Don't confuse _SCREEN with _VFP. That variable gives you access to the VFP Application object, an automation server with a whole bunch of PEMs of its own. While we primarily used _SCREEN as the "top" object in VFP 3.0 _SCREEN-based systems, with the introduction of top-level forms and Automation servers, we're more likely to use the Application object.

Example

```
* Personalize the screen
_SCREEN.Caption = "Hacker's Visual FoxPro"
_SCREEN.BackColor = RGB(0,0,255)
_SCREEN.ForeColor = RGB(255,255,255)

* Call a method of the active form without knowing what form
* is in charge
_SCREEN.ActiveForm.SaveRecord()
```

See Also ActiveForm, Modify Window, SaveAsClass, _VFP

Scroll

Don't confuse the useful Scrolled event with this legacy command. While it's a neat command, we don't expect anyone to use it in VFP.

Usage

```
SCROLL nTopRow, nLeftCol, nBottRow,
       nRightCol, nRowChange [, nColChange ]
```

Parameter	Value	Meaning
nTopRow	Numeric	Top row of area to be scrolled.
nLeftCol	Numeric	Leftmost column of area to be scrolled.
nBottRow	Numeric	Bottom row of scrolled area.
nRightCol	Numeric	Rightmost column of area to be scrolled.
nRowChange	Numeric	Number of rows to move either up (negative) or down (positive).
nColChange	Numeric	Number of columns to scroll area either right (positive) or left (negative).

Text and images on the screen or active output window can be moved around using this command. Areas they leave behind are erased. Text and graphics that scroll beyond the specified boundaries are lost and cannot be retrieved by scrolling in the opposite direction.

Specifying an nRowChange value of zero with no nColChange value (or a value of zero) erases the area within the specified row and column boundaries. However, an nColChange setting of zero scrolls the area only vertically. We feel that specifying changes of zero ("no change") should result in, well, no change.

Visual FoxPro translates the rows and columns specified into those based on the current output font; funny effects can result from screens that may have looked okay in DOS. This command was developed long ago for DOS-based products; we're surprised to find it works at all.

Example

```
CLEAR
@ 5,5 SAY "C:\WINDOWS\WINLOGO.BMP" BITMAP
@ 10, 10 SAY "Way Cool Effects" ;
         FONT "Times",16 STYLE "T" COLOR R+
SCROLL 0,0,20,15,2
SCROLL 5,16,20,21,-2
FOR i = 4 TO -8 STEP -1
  IF i # 0
    SCROLL 0,26-i,20,26-i,i*.1
  ENDIF
NEXT
```

See Also @ ... Say

ScrollBars, Scrolled

The ScrollBars property determines whether an edit box, form or grid displays a scrollbar. The Scrolled event fires each time the user clicks either the horizontal or vertical scrollbars, or drags either scroll button (the "thumb") on the grid or form. It also fires when the DoScroll method is called programmatically. The Scrolled event applies only to grids and forms, not to edit boxes.

Usage
```
oObject.ScrollBars = nScrollBar
nScrollBars = oObject.ScrollBars
```

Parameter	Value	Meaning
nScrollBar	0	None.
	1	Horizontal bars only—grids and forms.
	2	Vertical bars only.
	3	Both horizontal and vertical bars—grids and forms only.

Scrollbars were added to Visual FoxPro forms in version 6.0, as part of the support for Active Documents. We greet this new capability with mixed feelings—it is always good to have a more flexible programming model, but some features are just too likely to be abused. We don't believe scrolling forms are a particularly good user interface, and strongly recommend you consider alternatives before settling on them. (We came across one piece of research that says only 10 percent of users scroll beyond the first screen of information on a Web page. It's stuff like that that makes us think scrollable forms don't belong in most applications.)

On the other hand, we think data entry operators using a scrollable form that more accurately depicts the data entry form they are working from (say, a Form 1040) is preferable to learning different navigation for the form than for the paper document. Also, if managed correctly, tabbing down through a document, paging up and down, and moving top to bottom in a document with the document metaphor could make scrollbars appropriate for some applications. Since DoScroll doesn't work for forms (only grids), you'll need to consider some tricks with GotFocus() and SetViewPort(). Scrolling can be a tedious thing, and that's why we suspect most Web surfers aren't inclined to do so. Ensure that, if you decide to incorporate scrolling forms in your design, you make them easy to use from the keyboard as well as with a mouse.

Usage
```
object.Scrolled()
Procedure object.Scrolled()
LPARAMETERS [ nIndex, ] [ nWhichWay ]
```

Parameter	Value	Meaning
nIndex	Integer	The index into this control, if used as part of a control array.
nWhichWay	0	User clicked the up arrow button or dragged the thumb upward.
	1	User clicked the down arrow button or dragged the thumb downward.
	2	User clicked in the space above the thumb.
	3	User clicked in the space below the thumb.
	4	User clicked the left arrow button or dragged the thumb to the left.
	5	User clicked the right arrow or dragged the thumb to the right.
	6	User clicked in the space to the left of the thumb.
	7	User clicked in the space to the right of the thumb.

The Scrolled event gives you an opportunity to rearrange the display as the user scrolls from one part of a grid or form to another. We haven't found a whole bunch of uses for this event yet, but we're sure we'll find some good stuff.

The directional feedback is confusing to a lot of people. The "arrow" values are returned if the user clicks on the buttons located at either end of the scrollbar, or if she grabs the "thumb" in the middle of the scrollbar and positions it where she wants it to be. We find it rather confusing that two very different physical events can't be distinguished this way. Even more confusing, you can change the magnitude of scrolling with the buttons, but not the precision of moving the thumb, by changing the "SmallChange" properties (does this mean we're getting nickeled and dimed? That this is a penny-ante feature? Let's change the subject…). The other four values are returned when the user clicks on the "background" of the scrollbar in order to move the thumb toward the position he clicked. Confusing as all this is, it is consistent, and it follows with the rest of the Windows scrolling window model.

Example
```
ThisForm.grdGrid1.Scrolled()
```

See Also ContinuousScroll, DoScroll, Edit box, Form, Grid, HScrollSmallChange, ScaleMode, SetViewPort, ViewPortHeight, ViewPortLeft, ViewPortTop, ViewPortWidth, VScrollSmallChange

Sec() See Hour().

Seconds See Set Seconds.

Seconds(), Sys(2)

SECONDS() returns a numeric value of the number of seconds since midnight, with a resolution of one millisecond. SYS(2) returns a character string of the same number, formatted as five digits with no decimal places.

Usage
```
nRetVal = SECONDS()
cTime = SYS(2)
```

Very useful for benchmarking the time to complete a task—record the start time, do the task, then subtract the start time from the end time to calculate the duration of the task. Don't confuse this with the SEC() function used to extract the seconds portion of a datetime.

The SECONDS() function grabs the time when FoxPro starts and stores it in some hidden nook or cranny. Changing the system time while FoxPro is running is not reflected in the SECONDS() function, although TIME() and DATETIME() do seem to pick it up.

Strangely enough, the SECONDS() function, while ignoring other changes, does note that midnight has passed during the current session and resets SECONDS() to zero. This can be very useful if you are capturing seconds since midnight in an application that might need to run for several days. This was a notorious 2.x bug, squashed finally in 3.0.

SYS(2) does reflect changes made to the system time while Visual FoxPro is running, although we don't advise doing this—it can make it awfully difficult to determine which source code is the most recent when the time keeps shifting! SYS(2), like the newly improved SECONDS(), will reset on the stroke of midnight.

Example
```
lcStopTime = SYS(2)
lnStartTime = SECONDS()
```

See Also DateTime(), Sec(), Time()

Seek, Seek(), IndexSeek(), Find

Seek, and ye shall find.

The Bible

These commands and functions all search for data in an indexed table. SEEK and SEEK() provide the fastest way to find a single record, if an index exists for the desired data. INDEXSEEK() lets you find out whether a particular record exists, without moving the record pointer. FIND is an ancient relic, but still handy in the Command Window, if you can remember to use it.

Usage

```
FIND cExpression
SEEK uExpression
     [ ORDER nIndexNumber | IDXFile
      | [ TAG ] TagName [ OF CDXFile ]
      [ ASCENDING | DESCENDING ] ]
     [ IN cAlias | nWorkArea ]
lFound = SEEK( uExpression [, cAlias | nWorkArea
               [, nIndexNumber | cIDXFile | cTagName ] ] )
lFound = INDEXSEEK( uExpression [, lMovePointer
                    [, cAlias | nWorkarea
                    [, nIndexNumber | cIDXFile | cTagName ] ] ] )
```

Parameter	Value	Meaning
cExpression, uExpression		The value to search for.
nIndexNumber	Numeric	The position of the index to use among the open indexes.
IDXFile or cIDXFile	Filename or Character	The stand-alone IDX file in which to search.
TagName or cTagName	Name or Character	The index tag in which to search.
CDXFile or cCDXFile	Filename or Character	The CDX index file containing the specified tag.
cAlias	Character	The alias of the table in which to search.
	Omitted	If nWorkArea is also omitted, search in the current work area.
nWorkArea	Numeric	The work area in which to search.
	Omitted	If cAlias is also omitted, search in the current work area.
lMovePointer	.T.	Move the record pointer to either the matching record or to EOF, if there is no matching record.
	.F.	Don't move the record pointer, whether or not a match is found.
lFound	.T.	uExpression was found.
	.F.	uExpression was not found.

Let's start with the most basic item here. FIND is obsolete. Don't use it in applications. It is handy when you're working in the Command Window and need to search for a particular string because you can omit the quotes around the string.

Before VFP, SEEK insisted that you be in the right work area with order set to the right order. Now you can specify the table and index you want to use for the search right in the command.

With those additions, SEEK is slightly more capable than SEEK(), because SEEK lets you specify which CDX file contains the tag you want, while SEEK() doesn't. However, SEEK() lets you omit the step of checking FOUND() to see if the search was successful. But SEEK lets you indicate whether to use the tag in ascending or descending order. The specification of ASCENDING or DESCENDING is independent of both the current index direction and the direction in which the index was created.

INDEXSEEK(), added in VFP 6, is a solution to a problem that didn't exist before Visual FoxPro. Both SEEK and SEEK() move the record pointer in the specified table (whether or not they find a match). The addition of database rules and triggers, as well as row buffering, means we often want to search for an item without moving the record pointer. That's INDEXSEEK()'s main purpose. It's what KEYMATCH() should have been, but isn't. Use INDEXSEEK() when you want to find out if a value is already in a table, but don't want to commit the record you're working on.

We're a little puzzled by INDEXSEEK()'s lMovePointer parameter. The whole point of the function is not to move the record pointer, so why make it an option? We suspect it's because Microsoft expects us all to stop using SEEK and SEEK() and simply switch to INDEXSEEK() in new code.

None of these items permanently affects the current work area or the current index order for the table. Changes are made behind the scenes as necessary, then things change back to the way they were found. This means you can, for example, search the target table of a relation based on a tag other than the one controlling the relation without having to reset the relation afterwards. Very handy.

As we've mentioned elsewhere, we don't find the nIndexNumber feature to be high on our list of preferred methods for identifying indexes, since modifications to the index or creation of a temporary .IDX file can skew the index numbers. It is preferable (and more self-documenting) to use the tag names, when you know them.

Example

```
* This is handy in the command window
USE Customer ORDER Company_Na
FIND AROUND THE HORN

USE Customer  && No order set

* Company_Na is a tag on UPPER(Company_Name)
SEEK "AROUND THE HORN" ORDER Company_Na
? FOUND()  && Returns .T.

SELECT 0  && change work areas
* Use nIndexNumber
? SEEK("ERNST HANDEL", "Customer", 1) && Returns .T.
* Use cTagName
? SEEK("ERNST HANDEL", "Customer", "Company_Na") && Returns .T.

SELECT Customer
SEEK "H" ORDER Company_Na DESCENDING  && Last "H" name
* Positions pointer on record for Hungry Owl All-Night Grocers

SET ORDER TO Company_Na
GO TOP
? INDEXSEEK("ERNST HANDEL")  && Returns .T.
? RECNO()  && Returns 1, because pointer didn't move
```

See Also Found(), Index, KeyMatch(), Locate, Recno(), Set Near

Select

This command changes the current work area. Don't confuse this command with the SELECT-SQL command or with the SELECT() function.

Usage `SELECT cAlias | nWorkArea`

SELECT makes the specified work area current. If nWork area is 0, SELECT switches to the lowest-numbered unused work area. This is handy when opening a series of tables.

We recommend that you never use SELECT with an explicitly numbered work area (i.e., SELECT 5). There's no reason on earth to have any idea which work area a particular table is open in.

Example

```
SELECT 0          && move to a new work area
USE Customer
* Move to another area and open another table
SELECT 0
USE Orders
* Switch back to Customer
SELECT Customer
* At the beginning of a "black box" routine,
* it's good to save the work area; then,
* at the end, restore it.
LOCAL nSelect
nSelect = SELECT()
* now do some processing that changes the work area
* now restore using indirect reference
SELECT (nSelect)
```

The last line of the example makes it look as if SELECT is doing name evaluation and getting a number. In fact, what's really going on is that the parentheses are forcing nSelect to be evaluated before it's used in the command. Without the parentheses, VFP would try to find a work area with an alias of nSelect.

It's also worth noting that, generally, it's better to save the work area using SELECT() than using ALIAS(). With ALIAS(), you have to check whether the variable is empty before restoring the work area; since SELECT() always returns the number of a valid work area, it doesn't require that extra check.

See Also (), Select-SQL, Select(), Use

Select() See Alias().

Select-SQL

SELECT-SQL is one of our favorite commands. It lets you create an output set from one or more tables based on various criteria and send it to one of several locations. What makes SELECT so cool is that you specify what you want rather than how to get it—FoxPro figures out how to get it internally.

A SELECT-SQL statement is often called a query because you're querying the database.

Usage

```
SELECT [ ALL | DISTINCT ]
       [ TOP nHowMany [ PERCENT ] ]
        eColumn1 [ AS ColumnName1 ]
             [, eColumn2 [ AS ColumnName2 ] ... ]
       FROM [ FORCE ]
            [ Database1! ]Table1 [ LocalAlias1 ]
              [ [ INNER | LEFT [ OUTER ] | RIGHT [ OUTER ]
               | FULL [ OUTER ] ] JOIN
               [ Database2! ]Table2 [ LocalAlias2 ]
                 [ ... ]
               [ ON lJoinCondition1 ]
               | , [ Database3! ]Table3 [ LocalAlias3 ]
```

```
          [ ... ] ]
[ WHERE lConditions ]
[ GROUP BY GroupColumn1 [, GroupColumn2 ... ] ]
[ HAVING lGroupFilter ]
[ UNION [ ALL | DISTINCT ] SELECT ... ]
[ ORDER BY OrderCriteria1 [ ASC | DESC ]
     [, OrderCriteria2 [ ASC | DESC ] ... ] ]
[INTO CURSOR CursorName [ NOFILTER ]
 | INTO TABLE | DBF TableName
 | INTO ARRAY ArrayName
 | TO FILE FileName [ ADDITIVE ]
 | TO PRINTER [ PROMPT ]
 | TO SCREEN ]
[ PREFERENCE PreferenceName ]
[ NOCONSOLE ]
[ PLAIN ]
[ NOWAIT ]
```

Parameter	Value	Meaning
nHowMany	Numeric	The number of records or percentage of the records to include in the final result.
eColumn*x*	Expression	An expression showing how to compute the data to go into the *x*th column of the result. Fields in the expression may be aliased. The expression should be written so that all values are the same length (in characters).
ColumnName*x*	Name	A name to assign to the *x*th field in the result set. Follows all the usual FoxPro field naming rules.
Database*x*	Name	The database containing the *x*th table in the query.
Table*x*	Name	The *x*th table to join into the query.
LocalAlias*x*	Name	An alias to use within the query for the *x*th table in the FROM clause.
lJoinCondition*x*	Logical	An expression (most likely, a comparison) that provides the join conditions for the *x*th join listed.
lConditions	Logical	The conditions used to choose the records that go into the result set. There are two types of conditions: join conditions involving fields from more than one table (though joins can also be handled in the FROM clause) and filter conditions involving fields from a single table.
GroupColumn*x*	Numeric	The number of the column in the result which is to be used as the *x*th grouping criterion.
	Name	The column name of the column to be used as the *x*th grouping criterion.
lGroupFilter	Logical	An expression on which to filter the results of grouping. This condition is applied to the intermediate results (normally following GROUPing) of the query.

Parameter	Value	Meaning
OrderCriteria*x*	Numeric	The number of the column in the result to use as the *x*th ordering criterion.
	Name	The name of a column to use as the *x*th ordering criterion.
CursorName	Name	A name for the cursor containing the result set.
TableName	Name	A name for the table containing the result set.
ArrayName	Array	An array to contain the result set.
FileName	Name	The name of a file into which a list of the result set should be dumped. The format is the same as using the LIST command.
PreferenceName	Name	A name for a BROWSE Preference to be used or created for the results. This is useful only when results go to the default Browse. You need an active resource file to do this.

Frankly, we don't think a syntax diagram is a very good way to learn SELECT-SQL. It's just too complex for that. One good way is to play with the Query Designer, though it can't handle all the queries you can write by hand. (In particular, it has trouble with certain kinds of joins.) Open the SQL window, so you can see the generated statements, then try different choices and see what happens. Once you're comfortable with the basic clauses and options, you can move on to writing your own queries and try out the more complicated stuff.

Nonetheless, let's try to make sense of this whole-language-in-one command. Like the other SQL commands, SELECT is non-procedural, which means you specify what you want, but you don't have to tell FoxPro how to get it. SELECT processes one or more tables, producing what's called a *result set*. In FoxPro, you have many alternatives of what to do with the result set. The default (from FoxPro 2.5 on) is to store it in a cursor and BROWSE the cursor. The PREFERENCE and NOWAIT options listed above apply only in that case and behave as they do for BROWSE.

Fielding a Team

There are two clauses required in every query: the field list, specified immediately after the SELECT, and the table list, which goes in the FROM clause. The field list contains a list of expressions, which create the result set. The simplest version is to put just "*", which means "include every field from every listed table." Otherwise, each expression can be as simple as a single field or can be a complex computation. You can mix and match the "*" with a field list, including all fields from some tables with selected fields from others, just by using an alias in front of the "*" to specify the table.

There are a few ground rules. While you can call both built-in functions and UDFs in field expressions, you need to be careful about them. Check out Help for some fair warnings on this. Because SELECT is non-procedural, you can't count on things happening in a particular order. Don't expect to find the record pointer in a particular location, but do be sure to put it back if you move it.

The first record the query finds (which could be almost any) defines the type and size for each field in the result set. So, it's important for that record to have the appropriate shape for the results you want to generate. For example, you might use an expression like:

```
IIF(SomeField, SomeOtherField, "X")
```

The problem is what happens if SomeField is .F. for the first record generated. The result is created with a one-character field rather than one the width of SomeOtherField. A better expression is:

```
IIF(SomeField, SomeOtherField, PADR("X", LEN(SomeOtherField)))
```

In the case of numeric fields, use a "picture" to show the size and decimals of the number. For example, the following forces FoxPro to create a 9-byte numeric field with two decimal places:

```
IIF(SomeField, SomeOtherField, 000000.00)
```

The AS clause lets you assign a field name of your choice (rather than FoxPro's choice) to a field of the result set. FoxPro's choice depends on the expression used for the field. If it's just a field name, the resulting column has the same name (unless multiple columns of the result originate from same-named fields). If it's an expression, FoxPro chooses a name like EXP_1 for a simple expression or function_EXP_1 when one of the built-in functions is used (like SUM_EXP_1). Frequently, the field names in the result set are unimportant and you can just let FoxPro do its thing. But, at other times, you need to know the name of the resulting field—in those cases, AS is worth its weight in gold (of course, "AS" wouldn't be that heavy in gold, so maybe we're damning with faint praise here).

You come FROM where?

The second required clause is a list of tables used in the query. In Visual FoxPro, table names can be qualified by the containing database, like TasTrade!Customer. This lets you use same-named tables from multiple databases in a query. For example, you might compare customer lists from two different databases. It also lets you use tables without having to explicitly open the database first.

The FROM clause also lets you assign a local alias to a table. The local alias is used only within the query. We've found two good uses for local aliases. The first is when we need to use multiple tables of the same name or to use the same table more than once in a query (the latter is called a self-join, by the way). In this case, the local alias is pretty much required. The second case is when the name of a table is long—sometimes, we assign a shorter local alias just to cut down on typing. One warning here: single-letter local aliases can sometimes confuse FoxPro because the single letters from A through J also refer to the first 10 work areas. We recommend you stick to aliases of two letters or more.

The optional FORCE clause is for times when you know better than VFP what order the tables should be joined in for optimal results. When you include FORCE, the joins are performed in the order specified in the FROM clause without any attempt to optimize. See "Faster than a Speeding Bullet" for more query optimization.

May I JOIN You?

When a query contains more than one table, you have to (well, you don't *have* to, but you'll be sorry if you don't) provide a way for FoxPro to match up records in the tables. SELECT's default behavior is to pair every record in each table with every record in every other table. That is, by default, the number of records in the result is the product of the number of records in each table. For example, if you have 500 Customers in one table and 2000 Orders in another, by default, the result set of a query listing Customers and Orders in the FROM clause would contain 500*2000 = 1,000,000 records.

You'll rarely want this default result (called a Cartesian join), of course. Normally, when you include two (or more) tables in a query, there's some data in the tables that determines which records match up. In the Customers and Orders example, both tables probably include a Customer ID field and you only want to match each customer record to the Orders for that customer. That's a join condition. It tells how to join two tables so that the results are meaningful. Normally, for a query involving N tables, you have at least N-1 join conditions.

Most often, the join conditions for two tables are the same as the persistent relation between them, but not always. Some of the most interesting queries we've written involve creative and complex join conditions. For example, a self-join might pair a daily sales record with the corresponding record from the previous year.

There are two ways to specify join conditions. All versions of FoxPro (back to 2.0 where SELECT was introduced) allow you to put join conditions in the WHERE clause discussed below. Starting in VFP 5, however, joins have their own place, as well, as part of the FROM clause. You do have to do it one way or the other, though. Either all your joins go in the FROM clause or they all go in the WHERE—there's no mix-and-match permitted.

When joins are specified in the FROM clause, the join condition follows the ON keyword; the actual expression you put there is no different than what you'd put in the WHERE clause.

When you put your joins in the FROM clause, however, you have some options you don't get when they're in the WHERE clause. Joins fall into two types—inner and outer—and outer joins can be further divided into left, right and full. (Funny, you'll find all those types as keywords in the syntax diagram.) In an inner join, only those records in one table that match up to a record in the other table are included in the result. For example, if you use an inner join for customers and orders, the result set includes only those customers who have actually placed an order. The WHERE clause can only handle inner joins. Developers working in VFP 3 and earlier need to create an outer join by using the UNION keyword to join two or more SELECT statements to gather those records that match and those that don't. The new JOIN syntax is a welcome relief from that challenge.

Outer joins let you deal with unmatched records. In a left outer join, all the records from the table on the left (that is, before the JOIN keyword) are included along with whichever records from the table on the right match up. If a record on the left has no match on the right, any fields in the result that are based on the table on the right are given a null value. A left outer join of customers and orders (in that order) includes all customers and their corresponding orders; customers who've placed no orders show up, but any fields related to orders are null.

A right outer join is the same thing in reverse. All the records from the table on the right (that is, after the JOIN keyword) are included along with any matching records on the right.

A full outer join includes all records from both tables, matched appropriately.

If queries were limited to two tables, we'd be done. However, you can put as many tables as you want in a query (subject to work area, command length and file handle limitations). So we need a way to specify joins involving three or more tables. In fact, any given join actually joins the result so far (which is a cursor) to a single table. Logically, we join multiple tables by doing a series of individual joins, each one adding another table to the results so far.

There are two ways to specify that series of joins, however, and to make matters more complicated, a single query can include both approaches.

The first way (which is the only one the Query Designer knows how to do) is to nest the joins. You list all the tables separated by their appropriate JOIN keywords and follow them with the ON clauses in reverse order. That is, the first ON clause matches up to the last JOIN listed. We call the "nested syntax" and we tend to indent it to show the nesting. The nested syntax is great for hierarchical relationships, like Customer to Orders to Order_Line_Items to Products, where the FROM clause might look like:

```
FROM Customer ;
   JOIN Orders ;
      JOIN Order_Line_Items ;
         JOIN Products ;
           ON Order_Line_Items.Product_Id = Products.Product_Id ;
        ON Orders.Order_Id = Order_Line_Items.Order_Id ;
     ON Customer.Customer_Id = Orders.Customer_Id
```

But not all the relationships you want to deal with in a query are hierarchical. Suppose you want to join an order to the customer who placed the order, the employee who took the order and the shipper used to send the order. While the order table serves as a parent to the customer, employee and shipper tables, there's no relationship among the three child tables. (We call these "unrelated siblings," and it mirrors the way we occasionally feel about our own siblings.)

While you can use the nested syntax for unrelated siblings, the resulting query is hard to read and hard to maintain. We prefer to use the less documented, but more readable, "sequential syntax." In this form, each JOIN is immediately followed by its corresponding ON clause. You can put as many of these in a row as you want and they're performed in the order listed. (Actually, joins may be performed in weird orders for optimization reasons, but from a logical perspective, sequential joins happen from top to bottom.) The join between Orders, Customer, Employee and Shippers might look like this:

```
FROM Orders ;
   JOIN Customer ;
     ON Orders.Customer_Id = Customer.Customer_Id ;
   JOIN Employee ;
     ON Orders.Employee_Id = Employee.Employee_Id ;
   JOIN Shippers ;
     ON Orders.Shipper_Id = Shippers.Shipper_Id
```

Outer joins are a little trickier to manage than inner joins. Once you've performed an outer join, you need to remember that you've done so and ensure that subsequent joins carry along the extra results. In many cases, that turns out to mean that each join that logically follows an outer join also needs to be an outer join.

WHERE, Oh, Where Can My Data Be?

Once you match up corresponding records, the next thing is to include only those records with relevant data. Filter conditions do this job—they live in the WHERE clause. This is where you specify things like "only orders this year" or "only customers in Pennsylvania." A query may have no filter conditions or many, complex filter conditions.

Both join conditions and filter conditions are Rushmore optimizable. See the section "Faster Than a Speeding Bullet" for clues on speeding up your queries.

WHERE has two comparison operators not found elsewhere in FoxPro: IN and BETWEEN. IN checks whether the specified field or expression is contained in a given list. (IN is a lot like FoxPro's INLIST() function.) It's handy for checking things like whether the customer's state is one of some subset, like ("PA", "NJ", "DE"). BETWEEN checks whether the field or expression is in the specified range—it works pretty much like FoxPro's BETWEEN() function and they seem to be equally fast. Both BETWEEN and BETWEEN() are inclusive, meaning that matches to the specified boundaries are included in the result. Like FoxPro's BETWEEN(), the BETWEEN clause does require proper placement of the lower and upper boundaries—it won't work if you reverse them.

The WHERE clause also may contain sub-queries, which are simply queries within another query. The sub-query is executed and then some comparison is made to its results. SELECT has several special operators for performing these comparisons: IN, EXISTS, ALL, and ANY or SOME. Of these, we've only found a real need for IN, which lets you see whether a particular value occurs in the results of a sub-query. We're actually far more likely to use NOT IN to find records that don't have a match in a sub-query. This is the best way to find the differences between two tables—all the records contained in one, but not in the other.

All the clauses discussed above relate to original data. The next few clauses work on the intermediate results obtained by joining the records, applying the WHERE clause and computing the expressions in the field list, or on even later results.

Just One of the GROUP

The GROUP BY clause lets you consolidate groups of records into a single result. For example, you might combine all the orders for each customer into a single customer order summary. Or you might count the number of customers by country. There's a trap here for the unwary—the term "group" in SELECT has a different meaning than "group" in a report. (In a report, grouping simply refers to layout; it doesn't consolidate.)

When you include GROUP BY in a query, all records whose values exactly match in all fields listed in the GROUP BY clause are consolidated into a single record.

Normally, you use GROUP BY together with a set of functions built into the SELECT command: COUNT(), SUM(), AVG(), MAX() and MIN(). These compute the specified function for the records in a group. You can put either a field name or a more complex expression inside the field. We refer to these as *aggregate* functions because they compute aggregate results.

All the aggregate functions operate correctly by ignoring null values. So, AVG(SomeField) is really the average of the non-null values of SomeField. This is a welcome change from older versions of FoxPro, which didn't recognize nulls, and brings FoxPro into line with other languages that speak SQL.

The biggest beneficiary of this change may be COUNT(), which accepts "*" as its parameter to give you the number of records in the group. In older versions of FoxPro, it didn't matter whether you put "*" or the name of a field inside COUNT()—the results were the same. In VFP 3 and later, COUNT(SomeField) tells you the number of records in the group with a non-null value for SomeField while COUNT(*) still gives you the number of records in the group.

If you use one of the aggregate functions without a GROUP BY clause, the result set contains a single record. It's as if you specified a grouping expression that put all the records in a single group.

Once you've done the grouping, you may want to omit some of the groups. The HAVING clause does that for you. It gives you another chance to filter the results, this time looking at intermediate data rather than original data. HAVING accepts the special IN and BETWEEN operators, but doesn't accept sub-queries.

Never use HAVING without GROUP BY. If you're not grouping results, you should be able to move the conditions to the WHERE clause, instead. Since WHERE is Rushmore-optimizable and HAVING is not, this can make an enormously significant speed difference. Actually, we have heard of a very few cases where you'd use HAVING without GROUP BY, though we've never run into one ourselves.

When you have the results you want, whether grouped or not, you might want to put them in a particular order. It happens that, in some cases (such as UNIONed or GROUPed queries or single-table queries where the original is ordered appropriately), results come out in order anyway. Don't count on this, though; it's an artifact of the way FoxPro performs the query and might change in future versions or perhaps even under unusual conditions in the current version.

By ORDER of the King

Instead, when you need to be sure that query results are in a particular order, use the ORDER BY clause. ORDER BY says to sort the results (after filtering, grouping and filtering again) based on the fields listed. Records are sorted on the first field listed. Then, those that match in the first field are sorted on the second field listed. Then, those that match in the first and second fields are sorted on the third, and so on.

Interestingly, any field from any table in the FROM clause can be used here. However, you cannot put an expression in this clause. So, if you want to sort on a result field that's based on an expression, you have to either rename that field with AS (a pretty good idea, anyway) or specify it by its numeric position in the result set.

Each field in the ORDER BY clause can be applied in either ascending or descending order. So, you could show Customer and Orders, in alphabetical order by customer, then from most recent to oldest (descending date) order within each customer.

Ordering can be pretty slow, especially if the result set is large. In some cases, it may be better to omit ORDER BY from the query and create an index afterwards. (You can create one index tag against a read-only cursor created by SELECT.) With arrays, it's almost always better to apply ASORT() after the query—the exception is when you need to sort on multiple fields, because ASORT() can't do that.

Once you've put the results in order, you can eliminate some of them. The TOP clause, added in VFP 5, says to include on the first nHowMany records or first nHowMany percent of the records in the final result. The records are selected based on the order specified.

While the TOP clause is handy occasionally, it's not really that useful for two reasons. First, it applies to the overall result set—you can't choose the first nHowMany records in each group. So you can't, for example, return the five most recent orders for each customer. Second, it isn't applied until the whole result set has been accumulated, so it doesn't make things any faster.

Let's Not Get INTO That

In any case, after all this, you've got a nice result set. Now where do you put it? FoxPro gives you a whole bunch of choices. One group of choices is more Xbase-ish while the other is SQL-like.

The Xbase group uses the TO clause, which is almost like the TO clause of the various Xbase commands. (DISPLAY and LIST come to mind.) You can choose to send the results to a file, to the printer or to the screen. The TO SCREEN option is the one that makes this different from the usual Xbase TO—it's needed for two reasons. First, the default for SELECT, unlike Xbase commands, is to put results in a cursor and BROWSE the cursor. The second, important reason for the TO SCREEN option is that putting the results directly on the screen was the default in FoxPro 2.0, and there's always the off-chance that somebody's application depends on this ability.

The NOCONSOLE and PLAIN options apply only when you're using TO and behave as they do elsewhere. NOCONSOLE keeps the output from appearing in the active window. PLAIN omits column headings.

We use the TO options only for interactive, quick-and-dirty work, never in applications. For example, naturally we used a table to track the progress of this book. SELECT ... TO FILE gave us a quick way to get a list of all sections ready for some processing—for example, to go to our technical editor.

Outside that kind of situation, we can't imagine using SELECT ... TO any more than we'd use DISPLAY or LIST in an application.

So what do we do with query results? The SQL INTO clause gives us three options: save them in a cursor, save them in a table, or save them in an array. The array bit is actually a FoxPro extension not usually available in SQL. We're really glad it's there, though—we use it a lot. SELECT ... INTO ARRAY is really handy for populating things like listboxes and comboboxes.

The difference between INTO CURSOR and INTO TABLE is that the cursor goes away when we're done with it while the table sticks around. Each has its uses.

The most important fact about cursors created by SELECT-SQL is that they're read-only. You can't change the data in them either interactively or programmatically. In FoxPro 2.x, this was an important, frustrating limitation. In Visual FoxPro, it doesn't matter anymore. If you need to be able to update cursor contents, use a view instead of a query to create the cursor. (There is actually a way around this limit. As long as the query creates a "real" cursor and not just a filter of the original table, you can USE the cursor AGAIN in another work area and it's read-write there.) Another VFP 5 addition is the NOFILTER clause for INTO CURSOR. In order to do things as fast as it can, FoxPro pulls a little trick. If a query involves only a single table, has no calculated fields, is fully optimizable, and is sent to a cursor, rather than going to the trouble of creating a whole new cursor, FoxPro simply filters the original table. Often, that's good enough for whatever you have in mind. However, in some situations, especially those where the query result is then used in a subsequent query or where you want to index the cursor, having only a filtered view of the original causes problems. In VFP 3 and earlier versions, you worked around this by putting something in the query that outwitted FoxPro. Starting in VFP 5, it's a lot easier—just add NOFILTER to the query and FoxPro always creates a real cursor. (Doesn't "real cursor" sound like an oxymoron?)

Odds and Ends

The ALL and DISTINCT keywords determine whether the result set contains every record found or only a unique set of records. When you specify DISTINCT, every field is compared; records that exactly match another record in the set are eliminated, so that each unique combination appears only once. If this sounds slow, it's because it is slow. Since you rarely want to match up every single field, you're usually better off culling duplicates with GROUP BY.

DISTINCT does have another use. You can put it inside the aggregate functions so they only compute whatever against unique values of the field. For example, you can count the number of unique hire dates among the TasTrade employees by including COUNT(DISTINCT Hire_Date).

If you've been following along, you'll notice we've mentioned every clause listed above except UNION. This clause lets you put the results of several queries into a single result set. It's kind of like a built-in APPEND command. Each query is executed, then all the results are stuck together in a single cursor or table or array (or output together if you insist on using the TO clause).

There's one important set of rules for UNIONing queries. The field list for each query in the UNION must have the same number of items. Corresponding items must be the same type. The first query in the UNION creates the template for the result, so fields in subsequent queries must be no larger than those in the first query. (They can be smaller.) If you think about what's going on here, the whole set of rules makes sense.

By default, a UNION includes only DISTINCT records—just like including the DISTINCT clause in a single query, UNION automatically culls out exact duplicates. There are two reasons this can be a problem. First, UNION doesn't bother to check whether the duplicates originated in the same table—they're still eliminated. Second, culling duplicates this way is slow. Our recommendation is to use UNION ALL except when you know you want duplicates removed.

There's a limit of nine UNIONs in a single query. That is, you can't combine more than 10 individual queries at once. We've never considered this a problem for two reasons. First, we've never needed to combine more than three or four queries at once. Second, you can simply break a larger problem into smaller parts. If you should need to combine the results of 20 queries (we can't imagine why), do two 10-table UNIONs, placing each in a cursor. Then, UNION those two results.

Because ORDER BY and TO/INTO are post-processing clauses, a UNIONed query should contain only one of each of these. The other clauses can be applied separately to each query in the UNION.

In VFP 3 and earlier, UNION was often used to simulate outer joins.

Example

```
* Compute the number of 1994 orders for each customer
* in the TasTrade customer list, but keep only those with
* 10 or more. Note that you can't use the TOP clause
* for this.
SELECT Customer.Customer_ID, COUNT(*) ;
   FROM TasTrade!Customer ;
     JOIN TasTrade!Orders ;
       ON Customer.Customer_ID=Orders.Customer_ID ;
   WHERE YEAR(Orders.Order_Date)=1994 ;
   GROUP BY 1 ;
   HAVING COUNT(*)>=10 ;
   INTO CURSOR OrderCount

* Find all the customers with no orders
SELECT * FROM Customer ;
  WHERE Customer_ID NOT IN (SELECT Customer_ID FROM Orders)

* Join Orders with Customer, Employee and Shipper
* Here's the nested syntax - does the order of the joins
* make sense to you? It doesn't to us.
SELECT Customer.company_name, ;
       Orders.order_date, ;
       Employee.last_name,;
       Shippers.company_name AS Shipper_Name;
  FROM tastrade!customer ;
    JOIN tastrade!employee;
      JOIN tastrade!shippers ;
        JOIN tastrade!orders ;
        ON Shippers.shipper_id = Orders.shipper_id ;
      ON Employee.employee_id = Orders.employee_id ;
```

```
   ON Customer.customer_id = Orders.customer_id

* Here's the same query using the sequential syntax.
* We think it's a lot more readable.
SELECT Customer.company_name, ;
       Orders.order_date, ;
       Employee.last_name,;
       Shippers.company_name AS Shipper_Name ;
 FROM tastrade!orders ;
   JOIN tastrade!customer ;
     ON Customer.customer_id = Orders.customer_id ;
   JOIN tastrade!employee  ;
     ON Employee.employee_id = Orders.employee_id ;
   JOIN tastrade!shippers ;
     ON Shippers.shipper_id = Orders.shipper_id

* Here's an example where the nested syntax makes sense
* because the tables have a hierarchical relationship.
SELECT Company_Name, Order_Date, Product_Name ;
 FROM Customer ;
   JOIN Orders ;
     JOIN Order_Line_Items ;
       JOIN Products ;
         ON Order_Line_Items.Product_Id = Products.Product_Id ;
     ON Orders.Order_Id = Order_Line_Items.Order_Id ;
   ON Customer.Customer_Id = Orders.Customer_Id


* What if we want to see all the customers in that query?
* We need an outer join between Customer and Orders
SELECT Company_Name, Order_Date, Product_Name ;
 FROM Customer ;
   LEFT JOIN Orders ;
     JOIN Order_Line_Items ;
       JOIN Products ;
         ON Order_Line_Items.Product_Id = Products.Product_Id ;
       ON Orders.Order_Id = Order_Line_Items.Order_Id ;
     ON Customer.Customer_Id = Orders.Customer_Id
```

See Also Create Cursor, Create SQL View, Set ANSI

Selected, SelectedId

These properties tell you which items in a list or combo are highlighted.

Usage

```
lIsHighlighted = oObject.Selected( nIndex )
oObject.Selected( nIndex ) = lIsHighlighted
lIsHighlighted = oObject.SelectedId( nItemId )
oObject.SelectedId( nItemId ) = lIsHighlighted
```

These two array properties let you figure out which items in a list or combo are highlighted and let you highlight items. Like the other properties related to lists, there are two of these because one gives you access via the item's Index and the other lets you use the item's unique ItemId. (See AddItem for more on this topic.)

In VFP 3, SelectedId doesn't work at all. Ever. No matter what's highlighted or which value you check, SelectedId is always .F. Unless you explicitly set it to .T. But that doesn't do much good, because the item still doesn't get highlighted. In addition, neither of these properties works for combos in VFP 3. Both bugs are fixed in VFP 5.

Selected is most useful when MultiSelect is .T. Then it lets you find all the highlighted items. With MultiSelect set to .F., you can find a single highlighted item with ListIndex or ListItemId—no need to check Selected or SelectedId. For the same reason, these properties aren't terribly useful with combos.

Example

```
* Set up a multiselect listbox with Employees
* Preselect all those located in the USA
* Set these properties in the Prop Sheet
MultiSelect = .T.
RowSourceType = 2   && Alias
RowSource = "Employee"
ColumnCount = 3
ColumnWidths = 80,40,70

* In the Init for the list:
LOCAL nCount

SELECT Employee
nCount = 1
SCAN
   IF Country = "USA"
      This.Selected[nCount] = .T.
   ENDIF
   nCount = nCount + 1
ENDSCAN
```

Be aware that, in VFP 3, no more than 60 items can be selected at the same time. See MultiSelect for more on this bug.

See Also AddItem, ComboBox, ListBox, ListIndex, ListItemId, MultiSelect

SelectedBackColor, SelectedForeColor

These properties determine the colors used to highlight text.

Usage

```
oObject.SelectedBackColor = nBackColor
nBackColor = oObject.SelectedBackColor
oObject.SelectedForeColor = nForeColor
nForeColor = oObjected.SelectedForeColor
```

Only a few controls (Edit box, Text box, Spinner, ComboBox) allow you to select text. These properties determine what colors are used for the selected text.

In a combo box, the selected colors affect only the text in the text box portion, not the drop-down list (where ItemBackColor, ItemForeColor, SelectedItemBackColor and SelectedItemForeColor hold sway). Plus, there's a very interesting effect. The current item shows up with a background of SelectedBackColor, but there's a small border around it in the combo's BackColor. (When Style = 2—drop-down list, the text in the text box portion is always selected.) You can make some pretty sharp looking effects with this (or you can set it up to be not noticeable).

Example

```
* Change the defaults for all objects
* to black on red
ThisForm.SetAll("SelectedBackColor",RGB(255,0,0))
ThisForm.SetAll("SelectedForeColor",RGB(0,0,0))
```

See Also BackColor, ForeColor, ItemBackColor, ItemForeColor, SelectedItemBackColor, SelectedItemForeColor, SelLength, SelStart, SelText

SelectedItemBackColor, SelectedItemForeColor

These properties determine the colors used for the items currently highlighted in a list or combo box.

Usage

```
oObject.SelectedItemBackColor = nBackColor
nBackColor = oObject.SelectedItemBackColor
oObject.SelectedItemForeColor = nForeColor
nForeColor = oObject.SelectedItemForeColor
```

These colors are used for whatever's currently highlighted in the list or combo box. In a list box with multi-select, all the highlighted items use these colors.

In a combo box, these colors apply only to the drop-down portion. The part that's always visible uses BackColor and ForeColor (or, when selected, SelectedBackColor and SelectedForeColor).

Example
```
ThisForm.lstFriends.SelectedItemBackColor = RGB(0,0,255)
ThisForm.lstFriends.SelectedItemForeColor = RGB(255,255,255)
```

See Also BackColor, ForeColor, ItemBackColor, ItemForeColor, SelectedBackColor, SelectedForeColor

SelectOnEntry

This property determines whether the text in a grid column, text box or edit box gets highlighted when the user uses the keyboard to move into the control.

Usage
```
oObject.SelectOnEntry = lHighlightIt
lHighlightIt = oObject.SelectOnEntry
```

The docs don't make it clear that SelectOnEntry is relevant only when the user tabs into a control, not when the user clicks into the control. In fact, clicking into an item has never highlighted it in FoxPro. (Double- or triple-clicking does let you select all, however.)

In a grid, SelectOnEntry only matters, of course, if the control in the cell is one that contains text. If there's no text to select, it's ignored.

In addition, there's interaction between the grid's Highlight property and the individual columns' SelectOnEntry. When Highlight is .F., SelectOnEntry is ignored and no text is highlighted on entry to a cell.

For text boxes and edit boxes, setting SelectOnEntry is a more readable alternative to using K in the Format property, which is no doubt why they acquired this property in VFP 5.

Example
```
ThisForm.grdMyGrid.colThree.SelectOnEntry = .F.
```

See Also Column, EditBox, Format, Grid, Highlight, TextBox

SelLength, SelStart, SelText

These three properties control selected text in those controls where textual entry is permitted: text boxes, edit boxes, spinners and combo boxes. You can figure out what the user highlighted or you can highlight text programmatically.

Usage
```
oObject.SelLength = nNumCharsHighlighted
nNumCharsHighlighted = oObject.SelLength
oObject.SelStart = nFirstCharHighlighted
nFirstCharHighlighted = oObject.SelStart
oObject.SelText = cCharsHighlighted
cCharsHighlighted = oObject.SelText
```

When no text is highlighted, SelStart indicates the position of the cursor in the text. In that case, SelLength is 0. Otherwise, SelStart is the start of the highlighted text and SelLength is the number of highlighted characters.

You can change the position of the highlight by manipulating SelStart and SelLength. Even cooler, you can actually change the text itself by manipulating SelText. You can put any text you want right into the control (except that, with spinners, it has to be digits). This solves one of the trickiest problems we had with FoxPro 2.x—getting our hands on selected text and modifying it in some way.

Except for spinners, the selection is maintained even when that control isn't the active control. When you return to the control (by tabbing), the same text is highlighted.

Spinners act really weird. If you type into a spinner, the digits aren't all the way against the arrows. If you highlight some of the text you've typed while you're still there, it becomes SelText, but as soon as you tab out of the spinner, the text you typed moves to the right and SelText changes to the characters now in the position specified by SelStart and SelLength.

Finally, combo boxes only let you fiddle with these properties when their Style is 0 for combo. If you use the drop-down style (2), the entire length of the current item is highlighted regardless of these properties.

It's okay that you can't change these properties for combos set up as drop-down lists. What's not okay is that they don't tell you anything in that case. They should provide the information about the currently selected item.

Example

```
* Change the current selection of a control
* to lowercase. Assume we're in a method of
* the control.
This.SelText = LOWER(This.SelText)

* Highlight the 5th through 10th characters
* of edit box EDIT1 on the current form
ThisForm.Edit1.SelStart = 5
ThisForm.Edit1.SelLength = 6
```

See Also ComboBox, EditBox, HideSelection, Spinner, TextBox

Separator See Toolbar.

Server

Server is a new object, exposed within the Project object to allow us to view and manipulate all of the server information within the project programmatically.

Property	Value	Purpose
CLSID	Character	The COM unique identifier used to access your server from other applications.
Description	Character	The description of the server, as entered on the Servers page of the Project Info dialog.
HelpContextID	Integer	The topic in the associated help file to be invoked from this object.
Instancing	Numeric	Determines whether the class can be instantiated and, if so, whether the same server can serve multiple applications.
ProgID	Character	The name of the class as it would be used in CreateObject().
ServerClass	Character	Returns the class name of the server.
ServerClassLibrary	Character	The Class Library where the class is defined. Returns the PRG name if the class is defined in code, or the VCX name if it was defined visually.

You can use the new Server interface to examine all of the properties of COM objects within your project. Combined with the Project object and ProjectHooks, we can envision some pretty cool builders to document your application, or to use properties like the CLSID to tweak Registry settings.

Server is not a new FoxPro base class, but rather a COM interface exposed by Visual FoxPro. That means there's no way to subclass the Server objects. Also, since the Project Manager doesn't examine the files added to it until a build is performed, don't expect to see new Server objects until you build the project for the first time.

Example

```
MODIFY PROJECT MySample NOWAIT
oProject = _VFP.ActiveProject
? oProject.Servers.Count  && displays the # of servers available
FOR EACH oServer in oProject.Servers
  ? oServer.CLSID         && display the Class ID for each
NEXT
```

See Also CLSID, Description, HelpContextID, Instancing, ProgID, Project, ServerClass, ServerClassLibrary, Servers

ServerClass, ServerClassLibrary

These properties tell you the lineage of the server you're examining within the Project object.

Usage

```
cServerClass = oServer.ServerClass
cSCLibrary = oServer.ServerClassLibrary
```

These two properties of the Server object, which is available through the Project hierarchy, tell you the class definition and the library location of a class defined as OLEPublic. If the class definition is in code, the class name is the name supplied in DEFINE CLASS and the class library is the fully qualified name of the program where the definition resides. In the more common case of a visual class, the ServerClass is the class' Name and the ServerClassLibrary is the fully pathed name of the VCX.

Example

```
* Created a test class "fred" in the SYS2335 program
? oProj.servers.item[1].ServerClass        && "fred"
? oProj.servers.item[1].ServerClassLibrary
* Returns "C:\test\sys2335.prg"
```

See Also Project, Server

ServerHelpFile, ServerProject

These properties of the Project object let you set and query the name of the help file invoked for the COM servers in the project, and the first part of the name used to create the COM objects.

Usage

```
prjProject.ServerHelpFile = cHelpFileName
cHelpFileName = prjProject.ServerHelpFile
prjProject.ServerProject = cProjectName
cProjectName = prjProject.ServerProject
```

Parameter	Value	Meaning
cHelpFileName	Character	The path and filename of the help file invoked from an object or class browser when examining the COM object.
	Empty string	There is no help file for the servers in this project. (Not a great idea, of course.)
cProjectName	Character	The first portion of the ProgID, the programmatic identifier that uniquely identifies the server.

If you are creating a set of COM objects to be used by others, or even if you want to remember what they do a few months down the line, you can add a reference to a help file to the COM object and its type library. When the type library is examined (in the Class Browser or other object browsers), the help file can be invoked to provide documentation for your classes. We were a little surprised to find that the help file is at the *project* level and not set up so each server could have its own. But, realistically, you're most likely to set up individual projects for each server you plan to distribute separately, since the project generates one EXE or DLL file.

The ServerProject property determines the first half of the name you use when creating the server objects using CreateObject() or NewObject(). ServerProject is the object name up to the period. This name defaults to the name of your project, but if you'd prefer to have your developers invoking CreateObject("CoolThing.MyServer") rather than CreateObject("YetAnotherProject.MyServer"), you can change it programmatically with this property, or graphically in the Servers tab of the Project Info dialog.

Example

```
* This command returns the current help file for Project oProj:
? oProj.ServerHelpFile
* This command changes the server name in all ProgIDs
oProj.ServerProject = "MyTestServerProject"
```

See Also Project, ProgID, Server

ServerName

This property stores the name of the program used to start the current application. This can be handy for determining the pathing needed to reach other components.

Usage

```
cServerName = appObject.ServerName
```

When starting your COM server as either a DLL or an EXE, its HOME() and SYS(2004) values might not give you the information you need. For an EXE, those functions often point at the Windows System directory. For a DLL, they point to the same settings as the application in which the DLL is running, since they share the same space. To know the location of the file that was started, and hence more easily find local resources it might need, such as an INI file or a resource file, test ServerName. This returns a full path and filename of the file that started the current application object.

Example

```
? _VFP.ServerName  && in development, returns the path to VFP
```

See Also Application, Server, _VFP

ServerProject See ServerHelpFile.

Servers

Servers presents a collection interface to use within a Project object. It exposes each of the OLE servers defined within your project

Usage

```
oServer = oProject.Servers.Item[ nIndex ] |
          oProject.Servers[ nIndex ]
nCount = oProject.Servers.Count
```

Parameter	Value	Meaning
nIndex	Positive Integer	Enumerates a server item within the project.
oServer	Server object	The server object returned from the collection.
nCount	Integer	The number of servers defined within the project.

The Servers collection is another of those strange COM collections we are meeting more and more within VFP. It's not exactly an array of items, as it has properties of its own, such as Count, but it's not a full-fledged object either, really, because it doesn't really *do* anything itself. We'd better get used to these—the world of COM is full of them.

In this case, Servers is a collection of all OLEPublic interfaces exposed within the Project. Count tells you how many there are. The Item method can be used to access its contained servers, though a subscript on the Servers collection itself does the same thing, as shown in the Usage.

One thing that confused us about Servers at first: The collection doesn't show your server objects until the project has been built at least once. That makes some sense if you consider that it's only during the build process that the Project Manager actually scans the code.

Example

```
MODIFY PROJECT MySample NOWAIT
oProject = _VFP.ActiveProject
? oProject.Servers.Count  && displays the servers available
FOR EACH oServer in oProject.Servers
  ? oServer.CLSID         && display the Class ID for each
NEXT
```

See Also Count, Item, Project, Server

Set, Set(), SYS(2001)

Probably the single most destructive command in the language, the SET command gives Visual FoxPro much of its power and much of its flakiness.

Usage

```
SET SettingName ON | OFF
SET SettingName TO uExpression
```

SET is a tremendously powerful command to change the behavior of FoxPro, while at the same time it can be a frustrating tool to work with. Don't think so? Add one line to your startup program—SET EXACT ON—and watch your system fall to pieces. Computer language purists object to SET commands for a pretty straightforward reason: the formation of the infinite-state machine. Although that sounds cool, it isn't the machine you want to try to make a living on. A finite-state machine may be in a fixed number of predictable states, and therefore results may always be predicted from the current state. Now, however, introduce a single SET command, say, EXACT. Now there are two states for all the code within your system—one set of behaviors for EXACT ON and one for EXACT OFF. That's easy enough—you can code for this eventuality, by testing SET("EXACT") before any test that depends on it. But add a second SET command, say, TALK, and you now have four states to test. Another SET command, such as DATE, introduces 11 different states all by itself, and in combination with SET CENTURY and SET MARK TO, a dazzling assortment may be formed.

So should we avoid SET commands altogether? No, we just need to use them carefully. Along with bringing confusion to the possible states in which Visual FoxPro can find itself, the SET command gives Visual FoxPro the flexibility to globally configure itself to behave in a number of rational ways. Unfortunately, these "rational ways" can often be rent asunder by one bad bit of coding that leaves the application in an unusual state. A subroutine you mug off CompuServe that inadvertently leaves SET EXACT ON will suddenly make your most rock-solid code roll over on its back, eyes bulging. Perform a SEEK on "A," hoping to find the first record beginning with "A," and nothing comes back. SETs are definitely two-edged swords.

However, the use of SET commands can simplify application development. For example, rather than continuously having to check the proper display of a currency figure, one set of SET CURRENCY, SET SEPARATOR, SET POINT commands can cause all (or almost all) FoxPro commands to behave appropriately without further intervention on your part. So they are useful while at the same time infuriating.

SET commands are global in scope. Before Visual FoxPro, this was absolute—one SET command affected all following code—but now some SET commands have been limited to affecting only a single data session, but everything within that session is affected. These "semi-global" commands are:

ANSI	CENTURY	DATABASE	DELIMITERS
AUTOSAVE	COLLATE	DATE	EXACT
BLOCKSIZE	CONFIRM	DECIMALS	EXCLUSIVE
CARRY	CURRENCY	DELETED	FIELDS

FIXED	MULTILOCKS	REFRESH	SEPARATOR
HOURS	NEAR	REPROCESS	SYSFORMATS
LOCK	NULL	SAFETY	TALK
MARK TO	POINT	SET SECONDS	UNIQUE
MEMOWIDTH			

SET commands range from SET ALTERNATE to SET XCMDFILE. We won't cover all of them here, but we'll point out some generalities. To every rule there is an exception, and SET commands prove this time and time again.

In general, there are two ways you'd want to use a SET command: globally, so that it takes effect, and you can assume that condition, throughout your application; and locally, in order to take advantage of a feature only available within one SET mode. Let's talk about each of these needs and strategies for achieving them.

Global settings are settings you would probably like to establish once and be done with it. FoxPro offers three ways for you to accomplish this. First, many settings are available through the Tools-Options dialog and are stored in the Windows Registry (for more details, see "Registration Database"). Second, all settings stored within the CONFIG.FPW file are read on setup and are in effect for the entire session, unless reset, or unless you've accidentally specified the wrong configuration file (check "Configuration Files" for more details on this). Finally, you can set up a program to explicitly issue the appropriate SET commands. Depending on your specific needs, each of these methods may be best for you.

Using the Registry is great. It's consistent with other Windows applications. The Registry functions and structure allow you to set up more than one user on the same hardware, each with her own settings. The latest versions of Windows 95 and NT provide the ability for administrators to manage Registry entries across the network. However, Registry settings are not read at startup by runtime modules, so you'll need to resort to alternative methods for runtime environments. However, don't give up on the Registry altogether. Even if you decide to programmatically load your settings, you might want to consider keeping these settings in the Registry.

In many cases, it can be simpler to embed a CONFIG.FPW file into your .EXE, especially for settings you will not allow users to change. Add the CONFIG.FPW (this *must* be its name) to the Project Manager as a file, and the settings are read on startup. If you do want or need the users to change settings in the CONFIG.FPW, you can include the file by any name on the disk and point to it with the -C startup switch—see "CONFIG.FPW" for details.

Finally, the programmatic method offers a lot of flexibility. Store all your settings in a table, perhaps stored centrally for ease of maintenance and to allow your users to move from machine to machine, and read each of the settings and process them. You might consider this method with the Registry as your centralized database—if you're using Windows 95 and/or Microsoft's System Management Server. Local settings, on the other hand, are those you need in effect for one small set of commands to ensure they work correctly. The *safest,* though not necessarily bulletproof, method of manipulating SET commands within a "black box" function is to preserve the initial value, change the setting to the desired one, perform the SET-dependent function, and then immediately restore the setting, as in the following code snippet:

```
cDateSet = SET("DATE")
SET DATE ANSI
sMyDate = CTOD(cYear+"."+cMonth+"."+cDay)
SET DATE &cDateSet
```

The local setting method above does have its hazards. If any function or command can interrupt the execution of this snippet, you're back into the infinite-state machine—who knows what will happen? Two situations where we know this may happen are the execution of ON KEY LABEL functions and the automatic refreshing of a Grid/Browse. As usual, a little defensive programming can minimize the hazards. Within code called by ON KEY LABEL, use the same technique as above to save-change-restore any settings you need to work. Grids/Browses are a little trickier—the danger occurs if you change a setting that the grid depends upon for a display function, such as the SET DATE function above. The only work-around we know of is to use naming conventions in such a way that you'll know when it is unwise to make such changes. An alternative is not to use specific SET commands, such as SET DATE, within your routines if you plan to use grids—instead, use CASE statements to determine the current environment and use those settings to properly process your routine. Take a look at the examples included with the BITx() functions for some ideas on how to do this.

Usage

```
uRetVal = SET( cSetting [, 1 | 2 | 3 ] )
uRetVal = SYS( 2001, cSetting [, 1 | 2 | 3 ] )
```

The SET() and identical SYS(2001) functions return the values of a setting. All but a few—(SET("MOUSE",1), SET("HOURS") and SET("DECIMALS"), for example) return character strings. A numeric argument of 1 or 2 returns additional information in some cases, and 3 works for SET("PRINTER"). In those cases where there are only two settings to return—one with and one without the parameter—you can substitute almost anything for the second parameter and get the same result. "FRED," $123.45, DATE(), .T., and .NULL. all seem to work for us. A few SET commands, such as SET FUNCTION TO, cannot be detected with a matching SET() function.

Many of the SET commands are overloaded. SET FIELDS, for example, can be ON or OFF, or it can be a field list, or it can be LOCAL or GLOBAL. So how do you determine which of these values is returned by the SET() command? –Easy—overload that function as well. SET("FIELDS") returns "ON" or "OFF," SET("FIELDS",1) returns the list of fields upon which commands such as EDIT and BROWSE work, and SET("FIELDS",2) returns either GLOBAL (fields can be in more than one table and can contain calculated fields) or LOCAL (only fields from the current table can be used). Whew! Got all that?

The options for each SET() function are described with that SET command.

Example

```
cDelSet = SET("DELETED")
```

See Also Display Status, Configuration Files, Registration Database

Set Alternate, Set("Alternate")

The SET ALTERNATE commands let you send certain kinds of output to a file as well as to the screen. Think of the output it creates as a "log file" (but don't confuse it with the log files created by the Coverage Logging option in the Debugger).

Usage

```
SET ALTERNATE TO [ FileName [ ADDITIVE ] ]
SET ALTERNATE ON | OFF
cOnOrOff = SET("ALTERNATE")
cFileName = SET("ALTERNATE",1)
```

Back when Tamar used to teach dBase, she needed a way for students to perform a series of commands and turn something in that showed they'd done it right. Fortunately, someone had added SET ALTERNATE to the language. The students could see their output on screen, but a duplicate of it appeared in a file that could be printed out and turned in. Other than that, we've never found much use for these commands. Back in ancient Xbase history, before the TextMerge commands came along, SET ALTERNATE was handy for creating text files.

SET ALTERNATE is confusing to use. (The students certainly found it so.) It's a two-step process to turn it on and a two-step process to turn it off (unless you use CLOSE ALTERNATE). SET ALTERNATE TO lets you specify a file to contain the output. That file stays in effect until you issue the command without a file or SET ALTERNATE TO a different file. Actually, of course, it's all analogous to the SET PRINT commands and provides you an alternate output file.

Once you've established an alternate file, SET ALTERNATE ON or OFF determines whether eligible output goes to that file. (Output from ?, ??, DISPLAY and LIST is eligible.) The text you send to the file is echoed to the active window unless you SET CONSOLE OFF.

Example

```
SET ALTERNATE TO Test.TXT
USE Employee
* Start logging
SET ALTERNATE ON
LIST First_Name,Last_Name
```

```
* Stop logging
SET ALTERNATE OFF
LIST Birth_Date
* Turn off log file
SET ALTERNATE TO
```

See Also Close Alternate, Set, Set Console, Set Device, Set Print, Set TextMerge, StrToFile()

Set ANSI, Set Exact

These two commands do almost the same thing, but in different situations. They both control the way string comparisons are performed. SET ANSI affects SQL commands; SET EXACT affects Xbase commands.

Usage

```
SET ANSI ON | OFF
SET EXACT ON | OFF
```

Xbase started life as an interpreted language whose commands were meant to be entered interactively. In that situation, it was handy to be able to type something like SEEK "SM" and move the record pointer to the first "SMITH" (or whatever happened to be the first record starting with "SM"). It was especially convenient to be able to do similar things in FOR clauses, so you could list all the people whose names started with "S" or all the parts whose part numbers began with "124".

To make those kinds of things possible, the default behavior of the "=" operator is to compare strings only until the end of the string on the right-hand side. That is, in Xbase, "123"="12" and "Smithsonian"="Smith". But "Smith"<>"Smithsonian". Pretty weird.

SET EXACT controls this behavior. When it's OFF (the default), you get the partial comparisons. When EXACT is ON, strings have to match exactly. You can also use the "==" operator to test for exact equality. (In fact, we read "==" as "exactly equals.")

Once upon a time, the double equal sign operator wasn't optimizable, but it has been for a lot of versions already. So, we prefer to leave EXACT OFF and use the double equal sign because it's a local solution to a local problem.

SET ANSI, which also defaults to OFF, is almost the same. It affects FoxPro's SQL commands: SELECT, DELETE-SQL and UPDATE-SQL. There's one subtle difference. With SET EXACT OFF, it matters which side of the "=" is shorter. With SET ANSI OFF, it doesn't matter. The strings are compared to the end of the shorter string, whichever side it's on. So, in SQL commands, "Smithsonian"="Smith" and "Smith"="Smithsonian".

The exactly equals operator isn't as strict in SQL commands as it is in Xbase commands. Regardless of the setting of ANSI, in a SQL command, == ignores trailing blanks.

One final note. Keep in mind that the "not equals" operator "<>" is also affected by SET EXACT.

Both SET EXACT and SET ANSI are scoped to the data session.

Example

```
USE Customer
SET EXACT OFF                      && the default
BROWSE FOR Company_Name = "G"      && You get all the companies
                                   && that start with "G"
SET EXACT ON
BROWSE FOR Company_Name = "G"      && Empty Browse
```

See Also Delete-SQL, Select-SQL, Update-SQL

Set AplAbout **See On AplAbout.**

Set Asserts **See Assert.**

Set Autosave **See Flush.**

Set Bell, Set("Bell")

SET BELL can be toggled to determine if you want to annoy your end users endlessly and drive them to an early grave by beeping at them when they reach the end of a field. To further annoy them, you can change the bell's exact sound (or the sound file it plays) as well. The chosen sound is also played when the CHR(7) character is displayed to the screen.

Usage

```
SET BELL ON | OFF
SET BELL TO [ nFreq, nSeconds ]     && MS-DOS version
SET BELL TO [ cWavFile, nNothing ] && Windows, VFP 3 & 5 version
SET BELL TO [ cWavFile ]           && VFP 6, at last!
cBellOnOff = SET( "BELL" )
cWavFile = SET( "BELL" , 1 )
```

Parameter	Value	Meaning
nFreq	Numeric	Approximate frequency of the bell sounds, in Hertz, range 19 to 10,000—MS-DOS ONLY!!!
nSeconds	Numeric	Length of time the annoying tone plays, in seconds—MS-DOS ONLY!!!
cWavFile	Character	Name of a sound file, with path if necessary or, in FoxPro/Windows, the name of a pre-defined sound in the [Sound] section of WIN.INI.
nNothing	Numeric	This parameter is ignored, but an error, "Missing expression", occurs if not passed. Useless.
Omitted		Restores the bell to its "normal" condition—a bell sound in DOS and the system setting for the bell under Windows.

We have yet to meet an end user who prefers to be beeped at when the normal end of each field is reached. SET BELL OFF!

Prior to VFP 6, there was no way to determine what settings are in place, beyond SET("BELL") returning "ON" or "OFF." VFP 6 introduced SET("BELL",1) to return the name of the WAV file, if one is set.

Two different methods exist for specifying a sound file. You can supply either a specific filename and path, or the name of a Windows event may be given. If you want to play a specific sound file, make sure it exists by using the FILE() function. If you choose to be consistent with other applications, check the user's Registry for the entry you wish to use before specifying it. Otherwise, the default system sound (typically a beep, but it also can be changed by the user in Control Panel or Registry) plays. See the Control Panel's Sound applet and the Registry key mentioned below for some ideas and the name of events you might want to hook into.

The Help files for VFP 3 and 5 were out to lunch when they talked about the [Sounds] entry of WIN.INI as the source of system-event sounds. WIN.INI's old, everything is in the Registry now. Worse, when the Sounds moved to the Registry, we lost the ability to use them natively. "Sound Schemes" are stored in the Registry in all Win32 environments (the only ones in which VFP 5 and VFP 6 can run) under the key HKEY_CURRENT_USER\AppEvents\Schemes\Apps \.Default. (Note the dot (".") before "Default" in that path.) See the third example below for some ideas for using these.

You may want to warn the user that a sound driver must be in place, and give them an option to turn off these sounds. Specifying a WAV file when no driver is available results in no sounds at all.

Example

```
SET BELL TO "C:\WINDOWS\TADA.WAV",11
?? CHR(07)  && the WAV file is played.
? SET("BELL", 1)  && Returns "C:\WINDOWS\TADA.WAV",11

* This is how easy it should be. This works in FPW:
SET BELL TO "SystemExclamation",5
?? CHR(07)  && user-defined sound is played.

* This is how easy it is?:
SET PROCEDURE TO SAMPLES\CLASSES\Registry.PRG ADDITIVE
oRegistry = CREATEOBJECT("Registry")
HKEY_CURRENT_USER = -2147483647  && BITSET(0,31)+1
cValue = SPACE(255)
oRegistry.GetRegKey("",@cValue,;
 "AppEvents\Schemes\Apps\.Default\SystemExclamation\.Current";
 , HKEY_CURRENT_USER)
IF "\" $ cValue
  * This is an explicit path
  * The Windows\media Path is assumed if not supplied
ELSE
  cValue = "C:\WINNT\Media\" + cValue
ENDIF
IF FILE(cValue)
  SET BELL TO cValue, 0
ENDIF
?? CHR(07)
```

See Also INI Files, Registration Database

Set Blink, Set Intensity, Set("Blink"), Set("Intensity")

Two settings for the DOS screen, supported but ignored in Visual FoxPro, with one small exception.

Usage

```
SET BLINK ON | OFF
SET INTENSITY ON | OFF
cBlinkOnorOff = SET( "BLINK" )
cIntenseOnorOff = SET( "INTENSITY" )
```

SET BLINK is a setting for the DOS VGA and EGA screen modes that support blinking. Blinking is unsupported in Windows as an interface standard, and ignored in Visual FoxPro. We miss the easy-to-code "Please Wait..." messages we could get with SET BLINK.

SET INTENSITY was the flip side of the same DOS coin—if blinking were turned off, manipulating the intensity of some objects would give you twice the colors of the standard 16-color palette, a feature we used to our advantage in some FoxPro DOS screens. It would make sense that this functionality would also be ignored in Visual FoxPro, and it is, with one small exception.

SET INTENSITY ON, the default, sets the background color of explicitly issued @ ... GET commands to the color Windows has set for its button faces. If INTENSITY is set OFF, the background of the GET is transparent.

See Also Set, Set Color of Scheme

Set BlockSize, Set("Blocksize"), Sys(2012)

BLOCKSIZE specifies the size of the individual blocks used to store memo and general field data for the current DataSession. SYS(2012) reports on what setting is in effect for an individual file.

Usage

```
SET BLOCKSIZE TO nSize
nSizeInBytes = SET( "BLOCKSIZE" )
nSizeInBytes = SYS( 2012 [, nArea | cAlias ] )
```

Parameter	Value	Meaning
nSize	0	Specifies that memo fields are stored in blocks of one byte.
	1–32	Specifies that memo fields are stored in large blocks of nSize times 512 bytes, that is, blocks ranging from 512 bytes to 16 kilobytes.
	33–32,768	Specifies that memo field disk space is allocated in blocks of nSize bytes.
nArea	Numeric	Specifies the work area for the table to be examined.
	Omitted	If cAlias is also omitted, the table in the current work area is examined.
cAlias	Character	Specifies the table alias to report on.
	Omitted	If nArea is also omitted, the table within the current work area is examined.
nSizeInBytes	Numeric	The current blocksize in bytes, or zero if no memo field exists in the current work area.

BLOCKSIZE can have quite an effect on the size of your application, especially if several VCXs and SCXs are included in the final EXE. Visual FoxPro uses memo field blocks like they're going out of style. When editing data in shared tables, every time the contents of a memo field are changed, the entire contents of that memo field are written out again to the end of the file, and the original blocks used to store the data are flagged as unused. This space is not reclaimed by Visual FoxPro until the file is re-COPY'd or PACK'd (we prefer the former). In the less common case of using a file exclusively, additional blocks are allocated only once the current block has been completely filled.

The choice of BLOCKSIZE is one that varies depending on the exact circumstances in which you're using the memo field. One-byte blocks are the most efficient for space storage, if that is the overriding consideration. There must be a small amount of overhead in using single-byte blocks, we're sure, and under some circumstances (like editing multi-megabyte general fields), that overhead could become the most significant factor. If, on the other hand, you expect to store, and not edit, small memos of a predictable size, it probably makes more sense to allocate blocks in a multiple of the most common size, say, 64-byte blocks if most memos are 128 bytes or less. The performance of your hardware, both in the storage and retrieval of blocks, as well as the CPU overhead in tracking them all, could be the most important factor in other cases. Our advice: your mileage may vary. Test the file's BLOCKSIZE under the hardware conditions and with the data it will be storing, and benchmark its performance.

SET("BLOCKSIZE") is the current setting and has nothing to do with individual tables. Each individual table's block size is stored in the header of the memo file, and may be retrieved with SYS(2012). The SET command only comes into play for tables (and cursors) created or rewritten within this data session. This is dumb—we think that block size should be settable for each individual table.

Another annoying thing about these functions is that since SYS(2012) always returns its value in bytes, but SET BLOCKSIZE uses three different schemes—blocks of 512 bytes for 1–32, explicit bytes for 33–32,768 and zero for one byte—the routine to decode them and calculate what value you want to pass to SET BLOCKSIZE seems like a pain. It isn't, really. If you originally SET BLOCKSIZE TO 32, then used SYS(2012) to obtain the current setting (16384) and then reissued SET BLOCKSIZE with the 16384 figure, the effect would be the same. The only gotcha is if SET("BLOCKSIZE") is zero, then SYS(2012) would return a 1. So, the function to return the appropriate BLOCKSIZE from a SYS(2012) value would be:

```
lcSetBlockSize = IIF(SYS(2012) = 1, 0, SYS(2012))
```

A table retains its block size unless it is rewritten while there is a different block size in effect. A number of commands can cause this: ALTER TABLE, COPY, CREATE TABLE, MODIFY STRUCTURE, PACK, or even SELECT … INTO TABLE. Like most SET commands, our preference is to decide the right way it should be throughout your application, set it that way, and leave it alone.

Example

```
SET BLOCKSIZE TO 0
? SYS( 2012 )    && returns the block size of the current file
? SET( "BLOCKSIZE" )  && returns the global or datasession-specific setting
```

See Also Alter Table, Copy, Create Table, Pack, Set DataSession

Set Border

This is yet another command that used to be useful but we can't imagine using today. SET BORDER determines the type of border that surrounds windows, popups and boxes that you create. Several of its options are ignored in Visual FoxPro, and there's not much reason to use the others.

Usage

```
SET BORDER TO SINGLE | DOUBLE | PANEL | NONE
         | nBorderString1 [ , nBorderString2 ]
```

Parameter	Value	Meaning
nBorderString*n*	List of numbers	A comma-delimited list of up to eight ASCII character values used to specify the various parts of the border. nBorderString2 applies only to inactive windows. Both border strings are ignored in Visual FoxPro.

SINGLE provides a single border window, as you'd expect. Both DOUBLE and PANEL provide a half-size, panel-type border. NONE, not surprisingly, produces objects with no border. If you specify a border string, it's totally ignored and you get a single border anyway. Adding border characteristics such as GROW or MINIMIZE to the window definition forces the border back to the Windows look, while FLOAT or CLOSE forces the top border to show a control menu icon and/or close icon.

We don't create the kinds of objects that use the value of SET BORDER very much in Visual FoxPro.

Example

```
SET BORDER TO PANEL
DEFINE WINDOW test FROM 10,10 TO 20,60
ACTIVATE WINDOW test
```

See Also @ ... TO, BorderStyle, Define Popup, Define Window, Set

Set BrowseIME, Set("BrowseIME")

This setting and its accompanying function are for those working with double-byte character sets. They determine and indicate, respectively, whether an Input Method Editor (IME) opens automatically when you land in a text box in a Browse.

Usage

```
SET BROWSEIME ON | OFF
cOnOrOff = SET( "BROWSEIME" )
```

An IME is used for entering characters in Eastern languages like Chinese and Korean. For a full explanation of IME's (well, as full as we can give from our Western perspective), see IMEStatus().

With single-byte character sets, this setting is ignored.

See Also Double-Byte Character Sets, IMEStatus

Set BrStatus See Browse.

Set Carry, Set("Carry")

SET CARRY lets you specify that the values of certain fields should be repeated in newly added records. SET("CARRY") indicates whether you're working in that mode.

Usage

```
SET CARRY ON | OFF
SET CARRY TO [ FieldList [ ADDITIVE ] ]
cCarry = SET( "CARRY" )
```

Parameter	Value	Meaning
FieldList	Comma-delimited list of fields	The fields whose values should be carried forward to new records.
	Omitted	Resets the list of fields to be carried forward to include all fields.
cCarry	"ON"	CARRY is currently ON.
	"OFF"	CARRY is currently OFF.

When you SET CARRY ON, the values of the specified fields are copied into new records. SET CARRY affects records added with INSERT and APPEND, and records added in a grid, BROWSE (or EDIT).

Issuing SET CARRY TO automatically turns CARRY ON. The ADDITIVE clause says to add the fields in FieldList to the existing list of fields to be carried forward. If you omit ADDITIVE, the new list replaces the current list.

SET CARRY ON or OFF affects all open tables, but the list of fields applies only to the table in the current work area and is maintained separately for each data session. (That last seems pretty funny since we can't actually imagine giving an end user access to anything that respects SET CARRY.) SET CARRY does not apply to grids.

You can list memo fields in SET CARRY, but their values aren't carried forward.

SET CARRY can be very handy for interactive data entry, but we don't think it belongs in an application.

Example

```
USE MyLogTable           && a table for logging hours spent
SET CARRY TO dLogDate
BROWSE                   && now enter today's log entries
```

SET("CARRY") returns either "ON" or "OFF" to indicate the current setting.

Unfortunately, although you can pass a second (numeric) parameter, it still returns "ON" or "OFF". There's no way to get the current list of fields to carry forward. Seems to us that SET("CARRY",1) ought to do this.

See Also Append, Browse, Insert, Set, Set()

Set Catalog See Access().

Set Century See Set Date.

Set ClassLib, Set("ClassLib"), Release ClassLib

Set ClassLib lets you add class libraries to the list of places FoxPro looks for class definitions when you refer to one. Release ClassLib removes a class library from that list. Set("ClassLib") shows you the current list.

Usage

```
Set ClassLib To [ ClassLibrary1 [ IN AppOrExeFile1 ]
                [ ALIAS ClassAlias1 ]
                [, ClassLibrary2 [ IN AppOrExeFile2 ]
                [ ALIAS ClassAlias2 ] [ ... ] ]
                [ ADDITIVE ] ]
cClassList = SET( "CLASSLIB" )
Release ClassLib ClassLibrary1 | ALIAS ClassAlias1
                 [ IN AppOrExeFile1 ]
                 [, ClassLibrary2 | ALIAS ClassAlias2
                 [ IN AppOrExeFile2 ] [ ... ] ]
```

Parameter	Value	Meaning
ClassLibrary*x*	Name	The filename of a class library to add to or remove from the search chain. For SET CLASSLIB, include the path if it's not in the FoxPro path.
	Omitted	In SET CLASSLIB, remove all libraries from the search path.
AppOrExeFile*x*	Name	The name of an APP or EXE file into which the class library is built.
	Omitted	Look for the class library as a separate file on disk, or in the current EXE or APP.
ClassAlias*x*	Name	An alias by which to refer to the class library.
	Omitted	Use the filename (first part up to the ".") as the alias. If you use spaces in the filename (and please reconsider if you do!), they are replaced with underscores in the alias.
cClassList	Character	The complete list of class libraries that are currently being used, including paths and aliases.
	Empty	No class libraries are in the search path.

The alias gives you an alternate name for the library, which you can use in CreateObject() to distinguish among classes with the same name in different libraries.

Setting class libraries normally removes previous settings. Use ADDITIVE to add to the current list. Set ClassLib To without a list is like issuing Release ClassLib for the whole list.

The IN clause, added in VFP 5, lets you add libraries that exist only as part of an application to the search path. It also protects you when the same name is used for a class library found in an application and on the disk.

Class libraries are searched in the order they're added to the search list. Adding a library to the list that's already there doesn't change the search order.

The Help for Set ClassLib says that classes loaded in memory are searched pretty early in the search chain. We haven't been able to find a way to get a class to hang around in memory once the source for it (whether a program, class library or procedure file) is removed.

However, once you've instantiated a class, you can release the class library. The class can still find its code. We're not sure whether the instance carries a copy of its code with it at all times or goes back to the class library to find it. Our instinctive feeling is the former, but a class library cannot be deleted while an object inheriting from it is instantiated, so objects do maintain some hold on their classes. And clearly, VFP has some mechanism to look in class libraries for code, because it can find its way up the inheritance tree without our help.

RELEASE CLASSLIB was enhanced in a couple of ways in VFP 5, but they didn't do a very good job of it. The IN clause was added to allow you to release class libraries that are built into applications. However, using it gives an error unless there's a classlib of the same name in the directory from which you SET the CLASSLIB. You have to use the ALIAS form of the command to release such a class library.

But wait, there's more. You can only use the IN clause once in RELEASE CLASSLIB, and it must be the last clause. Any libraries you list after the IN clause are ignored. Although it's documented that way, we consider this a bug because there's no logical reason for the command to behave this way.

With the addition of NewObject(), we suspect we'll be using these commands a lot less than we used to.

Example

```
SET CLASSLIB TO CoolStuf
CREATE CLASS MyDateSpinner OF MyStuff AS DateSpinner
RELEASE CLASSLIB CoolStuf

cOldClassLib = SET("CLASSLIB")
SET CLASSLIB TO Connect ADDITIVE
oConn = CreateObject("ConnMgr")
SET CLASSLIB TO &cOldClassLib
```

See Also Create ClassLib, CreateObject(), NewObject(), Release Library, Set Library, Set Path, Set Procedure

Set Clear

This is an obscure command related to an obsolete capability. It determines whether or not the main window is cleared when you use a format file.

Usage

```
SET CLEAR ON | OFF
```

Format files were perhaps the first attempt at making it easy to provide attractive input screens. A format file contains a bunch of SAYs and GETs, which are used as a template for the EDIT command (and some other related commands). You establish the format file with SET FORMAT, then when you issue EDIT or APPEND, the input fields conform to the definitions in the format file.

SET CLEAR ON indicates that the main window should be cleared when you use the format file.

SET CLEAR OFF leaves the main window alone.

We can't see any reason to use this command. Format files are several generations obsolete.

See Also Set, Set Format

Set Clock, Set("Clock")

This command controls both the location and visibility of the system clock. It allows you to turn the clock on and off and to position it either on the status bar or anywhere you want on the screen.

Usage

```
SET CLOCK ON | OFF
SET CLOCK STATUS | TO [ nRow, nCol ]
```

Parameter	Value	Meaning
ON		Turn on display of the system clock at its last location.
OFF		Turn off display of the system clock.
STATUS		Turn on display of the system clock in the status bar.
nRow, nCol	Numeric	The position on the main FoxPro screen to display the system clock. Turns the clock on.
	Omitted	Return the system clock to its default position in the upper right corner. Turns the clock on.

Every version of SET CLOCK except SET CLOCK OFF turns the system clock on, in addition to anything else it does. You can also turn the clock on and off, though not control its location, in the View tab of the Options dialog.

With CLOCK set to STATUS, if you turn off the system status bar, the clock can't be seen.

The clock honors the current SET HOURS setting, but ignores SET SECONDS.

In the default location, the clock makes some assumptions about the size of the VFP window. It's happiest when the VFP window is maximized and may not show up at all or may be cut off if the window isn't maximized. Tamar habitually works with all her applications sized to fill the screen vertically, but not horizontally (and shortcuts on the rightmost section of her desktop)—in her default setup, the clock gets cut off.

Example

```
SET CLOCK ON        && make clock visible in last location
SET CLOCK STATUS    && move the clock to the status bar
SET CLOCK OFF       && turn the clock off
SET CLOCK ON        && turn the clock on - in the status bar
SET CLOCK TO 0,0    && move the clock to the upper left corner

* have some fun with the clock
=rand(-1)
for nTimes=1 to 10
    SET CLOCK TO SROWS()*RAND(),SCOLS()*RAND()
    =INKEY(1)
endfor
```

Usage

```
cClockStatus = SET( "CLOCK" )
cClockPosition = SET( "CLOCK", 1 )
```

Like most of the SET commands, the corresponding function returns the current settings. SET("CLOCK") returns "ON", "OFF" or "STATUS", while passing a second parameter returns the position of the clock. While the syntax diagram shows a second parameter of 1, in fact, any number or string will do. The position is returned as a comma-separated string. If you haven't specified a position, the empty string is returned.

Example

```
SET CLOCK ON
? SET("CLOCK")      && Displays ON
? SET("CLOCK",1)    && Displays the empty string
SET CLOCK TO 0,0
? SET("CLOCK",1)    && Displays 0.000,    0.000
```

See Also Set, Set Hours, Set Status Bar

Set Collate See CPConvert().

Set Color Set, Set Color Of Scheme, Scheme(), RGBScheme(), Set Color Of, Set Color To

These commands and functions all relate to old ways of setting colors. The first four are all part of the elaborate coloring system designed for FoxPro/DOS. See CREATE COLOR SET for an explanation of that system.

SET COLOR OF and SET COLOR TO date back even before the FP/DOS color system and are totally obsolete. Don't use them. They'll just get you in trouble.

Usage

```
SET COLOR SET TO [ ColorSetName ]
```

This command loads the named color set from the resource file and puts it into effect. Before you can use it, you need to have created a color set (with CREATE COLOR SET).

Usage

```
SET COLOR OF SCHEME nScheme TO
        [ ColorPairList | SCHEME nSourceScheme ]
cColorPairList = SCHEME( nScheme [, nColorPair ] )
cRGBColorList = RGBSCHEME( nScheme [, nColor Pair ] )
```

Parameter	Value	Meaning
nScheme	Numeric	A color scheme number from 1 to 24.
ColorPairList	List of color pairs	A comma-delimited list of up to 10 color pairs to use for the specified scheme.
nSourceScheme	Numeric	A color scheme number from 1 to 24 whose colors should be copied to the specified scheme.
nColorPair	Numeric	Which color pair should be returned?
	Omitted	Return the entire list of color pairs.
cColorPairList	Character	A list of 10 color pairs plus a shadow indicator.
cRGBColorList	Character	A list of 10 RGB color pairs plus a shadow indicator.

A color scheme is a set of 10 color pairs used for some aspect of the FoxPro interface. FoxPro has 24 color schemes, of which we're allowed to change 20 or so—a group of schemes in the middle is reserved (in VFP 3, it's 13 to 16; in VFP 5 and VFP 6, it's 13 to 15). In FoxPro for DOS, there was wide variation from one color scheme to the next. In Windows, by default, the differences are small. Using the Windows default colors, most color schemes contain black, white and an assortment of grays, with maybe the occasional blue thrown in.

There are two ways to indicate colors in FoxPro. The modern Windows way is by using the RGB color definitions. (See RGB() for details.) The traditional Fox way uses a set of letters and symbols in which, for example, blue is represented by "B", black by "N" and yellow by "GR+". Not exactly intuitive—we've never managed to learn these and don't plan to now.

SET COLOR OF SCHEME lets you change the colors assigned to a particular scheme. You can either make the scheme exactly match another color scheme or you can specify all 10 color pairs, either in RGB format or using the old letter system. The RGB format used in this command is different than anywhere else in FoxPro—instead of three numbers inside the RGB() function, you put six. The first three are the foreground and the last three are the background. This way, a single RGB() gives a color pair rather than a single color.

SCHEME() and RGBSCHEME() let you find out what colors are assigned to a particular scheme. You can return the entire list or a single color pair. No matter which format you choose, after the 10 color pairs, you see an extra comma followed by either "+" or "-". (Actually, in Visual FoxPro, we've only ever seen the "+".) That last character indicates whether objects using that color scheme cast a shadow or not. Since nothing casts a shadow in Visual FoxPro for Windows, you can safely ignore this value.

Color handling in Visual FoxPro (and in FoxPro 2.x for Windows) is significantly more trouble than in FoxPro for DOS with its complex, but powerful, colorset mechanism. You can use the DOS system in Visual FoxPro, but setting colors at the application level detaches those colors from the Windows colors, so they don't change when the user changes Windows color schemes. This is clearly a violation of the Windows Interface Guidelines. On the whole, your best bet in VFP is to totally ignore colors and color schemes and rely on the user to set appropriate colors at the Windows level. Doing anything else tells the user that his opinion doesn't count.

Example

```
SET COLOR SET TO MyColors  && Previously saved
? SCHEME(1)                && Return colors for scheme 1
? RGBSCHEME(4,3)           && Return 3rd color pair of scheme 4
* Copy colors from scheme 10 to scheme 7
SET COLOR OF SCHEME 7 TO SCHEME 10
```

See Also BackColor, ColorSource, Create Color Set, ForeColor, RGB(), Set

Set Compatible, Set("Compatible")

A SET command that toggles the behavior of many other commands and functions from their "normal" value to those more like dBASE IV's behavior. This is a dangerous command.

Usage

```
SET COMPATIBLE ON | DB4 | OFF | FOXPLUS
      [ PROMPT | NOPROMPT ]
lcCompSet = SET("COMPATIBLE") && returns "ON" or  OFF"
```

ON and DB4 are identical, as are OFF and FOXPLUS. The PROMPT | NOPROMPT option is kind of like a SET SAFETY for dBASE IV memo files.

When Fox Software first came on the scene with FoxBASE, its goal was to emulate dBASE II, only faster. As time went on, Fox began to add new features to the language. There was always the danger that a new feature added by Fox would conflict with a command of the same name in the next release from Ashton-Tate, and in fact, this happened several times. SET COMPATIBLE was an attempt by Fox Software to maintain its goal of 100% compatibility with dBASE, while still innovating within Xbase language. The manuals and help files supplied with Visual FoxPro cover the scope of this command pretty thoroughly, and we haven't found any funny behaviors beyond those described in "Commands and Functions Affected by SET COMPATIBLE" in the Help file.

Hardly anyone remembers off the top of their heads all the things that get funky if you flip the compatibility toggle. Although this function can be used as a stopgap measure by developers while converting a system from dBASE to Fox, we strongly urge all developers to use the native functionality of FoxPro, and to maintain COMPATIBLE FOXPLUS.

The PROMPT option is to determine whether a confirming dialog appears before a dBASE IV table with memo fields is converted to a VFP table. VFP lacks the ability to work with dBASE IV tables natively, although it does fine with dBASE III tables. We suspect that this is a marketing, and not a technological, limitation.

The PROMPT dialog that comes up is a bit confused. First, pressing the Help key is the same as the No key. Second, the dialog states that "This can later be reversed with COPY TO … TYPE FOXPLUS." This is not exactly true—that command will create a dBASE III, not dBASE IV, memo field. Finally, clicking on No errors the system with "Not a table."

If you choose to convert the dBASE IV file, a follow-up dialog prompts you to strip the "soft returns" from the memo fields. Soft returns are CHR(141)'s that dBASE added into a file to do word wrap. Select Yes only in those cases where text is stored in this field—always answer No if the memo field contains binary data.

See Also Set

Set Confirm, Set("Confirm")

SET CONFIRM determines whether or not the user has to press a cursor-movement key to complete a text entry. In some cases, it also controls whether you can choose a menu item by just pressing the first letter or if you need to press Enter, too.

Usage

```
SET CONFIRM ON | OFF
cConfirm = SET( "CONFIRM" )
```

With CONFIRM ON, the user must explicitly complete an entry in a text box or spinner by pressing Enter, Tab or a navigation key. When CONFIRM is OFF, filling a text box or spinner (by entering either as many characters as the InputMask calls for or as many as will fit) moves the cursor to the beginning of the next input field automatically.

We can make pretty good arguments for each setting of CONFIRM. In heads-down data entry, with CONFIRM OFF, it's easy to overwrite data accidentally. On the other hand, with CONFIRM ON, you have an extra keystroke after each field. You need to figure out which of these techniques makes sense in your application and then do it the same way throughout. One factor to consider is whether the user will normally completely fill each field. In that case, CONFIRM OFF can be a real time-saver and the user should be aware of the consequences of overlong entries. If some fields get filled and others don't, CONFIRM OFF can be very confusing since the user sometimes has to use Tab or Enter and other times doesn't. Best of all, of course, is to let each user decide which setting works for her.

With menus, SET CONFIRM only makes a difference on menu popups with no defined hotkeys. In that case, CONFIRM OFF means pressing the first letter of an item immediately executes the first item beginning with that letter. This can be confusing to users unless you're careful not to start two items on the same menu with the same letter—the first one catches all the keystrokes, and the second one can only be chosen by navigating to it and pressing Enter. (Actually, it's not quite that simple. Whenever you press the key, the next occurrence of an item beginning with that letter is chosen. If you happen to be already sitting on such an item, it doesn't get chosen. The next item with that letter is picked.) With CONFIRM OFF, pressing the first letter simply moves focus to that item.

In a Windows world, a popup where no item contains a hotkey is so rare that this feature is likely to be irrelevant in just about every application.

SET CONFIRM is scoped to individual data sessions, so it's no longer good enough to set it in your application's startup code.

See Also Define Popup, Set, Spinner, Text box

Set Console, Set("Console"), Sys(100)

This command determines whether the output from certain commands appears in the active window. The two functions let you find the current setting.

Usage

```
SET CONSOLE ON | OFF
cConsole = SET( "CONSOLE" )
cConsole = SYS(100)
```

We've never really been sure exactly which commands are affected by SET CONSOLE since we've never wanted to turn it off. Some of the affected commands are DISPLAY and LIST, ? and ??, SUM, AVERAGE and CALCULATE. Interestingly, SETting TALK OFF affects all of those commands except ? and ??. Maybe that's why we've never looked too hard at CONSOLE. The one place we find it really handy is for reports. If we SET CONSOLE OFF, we don't have to remember to put REPORT FORM whatever NOCONSOLE in our programs.

The two functions behave slightly differently. SET("CONSOLE") reflects the current status wherever you are, while SYS(100) tells you what's going on in a program. Since SET CONSOLE OFF is ignored in the Command Window, when you issue SET("CONSOLE") from there, you always get back "ON". In a program, it properly tells you the current setting. When you issue SYS(100) from the Command Window, it tells you how CONSOLE was set the last time you ran a program.

One thing that trips up a lot of people is that errors always turn CONSOLE on. There's no way to detect the old setting and restore it at the end of your error handler. By the time you get into the error handler, it's too late. As a standard, we SET CONSOLE OFF in the global environment-setting routine at the start of our applications, and forget about it after that.

Example

```
SET CONSOLE OFF
```

See Also Set, Set Talk

Set Coverage, Set("Coverage"), _Coverage

These cool features let you keep track of what code has been executed.

Usage

```
SET COVERAGE TO [ cFileName [ ADDITIVE ] ]
cFileName = SET( "COVERAGE" )
_COVERAGE = cCoverageApp
cCoverageApp = _COVERAGE
DO ( _COVERAGE) [ WITH cLogFile [, lHide ] [, cAddIn ] ]
```

Parameter	Value	Meaning
cFileName	Character	The name of a file to hold the coverage log.
	Omitted	Turn off coverage logging.
cCoverageApp	Character	The program file to use to analyze a coverage log.
cLogFile	Character	The name of the file containing the coverage information to process. (The cFileName from SET COVERAGE.)
lHide	.F. or omitted	The Coverage Analyzer is displayed.
	.T.	The Coverage Analyzer is hidden.
cAddIn	Character	The path and filename of an add-in utility.
	Omitted	No add-in is specified.

Code coverage was introduced as a partially completed feature in VFP 5.0. While the code coverage logging worked most of the time, Microsoft documented but failed to ship a code coverage analyzer. In addition, there were problems with incorrectly reported form and class methods in version 5.0. Coverage is now fully functional in VFP 6.

The idea behind code coverage is to document every line of code that gets executed in a routine to ensure that all cases have been tested as part of your testing routine. The first step is logging. Issue SET COVERAGE TO YourFileName to begin the process. Each line of code that executes adds a line to this ASCII text file, recording the filename, line, procedure, class and amount of time to execute. When your routine has finished, issue SET COVERAGE TO with no argument to stop recording and close the file. If you want to add to the same file, use the ADDITIVE keyword.

Now that you have this humongous text file, what to do with it? Run the code coverage analyzer, available on the

Tools menu, to read in the file and analyze the results.

The Code Coverage Analyzer is actually two pieces—an Engine and an Application. The engine does the heavy lifting of parsing the log file, while the Application presents the user interface. Realize that you can use the engine, but develop your own interface, to draw out the statistics you need. You could write your own components to do this, or you could consider writing an Add-In. Your add-in can be a program, form, APP, EXE, menu or query. You pass the name of your add-in to the Analyzer, and it is invoked after the Analyzer has been instantiated. An object reference to the Analyzer tool is passed to your add-in. At this point, your routine can do whatever it needs to do—change the file to be parsed, add controls to the analyzer form or present your own form instead. Fortunately, Microsoft has included well-commented source code for all parts of the Coverage application in the Tools\XSource directory, so writing add-ins shouldn't be too difficult.

Example

```
SET COVERAGE TO MYCOVER.LOG
DO MYCODE
SET COVERAGE TO
DO (_COVERAGE) WITH "MYCOVER.LOG"
```

Set CPCompile, Set("CPCompile"), Set CPDialog, Set("CPDialog")

The first of these commands determines the code page with which each compiled fragment of an application is marked. The second command specifies whether a confirmation dialog should be displayed whenever a table not marked with a code page is opened exclusively.

Usage

```
SET CPCompile TO [ nCodePage ]
nCodePage = SET(  "CPCompile")
SET CPDialog ON | OFF
cOnOrOff = SET( "CPDialog" )
```

By default, compiled elements of an application—programs, forms, and classes—are flagged with the current code page. Use this setting to override that marking. An element can still be flagged with its own code page by using the AS clause of the COMPILE command.

When a table is opened, Visual FoxPro reads the file's header to determine which code page the data needs to be represented in. (See "DBF, FPT, CDX, DBC—Hike!" for details.) If the code page flag is blank, and the file is opened exclusively (so Visual FoxPro can write to the file header), the GetCP() dialog appears, asking you to choose the original code page of the file. You probably want to have this dialog appear during development, and might need it as part of an import routine, but we would typically leave this setting OFF in most of our applications. The CPZero.PRG utility, included with every version of Visual FoxPro, in the HOME() + "\Tools\CPZero\" subdirectory, shows how you can blank out or update any table with its proper code page flag.

Example

```
cCPDialog = SET("CPDialog")   && preserve the setting
* do some processing here
SET CPDIALOG &cCPDialog       && restore the setting here
```

See Also Compile, CPConvert(), CPCurrent(), CPDBF(), GetCP()

Set Currency, Set("Currency")

SET CURRENCY dictates the format in which currency values are displayed.

Usage

```
SET CURRENCY TO LEFT | RIGHT
SET CURRENCY TO cSymbol
cLeftOrRight = SET( "CURRENCY" )
cSymbol = SET( "CURRENCY", 1 )
```

SET CURRENCY specifies whether the currency symbol should precede or follow the number, and what that symbol should be. These settings are used for any numeric field where the Format property includes the "$" symbol, or if you're using the Transform() function either on a currency value or with an "@$" format clause.

In VFP 5 and earlier, when the currency symbol is more than one character long and placed to the left of the number, it can be truncated if the InputMask does not provide sufficient space for the entire expression. For example, with currency set to "SEK" to the left of the number, TRANSFORM(12345.6789, "@$999999.9999") returns "K12345.6789" This was fixed in VFP 6.0

Example

```
SET CURRENCY TO " DMK"
SET CURRENCY RIGHT
* The @$ function is the older equivalent of Format
@ 1,1 SAY 12345.6789 PICTURE "@$99999.9999" && DISPLAYS "12345.6789 DMK"
```

SET("CURRENCY") returns either "RIGHT" or "LEFT", while SET("CURRENCY",1) returns the currency symbol.

See Also Configuration Files, Format, InputMask, Transform(), Set Point, Set Separator, Set SysFormats

Set Cursor, Sys(2002), Sys(2008), Sys(2009)

These commands and functions all relate to the keyboard cursor. SET CURSOR and SYS(2002) let you turn it on and off under certain circumstances. The other two don't do anything in Visual FoxPro (or FoxPro for Windows)—in FoxPro for DOS, they let you change the cursor shape.

Usage

```
SET CURSOR ON | OFF
SYS(2002 [, 1 ] )
```

Without the optional parameter, SYS(2002) is identical to SET CURSOR OFF—both turn off the keyboard cursor. (They don't affect the mouse cursor.) With the parameter, it turns it back on, just like SET CURSOR ON. However, they affect the cursor only when certain commands are executing. The only one of those commands you're likely to use in VFP is WAIT, but only its most basic form is affected; if you use WAIT WINDOW, these commands don't affect you.

Way back in FoxBase+ days, we used this stuff occasionally to exercise more control over what the user saw. In Windows, it doesn't make any sense at all. Don't do this.

See Also DragIcon, MousePointer, Set, Set Mouse

Set Database, DBC(), Set("Database")

SET DATABASE lets you specify which database should be current, while DBC() and SET("DATABASE") tell you which database is currently selected.

Usage

```
SET DATABASE TO [ Name ]
```

Omitting Name deselects the currently selected database without selecting another.

Why would you want to select a particular database anyway? There aren't a whole lot of reasons, but there are some commands and functions (like ADD TABLE, MODIFY DATABASE, PACK DATABASE, and DBGetProp()) that require the database to be current and others (like CLOSE DATABASES) that behave differently when no database is selected. Opening a table in a database opens the database, but doesn't make it current. If you want to use DBGetProp() or one of the other DBC-dependent functions, you need the database to be current.

Note, however, that some of the things you'd expect to need the database to be current, such as stored procedures, don't. There's no problem finding and executing them, even if they reference tables and fields in the database without specifying the database name. We're pretty impressed by VFP's versatility in this case.

Some commands (like CLOSE DATABASES) can leave you with no current database.

Usage

```
cDatabase = DBC()
cDatabaseStemOnly = SET( "DATABASE" )
```

DBC() returns the name of the current database. If FULLPATH is ON, the return value includes the complete path to the database. If FULLPATH is OFF, it returns only the drive and filename. If no database is current, DBC() returns the empty string. SET("DATABASE") returns only the name portion of the current database. That is, it omits the drive, path and extension.

Example

```
OPEN DATABASE MyData
? DBC()            && Returns "H:\HACKER\TEST\MYDATA.DBC"
? SET("DATABASE")  && Returns "MYDATA"
OPEN DATABASE MoreData
? DBC()            && Returns "H:\HACKER\TEST\MOREDATA.DBC
? SET("DATABASE")  && Returns "MOREDATA"
SET DATABASE TO
? DBC()            && Returns ""
? SET("DATABASE")  && Returns ""
CLOSE DATABASES
* all open free tables are closed
SET FULLPATH OFF
SET DATABASE TO MyData
? DBC()            && Returns "H:MYDATA.DBC"
CLOSE DATABASES
? DBC()            && Returns ""
```

See Also ADatabases(), Close Database, Create Database, DBC(), Delete Database, Modify Database, Open Database, Pack Database, Validate Database

Set DataSession **See DataSession.**

Set Date, DateFormat, Set Century, Century, Set Mark To, DateMark

These three SET commands and their equivalent local properties for text boxes combine to change the way that dates are displayed in your application. These settings are for display only, and make no difference in how the date is actually stored in the machine. (FoxPro always stores the full four-digit year; see "DBF, FPT, CDX, DBC—Hike!" for a description of the actual disk storage.)

Each of the SET commands may also be performed in the Tools-Options dialog, under the Regional tab. Within the development product, if saved as the default, they are stored in the Registry. They may be overridden at startup with commands in the configuration file CONFIG.FPW or programmatically at any time. Each of these SET commands is scoped to a private data session. SET SYSFORMATS ON causes FoxPro to ignore their settings and use the Control Panel's Regional settings instead.

As with most SET commands, we feel that you should set them and forget them—leave them the same for the entire application if at all possible. Use the local equivalents to get local exceptional behavior. If possible, consider using the user's preferences for date display, as set in the Control Panel Regional applet, using SET SYSFORMATS. Check out that topic for the care you'll need to take with that command.

Usage

```
SET CENTURY ON | OFF | TO [ nCentury [ ROLLOVER nRollOver ] ]
cOnOrOff = SET( "CENTURY" )
nCentury - SET( "CENTURY", 1 )
nYear = SET( "CENTURY", 2 )
TextBox.Century = nCenturySetting
```

Parameter	Value	Meaning
nCentury	1 to 99	The century to stick in front of two-digit years when converting to dates using the {} delimiters or the CTOD() and CTOT() functions.

Parameter	Value	Meaning
nCentury	Omitted	nCentury defaults to 19 (even if the system date is 2001!) and nRollOver defaults to 0.
nRollOver	0 to 99	Assume when converting two-digit years that years less than nRollOver occur in nCentury plus one.
	Omitted	Rollover behavior defaults to setting of zero.
nCenturySetting	0	Century is OFF for this text box.
	1	Century is ON for this text box.
	2	Default—display or hide century depending on the global (if no private datasession) or form-wide setting of SET CENTURY.

SET CENTURY determines whether dates and datetimes should be displayed with two-digit years (OFF) or four-digit years (ON). It is the opinion of your authors that you had better be planning (or at least let your clients think you're planning) applications which last into the next millennium. Unless you really can't afford the screen space, SET CENTURY ON. TextBoxes and GET fields with CENTURY set ON accept two digits in the year portion of a date and add the correct century based on the TO and optional ROLLOVER setting.

The TO and ROLLOVER settings (and the corresponding options for SET("CENTURY")) were introduced in VFP 5 and bear some explanation. SET CENTURY TO tells VFP which century number to assign to the date if the date is supplied with only a two-digit year, during data entry or conversion. The ROLLOVER portion allows you to split up the dates, so that those on or after a certain year fall in the century specified, and those less are assumed to be in the next century. In many cases, these two settings can alleviate the need to require four-digit dates. However, in some cases, such as the lady born in 1898 whose license next expires in 2003, a single 100-year range may not be sufficient.

Example

```
SET CENTURY ON
SET CENTURY TO 19 ROLLOVER 50
? {12/7/41}  && displays 12/07/2041
? {12/7/63}  && displays 12/07/1963
```

Usage

```
SET DATE [TO] cDateFormat
cDateFormat = SET( "DATE" )
nOrder = SET( "DATE", 1 )
TextBox.DateFormat = nFormat
```

Parameter	Value	Meaning
cDateFormat	AMERICAN or MDY	Month-day-year order. MARK is a slash if not overridden by SET MARK.
	ANSI	Year-month-day order with the period as the default MARK.
	BRITISH, FRENCH or DMY	Day-month-year order with the slash as the default MARK.
	GERMAN	Day-month-year with the period as the default MARK.
	ITALIAN	Day-month-year with the dash as the default MARK.

Parameter	Value	Meaning
cDateFormat	JAPAN or TAIWAN or YMD	Year-month-day with slashes as the default MARK.
	LONG or SHORT	The Date format is in accordance with the long or short settings in the Windows Control Panel Regional applet. These settings override the settings, whether made before or after SET DATE, of HOURS, CENTURY, MARK and SECONDS.
	USA	Month-day-year with the dash as the default MARK.
nOrder	0	MDY
	1	DMY
	2	YMD
nFormat	Numeric	The format to use, based on this list: 1: American 2: ANSI 3: British 4: French 5: Italian 6: German 7: Japan 8: Taiwan 9: USA 10: MDY 11: DMY 12: YMD 13: Short 14: Long

SET DATE sets the date format to a specific pattern. Remember that this format is for display purposes only and does not affect the way the date is stored or manipulated internally. However, if your code assumes it can grab the numeric day of the month by calculating VAL(SUBSTR(DTOC(DATE()),4,2)), you're in trouble. Use DAY() instead, or an appropriate function which does not assume a DATE setting.

The SHORT and LONG options were added in VFP 5. These let the display settings used in FoxPro be controlled by the Windows Control Panel Regional applet. While we're all in favor of empowering the end users (it usually is their machine, after all), there are practical limitations to how far we'll customize our application to support their needs. Dynamically resizing all of our text boxes to support date entry of "09/08/43" as well as "Wednesday, September 08, 1943" is a bit too much for us.

The introduction of nFormat as a property of text boxes lets us set the display format of individual text boxes. Unfortunately, Microsoft chose to make this property a numeric value, which makes it more difficult for a developer to recognize what format is in effect. We suspect that the numeric format was chosen to make localization easier, but at a cost of more difficult maintenance. We'd like to see the numeric constants added to FOXPRO.H so that code can be written as:

```
txtMyDate.DateFormat = C_GERMANDATE
```

If you *have* to know the position of the various components within the date, Microsoft introduced the ,1 argument to SET("DATE") in VFP 5.

Usage
```
SET MARK TO [ cExpression ]
cMark = SET( "MARK" )
TextBox.DateMark = cMark
```

SET MARK TO is a bit curious. There is always a date delimiter in place. SET MARK TO only overrides the existing date separator. If not specified, the delimiter is the default for the SET DATE in effect. So, if you are trying to determine the delimiter currently used, you need to check both SET("MARK") and, if that is empty, the underlying SET("DATE"). See the example below.

Help seems to indicate that the delimiter is changed, from dashes to slashes to dots, using SET DATE. This is only the case if a MARK has not already been SET, either explicitly or by FoxPro reading a set of defaults from the Registration Database on startup. To be certain you change both the order and the mark of the date display, you must explicitly issue a separate SET MARK TO command with no argument (see below).

Note that there are two SET MARK commands: SET MARK OF turns on and off marks associated with menu bars—see SET MARK OF for that one. SET MARK TO is the one associated with dates. SET MARK TO sets the delimiter between day, month and year to a particular character. While dashes, slashes and dots are typical, all character values seem to work.

Help claims that omitting cExpression resets the mark to a slash. It doesn't—it resets the mark character to the default for the current setting of DATE. If SET("DATE") = "GERMAN" and you issue the command SET MARK TO, the mark is now a dot.

Example
```
SET MARK TO "#"
SET DATE TO ANSI
? DATE()              && returns date with # delimiters
SET MARK TO
? DATE()              && returns date with ANSI "." delimiter
```

See Also Century, Date(), Day(), DMY(), DoW(), GoMonth(), MDY(), Month(), Set Hours, Set Seconds, Set SysFormats, StrictDateEntry, Year()

Set DBTrap See Access().

Set Debug, Set Echo, Set Step, Set TrBetween, _Throttle, Set("Debug"), Set("Echo"), Set("Step"), Set("TrBetween")

These items are all related to debugging, a necessary evil. They used to let you set up your environment to make debugging easier (or harder), but several of them are meaningless in VFP 5 and later.

Usage
```
SET DEBUG ON | OFF
cDebugFromMenu = SET( "DEBUG" )
```

In VFP 3 and earlier versions, SET DEBUG determines whether the Trace and Debug windows are available from the menu. In VFP 5 and VFP 6, SET DEBUG OFF is ignored—instead, the new DEBUG command controls the debugger.

SET("DEBUG") tells you the current setting of SET DEBUG.

Usage
```
SET ECHO ON | OFF
cEchoMode = SET( "ECHO" )
SET STEP ON | OFF
cStepMode = SET( "STEP" )
```

In VFP 3 and earlier, SET ECHO ON opens the Trace window without pausing; in VFP 5 and later, it's ignored. SET STEP ON opens the Trace window and suspends execution of the program. SET ECHO OFF and SET STEP

OFF don't do anything.

SET("ECHO") returns "ON" when the Trace window is open, and "OFF" otherwise. SET("STEP") returns "OFF" regardless of the last setting of STEP.

The relationship between SET STEP and the Trace window is a little strange. Issuing SET STEP ON, whether in a program or from the Command Window, opens Trace and gives it focus. If a program is running, it's suspended at the line following SET STEP ON. You can then use the menu to step through the code.

On the whole, it's better to open the Debugger, set some breakpoints, and run an unmodified program than to insert SET STEP ON (or SUSPEND) in a program.

Usage
```
SET TRBETWEEN ON | OFF
cTraceBetween = SET( "TRBETWEEN" )
```

SET TRBETWEEN gives you programmatic control over the Trace Between Breaks setting in the Debugger. Issuing SET TRBETWEEN ON is the same as checking that item. In both cases, every line of the program is shown and highlighted when the Trace window is visible. With TRBETWEEN set to OFF or the item unchecked, no code is highlighted until a breakpoint is reached. Setting TRBETWEEN OFF executes the program faster, since no visual updates are needed.

SET("TRBETWEEN") tells you the last setting of SET TRBETWEEN. In VFP 3, it didn't properly reflect changes made with the menu. Fortunately, this bug is fixed in later versions.

Usage
```
_THROTTLE = nStepSpeed
nStepSpeed = _THROTTLE
```

The _THROTTLE system variable determines how quickly a program executes when the Trace window is open. In some cases, especially if a program is making decisions based on keystrokes and mouse clicks, stepping through a program makes it too difficult to see what's going on. Instead, it's better to slow the program down so you can see what happens each step of the way. _THROTTLE lets you do that by specifying a delay of anywhere from 0 to 5.5 seconds between consecutive commands. In VFP 5 and later, of course, you can turn on Coverage and/or Event Tracking in the Debugger to get a log of what's going on. Which tool is best depends on what kind of thing you're debugging and what kind of problems you're having.

You can set _THROTTLE programmatically or through the Throttle item on the Trace window's context menu.

The setting of _THROTTLE is ignored unless the Trace window is open and Trace Between Breaks is ON.

Example
```
_THROTTLE = .5    && half-second between commands
```

See Also Debug, Resume, Set, Set Coverage, Set EventList, Set EventTracking, Set Talk, Suspend

Set DebugOut See DebugOut.

Set Decimals, Set Fixed, Set("Decimals"), Set("Fixed")

These two commands determine display and calculation of numbers involving decimals. SET DECIMALS determines the minimum number of decimals used and displayed. SET FIXED determines whether the SET DECIMALS value is also the maximum number displayed.

Usage
```
SET DECIMALS TO [ nDecimals ]
SET FIXED ON | OFF
nDecimalSetting = SET( "DECIMALS" )
cIsItFixed = SET( "FIXED" )
```

When you perform a calculation involving decimal numbers, SET DECIMALS sort of determines the number of decimal places in the result. To be more specific, it determines the number of decimal places you'll see in the result, if the result has more places than the current setting. The correct calculation is performed and stored internally, but all subsequent displays of the result use the DECIMALS setting at the time the number was calculated. (If the result has fewer places than the DECIMALS setting and FIXED is OFF, the result is not padded with zeroes.)

If that sounds confusing, it's because it is. Try this:

```
X1 = 10/3          && with default DECIMALS setting of 2
? X1               && 3.33, as expected
SET DECIMALS TO 5
X2 = 10/3
? X2               && 3.33333 - so far, so good
DISPLAY MEMORY LIKE X*
```

Interesting—X1 shows up as 3.33 while X2 is 3.33333. But it gets stranger.

```
? X1*2             && 6.67
? X2*2             && 6.66667
SET DECIMALS TO 18
? X1*2             && 6.67
? X2*2             && 6.66667
? X1*3             && 10.00
? X2*3             && 10.00000 - so no precision was lost in either case
```

The variables remember how many decimal places they were created with, even though you can see in the memory listing that the internal representations are the same.

What does all this mean for you? That you should choose a decimals setting for your application and use it throughout.

SET DECIMALS TO without a number resets you to the default of 2, even if you've set a different default through the Tools-Options dialog.

SET FIXED is much easier. When you turn it on, every number is displayed with the DECIMALS setting, even if the actual result is shorter or longer. That is, it rounds or pads numbers to exactly the specified number of decimal places.

SET DECIMALS affects Currency and Integer values only when SET FIXED is ON. In that case, Integer values are shown with the number of decimal places indicated by SET("DECIMALS"). Currency is more interesting—ththe number of decimal places shown can be decreased if SET("DECIMALS") is less than four, but it never goes above four.

Both FIXED and DECIMALS are scoped to data sessions.

Example

```
* Using X1 and X2 created above
SET DECIMALS TO 3
SET FIXED ON
? X1         && 3.333
? X2         && 3.333
? X1*2       && 6.667
yMoney = $37.5837
? yMoney     && 37.584
SET DECIMALS TO 7
? yMoney     && 37.5837
```

See Also Set, Set SysFormats

Set Default **See CD.**

Set Deleted **See Delete.**

Set Delimiters, Set ReadBorder, Set("Delimiters"), Set("ReadBorder")

These two commands relate to old ways of indicating the bounds of a text box. They're pretty much irrelevant in Visual FoxPro.

Usage

```
SET DELIMITERS ON | OFF
SET DELIMITERS TO cDelimiters | TO DEFAULT
cOnOrOff = SET( "DELIMITERS" )
cDelimiters = SET( "DELIMITERS", 1 )
SET READBORDER ON | OFF
cOnOrOff = SET( "READBORDER" )
```

SET DELIMITERS goes back to the very early days of Xbase. It allows you to put either colons or a pair of characters of your choice at either end of a text box (or its predecessor, the @ .. GET). It was handy in the days when you had neither color differences nor border lines to distinguish the endpoints. Although it sort of works in Visual FoxPro, there's no reason to use delimiters—just specify BorderStyle = 1 to put a nice border around a text box.

SET READBORDER applies only to @ .. GETs and serves the same purpose as BorderStyle, except that it applies to all the @ .. GETs within a screen. Like most SET commands, we think it can be far more trouble than it's worth, and recommend you stay away from it.

See Also BorderStyle

Set Design See Access().

Set Development, Set("Development"), Set DoHistory, Set("DoHistory")

These commands are debugging aids. One big difference between them is that SET DEVELOPMENT is somewhat useful, while SET DOHISTORY is a nearly unusable relic.

Usage

```
SET DEVELOPMENT ON | OFF
cDevelSetting = SET( "DEVELOPMENT" )
```

SET DEVELOPMENT is most useful when you use a program editor other than the built-in FoxPro editor and when you don't use Project Manager. Because we recommend the built-in editor and Project Manager, our view is that SET DEVELOPMENT's usefulness is fairly limited.

When you use VFP's built-in editor, something internal to the product makes sure that you always run the more recent version of the code; that is, code gets recompiled after it's changed. With an outside editor, that internal process doesn't occur. SET DEVELOPMENT ON tells VFP to check whether the source file is more recent than the compiled version of a program, and, if so, to compile it before running it. Of course, building an app with Project Manager does the same thing.

In older versions (before VFP 5), SET DEVELOPMENT had a couple of other, pretty much unrelated, behaviors. When it was ON, the Cancel item on the Program pad was enabled while a form or READ was active. In addition, with DEVELOPMENT ON, the Trace window opened automatically when a form hit a bug. In other words, life was a little simpler for you as the developer. That was the point. These behaviors appear to be gone in recent versions and we're not sure we really care.

We recommend DEVELOPMENT ON while you're developing and OFF in applications distributed to users. Consider using the value of VERSION(2) to toggle SET DEVELOPMENT in runtime environments.

Usage

```
SET DOHISTORY ON | OFF
SET DOHISTORY TO [ HistoryFile [ ADDITIVE ] ]
cHistSetting = SET("DOHISTORY" [, 1 ] )
```

SET DOHISTORY was a very cool command back in ancient Xbase times. It let you trace through a program and see the exact sequence of commands executed. We used it a lot in those days. But DOHISTORY's days ended with the addition of the Trace window. Now, you can not only see what's happening, but interact with it.

But why not produce a history file anyway? That's what you're thinking, right? Because it's slow. In VFP 6, a very simple test, just looping and displaying the loop counter, was slightly longer with DOHISTORY ON and set to a file. With DOHISTORY defaulted to the Command Window, though, it took about 1.5 times as long. Not so bad, right? But that was an I/O-bound process. We took the display out of the loop, so all we were doing was counting internally. With DOHISTORY ON, the loop took anywhere from 13 to 32 times as long, depending where the history was directed. (However, this is a tremendous improvement over VFP 3, in which the second test was 20,000 times as long with DOHISTORY ON.) Besides, beginning in VFP 5, you can use Coverage and Event Tracking to see what's going on. While VFP 5 didn't provide a Coverage Analysis tool, just the raw logging capability, it appears the Coverage Analyzer in VFP 6 will make Coverage Analysis a regular part of our routine.

Like SET ALTERNATE, the two forms of SET DOHISTORY are independent of each other. To turn on history tracking and set it to a file, you have to issue both SET DOHISTORY ON and SET DOHISTORY TO a file. But don't.

See Also Set, Set Debug, Set Echo, Set Step, Set Talk, Version()

Set Device, Set("Device"), Sys(101)

This group is more old Xbase baggage. SET DEVICE lets you redirect the output of @ .. SAYs while the two functions tell where that output is going at the moment.

Usage

```
SET DEVICE TO SCREEN | PRINTER [ PROMPT ] | FILE FileName
cCurDevice = SET( "DEVICE" [, 1 ] )
cCurDevice = SYS( 101 )
```

Once upon a time, the @ .. SAY command was one way to produce reports. By twiddling the DEVICE setting, you could have the report appear either on screen, on paper or in a file. With SET("DEVICE") or SYS(101), you could even remember how it was set beforehand and restore it. If you designate a file destination, SET("DEVICE") returns "FILE" and SET("DEVICE",1) returns the destination filename.

In Visual FoxPro, @ .. SAY is a terrible way to produce reports, so there's not much reason to touch the DEVICE setting.

Incidentally, if you SET DEVICE TO PRINT, the actual output location is controlled by the setting of SET PRINT TO.

Example

```
SET DEVICE TO PRINT
* Issue @ .. SAYs to send a report to the printer
SET DEVICE TO SCREEN
```

See Also @ ... Say, Set, Set Print

Set Display, Set("Display")

This was a tremendously useful command in FoxPro for DOS. Although it does some things in Visual FoxPro for Windows, it has lost most of its utility. SET DISPLAY changes the video display mode to a specified mode.

Usage

```
SET DISPLAY TO CGA | COLOR | EGA25 | EGA43 | MONO | VGA25 | VGA50
cCurrentMode = SET( "DISPLAY" )
```

Changing the display mode makes a number of changes to the environment. The screen font is changed to FoxFont and the font size changes to provide approximately the number of lines specified for the display mode—9 point for 25-line displays and 7 point for 43- and 50-line modes. If the main window is less than full-size, it may be expanded to accommodate the correct number of screen rows. The Windows-style status bar is turned off.

The docs say you'll get an error message if you specify any video mode that's not available. In our tests, that's always COLOR and MONO. We also notice that SET("DISPLAY") returns "VGA25" whether we specify

"CGA", "EGA25" or "VGA25", and "VGA50" for either "EGA43" or "VGA50".

Using SET DISPLAY in a Windows app is totally inappropriate. As with other aspects of the visual environment, in Windows the user controls the display settings.

Example
```
SET DISPLAY TO VGA50  && yields 7-point FoxFont
```

See Also FontName, FontSize, IsColor(), Modify Window, SCols(), Set, Set Status Bar, SRows(), Sys(2006), SysMetric

Set DoHistory See Set Development.

Set Echo See Set Debug.

Set Escape, Set("Escape")

This command controls whether the Esc key interrupts program execution. It doesn't control whether Esc closes windows, chooses Cancel buttons, and so forth.

Usage
```
SET ESCAPE ON | OFF
cOnOrOff = SET("ESCAPE")
```

SET ESCAPE also controls ON ESCAPE. When ESCAPE is OFF, the escape handler specified with ON ESCAPE is ignored.

SET ESCAPE is only one part of turning off the Esc key in an application. It keeps the user from interrupting your program—generally a good thing to do. But it still leaves Esc available in forms and Browses and other places. This is usually what we want (once we've finished debugging the application, anyway).

If you really want to make Esc dead, dead, dead, SET ESCAPE OFF and issue ON KEY LABEL ESCAPE *, which tells FoxPro to execute a comment when the user presses Esc.

Example
```
SET ESCAPE OFF
```

See Also Cancel, On Escape, On Key Label

Set EventTracking, Set("EventTracking"), Set EventList, Set("EventList")

These commands let you programmatically control all the same features managed by the Debugger's Event Tracking dialog. Well, almost all of them, anyway.

Usage
```
SET EVENTTRACKING ON | OFF | PROMPT
cTrackingStatus = SET( "EVENTTRACKING" )
SET EVENTTRACKING TO [ FileName [ ADDITIVE ] ]
cTrackingFile = SET( "EVENTTRACKING", 1 )
SET EVENTLIST TO [ EventList [ ADDITIVE ] ]
cEventsTracked = SET( "EVENTLIST" )
```

Let's get the most important item out of the way first. SET EVENTLIST and SET EVENTTRACKING have the same four-letter (and, in fact, five-letter) abbreviation. Which one wins if you type just SET EVEN or SET EVENT? SET EVENTTRACKING. You need at least SET EVENTL for SET EVENTLIST.

When you're trying desperately to figure out what's going wrong in a program, event tracking can be a lifesaver. It lets you see what events are firing, in which order, without having to go into each one of them and add a DEBUGOUT statement. However, given the incredible assortment of events available, you don't really want to see all of them. Consider the number of MouseMove events fired by a single move of the mouse from one object to another, for example. So SET EVENTLIST lets you decide which events should be tracked. Use the

ADDITIVE keyword to add another event or two to the current list. Unfortunately, there's no easy way to remove just one or two events, but leave the rest. (You have to either retype the list or grab the current list with SET("EVENTLIST"), use STRTRAN() to remove the offender, and issue a new SET EVENTLIST.)

We ran into one interesting trap with SET EVENTLIST. If you specify only a single event, you can put quotes around the event name or not—your choice. As soon as you have more than one in the list, surrounding it with quotes gets you a Syntax Error. (However, if you really like typing extra characters, you can surround the individual items in the list with quotes. Just make sure the commas are outside the quote marks. Not that we can think of any reason to do it this way.)

So, once you've set the event list to the ones you care about, how do you actually track them? First, you have to actually turn on event tracking. Ordinarily, it's off.

By default, the messages indicating which event of which object fired appear in the DebugOutput window. There are two ways to get that information into a text file instead. You can redirect all the Debug Output information with the SET DEBUGOUT command. If all you want to put in a file is event-tracking data, use SET EVENTTRACKING TO filename, instead. ADDITIVE, of course, says to leave the file alone and just stick the new information at the end.

Once you put the event data in a text file, you can, if you want, do things like import that data into a table and compute various statistics. This might be a good choice when you're trying to figure out which methods are worth optimizing. Find out which ones fire the most and slim them down. Take a look at SET COVERAGE for more help in this regard. The PROMPT option of SET EVENTTRACKING brings up the Event Tracking dialog. If the Debugger is open in its own frame, that frame comes to the top. You can't combine the PROMPT option with either ON or OFF. The keyword that appears first takes precedence and the other is ignored.

One item in the Event Tracking dialog isn't accessible by command. With the dialog, you can specify that the data goes *only* to the file you name and not to the Debug Output window. There's no command equivalent for that one.

Example

```
SET EVENTLIST TO Load, Init, Click
SET EVENTTRACKING ON
* Run a form
SET EVENTTRACKING OFF
SET EVENTLIST TO

* To remove a specific event from the
* tracking list, do something like:
cList = SET("EVENTLIST")
cList = STRTRAN(cList,cEvent,"")
cList = STRTRAN(cList,", ,",",")
SET EVENTLIST TO &cList
```

See Also Debug, DebugOut, Set Coverage,

Set Exact See Set ANSI.

Set Exclusive, Set("Exclusive")

This command determines whether the default mode for opening tables is exclusive or shared access.

Usage

```
SET EXCLUSIVE ON | OFF
cIsItExclusive = SET( "EXCLUSIVE" )
```

Parameter	Value	Meaning
cIsItExclusive	"ON"	Unless otherwise specified, open tables exclusive.
	"OFF"	Unless otherwise specified, open tables shared.

Opening a table for exclusive access makes it totally unavailable to other users, even to other applications on the same machine or other forms with private data sessions in the same application. You can't even read the data for reporting or queries. So you only want to do it when you have to—such as when you need to perform maintenance that requires exclusive access. (For example, you need exclusive access to rebuild indexes, change table structures, and so on.)

EXCLUSIVE can improve system performance tremendously, and should be considered for single-user applications running in a non-networked environment.

EXCLUSIVE can be set differently for each data session. By default, it's ON for the global, default data session, and OFF for all private data sessions.

The current SET EXCLUSIVE setting is used for all kinds of operations that open tables, including SELECT-SQL, CREATE, INSERT INTO, and any other command that opens a table to do its work. The only way to override the current setting is to open the table with USE and add either the SHARED or EXCLUSIVE keyword. SET EXCLUSIVE also affects opening databases with OPEN DATABASE or MODIFY DATABASE. Again, you can override the default in the OPEN DATABASE command.

SET("EXCLUSIVE") tells you the current setting.

Example

```
SET EXCLUSIVE ON
USE Employee
INDEX ON UPPER(Last_Name+First_Name) TAG Name
```

See Also FLock(), IsExclusive(), Modify Database, Open Database, RLock(),Use

Set FDoW, Set FWeek, Set("FDoW"), Set("FWeek")

FDoW sets the first day of the week, used to calculate DoW() (day of week) and Week(). FWeek determines how to compute the first week of the year for the Week() function.

Usage

```
SET FDOW TO [ nFirstDayOfWeek ]
nFirstDayOfWeek = SET( "FDOW" )
SET FWEEK TO [ nFirstWeek ]
nFirstWeek = SET( "FWEEK" )
```

Parameter	Value	Meaning
nFirstDayOfWeek	Omitted or 1	Sunday is the first day of the week.
	2 – 7	Use days Monday – Saturday as the first day.
nFirstWeek	Omitted or 1	The week containing January 1 is week 1.
	2	The week containing at least four days in the new year is week 1.
	3	Week 1 is the first week completely within the new year.

These functions come in handy for calculations involving work scheduling. You'll want to ensure your application SETs these explicitly in code or the CONFIG.FPW file if you plan to do calculations on these dates, because many manufacturing firms use week numbers as a key part of planning and scheduling.

Example

```
SET FWEEK to 3  && First week is a full seven days
SET FDOW to 4   && Set the first day to Wednesday
```

The example above sets the first week of the year to the first week that falls entirely within the new year. FWEEK determines what day the week starts on from the setting of SET FDOW. Executing SET FWEEK overrides a setting previously set on the International tab of the Options screen, or the default read from the Registration Database. The Registry values are only read in the development version of VFP.

See Also Date(), Day(), DMY(), DoW(), GoMonth(), MDY(), Month(), Set Century, Set Date, Set Mark, Set FDow, Week(), Year()

Set Fields, Set("Fields"), FldList()

SET FIELDS lets you limit some commands to dealing with only a subset of the fields in a table or even a group of fields drawn from several tables. The two functions give you information about the current settings. SET FIELDS affects those commands that let you specify a field list with the FIELDS clause, as well as INSERT INTO in its FROM MEMVAR and FROM ARRAY forms.

Although the things you can do with SET FIELDS are pretty cool, we've never used it much and don't expect to now. Pretty much everything you can do with SET FIELDS, you can also do with views (the SQL kind, not the CREATE VIEW kind).

Usage

```
SET FIELDS ON | OFF
SET FIELDS LOCAL | GLOBAL
SET FIELDS TO [ FieldList | ALL [ LIKE | EXCEPT Skeleton ] ]
```

As the syntax shows, the command has three forms. The ON/OFF version determines whether the SET FIELDS setting is used. The second form, LOCAL/GLOBAL, determines whether each table has its own setting for SET FIELDS or if there's a single field list across all work areas (in the data session). SETting FIELDS GLOBAL can be pretty neat, since it lets you refer to fields from other work areas without preceding them with an alias. With the right settings, you can put up a one-to-many browse without a FIELDS clause—it works for grids, too.

SET FIELDS TO lets you specify a list of fields to be included. Unlike most SET x TO commands in FoxPro, the list is additive. That means each time you issue SET FIELDS, the fields you list are added to the current field list. The list can include calculated fields—use the same format you do in a BROWSE. The LIKE and EXCEPT let you rule fields in or out based on their names—they're useful only if you have a strict naming convention. Any form of SET FIELDS TO with anything after TO also SETs FIELDS ON. SET FIELDS TO with nothing following it, however, doesn't use the additive rule. It empties the field list and subsequent commands complain of "No fields found to process."

SET FIELDS TO ALL is a little strange—it behaves differently depending on the LOCAL/GLOBAL setting. With LOCAL, it restores the field list to the entire table. With GLOBAL, ALL adds all the fields in the current table to the current list of fields, which means some may be listed more than once.

Usage

```
cOnOrOff = SET("FIELDS")
cListOfFields = SET("FIELDS", 1)
cLocalOrGlobal = SET("FIELDS", 2)
cListOfFields = FLDLIST()
cFieldName = FLDLIST( nWhichField )
```

SET("FIELDS") and FLDLIST() tell you all about the current fields set up. SET("FIELDS", 1) and FLDLIST() both return the list of fields, but FLDLIST() always includes the alias while SET("FIELDS", 1) includes the alias only when FIELDS is set to GLOBAL. If you SET FIELDS TO ALL, SET("FIELDS", 1) returns "ALL," while FLDLIST() spells them all out. Passing a numeric parameter to FLDLIST() lets you pull out the individual fields in the list. A parameter beyond the number of fields causes FLDLIST() to return an empty string.

Example

```
USE Customer
SET FIELDS TO Company_Name, Customer_Id
BROW                  && Notice that only name and id show up
? SET("FIELDS")       && Returns "ON"
? SET("FIELDS", 1)    && Returns "COMPANY_NAME,CUSTOMER_ID"
? FLDLIST()           && Returns "CUSTOMER.COMPANY_NAME,CUSTOMER.CUSTOMER_ID"
? SET("FIELDS", 2)    && Returns "LOCAL"
```

See Also AFields(), Append From, Blank, Browse, Copy Structure, Copy To, Display, Export, Gather, Insert-SQL, List, Replace From Array, Scatter, Sort

Set Filter, Set("Filter"), Filter()

SET FILTER lets you hide some of the records in a table based on specific criteria. SET("FILTER") and FILTER() tell you what the current criteria are.

Usage
```
SET FILTER TO [ lFilterExpression ]
```

All records for which lFilterExpression returns .T. are visible. Those where lFilterExpression evaluates to .F. are hidden. Hidden records are ignored by almost every command. (You can still GO to the record number of a hidden record, but if you then issue BROWSE or EDIT, you won't see the record you expect. More important is that SELECT-SQL ignores filters placed with SET FILTER.)

You must move the record pointer for a filter to take effect. Until you do, the current record is still visible even if it doesn't match the filter condition. We usually use LOCATE with no FOR clause for this, which moves us to the first record that meets the filter condition. (Issuing BROWSE is another way of moving the record pointer, but not usually a good choice in applications.)

In FoxPro 2.x, SET FILTER was one of the few places in FoxPro where you couldn't use a UDF. In VFP, however, you can use your own functions in filter conditions—the function is evaluated for each record in the table to determine whether that record should be visible.

Omit lFilterExpression to turn the filter off and make all records visible.

Example
```
USE Customer
* look at customers in the UK
SET FILTER TO Country = "UK"
BROWSE
```

Before Rushmore, you just didn't use filters. They were slooooow. With Rushmore, if you're careful, filters can be a useful tool. For a filter to be optimized, the left-hand side of each comparison must exactly match the key expression of an open index. "Exactly" here really means *exactly*, not more or less. If the tag is on UPPER(LastName), your filter expression must refer to UPPER(LastName)—a filter on LastName won't be optimized.

We often hear people complaining about filters being slow. After making sure the filter expression is optimizable (by ensuring that tags are available for each part of the expression and that there's a tag on DELETED(), if SET DELETED is ON), the next thing we always check is how they're moving around in the filtered table. Only commands that normally take a FOR clause are optimized by Rushmore when there's a filter in place. This means, in particular, that GO TOP, GO BOTTOM and SKIP aren't optimized. For more on this and some optimizable work-arounds, see "Faster Than a Speeding Bullet" in "Franz and Other Lists."

It's worth mentioning here that, while indexes are essential for optimizing filters, filtered indexes (those created with the FOR clause of INDEX) don't aid in optimization. When such a filter is in control, though, records are hidden just as if a filter were in place.

Usage
```
cCurrentFilter = SET("FILTER")
cCurrentFilter = FILTER()
```

Both SET("FILTER") and FILTER() return the current filter expression as a string. This is handy when you want to save it while you set a different filter, then restore it later.

Usually, when there are two identical ways to do something, we feel pretty strongly that one or the other is a better choice. But this case leaves us puzzled. Usually we prefer the more mnemonic approach (so, for example, KEY() is much better than SYS(14)), but there's a certain symmetry about using SET("something") to see what you SET something to. You can't go wrong either way, in this case.

Example
```
* preserve the original filter, if any
cCurrentFilter = FILTER()
* Look at Customers in France
SET FILTER TO UPPER(Country)="FRANCE"
```

```
* do some processing here, then restore the filter
SET FILTER TO &cCurrentFilter
```

Although the docs don't say anything about it, SET FILTER is scoped to private data sessions, meaning you can have the same table open in different forms (or different copies of the same form) and specify a different filter in each case. Also undocumented is that you can specify filters for views as well as tables.

In forms and reports, you can handle filters through the Filter property of cursors in the Data environment. This is an OOPier approach. On the whole, we prefer to use OOP-based approaches rather than SET commands whenever possible.

See Also Filter, Index, Set Deleted

Set Fixed See Set Decimals.

Set Format, Set("Format"), Sys(7)

These commands control the use of format files. SET FORMAT lets you specify a format file, while SET("FORMAT") and SYS(7) tell you the name of the current format file.

Usage

```
SET FORMAT TO [ cFileName | ? ]
cFormatFile = SET( "FORMAT" )
cFormatFile = SYS( 7 [, nWorkArea ] )
```

Way back in Xbase history, someone had the bright idea of letting users specify formatting and validation information about fields once, then be able to use that information with the built-in input commands. The result was the format file, a collection of SAYs and GETs, with no READ in sight. You SET FORMAT TO such a file (which normally has a .FMT extension), then issue EDIT, APPEND or INSERT. Instead of the default appearance, those commands use the SAYs and GETs to present a formatted screen. It was actually quite a good idea ... at the time.

Once the Screen Builder appeared in FoxPro 2, format files were rendered obsolete. Visual FoxPro drove another nail into the coffin with its OOP Form Designer.

SET FORMAT TO some filename specifies the format file to use. SET FORMAT TO with no file turns it off.

Don't bother. Use the Form Designer.

For every action, there's an equal and opposite reaction. If we can specify a format file, there must be a way to find out what it is. This being FoxPro, there are two ways. SET("FORMAT") and SYS(7) are nearly identical. Like so many of the SET() functions, SET("FORMAT") is undocumented. Both return the fully qualified path and file name for the format file in the current work area. SYS(7) can look at other work areas as well, if you add the second parameter.

See Also Set, Set Clear

Set FullPath, Set("FullPath")

This setting determines whether a few functions return a complete path with their results or only the drive and filename. The function returns the current setting.

Usage

```
SET FULLPATH ON | OFF
cOnOrOff = SET( "FULLPATH" )
```

This setting affects the various functions that return filenames for open tables and databases. In addition to the ones listed in Help (DBF(), CDX(), MDX() and NDX()), it also applies to DBC().

We're mystified as to why anyone would ever want this turned off. What good does "F:CUSTOMER.DBF" do you? Guess you might parse the drive name off to get just the filename, but even that's no big deal anymore now that JustDrive()'s been added to the language.

Example

```
USE HOME()+"FoxUser" AGAIN
? DBF(1) && Returns something like G:\VFP 6\FOXUSER.DBF
SET FULLPATH OFF
? DBF(1) && Returns something like G:FOXUSER.DBF
```

See Also CDX(), DBC(), DBF(), JustDrive(), MDX(), NDX()

Set Function See FkMax().

Set FWeek See Set FDoW.

Set Headings, Set("Headings")

This is a schizophrenic command that controls two similar, but unrelated, things. SET HEADINGS determines whether column headings appear in the output of commands that list fields. It also determines whether TYPEing a file includes the name of the file and the date. Why are these things linked together? Who knows?

Usage

```
SET HEADINGS ON | OFF
cCurrentHeadings = SET("HEADINGS")
```

In its first incarnation (column headings for listing commands), SET HEADINGS affects DISPLAY, LIST, AVERAGE, CALCULATE and SUM.

Example

```
cOldHead=SET("HEADINGS")
SET HEADINGS OFF
USE Employee
* Rough average age
AVERAGE YEAR(DATE())-YEAR(Birth_Date) FOR NOT EMPTY(Birth_Date)
SET HEADINGS &cOldHead
```

See Also Average, Calculate, Display, List, Set, Sum, Type

Set Help, Set HelpFilter See Help.

Set Hours, Hours

Sets the time to 12- or 24-hour format for the clock display and also for the entry and display of datetime fields. Hours is a property of text boxes that lets you set an individual text box to be different from the rest of the application. In either case, full accuracy is retained in the data that is stored; the command and property specify only a display picture.

Usage

```
SET HOURS TO [ 12 | 24 ]
cTime = SET( "HOURS" )
TextBox.Hours = 0 | 12 | 24
```

Issuing SET HOURS TO with no argument resets it to the default 12-hour setting. SET HOURS and the Hours property affect only datetimes and FoxPro's built-in system clock. Other functions, like TIME(), continue to return the same values.

Setting Hours to 0 (the default) uses the SET HOURS setting.

Example

```
SET HOURS TO 12
THISFORM.txtSample.Hours = 12
```

See Also DateTime(), Set Clock, Set SysFormats, Text box, Time()

Set IBlock See Access().

Set Index See Order().

Set Instruct See Access().

Set Intensity See Set Blink.

Set Key, Set("Key")

This command is a good alternative to setting a filter when you want to narrow down the visible records based on the current index. It lets you specify an index key or range of keys to be filtered in.

Usage

```
SET KEY TO [ uKeyValue ] [ IN cAlias | nWorkArea ]
SET KEY TO RANGE  uLowKey,  uHighKey
         | RANGE uLowKey, | RANGE , uHighKey
           [ IN cAlias | nWorkArea ]
cKeyValues = SET( "KEY" )
cLowKcy = SET( "KEY", 1)
cHighKey = SET( "KEY", 2)
```

SET KEY is similar to SET FILTER, except that it uses the current index order. And except that, used with grids (where filters aren't optimized), SET KEY is much, much, much faster than the equivalent filter.

There are two flavors of SET KEY. You can allow only records with a particular key value or you can limit it to a range of values. It turns out, though, that often there's not a lot of difference because, with SET EXACT OFF, you can specify partial key values, too. As with filters, you have to do something to move the record pointer to the first matching record.

The optional IN clause lets you SET KEY in any work area, not just the current one. To turn off a character key filter in another work area, you can SET KEY TO "" IN ThatArea, but we can't figure out how to turn off other key filters remotely.

Changing the index order turns off the key filter, which makes sense since it's based on the active index. If you need to temporarily change order, be sure to save and restore the KEY setting.

SET("KEY") lets you find out the current settings. With no second parameter, it returns the whole range. Pass either 1 or 2 to find out the lower or upper bound of the range. If you only set a single value (by omitting the RANGE keyword), the single value is used as both the lower and upper bound and is returned by both SET("KEY",1) and SET("KEY",2). However, if you use the RANGE keyword and omit either boundary, that version of the function returns a string of spaces.

Example

```
USE Customer
SET ORDER TO Company_Na
* limit to customers beginning with "G"
SET KEY TO "G"
? SET("KEY")     && Returns "G, G"
? SET("KEY",1)   && Returns "G"
? SET("KEY",2)   && Returns "G"
* limit to customers between "Fo" and "Fu"
SET KEY TO RANGE "Fo","Fu"
? SET("KEY")     && Returns "Fo, Fu"
? SET("KEY",1)   && Returns "Fo"
? SET("KEY",2)   && Returns "Fu"
* limit to customers up to "K"
SET KEY TO RANGE , "K"
? SET("KEY")     && Returns ",K"
? SET("KEY",1)   && Returns "              "
? SET("KEY",2)   && Returns "K"
* make all customers visible
SET KEY TO
```

See Also Filter, Index, Order, Set Filter, Set Order

Set KeyComp, Set("KeyComp")

"KeyComp" is short for Keyboard Compatibility. This command lets you decide whether to make the keyboard work more or less as it does in FoxPro/DOS or adhere to Windows standards. These days, we generally choose the latter, except in very special circumstances.

Usage

```
SET KEYCOMP TO DOS | WINDOWS | MAC
cKeyComp = SET( "KEYCOMP" )
```

Let's start with the easy one. SET KEYCOMP TO MAC is ignored in Visual FoxPro for Windows. There's no easy way to make a Windows app behave like a Mac app (not to mention that our Windows users would have a terrible time with our apps if we could).

The differences between the other two settings break into a few categories. The most important are default buttons and hotkeys.

One of the changes DOS users find most difficult to adapt to when they start working in Windows is the behavior of default buttons. Before the Windows standards came along, you pressed Enter to move from field to field in a form. In Windows, Enter chooses the default button. (Be aware that any button that has focus becomes the default button. When focus moves to an object other than a button, the button whose Default property is .T. once again becomes the default. In other words, when a button has focus, pressing Enter chooses that button, no matter which button is designated as the default.) If you SET KEYCOMP TO DOS, Enter doesn't do that anymore—you have to use CTRL+Enter.

In FoxPro/DOS, hotkeys on buttons and check boxes are only available when the focus is on that kind of object. When focus is in a text box or edit box or listbox (actually, their 2.x equivalents, of course), hotkeys aren't available. SETting KEYCOMP TO DOS lets Visual FoxPro behave the same way. In addition, with that setting, ALT+hotkey doesn't do anything.

Somehow, the setting of KEYCOMP seemed much more important in FoxPro 2.x. Maybe that's because there was a DOS version we needed to maintain compatibility with. The farther we get from that version, the more strongly we feel that this is a command to forget.

Example

```
SET KEYCOMP TO DOS
```

See Also Caption, Default

Set LdCheck See Access().

Set Library See Set Procedure.

Set Lock, Set("Lock"), Set Reprocess, Set("Reprocess")

SET LOCK determines whether a number of read-only commands automatically lock records in the table they're reporting on. SET REPROCESS determines the behavior that should occur when a lock cannot be placed.

Usage

```
SET LOCK ON | OFF
cLockOnOrOff = SET( "LOCK ")
```

If a record is locked, other stations may not see changes to a record until they themselves lock the record. Data is cached at each local workstation and is not refreshed if another workstation locks, changes and unlocks one of those records on a shared table. SET LOCK ON forces a brief LOCK/UNLOCK pair on each record for many commands that otherwise would just report from cached data. These commands are listed in the documentation and include the mathematical AVERAGE, CALCULATE, SUM and TOTAL, as well as the output commands DISPLAY, LABEL, LIST and REPORT. If exactly up-to-the-minute data is critical, you may want to consider this command.

On the other hand, this command can really foul up a locking scheme. Setting LOCK ON means that these commands also release any pre-existing locks when they are run, as if UNLOCK ALL had been issued. See the first example below. If you really need this setting, we recommend that you wrap the individual needy commands in a SET/reSET pair to avoid problems with locking, as we show in the second example.

Example

```
SET MULTILOCKS ON
SET LOCK ON
? RLOCK("2,4,6,8",ALIAS()) && lock four records
LIST FOR SYS(2011) = "Record Locked"  && Nothing!
SET LOCK OFF
? RLOCK("2,4,6,8",ALIAS()) && lock four records
LIST FOR SYS(2011) = "Record Locked"  && Lists the four records

cSetLock = SET("LOCK")
SET LOCK ON
CALCULATE AVG(nAge), MAX(nAge) to nAvg, nEldest
SET LOCK &cSetLock

* also see the combined example with SET REPROCESS below
```

Usage

```
SET REPROCESS TO nAttempts | nTime SECONDS | AUTOMATIC
nSetting = SET("REPROCESS")
```

Parameter	Value	Meaning
nAttempts	–2	This is the same as SET REPROCESS TO AUTOMATIC. When a command requiring a lock is issued, and the lock cannot be placed, the lock is retried forever (with the status bar prompt "Attempting to lock... Press ESC to cancel.") unless the user presses Escape to end the retries. If the user terminates the lock attempt and it came from a command that automatically places a lock, the ON ERROR handler receives the failed lock error. On the other hand, if a function such as LOCK() is placing the lock, the values .T. and .F. are returned to indicate the success of the operation, and the error handler is not called.
	–1	One of the easiest ways to get your user to turn the computer off. If a lock cannot be made, the message "Waiting for lock..." is displayed and there is nothing—nothing—the user can do. If the user with the lock on the file or record of interest is off on vacation this week, you might as well take this week off. The main FoxPro window cannot be minimized or closed. There has to be a better way—we can't think of a worse one.
	0	This one's a doozy, folks: If an ON ERROR command is in effect, no attempts at retrying are performed. If a lock cannot be made, .F. is returned if a function tried to place the lock. If a command attempted the lock, an error is generated. But, if there is no ON ERROR command in effect, both commands and functions behave just like AUTOMATIC locking.
	Positive integer	The number of times to attempt to place the lock before giving up.

Parameter	Value	Meaning
nTime	Positive integer	The number of seconds during which to continuously retry the lock.
nSetting	Integer	Returns the values set above, returning –2 for AUTOMATIC, and not distinguishing between settings of nAttempts and nTime.

This can be a very confusing command. The results often surprise the developer, because there are several conditions that determine the outcome of an unsuccessful lock attempt. Mostly, we feel this is a documentation issue. The help file entry is so bad that we no longer understood the function after reading the topic. But we've gotten over it, and we hope we can help you to get over it, too.

First, if you are attempting to get a lock explicitly with functions such as FLOCK() or LOCK(), the functions return a logical value to tell you if you were successful. Your function gets control back after the time or number of retries expire, if this is specified. If automatic locking is chosen, your function gets the return after the lock is made, or if the user chooses not to wait for the lock and presses Escape.

If a command rather than a locking function is placing the lock, there's no way for FoxPro to signal the command that a lock has failed, except by generating an error. Your ON ERROR handler should be written to handle these errors, offering the user the options of trying again or canceling the operation. If the user has the option of canceling, you need to consider how best to gracefully recover from this unstable condition, reset the environment, and restart the application. In a procedure where this error wouldn't be unusual, we often install a local ON ERROR handler that can properly reset the environment if records are unavailable. In a global ON ERROR handler, it can be far more difficult. We might consider resorting to RETURN TO MASTER in this case, effectively shutting down and restarting the application.

In general, we try to avoid the second situation altogether by using explicit record locking and pessimistic buffering to reduce the potential loss of data. If we need to SET LOCK ON for some particular purpose, we often reset REPROCESS to AUTOMATIC for the length of that procedure, with a custom ON ERROR handler to handle unavailable data, but generally we leave REPROCESS at 0, and LOCK OFF.

Example

```
USE AGES
lcOnError = ON("ERROR")
lcSetLock = SET("LOCK")
lnSetRepr = SET("REPROCESS")
SET LOCK ON
SET REPROCESS TO -2
ON ERROR DO lErrHand with ERROR(), MESSAGE()
AVERAGE AGES TO nAges
ON ERROR &lcOnError
SET REPROCESS TO (lnSetRepr)
SET LOCK &lcSetLock

Procedure lErrHand(nErr, cMessage)
IF nErr = 108 or nErr = 109
  WAIT WINDOW "Some records were not available." + chr(13) + ;
              "Try again later. Press any key to continue..."
  RETURN
ENDIF
ENDPROC
```

See Also Error(), FLock(), IsFLocked(), Lock(), SYS(2011)

Set LogErrors See Compile.

Set MacDesktop, Set MacHelp See On AplAbout.

Set MacKey See Clear Macros.

Set Margin See _PLOffset.

Set Mark Of, MrkBar(), MrkPad()

The SET MARK OF command (not to be confused with SET MARK TO) lets you put a checkmark next to a menu bar or pad. The two functions ask whether an item is marked.

Usage

```
SET MARK OF MENU MenuName [ TO ] cMark | lMarkIt
SET MARK OF PAD PadName OF MenuName [ TO ] cMark | lMarkIt
SET MARK OF POPUP PopupName [ TO ] cMark | lMarkIt
SET MARK OF BAR nBar OF PopupName [ TO ] cMark | lMarkIt
```

SET MARK OF can be divided up two different ways. First, there are two kinds of values you can hand it: character and logical. In Visual FoxPro, the character values are ignored. (In FoxPro 2.x, they let you specify the mark character.)

The logical value determines whether the specified item has a checkmark character (like, for example, the item for the active window in Visual FoxPro's Window menu). When lMarkIt evaluates to .T., the item is checked.

However, like other menu commands, the MENU and POPUP versions of SET MARK propagate downward. If you SET MARK OF a popup to .T., all the bars on that popup get marked unless you issue a separate SET MARK OF BAR command to turn off particular bars. Similarly, SETting MARK OF a menu to .T. marks all the pads.

You can mark system menu items, either at the popup or the bar level. The secret is to use their built-in names. For example, to mark all the bars of the Edit menu, you'd use SET MARK OF POPUP _MEdit .T. To mark individual bars, you have to use their bar numbers. For example, use SET MARK OF BAR _med_undo .T. to mark the Edit-Undo menu bar. Of course, we have no idea why you'd ever want to mark system menu bars.

Incidentally, although Microsoft has chosen not to document it anymore, there *is* a SET MARK OF PAD command, and it does work for menu pads you define yourself.

Example

```
SET MARK OF BAR 3 OF MyPopup TO .T.
```

Usage

```
lIsMarked = MRKBAR( cPopupName, nBar | SystemBarName )
lIsMarked = MRKPAD( cMenuName, cPadName)
```

MRKBAR() and MRKPAD() report whether the specified bar or pad has been marked. For system menu bars, you have to use the bar name, not in quotes. (Actually, that bar name is a number, a very negative number.)

Example

```
* See GETBAR()
```

See Also Define Bar, Define Menu, Define Pad, Define Popup, GetBar(), GetPad(), Menus

Set Mark To See Set Date.

Set MBlock See Access().

Set MemoWidth, Set("MemoWidth")

SET MEMOWIDTH lets you specify the number of characters per line for output and processing of memo fields and multiline strings. SET("MEMOWIDTH") tells you the current setting.

Usage

```
SET MEMOWIDTH TO nWidth
? nMemoWidth = SET( "MEMOWIDTH" )
```

The default memowidth is 50 characters per line. You can set it to anything from 8 to 256, in FP2.x and VFP 3, and 8 to 1024 in later versions. Settings of nWidth less than 8 result in an error message; specifying nWidth more than the maximum allowed gives you the maximum anyway, without an error message.

The memowidth setting affects almost all operations in which memos or character strings are divided into lines. The result of a function like MEMLINES() varies, based on the current setting of memowidth. The following functions and commands are affected by memowidth: ATCLINE(), ATLINE(), RATLINE(), MEMLINES(), MLINE(), ?, ??, DISPLAY, LIST. For ?, ??, DISPLAY and LIST, memowidth affects only memo fields and character strings longer than 256 characters. The other functions apply memowidth to shorter character strings as well. Note that the ALines() function, added in VFP 6, is *not* affected by this setting.

SET("MEMOWIDTH") lets you determine the current setting for memowidth. Like most of the SET() functions, it's handy for changing, then restoring the old setting.

Each data session gets its own setting for memowidth.

Example

```
cLong="This is a long enough string to have some word wrap"
SET MEMOWIDTH TO 20
? MEMLINES(cLong)     && Returns 3
SET MEMOWIDTH TO 50
? MEMLINES(cLong)     && Returns 2
SET MEMOWIDTH TO 256
? MEMLINES(cLong)     && Returns 1

* save old setting
nOldWidth=SET("MEMOWIDTH")
SET MEMOWIDTH TO 80
DISPLAY notes OFF
SET MEMOWIDTH TO nOldWidth
```

See Also ?, ??, ALines(), AtCLine(), AtLine(), Display, List, MemLines(), MLine(), _MLine, RAtLine(), Set()

Set Message, Set("Message")

SET MESSAGE controls the location of messages coming from menus and old-style controls (@ ... GET and @ ... EDIT). It also lets you explicitly specify a message. This one got weird in the move to Windows and hasn't gotten any better in Visual FoxPro.

Usage

```
SET MESSAGE TO cMessage
SET MESSAGE TO nRow [ LEFT | CENTER | RIGHT ]
SET MESSAGE WINDOW MessageWindow
nMessageRow = SET( "MESSAGE" )
cMessage = SET( "MESSAGE", 1 )
```

SET MESSAGE is pretty wimpy in Visual FoxPro. This set of commands was quite handy in FoxPro for DOS, where it gave you lots of control over the messages associated with input controls and menu items and even let you show a message totally unrelated to screens or menus. But something was lost in the translation to Windows.

SET MESSAGE WINDOW is ignored in Visual FoxPro or in FoxPro 2.x for Windows. Messages still appear in the Windows-style status bar. If you turn that off, too, your messages go straight to oblivion.

SETting MESSAGE to a particular row works only when you have the Xbase-style status bar turned on. That's the one controlled by SET STATUS, not the Windows-type bar controlled by SET STATUS BAR.

SET("MESSAGE") returns only the row to which MESSAGE has been set. When you SET MESSAGE to a window, there's nothing that lets you know that. Interestingly, when MESSAGE is set to the Windows-style status bar, the row returned appears to reflect the bar's position. If you resize the main VFP window, the value returned changes.

Fortunately, none of the problems here is that severe because good Windows applications put their messages in the Windows-style status bar, not in miscellaneous windows or random locations on screen. Plus, the StatusBarText property is a much easier way to associate some text with each object. If what you're really trying to do is give controls those neat little messages that all recent Microsoft applications have, take a look at the ToolTips and ItemTips properties. If you want to throw system messages on the screen, use MESSAGEBOX().

See Also ItemTips, MessageBox(), Set, StatusBarText, ToolTipText

Set Mouse

This command doesn't do anything in Visual FoxPro and, in fact, it's not even listed in the Help file beginning in VFP 5.

See Also Set, Sys(2002)

Set MultiLocks See Lock().

Set Near, Set("Near")

> Peace to him that is far off, and to him that is near.
>
> *The Bible*

This command determines what happens when a search fails. With SET NEAR OFF, the record pointer goes to end of file. SET NEAR ON moves the record pointer to the closest matching record.

Usage

```
SET NEAR ON | OFF
cNear = SET( "NEAR" )
```

SET NEAR applies only to searches involving SEEK (and its cousins, SEEK() and INDEXSEEK()), plus the antique FIND. Searches with LOCATE and implied searches due to relations between tables ignore SET NEAR.

"Closest matching record" means the first record after the desired value, that is, the next highest value in an ascending index and the next lowest in descending order. With NEAR OFF, you can use RECNO(0) to explicitly move the record pointer to where you'd have been with NEAR ON.

SET("NEAR") tells you the current setting, so you can change it, then reset it. SET NEAR is one of the many settings scoped to a data session.

Example

```
SET NEAR ON
USE Employee ORDER Last_Name
* An honest man would be handy
SEEK "DIOGENES"
BROWSE  && Record pointer is on record for Anne Dodsworth
```

See Also Find, RecNo(), Seek, Set, Set Exact, Set Order

Set NoCPTrans See CPConvert().

Set Notify, Set("Notify")

This command determines whether an assortment of system messages are displayed. In Visual FoxPro, it seems as though there's no rhyme nor reason as to which messages are covered by NOTIFY, but the secret is that, back in FoxPro/DOS days, all of these appeared in a WAIT WINDOW. Some of these messages have moved to the status bar (when it's available), but they're still affected by this setting.

Usage
```
SET NOTIFY ON | OFF
cNotifySetting = SET( "NOTIFY" )
```

Among the messages controlled by SET NOTIFY are the automatic messages associated with input, such as the "Range" message for spinners (or text boxes with Range events) and the "Invalid Input", "Invalid Date" and "Invalid Date/Time" messages. Because of this, you'll usually want to SET NOTIFY OFF in your applications.

Example
```
SET NOTIFY OFF
```

See Also Set, Set Status Bar, Set Talk

Set Null, Set("Null")

Judicious absence is a weapon.

Charles Reade

This command determines whether or not fields added or modified with CREATE TABLE and ALTER TABLE default to accepting nulls, and whether unspecified fields in INSERT-SQL are filled with null or empty values. The function returns the current setting.

Usage
```
SET NULL ON | OFF
cOnOrOff = SET( "NULL" )
```

When SET NULL is ON, all fields added in CREATE TABLE and ALTER TABLE and those respecified with ALTER TABLE allow nulls unless you include the NOT NULL clause. Conversely, when SET NULL is OFF, those fields don't accept nulls unless you explicitly allow them by including the NULL clause in the definition. Boy, does that sound confusing, but it isn't really. This command lets you set up a default, which applies unless you explicitly override it in the command.

The interaction of SET NULL with INSERT is really interesting. When you issue INSERT INTO a table, if you choose, you can provide values for only a subset of the fields. However, when you do that, the other fields still have to get created. Before Visual FoxPro, the value inserted into those fields was blank—that is, you could test ISBLANK() on the omitted fields and get .T. With SET NULL OFF, that's still what you get. But when you SET NULL ON, those fields that accept nulls have them inserted.

Our advice (like that for many SET commands): Establish a standard for your entire application, set it once, and leave it that way. Toggling this on and off inside an application must be done with a lot of care.

Example
```
SET NULL OFF
CREATE TABLE Test1 (cfld C(3), nfld N(4) NULL)
* cfld doesn't accept nulls, but nfld does
SET NULL ON
CREATE TABLE Test2 (cfld C(3) NOT NULL, nfld N(4))
* same as above - no nulls for cfld, but nfld accepts them

* now let's put some data in
* NULL is still ON
INSERT INTO Test1 (cfld) VALUES ("abc")
SELECT Test1
? ISNULL(nfld)    && returns .t.
? ISBLANK(nfld)   && returns .f.
SET NULL OFF
INSERT INTO Test1 (cfld) VALUES ("def")
? ISNULL(nfld)    && returns .f.
? ISBLANK(nfld)   && returns .t.
```

See Also Alter Table, Blank, Create Table, Insert-SQL, IsBlank(), IsNull(), Set Commands

Set NullDisplay See NullDisplay.

Set Odometer See Set Talk.

Set OLEObject, Set("OLEObject")

This setting determines whether OLE objects can be created and manipulated in the application.

Usage
```
SET OLEOBJECT ON | OFF
cOLEObject = SET( "OLEOBJECT" )
```

Whenever you create an object in VFP using CreateObject(), NewObject(), or AddObject(), FoxPro searches for a class definition that matches the name of the class you supply. It searches the FoxPro base classes, class definitions already in memory, the current program, the CLASSLIB setting, the PROCEDURE setting, the program stack, and then, finally, the Registry. With OLEOBJECT set ON (the default and the setting we recommend), OLE class definitions in the Registry are included in the search whenever an attempt is made to create an object.

With SET OLEOBJECT OFF, the Windows Registry is not used as the last item in the search path of the CreateObject(), AddObject() or NewObject() functions, effectively turning off OLE Automation. While this lowers the memory overhead needed to run Visual FoxPro on a workstation, we suspect this overhead isn't as much of a problem as trying to figure out why OLE Automation doesn't work.

If a mistyped class definition causes the Registry to be searched, even though the class should have been found within your application, a small bit of time will certainly be consumed with this search. However, we think that given how few times this will occur, the overhead is negligible—you're about to blow up anyway, right? On the other hand, picture yourself banging your head bloody against the client's monitor at three in the morning screaming, "But it worked on my machine!" when this setting gets toggled off by some rogue routine at your client's site. Whether or not you intend to use OLE Automation in your application, we suggest you leave this setting at its default ON setting.

This setting has no effect on general fields, or OLE objects on forms. OLE support is automatically loaded if a general field is detected in a table, or if an OLE object is detected while loading a form.

Example
```
SET OLEOBJECT ON
```

See Also Set, Set()

Set Optimize, Set("Optimize")

Here's another command to add to your "Don't ever use this" list. Even on those rare occasions when you might need the effects of SET OPTIMIZE OFF, it's better to localize it by adding NOOPTIMIZE to the relevant commands than to make a global change.

SET OPTIMIZE determines whether FoxPro attempts to use Rushmore to optimize commands. The default is ON, as it should be. SET OPTIMIZE affects all commands with FOR clauses.

Usage
```
SET OPTIMIZE ON | OFF
cOptimizeSetting = SET( "OPTIMIZE" )
```

We had a hard time imagining any case where you'd want to SET OPTIMIZE OFF, but we asked around and heard a few stories. Basically, very, very rarely, you may have a large enough data set and a complicated enough condition that Rushmore can't figure out what to do with it and gets bogged down. In such cases, turning optimization off results in better performance because FoxPro doesn't bother to try to figure out how to optimize. (Two of our reporters indicated they had problems with complex combinations of SCAN FOR and SET FILTER, which actually gave bad results because of Rushmore failing.) Similarly, when dealing with a view that has no indexes, turning off Rushmore may speed things up because FoxPro doesn't even bother to see whether it can optimize.

Another time to consider turning off optimization is when memory and disk space are insufficient for Rushmore to do its thing. Again, setting OPTIMIZE OFF in that case prevents Rushmore from giving it the old college try before doing it the slow way.

The bottom line here is that SET OPTIMIZE OFF or NOOPTIMIZE is something to try when all else has failed. Before you do so, try rebuilding your indexes; the problem may be corrupted indexes.

Finally, the documentation talks about possibly needing to turn off optimization in cases where you change the value of an index tag used for optimization. We tried to get bad results in such a case and found that FoxPro seemed to be smart enough to rebuild its bitmap along the way.

As for SET("OPTIMIZE"), it returns the current setting, so you can save it and reset it later.

See Also Set, Set()

Set Order See Order().

Set Palette

SET PALETTE determines whether graphics are displayed using the native color palette from the first displayed graphic or from the Visual FoxPro palette.

Usage
```
SET PALETTE ON | OFF
lcPalette = SET("PALETTE")
```

Visual FoxPro has its own built-in palette for displaying graphics. This palette is optimized for displaying multiple graphics on the screen at one time. However, in order to do this, Visual FoxPro approximates the colors in each image using colors from its own palette. Consequently, each image may be displayed somewhat "off-color" from its true value—and surely an equal-opportunity company like Microsoft is going to avoid anything off-color in its PC software! SETting PALETTE ON may cause multiple images shown at the same time to appear quite differently from their expected colors.

If you need to display images at their highest resolution and with their true colors, plan to display only one on the screen at a time, with SET PALETTE OFF. If your application demands more than one image on the screen at once, you'll need to accept the limitations of SET PALETTE ON.

SET("PALETTE"), of course, tells you the current setting.

See Also Image Control, OLEControl

Set Path, Set("Path")

This command lets you specify a series of directories that FoxPro should search when you ask for a file. Although it serves the same purpose, it's not connected to the DOS search path.

Usage
```
SET PATH TO [ ListOfDirectories ]
cCurrentPath = SET( "PATH" )
```

You can have a default path stored in the Registry. Just specify a path and bring up the Tools-Options dialog (or specify the path in the File Locations tab there). Choose Set as Default, and the specified path (along with anything else you've changed) is saved. When you start Visual FoxPro, that path is already set.

As with so many of the SET commands, you can omit the parameter to reset the path. However, it gets reset to empty, not to the stored default. Resetting to the saved path requires you to issue the SYS(3056) function, which resets *all* the settings stored in the Tools-Options dialog—that's a little severe. Bottom line: Be sure to save the current path before you start fiddling if it's important to you.

The list of directories is a little strange. It's a comma-delimited or semicolon-delimited list—in fact, you can mix the separators. But it's never checked for validity. You can SET PATH TO any sort of garbage at all and FoxPro never blinks.

To make things more complicated, you can use a macro (&) or indirect reference (parens) to set the path to the list of directories contained in a string. But you can't use EVAL()—you get an error message in VFP 5 and VFP 6. (In VFP 3, if you SET PATH TO EVAL(cList), then check SET("PATH"), you'll see that FoxPro took you literally and set the path to "EVAL(cList)"—not quite what you had in mind.)

When you use a macro or indirect reference, you can't put anything that needs to be evaluated in the list. For example, the following:

```
cList = "C:\WINDOWS,SYS(2004)"
SET PATH TO (cList)
```

results in a path of:

```
C:\WINDOWS,SYS(2004)
```

Even using a macro instead of indirect reference has the same result. To get the desired effect, you have to make sure the function is evaluated before you get to the SET PATH line:

```
cList = "C:\WINDOWS,"+SYS(2004)
SET PATH TO (cList)
```

Unless there's only one directory in the list, you can't include the function call right in the SET PATH line.

To our utter astonishment, SET PATH can handle directories with embedded spaces without having to surround them with quotes. We had no problem SETting PATH TO C:\Program Files (perhaps our least favorite directory ever). It kind of makes sense, since SET PATH doesn't see a space as a delimiter, but it sure is different than the way VFP handles embedded spaces elsewhere.

Example

```
SET PATH TO C:\WINDOWS, F:\VFP
? SET("PATH")     && Returns "C:\WINDOWS,F:\VFP"
* Can use function call for one item
SET PATH TO (SYS(2004) + "\DATA")
* But the following DOESN'T work as you'd expect
SET PATH TO (SYS(2004) + "DATA"), C:\WINDOWS
* Do it this way instead
cList = (SYS(2004) + "DATA")+", C:\WINDOWS"
SET PATH TO (cList)
```

See Also ChDir, FullPath(), Set Default, SYS(3056)

Set PDSetup, _GenPD, _PDriver, _PDSetup, Set("PDSetup")

These three system memory variables and one command set up a pretty sophisticated printing system under earlier DOS versions of FoxPro. While they may still be usable in Visual FoxPro, we are hard-pressed to think of why you might want to use them.

Usage

```
_GENPD = cGenerator
cGenerator = _GENPD
_PDRIVER = cDriverName
cDriverName = _PDRIVER
_PDSETUP = cSavedSetup
cSavedSetup = _PDSETUP
SET PDSETUP TO cSavedSetup
cSavedSetup = SET("PDSETUP")
```

Parameter	Value	Meaning
cGenerator	Character	The name of the program to run when creating or changing a printer driver setting.

Parameter	Value	Meaning
cDriverName	Character	The name of the program or C routine (PLB/FLL) built into Genpd.APP used to perform the actual row-by-row, character-by-character printing. PS.PRG was used for PostScript printing, while Driver.PRG was used for all others.
cSavedSetup	Character	The name of a previously defined printer setup, which could store information on the printer brand and model (and consequently the language), margins, font sizes and orientation. Setting PDSetup to a single blank character brings up the printer driver setup dialog.

Using these capabilities within Visual FoxPro is depending on too much backward compatibility, in our opinion. Check out the *Hacker's Guide to Visual FoxPro 3.0* or some of the 2.x references in this book's appendices if you need to transport stuff using these commands and settings to Visual FoxPro; don't even consider using them there.

See Also _ASCIICols, _ASCIIRows, Report, Set Printer, Set Resource, Version()

Set Point, Set("Point"), Set Separator, Set("Separator")

These commands control the characters used for the decimal point and to separate groups of digits.

Usage

```
SET POINT TO [ cPointChar ]
cPointChar = SET( "POINT" )
SET SEPARATOR TO [ cSeparatorChar ]
cSeparatorChar = SET( "SEPARATOR" )
```

SET POINT controls the decimal point. SET SEPARATOR controls the character that goes between groups of digits (when you format a number that way). In the default U.S. setup, the point character is "." while the separator is ",". In much of the rest of the world, they use exactly the opposite.

Regardless of these settings, you must do it the U.S. way in code. Any numeric constants use a period for the decimal point. InputMasks use "." and "," for the decimal point and separator, respectively. (The "." and "," get translated to the appropriate POINT and SEPARATOR characters when you run the form.) While this is no doubt annoying to non-Americans writing code, it is actually a sensible choice. The point and separator characters can be changed many ways—you wouldn't want the interpretation of code to depend on the current settings. (There's a similar problem with date constants. They're interpreted according to the SET DATE setting when the code is compiled, not when it's executed.)

These two settings respect SET SYSFORMATS. When that setting is ON, they draw their values from the Windows settings. Otherwise, they use the established FoxPro settings (the defaults or those saved in the Registry or specified in a Config.FPW file). However, if you SET SYSFORMATS OFF, SET POINT and SET SEPARATOR do not revert to their FoxPro defaults. You have to issue SET POINT TO and SET SEPARATOR TO to restore the defaults.

Example

```
* set up European settings
SET POINT TO ","
SET SEPARATOR TO "."
```

See Also Configuration Files, InputMask, Set, Registration Database, Set SysFormats

Set Precision See Access().

Set Printer, Set("Printer"), Sys(102), Sys(6)

SET PRINTER is another "can of oil" command—three in one. It lets you send output to the printer, choose a printer for output, and specify a default font for output. The functions provide information about the current print setup.

Usage

```
SET PRINTER ON [ PROMPT ] | OFF
SET PRINTER TO [ FileName [ ADDITIVE ] | DEFAULT
       | NAME WindowsPrinterName | \\MachineName\PrinterName ]
SET PRINTER FONT cFontName [, nFontSize ] [ STYLE cStyleCodes ]
```

We've never used the full name of this command. In fact, we've never seen SET PRINTER anywhere but in the documentation. It's universally called SET PRINT.

SET PRINT ON starts queuing output for the current printer. SET PRINT OFF stops queuing output. The queued output is actually sent to the printer (well, to Print Manager anyway) by issuing SET PRINT TO without anything after it.

SET PRINT ON PROMPT brings up the printer setup dialog only some of the time. PRINT has to be OFF. If it was previously ON, both SET PRINT OFF and SET PRINT TO have to run, in that order, before FoxPro pays attention to the PROMPT clause. This is true even if the user cancels out of the printer setup dialog.

In addition, you have to have at least one printer installed to use the PROMPT clause; with no printers installed (as, say, on a notebook that's never used for printing), using the PROMPT clause brings up a pair of error messages. Check NOT EMPTY(aPrinters(laTemp)) to make sure a printer is available.

The various forms of SET PRINT TO route output to different places. You can specify a filename, the Windows default printer, a specific Windows printer or, in networks that support the Universal Naming Convention (UNC), a specific network printer. (A couple of other forms aren't relevant in Windows, so we've omitted them from the syntax diagram.)

Finally, SET PRINT lets you establish a default printer font that's used when you don't specify a font for an output item.

Normally, SET PRINT affects only output from ? and ?? and commands with the TO PRINT clause, but combined with SET DEVICE, you can also redirect @ .. SAY output.

Usage

```
cOnOrOff = SET( "PRINTER" ) | SYS(102)
cPrintFile = SET( "PRINTER", 1 ) | SYS(6)
cCurrentPrinter = SET( "PRINTER", 2)
cDefaultPrinter = SET( "PRINTER", 3)
```

The functions tell you the current state of printer affairs. It takes several of them together before you can figure out where output is likely to go at this moment. SET("PRINT") by itself just tells you "ON" or "OFF". So far, so good. SET("PRINT",1) and SYS(6) tell you if you've SET PRINT TO a file, including a UNC file name, or if you've SET PRINT TO a port (like SET PRINT TO LPT1).

SET(PRINT",2) and SET("PRINT",3) tell you about default printers. SET("PRINT",2), added in VFP 5, tells you about the Windows default printer. Finally, SET("PRINT",3), new in VFP 6, tells you which printer VFP considers its default (current destination) printer.

Example

```
SET PRINT TO DEFAULT
SET PRINT ON
? "This is a test of the emergency printer system"
? "This is only a test."
? "In the event of a real emergency, these words would"
?? "be much larger and louder"
SET PRINT OFF
SET PRINT TO

SET PRINT TO Test.Txt
SET PRINT ON
? SET("PRINT")
? SET("PRINT",1)
```

See Also ?, ??, APrinters(), GetPrinter(), PrtInfo(), Set Device, Sys(1037)

Set Procedure, Set Library, Release Procedure, Release Library, Set("Procedure"), Set("Library")

These commands tell FoxPro where to look for procedures and functions used in your code. SET PROCEDURE refers only to FoxPro routines, while SET LIBRARY can access both FoxPro code and routines in external libraries.

Usage

```
SET PROCEDURE TO [ FileName1 [, FileName2 [, .. ] ] [ ADDITIVE ] ]
SET LIBRARY TO [ FileName [ ADDITIVE ] ]
cProcFiles = SET( "PROCEDURE" )
cLibFiles = SET( "LIBRARY" )
```

Back in the days before the Project Manager, programmers needed a way to tell FoxPro (and FoxBase before it) where to find those well-debugged routines called by various programs in an application. There were two basic solutions to the problem: You could store each routine in a separate PRG file and make sure it was on the FoxPro path, or you could put your common code into a "procedure file" and SET PROCEDURE TO that file. You could only use one procedure file at a time, so these files were often massive. Like so many other choices in FoxPro, this one became almost a religious issue for many people.

Then along came the Project Manager and the issue was moot. The PM could find all your code and bind it together neatly into an APP or EXE. Procedure files were out in the cold.

Like the phoenix, procedure files were reborn with VFP. With the ADDITIVE clause, plus the need to make class definitions available to the code that depends on them, SET PROCEDURE once again found its way into lots of applications. VFP 6's NewObject() function, though, may mean that, while procedure files are still used, SET PROCEDURE starts disappearing again.

SET LIBRARY's story is a little different. When it was first added to FoxPro, its sole purpose was to provide access to external library files built with the Library Construction Kit (PLBs for FoxPro/DOS, FLLs for FoxPro/Windows). But SET LIBRARY was enhanced as part of the dBASE compatibility campaign in FoxPro 2.6.

In dBASE and now in FoxPro, as well, you can SET LIBRARY to either an external library or to a procedure file. In fact, using the ADDITIVE clause, you can have both at once—despite the documentation. However, SET LIBRARY can handle only one procedure file at a time, though you can open multiple external libraries.

Procedure files are searched earlier in the search order than external libraries.

We suggest you stick with SET PROCEDURE for procedure files, unless you absolutely need the later search of SET LIBRARY. Then, proceed with caution, but remember that the ability to open a procedure file simultaneously with library files is undocumented and may someday no longer work.

One more warning. SET("LIBRARY") tells you about a procedure file opened with SET LIBRARY only if there are no external libraries open. As soon as you SET LIBRARY TO an FLL, you can't find out about a procedure file you SET LIBRARY TO.

As with so many other SET commands, SETting LIBRARY or PROCEDURE TO without listing a file clears the current setting.

Usage

```
RELEASE PROCEDURE ProcedureFile
RELEASE LIBRARY LibraryFile
```

These commands let you remove procedure and libraries files from memory. Both insist you provide the path to the file, if it's not in the current FoxPro search path.

You can't release a procedure file set with SET LIBRARY. When you issue RELEASE LIBRARY with a procedure filename, you get the error "API library not found." Not very helpful, is it? As far as we're concerned, this is just one more reason not to use SET LIBRARY to do SET PROCEDURE's job.

Example

```
SET LIBRARY TO HOME()+"FoxTools"            && provided with VFP
? WORDS("How many words in this line?")   && returns 6
RELEASE LIBRARY HOME()+"FoxTools"

* Open some programmatic class libraries without closing
* other procedure files
SET PROCEDURE TO AppClasses, MoreClasses ADDITIVE
```

See Also Call, CreateObject(), Declare-DLL, FoxTools, Load, NewObject(), Set Path

Set ReadBorder See Set Delimiters.

Set Refresh

Determines how often data shared on a multi-user system is refreshed within a BROWSE and how often local data caches are refreshed from the server.

Usage

```
SET REFRESH TO nRefreshDisplay [, nRefreshBuffers ]
nRefreshDisplay = SET( "REFRESH" )
nRefreshBuffers = SET( "REFRESH",1 )
```

Parameter	Value	Meaning
nRefreshDisplay	0	The local engine does not check for changes made to the displayed data.
	Integer	The local display is refreshed every nRefreshDisplay seconds.
nRefreshBuffers	0	Local data buffers are not refreshed.
	Integer	Local data buffers are refreshed every nRefreshBuffers seconds.
	Omitted	If nRefreshDisplay is set to anything other than 0, nRefreshBuffers is set to the same setting as nRefreshDisplay. If nRefreshDisplay is set to 0, nRefreshBuffers defaults to 5.

A BROWSE shows a number of records on the screen at any one time, but other users might be changing those records as you watch. If REFRESH is left at its default state of 0,5, these changes are never displayed. For table fields displayed with other controls, you must lock a record to be sure the fields display the actual values stored on disk, but REFRESH can "read through locks" to show you the most up-to-date information available while within a BROWSE.

We generally feel that BROWSEs should not be used in applications; instead, they should be replaced by the far more controllable Grid. See "Commands Never to Use" for more details. Grids don't seem to be affected by the setting of REFRESH, requiring either that the row receive the focus, the form's Activate event occur, or the form's Refresh method be called in order for data to be properly displayed.

The second parameter is less well documented. This parameter supposedly determines how often the locally cached data buffers should be updated with new data. Don't ever set this parameter to zero, or you won't see changes made to records displayed on screen until the records are locked.

It seems to us that the default setting of 5 seconds should beat the server to death with so many requests to update data that the entire system would come crashing down, but that hasn't been our experience. On very large systems or WANs where network bandwidth is a precious commodity, we recommend you try raising the refresh level by doubling it and checking the performance change to the network and application. Ten, 20 or even 40 seconds between updates might not make that much difference in the appearance of your application, but could significantly affect other network performance criteria. As always, your mileage may vary; test your application under your environment to be sure of optimal performance.

Example
```
SET REFRESH TO 30
```

See Also Browse, Grid, Lock

Set Relation, Set("Relation"), Set Skip, Set("Skip")

The two commands here control temporary relations—that is, relations you set up in a program for a particular purpose, while the corresponding functions tell you about those relations. They have no connection with persistent relations stored as part of a database (except that they may involve the same tables).

SET RELATION turns relations on and off while SET SKIP indicates that a relation is one-to-many. Don't confuse this form of SET SKIP (SET SKIP TO) with the other version (SET SKIP OF), which affects menus and popups.

Usage
```
SET RELATION TO [ eExpr1 INTO cAlias1 | nWorkArea1
        [, eExpr2 INTO cAlias2 | nWorkArea2 [, ... ] ]
        [ IN cParentAlias | nParentWorkArea ]
        [ ADDITIVE ] ]
SET RELATION OFF INTO [ cAlias | nWorkArea ]
```

SET RELATION TO establishes temporary relations. There are two ways to define these relationships between two tables. One of them harks back to the early days of Xbase. In both cases, two tables are involved: a "parent" or controlling table and a "child" or controlled table. Once the relation is established, moving the record pointer in the parent table automatically moves the record pointer in the child table.

The usual way connects an expression from the parent record to an index key of the child record. The order of the child table must be set to the appropriate index before SET RELATION is issued. Once you set the relation, moving the record pointer in the parent issues an implied SEEK eExpr*n* in the child work area. If there is no related record, the child's record pointer ends up at EOF().

Example
```
USE Customer
USE Orders IN 0 ORDER Customer_I
SET RELATION TO Customer_Id INTO Orders
* Now moving in Customer moves the record pointer in
* Orders to the first order for that customer
```

We've run across a number of people who think a relation can be based only on a single field or that the related fields of the child and the parent have to have the same name. Neither of these is true. The important thing is that the parent must have appropriate fields to create an expression that is the same as the key for some tag of the child. In some situations, you want to set things up with an expression in the parent that's only part of the key expression. For example, say the parent is customer and the child is invoice. The invoice table may have a tag on customer_id plus invoice date (CUSTOMER_ID+DTOS(INV_DATE)). As long as SET EXACT is OFF, you can establish a relation based on just the customer_id; you'll then be able to see the invoices for each customer in date order.

The old, old way of setting a relation uses the record number of the child to connect to the parent. In this case, no order is set in the child table and the relational expression eExpr*n* must be numeric. When the record pointer moves in the parent, an implied GOTO is issued in the child. We use this technique very, very occasionally to connect query results to the original data. (It's usually better, though, because of the unreliability of record numbers, to include the primary key in the query and base a relation on that field.)

Family relations are more fluid in the database world than in the real world. One table might act as the parent (or controlling) table of another at one time, then the relationship may be reversed later. The terms "parent" and "child" refer to what's going on at this moment rather than to a permanent state of affairs.

You can establish multiple relations at the same time. That is, one parent can control several children (this works better in FoxPro than in real life). There are two ways to do this. First, you can list several pairs of relational expressions and controlled tables in a single SET RELATION. Alternatively, you can use the ADDITIVE clause to allow new relations to be added without closing existing relations. The example below shows both techniques.

Example

```
* Open the TasTrade Orders table and relate it to
* the Line items and Shippers tables
OPEN DATA TasTrade
USE Orders
USE Order_Line_Items IN 0 ORDER Order_id
USE Shippers IN 0 ORDER Shipper_Id

* Here's both relations set at once
SET RELATION TO Order_Id INTO Order_line items, ;
                Shipper_Id INTO Shippers

* This time, the two relations are set separately
SET RELATION TO Order_Id INTO Order_line_items
SET RELATION TO Shipper_Id INTO Shippers ADDITIVE
```

Issuing SET RELATION TO without any parameters turns off all relations for the current work area. To turn off relations selectively, use SET RELATION OFF and specify which relation is being terminated.

Example

```
* Turn off the relation into line items
SET RELATION OFF INTO Order_line_items
```

The optional IN clause lets you establish relations where the parent is in a work area other than the current work area. You can't turn relations off this way, though—for that, you have to be in the right work area. We find this clause most useful when establishing several levels of relationships. Using IN, all the work can be done without changing work areas.

Multiple levels of relations can be specified. Think of parent–child–grandchild–great-grandchild, and so on. For example, in TasTrade, you might set up relationships from Customers into Orders, then from Orders into Order_Line_Items and then from Order_Line_Items into Products. Moving the record pointer in Customers would then move the record pointers for Orders, Order_Line_Items and Products.

Usage

```
SET SKIP TO [ cAlias1 [, cAlias2 [ , ... ] ] ]
```

This command turns a relation into a one-to-many relation. It indicates that issuing SKIP in the parent should proceed to the next record in the child and not go on to the next parent record until there are no more child records for this parent. This allows you to process all the children for a given parent. SET SKIP TO by itself changes the relation back to one-to-one.

SET SKIP is most useful for Browses and reports, where it lets you display all the children of a parent.

Example

```
* Set up a one-to-many relation
* between Customers and Orders
USE Customer
USE Orders IN 0 ORDER Customer_I
SET RELATION TO Customer_Id INTO Orders
* This Browse shows the first order for each company
BROWSE FIELDS Company_Name, ;
              Orders.Order_Number,Orders.Order_Date
* Now make it one-to-many
SET SKIP TO Orders
* This Browse shows all orders for each company
* and shows each company name only once
BROWSE FIELDS Company_Name, ;
              Orders.Order_Number,Orders.Order_Date
```

When multiple levels of relations are in place, you can set one-to-many relations at any level. To make all the relations in the chain one-to-many, issue SET SKIP TO followed by the alias of each table other than the parent. In the example above with Customers, Orders, Order_Line_Items and Products, to make all three relations one-to-many, you'd issue:

```
SET SKIP TO Orders,Order_Line_Items,Products
```

You can mix and match relations, making some relations in a chain one-to-one and others one-to-many. The best way to see the differences is to open a few tables, set the relations, then try different parameters to SET SKIP, issuing BROWSE each time to see the result.

Usage

```
cRelationPhrase = SET( "RELATION" )
```

The undocumented SET("RELATION") function returns a string that's exactly what you need to put in the SET RELATION command to establish the existing relationships for the current work area. The string shows every existing relation, including both the relational expression and the target.

The function accepts a second parameter, but it doesn't change the output.

Example

```
OPEN DATA TasTrade
USE Orders
USE Order_Line_Items IN 0 ORDER Order_Id
USE Shippers IN 0 ORDER Shipper_Id
SET RELATION TO Order_Id INTO Order_Line_Items
SET RELATION TO Shipper_Id INTO Shippers ADDITIVE

?SET("RELATION")  && "shipper_id INTO shippers, order_id INTO order_line_items"
```

You can use SET("RELATION") to store the existing relations for a table while you set different ones, then restore the old ones when you're done. To get the same information broken into its components, use TARGET() and RELATION().

Usage

```
cSkipAliases = SET("SKIP")
```

SET("SKIP") is also undocumented. It tells you which child tables have one-to-many relationships with the current table. Like SET("RELATION"), it returns a character string that you can plug into the corresponding command. In this case, the string is a comma-delimited list of aliases.

Example

```
OPEN DATA TasTrade
USE Orders
USE Order_Line_Items IN 0 ORDER Order_Id
USE Shippers IN 0 ORDER Shipper_Id
SET RELATION TO Order_Id INTO Order_Line_Items
SET RELATION TO Shipper_Id INTO Shippers ADDITIVE

SET SKIP TO Order_Line_Items
?SET("SKIP")        && Returns "Order_line_items"
```

As with SET("RELATION"), you can use SET("SKIP") to grab current information before you change it, then restore it later. Unlike SET("RELATION"), there's no other way to get the data returned by SET("SKIP").

See Also Alter Table, Create Table, Relation(), Set Order, Target(), Use

Set Reprocess See Set Lock.

Set Resource, Sys(2005), Set("Resource")

Usage

```
SET RESOURCE [ ON | OFF ] | [ TO FileName ]
cFileName = SET( "RESOURCE" ) | SYS( 2005 )
```

The FoxPro resource file, by default named FOXUSER.DBF, stores the size and position settings of all windows and toolbars. It also stores diary entries, and other miscellaneous entries such as the location of the builder registration table and the most recently used projects. Earlier versions of FoxPro used this file to store additional information such as printer settings, label layouts, and other data used only for the DOS product.

Nowhere does it say that you have to use a resource file. While it is nice to let your users resize windows and have them reappear in the same place, it does add another management issue to your application framework. Many cool features, like color sets and printer drivers, useful in the DOS product, have been assumed by the operating system. Unless your users have a need for it, consider delivering your application to them with SET RESOURCE OFF. Saving and restoring form positions is easily accomplished in your base classes, and you can eliminate the hassle of managing resource files.

A FoxPro resource file is opened exclusively by the first user to get to it, and cannot be shared. Our usual method of handling this is to bundle a "seed" resource file within our application, and install a copy of this file for each user.

Because every window that's been opened stores a record within this file, we regularly browse the file and clean out deadwood, packing the file.

SET("RESOURCE") returns the current status, ON or OFF, and SET("RESOURCE",1) and the synonymous SYS(2005) return the path and filename of the current resource file. We prefer the first format, SET("RESOURCE",1), because it's a wee bit more self-documenting.

Example

```
SET RESOURCE OFF
SET RESOURCE TO C:\MYAPP\MYRSRC.DBF
```

See Also Calendar/Diary, Configuration Files

Set Safety, Set("Safety")

This is a rather friendly command. It can keep you from doing some really stupid things. When SAFETY is ON, FoxPro prompts you before overwriting files in most cases.

Usage

```
SET SAFETY ON | OFF
cSafetySetting = SET( "SAFETY" )
```

With SET SAFETY ON, commands that completely overwrite a file bring up a dialog that tells you the file already exists and asks for permission to overwrite it. If you choose "No," the operation is canceled. SET SAFETY OFF bypasses that dialog.

The only problem with SET SAFETY is that some file-writing commands bypass it. The low-level file functions ignore SET SAFETY, as do DDE commands (which have their own safety option).

SET("SAFETY"), of course, gives you the current setting, as either "ON" or "OFF".

Example

```
* preserve old setting
cOldSafety=SET("SAFETY")

USE MyData

* turn it off
SET SAFETY OFF
COPY TO olddata FOR NOT DELETED()

* reset it
SET SAFETY &cOldSafety
```

SET SAFETY ON can be a lifesaver while you're doing development and testing from the command prompt, but we think it shouldn't usually be used in an application. We understand what's happening when a dialog box leaps to the fore and asks "Overwrite A837492484.TMP?", but we should probably spare our end users these confusing and sometimes misleading dialogs. The exception is when the user is given the control to modify something and should be allowed to either rename or overwrite, just as he or she would in, say, a word processor. Check out the FILE() function to determine whether or not you're going to overwrite a file.

SAFETY is one of the many settings scoped to a data session, so you have to remember to turn it off somewhere early in your form class.

See Also DDESetOption(), File(), Set

Set Scoreboard See Set Status Bar.

Set Seconds, Set("Seconds"), Seconds

This setting and property determine whether datetime output includes the seconds portion of the time. The function returns the current setting.

Usage

```
SET SECONDS ON | OFF
cOnOrOff = SET( "SECONDS" )
txtTextbox.Seconds = nSecondsSetting
nSecondsSetting = txtTextbox.Seconds
```

Parameter	Value	Meaning
nSecondsSetting	0	Don't show seconds.
	1	Show seconds.
	2	Use SET SECONDS setting.

As in so many places in VFP, the SET command here is global (actually, data session wide), while the property is local.

SET SECONDS also affects conversion of datetimes with TTOC(). When SECONDS is OFF, the converted value doesn't include the seconds portion. This setting doesn't affect precision going the other direction, though. CTOT("12/31/1999 23:59:59") always stores the seconds internally, regardless of the SECONDS setting.

Example

```
SET SECONDS ON      && Default value
? DATETIME()        && Displays 09/15/95 04:30:21 PM
SET SECONDS OFF
? DATETIME()        && Displays 09/15/95 04:30 PM

This.Seconds = 1    && Turn on seconds in textbox code
```

See Also DateTime(), Hours, Set Hours, TToC()

Set Separator See Set Point.

Set Shadows

Here's another command for your "never mind" list. This one doesn't do anything in Visual FoxPro. In fact, it didn't do anything in FoxPro for Windows either.

Set Skip See Set Relation.

Set Skip Of, SkpBar(), SkpPad()

Here's another command that's easy to confuse. SET SKIP OF is about menus. SET SKIP TO is about relations. We're interested in menus right now.

SET SKIP OF lets you turn individual menu components on and off. When a component is turned off, its prompt dims and the user can't choose it—sort of. SKPBAR() and SKPPAD() tell you the status of individual bars and pads.

Usage

```
SET SKIP OF MENU MenuName lSkipIt
SET SKIP OF PAD PadName OF MenuName lSkipIt
SET SKIP OF POPUP PopupName lSkipIt
SET SKIP OF BAR nBar OF PopupName lSkipIt
```

These commands work inside out—when you SET SKIP of some component to .T., it gets disabled. In fact, it works the same way as the SKIP FOR clause of the various DEFINE commands for menu components. Like SET DELETED, it's just one of those things that's backward. Consider it sort of a Disabled property—then the double-negatives make some sense!

Like so many other menu commands, the MENU and POPUP versions of this one propagate downward. SET SKIP OF a popup to .T. and every bar on the popup is disabled. You can then enable individual bars with SET SKIP OF BAR.

Unlike SKIP FOR, SET SKIP OF is not dynamically evaluated. That is, lSkipIt is evaluated when you issue the command and the item's status is set accordingly. But changes to lSkipIt after that do not affect that menu item. Use SKIP FOR to set up conditions that are evaluated repeatedly. (You can refresh the menu and update the SKIP status by issuing ACTIVATE MENU MenuName NOWAIT.)

In the system menu, disabling a pad prevents you from opening that pad, so you can't get to the items on the pad's associated popup. In non-system menus, that's not the case. To disable all the items below a pad, you have to SET SKIP OF the pad and of the popup associated with it.

Example

```
* Turn off the view menu
SET SKIP OF PAD _MSM_View OF _MSysMenu .T.
```

Usage

```
lIsSkipped = SKPBAR( cPopupName, nBar )
lIsSkipped = SKPPAD( cMenuName, cPadName )
```

When you need to know if a menu item is available at the moment, these two are the ticket. The results are changed by the SET SKIP OF commands and the SKIP FOR clause of the various DEFINE commands.

As with MRKBAR(), to check SKPBAR() for bars of the system menu, you need to specify the bar name, which is really a negative number. (Being able to check the system menu bars lets you set up buttons that are enabled and disabled based on the corresponding menu item. You're most likely to use this with a toolbar so you can, for example, have Cut, Copy and Paste buttons that are enabled only when they're relevant.)

Example

```
? SKPPAD("_MsysMenu", "_MSM_View") && Returns .T. after above
? SKPBAR("_Medit",_Med_Undo)       && Test whether Undo is disabled
```

See Also Define Bar, Define Menu, Define Pad, Define Popup, Menus

Set Space See ?.

Set SQL See Access().

Set Status See Set Status Bar.

Set Status Bar, Set Status, Set Scoreboard, Set("Status Bar"), Set("Status"), Set("Scoreboard")

The first two commands here control the status bar at the bottom of the screen. SET SCOREBOARD doesn't do anything, but it's historically related to the other two.

Usage

```
SET STATUS BAR ON | OFF
SET STATUS ON | OFF
SET STATUS TIMEOUT TO [ nSeconds ]
cStatusBarOn = SET("STATUS BAR")
cStatusOn = SET("STATUS")
```

FoxPro has two different status bars. From way back into Xbase history, there's the traditional Xbase status bar. It appears two lines above the bottom of the screen. In dot-prompt days, two different kinds of messages appeared under the status bar. When FoxPro moved into the Windows world, it acquired a Windows-type status bar (Help refers to it as the "graphical status bar"). This one goes at the very bottom of the screen and is much less dorky-looking than the old one.

The two status bars are mutually exclusive. Turning one on turns the other off. There are also a number of items that behave differently depending on which status bar is displayed. (See SET TALK for one example.) We recommend you use the Windows-style status bar in Windows applications. As always, it's better to stick with a standard.

SET STATUS TIMEOUT has nothing to do with the Xbase-style status bar, despite the command it looks like, and despite its misplacement in the VFP 3 Help file. (It's undocumented in VFP 5 and VFP 6.) Just another case of overloading. Certain messages (like SET TALK output) appear in the Windows-style status bar. This command lets you determine how long they stay there before the normal status information returns. Leave out nSeconds to reset to the five-second default. The maximum value accepted is 2,147,483,647 and, no, we didn't test it. Well, just a little. Numbers over a few million seem to be ignored.

The SET() functions let you figure out which status bar (if either) is on. We haven't found a way to determine the status timeout setting.

SET SCOREBOARD is totally ignored in Visual FoxPro. Way back when, it determined where the CapsLock, NumLock and Insert indicators appeared.

Example

```
SET STATUS TIMEOUT TO 2
SET STATUS BAR ON
```

See Also Set Clock, Set Notify, Set Talk

Set Step See Set Debug.

Set Sticky, Set("Sticky")

Yet another setting that's ignored in Visual FoxPro. In DOS and on the Mac, this one controls whether menu popups stay open if you release the mouse button.

Set StrictDate, Set("StrictDate")

While the SET command is new to VFP 6.0, the concept of strict dates was introduced in VFP 5.0. This command makes it easier to transition legacy code and also allows you to ensure Year 2000 compliance.

Usage

```
SET STRICTDATE TO [ 0 | 1 | 2 ]
nStrictLevel = SET("STRICTDATE")
```

Parameter	Value	Meaning
nStrictLevel	0 or omitted (at runtime)	Off. No strict date checking is done. To avoid problems with running legacy code, this is the default setting for ODBC and runtime modules. Code compiled in this mode will not generate an error, regardless of the runtime setting.

Parameter	Value	Meaning
nStrictLevel	1 or omitted (at design time)	On. Verifies that all date and datetime constants are non-ambiguous. Otherwise, this setting generates an error in development or runtime modes. Code must be recompiled in 6.0 in order for the error detection to work, even at runtime.
	2	CTO-hostile. This setting incorporates all of the behaviors of level 1, but also squawks when it runs into a CTOD() or CTOT() function, warning that they "can produce incorrect results."

Strict date formatting was introduced in Visual FoxPro 5.0, with the StrictDateEntry property available for text boxes. However, it's with the introduction of the SET command in VFP 6.0 that this feature really comes into its own.

A strict date is a constant or date expression that can be interpreted only one way. The format for strict dates is:

```
{^YYYY-MM-DD [ , ] [ HH [ :MM [ :SS ] ] [ A | P ] ] }
```

where the separators can be any combination of dashes, forward slashes or dots. The year must be four digits in order to be unambiguous. The time portion looks really messy when expressed in the standard syntax, but all it means is that you express only as much time precision as you need—hours, minutes or seconds—and add the optional "a" or "p" on the end (AM is assumed). Hmmm ... doesn't this mean the time is still ambiguous? We think so, but let's not tell Microsoft—they tried so hard!

One thing tripped us up while trying all the variations of the optional sections of this expression. If you want to specify time after the date, you must include either a colon after the hours, or the comma separating the date from the time.

At first, we thought SET STRICTDATE was a compile-time setting only, then we started seeing runtime effects, then we just got totally confused. Let's see if we can clarify what might be the single most important Y2K feature in the language.

First, let's talk about the compile-time effects. These are pretty clearly documented—0 is the equivalent of "Shut up," 1 generates errors when compiling code and running that compiled code, and 2 does all that 1 does, but also objects to the CTOT() and CTOD() functions. All pretty straightforward. Our general feeling is that we will develop with STRICTDATE set to 2 all the time, a setting even more conservative than the default development setting of 1. After all, if we can build features into our products that will make it easier for us to produce both internationally consistent and Year-2000-safe code, why not take advantage of what is there?

Setting STRICTDATE to its various settings also changes the size of the resulting object code. Code with CTOD() is larger when compiled with STRICTDATE equal to 2—it appears that the entire line of suspicious code is preserved for the runtime environment to evaluate, and to generate errors if STRICTDATE is still not met.

If the compile-time environment is set to 0, the code will never generate an error at runtime, regardless of the runtime setting of STRICTDATE. With compile-time STRICTDATE of 1 or 2, the runtime setting of 1 or 2 generates errors, but 0 is silent if errors are present. So what does this mean? The compiler has the brains, not the runtime. The compiler flags code as suspicious, and if the runtime isn't set up to be silent, it alarms when that code is hit.

What came next really caught us by surprise. We tested a routine that tells us how many days until DevCon and updated it to show the days until the then-just-announced 1999 conference. Compiling the program led to an error message, because dates were in the American and not strict format, and running the program also gave warnings until the code was rewritten. But here's the kicker: the code had been running for months in Visual FoxPro 6.0

without a peep! It had to be recompiled in 6.0 before it would generate an error. So, 5.0 code with ambiguous dates will not error under 6.0 until recompiled in 6.0.

In runtime, we'll set STRICTDATE as strictly as we can—in most cases, at 2, but perhaps at 0 in situations where we are still bringing the code into Y2K compliance. STRICTDATE is set by default at 0 in runtime environments, for the maximum backward compatibility; code in previous versions should compile and run with no change in behavior. But you'll want to boost STRICTDATE up to 2 as soon as you've ironed out the issues in your code.

Strict dates solve the problem of source code changing its behavior unexpectedly when recompiled, only because the developer changed the settings for date interpretation. For example, changing SET CENTURY from 19 ROLLOVER 50 to 19 ROLLOVER 60, or changing SET DATE from MDY to DMY, changes the interpretation of the constant {10/12/55} embedded within the code the developer recompiles. This is almost always not intended, and can lead to code breaking under "normal" circumstances. The primary purpose of SET STRICTDATE is to sound alarms at compile time to alert the developer to a potential problem.

The highest setting, SET STRICTDATE TO 2, essentially eliminates the use of the CTOT() and CTOD() functions. Because these functions evaluate a string parameter at runtime and interpret their value as dates based on the current SET DATE settings, it is possible for these functions to return a value unanticipated by the developer. Instead, we agree with the Microsoft recommendation to use the newly revised DATE() and DATETIME() functions to create unambiguous dates.

Example

```
SET STRICTDATE TO 2
? CTOT("01/01/1950")  && error 2033, "CTOD and CTOT can produce
                      && incorrect results…"
SET STRICTDATE TO 1
? {^1998-05-17 14}   && errors if lacking colon or comma
? {^1958-05-17 14:}  && works correctly
? {^1958-05-17, 14}  && also works
```

See Also CToT(), CToD(), Date(), DateTime(), Set Commands, StrictDateEntry

Set SysFormats, Set("SysFormats")

This command yields the control of the date and time formats from the developer to the end user, a goal we find laudable.

Usage

```
SET SYSFORMATS ON | OFF
cOnOrOff   = SET( "SYSFORMATS" )
```

We think it's a good idea to let users choose the settings with which they are most comfortable. We should preserve their window positions, respect their color settings, and work with the screen resolution as configured. Set SysFormats has that attitude as well, yielding control of the date, currency, time and numeric formats to the Regional applet in the Windows Control Panel.

Help states that the Windows settings can be overridden by issuing the associated SET commands. It's not as simple as that. When SET SYSFORMATS is set ON, three of the settings get weird. MARK is explicitly set, even if it's the same as the underlying format. The display of CENTURY is also determined by the Control Panel settings and not properly reflected in SET("CENTURY"). SET HOURS is similarly overridden by the Control Panel setting and VFP's settings ignored. SETting CENTURY TO and ROLLOVER clauses, on the other hand, are properly respected. Most of the other SET commands affected by this command—CURRENCY, DATE, DECIMALS, POINT and the undocumented SEPARATOR—seem to behave in a more rational manner: the Control Panel sets them, the SET() function reflects the setting, and VFP's SET command is capable of overriding them.

But it's very challenging to work in a system where you cannot determine the current settings. Generic date-parsing routines will have to be revised to more carefully manipulate the date setting, not to depend on switching and restoring SET DATE. (Hint: If the setting of SYSFORMATS is ON and the DATE is SET to SHORT, you need to preserve and restore SET MARK TO and/or turn on and off SYSFORMATS to parse the date.) Routines to automatically size a text box to fit the date cannot depend on SET("CENTURY"). A routine that sets data session-scoped commands (as all of these are) to the default data session settings cannot always determine what these commands are set to. This command is a good idea; we'll be pleased when it is fully implemented.

Example

```
SET SYSFORMATS ON
* IN THE CONTROL PANEL, SET THE SHORT DATE TO 'M/d/yy'
SET CENTURY ON
? SET("CENTURY")  && "ON"
? DATE()  && Yields a date in MM/DD/YY format.
```

See Also Set Century, Set Date, Set Hour, Set Mark, Set Seconds

Set SysMenu

This command (actually, it's more like a collection of commands) lets you make changes to the system menu. There are a surprising number of alternatives.

Usage

```
SET SYSMENU ON | OFF | AUTOMATIC
SET SYSMENU TO [ PadList | PopupList | DEFAULT ]
               [ SAVE | NOSAVE ]
```

We've divided the command into two parts. ON and OFF are pretty much obsolete in a Windows application—they work, but you wouldn't want to use them. Just leave SYSMENU set to AUTOMATIC.

SET SYSMENU TO has some interesting things going on. The setting we use the most is DEFAULT to restore the regular menu when we've changed it somehow. Any app that runs in the interactive version of VFP and installs its own menu should be sure to SET SYSMENU TO DEFAULT on the way out.

You can also specify that the menu should be composed of specific system pads or popups. You can look up the names of system pads and popups in Help or by parsing SYS(2013). SET SYSMENU TO by itself empties the menu. From the Command Window, it's pretty funny though, because no sooner have you removed everything than the Format menu pops up, because it's always available when you're in an editing window (like the Command Window).

Perhaps you have certain items you always add to the menu and/or others you always remove. It gets pretty tedious having to fiddle every time you SET SYSMENU TO DEFAULT. So don't. Instead, set up the menu the way you want it, then issue SET SYSMENU SAVE. From then on, SET SYSMENU TO DEFAULT restores the menu the way you modified it, not the bare-bones VFP menu.

Tired of your changed menu? SET SYSMENU NOSAVE and you're back to basics. One warning: In the professional edition of VFP 3, if you use the default Config.FPW, which calls VFPStart.PRG, VFP adds the Class Browser to the Tools menu on the way in. SET SYSMENU NOSAVE removes that bar. No such add-ins exist with VFP 6.

Example

```
* Generated menus begin with:
SET SYSMENU TO
SET SYSMENU AUTOMATIC
```

See Also Menus, Sys(1500), Sys(2013)

Set Talk, Set("Talk"), Sys(103), Set Odometer, Set("Odometer")

These commands control the display of messages from various record-processing commands.

Usage

```
SET TALK ON | OFF
SET TALK WINDOW [ WindowName ] | NOWINDOW
cOnOrOff = SET( "TALK" )
cNoWindow = SET( "TALK", 1 )
cOnOrOff = SYS( 103 )
```

```
SET ODOMETER TO [ nRecords ]
nRecords = SET( "ODOMETER" )
```

A whole bunch of commands that can process bunches of records (like REPLACE, DELETE, COUNT, and so forth) provide feedback by showing how many records they've processed. When you're working interactively, this feedback is a big help. In applications, it can provide a very basic kind of "user pacifier." However, other feedback (like the record number a LOCATE lands on) is never welcome in an application. All of this output is controlled by SET TALK. Normally, you'll turn it OFF in an application, though you might turn it on briefly to keep the user from rebooting while performing a long process. (Of course, an attractive progress bar is a much better choice and there are plenty of ActiveX progress bars to choose from.)

The second form of SET TALK specifies where the feedback appears. By default, it appears in the Windows-style status bar. If you use WINDOW and specify a defined window, it works as long as you remember to ACTIVATE the window. The other two forms, though, SET TALK WINDOW and SET TALK NOWINDOW, only make sense if you turn off the Windows-style status bar. Then, WINDOW puts the talk in a WAIT WINDOW and NOWINDOW sends it to the main FoxPro window.

When TALK is on, if you're dealing with enough records and your machine is slow or you watch carefully, you can see the number of records processed accumulating. By default, FoxPro counts by hundreds. SET ODOMETER controls that setting. Set it to a higher number and there's less frequent output; set it lower and you get updated more often. In Windows, where screen updates are much slower than record processing, it pays to set ODOMETER as high as you can stand it, if you're going to keep TALK on. SET ODOMETER TO without a number resets it to the default.

Example

```
SET ODOMETER TO 500
SET TALK ON
```

See Also Set, Set Notify, Set Status Bar

Set TextMerge, Set("TextMerge"), \, \\, _PreText, _Text, Set TextMerge Delimiters

Textmerge is a combination of several of FoxPro's best features—it creates low-level file output, performs runtime evaluation and eases formatting of different types of data. \ and \\ are the textmerge equivalents of ? and ??, outputting to the destination specified by SET TEXTMERGE TO, rather than SET DEVICE TO.

Usage

```
SET TEXTMERGE [ ON | OFF ] |
          [ TO FileName [ ADDITIVE ] ]
          [ WINDOW WindowName ]
          [ SHOW | NOSHOW ]
cOnOrOff = SET( "TEXTMERGE" )
```

Here's the deal. When you issue the command SET TEXTMERGE TO Filename, a low-level file channel is opened and the file Filename is opened or created. The low-level file handle is stored in the system memory variable _TEXT. Output created with the single or double backslash (\ or \\) is echoed to the file with \ issuing a carriage return before outputting the remainder of the line, and \\ issuing its characters immediately following the text that had been output before. "Big deal," you say. "I can do the same thing with SET ALTERNATE or SET PRINTER." Yes, BUT! Textmerge really shines when TEXTMERGE is set ON.

SET TEXTMERGE ON tells FoxPro to examine each line of output for expressions encased in textmerge delimiters. If these are found, the expression within delimiters is evaluated, and the result of that expression is output. Still not impressed? Here's the key: the result of the expressions are converted to text automatically—dates, numerics, datetimes, whatever. To output a line containing a number, date, datetime and page number, you would have to convert each one, as in:

```
?  LTRIM(STR(nNumber,4)) + space(6) + ;
   DTOC(Date()) + SPACE(7) + ;
   TTOC(DateTime()) + SPACE(4) + ;
   "Page #" + ltrim(_PAGENO)
```

In a textmerge document, you would just say:

```
\<<nNumber>>        <<Date()>>        <<Datetime()>>     Page # <<_PAGENO>>
```

Now which would you prefer to have to decode and maintain six months after you wrote it?

SET TEXTMERGE is different from SET ALTERNATE or SET PRINT in that you can both SET TEXTMERGE TO and ON in a single line. For ease of maintenance, we advise you to splurge on the two lines of code to SET TEXTMERGE TO and ON.

Unlike the command to SET TEXTMERGE ON and SET TEXTMERGE TO, you MUST write two separate lines of code to SET TEXTMERGE OFF and SET TEXTMERGE TO, so that's an even a better reason to have two matching pairs of commands.

And textmerge is *fast!* Ted recently wrote some processing code to read through 800 HTML documents, parse the contents, and generate an HTML Help index in SiteMap format. Processing all of the files took eight seconds! One key factor was to set NOSHOW. With the text scrolling past on the screen, it took eight *minutes* for the same process.

The remaining optional clauses are pretty straightforward. ADDITIVE specifies that output is appended to the end of an existing file. WINDOW WindowName allows you to specify an output window where the echoed textmerge text should appear. We recommend you always specify a window if you want the output echoed, for two reasons. First, in Visual FoxPro 5 and greater, it's possible to release the main FoxPro window and run your application as a top-level form. In that case, your output might be lost. Secondly, it's been our experience that Windows seems to slow down when outputting scrolling text to the screen or a window not on top. If you create a specific window for your textmerge, you can force it to be WONTOP() for the operation.

SHOW | NOSHOW specifies whether text output to the merge file should also be echoed to the screen or optional window.

The help file claims that SHOW is the default—that's true the first time SET TEXTMERGE is issued. After that, the default appears to be the last setting used—that is, if NOSHOW was issued with the previous command, text will not be echoed unless SHOW is explicitly specified. So this isn't really a "default" behavior, it's more like a global SET behavior. Always specify SHOW or NOSHOW and you won't have a problem.

Rather than using SET TEXTMERGE TO a particular file, we suggest you use FCREATE() or FOPEN() to access the file. Why? If SAFETY is ON, SET TEXTMERGE generates a confirmation dialog to overwrite the file. Any number of errors can prevent the file from being created—improper filenames, bad drive designator, lack of rights—but FCREATE() and FOPEN() allow you to handle the errors using the simpler low-level error handler FERROR(), rather than the massive CASE statement needed to process all of FoxPro's possible file errors, or dropping though to your global error handler. If the low-level function was successful, you can set _TEXT to the file handle returned from these low-level file functions.

There are other neat commands to use with text merging. TEXT...ENDTEXT allows you to include a block of text right in your program; it obeys the settings of _PRETEXT and evaluates any expressions within delimiters.

Example

```
* The *best* examples of textmerge are available in your main
* Visual FoxPro directory - check out GENMENU.PRG and others
* But here's something for you to try
LOCAL lcOldPreText

* SET TEXTMERGE ON TO textmerg.txt NOSHOW  && don't do this!
SET TEXTMERGE TO textmerg.txt
SET TEXTMERGE ON NOSHOW

\Generated at <<DATE()>> <<TIME()>>
\
```

```
TEXT
This is a block of text with
no comments or anything before
it
ENDTEXT
\
\Now we add a pretext
\
lcOldPreText = _PRETEXT
_PRETEXT = "*"+CHR(09)
TEXT
Four score and seven years ago,
our forefathers (and mothers) brought
forth upon this continent a new nation,
ENDTEXT
_PRETEXT = lcOldPreText
\
\ And delimiters are evaluated within TEXT...ENDTEXT
\
TEXT
Today is <<DATE()>> and the time is <<TIME()>>
ENDTEXT
SET TEXTMERGE OFF
SET TEXTMERGE TO
MODI FILE textmerg.txt
```

Usage

```
_PRETEXT = cTextToPrecede
cTextToPrecede = _PRETEXT
_TEXT = nHandle
nHandle = _TEXT
```

_PRETEXT is not a system-generated excuse like "I just happened to be in the neighborhood," but a system memory variable which holds a character expression. This expression is inserted at the beginning of each line of text generated by the textmerge commands. Set _PRETEXT to "*" to comment a block of code, or to a set of tabs to indent a block.

_TEXT is a built-in FoxPro system memory variable. It contains the low-level file handle of the destination of textmerged output. Set _TEXT to –1 (negative one) to temporarily shut off output to the designated file. Since _TEXT stores the number of a low-level file handle opened for output, switching _TEXT programmatically allows you to switch output back and forth between several destinations, a trick the FoxPro 2.x screen generator used to separate startup and cleanup code.

Example

```
_PRETEXT = "*" + CHR(9)   && comment and indent merged text
SET TEXTMERGE TO D:\TEXTMERG.TXT
? _TEXT  && displays the opened file handle
```

Usage

```
SET TEXTMERGE DELIMITERS TO [ cLeftExp [, cRightExp ] ]
cAllDelimiters = SET( "TEXTMERGE", 1 )
```

Delimiters specified with this command tell FoxPro what to look for when outputting a line with the textmerge commands \, \\ or TEXT. Expressions contained within the delimiters are evaluated when TEXTMERGE is SET ON. If no delimiters are specified, they default to << and >>, respectively. If a single character expression is specified, it's used for both the left and right delimiters. Avoid using those single characters already used by other FoxPro functions—%, &, $, *, (, or). Colons, used singly or doubly, are probably a safe bet, as long as you don't use the scope resolution operator in the code. It's best to leave the delimiters as is, unless you need to output the << or >> characters themselves. Each delimiter expression can be either one or two characters in length.

This means that you can't really parse the return value of the SET() function and be sure where the first delimiter ends and the second begins—see the second example below. This means a "black box" routine cannot mess with these values. A return of LEN(SET("TEXT",1)) = 3 means you're doomed. It would be better if this SET() function, like most of them, returned the explicit string that we could use to SET TEXTMERGE DELIMITERS TO &OurString, and leave the parsing to us. Our advice: don't do this. Leave the delimiters as they are, or if you must change them, change them to something simple like a matched pair of single or double curly braces or something.

Example

```
SET TEXTMERGE DELIMITERS TO "::", "::"

SET TEXTMERGE DELIMITERS TO "@~","@"
? SET("TEXTMERGE",1)  && returns "@~@" - but which is which?
```

See Also FError(), Low-Level File Functions, Set Alternate, Set Printer, Text

Set Topic, Set Topic ID See Help.

Set Trap See Access().

Set TrBetween See Set Debug.

Set TypeAhead, Set("TypeAhead")

SET TYPEAHEAD determines the maximum number of characters Visual FoxPro can capture and hold for the next input event.

Usage

```
SET TYPEAHEAD to nKeyStrokes
nKeyStrokes = SET("TYPEAHEAD")
```

Parameter	Value	Meaning
nKeyStrokes	Numeric	How many characters Visual FoxPro will buffer.

Legitimate values to supply range from zero to 32,000, according to the documentation. The default is 20, enough for all but the fastest typists. We haven't tried to test the upper range, and can't imagine why you'd want to hold on to that many. Setting TYPEAHEAD to 0 means that Visual FoxPro doesn't preserve any characters for the next input event, effectively disabling the INKEY() function and ON KEY commands. Functions and methods only available within an input event (such as the KeyPress event) are not affected, since the READ EVENTS in effect immediately picks up any key pressed.

Example

```
SET TYPEAHEAD TO 0 && clear the buffer
SET TYPEAHEAD TO 100 && for real fast typists!
```

See Also Clear TypeAhead, InKey(), On KEY

Set UdfParms See LParameters.

Set Unique See Index.

Set View See Create View.

Set Volume, Sys(2027)

These commands were meant to help you handle the differences between directory (folder) conventions on PCs and Macs. Of course, with Visual FoxPro/Mac available only in Version 3, this isn't much of an issue anymore. In fact, these two aren't even included in the VFP 5 or VFP 6 Help files.

SET VOLUME lets you assign a DOS-type drive name to a Mac volume or folder. SYS(2027) is supposed to convert from DOS notation to Mac notation, but it doesn't.

Usage

```
SET VOLUME DriveName TO FolderName
cMacPath = SYS( 2027, cDOSPath)
```

SET VOLUME is really pretty cool. It works in the Windows versions of VFP, too, not just on the Mac. You can use it to assign a shorthand drive name to a particular directory, then refer to that directory using the drive name. We don't think we'd do this in an application, but it is pretty neat while you're developing. Our tests indicate some problems in network situations, but everything seems to work properly on local drives. On the Mac, it's an essential part of a cross-platform strategy.

There's no way in Visual FoxPro to see what mappings you've created, unfortunately. SET("VOLUME") doesn't work. Help says the mappings show up in DISPLAY STATUS, but they don't.

SYS(2027) doesn't work in Visual FoxPro. Hand it a path and you get back the same path in the same old DOS notation.

Example

```
SET VOLUME q: TO _SAMPLES+"Tastrade"
MODI PROJ Q:TasTrade
```

See Also Set Default, Set Path

Set Window Of Memo See Modify Memo.

Set XcmdFile See On AplAbout.

SetAll

This is a very cool method. It lets you change the same property of many objects at once. Of course, there are a few rules.

Usage

```
oContainer.SetAll( cProperty, uValue [, cClass ] )
```

Parameter	Value	Meaning
cProperty	Character	The property to be changed.
uValue	Expression	The new value.
cClass	Character	Restrict the change only to members of the specified class.

All the container classes have SetAll. Use it to make some change to all the objects contained within the container or, if you want, only to those members that are based on a particular class. For example, you can change the Enabled status of every control on a form or you could change only the command buttons.

SetAll drills down within the container to the very lowest level. For example, calling a grid's SetAll method affects every control in the grid, as well as the headers and columns (unless you restrict it to a particular class). If the grid contains another grid, the columns, headers and controls in that grid are affected, too.

Note that the object itself is not affected by the SetAll call. That is, if you use SetAll to change the BackColor of controls on a form, the form's BackColor doesn't change.

Unfortunately, SetAll isn't as cool as it could be. Although you can specify that all objects of a particular class are changed, you can't specify that all objects that have a particular class somewhere in their class hierarchy or even all objects based on a particular base class should be affected. Since we rarely use objects based on the VFP base classes, and work with an assortment of classes derived from each base class, using SetAll to make a change to all the buttons or all the combos on a form is harder than we'd like.

Check out "Builders and Wizards (and Bears, Oh My!)" on the CD for more on this method.

Example

```
* Enable all the text boxes on a form from within a method
* of the form
This.SetAll("Enabled",.T.,"TextBox")
```

See Also Controls

SetData See ClearData.

SetFldState() See GetFldState().

SetFocus

This method is Visual FoxPro's answer to _CUROBJ. It allows you to set the focus to any control.

Usage `oObject.SetFocus()`

SetFocus works kind of inside out from the way _CUROBJ does its stuff. With _CUROBJ, you assign a value that leads to the object you want. In the new, OOP paradigm, you call the SetFocus method for the object you want to receive focus.

SetFocus can't be called from some methods. The ones you're likely to run into are When and Valid. Make your calls from GotFocus and LostFocus instead.

Example

```
* In a form to edit Employee records,
* the Click method for the "Edit" button might:
ThisForm.First_Name.SetFocus()
```

See Also GotFocus, LostFocus, _CurObj

SetFormat See GetFormat.

SetMain See MainFile.

SetVar See DoCmd.

SetViewPort

This form method lets you decide which part of a form is visible.

Usage `frmForm.SetViewPort( nNewViewPortLeft, nNewViewPortTop )`

In a form with scrollbars, only a portion of the form is visible at any time. The ViewPortLeft and ViewPortTop properties indicate what portion it is. This method sets those properties (which are read-only).

If the values you pass are too big, the form scrolls as far to the right or the bottom as possible. "Too big" here means that listening to you would result in showing an area beyond the form's boundaries. The key point is that you can't assume that ViewPortLeft and ViewPortTop always contain the values you passed, even before the user gets an opportunity to scroll.

This method accepts negative parameters. It shouldn't, since the form begins at 0,0. It scrolls the appropriate amount, revealing empty negative space. At least some of the time, the refresh from such a call is incomplete and, in some cases, clicking on the form moves things back to where they were. All in all, an ugly mess. Don't do this!

Example

```
* Force the user to look at the upper-left corner
ThisForm.SetViewPort(0,0)
```

See Also Form, ViewPortLeft, ViewPortTop

Shape

No, this isn't fitness advice. It's a full-fledged control that displays rectangles, circles and shapes in between and lets them react when acted upon. Shapes can give regions of your interfaces "hotspots," like the invisible buttons of FoxPro 2.x but with the fine control of a Visual FoxPro object.

Property	Value	Purpose
BackStyle	Numeric	Determines whether you can see through the shape.
BorderColor	Numeric	The color of the shape's border.
BorderStyle	Numeric	Specifies the type of border used for the shape. Options include dotted, dashed and so forth. Ignored unless BorderWidth is 1.
BorderWidth	Numeric	The width in pixels of the shape's border.
Curvature	Numeric	Determines the actual shape of the object. Set it to 0 for a rectangle, 99 for a circle or anything in between for various rounded rectangles.
DrawMode	Numeric	Determines how the shape's colors interact with the colors of the objects beneath it.
FillColor	Numeric	The color of the shape's interior.
FillStyle	Numeric	The type of pattern used for the interior of the shape. Various types of lines and "hatching" are available.

Shapes respond to the usual events like Click and DragOver, and have the run-of-the-mill methods like Drag and Move. This is a big improvement over FoxPro 2.x where shapes (and lines) were just so much dead space on your form. The ability to manipulate properties at runtime make these so much better than what you can make with the form's drawing methods. Consider a shape with Transparent BackStyle and no border for invisible regions you can place over controls (using ZOrder) to catch mouse movements without having to write the code for every control; Ted used this trick to make a read-only, unclickable grid.

Example

```
* Here's the red circle that's used in so many examples of OOP.
* It responds when clicked.
DEFINE CLASS RedCircle AS Shape

   Curvature = 90
   BorderColor = RGB(255,0,0)
   FillColor = RGB(255,0,0)
   FillStyle = 0

   PROCEDURE Click
      WAIT WINDOW "Who's that knocking on my door?"
```

```
    ENDPROC
ENDDEFINE
```

See Also BackStyle, BorderColor, BorderStyle, BorderWidth, Box, Circle, Curvature, DrawMode, FillColor, FillStyle, Line

_Shell

_SHELL can be used to replace the command window with a different program shell.

Usage

```
_SHELL = cCommand
cCommand = _SHELL
```

Some users, we've observed, are just not safe with the interactive development version of Visual FoxPro. (Some of them aren't safe with computers at all, but that's another topic...) To think about one of these folks getting access to the Command Window makes us wonder why we didn't get into some safe profession, like bungee testing. If the user absolutely, positively has to have the development version of Visual FoxPro, you can use the _SHELL variable to always run your program instead of dropping back to the Command Window. You can set this in your configuration file with the equivalent _SHELL command.

Each time _SHELL is invoked, it clears the _SHELL setting, so you'll need to reset it in your application.

If you think your users are absolutely, completely safe with your application while they run the interactive version, think about these three little letters: Z...A...P...

Example

```
_SHELL = "DO SAFEMENU.PRG"
```

See Also _Assist, RUN

Show, Hide

These methods both activate and deactivate forms, formsets and toolbars, and make them visible or invisible. Show also lets you override a form's WindowType property and indicate whether a form is modal or modeless.

Usage

```
oObject.Show( [ nWindowType ] )
oObject.Hide
```

Parameter	Value	Meaning
nWindowType	1	Make the form or formset modal.
	2	Make the form or formset modeless.

Showing an object does two things: It makes it visible and it activates it, firing the Activate event along the way. Applying Hide to the object makes it invisible and deactivates it, firing Deactivate. Changing the Visible property has the same effect—some of the time. Or, to be more accurate, changing the Visible property has the same effect, if it's done from a method of the form. But if Visible already had the value you assign, Activate or Deactivate doesn't fire. That is, if Visible was .T. and you set it to .F., the object becomes invisible and Deactivate fires. But if Visible is .T. and you set it to .T., nothing happens at all. In addition, Activate and Deactivate don't fire when you change Visible from another object, so the active status of the form doesn't change.

Why are the values for nWindowType different from the ones for the WindowType property? Why is the sky blue? Why is the Pope Catholic? Just because.

nWindowType is ignored for toolbars, since there's no such thing as a modal toolbar.

Making a form modal means that no other form can gain focus until you dispatch the one you're working on. Similarly, with a modal formset, only the forms in the set are accessible—other forms won't respond. Toolbars aren't affected, though—you can access them even with a modal form or formset around. Frankly, we think it's kind of odd, since much of the menu is disabled by a modal form and we tend to think of a toolbar as mouse shortcuts for the menu.

Example

```
oForm = CreateObject("Form")
oForm.Show()

* Clicking a particular button might hide one form in a formset
* The button's Click would contain:
ThisFormSet.frmMysterious.Hide()
```

See Also Activate, Deactivate, Visible, WindowType

Show Get, Show Object

These two commands were essential in the READ-oriented world of 2.x. They refresh the display of individual controls. SHOW GET references the control by the name of the underlying variable, while SHOW OBJECT refers to it by its unique object number.

SHOW GET and SHOW OBJECT also let you change the caption of a button or check box, enable or disable a control, and change a control's colors.

In Visual FoxPro, these commands are only relevant for old code. In new code, use Visual FoxPro's controls and manipulate their properties directly. To update the display of a control, use its Refresh method.

See Also @ Commands, BackColor, Caption, Enabled, ForeColor, Refresh

Show Gets, Sys(2016)

SHOW GETS refreshes the display of all the controls in a READ-style screen, as well as executing the READ's SHOW clause. This was the key mechanism for updating the display in FoxPro 2.x. SYS(2016) returns the name of the last window named in a SHOW GETS command—we never found a use for this function in 2.x (though GENSCRN, the screen-generation program, generated code that used it.)

Of course, in Visual FoxPro, SHOW GETS is obsolete. Use the form's Refresh method instead. Initiating the Refresh method of a form or container also fires the Refresh methods of any contained controls. SHOW GETS also lets you enable or disable entire screens or change their colors. You can simply manipulate a form's properties to do these.

See Also @ Commands, BackColor, ColorScheme, Enabled, ForeColor, Refresh, Show

Show Menu See Hide Menu.

Show Object See Show Get.

Show Popup See Hide Menu.

Show Window See Define Window.

ShowDoc, HideDoc

These events fire when an ActiveDoc is first displayed, and when the user navigates away from it, respectively.

Usage

```
PROCEDURE acdActiveDoc.ShowDoc
PROCEDURE acdActiveDoc.HideDoc
```

As far as we can tell, using IE 4, ShowDoc always fires after Init for the ActiveDoc. We suspect that in IE 3, with its cache that lets you go back to an ActiveDoc application after navigating elsewhere, ShowDoc also fires when you do, so it's sort of an application-level Activate.

HideDoc fires when you navigate away from the ActiveDoc in the Browser. Since you can arrange to have an independent VFP window open up at that point to host the application, that means you can't assume that HideDoc firing indicates that the ActiveDoc is about to be destroyed. And, in fact, you can't even assume that HideDoc always fires. If you run an active doc application in VFP rather than a browser, HideDoc never fires. (This is even odder than it sounds because ShowDoc fires, regardless of the host.)

We suspect that ShowDoc isn't really terribly useful, except when you're running in IE 3 or another browser with a cache. In that case, it lets you know when you've returned to the application from some other page. We can't think of many reasons to use HideDoc, either. The one time we might want to put some code in it, when the app is jumping from the browser to VFP, we can just as well use ContainerRelease. However, we'll never turn up our noses at "extra" events. Sooner or later, there's a time when they come in handy.

Example

```
PROCEDURE ShowDoc
WAIT WINDOW "ShowDoc is firing"
ENDPROC

PROCEDURE HideDoc
WAIT WINDOW "HideDoc is firing"
ENDPROC
```

See Also ActiveDoc, ContainerRelease, Destroy, Init

ShowTips, ToolTipText

We really love tooltips—they're the little messages that appear when you pause over a toolbar button in almost any Windows app that's been released in the last few years. (We especially love them because we often can't tell what a lot of the icons are meant to be.) On the other hand, occasionally they get in our way. So, we think this pair of properties is really cool. ToolTipText lets you specify tooltips for pretty much any native control. ShowTips determines, on a form-wide basis, whether the messages show.

Usage

```
oObject.ShowTips = lShowTips
lShowTips = oObject.ShowTips
oObject.ToolTipText = cToolTipMessage
cToolTipMessage = oObject.ToolTipText
```

All the native controls that accept focus plus shapes let you specify tooltips. However, when you embed a control in a grid, the only time the tooltip shows is when that control actually has focus and you pause the mouse there. Since we're not really convinced you'd ever want tooltips in a grid (see below), we don't think this is too much of a limitation.

Tooltips are limited to 50 characters in VFP 3 and 127 in later versions. In VFP 3, you can specify a longer tip, but nothing at all shows up for that control. In VFP 5 and VFP 6, you can't specify a tip that's too long—you get an error message. The length restriction, especially at 127, isn't so limiting—these are just meant to be quick reminders of a control's functions, not full-blown help. If you want to specify something longer than that, consider using StatusBarText, which lets you put a message in the status bar when the control has focus, or WhatsThisHelp. One hundred and twenty-seven characters in a little yellow ribbon across the screen is unreadable, annoying and amateurish.

Only forms and toolbars have the ShowTips property because they're an all-or-nothing proposition. The default is different, though, for the two types of objects. By default, forms have tooltips off while toolbars have them on.

The defaults pretty much match our view of when to use tooltips. Controls in toolbars should have them. Most items in forms should not. One way to look at it is that "tools" should have tooltips. Another view, and the one we feel most comfortable with, is that controls that present only an icon to the world should have tooltips. Textual controls like an "OK" button don't need a tooltip—if "OK" isn't clear enough, use a different prompt.

Every rule has its exception, and this one does, too. While it is not difficult to design forms with separate toolbars, there are still a number of developers who prefer their tools to be embedded in their forms. Witness the "Next," "Previous," "Top" button bar embedded in the standard Form Wizard-generated form, or the control panel of buttons at the top of the Class Browser. Both have ShowTips on by default (actually, the Wizard form does that only if you choose picture buttons), and we cannot argue with that choice. As always, with user interface issues, establish a standard for your applications and stick with it.

Don't confuse tooltips with the little tips that pop up when you can't see all of an entry in a list box. Those are ItemTips.

Example

```
ThisForm.cmdQuit.ToolTipText = "Exit this application"
ThisForm.cmdSave.ToolTipText = "Save current record"
ThisForm.ShowTips = .T.
```

See Also ItemTips, StatusBarText, WhatsThisHelp

ShowWhatsThis See WhatsThisButton.

ShowWindow

This property, added in VFP 5, determines who owns a form or toolbar. Together with the Desktop property, it also determines where the form or toolbar appears.

Usage `nWindowOwner = oObject.ShowWindow`

Parameter	Value	Meaning
nWindowOwner	0	The main VFP window (_SCREEN) owns the form or toolbar.
	1	A VFP-created top-level form owns the form or toolbar.
	2	Windows owns the form—it's a top-level form.

Why does it matter who owns a form or toolbar? There are a couple of reasons, but the biggest is professionalism. Having your whole application contained in the main VFP window just doesn't look very good. Even if you set Desktop to .T. so the window can go anywhere, it still belongs to the main VFP window—when you minimize VFP, it goes along. That's not the way serious applications work. ShowWindow lets you create an independent window for your application and have it appear in the taskbar and behave independently from the main VFP window.

So the next question is, to quote George Carlin, "Why are there three?" The answer is that, once you've created your top-level form to host your application, you may want to have it contain other windows (children). Even if you don't, you probably do want it to own a toolbar. The forms and toolbars that belong to a top-level form need ShowWindow set to 1.

Setting ShowWindow to 1 only partly determines where a child form appears. If Desktop is .T., the child form belongs to the top-level form, but can appear anywhere. However, when you minimize the top-level form, the child form goes with it, even if it's physically elsewhere.

If you create a toolbar as a child of a top-level form too early in the form's existence, the toolbar is confined to the main VFP window rather than the top-level form. Load and Init are definitely too early. Activate is late enough—just remember to add some code so you only create the toolbar once.

Example

```
IF This.ShowWindow = 2
   This.Caption = "You don't own me!"
ENDIF
```

See Also AlwaysOnBottom, AlwaysOnTop, Desktop, MDIForm, _Screen

Sign() See Abs().

Sin() See Cos().

Sizable

Sizable allows you to resize an OLEBoundControl, OLEControl or toolbar.

Usage
```
oObject.Sizable = lResizable
lResizable = oObject.Sizable
```

When Sizable is set true, a toolbar can be resized by clicking and dragging the mouse over any of its borders.

Even if a toolbar's Sizable property is .F., the mouse pointer still displays double-headed arrows when floated over the borders. Even more difficult to deal with is that, while the user cannot reshape a toolbar, docking (particularly docking on the vertical edges) reshapes the toolbar. Since this is bound to frustrate your users to no end, we recommend you leave this as the default .T.

For an OLE object, Sizable determines if the object within the control can be resized. When the object is activated, by double-clicking or using the DoVerb method, the border around the object shows drag handles on the corners and centers of each border. A user can then resize an OLE object to obscure other controls on the form, but only until the control loses the focus—then the OLE object is cropped to fit within its original size. Similarly, shrinking the OLE object does not change the active, clickable area of the OLE control. However, if AutoSize is also true, the entire control resizes to accommodate the resized OLE object. We can't imagine a situation where we would want the end user to have that much control. Sizable is a good feature, but not when it's combined with AutoSize.

Example
```
oForm.OLEControl.Sizable = .T.
```

See Also AutoSize, Dock(), DoVerb, OLEBoundControl, OLEControl, Toolbar, UnDock()

Size Popup See Hide Menu.

Size Window, Zoom Window

These commands change the size of a window from maximum to minimum or any specified size in between. This is the old FoxPro 2.x way of changing window size. We recommend you use a form's Height, Width and WindowState properties instead.

Usage
```
SIZE WINDOW WindowName TO nNewHeight, nNewWidth
                     | BY nRowIncrement, nColumnIncrement
ZOOM WINDOW WindowName
        MIN [ AUTO ] | MAX | NORM
        [ AT | FROM nTopRow, nLeftColumn
        [ SIZE nNewHeight, nNewWidth
          | TO nBottomRow, nRightColumn ] ]
```

The SIZE WINDOW command lets you resize any user-defined window or resizable FoxPro system window either to specified proportions or by specified increments. This command doesn't provide any functionality you can't get using ZOOM WINDOW NORM.

MIN minimizes the form. The AUTO keyword is only applicable to the DOS version of FoxPro 2.x, where it docks the form. MAX maximizes the form, within the limits of its parent window, or the Visual FoxPro application window. NORM is used for most of the rest of the keywords shown above, because it doesn't make much sense to try to position a zoomed form—it takes up the whole window. Similarly, a minimized form parks itself on the bottom of the window, regardless of where you tell it to be placed.

Some form windows are restricted in size by the MaxHeight and MaxWidth properties, as well as their counterparts MinHeight and MinWidth. Typically, no error is generated, but the window fails to be resized if these bounds are exceeded. For this reason, we recommend using the WindowState property to manipulate the windows rather than using this antiquated command.

ZOOM WINDOW MIN and MAX fire the form's Resize event and Refresh method, but ZOOM WINDOW NORM does not. This is another reason, in your authors' opinion, to manipulate WindowState rather than use this command.

Example

```
ACTIVATE WINDOW CALENDAR  && Open the calendar/diary
ZOOM WINDOW CALENDAR ;
  NORM AT 3,3 ;
  SIZE 0,100  && Widen the diary
```

See Also Height, Left, MaxHeight, MaxWidth, MinHeight, MinWidth, Resize, Top, Width, WindowState

SizeBox, ZoomBox

You'll have to use Visual FoxPro for the Mac for these properties (added in version 3.0b) to do something useful. There, they control whether a form has the Mac-style controls for resizing and zooming windows. They're ignored in the Windows version.

See Also BorderStyle, MaxButton, MinButton, Sizable, WindowState

Skip See Go.

SkpBar(), SkpPad() See Set Skip Of.

Sort

This is an oldie-but-baddie command. Back in the days before indexes, it was an awfully important command, but it's been superseded so many times, we've lost count.

SORT makes a copy of a table, physically ordering the records in the new table according to specified criteria. SORT is a resource hog—it can require as much as three times the disk space occupied by the table to do the copying. Because you can do the same thing with COPY TO and an index, or SELECT-SQL, there's not much reason to use SORT.

In Visual FoxPro, SORT does have one pair of cool new clauses (FIELDS LIKE, FIELDS EXCEPT), but COPY TO has them, too. (Actually, FIELDS LIKE and FIELDS EXCEPT were added in FoxPro 2.6, but Microsoft didn't bother to tell very many people about them, then.)

Usage

```
SORT TO cTable
        ON uFieldName1 [ / A | D ] [ /C ]
        [, uFieldName2 [ /A | D ] [ /C ]  [ , ... ] ]
        [ ASCENDING | DESCENDING ]
        [ Scope ]
        [ FOR lForExpression ]
        [ WHILE lWhileExpression ]
        [ FIELDS cFieldList | LIKE cInclude | EXCEPT cExclude ]
        [ NOOPTIMIZE ]
```

We believe SORT has no place in any application, so we're not going to review all the clauses in detail. In brief, here's what SORT does.

Those records of the table open in the current work area that meet the Scope, FOR and WHILE clauses are copied to cTable. Only those fields either listed in cFieldList or included by the FIELDS LIKE and FIELDS EXCEPT clauses are copied.

The new table is ordered based on the ON clause. Records are sorted first by uFieldName1. Where that field is identical, records are sorted on uFieldName2. Where both are identical, the next listed field is used, and so forth. For each sort field, you specify independently where it should be applied in ascending (/A) or descending (/D) order, and whether the sort is case-insensitive (/C). The default is ascending order and case-sensitive. Combine A or D with C behind a single slash (/AC or /DC).

The ASCENDING and DESCENDING clauses determine the sort order for fields that don't specify it explicitly.

As always, NOOPTIMIZE is mostly useless.

Example

```
USE Employee   && small enough to make this not too painful
SORT ON Last_Name /C, First_Name /C TO EmpName

* Here's a better way to do that
SELECT * FROM Employee ;
   ORDER BY Last_Name, First_Name ;
   INTO TABLE EmpName
```

See Also Copy To, Index, Select-SQL, Set Optimize

Sorted

This property determines whether the items in a combo or list box are sorted alphabetically.

Usage

```
oObject.Sorted = lSortThem
lSortThem = oObject.Sorted
```

Help says that Sorted applies only if RowSourceType is 0 or 1, meaning you're either adding the items with AddItems or providing them explicitly. What it doesn't say is that you can't even set Sorted to .T. for any other RowSourceType—you can't.

Changing Sorted changes the ListIndexes (but not the ListItemIds) of the items in the list or combo. Also, when Sorted is .T., new items are added at the correct index in the list, which means the index of other items can change.

Beware—the sort is case-sensitive (unless you SET COLLATE TO "GENERAL", which is not generally a good idea).

One interesting point here. If you set Sorted to .T., then later change it to .F., the items stay in sorted order until you do something that changes their order. This does offer the possibility of a neat trick for getting a case-insensitive sort. SET COLLATE TO "GENERAL", turn Sorted on, then SET COLLATE back to "MACHINE" where you usually want to keep it. (Just be careful not to do anything you don't mean while COLLATE is at "GENERAL".) Of course, this only works if you have a fixed list.

Example

```
lstFlavors.RowSourceType = 1  && explicit list
lstFlavors.RowSource = "Chocolate,Vanilla,Strawberry," + ;
                       "Butter Pecan,Cherry Vanilla,Coffee"
lstFlavors.Sorted = .T.
```

See Also AddItem, AddListItem, ComboBox, ListBox, ListIndex, ListItemId, RemoveItem, RemoveListItem, RowSource, RowSourceType

Soundex(), Difference()

These two functions are both for comparing character strings and they're both pretty useless. By now, they're just being dragged along into new versions for backward compatibility.

Both DIFFERENCE() and SOUNDEX() are intended to help find matches when strings might be misspelled. SOUNDEX() applies a coding scheme also called Soundex to a string and returns a four-character string consisting of a letter and three digits. The Soundex encoding is meant to give matching results for strings that are phonetically identical or nearly so. So, for example, SOUNDEX("Smith") and SOUNDEX("Schmidt") both return "S530." However, the scheme isn't really good enough to be useful in practice. Among other things, the letter returned is always the first letter of the original string, so "Knowles" and "Noles" return two different values.

DIFFERENCE() takes two strings and returns a number between 0 and 4, measuring the phonetic difference between the strings. A value of 0 means the strings are very different, while 4 means they're quite similar. Unfortunately, like SOUNDEX(), DIFFERENCE() isn't very smart. It also doesn't know about things like "kn" or that "ph" sounds like "f." We've never found a reason to use DIFFERENCE().

If you really need to match strings that might be misspelled, take a look at a terrific library for Visual FoxPro called PhDbase by Korenthal Associates. It handles "fuzzy" search, as well as quick searches of full text. That's what we use when we need those abilities.

Usage

```
cReturnValue=SOUNDEX(cString)
nReturnValue=DIFFERENCE(cString1, cString2)
```

Example

```
? SOUNDEX("Tamar")     && returns "T560"
? SOUNDEX("ted")       && returns "T300"
? DIFFERENCE("tamar","ted")    && returns 2
? DIFFERENCE("ted","teddy")    && returns 4
```

See Also Like()

Space()

This is a function that has pretty much outlived its usefulness. It returns a string composed of a specified number of blanks (CHR(32)).

Usage

```
cMyString = SPACE( nLength )
```

Before EMPTY() was added to FoxPro, to determine if a character field had any data in it, you'd compare it to SPACE(LEN(fieldname)). This was considered a forward-thinking solution since it would continue to work even if the field's size was increased. But EMPTY() performs the same test more quickly and is more readable.

The only use left for SPACE() is for initializing variables to a certain size.

Example

```
cLastName = SPACE(30)   && sets variable cLastName to 30 spaces
```

See Also Empty(), Len(), Replicate()

Sparse See CurrentControl.

SpecialEffect

This property determines whether various controls have a 3-D look. For a few, it also determines the type of 3-D.

Usage

```
oObject.SpecialEffect = nEffect
nEffect = oObject.SpecialEffect
```

The values of nEffect are different for page frames, containers and controls than for other objects with this property. Most annoying, those three baseclasses use 2 for non-3-D while everyone else uses 1 for it. Why not make that one 0 and let other values represent other possibilities?

Visual FoxPro doesn't offer a lot of choice in 3-D. Only page frames, Containers and Controls really have options, and that's only if you don't have tabs on them. For page frames, when Tabs is .F., SpecialEffect is honored and interacts with BorderWidth to raise or sink the page by different amounts. The Container and Control classes also let you create raised and sunken effects in the same way.

For most of the controls that have SpecialEffect, it primarily affects the border of the object. For example, 3-D text boxes look sunken inside their borders. For option buttons and check boxes, SpecialEffect controls the actual graphical element that represents the control (the little circle or the check box itself).

For some objects such as page frames and Containers, the illusion used to make them look sunken and raised doesn't work very well once BorderWidth gets past 2 or 3. In particular, the color used to provide the brightening for the right and bottom edges of a sunken control or the left and top edges of a raised control is the default gray back color. You can prove this by changing the appropriate BackColor and noting that the BorderWidth is what you specified. We think a couple of shades lighter would be more effective. (We also note that, in VFP 3, this actually worked better for page frames than it does in versions 5 or 6.)

Example

```
* Use a sunken page frame
This.Tabs = .F.
This.SpecialEffect = 1
This.BorderWidth = 5
```

See Also BorderColor, BorderWidth, Container, Control, Page, Pageframe, Tabs

_SpellChk **See _Beautify.**

Spinner Control

A spinner is a gadget dedicated to entering numbers. It lets you enter them directly as well as increment or decrement the current value with either the mouse or the keyboard. FoxPro 2.x had spinners, but they were really just fancy text boxes. These spinners are much better because they give you tremendous control over what's going on.

Property	Value	Purpose
Increment	Numeric	Determines the amount the value changes with a click of an arrow or pressing an arrow key.
KeyboardHighValue, KeyboardLowValue	Numeric	Determine the highest and lowest numbers that can be entered from the keyboard.
SpinnerHighValue, SpinnerLowValue	Numeric	Determine the highest and lowest numbers that can be entered by "spinning."
Text	Character	Contains the spinner value as an unformatted character string.
Event	**Purpose**	
DownClick, UpClick	Occur when the down-arrow or up-arrow is clicked or the keyboard arrows are used.	
RangeLow, RangeHigh	Occur when the spinner tries to lose focus. Each can return a value, and the spinner's value must be between those two values for it to lose focus.	

Check out Increment for an example of a spinner whose increment changes as the value changes.

Example

```
* Set up a spinner class that counts
* by 100's between 1000 and 20000
```

```
* and annoyingly beeps when you use the spinner arrows
oForm = CREATEOBJECT("Form")
oForm.AddObject("spnBigSpin", "BigSpinner")
oForm.spnBigSpin.Visible = .T.
oForm.SHOW()

DEFINE CLASS BigSpinner AS Spinner

   Value = 1000
   Increment = 100
   KeyboardLowValue = 1000
   SpinnerLowValue = 1000
   KeyboardHighValue = 20000
   SpinnerHighValue = 20000

   PROCEDURE DownClick
   ?? CHR(7)
   ENDPROC

   PROCEDURE UpClick
   ?? CHR(7)
   ENDPROC
ENDDEFINE
```

See Also DownClick, Increment, KeyboardHighValue, KeyboardLowValue, RangeHigh, RangeLow, SpinnerHighValue, SpinnerLowValue, Text, UpClick

SpinnerHighValue, SpinnerLowValue See KeyboardHighValue.

SplitBar

This property lets you decide whether the user should be allowed to split a grid into two panels. It's one of a number of properties added in version 5.0 to which our reaction was: "Of course."

Usage `lUserCanSplit = grdGrid.SplitBar`

You have to decide this one at design-time—it can't be changed on the fly. When you turn SplitBar off, the scrollbar widens to fill the black space normally allocated for splitting the grid.

We thought it would be cool to be able to partition a grid at design-time, then turn SplitBar off to prevent users from messing with our careful setup. Alas, setting SplitBar to .F. returns Partition to 0 (although it doesn't happen until you save the form). We can't quite bring ourselves to call this one a bug since we suspect it's simply outside the design of the grid. No SplitBar means no partition.

Example

```
* You might set this one in a builder based
* on user input
oGrid.SplitBars = lAllowSplit
```

See Also Panel, PanelLink, Partition

SQLCancel()

This function quits execution of a command you've passed to the server. It's relevant only when you're in asynchronous mode.

Usage `nSuccess = SQLCancel( nConnectionHandle )`

As far as we can tell, SQLCancel() always returns 1 as long as you give it a valid connection handle. It doesn't matter if there's actually something to cancel, or even if you're in asynchronous mode.

Use this function when you've started a process and realize that it's not such a good idea. We can think of a couple of handy ways to use this. For example, you might set up a timer and cancel after the specified time has elapsed. Or you might put up a message to the user indicating what's happening and including a Cancel button. If the user presses Cancel, you use SQLCancel() to kill the process.

Example

```
nHandle = SQLConnect("Northwinds")
= SQLSetProp(nHandle, "Asynchronous", .T.)
= SQLExec(nHandle, "Select * FROM Customers,Orders")
* Oh, my goodness, it has no join condition!
= SQLCancel(nHandle)
```

See Also SQLConnect(), SQLExec(), SQLPrepare(), SQLSetProp()

SQLColumns() See SQLTables().

SQLCommit(), SQLRollback()

These functions control updates to a remote server when you're working with manual transactions. They're the SQL Pass Through equivalents to END TRANSACTION and ROLLBACK.

Usage

```
nSuccess = SQLCommit( nConnectionHandle )
nSuccess = SQLRollback( nConnectionHandle )
```

By default, SQL Pass Through (see "Your Server Will Be With You in a Moment") uses automatic transaction handling, which wraps each individual update in a transaction and sends it along. You can choose to manage your own transactions by setting the connection's Transactions property to 2 (for Manual) using SQLSetProp(). If you do so, then SQLCommit() actually passes updates to the server while SQLRollback() cancels the queued updates.

Doing things this way means updating is a two-step process. TableUpdate() commits the changes locally and queues them for the server, but they don't actually get sent until you issue SQLCommit().

From our tests, it appears that SQLRollback() can leave your local cursors out of synch with the original remote data. This makes sense because you've committed the changes locally, but then reverted them at the server level. It's too late to revert them locally, but a call to Refresh() for each cursor affected seems to solve that problem.

SQLCommit() and SQLRollback() are generic ODBC calls you can use with any ODBC driver that supports them. That's good if you are working in an environment with multiple flavors of back-end servers. If, however, you're in a shop with only one server, check to see if the server can support manual transactions internally. We've found some benefits to using nothing but SQLExec() commands to control the beginning, end or rollback of transactions on the server side. This way, you can leave the connection's Transaction property set to Automatic and use it to send one-shot, atomic, transaction-wrapped updates, but also send your own "Start," "End" or "Rollback" commands as needed—a far more flexible model.

Example

```
* You can run this code from the Command Window
* to see how this stuff works.
* Our "Northwinds" datasource is
* described in "Your Server Will Be With You in a Moment"

nHandle = SQLConnect("Northwinds")
? SQLSetProp(nHandle, "Transactions", 2)
? SQLExec(nHandle, "SELECT * FROM Customers")
* make the cursor updatable
? CursorSetProp("Tables", "customers")
? CursorSetProp("KeyFieldList", "customerid")
? CursorSetProp("UpdatableFieldList", "companyname")
? CursorSetProp("SendUpdates", .t.)
? CursorSetProp("UpdateNameList", ;
                "customerid customers.customerid, ;
                companyname customers.companyname")
* Now change something
GO 4
REPLACE CompanyName WITH "Around the Horn and Back"
* Update locally
```

```
? TableUpdate()
* Go over to Access and note that the record hasn't been changed
? SQLCommit(nHandle)
* Now the table in Access should reflect the change
* Clean up
? SQLDisconnect(nHandle)
```

See Also CursorSetProp(), SQLConnect(), SQLDisconnect(), SQLExec(), SQLSetProp(), TableUpdate()

SQLConnect(), SQLDisconnect(), SQLStringConnect()

These functions are the first and last ones you'll need to use SQL Pass-Through (the client-server mode in which you send commands directly to the back end). SQLConnect() and SQLStringConnect() let you hook up with remote data via ODBC. SQLDisconnect() closes a connection opened by one of the others. Think of SQLConnect() and SQLStringConnect() as dialing a phone and SQLDisconnect() as hanging up the phone.

Usage

```
nConnectionHandle = SQLCONNECT( cDataSource [, cUserId [, cPassword ] ] )
nConnectionHandle = SQLCONNECT( [ cNamedConnection ] )
nConnectionHandle = SQLSTRINGCONNECT( [ cConnectionString ] )
```

Parameter	Value	Meaning
cDataSource	Character	The name of a data source as seen in the ODBC Administrator.
cUserId	Character	The user ID with which to log in to the server.
cPassword	Character	The password with which to log in to the server.
cNamedConnection	Character	A named connection from the current database.
	Omitted	Presents an ODBC dialog allowing the user to choose which ODBC Connection or Data Source to use.
cConnectionString	Character	A complete connection string, as needed to connect to the desired server. Specify the data source by including "dsn=cDataSource" in the string.
	Omitted	A different dialog box than the one above is presented, allowing the operator to choose among file and machine data sources.
nConnectionHandle	-1	Connection attempt failed
	Positive Number	Connection succeeded and can be accessed through nConnectionHandle.

Continuing the phone analogy, using SQLConnect() with a named connection is like pushing your speed dial button. Using SQLConnect() with a separate data source, user ID and password is like pushing all the buttons yourself. Using SQLStringConnect() is like calling the operator and giving her all the information.

If you omit the parameters, the two functions behave slightly differently. SQLConnect() brings up the "Select Connection or DataSource" dialog, letting you pick either. However, SQLStringConnect() offers the SQL Data Sources dialog, letting you choose from the existing ODBC data sources. Pressing Cancel in either dialog aborts the process, returning -1 to indicate no connection was established.

Be sure to hold on to the return value of these functions. The return value is your key to doing anything useful. All the other SQL Pass-Through functions take the connection handle as the first parameter. If you lose track of your connection handles, there's no way to find out what handles are out there, short of trying to use one and trapping for an error. The example at the end of this section remedies this problem—it shows a connection manager class that keeps track of connections for you. You instantiate the class once, and then let it manage all your connections. Using this class, you'd never call SQLConnect() or SQLStringConnect() yourself.

Usage `nReturnValue = SQLDISCONNECT( nConnectionHandle )`

Parameter	Value	Meaning
nConnectionHandle	Positive	The connection handle for the connection to be closed.
	0	Close all open connections.
nReturnValue	1	Connection successfully closed.
	-1	Connection level error.
	-2	Environmental error.

SQLDisconnect()is the function to hang up the phone. You pass the handle and FoxPro says "goodbye" for you.

The documentation says this function returns -1 when it can't close the connection. We haven't seen that in practice. Our experience is that, if something's going on our end that prevents us from closing the connection (like an asynchronous command is still executing), we get an error message, not a return value of -1.

Example

```
* We recommend you use something like the Connection Manager
* class shown here to manage your connections. This solves
* the problem of there being no way to find out what connections
* exist. You'll probably want to beef this class up, at least
* with a custom error handler.
* We created this class as a visual class. The code shown here
* was exported by the Class Browser. You'll find this class
* on the disk in Connect.VCX.
**************************************************
*-- Class:        connmgr (h:\hacker\testcode\connect.vcx)
*-- ParentClass:  custom
*-- BaseClass:    custom
*-- Connection Manager. Used to keep track of all active
*-- connections.
*
DEFINE CLASS connmgr AS custom


   *-- The number of open connections
   PROTECTED nconnectioncount
   nconnectioncount = 0
   Name = "connmgr"

   *-- Holds the open connections
   PROTECTED aconnections[1]


   *-- Open a connection
   PROCEDURE openconnection
      * Open a connection - based on parameters
      LPARAMETERS cSource, cUserId, cPassword
         * cSource is either datasource name or named connection

      LOCAL nHandle

      IF NOT EMPTY(DBC()) AND INDBC(cSource, "CONNECTION")
         * named connection - go for it
         nHandle = SQLCONNECT(cSource)
      ELSE
```

```
      DO CASE
      CASE TYPE("cUserId") = "C" AND TYPE("cPassword") = "C"
         nHandle = SQLCONNECT(cSource, cUserId, cPassword)
      CASE TYPE("cUserId") = "C"
         nHandle = SQLCONNECT(cSource, cUserId)
      CASE TYPE("cPassword") = "C"
          nHandle = SQLCONNECT(cSource, "", cPassword)
      OTHERWISE
         nHandle = SQLCONNECT(cSource)
      ENDCASE
   ENDIF

   IF nHandle > 0
      * successful connection
      * so add this connection to our list
      This.nConnectionCount = This.nConnectionCount+1
      DIMENSION This.aConnections[This.nConnectionCount, 4]
      This.aConnections[This.nConnectionCount,1] = nHandle
      This.aConnections[This.nConnectionCount,2] = cSource
      This.aConnections[This.nConnectionCount,3] = cUserId
      This.aConnections[This.nConnectionCount,4] = cPassword

   ENDIF
   RETURN nHandle
ENDPROC


*-- Close an open connection
PROCEDURE closeconnection
   * Close an open connection. Make sure to remove it from
   * the open list
   LPARAMETERS nHandle
      * Which connection to close

   * Find out if we have such a connection
   LOCAL nConnectionRow
   nConnectionRow = ASUBSCRIPT(This.aConnections, ;
                    ASCAN(This.aConnections,nHandle), 1)
   IF nConnectionRow > 0
      * found it, now get rid of it
      nResult = SQLDISCONNECT(nHandle)
      = ADEL(This.aConnections, nConnectionRow)
      This.nConnectionCount = This.nConnectionCount-1
      IF This.nConnectionCount > 0
         DIMENSION This.aConnections[This.nConnectionCount,4]
      ENDIF
   ELSE
      * Turn off the error handler and send the code for
      * error we want. This lets AERROR() return the right
      * information, but keeps the user from seeing a
      * message.
      LOCAL cOldError
      cOldError=ON("ERROR")
      ON ERROR *
      ERROR 1466
      ON ERROR &cOldError
      nResult = -2
   ENDIF

   RETURN nResult

ENDPROC


*-- List all open connections
PROCEDURE list
   * List the open connections in the active window
```

```
      ?"Connection handle", ;
       "Data Source/Connection","Userid","Password"

      IF This.nConnectionCount>0
         LOCAL nConn
         FOR nConn = 1 TO This.nConnectionCount
            ? This.aConnections[nConn, 1]
            ?? This.aConnections[nConn, 2] AT 19
            IF TYPE("This.aConnections[nConn, 3]") = "C"
               ?? This.aConnections[nConn, 3] AT 42
            ENDIF
            IF TYPE("This.aConnections[nConn, 4]") = "C"
               ?? This.aConnections[nConn, 4] AT 49
            ENDIF
         ENDFOR

      ELSE
         ? "No Open Connections"
      ENDIF
   ENDPROC


   PROCEDURE count
      * return the number of connections
      RETURN This.nConnectionCount
   ENDPROC


   PROCEDURE aconnect
      * Return an array containing all active connection
      * information.
      * Since we're already storing it in an array,
      * this is as simple as copying the array

      PARAMETER aReturn
      EXTERNAL ARRAY aReturn

      LOCAL nReturn   && return value is # of rows or -1

      IF TYPE("aReturn[1]") = "U"
         * Bad parameter, can't do it
         nReturn = -1
      ELSE
         IF This.nConnectionCount = 0
            nReturn = 0
         ELSE
            * redim the array to get rid of old data
            DIMENSION aReturn[1]
            * Copy from the property into the parameter
            = ACOPY(This.aConnections, aReturn)
            nReturn = ALEN(aReturn, 1)
         ENDIF
      ENDIF

      RETURN nReturn
   ENDPROC

ENDDEFINE
*
*-- EndDefine: connmgr
*************************************************
```

See Also Create Connection, SQLGetProp(), SQLSetProp()

SQLExec(), SQLPrepare()

The "exec" here stands for "execute". SQLExec() sends commands to the server to be executed. SQLPrepare() lets you speed up that execution by compiling the command before it's executed. You send it on ahead to the server, which compiles it and keeps it ready to go.

Usage

```
nSuccess = SQLExec( nConnectionHandle [, cCommand
                    [, cResultCursor ] )
nSuccess = SQLPrepare( nConnectionHandle, cCommand
                       [, cResultCursor ] )
```

Parameter	Value	Meaning
nConnectionHandle	Numeric	The existing connection handle for the remote database being queried.
cCommand	Character	The command or commands to pass to the server.
	Omitted	Execute a command previously passed to the server with SQLPrepare().
cResultCursor	Character	The name of a cursor in which to store the results of cCommand.
	Omitted	Name the result cursor SQLResult.
nSuccess	Positive	The number of result sets returned.
	0	Still executing commands.
	-1	An error occurred.

If the server can handle it, you can pass multiple commands with a single SQLExec(). In this case, there may be multiple result sets to return. The way SQLExec() handles this depends on the settings for both Asynchronous and Batch—see "Your Server Will be With You in a Moment" for an explanation of these settings; you actually set them with SQLSetProp().

When you're using asynchronous mode, you call SQLExec() over and over until it returns something other than 0. If you're also in batch mode, you then use SQLMoreResults() to retrieve additional result sets.

The first result set returned goes in a cursor named SQLResult, unless you pass a different name in cResultCursor. In batch mode, additional results simply tack a digit on the end of the first cursor name. You can do the same thing in non-batch mode or you can pass a different cursor name with SQLMoreResults().

SQLPrepare() is handy for times when you'll want to execute the same command over and over. Send it to the server once and get it compiled, then execute it as needed. It lets you create the equivalent of a parameterized view, but manage it with SPT. The biggest downside we see is that the compiled command is available only until you send along a different command.

In asynchronous mode, you can cancel a command before it finishes with SQLCancel().

If you're an old FoxPro hacker, like we are, there's one gotcha in passing commands to the server. ODBC doesn't understand the abbreviations of FoxPro commands we're all accustomed to. If you pass a query like "SELE * FROM Customers," it'll fail because ODBC has no clue what SELE means.

Example

```
* In synchronous mode
nHandle = SQLConnect("Northwinds")
IF nHandle > 0
   IF SQLExec(nHandle, "Select * FROM Customers") = 1
```

```
      BROWSE
   ELSE
      WAIT WINDOW "Trouble at the pass"
   ENDIF
ELSE
   WAIT WINDOW "Can't connect"
ENDIF

* Set up a parameterized SPT command
* Use the same connection as above
cCountry = ""
IF SQLPrepare(nHandle, ;
      "SELECT * FROM Customers WHERE Country = ?cCountry") = 1
   cCountry = "UK"
   IF SQLExec(nHandle) = 1
      * Got all UK Customers
      BROWSE TITLE "Customers in the UK"
   ENDIF
   cCountry = "USA"
   IF SQLExec(nHandle) = 1
      * Got all US Customers
      BROWSE TITLE "Customers in the USA"
   ENDIF
ENDIF
```

See Also SQLCancel(), SQLConnect(), SQLDisconnect(), SQLGetProp(), SQLMoreResults(), SQLSetProp()

SQLGetProp(), SQLSetProp()

These two functions let you check and change properties of a remote connection. Unlike the other functions whose names begin with SQL, these apply both to views and to SQL Pass-Through, though some properties are relevant really for only one or the other.

Usage

```
uResult = SQLGetProp( nConnectionHandle, cProperty )
nSuccess = SQLSetProp( nConnectionHandle, cProperty
                       [, uValue ] )
```

Parameter	Value	Meaning
nConnectionHandle	Positive Integer	Check or change properties for an existing connection with this handle.
	0	Check or change default properties used for creation of new connections.
cProperty	Character—See list in Help	The property whose value is to be checked or changed.
uValue	The type indicated by cProperty	The new value to assign to cProperty.
	Omitted	See below for further discussion. In theory, omitting this value resets the property to its default.
uResult	Character, Numeric or Logical	The current value of cProperty for the specified connection.

Parameter	Value	Meaning
nSuccess	1	Change was successful.
	Negative value	An error occurred.

A connection is Visual FoxPro's way of communicating with ODBC and the back-end server. It has an assortment of properties that determine how the communication proceeds. The term "property" is used here somewhat loosely. Connections are not objects in the OOP sense. But these properties are characteristics of the connection, so it's not a big stretch.

The help file has a pretty good list of the meanings for these items and their legal values, so we won't repeat that here. Instead, we'll focus on the mistakes.

In VFP 3, the optional third parameter in SQLSetProp() is a real hit-or-miss proposition. Sometimes when you omit it, things work as documented—the specified property gets restored to its default value. For WaitTime and BatchMode, the property changes, but the value it changes to is not the documented default. (WaitTime goes to 0; BatchMode goes to .F.) In the worst cases, you get an error message telling you "Property value is out of bounds"—we see this for Transactions and DispLogin. In Visual FoxPro 5 and 6, these problems are fixed.

Some of these problems may be bad documentation, while others may reflect differences in ODBC drivers or servers. But the bottom line is the omitted third parameter doesn't work as advertised in VFP 3.

DataSource is documented as read-write, but we haven't been able to change it—we suspect the docs are wrong, not the product. QueryTimeOut and PacketSize are also documented as read-write. They are, but only for a connection handle of 0 to let you change the defaults. They're read-only for an existing connection.

The optional 0 parameter for nConnectHandle lets you cut down on labor. If you always want asynchronous, non-batch connections, change your default and then all the new connections you create in this session will use the new defaults. The only way we've found to make these changes persist across sessions is to use the Tools-Options dialog. Set them there, then choose Set as Default, and your choices get saved in the Registry.

We'd advise you not to cut down on labor within your programs by trying to abbreviate the Property keywords, however, even though FoxPro seems perfectly willing to let you. You can reduce the property names to the minimum unique characters—DispLogin and DispWarnings can be abbreviated to DispL and DispW, while ConnectString and ConnectTimeOut can only be reduced to ConnectS and ConnectT, and QueryTimeOut can be reduced to the preposterous Q. C'mon, folks, translating this code into English is hard enough without cryptic pseudo-savings. In the Command Window, we'll never type an extra character, either, but don't let this unreadable gobbledygook enter your code!

Example

```
nHandle = SQLConnect("Northwinds")
? SQLGetProp(nHandle,"Asynchronous")  && Displays .F., the default
* Make it asynchronous
? SETSetProp(nHandle,"Asynchronous",.T.)
```

See Also Create Connection, CursorGetProp(), CursorSetProp(), DBGetProp(), DBSetProp(), SQLConnect()

SQLMoreResults()

This long-named function is used only in non-batch mode with SQL Pass-Through. It asks ODBC for the next set of results when you've sent a bunch of commands to the server at once.

Usage

```
nResult = SQLMoreResults( nConnectionHandle [, cCursor ] )
```

Parameter	Value	Meaning
nConnectionHandle	Numeric	The existing connection handle for the remote database being queried.
cCursor	Character	The name of a cursor in which to put the query results.
	Omitted	Use the name passed with the original SQLExec. If that was omitted, too, use "SQLResult".
nResult	0	The command is still executing.
	1	The current command has finished.
	2	All commands have finished.
	Negative	An error occurred.

To the extent we've been able to test, it appears to work as advertised, except for the completely undocumented cCursor parameter. The cursor name is limited to 10 characters.

Example

```
* This example uses the ever-popular PUBS database
nConn = SQLConnect("LocalServer")
* Turn batch mode off
SQLSetProp(nConn, "BatchMode",.F.)
* Here the first Query returns SQLResult cursor of authors
SQLEXEC(nConn, "select * from authors;" + ;
               " select * from publishers")
* Now we direct the second result set to the named cursor
? SQLMoreResults(nConn, "rv_Publs")
```

See Also SQLConnect(), SQLExec(), SQLGetProp(), SQLSetProp()

SQLPrepare() See SQLExec().

SQLRollback() See SQLCommit().

SQLSetProp() See SQLGetProp().

SQLStringConnect() See SQLConnect().

SQLTables(), SQLColumns()

These two functions let you collect information about the remote data being accessed via SQL Pass-Through. SQLTables() gives you a list of tables in the remote database, while SQLColumns() tells you about the fields of an individual table.

Usage

```
nSuccess = SQLTables( nConnectionHandle [, cTypeOfTables
                      [, cResultCursor ] ] )
```

Parameter	Value	Meaning
nConnectionHandle	Numeric	The existing connection handle for the remote database being queried.

Parameter	Value	Meaning
cTypeOfTables	Character	A comma-delimited list of table types. The list can include "View", "Table" and "System Table." Some servers support other types.
	Omitted or Empty	Include all table types.
cResultCursor	Character	The name of a cursor to contain the list of tables.
	Omitted	Put results in a cursor called SQLResult.
nSuccess	1	The command completed successfully.
	0	The command is still executing (in asynchronous mode).
	Negative	An error occurred.

The cursor created by SQLTables() has five fields. The most important one is the third, which contains the name of the table. The other fields provide information that doesn't have counterparts in FoxPro, like the table's owner and type.

Usage

```
nSuccess = SQLColumns( nConnectionHandle, cTable
                      [, cFormat  [, cResultCursor ] ] )
```

Parameter	Value	Meaning
nConnectionHandle	Numeric	The existing connection handle for the remote database being queried.
cTable	Character	The name of the table for which to return a list of fields (columns).
cFormat	"FOXPRO" or omitted	Return field information in FoxPro's usual structure format.
	"NATIVE"	Return field information in the server's native structure format.
cResultCursor	Character	The name of a cursor to contain the list of fields.
	Omitted	Put results in a cursor called SQLResult.
nSuccess	1	The command completed successfully.
	0	The command is still executing (in asynchronous mode).
	Negative	An error occurred.

The structure of the cursor created by SQLColumns() depends on what you pass for cFormat. With "FoxPro," you get a cursor with four columns containing field name, type, size and decimals, pretty much the usual, old-fashioned, structure information for FoxPro. (Seems to us it ought to have a lot more fields now to match the table structure used in Visual FoxPro.) When cFormat is "Native," the exact structure depends on the server—Help shows a fairly common structure.

Using SQLTables() and SQLColumns() together, you can build a local data dictionary for a remote database.

Example

```
nResult = SQLTables(nHandle, "", "TableList")
* Now use the name of the table stored in TableList to
* extract the columns of the table.
nResult = SQLColumns(nHandle, TableList.TableName)
```

See Also SQLCancel(), SQLConnect(), SQLExec()

Sqrt()

This function computes the square root of a number. It can operate on numeric, currency, integer and double values, but always returns a numeric value.

Usage

```
nResult = SQRT(nValue)
```

Since square roots aren't defined for negative numbers, VFP returns an error if you pass it a negative number.

Example

```
?SQRT(49)    && returns 7
?SQRT($81)   && returns 9
```

SRows() See SCols().

StartMode

This property of the Application object lets you determine how the application was started, so you can decide on the right course of action depending on the facilities available.

Usage

```
nRetVal = Application.StartMode
```

Parameter	Value	Meaning
nRetVal	0	Normal VFP interactive session.
	1	Out-of-process (EXE) OLE Server.
	2	Runtime out-of-process OLE Server.
	3	Runtime in-process OLE Server.

Use the StartMode property to determine what capabilities are available to you. For example, you don't want to raise an error on your big, fancy error-handling form if the application is running as an out-of-process server where you don't have access to the user interface.

Example

```
? _VFP.StartMode  && 0, from the Command Window
* FoxMind.Remind is a simple test server, created as an EXE
oDear = CreateObject("FoxMind.Remind")
? oDear.Application.StartMode  && returns 2
* Rebuild the server as a DLL
? oDear.Application.StartMode  && returns 3
```

See Also Application, _VFP

_StartUp

This system variable lets you specify a program to run when FoxPro starts up. You specify it in the CONFIG.FPW file.

Usage

```
_STARTUP = cProgram
```

This variable was added in FoxPro 2.6 to enable the Catalog Manager to be up and running when FoxPro opened.

The specified program is run before a command specified by COMMAND=.

Changes to _STARTUP once FoxPro is running don't have any automatic effects. But because this is a system variable that can't be cleared, it's another hook you can grab to use for your own purposes. See _ASSIST for ideas about how to use these hooks.

Example
```
* The next line would appear in CONFIG.FPW.
_STARTUP = MyStart.PRG
```

See Also _Assist, Configuration Files, _Shell

StatusBar, StatusBarText

These properties control the contents of the status bar. StatusBar is an application property that sends a message to the status bar. StatusBarText lets you specify some text to appear when a control has focus. It's a cousin to ToolTipText, but more useful for overall data entry. Use StatusBarText to give the user more information about what needs to be entered than the control or its associated label holds. Think of this as the first level of online Help. Like the messages associated with menu items, StatusBarText is there all the time, but is so unobtrusive that it won't bother the most experienced user.

Usage
```
oApp.StatusBar = cHelpText
cHelpText = oApp.StatusBar
oObject.StatusBarText = cHelpText
cHelpText = oObject.StatusBarText
```

StatusBar entered the language in VFP 5 as a property of the application object. When you change its value, the new value is displayed on the status bar. But it's erratic. Lots of things clear it and restore the default value. We haven't been able to find any rhyme or reason to what changes the status bar and what doesn't. (In fact, we think the VFP developers have some trouble with this, too, because we've seen some pretty strange behavior in development mode. Without doing anything she knows of to cause it and without the mouse positioned over the standard toolbar, Tamar often sees the string "Standard" in the status bar for long periods of time. At other times, the StatusBarText from one of the buttons on that toolbar sticks around, even after the mouse is moved. In both cases, issuing SET STATUSBAR ON reactivates the status bar.)

StatusBarText is a property of individual controls. There's a gotcha when you enter StatusBarText (and other strings) through the Property Sheet. Don't surround the text with quotes (yeah, we know it feels unnatural)—if you do, the quotes show up when you run the form. On the other hand, when you assign StatusBarText in code, you do need the quotes. It makes sense (because the Property Sheet, like the Query Designer, is smart enough to figure out what type of data it wants and deal with it appropriately), but it's really disconcerting with a property as text-oriented as this one.

Grids have StatusBarText, but it appears only when the grid first receives focus and only if you land on a control in the grid that doesn't have its own StatusBarText. As you move around in the grid, the grid's StatusBarText does not reappear. You see it again only when focus moves to another control and then back to the grid. We'd like the grid's StatusBarText to appear anytime focus is on a column whose control doesn't have any StatusBarText. That would be truly useful. As is, a grid's StatusBarText seems pretty useless.

Example
```
* For a Save button, you might set:
This.StatusBarText = " Save the Current Record"
```

See Also ErrorMessage, Message, ToolTipText

Store See =.

Str(), Val()

Str() and Val() are reciprocal functions for converting numeric values to strings and vice versa. Both process null values correctly, returning nulls.

Usage

```
cReturn = Str( nNumeric, [ nLength [, nDecimals ] ] )
nReturn = Val( cString )
```

Parameter	Value	Meaning
nNumeric	Numeric	The numeric value to be converted.
nLength	Numeric	The overall length of the resulting field, including preceding minus signs and any decimal places. Defaults to 10 if not specified. Limited to a maximum of 237.
nDecimals	Numeric	Number of decimal places to be returned. If nDecimals is greater than (nLength minus 2), the length takes priority and no more than (nLength minus 2) decimal places are returned. Defaults to zero if not specified. Limited to a maximum of 18.
cString	Character	A numeric value expressed in a string. Preceding plus or minus signs recognized. 16-character limit.

Str() takes a numeric value and returns a character value. Optionally, the length and number of decimal places of the field may be specified. If the length is less than the number of digits to the left of the decimal place, one of two things happens. If the number is less than 10 billion or the specified size is less than seven characters, asterisks are returned. But wait. If the numeric value has 10 digits to the left of the decimal place and the resulting string length is specified as at least seven, one of two things happens. In all cases, a string is returned in scientific notation. However, the string disagrees slightly between VFP 3 and later versions. Both versions are mathematically correct, but the string returned by the later versions more closely resembles what we learned was "scientific notation" in school:

```
? Str(1234567890123,7)   && returns ".1E+13" in VFP3
? Str(1234567890123,7)   && returns "1.E+12" in VFP5 and VFP 6

? Str(1234567890123,12)  && returns ".123456E+13" in VFP3
? Str(1234567890123,12)  && returns "1.23456E+12" in VFP5 and VFP 6
```

This can be as useless as asterisks, because the exact value of the number has been lost for display purposes. If you're performing bulk conversions of numeric data to strings, make sure that you check for a return of asterisks or one containing the letter "E".

Str() rounds fractional values ending in .50 up and .49 down. The online help claims the function truncates values, but Str(12345.6789,5) returns "12346", not 12345, and Str(12345.6789,7,2) returns "12345.7".

Str() first fits the whole number portion into the string, and what is left over is used for the decimal portion. You cannot assume that an expression Str(x,8,3) will always have the decimal point four spaces from the right end of the string—Str(1234.567,8,3) returns "1234.567", but Str(123456.7,8,3) returns "123456.7". We think this should result in a "Numeric Overflow" error, not in a string that looks different from the others.

Val() returns a number based on its evaluation of the numeric portion of a string. Val() ignores alphabetic characters after the number, converting Val("234abc") to 234. Val() recognizes and correctly parses leading spaces, and plus and minus signs. Val() also understands scientific notation, properly converting character expressions in the form "xE±z".

Val() converts nearly all character strings to numbers—the only problem is that some of these numbers may be beyond the range FoxPro can actually work with. Val("1E+307") creates a numeric without an error message, but this value cannot be stored in a numeric, double, float or integer field, nor can you do much useful processing on it. If you are converting character data to numeric in your applications, you need to range-check the result to ensure you are working with legitimate numbers.

Like other functions which depend on settings and symbols that vary by country, Val() correctly respects the settings of SET("POINT") to display and parse decimal points. If your application is likely to be used with data that may have been saved with another decimal point mark, make sure you have a way of detecting this. Similarly, if your users can customize your application to their native settings, you need to bracket code where you assume the setting of POINT.

Example

```
nHardDriveSize = Val(SYS(2020))
cPageNum = "Page "+LTRIM(Str(_PAGENO))
lnWrongVal = Val("123,456")  && what's this value?

lcPointSet = SET("POINT")   && preserve the setting
SET POINT TO "."            && set to known value
lnMyVal = Val("12345.67")   && use it
SET POINT TO lcPointSet     && restore the setting
```

The first example shows how Val() can return a numeric value from one of the SYS() functions, which typically return their values as character strings. The second example shows one of the most common uses of the Str() function—converting the system memory variable _PAGENO, representing the current page being printed, to a string to use as part of your report header or footer. The third example, lnWrongVal, shows a killer mistake. In the U.S., this number is parsed up to the alphabetic comma and is evaluated as exactly one hundred twenty-three. In most of Europe, where the POINT is typically a comma and the thousands separator a period, this value has a potentially significant decimal portion. Miscalculations at this level can be disastrous, and a bear to track down. The last example shows an example of the right way to capture the POINT setting, change it, perform your function, and restore it.

See Also Asc(), Chr(), Round(), Transform(), Set Point

StrConv()

This function, added in version 3.0b, performs an assortment of conversions between different character sets. Among other things, it can be used in place of LOWER() and UPPER(). The parts we're able to test without having double-byte data at hand seem to work.

Usage

```
cConvertedString = STRCONV( cOriginalString, nConversionType
                            [, nLocaleId ] )
```

Parameter	Value	Meaning
cOriginalString	Character	The data you want to convert.
nConversionType	1	Change single-byte to double-byte.
	2	Change double-byte to single-byte.
	3, 4	Change between the two Japanese forms.
	5	Change double-byte to Unicode.
	6	Change Unicode to double-byte.

Parameter	Value	Meaning
nConversionType	7	Change to appropriate lowercase for nLocaleId.
	8	Change to appropriate uppercase for nLocaleId.
nLocaleId	Numeric	Specifies the locale for lowercase and uppercase conversion.
cConvertedString	Character	The original string after the specified conversion has been performed.

The nLocaleId parameter was added in VFP 6. In English, there's a one-to-one correspondence between lowercase and uppercase letters. However, in some languages, where some characters take accents, it's not that simple. Specifying the locale you're interested in makes it possible to handle these cases. Unfortunately, it doesn't look as though you can simply pass any locale ID to see how your string would be converted—your version of Windows has to support that locale.

Example

```
? STRCONV("This is a test", 7)  && Returns "this is a test"
```

See Also Double-Byte Character Sets, Lower(), Upper()

Stretch

This property determines how an Image or OLE control is displayed. The image can be displayed in three different ways: at its full resolution where it might be cropped to fit within the space allowed; stretched or shrunk to fit the space but maintain its proportions; or distorted so that all of the image is squashed into the space allowed

Usage

```
oObject.Stretch = nStretchValue
nStretchValue = oObject.Stretch
```

Parameter	Value	Meaning
nStretchValue	0	Clip. No change to the original pixels of the original image. If the image is larger than the space allowed, the upper-left corner of the image is displayed.
	1	Isometric. The image is stretched or shrunk to show the best proportional image possible within the space allowed.
	2	Stretch. The image is stretched or shrunk to fit the space.

Figure 4-10 illustrates the results of the three different settings. We hardly ever use anything other than the Isometric setting, but Microsoft chose the Clip option as the default. We suspect they did this because that setting requires the least processing.

Example

```
imgImage.Stretch = 1
```

See Also Image, OLEBoundControl, OLEControl

StrictDateEntry

This text box property, added in Visual FoxPro 5.0, allows several shortcuts to date and datetime entry.

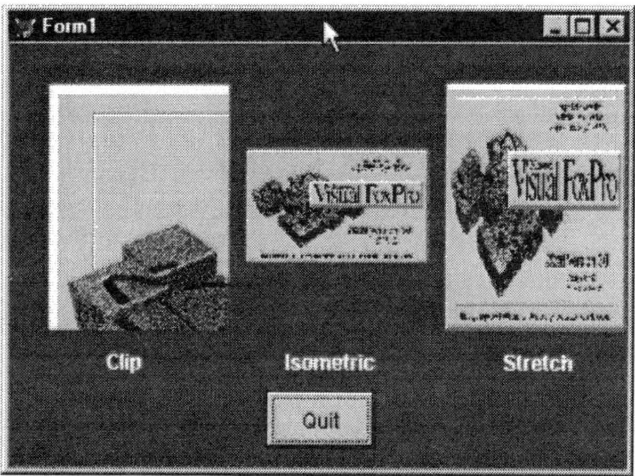

Figure 4-10: Different settings of Stretch result in markedly different results!

Usage

```
txtDateTime.StrictDataEntry = nOption
nOption = txtDateTime.StrictDataEntry
```

Parameter	Value	Meaning
nOption	0	Loose, allowing several shortcuts and new key characters.
	1 (default)	Strict. Same as previous (VFP 3.0 and before).

Loose data entry allows a couple of cool shortcuts. The year is assumed if not supplied. The caret (^) forces date entry into YY-MM-DD format, regardless of SET DATE or the DateFormat property. Dates can be typed in delimited with all of the standard delimiters (the period, slash, hyphen) as well as whatever has been set globally with SET MARK or locally with DateMark.

We've got mixed feelings about this new feature. First, we never found it that hard to do date entry the old way. "If it was hard to write, it should be hard to use" is not our development philosophy, however, and especially in heads-down data-entry situations, it can be simpler to enter fewer characters. There is more burden upon the developer, too, because an incorrectly entered date will not generate an internal error, but rather force the text box's value to an empty datetime. Validation must be performed by the developer if required. In balancing the user convenience against the cost of development, testing and maintenance, we'll recommend this only for clients where it can offer a compelling advantage.

Example

```
oForm = createobject("form")
oForm.AddObject("txtDateEntry","TextBox")
WITH oForm.txtDateEntry
   .Visible = .t.
   .DateFormat = 14  && long
   .Width = 312
   .Value = DATETIME()
   .StrictDateEntry = 0
ENDWITH
oForm.Show()
* Key in a value, such as ^-2-14, and press tab to observe the
* string properly translated.
```

The caret overrides your ability to skip the year. If the operator enters a caret, they must put in the full year-month-day sequence.

See Also DateFormat, DateMark, Set Date, Set Mark, Set SysFormats

StrToFile() See FileToStr().

StrTran(), Stuff() See ChrTran().

StuffC() See ChrTranC().

Style

This property is a prime example of polymorphism at work. Five different controls have it, and it has four different interpretations.

Usage

```
oObject.Style = nStyle
nStyle = oObject.Style
```

For combos, Style determines whether you get a drop-down list or a real combo (called a "drop-down combo") that lets you type in new data. With a drop-down combo, new items aren't automatically added to the combo's list. You'll have to handle them in code—see DisplayValue for details. Combos are the only control where the choices are 0 and 2. We do wonder what they have in mind for Style = 1.

For check boxes and option buttons, Style distinguishes graphical objects from textual ones. Unless Style is 1-graphical, any pictures you specify are ignored.

Style for command buttons lets you make some of them "invisible"—one way to create a "hot spot" on a form. Although invisible buttons have no physical presence on a form, they can still gain focus complete with a focus rectangle. Consider setting TabStop to .F. for invisible buttons to make them mouse-only.

Finally, there's one backward-compatibility choice here. Set a text box's Style to 1 if you want it to behave more or less like an @ ... SAY in FoxPro 2.x. We haven't found a way to refresh these text boxes (when the value is an expression) other than reassigning the original value. Guess they really are like @ ... SAYs.

Example

```
* Normally, you'll set this property at design time. But let's
* change a combo to drop-down list.
ThisForm.cboMyCombo.Style = 2
```

See Also DisabledPicture, DisplayValue, DownPicture, Picture, SpecialEffect, Valid

SubStr() See Left().

SubStrC() See LeftC().

Sum See Average.

Suspend See Cancel.

Sys(0)

SYS(0) returns the machine identification number and the identification of the user, if your network shell supports this functionality.

Usage

```
cID = SYS(0)
```

We usually don't depend on this information being available. Single-user installations may not give us useful information. Under some network operating systems, SYS(0) is blank unless specific changes are made to the NOS configurations—changes our clients may be unwilling or unable to do. Some network shells do not provide this information, causing the function to return SPACE(15)+"#"+SPACE(1). Stand-alone installations (including those that have not started the network shell) return "1". Bottom line: you need to test if this information is available on the specific installation you are working on. In a shrink-wrapped application, or one where you don't configure the client's workstation, count on SYS(0) returning blank information, somewhere, sometime.

Example

```
? SYS(0)          && "PROMETHEUS # troche" on Ted's NT machine
? SYS(0)          && "TAMAR'S DELL#Tamar " on Tamar's NT machine
```

See Also User()

Sys(1), Sys(10), Sys(11)

To everything there is a purpose, and a time to everything under heaven.

Ecclesiastes

If you are like us and never had a need to use the Julian date system, you've probably assumed that it was named for some dead Roman emperor, Julius somebody, and was based on some arcane mythology or astrological event. Not so, bucko.

While many of us prefer to count the days, weeks, fortnights, months and years as they go by, some scientists prefer to just have a serial number to distinguish today from yesterday, this night from one a hundred days ago. They may have a point. Joseph Scaliger in 1582 devised a numbering scheme based on the intersection of three major cycles: the 28-year solar cycle, the 19-year lunar cycle and the 15-year indiction cycle (the tax period used in the Ancient Roman Empire) and determined that the last date on which all these cycles started on the same date was January 1, 4713 B.C., and therefore called this Julian Day One. He named it Julian after his father, Julius. And we've been counting ever since.

At least that's one story we've read. Another is that these are sequential numbers since the date of the Great Flood. Since we weren't around for either of these events, we're not too worried about the truth of them, just what FoxPro can do with these numbers.

The Visual FoxPro facility for dates, as we mentioned in "DBF, FPT, CDX, DBC—Hike!" is accurate only back to 1752. The FoxPro help file cautiously points out that this is true only in the United States. We suspect it is also as accurate in the British Empire and former colonies, but know it took the Russian Revolution of 1918 to bring that region into compliance. If you're implementing an application outside the U.S. and need historical accuracy, you'd be wise to consult your neighborhood chronologist.

So the Julian numbering scheme may be a good way to get around all these local squabbles about what day it is. For dates in the distant past, though, you may need to devise your own algorithm, but once it's created, math on those numbers will be accurate against the values returned by these functions.

Usage

```
cDateJ = SYS( 1 )
cJtoC = SYS( 10, nExpression )
cDtoJ = SYS( 11, dExpression | tExpression | cExpression )
```

SYS(1) returns a character string containing the Julian number of today's date, sort of a DATEJ() function.

SYS(10) converts a numeric Julian number to a character string that looks an awful lot like a date, so it could be called JTOC(). While this function accepts arguments as low as 1,721,119 (which returns the silly string of 03/00/0000), it makes no allowance for the vagaries of the Gregorian calendar and is not accurate before the last zigzag of that counting method—September 14, 1752 for the U.S. and the British Empire.

SYS(11) converts a date or a datetime or a character string that looks like a date to a string containing the equivalent Julian number, so we'd make this into both the DTOJ() and TTOJ() functions. This is a pretty robust function, converting numbers with and without preceding zeroes without a complaint, digesting the entire assortment of standard date delimiters—slashes and dashes and dots—as well as the current SET("MARK") without a noise, but it does barf on a string containing both the date and time, such as the string returned by TTOC(). However, with all the other expressions that SYS(11) can convert correctly, you should be able to convert pretty much anything to a format acceptable by this function.

Conversions respect the settings of SET CENTURY, SET DATE and SET MARK TO, so don't assume a positional value or length unless you've explicitly set those settings beforehand.

See Also Date(), DateTime(), Set Century, Set Date, Set Mark

Sys(2) See Seconds().

Sys(3), Sys(2015)

These two functions generate random strings. SYS(3) returns an 8-character string suitable for a filename. SYS(2015) returns a 10-character string handy for a procedure or function name—it was added in FoxPro 2.0 to allow GENSCRN, the 2.x screen generator, to generate procedure names for snippet code.

Usage

```
cString = SYS(3)
cString = SYS(2015)
```

SYS(3) is driven by the system clock and has a big problem. If you call it in succession too quickly, you can get the same string back. On a Pentium/90 with 24MB memory, calling SYS(3) a thousand times in a tight loop produced only 134 different values, each of them seven or eight times. On a Pentium Pro/200 with 64MB of memory, the same code produced only 82 distinct values, most of them 12 or 13 times. On the other hand, using SYS(2015) in the same loop produced 1,000 different values on both machines.

Also, keep in mind that two workstations calling one of these functions at the same time will get the same value. They're not suited to generating unique IDs.

You do occasionally need a name for a temporary file. Your best bet is to use SYS(3) or SYS(2015) in a loop until you get one that doesn't exist. See the example.

Beware: The strings returned by SYS(3) always are composed entirely of digits. This means they can't serve as aliases for tables. So, while you can create a table named with the value returned, when you open it, you'll want to specify a legal alias. If you don't, VFP assigns the table an alias based on the work area in which it's opened.

Example

```
* Get a unique filename for a text file
* On a busy network, you may want to try to FCREATE()
* the file inside the loop to make sure someone else hasn't
* just grabbed the same name.
cFile = SYS(3)
DO WHILE NOT FILE(cFile+".TXT")
   cFile = SYS(3)
ENDDO
```

See Also File(), Rand()

Sys(5) See CurDir().

Sys(6) See Set Printer.

Sys(7) See Set Format.

Sys(9) See OS().

Sys(10), Sys(11) See Sys(1).

Sys(12) See Memory().

Sys(13) See PrintStatus().

Sys(14) See Candidate().

Sys(15) See ChrTran().

Sys(16) See Program().

Sys(17) See DiskSpace().

Sys(18), VarRead()

These two identical functions tell you the name of the current field in a READ or Browse. In a Visual FoxPro form, they return the ControlSource of the current control, but without any of the container hierarchy that identifies it.

Usage

```
cCurrentField = SYS(18)
cCurrentField = VARREAD()
```

In a FoxPro 2.x-style READ and a Browse, VARREAD() is handy for finding out where the cursor is sitting, so you can act on that field. (We much prefer the mnemonic VARREAD() to the cryptic SYS(18).) A common use of VARREAD() in 2.x apps was to provide context-sensitive help (ON KEY LABEL F1 DO GetHelp WITH VARREAD()).

In Visual FoxPro, the ActiveControl property of a form gives much broader access to the information, since you can use it to check information about any property of the current control. (Unfortunately, ActiveControl isn't always available.)

In READ and forms, the field/control name is returned in uppercase. In Browse in FoxPro 2.x, the field name returned had the first letter in uppercase and the rest in lowercase. This made it easy for a routine to tell whether it was called by a Browse or a form/screen. However, in VFP, the name is always returned in uppercase, even in a Browse. This makes sense because Browse is really a grid.

In a form, the value returned by VARREAD() and SYS(18) contains just the ControlSource of the current object; it doesn't contain a complete path to the ControlSource. If the ControlSource is a property of some object, the name alone doesn't do you much good.

In new forms, we recommend using the OOP way whenever possible and leaving VARREAD() for Browse code. As for SYS(18), don't ever use it—it's unreadable.

Example

```
* To see what the current field is in a Browse
ON KEY LABEL F2 WAIT WINDOW VARREAD()
USE Customer
BROWSE
* Now move around and press F2
```

See Also ActiveControl, ControlSource, Name

Sys(20) See ChrTran().

Sys(21), Sys(22) See Order().

Sys(23), Sys(24) See Memory().

Sys(100) See Set Console.

Sys(101) See Set Device.

Sys(102) See Set Printer.

Sys(103) See Set Talk.

Sys(1001), Sys(1016) See Memory().

Sys(1023), Sys(1024)

These two functions allow you to toggle on and off a special debugging mode for monitoring the interaction of your application and help files. This can be very useful in ensuring that you provide help for built-in dialogs you include in your application.

Usage

```
SYS( 1023 )   && turn on diagnostic mode
SYS( 1024 )   && return to normal mode
```

Help can be invoked in a number of ways within an application. For example, F1 can be pressed to bring up help, passing information about the item with focus or the text that is highlighted. Shift+F1 or WhatsThisHelp passes the WhatsThisHelpID of the item clicked on when in WhatsThisHelp Mode. Within the Command Window, a developer can type HELP and the name of the topic for which he wants help. For all of these cases, these two SYS() functions allow you to see the information passed to the Help engine.

As we discuss in the HelpContextID section, the ID is a unique address for a help topic in the help file. For controls that you build, the HelpContextID is a property you assign in the Form and Class Designers, but for other built-in elements, like the "Minimize" option on the active window control menu, the ID is already coded for you—one job of these functions is to determine and display that ID for you.

Designed long before Windows became the sole platform for VFP, SET TOPIC can accept either a numeric or a string argument. Similarly, Windows Help and HTML Help can be invoked passing either a string or a number, accepting either integers (HelpContextIDs) or strings (Help topics) through the same API call. (Internally, FoxPro passes an additional argument to Help to tell it whether to expect a string or an ID integer.) While the Windows Way to do things is to assign every control a HelpContextID, it's also possible to assign the topic using SET TOPIC, perhaps in GotFocus and LostFocus. These SYS() functions display either the ID or string passed to help. In a remarkable coincidence, this technique works for all of the flavors of help: DBF, WinHelp and HTML Help.

These functions accept no parameters and return the empty string. When diagnostic mode is running, any call to help pops up a Yes/No message box, telling you the information to be passed to the Help engine and allowing you to decide to continue or abandon the operation. Pressing F1 while an object has the focus (or a menu pad is highlighted) displays the HelpContextID for that item. Typing HELP and the thing you want help on offers to pass the string you type to the Help engine. For example, issuing the command HELP TableUpdate passes the string 'TableUpdate' to the Help engine. Alternatively, selecting File-New from the menu and pressing F1 displays the HelpContextID (both in decimal and hexadecimal format) sent to the Help engine.

Don't forget when designing and testing your coverage of HelpContextIDs in your application to cover the built-in dialogs, like GetCP() and LocFile(), as well as the window and application control menus. In addition, you'll want to make sure you've tested and created help for all of the HelpContextIDs for Windows Common Dialogs or any OCXs your application uses. SYS(1023) can supply you with those HelpContextIDs as well.

See Also Help, HelpContextID, Set Help, Set Topic, WhatsThisHelp

Sys(1037) See GetPrinter().

Sys(1269)

SYS(1269) returns information about an object's properties. It provides two pieces of information about each—whether it's been changed from the default and whether it's read-only. Broken in VFP 3.0, it has been superseded in later versions by the preferable PEMStatus().

later versions by the preferable PEMStatus().

Usage

```
lPropertyHasAttribute = SYS( 1269, oObject, cProperty,
                             nAttribute )
```

Parameter	Value	Meaning
oObject	Object	The object whose properties are to be checked.
cProperty	Character	The name of the property to check.
nAttribute	0	Has the property changed from its default value?
	1	Is the property read-only?

SYS(1269) was a very late addition to VFP 3; in fact, it was added to the product so late that it didn't get into the docs. It didn't work so well in that version, either, but by 3.0b was performing as advertised. However, by that point, the facilities it offered were so clearly needed that they got incorporated in a real, mnemonically (well, almost mnemonically) named function—PEMStatus(). So, in practice, there's never any reason to use SYS(1269), except in VFP 3.0, where it doesn't work right. (Specifically, in that version, passing nAttribute for 1 always returns .F., whether or not the property is read-only.)

When you pass 0 for nAttribute, SYS(1269) returns .T. only if the property has changed by being explicitly set. For example, if you add an object to a form, so ControlCount changes from 0 to 1, SYS(1269,oForm,"ControlCount",0) returns .F., not .T. as we'd expect. It's possible, though, that it's meant to reflect only changes due to direct assignments. Similarly, SYS(1269) returns .F. when a property was changed in the class on which the object is based, but not in this instance of the object.

Example

```
oForm = CreateObject('Form')
? SYS(1269, oForm, "Left", 0)       && Returns .F.
oForm.Left = 50
? SYS(1269, oForm, "Left", 0)       && Returns .T.
? SYS(1269, oForm, "BaseClass", 1)  && Returns .T.
                                    && except in VFP 3.0
```

See Also AMembers(), PEMStatus()

Sys(1270)

This function gives you a reference to the object located at either the mouse position or a specified position. The way you specify positions, however, is fairly ridiculous.

Usage

```
uObject = SYS( 1270 [, nXCoord, nYCoord ] )
```

Parameter	Value	Meaning
nXCoord, nYCoord	Numeric	The position for which you want an object reference.
	Omitted	Return a reference to the object under the mouse pointer.
uObject	Object	A reference to the object at the current or specified position.
	.F.	No object was found at the current or specified position.

SYS(1270) is a lot like ASelObj() except that it doesn't require you to actually click on anything—you can just grab whatever's under the mouse pointer. Like so many SYS() functions before it, now that Microsoft has seen that this one is really useful, in VFP 6 they've given us a new and improved version—check out AMouseObj().

If you omit the parameters, this function works as advertised. It gives you a reference to the object the mouse is over. This is especially handy for debugging.

When you pass the optional coordinates, they're measured from the upper-left corner of your screen. That's right, not the VFP main window, but the screen itself. So, if you move VFP, you have to change the parameters to this function. We can't think of any reason why this function is interested in the outside world since it can't give us information about what's out there.

We're also baffled as to why the function has two different return types. Why not return .NULL. when there's no object there? Having an object reference in one case and .F. in the other makes it a pain to write code that uses the function. We have to check VarType() of the return value before we do anything.

Example

```
oCurrent = SYS(1270)

* A lot of people set up something like this to make debugging
* easier. The second line is needed so forms will close.
ON KEY LABEL F11 o = SYS(1270)
ON KEY LABEL F12 o = .null.
```

See Also AMouseObj(), ASelObj(), MCol(), Mouse, MRow(), Point, PSet

Sys(1271)

This function, also a late addition to VFP 3, tells you the name of the form in which an instantiated object is stored.

Usage `uFileName = SYS( 1271, oObject )`

Property	Value	Purpose
oObject	Object	The object for which you want to know the filename.
uFileName	Character	The complete path and filename for the form containing oObject.
	.F.	oObject doesn't come from a form stored in an SCX file.

We can't quite see why they added this function to the language. If you could hand it any object and find out where it comes from, it would be useful, but it only handles forms created as SCX files and the objects those forms contain. On the other hand, we can't see any other way of getting to this information, so maybe there are some cases where it's useful. Our venerable tech editor says he uses it when working with multiple instances of the same form. His code renames each instance to have a unique Name, so SYS(1271) lets him figure out that they're all the same form.

Like SYS(1270), this one returns values of two different types for no reason we can see.

Example

```
DO FORM Test
? SYS(1271, _SCREEN.ActiveForm)
```

See Also Do Form, PEMStatus(),Sys(1270)

Sys(1272)

This function gives you the complete containment hierarchy for any object. In other words, you hand it an object reference and it'll tell you exactly how to address that object. It's sort of the object version of FULLPATH().

Usage `cCompleteReference = SYS( 1272, oObject )`

One of the difficulties in the OOP world is literally getting a handle on things. When you run a form, you may not know the name of the form. _SCREEN.ActiveForm is one solution to this problem, but SYS(1272) gives you more leeway because you can grab the exact reference needed. To see the exact hierarchy for the object with focus, try SYS(1272, _SCREEN.ActiveForm.ActiveControl).

This function seems useful mostly for debugging and for developer tools, not in production code.

Example

```
* To see exactly where you are while debugging, try this
* in the Watch window:
SYS(1272, SYS(1270))
* As you move the mouse, you can see exactly which control
* you're over with its entire hierarchy.
```

If you use the example, remember to remove it from the Watch window before you try to close the form. The reference it creates keeps the form from closing.

See Also ActiveControl, ActiveForm, Sys(1270)

Sys(1500)

This is one of the coolest of the SYS() functions. Added in version 5.0, it lets us call system menu bars without having to KEYBOARD their hot keys or shortcuts. It's especially useful for toolbars and context menus.

Usage `cEmptyString = SYS(1500, cMenuBarName, cMenuPopupName)`

Parameter	Value	Meaning
cMenuBarName	Character	The name (not the prompt) of the actual menu item you want to use.
cMenuPopupName	Character	The name (not the prompt) of the menu popup that contains the item.
cEmptyString	Character	No matter what it does or doesn't do, the function returns the empty string.

The system menu has some great capabilities built into it, things like undo/redo and cut/copy/paste. We often want to include these items in our applications but call on them from places other than the menu, such as a standard toolbar or a context (right-click) menu. Before SYS(1500) came along, we either had to write our own code to emulate VFP's or KEYBOARD appropriate keystrokes to call the menu item. In many cases, writing our own code was a truly daunting task. As for KEYBOARDing the right keystrokes, we could and did do it, but it was one more thing that made our apps more fragile than necessary. Among other things, the hot keys for different items vary in different languages.

SYS(1500) provides a simple, straightforward solution. Just call on the menu item directly. There is one caveat. As with the KEYBOARD approach, the menu item must be available. If you haven't included _MED_UNDO on the Edit popup (_MEDIT), you can't issue SYS(1500,"_MED_UNDO","_MEDIT"). However, as with other menu tricks, the item doesn't actually have to be visible to be used; it only has to be defined.

VFP provides somewhat more flexibility here than we expected. The menu bar itself has to have its usual assigned name (like _MED_UNDO), but the popup can have any name. In addition, the menu bar *doesn't* have to be on the popup where it's usually found. You can rename the popup or move the item to a different popup and still use this function. Just make sure to specify the right popup name in the function call. (Of course, there are user interface reasons why you normally want to leave the bars on their default menu popups.)

Be aware that the function doesn't give you a clue whether or not it was successful. If you pass it a nonexistent menu bar or popup, there's no error message, no special return value, no nothing. If it's important to make sure the action you're calling on happens, you'll want to test for the existence of the appropriate menu bar/popup pair beforehand. Check out POPUP and GETBAR() for some ideas how to do that.

Example

```
* The Click method for a Paste button might contain:
SYS(1500,"_MED_PASTE","_MEDIT")
```

See Also GetBar(), Menus, Popup()

Sys(2000)

This is a nice little function that's been mostly superseded by later additions to the language. It returns the name of a file matching a skeleton. You can use it in a loop to find all files that match a given skeleton.

Usage `cFileName = SYS( 2000, cSkeleton [ ,1 ] )`

Parameter	Value	Meaning
cSkeleton	Character	A file specification. It can contain the DOS wildcards "?" and "*".
1	Included	Find the next matching file.
	Omitted	Find the first matching file.

The order in which filenames are returned is the order they appear in a DOS DIR listing. Of course, this is a pretty useless order. ADIR(), which is generally a better choice than SYS(2000), also uses the DOS order, but you can then ASORT() to get some useful order. The only situation where we've found a use for the SYS(2000) function is one where we are polling a directory for the next file matching a skeleton, grabbing it for processing, and immediately deleting or renaming it. Multiple machines can poll the same directory, and each will get the name of the next file in queue. Grabbing the first available name is faster than searching an entire directory listing, particularly on slower hardware.

Example

```
* Our own version of ADIR() - no reason to use it
* Assume cSkel is the file skeleton
LOCAL nFileCount, cFileName, aFiles[1]

cFileName=SYS(2000,cSkel)
nFileCount=0
DO WHILE NOT EMPTY(cFileName)
   nFileCount = nFileCount + 1
   DIMENSION aFiles[nFileCount]
   aFiles[nFileCount] = cFileName
   cFileName = SYS(2000,cSkel,1)
ENDDO
```

See Also ADir(), Dir, Display Files, List Files

SYS(2001) See Set.

Sys(2002) See Set Cursor.

Sys(2003) See CurDir().

Sys(2004) See Home().

Sys(2005) See Set Resource.

Sys(2006) See DiskSpace().

Sys(2007)

SYS(2007) returns a checksum that you can use to "fingerprint" a character string. This checksum can be used later to check if the value of the character string has changed. This function is the source of the CkVal field in the FoxPro resource file. Checksums are related to the original character field by some magical formula, which returns a number from zero to 65,535. Obviously, with only 65,536 combinations to choose from, SYS(2007) does not create a perfect, unique entry. For example, checksums run on the Details field of VFP 3's FoxHelp.DBF yield 72 duplicates on fewer than 3,000 records. But as a flag to determine if a single field has changed, it's suitable for many functions.

Usage

```
cReturn = SYS( 2007, cString )
```

Parameter	Value	Meaning
cString	Character	Value to be checksummed.
cReturn	Character	5 characters containing a left-justified number.

Example

```
cCkVal = SYS(2007,Foxuser.Data)

* * LogTime.PRG - time entry into resource diary
PARAMETERS tcLogMessage
PRIVATE ALL LIKE l*
IF EMPTY(SET('RESOURCE',1))
  WAIT WINDOW PROGRAM() + ": No resource in use!"
  RETURN .F.
ELSE
  lcResSet = SET('RESOURCE')
  SET RESOURCE OFF
ENDIF

lnSelect = SELECT()
SELECT 0
USE SET('RESOURCE',1) AGAIN ALIAS Diary
LOCATE FOR TYPE = "DATA" AND ;
           ID   = "DIARYDATA" AND ;
           NAME = DTOS(DATE())

IF NOT FOUND()
  INSERT INTO Diary VALUES ("DATA", "DIARYDATA", ;
                            DTOS(DATE()),.F., 0, TIME() + ;
                            " " + tcLogMessage, DATE())
ELSE
  REPLACE DATA WITH DATA + CHR(13) + TIME() + " " + tcLogMessage
ENDIF

REPLACE CkVal WITH VAL(SYS(2007, DATA))
USE IN Diary
SELECT (lnSelect)
SET RESOURCE &lcResSet
RETURN
```

The second example posts the message passed to the function as a calendar entry, appending to an existing entry or creating a new one. It uses SYS(2007) to update the CkVal field. (Hint: If you want to hide a calendar entry, just change its checksum.) If this code looks a little funny, it's because it is essentially unchanged since (and still runs in) FoxPro 2.0, despite a few changes to the resource file's structure.

See Also Set Resource, Val()

Sys(2008), Sys(2009) See Set Cursor.

Sys(2010) See DiskSpace().

Sys(2011) See FLock().

Sys(2012) See Set BlockSize.

Sys(2013)

This function gives you a character string containing the pad and bar names of all the system menu items. We haven't found much use for it over the years, especially since the same information is available in the online help in a much easier to read format.

Usage `cMenuItems = SYS(2013)`

The list is space-delimited.

It seems to us that this list might be more useful if it were contained in an array rather than a single character variable. So the example below shows a function which parses the list into an array.

Example

```
* MakeMArr.PRG
* make an array out of the system menu pad and bar names
* Returns the number of items found
* If there's a parameter problem, returns -1.
* Sample Call:
*        nMenuCnt = MakeMArr(@aMenuItems)

PARAMETERS aMenuArr
* Have to pass menu in so it exists in calling program.

LOCAL cMenuString,nCnt,nNextPos
* cMenuString holds SYS(2013) return
* nCnt is a counter
* nNextPos = position of next blank in string

* Make sure we've got an array
IF TYPE("aMenuArr[1]")="U"
* bail out
   RETURN -1
ENDIF

cMenuString=SYS(2013)

* Now parse the string
* and create an array item for each item there
nCnt=0
DO WHILE NOT EMPTY(cMenuString)
   nNextPos=AT(" ",cMenuString)
   IF nNextPos<>0
      nCnt=nCnt+1
      DIMENSION aMenuArr[nCnt]
      aMenuArr[nCnt]=LEFT(cMenuString,nNextPos-1)
      IF nNextPos<LEN(cMenuString)
         cMenuString=SUBSTR(cMenuString,nNextPos+1)
      ELSE
         cMenuString=""
      ENDIF
   ENDIF
ENDDO
RETURN nCnt
```

See Also Define Bar, Define Menu, Define Pad, Define Popup

Sys(2014) See FullPath().

Sys(2015) See Sys(3).

Sys(2016) See Show Gets.

Sys(2017)

This function doesn't do anything. Really. In FoxPro 2.x, it displayed the FoxPro startup screen, but Visual FoxPro doesn't have one.

Usage
```
cResult = SYS(2017) && cResult is a zero-length character,
                    && but who cares?
```

Sys(2018) See Error.

Sys(2019), Sys(2023)

SYS(2019) tells you where your configuration file is located. SYS(2023) tells you where temporary files are stored.

Usage
```
cConFigFile = SYS( 2019 )
cTempFileDir = SYS( 2023 )
```

The SYS(2019) function returns the path and filename of the configuration file that was read on startup. One of the best ways to get yourself totally confused is to think that you're using one CONFIG file when, in fact, you're using another. Visual FoxPro searches for the configuration file in this order:

- a file specified using the -C startup command line option
- a file specified using the FOXPROWCFG environment variable
- a file named CONFIG.FPW in the current directory
- a file named CONFIG.FPW anywhere along the DOS search PATH

If a CONFIG.FPW is not found, Visual FoxPro is pretty vigorous about searching the path to find one, oftentimes with surprising results. Our advice: Avoid headaches and always explicitly specify a CONFIG.FPW file on startup.

SYS(2023) returns the drive and directory path where temporary files are stored.

Example
```
WAIT WINDOW SYS(2019)  && displays current config file
MODI COMM SYS(2019)    && edits the configuration file
? SYS(2023)       && displays "C:\TEMP\TMPFILES" on Ted's machine
```

SYS(2023) behaves differently in DOS and Windows in the 2.x products—DOS returns only the drive letter and a colon, whereas Windows returns the whole path. Because we doubt we'll see another DOS product, this has certainly become less of an issue. Just bear this in mind when converting DOS code to VFP.

See Also Configuration Files

Sys(2020) See DiskSpace().

Sys(2021) See Candidate().

See Candidate().

Sys(2022) See DiskSpace().

Sys(2027) See Set Volume.

Sys(2029)

This function returns the type and some clues to the origin of a DBF table.

Usage `cTableType = SYS( 2029 [, nWorkArea | cAlias ] )`

You can see the return values in the FoxPro help file and documentation: "0," "48," and "245" for "No table open," "FoxPro 3.0 table," and "FoxPro 2.x with memo field," respectively. Why these bizarre values? The secret to these weird values is that the values are the decimal equivalent of the very first byte of the file, established by Ashton-Tate and Fox Software over the years as the flag that these files contain their proprietary structures.

Example `? SYS(2029)`

See Also FCount(), FSize(), Header(), RecSize()

Sys(2333)

SYS(2333) allows Visual FoxPro to take advantage of ActiveX controls that support the new (as of OLE 2) VTable binding feature, an interface that can speed processing. Unfortunately, many controls fail when this interface is enabled.

Usage `cSetting = SYS( 2333 [, nSetting ] )`

Parameter	Value	Meaning
cSetting	Character	The resultant setting after the function runs as a one-character string (not an integer).
nSetting	0 or omitted	Interface is disabled. This is VFP 6's default.
	1	Interface is enabled. This is VFP 5's default, and it seemed like a good idea at the time.
	2	Returns the current setting.

VTable binding is a faster method of talking with ActiveX controls. Controls supporting this feature store a virtual table of their internal functions and allow more direct access to those functions. Without VTable binding, every call to an ActiveX control has to go through several steps to access the function it calls. While VTable binding is a great idea, far too few of the third-party controls implement the interface correctly, leading to lots of problems when VFP 5 developers attempt to integrate those controls into their applications. For this reason, Microsoft chose to change the default behavior of Visual FoxPro in the 6.0 product to disable this interface.

If you know the control you are working with supports VTable binding, try turning on SYS(2333) to see if it improves performance. But if you run into crashes and weird behaviors, be prepared to turn it off again.

Example

```
? SYS(2333)     && sets and returns the default "0"
? SYS(2333,0)   && same effect as the previous command
? SYS(2333,1)   && enables VTable binding and returns "1"
? SYS(2333,2)   && returns the current setting, "1"
```

See Also AutoYield, Sys(2334)

Sys(2334)

SYS(2334) reports the Automation server's invocation mode. This function tells you how any method of your Automation server was invoked.

Usage `cStartedAs = SYS( 2334 )`

Parameter	Value	Meaning
cStartedAs	Empty string or 0	Unknown. The method might be running as part of the initialization of the object (called from Init) or as a standalone EXE.
	1	This method was called as part of an application server supporting VTable binding.
	2	This method was called as part of an application server not supporting VTable binding, via the older IDispatch interface.

It might be important to your COM server's behavior to determine how it was invoked, although we haven't thought up a case for this yet. We're more likely to use StartMode to determine the environment in which the code is running, but if you need to distinguish between VTable and IDispatch invocations, here's the way to do it.

It's not documented, but SYS(2334) returns an empty string if you call it at times when none of the values are appropriate—for example, from the command line or within a routine that's not running as part of an OLEPUBLIC method. It returns 0 when operating as an Automation server in those methods that don't use either interface—for example, Init, Error or Destroy.

Example `IF SYS(2334) = "2"  && IDispatch call`

See Also StartMode, SYS(2333)

Sys(2335)

This function gives us the ability to turn off the dialog boxes that hang our EXE servers, so that we can trap problems with the error handler instead.

Usage `nSetting = SYS(2335 [, nNewSetting ] )`

Parameter	Value	Meaning
nNewSetting	Omitted	Returns the current setting of SYS(2335), in VFP runtime only. In the development environment, returns the empty string.
	0	Unattended mode. If a dialog attempts to force your EXE into a modal condition, an error (number 2031, "User Interface operation not allowed at this time") is generated instead.
	1	Normal mode. This is the default, where dialogs can interrupt the operation of your application.
nSetting	Empty String	Returned in development mode.

Parameter	Value	Meaning
nSetting	"0" or "1"	Returns the current mode of the EXE—not the previous mode, but the mode after the SYS() function has been executed.

Ted once wrote a Remote Automation server, and had lots of problems trying to figure out why the process kept hanging after some modifications to the code. It turned out, if you watched the task bar while starting the server, a task named "Open" would appear, but there was no way to activate that task, no way to bring it forward, nothing to do but halt the task. Finally, after some detailed code review, the line SET HELP TO was found, which of course does not set help off, but rather tries to set help to the FoxHelp file. Since this was a production machine with no such file, a friendly FoxPro locate dialog would appear. However, since this was a Remote Automation server, it had no interface. Hang city.

SYS(2335) allows us to avoid all that trouble. If you are developing COM EXEs and want to make sure they don't attempt to create a dialog, hanging your server, set SYS(2335) as soon as possible in the code that starts your server.

SYS(2335) reports that a DLL starts out in mode 1, but that is incorrect. An attempt to start a dialog within an in-process DLL always fires an error 2031. We think SYS(2335) should report that you are in unattended mode. Instead, you need to check both this function and the StartMode property to determine if your application has started as an EXE or DLL.

Example

```
lnOldMode = SYS(2335)   && preserve the old mode
lnNewMode = SYS(2335,0)   && and set it as desired.
```

See Also Error, On Error, StartMode

Sys(3004), Sys(3005), Sys(3006)

These functions are relevant only if you need to deal with localized versions of applications, something we have no experience with. When you want FoxPro to talk to, say, the French version of Excel via OLE, you have to tell OLE what language you're sending the commands in.

Usage

```
cLocale = SYS( 3004 )
cResult = SYS( 3005, nLocaleId )
cResult = SYS( 3006, nLanguageId )
```

SYS(3004) tells you what language OLE currently expects. SYS(3005) lets you change that language. Its nLocaleId parameter is the same as the cLocale return value of SYS(3004) except for the data type. Seems pretty dumb for one to return character while the other expects numeric, but we've noticed that something in the SYS() engine seems to always prefer character returns.

SYS(3006) is a little more complex and is not for the faint-hearted. nLanguageId is a code based on both the language and the sort order. We don't think it's an accident that the codes are not included in Help. This is the kind of stuff usually only C programmers mess with. We went looking for them and eventually found them in the Developer's Library buried in information on the Win32 Software Development Kit. Microsoft recommends you switch these settings using DefOLELCID instead. We're in pretty much over our heads here, so we're inclined to go along with them.

It's pretty odd to have SYS() functions that actually change something, not just return information, but we suspect the idea here was to bury these where only the folks who really need them would find them.

Both SYS(3005) and SYS(3006) return the empty string.

Example

```
? SYS(3004)    && Returns 1033, the code for English
```

See Also DefOLELCID, Set Collate

Sys(3050)

This obscurely named function lets you specify how much memory Visual FoxPro can grab. It has separate settings for foreground memory (when VFP's in control) and background memory (when you leave VFP running while you do something else). The function can also tell you the current settings.

Usage `cMemoryInBytes = SYS(3050, nType [, nMemoryInBytes ] )`

Parameter	Value	Meaning
nType	1	Inquire about or change foreground memory.
	2	Inquire about or change background memory.
nMemoryInBytes	0	Reset to startup value for your system.
	Positive number	Round down to nearest 256K and allow VFP to use that much memory.
cMemoryInBytes	String of digits	The actual amount of memory VFP can use.

FoxPro loves memory—it always has. All other things being equal, FoxPro wants to grab as much memory as it can get. In Windows, that's not always a very nice thing to do. FoxPro 2.x for Windows included the MemLimit setting in the Config.FPW file to put a limit on FoxPro's appetite for memory. MemLimit doesn't do a thing in VFP, but SYS(3050) takes its place. Use it to cap the amount of memory Visual FoxPro can grab (or to let it have more than the default, if you know you won't be running other apps.) Our friend Mac Rubel has spent a lot of time testing VFP's behavior with different amounts of memory. His conclusion is that allocating too much memory can slow things down more than allocating not enough, so watch out with these settings.

Memory is allocated to FoxPro in chunks of 256K bytes. The number you pass to SYS(3050) is rounded down (unless it's less than 256, in which case it's rounded up). Pass the number (or divide the return value) as a multiple of 1024 for "K" or 1024^2 for megabytes.

We haven't figured out yet where VFP gets the initial values. Let us know if you've worked it out.

Example

```
? SYS(3050,1,2000000)       && Returns 1835008, much too little
? VAL(SYS(3050,1))/1024^2   && Returns 1.75 Mb
```

See Also Sys(1001), Sys(1016)

Sys(3051), Sys(3052)

The goal of these two functions is to give you increased control over file and record locking. SYS(3051) supposedly lets you specify the length of time FoxPro waits before trying again to lock a file. SYS(3052) lets you decide what FoxPro does if an index or memo file is locked and you want to lock it.

Usage `cWaitTime = SYS( 3051 [, nWaitTime ] )`

Parameter	Value	Meaning
nWaitTime	0	Reset to default (333 milliseconds).

Parameter	Value	Meaning
nWaitTime	100 to 1000	The time, in milliseconds, FoxPro should wait between attempts to lock a file or record, if SET REPROCESS calls for multiple attempts.
	Omitted	Return the current setting.
cWaitTime	Character	The current setting for wait time. If you pass a legal value for nWaitTime, returns the new setting as a character string.

Various settings for SET REPROCESS tell FoxPro to keep trying to lock something, either indefinitely or a certain number of times or for a certain length of time. Trying over and over and over without pausing for breath is sort of like continuously dialing a phone number that's giving you a busy signal. All it does is tie up the phone lines. It makes more sense to wait a minute to let the person get off the phone. Similarly, it makes sense to wait between locking attempts to let the other user finish with whatever you're trying to lock. That's what this function is all about. We had a hard time seeing the effects of this function. It turns out that you really need to have two separate VFP sessions for it to make a difference. It's not good enough to test with different aliases in the same work area or even with private data sessions.

Usage

```
cHonorReprocess = SYS( 3052, nFileType [, lHonorReprocess ] )
```

Parameter	Value	Meaning
nFileType	1	Index Files
	2	Memo Files
lHonorReprocess	Logical	Should attempts to lock the specified file type honor the current reprocess setting?
	Omitted	Return the current setting for the specified file type.
cHonorReprocess	"0"	VFP doesn't honor the reprocess setting for the specified file type.
	"1"	VFP honors the reprocess setting for the specified file type.

We've heard of just a few applications that, every once in a while, have a problem locking an index file. We suspect there may be some differences in the mechanisms used to lock individual records and those used for their counterparts in memo and index files that lead to such problems. If our speculations are true, this function was designed to remedy such problems.

By default, FoxPro tries over and over and over to lock the index or memo files it needs. This function lets you set some limits on those attempts.

We should add that we've been unable to come up with a situation in which this function makes a difference, but we think it might for those applications we mentioned above. We asked around but couldn't find anyone who's ever needed to actually use this function, though.

Both of these functions, by the way, like just about all the SYS() functions, remind us that the FoxPro team is composed of C programmers. Return numeric and logical values as character? C'mon, get real!

Example

```
* Lengthen the reprocess delay
= SYS(3051,1000)
```

See Also Set Reprocess

Sys(3053)

This one is only for those brave souls who've mastered the mysteries of ODBC (Open DataBase Connectivity, Microsoft's contribution to the client-server world). It opens a connection to ODBC and returns the handle to that connection. The handle can then be used in calls to the ODBC API (Application Programming Interface).

Usage `nODBCHandle = SYS(3053)`

We don't know too many people who make direct calls to ODBC. Unless you've paid your dues with the ODBC SDK (boy, Microsoft really is into three- and four-letter acronyms, isn't it?), we suggest you don't do this.

Example `nHandle = SYS(3053)`

See Also Declare-DLL, Set Library

SYS(3054)

This cool function, introduced in VFP 5, makes it easier to tell whether your queries are as fast as they could be. It displays optimization information (known as "SQL ShowPlan") in the main VFP window.

Usage `cSetting = SYS( 3054 [, nSetting ] )`

Parameter	Value	Meaning
nSetting	0	Turn on SQL ShowPlan.
	1	Turn on SQL ShowPlan for filters only.
	11	Turn on SQL ShowPlan for filters and joins.
	Omitted	In VFP 6, return the current ShowPlan setting. In VFP 5, same as passing 1.
cSetting	Character	In VFP 6, the value of nSetting passed in, as a character string. In VFP 5, the empty string.

Have you ever had a query that was much slower than you expected it to be and you couldn't figure out what was slowing it down? We sure have. SYS(3054) is the ticket to solving these problems. When you turn it on and run a query, VFP shows you exactly how it's optimizing the query. The feedback tells you which tags it's using and how well things are optimized. For joins, it tells you which tag is being used to optimize the join.

At first glance, it seems odd that there are three settings for this function. Actually, it seems that way on second glance, too. Usually, when we work with SYS(3054), we want to know about both joins and filters. However, the designers of VFP thought you might want filter information only. In fact, the parameter 11 for filter and join information isn't documented in VFP 5. For some reason, there's no way to get join information only.

In VFP 5, issuing SYS(3054) always echoes some feedback to the active window ("SQL ShowPlan is enabled" for SYS(3054,1)). In VFP 6, that feedback is gone; instead, the function returns the value you pass it.

Once you turn on SQL ShowPlan, each time you execute a query, optimization information appears in the active window. For each table in the query, you get a report of whether it's fully, partially, or not optimized, as well as the name of the tag or tags used to optimize it.

For each join, there's a line indicating what tag is used to optimize the join. In some cases, VFP decides to build a temporary tag and use that—when it does, it tells you. Join information appears in the order in which the joins are physically performed, which often doesn't correspond to the logical order in the query. See "Faster than a Speeding Bullet" in "Franz and Other Lists" for information about speeding up your queries and using SYS(3054) to figure out what's wrong.

Example

```
?SYS(3054,11)    && echoes 11 in VFP 6
* Using TasTrade data
SELECT * ;
   FROM customer JOIN orders ;
     ON customer.customer_id = orders.customer_id ;
   WHERE UPPER(company_name) = "C" ;
   INTO CURSOR test
?SYS(3054,0)
```

See Also Select-SQL

Sys(3055)

This function, new in VFP 6, lets you decide how much of your resources (okay, FoxPro's resources) should be available for parsing complex FOR and WHERE clauses. You'll rarely need it, but when you do, you'll sure be glad they added it.

Usage

```
nPreviousAllocation = SYS( 3055 [, nNewAllocation ] )
```

One of the cooler things about VFP is the ability to work against views and not have to think about whether data is local or remote. In previous versions of VFP, this ability was severely limited. If a local view was updateable and set for the WHERE clause to check "key and modified fields" (or "key and updateable fields"), you were limited to changing 23 or fewer fields at a time. If you changed more than that, you'd get error 1812—SQL Statement Too Long. (And when it happened to you, you felt a lot like Napoleon on the road to Moscow.)

It turns out that this was a trade-off made by the VFP team. (We think it's a memory issue, though we couldn't detect memory consequences.) As of VFP 6, they've put the trade-off in our hands instead. First, they raised the initial limit. The new default, and the lower limit the function will accept, is 40 changed fields. If you know you need to handle more than that, you can call SYS(3055) to up the limit. Pass it eight times the number of fields you want to handle. The maximum is 2040, which is conveniently 255*8.

We've also heard occasionally of people getting the same or similar error messages in other situations. This function should help there, too. You may need to experiment to find the right setting in that case.

Our friends at Microsoft tell us there can be performance consequences from raising this value. In our tests here at Hacker Labs, we found that the time to update from a view to a table did increase a little with higher values of SYS(3055), but the increases were so tiny you won't see them unless you're doing a ton of updates. (With 1000 updates of a record with 48 fields, the total time increased by about three seconds when we went from the minimum SYS(3055) setting that would do the job to the maximum setting. Interestingly, the increase wasn't a straight line—some lower SYS(3055) values resulted in more time than higher ones—but that could reflect other things going on with the test machine. Also interestingly, we saw no difference in memory usage with the different settings.) Bottom line: Raise this one if you need it, but don't bother if it's not relevant to your situation.

We also note that the term "complexity," used to describe this function in the docs, is something of a misnomer in this context. The WHERE clause generated by a TableUpdate() is never complex, just long.

Example

```
* Handle TableUpdate() for a query with 100 modifiable fields.
SYS(3055, 800)
```

See Also DBSetProp(), Sys(3054), TableUpdate()

Sys(3056)

SYS(3056) allows you to make temporary changes to your Visual FoxPro configuration, and then issue this function to restore the values you've established in the Registry and Config.FPWfiles.

Usage `SYS( 3056 [, nSkipSets ] )`

Parameter	Value	Meaning
nSkipSets	1	Restore the current environment to those settings stored in the Registry, but do not modify the SET commands and do not read the Config,FPW file.
	0 or Omitted	Restore all settings in the current VFP environment by reading them first from the Registry, including SET commands, and then reading the current Config.FPW file.

The Options dialog of the Tools menu puts a fascinating assortment of information into the Registry: many SET settings (including those that used to be available from the View window), default file locations, IntelliDrop field mappings, ActiveX controls, Syntax Coloring and all sorts of neat other options. SYS(3056) is the programmatic way to get VFP to read all of these settings we've stored. We see this being handy in two situations. First, it allows us to restore all settings to their "Saved as Default" values when we are messing around. Second, it allows us to twiddle the Registry to set those settings like Syntax Coloring or SCC settings that don't have a matching VFP SET command, and then issue SYS(3056) to force VFP to read the changes we've made.

These options are stored to HKEY_CURRENT_USER\Software\Microsoft\VisualFoxPro\ 6.0\Options. You can use the native tools of your platform—RegEdit and RegEdt32—or a number of third-party tools to edit these settings, but do so with caution. Backups of the Registry should be a routine and regular task in your shop, and consider copying the set of keys you're working on to a REG file before messing with them.

Note that options listed in the Registry in all uppercase (like NOTIFY) correspond to SET commands, whereas the mixed-case options (like EditorCommentColor) do not have a matching SET command.

SYS(3056) affects only those settings stored in the Registry key above, and not the subfolders of that key. That means that there are problems with Intellidrop (field-mapping) classes, Visual FoxPro classes (those shown on the Form and Class Control toolbars), and ActiveX controls. There are actually two different problems here: Intellidrop settings are immediately written to the Registry when you use the Options dialog, even if you don't press the Set As Default button, so issuing SYS(3056) just reads them back. This can still be an advantage to you: If you set the settings in the Registry programmatically, SYS(3056) will read them for you. But you can't experiment with these settings and then just issue SYS(3056) to restore to the previous settings. Once they're chosen, you need to remember the original settings to restore them.

The second problem is that the ActiveX and Visual Class Libraries available on the Controls tab of the Options dialog are never re-read. All of the other options displayed in the Options dialog do get re-read from the Registry by this function.

Example

```
SYS(3056,1)   && restore file locations, but not SETs
```

See Also Configuration Files, Registration Database, Set, Set Resource, SYS(2019)

Sys(4204) See _RunActiveDoc.

SysMetric() See FontMetric().

TabIndex

This property determines the tab order of controls within a container. It's maintained separately for different containers, so you can do things like order the buttons in a group separately from the order of controls on the form.

Usage
```
oObject.TabIndex = nTabOrder
nTabOrder = oObject.TabIndex
```

This property determines the sequence of data entry in your form—the route through the controls the user will take if she presses the arrow keys or Tab to move from one control to the next. The order in which a user tabs through the controls in a form does not have to be the same as the creation order of the controls. TabIndex lets you determine the tab order. Every container except grids and page frames, which have different properties for this (so much for polymorphism), lets you set TabIndex for each control inside that accepts focus. When you tab (or arrow, in some cases) through the controls in that container, the order you see is the TabIndex order of those controls.

The structure used here is well thought out. Rather than numbering every control on a form in one sequence at the form level, you specify the order only for those controls directly contained on the form. If some of those controls contain others (for example, command groups contain command buttons), you number the items inside that container independently from the form. So each command group, option group and page has its own numbering sequence, no matter how deeply it's nested. The container has a TabIndex (or in the case of pages, PageOrder) that determines its sequence within the form or page that holds the container. This approach makes it easy to reorder things without fouling up the work you've already done.

At design time, the Tab Order option on the View menu lets you manipulate TabIndex without having to fiddle in the Property Sheet. Think of it as an "Order Builder."

We suggest you use the Tab Order menu option, rather than manipulating values on the Property Sheet. There are two methods of ordering available at design time. You choose the one you want in the Tools-Options dialog, under the Forms tab. You can set Tab Ordering to be either "Interactive" or "By List," our preference. It's easy to get confused about the TabIndexes of objects in a group. When you change one, the others don't change to fill in the gaps, so you can end up with several objects with identical TabIndexes. (Don't know why VFP can't adjust them. Other properties like PageOrder are smart enough to do this. On the other hand, that automatic adjustment makes manipulating PageOrder really tough, so maybe there's no good solution to this one.)

You can use the Tab Order dialog to reorder at any level. Just right-click, Edit on the container you want to reorder, then choose View-Tab Order from the menu. The dialog lets you reorder the objects inside the chosen container. Very cool!

You can change the TabIndex at runtime, too (though it suffers from the same confusion as at design time), but we suggest you don't. Except in very unusual circumstances, changing the order in which the user tabs through the controls definitely falls into the category of a user-hostile interface.

Example
```
ThisForm.cmgNavButtons.cmdTop.TabIndex = 1
```

See Also ColumnOrder, CommandGroup, OptionGroup, Page, PageOrder, ZOrder

TableUpdate(), TableRevert()

These functions commit or discard changes to buffered data.

Usage

```
lSuccess = TableUpdate( [ lAll | nUpdateWhat [, lForce
                        [, cAlias | nWorkArea
                        [, ErrorRecordsArray ] ] ] ] )
nAffected = TableRevert( [ lAll [, cAlias | nWorkArea ] ] )
```

Parameter	Value	Meaning
lAll	Logical	Should we update or revert all records or just the current record? Relevant only when using table buffering.
nUpdateWhat	0	Update only the current row.
	1	If table buffering is on, update all rows. If row buffering is on, update the current row. Give up as soon as an error occurs, leaving whatever has already been updated changed.
	2	Same as 1, except if an error occurs, log it in aErrorRecords and continue.
lForce	Logical	Should we insist on our changes going through, even if others have changed the record in the meantime?
cAlias	Character	Commit or discard changes for table cAlias.
	Omitted	If nWorkArea is also omitted, commit or discard changes for the table in the current work area.
nWorkArea	Numeric	The work area containing the table to have changes committed or discarded.
	Omitted	If cAlias is also omitted, commit or discard changes for the table in the current work area.
ErrorRecordsArray	Array Name	If nUpdateWhat is 2, contains a list of record numbers for which the update was unsuccessful.
lSuccess	.T.	All changes were successfully committed.
	.F.	Some changes could not be committed.
nAffected	Numeric	The number of records for which changes were discarded.

When you're working with buffered data, sooner or later you need to either copy the data from the buffer to the original table or view, or throw away the changes and restore the original data. That's what these two functions are about.

TableRevert() is simpler. It's the one you want when the user presses Cancel. You might also use it when you encounter a conflict and the user chooses to keep the other guy's changes. (You could also handle that case on a field-by-field basis—see GetFldState().)

For both functions, the lAll parameter is relevant only when you're using table buffering. With row buffering, whichever value you pass, you still affect only the current record. TableUpdate() offers an alternative approach to specifying what to update, too. You can pass 0, 1 or 2 for nUpdateWhat. 0's easy—it means update only the current row and corresponds to passing .F. for lAll. 1 is the same as passing .T. for lAll—it says to try to update all the records, but give up as soon as any record can't be committed. The problem with this approach is that it can leave you with some records updated and some not updated. Unless you're wrapped in a transaction, this is a recipe for disaster.

Fortunately, in VFP 5 and VFP 6, you have another alternative. Passing 2 for nUpdateWhat says to go ahead and commit all the changes you can, and create a log of the records that couldn't be changed. ErrorRecordsArray is a one-column array containing the record pointers for all those records.

The lForce parameter offers two attitudes toward updating. You can be polite and check whether anyone else has changed the data in the meantime, or you can be rude and ride roughshod over other people's changes.

Your application can approach updates from two perspectives. You can give it a shot and cope if the update fails. In this case, you'll probably want lForce to be .F. The other choice is to check for conflicts first and resolve them, then commit your changes with lForce = .T. when you've taken care of all the problems.

In VFP 3, when you use table buffering, you have to either commit or revert changes before you can close the form. Otherwise, you get an error message—fair enough. What isn't fair is that when you're using a private data session, the form goes ahead and closes and leaves you with a data session labeled "Unknown" with the offending table still open. In fact, anything that prevents a table from closing (like a trigger failing) when you close the form causes the same problem. The moral is that you must be sure to either commit or revert changes as part of a form close. If you should get caught in this situation, you can go to the View window, choose the Unknown data session, select the open table, issue TableRevert(.T.), then close the table. Once you've closed every table in the Unknown data session (any relation to the Unknown Soldier?), the session goes away.

In later versions of VFP, failing to either commit or revert changes before closing a form is the same as reverting the changes.

Example

```
* Click code for a cancel button may be as simple as:
=TableRevert()

* For a Save button, there are several approaches. If you choose
* to resolve conflicts first (see GETFLDSTATE() for one way to
* do so for a single record), you can finish up with a call
* to TableUpdate():
IF NOT TableUpdate(2, .T., ALIAS(),aSaveErrors)
   * force changes on all rows, but just in case, track
   * any errors in an array
   * You'll want something a little more sophisticated here.
   WAIT WINDOW "Unexpected problem with " + ;
               ALEN(aSaveErrors,1) + " records"
ENDIF
```

See Also Buffering, CurVal(), GetFldState(), GetNextModified(), OldVal()

Tabs

This property determines whether or not the pages in a page frame have tabs. Tabs let the user click on a page to bring it to the top. Without tabs, the pages sit one on top of the other and you have to bring different pages to the top programmatically (by changing ActivePage).

Usage

```
pgfPageFrame.Tabs = lHasTabs
lHasTabs = pgfPageFrame.Tabs
```

If Tabs is .T., the setting of BorderWidth is ignored and a border width of 1 pixel is used.

If you use tabs, you can force them to stay in a single row or let them get stacked as in the Tools-Options dialog. Check out TabStretch.

In VFP 5 and later, TabStyle lets you base the width of each tab on its contents.

Tabs can only be at the top of the page frame—if you need something else, check out some of the ActiveX controls around.

Example
```
ThisForm.pgfDays.Tabs = .T.
```

See Also ActivePage, BorderWidth, Page, Page frame, TabStretch, TabStyle

_Tabs **See _Alignment.**

TabStop

This property determines whether you can get to a control with the keyboard.

Usage
```
oObject.TabStop = lCanTabHere
lCanTabHere = oObject.TabStop
```

You can use TabStop to make some items mouse-only. For example, you can emulate the Mac interface by setting TabStop to .F. for all buttons, check boxes and the like. (We can't imagine why anybody would want to work that way, but it *is* the Mac standard.) If your users demand this interface convention, make sure all of your graphical controls have hot keys, so reaching for the mouse isn't mandatory to make it through a form.

TabStop is most useful when you want, for example, to let the user tab through the data-entry fields without having to tab through all the buttons, too. The downside of this, of course, is that the user then has to resort to button hot keys or switch to the mouse to save her data.

You can change TabStop at runtime, but we don't recommend it. It seems like a good way to terminally confuse your users.

TabStop is ignored for controls in a column of a grid. The docs say that it's read-only in that case, but in fact you can change it. Your changes are ignored, however. Seems that controls in a grid, if available, must be tab-able.

Example
```
* Keep user from tabbing into all buttons on a form
* Actually this only affects buttons based on the base classes
ThisForm.SetAll("TabStop", .F., "CommandButton")
ThisForm.SetAll("TabStop", .F., "OptionButton")
```

See Also Enabled, ReadOnly, TabIndex

TabStretch, TabStyle

These page frame properties determine whether the pages are kept in a single row or stacked in multiple rows (like the Tools-Options dialog) if the captions don't all fit in a single row, and whether all the tabs are the same size or if they adjust to fit their captions.

Usage
```
pgfPageFrame.TabStretch = nStackOrClip
nStackOrClip = pgfPageFrame.TabStretch
pgfPageFrame.TabStyle = nFixedOrNot
nFixedOrNot = pgfPageFrame.TabStyle
```

We guess Microsoft figures there might be some other choices for these properties someday. It's the only reason we can think of for making them numeric instead of logical. Visual SourceSafe shows one such possibility—a "ragged row" of tabs, with forward/back buttons to scroll through the tabs, looking sort of like a spinner on its side. It does free up some screen real estate, but it doesn't do much for us.

VFP 5 and VFP 6 are smarter than VFP 3 in deciding what constitutes the tabs fitting. We suspect that's due to the addition of TabStyle, which no doubt necessitated some work in the calculation of tab sizes. In VFP 3, there's no way to control the size of the tabs, so it's not like FoxPro says, "I can only fit this many of your desired tab width in the allocated space." We've seen tabs get stacked in that version even when there appeared to be plenty of white space on either side of every tab caption. In these cases, we can set TabStretch to "clip" and still see the complete caption for every tab. Fortunately, VFP 5 and VFP 6 seem to do a much better job of this.

When you do stack tabs, be sure to leave TabStyle at the default, 0-Justified. (For a good laugh, create a page frame with a whole bunch of pages with different caption widths, then set TabStretch to 0-Multiple Rows and TabStyle to 1-Nonjustified.) In VFP 3, you'll want to fiddle with the page frame's size to be sure every row has the same number of pages. The look of a page frame with an odd number in the last row is really strange.

Example

```
ThisForm.pgfQuarters.TabStretch = 0  && but you'll usually set
ThisForm.pgfQuarters.TabStyle = 0    && these in the PropSheet
```

See Also Page, PageCount, Page frame, Tabs

Tag See Comment.

Tag() See Candidate().

TagCount(), TagNo()

> He telleth the number of the stars; he calleth them all by their names.
>
> *The Book of Psalms* 147:4

This pair of functions was added to FoxPro 2.6 for compatibility with dBase. Despite the short shrift they're given in the documentation, they're both fairly useful. TAGCOUNT() tells you the number of tags and stand-alone indexes open for a table, while TAGNO() identifies the position of a tag or index in the list of open indexes.

Usage

```
nTotalTags = TAGCOUNT( [ cIndexFile [, nWorkArea | cAlias ] ] )
```

Parameter	Value	Meaning
cIndexFile	Character	Name of the CDX file for which to return a tag count.
	Omitted or Empty	Return the total open tag count for the table.
nWorkArea	Numeric	Return information about the table open in work area nWorkArea.
	Omitted	If cAlias is also omitted, return information about the table open in the current work area.
cAlias	Character	Return information about the table open as cAlias.
	Omitted	If nWorkArea is also omitted, return information about the table open in the current work area.

TAGCOUNT() tells you either how many tags are in a specified index file or the total number of tags and stand-alone indexes open for a table. Despite its documentation, you can pass the name of a stand-alone index file (IDX) for cIndexFile. One use for this capability is to see whether a particular index file is open. If so, TAGCOUNT() returns 1; if the index isn't open or doesn't exist, TAGCOUNT() returns 0.

There's a secret to making TAGCOUNT() useful in work areas other than the current work area. The order of parameters makes it seem that you have to inquire about a particular index file in another work area, but passing the empty string for cIndexFile causes the function to return all tag information.

Example

```
USE Employee     && TasTrade employee table
? TAGCOUNT()     && Returns 3
SELECT 0         && move to another work area
? TAGCOUNT("","Employee")           && Returns 3
? TAGCOUNT("Employee","Employee")   && Returns 3
```

Usage

```
nTagNumber = TAGNO( [ cIndexName [, cIndexFile
                    [, nWorkArea | cAlias ] ] ] )
```

Parameter	Value	Meaning
cIndexName	Character	Name of the stand-alone index or tag whose position is to be returned.
	Omitted	Return the position of the current master index.
cIndexFile	Character	Name of the CDX file about which to return information.
	Omitted	Return the position of the current master index.
nWorkArea	Numeric	Return information about the table open in work area nWorkArea.
	Omitted	If cAlias is also omitted, return information about the table open in the current work area.
cAlias	Character	Return information about the table open as cAlias.
	Omitted	If nWorkArea is also omitted, return information about the table open in the current work area.

The tags and stand-alone indexes open at any time have position numbers assigned to them (based on the order in which they were opened—for more on these, see CANDIDATE()). Many of the index information functions (for example, TAG() and KEY()) accept these position numbers to indicate which tag or index you want information about. TAGNO() takes a tag or index name and tells you its current index number.

As with TAGCOUNT(), you can pass the name of a stand-alone index for cIndexFile, but we really can't see any reason you'd want to, since you have to pass the same name for cIndexName.

Both TAGCOUNT() and TAGNO() simply return 0 if the named index or file doesn't exist.

Example

```
USE Employee
? TAGNO("Last_Name")  && Returns 2
? TAGNO("Group_Id")   && Returns 1
SELECT 0              && Go to another work area
? TAGNO("Last_Name","","Employee")  && Returns 2
```

See Also Candidate(), Index, Key(), Tag()

_Tally

This system variable tells you how many records were processed by the last command that affects it. The most common use for _TALLY is to check how many records were returned by a SQL-SELECT, but it actually works with many Xbase commands and the other SQL commands.

Usage `nNumAffected = _TALLY`

Here is the complete list of commands that change _TALLY (well, we think it's complete—we tried a bunch of undocumented stuff):

Append From	Delete	Replace
Average	Delete-SQL	Replace From Array
Blank	Export	Select-SQL
Calculate	Index	Sort
Copy To	Pack	Sum
Copy To Array	Recall	Update-SQL
Count	Reindex	

Actually, JOIN, TOTAL and UPDATE are documented as changing _TALLY, too, but they're so obsolete, we didn't even test them. A good thumbrule is that _TALLY is updated by every command that displays a record count when TALK is ON.

Generally, _TALLY contains the number of records affected by the command. So, after DELETE, it has the number of records deleted; after REPLACE, _TALLY contains the number of records that had a field replaced.

However, there's one real oddity on this list. _TALLY after REINDEX contains the number of records for which the last tag indexed applies. If you have filtered tags (indexes using a FOR clause), _TALLY returns the number of records contained in the last index. "Last" here refers to the creation order of the tags, since they're re-created in the same order. This isn't really a big problem since we suggest you never use REINDEX anyway.

In VFP 3 and VFP 5, when TALK is OFF, INDEX and REINDEX don't update _TALLY. This bug is fixed in VFP 6.

Example

```
SELECT First_Name, Last_Name FROM Employee ;
   WHERE MONTH(Birth_Date)=MONTH(DATE()) ;
   INTO ARRAY aThisMonth
* Check if any records met the criteria
IF _TALLY=0
   * If not, create the array with blank values
   DIMENSION aThisMonth[1,2]
   aThisMonth = ""
ENDIF
```

This example shows perhaps the most common use of _TALLY. When you SELECT INTO an array and no records are selected, the array doesn't get created. So, it's usual to test _TALLY right afterwards and, if necessary, create the array.

However, the wide range of commands that affect _TALLY lends itself to all kinds of possibilities. We bet most of you have sections of code that perform one of the commands above, then use COUNT or RECCOUNT() or ALEN() to see how many records were affected (we sure do). And there was _TALLY just waiting to give you the answer. Here's a simple example:

```
USE Employee
COUNT FOR MONTH(Birth_Date)=MONTH(DATE())
WAIT WINDOW ;
     LTRIM(STR(_TALLY))+" employees have birthdays this month"
```

Do watch out for one thing with _TALLY. Because so many commands affect it, it's important to grab the value right away if you want to keep using it. Otherwise, you run the risk that a later command will overwrite the value.

See Also Append From, Average, Blank, Calculate, Copy To, Copy To Array, Count, Delete, Delete-SQL, Export, Index, Join, Pack, Recall, Reindex, Replace, Replace From Array, Select-SQL, Sort, Sum, Total, Update, Update-SQL

Tan() See Cos().

Target() See Relation().

TerminateRead

This is another property included only for conversion of FoxPro 2.x screen sets. It corresponds to the Terminate Read option offered by several 2.x controls. When this property is .T. for a control, using that control shuts down the formset.

Usage
```
oObject.TerminateRead = lEndItAll
lEndItAll = oObject.TerminateRead
```

This property is relevant only for formsets running in one of the READ compatibility modes (with WindowType = 2 or 3). It's ignored otherwise.

See Also Release, WindowType

_Text See Set TextMerge.

Text See Value.

Text ... EndText

This delimiter pair lets you specify a block of text to be sent somewhere (where depends on other settings) without having to put quotes around it or use a printing command like ?. It's most useful with text merge.

Usage
```
TEXT
OutputText
ENDTEXT
```

When FoxPro hits a TEXT block, it sends the enclosed text to the current output location, usually the active window. The text can be redirected several different ways. The most common and useful is with SET TEXTMERGE. This sends the text to the current textmerge output file and indicates that any items enclosed in the textmerge delimiters ("<<" and ">>", by default) should be evaluated before being output.

Text can also be redirected with SET PRINT or by assigning a file handle to the _TEXT system variable. However, in this case, expressions in textmerge delimiters are not evaluated; they're simply copied.

Example
```
SET TEXTMERGE TO Text.TXT
SET TEXTMERGE ON NOSHOW
TEXT
This text ends up in the output file.
Any variables or functions enclosed in the delimiters will be
evaluated. For example, today is <<DATE()>>.
ENDTEXT
SET TEXTMERGE OFF
SET TEXTMERGE TO
```

See Also Set Print, Set TextMerge, _Text

TextBox

The text box is Visual FoxPro's answer to the @...GET of old. It lets you enter any alphanumeric data, and can store it as any data type.

Property	Value	Purpose
Format	Character	Contains a string of formatting codes to be applied to the entire text box contents.
HideSelection	Logical	Determines whether selected text keeps its highlight when focus moves to another control.
InputMask	Character	Contains a string of format characters that specify a template for the input value.
Margin	Numeric	Specifies the size of the margin around the entire interior of the text box.
MemoWindow	Character	Specifies the name of a window to be used for expanding the text, if the ControlSource is a memo field. Backward compatibility only.
OpenWindow	Logical	Supposed to specify whether the MemoWindow opens automatically when focus lands on the text box. Doesn't. Backward (and badly implemented) compatibility only.
PasswordChar	Character	Specifies a character to display instead of the user's input. Allows text boxes to be used for input of passwords.
SelectOnEntry	Logical	Determines whether the text in the text box is highlighted when the user tabs into it. Has no effect when the user clicks to get in.
SelLength, SelStart	Numeric	Length and starting position of the currently selected text.
SelText	Character	Currently selected text.
Text	Character	Contains a character representation of the value of the text box with no formatting.

Event	Purpose
KeyPress	The user pressed a key while focus was in the text box.

Example

```
* The class here is designed for collecting
* US and Canadian phone numbers.
DEFINE CLASS PhoneText AS TextBox

  Format = "R"
  InputMask = "(999)999-9999"

ENDDEFINE
```

See Also Edit box, Format, HideSelection, InputMask, KeyPress, Margin, MemoWindow, OpenWindow, PasswordChar, SelectOnEntry, SelLength, SelStart, SelText, Text

TextHeight, TextWidth

The TextHeight and TextWidth methods return the size of a supplied text string, in pixels.

Usage
```
nHeight = objFormOrScreen.TextWidth( cString )
nWidth = objFormOrScreen.TextHeight( cString )
```

These methods are handier versions of the TxtWidth() and FontMetric() functions. They return the size a text string will take up on a Form or on the _SCREEN, expressed in pixels. The calculation is based on the current output window's text name, size and style.

TextWidth returns the length of the longest line of text, if carriage returns are included in the supplied string. TextHeight increases correctly as well, but only if the string includes linefeed characters. This is not the case with VFP 3.x, where TextWidth returns the width for the whole string, as if the carriage returns were printable characters. For VFP 3.x, use MemLines() and MLine() to parse the string into individual lines and pass them to TextWidth(). With VFP 5.0 and later, this bug has been squashed.

Example
```
_SCREEN.FontName = "Arial"
_SCREEN.FontSize = 10
nHowWide = _SCREEN.TextWidth("How wide is my string?")   && 134
nHowHigh = _SCREEN.TextHeight("How high is my string?")  && 16
```

See Also FontMetric, MemLines(), MLine(), TxtWidth(), ScaleMode

This, ThisForm, ThisFormSet

The documentation refers to these three as "object references" and we can't think of anything better. They're not commands nor functions; neither are they properties, events nor methods. And they're not exactly variables, either. What they are, in an informal sense, is handles. They let you grab onto objects without knowing the names of the objects.

Usage
```
This.Property | Method | MemberName
ThisForm.Property | Method | MemberName
ThisFormSet.Property | Method | MemberName
```

When you're writing method code for an object, you often need to refer to properties and methods of that object and of other related objects. But you don't know what the name of the object will be when it's instantiated. So you often can't write something like MyWonderfulObject.Caption.

Even when you do know the name (for example, when you're designing a form that will have only one instance), it's not a good idea to refer to the object by name. Doing so limits the reusability of the object.

Similarly, in a method of a form or formset, you don't want to refer to it by name since you may instantiate it more than once, with a different name for each instance.

The three object references are the way to avoid the problem. THIS refers to the current object. When you're in a method of a control, THIS is the control itself. In a method of a form, THIS is the form. In a method of a formset, THIS is the formset, and so on. The same idea applies to non-visual objects as well. THIS is always the object whose method you're in.

ThisForm, then, is the form containing the object. In a method of a control, ThisForm refers to the form containing the control. In a method of a form, ThisForm and THIS both refer to the form. Finally, ThisFormSet refers to the form set containing the object whose method you're in.

Example
```
oTest=CREATEOBJECT("TestForm")
oTest.SHOW()
READ EVENTS

DEFINE CLASS TestForm AS Form

   ScaleMode = 0  && Foxels just to make it easier
                  && to position things
   ADD OBJECT txtUpdate AS Updater
   ADD OBJECT cmdClear AS ClearButton
   ADD OBJECT cmdQuit AS QuitButton
```

```
PROCEDURE Init

   * set up Clear button to clear textbox
   This.cmdClear.cWhatToClear="txtUpdate"

   * position things
   This.Height=10
   This.Width=30
   This.AutoCenter=.T.

   This.txtUpdate.Left=5
   This.txtUpdate.Top=2

   This.cmdClear.Left=5
   This.cmdClear.Top=5

   This.cmdQuit.Left=15
   This.cmdQuit.Top=5

ENDPROC

ENDDEFINE

DEFINE CLASS Updater AS Textbox

   Width=20
   Height=1.5

PROCEDURE InteractiveChange
  * change the form caption

   ThisForm.Caption=This.Value

ENDPROC

PROCEDURE ProgrammaticChange
   * revert the form caption

   ThisForm.Caption="TestForm"

ENDPROC

ENDDEFINE

DEFINE CLASS ClearButton AS CommandButton

   Width=7
   Height=1.5
   Caption="Clear"

   * add a custom property
   cWhatToClear=""

PROCEDURE Click
    LOCAL cClearWhat
    cClearWhat=This.cWhatToClear
    ThisFORM.&cClearWhat..Value=""
ENDPROC

ENDDEFINE

DEFINE CLASS QuitButton AS CommandButton

   Caption="Quit"
   Width=7
   Height=1.5
```

```
PROCEDURE Click

   CLEAR EVENTS

ENDPROC

PROCEDURE Destroy

   CLEAR EVENTS

ENDPROC
ENDDEFINE
```

The example includes several class definitions, three of them controls (two buttons and a text box) and one for a form class. In the form's Init method, we can change properties of the form using THIS.property (for example, THIS.Height=10). But, in the Text box's InteractiveChange event, to change the form's caption, we need to use ThisForm.Caption, indicating that FoxPro should look outside the current object (the text box) to see the containing form.

We should point out that this sample does something we never actually do—it uses foxels. We always work in pixels. But for a hand-coded sample like this, foxels make things much easier.

See Also CreateObject(), Define Class

_Throttle See Set Debug.

Time() See Date().

Timer Control

The Timer Control is a cool little device for creating events that fire at predetermined intervals. This is a great replacement for DO...WHILE and INKEY() loops, which chew up a whole bunch of processor time counting milliseconds. The timer control is flaky and unpredictable in VFP 3.x. The Fox team has done a great job of bringing this one under control in VFP 5 and 6.

Property	Value	Purpose
Interval	Numeric	Determines length of time (in milliseconds) between Timer events.
	0	Timer is disabled.
Enabled	.T.	Timer counts down Interval milliseconds and then fires the Timer event.
	.F.	Timer does nothing.
Event	**Purpose**	
Timer	Code to be executed when event occurs.	
Method	**Purpose**	
Reset	Resets the countdown to Interval; does not change Enabled state.	

The timer is a control with no visible presence at runtime, but fires its Timer event at a regular, defined Interval. If you used READ TIMEOUT clauses in version 2.x, and hoped that these controls would solve some of the issues with that clause, we think you'll find this is a much better way to go. If you messed with this control in VFP 3 and got frustrated, give it another shot. We have to give Microsoft credit where credit is due, and they did a great job with Timer. In the original version of this book, which covered Visual FoxPro 3.0, Timer got credit for a lot of bugs—even the dreaded double-bug icon—but in 6.0, it appears vastly improved.

Timers fire when the menu is dropped down. They didn't in VFP 3.0. Timers fire in toolbars. Timers fire when a form is being dragged around. Timers fire when another application window is resized, or when Fox's window is resized. Timers fire when your application displays a message box. Awesome!

Example

```
* RemindMe.Prg
* This is a pretty trivial example of a program that accepts
* a message and the number of seconds to wait to display that
* message. In the meantime, processing can go on as normal in
* the foreground.
* Pass the message to display, and the
* Number of seconds to wait to display it
LParameters tcMessage, tnTime

_SCREEN.AddProperty("oTimer")
_SCREEN.oTimer = CreateObject("RemindTime", ;
                              tcMessage, ;
                              tnTime * 1000)   && convert to
                                               && milliseconds
RETURN

DEFINE CLASS RemindTime AS Timer
  cMessage = ""
  nTime = 0
  Interval = 5000  && check every 5 seconds
  Procedure Init(tcMessage, tnTime)
    This.cMessage = tcMessage
    This.nTime = tnTime
  EndProc
  Procedure Timer
    This.nTime = This.nTime - This.Interval
    IF This.nTime < 0  && we've exceed the interval
      MessageBox(This.cMessage)
      This.Enabled = .F.
      RELEASE This
    ENDIF
  EndProc
EndDefine
```

See Also Interval, Timer Event, Reset

Timer

The Timer event fires each time a Timer has counted down the specified Interval of time.

Usage `Procedure tmrTimer.Timer`

The Timer procedure is the place you put the code you want to run after each Timer event has been reached. The Timer's interval is specified (in milliseconds) with the Timer's Interval property; a Timer is enabled if its Enabled property is .T. and the Interval is greater than 0.

Example

```
PROCEDURE Timer1.Timer
  WAIT WINDOW NOWAIT "Time's Up!"
ENDPROC
```

See Also Interval, Timer Control

TitleBar

This property, added in VFP 6, makes creating a form without a title bar a whole lot easier.

Usage

```
oForm.TitleBar = nHasTitleBar
nHasTitleBar = oForm.TitleBar
```

Parameter	Value	Meaning
nHasTitleBar	0	The form has no title bar.
	1	The form has a title bar.

Before this property was added, removing the title bar from a form (say, to create a splash screen) was a pain. You had to set a whole bunch of properties. (See BorderStyle for the whole list.) Now you need just one, and all the others don't matter.

This property is another case of a C influence on VFP. There's no reason on earth why this property should be numeric. There are only two possible values. Unless, of course, the designers are thinking of giving us other choices here, like, say, title bars at the bottom or on the sides.

What we want to use this property for most is creating splash screens. Unfortunately, a bug means we can't create a generalized splash screen class. When a form class has TitleBar set to 0 and ShowWindow set to 2 ("as top-level form"), forms instantiated from that class have a title bar anyway. (VFP 5 has the same bug, except that to see it, you have to set that whole collection of properties that give a form without a title bar.)

Oddly, forms (the DO FORM kind) created with TitleBar = 0 and ShowWindow = 2 work just fine.

Example

```
* Check whether the active window has a title bar
IF _SCREEN.ActiveForm.TitleBar = 1
   _SCREEN.ActiveForm.Caption = "April Fool!"
ENDIF
```

See Also BorderStyle, Caption, Closable, ControlBox, MaxButton, MinButton, Movable, ShowWindow

Toolbar, Separator

Toolbars are unique in Visual FoxPro. They're neither controls nor forms, yet they have some of the behaviors of each. But they also have some behaviors all their own. A toolbar is truly a bar (not a form) full of tools. Separators are special objects that can exist only in toolbars—their role in life is to put some space between different groups of controls on the toolbar.

From the user's point of view, think of toolbars as mouse shortcuts. Instead of opening a menu popup and clicking on the desired item, the user can choose from the toolbar. Good interface design says that anything the user can do with the mouse, she can do with the keyboard, too, so don't view toolbar items as replacements for menu items—only as other ways to access them. Sadly, the Visual FoxPro interface itself breaks this rule all the time, and toolbars are one of the worst culprits. The Form Controls toolbar, for example, has no menu counterparts—if you can't use a mouse, you can't design forms in Visual FoxPro. That's inexcusable.

Toolbars are containers—they hold controls. You can put just about any control in a toolbar, but we recommend you limit yourself to command buttons, option buttons, check boxes, combo boxes, timers and maybe some ActiveX controls. (For option buttons and check boxes, you'll probably want the graphical kind.) The others are just too unwieldy for toolbars.

Like forms, toolbars can exist on their own. You can create a toolbar, then Show it and it's a live object. Toolbars can be added to form sets, but not forms. Adding a toolbar to a form set is weird, though. Once you've turned the individual form into a form set (by choosing Create Form Set from the Form menu), you add a toolbar by choosing it from the Form Controls toolbar as if it were a control. But the toolbar doesn't go onto another form—it becomes an independent member of the form set.

Toolbars can be "docked" at any side of the screen. Docking a toolbar means attaching it so it becomes part of the border. When you dock a toolbar, it reshapes itself to be as narrow as possible against the screen edge. That is, when you dock it at top or bottom, it gets as short as possible. When you dock it at either side, it gets as narrow as possible. Docked toolbars have no title bar. The user can dock toolbars by dragging the title bar to a screen edge, or by double-clicking on the title bar or any space not occupied by a control. Similarly, double-clicking on empty space or dragging that space off the edge will undock a toolbar.

A toolbar's size is determined by what it contains. When a toolbar is undocked, you can reshape it. Dragging on a side or corner doesn't enlarge or shrink the toolbar—it changes its shape. Changes to its Height and Width might reshape it, but the actual values you get for Height and Width are determined by the contents.

A toolbar can get focus only if it contains a control that allows text input (text box, edit box, spinner, or combo box). Clicking into one of those objects moves focus to the toolbar. Clicking on any other control on a toolbar leaves focus where it was before (unless the clicked control changes the focus). Even when a control on a toolbar has focus, the toolbar itself is never _SCREEN.ActiveForm. You cannot tab between controls on a toolbar even if they can get focus.

Toolbar

Property	Value	Purpose
ActiveControl	Object	References the control on the toolbar that has focus. Normally, this property contains a value only briefly while the control responds to being clicked. A few controls can actually hold focus and stay ActiveControl for more than an instant.
ControlBox	Logical	Determines whether the toolbar (when undocked) has a Close button in the upper right corner. Make sure that users can recall toolbars if they close them inadvertently. Since we think users should generally have control of their environment, we suggest you set this to .F. only in unusual circumstances.
ControlCount	Numeric	The number of controls on the toolbar.
Controls	Collection	References to the controls on the toolbar.
DataSession	Numeric	Determines whether the toolbar has its own private data session.
DataSessionId	Numeric	The ID number of the toolbar's data session.
Docked	Logical	Indicates whether the toolbar is currently docked.
DockPosition	Numeric	Determines whether the toolbar is currently docked and, if so, at which side.
KeyPreview	Logical	Supposedly determines whether controls see keypresses right away or the toolbar gets them first. But there's no corresponding KeyPress event for toolbars, so setting this is useless.
ShowTips	Logical	Determines whether tooltips for the controls on the toolbar are displayed.

Event	Purpose
AfterDock	Fires after the toolbar has been docked.
BeforeDock	Fires when the toolbar is asked to dock or undock.
Undock	Fires after the toolbar has been undocked, but before it redisplays.
Method	**Purpose**
Dock	Docks or undocks the toolbar at a specified location and position.

The ActiveControl property of a toolbar should contain an object reference only briefly, while a control is in use. But if the toolbar contains a control that can get focus (like a text box), it's possible for ActiveControl to get confused. If the text box (or whatever) has focus and you click on another control on the toolbar, ActiveControl becomes more persistent and doesn't always point to the right control.

In VFP 3 and VFP 5, timers in toolbars never fire. (Actually, we've heard they fire under some very specific, very weird circumstances, but that's maybe even worse than never.) In those versions, don't put a timer in a toolbar. However, you can create a timer and store a reference in a property of the toolbar. Tamar wrote an article about toolbars that enable and disable their controls using a timer this way (see the November '97 issue of *FoxPro Advisor*) . The good news is that this bug is fixed, so timers in toolbars do fire in VFP 6.

Separator

If toolbars are hybrid objects, separators are just barely objects at all. You stick them into toolbars to visually separate consecutive controls. They let you group similar functions together and keep them apart from other groups. All in all, pretty useful.

But separators are pretty basic. In VFP 6, they're up to a grand total of 19 PEMs, the fewest of any of FoxPro's base classes. Even though they have a position on a toolbar, separators don't have Left or Top properties—their position is determined by the position of the objects around them. You can't determine anything about their appearance (or is that lack of appearance).

Separators are actually a lot more capable in VFP 6 than in previous versions. In this version, they have their own Init, Error and Destroy events. (Actually, we suspect all VFP classes are now derived from a single base class that includes these events.) Though we've never subclassed separators except for testing purposes, the new additions make it more likely that we'll do so, in the future, just as soon as we figure out what we'd want a separator subclass to do.

Example

```
* Set up a toolbar class that keeps the user informed
* as it docks and undocks.
DEFINE CLASS AnnoyingToolBar AS ToolBar

PROCEDURE BeforeDock
   LPARAMETERS nLocation

   LOCAL cLocation

   DO CASE
   CASE nLocation = 0
      cLocation = "Top"
   CASE nLocation = 1
      cLocation = "Left"
   CASE nLocation = 2
      cLocation = "Right"
```

```
      CASE nLocation = 3
         cLocation = "Bottom"
      ENDCASE

      IF nLocation = -1
         WAIT WINDOW "Hey, I'm undocked!"
      ELSE
         WAIT WINDOW "Getting ready to dock at "+cLocation
      ENDIF

   ENDPROC

   PROCEDURE AfterDock

      WAIT WINDOW "Finished docking"

   ENDPROC

   PROCEDURE UnDock

      WAIT WINDOW "Undocked"

   ENDPROC
   ENDDEFINE
```

Other than being annoying, the class in the example is good for showing the sequence of toolbar events. When you dock the toolbar, BeforeDock fires before AfterDock (well, that makes sense). But when you undock a toolbar, Undock fires before BeforeDock. Got that?

The firing sequence was different in VFP 3. See BeforeDock for the details.

See Also ActiveControl, AfterDock, BeforeDock, ControlBox, ControlCount, Controls, Dock, Docked, DockPosition, FormCount, Forms, Undock

ToolTipText See ShowTips.

Top See Left.

TopIndex, TopItemId

These properties tell you which item in a list or combo box is at the top of the displayed list. This is one of those things people were always trying to figure out how to do in FoxPro 2.x but it couldn't be done. In Visual FoxPro, not only can you do it, but it's as simple as checking a single property!

For lists only, you can change these properties to change the display.

Usage

```
lstList.TopIndex = nIndexOfTopItem
nIndexOfTopItem = oObject.TopIndex
lstList.TopItemid = nItemIdOfTopItem
nItemIdOfTopItem = oObject.TopItemid
```

For the difference between an Index and an ItemId, see the entry for AddItem.

The docs through VFP 5.0a say you can change this property for both combos and list boxes. 'Tain't so. The docs for VFP 6 say that TopIndex is read-only at runtime, while TopItemId is read-write. That's wrong, too.

For combos, these properties are read-only. Our take is that this is a bug in the docs, not in the product. The nature of combo boxes is that they always open with the current value displayed in the visible portion of the scrollable part, so the ability to change the top item doesn't make sense.

Example `frmMyForm.lstMyList.TopItemId = 37`

See Also AddItem, ComboBox, ListBox, ListIndex, ListItemId

Total See Join.

Transform()

This function formats a numeric or character expression using the picture and function clauses available with the Format and InputMask properties.

Usage `cRetVal = TRANSFORM( uExpression [, cFormat ] )`

Parameter	Value	Meaning
eExpression	Any field types except memo, picture and general	Expression to be transformed.
cFormat	Character	Format codes, preceded by the @ symbol, and InputMask codes.
	Omitted (VFP 6 only)	Transforms any data type sent to it with a default format, specified in the Help file.
cRetVal	Character	A character string resulting from the formatting.

TRANSFORM() can be a very handy way to express a special coding system—such as currency, ID numbers or stock numbers—with a defined picture, without having to store the formatting with each field. In addition, TRANSFORM() is useful as a generic translator of any type of data, as it accepts all but general and picture fields as expressions, and always returns a character field.

Any attempt to TRANSFORM the contents of a memo field by specifying a format code results in a return of the string "Memo," a useless result as far as we are concerned. Apply ALLTRIM() to the memo field to get the result you want. Omitting the format code in VFP 6 returns the same result as ALLTRIM() but what's the point?

Example

```
cRetVal = TRANSFORM("6175551212", "@R (999) 999-9999" )
* returns "(617) 555-1212"
? TRANSFORM(12345,"@B, $$ 9,999,999")
* left-justified, floating $ sign: "$12,345"
? TRANSFORM(date(),"@E")  && returns string of format DD/MM/YY
? TRANSFORM(PRINTSTATUS(),"Y")  && displays "Y" or "N"
* The hexadecimal display was introduced in VFP 5.0:
? TRANSFORM(12345, "@0" )  && "at zero" yields "0x00003039"
* Assume that Notes is a memo field
? TRANSFORM(Notes, "@!")  && returns "Memo" - Doh!
? TRANSFORM(ALLTRIM(Notes), "@!") && returns the memo all caps
? TRANSFORM(Notes)          && in VFP 6, returns the memo value
```

See Also DToC(), DynamicInputMask, InputMask, Format, Str(), TToC(), Val()

_Transport See _Beautify.

_TriggerLevel

_TriggerLevel lets you know if a trigger is firing because an event is taking place on the table directly, or if the trigger is firing because it was called from another trigger.

Usage `nLevel = _TRIGGERLEVEL`

Parameter	Value	Meaning
nLevel	0	No trigger is in effect.
	1	A top-level trigger event is executing.
	2 or more	A trigger procedure is running within another trigger.

Using the Relational Integrity Builder or your own homegrown version, one trigger can call another. In a one-to-many relationship with cascaded deletion enabled, deleting a parent record fires the delete trigger procedure of the parent, which in turn attempts to delete the child records. This fires the delete trigger in the child table. _TriggerLevel in the parent procedure is 1; it is 2 when it reaches the child. Similarly, in a cascaded update, a change to the parent's primary key fires the update trigger procedure first of the parent, at _TriggerLevel 1, then the child's update trigger, at _TriggerLevel 2.

We can envision many circumstances where it would be important to know if the individual trigger is being fired, or if the trigger is being fired as part of a cascade. In the classic order entry scenario of an order header and many order detail records, you may want the delete trigger of the order detail record to confirm that the user really wants to delete a line item, perhaps with a MessageBox(). If, however, an entire order is to be deleted, you don't want to ask the order entry clerk to confirm every detail line deletion, but rather ask once at the order level to confirm that the entire order is to be deleted. Checking _TriggerLevel in the order detail table's delete trigger will tell you if the individual line is being deleted, or if the entire order is on its way out.

Example
```
IF _TRIGGERLEVEL > 1  && called from another trigger
```

See Also Append Procedure, Create Trigger, Modify Procedure

Trim() See AllTrim().

TToC(), TToD() See CToT().

TxnLevel() See Begin Transaction.

TxtWidth()

TXTWIDTH() returns the length in character columns that a string will take up on the current output window (or desktop), based on the specified font and style or the current default font.

Usage `nWidth = TXTWIDTH( cString [, cFont, nSize [, cStyle] ] )`

Parameter	Value	Meaning
cString	Character	The string whose length is to be calculated.
cFont	Character	The name of the font in which the string should appear.

Parameter	Value	Meaning
cFont	Omitted	Use the current output window's defined font.
nSize	Numeric	The size of the font in points.
	Omitted	Use the current output window's defined font size.
cStyle	Character	A character expression specifying the style, or combination of styles, that the string will use (see WFONT() for a listing of styles).
	Omitted	If both cFont and nSize are omitted, cStyle defaults to the current output window's defined style. If cFont and nSize are specified, the normal font style for that font is used. "Normal" is a bit misleading here, because it does not necessarily mean "plain." If a font is constructed with built-in attributes, the "normal" style for that font includes the attribute. Fox example, there is no difference in TXTWIDTH(), nor in appearance, between a display in "Arial Rounded MT Bold" when the bold attribute is set on or when it's left in its "normal" style.
nWidth	Numeric	Visual FoxPro's best guess on the size of the string, expressed in columns of the current output window's font.

TXTWIDTH() calculates the length a string will occupy in the current output window, expressed in terms of columns of the output window's font (returned by WFONT()). This is more accurate than messing with FONTMETRIC(6) values for the average character width for both fonts involved.

TXTWIDTH() can be used to do FONTMETRIC() one better, by providing the length of each character within a font, a capability sadly lacking from the latter function. Rather than using FONTMETRIC's feeble "average width," TXTWIDTH() can be used when precision is needed.

When working with varied font types and sizes, TXTWIDTH() is usually the easiest to use. But when you're working within a form and working in the default font, don't overlook the possibility of using the TextWidth and TextHeight methods instead.

Example

```
? TXTWIDTH("Hello World!", "Arial",10,"B")

* The example in Visual FoxPro's Help file for centered text
* doesn't work. They added an extra space after the font name.
* This example centers the text within the current window,
* horizontally & vertically, displays overwriting in a variety
* of colors & sizes - neat effects for logos & splash screens.

cfontname = "Arial"
do Hello with 'Hello!',cFontName,36,"RB/W"
do Hello with 'Hello!',cFontName,30,"R/W"
do Hello with 'Hello!',cFontname,24,"RG+/W"
do Hello with 'Hello!',cFontName,18,"G/W"

procedure Hello (cWhatToSay, cFontName, nFontSize, cFontColor)
@ WROWS()/2, ;
  (WCOLS( )-TXTWIDTH(cWhatToSay, cFontName,nFontSize)* ;
   FONTMETRIC(6,cFontName,nFontSize)/FONTMETRIC(6))/2  ;
  SAY cWhatToSay ;
  FONT cFontName,nFontSize ;
  COLOR (cFontColor) ;
  STYLE "T"
return
```

See Also FontMetric(), SysMetric(), TextWidth, TextHeight, WFont()

Type

This command is a lot like the DOS TYPE command, only smarter. It lets you display a text file on screen or send it to the printer or another file (though why you'd want to scroll one file to another is a mystery to us).

Usage

```
TYPE cFileName
     [ AUTO ] [ WRAP ]
     [ TO PRINTER [ PROMPT ] ]
     | [ TO FILE cOutputFile [ ADDITIVE ] ]
     [ NUMBER ]
```

Keyword	Meaning
AUTO	Turn on automatic indentation. Each paragraph is indented to the level of the first line of the paragraph.
WRAP	Turn on automatic word-wrapping.
TO PRINTER	Send the file to the printer.
PROMPT	Display the Windows Print dialog before printing.
TO FILE	Send the output to the named file.
ADDITIVE	Add to the named file instead of overwriting it.
NUMBER	Precede each line with a number.

AUTO needs to be used with WRAP. By itself, it doesn't appear to do anything. Together, the result is pretty cool. Both AUTO and WRAP use the word-processing definition of a "paragraph"—everything up to a hard return. So, files containing hard returns (CHR(13) at the end of each line) either wrap badly or not at all, depending on the original line length. Wrapping is based on an 80-character line. We don't see why TYPE doesn't respect SET MEMOWIDTH, but it doesn't.

TYPE can't handle long files with no returns in them unless you use WRAP. Without WRAP, they get cut off after 256 characters. Every version of FoxPro for Windows we tested showed the same bug, though it works properly in FoxPro for DOS.

If you specify AUTO WRAP NUMBER, be sure that none of the paragraphs begin with spaces. Lines in those paragraphs don't get numbered. We're not sure how much we care since we can't see *why* you'd want to combine those options, but we figured we ought to tell you.

As with many commands that send output to a file, the ADDITIVE clause works but is undocumented.

Whether or not you specify TO PRINTER or TO FILE, the output of TYPE scrolls in the active window. Unfortunately, TYPE ignores the setting of SET CONSOLE, so there's no direct way to prevent this. You can define and activate a window NOSHOW (or off-screen) to hide the output, but you shouldn't have to.

When SET HEADING is ON, TYPE's output includes a heading consisting of the filename, the date and a page number.

Example

```
TYPE README.TXT
TYPE BUGGY.PRG TO PRINT NUMBER
```

See Also ?, ??, ???, @ ... Say, FileToStr(), Low-Level File Functions, Set Alternate, Set Console, Set Heading, Set Printer, Set TextMerge

Type

Every item in a project has some native type, like form, menu, free table, and so forth. The Type property indicates that type.

Usage

```
cTypeChar = filFile.Type
```

Each type is indicated by a single character. Some of them make intuitive sense, like "Q" for query or "R" for report. Others are a bit of a stretch, like "D" for free table (that is, "DBF") and "V" for class library ("VCX") and a few make no sense at all: "K" for form? Maybe it stands for "sKreen"? Or maybe it's "Kouldn't find a letter we weren't already using?"

You can find the complete list in the Help file.

Type is read-write! You can change the type of a file. VFP seems amazingly immune to weird values in the Type field. We were able to change the type of a program from "P" to "D" and then call the Modify method without trashing the project or crashing the product. Not only that, but the appropriate editing window opened up. It does make you wonder what the point of the Type field is, though. It also means you need to be pretty careful about code like the example, since Type may not accurately identify the file type. Our view is that changing this property is a really bad idea. Just because they let you doesn't mean you have to do it.

Example

```
* Use Type to figure out whether or how you want to process
* each file in a project. Here we'll open forms and programs,
* and ignore everything else
oProj = _VFP.ActiveProject
FOR EACH oFile IN oProj
   IF oFile.Type $ "PK"  && Program or Form
      oFile.Modify()
   ENDIF
ENDFOR
```

See Also File, Project

Type(), VarType()

TYPE() returns the data type of the variable or field passed to it. One of the most common errors in coding FoxPro has been to forget the quotes required around the parameter for the TYPE() function. VARTYPE(), introduced in VFP 98, doesn't require quotes, is significantly faster, and provides better reporting of whether the expression is null, but it has its own idiosyncrasies. Since neither function detects code page translation flags, nor can they distinguish the many numeric field types, sometimes AFIELDS() is far more useful.

Usage

```
cValue = TYPE( cExpression )
cValue = VARTYPE( eExpression [, lIgnoreNull ] )
```

Parameter	Value	Meaning
cExpression	Character	A string that can be evaluated to a legitimate variable or field name, or a valid expression.
eExpression	Expression	Expression that evaluates to an existing variable, object or field expression.

Parameter	Value	Meaning
lIgnoreNull	.F. or omitted	Return "X" if eExpression is null.
	.T.	Return the underlying object, field or variable type if eExpression is null.
cValue	Single character	The type of the expression returned.

TYPE() and VARTYPE() return identical values except for three cases: VARTYPE() returns "X" if the expression is .NULL. and you haven't specified the optional lIgnoreNull parameter. VARTYPE() does not distinguish memos from strings, returning "C" for both, where TYPE() returns "M" and "C", respectively. Finally, VARTYPE() does not recognize Screen-type variables.

Passing a variable of type "S" (see "SAVE SCREEN") to VARTYPE() results in error 19, "Data type mismatch." The TYPE() function properly returns "S".

Note that Character fields and memory variables and Character/Binary fields both return "C," not giving you a clue that the field is stored NOCPTRANS. This is because, despite the Table Designer's popup, Character/Binary is not really a field type but the combination of type and the NOCPTRANS property. Adding it to the Designer's popup but not adding it as a new TYPE() is an inconsistency worthy of the term *bug*. Same deal for Memo fields and Memo/Binary. Bogus.

Returning the TYPE() or VARTYPE() of integer, numeric, double and float fields all as "N" is a bug. While all are treated the same way when used as memory variables, the storage and precision of integers and doubles are significantly different than the other two. A work-around is to use AFIELDS() to determine which field type you're working with, and reserve the use of TYPE() for memory variables.

Because VARTYPE() explicitly passes the expression to test as a parameter, it fails if an expression cannot be evaluated, causing an error 12, "Variable not found"—you'll still want to use TYPE() to check if a variable exists. VARTYPE() is preferred, though, if you know the variable does exist (because your code just declared it or received it as a parameter) and just need to know what type it is. In our informal tests, VARTYPE() was five or six times faster than TYPE() in most situations. Curiously, both functions seem to slow down immensely when you start to test large strings (10,000 characters and up), so you'll want to avoid repetitive testing on multi-megabyte memo fields if you can avoid it.

Example

```
? TYPE("_VFP.Name")  && returns "C"
oThing = CREATEOBJECT("Form")          && create a form object
cName = "oThing"                       && store the variable name
? TYPE("oThing")   && returns "O"
? TYPE(cName)      && also returns "O"
? ISNULL(oThing)   && returns .F.
? VARTYPE(oThing)  && returns "O"
? VARTYPE(cName)   && cName returns "C"
oThing.Release()   && make it go away
? TYPE("oThing")   && still "O"
? ISNULL(oThing)   && now .T.
? VARTYPE(oThing)  && now "X"
```

See Also AFields(), Evaluate(), IsNull(), Save Screen

TypeLibCLSID, TypeLibDesc, TypeLibName

These three properties of the Project object describe the Type Library, created to describe COM components.

Usage

```
cClassID = prjProject.TypeLibCLSID
cDescription = prjProject.TypeLibDesc
prjProject.TypeLibDesc = cDescription
cName = prjProject.TypeLibName
```

Parameter	Value	Meaning
cClassID	Character	The ClassID of the type library. This is the 16-byte unique ID for this class, represented in hexadecimal, with curly braces and hyphens added for better (but not much!) readability
cDescription	Character	The description of the servers in the type library. Set this on the Servers tab of the Project Info dialog, or programmatically via this property.
cName	Character	The name of the type library, without the TLB or VBR extension. Typically, the name of the project.

These three properties are associated with the type library, which is a file or set of files used by COM to communicate the interfaces and capabilities of an object. Type libraries are used internally by COM to register new servers on the system, and by object browsers to display the information about a server to a developer. TypeLibCLSID and TypeLibName are read-only, generated by the system, but TypeLibDesc is yet another place to store comments.

TypeLibCLSID is a number—unique across space and time (we can almost hear Rod Serling or someone like that intoning those words gravely)—generated by VFP that identifies the set of interfaces present in this project. The number is re-created each time you select "Recreate Component IDs" from the build dialog, or send .T. for the optional fifth parameter to the Build method. This class ID is used as a unique key into the Registry to store project-level information on your servers, such as the type library description and the locations of the type library and help file.

TypeLibName is the name of the generated TLB and VBR files. All the ones we generate take on the same name as the project in which they are contained.

TypeLibDesc is read-write at design time, and gives you a place to add a brief description of the servers in the type library.

Trying to set the description to more than 126 characters programmatically causes problems. If you set TypeLibDesc to 127 characters or more, you get back an empty string on testing the value from the Project. But look in the Project Info dialog and the value is there. Typing more than a couple hundred characters into the field crashes FoxPro with a nasty GPF. Don't do that!

Example

```
? oProject.TypeLibCLSID
? oProject.TypeLibName
oProject.TypeLibDesc = "My servers for testing"
```

See Also Project, Server

UIEnable

This event gives you a hook into the controls on a page when the page is activated or deactivated. It fires for each control on the page on the way into and on the way out of the page. It took us awhile to "get" this one, but it's actually pretty cool.

Usage

```
PROCEDURE oObject.UIEnable
LPARAMETERS [ nControlIndex ,] lComingIn
```

Parameter	Value	Meaning
nControlIndex	Numeric	If the control is contained in an array, indicates which element of the array fired the event.
	Omitted	The control is not part of a control array.
lComingIn	.T.	The event fired because the page containing this control is being activated.
	.F.	The event fired because the page containing this control is being deactivated.

The firing of this event is tricky. First, it fires not for the page frame, nor for the page (in fact, pages don't even have a UIEnable event), but for the controls contained on the page becoming active or inactive. That is, when a page comes to the top, the UIEnable events of the controls for the page that was on top fire, then the UIEnable events for the controls on the page that's now on top fire.

In addition, UIEnable fires only on changes to the active page. If focus leaves the page frame, it doesn't fire. Nor does it fire when focus returns to the page frame. It fires only when a different page of the page frame comes to the top.

When would you use this event? When you want to check something about some control whenever its page comes to the top. If a control on one page depends on several other controls in the page frame, UIEnable lets you update it once—when you need it to be right. For example, suppose a list is based on a view and the view parameters are specified on the other pages. You don't want to requery the view and the list every time one of the parameters changes—that would be horribly slow. Instead, you can put the calls to the REQUERY() function to update the view and the Requery method to update the list in the UIEnable method of the list and it'll be updated whenever that page comes to the top.

You might also take advantage of this event to refresh pages when they come to the top. Our tech editor tells us he adds a custom object to each page in a page frame with the UIEnable method set to call the page's Refresh method on the way in. (The adding is done in the Init method.)

This event is really elegant. On the other hand, we can't figure where its name came from. Probably from some other Microsoft language. We think PageActivate and PageDeactivate (or OnPageActivate and OnPageDeactivate) would be just a wee bit more intuitive.

Example

```
* In a simplified version of the example above, assume one page
* of a pageframe contains a list based on a query (RowSourceType=3)
* and that the query conditions include some variables
* which are the ControlSources of controls on other pages.
*
* To update the list when its page comes to
* the top, you'd have the following in
* the list's UIEnable event:
IF lEnable   && only on the way in
  This.Requery()
ENDIF
```

See Also Page, Page frame, Refresh

#UnDef See #Define.

UndoCheckOut See CheckIn.

Undock See BeforeDock.

Unique() See Candidate().

_Unix See _Dos.

Unload See Load.

Unlock See Lock().

UpClick, DownClick

These events fire when you click the little arrow characters in a spinner or when you use the arrow keys to change the spinner value. They also fire when you use the arrows to scroll the drop-down portion of a combo box. Despite documentation to the contrary in some versions, these events never fire for list boxes.

Usage

```
PROCEDURE oObject.UpClick
[LPARAMETERS nIndex]

PROCEDURE oObject.DownClick
[LPARAMETERS nIndex]
```

You only need to include the nIndex parameter when you're dealing with a group of objects held in a control array. In that case, nIndex tells you which of those objects triggered the event.

Don't get fooled about when these events fire. First, for combos, they fire not when you drop the combo open, but when the combo has more than DisplayCount items and you use the scroll bar in the drop-down portion. These events also don't happen until you release the mouse button to complete the click. (This is in line with the timing of the Click event—we've got no complaints about it.) This means you could wind through dozens of values in the spinner or scroll the combo a long way before the UpClick or DownClick fires. If you need to take action as soon as the spinner's value changes, use InteractiveChange instead. For combos, you're out of luck—there's nothing you can do until the user chooses a value.

Also, keep in mind that UpClick and DownClick don't discriminate between the arrows on the spinner and the arrow keys. They fire in either case.

Example

```
* Give the user some feedback
PROCEDURE spnSpinner.UpClick
   WAIT WINDOW "You clicked the up arrow" NOWAIT
ENDPROC
```

See Also ComboBox, DropDown, InteractiveChange, ListBox, Spinner

Update See Join.

Update-SQL

This is one of several SQL commands added in Visual FoxPro. This one behaves pretty much like the Xbase REPLACE command—it updates one or more fields in one or more records of a single table.

Usage

```
UPDATE [ DatabaseName! ] TableName
          SET FieldName1 = uExpr1
          [, FieldName2 = uExpr2 [, ... ] ]
          [ WHERE lCondition ]
```

Parameter	Value	Meaning
DatabaseName	Name	Name of the database containing TableName.
TableName	Name	The table containing the fields to be updated.
FieldName*x*	Name	The *x*th field to be updated.
uExpr*x*	Same type as FieldName*x*	An expression to evaluate to assign a value to FieldName*x*.
lCondition	Logical	An expression determining which records get updated.

Except in a few minor details, UPDATE in Visual FoxPro acts like the Xbase REPLACE command. The SET clause takes the place of the "field WITH value" piece and the WHERE clause fills in for the FOR clause. In fact, REPLACE seems more powerful since it also supports scope and WHILE clauses (not to mention replacing in multiple tables at once, though that's not a very good idea). On the other hand, by using a sub-query in the WHERE clause, you can do some pretty powerful things with UPDATE.

Beware of one big difference between them. If you REPLACE without indicating what records you're interested in, only the current record is affected. UPDATE with no WHERE clause changes every record in the table.

The help hints and our tests confirm that REPLACE is generally faster than UPDATE. In exclusive mode, the differences are small, but with shared tables, we see tremendous differences. The reason for the difference is that UPDATE uses record locking while REPLACE locks the entire table. There may be cases where you can't lock the table, so UPDATE's behavior can save your skin in spite of its performance consequences.

UPDATE isn't affected by the weird Xbase behavior that afflicts REPLACE when you're changing a value in another work area and the current work area is at EOF(). UPDATE is unaffected by this nonsense. See REPLACE for a full explanation of the problem.

Example

```
* This is the same example given for REPLACE.
* Here's the equivalent using UPDATE.

* Suppose the area code for a bunch of phone numbers
* changes. You need to update those records.
* Assume you've stored the exchanges that are changing
* in a table, EXCHANGES, with one field, Exchange, and
* a tag on that field.
* The old area code is stored in cOldCode.
* The new area code is stored in cNewCode
USE PhoneList
UPDATE SET AreaCode = cNewCode ;
   WHERE AreaCode = cOldCode ;
   AND LEFT(Phone,3) IN (SELECT Exchange FROM Exchanges)
```

See Also Delete-SQL, Replace, Select-SQL

Updated()

UPDATED() ostensibly tells you whether any of the data in a form has changed since you last saved it. But it doesn't work right for its purpose.

Usage

```
lAnythingNew = UPDATED()
```

Way back in the dark, murky mists of Xbase history, UPDATED() was a useful function. It told you whether any of the items in a READ had been changed, so you could, for example, know whether to prompt the user to save changes when he pressed Escape.

In FoxPro 1.0, a cool new function code was added to @GET. FUNCTION "@M" let you specify a list of valid inputs and force the user to choose from the list. With that function code, UPDATED() began to lose its shine because simply moving through the list of valid inputs set UPDATED() to .T. FoxPro 2 just made things worse—clicking a button, even an OK or Cancel button, set UPDATED() to .T. So did checking or unchecking a check box, or choosing from a list or popup. Most folks wrote their own function to figure out whether a save was needed.

Visual FoxPro's buffering makes all this a lot easier. With GETNEXTMODIFIED() and GETFLDSTATE(), you can see exactly what's been changed.

InteractiveChange and ProgrammaticChange let you act as soon as a change occurs, and KeyPress together with KeyPreview lets you figure out what the user is actually doing.

We told people to stay away from UPDATED() in FoxPro 2.x. Lots of things have changed, but this isn't one of them—stay away from UPDATED().

Example

```
* This is how you should be able to use UPDATED(), but can't
* This code might go in a Cancel button's Click
* Assume FoxPro.H has been included in the form
* Display the standard 'Save your changes (Y/N)' routine
IF UPDATED()
   nResult = MESSAGEBOX("Save changes", MB_YESNO + ;
                        MB_ICONQUESTION + MB_DEFBUTTON1)
   IF nResult = IDYES
      * call the save routine
   ENDIF
ENDIF
```

See Also GetFldState(), GetNextModified(), InteractiveChange, KeyPress, KeyPreview, ProgrammaticChange

Upper() See Lower().

Use

This command opens and closes tables. It has myriad clauses that let you vary the way it works.

Usage

```
USE [ [ Database! ] TableName | [ Database! ] ViewName | ? ]
    [ IN nWorkArea | cAlias ]
    [ AGAIN ]
    [ ONLINE ]
    [ ADMIN ]
    [ ALIAS AliasName ]
    [ NOREQUERY [ nDataSession ] ]
    [ NODATA ]
    [ INDEX IndexFileList | ? ]
    [ ORDER [ nIndex | IDXFileName
     | [ TAG ] TagName [ OF CDXFileName ]
       [ ASCENDING | DESCENDING] ]
    [ EXCLUSIVE | SHARED ]
    [ NOUPDATE ]
```

Parameter	Value	Meaning
TableName	Name	The name of an existing table to open. Can include a path. If the table is part of an open database, use the long name specified in the database, not the filename. If the name or path includes spaces, enclose it in quotes.
ViewName	Name	The name of an existing view to open. Must either be in the current database or be aliased by the database. If the name includes spaces, enclose it in quotes.
nWorkArea	0	Open the table in an unused work area.
	Numeric other than 0	Open or close the table in the specified work area.
	Omitted	If cAlias is also omitted, open or close the table or view in the current work area.
cAlias	Character	Open or close the table or view in the specified work area.
	Omitted	If nWorkArea is also omitted, open or close the table or view in the current work area.
AliasName	Name	The alias to assign the newly opened table or view.
	Omitted	The alias is the same as the table or view name in most cases. If the table or view name includes spaces, they're changed to underscores in the alias. If the table or view name can't be used as an alias, VFP creates an alias. If the table is opened in one of the first 10 work areas, the alias is one of the letters A through J (with A for work area 1, B for 2, and so on). If the table is opened in any other work area, the alias is the letter W followed by the work area number, such as W1834.
nDataSession	Numeric	Used with NoRequery, tells the view to get its data from an open copy of the same view in the specified data session.
IndexFileList	List of Names	A comma-delimited list of index files to open with the table.
nIndex	Numeric	The position in the index list of the index by which the table should be initially ordered. See CANDIDATE() for a discussion of index numbers.
IDXFileName	Name	The name of the stand-alone index by which the table should be initially ordered.
TagName	Name	The name of the tag by which the table should be initially ordered.
CDXFileName	Name	The name of the compound index file containing TagName.

One of the cool things in Visual FoxPro is the ability to treat query results just like a table by defining a view. This means that, instead of running a query to get the results, you simply open the view with USE. Looking at the code, you usually can't even tell whether it's a table or a view.

USE actually both opens and closes tables and views. If a table or view name or ? is specified, USE opens that table. (We'll use the word "table" in this discussion to mean "table or view," unless we tell you.) If all of those are omitted, USE closes the table. In fact, if there's a table already open in the work area you specify (or the current work area, if you don't specify), USE closes it before opening the table you name.

When you USE a local view, it also opens (and leaves open) the tables the view is based on.

USE closes any open table in the specified work area before it checks whether it can open the new one. If the open fails, the work area is left with no table open.

If you don't specify otherwise, USE operates on the current work area. As with other Xbase commands, you can specify a work area by providing its number or the alias of the table currently open there. But USE offers one more option—if you say IN 0, it finds the lowest unused work area and opens the table there. Watch out when you use this option—like the IN clause of other commands, USE doesn't change the current work area. The table gets opened, but you're not sitting on it until you SELECT the new work area. The IN 0 option is most useful when you want to open a series of tables.

You can close a table without SELECTing its work area first. Just USE IN cAlias to close the table open as cAlias.

Any table can be opened many times, using only a single file handle. That's what AGAIN is all about. One warning—if you USE a table twice and SET ORDER to the same thing in both work areas, both work areas have to be either ascending or descending. You can't have one ascending and the other descending using the same index. This is true even if the two uses of the table are in different data sessions!

NOREQUERY and NODATA are both supposed to speed up opening of views. Neither behaves quite as documented. NODATA tells FoxPro to create a cursor for the view, but don't populate it yet. The idea is that getting just the structure should be faster than actually moving the data. In fact, that's true only when dealing with an intelligent server. Some servers will fulfill this request by retrieving all records, then throwing them out.

NOREQUERY, on the other hand, is utterly useless by itself. It's supposed to prevent data from being loaded a second time when you open a view AGAIN. Great idea, but as far as we can tell, that's what happens automatically when you USE a view AGAIN. You don't need NOREQUERY for that.

With the optional nDataSession parameter, NOREQUERY is pretty cool. If you have the same view open in several data sessions, you can open it again and specify which data session's version of the view should be "borrowed" to populate the newly opened view. With a parameterized view, each data session might contain a different set of records, so you can decide which set you want. The newly opened view is populated with the last committed data from the specified view—what we'd see with OldVal(), not the current data in that view. If the user has changed some data but the changes haven't been saved to the original data source, the new view doesn't see those changes (which is as it should be).

The ONLINE and ADMIN options are for offline views. These views let you detach data from the database and take it on the road without having to have all the data along. You take a view offline with the CREATEOFFLINE() command. Once you've done so, the view can be treated like a table, opened with USE, and so forth. These options are for using the offline view in the presence of the original database. ONLINE says to open the view and prepare to reattach it to the actual data. Once you USE a view ONLINE, you need to either commit or revert the changes in the data. ADMIN lets you open the offline view without having to update the actual data—you can, for example, simply examine the changed data to see what you want to do with it.

The INDEX and ORDER clauses are really a shortcut for the SET INDEX and SET ORDER commands. They do the same thing as those commands right in the USE.

EXCLUSIVE and SHARED let you override the SET EXCLUSIVE setting when necessary. NOUPDATE lets you open a table in "look, but don't touch" mode—a feature we use all the time when peeking at the tables underlying the Form, Class and Menu power tools.

Example

```
* Open a table in an unused work area in a specified order
USE Employee IN 0 ORDER Last_Name

* Open a view
OPEN DATA TasTrade
* Quotes are needed below because of embedded blank, so we'll
* assign an alias.
USE "Product Listing" ALIAS Prods
```

See Also Candidate(), CreateOffline(), NoDataOnLoad, OldVal(), Select, Set Exclusive, Set Index, Set Order, Used()

Used() See Alias().

User() See Access().

Val() See Str().

Valid See When.

Validate Database

This command is a rescue mission. It lets you check whether a database is damaged and, as much as possible, repair the damage.

Usage

```
VALIDATE DATABASE [ RECOVER ]
          [ NOCONSOLE ]
          [ TO PRINT [ PROMPT ] | TO [ FILE ] FileName ]
```

By itself, VALIDATE DATABASE examines the current database and reports any problems it finds. Problems can occur if you delete files that belong to the database without removing them first (for example, if you delete a table using Explorer). You can also wreak havoc by manipulating the DBC as a table, if you're not careful. VALIDATE DATABASE lets you know what's wrong.

You can actually issue VALIDATE DATABASE on a database that's not open exclusively, but all you can get from that is a report as to whether maintenance is needed. With exclusive access, the database's index gets rebuilt as well.

The RECOVER clause lets you become part of the solution instead of part of the problem. For each inconsistency, you're prompted to either locate the missing file or delete the offending item from the database. More often than not, it seems the only choice is to remove the offender—we sure wish this command was smarter. Since it's not, your best bet is often to ignore the errors and open the DBC as a table, then try to repair the problems manually. As an alternative, you may want to keep Stonefield Database Toolkit or another tool that can repair tables and databases in your arsenal.

Much to our dismay, VALIDATE DATABASE RECOVER is available only from the Command Window. You can't use it in a program. If you do, you get an error message. What a shame!

By default, the validation report appears in the active window. The remaining options let you send it elsewhere.

Example

```
CREATE DATABASE ValTest
CREATE TABLE Test1 (cFld C(1))
INDEX ON cFld TAG cFld
USE
CREATE SQL VIEW TestView AS SELECT * FROM Test1

* okay, now we've got data. Validate.
VALIDATE DATABASE  && Should return "Database is Valid"

* now let's see what kind of trouble we can cause
CLOSE DATA
DELETE FILE Test1.CDX
USE ValTest.DBC
LOCATE FOR ObjectType="View"
REPLACE ObjectType WITH "Not a View"
USE

* Now open the database again and see what happens
OPEN DATA ValTest EXCLUSIVE
VALIDATE DATABASE          && Reports lots of problems
VALIDATE DATABASE RECOVER  && prompts you to fix things up
```

See Also Open Database, Remove Table, Set Database

Value, Text

Value is a wonderfully overloaded property that, in one way or another, tells you the current value of a control. The type and interpretation of the value changes, depending on the control involved. Text is a handy corollary to Value, giving you a textual version of the value, in case it's not character. Text applies only to the controls that allow textual input.

Usage

```
oObject.Value = uControlValue
uControlValue = oObject.Value
cValueText = oObject.Text
```

You can change the Value of a control and see your changes reflected in the display. In some cases, changing the Value can have profound effects. In at least one, it can cause ugly behavior.

The simplest cases are text boxes, edit boxes and spinners. In that case, what you see is what you get. Value contains the actual value displayed.

Except for a couple of things. If an edit box has MaxLength set so you can only see part of the data, Value still contains the entire string. Watch out, though: as soon as you start fiddling with the data in the edit box, the data is truncated to MaxLength characters. If the edit box is bound to a field, the data in the field changes, too.

Value's type for these controls is determined by the control's ControlSource, if there is one. If not, Value is character for text and edit boxes and numeric for spinners.

These controls plus combo boxes are the ones that have the Text property. Most of the time, Text contains what you'd get if you applied TRANSFORM() to Value; that is, a character string that looks like the value. However, some of the Format options change that. For example, when Format includes "R", Text includes the extra formatting characters, while Value does not. When Format includes "E" (for British dates), Text contains the date in the DD/MM/YY format rather than the current date format.

On to buttons. Command buttons don't have a Value. Only CommandGroups do. The value can be either numeric or character. If it's numeric, it contains the position in the group of the button last chosen. (Position is based on the buttons' order in the Buttons collection.) If Value is character, it contains the Caption of the last chosen button.

OptionGroups work the same way, allowing either numeric or character Values. However, individual option buttons also have a Value property. It's 1 if that button is chosen and 0 if it isn't.

You can set the Value of more than one option button in an option group to 1, so that multiple options appear to be chosen. You can also set them all to 0, so that no buttons are chosen. Individual option buttons shouldn't even have a Value property, but since they do, it ought to work right.

Check boxes are pretty simple, too. Their Value can be numeric or logical, with 0 = .F. = unchecked and 1 = .T. = checked. There's one complication: A check box can also show a null value. Set Value to 2 or .NULL. and the check box turns gray. Watch out. Just because it's gray doesn't mean it can't be clicked—it can. Use Enabled to make it unclickable.

For combo and list boxes, things get interesting. Value can be either character or numeric. If it's character, it contains the actual text of the chosen item—as a character string. Even if the RowSource data is something other than character, when it's placed in a list or combo, it's converted to character there. If Value is numeric, it's the Index in the list or combo of the chosen item. In VFP 5 and VFP 6, you can put a numeric data item in Value (as a character string, of course) by setting the list or combo's BoundTo property to .T. In VFP 3, there's no way to use numeric data for the Value of a list or combo. This lets you show a description in the list while saving a numeric ID for the Value.

For multi-column lists and combos, Value (when character) contains the contents of BoundColumn for the chosen item. DisplayValue, however, always contains the contents of the first column, unless you make it numeric.

Finally, the one that surprised the heck out of us. Grids have Values. The Value is only available when the grid has focus, but then it contains the value of the cell with focus. The type of Value changes to match the current column. When the grid doesn't have focus, its Value is 0.

Don't change a grid's Value—doing so unlinks the connection between the grid contents and the Value property. Once you do it, Value is no longer updated by moving in the grid.

Beware. When a control has a ControlSource, the new Value doesn't reach the ControlSource until just before the control's Valid. If you check the value of the ControlSource in InteractiveChange, you won't see the new value. That is, in InteractiveChange, Value shows one thing and the value of the ControlSource shows something else. Yet another reason to always refer to Value, not the actual ControlSource to which the control is bound.

Example

```
* Initialize a list to a particular item
This.Value = cCurrentChoice
```

See Also BoundColumn, Buttons, Caption, ControlSource, DisplayValue, Enabled

VarRead() See Sys(18).

VarType() See Type().

Version, Version() See OS().

VersionComments, VersionCompany, VersionCopyright, VersionDescription, VersionLanguage, VersionNumber, VersionProduct, VersionTrademarks

These project properties give you programmatic access to the version information from the EXE Version dialog.

Usage

```
cVersionComments = prjProject.VersionComments
prjProject.VersionComments = cVersionComments
```

```
cVersionCompany = prjProject.VersionCompany
prjProject.VersionCompany = cVersionCompany
cVersionCopyright = prjProject.VersionCopyright
prjProject.VersionCopyright = cVersionCopyright
cVersionDescription = prjProject.VersionDescription
prjProject.VersionDescription = cVersionDescription
nVersionLanguage = prjProject.VersionLanguage
prjProject.VersionLanguage = nVersionLanguage
cVersionNumber = prjProject.VersionNumber
prjProject.VersionNumber = cVersionNumber
cVersionProduct = prjProject.VersionProduct
prjProject.VersionProduct = cVersionProduct
cVersionTrademarks = prjProject.VersionTrademarks
prjProject.VersionTrademarks = cVersionTrademarks
```

There's one property for each piece of information you can store about the executable. This is the information that's available by pressing the Version button from the Build dialog of the Project Manager—don't confuse it with the stuff in the Project Info dialog. Once you build an EXE or DLL, you can retrieve the information with the GetFileVersion() API function or the new AGetFileVersion() function. Then you can use it in About dialogs or wherever to tell users all about the application.

Except for VersionLanguage and VersionNumber, these items are all ordinary character fields. They accept whatever characters you send them, including multiple lines. VersionLanguage is numeric—the reasonable values are listed in FoxPro.H. There's quite an amazing list of local variations there.

VersionNumber is different from all the others. The version number of a project has three sections, separated by periods, such as "2.17.2837". Each section can hold up to four digits.

However, setting VersionNumber programmatically is a little strange. You must pass at least the two periods—if that's all you pass, the first section keeps its old value, while the other two are reset to 0. If you pass more than four characters for any section, the result depends on exactly what you do. If you pass too much for the first section, the first four characters of the section are used, along with whatever you specify for the other sections. Passing too much for the second or third section results in an error message.

Example

```
oProj.Product = "My Wonderful App 98"
oProj.VersionNumber = "7.0.1"
```

See Also AGetFileVersion(), AutoIncrement, FoxTools, Project

_VFP **See Application.**

View **See Panel.**

ViewPortHeight, ViewPortWidth

These properties tell you the dimensions of the visible portion of a form. They're really only relevant when the form has scrollbars.

Usage

```
nVisibleHeight = frmForm.ViewPortHeight
nVisibleWidth = frmForm.ViewPortWidth
```

When a form has scrollbars, some portion of it is hidden. (We almost said "may be hidden," but the way scrollbars work, they only appear if a portion of the form is actually hidden.) These two properties let you know the size of the part of the form the user can see.

Although the "inside area" of the form accounts for a title bar, if there is one, it doesn't consider scrollbars. So, if you resize a form vertically and make a scrollbar appear, ViewPortWidth doesn't change, even though less of the actual form is now visible to the user. Oddly, Height and Width, which we'd expect to include every little bit of real estate occupied by the form, do consider both a title bar and scrollbars. So, the Height of a form can be less than its ViewPortHeight. Weird.

Example

```
IF This.ViewPortWidth > nSomeMagicValue
   * There's enough room to do something special
   This.oleGreatPicture.Visible = .T.
ENDIF
```

See Also Form, Height, ViewPortLeft, ViewPortTop, Width

ViewPortLeft, ViewPortTop

These two properties tell you what part of a form is currently visible. Well, actually, they tell you where the visible part starts—you need to combine them with some others to figure out the whole visible portion.

Usage

```
nVisibleLeft = frmForm.ViewPortLeft
nVisibleTop = frmForm.ViewPortTop
```

For a form with scrollbars, you sometimes need to know which part of the form the user can see at this moment. These two get you started by telling you the upper-left corner of the part you can see. Add Height and Width to these to see where the visible area ends.

You can't set these directly. To change the position of the viewport, call the SetViewPort method.

Example

```
* A control can figure out whether it can be seen
IF NOT BETWEEN(This.Left,ThisForm.ViewPortLeft, ;
               ThisForm.ViewPortLeft + ThisForm.Width)
   * Hmmm, I can't be seen. What should I do?
   * I know. I'll be obnoxious!
   MESSAGEBOX("Hey, you can't see me! Try scrolling.", 64, ;
              This.Name)
ENDIF
```

See Also Form, Height, SetViewPort, ViewPortHeight, ViewPortWidth, Width

ViewPortWidth See ViewPortHeight.

Visible

> As I was going up the stair
> I met a man who wasn't there
>
> Hughes Mearns, *The Psychoed*

This property lets you turn things on and off visually. Now you see it, now you don't.

Usage

```
oObject.Visible = lIsVisible
lIsVisible = oObject.Visible
```

Objects that are invisible can't receive focus. Makes sense to us—it would be really hard to tell that your cursor's on an object that isn't there.

Containers take their contents with them when you make them visible or invisible. That is, if you make a form invisible, all the controls disappear, too. When you make the form visible, you can see all the controls on it that were visible in the first place. The Visible property of the individual controls doesn't change, though. The same thing applies to all the other containers, like page frames, grids, command groups, and so on.

The interaction of Visible with grids is a little strange. Setting the grid's Visible to .F. acts as you'd expect—the grid disappears along with all its contents. But when you set Visible to .F. for a column, the column empties out but doesn't disappear. This doesn't surprise us—what does is that columns have a Visible property in the first place. Pages don't because it doesn't make sense to make a single page of a page frame disappear. Why does this make any more sense for columns?

Visible interacts with Sparse, so you can get some pretty weird results with the controls in columns, too. If Sparse is .T. and you set Visible .F. for the control in a column, the control disappears, but only when it has focus! To get the controls to disappear for all rows, you have to have Sparse set to .F., not that we can imagine why you'd want to do this.

On the whole, we don't think we'll be fiddling with Visible for members of grids too much.

Setting Visible to .T. for a form is not the same as showing the form. It doesn't activate the form, just makes it visible. Form.Show() is really a combination of setting Visible to .T. and activating the form.

When you add an object to a container with AddObject, it starts out with Visible set to .F., regardless of the way it's set in the class the object is based on. This lets you fiddle with the object before the user can see it. Get in the habit of following every AddObject call with Visible=.T. for the object. (It's not good enough to do it in the object's Init—it gets changed back after that.) Objects created with CreateObject() also start with Visible set to .F.

It's tempting to use Visible a lot to turn things on and off as context changes. Be careful how much you do this. Users can get really confused if a form looks different every time they look at it. Don't have buttons and the like disappearing unless you're into user-hostile interfaces. Use Enabled to make things inaccessible when they don't apply at the moment. Reserve twiddling Visible for cases like entire forms that don't apply for a particular record.

Example

```
* Make an object invisible because of a field value
IF lIsMale
   ThisFormSet.frmPregnancies.Visible = .F.
ENDIF
```

See Also Enabled, Hide, Show

VScrollSmallChange See HScrollSmallChange.

Wait

WAIT is a simple little command, but with nice effect. Its primary mission in life is to display a message. By default, a WAIT WINDOW command appears in the upper right corner of the active screen, below the toolbars, while a plain WAIT is displayed in the current output window.

Usage

```
WAIT [ CLEAR ] | [ cMessage ][ TO cResponse ]
[ WINDOW [ AT nRow, nColumn ] [ NOWAIT ] [ NOCLEAR ] ]
[ TIMEOUT nTime ]
```

Parameter	Value	Meaning
CLEAR		Clears any existing WAIT WINDOW. Cannot be used with any other keywords or arguments!
cMessage	Character	The message to be displayed. Multiple lines can be specified by separating strings with carriage returns (CHR(13)'s). More than 254 characters generates error 1903, "String too long to fit."
	Omitted	Display "Press any key to continue..."

Parameter	Value	Meaning
cMessage	Empty String	Show the cursor, blinking, at the last output location, unless you have SET CURSOR OFF.
cResponse	Character	Receives a one-character alphanumeric response. Blank is returned for nonprintable characters or mouse clicks. The specified memory variable is created if it doesn't exist. If it does exist, its type is changed to character, if necessary, and its value is overwritten.
nRow	Numeric	The row where the window should appear. The row number is based on the screen font (see WFONT()). Numbers less than 0 are ignored.
nColumn	Numeric	The column where the window should appear. The column number is based on the screen font (see WFONT()). Columns less than 0 are ignored.
NOWAIT		Continues processing immediately.
NOCLEAR		WAIT WINDOW remains until another WAIT WINDOW command or WAIT CLEAR is issued. Without this clause, the window clears when a keystroke or mouse click is received.
nTime	Numeric	The time to wait in seconds before continuing processing. Ignored if NOWAIT is specified.

Note that CLEAR and NOCLEAR are not a pair, as the Help would have you believe. CLEAR must be used alone to clear an existing window; any other use results in a syntax error. NOCLEAR is new to Visual FoxPro—it keeps a window on the screen even if a keystroke is pressed.

The many clauses of WAIT that were added over the years can lead to some commands that look like they should work, and don't cause an error message, but don't give the expected response. For example,

```
WAIT WINDOW NOWAIT "Processing..." TIMEOUT 30
```

might be interpreted as "Display this message, let me continue processing, and then clear the message after 30 seconds." In fact, the TIMEOUT clause is ignored if NOWAIT is specified, and the message clears only if a keystroke is pressed or a WAIT CLEAR command is issued.

WAIT is getting dated. For input, consider instead a MessageBox or custom form. To keep the user informed of processing status, a custom form with the new ProgressBar control is more informative and more standard. Finally, look at the many options to update messages on the application status bar as well. WAIT WINDOWs give away that a FoxPro app is running—not necessarily a bad thing, but a non-standard interface that could confuse new users.

WAIT "" produces a blinking cursor in the screen or current output window. WAIT WINDOW "" does the same—where's the WINDOW? There ain't one.

WAIT "" NOWAIT immediately executes the next command, with no display as you might expect. However, WAIT "xxx" NOWAIT leaves the cursor blinking on the "xxx" message and needs a key to return control to the program, ignoring the NOWAIT clause. In fact, even WAIT NOWAIT with no string waits. We hardly ever use NOWAITs without WINDOWs, because the window, particularly with the AT clause, is so cool. But if you're going to use it (consider using ? instead), or are porting code that uses it, don't expect it to NOWAIT just because you told it to.

Example
```
WAIT WINDOW "Sorry, Dave, I can't do that." NOWAIT NOCLEAR
```

See Also Accept, Input, MessageBox(), SysMetric(), WFont()

WBorder(), WCols(), WFont(), WLCol(), WLRow(), WRows(), WTitle()

One may know the world without going out of doors.
One may see the Way of Heaven without looking through the windows.
The further one goes, the less one knows.

Lao-tzu

This group of functions tells you about the position and appearance of a window. Using them, you can retrieve almost enough information to re-create the window. Of course, it would be nice if you could retrieve all the information you need.

All of these functions work on the active window unless you pass the name of another window. If no window is active and you don't name a window, the functions return information for the main FoxPro window. All work on both built-in and user-defined windows, as well as toolbars.

For forms and the main FoxPro window, much of the information returned by these functions can also be found using an assortment of form-level properties.

Usage
```
lHasBorder = WBORDER( [ cWindow ] )
```

WBORDER() returns .T. if the specified window has a border and .F. if it doesn't. The only way a window can have no border is if it was defined with the NONE clause. All system windows have borders.

There's no way to find out what kind of a border a window has, only whether or not it has one. This is one reason you can't gather enough information to re-create a window. (The other big problem is that there is no way to determine whether the window was defined with the keywords CLOSE, ZOOM, MINIMIZE, and so forth.)

Example
```
? WBORDER("command")   && Returns .T.
DEFINE WINDOW Test FROM 0,0 TO 10,60 NONE
? WBORDER("test")      && Returns .F.
```

Usage
```
nNumberOfColumns = WCOLS( [ cWindow ] )
nNumberOfRows = WROWS( [ cWindow ] )
```

WCOLS() and WROWS() tell you the size of the window, returning the number of rows and columns, respectively. The size returned is relative to the font used to define the window (see WFONT(), below) and represents the amount of space inside the border.

Example
```
DEFINE WINDOW test FROM 0,0 TO 10,10 FONT "Arial",10
? WROWS("test") && Return values depending on the Screen font
? WCOLS("test")
```

Usage
```
uReturnValue = WFONT( nAttribute [, cWindow ] )
```

Parameter	Value	Meaning
nAttribute	1	Return the name of the font for the specified window.

Parameter	Value	Meaning
nAttribute	2	Return the font size for the specified window.
	3	Return the font style for the specified window.
cWindow	Character	The window for which to return font information.
	Omitted	Return information for the active window. If no window is active, return font information for the main FoxPro window.

WFONT() tells you about the font specified for the window. With three calls to WFONT(), you can find out everything there is to know about the font. Passing 3 for nAttribute returns one or more style codes, as shown in the following table.

Style Code	Meaning
B	Bold
I	Italic
N	Normal—none of the other options
O	Outline
Q	Opaque
S	Shadow
-	Strikeout
T	Transparent
U	Underline

Example

```
DEFINE WINDOW test FROM 0,0 to 10,40 ;
        FONT "WingDings",12 STYLE "BI"
? WFONT(1, "test")  && Returns "wingdings"
? WFONT(2, "test")  && Returns 12
? WFONT(3, "test")  && Returns "BI"
```

Usage

```
nLeftCol = WLCOL( [ cWindow ] )
nTopRow = WLROW( [ cWindow ] )
```

This pair of functions tells you where it's at—the specified window, that is. They return the column and row, respectively, of the upper left corner of the window. This is the information you'd need for the FROM or AT clause of a DEFINE WINDOW command.

The name WLCOL() is nice and logical—you can read it as "Window Left Column." But WLROW() is absurd—what's "Window Left Row?" Technically, it should be WUROW() for "Window Upper Row." However, we can see the appeal of a matching set here.

The values returned by these functions depend on the font of the window that contains the window you're asking about. Often, that'll be the main FoxPro window. If you change the font of a window, the relative coordinates of windows in that window change.

Example

```
DEFINE WINDOW test FROM 10,10 TO 20,40
? WLCOL("test")  && Returns 10
? WLROW("test")  && Returns 10
MODIFY WINDOW screen FONT "arial",8
? WLCOL("test")  && Return values depending on
? WLROW("test")  && the original font for the screen
```

Usage `cWindowTitle = WTITLE( [ cWindow ] )`

WTITLE() tells you the defined title of a window. For system windows, the title and the name are the same. For example, both the title and the name of the standard toolbar are "STANDARD". For a user-defined window, the title is specified by the TITLE clause of DEFINE WINDOW or MODIFY WINDOW. If no TITLE clause is included, the window has no title.

Things are more complicated for a Browse window. This has been a source of confusion in FoxPro for years, since some commands require you to refer to a window by name, not title. If you issue BROWSE without a WINDOW or TITLE clause, both the name and the title of the Browse window are the alias of the table being browsed. If a TITLE clause is included in BROWSE, the window title is that specified string, but the window name is the first word of the title (from the first non-blank up to the first punctuation mark). For example, if you issue:

```
USE Employee
BROWSE TITLE "My Employees"
```

the window title is "My Employees", but the window name is "My". To move this Browse, you'd issue something like:

```
MOVE WINDOW my BY 5,5
```

If you issue BROWSE with a WINDOW clause and no TITLE clause, and the specified window has a title, the Browse window inherits that title. As before, the portion up to the first blank becomes the window name.

Designer or editing windows draw their titles from the object being edited. For some, like MODIFY COMMAND and MODIFY FILE, the title is just the name of the file being edited. For others, like reports and forms, the title includes the name of the tool in use. If the word "Designer" appears in the name of the tool, the tool name is at the beginning of the window title. Usually, the name of the object being edited is part of the title, too; for example, "Report Designer - Report2". In all these cases, though, the window name is the first word in the title.

To confuse matters more, the list on the Window pad shows window titles for system windows, but window names for user-defined windows. This is just plain confusing.

WTITLE() returns all caps for some windows, but certain system window titles are returned in mixed case. Titles defined with a TITLE clause are returned as they were specified. (That's a good thing, not a bug.) For this reason, it's a good idea to apply UPPER() or LOWER() to the results of WTITLE() and compare to all uppercase or lowercase strings.

Example

```
DEFINE WINDOW test FROM 0,0 TO 10,20 TITLE "My Test Window"
? WTITLE("test")    && Returns "My Test Window"
? WTITLE("command") && Returns "Command"
```

See Also BorderStyle, Caption, Define Window, FontBold, FontItalic, FontName, FontOutline, FontShadow, FontSize, FontStrikethru, FontUnderline, Height, Left, Modify Window, Top, WExist(), Width, WMaximum(), WMinimum(), WOnTop(), WOutput(), WVisible(), Zoom Window

WChild(), WParent()

These functions let you figure out who's who among the window set. WCHILD() lets you find the child windows of a window, while WPARENT() gives you the parent window.

Usage

```
cParentWindow = WPARENT( [ cWindowName ] )
nChildCount = WCHILD( [ cWindowName ] )
cNextChild = WCHILD( [ cWindowName, ] nCounter )
```

Parameter	Value	Meaning
cWindowName	Character	The window about which you want parent or child information.
	Omitted	Return information about the current output window.
cParentWindow	Character	The name of the parent window of the specified window.
	Empty	The specified window sits right in the main Visual FoxPro window.
nChildCount	Numeric	The number of child windows for the specified window.
nCounter	0	Return the name of the first child window.
	Any other number	Return the name of the next child window—the first call with nCounter included returns the first child.
cNextChild	Character	The name of the next child window of the specified window.
	Empty	There are no more child windows for the specified window.

All windows that aren't defined IN some other window and aren't defined IN DESKTOP are children of the main Visual FoxPro window. So are undocked toolbars. WPARENT() returns the empty string for such windows. Windows defined IN DESKTOP have no parent and again, WPARENT() returns the empty string.

WCHILD() is a weird function. When you omit the numeric parameter, it's simple enough. It tells you how many children a particular window has. But when you pass a number, it's downright strange. It lets you go through the list of children, but it's kind of touchy.

Here's the story. Pass 0 and you get the "first" child window—the child that's first on the list in the Window menu. Pass any other number and you start cycling. Each time you call WCHILD() with any number other than 0, you get the next child window. You get the empty string as a return value when you're out of child windows. To go back to the beginning, you have to use WCHILD(0), but that counts as the first call, and the next WCHILD() call with anything other than 0 continues cycling. Be sure to save the result whenever you call WCHILD() with a number, because the cycling process means you won't get the same window again (except for successive calls to WCHILD(0)).

In VFP 5.0a and earlier, issuing a series of calls to WCHILD(<number>) on a window other than the main VFP window runs out of windows too soon. The last child window doesn't get reported.

To get children of the main Visual FoxPro window, either ACTIVATE SCREEN or pass the name of the main window. FoxPro is actually pretty flexible about what you can pass here: "SCREEN" works, so does _SCREEN.Caption, and if you haven't changed the caption, "Microsoft" is effective, too. Of course, you could just use FormCount and the Forms collection of _SCREEN instead.

Example

```
* The most common thing to do is to loop through and find
* all the children.
* This example works on the active window.
nChildCnt = WCHILD()
WAIT WINDOW "This window has " + ;
            PADL(nChildCnt, 3) + " children."
```

```
cChildName = WCHILD(0)
DO WHILE NOT EMPTY(cChildName)
   WAIT WINDOW "One child is " + cChildName
   cChildName = WCHILD(1)
ENDDO
```

See Also Define Window, WTitle()

WCols() See WBorder().

Week() See DoW().

WExist(), WMaximum(), WMinimum(), WRead(), WVisible()

The windows of my soul I throw
Wide open to the sun.

John Greenleaf Whittier, *My Psalm*

These functions tell you about the current status of a window. All accept a parameter specifying the window; pass the name (not the title—see WTITLE()) of the window. For some, the window parameter is optional. Those functions return information about the active window if no window is specified.

These functions return information about user-defined windows, system windows and toolbars. With forms, the WindowState and Visible properties provide much of the same information, while MaxButton and MinButton let you find out if a form can be maximized or minimized.

Usage

```
lWindowExists = WEXIST( cWindow )
```

For user-defined windows, WEXIST() tells you whether a window has been defined. If so, the function returns .T. It doesn't matter whether the window has ever been activated or whether it's visible; it just needs to have been defined. You must name a window for this command since, by definition, the active window exists.

For system windows, WEXIST() indicates whether the window is active. It need not be visible (it could be hidden), but it must be active for WEXIST() to return .T.

In earlier versions of VFP, there were two exceptions. WEXIST("Command") always returned .T., even in a runtime executable. WEXIST("Debug") always returned .T. once the Debug window had been opened in a session, regardless of its current state. In VFP 6 and VFP 5, both calls return .F.

Example

```
* first, a user-defined window
CLEAR ALL
? WEXIST("test")    && Returns .F.
DEFINE WINDOW test FROM 0,0 TO 10,10
? WEXIST("test")    && Returns .T.

* now a system window
CLEAR ALL
? WEXIST("Trace")    && Returns .F.
ACTIVATE WINDOW Trace
? WEXIST("Trace")    && Returns .T.
HIDE WINDOW Trace
? WEXIST("Trace")    && Returns .T.
RELEASE WINDOW Trace
? WEXIST("Trace")    && Returns .F.
```

Usage

```
lIsMaximized = WMAXIMUM( [ cWindow ] )
lIsMinimized = WMINIMUM( [ cWindow ] )
```

This pair of functions tells you whether the specified window is maximized or minimized, respectively. They always return .F. for toolbars because toolbars can't be minimized or maximized.

A user-defined window can only be maximized if it was defined with the ZOOM keyword. Similarly, it can only be minimized if it was defined with the MINIMIZE keyword.

Example

```
DEFINE WINDOW test FROM 0,0 TO 10,40 ZOOM MINIMIZE
ACTIVATE WINDOW test
? WMAXIMUM("test")    && Returns .F.
? WMINIMUM("test")    && Returns .F.
ZOOM WINDOW test MAX
? WMAXIMUM("test")    && Returns .T.
ZOOM WINDOW test MIN
? WMINIMUM("test")    && Returns .T.
```

Usage `lInRead = WREAD( [ cWindow ] )`

WREAD() tells you whether the specified window is part of the active FoxPro 2.x style READ. WREAD() returns .T. if there is an active READ and the window either contains at least one @..GET or @..EDIT object from that READ, or is listed in the WITH clause for the READ.

WREAD() was important in some of the schemes for event-driven applications necessary in 2.x. We can't see much reason to use it in Visual FoxPro, except in legacy applications.

Example

```
* Before entering the following code in the command window,
* open the Debugger and put the string
* WREAD("test")
* in the Watch window
DEFINE WINDOW test FROM 0,0 TO 10,40
ACTIVATE WINDOW test
* Note that WREAD("test") is .F.
CLEAR
@0,0 GET x DEFAULT "abc"
READ
* Now WREAD("test") is .T.
```

Usage `lIsVisible = WVISIBLE( cWindow )`

WVISIBLE() tells you whether the specified window is visible right now. Like WEXIST(), it requires you to name a window, presumably on the principle that you can see the active window, so you know it's visible.

WVISIBLE() returns .T. if the window has been activated and hasn't been hidden. Otherwise, it returns .F. WVISIBLE() doesn't care if the window is in the viewable area of the screen, only that it's active and not hidden. So a window with negative coordinates is WVISIBLE().

Example

```
DEFINE WINDOW test FROM 0,0 TO 10,40
? WVISIBLE("test")    && Returns .F.
ACTIVATE WINDOW test
? WVISIBLE("test")    && Returns .T.
HIDE WINDOW test
? WVISIBLE("test")    && Returns .F.
SHOW WINDOW test
? WVISIBLE("test")    && Returns .T.
```

See Also Activate Window, Deactivate Window, Define Window, Hide Window, Modify Window, Read, Release Window, Show Window, Visible, WindowState, WTitle(), Zoom Window

WFont() See WBorder().

WhatsThisButton, WhatsThisHelp, ShowWhatsThis, WhatsThisHelpID, WhatsThisMode

WhatsThisHelp is a Windows feature meant to serve as an intermediate level of help between ToolTips and the full-fledged Help system. These three properties and two methods control it.

Usage

```
frmForm.WhatsThisButton = lToShowOrNot
lToShowOrNot = frmForm.WhatsThisButton
frmForm.WhatsThisHelp = lWhichHelpToShow
lWhichHelpToShow = frmForm.WhatsThisHelp
oObject.WhatsThisHelpID = nWTContextID
nWTContextID = oObject.WhatsThisHelpID
```

Parameter	Value	Meaning
lToShowOrNot	.T.	Display the WhatsThisHelpButton, provided all the other criteria are met. See below for details.
	.F.	Don't display the button.
lWhichHelpToShow	.T.	Allows the display of the WhatsThisHelp button on the form's title bar, and allows invoking of the form's ShowWhatsThis and WhatsThisMode methods. When WhatsThisHelp is invoked (through the WhatsThisHelpButton, Shift+F1, or pressing F1 when focus is on an object with a non-zero WhatsThisHelpID), VFP calls the default help file, specified by SET("HELP",1), passing it the WhatsThisHelpID. If the help file is a Windows Help file, WhatsThisHelp appears in a small yellow popup window. If it's HTML or DBF Help, the full help screen is invoked.
	.F.	Displays conventional, rather than WhatsThisHelp, help. The form uses the default help file, as indicated by SET("HELP", 1) and passes the context ID specified by the HelpContextID. WhatsThisHelp is disabled. The WhatsThisHelp button does not appear.
nWTContextID	Negative	No WhatsThisHelp is available for this item. When a negative number is sent to the help engine, it displays a message to that effect.
	0	When help is requested for oObject, search the container hierarchy, starting with the object and moving through its Parent, then the Parent's Parent, and so forth until a positive ContextID is located. Send the result of the search to the Help engine, which displays that help topic if it's found or the usual "No topic" message if a negative ID is found, but is silent if no non-zero IDs can be located.
	Positive	Passes on the ID to the Help engine.

WhatsThisHelp is the little button with the question mark that appears in the titlebar of forms. By design, WhatsThisHelp is available only when the form's Maximize and Minimize buttons have been disabled, WhatsThisHelp has been set to .T., and the form has a BorderWidth set to any choice other than 0 – No Border. Undocumented is that TitleBar needs to be set .T. also, obviously. We suspect that WhatsThisHelp was originally intended for modal dialogs, where the Help menu was inaccessible, but we have yet to see an interface specification that states that.

When either MaxButton or MinButton (not both) is .T. and all of the other conditions are met, the WhatsThisHelp button appears, shifted a bit to the left, and doesn't work. It shouldn't appear at all.

Usage

```
oObject.WhatsThisMode( )
PROCEDURE oObject.ShowWhatsThis
LPARAMETERS nWhatsThisHelpID
```

WhatsThisMode is a method that invokes WhatThisHelp, turning the cursor into a question mark and arrow. Adding NODEFAULT to the method code prevents WhatsThisHelp from starting. Be aware that this is a method, and not a hook to the event occurring. You can call this method to invoke WhatsThisHelp mode, but it doesn't fire each time WhatsThisHelp is invoked.

ShowWhatsThis is the opposite. It's called after the context ID has been determined and after the choice of help files has been made. If you want to override the default help display for some controls, you can intercept the ID in this routine and perform the functions you want here. You might, for instance, bring up a custom "help" dialog or a message box. ShowWhatsThis fires if you call WhatsThisHelp with a positive or negative ID and receives the ID, but doesn't fire if the ID is zero and no non-negative ID can be located in the containership hierarchy.

Example

```
* Check out the Solutions Sample that comes with VFP
DO HOME(2) + "\Solution\Solution.App"
* Under "Form" select "Provide What's This Help on a Form"
```

See Also Help, Set Help, ToolTips

When, Valid

These two events are just about the only carryovers from FoxPro 2.x's READ that are still useful. When fires when a control is offered focus. If When returns .T., the control can have the focus and its GotFocus event fires. (When also fires at a few other times—see below.) A good rule of thumb is for textual controls (text box, edit box, spinner), Valid fires whenever the control loses focus and determines whether it's allowed to lose focus. If so, the control's LostFocus fires. For non-textual controls, Valid fires when the user does something that could change the control's Value.

Usage

```
PROCEDURE oObject.When | oObject.Valid
[ LPARAMETERS nIndex ]
```

The nIndex parameter is passed when oObject is a control array. That's as it should be. What isn't as it should be is that, when some types of controls are placed in a control array, the When and Valid for the control array fire only if a procedure actually exists for the same event in the class definition for the control. That's right—it's not enough to define When and Valid for the control array. At least some of the time, you have to do so for the types of objects in the array, too, even though that code never executes. (ErrorMessage and Message have the same weird behavior. We haven't tested every type of control in this scenario, but the problem occurs at least for text boxes, edit boxes, spinners and check boxes.)

When is pretty simple. It fires when you head for the object. There are only a few surprises. First, the When for a list box fires every time you move the highlight in the list. This behavior is the same as that of lists in 2.x and is very handy. It lets you do something, like update other controls, as the user moves through the list.

Second, the When for some controls fires more than once when you use the control. When you use a button (command or option), check box, or combo, if focus will still be on that control afterwards, the When fires following the Valid. If you click on the control, you get the following sequence: When, GotFocus, Valid, When.

Finally, ActiveControl doesn't point to the control whose When you're executing. The control doesn't become ActiveControl until When returns .T. and GotFocus fires.

Valid is trickier. It can return either a logical or a numeric value. Many controls ignore most of the return values. Only textual controls (text box, edit box, spinner and combo box with Style = 0) pay attention to a return value of .F. or 0. For other controls, despite Help to the contrary, no matter what you return, focus is permitted to leave the object. Since the other controls present only valid options in the first place, this is appropriate behavior—it's just documented wrong.

Returning a non-zero value is even trickier. Lists and option buttons totally ignore numeric returns, as do controls in a grid. Other controls do move the focus forward or backward the specified amount. However, we strongly recommend you stay away from this approach—it's just plain too confusing. It's kind of a shame this technique isn't easier to use, because it's one way to work around the fact that you can't call SetFocus from the Valid method of a textual control—in other words, from those controls where Valid really means a validity check.

Figuring out when the Valid for an object fires was confusing in FoxPro 2.x and it's still somewhat confusing. For controls that accept text (the same ones that pay attention to Return .F.), it's easy—it always fires when you leave, whether you click, tab, press Enter, or do something else.

Other controls fire their Valids only when they feel used. Clicking on a button or check box fires its Valid. So does pressing Spacebar or Enter. For a combo (with Style set to either combo or dropdown), Valid fires when you choose something from the list with the mouse or with Spacebar or Enter. A list's Valid fires only when you double-click an item or press Enter.

Watch out for this one. The Valid and the LostFocus of a control don't fire if the user action doesn't cause the control to lose focus. We know that sounds obvious, but what might not be so obvious is the list of things that *don't* take focus from a control. For example, clicking a button on a toolbar doesn't take focus from the control that had it. Neither does making a menu selection. So why don't we have a bug icon on this one? Because it's not a bug. Some of the things that are on menus and toolbars shouldn't change the focus. Think of choosing, say, Edit-Cut from the menu or clicking a Cut button. Do you want the focus to leave the control you're on? Of course not. But if you're coding toolbar buttons to close forms, or menu options to bring up other forms, you may want to consider forcing the last item's Valid to fire to ensure that you're not leaving invalid data behind. See "It's a Feature, Not a Bug" for more on this issue.

As an extra added attraction, several of the containers have When and Valid events of their own. The events for button groups fire right after the same event for the button itself. A grid's When fires when you first enter the grid. The grid's Valid fires when you leave the grid.

Finally, all the comments about which keystrokes fire Valids apply only when KEYCOMP is set to Windows. With KEYCOMP set to DOS, some different keystrokes fire objects' Valids.

Last but not least (didn't we just say "finally"?), if SET NOTIFY is ON (not something we generally recommend), when a Valid returns .F., a wait window saying "Invalid Input" appears. If there's code in the control's ErrorMessage, that runs first, but then the "Invalid Input" window appears. To avoid this, either SET NOTIFY OFF or RETURN 0 rather than .F. from the Valid.

Using WAIT WINDOW in the When of some controls interferes with the control's operation. For example, a WAIT WINDOW in a check box's When prevents the check box from changing value when you click it (though it does get focus). We think that the action needed to clear the WAIT WINDOW fouls things up. WAIT WINDOW NOWAIT is fine, though.

Example

```
* See if user input is acceptable in a textbox for grade entry
PROCEDURE txtGrade.Valid

IF BETWEEN(This.Value,"A","F")
   RETURN .T.
ELSE
   WAIT WINDOW "Invalid grade. Try again" NOWAIT
```

```
    RETURN .F.
ENDIF
```

See Also Control Arrays, ErrorMessage, GotFocus, LostFocus, Set KeyComp, Set Notify

Width See Height.

WindowList

Yet another conversion-related property. This one replaces the WITH clause of READ, listing windows that are to be treated as part of the formset even though they're not forms.

Usage
```
frsFormSet.WindowList = cListOfAssociatedWindows
cListOfAssociatedWindows = frsFormSet.WindowList
```

Associated windows are relevant only in modal situations. You need to tell FoxPro that some windows are accessible, so the user can touch those even though the current form is modal. For example, you might make the Calculator available during entry of line items. Normally, in a modal READ, only the windows controlled by the READ are accessible.

The Converter doesn't get this one quite right. When READ has a WITH clause, it's automatically modal even without the MODAL keyword. Faced with a screen that has a list of associated windows but doesn't have MODAL checked (in the 2.x Project Manager's Edit Screen Set dialog), the Converter copies the list of windows to WindowList, but sets WindowType to 2 rather than 3, the modal choice for READ-type windows.

Like the other conversion stuff, this one's relevant only when WindowType is one of the READ compatibility types. It's totally ignored for real VFP forms.

Example
```
This.WindowList = "Customers"
```

See Also WindowType

_Windows See _Dos.

WindowState

This property determines whether a form is minimized, maximized or shown at its normal size.

Usage
```
frmForm.WindowState = nWindowState
nWindowState = frmForm.WindowState
```

Parameter	Value	Meaning
nWindowState	0	Normal—the current defined size.
	1	Minimize to an icon.
	2	Maximize to the size specified by MaxHeight and MaxWidth, or to fill the Visual FoxPro window.

You can achieve the same effects with ZOOM WINDOW, but changing WindowState is the OOP way to do this.

You can use WindowState to minimize and maximize a form even if it doesn't have Min and Max buttons and even if the window can't be sized because of its BorderStyle. Changes to WindowState fire the form's Resize event, so you can take appropriate action.

One weird behavior. If you maximize, then minimize a form, when you then set WindowState to 0 to restore the form, Resize fires twice because the form first maximizes, then returns to its original size.

Example

```
* This code might be in a form's Resize event (if you're
* using formsets, which we don't)
IF This.WindowState = 2   && maximized
   * move things around so they can be seen
   ThisFormSet.Form2.Left = This.MaxLeft + This.Width
ENDIF
```

See Also BorderStyle, MaxButton, MaxHeight, MaxWidth, MinButton, Zoom Window

WindowType

This property determines whether a form or formset is modal or modeless. It also determines whether it's a real Visual FoxPro form or a backward-compatibility READ form.

Usage

```
oObject.WindowType = nWindowType
nWindowType = oObject.WindowType
```

There are four choices for WindowType, but you'll only want to use two of them in forms you create in Visual FoxPro. Types 2 and 3 are for forms converted from FoxPro 2.x—2 is modeless READ-type, and 3 is modal READ-type. In fact, you can't even choose these two in the Property Sheet. Because no one (okay, no one except the people who wrote the code in the first place) knows how they work, we urge you to forget you ever read about them.

When you create forms and formsets with CreateObject(), you can set WindowType before you Show the thing. Or you can just pass the appropriate parameter to the Show method.

You can't change WindowType while the form is displayed, but you can change it while it's hidden. However, we can't imagine why you'd want to change an existing form from modal to modeless or vice versa. That's bound to confuse the heck out of your users.

Most forms are either modal or modeless all the time. Either it's a dialog or a document. You can set WindowType in the Form Designer and be done with it.

We have occasionally run into a form that's usually a document, but once in a while needs to be called modally from another form. That's where the opportunity to change WindowType (or pass the parameter to Show) at runtime comes in handy.

Example

```
oForm = CreateObject("Form")
oForm.WindowType = 1   && Make form modal
oForm.Show()
```

See Also Show

With ... EndWith

This command doesn't let you do anything new. It just makes it easier to refer to a bunch of properties of the same object.

Usage

```
WITH oObject
   [ Statements ]
ENDWITH
```

It can be pretty tedious to assign new values to a bunch of properties. Say you're working on a check box embedded in a grid, which in turn is embedded in a page of a page frame, but you're doing the manipulation at the form level. To change its caption, you'd need something like:

```
ThisForm.pgfMyFrame.pagPage1.grdMyGrid.grcColumn1.chkMyCheck.Caption = ;
   "Wowza!"
```

Imagine changing eight or 10 properties this way. WITH is a better way. You write all that out once and then Visual FoxPro understands what you mean:

```
WITH ThisForm.pgfMyFrame.pagPage1.grdMyGrid.grcColumn1.chkMyCheck
    * manipulate as many properties as you want
    .Caption="Wowza!"
    .Enabled=.T.
    .Value=.T.
ENDWITH
```

In our tests here at Hacker's Labs, we found that using the WITH version was also slightly faster than the long form. The difference isn't enough to matter in most situations, but might be handy when you're trying to squeeze that last little bit of performance out of your app. Keep in mind, too, that the more properties you're setting, the more improvement you get.

You might think the only statements you can put inside the WITH would be property assignments and that each line must begin with the "." to set off the property, but you'd be wrong. In fact, pretty much any command can go in there. Not only that, but you can refer to properties anywhere in the command line without prefacing them with the object name. Both stand-alone and end-line comments (with &&) are permitted. Finally, you can nest WITH statements so that inside a WITH, you can add another level or two of referencing and speak directly to a lower-level object.

Note that we said "you can" do all those things. That doesn't mean you should. It wouldn't take much to end up with an unreadable mess. We think WITH is pretty good for what it's intended for, letting you cut down on complicated references. But, mixing a lot of other code in with this isn't a good idea. Remember, overly clever code leads to support calls.

Example

```
frmMyForm=CREATEOBJECT("Form")
* code like this is an okay idea
WITH frmMyForm
   .Height = 200
   .Width = 100
   .Caption = "Form to demonstrate WITH command"
ENDWITH

* code like the following is a not-so-great idea
WITH frmMyForm
   .Show()
   .AddObject("txtMyText","textbox")
   WITH .txtMyText
      .Height = .Parent.Height/10
      .Width = .Parent.Width/2
      .Visible = .T.
   ENDWITH
ENDWITH
```

_Wizard See _Beautify.

WLast(), WOnTop(), WOutput()

These three functions tell you about active windows and where output is going. WONTOP() tells you which window is active now. WLAST() tells you which window was active before the one that's active now. WOUTPUT() tells you where output is going now.

All three of these functions can either give you the name of the window that has the specified status (last active, currently active, receiving output) or tell you whether a particular window has that status.

Usage

```
cReturnValue = WLAST()
lReturnValue = WLAST( cWindow )
cReturnValue = WONTOP()
lReturnValue = WONTOP( cWindow )
```

WONTOP() without a parameter returns the name of the window that's "on top," that is, the active window. Normally, you can identify this window because its title bar is a different color than other windows' title bars. If you pass a window name, WONTOP() tells you whether or not it's on top. Toolbars can never be WONTOP(), though other system windows can. The Command Window is also never WONTOP().

If the parameter is omitted, WLAST() returns the name of the window that was active just before the current active window (the previous WONTOP()). If you pass the name of a window, the return value tells whether that window was active just before the current active window.

When you click from one window to another, the window you click on becomes WONTOP(), while the one you left becomes WLAST(). Issuing ACTIVATE WINDOW makes the named window WONTOP(). However, the Command Window is never WONTOP() or WLAST().

There's a subtle point when using a form set (or a 2.x screen set). When you move from one form to another in the set, the DEACTIVATE method of the form you're leaving fires. By the time that happens, the form you're leaving has become WLAST() and the new form is WONTOP(). When using 2.x-style screen sets, the same thing is true for the DEACTIVATE clause of the READ command—by the time it executes, the new window is WONTOP() and the one you're leaving is WLAST().

However, except when building developer's tools, checking WONTOP() and WLAST() and changing them with ACTIVATE WINDOW should be much less common in Visual FoxPro than in FoxPro 2.x. Since pretty much every window involved in an application will be a form, you can do these manipulations using form and formset properties and methods instead.

A hidden window can't be WONTOP() even if you use the optional SAME clause of HIDE WINDOW. A window must be visible to be WONTOP().

Example

```
* Open the Watch window
* window and put WONTOP() and WLAST() in it
* Then, try this:
DEFINE WINDOW test1 FROM 0,0 TO 10,30
DEFINE WINDOW test2 FROM 0,40 TO 10,70
ACTIVATE WINDOW test1
* notice that WONTOP() is now "TEST1"
* click into the Command window
* now WLAST() is "TEST1", too
ACTIVATE WINDOW test2
* WONTOP() becomes "TEST2"
* Click between the two windows and watch what happens.
* Note that clicking on a window doesn't make it WONTOP().
* This isn't true with forms.
```

Usage

```
cReturnValue = WOUTPUT()
lReturnValue = WOUTPUT( cWindow )
```

Without a parameter, WOUTPUT() tells you the name of the window to which any output will be sent (the "output window"). If you pass a window name, you find out whether that window is the output window.

Issuing ACTIVATE WINDOW changes WOUTPUT() to the named window, if it's capable of receiving output. Clicking on a window created with DEFINE WINDOW does *not* make it WOUTPUT(), but clicking on a form does.

WONTOP() and WOUTPUT() often have the same value, but not always. There are many windows that cannot be WOUTPUT() because they can't receive output. This is true of all system windows and of Browse windows. (In FoxPro 2.x, comparing WONTOP() to WOUTPUT() was one way of determining whether a Browse or a READ window was active when coordinating Browse with READ.)

Output from commands (like DIR, ?, and COUNT) that you probably think of as going to the main FoxPro window actually goes to WOUTPUT(). To have this output go to the main FoxPro window, you can issue ACTIVATE SCREEN before the command that generates the output. However, as we've mentioned elsewhere, using the Screen raises various issues, because some applications may use only top-level windows and dispense with the Screen entirely.

WOUTPUT() can point to a hidden window, which can be confusing when your output seems to disappear entirely.

Example

```
* open the Watch window and put WOUTPUT() in it
* Then:
DEFINE WINDOW test1 FROM 0,0 TO 10,30
DEFINE WINDOW test2 FROM 0,40 TO 10,70
ACTIVATE WINDOW test1
* note that WOUTPUT() is now "TEST1"
ACTIVATE WINDOW test2
* WOUTPUT() is now "TEST2"
* Click on Debug Window - WOUTPUT() doesn't change
* Click between the windows - WOUTPUT() doesn't change
```

See Also Activate Screen, Activate Window, ActiveForm, Define Window, Hide Window, Show, Show Window, WTitle()

WLCol(), WLRow() See WBorder().

WMaximum(), WMinimum() See WExist().

WordWrap

This is a property of the label control, which should allow it to dynamically resize vertically. Handled carefully, it will do that.

Usage

```
lblLabel.WordWrap = lWordWrap
lWordWrap = lblLabel.WordWrap
```

In theory and from reading the Help file, you might think that WordWrap would turn on and off the capability to wrap a label around, so as it changes it does not take up any more space horizontally, but rather rubber-band-stretches vertically by wrapping words. We initially viewed this as "Vertical AutoSize," but that's not exactly how it works.

Setting WordWrap True doesn't automatically wrap your text to a previously set Width. You need to either manually set Height of the label, or turn on AutoSize *after* setting WordWrap .T. before the text will wrap. We expected that WordWrap would cause Height to automatically resize to fit the text, but Microsoft's solution to this makes sense, too.

Example

```
* Try these from the command window
x=createobject("form")
x.visible = .t.
x.addobject("MyLabel","Label")
x.mylabel.visible = .t.
x.mylabel.caption = "Now I can wrap enough words to occupy " ;
                  + "four lines of text"
* Only as much text as can fit in the default size appears
x.mylabel.wordwrap = .t.              && Still no more text
x.mylabel.height = 4*x.mylabel.height  && Now it appears!
```

See Also AutoSize, Height, Label, Width

WOutput() See WLast().

WParent() See WChild().

_Wrap

This remnant of the printer variable system actually does something. It determines whether output produced by ? and ?? pays attention to _RMARGIN or not. If _WRAP is .T., output stops at _RMARGIN and wraps to the next line.

Usage `_WRAP = lWrapIt`

One other kink feels like a bug, but actually makes sense. When _WRAP is .T., output from ?? is stored up until either the right margin is reached or a ? command is issued. The characters aren't sent to the device until that time. Where this catches us is when we are trying to ring the bell with ?? CHR(07). Remember to turn _WRAP off before issuing that command.

Example
```
_WRAP = .T.
_RMARGIN = 20
? "This long string will be wrapped when you see it"
_WRAP = .F.
? "This one won't be wrapped because _WRAP is .F."
```

See Also _Alignment, _Indent, _LMargin, _RMargin

WRead() See WExist().

WriteExpression, WriteMethod See ReadExpression.

WRows(), WTitle() See WBorder().

WVisible() See WExist().

Year() See CDoW().

ZAP

This may be the single most dangerous command in all of FoxPro, but it's incredibly handy when you're working interactively. ZAP permanently removes all records from a table. The name supposedly stands for "Zero And Pack." ZAPped records cannot be recalled.

Usage `ZAP [ IN cAlias | nWorkArea ]`

Although you can ZAP in a work area other than the current one, we really don't recommend it. Using this command by itself is like striking matches; using it in another work area is like striking matches in a gas station.

ZAP is not a good database citizen. It doesn't call the Delete trigger for a table in a database. Instead, it neatly avoids all the work you've done to make sure the integrity of your database is maintained. This is a major flaw.

Due to the above and for lots of other reasons, never use ZAP in a program. It's just too risky. See PACK for suggestions on alternatives. Actually, the one case where ZAP might be acceptable is when you're working on a temporary file in the first place, so no permanent data is at risk. Even so, there's usually a safer way.

So why do we think it's incredibly handy? When you're manipulating data manually—perhaps parsing older data to create a normalized database—it's clean and simple to ZAP the target table between tests. Outside this kind of situation, we strongly recommend you avoid ZAP.

ZAP does respect SET SAFETY, so if you have it on, you are warned before you throw all your data in the garbage can.

Example
```
USE TestData
ZAP
```

See Also Delete, Pack, Recall, Set Safety

Zoom Window See Size Window.

ZoomBox See SizeBox.

ZOrder

ZOrder is a method of controls that manipulates which control is on top of a stack of overlying controls, but, far more importantly (and far less documented!), also controls the firing order of key events for a set of controls on a form. The fact that there's no equivalent property for finding out who's on top makes this a pain in the neck to work with.

Usage `oControl.ZOrder( nWhichWay )`

Parameter	Value	Meaning
nWhichWay	0	Bring the designated control to the top of the stack.
	1	Push the designated control to the bottom of the stack.

As is badly explained in the Help file, ZOrder does actually maintain the visual order of controls that might partially overlay each other. It could be incorrectly postulated from the tone of the topic that there might be an equivalent method for the graphical elements drawn on a form with the Line, Box and Circle methods. Nope. As we explain in the reference sections for those elements, graphical elements drawn with these methods are completely passive. Although they appear to be on top of our controls when drawn, they are, in fact, just the last thing to be drawn on the form. As the controls that appear to be underneath them become active or refresh, the drawings are erased. Moving a control that has been drawn over shows that nothing remains of the drawing underneath the control.

ZOrder serves a second function, one that has bollixed us good on a few occasions. ZOrder not only controls the appearance of controls within a form, it also controls the firing order of those controls during key events such as Init, Refresh and Destroy. This can be a distinct and separate order from the TabIndex, which determines the order in which an operator moves from control to control. It is also different from the PageOrder property of Page frames, which determines the internal organization of pages within the page frame. ZOrder'ing a page to the front brings it to the top, but does not alter its order within the Page frame.

We suppose that, by necessity, there must be some logic to the firing order of controls. FoxPro must keep a list somewhere of all the controls it needs to work with, because it needs to go through that list and run them all. As explained in "A Gala Event," controls fire Init events from the innermost level out—a text box contained within a column within a grid within a page frame fires first, followed by the column, grid and page frame, in that order. During the Destroy process, the opposite occurs—events fire inward, as if the form implodes. But what of controls on the same level? If three text boxes are placed on a form, which fires first?

Some of the answer can be found within the ZOrder method. Controls on the same level of a container—form, formset, page, whatever—fire in the order they were added to the form, unless they have been moved from that order. In design mode, the "Send to Back" and "Bring to Front" options manipulate this order. This order is saved, not as an explicit property of our controls, but rather is implied in the order in which controls are saved—the actual record order of the SCX or VCX. In a runtime environment, the ZOrder method provides the same ordering function. The frustrating thing is that we don't ever get to directly determine where we are in this list, only push a control to the front or back.

Have some patience with our explanation and we hope all will be clear when we're done. It's really not that bad.

On a visually designed form, the controls' Init events fire in the order they were added to a form. This is also the default TabIndex order, the order in which the operator will move through the form if he presses Tab to go from control to control. Fine. The TabIndex order can be rearranged by using the Tab Order option on the View menu pad or by directly changing the TabIndex property of each control. This does not change the ZOrder. On the other hand, using the "Send to Back" and "Bring to Front" options on the Format menu changes the ZOrder of the controls. A control sent to the front is the last to fire its Init, and the first to be destroyed. An element sent to the back acts as if it were the oldest element on the form, firing its Init first, and being the last control to be destroyed.

If the form is generated from code rather than an SCX, each Init fires in the order it's specified with ADD OBJECT in the form's definition, and is unaffected by ZOrder. Our third example demonstrates this. In a coded form, all the Inits still fire, regardless of whether you ZOrder a control to the top of the stack. In a visually designed form (an SCX), an Init that forces its control to the front (by issuing the command This.ZORDER(0)) prevents the other controls' Inits from running. Bear this in mind if you mess with ZOrder and try to convert a form from visual to hand-coded.

While a form is up and running, a control can be programmatically sent to front by calling the control's ZOrder(0), or to back with ZOrder(1). This has a crucial message for us: Don't mess with the ZOrder while program execution is within one of those events that fires in ZOrder order—Init, Destroy, Refresh and perhaps others—without a great deal of care. As shown in the example below, it's relatively easy to get stuck in a loop with two controls insisting "Oh, no, after you," like Chip 'n Dale. The flip side of this is that a control which teleports itself to the "top" of the stack of controls can short-circuit the stack of other controls waiting to fire their methods, causing a debugging nightmare. Sometimes a Refresh will fire and sometimes it won't. We can see some nice possibilities for this, but if you decide to resort to this tricky method, document it explicitly. Remember—some poor fool, perhaps even you, is going to have to debug this monster long after you've forgotten this trick.

Finally, Destroy events fire in the sequence of ZOrder in effect at the time the Destroy sequence starts. Mess with them within the Destroy event at the risk of your sanity.

During the Destroy events, attempting to push the ZOrder of a control back "over" controls that may have already been destroyed can crash FoxPro with an "Invalid Page Fault."

Example

```
* Here's a sample program that tests what ZOrder() will do
* The first creates an infinite loop, the second misses
* firing the Refresh() of one of the controls, and the third
* shows how the rules are different for Init()s in coded (vs.
* graphically designed) forms.
PRIVATE nDirection

* 1st example: Looping form
* Press any key other than Enter or Spacebar to stop the show.
WAIT WINDOW "An infinitely looping form"
nDirection = 1  && force the control to the back
oForm = CREATEOBJECT('BadForm')
oForm.Show()
oForm.Release()

* Second example: Button2's Refresh never fires
WAIT WINDOW "Form that skips Button2's Refresh"
nDirection = 0  && force the control to the front
oForm = CREATEOBJECT('BadForm')
oForm.Show()
oForm.Release()

* Last example: Inits in coded forms all fire
WAIT WINDOW "Form with Inits that should skip but don't"
nDirection = 0  && force the control to the front during Init
```

```
oForm = CREATEOBJECT('BadForm2')
oForm.Show()
oForm.Release()

RETURN

DEFINE CLASS BadForm AS Form
  ADD OBJECT btnCommandOne AS btnCommand WITH Top = 10
  ADD OBJECT btnCommandTwo AS btnCommand WITH Top = 50
ENDDEFINE

DEFINE CLASS btnCommand AS CommandButton
  PROCEDURE Refresh
   WAIT WINDOW "Hello, I'm " + this.name + ;
      "'s Refresh Event" + chr(13) + ;
      "Refresh Events fire in ZOrder()." + chr(13) + ;
      "Press Enter to continue," + ;
      " any other key to quit " ;
      TO cTheirAnswer
   IF EMPTY(cTheirAnswer)
      This.ZOrder(nDirection)  && change order
   ENDIF
  ENDPROC
ENDDEFINE

DEFINE CLASS BadForm2 AS Form
  ADD OBJECT btnCommandOne AS btnCommand2 WITH Top = 10
  ADD OBJECT btnCommandTwo AS btnCommand2 WITH Top = 50
ENDDEFINE

DEFINE CLASS btnCommand2 AS CommandButton
  PROCEDURE Init
   WAIT WINDOW "Hello, I'm " + this.name + ;
      "'s Init Event" + chr(13) + ;
      "Hand-coded Init Events all fire " + ;
      "regardless of ZOrder()." + chr(13) + ;
      "Press Enter to continue"
   This.ZOrder(nDirection)  && change order
  ENDPROC
ENDDEFINE
```

See Also Box, Circle, Line, PageOrder, TabIndex

Section 5: But Wait, There's More!

We will now discuss in a little more detail the Struggle for Existence.

Charles Robert Darwin, *The Origin of Species*, 1859

We've sliced, we've diced, we've chopped Visual FoxPro into little pieces. But there's still more to say. A few features are so cool, they warrant their own chapters. This section goes into detail on the ActiveX technologies, the Object Browser and Component Gallery. In addition, there's a bonus chapter on hacking the Wizards and Builders in the HackFox Help file on the CD.

Active Something

True contentment is a thing as active as agriculture.

G. K. Chesterton, *A Miscellany of Men*, 1912

Active is the buzzword every new Microsoft technology seems to be getting stuck with these days. Is this just a marketing term or is there something behind all this?

In the original *Hacker's Guide to Visual FoxPro 3.0,* we included a chapter "OLE, OLE, Oxen Free!" that talked about the brave new world of OLE. Even at that time, OLE was not that new, but it was just catching on in the developer community. FoxPro 2.x provided support only for OLE 1.0 in its implementation, and that was pretty weak. Visual FoxPro supported OLE 2.0 but, like many "point zero" releases, there were a lot of incompatible products released under the 2.0 banner.

We've made a somewhat arbitrary decision to divide the ever-expanding subject of OLE, er, COM, into several pieces. "It was Automation, You Know" covers those technologies formerly known as OLE Automation, now simply Automation, as well as the brave new world of Automation servers created with Visual FoxPro. In this section, we take on a few of the other aspects of the technology, and look at the Registry, Linking and Embedding, and ActiveX Controls.

OLE History

"In the beginning, there was DOS. And it was good..."

Well, maybe not that good. People wanted computers to be able to do more and more, and DOS just didn't cut it. So then GUIs (Graphical User Interfaces) were invented, to allow users to create better looking documents in an easier-to-use environment. And it was good. Well, maybe not that good. Users now wanted to be able to copy a portion of one document and place it in another. Cut-and-paste was invented to fill this need. And it was...okay, but not enough. Now that a user could create an item in one application and paste it into another, they wanted to go back to the first document, update the data, and have the second document reflect the changes made in the first. So DDE, with its hot-links, cold-links, warm-links and lukewarm-links, was invented to fill this gap. And DDE was...well, it was...anyway, we learned to work with it.

OLE was next in this genesis—Object Linking and Embedding—a method used to actually embed the data and a link to the originating document in a final document in a visual manner. OLE 1.0 was a clumsy and error-prone architecture. OLE 2.0 introduced far more stability into the structure. And with OLE 2.0, sounding like Monty Python's Knight Who Says "Ni," Microsoft declared that OLE was no longer "Object Linking and Embedding" but should henceforth be referred to only as "OLE." Not long after that, "OLE Automation" became simply "Automation" and OCXs (which started as OLE Controls) were declared to be "ActiveX Controls." More recently, the term "OLE" was considered too passé, and "COM" became the new rage. (Who knows what Microsoft will be calling this technology by the time you read this book?)

There really and truly is something to COM that's different from ActiveX or OLE. COM, the Component Object Model, is at the very base of all of Microsoft's designs for object interaction. OLE and all of the Active technologies are built on the base of COM object design. But for Microsoft to distinguish that this year's solution is "COM" is, to us, more of a marketing issue than a factual one.

Windows Registry

> I know not anything more pleasant, or more instructive, than to compare experience with expectation, or to register from time to time the difference between idea and reality. It is by this kind of observation that we grow daily less liable to be disappointed.
>
> Samuel Johnson

The Windows Registry is the source of all information linking applications together. The Registry is a structured collection of "key" values, each of which may have one or more settings. Understanding how to read and work with Registry entries is crucial for understanding the nuances of COM.

The Registry can be viewed with a Microsoft-supplied viewer program, Regedit.EXE (on Win9x platforms) or Regedt32.EXE (for Windows NT)—see Figures 5-1 and 5-2. Tracing your way through the networked set of keys can tell you the verbs appropriate to use with a server, the paths to the server, and how to match extensions to their executables. A set of registration keys can be exported from the registration file to an editable text format (usually with a .REG extension) and imported into the same or a different Registry.

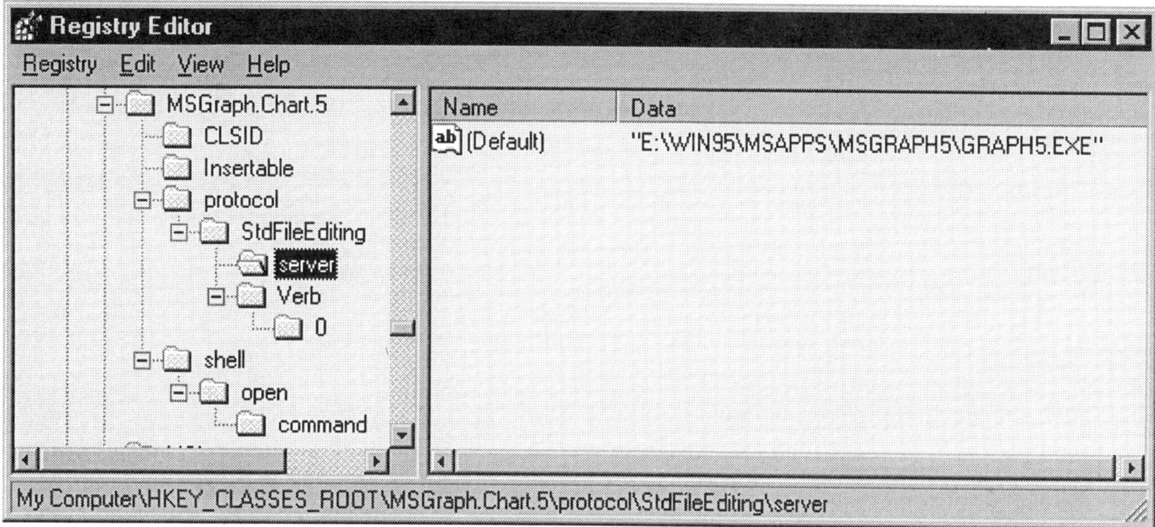

Figure 5-1: A view of the Windows 95 Registration Editor, showing entries for the MSGraph 5.0 applet.

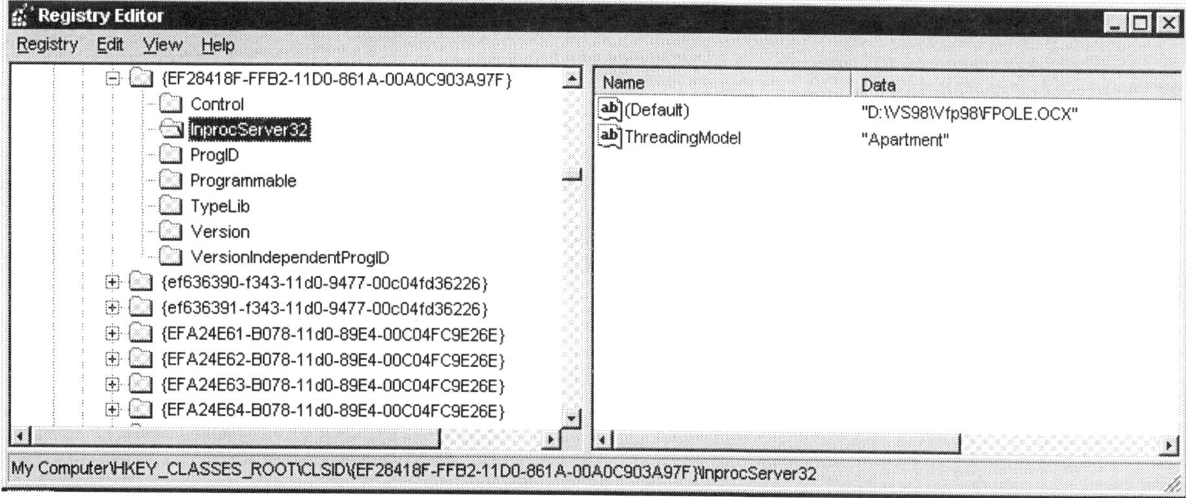

Figure 5-2: The Windows NT 4.0 Registration Editor, showing the settings for VFP's FPOLE interface.

Two words of caution (based on painful experience!) for working with the Registry: Make backups! A badly planned entry in the Registry can cause your applications or even Windows itself to fail. Some backup programs fail to back up the Registry, because the file is always open while Windows is running. Make sure your backup program knows how to back up the Registry. In addition, look for utilities specifically designed to restore the Registry when the operating system is no longer bootable. Rdisk.EXE comes with Windows NT. Emergency startup disks can be made for Windows 95/98. In addition, the Resource Kits for each operating system come with additional Registry tools. Check 'em out.

Linking and Embedding

> There is no object so soft but it makes a hub for the wheel'd universe.
>
> Walt Whitman

The simplest form of OLE is the ability to place data and images from one application into another. This ability to embed or link objects within FoxPro is cleverly called "Object Linking and Embedding." Bet someone stayed up all night thinking that one up! Linking and embedding objects is a feature that was available in FoxPro 2.5 and 2.6 for Windows, but there have been significant enhancements in Visual FoxPro.

FoxPro stores the object, or the links to the object, in a General field. General fields are nothing more than enhanced memo fields, and they share many characteristics with them. Among other things, for a given table, they're both stored in a single FPT file. A General field is made of several components. First, there's the binary data needed to tell FoxPro what this data is. This key refers FoxPro to the Registry (see the Reference section), which stores the name of the server (originating) application and the capabilities of the server. Also stored within the General field is the "display data," a bitmap or metafile which gives FoxPro an image to display when the General field is shown in a MODIFY GENERAL window or an OLEBoundControl. Finally, if the data is linked from a file on disk, the path and filename of the original file are stored in the General field. If the data is embedded rather than linked, the actual data is also included within the General field.

When should data be embedded and when should it be linked? The answer, as with most things in the design of a FoxPro application, is "it depends." Some OLE servers, like MSGraph, don't have the ability to store freestanding files, but can only operate within another application. For these servers, the decision has been made for you. On the other hand, if you're working with data that needs to be accessed and manipulated from another application, such as a Paintbrush file that will change over time, the data should be linked so the other applications will be able to find it on disk. The flip side of the same coin is that embedding data within a General field protects it from unauthorized changes, so it's editable only within your application or another FoxPro application with appropriate access to your data.

Disk space is another consideration. Since OLE generates display data as well as storing embedded data within a file, large, high-color, detailed graphic images can consume very large amounts of disk space. Display data is typically stored in a bitmap-type format: several bytes of color information for each pixel. So, even if the original image is deeply compressed, like a JPG or PNG image, the resulting display data can take megabytes of space. We know of some applications where the decision was made to bypass general fields for storing the image altogether. The path to the actual data is stored in a character or memo field, and the data is brought into the general field of a temporary cursor when it needs to be manipulated. So the decision to link or embed, either permanently or temporarily, or none of the above, is one that needs to be made based on the best compromise of your application's need for access, security and disk space issues.

Data is attached to a General field with the APPEND GENERAL command. It can be displayed with the legacy MODIFY GENERAL or @...SAY commands, or preferably with the more capable and controllable OLEControl and OLEBoundControl. See the Reference section for more on these commands.

Like memo fields, General fields suffer from "memo bloat." When changes are made to information stored within the memo file, new blocks of information are written at the end of the file, then the original blocks are marked as no longer in use. These blocks are never reused. It is necessary to PACK MEMO (we dislike PACK—see "Commands Never to Use" earlier in the book for some good workarounds) or COPY the table to eliminate the wasted space.

In-Place, er, In-Situ Activation, er, Visual Editing

> To a philosopher all *news*, as it is called, is gossip, and they who edit it and read it are old women over their tea.
>
> Henry David Thoreau, *Walden*, 1854

The confused topic title is typical of this confused topic. Microsoft fumbled the ball in a major way when rolling out this feature, changing its name three times in the process. In-situ is wonderful for those Ivy League Latin scholars among us, but we can't see this catching on with the MTV crowd—it sounds more like a sneeze than a feature. "In-Place" says what it does and will probably be popular with programmers for years to come, because it tells us what it is. Visual Editing, however, is what Microsoft decided to call it, a phrase that flows off the tongue of the sales reps easily enough, and one that looks good in print. But what does it mean to do "visual editing"—that you look at the screen while you type?

What it does is far easier to explain than trying to come up with a name for it. Visual Editing is a better user interface to allow users to manipulate data from one application while running another. Microsoft has discovered through usability studies that users are uncomfortable and disconcerted when they're working in an application and a second application's interface—a new window, menu and toolbars—leaps to the front when the second application's data is called up. For example, a user might want to place a graph of quarterly sales on a page in the annual report. In earlier versions of OLE, placing a graph in a document and calling it up for editing brought up the entire MS Graph interface, with its own menus, toolbars and separate graph and datasheet windows. The document the hapless user was working on was shoved far to the back, out of the way and inaccessible.

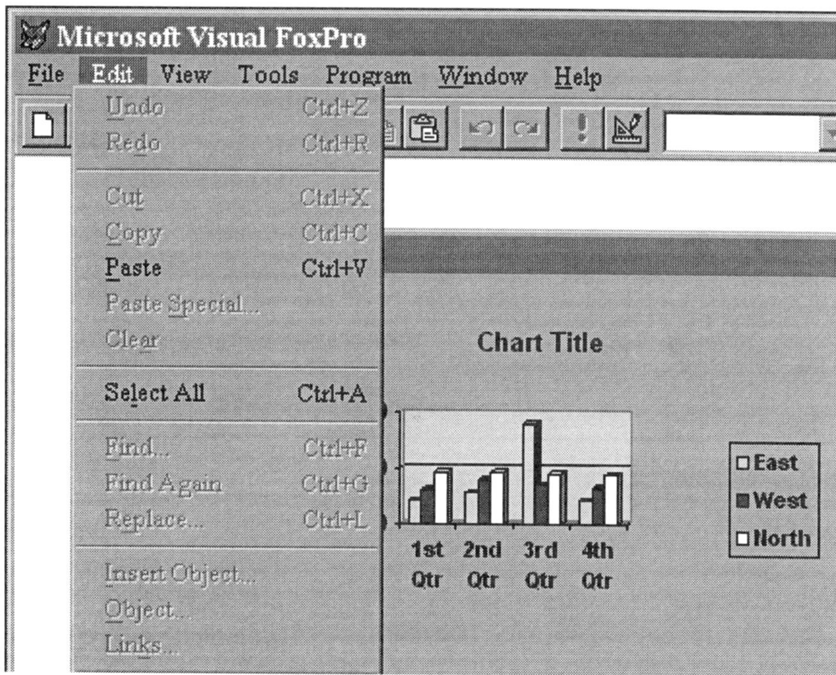

Figure 5-3: The native FoxPro menu before OLE activation.

With Visual Editing, the graph doesn't come up with its own window, but rather is activated in place (get it?), maintaining its position and relative size within the document. The toolbars of the host application are replaced with the toolbars of MSGraph, in a manner similar to the way that Visual FoxPro brings up and removes its own toolbars as the various power tools are called into play. The menus also change. Those menus that are more the concern of the containing application remain the same. That includes the File menu, with its options to Open, Close and Exit, and the Window menu, with its choices for arranging the various windows on the screen. The remaining menu pads are up for negotiation between the contained application and its container. The Edit menu is a good candidate for replacement, so that it can offer features unique to the application. The Help menu is taken over by the embedded application, allowing it to offer context-sensitive help. Any menus you create that should participate in this negotiation process should include the NEGOTIATE keyword (see the Reference section on DEFINE PAD for details). Figures 5-3 and 5-4 illustrate the menu negotiation with before-activation and after-activation pictures of an MSGraph application.

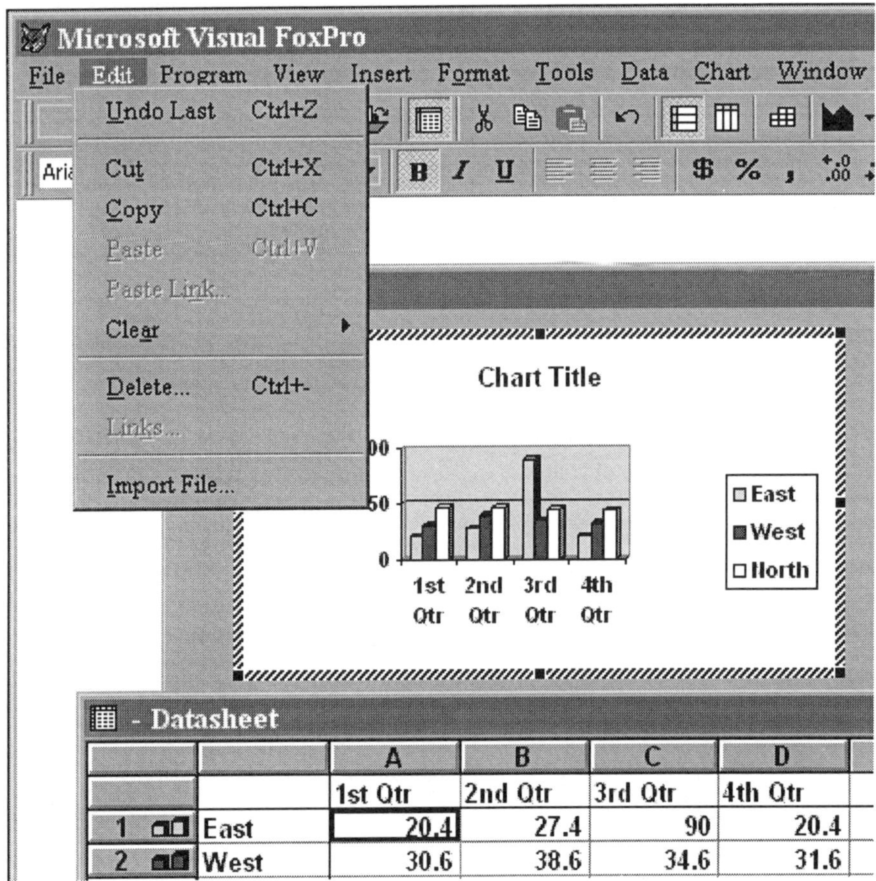

Figure 5-4: After In Place Editing. Note new toolbar and menu pads and bars.

One significant limitation of this method is that Visual Editing is available only for embedded objects. Microsoft claims this is to avoid having multiple users attempting to make changes to a file simultaneously. We find it astounding that no one considered implementing a locking scheme as part of the logic of Visual Editing. So, you need to either embed data you want to allow your clients to edit, or run the linked application directly rather than use Visual Editing.

Last words of warning before you leap into implementing this feature: Visual Editing, like most of OLE, is resource-intensive. Ensure that you test and evaluate the features on a minimally acceptable system before committing to a large project dependent on this feature. OLE is very cool, but that coolness comes at a cost. While it may be theoretically possible to implement a Visual FoxPro system with Visual Editing on a 12 Mb 486 system, it would not be a pretty thing. Data entry clerks would get into the habit of calling up a Visual Editing situation just before going to lunch, so it might be ready for them upon their return. Sixteen megabytes is probably a good minimum system for OLE work, and more is better. For more of our hardware recommendations, check out "Hardware and Software Recommendations" in the earlier part of the book.

ActiveX Controls, aka OLE Custom Controls, aka OCXs

> Any technology sufficiently advanced is indistinguishable from magic.
>
> Sir Arthur C. Clarke, *Clarke's Law*

Sometimes it's hard to believe things accomplished by our computers are not simply magic. ActiveX Controls often seem to take on that aura. An ActiveX Control is an add-on for Windows32 applications that gives our applications capabilities not imagined by the authors of Visual FoxPro (or sometimes just better versions of the ones they did imagine). ActiveX Controls, or, more familiarly, OCXs (named for their usual extension), can be added to a development environment like Visual FoxPro in such a way that they seem like just another control. They have properties, events and methods. They can be selected from the Form Controls toolbar and placed on forms. They can be manipulated in code through the usual Formset.Form.Object.Property addressing scheme. Events and methods can be initiated as with any native control. But the ActiveX Control can be written by a third party. This is a tremendous avenue of possible add-on tools for Visual FoxPro.

Not only that, but ActiveX Controls are designed to be available to any tool that supports the OLE Custom Control interface. ActiveX Controls developed for other tools, such as Visual Basic, Access, or Visual C++, should be compatible ("should be" is the key here—see below) with the FoxPro environment. This larger market for selling tools can only help to bring more and better developers into this field. ActiveX Controls from a variety of manufacturers are already available for graphing, displaying calendars and acquiring analog data. We expect to see much more in this field.

ActiveX Controls originated with the VBX, or Visual Basic eXtension, feature added in Visual Basic 3.0. These add-ons were specifically designed to take advantage of the VB environment, and had a number of limitations that made them difficult to use in other development environments or to add to other platforms. Access 2.0 featured the ability to use the second generation of VBXs, 16-bit OCXs. However, this still wasn't enough, and 32-bit ActiveX Controls were developed to address those needs. 32-bit ActiveX Controls are the only format supported by Visual FoxPro, and VFP was the first released application to use them. Since the release of Visual FoxPro, additional platforms for 32-bit ActiveX Controls have appeared—most notably, Visual Basic 4.0 and later.

With the proliferation of ActiveX Controls for the much larger developer market, the reality behind the promise came to light. ActiveX Controls *should* be the same, the interfaces *should* all work the same, and everybody *should* just get along fine. Uh-huh. Well, the ugly truth is that VFP, first out of the gate with OCX support, was developed with a preliminary specification. Last-minute changes defeated some of the compatibility the VFP team tried so hard to achieve. Developers of VB, in an effort to make OCXs most useful on their platform, interpreted the specification to let them introduce some custom interfaces, rendering controls that used those interfaces inoperable in other platforms. Finally, OCXs shipping to support the interface in VB lacked key elements needed to support the faster VTable binding, forcing the VFP development team to create the SYS(2333) function to turn off that feature.

Like many other features of OLE 2.0, ActiveX Controls are a mish-mash of feature sets and optional APIs. Visual Basic, Access and other development platforms supporting ActiveX Controls reveal incompatibility problems, with controls running with one and not other platforms of this "standard." We really hope that Microsoft gets their act together on this one and finds a way to deliver the same support, using the same APIs, across their entire product line of development systems. If Microsoft can't even do this internally, third-party vendors stand no chance of supporting the OCX specification. And if there isn't a large demand for ActiveX Controls, the promising market for innovative, high-quality, high-performance ActiveX Controls will wither and die, making our job of delivering the best bang for the buck that much harder.

The number of OCXs bundled with Visual Studio is pretty dazzling, and really beyond the scope of what we want to cover here. In the following sections, we'll talk a little bit about how ActiveX Controls are used in VFP, and some important controls VFP provides.

How to use ActiveX Controls in Visual FoxPro

Just as with FoxPro's base class controls, the first thing you want to do with these controls is to subclass them, and use your subclasses in forms. The reason for this is that it's not possible to add custom properties and methods to the base classes. There will come a time when you have designed the coolest form and realize that you need to add some feature to the control. With subclassed controls, this is easy.

The properties of these controls are accessible in curious ways. Right-clicking on most ActiveX Controls will bring up a context-sensitive menu with two "Properties" options: one labeled just "Properties" that brings up the native VFP property sheet, and a second one, usually labeled "*Control* Properties" that brings up the control's property sheet. The control's own property sheet is often the only way to see some of the properties of the control. If they appear at all, many of the control's properties show up only on the "All" tab and not on the "Other" tab of VFP's Property Sheet.

You'll also note that few ActiveX Controls have data binding features. If you need to add, say, a table of data, you'll have to use AddItem to do it one at a time. This can seriously limit the capacity of the controls to work with large data sets. We have seen a few controls with data binding features, using ODBC or ADO to link to the underlying data sources. These can be problematic, because their implementation really makes them stand-alone data applications plunked in the middle of our apps—they're not sharing data with the host VFP application. That means these controls are usually pretty heavy consumers of resources, and aren't going to recognize changing data within the application until it's committed to the data source and the control's data is requeried. Rumors abound that a group at Microsoft is hard at work on the next OCX standard with a data-bound feature; we look forward to that possibility. For now, if you need to data-bind an OCX, you might have to write the code yourself, perhaps in a data-binding wrapper class definition.

Almost all of the controls we discuss below have an AboutBox method, which displays an application-modal dialog crediting the authors. A word of caution: All of the controls we're mentioning here are labeled "Version 1.0." Even Ashton-Tate knew better, back in the dBASE II days, than to offer version 1.0 of a product!

FoxhWnd

hWnd is the Windows API short name for a handle to a window. Handles, in Win32 API talk, are numbers that specify a memory location or structure within memory. Much of the Windows API is based on passing the hWnd of an object. Most controls in languages such as VB or VC++ are, in fact, windows with their own hWnds. Visual FoxPro does not follow the style of using hWnds for each control, instead assuming responsibility for drawing and redrawing the entire "client area" of the application. This decision was made long ago, when FoxPro was a multi-platform client, and writing platform-specific code for Windows would have been inefficient. Now that FoxPro is down to supporting only the Win32 platform, that decision seems more unfortunate than it did at the time. Hindsight is 20/20.

So what does lacking a bunch of Windows handles mean to us? Windows calls that depend on having a handle to the calling application can be treated two ways. One way is to ignore the request for a handle and pass zero instead. The other is to determine the handle of the main FoxPro window, and pass that one as a proxy for the specific handle the routine might be looking for. In order to determine the FoxPro main window handle, you need to load FoxTools and invoke the MainHWnd() function.

Some Windows API calls just won't settle for either of these alternatives, though, and the FoxhWnd ActiveX Control was introduced to solve their needs. The Solutions Samples included with VFP have a demonstration of FoxhWnd. It's in the first section of ActiveX Controls, and is called "Play an AVI in an ActiveX control."

Filer

Filer used to be a handy "desktop accessory" tool built into FoxPro, great for finding all those times you misspelled "license" and opening all the programs in the native FoxPro editor. Alas, time and politics killed poor Filer, eliminated from the feature list for VFP 5.0. Rumors abound as to the real cause of its demise. We can't say for sure, but we suspect it wasn't really long filenames that killed it.

Filer returned, not too long after the shipping of VFP 5.0a, but in a new guise: as a FoxPro form and a COM object containing the core file-searching capabilities. The source code for the Filer form is provided, and we've seen several variations of the Filer form in *FoxPro Advisor* magazine as well as out on the Web. In VFP 6, you'll find the form and DLL in HOME() + "\Tools\Filer".

Did we say DLL? Yes, the Filer functionality comes to us in DLL format this time. But, you might ask, is a DLL an ActiveX Control? Well, no, strictly speaking. By Microsoft's definitions this month, ActiveX Controls are COM components with a design-time user interface: an OCX. (We mean that about Microsoft definitions: COM was the Common Object Model when we started this book, but it's the Component Object Model now. Just ask Microsoft.) But this chapter is "Active Something" and, like many of the other Active technologies Microsoft is shipping these days, Filer is a COM component accessible from many languages but lacking a design-time user interface. We feel the control needs to be featured, and this was the best place for it.

Here's a quick idea of what Filer can do for you:

```
oFiler = CREATEOBJECT("filer.fileutil")
oFiler.SearchPath = "C:\Temp"   && path can be separated with commas
oFiler.FileExpression = "*.*"   && wildcards and multiple file
                                && expressions, separated with semicolons
oFiler.SubFolder = .T.          && search subfolders
oFiler.SearchText1 = ""         && the text to search for
oFiler.SearchText2 = ""
oFiler.SearchText3 = ""
oFiler.IgnoreCase = .T.         && ignore the case
oFiler.WholeWords = .T.         && find only whole words
oFiler.Find(0)                  && 0: new search, 1: add to results
oFiler.Files.Count              && returns count of files found
oFiler.Files[2].Name            && returns name of file
oFiler.Editor = "notepad"       && specify an external editor
oFiler.IsHostedByFox = 0        && use the specified editor, not internal
```

Now, you could probably write all of the code to perform the searching functions in VFP—ADIR() and a little recursion get you most of the way there. Processing the text searching is easy with FileToStr(), ANDing and ORing results would be tiresome but manageable—but why bother? You've already got the functionality you need, in a compact little utility, listed as being freely distributable (at least in our licenses—you need to check yours).

FoxTLib

The FoxTLib OCX is a handy utility for reading and parsing ActiveX Type Libraries. A Type Library describes the functionality of its associated component, going into detail on the interface. It can be important to browse type libraries, as we discuss in "It Was Automation, You Know," to determine the method names, parameters and constants required by a function. FoxTLib supplies all of the information in an easy-to-use format. Check out the VFP Help for the details on FoxTLib, and check out the sample class Typelib.VCX (original, huh?) included in the _SAMPLES + "Classes\" directory.

FPOLE

Some people are still out there programming in a language not capable of working with all of Microsoft's technologies (actually, come to think about it, we suspect we all are). For them, the VFP team included a DLL in VFP 5, and a DLL-OCX pair in VFP 6, that allows them to access FoxPro's internal functionality even if their language is not capable of using Automation directly. It is called FPOLE, and it presents several methods. FoxDoCmd() allows you to pass a single command to FoxPro and have it execute it. This is the technique used within the Visual FoxPro HTML Help to run the FoxPro Solution Samples. (To check that out, go to the VFP Home Page, select "Samples" from the list on the right, right-click in the right viewer pane and select "View Source.") Other methods include FoxEval() to evaluate an expression, SetOLEObject() to specify the class used in the methods above, and several other methods for error handling.

Wrap it Up

> There is not a fiercer hell than the failure in a great object.
>
> John Keats

ActiveX offers some great challenges. Integrating the functionality available only through OLE can allow you to create easier-to-use, easier-to-maintain, richer interfaces with less coding and maintenance. Embedded and linked data can maintain the inter-application links from one session to the next. Visual Editing allows the presentation of data from foreign sources within the comfortable context of your own application.

But the reality of the situation is that many of these new capabilities are still being worked out. The perfect OCX for the job might work well under Visual Basic but may not have been tested under Visual FoxPro. Your clients might be surprised to hear that some functionality is available only under specific variations of the operating systems, or that 16 megabytes of RAM is good for a "starter" system. Each and every application you work with will require a different command set, different syntax, perhaps a different sequence of steps. Be prepared to face these challenges, and you will create some very cool COM/OLE/ActiveX-based systems.

Hacking the Class Browser and the Component Gallery

Visual FoxPro's Class Browser and new Component Gallery (or just "Browser" and "Gallery") are valuable development tools; most self-respecting VFP hacks will want to know them well.

Most of Visual FoxPro's ancillary tools, like Browser and Gallery, are actually written in Visual FoxPro. (Surprised?) Starting with VFP 6, the source code for all the VFP-coded tools is included. This is great news for VFP developers because the source for these tools provides some great (and occasionally not so great) examples. If you search carefully, you may even find an astonishing feat of software prowess: a comment in the source code.

Lack of comments aside, if you've ever wondered just how a particular wizard or service works, you can now easily and legally reverse-engineer it.

The source for VFP's tools is kept in a ZIP file in the HOME()+"Tools\XSource" directory. If this directory doesn't exist on your system, it's possible that you chose to omit some tools during installation. The Browser and Gallery source can be found in the HOME() + "Tools\XSource\vfpsource\Browser" directory. The most interesting file in this directory is the form Browser.SCX. The Browser and the Gallery share the same SCX file, and many of the methods therein serve both the Browser and the Gallery.

Let's look first at the Browser, and then we'll explore the new Gallery.

The Class Browser

The Browser is useful for a variety of development purposes. These include, among others:

- Managing classes and class libraries, including adding, deleting, renaming and redefining classes.
- Generating equivalent code for visual classes.
- Creating running instances at design time.
- Browsing all the classes and libraries used by a project.
- Browsing the interfaces of ActiveX and COM components.

What's New in VFP 6

The Class Browser remained mostly unchanged from VFP 3 to VFP 5, except they removed most of the GPFs. The changes to the VFP 6 Browser enhance its usability. The following enhancements to the VFP Browser are roundly welcomed.

- A new button (named cmdBrowser) has been added to the toolbar; its function is to toggle the Browser to display the Gallery.
- The "Type" drop-down combo control is now located on the same line as the Browser toolbar, resulting in more efficient use of display real estate.
- You can resize the individual panes in the Browser by dragging the boundaries between panes.
- The Browser shortcut menu has been endowed with new options. You can now toggle the visibility of the Parent Class toolbar, open a new instance of the Browser, open a new instance of the Gallery, and force the Browser display to refresh.
- The items in the methods and properties pane now display little icons to show the status (public, private, or hidden) of these members. These icons are consistent with those used in Visual Modeler.
- The Redefine dialog uses a conventional class specification dialog rather than requiring you to type the class name, and lets you use the Open Class dialog to specify the new parent class and class library.
- The typelib information shown for TLB, DLL, OLB, or OCX files includes much more detail than before, including type information for properties and interface specification of methods. Tip: A lot of useful information appears in the lower right description pane, so make sure you use the Browser's shortcut menu to turn on the description panes.
- If the TLB, DLL, OLB, or OCX file currently displayed in the Browser has an associated help file, double-clicking or pressing the spacebar brings up help for the highlighted item.
- You can export code to HTML with a right click on the View Class Code button. This invokes your Web browser and places it over the Browser's right pane.
- The View Code window is modeless.
- Right-click the Gallery/Browser button to see a history of previously selected items (not files—items). Nice!
- Here's one you probably wouldn't otherwise discover: With a class selected, pressing Ctrl and right-clicking on the class icon image gives you a new object instance created in the Command Window, complete with an object reference.
- Low-resolution users will note that the Browser can now be resized to a smaller size than was possible before. The Browser's minimum dimensions in VFP 5 are 123x252 pixels with two lines of display; in VFP 6, the Browser can shrink to 131x155 pixels with five lines of display, with Browser using one-third less real estate.

Of course, the big change in the Browser is integration with the new Gallery.

Starting the Class Browser

There are three ways to start the Browser. From the Tools menu, select Class Browser. Another way is to use the _BROWSER system variable. _BROWSER defaults to "Browser.APP", which is located in the Visual FoxPro home directory. Issuing the command:

```
DO (_BROWSER)
```

is equivalent to using the menu. In addition, you can pass a parameter containing the name of the class library to load. For example, this code:

```
DO (_BROWSER) WITH HOME(2)+"tastrade\libs\about"
```

loads About.VCX for the TASTRADE sample application. Add a second parameter to the command to select a particular class in the list. For example, this code:

```
DO (_BROWSER) WITH HOME(2)+"tastrade\libs\about", "aboutbox"
```

loads the About library and selects the class called AboutBox. Specifying a form filename directly works, too:

```
DO (_BROWSER) WITH HOME(2)+"tastrade\forms\customer.scx"
```

starts the Browser with the form Customer.SCX loaded.

Finally, if the Gallery is running, you can just press the Browser button to show the Browser.

The Browser Interface

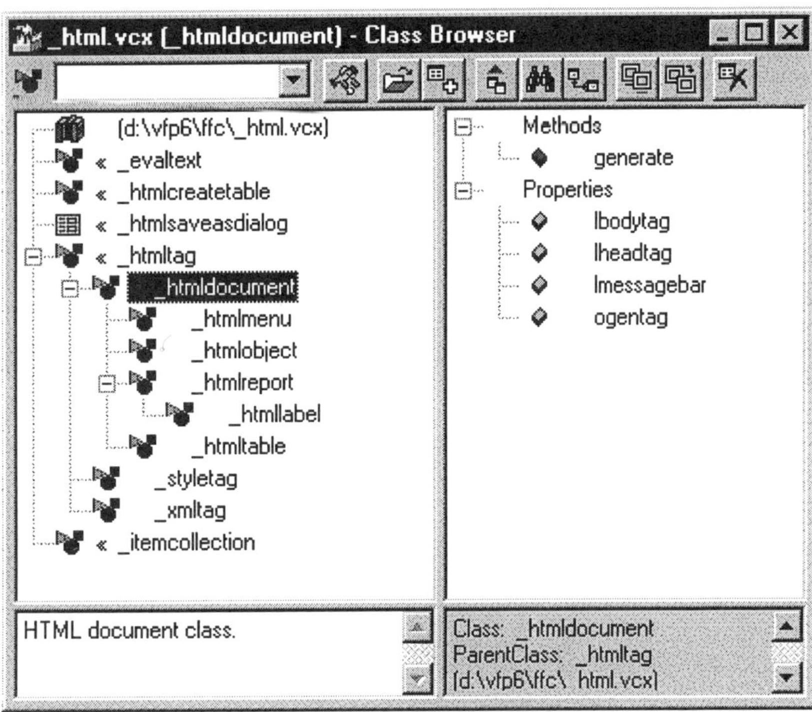

Figure 5-5 Just browsing, thanks. The Class Browser interface.

Figure 5-5 shows the Browser. Here are a few things you should know about the Browser to increase your productivity with this tool.

Click this button to see the class code. Note that in some cases, the code shown can't be executed correctly. (This happens if the class is a container of other classes.) Right-click this button and see the class code in HTML format. This isn't obvious, but the window that appears is actually an instance of your HTML browser, wherein you can use the shortcut menu to view the HTML source for displaying the source.

Use this button to create a new class. This new class can be a subclass of the currently selected class, a subclass of any other class, or a subclass of a VFP base class.

You can redefine classes (that is, change the parent class) in the Browser with this icon. In VFP 6, you can even redefine a class to use a different base class, after being warned that some intrinsic methods and properties will be understandably lost in the process.

When you have a method code window open, this button (which floats or docks independently of the Browser on a one-button toolbar) allows you to view the code up the class hierarchy in parent class methods. You can't close this toolbar with the mouse because it doesn't have a Close button.

View More Than Class Libraries

In the Browser's open dialog, note the different types of files that are supported. Figure 5-6 shows the Browser's open dialog with the drop-down expanded to show the sorts of things you can display in the Browser.

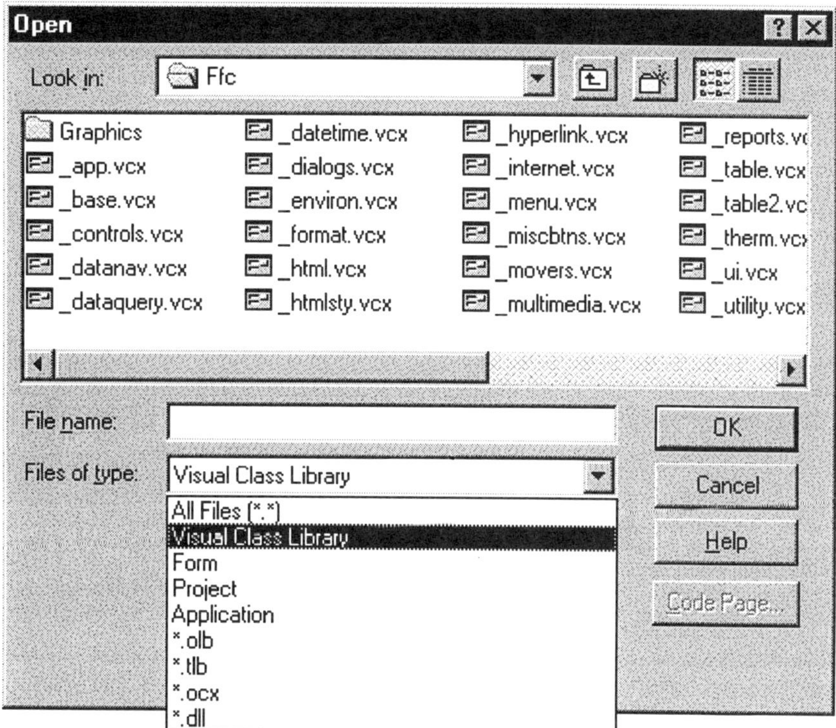

Figure 5-6 Open sesame! The Class Browser's Open dialog shows that you can view more than just class libraries in the "Class" Browser.

You can open VFP forms in the Browser; many of the features, such as showing code, work as you might expect. This is very handy for communicating your code examples with other users via e-mail.

If you open a VFP project file, all the class libraries in that project are visible in a single view. This is great if your project contains hundreds of classes and you have no idea which library a particular class belongs to.

You can open all manner of EXEs and OLE files, and the Browser displays their public interfaces. If help is available, double-clicking an item or pressing the spacebar invokes it.

Clever Tricks

To add controls to a form or class, in the Browser open the VCX (class library) containing the class of the object you want to add to the form, select the class, and then drag and drop the class icon to the design surface. You can also drop a control on the desktop, and you'll get a running instance of that class.

To quickly get to a class you're using, in the Form or Class Designer select an object. Open the Browser. It opens with the class library of the selected class loaded, and with the selected class highlighted.

Except for one thing. When no object on the form is selected, the Browser opens with the library containing the open form class, but it doesn't highlight the form class.

Class Management

Here's a synopsis of what you can do with classes using either VFP commands or the Browser.

Action	VFP Command	Class Browser Action
Clean up a class library	Compile Classlib or open the VCX as a table and issue a PACK command.	Highlight a class or class library file in the Browser and press the Clean Up Class Library button.
Copy a class from one class library to another	Add Class	Open two copies of the Browser, with one pointing to the class to be copied and the other containing the destination class library. Ctrl+drag the class from one Browser instance to another.
Create a class library	Create Classlib or Create Class using a new class library.	Click the New Class icon and specify the new class library name in the New Class dialog.
Create a new class	Create Class	Select the parent class in the Browser and click the New Class button.
Move a class between class libraries	No single command exists to move a class. Instead, copy the class to a second library (Add Class), and then remove it from the first.	Drag the class from one Browser instance to another. If subclasses of the moved class are open in any open Browser instances, the subclasses are automatically remapped to the parent class's new class library. If subclasses of the moved classes aren't open in another Class Browser instance, you've just corrupted your class hierarchy. Watch out!
Open a class in the Class Designer	Modify Class	Select the class in the class library. Then double-click it, select Modify from the shortcut menu, or press the spacebar.
Remove a class from a class library	Remove Class	Select the class, and then select Remove from the shortcut menu.
Rename a class	Rename Class VFP does not adjust classes below the renamed class in the class hierarchy.	Select the class, and then select Rename from the shortcut menu. The Browser adjusts classes below the renamed class in the class hierarchy if they're displayed in the Browser.
View class code	There's no command or series of commands to do this, short of a complex program.	Select the class and press the View Class Codebutton.

Programming the Class Browser with Add-Ins

The VFP Browser is designed for extendibility. It has a rich programming interface, and it exposes its complete object model. The usual way to program the Browser is by hooking its events and methods with Browser add-ins.

An add-in is a program that you create (or download) and then register with the Browser. Once registered, the add-in can be invoked automatically by Browser events or methods. If the add-in is not assigned to a particular event or method, it can be invoked by the user.

Here is an example Browser add-in that demonstrates some of the most important qualities of add-ins.

```
* Program Add-InSample1.PRG
* This program echoes class information to
* the debug output window

#DEFINE DEBUGWINDOW  "Debug Output"

LPARAMETERS oBrowser

IF ! oBrowser.lFileMode AND !EMPTY(oBrowser.cClass)
 ACTIVATE WINDOW DEBUGWINDOW

  *-- Output the class name
  DEBUGOUT "Class Name: "+ oBrowser.cClass

  *-- Output the class library name
  DEBUGOUT "Class Library: "+ oBrowser.cFileName

  *-- Output the class's timestamp
  DEBUGOUT "Timestamp: "+ PADR(oBrowser.nTimeStamp,25)

  *-- Display the entire class pedigree
  DO WHILE oBrowser.SeekParentClass()
      *-- Output the parentclass name
      DEBUGOUT "Parent Class: "+ oBrowser.cClass
  ENDDO
ELSE
  WAIT WINDOW "Please select a class and try again"
ENDIF
```

Observe the following points about the sample add-in above: The Browser passes a reference to itself as a parameter to the add-in. This means that all of the Browser's members are available for reference. The example above demonstrates the Browser's cClass, cFileName, and nTimeStamp properties, and its SeekParentClass() method.

Now, with the Browser running, register the add-in as follows:

```
_oBrowser.AddIn("Sample Add-In", "Add-InSample1.PRG")
```

While the Browser form is running, you can refer to it with a memory variable named _oBrowser.

The Browser's AddIn() method registers add-ins. The syntax shown here specifies a name for the add-in and the program to run. An optional third parameter specifies the event or method to which the add-in gets assigned.

If a Browser event is assigned to the add-in, then the add-in is invoked automatically near the beginning of that event's execution. If a Browser method is assigned to the add-in, then the add-in is invoked near the end of that method's execution.

In the example above, since no method or event is specified, the add-in is listed in the Browser's add-in shortcut menu.

The Add-In option doesn't always appear on the shortcut menu. When the mouse is over the classes or members panes, right-clicks don't show add-ins among the choices. You have to right-click on either of the description pages or the top of the Browser, where the buttons are, or over the Browser form itself, to see the add-in item.

Alternately, passing the name of an add-in to the Browser's DoAddIn() method runs that add-in.

Tell me more! Tell me more!

The Browser is extensively documented under "Class Browser" in VFP help. Also take a look at the following topics: "Class Browser Buttons", "Class Browser Methods", and "Class Browser Properties.". For more information on add-ins, see also the white papers section of the Visual FoxPro pages on the Microsoft Web site.

Having Trouble with the Class Browser's ActiveX Controls

Some people complain that the Class Browser crashes a lot. If the Browser is prone to instability on your system, try invoking it with the optional third parameter set to .T.:

```
DO (_BROWSER) WITH FileName, , .T.
```

This opens the Browser in "listbox" mode with the treeview control replaced by a VFP listbox. It's not as pretty looking, but it may work better for you. (This is a legacy feature from VFP 3, which had a Mac version; the listbox is a substitute for the outline OLE control, which doesn't have a Mac counterpart.)

Having said all that, it's worth noting that fellow hacker Steve Black uses the Browser extensively running the latest build of FoxPro and NT4 SP3 on a completely NT-compliant machine and has no stability problems whatsoever with the Browser. None.

The VFP Component Gallery

The Gallery is the Browser's companion. Both share the same display surface, and you can toggle between them with a handy command button.

The Gallery is a flexible and programmable shortcut manager. Because it works with shortcuts, you can't hose a file using the Gallery; when you delete a shortcut from the Gallery, the underlying file is not deleted.

The Gallery can be used to categorize and display almost anything, and its strength is in grouping the various resources used in software development. With the Gallery, you can create and display your own abstractions, organized as you wish, with event behavior—such as click, right-click, double-click—that you can innovate and control. Moreover, the Gallery also has *dynamic folders*, which we'll discuss in a minute, which have the ability to hold all the contents of VFP projects, class libraries, and directories.

Now, you could use the "other" section of the "other" tab in Project Manager to do some of this, but that's primitive, inflexible, and—let's face it—low tech.

What's What in the Gallery

It's probably a good idea to explain a few things before going further.

A **catalog** is both a DBF table and the highest-level element of the Gallery. A catalog's records define the shortcut items you see in the right-hand pane in the Gallery.

A **folder** is simply a logical package of items and possibly other folders. (Folders look just like subdirectories and that abstraction works for us.) Folders are either *static* or *dynamic*. A static folder contains predefined shortcuts to items. A dynamic folder determines its contents each time the Gallery is refreshed. A dynamic folder could be defined as a directory ("C:\Projects*.*"), a VFP project, or a class library.

An **item** is a shortcut to a particular file or URL.

An **item type** defines the behavior of particular items in the catalog. Item types are stored in the HOME()+"Gallery\VfpGlry.VCX" class library, and are configurable through the Properties dialog for each catalog. The root catalog, named "Catalogs", contains the default item types that apply to all catalogs. See "Understanding Item Types" below for more on item types.

Start Me Up!

VFP 6 has a system memory variable named _GALLERY to identify the Gallery application. By default, it's "Gallery.App" in your HOME() directory. You can replace or "wrap" the Gallery application by changing the value of _GALLERY.

You can use the _GALLERY memory variable to invoke the Gallery, like this:

```
DO (_GALLERY)
```

In addition, you can pass a parameter containing the name of the catalog to load. For example, this code:

```
DO (_GALLERY) WITH HOME()+"Gallery\Vfp Catalog"
```

loads Vfp Catalog.DBF.

You can also start the Gallery from the Tools menu, or press the Gallery button in the Browser.

The Component Gallery Interface

If you're comfortable with Explorer-type interfaces, the basic features of the Gallery (shown in Figure 5-7) will work pretty much as you'd expect.

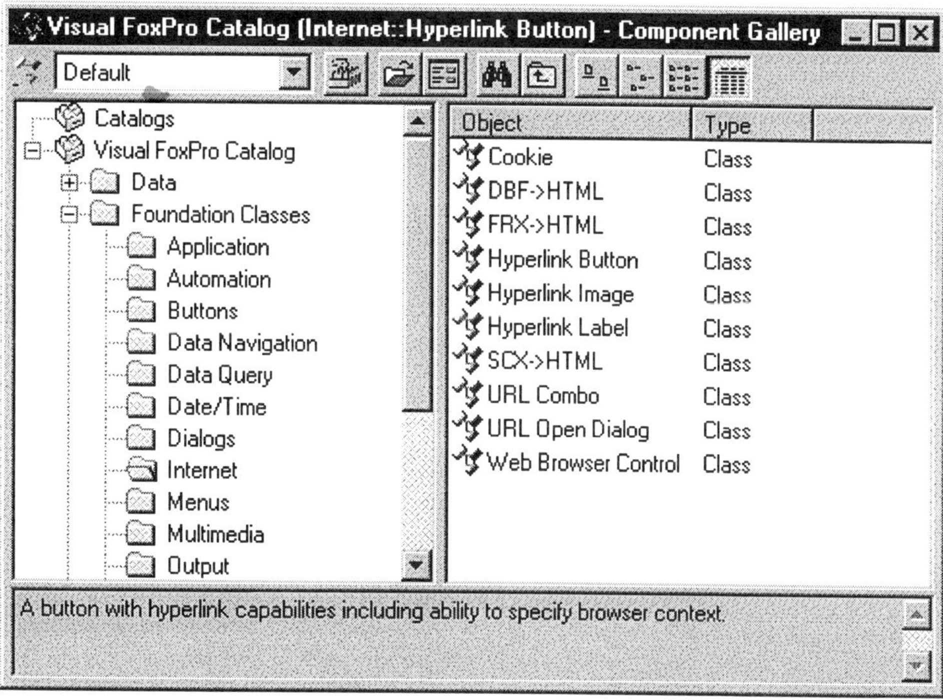

Figure 5-7: The Component Gallery interface—Yet another Explorer-type interface

The Gallery is segmented into two panes. The catalog pane, on the left, lists the folder hierarchies within the currently open catalogs. The items pane, on the right, shows the items in the current catalog or folder. Both panes are endowed with item-sensitive context menus to do the usual useful things such as cut, copy, paste, rename, and so on. You can also invoke item-sensitive property dialogs for selections in the left or right panes. Moreover, the entire Gallery is enabled for both regular and OLE drag and drop.

Pressing almost any key when focus is in the left pane closes the Gallery. Oops!

As in the Browser, the Move icon—the top-left icon in the Gallery form (which changes based on the highlighted item)—can be used to drag the currently selected item to the desktop, a design surface, or a project. Right-clicking the Move icon invokes a GetPict() dialog to change the icon. There's a nice touch here: When you select Cancel in the GetPict() dialog, you get the option to reset the icon to the default for that item.

The View Type drop-down lets you choose among different views of the Gallery. For example, in the VFP Catalog, selecting "Internet" filters the catalogs to display Internet items only. To create your own custom views, use the Dynamic Views tab in the Gallery Options dialog—we'll look at that in more detail in a minute. The Browser button toggles the view back to the standard Browser. Neat touch here: Right-clicking the Browser button brings up a nice long list of the previously opened folders.

The Open button is for opening new catalogs. The open dialog (Figure 5-8) is a little unconventional and merits explanation. In the process, we'll take our first look at the Gallery internals.

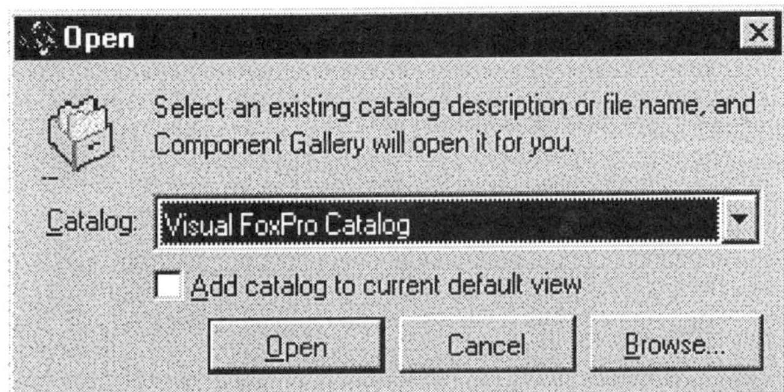

Figure 5-8: An Open dialog like no other. The Component Gallery's Open dialog is different because it offers catalog tables, and those references are kept in Browser.DBF.

This isn't your garden-variety Open dialog. The catalog drop-down control displays the catalogs currently registered on your system. The catalog names are kept in the Browser.DBF table. If you ever clean out or lose Browser.DBF, you can use the Browse button to select an existing catalog file that isn't listed in the catalog drop-down. The Add catalog check box control adds the contents of the catalog to the current view (the default is to close the current catalog and open the one you specify).

The Options button brings you to a three-tabbed dialog (Figure 5-9) where you can set certain Gallery properties.

The Standard tab displays the general defaults for the Gallery itself. Like some of the Tools/Options dialog options, these brief labels can be pretty obscure until you understand the product well:

- The "Enable item renaming" check box determines if clicking and then hovering over the item puts you in a name edit mode, just as it works in Explorer.
- The "FFC Builder Lock" check box will, if checked, automatically invoke builders for new objects you create with the Gallery. If they have a builder, that is. Some do, some don't.
- The "Drag and drop to desktop" check box enables dragging and dropping to the desktop, just like it works in the Class Browser.
- The "Advanced editing enabled" check box is a killer. If this option isn't checked, that explains why you can't do half the stuff we're talking about in this chapter.

Checking the "Advanced editing enabled" check box gives you access to advanced features of Gallery property dialogs. This is where the Gallery really starts to shine!

- The "Catalog default behavior" option determines whether new catalogs are appended to, or replace, the current visible collection of catalogs.
- The "Item default behavior" option determines whether a double-click on an item opens or edits an item by default. This applies only to items that can be edited in VFP, of course. Otherwise, the selection will simply run regardless of what you've specified here.

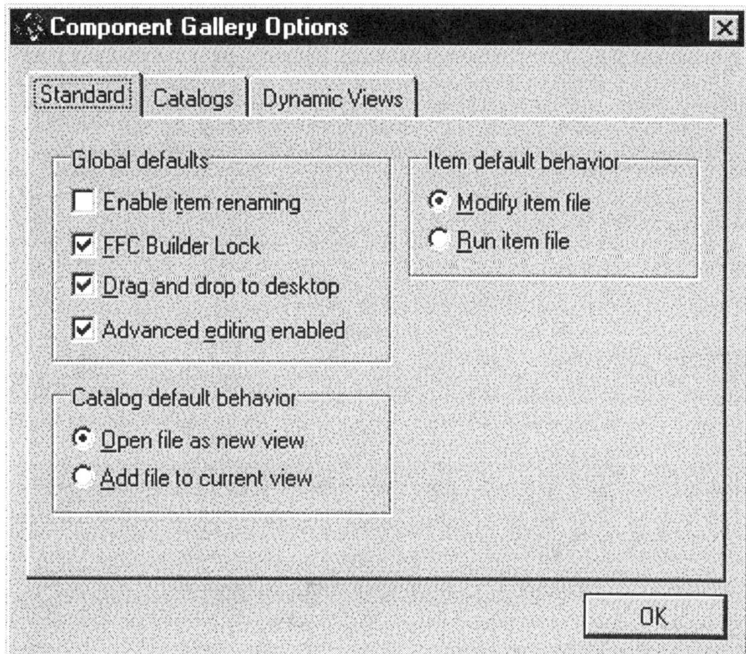

Figure 5-9: I need options. The component gallery comes with its own options; this figure shows the Standard options page.

Use the Catalogs tab (figure 5-10) to maintain the list of catalogs that appear in the catalog drop-down in the Catalog Open dialog.

The New button is only enabled when at least one catalog is loaded in the Catalogs pane. We don't know why we need to load a catalog before we can create a new one, and frankly this behavior seems wrong. Nonetheless, in VFP 6.0, that's the way it is.

The Global and Default check boxes let you set the persistent visibility of each catalog. A Global catalog is always visible in the Catalogs pane, regardless of which catalogs you open for display. You may want to mark the Favorites catalog as a global catalog so you always have access to your favorite things. A Default catalog is the one that's active and current whenever the Gallery is invoked programmatically. You can have any number of default catalogs.

When you invoke the Gallery from the Browser, it always comes up empty. The only way the Gallery appears initially populated with the default catalogs is when it's originally opened with DO (_Gallery) or with Tools/Component Gallery.

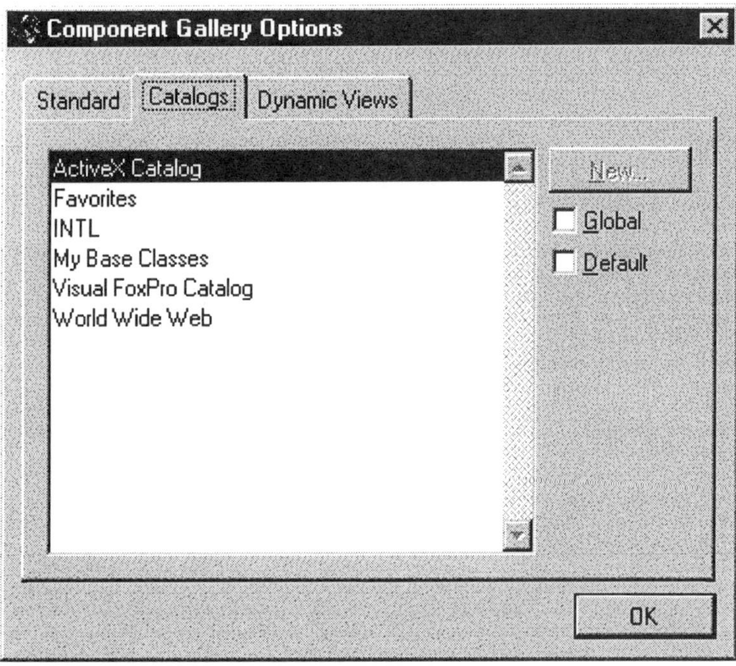

Figure 5-10: What, no underwear ads? A catalog page suitable for family viewing.

The Dynamic Views tab lets you create your own custom, live views of your catalogs. Figures 5-11 and 5-12 show how to create or edit a new dynamic view called "Excel Spreadsheets" that displays all items of type "file" that contain ".XLS" in their names.

We think Dynamic Views are ultra cool. This adds a second powerful dimension to the Gallery. The first dimension is the obvious one: Catalogs and folders that logically segment things as you choose. But Dynamic Views permit you to see all the items of a particular type (you define), regardless of their logical placement within a catalog.

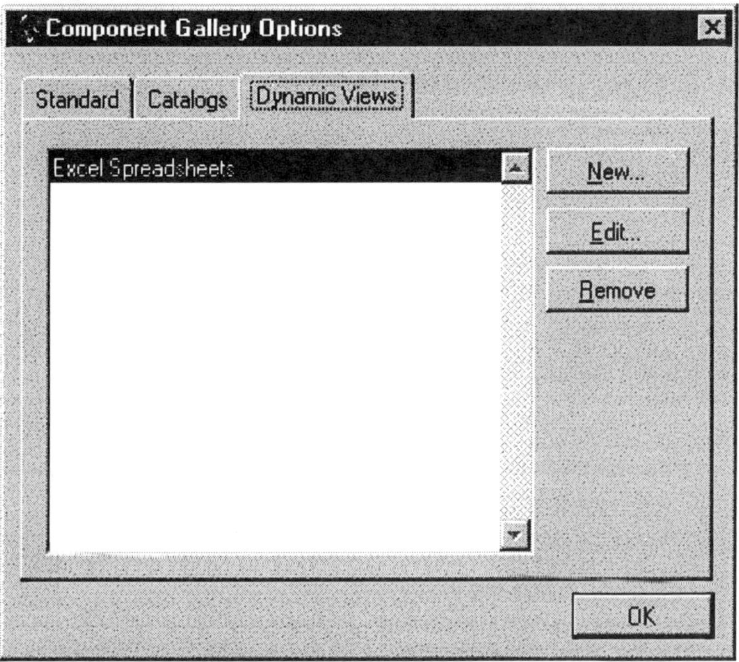

Figure 5-11: Select the New button to create a new View, or the Edit button to bring up the dialog below.

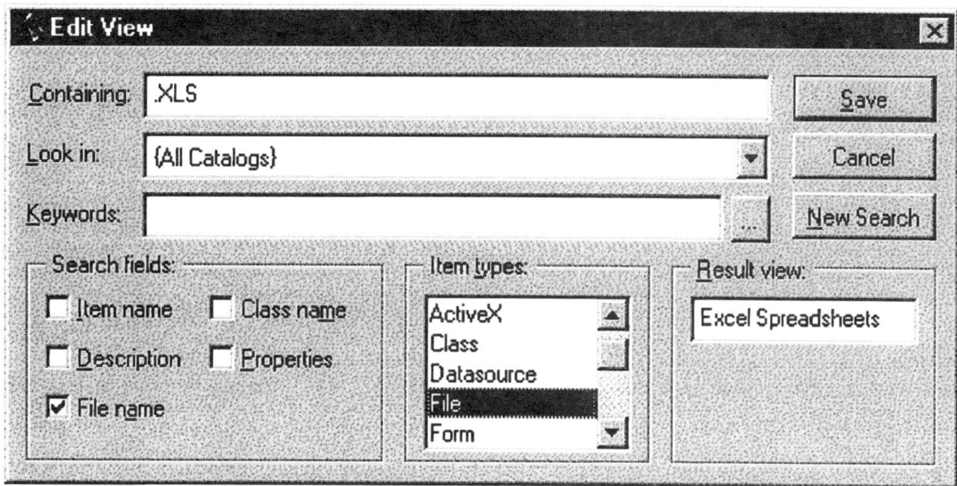

Figure 5-12: A different view of things. This is where you define and edit dynamic views.

Figure 5-13 shows the Keywords dialog, accessible from a button in the Edit View dialog. This dialog lets us create dynamic views based on keywords used to describe them. The keywords displayed in this list are stored in a table called Keywords.DBF. You can use keywords to further expand the power of the Gallery's dynamic views.

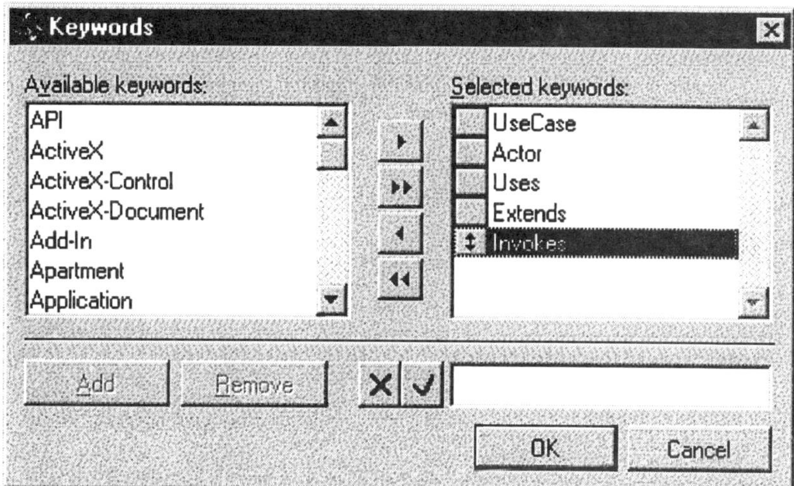

Figure 5-13: Views can be based on keywords you specify.

In order to add a keyword, you must first have a catalog loaded in the Gallery. When we instructed the underpaid workers at Hacker Laboratories to take the screen shot shown in Figure 5-13, we forgot to mention that, so that's why the Add and Remove buttons look disabled.

We think all the things you can do in the Options dialog are a good idea. But we cannot fathom why the Catalogs page is in that dialog. More specifically, we can't understand why the New button is in that dialog. This isn't an option, it's an action. Options are choices you make about how things look or operate. It's as if the New button in the Project Manager could only be accessed from the Project Info dialog. We'd feel the same way about the Dynamic Views page, except for one thing.

Surprise! The Find button works just like choosing New… on the Dynamic Views page! In effect, when you choose Find, you create a new persistent view. We're not really crazy about this; after all, cluttering our dynamic views every time we go searching is a bit much. However, it's easy enough to clean up the list of dynamic views using the Dynamic Views page.

Understanding Item Types

So, how does the gallery work internally, you ask?

The behavior of a Gallery item, like what happens when you click or drag it, is defined by its item type. The class library Gallery\VfpGlry.VCX stores the item types supplied by Microsoft, and you can modify, subclass, or simply copy these classes to create your own types. If you develop your own custom item types, it's probably a good idea to store them in some other VCX, such as *My_VfpGlry.VCX*. This allows you to later update the Gallery's class libraries without fear of clobbering your work.

Figure 5-14 shows the hierarchy of the Gallery item types as supplied by Microsoft. The _item and _folder classes live in _Gallery.VCX. All other classes are defined in VfpGlry.VCX.

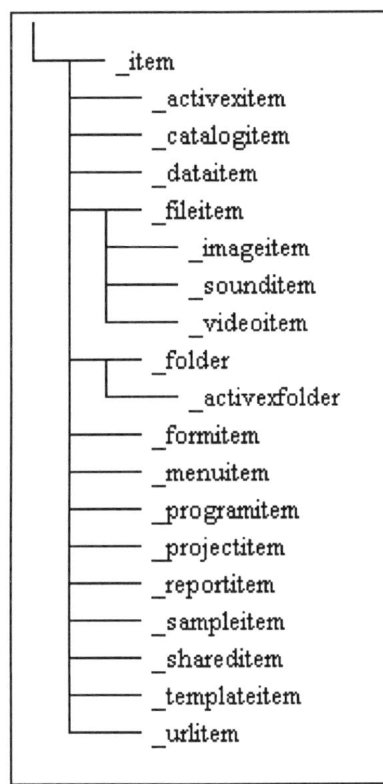

Figure 5-14: Type-o-rama! The Item Types hierarchy provided by Microsoft.

When creating your own item types, the most flexible base type is the _fileitem. In fact, _fileitem should serve most of your needs because its behavior is to simply invoke the Windows file associations. Moreover, the _fileitem type has the ability to redirect popular file extensions to other file types. We'll talk more about redirection in a minute.

Item types can be tied to particular catalogs. The root catalog, which is always named "Catalog", serves as the basis for all catalogs. If you select the Item Types tab of the properties of the root catalog, you'll get something like the dialog in Figure 5-15 once you've turned on the Advanced Editing option on the Class Browser's option dialog. Do it now! C'mon, you're reading the *Hacker's Guide*! That alone qualifies you as "Advanced!"

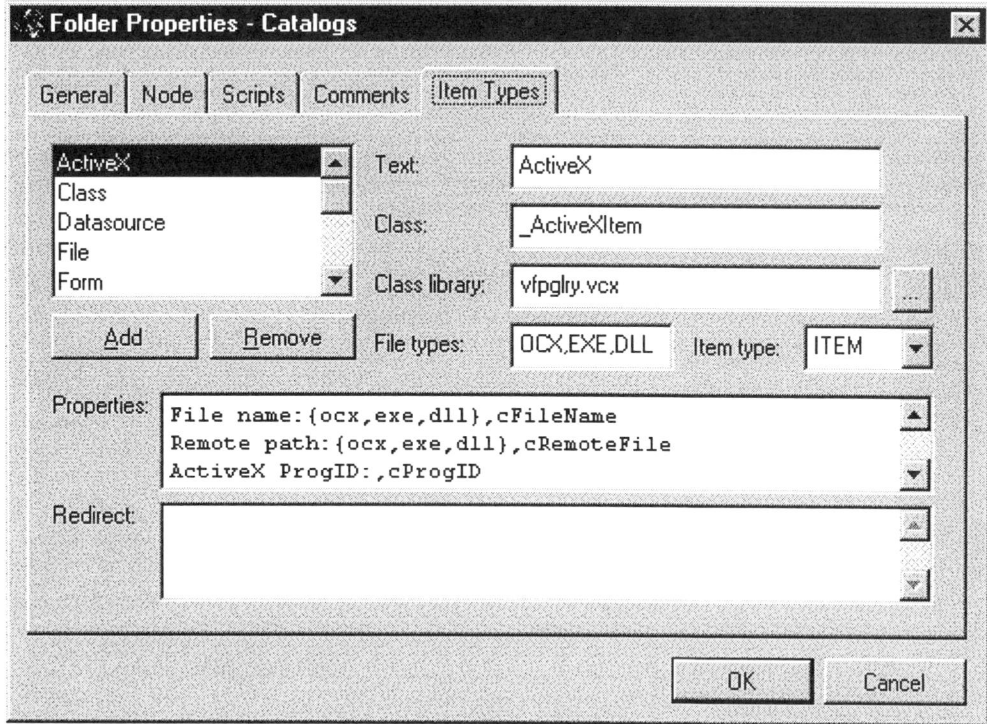

Figure 5-15: Catalog Properties, Item Types.

Note the following things about the Item Types page in this dialog:

- The list of item types matches the item types you see in the New Item shortcut menu. To modify the New Item shortcut menu, simply edit this list.
- Each item type can be associated with display text, a class, and a class library. In this case the display text is "ActiveX", the class is _ActiveXItem, and the class library is VfpGlry.VCX.
- The lines in the Properties edit box specify what's displayed in the final page of the item's Properties dialog. For example, for the ActiveX item type pictured in Figure 5-15, when you examine the properties of an ActiveX item in the component gallery you'll see the following:
  - File name: with an associated Open dialog initialized with OCX, EXE, and DLL files, and the filename specified will be stored in the item's cFileName property.
  - Remote path: with an associated open dialog initialized with OCX, EXE, and DLL files, and the filename specified will be stored in the item's cRemoteFile property.
  - Other lines in the edit box can't be seen in Figure 5-15. They include entries for Class, Class Library, Source project, and Associated file; these all work the same as described above for the corresponding text box entries.
- If you create your own item types, you make them available by clicking the Add button and filling in the specifics of your new item type.

The properties for the _fileitem item type are worth a look because, in addition to showing custom properties, they show an example of item redirection. See the Redirect field in Figure 5-16.

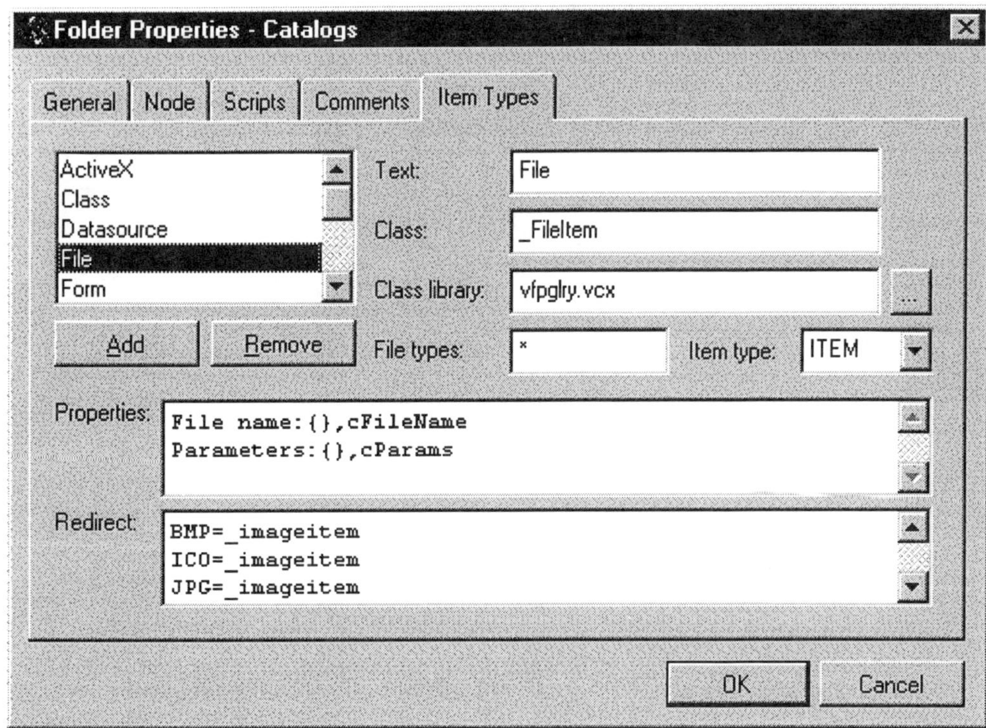

Figure 5-16: Item Types.

Here is the full list of redirections:

BMP=_imageitem, ICO=_imageitem, JPG=_imageitem, GIF=_imageitem, WAV=_sounditem, RMI=_sounditem, AVI=_videoitem, DBF=_dataitem, SCX=_formitem, MNX=_menuitem, FRX=_reportitem, LBX=_reportitem, PRG=_programitem, APP=_sampleitem, OCX=_activexitem, HTM=_urlitem, HTML=_urlitem, PJX=_projectitem, TXT=_programitem, LOG=_programitem, H=_programitem.

You can probably guess how redirections work: When an item with any of those file extensions is created, the designated item type is created instead. For example, if you try to add a PRG as a file item, the Gallery notices the PRG redirection and creates a _programitem instead of a _fileitem. This is why the _fileitem item type is so flexible; it has the ability to properly redirect new items to the correct item type.

Note that dragging VCX or PJX files from the Windows Explorer just creates a regular file shortcut, and not a dynamic folder. We think VFP's Gallery should be able to recognize VFP's own components.

I Never Metadata I Didn't Like

Here's a brief description of the data structures used by the Browser and the Gallery.

Browser.DBF

The Browser stores all its metadata in a table named Browser.DBF found in the VFP home directory. The Gallery also uses Browser.DBF to store its catalog-related information. The following table shows a field-by-field description of Browser.DBF.

Field	Description	Used by (B)rowser (G)allery
PLATFORM	"WINDOWS" or blank when Type="ADDIN". We suspect this is left over from the VFP 3 days when there was something other than Windows, and that it was retained for backward compatibility.	BG
TYPE	Records with type field value "PREFW" store Browser and Gallery preferences. Records with type field value "ADDIN" store add-in information.	BG
ID	"FORMINFO" records are used by the Browser to store form preferences and by the Gallery to store information about your catalogs. The only way to tell the difference is that Gallery records contain the string ".dbf" in the Name field. "BROWSER" records contain default settings for the Gallery (not the Browser!). See the Properties field for this record to see these default properties. These get set in the Gallery Options dialog. "METHOD" records store Browser add-ins that are tied to a particular Browser event or method. "MENU" records store Browser add-ins that are not tied to a particular Browser event or method, and are thus available on the add-in shortcut menu.	BG
DEFAULT	True for the default Gallery catalog.	G
GLOBAL	Applies to Gallery catalog records. True if the catalog is global. By default, new catalogs are not global. To make a catalog global, check the appropriate check box in the Catalogs tab in the Gallery's Options dialog.	G
BACKUP	When Gallery opens a catalog or a VCX, this field in the associated Browser.DBF record is queried. If the value is True, the Gallery checks to see if a file of the same name exists in the backup subfolder below that one. If the backup file doesn't exist, it is automatically created (as is a subfolder called Backup if needed). Then the Backup field is set to .F. This field can be set programmatically to force the Gallery to automatically back up a file the next time—and only the next time—that file is opened. You can set this field via add-in hooks, or with a program that opens and updates Browser.DBF. Note that Gallery doesn't automatically back up your work. You can force a backup at any time by selecting Backup on the catalog item shortcut menus. This feature is used internally in one special case. When Browser.DBF is first created after VFP is installed, a new Browser.DBF is created with the default catalogs (around five or so). The Backup field is set to .T. so that each catalog gets backed up the very first time it is opened, since VFP doesn't install the associated backup catalog tables. Beyond that special function, it can be used at will by developers for their own purposes.	G

Field	Description	Used by (B)rowser (G)allery
NAME	The filename that relates to this record. For a Browser record, the file type could be, among other things, VCX, PJX, SCX, OCX, DLL, EXE, or APP. For Gallery records, the file type is DBF. In the case of Browser and Gallery add-ins, the Name field stores the name of the add-in. This is what appears in the add-in shortcut menu if the add-in is not tied to an event or method.	BG
DESC	Used only by the Gallery, it stores the description of the catalog referred to in the Name field.	G
METHOD	Stores the name of the method to which an add-in is tied. If the Method field equals "*", the add-in executes for all methods.	BG
PROPERTIES	Used by the Browser to store default settings.	B
SCRIPT	According to our sources at Microsoft, this field is used by code deep within the Gallery and is for internal use only.	G
PROGRAM	Stores the name of the program to execute by PRG-based add-in.	BG
CLASSLIB	Stores the name of the class library in the case of a VCX-based add-in.	BG
CLASSNAME	Stores the name of the class to execute in the case of a VCX-based add-in.	BG
FILEFILTER	Used by add-in records to specify file masks for which the add-in applies. The FileFilter is specified in the fourth parameter of the AddIn method.	B
DISPMODE	Hierarchical/alphabetic listing display mode for the Browser (numeric).	B
TOP	The stored top coordinate for the Browser/Gallery form. All stored coordinates and sizes apply only if you include the filename when you open the Browser/Gallery. When you use the Open button, you get whatever settings are currently in effect.	BG
LEFT	The stored left coordinate for the Browser/Gallery form.	BG
HEIGHT	The stored height of the Browser/Gallery form.	BG
WIDTH	The stored width of the Browser/Gallery form.	BG
HEIGHT1	The stored height of the class and member description panes in the Browser.	BG

Field	Description	Used by (B)rowser (G)allery
WIDTH1	The stored width of the class and member description panes in the Browser.	BG
HEIGHT2	The height of the item description pane in the Gallery.	G
WIDTH2	The width of the item description pane in the Gallery.	G
WINDOWSTAT	0—Window is zoomed normal; 1—Window is minimized; 2—Window is maximized.	BG
PROTECTED	True if protected members are to be displayed in the right-hand Browser pane.	B
EMPTY	True if empty methods are to be displayed in the right-hand Browser pane.	B
HIDDEN	True if hidden members are to be displayed in the right-hand Browser pane.	B
DESCBOXES	True if description panels are to be displayed.	BG
AUTOEXPAND	True if hierarchical items are to be displayed automatically expanded in the left-hand pane.	BG
PUSHPIN	True if the display is always on top.	BG
PCBROWSER	Parent class toolbar flag. If true for a file item, the toolbar is on for that file. If you close the parent class toolbar, this field is set to .F. for all open VCXs.	B
VIEWMODE	Indicates whether the items pane of the Gallery displays large icons, small icons, or a list.	G
FONTINFO	Stores the display font preference.	BG
FORMCOUNT	Used internally by the Browser to track the number of Browser instances where this record's class library is being displayed.	G
UPDATED	The datetime this record was last updated.	BG
COMMENT	A comment field for your use.	BG
USER1,2,3,4	Not used; there for your use.	BG

Additional Component Gallery Data Structures

Here's a brief overview of Gallery-specific structures. The Gallery distributes its metadata in several locations.

Like the Browser, the Gallery keeps some of its metadata in Browser.DBF (described above). That data stores references to the available catalogs, as well as some properties such as whether the catalog is a global one (auto-open and always in view) or default (in the default view). Delete a Gallery catalog record from Browser.DBF and it won't appear in the Gallery Open dialog. The Gallery catalog records in Browser.DBF contain ".dbf" in their Name field. Since this field is of type memo, you can't easily identify Gallery records in a simple browse of Browser.DBF—what a pain.

The rest of the Gallery metadata is stored in VfpGlry.DBF, which lives in the Gallery subdirectory below the VFP root. VfpGlry.DBF defines the default display and behavior of the Gallery. When you look at the Gallery, you are looking at catalogs whose items are defined in the particular catalog tables, but whose default behavior emanates from definitions in VfpGlry.DBF.

In fact, delete all Gallery records from Browser.DBF and the Gallery will re-initialize the root catalog from data in VfpGlry.DBF.

Many of the records in VfpGlry.DBF point to behavior classes stored in VfpGlry.VCX through fields named ClassLib and ClassName. Thus the records in VfpGlry.DBF are pointers to the behavior classes that, in the case of the native VFP-supplied behaviors, live in VfpGlry.VCX. Of course, any custom gallery behavior you define or modify can live in any VCX you choose. In fact, if you define custom Gallery behavior classes or modify existing ones, we suggest that you keep these in a different class library so that future upgrades of VFP don't clobber your work.

To illustrate some of the functionality of VfpGlry.DBF, we'll examine some of the fields in a representative record—the one with Id = "fileitem".

Field	Value	Meaning
Type	"FOLDER", "CLASS", "ITEM" or "OBJECT"	The Type field indicates what type of record this is. You'll surely be stunned to find out that "FOLDER" types are folders. "CLASS" items define the metadata for the various types of things the Gallery can display. "ITEM" types define the native catalogs that ship with VFP. "OBJECT" types are objects attached to the Gallery when it's instanced.
Id	"fileitem"	The unique identifier for this type of item.
Text	"File"	The item display text.
Typedesc	"Item"	That is, not a "Folder".
Desc	Text	The text appearing in the item description pane.
Properties	File name:{},cFileName Parameters:{},cParams	Specification for input fields that appear in the Properties dialog for items of this type. Values inside the curly braces are used as the parameter in GetFile() dialogs.
Classlib	Vfpglry.vcx	The class library where the item's behavior class is stored.
Classname	_fileitem	The default class that embodies this catalog item.
Itemtpdesc	BMP=_imageitem ICO=_imageitem JPG=_imageitem GIF=_imageitem WAV=_sounditem	Alternate classes to embody file items of these particular types.

Field	Value	Meaning
Itemtpdesc	RMI=_sounditem AVI=_videoitem DBF=_dataitem SCX=_formitem MNX=_menuitem FRX=_reportitem LBX=_reportitem PRG=_programitem APP=_sampleitem OCX=_activexitem HTM=_urlitem HTML=_urlitem PJX=_projectitem TXT=_programitem LOG=_programitem H=_programitem	

Other records may use different fields and different values, but this representative record is enough to get you started in hacking the Gallery.

Catalog tables contain records that reference actual catalog items. The main native catalog is called "Visual FoxPro Catalog" and is kept in "VFP Catalog.DBF." All VFP 6 foundation classes, for example, are cataloged there.

The structure of catalog tables is the same as that of VfpGlry.DBF, so much of what we've already seen also applies here. This is a good opportunity to look at a few other metadata fields and how they work. The following table shows the record with Id = "clireg" in "ActiveX Catalog.DBF." This item allows you to register a custom VFP Automation server remotely using its generated VBR file.

Field	Value	Meaning
Type	"ITEM"	
Id	"clireg"	This item's ID.
Parent	"actxtools"	ID of the parent catalog record; in this case, it corresponds to a folder named "Tools".
Desc	"This tool allows you to register a custom VFP automation server remotely using the generated VBR file."	The description window text.
Properties	cDblClick=<>	You can override the events (KeyPress, Click, DblClick, RightClick) by setting the c[EventName] property. If it's something like cDblClick=DO Foo.PRG, then double-clicking on the item in the Gallery runs that line. If you set cDblClick=<testscript>, then double-clicking runs the code in the Script memo field of the record with Id= "testscript". If you set cDblClick=<>, double-clicking runs the code in the Script memo field of

Field	Value	Meaning
		the current record. In this case, DblClick runs the code in the Script field below.
Filename	(HOME(6) + "CLIREG\CLIREG32.EXE")	The filename to execute when the item is double-clicked. This value is stored in the oTHIS.cFileName reference, which you can use in scripts. See the Script field below. Note that the whole behavior of this item is defined by the filename field and, in this case, also the Script field. The ClassName and ClassLib fields are blank in this record.

Script	`cVBRFile = GETFILE("VBR")`
	`cCliReg = oThis.cFileName`
	
	`IF !FILE(m.cCliReg)`
	`  RETURN .F.`
	`ENDIF`
	
	`IF EMPTY(m.cVBRFile) OR ;`
	`  UPPER(JUSTEXT(m.cVBRFile)) #;`
	`    "VBR"`
	`  RETURN .F.`
	`ENDIF`
	`oThis.Runcode( [RUN /N  &cCliReg. "&cVBRFile." -NOLOGO])`
		The Script field gives you control over what happens when the user runs the item. Here this scripting code will run when the user double-clicks (see the Property field) items of this type in the Gallery.
		
		Note that, in this version of VFP, there is no script equivalent of DODEFAULT() so if you script an event, the default behavior for that event will not execute.

Back o' da Book

Great is the art of beginning, but greater the art is of ending;
Many a poem is marred by a superfluous verse.

Henry Wadsworth Longfellow

Here we are at the end of the book. But there are still a couple of things left to do. Appendix 1 is a list of resources: books, periodicals, and people. Appendix 2 tells you what's on the CD so you know whether to stick it in your drive—we bet you will. (Of course, if you're reading the CD version of this book, you've already done so.)

Resource File

In this section we list many resources we think may be of benefit to you. These include books worth reading, either for their value as a reference or as food for thought. Following that list is a list of FoxPro 2.x books to aid in your understanding of "legacy" code and techniques. Included at the end is a list of other resources worth checking into.

Suggested Reading

Alciere, Rose Mary, *Creating Help for Windows™ Applications*, Wordware Publishing, Inc., 1995, ISBN 1-55622-448-6. A great introductory book on how Windows Help is made. Intended primarily for Windows 3.1, it even includes a chapter specifically aimed at making the Windows API function WinHelp() work with FoxPro for Windows 2.x! The API functions and basics of WinHelp still apply, should you choose WinHelp over HTML Help.

Brentnall, Savannah, *Object Orientation in Visual FoxPro,* Addison-Wesley, 1996, ISBN 0-20147-943-5. An excellent primer on the ideas of object-oriented programming and how they apply to Visual FoxPro. Introduction by Ken Levy—we didn't know he could write comments!

Cooper, Alan, *About Face, The Essentials of User Interface Design*, IDG Books, 1995, ISBN 1-56884-322-4. This must-read book makes you think long and hard about how user interfaces work—not just the ones you write, but the ones you use every day. While you may not agree with everything Cooper suggests, you'll be forced to question your assumptions. Best of all, Cooper is a great writer.

Booch, Grady, *Object Oriented Analysis & Design*, Benjamin Cummings, 1994, ISBN 0-8053-5340-2. One of the heavies of the industry on analysis and design issues. When you're done playing with all the new cool things in VFP and it's time to get back to work, here's one of the tomes to be studying.

Brockschmidt, Kraig, *OLE Programmer's Reference* Volumes 1 and 2, and *Inside OLE*, all by Microsoft Press: Great stuff, but pretty deep for us high-level language application developers. Mostly deals with the inner workings of OLE.

Jacobson, Ivar, *Object-Oriented Software Engineering*, Addison-Wesley, 1992, ISBN 0-201-54435-0. Some really cool stuff here. In-depth examination of Jacobson's own Objectory system, with good overviews of object-oriented analysis and design and a comparison of several methodologies out there.

KNOWware, *HTML Help in a Hurry™ Course Book,* available from KNOWware, (800) 566-9927 or http://www.kware.com, 1997. This was the first book available for HTML Help, and the KNOWware team, led by HTML Help MVP Mary Deaton, used the materials to teach Microsoft staff worldwide the basics of HTML Help. The course book is very short (38 pages), but a good basic start.

Gamma, Erich, Richard Helm, Ralph Johnson, John Vlissides, *Design Patterns: Elements of Reusable Object-Oriented Software,* Addison-Wesley, 1994, ISBN 0-20163-361-2. Often referred to as "The Gang of Four" or "Gamma and Helm" for short, this is *the* book that defined what object design patterns were and how to use them. Our good friend Alan Schwartz advises that, in order to really *get it,* consider reading the core text (about 70 pages) four times. The book contains a catalog of design patterns, explanation of their use, benefits, liabilities and great discussion. Design patterns are not so much "the latest thing" in programming, as much as they are a new vocabulary we can use to express what we have been doing all along.

Humphrey, Watts, *Managing the Software Process,* Addison-Wesley, 1989, ISBN 0-201-18095-2. From one of the key players in the Software Engineering Institute at Carnegie Mellon University, this book (like most of his books) is worth a read. Watts and the SEI are at the cutting edge of real software engineering.

Maguire, Steve, *Debugging the Development Process: Practical Strategies for Staying Focused, Hitting Ship*

Dates, and Building Solid Teams, Microsoft Press, 1994, ISBN 1-55615-650-2. The other "Steve M" from Microsoft has some excellent observations on the development process. Not only is this information applicable to our FoxPro development, but many of the examples give us insight into just what they are thinking at Microsoft.

McCarthy, Jim, and Denis Gilbert, *Dynamics of Software Development,* Microsoft Press, 1995, ISBN 1-55615-823-8. Another view inside Microsoft and another good volume on what is involved in software development.

McConnell, Steve, *Code Complete*, Microsoft Press, 1993, ISBN 1-55615-484-4. Written before the era of Visual FoxPro, this book nonetheless has tremendous relevance for those of us who need to produce long-lasting, reliable and robust code. Steve explores the art and craft of programming, reflecting on the philosophical implications of many of the designs of coding. An awesome book.

McConnell, Steve, *Rapid Development,* Microsoft Press, 1996, ISBN 1-55615-900-5. Excellent material from a top-notch author on the trials and tribulations of software development. Includes a number of case studies and lists of pitfalls to avoid.

McConnell, Steve, *Software Project Survival Guide,* Microsoft Press, 1997, ISBN 1-57231-621-7. Steve can't stop writing and we can't stop reading! Yet another great book, with excellent supporting materials available on his Web site. A must read.

Microsoft Windows ??? Resource Kit, Microsoft Press—fill in the ??? yourself—"3.1," "For WorkGroups 3.11," "95," "98," or "NT" depending on your (and your clients') particular flavor(s) of Windows. Invaluable books (sometimes in more than one sense), these can be tremendous aids in troubleshooting problems with the underlying Windows system. They typically include manuals and disks with some handy utilities and reference materials.

MSDN—The Microsoft Developer's Network—a series of CDs released quarterly. Depending on the level of participation (there are currently three levels, but Microsoft changes programs like these so often it makes our heads spin), a very large variety of information can be found, including the ADO Software Development Kit, documentation on disk for several of the other SDKs, relevant KnowledgeBase articles, and sample code. Utilities and sample code alone pays for the subscription. Having these disks is like carrying around the Microsoft Web site with you—an excellent resource when you need information fast, especially if you can't connect to the Web.

Norman, Donald, *The Design of Everyday Things*, Doubleday, 1988, ISBN 0-385-26774-6. Formerly published as the poorly selling *The Psychology of Everyday Things*, this book is a self-fulfilling example of the fact that books are judged by their covers and user interfaces by their utility. Excellent examples and discussions about why some designs work and others fail. Thought-provoking material for anyone who wants to write a system that others can use.

Plauger, P.J., *Programming on Purpose*, PTR Prentice Hall, 1993, ISBN 0-13-721-374-3. Author of the popular column of the same name in *Computer Language*, Plauger revises and expands some of his best columns into a wonderfully entertaining series of essays on the whys and wherefores of analysis, design and software engineering.

Sessions, Roger, *COM and DCOM: Microsoft's Vision for Distributed Objects,* Wiley Computer Publishing, 1998, ISBN 0-471-19381-X. An excellent book to introduce the concepts of distributed computing using Microsoft's latest technologies. The author doesn't get bogged down in the details of Microsoft Transaction Server or Message Queue, but rather explains the use of these technologies at an understandable level.

Shneiderman, Ben, *Designing the User Interface*, Addison-Wesley, 1998, ISBN 0-201-69497-2. Shneiderman is one of the fathers of the science of Computer-Human Interaction. This book is the third edition of what was originally written as a college text. Like the original, it has plenty of advice, backed up with empirical research, on how to organize user interfaces.

Taylor, David, *Object Oriented Technology: A Manager's Guide*, Servio-Addison-Wesley, ISBN 0-201-56358-4. OOP in 128 pages. An excellent overview of why anyone would want to OOPify their code. A good primer, a good start as the first book in your OOP-reading series, and a great book to hand to your boss when asked to justify OOPification.

TechNet—Similar to MSDN above, this is also a CD-based product available from Microsoft. TechNet seems to be more focused on the support professional than the developer, although we have found very good information on these discs as well. Published monthly. If your primary interests include support, the need for new drivers, and workarounds, this disc set can save you several hundred dollars as compared to the cost of MSDN.

Tognazzini, Bruce, *TOG on Interface*, Addison-Wesley, 1992, ISBN 0-201-60842-1. The man who made the Macintosh user interface the shining example it is writes on the many issues surrounding the human computer interface in a fresh and engaging way. A book that's hard to put down. Very useful knowledge for user interface designers.

Tufte, Edward, *Visual Explanations,* 1998, *Envisioning Information*, 1990, and *The Visual Display of Quantitative Information*, 1983—all from Graphics Press. Three of the most beautiful books we own. While not specifically aimed at computer graphics, these books can give you some great ideas about what makes a graph worth making, and common mistakes made in graphical presentations and how to avoid them. Applicable both for folks designing graphs and those designing graphical user interfaces.

Wexler, Steve, *Official Microsoft HTML Help Authoring Kit,* Microsoft Press, 1998, ISBN 1-57231-603-9. Steve Wexler is a principal in WexTech Systems, Inc., makers of Doc-To-Help, and has been in the help business for quite some time. He writes well and expresses the complexities of HTML Help in an understandable fashion. Written between versions 1.0 and 1.2, there may be some items out of date, but overall, you can pick up a lot from the book.

Yourdan, Edward, *The Decline and Fall of the American Programmer*, Yourdan Press (Prentice Hall), 1993, ISBN 0-13-191958-X. A sweeping survey of the entire software industry, with some very intriguing observations and predictions. Worth the read for anyone considering a career in the industry over the next few decades. Yourdan has a follow-up book, *Rise and Resurrection,* that we haven't gotten around to reading yet, so don't give up hope!

FoxPro 2.x Resources

In a number of places in the book, we refer to the "2.x way of doing things" or the "Xbase way" and refer you here. These are, in our opinions, some of the finest books written on those languages, and serve as a great reference to understanding the many aspects of the product which continue to be supported, unchanged, in the 3.x series, as well as those which have undergone radical transformations.

Adams, Pat and Powell, Jordan, *FoxPro Windows Advanced Multi-User Developer's Handbook*, Brady, 1994, ISBN 1-56686-100-4. The authority on multiuser issues, and the tuning and configuration of workstations for optimal performance. Also includes the enormous FPWeror.PRG, a great error-handler for 2.x systems.

Griver, Y. Alan, *The FoxPro 2.6 CodeBook*, Sybex, 1994, ISBN 0-7821-1551-9. We suspect more applications out there are based on this framework than on any other. A simple, straightforward but elegant solution to many of the problems of application development posed by version 2.x.

Hawkins, John, *FoxPro 2.5 Programmer's Reference*, Que, 1993, ISBN 1-56529-210-3. An encyclopedia of FoxPro 2.x commands, this book was (innovatively, we think) organized into more than 40 chapters by separating the commands and functions into logical groups. A great resource when you run into unfamiliar commands or unusual needs.

Slater, Lisa and Arnott, Steven, *Using FoxPro 2.5 for Windows*, Que, 1993, ISBN 1-56529-002-X. When we are asked for the best way to do something, we often find ourselves reaching for this well-worn tome and invoking, "Well, Lisa says...". (Sorry, Steve.) One of the best tutorials around, with remarkable depth as well.

Slater, Lisa, with J. Randolph Brown, Andy Griebel, John R. Livingston, *FoxPro MAChete: Hacking FoxPro,*

Hayden Books, 1994, ISBN 1-56830-034-4. This book was our best introduction to the world of the Mac. Three separate chapters introduce FoxPro folk to the Mac, FoxBase/Mac people to FoxPro, and non-Fox, Mac users to FoxPro. The rest of the book focuses on a rapid application development approach that's appropriate for all versions of FoxPro 2.x and the Mac-specific aspects of FoxPro 2.x.

Other Resources

Magazines

All of the magazines below have very good material. The focus of each magazine is a little different, and their editorial style changes over time. We recommend you order a copy of two of each (or get them from the newsstand) and choose the periodical that's right for you. (Just to come clean, Tamar is the editor and Ted is a contributing editor for *FoxPro Advisor*. Our publisher, Whil Hentzen, is the editor of *FoxTalk*.)

FoxPro Advisor, published by Advisor Publications, Inc., 4010 Morena Blvd., P.O. Box 17902, San Diego, CA, 92177. (800) 336-6060 in the U.S., (619) 483-6400.

FoxTalk, published by Pinnacle Publishing, 1503 Johnson Ferry Rd. #100, Marietta, GA, 30062. (800) 788-1900, (770) 565-1763.

Pinter FoxPro Letter, published by Les Pinter, P.O. Box 10349, Truckee, CA, 96162. (800) 995-2797.

Online Resources

CompuServe is far and away our favorite online service for FoxPro technical support. This is no doubt due, at least in part, to the fact that once Fox Software and later, Microsoft, provided their official online presence here. Questions are answered both rapidly and accurately by peer support, as well, often in a matter of hours (sometimes even minutes). Hundreds of files containing helpful hints, cool programming tricks, utilities and work-arounds are available in the libraries on the forums. Recently, the activists have started new collections of "FreeHelp" utilities that are free for the downloading, and have revived the process of archiving forum messages and making them available for download. GO FOXUSER for support of the FoxPro 2.x (and earlier) products on the DOS, Windows, Mac and Unix platforms, help wanted messages, professional advice, and great bull sessions. GO VFOX for excellent peer support for all versions of Visual FoxPro.

On the Internet, check out comp.database.xbase.fox or Microsoft's microsoft.public.fox.* groups for the latest FoxPro news in a Usenet newsgroup.

The World Wide Web has a very high turnover rate, but we hope one or two of the following addresses will still be in business when you get there:

http://www.wji.com/fox/homepage.html has links to many pages of resources, user group listings, sample source code, and more.

http://www.universalthread.com: Probably the most popular Fox-based Web site. This Web-based service features many of the forum basics: threading, private messages, etc. Basic membership is free, but many people are attracted to the "Premier" memberships.

http://www.state.sd.us/people/colink/foxpage.htm—Colin Keeler manages the finances of South Dakota and maintains this page on the side. Good stuff, with links to great pages.

http://msdn.microsoft.com/vfoxpro—get the scoop straight from the horse's mouth. This is Microsoft's official site for FoxPro information. Lots of good links and information available nowhere else. Make sure to register your purchase of Visual FoxPro in order to get access to the Owner's Area.

User Groups, Conferences and Professional Associations

Ted has been involved with user groups for 10 years in the positions of founder, president, newsletter editor, bulletin board system operator, master of ceremonies, and flunky, sometimes all at the same time. Tamar has been more sane in her active participation, but both of us agree that user groups are an excellent opportunity to meet people of similar interests, seek support for vexing problems, share your knowledge, and see some of the new innovations.

We both visit (Ted more often than Tamar) the user groups in our backyards, but that doesn't do you much good, unless you happen to live nearby. However, finding a group near you could make your life much better. The best user group list we know of was maintained by our friend and publisher Whil Hentzen—check out the file Ugstuf.EXE in the libraries of the various Fox fora on CompuServe. Maintaining such a list is a full-time task, and with the plethora of search engines available on the Web, that may be a preferable choice if available.

Professional conferences are one of our favorite ways to get up to speed quickly. Despite the loss of billable hours as well as the costs of travel, lodging and the conference admission, we are certain that we make money by going to conferences. We meet potential clients, business partners (not to mention co-authors), employee candidates, and resources that advance our careers, at the same time as we learn from some of the most advanced members of our community. Taking an hour-long session from one of the "gurus" can save you weeks of painful trial-and-error research.

Several conferences take place each year. Microsoft has continued the tradition started by Fox Software of an (almost) annual Developer's Conference (we say *almost* because October '93 saw us in Orlando; 15 months later, January '95 found us in San Diego). The June '99 conference will mark the 10th FoxPro DevCon. Other regional conferences have been very successful the last few years. These more local events can save a great deal of expense in terms of travel, lodging and admission costs, with a somewhat more limited schedule of events and a smaller speaker list.

ACM, the Association for Computer Machinery (yeah, we're not machinery either, but we're members), is the granddaddy of professional associations for computer folks. With both local chapters and a couple of dozen special interest groups (known as "SIGs"), it has something for everyone who's serious about computers. You can contact them at (800) 342-6626 or acmhelp@acm.org in the U.S. and Canada, 32-2-774-9602 or acm_europe@acm.org in Europe. ACM also has a Web page at http://www.acm.org.

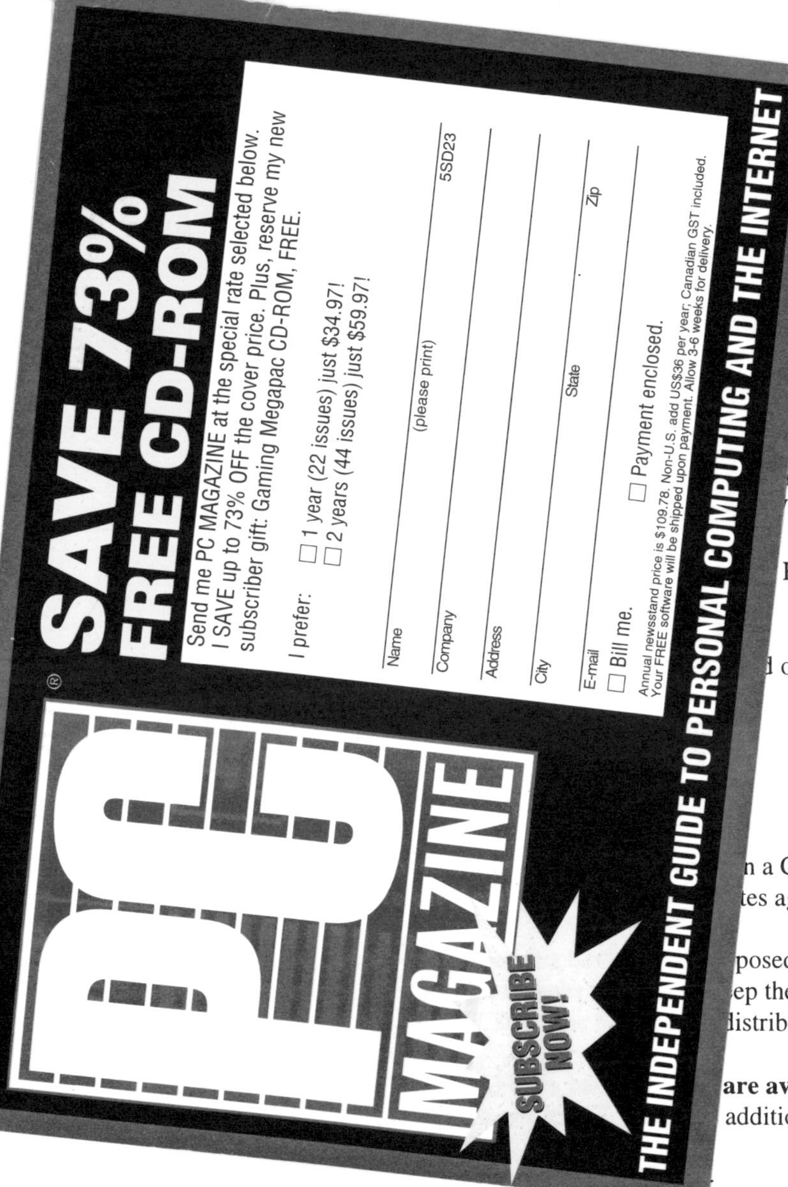

What's on the CD?

… us to provide the *Hacker's Guide* in an online … HTML Help version of this book.

… that this section in the HTML Help version contains a … unity to keep adding things until the last possible … additional chapter that's not in the printed version - … Wizards.

… Help file for HTML Help. (You'll also find some clues to …

… d other goodies. For the complete list, see this chapter in …

Publisher's Note

… n a CD. After all, who needs another CD to clutter things up. … tes ago. The Internet is where it's at. Just ask BILL <g>.

… posed to be 1000 pages in a 7x9 format. It ended up being … ep the extra content (and go to a larger, more expensive … distributing the .CHM file. We chose to keep the content.

… **are available by download from our website.** Using our … additions or corrections in a timely and cost efficient manner.

How to Download the Files

To download the files:

1. Go to our website:

   www.hentzenwerke.com

2. Click on the **Books by Hentzenwerke Publishing** hyperlink. Then click on **Download Pre-release Versions or Source Code and Final .CHM File.**

3. If you ordered the book from Hentzenwerke and were issued a Username and Password, you can use them here. That's all you need.

   If you do not have a Username and Password, follow the directions on the screen. As a protection to your investment, there is a password scheme in place to prevent the downloading of these files without purchasing the book.

You will need to have the book with you in order to download the files!

About the Authors

Tamar E. Granor

Tamar E. Granor is the Editor of *FoxPro Advisor* magazine and co-author of its "Ask Advisor" column. She is a Microsoft Support Most Valuable Professional for her contributions to CompuServe's FoxPro forums. Tamar is a frequent speaker at FoxPro conferences including Microsoft's FoxPro Developer's Conference. She has developed and enhanced numerous FoxPro applications for businesses and other organizations.

Ted Roche

Ted Roche is the director of development at Blackstone Incorporated, a Microsoft Solution Provider based in Waltham, Massachusetts. Ted is a Contributing Editor of *FoxPro Advisor* magazine and co-authors the "Ask Advisor" column. He is a Microsoft Certified Solution Developer, a Microsoft Support Most Valuable Professional and a CompuServe Support Partner. Ted is also a frequent speaker at FoxPro conferences, including Microsoft's FoxPro Developer's Conference.

Doug Hennig, Technical Editor

Doug Hennig is a partner with Stonefield Systems Group Inc. in Regina, Saskatchewan, Canada. He's the author of Stonefield's Database Toolkit for Visual FoxPro and Stonefield Data Dictionary for FoxPro 2.x. He's also the author of *The Visual FoxPro Data Dictionary* in Pinnacle Publishing's *The Pros Talk Visual FoxPro* series. Doug has spoken at user groups and regional conferences all over North America, and at the 1997 Microsoft FoxPro Developers Conference. He's a Microsoft Most Valuable Professional (MVP).